A volume of a series in English,
edited by ERNEST BERNBAUM

Victorian Poetry

A Companion Volume to

VICTORIAN PROSE

Edited by Frederick William Roe

VICTORIAN POETRY

Edited by

E. K. BROWN

UNIVERSITY OF CHICAGO

THE RONALD PRESS COMPANY

NEW YORK

4

PRINTED IN THE UNITED STATES OF AMERICA

PREFACE

The main purpose of this anthology is to represent liberally the principal poets of the Victorian age. Most of the space has been given to Tennyson, Browning, Arnold, Swinburne, and Dante Gabriel Rossetti; the remainder is occupied by selections, relatively few and in the main brief, from nine other poets of unquestionable distinction and importance, but less various in their excellence, and less central to the art-currents of the period. I have had in mind the needs of advanced undergraduate courses in Victorian poetry, and have compiled the anthology with the conviction that such courses are coming more and more to concentrate on the performance of the major figures, and to present the others briefly. An attempt has been made to include a quite unusual number of long works, for example *Atalanta in Calydon, The House of Life* and *Modern Love,* seldom if ever given in full in an anthology, along with *In Memoriam, Maud,* two of the *Idylls of the King,* two monologues from *The Ring and the Book, Bishop Blougram's Apology, Sohrab and Rustum, Tristram and Iseult, Monna Innominata,* and one of the tales from *The Earthly Paradise.* In preparing the bibliographies and annotations I have sought to serve the interests of advanced undergraduates; but in the annotations it has seemed wiser to be too full rather than too meager.

In the preparation of the book help of many kinds has been generously given by many colleagues and friends, especially by Gilbert Norwood and A. S. P. Woodhouse of the University of Toronto, W. C. DeVane of Yale University, and Frederick W. Roe of the University of Wisconsin, who has in the making a companion volume of selections from Victorian prose. Mr. Roe has been untiring in his interest, encouragement, and kindly labors, and, to its great profit, has read the introduction. In the approach to the subject I am conscious of a profound debt to two former teachers, W. J. Alexander, who introduced me to the principal Victorian writers in a course at the University of Toronto, and Louis Cazamian, who, in lectures *en Sorbonne,* impressed upon me the organic wholeness of the literature of the nineteenth century. Without the many-sided help of my wife the production of the book would have been long delayed.

ACKNOWLEDGMENTS

The poems of Thomas Hardy are reprinted from his COLLECTED POEMS, 1928, by permission of the Macmillan Company, New York, publishers.

The poems of Gerard Manley Hopkins are reprinted from his POEMS, 1918, by permission of his heirs and the Oxford University Press, London, publishers.

The poems of A. E. Housman are reprinted from LAST POEMS, by permission of Henry Holt, New York, publishers.

TABLE OF CONTENTS

PREFACE iii
INTRODUCTION xi
ALFRED TENNYSON
Claribel 2
Mariana 2
The Poet 3
To J. M. K. 4
The Lady of Shalott 4
Œnone 6
To– 10
The Palace of Art 10
The Lotos-Eaters 14
A Dream of Fair Women 17
You Ask Me, Why, tho' Ill at Ease 21
Of Old Sat Freedom on the Heights 22
Love Thou Thy Land with Love Far-brought 22
Morte d'Arthur 23
Ulysses 27
Tithonus 28
Locksley Hall 29
St. Agnes' Eve 34
Sir Galahad 34
The Vision of Sin 35
Break, Break, Break 38
Songs from *The Princess* 38
In Memoriam A. H. H. 41
The Eagle 77
Come Not, When I Am Dead 77
Ode on the Death of the Duke of Wellington 77
Maud; a Monodrama 81
Northern Farmer, Old Style 101
Northern Farmer, New Style 103
In the Valley of Cauteretz 105
The Higher Pantheism 105
Flower in the Crannied Wall 106
In the Garden at Swainston 106
From Idylls of the King
Lancelot and Elaine 106
The Holy Grail 127
The Last Tournament 139
Lucretius 151
The Revenge 155
'Frater Ave Atque Vale' 157
To Virgil 157
Locksley Hall Sixty Years After 158
Far-Far-Away 166
Crossing the Bar 166

ROBERT BROWNING

Johannes Agricola in Meditation 168
Porphyria's Lover 168
Cavalier Tunes 169
My Last Duchess 171
Soliloquy of the Spanish Cloister 172
In a Gondola 173
Cristina 176
The Laboratory 177
The Bishop Orders His Tomb at St. Praxed's Church 178
"How They Brought the Good News from Ghent to Aix" 181
Pictor Ignotus 182
The Italian in England 184
The Englishman in Italy 185
The Lost Leader 189
Home-Thoughts, from Abroad 189
"Here's to Nelson's Memory" 190
Home-Thoughts, from the Sea 190
Meeting at Night 190
Parting at Morning 190
Saul 190
Love among the Ruins 198
Evelyn Hope 199
Up at a Villa—Down in the City 201
A Woman's Last Word 203
Fra Lippo Lippi 203
A Toccata of Galuppi's 210
An Epistle 212
My Star 216
"Childe Roland to the Dark Tower Came" 216
How It Strikes a Contemporary 220
Bishop Blougram's Apology 221
Memorabilia 241
Andrea del Sarto 241
"De Gustibus—" 245
Cleon 246
A Grammarian's Funeral 250
Two in the Campagna 253
Abt Vogler 254
Rabbi Ben Ezra 256
Caliban upon Setebos 259
Confessions 264
Youth and Art 264
Prospice 265
Epilogue 266
From The Ring and the Book
Pompilia 269
The Pope 304
House 345
Shop 346
Echetlos 349
Never the Time and the Place 350
Prologue to "Asolando" 350

Dubiety 351
Epilogue to "Asolando" 351

ELIZABETH BARRETT BROWNING
Cowper's Grave 353
The Cry of the Children 354
Grief 358
The Dead Pan 358
From Sonnets from the Portuguese 361
A Musical Instrument 365
Bianca among the Nightingales 366

EDWARD FITZGERALD
Rubáiyát of Omar Khayyám of Naishápúr 369

ARTHUR HUGH CLOUGH
In a Lecture-Room 382
Τὸ Καλόν 382
Qua Cursum Ventus 382
The New Sinai 383
The Latest Decalogue 384
At Venice 384
Peschiera 385
Qui Laborat, Orat 386
"With Whom Is No Variableness, neither Shadow of Turning." 387
Say Not, the Struggle Nought Availeth 387
Where Lies the Land to Which the Ship Would Go? 387

MATTHEW ARNOLD
Short ones—All
Mycerinus 389
✓The Strayed Reveller 392
✓To a Friend 395
✓Shakespeare 396
✓The Forsaken Merman 396
✓Memorial Verses 399
Cadmus and Harmonia 400
Apollo 400
To Marguerite—*Continued* 401
✓Tristram and Iseult 401
A Summer Night 417
The Buried Life 419
Stanzas in Memory of the Author of "Obermann" 421
Consolation 423
Lines Written in Kensington Gardens 424
The Future 425
Morality 426
✓Sohrab and Rustum 427
Philomela 443
Requiescat 444
✓The Scholar Gipsy 444
Stanzas from the Grande Chartreuse 449
A Southern Night 452
✓Thyrsis ... Arthur Hugh Clough—elegy 453
✓Dover Beach 458

The Last Word 459
Rugby Chapel 459
Westminster Abbey 461

DANTE GABRIEL ROSSETTI
The Blessed Damozel 467
My Sister's Sleep 469
The Portrait 469
Jenny 471
The Card-Dealer 475
Sister Helen 475
Troy Town 479
Ave 480
The House of Life 481
The King's Tragedy 517

CHRISTINA ROSSETTI
Dream Land 528
Song (Oh roses for the flush of youth) 529
Up-Hill 529
A Birthday 529
Song (When I am dead, my dearest) 529
The Three Enemies 530
Echo 530
Goblin Market 531
A Better Resurrection 536
Passing Away, Saith the World 537
Wife to Husband 537
Amor Mundi 538
Paradise: in a Dream 538
Somewhere or Other 539
Weary in Well-doing 539
The Lowest Place 539
A Dirge 539
Bird Raptures 539
Monna Innominata 540

GEORGE MEREDITH
Love in the Valley 545
Juggling Jerry 550
Modern Love 551
The Woods of Westermain 568
Earth and Man 572
Lucifer in Starlight 576
The Spirit of Shakespeare 576

WILLIAM MORRIS
Riding Together 578
The Chapel in Lyoness 579
Summer Dawn 580
The Defence of Guenevere 580
Concerning Geffray Teste Noire 587
Old Love 593
The Gilliflower of Gold 593

Shameful Death 594
The Eve of Crecy 594
The Blue Closet 596
The Haystack in the Flood 598
Sir Giles' War-Song 599
Praise of My Lady 600
Songs from the *Life and Death of Jason* 601
The Earthly Paradise 602
    Atalanta's Race 603
    February 617
    June 618
    November 618
    L'Envoi 619
From Sigurd the Volsung 620
The Day Is Coming 624

A. C. SWINBURNE

Atalanta in Calydon 627
Dedication to Poems and Ballads 680
The Triumph of Time 681
Itylus 687
Hymn to Proserpine 688
Faustine 690
Dolores 692
The Garden of Proserpine 698
Sapphics 699
Prelude to Songs before Sunrise 700
Super Flumina Babylonis 702
Hertha 705
To Walt Whitman in America 710
Siena 711
Cor Cordium 715
Messidor 715
A Forsaken Garden 716
For the Feast of Giordano Bruno 718
The Higher Pantheism in a Nutshell 718
Nephelidia 719
After Looking into Carlyle's Reminiscences 720
Neap-tide 721
England: an Ode 722

THOMAS HARDY

Hap 725
Nature's Questioning 725
The Impercipient 726
Drummer Hodge 726
Lausanne 727
"I Said to Love" 727
By the Earth's Corpse 727
Mute Opinion 728
A Broken Appointment 728
The Darkling Thrush 729
In Tenebris 729
When I Set Out for Lyonesse 731

GERARD MANLEY HOPKINS
The Windhover 733
Pied Beauty 733
Felix Randal 733
The Leaden Echo and the Golden Echo 734
Carrion Comfort 735

A. E. HOUSMAN
From A Shropshire Lad 737
From Last Poems 743

BIBLIOGRAPHICAL AND EXPLANATORY NOTES 745

INDEX 907

INTRODUCTION

VICTORIAN poetry is essentially a continuation of the poetry of the romantic movement. Between the poetry of Tennyson, Browning and Arnold and that of Byron, Shelley and Keats, there is no greater difference than that which separates the poetry of the young men of the second romantic generation from the poetry of their seniors, Wordsworth, Coleridge and Scott. The elements common to romantic and Victorian poetry are fundamental and patent: a persistent concern with nature, a quest of the strange and extreme, a nostalgia for a golden past, a prophecy of a golden future, a determination to feel, a harrowing anxiety about the nature of things, an ability to invent new poetic forms and subtle variations of the old. Not only are these elements common to both: in the Victorian approach to them, indebtedness to the romantic poets is clear. The most original and powerful poets of our time make very grave reservations about the great Victorians; and in general they have approached the subjects studied by the Victorians in a manner which gives little or no evidence of Victorian influence. Quite different was the Victorians' attitude towards their immediate predecessors: Browning's veneration for Shelley, Arnold's veneration for Wordsworth, Rossetti's veneration for Keats would of themselves establish the continuity of the poetry of the nineteenth century. Can one imagine Mr. Eliot writing of Swinburne:

> Sun-treader, life and light be thine forever!
> Thou art gone from us; years go by and spring
> Gladdens and the young earth is beautiful,
> Yet thy songs come not, other bards arise
> But none like thee. . .
> Yet, sun-treader, all hail! From my heart's heart
> I bid thee hail! E'en in my wildest dreams,
> I proudly feel I would have thrown to dust
> The wreaths of fame which seem'd o'erhanging me
> To see thee for a moment as thou art. . . .

But that is how Browning addressed the spirit of Shelley. Or can one imagine Edward Thomas or Mr. Frost saying of Arnold what Arnold said of Wordsworth:

> He found us when the age had bound
> Our souls in its benumbing round;
> He spoke and loosed our heart in tears.
> He laid us as we lay at birth
> On the cool flowery lap of earth,
> Smiles broke from us and we had ease. . . .
> Our youth returned; for there was shed
> On spirits that had long been dead,
> Spirits dried up and closely furl'd,
> The freshness of the early world. . . .
> Time may restore us in his course
> Goethe's sage mind and Byron's force;
> But where will Europe's latter hour
> Again find Wordsworth's healing power?

These passages are not exceptional: Swinburne used such language of Shelley, Arnold of Byron; Tennyson of Wordsworth. Nor was such homage addressed to the romantic poets simply as minds, as teachers. The forms of the Victorian poets exhibit a careful study of their immediate predecessors. "The Scholar Gipsy" and "Thyrsis" show a penetration into the secrets of Keats's art; "Hertha" and others among the *Songs before Sunrise* show with what profound understanding Swinburne had immersed himself in the lyrics of Shelley; the blank verse of "Morte d'Arthur" points to an intensive study of *Hyperion,* and of Wordsworth.

I. REALISM

Nevertheless the Victorian poets, employing much the same forms, and dealing with much the same themes, were far too original, far too powerful, far too much in accord with the developments of their time, to lapse into imitation. The breath of realism which was animating the literature of France during the middle years of the nineteenth century blew also in England. Realism shaped the novels of social description and social protest—such novels as Mrs. Gaskell's *North and South* (1853) Charles Kingsley's *Yeast* (1848) and *Alton Locke* (1850) and most of the vast production of Charles Reade. Thackeray was restless within the bounds of conventions which prevented him, as he thought, from vying with Fielding in drawing a full man; within those bounds Dickens managed to remain only by resorting to humorous transpositions of material which in itself was often unutterably sordid. In a famous chapter of *Adam Bede* George Eliot defined the function of fiction in terms which would have covered anything that Zola ever wrote; and if George Eliot's practice fell far short of the bold theorizing she allowed herself, the root of her timidities was in the depths of a personality grievously wounded by the consequences of her reluctant defiance of Victorian convention. Inevitably the realism which was either evident or latent in Victorian fiction entered Victorian poetry.

Its traces are conspicuous in Browning. The Victorian poem which is to be set beside *Paradise Lost, The Faerie Queene* and the *Canterbury Tales* is *The Ring and the Book;* and the distinctive mark of *The Ring and the Book* is its realism relieved by grotesqueness. The sordid event which is at the centre of the poem; the gallery of rogues who do the devil's work in the world; the shallow, scheming and grasping lawyers through whom the pleas of innocent and guilty alike are made; the racy earthy details in which the book abounds; the persistent stress on the particular and peculiar in place and time and person; —all these elements are parts of the realistic formula of fiction. There is indeed no mid-Victorian novel in which there are so many isolated passages at which a Victorian maiden might blush; and one is at times driven to the conviction that only in poetry could such frankness have been achieved. In this, as in almost everything else, *The Ring and the Book* is the consummation of Browning's art: in his monologues and in his plays, the realistic formula also operates, perhaps not with such continuous power Nevertheless, among English poets no one since Chaucer had written so much and so well within the limits of realism. One has but to formulate the types of character with whom he dealt most successfully to be persuaded of this: a monastic painter craving the pleasures of the senses and of purely human emotions (Fra Lippo Lippi) ; a prelate who quiets his doubts by assuring himself that neither faith nor infidelity is demonstrable, and faith is better than infidelity in supplying the good things of the earthly life (Blougram) ; a lord narrow in mind and soul, taking terrible vengeance on a wife who violates the few principles his mind and soul can grasp (the Duke, in "My Last Duchess") ; another lord, cruel, cunning, cold and cynical, and acting out all these qualities (Guido Franceschini) . Bishop Westcott remarked: "He has laid bare what there is in man of sordid, selfish, impure, corrupt, brutish. . . . Browning has dared to look on the darkest and meanest forms of action and passion, from which we commonly and rightly turn our eyes. . . ." Nor is Browning's realism simply in his substance: his style similarly falls within the realistic formula. The man who in a letter to a woman friend could say of common acquaintances: "I always knew how to play with a snake and could manage a dozen like her" or "I spit at him and have done with it," carried into his mature poetry the same note of homely vehement naturalness. Other poets who have dealt with the materials of realism as frequently as Browning have usually sought to purify or dignify that material by a noble style. Browning's style is noble only when the substance requires nobility for adequate expression.

Realism is dominant in other Victorian poets. It is dominant in Clough: much of the *Bothie's* charm derives from the choice of a *real* subject—a reading party of Oxford undergraduates in the Scottish highlands—and a humorous realism of treatment. The appeal of this poem is essentially the same as that made by a realistic novel. Clough is no less a realist in his treatment of mental states: however complex or subtle his psychological analysis may become, it remains severely that of a realistic anatomist of the mind, and it is almost always expressed in a style which is conscientiously stripped of adventitious ornament, indeed of all superficial beauty. If in other poets realism is not so clearly dominant, critics have failed to give enough emphasis to its presence. Every reader of Tennyson knows and likes his two poems on the Northern Farmer; but few appreciate that these two poems are not isolated: few read "The Northern Cobbler," "The Spinster's Sweet 'Arts," "Owd Roä" and other poems of the same richly savoury realism. To achieve excellence in realistic representation Tennyson required the help of dialect: only dialect could free him completely from the jewelled, alembicated style. The use of realistic material in poems written in this style led him to many of his most notorious absurdities; to the description of a moustache as "the knightly growth that fringed his lips," of a fish-basket as "ocean-smelling osier." More elusive of definition is the realism of Rossetti. Realism was a fundamental principle of the Pre-Raphaelite Brotherhood. The members of that group believed in the need for painting with unfailing accuracy and completeness all the details of their subjects: they despised the conventional foregrounds and backgrounds—the monotonously undulating rocks, the uniformly symmetrical trees—of modern academic painting. They held that if an object was to be introduced into a painting, however minor its function, it should be fully and faithfully presented. Rossetti's paintings and his poems abound in touches of full and faithful realization of detail. To take but one example, and that from his poetry, one may note the perfect realization of detail in these lines:

Your hands lie open in the long fresh grass—
    The finger-points look through like rosy blooms;
    Your eyes smile peace. The pasture gleams and glooms
'Neath billowing skies that scatter and amass;
All round our nest far as the eye can pass
    Are golden kingcup-fields with silver edge
    Where the cow-parsley skirts the hawthorn hedge.
'Tis visible silence, still as the hour-glass.

Deep in the sun-searched growths the dragon-fly
Hangs like a blue thread loosened from the sky—
    So this winged hour is dropt to us from above.
Oh! clasp we to our hearts, for deathless dower,
This close-companioned inarticulate hour
    When two-fold silence was the song of love.

There is much in these lines which is alien to realism; but they are within the realistic formula in so far as they have to do with particular objects, rather than with emotions. The fingerpoints, the skies that scatter and amass, the kingcup fields, cow-parsley and hawthorn hedge, and the dragon-fly, have along with a suggestive aura, full pictorial realization. Besides, the handling of the details illustrates the type of realism specific to the Pre-Raphaelites: the background and foreground are realized just as fully as the central figure. Although it would be a disastrous mistake to follow, without reservations, Ruskin in his view that Pre-Raphaelitism was essentially, if not indeed entirely, realistic, it is equally mistaken to allow one's awareness of the rich suggestive power of the Pre-Raphaelites to blind one to their realism.

Rossetti is also a realist in the main when he is describing human feelings. Much of his love-poetry was thought by Victorians, and is thought by some academic critics to-day, to be objectionably frank. Sonnets such as "Nuptial Sleep" and "Supreme Surrender" have a fullness in the description of emotion comparable with the fullness in the description of particular objects already noted. "Jenny" is one of the chief defiantly realistic poems of the century, far as it is from being completely successful.

Tennyson was a Pre-Raphaelite before the Pre-Raphaelite Brotherhood was founded and after its leader was dead. His poetic manner was not, as has been said, altogether appropriate to realism, except when he lapsed into dialect; still in such poems as "Mariana," "The Lady of Shalott," "Sir Galahad," "The Palace of Art," to speak only of his early works, the realization of natural objects has the fullness and accuracy of the best Pre-Raphaelite work (and other Pre-Raphaelite qualities as well): as in

With blackest moss the flower-plots
    Were thickly crusted, one and all:
The rusted nails fell from the knots
    That held the pear to the gable-wall.
The broken sheds looked sad and strange:
    Uplifted was the clinking latch. . . .

or

The hard brands shiver on the steel,
The splintered spear-shafts crack and fly. . . .

A barer realism than Tennyson or Rossetti ever achieved is to be found in those parts of Morris's early poems in which human cruelty and malice are evoked, in such passages as this from the incomparable "Haystack in the Floods":

From Robert's throat he loosed the bands
Of silk and mail; with empty hands
Held out she stood and gazed, and saw,
The long bright blade without a flaw
Glide out from Godmar's sheath, his hand
In Robert's hair; she saw him bend
Back Robert's head; she saw him send
The thin steel down; the blow told well,
Right backward the knight Robert fell
And moaned as dogs do, being half-dead. . . .

Among the poets of the nineteenth century Morris was the first to have a realistic imagination of the aspect of medieval life. He would have been one of the great realistic poets, had he not been helpless until towards the end of his poetic life in the bands of a somewhat pinchbeck romantic style. Not until long after 1858 could he free himself from inversions, archaisms and all the small change of the sham medievalism of the romantics.

Meredith and Hardy, however far they may at times have diverged from realism, allowed to it a larger and more central space in their poetry than most of their elders. Meredith's realism is most emphatic when his subject is human: to set *Modern Love* side by side with *The House of Life* is to be immediately convinced of Meredith's power to understand and to reveal individual character, of his power to probe strange involutions of feeling and to present the subtle mixtures of beauty and ugliness, nobility and baseness that make common human nature. Although his approach to the non-human world is also realistic in intention, the effect produced by his representations of it is usually intensely romantic. It is romantic because of the almost reeling intensity of his emotions, because of the richness of his imagery and diction, and because of the oracular pregnancy and obscurity of his thought. It is all in too high a key for realism.

The picture of life which Hardy gives, in verse as in prose, is heavily colored by a temperament so unusual as to be almost abnormal. Of the difference between his angle of vision and that of the majority of men he was clearly aware: and in expressing his awareness he curiously mingles pride, regret, resentment, and uneasiness. A highly peculiar temperament, of whose peculiarity its possessor is fully aware, is unlikely to express itself in realistic terms. Hardy, however, had the realist's desire for complete fidelity to fact, material fact and emotional and intellectual fact; and within him this desire to report with unwavering fidelity warred with a temperamental delight in the intense and exaggerated, just as it did in Browning. The mention of Browning establishes that out of such a conflict great successes in realistic representation can issue; and in Hardy as in Browning they did. However Hardy was much more preoccupied with himself than Browning, his knowledge of life and of earlier representations of life was much less; his sympathetic power if more intense was much narrower. Accordingly his achievements in realistic representation are fewer; and they are less complete. His desire for fidelity impressed itself strongly on his mode of representation: on his diction, his stanza-form, his rhythms. In these, like Clough, he is almost excessively a realist.

II. OBJECTIVITY

A dissatisfaction with subjectivism is an even more fundamental quality in Victorian poetry. In the romantic period, as Mr. Garrod has said, nearly every poet wrote, as one of his major achievements, a "history of his own soul"; in the process of his own intellectual, emotional and spiritual development lay the chief interest of each of the great romantics. It is not easy to find Victorian equivalents for *The Prelude, Childe Harold* and *Endymion:* to the Victorians such intimate disclosures were somewhat repulsive. Doubtless the pudency of the Victorians partially explains why they found such poetry repulsive; but to this factor too much weight has been given. In France a similar recoil from the poetry of intimate disclosure occurred: and among the Parnassians pudency (in a moral sense at least) was insignificant. Leconte de Lisle speaks for his English contemporaries as well as for his own countrymen when he attacks in his sonnet "Les Montreurs" the men who offer the world in a peep show the sight of their most intimate feelings. His great disciple, Jose Maria de Hérédia, in his discourse at the time of his reception into the French Academy, developed the Parnassian doctrine more clearly and fully. Speaking of his predecessor, de Mazade, he said: "He tried to get out of that personal manner into which poetry has been misled, that familiarity in baring one's heart before the public suitable only to a very few select spirits"; and more sharply he continued: "Public confessions, whether sincere or false, offend in us a profound modesty," and such confessions are contrary to the true aim of poetry which is "essentially simple, ancient and primitive." Summing up his position Hérédia contends that "The poet is the more truly and more completely human as he is more impersonal," the self being essentially odious.

Any glorification of the artist's self, whether by complacent exhibition of his power over his materials or by the imposition of a distorting set of values upon the objective world, is obnoxious to the great aesthetic thinker of the Victorian period, Ruskin. In his opinion, the greatest artist is he who has the greatest number of the greatest ideas; who paints man and nature with the strictest fidelity and the most penetrative insight. After looking at Giotto's frescoes in Santa Maria Novella at Florence, he formulates his aesthetic advice in three simple maxims: "You shall see things as they Are; and the least with the greatest, because God made them; and the greatest with the least, because God made *you,* and gave you eyes and a heart." The greatest critical document of the age, after *Modern Painters,* Matthew Arnold's preface to the *Poems* of 1853, is no less emphatic. It is a plea for poets to turn out of the path of lyricism into those of the epic or the drama, from the subjective to the objective.

False aims are now prescribed for poetry, Arnold contends. He represents a contemporary critic as saying: "A true allegory of the state of one's own mind in a representative history is perhaps the highest thing that one can attempt in the way of poetry." This he believes to be nonsense. "No great work," he retorts, "has ever been produced with such an aim. Faust itself in which something of the kind is attempted, wonderful passages as it contains, and in spite of the beauty of the scenes which relate to Margaret, *Faust* itself, judged as a whole, and judged strictly as a poetical work, is defective," *Faust,* he goes on to say is the work of "the greatest poet of modern times." The formula on which Goethe and the other romantic poets worked in their most ambitious poems is to Arnold a formula radically false. It is false because the aim it sets before the poet is that of a subjective poem rather than an objective. Steeped as he himself was in romanticism, deeply and incurably romantic as most of his own poetry is, he did attempt more than once to create outside the formula which he attacked. He attempted to escape in "Sohrab and Rustum," in "Balder Dead," in "Merope," and perhaps also in "Tristram and Iseult" and in "The Sick King in Bokhara." He valued such poems as these highly: he was gravely disappointed by the failure of "Merope" and the apathy of his readers towards "Balder Dead," and to Clough he complained about the scale of values which would set "The Scholar Gipsy" above "Sohrab and Rustum." Among lyric poets only Wordsworth and Goethe stood high in his regard: in the main his praise, his unqualified praise, was reserved for the poets who had treated of life in objective forms, in the tragedy and the epic.

Browning fully shared Arnold's revolt against the subjective. In theory he estimated the subjective poet more generously, it is true, as may be seen from his critical remarks in his essay on Shelley. The objective poet, he says, is "one whose endeavour is to reproduce things external (whether the phenomena of the scenic universe or the manifested action of human heart and brain) with an immediate reference in every case to the common eye and apprehension of his fellow-men. . . ." The subjective poet has to do "not with the combination of humanity in action but with the primal elements of humanity . . . and he digs where he stands, preferring to seek them in his own soul." Browning himself had the prophetic impulse of the subjective poet, but he was singularly reluctant to bare his own soul as the instrument of his discoveries among the primal elements of humanity. In him the objective poet was stronger: he very rarely speaks in his own person—for the lyrical monologue he substituted the dramatic monologue. That his adoption of the dramatic monologue was rooted in a reluctance to disclose the intimate secrets of his own personality is obvious to one who has read his bitter poem "House." In it he says:

> "A peep through my window, if folk prefer
> But please you, no foot over threshold of mine. . . .
>
> Outside should suffice for evidence:
> And whoso desires to penetrate
> Deeper, must dive by the spirit-sense . . .

To the claim that the greatest of English objective poets had flung open the doors of even the most secret apartment of his spiritual house he retorts:

> "'*With this same key*
> *Shakespeare unlocked his heart,*' once more!"
> Did Shakespeare? If so the less Shakespeare he!

The less an objective poet; and for Browning, the less admirable a person. It may be that through his dramatic monologues we may think we discern the contours of Browning's mind and heart: it is always open to Browning to deny our discoveries, and, what is more important, we never can feel that Browning is the *montreur* that the great romantics were.

The most complete of the many Victorian revolts against the subjectivism of the romantics is in the poetry of William Morris. Morris passed out of the manner of lyrical poetry into that of romantic idyllic narrative and then into that of the epic. Above all in *Sigurd the Volsung* he escapes from the romantic tradition into a simpler and purer air. No other Victorian poem will so fully satisfy the demand of Hérédia that poetry be "simple, ancient, primitive." In *Sigurd the Volsung* almost all the elements are simple and large. To come to it from Morris's intense and suffocating early poetry or from his sweet and gently sensuous idylls, is like suddenly breathing air from high mountains. The characters—

even those which are subsidiary or merely episodic—are energetic and grand in their vices as in their virtues; the conflicts are narrated with the leisureliness and spaciousness of the epic; and even the landscape abounds continuously in effects of largeness and spaciousness, a landscape of rugged mountains, trackless plains, and broad seas. Reference was made above to the inadequacy of Morris's style for a realistic effect; even in *Sigurd,* now and then, the style jars with the substance, and an edulcorated sensibility invades the poem impairing its objective purity. Heroic sadness dwindles into romantic melancholy, heroic love into romantic yearning. In the main, however, the poem is a triumphant return to an earlier mode of feeling and thinking, an earlier mode even of perceiving. The extent to which it breaks with the standards of its time is the chief explanation for the absurdly unintelligent neglect with which it has met. Apart from an archaism which detracts from their authenticity, what is more grandly realistic than the poem's great scenes of action? The awakening of Atli's lords after his wife Gudrun has set fire to the palace represents the manner in which Morris could combine the claims of realistic representation, those of objective narrative, and those of heightened poetic intensity:

> But the wine-drenched earls were awaking, and the sleep-dazed warriors stirred,
> And the light of their dawning was dreadful; wild voice of the day they heard,
> And they knew not where they were gotten, and their hearts were smitten with dread,
> And they deemed that their house was fallen to the innermost place of the dead,
> The hall for the traitors builded, the house of the changeless plain;
> They cried and their tongues were confounded, and none gave answer again:
> They rushed, and came nowhither; each man beheld his foe,
> And smote at the hopeless and dying, nor brother brother might know,
> The sons of one mother's sorrow in the fire-blast strove and smote,
> And the sword of the first begotten was thrust in the father's throat,
> And the father hewed at his stripling; the thrall at the war-king cried,
> And mocked the face of the mighty in that house of Atli's pride.

The correspondence or non-correspondence of this with the manner of the sagas is irrelevant to the judgment one passes upon it. The relevant comparison is with other attempts at objective narrative in the post-medieval period.

III. DRAMA AND DRAMATIC MONOLOGUE

The strong objective impulse in the Victorian poets ought to have produced a great age of poetic drama. The four greatest poets of the time were profoundly interested in the possibilities of dramatic composition.

Between 1875 and 1885 Tennyson published six plays; four of them were acted in commercial theatres during that decade; and one of the others was acted some years later. In *Harold, Becket,* and *Queen Mary,* as his son has said, he sought to round out the representation of English history supplied in the historical dramas of Shakespeare. Inevitably he wrote as a belated Elizabethan; and inevitably there was some artificiality in his work. Even in other plays when he was not so clearly under the Shakespearean influence, artificiality was obvious. He tried, for example, in *The Promise of May* to represent aspects of contemporary life in a somewhat realistic manner, but his success was slight, although a radical duke protested from the orchestra at his picture of an agitator. Audiences were found for the plays of the most popular poet of the age; great actors, of whom Irving was one, were happy to appear in them; but from the perspective of a later age it is clear that Tennyson lacked knowledge of the theatre, a clear and powerful dramatic idiom, and the truly dramatic temper.

Tennyson ventured to present and publish dramas only when his reputation was secure; it was as a dramatist Browning first attracted attention. The great actor Macready asked the author of *Pauline* to submit a play; and in 1837 *Strafford* was produced after Macready had submitted it to extensive alteration. Macready's awareness that there was a "sad want of judgment and tact in the whole composition" was shared by the public, as it was to be by Miss Barrett and by later and less partial critics. *Strafford* ran for only four nights: Browning's next play *King Victor and King Charles* Macready pronounced a *"great mistake"* and it was not produced at all. Another play met the same discouragement from the actor-manager. Browning's next venture, *A Blot in the 'Scutcheon* failed also; the conflict of interests and of tempers to which it led is an unpleasant and discreditable episode in the relation of literature and the theatre and ended the collaboration of Browning and Macready. It also ended the period of the poet's life in which the writing of plays with a view to their performance was the main interest. For his play *Colombe's Birthday* he had sought without success the interest of Kean; and when in 1853 this play was produced—it ran for seven performances—Browning's feet were already firmly set on the path which led to the dramatic monologue. Some of his plays were from time to time revived; but their success was never more than tepid, except with those who loved poetry and came to hear a great poet's lines declaimed.

The failure of Browning is more significant than the modest, temporary success of Tennyson. Had Browning succeeded in writing plays which held the boards, it is probable that he would have given his life to the drama. For dramatic composition he had high qualities: a deep sense of human nature, a delight in that nature in its most violent and exciting aspects, and the command of a language robust, coloured, and individuated. On Browning as on Tennyson the shadow of the Elizabethan age is perceptible; and his Elizabethanism is partially to blame for his failure.

Another and more important factor in his failure remains to be mentioned and may properly be introduced with a reference to Matthew Arnold. Arnold too was interested in drama. His one play, *Merope,* he mainly wished to be read although he would have been pleased, no doubt, if it had been acted on the London stage. *Merope* is completely divorced from the theatre of the period; it belongs with *Samson Agonistes,* as a revival of the form of Greek tragedy. Its divorce from the Victorian theatre is consistent with the opinion advanced by Arnold in his essay *The French Play in London* that if there was a modern English theatre there was no modern English drama.

It is in the absence of a modern English drama that a major—perhaps the profoundest reason for Browning's unhappy relations with the theatre is to be sought. There is no duller or weaker period in the history of the English drama than the thirty years which preceded the appearance of Tom Robertson's plays towards the end of the sixties. There was neither a powerful poetic drama nor a powerful drama in prose. It is impossible here to describe the condition in which the drama then languished; but no student of it would pretend that between its mediocrity and flatness and the genius of a Browning there was any conceivable relation.

The case of Swinburne is much less interesting. From his boyhood to his old age he wrote plays in verse, Elizabethan and classical; but the only stage on which he would have cared to have them produced was the stage of ancient Athens or the Globe Theatre as Shakespeare knew it. Some of his plays have high excellences; but they are the excellences not of drama but of poetry.

The frustration of the dramatic impulse in the great poets of the age is one of the saddest aspects of Victorian literature.

The deplorable severance of literature and the theatre had at least one notably good consequence: it aided the development of the dramatic monologue. Although poems of this type had appeared in earlier times—*The Wyf of Bath's Prologue* and *The Prisoner of Chillon* are eminent instances—the great triumphs and wide diffusion of the dramatic monologue are phenomena of the middle and closing thirds of the nineteenth century. It would be gross exaggeration to claim that the sole root of the dramatic monologue's life in the Victorian age lies in the illiteracy of the Victorian theatre; the approach to character which the monologue provides is not congenial to the stage drama. Sir Mungo MacCallum, in his profound Warton Lecture, *The Dramatic Monologue in the Victorian Period,* has differentiated the stage drama from the dramatic monologue in terms of characterization. Sir Mungo begins by quoting Browning's dedication of Sordello: "My stress lay on the incidents in the development of a soul: little else is worth study." He proceeds to Swinburne's phrase, "the most intricate and subtle sophistries of self-justified and self-conscious crime." One great interest of the Victorians lay, he says, in the exploration of such "incidents in the development of a soul," in such "intricate and subtle sophistries," as cannot easily be represented on the stage. Another lay in the exploration of unconscious virtue "when the workings of the soul are so akin to reflex action that it needs the lenses of analytic genius to detect them at all." In either of these domains, complex or simple, the dramatist is at a loss. "The impalpable suggestion," he concludes, "that moulds us at unawares, 'the thoughts that increase in the heart when the heart's self knows not,' the silent mutation that cometh not with observation, how can these things be represented on the stage or in the kind of composition that the stage prescribes?" In a word, the dramatic monologue will pierce to recesses so secret, so far within the physical appearance, the verbal expression, and even the subtlest play of feature that no actor can mirror them.

The distinctive triumphs of the dramatic monologue are won in the poems in which all the resources of the writer to analyze, to subtilize and to complicate, are brought into play. In essence the dramatic monologue is a highly intellectual kind of art; it justifies itself as a distinct genre in such poems as *Saul, An Epistle, Cleon,* and *Bishop Blougram's Apology,* where stage dramaturgy would have been entirely inadequate.

Still another impulse of the Victorian mind found expression in the dramatic monologue. Again Sir Mungo contrasts the drama and the dramatic monologue, finding the former unsuited to the expression of the impulse.

> There was in many quarters much curiosity about all sorts of people and opinions and sentiments, and a keen desire to have them explained from the angle of vision that would reveal their relative justification. There may have been less eagerness to know the absolute rights and wrongs of the question at issue; or perhaps it would be fairer to say, there may have been the feeling that these could not be ascertained without hearing all sides, and that meanwhile the main thing was to get the most cogent statement possible from every witness who could be called. This attitude was not very favourable to the drama; for the drama, despite all the free play it allows to the individual, and the impossibility of comment by the dramatist, still, if it be a great drama, will suggest the final imaginative truth of its theme, at least as seen by the author; but it was altogether favourable to the dramatic monologue, which sanctions and enjoins intimate and often special pleading for every variety of thought, conduct and character.

What Sir Mungo here asserts to be a resource of the dramatic monologue as a type, is essential to the appreciation of human character most congenial to the greatest of all masters of the monologue, Browning. No other interpreter of Browning has so well, and above all so briefly, suggested Browning's excellence and limitations as a portrayer of character, although almost every one who reads Browning perceives with more or less clearness just what the excellence and the limitations are.

> Like the Shakespeare of proven knowledge in his throng of creatures, he can habitually merge himself in this man or that; and like the Shakespeare of conjecture in Sonnets, he can on occasion deliver his own soul; but he does not impress one as exceptionably able to see life steadily and see it whole, as Shakespeare does in the scope and implications of his greater masterpieces. He loves to break the clear white light through the medium of his own or a borrowed ego, and seldom reaches finality, except in so far as clear insight into truth in one of its aspects means implicit perception of the rest.

IV. STANZA AND METRE

In his suggestive essay on Victorian poetry Mr. John Drinkwater has pointed out that the originalities and distinctions in form of that poetry were in diction rather than in metre or stanza.

Some originalities in metre and stanza there were, of which but a few can be noticed here. Arnold was the first English poet to experiment significantly in free verse. In his first collection, *The Strayed Reveller,* with its lines of varying length, unrhymed, and liberated from any defined stanzaic unit, disclosed a revolt from the poetry of the English romantics. It has been conjectured that his models here and in the subsequent poems in which he employed free verse were Goethe and Greek verse; and the conjecture is acceptable. The stanza of *In Memoriam,* although it had been occasionally and obscurely used in the Elizabethan age, Tennyson thought to be his own invention. The clue for the stanza of *The Rubáiyát* FitzGerald found in his Persian original; but to English poetry it was new. New also was the sixteen-line sonnet of Meredith's *Modern Love.*

In metre the great originality of the period was Hopkins's practice of *sprung rhythm.* This may be briefly described as a metre in which each foot has one stressed syllable, and may have unstressed syllables ranging from none at all to four, and for cogent reason even more than four. Hopkins points out that when common speech or prose has a perceptible rhythm it is of this kind; that such also is the usual rhythm in music; and finally that classical poets and such medieval poets as the author of *Piers Plowman* employ such a metre. He erred in supposing that it had lapsed from use in English poetry at the end of the sixteenth century; but there is no doubt that it had lapsed from common use when he wrote. How striking his employment of sprung rhythm could be a very simple instance will show. In the following line from "Hurrahing in Harvest" the second foot consists of the monosyllable "rears" and the third of the monosyllable "wings":

The heart rears wings bold and bolder.

He also believed that one might introduce into a line a syllable or a number of syllables for a special effect and yet ignore the addition in scanning the line. His sympathetic and discerning interpreter, Father G. F. Lahey, gives as a striking example of this innovation the following passage in which the addition is italicized:

I caught this morning, morning's minion, kingdom of daylight's dauphin, *dapple-dawn-drawn*
Falcon, in his riding.

These are but instances, and very simple instances of the innovating genius of Hopkins. When set side by side with his poetry, the work of Tennyson, Swinburne and Browning, perhaps the greatest of the more orthodox Victorian metrists seems highly traditional.

Of Swinburne it must however be said that his use of the anapaest was more powerful than any other poet's. From the choruses of *Atalanta in Calydon,* with such openings as

When the hounds of spring are on winter's traces,
The mother of months in meadow or plain
Fills the shadows and windy places
With lisp of leaves and ripple of rain . . .

through the great political and philosophical poetry, such as *Hertha:*

In the darkening and whitening
Abysses adored
With dayspring and lightning,
For lamp and for sword,
God thunders in heaven, and his angels are red with the wrath of the Lord . . .

to such late visions of natural beauty as *A Nympholept:*

I dare not sleep for delight of the perfect hour,
Lest God be wroth that his gift should be scorned of man.
The face of the warm bright world is the face of a flower,
The word of the wind and the leaves that the light winds fan . . .

in all his periods and in almost all his moods, it is Swinburne's command of the anapaest that most surely achieves the effect at which he aims. This excellence alone, without any consideration of his other metrical exploits, would entitle him to be placed among the great traditional metrists of the language.

Tennyson's metrical effects are more varied and more delicate than Swinburne's. His was the chief role in the evolution of blank verse which began in the massiveness of Wordsworth and the fluidity of Keats; so heavily did the author of "Œnone," "Morte D'Arthur," and the *Idylls* imprint his mastery on this medium that for decades no poet could use it without appearing to be his imitator. Tennyson was seldom quite original in his stanzas: it is typical of his art that he should have thought the stanza of *In Memoriam* his own invention whereas many earlier poets had used it and Dante Gabriel Rossetti was also reviving it in ignorance of Tennyson's intention. But if his originality was not absolute, his sense for the stanza which would best suit his feeling was almost unerring: from the "Lady of Shalott," through *In Memoriam* and the songs of *The Princess,* on to the tribute to Virgil and that no less lovely tribute to Catullus, what Tennyson has used, few dare use again.

Browning's innovations, if less fundamental than Hopkins's, are often scarcely less daring. Of all the Victorians he was most ingenious in inventing or adapting to his use stanza forms: as examples of his ingenuity one might mention "My Star," "A Grammarian's Funeral," "Rabbi Ben Ezra," and "Love Among the Ruins." The list could be almost indefinitely protracted; but it is necessary to say that the originality and intensity of his diction, his rhythms, and his rhymes distract the reader from the less obtrusive and less clearly original stanza forms. It is probable that in the total effect produced by Browning's best and most characteristic poems, the stanza form counts for little.

V. DICTION

In diction Browning is among the Victorian poets the greatest innovator. To understand the importance of Browning's innovations in diction one must look back to the diction of English poetry at the beginning of the century. Wordsworth is properly associated with three major changes in the language of English poetry. He removed the weight of the decorative and sonorous poetic diction of the eighteenth century; he fostered and exemplified a frank and liberal introduction into poetry of the names of commonplace objects and other common terms; and, obeying the law of his own temperament, he gave to the new diction a prevailing noble tone. Aware or not of Wordsworth's theories and respectful or scornful towards his practice, the romantic poets, along with the rejection of eighteenth century diction and the introduction of common terms, sought in their diction an effect of nobility. It was not nobility as the preceding century understood that chameleon expression; but it was a genuine nobility. The typical great lines of the romantic poets are elevated in effect, whether it be the elevation of austere simplicity as in

> The silence that is in the starry sky,
> The sleep that is among the lonely hills,

or the elevation of gorgeous fancy as in

> The same that oft-times hath
> Charm'd magic casements, opening on the foam
> Of perilous seas, in faery lands forlorn.

Byron is among the greater romantics the solitary exception: his diction rose and fell with his moods, and at its most effective often was far below nobility. But in form, at least, Byron was not in the succeeding age an important influence; belonging as he did to a period in which most poets were at times, if not always, great masters of poetic form, he was negligent and even offensively slovenly in expression. The Victorian inheritance from romantic poetry was in diction a delight in the exact word and the elevated tone.

Elevation has its obvious perils; it was by a straining after elevation that the eighteenth century had lapsed into the excesses of artificial diction. And in the Victorian age straining after elevation had effects only slightly less disastrous. Against the superstition that poetry should be elevated, Browning was the one sturdy irreducible enemy. In temperament he was quite unlike Wordsworth and the other masters of romantic poetry, Byron aside. The diction which satisfied Wordsworth, a man almost entirely unaware of the savoury incongruities of life, and with no capacity to delight in them, a man in whom a few massive and lofty feelings came and went with a noble slowness, could scarcely satisfy Browning's mind, so restless, and humorous, or Browning's feelings, which chased through his being one on the heels of the other in a devil's dance.

Browning required a diction far more varied in tone than the diction bequeathed by the romantics. He wished to be lofty in one line or one phrase; quaint or vulgar or freakish in the next. He was not at all disposed to think that expressions falling below the noble were out of place in a poem of which the central feeling or idea was serious, or affecting. An example of such a conviction on Browning's part is seen in "The Heretic's Tragedy," where he describes the burning at the stake of a medieval French priest. The speaker in this dramatic monologue is another priest, bitterly delighting in the suffering and the terror of the culprit; but the reader is not, of course, expected to delight in it. He is expected to be struck with some horror by the mood of the speaker and moved to some pity and some shuddering by the plight of John, the victim. The poem, then, cannot be regarded as falling short of seriousness in idea and emotion. Yet the fourth stanza will give a sample of the language used:

> Good sappy bavins that kindle forthwith;
> Billets that blaze substantial and slow;
> Pine-stump split deftly, dry as pith;
> Larch-heart that chars to a chalk-white glow:
> Then up they hoist me John in a chafe,
> Sling him fast like a hog to scorch,
> Spit in his face, then leap back safe,
> Sing "Laudes" and bid clap-to the torch.

No other poet of the age would have used such language to describe such an event: side by side with a line that almost any of the romantics might have envied for its combination of image and sound:

> Larch-heart that chars to a chalk-white glow

comes a line as easy as the most homely conversation:

> Then up they hoist me John in a chafe.

What the conjunction of these two lines represents is visible in all the lines and phrases of the stanza: Browning is eager for a range which far exceeds the range of expression of the romantics or of his fellow-Victorians.

For his variety of tone he was sharply criticized. Even so intelligent a critic as Bagehot spoke of much of his poetry as satisfactory to no *sane* taste. Formally it was in this grotesque variety he gave the greatest challenge to his age, if one excepts the challenge implied in the persistent difficulty of his poetry. It may be well then to look at one further example of his range. One of his most celebrated poems, "A Grammarian's Funeral," will supply an admirable one:

> That's the appropriate country; there, man's thought,
> Rarer, intenser,
> Self-gathered for an outbreak, as it ought,
> Chafes in the censer.
> Leave we the unlettered plain its herd and crop;
> Seek we sepulture,
> On a tall mountain, citied to the top,
> Crowded with culture!

Only Browning would have introduced into a grave funeral hymn such a grotesque phrase as "crowded with culture"; only he would have chosen such a moment to bring in a verbal use of "city."

Whatever objections Victorian critics might offer to his diction, it did not fail to affect the poetry of the younger Victorians, notably that of Hardy.

The unusualness of Hardy's diction is patent and multiform. His poetry abounds in archaisms, in words like "wight," and "witlessness," and "mumm"; in strange formations such as "enjailed," or "unblooms," or "anywhen"; in terms which verge at least on pedantry, and yet occur in poems of simple feeling, terms such as "retrocede," or "phasm." The effect of such expressions is to suggest a psychological distance between his subject and his feelings, a species of cosmic humor, as if, intense as was Hardy's sympathy for the miseries of man, he appreciated, even when recording his sympathy, how slight they were in the huge scheme of things.

An originality less vigorous but no less definite appears in the first collection of William Morris. It supposes a painter's eye: but it has little to do with what is ordinarily described as pictorial verse. Plainness and bareness are its marks, and its most extreme instances are in such expressions as:

Creeping o'er my *broad* eyelids unafraid

or

Why did your *long* lips cleave
In such strange way?

or

See through my *long* throat how the words go up
In *ripples* to my mouth.

or

. . . quiet groans
That swell not the *little* bones
Of my bosom.

Such simplicity is interwoven with expressions in which artifice is obtrusive. As Morris grows older the artifice and the simplicity fuse into a language apter for objective verse, but never again could Morris's diction jolt one's senses as these earlier lines do.

Most of the other Victorians used a diction either frankly romantic like Tennyson's or Swinburne's or Rossetti's, or else a development from romantic diction such as Arnold's. Arnold is Keatsian in his more elaborate poems such as "The Scholar Gipsy" and "Thyrsis," Wordsworthian in his more austere pieces, and exhibits a fusion of the two, with something of Byron added, in the poems where he most fully expresses his whole range of attitude.

VI. SOUND

Much more might be said of the diction of these and other Victorian poets; but it is more important to appreciate their use of sound. Two at least among them had a mastery of sounds original, powerful, and constant.

Tennyson was from the years of his apprenticeship much concerned with beauty of sound; and in his volumes of 1830 and 1832 many poems have their place solely as dexterous exercises in sound. Of these "Claribel" is the most strikingly pure example. The second stanza of this poem is a series of sounds and little else:

At eve the beetle boometh
Athwart the thicket lone:
At noon the wild bee hummeth
About the moss'd headstone:

At midnight the moon cometh,
And looketh down alone.
Her song the lintwhite swelleth,
The clear-voiced mavis dwelleth,
The callow throstle lispeth,
The slumbrous wave outwelleth,
The babbling runnel crispeth,
The hollow grot replieth
Where Claribel low-lieth.

Taken by itself an epithet such as "slumbrous," or a line such as "Athwart the thicket lone" may have a burden of meaning; but in the total effect even the sounds of beetle, wild bee, birds and water are deprived of their definiteness and become lost in the single musical effect which Tennyson is trying to attain. The stanza is an incantation rich and slow.

Even in poems where the weight of thought is comparable with that in Wordsworth's philosophical poetry, the preoccupation with sound continues. Let *In Memoriam* serve as an example: is not this lyric another incantation, solid as it is found to be when one stays to examine its substance?

Tho' truths in manhood darkly join,
Deep-seated in our mystic frame,
We yield all blessing to the name
Of Him that made them current coin;

For Wisdom dealt with mortal powers,
Where truth in closest words shall fail,
When truth embodied in a tale
Shall enter in at lowly doors.

And so the Word had breath, and wrought
With human hands the creed of creeds
In loveliness of perfect deeds,
More strong than all poetic thought;

Which he may read that binds the sheaf,
Or builds the house, or digs the grave,
And those wild eyes that watch the wave
In roarings round the coral reef.

The seamless fabric of the verse dazes one: it is only by a deliberate effort that one resists the succession of full rich vowels and liquid consonants to attend to the very important idea that Tennyson has uttered. Nothing else more adequately explains the dismissal of Tennyson as a poet of thought, perhaps, than the perfect vesture his thought wears.

It is the same with Swinburne. He was himself aware of the overluxuriance of his verse, as his self-parody "Nephelidia" so amusingly demonstrates. He begins:

From the depth of the dreamy decline of the
dawn through a notable nimbus of nebulous noonshine,
Pallid and pink as the palm of the flagflower
that flickers with fear of the flies as they float,
Are they looks of our lovers that lustrously lean
from a marvel of mystic miraculous moonshine. . . .

And "a marvel of mystic miraculous moonshine" his poetry may, much of it, appear to be. Some of his bitterest satire looses its edge, the sound is so richly melodious; reading it one appreciates why the Elizabethan satiric poets considered a certain roughness of style demanded by the satiric type.

Many of Swinburne's poems are almost pure music. He was, says Professor Cazamian, a symbolist poet "in everything but the name . . . the flood of his verse poured forth in a rush of rhythm and sound, guided by a haunting cadence." Mr. I. A. Richards quotes the following characteristic Swinburnian stanza from "Before the Mirror":

> There glowing ghosts of flowers
> Draw down, draw nigh;
> And wings of swift spent hours
> Take flight and fly;
> She sees by formless gleams,
> She hears across cold streams,
> Dead mouths of many dreams that sing and sigh.

The critic comments wisely: "Little beyond vague thoughts of the things the words stand for is required." In the same spirit Mr. Eliot singles out another characteristic passage:

> There lived a singer in France of old
> By the tideless dolorous midland sea.
> In a land of sand and ruin and gold
> There shone one woman, and none but she.

He goes on to remark; "It is the word that gives him the thrill and not the object." "Gold" and "dolorous" and "ruin" and "shone," the phrases "midland sea" and "France of old": it is on these and on the movement of the lines that Swinburne relies to communicate the mysterious sadness which is the soul of the passage. Across the Channel, Verlaine was using the same resources, and turning verse into verbal music, *romances sans paroles.*

English poetry has usually been marked by definite imagery; and at no time was such imagery more abundant or more striking than in the nineteenth century. The novelty of Swinburne's dependence on sound, of his reduction of imagery to brief and misted phrases, is one of the Victorian innovations which have most violently disturbed the national taste in poetry. Those who found it too much of a disturbance have accused Swinburne of intolerable monotony; and indeed a succession of such stanzas must be infinitely monotonous to any one who is in quest of a more precise sense than they possess. Once one appreciates that the power of the poem dwells in its sounds, that the meaning dwells there too, one will not press the charge of monotony. What one feels then is the power of the music, the power of the emotional meaning it conveys.

In sound-effects Housman is, whether the relation was conscious or not, Swinburne's disciple. It is significant that he should have remarked that among the English poets of the nineteenth century the most original were Wordsworth and Swinburne. Swinburne diffused his music through lingering feet, rich polysyllables, and interminable stanzas; but Housman concentrates his in regular and emphatic feet, resonant monosyllables, and stanzas as simple and brief as any one ever wrote. Still, the underlying likeness is profound and unmistakable. In lines such as

> If the heats of hate and lust
> In the house of flesh are strong,
> Let me mind the house of dust
> Where my sojourn shall be long,

despite the clarity of statement, the effect of pure sound is as overwhelming as in "The Triumph of Time" or "The Garden of Proserpine." It is in such passages as that quoted, rather than in his more rhetorical or more suggestive poems that Housman achieves his noblest and most intense effects.

At the very opposite pole from such emphatic music as Housman's is Morris's. Of the musical effect in the more striking pieces in his first collection, *The Defence of Guenevere and Other Poems,* Dixon Scott has finely said:

> It is worth while noting, too, how extraordinarily this plodding tick-tock of the metre, pursuing its way imperturbably, quite indifferent to the human stresses of the speaker's voice or the natural

modulations of the story, actually produces an effect of incommunicable tensions and mysterious significances by tugging the skin of the verse away from the simple underlying meaning. If the reader's voice obeys the injunctions of the rhythm, it often puts an emphasis on unimportant words—on words, certainly, that had no special meaning for Morris; and the result of this disparity between their sound-value and their sense-value is a strange acquisition of mystical momentousness as though they meant infinitely more than they said.

The subtle music of which Scott is here speaking is shown in the first stanza of "Concerning Geffray Teste Noire."

And if you meet the Canon of Chimay,
As going to Ortaise you well may do,
Greet him from John of Castel Neuf, and say
All that I tell you, for all this is true.

The tense quietness of this, partly metrical, partly verbal, is lost in the poetry that followed, in *The Life and Death of Jason* and *The Earthly Paradise;* and in the revisions to which Morris planned to submit his first collection it was to be nullified. It remains a unique moment in the development of English poetry. The large utterance of *Sigurd the Volsung* has no parallel more recent than Chapman's translation of Homer; and surpasses Chapman in swing and force of sound.

Again, as so often, it is with Morris that a survey of an aspect of Victorian poetry concludes.

VII. THOUGHT

Victorian poetry is in an unusual and even eminent degree a poetry of thought. Few complaints against its quality are more obstinate than the complaint that it is dragged down from the true heights of poetry by its load of thought. Of Browning and Tennyson Mr. F. L. Lucas has remarked: "Both . . . seem to me pure poets damaged by being too much honoured as prophets in their own country. In consequence they were led more and more to preach, where they should have sung. . . . Donne was wiser, who wrote lyrics in his youth and sermons in his old age; and so instead of muddling the two, made great literature of both." Against Arnold the same charge has been made, against Swinburne, against Meredith and against Hardy.

It is not baseless. The quality of thought in the greater Victorian poets is significantly dissimilar to that in the greater romantics. Mr. Herbert Read has written of the "felt thought" of Wordsworth; and Keats himself had spoken of the need to prove one's ideas upon the pulses if they are to be fully real. The greatest expressions of romantic thought are "felt": they have been proved upon the pulses. To limit oneself to two examples, a passage from "Tintern Abbey" and a passage from the "Ode to Autumn," the thought of Wordsworth and of Keats is easily shown to be a rich mixture of intellect, emotion, sensation and the supra-rational. The first passage is from "Tintern Abbey":

And I have felt
A presence that disturbs me with the joy
Of elevated thoughts; a sense sublime
Of something far more deeply interfused,
Whose dwelling is the light of setting suns,
And the round ocean and the living air,
And the blue sky, and in the mind of man:
A motion and a spirit, that impels
All thinking things, all objects of all thought,
And rolls through all things.

Take along with this the closing stanza of "To Autumn":

Where are the songs of Spring? Ay, where are they?
Think not of them, thou hast thy music too,—

While barred clouds bloom the soft-dying day,
And touch the stubble-plains with rosy hue;
Then in a wailful choir the small gnats mourn
Among the river sallows, borne aloft
Or sinking as the light wind lives or dies;
And full-grown lambs loud bleat from hilly bourn;
Hedge-crickets sing; and now with treble soft
The red-breast whistles from a garden-croft;
And gathering swallows twitter in the skies.

Set beside the lines in which Wordsworth expresses the divinity which he finds in the universe a noble and famous passage in which Browning is dealing with the divine:

Oh, speak through me now!
Would I suffer for him that I love? So would'st thou—
so wilt thou!
So shall crown thee the topmost, ineffablest, uttermost crown—
And thy love fill infinitude wholly, nor leave up nor down
One spot for the creature to stand in! It is by no breath,
Turn of eye, wave of hand, that salvation joins issue with death!
As thy Love is discovered almighty, almighty be proved
Thy power, that exists with and for it, of being Beloved!
He who did most shall bear most; the strongest shall stand
the most weak.
'Tis the weakness in strength, that I cry for! my flesh,
that I seek
In the Godhead! I seek and I find it. O Saul, it shall be
A Face like my face that receives thee; a Man like to me,
Thou shalt love and be loved by for ever: a Hand like this hand
Shall throw open the gates of new life to thee! See the Christ
stand!

It is a great passage, no doubt; in it there is feeling as well as thought, and a kind of intellectual imagination. But it is not felt thought: feeling and thought are both present and both are intense, but they have not coalesced.

Now set by the passage in which Keats expresses his resignation to the amalgam of good and evil, pleasure and grief in life, a passage in which Arnold does the same. It is from the impressive poem "Consolation":

Through sun-proof alleys
In a lone sand-hemm'd
City of Africa,
A blind, led beggar,
Age-bow'd, asks alms.

No bolder Robber
Erst abode ambush'd
Deep in the sandy waste:
No clearer eyesight
Spied prey afar.

Saharan sand-winds
Sear'd his keen eyeballs.
Spent is the spoil he won.
For him the present
Holds only pain.

Two young, fair lovers,
Where the warm June wind,

Fresh from the summer fields,
Plays fondly round them,
Stand, tranc'd in joy.

With sweet, join'd voices,
And with eyes brimming—
'Ah,' they cry, 'Destiny!
Prolong the present!
Time! stand still here!'

The prompt stern Goddess
Shakes her head, frowning.
Time gives his hour-glass
Its due reversal.
Their hour is gone.

It would be entirely false to dismiss this passage as in thought less noble, in feeling less intense than the stanza from Keats. Yet, as in the passages from Wordsworth and Browning, a differentiation is necessary. Arnold, like Browning, has not fused thought and feeling; it is possible to speak of a load of thought in his poem, a phrase which would be entirely inappropriate to the poem of Keats. Both Arnold and Keats in the passages quoted display a notable imaginative power; but from the imaginative passages Arnold proceeds to a deduction (the whole of which I have not quoted); Keats draws no deduction—his stanza must be apprehended as a whole, imagination, emotion, idea, mysteriously fused.

The above illustrations will serve a purpose if they throw a light on the operation of thought in Victorian poetry. The thought itself is illuminated by considering how the several poets of the time responded to the main currents of Victorian speculation.

VIII. THE IDEA OF EVOLUTION

Scientific thought is unquestionably one of those currents. In the nineteenth century the dominant concept in science is that of evolution. It is a concept which requires very careful handling if confusion is to be avoided. Many critics have coupled with the notion of evolution propounded by Darwin in his *Origin of Species* (1859) and subsequent works passages in the poets which merely express the more general and much older idea of development. A notable passage from *In Memoriam* is among those most often chosen:

They say,
The solid earth whereon we tread

In tracts of fluent heat began,
And grew to seeming-random forms,
The seeming prey of cyclic storms,
Till at the last arose the man;

Who throve and branched from clime to clime,
The herald of a higher race,
And of himself in higher place,
If so he type this work of time

Within himself, from more to more.

What Tennyson is asserting here is, first, the nebular hypothesis of the origin of the world, second, the geological explanation of the manner in which the world has come to its present form, third, the late appearance of man in the world, fourth, the process of development in which what is now humanity was once less developed and will some time be more developed. With this passage, written, one must remember, at least a decade befeore the *Origin of Species* was published, the conception Darwin was to set forth is compatible but not identical; it is incorrect to find in Tennyson's lines any striking anticipation of Darwin. Another passage also written before the *Origin of Species* was published comes in *Maud:*

> A monstrous eft was of old the Lord and Master of Earth,
> For him did his high sun flame, and his river billowing ran,
> And he felt himself in his force to be Nature's crowning race.
> As nine months go to the shaping an infant ripe for his birth,
> So many million of ages have gone to the making of man:
> He now is first, but is he the last? is he not too base?

The opinions expressed by the speaker in *Maud* cannot be taken as Tennyson's own, unless they are repeated in other poems where he speaks in his own person. Even if one puts aside the question whether the passage quoted represents Tennyson's opinion, one cannot find in it any evidence of belief in such a theory of evolution as Darwin's. All that one can find is a belief that man appeared late in the order of life in this world, that he followed other and lower beings, and that subsequent development may supersede man with beings higher than he is.

After the publication of the *Origin of Species,* another idea appears in Tennyson's poetry, the idea of a possible downward movement in the developing process. Nowhere is this idea expressed more clearly or more intensely than in "Locksley Hall Sixty Years After." Again one must hesitate before ascribing to Tennyson all the opinions expressed by the old man who speaks. But what he says can be at least in part confirmed from other poems in which the poet directly addresses us. Among the old man's utterances are these:

> Evolution ever climbing after some ideal Good,
> And Reversion ever dragging Evolution in the mud. . . .

and

> Many an Æon moulded earth before her highest, man, was born,
> Many an Æon too may pass when earth is manless and forlorn. . . .

It would be dangerous to assume that Darwin is in the background here: Darwin supplies no more reason for supposing that the curve of development may turn down than for supposing that it would rise upward eternally.

Tennyson has expressed in conversation or in letters some reservations about the Darwinian theory. "No evolutionist" he wrote "is able to explain the mind of man or how any possible physiological change of tissue can produce conscious thought." No one who fully accepted the Darwinian theory, or who was attuned to the scientific habit of mind so fully embodied in Charles Darwin would have written that sentence. What a scientific mind, sceptical of Darwin's theory, might have written is something like this: "No evolutionist has *so far* succeeded in explaining the origin and nature of human intelligence."

But if Tennyson is not correctly styled a follower of Darwin, he must be allowed to have known more of the science of his age than any other poet, to have in large measure merited Huxley's phrase of eulogy "a modern Lucretius." As a boy he was interested in science; and in long years after his leaving Cambridge and before his marriage when he gave so much of his time to study, the mornings went to science and only the afternoons to the humane letters. He read Lyell's epochal *Geology* in 1837; and in 1844 he ordered a copy of *Vestiges of Creation* before it appeared, as he was later to do for the *Origin of Species.* It was natural that Huxley should say at the time of Tennyson's death that he had known more of what his scientific contemporaries were doing than any other man of letters. No one was better qualified to pass judgment.

Something further must be allowed. For his belief in progress he sought the confirmation of science, that is to say he wished to find in scientific fact justification for such a flight of prophecy as he allowed himself in the first *Locksley Hall:*

For I dipt into the future, far as human eye could see,
Saw the Vision of the world, and all the wonder that would be. . . .

. . . I doubt not through the ages one increasing purpose runs,
And the thoughts of men are widened with the process of the suns.

Evolution or, better, development in the sense here indicated he did, when he was young, believe in; and he always wished to believe in it. If the scientists could furnish him with evidence that humanity had superseded a lower form of life, he would thank them.

He was not however content to believe that God was within nature. Nature was for him an expression of God—God was in nature; but God was outside it too, transcendent as well as immanent:

Out of darkness came the hands
That reach *through* nature moulding men.

With the scientific thought of his age Browning was much less conversant than Tennyson; but Browning was much occupied with the nature and value of the scientific habit of mind. *Paracelsus* is an example of his preoccupation. At the beginning of the poem Festus contrasts the method of Paracelsus with that of older students of the nature of things: they merely mused, Paracelsus investigates; they depended on past wisdom, Paracelsus strikes out a new path, lighted on his difficult way only by a hypothesis of his own engendering, the gift to him of his genius. Paracelsus distinguishes his position from that of his predecessors in a clear contrast:

I understand these fond fears just expressed.
And first; the lore you praise and I neglect,
The labours and the precepts of old time,
I have not lightly disesteemed. But, friends,
Truth is within ourselves; it takes no rise
From outward things, whate'er you may believe.
There is an inmost centre in us all,
Where truth abides in fullness. . . .
. . . and to KNOW
Rather consists in opening out a way
Whence the imprisoned splendour may escape,
Than in effecting entry for a light
Supposed to be without.

Paracelsus fails to achieve the complete success to which he and his friends had looked forward. His failure came of lack of love; from lack of love many disasters befall the operation of the intelligence. The man who lacks love cannot maintain in its strength that inmost centre of which we have heard Paracelsus speak; and when that centre decays insight, or the ability to frame original hypotheses, atrophies. Lack of love goes hand in hand with a greed for power; and it was such a greed which prompted in Paracelsus that scorn for the past of which he speaks, and which was in the end to cripple his thinking. Further, the man who lacks love will antagonize his fellows: in consequence they will not accept or develop his teachings.

Browning's verdict on the scientific habit of mind, as represented in Paracelsus, is in two parts. The first is that such a habit is incomplete and therefore distorting. The second part of the verdict is much more favorable. Whatever may have been Paracelsus's greed for power, one of his aims was to explore the secrets of the universe and thus furnish man with knowledge. Such an aim is noble; and noble is Paracelsus's exclusive devotion to an intellectual good. Whatever his weaknesses and errors, Paracelsus is a heroic figure.

Towards evolution and the more general notion of development Browning's attitude was almost identical with Tennyson's. Like Tennyson he conceived of man as the highest stage so far attained in the unrolling of the animated world. In *Paracelsus* he says—it is Paracelsus who speaks:

Thus [God] dwells in all,
From life's minute beginnings, up at last
To man—the consummation of this scheme
Of being, the completion of this sphere
Of life: whose attributes had here and there
Been scattered o'er the visible world before,
Asking to be combined, dim fragments meant
To be united in some wondrous whole,
Imperfect qualities throughout creation,
Suggesting some one creature yet to make,
Some point where all those scattered rays should meet
Convergent in the faculties of man.

Man will in turn be surpassed. The full possibilities of the human type have not yet been realized:

Man is not Man as yet.

Once those possibilities have been realized, a further objective will be attempted:

And, man produced, all has its end thus far:
But in completed man begins anew
A tendency to God.

Mr. Beach has warned against the assumption that such passages denote a belief in the scientific conception of evolution, wisely suggesting that they merely express a philosophic view of universal life, in which the simple and the complex, the high and the low forms of life are set together in an intellectually satisfying unity.

When Darwin formulated his doctrine, Browning did not accept it without grave reservations. He accepts that part of the doctrine which merely states "a conception familiar to me from the beginning: see in *Paracelsus* the progressive development from senseless matter to organized until man's appearance." But Browning is adamant against any conception of the process of life which would exclude belief in a cause exterior to matter and acting upon it. He tells us so in prose; and in the late "Parleying with Francis Furini" he insists:

Not inmost is the Cause Externe, fool, look and learn!

Like Tennyson, then, he declines to accept a doctrine which would either make an end of God or transfer Him to a point within nature. Like Tennyson he is not a scientific evolutionist.

Most of Arnold's poems were written before the publication of the *Origin of Species;* and neither before nor after he read that work was scientific thought a notable preoccupation of his. Indeed of all the Victorian masters Carlyle alone was less affected by scientific conclusions. Science was for Arnold a dead thing: it was powerless to stimulate his imagination, even to horrify it, and it was not science which dissolved his faith. The sources of his scepticism, which was profound, lay elsewhere, in the higher criticism, in philosophic history, in the main stream of European thinking about humanity.

To science he seldom refers in his poetry and it is in his prose that we must seek the clear expression of his doubts as to its worth to civilization and culture. As early as 1852, when science counted for little in the curricula of elementary schools or training schools he was shocked by the "utter disproportion between the amount of positive information and the low degree of mental culture and intelligence which [the pupil teachers] exhibit." In literature, for him the supreme instrument of education, he discerned the remedy for this disproportion; science would but increase it. Thirty years later, in his last report as an inspector he ends with a quotation of Bishop Butler's opinion: "Of education information is really the least part." Sometimes he paid a perfunctory compliment to the educative value of science, but the core of his estimate of this value is in the well-known passage in the essay "Literature and Science":

> "If one is driven to choose, I think I would rather have a young person ignorant about the moon's diameter, but aware that "Can you not wait upon the lunatic?" is bad [as a paraphrase of the line in Macbeth, "Canst thou not minister to a mind diseased?"] rather than a young person whose education had managed things the other way."

If one is driven to choose! One cannot doubt that Arnold thought England would be driven to choose, and that he greatly feared England would make the wrong choice.

However in Arnold's approach to the problems of his age, and especially in his approach to the religious problem, he adopted an attitude which was intimately allied with the discipline which science can give. In his theological writings he is perpetually protesting against "unverifiable" hypotheses and against "insane licence of affirmation." Religion cannot, he thinks, be securely founded upon the unverifiable; no conception of God which is not verifiable in human experience can possibly stand. It is perilous, however, to assume that Arnold absorbed such an insistence upon verification from the sciences, although he was clearly aware of the affinity between his demands and those which the scientific temper would impose.

Matthew Arnold was but six years the senior of George Meredith; and only two years separate their first collections of verse. The intellectual hiatus between the two poets is nevertheless astonishing. Meredith made peace with science, and made it easily; Arnold never did. Meredith was not merely content but delighted to consider man as wholly earth-bound; his confidence in the body of facts which he grouped in his recurring term Earth freed Meredith from the conflict which agonized Tennyson, Browning and Arnold. In Meredith's view of the universe there was no place for battle between spirit and body, divine and animal: for him all was a great and satisfying unity.

At the beginning of his account of Meredith's thought M. Photiadès has aptly set a quotation from *Lord Ormont and His Aminta:* "We do not get to any Heaven by renouncing the Mother we spring from; and when there is an eternal secret for us, it is best to believe that Earth knows, to keep near her, even in our utmost aspirations." However even if Man is disloyal to Earth, Earth will not disown him. In "Earth and Man" Meredith presents the disloyalty and the forgiveness

> . . . the wretch inclines
> Afresh to the Invisible, who, he saith,
> Can raise him high: with vows of living faith
> For little signs.
>
> Some signs he must demand,
> Some proofs of slaughtered nature; some prized few
> To satisfy the senses it is true,
> And in his hand. . . .
>
> From dust, of him abhorred,
> He would be snatched by Grace discovering worth.
> 'Sever me from the hollowness of earth!
> Me take, dear Lord.' . . .
>
> If he aloft for aid
> Imploring storms, her essence is the spur.
> His cry to heaven is a cry to her
> He would evade.

As Man engages in the hopeless quest of a super-terrestrial Spirit, Earth quietly observes her child and furnishes him his strength, confident that in the end he will recognize that Earth and Earth's issue alone exist.

Man is the child of Earth, not her foster child. Professor Trevelyan contrasts the doctrine of Wordsworth in the Intimations ode:

The homely nurse doth all she can
To make her foster-child, her inmate, Man,
Forget the glories he hath known
And that imperial palace whence he came

with that of Meredith, whose vision is clearest perhaps in "The Empty Purse" in which he celebrates the manifold excellence of Earth:

. . . Our Earth we have seen
Beneath and on surface, her deeds and designs;
Who gives us the man-loving Nazarene,
The martyrs, the poets, the corn and the vines.

The gap between Wordsworth and Meredith is roughly the gap between pre-evolutionary and post-evolutionary idealism. Meredith made no difficulty in accepting the teachings of Darwin and his expositors. He speaks in "The Woods of Westermain" of reading in the eyes of oxen

Back to hours when mind was mud.

It must be said that the poems from which Meredith's evolutionary naturalism may be clearly perceived are poems written as late as the eighties. Further, as Mr. Beach insists, it must be conceded that Swinburne, although he was nearly a decade younger than Meredith, long preceded him in a complete assimilation of the doctrine of evolution.

Swinburne was nine years younger than Meredith; but he was ready to announce his full adherence to evolutionary naturalism a decade earlier. The substance of his naturalism is scarcely distinguishable from the doctrines of Meredith which have been noted, and accordingly need not be expounded at length; but Swinburne's tone is different. Where Meredith is grave and quiet, Swinburne is defiant and stormy. In the "Prelude" to *Songs before Sunrise* he repudiates any framework for life beyond Earth:

He hath given himself to time, whose fold
Shuts in the mortal flock that lives
On its plain pasture's heat and cold.

There is no God, there never was:

Save his own soul's light overhead
None leads him and none ever led. . . .

The force from which all elements in the world derive he describes in "Hertha." Life was in the beginning something that drifted and swam on the waters, in the spring-coloured hours of the world's history flowers broke out, in which man was potential; finally man emerged. As in Meredith's vision man was disloyal to Earth, the source of all he is, Swinburne too shows man in quest of a super-terrestrial being whom he would worship. The difference in the temperaments of the poets appears in their renderings of Earth's attitude to her offspring's disloyalty. Meredith shows her patiently and assuredly awaiting Man's recovery; Swinburne shows her disillusioning man with his idol:

Lo, winged with world's wonders,
With miracles shod,
With the fires of his thunders
For raiment and rod,
God trembles in heaven, and his angels are white with the terror of God.

For his twilight is come on him,
His anguish is here;
And his spirits gaze dumb on him,
Grown grey from his fear;
And his hour taketh hold on him stricken, the last of his infinite year.

Thought made him and breaks him,
Truth slays and forgives;
But to him as time takes him
This new thing it gives,
Even love, the beloved Republic. . . .

The fundamental difference between Hardy's view of the universe and that held by the two poets just considered is one not of definition but of judgment. Meredith and Swinburne were happy in the natural order; they did not lament the disappearance of God, but rather judged that a universe ruled by the natural law was preferable to a universe ruled by such a God as earlier thinkers, Christian or non-Christian had conceived. The natural order did not so satisfy Hardy, and yet he was unable like Tennyson and Browning, whom it equally dissatisfied, to convince himself of the existence in the universe of a supra-natural force.

The intellectual drama in the poetry of Hardy is in essence that of the conflict within him of his reason, which told him that only a scientific conception of the universe was tenable, and his moral being which insisted that such a conception was too horrible to be true. It was too horrible because of the pain in which it involved humanity. The problem of pain had not been a pre-occupation of Meredith, whose fortitude and austerity forbade him to contemplate pain with the warm worried sympathy which it provoked in Hardy. Swinburne was much pre-occupied with pain; but, as recent biographers have demonstrated, pain was in his personality intimately related to love; and he delighted to imagine himself the recipient of savage cruelty. A universe in which savage cruelty abounded would not to him have been intolerable at all.

To Hardy it was intolerable. He sought many escapes from the conviction that man must suffer without reprieve. The most profound of his many escapist conceptions was that of a force within or behind nature which was slowly growing in consciousness and which when its consciousness was fully matured would perceive the roughness of humanity's fate and alter it. At times he repudiated this mildly hopeful conception of the force which determined the line of life; and it would be false to represent him as believing in it as he believed in the injustice and pain of human life. Nevertheless Hardy was indignant when the term pessimist was applied to him and, notably in the Apology which prefaces *Late Lyrics and Earlier,* undertook to define his creed as one of "evolutionary meliorism." The position of the evolutionary meliorist towards the human society he has expressed in the same apology:

"Looking down the future these few hold fast to the same: that whether the human and kindred animal races survive till the exhaustion or destruction of the globe, or whether these races perish and are succeeded by others before that conclusion comes, pain to all upon it, tongued or dumb, shall be kept down to a minimum by loving-kindness operating through scientific knowledge, and actuated by the modicum of free will conjecturally possessed by organic life when the mighty necessitating forces—unconscious or other—that have "the balancings of the clouds," happen to be in equilibrium, which may or may not be often."

The morality here set forth finds no sanction in the natural order: it is a specifically human contribution. Why man should so act Hardy does not make clear in so many words: but from his poetry it is easy to infer that man must so act if he would satisfy his own being and that if he fails so to act he outrages his humanity. Such a basis for a moral doctrine is extremely insecure; and to an observer of human life as acute as Hardy that insecurity was obvious. In it he could not rest from questioning the nature of the force which controlled the universe, in so far at least as he considered the universe is controlled.

When a reader of Hardy leaves the solid ground of his prose-statements to supplement from his verse what they tell us, caution must be his monitor. Hardy himself has warned against supposing that all his verses express his own views. In the preface to his first collection, *Wessex Poems,* he says: "The pieces are in a large degree dramatic or personative in conception; and this even when they are not obviously so." In the next collection, *Poems of the Past and Present,* he repeats the warning and goes on to insist that the book "will be found to possess little cohesion of thought or harmony of colouring." The last words in the introductory note to his final volume put forward the most impressive warning of all: "I also repeat what I have often stated on such occasions, that no harmonious philosophy is attempted in these pages, or in any bygone pages of mine, for that matter."

IX. THE HIGHER CRITICISM

Second only to the many-sided development of scientific thought was the progress in the critical study of the Bible. In Hardy's "Drinking Song" after the stanza on Darwin's doctrine:

> Next this strange message Darwin brings,
> (Though saying his say
> In a quiet way);
> We are all one with creeping things;
> And apes and men
> Blood-brethren,
> And likewise reptile forms with stings.

follows a stanza on the higher criticism as exemplified in Cheyne:

> And when this philosoph had done
> Came Doctor Cheyne:
> Speaking plain he
> Proved no virgin bore a son.
> "Such tale, indeed,
> Helps not our creed,"
> He said. "A tale long known to none."

Concern with the problem of the higher criticism began to diffuse itself a little later than concern with the problem of man's place in the animal creation.

In the thirties and forties men such as Julius Hare, Arthur Stanley and Stanley's master Dr. Thomas Arnold, had inklings of the revolution in English religious thought and life which would flow from knowledge of what in Germany had been said and written by Ewald, Baur, and Strauss. But it was not until in 1860 a group of seven Oxford men published the collection *Essays and Reviews* that any large number of Englishmen came face to face with the problem. The last and most persuasive of the essays in the volume was Benjamin Jowett's "On the Interpretation of Scriptures." Jowett points out that among German scholars in the nineteenth century "there is for the first time in the history of the world an approach to agreement and certainty" in the interpretation of Scripture; and that this approach to agreement and certainty springs from the willingness of the Germans to seek one thing and one thing only: "the original spirit and intention of the Authors" of Scripture. Jowett finds in their interpretation of Scripture the greatest advance in religious thought since the Reformation; and the implication is clear that the English who in the time of the Reformation had been among the party of progress in Europe are now among the party of reaction.

What the "Seven against Scripture" chiefly advocated was the application to the Bible of the methods of interpretation long used in classical scholarship: the aim of Biblical scholarship was, they said, to discover what had actually been written, when it had been written, and what to its original authors and audience it would mean. If such method of interpretation were to prevail in England, there was need of learning in philology and archaeology far beyond what then existed; and indeed none of the contributors to the symposium was himself qualified to undertake the work whose need they perceived. Nothing was to be hoped for from the Regius Professor of Hebrew at Oxford: Pusey had gone to Germany in the twenties with the intention "to devote my life to the Old Testament as I saw that this was the point of attack in our defences that would be most easily breached" and had returned knowing much but in no degree weakened in his orthodoxy.

The interpretation for which the essayists and reviewers looked came from an entirely unexpected champion, John William Colenso. "It was," says Cheyne, "John William Colenso who reopened the suspended intercourse between the critical students of England and the continent." Almost forty years of age when in 1853 he was elevated to the bishopric of Natal he had, despite his sympathy with reform, done nothing to indicate that in scholarship he would strike a resounding, and indeed a decisive blow. What books and articles he had written had to do with piety or mathematics. Questions asked of him by Zulus to whom he taught the Christian faith stirred in him a vague disquietude; with the habits of a scholar he turned to the German critics and far off in Natal he read them to greater advantage than bishops in England. He began to publish his views in 1862: "on the grapeshot of the *Essays and Reviews* followed the bombshell of Bishop Colenso's volume on *The Pentateuch and the Book of Joshua Critically Examined.*" J. M. Robertson suggests that although *Essays and Reviews* had passed through nine editions within a year of its publication, Colenso was more effective in dissolving the mists of indifference and ignorance which prevented the cultivated English public from grappling with the problem of Biblical interpretation. In producing the immense effect he did produce he was aided by his episcopal position and by his writing not as a scholarly recluse but as a missionary who in explaining Christian doctrine to black men had encountered difficulties which had led him to a critical study of the sacred text. He wrote that is to say as the result of an urgent practical dilemma: and as Cheyne says, he had "a plain practical characteristically English mind." Biblical criticism does not regard him as one of its masters; but it renders homage to his integrity and effectiveness.

With subsequent criticism the student of Victorian poetry need not be concerned; the great names of Robertson Smith, Driver and Cheyne himself are linked with the performance of what the essayists and reviewers advocated and Colenso began. Mention must, however, be made of the appearance in 1863, only one year after Colenso's first work, of Ernest Renan's *Vie de Jésus* which more powerfully affected European attitudes towards Christianity than anything since Strauss's *Leben Jesu* of 1835.

Far beyond all other Victorian poets Browning and Arnold were preoccupied with the higher criticism. Browning was in the main its resolute enemy, Arnold its worried advocate. Only these two will be considered here.

In one of the poems in *Dramatis Personae* (1864) Browning writes:

> The candid incline to surmise of late
> That the Christian faith proves false, I find;
> For our Essays-and-Reviews' debate
> Begins to tell on the public mind,
> And Colenso's words have weight:
>
> I still, to suppose it true, for my part
> See reasons and reasons; this, to begin:
> 'Tis the faith that launched point-blank her dart
> At the head of a lie—taught Original Sin
> The Corruption of Man's Heart.

In these two stanzas of "Gold Hair" the incompatibility between Browning's mind and that of a Biblical scholar is patent. The scholar inquires disinterestedly whether facts asserted in the Bible to have occurred did occur, and whether the evidence for authorship and period of composition supports the beliefs held: the plane along which his intelligence moves is the plane of patient laborious criticism. Browning's plane is quite another: his intelligence inquires into the adequacy of Christianity to the spiritual needs of man. Once convinced of the adequacy he could not believe that inquiry into the authorship and date of parts of the Bible could serve any valuable end.

Moreover Browning's Christianity insisted weightily upon the Divinity of Christ. He held that Christ was either the son of God or an impostor; and that the value of Christ lay not in his teaching but in his divinity. As divine he was the incontrovertible and supreme proof that God was a loving God: and that God was a loving God was Browning's main spiritual intuition, the root of his entire attitude towards the universe. The higher criticism seemed to him to tend toward the disallowance of Christ's divinity; if this were disallowed, the structure of Browning's optimism would have collapsed.

In *Christmas Eve and Easter Day* (1850) Browning's hostility to the higher criticism and the main ground for it appear. He presents himself—and this is one of the rare major poems in which he speaks without dramatic disguise—as visiting first a dissenting chapel in London, then St. Peter's at Rome, finally a lecture room in the theological faculty of Göttingen. The dissenting chapel is objectionable: the people are unloving, debased and ignorant, the preacher stupid and assured. The Basilica is the expression of a religion which has overlaid the original revelation of Christ with ceremonies and dogmas which conceal much of its reality. But it is for the theological lecturer that Browning reserves his heaviest objections. The lecture begins:

All settle themselves, the while ascends
By the creaking rail to the lecture desk,
    Step by step, deliberate
    Because of his cranium's over-freight,
Three parts sublime to one grotesque,
If I have proved an accurate guesser
The hawk-nosed high-cheek-boned professor.

That is the note of the treatment; but Browning was also critical of the appearance and manner of the dissenting preacher. The professor's purpose was to inquire into the origin of Christianity and above all into the nature of Christ. His major premise (which in the poem he makes no attempt to justify) is that

. . . plainly no such life was liveable

as the evangelists had reported. But he insisted that Christ was not a mere fabrication of his disciples. He had lived.

'Twas obviously as well to take
The popular story,—understanding
    How the ineptitude of the time,
And the penman's prejudice, expanding
    Fact into fable fit for the clime,
Had, by slow and sure degrees, translated it
    Into this myth, this Individuum,—
Which, when reason had strained and abated it
    Of foreign matter, left, for residuum,
A Man!—a right true man, however,
Whose work was worthy a man's endeavour:
Work, that gave warrant almost sufficient
    To his disciples, for rather believing
He was just omnipotent and omniscient. . . .

This was more than Browning could endure, and in the interval of a husky cough from the professor he fled from the room.

He tells us why it was more than he could endure. The intellect of Christ as man did not seem to Browning impressive:

Poor intellect for worship, truly,
Which tells me simply what was told . . .
Elsewhere by voices manifold.

Browning also felt that the professor's explanation raised the problem of Christ's good faith. Had he asserted that he was God when he was but man? If so, how could one have trust in his teaching?

All that he could respect in the criticism of Göttingen was its learning: but the learning which had laid the world under an obligation by its reconstruction of precious Greek masterpieces which otherwise we should not have had for our delight was wrongly applied to the sacred text. Those who shape their religion from the teachings of Göttingen err in calling themselves Christian. They worship what they have made:

> Nay, call yourselves, if the calling pleases you,
> "Christians,"—abhor the deist's pravity—
> Go on, you shall no more move my gravity
> Than, when I see boys ride a-cockhorse,
> I find it in my heart to embarrass them
> By hinting that their stick's a mock horse,
> And they really carry what they say carries them.

He returns to the dissenting chapel. The ugliness and narrowness which he has stressed in his earlier picture of it, and which he stresses boldly and provocatively in describing his return, is infinitely less objectionable than the proclamations of a dissolving criticism.

The tendencies of Biblical scholarship continued to disturb him in the fifties; and, notably in "Bishop Blougram's Apology," the collection *Men and Women* reveals his anxiety. However it is in *Dramatis Personae,* appearing just after the *Essays and Reviews,* the first volume of Colenso, and Renan's *Vie de Jésus* that his interest reaches its greatest intensity. In "A Death in the Desert," he faces, as in "Christmas Eve and Easter Day," what he believes to be the disastrous implications of the higher criticism for the conception of Christ. We have seen what he thought of *Essays and Reviews* and of Colenso. About Renan he uses in a letter to Miss Isa Blagden very vehement language. His book is "weaker and less honest than I had been led to expect"; "you could no more deduce the character of his text from the substance of his notes, than rewrite a novel from simply reading the mottoes at the head of each chapter"; one of Renan's inferences is "altogether too gross a blunder to be believed in a scholar"; and a parting remark is compact of angry contempt,—

> What do (you) think of the figure *he* cuts who makes his hero participate in the wretched affair with Lazarus, and then calls him all the pretty names that follow? Take away every claim to man's respect from Christ and then give him a wreath of gum-roses and calico lilies, or, as Constance says to Arthur in King John "Give Grannam King John and it grannam wil give it a plum, an apple and a fig."

Against Renan we are told that "A Death in the Desert" was not directed; but the authority is uncertain, and Mr. W. O. Raymond has established at least a high degree of probability that it was in part so directed. But Strauss's position—that the Fourth Gospel was not John's but the work of a Gnostic of the second century—is nearer to the position attacked in the poem. Either Christ was indeed God or the gospels are useless, Browning thinks; and in "A Death in the Desert" he makes the apostle John emphasize the view. Renan appears by name in the Epilogue as the speaker of the second lyric. The tenor of the lyric is that unless Christ indeed lived and was indeed the Son of God, he has no power to nerve or console man. Renan sees the Face, the personal reality, of Christ disappearing,

> Lost in the night at last.

But in the third lyric Browning speaks in his own behalf and replies:

> That one Face, far from vanish, rather grows,
> Or decomposes but to recompose,
> Become my universe that feels and knows.

The peculiarity of Browning's position is that despite his anger at interpretations which question the historical facts of the New Testament story his own emphasis was never upon the historicity of those facts: it was always upon the adequacy of Christianity to the spiritual nature of man. Conviction of this adequacy should, he thought, lead one to accept the New Testament story:

> . . . the acknowledgment of God in Christ
> Accepted by thy reason, solves for thee
> All questions in the earth and out of it,
> And has so far advanced thee to be wise.

It is, as Sir Henry Jones has said, what the heart tells us of Christianity, not what the head tells us, that was crucial to Browning. His anger at the higher criticism derived from his belief that it was assigning to the head the crucial role: the head, not the heart, would decide what the doctrine of Christ was, who he was, and the measure in which he and his doctrine might be accepted. Browning appears to have had no perception of the place left for "Christianity of the heart" by the higher criticism; he does not appear to have appreciated in the least that his Christianity grounded on a firm intuition of the nature of God and of the universe, was inviolable by the higher criticism: that to the centre of his Christian faith, no onslaught by unloving critical minds could ever penetrate. It is startling to find Browning unaware of the strength of his own position, and to find him opposing this second great strain in the intellectual development of the Victorian age as firmly as he had opposed the first, evolutionary science. It would seem that to Browning the observation of a mental exercise, purely rational and critical, alien entirely to the temper and habit of his own mind, was unbearably painful.

About Arnold's attitude towards the higher criticism English opinion was from the beginning confused and exasperated. Most of his studies in religious criticism appeared after his last collection of poems: *St. Paul and Protestantism* in 1870, *Literature and Dogma* in 1873, *God and the Bible* in 1875, *Last Essays on Church and Religion* in 1877. His deep interest in the problem of religious reform began much earlier, at least as early as the publication of *Essays and Reviews.* Writing to his mother in 1861, he makes plain his sympathy with the authors of that work, his awareness of the difficult position in which they will find themselves, and a not very firm belief that their way of introducing to the English public the conclusions of contemporary Biblical scholarship is the right way. "The wine of the Essays," he says, "is rather new and fermenting for the old bottles of Anglicanism. Still the tendency in England is so strong to admit novelties only through the channel of some old form, that perhaps it is in this way that religion in England is destined to renew itself." With the passage of the next ten years his mind hardened to a firm assurance that it was through the Church that England would move to the proper religious position, if she could reach that position at all. The *Essays and Reviews* interested him; but it was Colenso who drove him to speak out. Colenso seemed to him an accomplished example of the entirely wrong way of reforming opinion. "I think," he says in a letter written towards the end of 1862, "of doing what will be rather an interesting thing . . . contrasting Colenso and Co.'s jejune and technical manner of dealing with Biblical controversy with that of Spinoza in his famous treatise on the *Interpretation of Scripture,* with a view of showing how, the heresy on both sides being equal, Spinoza broaches his in that edifying and pious spirit by which alone the treatment of such matters can be made fruitful, while Colenso and the English Essayists, from their narrowness and want of power, more than from any other cause, do not." It is notable that his position towards the Essayists and Reviewers has stiffened; he never likened them to Colenso without serious qualifications, but he had come to think their emphasis mistaken. It is also notable that the religious critic who beyond all others of his time offended pious people by his unedifying manner of dealing with sacred subjects begins by reproaching others for their want of unction and edification.

The essay on "The Bishop and the Philosopher" to which he refers in this letter ap peared at the beginning of 1863; and was followed within that year by one on Spinoza alone and another on "Dean Stanley's Lectures on the Jewish Church." Stanley he found to have the qualities which he pronounced wanting in the other English reforming critics; and it is in his essay on Stanley that we may best find his conception of the ideal use of the conclusions of Biblical investigation.

In it Arnold asserts that scholars who live exclusively in the world of ideas and who communicate their ideas only to the slight audience of other scholars need no power of edification to perform their function. They may deal with religious problems in the severe and purely critical way in which they would approach any problem of the pure intelligence. Most scholars do not live in so purely intellectual a world; nor are they willing to speak to so small a congregation. They cannot then perform their function, which is partly a teacher's, without much more than merely intellectual power.

What must they have? They must be fit to carry out "one of the hardest tasks in the world: to make new intellectual ideas harmonize truly with the religious life, to place them in their right light for that life." It matters little, relatively, whether one originates an idea; what matters is that one should be able to make that idea useful in the religious development of the community. Colenso could not make his ideas useful. He would point out that "a priest could not have eaten, daily, eighty-eight pigeons for his own portion, 'in the most holy place' "; and he would conclude that the holy writer who mentioned the eaten pigeons erred and practised deception. It may have been, Colenso said, that to the holy writer embroidering fact with impossible trimmings seemed innocent; still he did deceive. Facts such as that of the pigeons were the substance of Colenso's book; and on it Arnold's remark is "Heaven and Earth, what a gospel!" Such a gospel, in a book intended for a general audience could do no good: it merely unsettled, and offered no new synthesis which might enable men to hold their sense of the worth of the Old Testament and at the same time accept the new view of that work which the discrepancies indicated would require.

Stanley did good. His stress fell not on discrepancies and difficulties although he perceived and admitted them; it fell on the essence of the Old Testament. Some critics reproached him for not grappling with more of the problems of fact: with that reproach Arnold was impatient. "Which are a man's deepest thoughts," he asks, "his thoughts whether it was 215 years, or 430, or 1000 that the Israelites sojourned in Egypt, or his thoughts on the moral lesson to be drawn from the story of the Israelites' deliverance?" No book on the Old Testament would satisfy Arnold if it was not concentrated on the great central fact of the Jewish quest for righteousness.

For him the error of the higher critics is one of emphasis; they have bent so long over the details, as to have forgotten why they began to study the Book in the first place. They are like critics of the *Iliad* and the *Odyssey* who wrestle with the problems of date and authorship and manuscript. When Arnold applied himself, in the series of works on religion which occupied him from 1870 to 1877, it was to just the same kind of interpretative effort, harmonizing the conclusions of Biblical investigation with the spiritual needs of his time.

Subsequent poetry was either, like Meredith's and Swinburne's, radically unChristian and, accordingly, unstirred by the issue of Biblical criticism, or fervidly Christian, like Patmore's, Hopkins's and Christina Rossetti's and, accordingly, untouched by it.

X. POLITICAL AND SOCIAL IDEAS

Wordsworth, Coleridge and Southey began by celebrating the French Revolution as the preface to a new and ideal world-order; but the savagery in the Reign of Terror, the execution of the King and Queen, the policy of aggressive expansion, and the military dictatorship of Napoleon blighted their hopes. They turned back to the glories and securities of the English past and contemplated these with a Burkean enthusiasm and veneration. Shelley and Byron were more nearly constant to the revolutionary hope and faith.

Victorian poetry has within it both the revolutionary and the conservative strains. Tennyson repeated the ideas held by the elder romantics in their sobered maturity. He was full of national pride, and prone to speak of other peoples in such terms as "the red foolfury of the Seine" and "the wild hysterics of the Celt." Still in his opinions on domestic affairs he was far indeed from blind Toryism. He even made it plain that his devotion to England was not unconditional:

Should banded unions persecute
Opinion, and induce a time
When single thought is civil crime,
And individual freedom mute;

Tho' Power should make from land to land
The name of Britain trebly great—
Tho' every channel of the State
Should fill and choke with golden sand—

Yet waft me from the harbour-mouth,
Wild wind! I seek a warmer sky,
And I will see before I die
The palms and temples of the South.

Nor was Tennyson one of those individualists who believed that the century's shibboleth of freedom was in itself sufficient to ensure to England a good society. Liberalism was, he was sure, an inadequate creed if it left untouched the miseries of the poor and the inequities of the economic order—the condition of England question, as his friend Carlyle called it. In "Locksley Hall Sixty Years After," on the very eve of the Golden Jubilee of the Queen, Tennyson attacked the Victorian failure in terms among the warmest in a period which abounded in vehement criticism. Against the parliamentary regime—the "tonguesters," against the tyranny of an unintelligent and sensual majority—"demos," against the absence of distinction and elevation in personal conduct, he lashed out in language which is not far from the diatribes of Carlyle and Ruskin. Pessimism and abhorrence of vulgarity, both rooted deep in Tennyson's temperament, combined to make his most explicit utterances on domestic affairs gloomy and fearful. Such an attitude survived in a number of the later poets; but Tennyson's national pride, although it was to be echoed noisily by Kipling and nobly by Housman, has never since found so adequate an organ.

Tennyson's preoccupation with public affairs is in sharpest contrast to Browning's almost-indifference. When Browning presents social and political matters in his poetry, it is almost always because of a psychological curiosity about the motives by which individuals are shaped to political and social attitudes. As always his concern is with the individual nature. He professed a liberal faith and wrote, late in his career, a sonnet to explain why he was a liberal; it would have been more interesting if he had explained why, at the time when English liberals were really tested by Gladstone's Irish policy, he dissented and became a Unionist.

If anything may be predicted of his wife, it may be said that she would not have accompanied him in such dissent. Among the major poets of the early Victorian time, she was the most passionately radical. Much of her radicalism was developed in Italy: in her collection of 1860, *Poems before Congress,* she is scarcely less violent than Swinburne was to be in his treatment of Italian themes a decade later. She believed that Italy must be freed from the Austrian oppression, unified, and republican; to attain these paradisal ends she hoped in Napoleon III, in whom she put her trust as in one who was not born to the purple but raised to his authority as the chosen leader of a nation; and her imagination was caught by the figure of the soldier-patriot Garibaldi. Her enthusiasm for the redemption of oppressed Italy was but a part, though a very large one, of an enthusiasm for freedom everywhere, always, for every one.

Her internationalism is the opposite of Tennyson's national pride. In the preface to *Poems before Congress* she wrote:

I confess that I dream of the day when an English statesman shall arise with a heart too large for England, having courage in the face of his countrymen to assert of some suggested policy . . . 'This is good for your trade: this is necessary for your domination; but it will vex a people hard by; it will hurt a people farther off; it will profit nothing to the general humanity: therefore, away with it—it is not for you or me.'

Before she went to Italy she had written "The Cry of the Children," one of the most affecting humanitarian poems in the language; in Italy she did not lose her concern for the oppressed classes at home, but wrote, among other social pieces, the powerful diatribe "A Curse for a Nation" (mistaken by many Americans with a heavy conscience for an attack on slave-holding and the acquiescence in it). Its real theme is the oppression of the English poor by the governing classes of a nation which abroad advocated liberty.

Her place as a radical, aflame with zeal for liberty at home and abroad, and as a bitter satirist of conservatism, was taken by Swinburne, whose *Songs before Sunrise* are the most impressive political verse of the period. Like Mrs. Browning he placed Italy in the foreground of his political preoccupation; but wherever there was oppression he was quick to chastise, just as he was quick to fan any spark of liberty, however faint. The absence of oppression was, for him as for John Stuart Mill, prerequisite to all virtue. It is instructive to consider his *Songs* as the rendering into poetry of Mill's essay *On Liberty,* of which Swinburne wrote some years later: "Ever since his *Liberty* came out it has been the text-book of my creed as to public morals and political faith." All the main aspects of Mill's essay are developed in the *Songs:* admiration of the Greek world; doubt as to the total effect of Christianity on the moral nature of man; hatred of the tyranny of the majority; insistence on the supreme value to the community and to the universe of freely developing individuals; almost mystical faith in the ideal of liberty, whether of thought, of discussion, or of action:

For where Freedom lives not, there live no good things.

To the spirit of the *Songs* the later political poetry of Swinburne appears to be in irreconcilable contrast. From a revolutionary idealist he appears to have become an aggressive nationalist, a jingo. It is true that in Europe liberty had won many victories and escaped many dangers: France became again a republic; Italy was unified, and if its regime was not republican, it was certainly in no important aspect oppressive. Swinburne continued to rage against continental tyrants, notably against the Czar. It was towards England that his attitude changed without any comparable change in the national regime. He was the enemy of the Irish and the Boers; he championed imperialistic adventures; he advocated strong measures against rival empires. The explanation perhaps lies in Swinburne's growing bookishness, and especially in his growing immersion in Elizabethan literature. He came to believe that Elizabethan drama was the greatest form of the greatest age of the greatest literature the world had ever seen. Between his mind and the brutal fact of oppression over Irish and Boers came the loved and shadowy figures of the Elizabethan dramatists. The proudest of all England's boasts must be, he thought, that she was Shakespeare's land. When Swinburne spoke of purely domestic affairs, he could still use radical language: he could taunt the House of Lords—which he conceived as an intolerable impediment to the popular will—as men

Who are Graces by grace of such mothers
As brightened the bed of King Charles.

Clough, too, allied himself with continental liberalism following with anxious interest the risings and revolutions from 1848 to the time of his death in 1861. His friend Matthew Arnold was, as an early sonnet shows, unable to keep pace with him: political and social matters occupied a great deal less space in the mind of the young Arnold, and it was not until after Clough's death that Arnold turned to them with the full power of his intelligence and his will. This is not the occasion for a survey of Arnold's political and social ideas: comment upon them will be found in the introduction to the companion volume of Victorian prose. Here it need only be said that Arnold lacked the confidence which burned unwaveringly in Mrs. Browning and Swinburne, and less surely in Clough: he never believed in seven-league boots, political or other. His hope was in the slow regeneration of individuals and the regeneration of the communities to which they belonged as the number of regenerate individuals grew. Meredith was nearer to Swinburne's hope, and more constant to it, if less fervid.

The political poetry of the period strikes its boldest note in the last poems of William Morris. After his conversion to socialism, Morris undertook party journalism and began to write in the socialist organs poems of a simple hortatory or laudatory sort in which he either celebrated the coming revolution in which the capitalist world would split asunder and give place to a socialist order, or else urged his comrades to persevere until the great change came, when in blood and fire the golden era would be born. His propagandist poetry is almost valueless: it has none of the qualities which make the rest of his work precious. In the poems of his middle years it is difficult—but by no means so difficult as certain critics suggest—to find the impress of his social hope. The kind of society he desired prior to his conversion to socialism is represented in the regime of Elf, the son of the Helper of Men:

> Peace lay on the land of the Helper and the house of Elf his son;
> There merry men went bedward when their tide of toil was done,
> And glad was the dawn's awakening, and the noon-tide fair and glad:
> There no great store had the franklin, and enough the hireling had;
> And a child might go unguarded the length and breadth of the land
> With a purse of gold at his girdle and gold rings on his hand.
> 'Twas a country of cunning craftsmen, and many a thing they wrought,
> That the lands of storm desired, and the homes of warfare sought.
> But men deemed it o'er-well warded by more than its stems of fight,
> And told how its earth-born watchers yet lived of plenteous might.

It is an ideal of small proprietors, each with his own rural home, supplemented by accomplished craftsmen, and guided by disinterested and companionable leaders; in such a regime war does not exist, and the conflicts which go on outside its borders are no threat to its security. When Morris set down such an ideal in *Sigurd the Volsung* (1876) he had not asked himself how it could be realized: it was when he asked such a question that he became a socialist, and becoming a socialist he was obliged to modify the ideal in the direction of communal authority.

XI. CONCLUSION

In substance, form and tone Victorian poetry is richly varied. Its variety is so marked that to some of the clearest-sighted Victorian critics it seemed almost a wilderness of unrelated experiments carried out by undisciplined and introverted individuals. In 1871, Henry Buxton Forman, the editor of Keats and Shelley, published a collection of essays entitled *Our Living Poets,* in which he sought to impose some order on what he believed to be chaos. "None of the arts as seen in this country to-day," was, he thought, "greatly coherent in the sense in which Greek sculpture, medieval Italian painting, modern German music, have been coherent. The art in which the English have excelled for centuries, the art of arts, Poetry, does not, it is true, present at this day, that compact appearance that the Elizabethan drama got from a national coherence of sentiment and habit. . . . From the lack of a universal ideal of life, the ideal in art is special to each great artist. This comes from the disintegration of society that has gone on a long while,—breaking and breaking old ideas and institutions and forms of thought." So much was Forman impressed by the eclecticism of Victorian poetry that he proposed an elaborate classification which would set Tennyson as the master of an "idyllic school," Browning as the master of a rival "psychological school," the Rossettis and Patmore in a "Pre-Raphaelite group" and in a fourth "Renaissance group" a very miscellaneous lot, among them Arnold, Swinburne, George Eliot, Morris and Sir Henry Taylor. Such desperate attempts to bring order out of a supposed chaos appear to-day fully ridiculous.

In some degree the poetry of any period is varied and eclectic. Critics such as Forman insisted, however, that the poetry of their age was specially marked by an absence of central moods, forms, and ideas. They looked back, longingly to the Elizabethan unity; and one at least among them, J. A. Symonds, towards 1890, attempted an elaborate contrast between the Elizabethan and the Victorian poetries. In the closing essay of his collection, *Essays Speculative and Suggestive,* he laid it down that whereas "Elizabethan literature has a marked unity of style," the heavy accumulation of knowledge and experience in the intervening centuries, along with a multitude of supporting factors, has made for a "diversity of style" in the Victorian period. Symonds is, however, aware that to a later age the differences among the Victorian poets may bulk less large than they did in their own lifetimes. "After the lapse of two centuries," he inquires, "will . . . Tennyson, William Morris, Swinburne, Clough, Rossetti, Browning, Mrs. Browning, Matthew Arnold, and the rest of them, seem singing to one dominant tune, in spite of their so obvious differences?" He does not really believe that posterity will perceive unity in Victorian poetry; but at least he conceives the possibility.

That possibility has become fact. Few literary periods have in retrospect seemed so unified. We do not believe that the Victorians moved each along his own peculiar line, that they suffered from a defective national coherence of sentiment or habit, or that they lived while a society or a national soul was disintegrating. In our view the Victorian age, in literature as in other aspects of its brilliant performance, is one of stability and unity, in which the structure of society and culture underwent a variety of shocks without its essential balance being imperiled.

In poetry it seems to have laid a consistent emphasis on thought, and in its thinking to have lingered anxiously and honestly over the ultimate problems—the nature of God, the nature of the universe, the relations between soul and soul, the place of man in the scheme of things, the probability of immortality and the nature of that immortality. It seems to have attached its principal emotions to such problems, rather than to the dramatic conflicts between man and man, or man and woman, finding that concrete emotions were for a number of reasons difficult to develop in their natural complexity. It seems to have sought technical excellence in a variety of directions, always remembering that the form of a poem should flow from its substance. And, finally in all its aims and achievements, in form or in thought or in feeling, it seems to have been mastered by the conviction that life was above all *important.*

The substance of the poetry written between the death of the queen and the outbreak of the first world war is almost imponderable; its form either craftily simple or else so nervously precise and strict as to fetter expression; its tone either relaxed or monotonously desperate. The clearest manifestation of its qualities appears in the group rather self-consciously styling themselves the "Georgians." In their anthologies, the first of which came out in 1912, the great issues are either avoided or touched briefly and coyly as if to grapple with them were either bad sense—or what, to this period, was worse—bad taste. The surface of nature is presented with a charming accuracy and suggestiveness: what lies behind or within is unsounded. In such an approach to nature, the theme of so much that is noblest and deepest in Victorian poetry the peculiar tone of the new period can be divined. That tone depends on a conviction that no tolerable solution of man's position in the universe is possible. Either the universe is unknowable to man, or else its nature is terrible to the degree that twentieth century man could not endure knowing it. In either event it seemed necessary to retreat from the Victorian contemplation of ultimates into a delight in surfaces. A brilliant amateur in literary criticism, Mr. George Dangerfield, has found phrases (in his *The Death of Liberal England*) which point to the essential weaknesses in pre-war poetry. "It was born old-fashioned . . . sought the refuge of the past and found in the sunlit ruins of the Romantic Revival a place where the encroaching sounds and fears of the twentieth century were quite unheard and unfelt . . . the rural England of Shakespeare and Milton and Wordsworth and Hopkins, gone very soft at the heart . . . where sorrow dies with sunset and even despair is crowned with new-mown hay." It is significant that such a body of poetry was contemporary with a general emphasis in English thought upon social problems rather than metaphysical, and with the emergence and popularity of the doctrine, preached passionately by Roger Fry and noisily by Clive Bell, that art constructs a self-contained world in which the emotions, if called by the same names as those which move man in the rest of his life, are really completely distinct from these. Literature was steadily depriving itself of its specific importance and influence. On the one side stood men like Davies and Monro and de la Mare acutely conscious of their own slightness and entirely satisfied to abdicate the high positions which the poets had claimed—and often held—in the nineteenth century; on the other stood men like Shaw and Wells and Lawrence who desired to hold the positions but were impatient of the methods of art, preferring the urgent, clamant tones of journalism and pamphleteering.

At the close of the period 1900–1914 the masters in poetry were those who were masters when the period began: Housman, who had published no verse since 1896; Hardy, who was sixty years old in 1900; Bridges who in that year was fifty-six, and whose first collection of verse had come out in the third quarter of the nineteenth century; and Yeats, who alone among the masters had published during the period poems showing a decisive development in his art and in his spirit. The young poets had awakened great expectations; but with the single exception of Masefield's narratives they had done nothing comparable with even the secondary successes of the Victorians. The period ended without any fundamental unification of tendencies: much that was Victorian persisted in an attenuated form; many new notes sounded, but in dissonant disorder; the one new type of poetry was slight and mannered.

The war brought sincerity, presenting to everyone a reality which seemed overwhelming and which, unlike the nature of the universe, no one at heart really wished to ignore. Its stimulus to poetry was sharp but brief: fatigue and cynicism followed from the spiritual over-exertion it required and the disillusionment with the treaty of Versailles. The acrid novels of Aldous Huxley, the acrid biographies of Lytton Strachey, the no less acrid fantasies of David Garnett, the tired and mannered introspections of Dorothy Richardson and Virginia Woolf exemplified the new tone. In poetry the old masters continued to dominate. No one seriously challenged the mastery of Hardy, Housman, Bridges, and Yeats until the poetry of T. S. Eliot slowly acquired an influence.

This influence was slight with the readers of poetry until the end of the twenties. Already, however, it was singularly potent with young writers whose spirit and technique were forming. Whatever estimate one may make of Mr. Eliot's poetry, this at least is indubitable—it was the chief influence toward the unification of the poetry of our time. Until its effect was felt, the twentieth century, in poetry, was a chaos, and most of the elements in that chaos had little separate significance. Mr. Eliot has clarified the issues: and he has contributed heavily toward the return of poetry to the great themes.

Again, as in the Victorian age, poets concern themselves honestly, sincerely and anxiously with the nature of the universe, the relation of man to it, the nature of the individual soul, and the subtlest relations between souls. Inevitably the preoccupation with great themes, in a tone of honesty and anxiety, will sooner or later restore the Victorians to critical favor and broad influence. Their hour is perhaps very near; and if a single prophetic word may be permitted, its sounding will probably be prefaced by the recognition that Browning's worth for this age is not notably less than his worth for his own time.

Toronto, August, 1941.

1809–1892

ALFRED TENNYSON

CHRONOLOGICAL TABLE

1809, August 6, born at Somersby in Lincolnshire where his father, a man of deep learning and warm devotion to natural beauty, was rector.
Educated at home, in private schools, and at Louth Grammar School.

1827 *Poems by Two Brothers* (anonymous), in collaboration with his brother Charles, later Charles Tennyson-Turner.

1828–31 At Trinity College, Cambridge.

1828 Meeting with Arthur Henry Hallam.

1830 *Poems Chiefly Lyrical.*
Journey to Spain with Hallam.

1832 *Poems* (dated 1833).

1833 Hallam dies at Vienna.
The Lover's Tale (privately printed).

1842 *Poems* (2 volumes).

1845 Pension of £200 awarded by the Government of Sir Robert Peel.

1847 *The Princess.*

1850 *In Memoriam* (at first anonymous).
Appointed Poet Laureate.
Marriage to Emily Sellwood, after a delay of almost twenty years.

1852 *Ode on the Death of the Duke of Wellington.*

1855 *Maud.*

1859 *Idylls of the King* (four idylls: "Enid" (later "Geraint and Enid"), "Vivien" (later "Merlin and Vivien"), "Elaine" (later "Lancelot and Elaine"), "Guinivere").

1862 *Ode for the Opening of the International Exhibition.*

1863 *Welcome to Alexandra.*

1864 *Enoch Arden and Other Poems.*

1869 *The Holy Grail and Other Poems* (including four poems later incorporated in the *Idylls:* "The Holy Grail," "The Coming of Arthur," "Pelleas and Ettarre," "The Passing of Arthur").

1872 *Gareth and Lynette and Other Poems* (including two poems later incorporated in the *Idylls:* "Gareth and Lynette," and "The Last Tournament.")

1874 Mrs. Tennyson becomes an invalid.

1875 *Queen Mary* (performed in 1876).

1876 *Harold.*

1880 *Ballads and Other Poems.*

1883 Elevated to the peerage as Baron Tennyson of Aldworth and Farringford.

1884 *The Cup* and *The Falcon.* (*The Falcon* was performed in 1879, *The Cup* in 1881.)
Becket.

1885 *Tiresias and Other Poems* (including "Balin and Balan," the last of the *Idylls* to appear).

1886 *Locksley Hall Sixty Years After and Other Poems.*

1889 *Demeter and Other Poems.*

1892, October 6, died at Aldworth; buried in Westminster Abbey.
The Death of Œnone and Other Poems.

In 1830 Tennyson brought himself to the notice of the chief reviews by his collection *Poems Chiefly Lyrical.* Already a group of his friends at Cambridge, among whom were Gladstone, Monckton Milnes, F. D. Maurice, and Hallam, had decided that he was to be the great poet of the post-romantic period; but from conservative reviewers the collection received sharp condemnation. The condemnation was even sharper when in 1832 he published another collection. Tennyson, shy and sensitive, wished to creep into his burrow and at all costs avoid a repetition of such merciless exposure. Still, he was a good enough judge of his own work to admit—to himself—that he had fallen into effeminacy, over-luxuriance, bathos, if not plain silliness; and in the decade which passed before he consented to publish another collection, he revised with unequalled tact and care many of the poems which had been most severely handled. Between 1832 and 1842 he published but two poems, both brief; but the small reading public of eager idealists had not forgotten him, and the generation whose taste the earlier reviewers represented was passing from the scene. The collection of 1842 was a popular and a critical success: a second edition was required in the following year, and when he was appointed to the laureateship eight years later the collection was in its sixth edition. Public recognition had come, prior to the laureateship, in the award of a pension; meanwhile many of the best minds of the time (notably among the clergy and in the House of Commons as well as among men of letters) found in Tennyson's lyrics the chief poetical achievement of the age.

Tennyson's reputation was deepened and broadened by *The Princess* and *In Memoriam:* with the latter he came to be accepted as a grave and profound thinker as well as the charming, moving lyrist who had won hearts and ears before. If it is admitted that *In Memoriam* fully merits the eulogies it received and long continued to receive, still it must be said that these eulogies, the appointment to the laureateship, and the adulation which streamed out from eminent people was in part injurious. Tennyson was driven—probably against his true nature—to believe that he had a high moral and intellectual commission to perform, to subordinate in most of his later poetry delight to instruction. He remained capable of independence, as he showed in *Maud,* a poem which baffled many of his admirers and dismayed others; and later poems such as *Lucretius* and even *Guinivere* establish that *Maud* was not an accident. Still he suffered, as Matthew Arnold ventured to say to Hallam Tennyson, from being the greatest popular poet of his age: how popular he was is clear from the sale in 1889 of twenty thousand copies of *Demeter and Other Poems* within a week of publication, how he suffered is shown by such poems as the bardic "Vastness" and the jingoistic "Hands All Round."

Only prejudice or satiety could blind any one to the beauty of Tennyson's art. In music, at his best—and he is very often at his best—Tennyson had among his contemporaries but one rival: Swinburne; in imagery, in structure he had none. Nor does his intelligence deserve the ridicule and gross abuse it has been the fashion to hurl at it. He grasped the fundamental ideas of Victorian science very clearly; and the men of science delighted to read him. He was a careful thinker and reader in the various departments of philosophy. It is true that his political conceptions were confused and founded only too often on undisciplined emotion; but, in his poetry at least, he was not disposed to exaggerate the importance of politics. His fundamental weakness is one of feeling, not of thought: often his feeling is inadequate to his subject, even more often it is shrill where it should have been deep, violent where it should have been intense. To most of his contemporaries the splendor of his art hid such weakness; in our time the weakness has hidden from most critics the splendor, perfect as that is in its tones and images.

CLARIBEL

A MELODY

I

Where Claribel low-lieth
The breezes pause and die,
Letting the rose-leaves fall:
But the solemn oak-tree sigheth,
Thick-leaved, ambrosial,
With an ancient melody
Of an inward agony,
Where Claribel low-lieth.

II

At eve the beetle boometh
Athwart the thicket lone:
At noon the wild bee hummeth
About the moss'd headstone:
At midnight the moon cometh,
And looketh down alone.
Her song the lintwhite swelleth,
The clear-voiced mavis dwelleth,
The callow throstle lispeth,
The slumbrous wave outwelleth,

The babbling runnel crispeth,
The hollow grot replieth
Where Claribel low-lieth.

[1830]

MARIANA

'Mariana in the moated grange.'
Measure for Measure.

With blackest moss the flower-plots
Were thickly crusted, one and all:
The rusted nails fell from the knots
That held the pear to the gable-wall.
The broken sheds look'd sad and strange:
Unlifted was the clinking latch;
Weeded and worn the ancient thatch
Upon the lonely moated grange.
She only said, 'My life is dreary,
He cometh not,' she said;
She said, 'I am aweary, aweary,
I would that I were dead!'

Her tears fell with the dews at even;
Her tears fell ere the dews were dried;

She could not look on the sweet heaven,
  Either at morn or eventide.
After the flitting of the bats,
  When thickest dark did trance the sky,
  She drew her casement-curtain by,
And glanced athwart the glooming flats.
    She only said, 'The night is dreary,
      He cometh not,' she said;
    She said, 'I am aweary, aweary,
      I would that I were dead!'

Upon the middle of the night,
  Waking she heard the night-fowl crow:
The cock sung out an hour ere light:
  From the dark fen the oxen's low
Came to her: without hope of change,
  In sleep she seem'd to walk forlorn,
  Till cold winds woke the gray-eyed morn
About the lonely moated grange.
    She only said, 'The day is dreary,
      He cometh not,' she said;
    She said, 'I am aweary, aweary,
      I would that I were dead!'

About a stone-cast from the wall
  A sluice with blacken'd waters slept,
And o'er it many, round and small,
  The cluster'd marish-mosses crept.
Hard by a poplar shook alway,
  All silver-green with gnarled bark:
  For leagues no other tree did mark
The level waste, the rounding gray.
    She only said, 'My life is dreary,
      He cometh not,' she said;
    She said, 'I am aweary, aweary,
      I would that I were dead!'

And ever when the moon was low,
  And the shrill winds were up and away,
In the white curtain, to and fro,
  She saw the gusty shadow sway.
But when the moon was very low,
  And wild winds bound within their cell,
  The shadow of the poplar fell
Upon her bed, across her brow.
    She only said, 'The night is dreary,
      He cometh not,' she said;
    She said, 'I am aweary, aweary,
      I would that I were dead!'

All day within the dreamy house,
  The doors upon their hinges creak'd;
The blue fly sung in the pane; the mouse
  Behind the mouldering wainscot shriek'd,
Or from the crevice peer'd about.
  Old faces glimmer'd thro' the doors,
  Old footsteps trod the upper floors,
Old voices called her from without.
    She only said, 'My life is dreary,
      He cometh not,' she said;
    She said, 'I am aweary, aweary,
      I would that I were dead!'

The sparrow's chirrup on the roof,
  The slow clock ticking, and the sound
Which to the wooing wind aloof
  The poplar made, did all confound
Her sense; but most she loathed the hour
  When the thick-moted sunbeam lay
  Athwart the chambers, and the day
Was sloping toward his western bower.
    Then, said she, 'I am very dreary,
      He will not come,' she said;
    She wept, 'I am aweary, aweary,
      Oh God, that I were dead!'

[1830]

THE POET

The poet in a golden clime was born,
  With golden stars above;
Dower'd with the hate of hate, the scorn of scorn,
  The love of love.

He saw thro' life and death, thro' good and ill,
  He saw thro' his own soul.
The marvel of the everlasting will,
  An open scroll,

Before him lay: with echoing feet he threaded
  The secretest walks of fame:
The viewless arrows of his thoughts were headed
  And wing'd with flame,

Like Indian reeds blown from his silver tongue,
  And of so fierce a flight,
From Calpe unto Caucasus they sung,
  Filling with light

And vagrant melodies the winds which bore
  Them earthward till they lit;

Then, like the arrow-seeds of the field flower,
The fruitful wit
Cleaving, took root, and springing forth anew
Where'er they fell, behold,
Like to the mother plant in semblance, grew
A flower all gold,

And bravely furnish'd all abroad to fling
The winged shafts of truth,
To throng with stately blooms the breathing spring
Of Hope and Youth.

So many minds did gird their orbs with beams,
Tho' one did fling the fire.
Heaven flow'd upon the soul in many dreams
Of high desire.

Thus truth was multiplied on truth, the world
Like one great garden show'd,
And thro' the wreaths of floating dark upcurl'd,
Rare sunrise flow'd.

And Freedom rear'd in that august sunrise
Her beautiful bold brow,
When rites and forms before his burning eyes
Melted like snow.

There was no blood upon her maiden robes
Sunn'd by those orient skies;
But round about the circles of the globes
Of her keen eyes

And in her raiment's hem was traced in flame
WISDOM, a name to shake
All evil dreams of power—a sacred name.
And when she spake,

Her words did gather thunder as they ran,
And as the lightning to the thunder
Which follows it, riving the spirit of man,
Making earth wonder,

So was their meaning to her words. No sword
Of wrath her right arm whirl'd,
But one poor poet's scroll, and with *his* word
She shook the world.

[1830]

TO J. M. K.

My hope and heart is with thee—thou wilt be
A latter Luther, and a soldier-priest
To scare church-harpies from the master's feast;
Our dusted velvets have much need of thee:
Thou art no sabbath-drawler of old saws,
Distill'd from some worm-canker'd homily;
But spurr'd at heart with fieriest energy
To embattail and to wall about thy cause
With iron-worded proof, hating to hark
The humming of the drowsy pulpit-drone
Half God's good sabbath, while the worn-out clerk
Brow-beats his desk below. Thou from a throne
Mounted in heaven wilt shoot into the dark
Arrows of lightnings. I will stand and mark.

[1830]

THE LADY OF SHALOTT

PART I

On either side the river lie
Long fields of barley and of rye,
That clothe the wold and meet the sky;
And thro' the field the road runs by
To many-tower'd Camelot;
And up and down the people go,
Gazing where the lilies blow
Round an island there below,
The island of Shalott.

Willows whiten, aspens quiver,
Little breezes dusk and shiver
Thro' the wave that runs for ever
By the island in the river
Flowing down to Camelot.
Four gray walls, and four gray towers,
Overlook a space of flowers,

And the silent isle imbowers
The Lady of Shalott.

By the margin, willow-veil'd,
Slide the heavy barges trail'd
By slow horses; and unhail'd
The shallop flitteth silken-sail'd
Skimming down to Camelot:
But who hath seen her wave her hand?
Or at the casement seen her stand?
Or is she known in all the land,
The Lady of Shalott?

Only reapers, reaping early
In among the bearded barley,
Hear a song that echoes cheerly
From the river winding clearly,
Down to tower'd Camelot:
And by the moon the reaper weary,
Piling sheaves in uplands airy,
Listening, whispers ' 'Tis the fairy
Lady of Shalott.'

PART II

There she weaves by night and day
A magic web with colours gay.
She has heard a whisper say,
A curse is on her if she stay
To look down to Camelot.
She knows not what the curse may be,
And so she weaveth steadily,
And little other care hath she,
The Lady of Shalott.

And moving thro' a mirror clear
That hangs before her all the year,
Shadows of the world appear.
There she sees the highway near
Winding down to Camelot:
There the river eddy whirls,
And there the surly village-churls,
And the red cloaks of market girls,
Pass onward from Shalott.

Sometimes a troop of damsels glad,
An abbot on an ambling pad,
Sometimes a curly shepherd-lad,
Or long-hair'd page in crimson clad,
Goes by to tower'd Camelot;
And sometimes thro' the mirror blue
The knights come riding two and two:
She hath no loyal knight and true,
The Lady of Shalott.

But in her web she still delights
To weave the mirror's magic sights,
For often thro' the silent nights
A funeral, with plumes and lights
And music, went to Camelot:
Or when the moon was overhead,
Came two young lovers lately wed;
'I am half sick of shadows,' said
The Lady of Shalott.

PART III

A bow-shot from her bower-eaves,
He rode between the barley-sheaves,
The sun came dazzling thro' the leaves,
And flamed upon the brazen greaves
Of bold Sir Lancelot.
A red-cross knight for ever kneel'd
To a lady in his shield,
That sparkled on the yellow field,
Beside remote Shalott.

The gemmy bridle glitter'd free,
Like to some branch of stars we see
Hung in the golden Galaxy.
The bridle bells rang merrily
As he rode down to Camelot:
And from his blazon'd baldric slung
A mighty silver bugle hung,
And as he rode his armour rung,
Beside remote Shalott.

All in the blue unclouded weather
Thick-jewell'd shone the saddle-leather,
The helmet and the helmet-feather
Burn'd like one burning flame together,
As he rode down to Camelot.
As often thro' the purple night,
Below the starry clusters bright,
Some bearded meteor, trailing light,
Moves over still Shalott.

His broad clear brow in sunlight glow'd;
On burnish'd hooves his war-horse trode;
From underneath his helmet flow'd
His coal-black curls as on he rode,
As he rode down to Camelot.
From the bank and from the river
He flash'd into the crystal mirror,
'Tirra lirra,' by the river
Sang Sir Lancelot.

She left the web, she left the loom,
She made three paces thro' the room,

She saw the water-lily bloom,
She saw the helmet and the plume,
She look'd down to Camelot.
Out flew the web and floated wide;
The mirror crack'd from side to side;
'The curse is come upon me,' cried
The Lady of Shalott.

PART IV

In the stormy east-wind straining,
The pale yellow woods were waning,
The broad stream in his banks complaining,
Heavily the low sky raining
Over tower'd Camelot;
Down she came and found a boat
Beneath a willow left afloat,
And round about the prow she wrote
The Lady of Shalott.

And down the river's dim expanse
Like some bold seër in a trance,
Seeing all his own mischance—
With a glassy countenance
Did she look to Camelot.
And at the closing of the day
She loosed the chain, and down she lay;
The broad stream bore her far away,
The Lady of Shalott.

Lying, robed in snowy white
That loosely flew to left and right—
The leaves upon her falling light—
Thro' the noises of the night
She floated down to Camelot:
And as the boat-head wound along
The willowy hills and fields among,
They heard her singing her last song,
The Lady of Shalott.

Heard a carol, mournful, holy,
Chanted loudly, chanted lowly,
Till her blood was frozen slowly,
And her eyes were darken'd wholly,
Turn'd to tower'd Camelot.
For ere she reach'd upon the tide
The first house by the water-side,
Singing in her song she died,
The Lady of Shalott.

Under tower and balcony,
By garden-wall and gallery,
A gleaming shape she floated by,
Dead-pale between the houses high,
Silent into Camelot.
Out upon the wharfs they came,
Knight and burgher, lord and dame,
And round the prow they read her name,
The Lady of Shalott.

Who is this? and what is here?
And in the lighted palace near
Died the sound of royal cheer;
And they cross'd themselves for fear,
All the knights at Camelot:
But Lancelot mused a little space;
He said, 'She has a lovely face;
God in his mercy lend her grace,
The Lady of Shalott.'

[1832, 1842]

ŒNONE

There lies a vale in Ida, lovelier
Than all the valleys of Ionian hills.
The swimming vapour slopes athwart the glen,
Puts forth an arm, and creeps from pine to pine,
And loiters, slowly drawn. On either hand
The lawns and meadow-ledges midway down
Hang rich in flowers, and far below them roars
The long brook falling thro' the clov'n ravine
In cataract after cataract to the sea.
Behind the valley topmost Gargarus
Stands up and takes the morning: but in front
The gorges, opening wide apart, reveal
Troas and Ilion's column'd citadel,
The crown of Troas.
Hither came at noon
Mournful Œnone, wandering forlorn
Of Paris, once her playmate on the hills.
Her cheek had lost the rose, and round her neck
Floated her hair or seem'd to float in rest.
She, leaning on a fragment twined with vine,
Sang to the stillness, till the mountain-shade
Sloped downward to her seat from the upper cliff.

'O mother Ida, many-fountain'd Ida,
Dear mother Ida, harken ere I die.
For now the noonday quiet holds the hill:

The grasshopper is silent in the grass:
The lizard, with his shadow on the stone,
Rests like a shadow, and the winds are dead.
The purple flower droops: the golden bee
Is lily-cradled: I alone awake.
My eyes are full of tears, my heart of love,
My heart is breaking, and my eyes are dim,
And I am all aweary of my life.

'O mother Ida, many-fountain'd Ida,
Dear mother Ida, harken ere I die.
Hear me, O Earth, hear me, O Hills, O Caves
That house the cold crown'd snake! O mountain brooks,
I am the daughter of a River-God,
Hear me, for I will speak, and build up all
My sorrow with my song, as yonder walls
Rose slowly to a music slowly breathed,
A cloud that gather'd shape: for it may be
That, while I speak of it, a little while
My heart may wander from its deeper woe.

'O mother Ida, many-fountain'd Ida,
Dear mother Ida, harken ere I die.
I waited underneath the dawning hills,
Aloft the mountain lawn was dewy-dark,
And dewy-dark aloft the mountain pine:
Beautiful Paris, evil-hearted Paris,
Leading a jet-black goat white-horn'd, white-hooved,
Came up from reedy Simois all alone.

'O mother Ida, harken ere I die.
Far-off the torrent call'd me from the cleft:
Far up the solitary morning smote
The streaks of virgin snow. With down-dropt eyes
I sat alone: white-breasted like a star
Fronting the dawn he moved; a leopard skin
Droop'd from his shoulder, but his sunny hair
Cluster'd about his temples like a God's.
And his cheek brighten'd as the foam-bow brightens
When the wind blows the foam, and all my heart
Went forth to embrace him coming ere he came.

'Dear mother Ida, harken ere I die.
He smiled, and opening out his milk-white palm
Disclosed a fruit of pure Hesperian gold,
That smelt ambrosially, and while I look'd
And listen'd, the full-flowing river of speech
Came down upon my heart.
'"My own Œnone,
Beautiful-brow'd Œnone, my own soul,
Behold this fruit, whose gleaming rind ingrav'n
'For the most fair,' would seem to award it thine,
As lovelier than whatever Oread haunt
The knolls of Ida, loveliest in all grace
Of movement, and the charm of married brows."

'Dear mother Ida, harken ere I die.
He prest the blossom of his lips to mine,
And added "This was cast upon the board,
When all the full-faced presence of the Gods
Ranged in the halls of Peleus; whereupon
Rose feud, with question unto whom 'twere due:
But light-foot Iris brought it yester-eve,
Delivering, that to me, by common voice
Elected umpire, Herè comes to-day,
Pallas and Aphroditè, claiming each
This meed of fairest. Thou, within the cave
Behind yon whispering tuft of oldest pine,
Mayst well behold them unbeheld, unheard
Hear all, and see thy Paris judge of Gods."

'Dear mother Ida, harken ere I die.
It was the deep midnoon: one silvery cloud
Had lost his way between the piney sides
Of this long glen. Then to the bower they came,
Naked they came to that smooth-swarded bower,
And at their feet the crocus brake like fire,
Violet, amaracus, and asphodel,
Lotos and lilies: and a wind arose,
And overhead the wandering ivy and vine,
This way and that, in many a wild festoon
Ran riot, garlanding the gnarled boughs
With bunch and berry and flower thro' and thro'.

'O mother Ida, harken ere I die.
On the tree-tops a crested peacock lit,
And o'er him flow'd a golden cloud, and lean'd
Upon him, slowly dropping fragrant dew.
Then first I heard the voice of her, to whom
Coming thro' Heaven, like a light that grows
Larger and clearer, with one mind the Gods
Rise up for reverence. She to Paris made
Proffer of royal power, ample rule
Unquestion'd, overflowing revenue
Wherewith to embellish state, "from many a vale
And river-sunder'd champaign clothed with corn,
Or labour'd mine undrainable of ore.
Honour," she said, "and homage, tax and toll,
From many an inland town and haven large,
Mast-throng'd beneath her shadowing citadel
In glassy bays among her tallest towers."

'O mother Ida, harken ere I die.
Still she spake on and still she spake of power,
"Which in all action is the end of all;
Power fitted to the season; wisdom-bred
And throned of wisdom—from all neighbour crowns
Alliance and allegiance, till thy hand
Fail from the sceptre-staff. Such boon from me,
From me, Heaven's Queen, Paris, to thee king-born,
A shepherd all thy life but yet king-born,
Should come most welcome, seeing men, in power
Only, are likest gods, who have attain'd
Rest in a happy place and quiet seats
Above the thunder, with undying bliss
In knowledge of their own supremacy."

'Dear mother Ida, harken ere I die.
She ceased, and Paris held the costly fruit
Out at arm's-length, so much the thought of power
Flatter'd his spirit; but Pallas where she stood
Somewhat apart, her clear and bared limbs
O'erthwarted with the brazen-headed spear
Upon her pearly shoulder leaning cold,
The while, above, her full and earnest eye
Over her snow-cold breast and angry cheek
Kept watch, waiting decision, made reply.

'"Self-reverence, self-knowledge, self-control,
These three alone lead life to sovereign power.
Yet not for power (power of herself
Would come uncall'd for) but to live by law,
Acting the law we live by without fear;
And, because right is right, to follow right
Were wisdom in the scorn of consequence."

'Dear mother Ida, harken ere I die.
Again she said: "I woo thee not with gifts.
Sequel of guerdon could not alter me
To fairer. Judge thou me by what I am,
So shalt thou find me fairest.
Yet, indeed,
If gazing on divinity disrobed
Thy mortal eyes are frail to judge of fair,
Unbias'd by self-profit, oh! rest thee sure
That I shall love thee well and cleave to thee
So that my vigor, wedded to thy blood,
Shall strike within thy pulses, like a God's,
To push thee forward thro' a life of shocks,
Dangers, and deeds, until endurance grow
Sinew'd with action, and the full-grown will,
Circled thro' all experiences, pure law,
Commeasure perfect freedom."
'Here she ceas'd,
And Paris ponder'd, and I cried, "O Paris,
Give it to Pallas!" but he heard me not,
Or hearing would not hear me, woe is me!

'O mother Ida, many-fountain'd Ida,
Dear mother Ida, harken ere I die.
Idalian Aphroditè beautiful,
Fresh as the foam, new-bathed in Paphian wells,
With rosy slender fingers backward drew
From her warm brows and bosom her deep hair

Ambrosial, golden round her lucid throat
And shoulder: from the violets her light foot
Shone rosy-white, and o'er her rounded form
Between the shadows of the vine-bunches
Floated the glowing sunlights, as she moved.

'Dear mother Ida, harken ere I die.
She with a subtle smile in her mild eyes,
The herald of her triumph, drawing nigh
Half-whisper'd in his ear, "I promise thee
The fairest and most loving wife in Greece,"
She spoke and laugh'd: I shut my sight for fear:
But when I look'd, Paris had raised his arm,
And I beheld great Herè's angry eyes,
As she withdrew into the golden cloud,
And I was left alone within the bower;
And from that time to this I am alone,
And I shall be alone until I die.

'Yet, mother Ida, harken ere I die.
Fairest—why fairest wife? am I not fair?
My love hath told me so a thousand times.
Methinks I must be fair, for yesterday,
When I past by, a wild and wanton pard,
Eyed like the evening star, with playful tail
Crouch'd fawning in the weed. Most loving is she?
Ah me, my mountain shepherd, that my arms
Were wound about thee, and my hot lips prest
Close, close to thine in that quick-falling dew
Of fruitful kisses, thick as Autumn rains
Flash in the pools of whirling Simois.

'O mother, hear me yet before I die.
They came, they cut away my tallest pines,
My tall dark pines, that plumed the craggy ledge
High over the blue gorge, and all between
The snowy peak and snow-white cataract
Foster'd the callow eaglet—from beneath
Whose thick mysterious boughs in the dark morn
The panther's roar came muffled, while I sat
Low in the valley. Never, never more
Shall lone Œnone see the morning mist
Sweep thro' them; never see them overlaid
With narrow moon-lit slips of silver cloud,
Between the loud stream and the trembling stars.

'O mother, hear me yet before I die.
I wish that somewhere in the ruin'd folds,
Among the fragments tumbled from the glens,
Or the dry thickets, I could meet with her
The Abominable, that uninvited came
Into the fair Peleïan banquet-hall,
And cast the golden fruit upon the board,
And bred this change; that I might speak my mind,
And tell her to her face how much I hate
Her presence, hated both of Gods and men.

'O mother, hear me yet before I die.
Hath he not sworn his love a thousand times,
In this green valley, under this green hill,
Ev'n on this hand, and sitting on this stone?
Seal'd it with kisses? water'd it with tears?
O happy tears, and how unlike to these!
O happy Heaven, how canst thou see my face?
O happy earth, how canst thou bear my weight?
O death, death, death, thou ever-floating cloud,
There are enough unhappy on this earth,
Pass by the happy souls, that love to live:
I pray thee, pass before my light of life,
And shadow all my soul, that I may die.
Thou weighest heavy on the heart within,
Weigh heavy on my eyelids: let me die.

'O mother, hear me yet before I die.
I will not die alone, for fiery thoughts
Do shape themselves within me, more and more,
Whereof I catch the issue, as I hear
Dead sounds at night come from the inmost hills,

Like footsteps upon wool. I dimly see
My far-off doubtful purpose, as a mother
Conjectures of the features of her child
Ere it is born: her child!—a shudder comes
Across me: never child be born of me,
Unblest, to vex me with his father's eyes!

'O mother, hear me yet before I die.
Hear me, O earth. I will not die alone,
Lest their shrill happy laughter come to me
Walking the cold and starless road of Death
Uncomforted, leaving my ancient love
With the Greek woman. I will rise and go
Down into Troy, and ere the stars come forth
Talk with the wild Cassandra, for she says
A fire dances before her, and a sound
Rings ever in her ears of armed men.
What this may be I know not, but I know
That, wheresoe'er I am by night and day,
All earth and air seem only burning fire.'

[1832, 1842]

TO ——

WITH THE FOLLOWING POEM

I send you here a sort of allegory,
(For you will understand it) of a soul,
A sinful soul possess'd of many gifts,
A spacious garden full of flowering weeds,
A glorious Devil, large in heart and brain,
That did love Beauty only, (Beauty seen
In all varieties of mould and mind)
And Knowledge for its beauty; or if Good,
Good only for its beauty, seeing not
That Beauty, Good, and Knowledge, are three sisters
That doat upon each other, friends to man,
Living together under the same roof,
And never can be sunder'd without tears.
And he that shuts Love out, in turn shall be
Shut out from Love, and on her threshold lie
Howling in outer darkness. Not for this
Was common clay ta'en from the common earth
Moulded by God, and temper'd with the tears
Of angels to the perfect shape of man.

THE PALACE OF ART

I built my soul a lordly pleasure-house,
Wherein at ease for aye to dwell.
I said, 'O Soul, make merry and carouse,
Dear soul, for all is well.'

A huge crag-platform, smooth as burnish'd brass
I chose. The ranged ramparts bright
From level meadow-bases of deep grass
Suddenly scaled the light.

Thereon I built it firm. Of ledge or shelf
The rock rose clear, or winding stair.
My soul would live alone unto herself
In her high palace there.

And 'while the world runs round and round,' I said,
'Reign thou apart, a quiet king,
Still as, while Saturn whirls, his stedfast shade
Sleeps on his luminous ring.'

To which my soul made answer readily:
'Trust me, in bliss I shall abide
In this great mansion, that is built for me,
So royal-rich and wide.'

* * * *
* * * *

Four courts I made, East, West and South and North,
In each a squared lawn, wherefrom
The golden gorge of dragons spouted forth
A flood of fountain-foam.

And round the cool green courts there ran a row
Of cloisters, branch'd like mighty woods,
Echoing all night to that sonorous flow
Of spouted fountain-floods.

And round the roofs a gilded gallery
That lent broad verge to distant lands
Far as the wild swan wings, to where the sky
Dipt down to sea and sands.

From those four jets four currents in one swell
Across the mountain stream'd below
In misty folds, that floating as they fell
Lit up a torrent-bow.

And high on every peak a statue seem'd
To hang on tiptoe, tossing up
A cloud of incense of all odour steam'd
From out a golden cup.

So that she thought, 'And who shall gaze upon
My palace with unblinded eyes,
While this great bow will waver in the sun,
And that sweet incense rise?'

For that sweet incense rose and never fail'd,
And, while day sank or mounted higher,
The light aërial gallery, golden-rail'd,
Burnt like a fringe of fire.

Likewise the deep-set windows, stain'd and traced,
Would seem slow-flaming crimson fires
From shadow'd grots of arches interlaced,
And tipt with frost-like spires.

* * * *
* * * *

Full of long-sounding corridors it was,
That over-vaulted grateful gloom,
Thro' which the livelong day my soul did pass,
Well-pleased, from room to room.

Full of great rooms and small the palace stood,
All various, each a perfect whole
From living Nature, fit for every mood
And change of my still soul.

For some were hung with arras green and blue,
Showing a gaudy summer-morn,
Where with puff'd cheek the belted hunter blew
His wreathed bugle-horn.

One seem'd all dark and red—a tract of sand,
And some one pacing there alone,
Who paced for ever in a glimmering land,
Lit with a low large moon.

One show'd an iron coast and angry waves.
You seem'd to hear them climb and fall
And roar rock-thwarted under bellowing caves,
Beneath the windy wall.

And one, a full-fed river winding slow
By herds upon an endless plain,
The ragged rims of thunder brooding low,
With shadow-streaks of rain.

And one, the reapers at their sultry toil.
In front they bound the sheaves. Behind
Were realms of upland, prodigal in oil,
And hoary to the wind.

And one a foreground black with stones and slags,
Beyond, a line of heights, and higher
All barr'd with long white cloud the scornful crags,
And highest, snow and fire.

And one, an English home—gray twilight pour'd
On dewy pastures, dewy trees,
Softer than sleep—all things in order stored,
A haunt of ancient Peace.

Nor these alone, but every landscape fair,
As fit for every mood of mind,
Or gay, or grave, or sweet, or stern, was there
Not less than truth design'd.

* * * *
* * * *

Or the maid-mother by a crucifix,
In tracts of pasture sunny-warm,
Beneath branch-work of costly sardonyx
Sat smiling, babe in arm.

Or in a clear-wall'd city on the sea,
Near gilded organ-pipes, her hair
Wound with white roses, slept St. Cecily;
An angel look'd at her.

Or thronging all one porch of Paradise
A group of Houris bow'd to see
The dying Islamite, with hands and eyes
That said, We wait for thee.

Or mythic Uther's deeply-wounded son
In some fair space of sloping greens
Lay, dozing in the vale of Avalon,
And watch'd by weeping queens.

Or hollowing one hand against his ear,
To list a foot-fall, ere he saw
The wood-nymph, stay'd the Ausonian king to hear
Of wisdom and of law.

Or over hills with peaky tops engrail'd,
And many a tract of palm and rice,
The throne of Indian Cama slowly sail'd
A summer fann'd with spice.

Or sweet Europa's mantle blew unclasp'd,
From off her shoulder backward borne:
From one hand droop'd a crocus: one hand grasp'd
The mild bull's golden horn.

Or else flush'd Ganymede, his rosy thigh
Half-buried in the Eagle's down,
Sole as a flying star shot thro' the sky
Above the pillar'd town.

Nor these alone: but every legend fair
Which the supreme Caucasian mind
Carved out of Nature for itself, was there,
Not less than life, design'd.

* * * *
* * * *

Then in the towers I placed great bells that swung,
Moved of themselves, with silver sound;
And with choice paintings of wise men I hung
The royal dais round.

For there was Milton like a seraph strong,
Beside him Shakespeare bland and mild;
And there the world-worn Dante grasp'd his song,
And somewhat grimly smiled.

And there the Ionian father of the rest;
A million wrinkles carved his skin;
A hundred winters snow'd upon his breast,
From cheek and throat and chin.

Above, the fair hall-ceiling stately-set
Many an arch high up did lift,
And angels rising and descending met
With interchange of gift.

Below was all mosaic choicely plann'd
With cycles of the human tale
Of this wide world, the times of every land
So wrought, they will not fail.

The people here, a beast of burden slow,
Toil'd onward, prick'd with goads and stings;
Here play'd, a tiger, rolling to and fro
The heads and crowns of kings;

Here rose, an athlete, strong to break or bind
All force in bonds that might endure,
And here once more like some sick man declined,
And trusted any cure.

But over these she trod: and those great bells
Began to chime. She took her throne:
She sat betwixt the shining Oriels,
To sing her songs alone.

And thro' the topmost Oriels' coloured flame
Two godlike faces gazed below;
Plato the wise, and large-brow'd Verulam,
The first of those who know.

And all those names, that in their motion were
Full-welling fountain-heads of change,
Betwixt the slender shafts were blazon'd fair
In diverse raiment strange:

Thro' which the lights, rose, amber, emerald, blue,
Flush'd in her temples and her eyes,
And from her lips, as morn from Memnon, drew
Rivers of melodies.

No nightingale delighteth to prolong
Her low preamble all alone,
More than my soul to hear her echo'd song
Throb thro' the ribbed stone;

Singing and murmuring in her feastful mirth,
Joying to feel herself alive,
Lord over Nature, Lord of the visible earth,
Lord of the senses five;

Communing with herself: "All these are mine,
And let the world have peace or wars,
'Tis one to me.' She—when young night divine
Crown'd dying day with stars,

Making sweet close of his delicious toils—
Lit light in wreaths and anadems,
And pure quintessences of precious oils
In hollow'd moons of gems,

To mimic heaven; and clapt her hands and cried,
'I marvel if my still delight
In this great house so royal-rich, and wide,
Be flatter'd to the height.

'O all things fair to sate my various eyes!
O shapes and hues that please me well!
O silent faces of the Great and Wise,
My Gods, with whom I dwell!

'O God-like isolation which art mine,
I can but count thee perfect gain,
What time I watch the darkening droves of swine
That range on yonder plain.

'In filthy sloughs they roll a prurient skin,
They graze and wallow, breed and sleep;
And oft some brainless devil enters in,
And drives them to the deep.'

Then of the moral instinct would she prate
And of the rising from the dead,
As hers by right of full-accomplish'd Fate;
And at the last she said:

'I take possession of man's mind and deed.
I care not what the sects may brawl.
I sit as God holding no form of creed,
But contemplating all.'

* * * *
* * * *

Full oft the riddle of the painful earth
Flash'd thro' her as she sat alone,
Yet not the less held she her solemn mirth,
And intellectual throne.

And so she throve and prosper'd: so three years
She prosper'd: on the fourth she fell,
Like Herod, when the shout was in his ears,
Struck thro' with pangs of hell.

Lest she should fail and perish utterly,
God, before whom ever lie bare
The abysmal deeps of Personality,
Plagued her with sore despair.

When she would think, where'er she turn'd her sight
The airy hand confusion wrought,
Wrote, 'Mene, mene,' and divided quite
The kingdom of her thought.

Deep dread and loathing of her solitude
Fell on her, from which mood was born
Scorn of herself; again, from out that mood
Laughter at her self-scorn.

'What! is not this my place of strength,' she said,
'My spacious mansion built for me,
Whereof the strong foundation-stones were laid
Since my first memory?'

But in dark corners of her palace stood
Uncertain shapes; and unawares
On white-eyed phantasms weeping tears of blood,
And horrible nightmares,

And hollow shades enclosing hearts of flame,
And, with dim fretted foreheads all,
On corpses three-months-old at noon she came,
That stood against the wall.

A spot of dull stagnation, without light
Or power of movement, seem'd my soul,
'Mid onward-sloping motions infinite
Making for one sure goal.

A still salt pool, lock'd in with bars of sand,
Left on the shore; that hears all night

The plunging seas draw backward from the land
Their moon-led waters white.

A star that with the choral starry dance
Join'd not, but stood, and standing saw
The hollow orb of moving Circumstance
Roll'd round by one fix'd law.

Back on herself her serpent pride had curl'd.
'No voice,' she shriek'd in that lone hall,
'No voice breaks thro' the stillness of this world:
One deep, deep silence all!'

She, mouldering with the dull earth's mouldering sod,
Inwrapt tenfold in slothful shame,
Lay there exiled from eternal God,
Lost to her place and name;

And death and life she hated equally,
And nothing saw, for her despair,
But dreadful time, dreadful eternity,
No comfort anywhere;

Remaining utterly confused with fears,
And ever worse with growing time,
And ever unrelieved by dismal tears,
And all alone in crime:

Shut up as in a crumbling tomb, girt round
With blackness as a solid wall,
Far off she seem'd to hear the dully sound
Of human footsteps fall.

As in strange lands a traveller walking slow,
In doubt and great perplexity,
A little before moon-rise hears the low
Moan of an unknown sea;

And knows not if it be thunder, or a sound
Of rocks thrown down, or one deep cry
Of great wild beasts; then thinketh, 'I have found
A new land, but I die.'

She howl'd aloud; 'I am on fire within.
There comes no murmur of reply.
What is it that will take away my sin,
And save me lest I die?'

So when four years were wholly finished,
She threw her royal robes away.
'Make me a cottage in the vale,' she said,
'Where I may mourn and pray.

'Yet pull not down my palace towers, that are
So lightly, beautifully built:
Perchance I may return with others there
When I have purged my guilt.'

[1832, 1842]

THE LOTOS-EATERS

'Courage!' he said, and pointed toward the land,
'This mounting wave will roll us shoreward soon.'
In the afternoon they came unto a land
In which it seemed always afternoon.
All round the coast the languid air did swoon,
Breathing like one that hath a weary dream,
Full-faced above the valley stood the moon;
And like a downward smoke, the slender stream
Along the cliff to fall and pause and fall did seem.

A land of streams! some, like a downward smoke,
Slow-dropping veils of thinnest lawn, did go;
And some thro' wavering lights and shadows broke,
Rolling a slumbrous sheet of foam below.
They saw the gleaming river seaward flow
From the inner land: far off, three mountain-tops,
Three silent pinnacles of aged snow,
Stood sunset-flush'd: and, dew'd with showery drops,
Up-clomb the shadowy pine above the woven copse.

The charmed sunset linger'd low adown
In the red West: thro' mountain clefts the dale
Was seen far inland, and the yellow down
Border'd with palm, and many a winding vale
And meadow, set with slender galingale;

A land where all things always seem'd the same!
And round about the keel with faces pale,
Dark faces pale against that rosy flame,
The mild-eyed melancholy Lotos-eaters came.

Branches they bore of that enchanted stem,
Laden with flower and fruit, whereof they gave
To each, but whoso did receive of them,
And taste, to him the gushing of the wave
Far far away did seem to mourn and rave
On alien shores; and if his fellow spake,
His voice was thin, as voices from the grave;
And deep-asleep he seem'd, yet all awake,
And music in his ears his beating heart did make.

They sat them down upon the yellow sand,
Between the sun and moon upon the shore;
And sweet it was to dream of Fatherland,
Of child, and wife, and slave; but evermore
Most weary seem'd the sea, weary the oar,
Weary the wandering fields of barren foam.
Then some one said, 'We will return no more;'
And all at once they sang, 'Our island home
Is far beyond the wave; we will no longer roam.'

CHORIC SONG

I

There is sweet music here that softer falls
Than petals from blown roses on the grass,
Or night-dews on still waters between walls
Of shadowy granite, in a gleaming pass;
Music that gentlier on the spirit lies,
Than tir'd eyelids upon tir'd eyes;
Music that brings sweet sleep down from the blissful skies.
Here are cool mosses deep,
And thro' the moss the ivies creep,
And in the stream the long-leaved flowers weep,
And from the craggy ledge the poppy hangs in sleep.

II

Why are we weigh'd upon with heaviness,
And utterly consumed with sharp distress,
While all things else have rest from weariness?
All things have rest: why should we toil alone,
We only toil, who are the first of things,
And make perpetual moan,
Still from one sorrow to another thrown:
Nor ever fold our wings,
And cease from wanderings,
Nor steep our brows in slumber's holy balm;
Nor harken what the inner spirit sings,
There is no joy but calm!'
Why should we only toil, the roof and crown of things?

III

Lo! in the middle of the wood,
The folded leaf is woo'd from out the bud
With winds upon the branch, and there
Grows green and broad, and takes no care,
Sun-steep'd at noon, and in the moon
Nightly dew-fed; and turning yellow
Falls, and floats adown the air.
Lo! sweeten'd with the summer light,
The full-juiced apple, waxing over-mellow,
Drops in a silent autumn night.
All its allotted length of days,
The flower ripens in its place,
Ripens and fades, and falls, and hath no toil,
Fast-rooted in the fruitful soil.

IV

Hateful is the dark-blue sky,
Vaulted o'er the dark-blue sea.
Death is the end of life; ah, why
Should life all labour be?
Let us alone. Time driveth onward fast,
And in a little while our lips are dumb.
Let us alone. What is it that will last?
All things are taken from us, and become
Portions and parcels of the dreadful Past.
Let us alone. What pleasure can we have
To war with evil? Is there any peace
In ever climbing up the climbing wave?
All things have rest, and ripen toward the grave
In silence; ripen, fall and cease:
Give us long rest or death, dark death, or dreamful ease.

V

How sweet it were, hearing the downward stream,
With half-shut eyes ever to seem
Falling asleep in a half-dream!
To dream and dream, like yonder amber light,
Which will not leave the myrrh-bush on the height;
To hear each other's whisper'd speech;
Eating the Lotos day by day,
To watch the crisping ripples on the beach,
And tender curving lines of creamy spray;
To lend our hearts and spirits wholly
To the influence of mild-minded melancholy;
To muse and brood and live again in memory,
With those old faces of our infancy
Heap'd over with a mound of grass,
Two handfuls of white dust, shut in an urn of brass!

VI

Dear is the memory of our wedded lives,
And dear the last embraces of our wives
And their warm tears: but all hath suffer'd change:
For surely now our household hearths are cold:
Our sons inherit us: our looks are strange:
And we should come like ghosts to trouble joy.
Or else the island princes over-bold
Have eat our substance, and the minstrel sings
Before them of the ten years' war in Troy,
And our great deeds, as half-forgotten things.
Is there confusion in the little isle?
Let what is broken so remain.
The Gods are hard to reconcile:
'Tis hard to settle order once again.
There *is* confusion worse than death,
Trouble on trouble, pain on pain,
Long labour unto aged breath,
Sore task to hearts worn out by many wars
And eyes grown dim with gazing on the pilot-stars.

VII

But, propt on beds of amaranth and moly,
How sweet (while warm airs lull us, blowing lowly)
With half-dropt eyelid still,
Beneath a heaven dark and holy,
To watch the long bright river drawing slowly
His waters from the purple hill—
To hear the dewy echoes calling
From cave to cave thro' the thick-twined vine—
To watch the emerald-colour'd water falling
Thro' many a wov'n acanthus-wreath divine!
Only to hear and see the far-off sparkling brine,
Only to hear were sweet, stretch'd out beneath the pine.

VIII

The Lotos blooms below the barren peak:
The Lotos blows by every winding creek:
All day the wind breaths low with mellower tone:
Thro' every hollow cave and alley lone
Round and round the spicy downs the yellow Lotos-dust is blown.
We have had enough of action, and of motion we,
Roll'd to starboard, roll'd to larboard, when the surge was seething free,
Where the wallowing monster spouted his foam-fountains in the sea.
Let us swear an oath, and keep it with an equal mind,
In the hollow Lotos-land to live and lie reclined
On the hills like Gods together, careless of mankind.
For they lie beside their nectar, and the bolts are hurl'd
Far below them in the valleys, and the clouds are lightly curl'd
Round their golden houses, girdled with the gleaming world:
Where they smile in secret, looking over wasted lands,
Blight and famine, plague and earthquake, roaring deeps and fiery sands,
Clanging fights, and flaming towns, and sinking ships, and praying hands.
But they smile, they find a music centred in a doleful song
Steaming up, a lamentation and an ancient tale of wrong,

Like a tale of little meaning tho' the words are strong;
Chanted from an ill-used race of men that cleave the soil,
Sow the seed, and reap the harvest with enduring toil,
Storing yearly little dues of wheat, and wine and oil;
Till they perish and they suffer—some, 'tis whisper'd—down in hell
Suffer endless anguish, others in Elysian valleys dwell,
Resting weary limbs at last on beds of asphodel.
Surely, surely, slumber is more sweet than toil, the shore
Than labour in the deep mid-ocean, wind and wave and oar;
Oh rest ye, brother mariners, we will not wander more.

[1832, 1842]

A DREAM OF FAIR WOMEN

I read, before my eyelids dropt their shade,
'*The Legend of Good Women,*' long ago
Sung by the morning star of song, who made
His music heard below;

Dan Chaucer, the first warbler, whose sweet breath
Preluded those melodious bursts that fill
The spacious times of great Elizabeth
With sounds that echo still.

And, for a while, the knowledge of his art
Held me above the subject, as strong gales
Hold swollen clouds from raining, tho' my heart,
Brimful of those wild tales,

Charged both mine eyes with tears. In every land
I saw, wherever light illumineth,
Beauty and anguish walking hand in hand
The downward slope to death.

Those far-renowned brides of ancient song
Peopled the hollow dark, like burning stars,
And I heard sounds of insult, shame, and wrong,
And trumpets blown for wars;

And clattering flints batter'd with clanging hoofs;
And I saw crowds in column'd sanctuaries;
And forms that pass'd at windows and on roofs
Of marble palaces;

Corpses across the threshold; heroes tall
Dislodging pinnacle and parapet
Upon the tortoise creeping to the wall;
Lances in ambush set;

And high shrine-doors burst thro' with heated blasts
That run before the fluttering tongues of fire;
White surf wind-scatter'd over sails and masts,
And ever climbing higher;

Squadrons and squares of men in brazen plates,
Scaffolds, still sheets of water, divers woes,
Ranges of glimmering vaults with iron grates,
And hush'd seraglios.

So shape chased shape as swift as, when to land
Bluster the winds and tides the self-same way,
Crisp foam-flakes scud along the level sand,
Torn from the fringe of spray.

I started once, or seem'd to start in pain,
Resolved on noble things, and strove to speak,
As when a great thought strikes along the brain,
And flushes all the cheek.

And once my arm was lifted to hew down
A cavalier from off his saddle-bow,
That bore a lady from a leaguer'd town;
And then, I know not how,

All those sharp fancies, by down-lapsing thought
Steam'd onward, lost their edges, and did creep
Roll'd on each other, rounded, smooth'd, and brought
Into the gulfs of sleep.

At last methought that I had wander'd far
In an old wood: fresh-wash'd in coolest dew
The maiden splendours of the morning star
Shook in the stedfast blue.

Enormous elm-tree-boles did stoop and lean
Upon the dusky brushwood underneath
Their broad curved branches, fledged with clearest green,
New from its silken sheath.

The dim red morn had died, her journey done,
And with dead lips smiled at the twilight plain,
Half-fall'n across the threshold of the sun,
Never to rise again.

There was no motion in the dumb dead air,
Not any song of bird or sound of rill;
Gross darkness of the inner sepulchre
Is not so deadly still

As that wide forest. Growths of jasmine turn'd
Their humid arms festooning tree to tree,
And at the root thro' lush green grasses burn'd
The red anemone.

I knew the flowers, I knew the leaves, I knew
The tearful glimmer of the languid dawn
On those long, rank, dark wood-walks drench'd in dew,
Leading from lawn to lawn.

The smell of violets, hidden in the green,
Pour'd back into my empty soul and frame
The times when I remembered to have been
Joyful and free from blame.

And from within me a clear under-tone
Thrill'd thro' mine ears in that unblissful clime,
'Pass freely thro': the wood is all thine own,
Until the end of time.'

At length I saw a lady within call,
Stiller than chisell'd marble, standing there;
A daughter of the gods, divinely tall,
And most divinely fair.

Her loveliness with shame and with surprise
Froze my swift speech: she turning on my face
The star-like sorrows of immortal eyes,
Spoke slowly in her place.

'I had great beauty: ask thou not my name:
No one can be more wise than destiny.
Many drew swords and died. Where'er I came
I brought calamity.'

'No marvel, sovereign lady: in fair field
Myself for such a face had boldly died,'
I answer'd free; and turning I appeal'd
To one that stood beside.

But she, with sick and scornful looks averse,
To her full height her stately stature draws;
'My youth,' she said, 'was blasted with a curse:
This woman was the cause.

'I was cut off from hope in that sad place,
Which men call'd Aulis in those iron years:
My father held his hand upon his face;
I, blinded with my tears,

'Still strove to speak: my voice was thick with sighs
As in a dream. Dimly I could descry
The stern black-bearded kings with wolfish eyes,
Waiting to see me die.

'The high masts flicker'd as they lay afloat;
The crowds, the temples, waver'd, and the shore;
The bright death quiver'd at the victim's throat;
Touch'd; and I knew no more.'

Whereto the other with a downward brow:
'I would the white cold heavy-plunging foam,
Whirl'd by the wind, had roll'd me deep below,
Then when I left my home.'

Her slow full words sank thro' the silence drear,
As thunder-drops fall on a sleeping sea:
Sudden I heard a voice that cried, 'Come here,
That I may look on thee.'

I turning saw, throned on a flowery rise,
One sitting on a crimson scarf unroll'd;
A queen, with swarthy cheeks and bold black eyes,
Brow-bound with burning gold.

She, flashing forth a haughty smile, began:
'I govern'd men by change, and so I sway'd
All moods. 'Tis long since I have seen a man.
Once, like the moon, I made

'The ever-shifting currents of the blood
According to my humour ebb and flow.
I have no men to govern in this wood:
That makes my only woe.

'Nay—yet it chafes me that I could not bend
One will; nor tame and tutor with mine eye
That dull cold-blooded Cæsar. Prythee, friend,
Where is Mark Antony?

'The man, my lover, with whom I rode sublime
On Fortune's neck: we sat as God by God:
The Nilus would have risen before his time
And flooded at our nod.

'We drank the Libyan Sun to sleep, and lit
Lamps which out-burn'd Canopus. O my life
In Egypt! O the dalliance and the wit,
The flattery and the strife,

'And the wild kiss, when fresh from war's alarms,
My Hercules, my Roman Antony,
My mailed Bacchus leapt into my arms,
Contented there to die!

'And there he died: and when I heard my name
Sigh'd forth with life I would not brook my fear
Of the other: with a worm I balk'd his fame.
What else was left? Look here!'

(With that she tore her robe apart, and half
The polish'd argent of her breast to sight
Laid bare. Thereto she pointed with a laugh,
Showing the aspick's bite.)

'I died a Queen. The Roman soldier found
Me lying dead, my crown about my brows,
A name for ever!—lying robed and crown'd
Worthy a Roman spouse.'

Her warbling voice, a lyre of widest range
Struck by all passion, did fall down and glance
From tone to tone, and glided thro' all change
Of liveliest utterance.

When she made pause I knew not for delight;
Because with sudden motion from the ground
She raised her piercing orbs, and fill'd with light
The interval of sound.

Still with their fires Love tipt his keenest darts;
As once they drew into two burning rings
All beams of Love, melting the mighty hearts
Of captains and of kings.

Slowly my sense undazzled. Then I heard
A noise of some one coming thro' the lawn,
And singing clearer than the crested bird
That claps his wings at dawn.

'The torrent brooks of hallow'd Israel
From craggy hollows pouring, late and soon,
Sound all night long, in falling thro' the dell,
Far-heard beneath the moon.

'The balmy moon of blessed Israel
Floods all the deep-blue gloom with beams divine:

All night the splinter'd crags that wall the dell
With spires of silver shine.'

As one that museth where broad sunshine laves
The lawn by some cathedral, thro' the door
Hearing the holy organ rolling waves
Of sound on roof and floor

Within, and anthem sung, is charm'd and tied
To where he stands,—so stood I, when that flow
Of music left the lips of her that died
To save her father's vow;

The daughter of the warrior Gileadite,
A maiden pure; as when she went along
From Mizpeh's tower'd gate with welcome light,
With timbrel and with song.

My words leapt forth: 'Heaven heads the count of crimes
With that wild oath.' She render'd answer high:
'Not so, nor once alone; a thousand times
I would be born and die.

'Single I grew, like some green plant, whose root
Creeps to the garden water-pipes beneath,
Feeding the flower; but ere my flower to fruit
Changed, I was ripe for death.

'My God, my land, my father—these did move
Me from my bliss of life, that Nature gave,
Lower'd softly with a threefold cord of love
Down to a silent grave.

'And I went mourning, "No fair Hebrew boy
Shall smile away my maiden blame among
The Hebrew mothers"—emptied of all joy,
Leaving the dance and song,

'Leaving the olive-gardens far below,
Leaving the promise of my bridal bower,
The valleys of grape-loaded vines that glow
Beneath the battled tower.

'The light white cloud swam over us. Anon
We heard the lion roaring from his den;
We saw the large white stars rise one by one,
Or, from the darken'd glen,

'Saw God divide the night with flying flame,
And thunder on the everlasting hills.
I heard Him, for He spake, and grief became
A solemn scorn of ills.

'When the next moon was roll'd into the sky,
Strength came to me that equall'd my desire.
How beautiful a thing it was to die
For God and for my sire!

'It comforts me in this one thought to dwell,
That I subdued me to my father's will;
Because the kiss he gave me, ere I fell,
Sweetens the spirit still.

'Moreover it is written that my race
Hew'd Ammon, hip and thigh, from Aroer
On Arnon unto Minneth.' Here her face
Glow'd, as I look'd at her.

She lock'd her lips: she left me where I stood:
'Glory to God,' she sang, and past afar,
Thridding the sombre boskage of the wood,
Toward the morning-star.

Losing her carol I stood pensively,
As one that from a casement leans his head,
When midnight bells cease ringing suddenly,
And the old year is dead.

'Alas! alas!' a low voice, full of care,
Murmur'd beside me: 'Turn and look on me:

I am that Rosamond, whom men call fair,
If what I was I be.

'Would I had been some maiden coarse and poor!
O me, that I should ever see the light!
Those dragon eyes of anger'd Eleanor
Do hunt me, day and night.'

She ceased in tears, fallen from hope and trust:
To whom the Egyptian: 'O, you tamely died!
You should have clung to Fulvia's waist, and thrust
The dagger thro' her side.'

With that sharp sound the white dawn's creeping beams,
Stol'n to my brain, dissolved the mystery
Of folded sleep. The captain of my dreams
Ruled in the eastern sky.

Morn broaden'd on the borders of the dark,
Ere I saw her, who clasp'd in her last trance
Her murder'd father's head, or Joan of Arc,
A light of ancient France;

Or her who knew that Love can vanquish Death,
Who kneeling, with one arm about her king,
Drew forth the poison with her balmy breath,
Sweet as new buds in Spring.

No memory labours longer from the deep
Gold-mines of thought to lift the hidden ore
That glimpses, moving up, than I from sleep
To gather and tell o'er

Each little sound and sight. With what dull pain
Compass'd, how eagerly I sought to strike
Into that wondrous track of dreams again!
But no two dreams are like.

As when a soul laments, which hath been blest,
Desiring what is mingled with past years,
In yearnings that can never be exprest
By sighs or groans or tears;

Because all words, tho' cull'd with choicest art,
Failing to give the bitter of the sweet,
Wither beneath the palate, and the heart
Faints, faded by its heat.

[1832, 1842, 1853]

YOU ASK ME, WHY, THO' ILL AT EASE

You ask me, why, tho' ill at ease,
Within this region I subsist,
Whose spirits falter in the mist,
And languish for the purple seas.

It is the land that freemen till,
That sober-suited Freedom chose,
The land, where girt with friends or foes
A man may speak the thing he will;

A land of settled government,
A land of just and old renown,
Where Freedom slowly broadens down
From precedent to precedent:

Where faction seldom gathers head,
But by degrees to fullness wrought,
The strength of some diffusive thought
Hath time and space to work and spread.

Should banded unions persecute
Opinion, and induce a time
When single thought is civil crime,
And individual freedom mute;

Tho' Power should make from land to land
The name of Britain trebly great—
Tho' every channel of the State
Should fill and choke with golden sand—

Yet waft me from the harbour-mouth,
Wild wind! I seek a warmer sky,
And I will see before I die
The palms and temples of the South.

[1842]

OF OLD SAT FREEDOM ON THE HEIGHTS

Of old sat freedom on the heights,
The thunders breaking at her feet:
Above her shook the starry lights:
She heard the torrents meet.

There in her place she did rejoice,
Self-gather'd in her prophet-mind,
But fragments of her mighty voice
Came rolling on the wind.

Then stept she down thro' town and field
To mingle with the human race,
And part by part to men reveal'd
The fullness of her face—

Grave mother of majestic works,
From her isle-altar gazing down,
Who, God-like, grasps the triple forks,
And, King-like, wears the crown:

Her open eyes desire the truth.
The wisdom of a thousand years
Is in them. May perpetual youth
Keep dry their light from tears;

That her fair form may stand and shine,
Make bright our days and light our dreams,
Turning to scorn with lips divine
The falsehood of extremes!

[1834?] [1842]

LOVE THOU THY LAND WITH LOVE FAR-BROUGHT

Love thou thy land, with love far-brought
From out the storied Past, and used
Within the Present, but transfused
Thro' future time by power of thought.

True love turn'd round on fixed poles,
Love, that endures not sordid ends,
For English natures, freemen, friends,
Thy brothers and immortal souls.

But pamper not a hasty time,
Nor feed with crude imaginings
The herd, wild hearts and feeble wings
That every sophister can lime.

Deliver not the tasks of might
To weakness, neither hide the ray
From those, not blind, who wait for day,
Tho' sitting girt with doubtful light.

Make knowledge circle with the winds;
But let her herald, Reverence, fly
Before her to whatever sky
Bear seed of men and growth of minds.

Watch what main-currents draw the years:
Cut Prejudice against the grain:
But gentle words are always gain:
Regard the weakness of thy peers:

Nor toil for title, place, or touch
Of pension, neither count on praise:
It grows to guerdon after-days:
Nor deal in watch-words overmuch:

Not clinging to some ancient saw;
Not master'd by some modern term;
Not swift nor slow to change, but firm:
And in its season bring the law;

That from Discussion's lip may fall
With Life, that, working strongly, binds—
Set in all lights by many minds,
To close the interests of all.

For Nature also, cold and warm,
And moist and dry, devising long,
Thro' many agents making strong,
Matures the individual form.

Meet is it changes should control
Our being, lest we rust in ease.
We all are changed by still degrees,
All but the basis of the soul.

So let the change which comes be free
To ingroove itself with that which flies,
And work, a joint of state, that plies
Its office, moved with sympathy.

A saying, hard to shape in act;
For all the past of Time reveals
A bridal dawn of thunder-peals,
Wherever Thought hath wedded Fact.

Ev'n now we hear with inward strife
A motion toiling in the gloom—
The Spirit of the years to come
Yearning to mix himself with Life.

A slow-develop'd strength awaits
Completion in a painful school;
Phantoms of other forms of rule,
New Majesties of mighty States—

The warders of the growing hour,
But vague in vapour, hard to mark;
And round them sea and air are dark
With great contrivances of Power.

Of many changes, aptly join'd,
Is bodied forth the second whole.
Regard gradation, lest the soul
Of Discord race the rising wind;

A wind to puff your idol-fires,
And heap their ashes on the head;
To shame the boast so often made,
That we are wiser than our sires.

Oh yet, if Nature's evil star
Drive men in manhood, as in youth,
To follow flying steps of Truth
Across the brazen bridge of war—

If New and Old, disastrous feud,
Must ever shock, like armed foes,
And this be true, till Time shall close,
That Principles are rain'd in blood;

Not yet the wise of heart would cease
To hold his hope thro' shame and guilt,
But with his hand against the hilt,
Would pace the troubled land, like Peace;

Not less, tho' dogs of Faction bay,
Would serve his kind in deed and word,
Certain, if knowledge bring the sword,
That knowledge takes the sword away—

Would love the gleams of good that broke
From either side, nor veil his eyes:
And if some dreadful need should rise
Would strike, and firmly, and one stroke:

To-morrow yet would reap to-day,
As we bear blossom of the dead;
Earn well the thrifty months, nor wed
Raw Haste, half-sister to Delay.

[1837] [1842]

MORTE D'ARTHUR

So all day long the noise of battle roll'd
Among the mountains by the winter sea;
Until King Arthur's table, man by man,
Had fallen in Lyonnesse about their Lord,
King Arthur: then, because his wound was deep,
The bold Sir Bedivere uplifted him,
Sir Bedivere, the last of all his knights,
And bore him to a chapel nigh the field,
A broken chancel with a broken cross,
That stood on a dark strait of barren land.
On one side lay the Ocean, and on one
Lay a great water, and the moon was full.
Then spake King Arthur to Sir Bedivere:
'The sequel of to-day unsolders all
The goodliest fellowship of famous knights
Whereof this world holds record. Such a sleep
They sleep—the men I loved. I think that we
Shall never more, at any future time,
Delight our souls with talk of knightly deeds,
Walking about the gardens and the halls
Of Camelot, as in the days that were.
I perish by this people which I made,—
Tho' Merlin sware that I should come again
To rule once more—but let what will be, be,
I am so deeply smitten thro' the helm
That without help I cannot last till morn.
Thou therefore take my brand Excalibur,
Which was my pride: for thou rememberest how
In those old days, one summer noon, an arm
Rose up from out the bosom of the lake,
Clothed in white samite, mystic, wonderful,
Holding the sword—and how I row'd across
And took it, and have worn it, like a king:
And, wheresoever I am sung or told
In aftertime, this also shall be known:
But now delay not: take Excalibur,
And fling him far into the middle mere:
Watch what thou seëst, and lightly bring me word.'
To him replied the bold Sir Bedivere:
'It is not meet, Sir King, to leave thee thus,
Aidless, alone, and smitten thro' the helm.
A little thing may harm a wounded man.
Yet I thy hest will all perform at full,

Watch what I see, and lightly bring thee word.'
So saying, from the ruin'd shrine he stept
And in the moon athwart the place of tombs,
Where lay the mighty bones of ancient men,
Old knights, and over them the sea-wind sang
Shrill, chill, with flakes of foam. He, stepping down
By zig-zag paths, and juts of pointed rock,
Came on the shining levels of the lake.
There drew he forth the brand Excalibur,
And o'er him, drawing it, the winter moon,
Brightening the skirts of a long cloud, ran forth
And sparkled keen with frost against the hilt:
For all the haft twinkled with diamond sparks,
Myriads of topaz-lights, and jacinth-work
Of subtlest jewellery. He gazed so long
That both his eyes were dazzled, as he stood,
This way and that dividing the swift mind,
In act to throw: but at the last it seem'd
Better to leave Excalibur conceal'd
There in the many-knotted waterflags,
That whistled stiff and dry about the marge.
So strode he back slow to the wounded King.
Then spake King Arthur to Sir Bedivere:
'Hast thou perform'd my mission which I gave?
What is it thou hast seen? or what hast heard?'
And answer made the bold Sir Bedivere:
'I heard the ripple washing in the reeds,
And the wild water lapping on the crag.'
To whom replied King Arthur, faint and pale:
'Thou hast betray'd thy nature and thy name,
Not rendering true answer, as beseem'd
Thy fealty, nor like a noble knight:
For surer sign had follow'd, either hand,
Or voice, or else a motion of the mere.
This is a shameful thing for men to lie.
Yet now, I charge thee, quickly go again
As thou art lief and dear, and do the thing
I bad thee, watch, and lightly bring me word.'
Then went Sir Bedivere the second time
Across the ridge, and paced beside the mere,
Counting the dewy pebbles, fix'd in thought;
But when he saw the wonder of the hilt,
How curiously and strangely chased, he smote
His palms together, and he cried aloud,
'And if indeed I cast the brand away,
Surely a precious thing, one worthy note,
Should thus be lost for ever from the earth,
Which might have pleased the eyes of many men.
What good should follow this, if this were done?
What harm, undone? deep harm to disobey,
Seeing obedience is the bond of rule.
Were it well to obey then, if a king demand
An act unprofitable, against himself?
The King is sick, and knows not what he does.
What record, or what relic of my lord
Should be to aftertime, but empty breath
And rumours of a doubt? but were this kept,
Stored in some treasure-house of mighty kings,
Some one might show it at a joust of arms,
Saying, "King Arthur's sword, Excalibur,
Wrought by the lonely maiden of the Lake.
Nine years she wrought it, sitting in the deeps
Upon the hidden bases of the hills."
So might some old man speak in the aftertime
To all the people, winning reverence.
But now much honour and much fame were lost.'
So spake he, clouded with his own conceit,
And hid Excalibur the second time,
And so strode back slow to the wounded King.
Then spoke King Arthur, breathing heavily:

'What is it thou hast seen? or what hast heard?'
  And answer made the bold Sir Bedivere:
'I heard the water lapping on the crag,
And the long ripple washing in the reeds.'
  To whom replied King Arthur, much in wrath:
'Ah, miserable and unkind, untrue,
Unknightly, traitor-hearted! Woe is me!
Authority forgets a dying king,
Laid widow'd of the power in his eye
That bow'd the will. I see thee what thou art,
For thou, the latest-left of all my knights,
In whom should meet the offices of all,
Thou wouldst betray me for the precious hilt;
Either from lust of gold, or like a girl
Valuing the giddy pleasure of the eyes.
Yet, for a man may fail in duty twice,
And the third time may prosper, get thee hence:
But, if thou spare to fling Excalibur,
I will arise and slay thee with my hands.'
  Then quickly rose Sir Bedivere, and ran,
And, leaping down the ridges lightly, plunged
Among the bulrush-beds, and clutch'd the sword,
And strongly wheel'd and threw it. The great brand
Made lightnings in the splendour of the moon,
And flashing round and round, and whirl'd in an arch,
Shot like a streamer of the northern morn,
Seen where the moving isles of winter shock
By night, with noises of the northern sea.
So flash'd and fell the brand Excalibur:
But ere he dipt the surface, rose an arm
Clothed in white samite, mystic, wonderful,
And caught him by the hilt, and brandish'd him
Three times, and drew him under in the mere.
And lightly went the other to the King.
  Then spoke King Arthur, drawing thicker breath:
'Now see I by thine eyes that this is done.
Speak out: what is it thou hast heard, or seen?'
  And answer made the bold Sir Bedivere:
'Sir King, I closed mine eyelids, lest the gems
Should blind my purpose, for I never saw,
Nor shall see, here or elsewhere, till I die,
Not tho' I live three lives of mortal men,
So great a miracle as yonder hilt.
Then with both hands I flung him, wheeling him;
But when I look'd again, behold an arm,
Clothed in white samite, mystic, wonderful,
That caught him by the hilt, and brandish'd him
Three times, and drew him under in the mere.'
  And answer made King Arthur, breathing hard:
'My end draws nigh; 'tis time that I were gone.
Make broad thy shoulders to receive my weight,
And bear me to the margin; yet I fear
My wound hath taken cold, and I shall die.'
  So saying, from the pavement he half rose,
Slowly, with pain, reclining on his arm,
And looking wistfully with wide blue eyes
As in a picture. Him Sir Bedivere
Remorsefully regarded thro' his tears,
And would have spoken, but he found not words,
Then took with care, and kneeling on one knee,
O'er both his shoulders drew the languid hands,
And rising bore him thro' the place of tombs.
  But, as he walk'd, King Arthur panted hard,
Like one that feels a nightmare on his bed
When all the house is mute. So sigh'd the King,
Muttering and murmuring at his ear, 'Quick, quick!
I fear it is too late, and I shall die.'
But the other swiftly strode from ridge to ridge,
Clothed with his breath, and looking, as he walk'd,
Larger than human on the frozen hills.
He heard the deep behind him, and a cry
Before. His own thought drove him, like a goad.
Dry clash'd his harness in the icy caves

And barren chasms, and all to left and right
The bare black cliff clang'd round him, as he based
His feet on juts of slippery crag that rang
Sharp-smitten with the dint of armed heels—
And on a sudden, lo! the level lake,
And the long glories of the winter moon.
Then saw they how there hove a dusky barge,
Dark as a funeral scarf from stem to stern,
Beneath them; and descending they were ware
That all the decks were dense with stately forms
Black-stoled, black-hooded, like a dream—by these
Three Queens with crowns of gold—and from them rose
A cry that shiver'd to the tingling stars,
And, as it were one voice, an agony
Of lamentation, like a wind, that shrills
All night in a waste land, where no one comes,
Or hath come, since the making of the world.
Then murmur'd Arthur, 'Place me in the barge,'
And to the barge they came. There those three Queens
Put forth their hands, and took the King, and wept.
But she, that rose the tallest of them all
And fairest, laid his head upon her lap,
And loosed the shatter'd casque, and chafed his hands,
And call'd him by his name, complaining loud,
And dropping bitter tears against his brow
Striped with dark blood: for all his face was white
And colourless, and like the wither'd moon
Smote by the fresh beam of the springing east;
And all his greaves and cuisses dash'd with drops
Of onset; and the light and lustrous curls—
That made his forehead like a rising sun
High from the daïs-throne—were parch'd with dust;
Or, clotted into points and hanging loose,
Mix'd with the knightly growth that fringed his lips.
So like a shatter'd column lay the King;
Not like that Arthur who, with lance in rest,
From spur to plume a star of tournament,
Shot thro' the lists at Camelot, and charged
Before the eyes of ladies and of kings.
Then loudly cried the bold Sir Bedivere,
'Ah! my Lord Arthur, whither shall I go?
Where shall I hide my forehead and my eyes?
For now I see the true old times are dead,
When every morning brought a noble chance,
And every chance brought out a noble knight.
Such times have been not since the light that led
The holy Elders with the gift of myrrh.
But now the whole ROUND TABLE is dissolved
Which was an image of the mighty world;
And I, the last, go forth companionless,
And the days darken round me, and the years,
Among new men, strange faces, other minds.'
And slowly answered Arthur from the barge:
'The old order changeth, yielding place to new,
And God fulfils Himself in many ways,
Lest one good custom should corrupt the world.
Comfort thyself: what comfort is in me?
I have lived my life, and that which I have done
May He within Himself make pure! but thou,
If thou shouldst never see my face again,
Pray for my soul. More things are wrought by prayer
Than this world dreams of. Wherefore, let thy voice
Rise like a fountain for me night and day.
For what are men better than sheep or goats
That nourish a blind life within the brain,
If, knowing God, they lift not hands of prayer
Both for themselves and those who call them friend?
For so the whole round earth is every way
Bound by gold chains about the feet of God.

But now farewell. I am going a long way
With these thou seëst—if indeed I go—
(For all my mind is clouded with a doubt)
To the island-valley of Avilion;
Where falls not hail, or rain, or any snow,
Nor ever wind blows loudly; but it lies
Deep-meadow'd, happy, fair with orchard-lawns
And bowery hollows crown'd with summer sea,
Where I will heal me of my grievous wound.'

So said he, and the barge with oar and sail
Moved from the brink, like some full-breasted swan
That, fluting a wild carol ere her death,
Ruffles her pure cold plume, and takes the flood
With swarthy webs. Long stood Sir Bedivere
Revolving many memories, till the hull
Look'd one black dot against the verge of dawn,
And on the mere the wailing died away.

[1835?] [1842]

ULYSSES

It little profits that an idle king,
By this still hearth, among these barren crags,
Match'd with an aged wife, I mete and dole
Unequal laws unto a savage race,
That hoard, and sleep, and feed, and know not me.

I cannot rest from travel: I will drink
Life to the lees: all times I have enjoy'd
Greatly, have suffer'd greatly, both with those
That loved me, and alone; on shore, and when
Thro' scudding drifts the rainy Hyades
Vext the dim sea: I am become a name;
For always roaming with a hungry heart
Much have I seen and known; cities of men
And manners, climates, councils, governments,
Myself not least, but honour'd of them all;
And drunk delight of battle with my peers,
Far on the ringing plains of windy Troy.
I am a part of all that I have met;
Yet all experience is an arch wherethro'
Gleams that untravell'd world, whose margin fades
For ever and for ever when I move.
How dull it is to pause, to make an end,
To rust unburnish'd, not to shine in use!
As tho' to breathe were life. Life piled on life
Were all too little, and of one to me
Little remains: but every hour is saved
From that eternal silence, something more,
A bringer of new things; and vile it were
For some three suns to store and hoard myself,
And this gray spirit yearning in desire
To follow knowledge like a sinking star,
Beyond the utmost bound of human thought.

This is my son, mine own Telemachus,
To whom I leave the sceptre and the isle—
Well-loved of me, discerning to fulfil
This labour, by slow prudence to make mild
A rugged people, and thro' soft degrees
Subdue them to the useful and the good.
Most blameless is he, centred in the sphere
Of common duties, decent not to fail
In offices of tenderness, and pay
Meet adoration to my household gods,
When I am gone. He works his work, I mine.

There lies the port; the vessel puffs her sail:
There gloom the dark broad seas. My mariners,
Souls that have toil'd, and wrought, and thought with me—
That ever with a frolic welcome took
The thunder and the sunshine, and opposed
Free hearts, free foreheads—you and I are old;
Old age hath yet his honour and his toil;
Death closes all: but something ere the end,
Some work of noble note, may yet be done,
Not unbecoming men that strove with Gods.
The lights begin to twinkle from the rocks:
The long day wanes: the slow moon climbs: the deep
Moans round with many voices. Come, my friends,

'Tis not too late to seek a newer world.
Push off, and sitting well in order smite
The sounding furrows; for my purpose holds
To sail beyond the sunset, and the baths
Of all the western stars, until I die.
It may be that the gulfs will wash us down:
It may be we shall touch the Happy Isles,
And see the great Achilles, whom we knew.
Tho' much is taken, much abides; and tho'
We are not now that strength which in old days
Moved earth and heaven; that which we are, we are;
One equal temper of heroic hearts,
Made weak by time and fate, but strong in will
To strive, to seek, to find, and not to yield.

[1842]

TITHONUS

The woods decay, the woods decay and fall,
The vapours weep their burthen to the ground,
Man comes and tills the field and lies beneath,
And after many a summer dies the swan.
Me only cruel immortality
Consumes: I wither slowly in thine arms,
Here at the quiet limit of the world,
A white-hair'd shadow roaming like a dream
The ever-silent spaces of the East,
Far-folded mists, and gleaming halls of morn.

Alas! for this gray shadow, once a man—
So glorious in his beauty and thy choice,
Who madest him thy chosen that he seem'd
To his great heart none other than a God!
I ask'd thee, 'Give me immortality.'
Then didst thou grant mine asking with a smile,
Like wealthy men who care not how they give.
But thy strong Hours indignant work'd their wills,
And beat me down and marr'd and wasted me,
And tho' they could not end me, left me maim'd
To dwell in presence of immortal youth,
Immortal age beside immortal youth,
And all I was, in ashes. Can thy love,
Thy beauty, make amends, tho' even now,
Close over us, the silver star, thy guide,
Shines in those tremulous eyes that fill with tears
To hear me? Let me go: take back thy gift:
Why should a man desire in any way
To vary from the kindly race of men,
Or pass beyond the goal of ordinance
Where all should pause, as is most meet for all?

A soft air fans the cloud apart; there comes
A glimpse of that dark world where I was born.
Once more the old mysterious glimmer steals
From thy pure brows, and from thy shoulders pure,
And bosom beating with a heart renew'd.
Thy cheek begins to redden thro' the gloom,
Thy sweet eyes brighten slowly close to mine,
Ere yet they blind the stars, and the wild team
Which love thee, yearning for thy yoke, arise,
And shake the darkness from their loosen'd manes,
And beat the twilight into flakes of fire.

Lo! ever thus thou growest beautiful
In silence, then before thine answer given
Departest, and thy tears are on my cheek.

Why wilt thou ever scare me with thy tears,
And make me tremble lest a saying learnt,
In days far-off, on that dark earth, be true?
'The Gods themselves cannot recall their gifts.'

Ay me! ay me! with what another heart
In days far-off, and with what other eyes
I used to watch—if I be he that watch'd—
The lucid outline forming round thee; saw
The dim curls kindle into sunny rings;
Changed with thy mystic change, and felt my blood
Glow with the glow that slowly crimson'd all

Thy presence and thy portals, while I lay,
Mouth, forehead, eyelids, growing dewy-warm
With kisses balmier than half-opening buds
Of April, and could hear the lips that kiss'd
Whispering I knew not what of wild and sweet,
Like that strange song I heard Apollo sing,
While Ilion like a mist rose into towers.

Yet hold me not for ever in thine East:
How can my nature longer mix with thine?
Coldly thy rosy shadows bathe me, cold
Are all thy lights, and cold my wrinkled feet
Upon thy glimmering thresholds, when the steam
Floats up from those dim fields about the homes
Of happy men that have the power to die,
And grassy barrows of the happier dead.
Release me, and restore me to the ground;
Thou seëst all things, thou wilt see my grave:
Thou wilt renew thy beauty morn by morn;
I earth in earth forget these empty courts,
And thee returning on thy silver wheels.

[c 1835] [1860]

LOCKSLEY HALL

Comrades, leave me here a little, while as yet 'tis early morn:
Leave me here, and when you want me, sound upon the bugle-horn.

'Tis the place, and all around it, as of old, the curlews call,
Dreary gleams about the moorland flying over Locksley Hall;

Locksley Hall, that in the distance overlooks the sandy tracts,
And the hollow ocean-ridges roaring into cataracts.

Many a night from yonder ivied casement, ere I went to rest,
Did I look on great Orion sloping slowly to the West.

Many a night I saw the Pleiads, rising thro' the mellow shade,
Glitter like a swarm of fire-flies tangled in a silver braid.

Here about the beach I wander'd, nourishing a youth sublime
With the fairy tales of science, and the long result of Time;

When the centuries behind me like a fruitful land reposed;
When I clung to all the present for the promise that it closed:

When I dipt into the future far as human eye could see;
Saw the Vision of the world, and all the wonder that would be.—

In the Spring a fuller crimson comes upon the robin's breast;
In the Spring the wanton lapwing gets himself another crest;

In the Spring a livelier iris changes on the burnish'd dove;
In the Spring a young man's fancy lightly turns to thoughts of love.

Then her cheek was pale and thinner than should be for one so young,
And her eyes on all my motions with a mute observance hung.

And I said, 'My cousin Amy, speak, and speak the truth to me,
Trust me, cousin, all the current of my being sets to thee.'

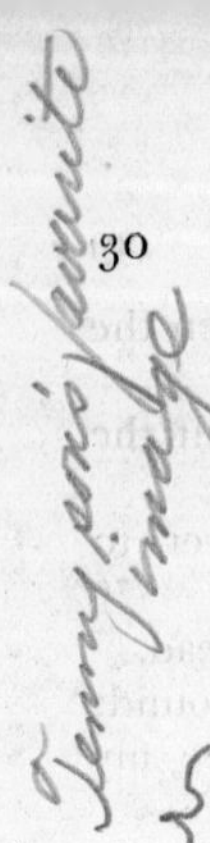

On her pallid cheek and forehead came a colour and a light,
As I have seen the rosy red flushing in the northern night.

And she turn'd—her bosom shaken with a sudden storm of sighs—
All the spirit deeply dawning in the dark of hazel eyes—

Saying, 'I have hid my feelings, fearing they should do me wrong;'
Saying, 'Dost thou love me, cousin?' weeping, 'I have loved thee long.'

Love took up the glass of Time, and turn'd it in his glowing hands;
Every moment, lightly shaken, ran itself in golden sands.

Love took up the harp of Life, and smote on all the chords with might;
Smote the chord of Self, that, trembling, pass'd in music out of sight.

Many a morning on the moorland did we hear the copses ring,
And her whisper throng'd my pulses with the fulness of the Spring.

Many an evening by the waters did we watch the stately ships,
And our spirits rush'd together at the touching of the lips.

O my cousin, shallow-hearted! O my Amy, mine no more!
O the dreary, dreary moorland! O the barren, barren shore!

Falser than all fancy fathoms, falser than all songs have sung,
Puppet to a father's threat, and servile to a shrewish tongue!

Is it well to wish thee happy?—having known me—to decline
On a range of lower feelings and a narrower heart than mine!

Yet it shall be: thou shalt lower to his level day by day,
What is fine within thee growing coarse to sympathise with clay.

As the husband is, the wife is: thou art mated with a clown,
And the grossness of his nature will have weight to drag thee down.

He will hold thee, when his passion shall have spent its novel force,
Something better than his dog, a little dearer than his horse.

What is this? his eyes are heavy: think not they are glazed with wine.
Go to him: it is thy duty: kiss him: take his hand in thine.

It may be my lord is weary, that his brain is overwrought:
Soothe him with thy finer fancies, touch him with thy lighter thought.

He will answer to the purpose, easy things to understand—
Better thou wert dead before me, tho' I slew thee with my hand!

Better thou and I were lying, hidden from the heart's disgrace,
Roll'd in one another's arms, and silent in a last embrace.

Cursed be the social wants that sin against the strength of youth!
Cursed be the social lies that warp us from living truth!

Cursed be the sickly forms that err from honest Nature's rule!
Cursed be the gold that gilds the straiten'd forehead of the fool!

Well—'tis well that I should bluster!—Hadst thou less unworthy proved—
Would to God—for I had loved thee more than ever wife was loved.

Am I mad, that I should cherish that which bears but bitter fruit?
I will pluck it from my bosom, tho' my heart be at the root.

Never, tho' my mortal summers to such length of years should come
As the many-winter'd crow that leads the clanging rookery home.

Where is comfort? in division of the records of the mind?
Can I part her from herself, and love her, as I knew her, kind?

I remember one that perish'd: sweetly did she speak and move:
Such a one do I remember, whom to look at was to love.

Can I think of her as dead, and love her for the love she bore?
No—she never loved me truly: love is love for evermore.

Comfort? comfort scorn'd of devils! this is truth the poet sings,
That a sorrow's crown of sorrow is remembering happier things.

Drug thy memories, lest thou learn it, lest thy heart be put to proof,
In the dead unhappy night, and when the rain is on the roof.

Like a dog, he hunts in dreams, and thou art staring at the wall,
Where the dying night-lamp flickers, and the shadows rise and fall.

Then a hand shall pass before thee, pointing to his drunken sleep,
To thy widow'd marriage-pillows, to the tears that thou wilt weep.

Thou shalt hear the 'Never, never,' whisper'd by the phantom years,
And a song from out the distance in the ringing of thine ears;

And an eye shall vex thee, looking ancient kindness on thy pain.
Turn thee, turn thee on thy pillow: get thee to thy rest again.

Nay, but Nature brings thee solace; for a tender voice will cry.
'Tis a purer life than thine; a lip to drain thy trouble dry.

Baby lips will laugh me down: my latest rival brings thee rest.
Baby fingers, waxen touches, press me from the mother's breast.

O, the child too clothes the father with a dearness not his due.
Half is thine and half is his: it will be worthy of the two.

O, I see thee old and formal, fitted to thy petty part,
With a little hoard of maxims preaching down a daughter's heart.

'They were dangerous guides the feelings—she herself was not exempt—
Truly, she herself had suffer'd'—Perish in thy self-contempt!

Overlive it—lower yet—be happy! wherefore should I care?
I myself must mix with action, lest I wither by despair.

What is that which I should turn to, lighting upon days like these?
Every door is barr'd with gold, and opens but to golden keys.

Every gate is throng'd with suitors, all the markets overflow.
I have but an angry fancy: what is that which I should do?

I had been content to perish, falling on the foeman's ground,
When the ranks are roll'd in vapour, and the winds are laid with sound.

But the jingling of the guinea helps the hurt that Honour feels,
And the nations do but murmur, snarling at each other's heels.

Can I but relive in sadness? I will turn that earlier page.
Hide me from my deep emotion, O thou wondrous Mother-Age!

Make me feel the wild pulsation that I felt before the strife,
When I heard my days before me, and the tumult of my life;

Yearning for the large excitement that the coming years would yield,
Eager-hearted as a boy when first he leaves his father's field,

And at night along the dusky highway near and nearer drawn,
Sees in heaven the light of London flaring like a dreary dawn;

And his spirit leaps within him to be gone before him then,
Underneath the light he looks at, in among the throngs of men:

Men, my brothers, men the workers, ever reaping something new:
That which they have done but earnest of the things that they shall do:

For I dipt into the future, far as human eye could see,
Saw the Vision of the world, and all the wonder that would be;

Saw the heavens fill with commerce, argosies of magic sails,
Pilots of the purple twilight, dropping down with costly bales;

Heard the heavens fill with shouting, and there rain'd a ghastly dew
From the nations' airy navies grappling in the central blue;

Far along the world-wide whisper of the south-wind rushing warm,
With the standards of the peoples plunging thro' the thunder-storm;

Till the war-drum throbb'd no longer, and the battle-flags were furl'd
In the Parliament of man, the Federation of the world.

There the common sense of most shall hold a fretful realm in awe,
And the kindly earth shall slumber, lapt in universal law.

So I triumph'd ere my passion sweeping thro' me left me dry,
Left me with the palsied heart, and left me with the jaundiced eye;

Eye, to which all order festers, all things here are out of joint:
Science moves, but slowly slowly, creeping on from point to point:

Slowly comes a hungry people, as a lion creeping nigher,
Glares at one that nods and winks behind a slowly-dying fire.

Yet I doubt not thro' the ages one increasing purpose runs,
And the thoughts of men are widen'd with the process of the suns.

What is that to him that reaps not harvest of his youthful joys,
Tho' the deep heart of existence beat for ever like a boy's?

Knowledge comes, but wisdom lingers, and I linger on the shore,
And the individual withers, and the world is more and more.

Knowledge comes, but wisdom lingers, and he bears a laden breast,
Full of sad experience, moving toward the stillness of his rest.

Hark, my merry comrades call me, sounding on the bugle-horn,
They to whom my foolish passion were a target for their scorn:

Shall it not be scorn to me to harp on such a moulder'd string?
I am shamed thro' all my nature to have loved so slight a thing.

Weakness to be wroth with weakness! woman's pleasure, woman's pain—
Nature made them blinder motions bounded in a shallower brain:

Woman is the lesser man, and all thy passions, match'd with mine,
Are as moonlight unto sunlight, and as water unto wine—

Here at least, where nature sickens, nothing. Ah, for some retreat
Deep in yonder shining Orient, where my life began to beat;

Where in wild Mahratta-battle fell my father evil-starr'd;—
I was left a trampled orphan, and a selfish uncle's ward.

Or to burst all links of habit—there to wander far away,
On from island unto island at the gateways of the day.

Larger constellations burning, mellow moons and happy skies,
Breadths of tropic shade and palms in cluster, knots of Paradise.

Never comes the trader, never floats an European flag,
Slides the bird o'er lustrous woodland, swings the trailer from the crag;

Droops the heavy-blossom'd bower, hangs the heavy-fruited tree—
Summer isles of Eden lying in dark-purple spheres of sea.

There methinks would be enjoyment more than in this march of mind,
In the steamship, in the railway, in the thoughts that shake mankind.

There the passions cramp'd no longer shall have scope and breathing space;
I will take some savage woman, she shall rear my dusky race.

Iron-jointed, supple-sinew'd, they shall dive, and they shall run,
Catch the wild goat by the hair, and hurl their lances in the sun;

Whistle back the parrot's call, and leap the rainbows of the brooks,
Not with blinded eyesight poring over miserable books—

Fool, again the dream, the fancy! but I *know* my words are wild,
But I count the gray barbarian lower than the Christian child.

I, to herd with narrow foreheads, vacant of our glorious gains,
Like a beast with lower pleasures, like a beast with lower pains!

Mated with a squalid savage—what to me were sun or clime?
I the heir of all the ages, in the foremost files of time—

I that rather held it better men should perish one by one,
Than that earth should stand at gaze like Joshua's moon in Ajalon!

Not in vain the distance beacons. Forward, forward let us range,
Let the great world spin for ever down the ringing grooves of change.

Thro' the shadow of the globe we sweep into the younger day:
Better fifty years of Europe than a cycle of Cathay.

Mother-Age (for mine I knew not) help me as when life begun:
Rift the hills, and roll the waters, flash the lightnings, weigh the Sun.

O, I see the crescent promise of my spirit hath not set.
Ancient founts of inspiration well thro' all my fancy yet.

Howsoever these things be, a long farewell to Locksley Hall!
Now for me the woods may wither, now for me the roof-tree fall.

Comes a vapour from the margin, blackening over heath and holt,
Cramming all the blast before it, in its breast a thunderbolt.

Let it fall on Locksley Hall, with rain or hail, or fire or snow;
For the mighty wind arises, roaring seaward, and I go.

[1842]

ST. AGNES' EVE

Deep on the convent-roof the snows
  Are sparkling to the moon:
My breath to heaven like vapour goes:
  May my soul follow soon!
The shadows of the convent-towers
  Slant down the snowy sward,
Still creeping with the creeping hours
  That lead me to my Lord:
Make Thou my spirit pure and clear
  As are the frosty skies,
Or this first snowdrop of the year
  That in my bosom lies.

As these white robes are soil'd and dark,
  To yonder shining ground;
As this pale taper's earthly spark,
  To yonder argent round;
So shows my soul before the Lamb,
  My spirit before Thee;
So in mine earthly house I am,
  To that I hope to be.
Break up the heavens, O Lord! and far,
  Thro' all yon starlight keen,
Draw me, thy bride, a glittering star,
  In raiment white and clean.

He lifts me to the golden doors;
  The flashes come and go;
All heaven bursts her starry floors,
  And strows her lights below,
And deepens on and up! the gates
  Roll back, and far within
For me the Heavenly Bridegroom waits,
  To make me pure of sin.
The sabbaths of Eternity,
  One sabbath deep and wide—
A light upon the shining sea—
  The Bridegroom with his bride!

[1834] [1837]

SIR GALAHAD

My good blade carves the casques of men,
  My tough lance thrusteth sure,
My strength is as the strength of ten,
  Because my heart is pure.
The shattering trumpet shrilleth high,
  The hard brands shiver on the steel,
The splinter'd spear-shafts crack and fly,
  The horse and rider reel:
They reel, they roll in clanging lists,
  And when the tide of combat stands,
Perfume and flowers fall in showers,
  That lightly rain from ladies' hands.

How sweet are looks that ladies bend
On whom their favours fall!
For them I battle till the end,
To save from shame and thrall:
But all my heart is drawn above,
My knees are bow'd in crypt and shrine:
I never felt the kiss of love,
Nor maiden's hand in mine.
More bounteous aspects on me beam,
Me mightier transports move and thrill;
So keep I fair thro' faith and prayer
A virgin heart in work and will.

When down the stormy crescent goes,
A light before me swims,
Between dark stems the forest glows,
I hear a noise of hymns:
Then by some secret shrine I ride;
I hear a voice but none are there;
The stalls are void, the doors are wide,
The tapers burning fair.
Fair gleams the snowy altar-cloth,
The silver vessels sparkle clean,
The shrill bell rings, the censer swings,
And solemn chaunts resound between.

Sometimes on lonely mountain-meres
I find a magic bark;
I leap on board: no helmsman steers:
I float till all is dark.
A gentle sound, an awful light!
Three angels bear the holy Grail:
With folded feet, in stoles of white,
On sleeping wings they sail.
Ah, blessed vision! blood of God!
My spirit beats her mortal bars,
As down dark tides the glory slides,
And star-like mingles with the stars.

When on my goodly charger borne
Thro' dreaming towns I go,
The cock crows ere the Christmas morn,
The streets are dumb with snow.
The tempest crackles on the leads,
And, ringing, springs from brand and mail;
But o'er the dark a glory spreads,
And gilds the driving hail.
I leave the plain, I climb the height;
No branchy thicket shelter yields;
But blessed forms in whistling storms
Fly o'er waste fens and windy fields.

A maiden knight—to me is given
Such hope, I know not fear;
I yearn to breathe the airs of heaven
That often meet me here.
I muse on joy that will not cease,
Pure spaces clothed in living beams,
Pure lilies of eternal peace,
Whose odours haunt my dreams;
And, stricken by an angel's hand,
This mortal armour that I wear,
This weight and size, this heart and eyes,
Are touch'd, are turn'd to finest air.

The clouds are broken in the sky,
And thro' the mountain-walls
A rolling organ-harmony
Swells up, and shakes and falls.
Then move the trees, the copses nod,
Wings flutter, voices hover clear:
'O just and faithful knight of God!
Ride on! the prize is near.'
So pass I hostel, hall, and grange;
By bridge and ford, by park and pale,
All-arm'd I ride, whate'er betide,
Until I find the holy Grail.

[1842]

THE VISION OF SIN

I

I had a vision when the night was late:
A youth came riding toward a palace-gate.
He rode a horse with wings, that would have flown,
But that his heavy rider kept him down.
And from the palace came a child of sin,
And took him by the curls, and led him in,
Where sat a company with heated eyes,
Expecting when a fountain should arise:
A sleepy light upon their brows and lips—
As when the sun, a crescent of eclipse,
Dreams over lake and lawn, and isles and capes—
Suffused them, sitting, lying, languid shapes,
By heaps of gourds, and skins of wine, and piles of grapes.

II

Then methought I heard a mellow sound,
Gathering up from all the lower ground;
Narrowing in to where they sat assembled
Low voluptuous music winding trembled,
Wov'n in circles: they that heard it sigh'd,
Panted hand-in-hand with faces pale,
Swung themselves, and in low tones replied;

Till the fountain spouted, showering wide
Sleet of diamond-drift and pearly hail;
Then the music touch'd the gates and died;
Rose again from where it seem'd to fail,
Storm'd in orbs of song, a growing gale;
Till thronging in and in, to where they waited,
As 'twere a hundred-throated nightingale,
The strong tempestuous treble throbb'd and palpitated;
Ran into its giddiest whirl of sound,
Caught the sparkles, and in circles,
Purple gauzes, golden hazes, liquid mazes,
Flung the torrent rainbow round:
Then they started from their places,
Moved with violence, changed in hue,
Caught each other with wild grimaces,
Half-invisible to the view,
Wheeling with precipitate paces
To the melody, till they flew,
Hair, and eyes, and limbs, and faces,
Twisted hard in fierce embraces,
Like to Furies, like to Graces,
Dash'd together in blinding dew:
Till, kill'd with some luxurious agony,
The nerve-dissolving melody
Flutter'd headlong from the sky.

III

And then I look'd up toward a mountain-tract,
That girt the region with high cliff and lawn:
I saw that every morning, far withdrawn
Beyond the darkness and the cataract,
God made Himself an awful rose of dawn,
Unheeded: and detaching, fold by fold,
From those still heights, and, slowly drawing near,
A vapour heavy, hueless, formless, cold,
Came floating on for many a month and year,
Unheeded: and I thought I would have spoken,
And warn'd that madman ere it grew too late:
But, as in dreams, I could not. Mine was broken,
When that cold vapour touch'd the palace gate,
And link'd again. I saw within my head
A gray and gap-tooth'd man as lean as death,
Who slowly rode across a wither'd heath,
And lighted at a ruin'd inn, and said:

IV

'Wrinkled ostler, grim and thin!
Here is custom come your way;
Take my brute, and lead him in,
Stuff his ribs with mouldy hay.

'Bitter barmaid, waning fast!
See that sheets are on my bed;
What! the flower of life is past:
It is long before you wed.

'Slip-shod waiter, lank and sour,
At the Dragon on the heath!
Let us have a quiet hour,
Let us hob-and-nob with Death.

'I am old, but let me drink;
Bring me spices, bring me wine;
I remember, when I think,
That my youth was half divine.

Wine is good for shrivell'd lips,
When a blanket wraps the day,
When the rotten woodland drips,
And the leaf is stamp'd in clay.

'Sit thee down, and have no shame,
Cheek by jowl, and knee by knee:
What care I for any name?
What for order or degree?

'Let me screw thee up a peg:
Let me loose thy tongue with wine:
Callest thou that thing a leg?
Which is thinnest? thine or mine?

'Thou shalt not be saved by works:
Thou hast been a sinner too:
Ruin'd trunks on wither'd forks,
Empty scarecrows, I and you!

'Fill the cup, and fill the can:
Have a rouse before the morn:
Every moment dies a man,
Every moment one is born.

'We are men of ruin'd blood;
Therefore comes it we are wise.
Fish are we that love the mud,
Rising to no fancy-flies.

IV Hopeless picture of life—negation of all that is in the rosy dawn. One last drink + he talks of sins.

'Name and fame! to fly sublime
  Thro' the courts, the camps, the schools,
Is to be the ball of Time,
  Bandied by the hands of fools.

'Friendship!—to be two in one—
  Let the canting liar pack!
Well I know, when I am gone,
  How she mouths behind my back.

'Virtue!—to be good and just—
  Every heart, when sifted well,
Is a clot of warmer dust,
  Mix'd with cunning sparks of hell.

'O! we two as well can look
  Whited thought and cleanly life
As the priest, above his book
  Leering at his neighbour's wife.

'Fill the cup, and fill the can:
  Have a rouse before the morn:
Every moment dies a man,
  Every moment one is born.

'Drink, and let the parties rave:
  They are fill'd with idle spleen;
Rising, falling, like a wave,
  For they know not what they mean.

'He that roars for liberty
  Faster binds a tyrant's power;
And the tyrant's cruel glee
  Forces on the freer hour.

'Fill the can, and fill the cup:
  All the windy ways of men
Are but dust that rises up,
  And is lightly laid again.

'Greet her with applausive breath,
  Freedom, gaily doth she tread;
In her right a civic wreath,
  In her left a human head.

'No, I love not what is new;
  She is of an ancient house:
And I think we know the hue
  Of that cap upon her brows.

'Let her go! her thirst she slakes
  Where the bloody conduit runs,
Then her sweetest meal she makes
  On the first-born of her sons.

'Drink to lofty hopes that cool—
  Visions of a perfect State:
Drink we, last, the public fool,
  Frantic love and frantic hate.

'Chant me now some wicked stave,
  Till thy drooping courage rise,
And the glow-worm of the grave
  Glimmer in thy rheumy eyes.

'Fear not thou to loose thy tongue;
  Set thy hoary fancies free;
What is loathsome to the young
  Savours well to thee and me.

'Change, reverting to the years,
  When thy nerves could understand
What there is in loving tears,
  And the warmth of hand in hand.

'Tell me tales of thy first love—
  April hopes, the fools of chance;
Till the graves begin to move,
  And the dead begin to dance.

'Fill the can, and fill the cup:
  All the windy ways of men
Are but dust that rises up,
  And is lightly laid again.

'Trooping from their mouldy dens
  The chap-fallen circle spreads:
Welcome, fellow-citizens,
  Hollow hearts and empty heads!

dance of death

'You are bones, and what of that?
  Every face, however full,
Padded round with flesh and fat,
  Is but modell'd on a skull.

'Death is king, and Vivat Rex![1]
  Tread a measure on the stones,
Madam—if I know your sex,
  From the fashion of your bones.

'No, I cannot praise the fire
  In your eye—nor yet your lip:
All the more do I admire
  Joints of cunning workmanship.

'Lo! God's likeness—the ground-plan—
  Neither modell'd, glazed, or framed:
Buss me thou rough sketch of man,
  Far too naked to be shamed!

[1] Long live the King.

'Drink to Fortune, drink to Chance,
  While we keep a little breath!
Drink to heavy Ignorance!
  Hob-and-nob with brother Death!

'Thou art mazed, the night is long,
  And the longer night is near:
What! I am not all as wrong
  As a bitter jest is dear.

'Youthful hopes, by scores, to all,
  When the locks are crisp and curl'd;
Unto me my maudlin gall
  And my mockeries of the world.

'Fill the cup, and fill the can!
  Mingle madness, mingle scorn!
Dregs of life, and less of man:
  Yet we will not die forlorn.'

V

The voice grew faint: there came a further change:
Once more uprose the mystic mountain-range:
Below were men and horses pierced with worms,
And slowly quickening into lower forms;
By shards and scurf of salt, and scum of dross,
Old plash of rains, and refuse patch'd with moss,
Then some one spake: "Behold! it was a crime
Of sense avenged by sense that wore with time."
Another said: "The crime of sense became
The crime of malice, and is equal blame."
And one: "He had not wholly quench'd his power;
A little grain of conscience made him sour:"
At last I heard a voice upon the slope
Cry to the summit, "Is there any hope?"
To which an answer peal'd from that high land,
But in a tongue no man could understand;
And on the glimmering limit far withdrawn
God made himself an awful rose of dawn.

[1842]

BREAK, BREAK, BREAK

Break, break, break,
  On thy cold gray stones, O Sea!
And I would that my tongue could utter
  The thoughts that arise in me.

O well for the fisherman's boy,
  That he shouts with his sister at play!
O well for the sailor lad,
  That he sings in his boat on the bay!

And the stately ships go on
  To their haven under the hill;
But O for the touch of a vanish'd hand,
  And the sound of a voice that is still!

Break, break, break,
  At the foot of thy crags, O Sea!
But the tender grace of a day that is dead
  Will never come back to me.

[1842]

SONGS FROM *THE PRINCESS*

I

As thro' the land at eve we went,
  And pluck'd the ripen'd ears,
We fell out, my wife and I,
O we fell out I know not why,
  And kiss'd again with tears.
And blessings on the falling out
  That all the more endears,
When we fall out with those we love
  And kiss again with tears!
For when we came where lies the child
  We lost in other years,
There above the little grave,
O there above the little grave,
  We kiss'd again with tears.

[1850]

II

Sweet and low, sweet and low,
  Wind of the western sea,
Low, low, breathe and blow,
  Wind of the western sea!
Over the rolling waters go,
Come from the dying moon, and blow,
  Blow him again to me;
While my little one, while my pretty one, sleeps.
Sleep and rest, sleep and rest,
  Father will come to thee soon;

Rest, rest, on mother's breast,
  Father will come to thee soon;
Father will come to his babe in the nest,
Silver sails all out of the west
  Under the silver moon:
Sleep, my little one, sleep, my pretty one, sleep.

[1850]

III

The splendour falls on castle walls
  And snowy summits old in story:
The long light shakes across the lakes,
  And the wild cataract leaps in glory.
Blow, bugle, blow, set the wild echoes flying,
Blow, bugle; answer, echoes, dying, dying, dying.

O hark, O hear! how thin and clear,
  And thinner, clearer, farther going!
O sweet and far from cliff and scar
  The horns of Elfland faintly blowing!
Blow, let us hear the purple glens replying:
Blow, bugle; answer, echoes, dying, dying, dying.

O love, they die in yon rich sky,
  They faint on hill or field or river:
Our echoes roll from soul to soul,
  And grow for ever and for ever.
Blow, bugle, blow, set the wild echoes flying,
And answer, echoes, answer, dying, dying, dying.

[1850]

IV

Tears, idle tears, I know not what they mean,
Tears from the depth of some divine despair
Rise in the heart, and gather to the eyes,
In looking on the happy Autumn-fields,
And thinking of the days that are no more.

Fresh as the first beam glittering on a sail,
That brings our friends up from the underworld,
Sad as the last which reddens over one
That sinks with all we love below the verge;
So sad, so fresh, the days that are no more.

Ah, sad and strange as in dark summer dawns
The earliest pipe of half-awaken'd birds
To dying ears, when unto dying eyes
The casement slowly grows a glimmering square;
So sad, so strange, the days that are no more.

Dear as remember'd kisses after death,
And sweet as those by hopeless fancy feign'd
On lips that are for others; deep as love,
Deep as first love, and wild with all regret;
O Death in Life, the days that are no more.

[1847]

V

O Swallow, Swallow, flying, flying South,
Fly to her, and fall upon her gilded eaves,
And tell her, tell her, what I tell to thee.

O tell her, Swallow, thou that knowest each,
That bright and fierce and fickle is the South,
And dark and true and tender is the North.

O Swallow, Swallow, if I could follow, and light
Upon her lattice, I would pipe and trill,
And cheep and twitter twenty million loves.

O were I thou that she might take me in,
And lay me on her bosom, and her heart
Would rock the snowy cradle till I died.

Why lingereth she to clothe her heart with love,
Delaying as the tender ash delays
To clothe herself, when all the woods are green?

O tell her, Swallow, that thy brood is flown:
Say to her, I do but wanton in the South.
But in the North long since my nest is made.

O tell her, brief is life but love is long
And brief the sun of summer in the North,
And brief the moon of beauty in the South.

O Swallow, flying from the golden woods,
Fly to her, and pipe and woo her, and make
her mine,
And tell her, tell her, that I follow thee.

[1847]

VI

Thy voice is heard thro' rolling drums,
That beat to battle where he stands;
Thy face across his fancy comes,
And gives the battle to his hands:
A moment, while the trumpets blow,
He sees his brood about thy knee;
The next, like fire he meets the foe,
And strikes him dead for thine and thee.

[1850]

VII

Home they brought her warrior dead:
She nor swoon'd nor utter'd cry:
All her maidens, watching, said,
"She must weep or she will die."

Then they praised him, soft and low,
Call'd him worthy to be loved,
Truest friend and noblest foe;
Yet she neither spoke nor moved.

Stole a maiden from her place,
Lightly to the warrior stept,
Took the face-cloth from the face;
Yet she neither moved nor wept.

Rose a nurse of ninety years,
Set his child upon her knee—
Like summer-tempest came her tears—
"Sweet my child, I live for thee."

[1850]

VIII

Ask me no more: the moon may draw the
sea;
The cloud may stoop from heaven and
take shape,
With fold to fold, of mountain or of
cape;
But O too fond, when have I answer'd thee?
Ask me no more.

Ask me no more: what answer should I
give?
I love not hollow cheek or faded eye:
Yet O my friend, I will not have thee
die!
Ask me no more, lest I should bid thee live;
Ask me no more.

Ask me no more: thy fate and mine are
seal'd:
I strove against the stream and all in
vain:
Let the great river take me to the main:
No more, dear love, for at a touch I yield;
Ask me no more.

[1850]

IX

Now sleeps the crimson petal, now the
white;
Nor waves the cypress in the palace walk;
Nor winks the gold fin in the porphyry
font:
The fire-fly wakens; waken thou with me.

Now droops the milk-white peacock like
a ghost,
And like a ghost she glimmers on to me.

Now lies the Earth all Danaë to the stars,
And all thy heart lies open unto me.

Now slides the silent meteor on, and leaves
A shining furrow, as thy thoughts in me.

Now folds the lily all her sweetness up,
And slips into the bosom of the lake.
So fold thyself, my dearest, thou, and slip
Into my bosom and be lost in me.

[1847]

X

Come down, O maid, from yonder moun-
tain height.
What pleasure lives in height (the shep-
herd sang),
In height and cold, the splendour of the
hills?
But cease to move so near the heavens, and
cease
To glide a sunbeam by the blasted pine,
To sit a star upon the sparkling spire;
And come, for Love is of the valley, come
For Love is of the valley, come thou down
And find him; by the happy threshold, he
Or hand in hand with Plenty in the
maize,
Or red with spirted purple of the vats,
Or foxlike in the vine; nor cares to walk

With Death and Morning on the Silver Horns,
Nor wilt thou snare him in the white ravine,
Nor find him dropt upon the firths of ice,
That huddling slant in furrow-cloven falls
To roll the torrent out of dusky doors.
But follow; let the torrent dance thee down
To find him in the valley; let the wild
Lean-headed eagles yelp alone, and leave
The monstrous ledges there to slope, and spill
Their thousand wreaths of dangling water-smoke,
That like a broken purpose waste in air.
So waste not thou, but come; for all the vales
Await thee; azure pillars of the hearth
Arise to thee; the children call, and I
Thy shepherd pipe, and sweet is every sound,
Sweeter thy voice, but every sound is sweet;
Myriads of rivulets hurrying through the lawn.
The moan of doves in immemorial elms,
And murmuring of innumerable bees.

[1847]

IN MEMORIAM A. H. H.

OBIIT MDCCCXXXIII

Strong Son of God, immortal Love,
    Whom we, that have not seen thy face,
    By faith, and faith alone, embrace,
Believing where we cannot prove;

Thine are these orbs of light and shade;
    Thou madest Life in man and brute;
    Thou madest Death; and lo, thy foot
Is on the skull which thou hast made.

Thou wilt not leave us in the dust:
    Thou madest man, he knows not why,
    He thinks he was not made to die;
And thou hast made him: thou art just.

Thou seemest human and divine,
    The highest, holiest manhood, thou:
    Our wills are ours, we know not how;
Our wills are ours, to make them thine.

Our little systems have their day;
    They have their day and cease to be:
    They are but broken lights of thee,
And thou, O Lord, art more than they.

We have but faith: we cannot know;
    For knowledge is of things we see;
    And yet we trust it comes from thee,
A beam in darkness: let it grow.

Let knowledge grow from more to more,
    But more of reverence in us dwell;
    That mind and soul, according well,
May make one music as before,

But vaster. We are fools and slight;
    We mock thee when we do not fear:
    But help thy foolish ones to bear;
Help thy vain worlds to bear thy light.

Forgive what seem'd my sin in me;
    What seem'd my worth since I began;
    For merit lives from man to man,
And not from man, O Lord, to thee.

Forgive my grief for one removed,
    Thy creature, whom I found so fair.
    I trust he lives in thee, and there
I find him worthier to be loved.

Forgive these wild and wandering cries,
    Confusions of a wasted youth;
    Forgive them where they fail in truth,
And in thy wisdom make me wise.

[1849]

I

I held it truth, with him who sings
    To one clear harp in divers tones,
    That men may rise on stepping-stones
Of their dead selves to higher things.

But who shall so forecast the years
And find in loss a gain to match?
Or reach a hand thro' time to catch
The far-off interest of tears?

Let Love clasp Grief lest both be drown'd,
Let darkness keep her raven gloss:
Ah, sweeter to be drunk with loss,
To dance with death, to beat the ground,

Than that the victor Hours should scorn
The long result of love, and boast,
'Behold the man that loved and lost,
But all he was is overworn.'

II

Old Yew, which graspest at the stones
That name the under-lying dead,
Thy fibres net the dreamless head,
Thy roots are wrapt about the bones.

The seasons bring the flower again,
And bring the firstling to the flock;
And in the dusk of thee, the clock
Beats out the little lives of men.

O not for thee the glow, the bloom,
Who changest not in any gale,
Nor branding summer suns avail
To touch thy thousand years of gloom:

And gazing on thee, sullen tree,
Sick for thy stubborn hardihood,
I seem to fail from out my blood
And grow incorporate into thee.

III

O Sorrow, cruel fellowship,
O Priestess in the vaults of Death,
O sweet and bitter in a breath,
What whispers from thy lying lip?

'The stars,' she whispers, 'blindly run;
A web is wov'n across the sky;
From our waste places comes a cry,
And murmurs from the dying sun:

'And all the phantom, Nature, stands—
With all the music in her tone,
A hollow echo of my own,—
A hollow form with empty hands.'

And shall I take a thing so blind,
Embrace her as my natural good;
Or crush her, like a vice of blood,
Upon the threshold of the mind?

IV

To Sleep I give my powers away;
My will is bondsman to the dark;
I sit within a helmless bark,
And with my heart I muse and say:

O heart, how fares it with thee now,
That thou should'st fail from thy desire,
Who scarcely darest to inquire,
'What is it makes me beat so low?'

Something it is which thou hast lost,
Some pleasure from thine early years.
Break, thou deep vase of chilling tears,
That grief hath shaken into frost!

Such clouds of nameless trouble cross
All night below the darken'd eyes;
With morning wakes the will, and cries,
'Thou shalt not be the fool of loss.'

V

I sometimes hold it half a sin
To put in words the grief I feel;
For words, like Nature, half reveal
And half conceal the Soul within.

But, for the unquiet heart and brain,
A use in measured language lies;
The sad mechanic exercise,
Like dull narcotics, numbing pain.

In words, like weeds, I'll wrap me o'er,
Like coarsest clothes against the cold:
But that large grief which these enfold
Is given in outline and no more.

VI

One writes, that 'Other friends remain,'
That 'Loss is common to the race'—
And common is the commonplace,
And vacant chaff well meant for grain.

That loss is common would not make
My own less bitter, rather more:
Too common! Never morning wore
To evening, but some heart did break.

O father, wheresoe'er thou be,
Who pledgest now thy gallant son;
A shot, ere half thy draught be done,
Hath still'd the life that beat from thee.

O mother, praying God will save
Thy sailor,—while thy head is bow'd,
His heavy-shotted hammock-shroud
Drops in his vast and wandering grave.

Ye know no more than I who wrought
At that last hour to please him well
Who mused on all I had to tell,
And something written, something thought;

Expecting still his advent home;
And ever met him on his way
With wishes, thinking, 'here to-day,'
Or 'here to-morrow will he come.'

O somewhere, meek, unconscious dove,
That sittest ranging golden hair;
And glad to find thyself so fair,
Poor child, that waitest for thy love!

For now her father's chimney glows
In expectation of a guest;
And thinking 'this will please him best,'
She takes a riband or a rose;

For he will see them on to-night;
And with the thought her colour burns;
And, having left the glass, she turns
Once more to set a ringlet right;

And, even when she turn'd, the curse
Had fallen, and her future Lord
Was drown'd in passing thro' the ford,
Or kill'd in falling from his horse.

O what to her shall be the end?
And what to me remains of good?
To her, perpetual maidenhood,
And unto me no second friend.

VII

Dark house, by which once more I stand
Here in the long unlovely street,
Doors, where my heart was used to beat
So quickly, waiting for a hand,

A hand that can be clasp'd no more—
Behold me, for I cannot sleep,
And like a guilty thing I creep
At earliest morning to the door.

He is not here; but far away
The noise of life begins again,
And ghastly thro' the drizzling rain
On the bald street breaks the blank day.

VIII

A happy lover who has come
To look on her that loves him well,
Who 'lights and rings the gateway bell,
And learns her gone and far from home;

He saddens, all the magic light
Dies off at once from bower and hall,
And all the place is dark, and all
The chambers emptied of delight:

So find I every pleasant spot
In which we two were wont to meet,
The field, the chamber and the street,
For all is dark where thou art not.

Yet as that other, wandering there
In those deserted walks, may find
A flower beat with rain and wind,
Which once she foster'd up with care;

So seems it in my deep regret,
O my forsaken heart, with thee
And this poor flower of poesy
Which little cared for fades not yet.

But since it pleased a vanish'd eye,
I go to plant it on his tomb,
That if it can it there may bloom,
Or dying, there at least may die.

IX

Fair ship, that from the Italian shore
Sailest the placid ocean-plains
With my lost Arthur's loved remains,
Spread thy full wings, and waft him o'er.

So draw him home to those that mourn
In vain; a favourable speed
Ruffle thy mirror'd mast, and lead
Thro' prosperous floods his holy urn.

All night no ruder air perplex
Thy sliding keel, till Phosphor, bright
As our pure love, thro' early light
Shall glimmer on the dewy decks.

Sphere all your lights around, above;
Sleep, gentle heavens, before the prow;
Sleep, gentle winds, as he sleeps now,
My friend, the brother of my love;

My Arthur, whom I shall not see
Till all my widow'd race be run;
Dear as the mother to the son,
More than my brothers are to me.

X

I hear the noise about thy keel;
I hear the bell struck in the night:
I see the cabin-window bright;
I see the sailor at the wheel.

Thou bring'st the sailor to his wife,
And travell'd men from foreign lands·
And letters unto trembling hands;
And, thy dark freight, a vanish'd life.

So bring him: we have idle dreams:
This look of quiet flatters thus
Our home-bred fancies: O to us,
The fools of habit, sweeter seems

To rest beneath the clover sod,
That takes the sunshine and the rains,
Or where the kneeling hamlet drains
The chalice of the grapes of God;

Than if with thee the roaring wells
Should gulf him fathom-deep in brine;
And hands so often clasp'd in mine,
Should toss with tangle and with shells.

XI

Calm is the morn without a sound,
Calm as to suit a calmer grief,
And only thro' the faded leaf
The chestnut pattering to the ground:

Calm and deep peace on this high wold,
And on these dews that drench the furze,
And all the silvery gossamers
That twinkle into green and gold:

Calm and still light on yon great plain
That sweeps with all its autumn bowers,
And crowded farms and lessening towers,
To mingle with the bounding main:

Calm and deep peace in this wide air,
These leaves that redden to the fall;
And in my heart, if calm at all,
If any calm, a calm despair:

Calm on the seas, and silver sleep,
And waves that sway themselves in rest,
And dead calm in that noble breast
Which heaves but with the heaving deep.

XII

Lo, as a dove when up she springs
To bear thro' Heaven a tale of woe,
Some dolorous message knit below
The wild pulsation of her wings;

Like her I go; I cannot stay;
I leave this mortal ark behind,
A weight of nerves without a mind,
And leave the cliffs, and haste away

O'er ocean-mirrors rounded large,
And reach the glow of southern skies,
And see the sails at distance rise,
And linger weeping on the marge,

And saying; 'Comes he thus, my friend?
Is this the end of all my care?'
And circle moaning in the air:
'Is this the end? Is this the end?'

And forward dart again, and play
About the prow, and back return
To where the body sits, and learn
That I have been an hour away.

XIII

Tears of the widower, when he sees
A late-lost form that sleep reveals,
And moves his doubtful arms, and feels
Her place is empty, fall like these;

Which weep a loss for ever new,
A void where heart on heart reposed;
And, where warm hands have prest and closed,
Silence, till I be silent too.

Which weep the comrade of my choice,
An awful thought, a life removed,
The human-hearted man I loved,
A Spirit, not a breathing voice.

Come Time, and teach me, many years,
I do not suffer in a dream;
For now so strange do these things seem,
Mine eyes have leisure for their tears;

My fancies time to rise on wing,
And glance about the approaching sails,
As tho' they brought but merchants' bales,
And not the burthen that they bring.

XIV

If one should bring me this report,
That thou hadst touch'd the land to-day,
And I went down unto the quay,
And found thee lying in the port;

And standing, muffled round with woe,
Should see thy passengers in rank
Come stepping lightly down the plank,
And beckoning unto those they know;

And if along with these should come
The man I held as half-divine;
Should strike a sudden hand in mine,
And ask a thousand things of home;

And I should tell him all my pain,
And how my life had droop'd of late,
And he should sorrow o'er my state
And marvel what possess'd my brain;

And I perceived no touch of change,
No hint of death in all his frame,
But found him all in all the same,
I should not feel it to be strange.

XV

To-night the winds begin to rise
And roar from yonder dropping day:
The last red leaf is whirl'd away,
The rooks are blown about the skies;

The forest crack'd, the waters curl'd,
The cattle huddled on the lea;
And wildly dash'd on tower and tree
The sunbeam strikes along the world:

And but for fancies, which aver
That all thy motions gently pass
Athwart a plane of molten glass,
I scarce could brook the strain and stir

That makes the barren branches loud;
And but for fear it is not so,
The wild unrest that lives in woe
Would dote and pore on yonder cloud

That rises upward always higher,
And onward drags a labouring breast,
And topples round the dreary west,
A looming bastion fringed with fire.

XVI

What words are these have fall'n from me?
Can calm despair and wild unrest
Be tenants of a single breast,
Or sorrow such a changeling be?

Or doth she only seem to take
The touch of change in calm or storm;
But knows no more of transient form
In her deep self, than some dead lake

That holds the shadow of a lark
Hung in the shadow of a heaven?
Or has the shock, so harshly given,
Confused me like the unhappy bark

That strikes by night a craggy shelf,
And staggers blindly ere she sink?
And stunn'd me from my power to think
And all my knowledge of myself;

And made me that delirious man
Whose fancy fuses old and new,
And flashes into false and true,
And mingles all without a plan?

XVII

Thou comest, much wept for: such a breeze
Compell'd thy canvas, and my prayer
Was as the whisper of an air
To breathe thee over lonely seas.

For I in spirit saw thee move
Thro' circles of the bounding sky,
Week after week: the days go by:
Come quick, thou bringest all I love.

Henceforth, wherever thou may'st roam,
My blessing, like a line of light,
Is on the waters day and night,
And like a beacon guards thee home.

So may whatever tempest mars
Mid-ocean, spare thee, sacred bark;
And balmy drops in summer dark
Slide from the bosom of the stars.

So kind an office hath been done,
Such precious relics brought by thee;
The dust of him I shall not see
Till all my widow'd race be run.

XVIII

'Tis well; 'tis something; we may stand
Where he in English earth is laid,
And from his ashes may be made
The violet of his native land.

'Tis little; but it looks in truth
As if the quiet bones were blest
Among familiar names to rest
And in the places of his youth.

Come then, pure hands, and bear the head
That sleeps or wears the mask of sleep,
And come, whatever loves to weep,
And hear the ritual of the dead.

Ah yet, ev'n yet, if this might be,
I, falling on his faithful heart,
Would breathing thro' his lips impart
The life that almost dies in me;

That dies not, but endures with pain,
And slowly forms the firmer mind,
Treasuring the look it cannot find,
The words that are not heard again.

XIX

The Danube to the Severn gave
The darken'd heart that beat no more;
They laid him by the pleasant shore,
And in the hearing of the wave.

There twice a day the Severn fills;
The salt sea-water passes by,
And hushes half the babbling Wye,
And makes a silence in the hills.

The Wye is hush'd nor moved along,
And hush'd my deepest grief of all,
When fill'd with tears that cannot fall,
I brim with sorrow drowning song.

The tide flows down, the wave again
Is vocal in its wooded walls;
My deeper anguish also falls,
And I can speak a little then.

XX

The lesser griefs that may be said,
That breathe a thousand tender vows,
Are but as servants in a house
Where lies the master newly dead;

Who speak their feeling as it is,
And weep the fulness from the mind:
'It will be hard,' they say, 'to find
Another service such as this.'

My lighter moods are like to these,
That out of words a comfort win;
But there are other griefs within,
And tears that at their fountain freeze;

For by the hearth the children sit
Cold in that atmosphere of Death,
And scarce endure to draw the breath,
Or like to noiseless phantoms flit:

But open converse is there none,
So much the vital spirits sink
To see the vacant chair, and think,
'How good! how kind! and he is gone.'

XXI

I sing to him that rests below,
And, since the grasses round me wave,
I take the grasses of the grave,
And make them pipes whereon to blow.

The traveller hears me now and then,
And sometimes harshly will he speak:
'This fellow would make weakness weak,
And melt the waxen hearts of men.'

Another answers, 'Let him be,
He loves to make parade of pain,
That with his piping he may gain
The praise that comes to constancy.'

A third is wroth: 'Is this an hour
For private sorrow's barren song,
When more and more the people throng
The chairs and thrones of civil power?

'A time to sicken and to swoon,
When Science reaches forth her arms
To feel from world to world, and charms
Her secret from the latest moon?'

Behold, ye speak an idle thing:
Ye never knew the sacred dust:
I do but sing because I must,
And pipe but as the linnets sing:

And one is glad; her note is gay,
For now her little ones have ranged;
And one is sad; her note is changed,
Because her brood is stol'n away.

XXII

The path by which we twain did go,
Which led by tracts that pleased us well,
Thro' four sweet years arose and fell,
From flower to flower, from snow to snow:

And we with singing cheer'd the way,
And, crown'd with all the season lent,
From April on to April went,
And glad at heart from May to May:

But where the path we walk'd began
To slant the fifth autumnal slope,
As we descended following Hope,
There sat the Shadow fear'd of man;

Who broke our fair companionship,
And spread his mantle dark and cold,
And wrapt thee formless in the fold,
And dull'd the murmur on thy lip,

And bore thee where I could not see
Nor follow, tho' I walk in haste,
And think, that somewhere in the waste
The Shadow sits and waits for me.

XXIII

Now, sometimes in my sorrow shut,
Or breaking into song by fits,
Alone, alone, to where he sits,
The Shadow cloak'd from head to foot,

Who keeps the keys of all the creeds,
I wander, often falling lame,
And looking back to whence I came,
Or on to where the pathway leads;

And crying, How changed from where it ran
Thro' lands where not a leaf was dumb;
But all the lavish hills would hum
The murmur of a happy Pan:

When each by turns was guide to each,
And Fancy light from Fancy caught,
And Thought leapt out to wed with Thought
Ere Thought could wed itself with Speech;

And all we met was fair and good,
And all was good that Time could bring,
And all the secret of the Spring
Moved in the chambers of the blood;

And many an old philosophy
On Argive heights divinely sang,
And round us all the thicket rang
To many a flute of Arcady.

XXIV

And was the day of my delight
As pure and perfect as I say?
The very source and fount of Day
Is dash'd with wandering isles of night.

If all was good and fair we met,
This earth had been the Paradise
It never look'd to human eyes
Since our first Sun arose and set.

And is it that the haze of grief
Makes former gladness loom so great?
The lowness of the present state,
That sets the past in this relief?

Or that the past will always win
A glory from its being far;
And orb into the perfect star
We saw not, when we moved therein?

XXV

I know that this was Life,—the track
Whereon with equal feet we fared;
And then, as now, the day prepared
The daily burden for the back.

But this it was that made me move
As light as carrier-birds in air;
I loved the weight I had to bear,
Because it needed help of Love:

Nor could I weary, heart or limb,
When mighty Love would cleave in twain
The lading of a single pain,
And part it, giving half to him.

XXVI

Still onward winds the dreary way;
I with it; for I long to prove
No lapse of moons can canker Love,
Whatever fickle tongues may say.

And if that eye which watches guilt
And goodness, and hath power to see
Within the green the moulder'd tree,
And towers fall'n as soon as built—

Oh, if indeed that eye foresee
Or see (in Him is no before)
In more of life true life no more
And Love the indifference to be,

Then might I find, ere yet the morn
Breaks hither over Indian seas,
That Shadow waiting with the keys,
To shroud me from my proper scorn.

XXVII

I envy not in any moods
The captive void of noble rage,
The linnet born within the cage,
That never knew the summer woods:

I envy not the beast that takes
His license in the field of time,
Unfetter'd by the sense of crime,
To whom a conscience never wakes;

Nor, what may count itself as blest,
The heart that never plighted troth
But stagnates in the weeds of sloth;
Nor any want-begotten rest.

I hold it true, whate'er befall;
I feel it, when I sorrow most;
'Tis better to have loved and lost
Than never to have loved at all.

XXVIII

The time draws near the birth of Christ:
The moon is hid; the night is still;
The Christmas bells from hill to hill
Answer each other in the mist.

Four voices of four hamlets round,
From far and near, on mead and moor,
Swell out and fail, as if a door
Were shut between me and the sound:

Each voice four changes on the wind,
That now dilate, and now decrease,
Peace and goodwill, goodwill and peace,
Peace and goodwill, to all mankind.

This year I slept and woke with pain,
I almost wish'd no more to wake,
And that my hold on life would break
Before I heard those bells again:

But they my troubled spirit rule,
For they controll'd me when a boy;
They bring me sorrow touch'd with joy,
The merry merry bells of Yule.

XXIX

With such compelling cause to grieve
As daily vexes household peace,
And chains regret to his decease,
How dare we keep our Christmas-eve;

Which brings no more a welcome guest
To enrich the threshold of the night
With shower'd largess of delight
In dance and song and game and jest?

Yet go, and while the holly boughs
Entwine the cold baptismal font,
Make one wreath more for Use and Wont,
That guard the portals of the house;

Old sisters of a day gone by,
Gray nurses, loving nothing new;
Why should they miss their yearly due
Before their time? They too will die.

XXX

With trembling fingers did we weave
The holly round the Christmas hearth;
A rainy cloud possess'd the earth,
And sadly fell our Christmas-eve.

At our old pastimes in the hall
We gambol'd, making vain pretence
Of gladness, with an awful sense
Of one mute Shadow watching all.

We paused: the winds were in the beech:
We heard them sweep the winter land;
And in a circle hand-in-hand
Sat silent, looking each at each.

Then echo-like our voices rang;
We sung, tho' every eye was dim,
A merry song we sang with him
Last year: impetuously we sang:

We ceased: a gentler feeling crept
Upon us: surely rest is meet:
'They rest,' we said, 'their sleep is sweet,'
And silence follow'd, and we wept.

Our voices took a higher range;
Once more we sang: 'They do not die
Nor lose their mortal sympathy,
Nor change to us, although they change;

'Rapt from the fickle and the frail
With gather'd power, yet the same,
Pierces the keen seraphic flame
From orb to orb, from veil to veil.'

Rise, happy morn, rise, holy morn,
Draw forth the cheerful day from night:
O Father, touch the east, and light
The light that shone when Hope was born.

XXXI

When Lazarus left his charnel-cave,
And home to Mary's house return'd,
Was this demanded—if he yearn'd
To hear her weeping by his grave?

'Where wert thou, brother, those four days?'
There lives no record of reply,
Which telling what it is to die
Had surely added praise to praise.

From every house the neighbours met,
The streets were fill'd with joyful sound,
A solemn gladness even crown'd
The purple brows of Olivet.

Behold a man raised up by Christ!
The rest remaineth unreveal'd;
He told it not; or something seal'd
The lips of that Evangelist.

XXXII

Her eyes are homes of silent prayer,
Nor other thought her mind admits
But, he was dead, and there he sits,
And he that brought him back is there.

Then one deep love doth supersede
All other, when her ardent gaze
Roves from the living brother's face,
And rests upon the Life indeed.

All subtle thought, all curious fears,
Borne down by gladness so complete,
She bows, she bathes the Saviour's feet
With costly spikenard and with tears.

Thrice blest whose lives are faithful prayers,
Whose loves in higher love endure;
What souls possess themselves so pure,
Or is there blessedness like theirs?

XXXIII

O thou that after toil and storm
Mayst seem to have reach'd a purer air,
Whose faith has centre everywhere,
Nor cares to fix itself to form,

Leave thou thy sister when she prays,
Her early Heaven, her happy views;
Nor thou with shadow'd hint confuse
A life that leads melodious days.

Her faith thro' form is pure as thine,
Her hands are quicker unto good:
Oh, sacred be the flesh and blood
To which she links a truth divine!

See thou, that countest reason ripe
In holding by the law within,
Thou fail not in a world of sin,
And ev'n for want of such a type.

XXXIV

My own dim life should teach me this,
That life shall live for evermore,
Else earth is darkness at the core,
And dust and ashes all that is;

This round of green, this orb of flame,
Fantastic beauty; such as lurks
In some wild Poet, when he works
Without a conscience or an aim.

What then were God to such as I?
'Twere hardly worth my while to choose
Of things all mortal, or to use
A little patience ere I die;

'Twere best at once to sink to peace,
Like birds the charming serpent draws,
To drop head-foremost in the jaws
Of vacant darkness and to cease.

XXXV

Yet if some voice that man could trust
Should murmur from the narrow house,
'The cheeks drop in; the body bows;
Man dies: nor is there hope in dust:'

Might I not say? 'Yet even here,
But for one hour, O Love, I strive
To keep so sweet a thing alive:'
But I should turn mine ears and hear

The moanings of the homeless sea,
The sound of streams that swift or slow
Draw down Æonian hills, and sow
The dust of continents to be;

And Love would answer with a sigh,
'The sound of that forgetful shore
Will change my sweetness more and more,
Half-dead to know that I shall die.'

O me, what profits it to put
An idle case? If Death were seen
At first as Death, Love had not been,
Or been in narrowest working shut,

Mere fellowship of sluggish moods,
Or in his coarsest Satyr-shape
Had bruised the herb and crush'd the grape,
And bask'd and batten'd in the woods.

XXXVI

Tho' truths in manhood darkly join,
Deep-seated in our mystic frame,
We yield all blessing to the name
Of Him that made them current coin;

For Wisdom dealt with mortal powers,
Where truth in closest words shall fail,
When truth embodied in a tale
Shall enter in at lowly doors.

And so the Word had breath, and wrought
With human hands the creed of creeds
In loveliness of perfect deeds,
More strong than all poetic thought;

Which he may read that binds the sheaf,
Or builds the house, or digs the grave,
And those wild eyes that watch the wave
In roarings round the coral reef.

XXXVII

Urania speaks with darken'd brow:
'Thou pratest here where thou art least;
This faith has many a purer priest,
And many an abler voice than thou.

'Go down beside thy native rill,
On thy Parnassus set thy feet,
And hear thy laurel whisper sweet
About the ledges of the hill.'

And my Melpomene replies,
A touch of shame upon her cheek:
'I am not worthy ev'n to speak
Of thy prevailing mysteries;

'For I am but an earthly Muse,
And owning but a little art
To lull with song an aching heart,
And render human love his dues;

'But brooding on the dear one dead,
And all he said of things divine,
(And dear to me as sacred wine
To dying lips is all he said),

'I murmur'd, as I came along,
Of comfort clasp'd in truth reveal'd;
And loiter'd in the master's field,
And darken'd sanctities with song.'

XXXVIII

With weary steps I loiter on,
Tho' always under alter'd skies
The purple from the distance dies,
My prospect and horizon gone.

No joy the blowing season gives,
The herald melodies of spring,
But in the songs I love to sing
A doubtful gleam of solace lives.

If any care for what is here
Survive in spirits render'd free,
Then are these songs I sing of thee
Not all ungrateful to thine ear.

XXXIX

Old warder of these buried bones,
And answering now my random stroke
With fruitful cloud and living smoke,
Dark yew, that graspest at the stones

And dippest toward the dreamless head,
To thee too comes the golden hour
When flower is feeling after flower;
But Sorrow—fixt upon the dead,

And darkening the dark graves of men,—
What whisper'd from her lying lips?
Thy gloom is kindled at the tips,
And passes into gloom again.

XL

Could we forget the widow'd hour
And look on Spirits breathed away,
As on a maiden in the day
When first she wears her orange-flower!

When crown'd with blessing she doth rise
To take her latest leave of home,
And hopes and light regrets that come
Make April of her tender eyes;

And doubtful joys the father move,
And tears are on the mother's face,
As parting with a long embrace
She enters other realms of love;

Her office there to rear, to teach,
Becoming as is meet and fit
A link among the days, to knit
The generations each with each;

And, doubtless, unto thee is given
A life that bears immortal fruit
In those great offices that suit
The full-grown energies of heaven.

Ay me, the difference I discern!
How often shall her old fireside
Be cheer'd with tidings of the bride,
How often she herself return,

And tell them all they would have told,
And bring her babe, and make her boast,
Till even those that miss'd her most
Shall count new things as dear as old:

But thou and I have shaken hands,
Till growing winters lay me low;
My paths are in the fields I know,
And thine in undiscover'd lands.

XLI

Thy spirit ere our fatal loss
Did ever rise from high to higher;
As mounts the heavenward altar-fire,
As flies the lighter thro' the gross.

But thou art turn'd to something strange,
And I have lost the links that bound
Thy changes; here upon the ground,
No more partaker of thy change.

Deep folly! yet that this could be—
That I could wing my will with might
To leap the grades of life and light,
And flash at once, my friend, to thee.

For tho' my nature rarely yields
To that vague fear implied in death;
Nor shudders at the gulfs beneath,
The howlings from forgotten fields;

Yet oft when sundown skirts the moor
An inner trouble I behold,
A spectral doubt which makes me cold,
That I shall be thy mate no more,

Tho' following with an upward mind
The wonders that have come to thee,
Thro' all the secular to-be,
But evermore a life behind.

XLII

I vex my heart with fancies dim:
He still outstript me in the race;
It was but unity of place
That made me dream I rank'd with him.

And so may Place retain us still,
And he the much-beloved again,
A lord of large experience, train
To riper growth the mind and will:

And what delights can equal those
That stir the spirit's inner deeps,
When one that loves but knows not, reaps
A truth from one that loves and knows?

XLIII

If Sleep and Death be truly one,
And every spirit's folded bloom
Thro' all its intervital gloom
In some long trance should slumber on;

Unconscious of the sliding hour,
Bare of the body, might it last,
And silent traces of the past
Be all the colour of the flower:

So then were nothing lost to man;
So that still garden of the souls
In many a figured leaf enrolls
The total world since life began;

And love will last as pure and whole
As when he loved me here in Time,
And at the spiritual prime
Rewaken with the dawning soul.

XLIV

How fares it with the happy dead?
For here the man is more and more;
But he forgets the days before
God shut the doorways of his head.

The days have vanish'd, tone and tint,
And yet perhaps the hoarding sense
Gives out at times (he knows not whence)
A little flash, a mystic hint;

And in the long harmonious years
(If Death so taste Lethean springs),
May some dim touch of earthly things
Surprise thee ranging with thy peers.

If such a dreamy touch should fall,
O turn thee round, resolve the doubt;
My guardian angel will speak out
In that high place, and tell thee all.

XLV

The baby new to earth and sky,
What time his tender palm is prest
Against the circle of the breast,
Has never thought that 'this is I':

But as he grows he gathers much,
And learns the use of 'I,' and 'me,'
And finds 'I am not what I see,
And other than the things I touch.'

So rounds he to a separate mind
From whence clear memory may begin,
As thro' the frame that binds him in
His isolation grows defined.

This use may lie in blood and breath,
Which else were fruitless of their due,
Had man to learn himself anew
Beyond the second birth of Death.

XLVI

We ranging down this lower track,
The path we came by, thorn and flower,
Is shadow'd by the growing hour,
Lest life should fail in looking back.

So be it: there no shade can last
In that deep dawn behind the tomb,
But clear from marge to marge shall bloom
The eternal landscape of the past;

A lifelong tract of time reveal'd;
The fruitful hours of still increase;
Days order'd in a wealthy peace,
And those five years its richest field.

O Love, thy province were not large,
A bounded field, nor stretching far;
Look also, Love, a brooding star,
A rosy warmth from marge to marge.

XLVII

That each, who seems a separate whole,
Should move his rounds, and fusing all
The skirts of self again, should fall
Remerging in the general Soul,

Is faith as vague as all unsweet:
Eternal form shall still divide
The eternal soul from all beside;
And I shall know him when we meet:

And we shall sit at endless feast,
Enjoying each the other's good:
What vaster dream can hit the mood
Of Love on earth? He seeks at least

Upon the last and sharpest height,
Before the spirits fade away,
Some landing-place, to clasp and say,
'Farewell! We lose ourselves in light.'

XLVIII

If these brief lays, of Sorrow born,
Were taken to be such as closed
Grave doubts and answers here proposed,
Then these were such as men might scorn:

Her care is not to part and prove;
She takes, when harsher moods remit,
What slender shade of doubt may flit,
And makes it vassal unto love:

And hence, indeed, she sports with words,
But better serves a wholesome law,
And holds it sin and shame to draw
The deepest measure from the chords:

Nor dare she trust a larger lay,
But rather loosens from the lip
Short swallow-flights of song, that dip
Their wings in tears, and skim away.

XLIX

From art, from nature, from the schools,
Let random influences glance,
Like light in many a shiver'd lance
That breaks about the dappled pools:

The lightest wave of thought shall lisp,
The fancy's tenderest eddy wreathe,
The slightest air of song shall breathe
To make the sullen surface crisp.

And look thy look, and go thy way,
But blame not thou the winds that make
The seeming-wanton ripple break,
The tender-pencil'd shadow play.

Beneath all fancied hopes and fears
Ay me, the sorrow deepens down,
Whose muffled motions blindly drown
The bases of my life in tears.

L

Be near me when my light is low,
When the blood creeps, and the nerves prick
And tingle; and the heart is sick,
And all the wheels of Being slow.

Be near me when the sensuous frame
Is rack'd with pangs that conquer trust;
And Time, a maniac scattering dust,
And Life, a Fury slinging flame.

Be near me when my faith is dry,
And men the flies of latter spring,
That lay their eggs, and sting and sing
And weave their petty cells and die.

Be near me when I fade away,
To point the term of human strife,
And on the low dark verge of life
The twilight of eternal day.

LI

Do we indeed desire the dead
Should still be near us at our side?
Is there no baseness we would hide?
No inner vileness that we dread?

Shall he for whose applause I strove,
I had such reverence for his blame,
See with clear eye some hidden shame
And I be lessen'd in his love?

I wrong the grave with fears untrue:
Shall love be blamed for want of faith?
There must be wisdom with great Death:
The dead shall look me thro' and thro'.

Be near us when we climb or fall:
Ye watch, like God, the rolling hours
With larger other eyes than ours,
To make allowance for us all.

LII

I cannot love thee as I ought,
For love reflects the thing beloved;
My words are only words, and moved
Upon the topmost froth of thought.

'Yet blame not thou thy plaintive song,'
The Spirit of true love replied;
'Thou canst not move me from thy side,
Nor human frailty do me wrong.

'What keeps a spirit wholly true
To that ideal which he bears?
What record? not the sinless years
That breathed beneath the Syrian blue:

'So fret not, like an idle girl,
That life is dash'd with flecks of sin.
Abide: thy wealth is gather'd in,
When Time hath sunder'd shell from pearl.'

LIII

How many a father have I seen,
A sober man, among his boys,
Whose youth was full of foolish noise,
Who wears his manhood hale and green:

And dare we to this fancy give,
That had the wild oat not been sown,
The soil, left barren, scarce had grown
The grain by which a man may live?

Or, if we held the doctrine sound
For life outliving heats of youth,
Yet who would preach it as a truth
To those that eddy round and round?

Hold thou the good: define it well:
For fear divine Philosophy
Should push beyond her mark, and be
Procuress to the Lords of Hell.

LIV

Oh yet we trust that somehow good
Will be the final goal of ill,
To pangs of nature, sins of will,
Defects of doubt, and taints of blood;

That nothing walks with aimless feet;
That not one life shall be destroy'd,
Or cast as rubbish to the void,
When God hath made the pile complete;

That not a worm is cloven in vain;
That not a moth with vain desire
Is shrivell'd in a fruitless fire,
Or but subserves another's gain.

Behold, we know not anything;
I can but trust that good shall fall
At last—far off—at last, to all,
And every winter change to spring.

So runs my dream: but what am I?
An infant crying in the night:
An infant crying for the light:
And with no language but a cry.

LV

The wish, that of the living whole
No life may fail beyond the grave,
Derives it not from what we have
The likest God within the soul?

Are God and Nature then at strife,
That Nature lends such evil dreams?
So careful of the type she seems,
So careless of the single life;

That I, considering everywhere
Her secret meaning in her deeds,
And finding that of fifty seeds
She often brings but one to bear,

I falter where I firmly trod,
And falling with my weight of cares
Upon the great world's altar-stairs
That slope thro' darkness up to God,

I stretch lame hands of faith, and grope,
And gather dust and chaff, and call
To what I feel is Lord of all,
And faintly trust the larger hope.

LVI

'So careful of the type?' but no.
From scarped cliff and quarried stone
She cries, 'A thousand types are gone:
I care for nothing, all shall go.

'Thou makest thine appeal to me:
I bring to life, I bring to death:
The spirit does but mean the breath:
I know no more.' And he, shall he,

Man, her last work, who seem'd so fair,
Such splendid purpose in his eyes,
Who roll'd the psalm to wintry skies,
Who built him fanes of fruitless prayer,

Who trusted God was love indeed
And love Creation's final law—
Tho' Nature, red in tooth and claw
With ravine, shriek'd against his creed—

Who loved, who suffer'd countless ills,
Who battled for the True, the Just,
Be blown about the desert dust,
Or seal'd within the iron hills?

No more? A monster then, a dream,
A discord. Dragons of the prime,
That tare each other in their slime,
Were mellow music match'd with him.

O life as futile, then, as frail!
O for thy voice to soothe and bless!
What hope of answer, or redress?
Behind the veil, behind the veil.

LVII

Peace; come away: the song of woe
Is after all an earthly song:
Peace; come away: we do him wrong
To sing so wildly: let us go.

Come; let us go: your cheeks are pale;
But half my life I leave behind:
Methinks my friend is richly shrined;
But I shall pass; my work will fail.

Yet in these ears, till hearing dies,
One set slow bell will seem to toll
The passing of the sweetest soul
That ever look d with human eyes.

I hear it now, and o'er and o'er,
Eternal greetings to the dead;
And 'Ave, Ave, Ave,'[1] said,
'Adieu, adieu' for evermore.

LVIII

In those sad words I took farewell:
Like echoes in sepulchral halls,
As drop by drop the water falls
In vaults and catacombs, they fell;

And, falling, idly broke the peace
Of hearts that beat from day to day,
Half-conscious of their dying clay,
And those cold crypts where they shall cease.

The high Muse answer'd: 'Wherefore grieve
Thy brethren with a fruitless tear?
Abide a little longer here,
And thou shalt take a nobler leave.'

[1] Hail, hail, hail.

LIX

O Sorrow, wilt thou live with me
No casual mistress, but a wife,
My bosom-friend and half of life;
As I confess it needs must be;

O Sorrow, wilt thou rule my blood,
Be sometimes lovely like a bride,
And put thy harsher moods aside,
If thou wilt have me wise and good.

My centred passion cannot move.
Nor will it lessen from to-day;
But I'll have leave at times to play
As with the creature of my love;

And set thee forth, for thou art mine,
With so much hope for years to come,
That, howsoe'er I know thee, some
Could hardly tell what name were thine.

LX

He past; a soul of nobler tone:
My spirit loved and loves him yet,
Like some poor girl whose heart is set
On one whose rank exceeds her own.

He mixing with his proper sphere,
She finds the baseness of her lot,
Half jealous of she knows not what,
And envying all that meet him there.

The little village looks forlorn;
She sighs amid her narrow days,
Moving about the household ways,
In that dark house where she was born.

The foolish neighbours come and go,
And tease her till the day draws by:
At night she weeps, 'How vain am I!
How should he love a thing so low?'

LXI

If, in thy second state sublime,
Thy ransom'd reason change replies
With all the circle of the wise,
The perfect flower of human time;

And if thou cast thine eyes below,
How dimly character'd and slight,
How dwarf'd a growth of cold and night,
How blanch'd with darkness must I grow!

Yet turn thee to the doubtful shore,
Where thy first form was made a man;
I loved thee, Spirit, and love, nor can
The soul of Shakspeare love thee more.

LXII

Tho' if an eye that's downward cast
Could make thee somewhat blench or fail,
Then be my love an idle tale,
And fading legend of the past;

And thou, as one that once declined,
When he was little more than boy,
On some unworthy heart with joy,
But lives to wed an equal mind;

And breathes a novel world, the while
His other passion wholly dies,
Or in the light of deeper eyes
Is matter for a flying smile.

LXIII

Yet pity for a horse o'er-driven,
And love in which my hound has part,
Can hang no weight upon my heart
In its assumptions up to heaven;

And I am so much more than these,
As thou, perchance, art more than I,
And yet I spare them sympathy,
And I would set their pains at ease.

So mayst thou watch me where I weep,
As, unto vaster motions bound,
The circuits of thine orbit round
A higher height, a deeper deep.

LXIV

Dost thou look back on what hath been,
As some divinely gifted man,
Whose life in low estate began
And on a simple village green;

Who breaks his birth's invidious bar,
And grasps the skirts of happy chance,
And breasts the blows of circumstance,
And grapples with his evil star;

Who makes by force his merit known
And lives to clutch the golden keys,
To mould a mighty state's decrees,
And shape the whisper of the throne;

And moving up from high to higher,
Becomes on Fortune's crowning slope
The pillar of a people's hope.
The centre of a world's desire;

Yet feels, as in a pensive dream,
When all his active powers are still,
A distant dearness in the hill,
A secret sweetness in the stream,

The limit of his narrower fate,
While yet beside its vocal springs
He play'd at counsellors and kings,
With one that was his earliest mate;

Who ploughs with pain his native lea
And reaps the labour of his hands,
Or in the furrow musing stands;
'Does my old friend remember me?'

LXV

Sweet soul, do with me as thou wilt;
I lull a fancy trouble-tost
With 'Love's too precious to be lost,
A little grain shall not be spilt.'

And in that solace can I sing,
Till out of painful phases wrought
There flutters up a happy thought,
Self-balanced on a lightsome wing:

Since we deserved the name of friends,
And thine effect so lives in me,
A part of mine may live in thee
And move thee on to noble ends.

LXVI

You thought my heart too far diseased;
You wonder when my fancies play
To find me gay among the gay,
Like one with any trifle pleased.

The shade by which my life was crost,
Which makes a desert in the mind,
Has made me kindly with my kind,
And like to him whose sight is lost;

Whose feet are guided thro' the land,
Whose jest among his friends is free,
Who takes the children on his knee,
And winds their curls about his hand:

He plays with threads, he beats his chair
For pastime, dreaming of the sky;
His inner day can never die,
His night of loss is always there.

LXVII

When on my bed the moonlight falls,
I know that in thy place of rest
By that broad water of the west,
There comes a glory on the walls:

Thy marble bright in dark appears,
As slowly steals a silver flame
Along the letters of thy name,
And o'er the number of thy years.

The mystic glory swims away;
From off my bed the moonlight dies;
And closing eaves of wearied eyes
I sleep till dusk is dipt in gray:

And then I know the mist is drawn
A lucid veil from coast to coast,
And in the dark church like a ghost
Thy tablet glimmers to the dawn.

LXVIII

When in the down I sink my head,
Sleep, Death's twin-brother, times my breath;
Sleep, Death's twin-brother, knows not Death,
Nor can I dream of thee as dead:

I walk as ere I walk'd forlorn,
When all our path was fresh with dew,
And all the bugle breezes blew
Reveillée to the breaking morn.

But what is this? I turn about,
I find a trouble in thine eye,
Which makes me sad I know not why,
Nor can my dream resolve the doubt:

But ere the lark hath left the lea
I wake, and I discern the truth;
It is the trouble of my youth
That foolish sleep transfers to thee.

LXIX

I dream'd there would be Spring no more,
That Nature's ancient power was lost:
The streets were black with smoke and frost,
They chatter'd trifles at the door:

I wander'd from the noisy town,
I found a wood with thorny boughs:
I took the thorns to bind my brows,
I wore them like a civic crown:

I met with scoffs, I met with scorns
From youth and babe and hoary hairs:
They call'd me in the public squares
The fool that wears a crown of thorns:

They call'd me fool, they call'd me child:
I found an angel of the night;
The voice was low, the look was bright;
He look'd upon my crown and smiled:

He reach'd the glory of a hand,
That seem'd to touch it into leaf:
The voice was not the voice of grief,
The words were hard to understand.

LXX

I cannot see the features right,
When on the gloom I strive to paint
The face I know; the hues are faint
And mix with hollow masks of night;

Cloud-towers by ghostly masons wrought,
A gulf that ever shuts and gapes,
A hand that points, and palled shapes
In shadowy thoroughfares of thought;

And crowds that stream from yawning doors,
And shoals of pucker'd faces drive;
Dark bulks that tumble half alive,
And lazy lengths on boundless shores;

Till all at once beyond the will
I hear a wizard music roll,
And thro' a lattice on the soul
Looks thy fair face and makes it still.

LXXI

Sleep, kinsman thou to death and trance
And madness, thou hast forged at last
A night-long Present of the Past
In which we went thro' summer France.

Hadst thou such credit with the soul?
Then bring an opiate trebly strong,
Drug down the blindfold sense of wrong
That so my pleasure may be whole;

While now we talk as once we talk'd
Of men and minds, the dust of change,
The days that grow to something strange,
In walking as of old we walk'd

Beside the river's wooded reach,
The fortress, and the mountain ridge,
The cataract flashing from the bridge,
The breaker breaking on the beach.

LXXII

Risest thou thus, dim dawn, again,
And howlest, issuing out of night,
With blasts that blow the poplar white,
And lash with storm the streaming pane?

Day, when my crown'd estate begun
To pine in that reverse of doom,
Which sicken'd every living bloom,
And blurr'd the splendour of the sun;

Who usherest in the dolorous hour
With thy quick tears that make the rose
Pull sideways, and the daisy close
Her crimson fringes to the shower;

Who might'st have heaved a windless flame
Up the deep East, or, whispering, play'd
A chequer-work of beam and shade
Along the hills, yet look'd the same,

As wan, as chill, as wild as now;
Day, mark'd as with some hideous crime,
When the dark hand struck down thro' time,
And cancell'd nature's best: but thou,

Lift as thou may'st thy burthen'd brows
Thro' clouds that drench the morning star,
And whirl the ungarner'd sheaf afar,
And sow the sky with flying boughs,

And up thy vault with roaring sound
Climb thy thick noon, disastrous day;
Touch thy dull goal of joyless gray,
And hide thy shame beneath the ground.

LXXIII

So many worlds, so much to do,
So little done, such things to be,
How know I what had need of thee,
For thou wert strong as thou wert true?

The fame is quench'd that I foresaw,
The head hath miss'd an earthly wreath:
I curse not nature, no, nor death;
For nothing is that errs from law.

We pass; the path that each man trod
Is dim, or will be dim, with weeds:
What fame is left for human deeds
In endless age? It rests with God.

O hollow wraith of dying fame,
Fade wholly, while the soul exults,
And self-infolds the large results
Of force that would have forged a name.

LXXIV

As sometimes in a dead man's face,
To those that watch it more and more,
A likeness, hardly seen before,
Comes out—to some one of his race:

So, dearest, now thy brows are cold,
I see thee what thou art, and know
Thy likeness to the wise below,
Thy kindred with the great of old.

But there is more than I can see,
And what I see I leave unsaid,
Nor speak it, knowing Death has made
His darkness beautiful with thee.

LXXV

I leave thy praises unexpress'd
In verse that brings myself relief,
And by the measure of my grief
I leave thy greatness to be guess'd;

What practice howsoe'er expert
In fitting aptest words to things,
Or voice the richest-toned that sings,
Hath power to give thee as thou wert?

I care not in these fading days
To raise a cry that lasts not long,
And round thee with the breeze of song
To stir a little dust of praise.

Thy leaf has perish'd in the green,
And, while we breathe beneath the sun,
The world which credits what is done
Is cold to all that might have been.

So here shall silence guard thy fame;
But somewhere, out of human view,
Whate'er thy hands are set to do
Is wrought with tumult of acclaim.

LXXVI

Take wings of fancy, and ascend,
And in a moment set thy face
Where all the starry heavens of space
Are sharpen'd to a needle's end;

Take wings of foresight; lighten thro'
The secular abyss to come,
And lo, thy deepest lays are dumb
Before the mouldering of a yew;

And if the matin songs, that woke
The darkness of our planet, last,
Thine own shall wither in the vast,
Ere half the lifetime of an oak.

Ere these have clothed their branchy bowers
With fifty Mays, thy songs are vain;
And what are they when these remain
The ruin'd shells of hollow towers?

LXXVII

What hope is here for modern rhyme
To him, who turns a musing eye
On songs, and deeds, and lives, that lie
Foreshorten'd in the tract of time?

These mortal lullabies of pain
May bind a book, may line a box,
May serve to curl a maiden's locks,
Or when a thousand moons shall wane

A man upon a stall may find,
And, passing, turn the page that tells
A grief, then changed to something else,
Sung by a long-forgotten mind.

But what of that? My darken'd ways
Shall ring with music all the same;
To breathe my loss is more than fame,
To utter love more sweet than praise.

LXXVIII

Again at Christmas did we weave
The holly round the Christmas hearth;
The silent snow possess'd the earth,
And calmly fell our Christmas-eve:

The yule-clog sparkled keen with frost,
No wing of wind the region swept,
But over all things brooding slept
The quiet sense of something lost.

As in the winters left behind,
Again our ancient games had place,
The mimic picture's breathing grace,
And dance and song and hoodman-blind.

Who show'd a token of distress?
No single tear, no mark of pain:
O sorrow, then can sorrow wane?
O grief, can grief be changed to less?

O last regret, regret can die!
No—mixt with all this mystic frame,
Her deep relations are the same,
But with long use her tears are dry.

LXXIX

'More than my brothers are to me,'—
Let this not vex thee, noble heart!
I know thee of what force thou art
To hold the costliest love in fee.

But thou and I are one in kind,
As moulded like in Nature's mint;
And hill and wood and field did print
The same sweet forms in either mind.

For us the same cold streamlet curl'd
Thro' all his eddying coves; the same
All winds that roam the twilight came
In whispers of the beauteous world.

At one dear knee we proffer'd vows,
One lesson from one book we learn'd,
Ere childhood's flaxen ringlet turn'd
To black and brown on kindred brows.

And so my wealth resembles thine,
But he was rich where I was poor,
And he supplied my want the more
As his unlikeness fitted mine.

LXXX

If any vague desire should rise,
That holy Death ere Arthur died
Had moved me kindly from his side,
And dropt the dust on tearless eyes;

Then fancy shapes, as fancy can,
The grief my loss in him had wrought,
A grief as deep as life or thought,
But stay'd in peace with God and man.

I make a picture in the brain;
I hear the sentence that he speaks;
He bears the burthen of the weeks
But turns his burthen into gain.

His credit thus shall set me free;
And, influence rich to soothe and save,
Unused example from the grave
Reach out dead hands to comfort me.

LXXXI

Could I have said while he was here,
'My love shall now no further range;
There cannot come a mellower change,
For now is love mature in ear.'

Love, then, had hope of richer store:
What end is here to my complaint?
This haunting whisper makes me faint,
'More years had made me love thee more.'

But Death returns an answer sweet:
'My sudden frost was sudden gain,
And gave all ripeness to the grain,
It might have drawn from after-heat.'

LXXXII

I wage not any feud with Death
For changes wrought on form and face;
No lower life that earth's embrace
May breed with him, can fright my faith.

Eternal process moving on,
From state to state the spirit walks;
And these are but the shatter'd stalks,
Or ruin'd chrysalis of one.

Nor blame I Death, because he bare
The use of virtue out of earth:
I know transplanted human worth
Will bloom to profit, otherwhere.

For this alone on Death I wreak
The wrath that garners in my heart;
He put our lives so far apart
We cannot hear each other speak.

LXXXIII

Dip down upon the northern shore,
O sweet new-year delaying long;
Thou doest expectant nature wrong;
Delaying long, delay no more.

What stays thee from the clouded noons,
Thy sweetness from its proper place?
Can trouble live with April days,
Or sadness in the summer moons?

Bring orchis, bring the foxglove spire,
The little speedwell's darling blue,
Deep tulips dash'd with fiery dew,
Laburnums, dropping-wells of fire.

O thou, new-year, delaying long,
Delayest the sorrow in my blood,
That longs to burst a frozen bud
And flood a fresher throat with song.

LXXXIV

When I contemplate all alone
The life that had been thine below,
And fix my thoughts on all the glow
To which thy crescent would have grown;

I see thee sitting crown'd with good,
A central warmth diffusing bliss
In glance and smile, and clasp and kiss,
On all the branches of thy blood;

Thy blood, my friend, and partly mine;
For now the day was drawing on,
When thou should'st link thy life with one
Of mine own house, and boys of thine

Had babbled 'Uncle' on my knee;
But that remorseless iron hour
Made cypress of her orange flower,
Despair of Hope, and earth of thee.

I seem to meet their least desire,
To clap their cheeks, to call them mine.
I see their unborn faces shine
Beside the never-lighted fire.

I see myself an honour'd guest,
Thy partner in the flowery walk
Of letters, genial table-talk,
Or deep dispute, and graceful jest;

While now thy prosperous labour fills
The lips of men with honest praise,
And sun by sun the happy days
Descend below the golden hills

With promise of a morn as fair;
And all the train of bounteous hours
Conduct by paths of growing powers,
To reverence and the silver hair;

Till slowly worn her earthly robe,
Her lavish mission richly wrought,
Leaving great legacies of thought,
Thy spirit should fail from off the globe;

What time mine own might also flee,
As link'd with thine in love and fate,
And, hovering o'er the dolorous strait
To the other shore, involved in thee,

Arrive at last the blessed goal,
And He that died in Holy Land
Would reach us out the shining hand,
And take us as a single soul.

What reed was that on which I leant?
Ah, backward fancy, wherefore wake
The old bitterness again, and break
The low beginnings of content.

LXXXV

This truth came borne with bier and pall,
I felt it, when I sorrow'd most,
'Tis better to have loved and lost,
Than never to have loved at all—

O true in word, and tried in deed,
Demanding, so to bring relief
To this which is our common grief,
What kind of life is that I lead;

And whether trust in things above
Be dimm'd of sorrow, or sustain'd;
And whether love for him have drain'd
My capabilities of love;

Your words have virtue such as draws
A faithful answer from the breast,
Thro' light reproaches, half exprest,
And loyal unto kindly laws.

My blood an even tenor kept,
Till on mine ear this message falls,
That in Vienna's fatal walls
God's finger touch'd him, and he slept.

The great Intelligences fair
That range above our mortal state,
In circle round the blessed gate,
Received and gave him welcome there;

And led him thro' the blissful climes,
And show'd him in the fountain fresh
All knowledge that the sons of flesh
Shall gather in the cycled times.

But I remain'd, whose hopes were dim,
Whose life, whose thoughts were little worth,
To wander on a darken'd earth,
Where all things round me breathed of him.

O friendship, equal-poised control,
O heart, with kindliest motion warm,
O sacred essence, other form,
O solemn ghost, O crowned soul!

Yet none could better know than I,
How much of act at human hands
The sense of human will demands
By which we dare to live or die.

Whatever way my days decline,
I felt and feel, tho' left alone,
His being working in mine own,
The footsteps of his life in mine;

A life that all the Muses deck'd
With gifts of grace, that might express
All-comprehensive tenderness,
All-subtilising intellect:

And so my passion hath not swerved
To works of weakness, but I find
An image comforting the mind,
And in my grief a strength reserved.

Likewise the imaginative woe,
That loved to handle spiritual strife,
Diffused the shock thro' all my life,
But in the present broke the blow.

My pulses therefore beat again
For other friends that once I met;
Nor can it suit me to forget
The mighty hopes that make us men.

I woo your love: I count it crime
To mourn for any overmuch;
I, the divided half of such
A friendship as had master'd Time;

Which masters Time indeed, and is
Eternal, separate from fears:
The all-assuming months and years
Can take no part away from this:

But Summer on the steaming floods,
And Spring that swells the narrow brooks,
And Autumn, with a noise of rooks,
That gather in the waning woods,

And every pulse of wind and wave
Recalls, in change of light or gloom,
My old affection of the tomb,
And my prime passion in the grave:

My old affection of the tomb,
A part of stillness, yearns to speak:
'Arise, and get thee forth and seek
A friendship for the years to come.

'I watch thee from the quiet shore;
Thy spirit up to mine can reach;
But in dear words of human speech
We two communicate no more.'

And I, 'Can clouds of nature stain
The starry clearness of the free?
How is it? Canst thou feel for me
Some painless sympathy with pain?'

And lightly does the whisper fall;
' 'Tis hard for thee to fathom this;
I triumph in conclusive bliss,
And that serene result of all.'

So hold I commerce with the dead;
Or so methinks the dead would say;
Or so shall grief with symbols play
And pining life be fancy-fed.

Now looking to some settled end,
That these things pass, and I shall prove
A meeting somewhere, love with love,
I crave your pardon, O my friend;

If not so fresh, with love as true,
I, clasping brother-hands, aver
I could not, if I would, transfer
The whole I felt for him to you.

For which be they that hold apart
The promise of the golden hours?
First love, first friendship, equal powers,
That marry with the virgin heart.

Still mine, that cannot but deplore,
That beats within a lonely place,
That yet remembers his embrace,
But at his footstep leaps no more,

My heart, tho' widow'd, may not rest
Quite in the love of what is gone,
But seeks to beat in time with one
That warms another living breast.

Ah, take the imperfect gift I bring,
Knowing the primrose yet is dear,
The primrose of the later year,
As not unlike to that of Spring.

LXXXVI

Sweet after showers, ambrosial air,
That rollest from the gorgeous gloom
Of evening over brake and bloom
And meadow, slowly breathing bare

The round of space, and rapt below
Thro' all the dewy-tassell'd wood,
And shadowing down the horned flood
In ripples, fan my brows and blow

The fever from my cheek, and sigh
The full new life that feeds thy breath
Throughout my frame, till Doubt and Death,
Ill brethren, let the fancy fly

From belt to belt of crimson seas
On leagues of odour streaming far,
To where in yonder orient star
A hundred spirits whisper 'Peace.'

LXXXVII

I past beside the reverend walls
In which of old I wore the gown;
I roved at random thro' the town,
And saw the tumult of the halls;

And heard once more in college fanes
The storm their high-built organs make,
And thunder-music, rolling, shake
The prophet blazon'd on the panes;

And caught once more the distant shout,
The measured pulse of racing oars
Among the willows; paced the shores
And many a bridge, and all about

The same gray flats again, and felt
The same, but not the same; and last
Up that long walk of limes I past
To see the rooms in which he dwelt.

Another name was on the door:
I linger'd; all within was noise
Of songs, and clapping hands, and boys
That crash'd the glass and beat the floor;

Where once we held debate, a band
Of youthful friends, on mind and art,
And labour, and the changing mart,
And all the framework of the land;

When one would aim on arrow fair,
But send it slackly from the string;
And one would pierce an outer ring,
And one an inner, here and there;

And last the master-bowman, he,
Would cleave the mark. A willing ear
We lent him. Who, but hung to hear
The rapt oration flowing free

From point to point, with power and grace
And music in the bounds of law,
To those conclusions when we saw
The God within him light his face,

And seem to lift the form, and glow
In azure orbits heavenly-wise;
And over those ethereal eyes
The bar of Michael Angelo.

LXXXVIII

Wild bird, whose warble, liquid sweet,
Rings Eden thro' the budded quicks,
O tell me where the senses mix,
O tell me where the passions meet,

Whence radiate: fierce extremes employ
Thy spirits in the darkening leaf,
And in the midmost heart of grief
Thy passion clasps a secret joy:

And I—my harp would prelude woe—
I cannot all command the strings;
The glory of the sum of things
Will flash along the chords and go.

LXXXIX

Witch-elms that counterchange the floor
Of this flat lawn with dusk and bright;
And thou, with all thy breadth and height
Of foliage, towering sycamore;

How often, hither wandering down,
My Arthur found your shadows fair,
And shook to all the liberal air
The dust and din and steam of town:

He brought an eye for all he saw;
He mixt in all our simple sports;
They pleased him, fresh from brawling courts
And dusty purlieus of the law.

O joy to him in this retreat,
Immantled in ambrosial dark,
To drink the cooler air, and mark
The landscape winking thro' the heat:

O sound to rout the brood of cares,
The sweep of scythe in morning dew,
The gust that round the garden flew,
And tumbled half the mellowing pears!

O bliss, when all in circle drawn
About him, heart and ear were fed
To hear him, as he lay and read
The Tuscan poets on the lawn:

Or in the all-golden afternoon
A guest, or happy sister, sung,
Or here she brought the harp and flung
A ballad to the brightening moon:

Nor less it pleased in livelier moods,
Beyond the bounding hill to stray,
And break the livelong summer day
With banquet in the distant woods;

Whereat we glanced from theme to theme,
Discuss'd the books to love or hate,
Or touch'd the changes of the state,
Or threaded some Socratic dream;

But if I praised the busy town,
He loved to rail against it still,
For 'ground in yonder social mill
We rub each other's angles down,

'And merge' he said 'in form and gloss
The picturesque of man and man.'
We talk'd: the stream beneath us ran,
The wine-flask lying couch'd in moss,

Or cool'd within the glooming wave;
And last, returning from afar,
Before the crimson-circled star
Had fall'n into her father's grave,

And brushing ankle-deep in flowers,
We heard behind the woodbine veil
The milk that bubbled in the pail,
And buzzings of the honied hours.

XC

He tasted love with half his mind,
Nor ever drank the inviolate spring
Where nighest heaven, who first could fling
This bitter seed among mankind;

That could the dead, whose dying eyes
Were closed with wail, resume their life,
They would but find in child and wife
An iron welcome when they rise:

'Twas well, indeed, when warm with wine,
To pledge them with a kindly tear,
To talk them o'er, to wish them here,
To count their memories half divine;

But if they came who past away,
Behold their brides in other hands;
The hard heir strides about their lands,
And will not yield them for a day.

Yea, tho' their sons were none of these,
Not less the yet-loved sire would make
Confusion worse than death, and shake
The pillars of domestic peace.

Ah dear, but come thou back to me:
Whatever change the years have wrought,
I find not yet one lonely thought
That cries against my wish for thee.

XCI

When rosy plumelets tuft the larch,
And rarely pipes the mounted thrush;
Or underneath the barren bush
Flits by the sea-blue bird of March;

Come, wear the form by which I know
Thy spirit in time among thy peers;
The hope of unaccomplish'd years
Be large and lucid round thy brow.

When summer's hourly-mellowing change
May breathe, with many roses sweet,
Upon the thousand waves of wheat,
That ripple round the lonely grange;

Come: not in watches of the night,
But where the sunbeam broodeth warm,
Come, beauteous in thine after form,
And like a finer light in light.

XCII

If any vision should reveal
Thy likeness, I might count it vain
As but the canker of the brain;
Yea, tho' it spake and made appeal

To chances where our lots were cast
Together in the days behind,
I might but say, I hear a wind
Of memory murmuring the past.

Yea, tho' it spake and bared to view
A fact within the coming year;
And tho' the months, revolving near,
Should prove the phantom-warning true,

They might not seem thy prophecies,
But spiritual presentiments,
And such refraction of events
As often rises ere they rise.

XCIII

I shall not see thee. Dare I say
No spirit ever brake the band
That stays him from the native land
Where first he walk'd when claspt in clay?

No visual shade of some one lost,
But he, the Spirit himself, may come
Where all the nerve of sense is numb;
Spirit to Spirit, Ghost to Ghost

O, therefore from thy sightless range
With gods in unconjectured bliss,
O, from the distance of the abyss
Of tenfold-complicated change,

Descend, and touch, and enter; hear
The wish too strong for words to name;
That in this blindness of the frame
My Ghost may feel that thine is near.

XCIV

How pure at heart and sound in head,
With what divine affections bold
Should be the man whose thought would hold
An hour's communion with the dead.

In vain shalt thou, or any, call
The spirits from their golden day,
Except, like them, thou too canst say,
My spirit is at peace with all.

They haunt the silence of the breast,
Imaginations calm and fair,
The memory like a cloudless air,
The conscience as a sea at rest:

But when the heart is full of din,
And doubt beside the portal waits,
They can but listen at the gates,
And hear the household jar within.

XCV

By night we linger'd on the lawn,
For underfoot the herb was dry;
And genial warmth; and o'er the sky
The silvery haze of summer drawn;

And calm that let the tapers burn
Unwavering: not a cricket chirr'd:
The brook alone far-off was heard,
And on the board the fluttering urn:

And bats went round in fragrant skies,
And wheel'd or lit the filmy shapes
That haunt the dusk, with ermine capes
And woolly breasts and beaded eyes;

While now we sang old songs that peal'd
From knoll to knoll, where, couch'd at ease,
The white kine glimmer'd, and the trees
Laid their dark arms about the field.

But when those others, one by one,
Withdrew themselves from me and night,
And in the house light after light
Went out, and I was all alone,

A hunger seized my heart; I read
Of that glad year which once had been,
In those fall'n leaves which kept their green,
The noble letters of the dead:

And strangely on the silence broke
The silent-speaking words, and strange
Was love's dumb cry defying change
To test his worth; and strangely spoke

The faith, the vigour, bold to dwell
On doubts that drive the coward back,
And keen thro' wordy snares to track
Suggestion to her inmost cell.

So word by word, and line by line,
The dead man touch'd me from the past,
And all at once it seem'd at last
The living soul was flash'd on mine,

And mine in this was wound, and whirl'd
About empyreal heights of thought,
And came on that which is, and caught
The deep pulsations of the world,

Æonian music measuring out
The steps of Time—the shocks of Chance—
The blows of Death. At length my trance
Was cancell'd, stricken thro' with doubt.

Vague words! but ah, how hard to frame
In matter-moulded forms of speech,
Or ev'n for intellect to reach
Thro' memory that which I became:

Till now the doubtful dusk reveal'd
The knolls once more where, couch'd at ease,
The white king glimmer'd, and the trees
Laid their dark arms about the field:

And suck'd from out the distant gloom
A breeze began to tremble o'er
The large leaves of the sycamore,
And fluctuate all the still perfume,

And gathering freshlier overhead,
Rock'd the full-foliaged elms, and swung
The heavy-folded rose, and flung
The lilies to and fro, and said

'The dawn, the dawn,' and died away;
And East and West, without a breath,
Mixt their dim lights, like life and death,
To broaden into boundless day.

XCVI

You say, but with no touch of scorn,
Sweet-hearted, you, whose light-blue eyes
Are tender over drowning flies,
You tell me, doubt is Devil-born.

I know not: one indeed I knew
In many a subtle question versed,
Who touch'd a jarring lyre at first,
But ever strove to make it true:

Perplext in faith, but pure in deeds,
At last he beat his music out.
There lives more faith in honest doubt,
Believe me, than in half the creeds.

He fought his doubts and gather'd strength,
He would not make his judgment blind,
He faced the spectres of the mind
And laid them: thus he came at length

To find a stronger faith his own;
And Power was with him in the night,
Which makes the darkness and the light,
And dwells not in the light alone,

But in the darkness and the cloud,
As over Sinaï's peaks of old,
While Israel made their gods of gold,
Altho' the trumpet blew so loud.

XCVII

My love has talk'd with rocks and trees;
He finds on misty mountain-ground
His own vast shadow glory-crown'd;
He sees himself in all he sees.

Two partners of a married life—
I look'd on these and thought of thee
In vastness and in mystery,
And of my spirit as of a wife.

These two—they dwelt with eye on eye,
Their hearts of old have beat in tune,
Their meetings made December June,
Their every parting was to die.

Their love has never past away;
The days she never can forget
Are earnest that he loves her yet,
Whate'er the faithless people say.

Her life is lone, he sits apart,
He loves her yet, she will not weep,
Tho' rapt in matters dark and deep
He seems to slight her simple heart.

He thrids the labyrinth of the mind,
He reads the secret of the star,
He seems so near and yet so far,
He looks so cold: she thinks him kind.

She keeps the gift of years before,
A wither'd violet is her bliss:
She knows not what his greatness is,
For that, for all, she loves him more.

For him she plays, to him she sings
Of early faith and plighted vows;
She knows but matters of the house,
And he, he knows a thousand things.

Her faith is fixt and cannot move,
She darkly feels him great and wise,
She dwells on him with faithful eyes,
'I cannot understand: I love.'

XCVIII

You leave us: you will see the Rhine,
And those fair hills I sail'd below,
When I was there with him; and go
By summer belts of wheat and vine

To where he breathed his latest breath,
That City. All her splendour seems
No livelier than the wisp that gleams
On Lethe in the eyes of Death.

Let her great Danube rolling fair
Enwind her isles, unmark'd of me:
I have not seen, I will not see
Vienna; rather dream that there,

A treble darkness, Evil haunts
The birth, the bridal; friend from friend
Is oftener parted, fathers bend
Above more graves, a thousand wants

Gnarr at the heels of men, and prey
By each cold hearth, and sadness flings
Her shadow on the blaze of kings:
And yet myself have heard him say,

That not in any mother town
With statelier progress to and fro
The double tides of chariots flow
By park and suburb under brown

Of lustier leaves; nor more content,
He told me, lives in any crowd,
When all is gay with lamps, and loud
With sport and song, in booth and tent,

Imperial halls, or open plain;
And wheels the circled dance, and breaks
The rocket molten into flakes
Of crimson or in emerald rain.

XCIX

Risest thou thus, dim dawn, again,
So loud with voices of the birds,
So thick with lowings of the herds,
Day, when I lost the flower of men;

Who tremblest thro' thy darkling red
On yon swoll'n brook that bubbles fast
By meadows breathing of the past,
And woodlands holy to the dead;

Who murmurest in the foliaged eaves
A song that slights the coming care,
And Autumn laying here and there
A fiery finger on the leaves;

Who wakenest with thy balmy breath
To myriads on the genial earth,
Memories of bridal, or of birth,
And unto myriads more, of death.

O wheresoever those may be,
Betwixt the slumber of the poles,
To-day they count as kindred souls;
They know me not, but mourn with me.

C

I climb the hill: from end to end
Of all the landscape underneath,
I find no place that does not breathe
Some gracious memory of my friend;

No gray old grange, or lonely fold,
Or low morass and whispering reed,
Or simple stile from mead to mead,
Or sheepwalk up the windy wold;

Nor hoary knoll of ash and haw
That hears the latest linnet trill,
Nor quarry trench'd along the hill
And haunted by the wrangling daw;

Nor runlet tinkling from the rock;
Nor pastoral rivulet that swerves
To left and right thro' meadowy curves,
That feed the mothers of the flock;

But each has pleased a kindred eye,
And each reflects a kindlier day;
And, leaving these, to pass away,
I think once more he seems to die.

CI

Unwatch'd, the garden bough shall sway,
The tender blossom flutter down,
Unloved, that beech will gather brown,
This maple burn itself away;

Unloved, the sun-flower, shining fair,
Ray round with flames her disk of seed,
And many a rose-carnation feed
With summer spice the humming air;

Unloved, by many a sandy bar,
The brook shall babble down the plain,
At noon or when the lesser wain
Is twisting round the polar star;

Uncared for, gird the windy grove,
And flood the haunts of hern and crake;
Or into silver arrows break
The sailing moon in creek and cove;

Till from the garden and the wild
A fresh association blow,
And year by year the landscape grow
Familiar to the stranger's child;

As year by year the labourer tills
His wonted glebe, or lops the glades;
And year by year our memory fades
From all the circle of the hills.

CII

We leave the well-beloved place
Where first we gazed upon the sky;
The roofs, that heard our earliest cry,
Will shelter one of stranger race.

We go, but ere we go from home,
As down the garden-walks I move,
Two spirits of a diverse love
Contend for loving masterdom.

One whispers, 'Here thy boyhood sung
Long since its matin song, and heard
The low love-language of the bird
In native hazels tassel-hung.'

The other answers, 'Yea, but here
Thy feet have stray'd in after hours
With thy lost friend among the bowers,
And this hath made them trebly dear.'

These two have striven half the day,
And each prefers his separate claim,
Poor rivals in a losing game,
That will not yield each other way.

I turn to go: my feet are set
To leave the pleasant fields and farms;
They mix in one another's arms
To one pure image of regret.

CIII

On that last night before we went
From out the doors where I was bred,
I dream'd a vision of the dead,
Which left my after-morn content.

Methought I dwelt within a hall,
And maidens with me: distant hills
From hidden summits fed with rills
A river sliding by the wall.

The hall with harp and carol rang.
They sang of what is wise and good
And graceful. In the centre stood
A statue veil'd, to which they sang;

And which, tho' veil'd, was known to me,
The shape of him I loved, and love
For ever: then flew in a dove
And brought a summons from the sea:

And when they learnt that I must go
They wept and wail'd, but led the way
To where a little shallop lay
At anchor in the flood below;

And on by many a level mead,
And shadowing bluff that made the banks,
We glided winding under ranks
Of iris, and the golden reed;

And still as vaster grew the shore
And roll'd the floods in grander space,
The maidens gather'd strength and grace
And presence, lordlier than before;

And I myself, who sat apart
And watch'd them, wax'd in every limb;
I felt the thews of Anakim,
The pulses of a Titan's heart;

As one would sing the death of war,
And one would chant the history
Of that great race, which is to be,
And one the shaping of a star;

Until the forward-creeping tides
Began to foam, and we to draw
From deep to deep, to where we saw
A great ship lift her shining sides.

The man we loved was there on deck,
But thrice as large as man he bent
To greet us. Up the side I went,
And fell in silence on his neck:

Whereat those maidens with one mind
Bewail'd their lot; I did them wrong:
'We served thee here,' they said, 'so long,
And wilt thou leave us now behind?'

So rapt I was, they could not win
An answer from my lips, but he
Replying, 'Enter likewise ye
And go with us': they enter'd in.

And while the wind began to sweep
A music out of sheet and shroud,
We steer'd her toward a crimson cloud
That landlike slept along the deep.

CIV

The time draws near the birth of Christ;
The moon is hid, the night is still;
A single church below the hill
Is pealing, folded in the mist.

A single peal of bells below,
That wakens at this hour of rest
A single murmur in the breast,
That these are not the bells I know.

Like strangers' voices here they sound,
In lands where not a memory strays,
Nor landmark breathes of other days,
But all is new unhallow'd ground.

CV

To-night ungather'd let us leave
This laurel, let this holly stand:
We live within the stranger's land,
And strangely falls our Christmas-eve.

Our father's dust is left alone
And silent under other snows:
There in due time the woodbine blows,
The violet comes, but we are gone.

No more shall wayward grief abuse
The genial hour with mask and mime;
For change of place, like growth of time,
Has broke the bond of dying use.

Let cares that petty shadows cast,
By which our lives are chiefly proved,
A little spare the night I loved,
And hold it solemn to the past.

But let no footstep beat the floor,
Nor bowl of wassail mantle warm;
For who would keep an ancient form
Thro' which the spirit breathes no more?

Be neither song, nor game, nor feast;
Nor harp be touch'd, nor flute be blown;
No dance, no motion, save alone
What lightens in the lucid east

Of rising worlds by yonder wood.
Long sleeps the summer in the seed;
Run out your measured arcs, and lead
The closing cycle rich in good.

CVI

Ring out, wild bells, to the wild sky,
The flying cloud, the frosty light:
The year is dying in the night;
Ring out, wild bells, and let him die.

Ring out the old, ring in the new,
Ring, happy, bells, across the snow:
The year is going, let him go;
Ring out the false, ring in the true.

Ring out the grief that saps the mind,
For those that here we see no more;
Ring out the feud of rich and poor,
Ring in redress to all mankind.

Ring out a slowly dying cause,
And ancient forms of party strife;
Ring in the nobler modes of life,
With sweeter manners, purer laws.

Ring out the want, the care, the sin,
The faithless coldness of the times;
Ring out, ring out my mournful rhymes,
But ring the fuller minstrel in.

Ring out false pride in place and blood,
The civic slander and the spite;
Ring in the love of truth and right,
Ring in the common love of good.

Ring out old shapes of foul disease;
Ring out the narrowing lust of gold;
Ring out the thousand wars of old,
Ring in the thousand years of peace.

Ring in the valiant man and free,
The larger heart, the kindlier hand;
Ring out the darkness of the land,
Ring in the Christ that is to be.

CVII

It is the day when he was born,
A bitter day that early sank
Behind a purple-frosty bank
Of vapour, leaving night forlorn.

The time admits not flowers or leaves
To deck the banquet. Fiercely flies
The blast of North and East, and ice
Makes daggers at the sharpen'd eaves,

And bristles all the brakes and thorns
To yon hard crescent, as she hangs
Above the wood which grides and clangs
Its leafless ribs and iron horns

Together, in the drifts that pass
To darken on the rolling brine
That breaks the coast. But fetch the wine,
Arrange the board and brim the glass;

Bring in great logs and let them lie,
To make a solid core of heat;
Be cheerful-minded, talk and treat
Of all things ev'n as he were by;

We keep the day. With festal cheer,
With books and music, surely we
Will drink to him, whate'er he be,
And sing the songs he loved to hear.

CVIII

I will not shut me from my kind,
And, lest I stiffen into stone,
I will not eat my heart alone,
Nor feed with sighs a passing wind:

What profit lies in barren faith,
And vacant yearning, tho' with might
To scale the heaven's highest height,
Or dive below the wells of Death?

What find I in the highest place,
But mine own phantom chanting hymns?
And on the depths of death there swims
The reflex of a human face.

I'll rather take what fruit may be
Of sorrow under human skies:
'Tis held that sorrow makes us wise,
Whatever wisdom sleep with thee.

CIX

Heart-affluence in discursive talk
From household fountains never dry;
The critic clearness of an eye,
That saw thro' all the Muses' walk;

Seraphic intellect and force
To seize and throw the doubts of man;
Impassion'd logic, which outran
The hearer in its fiery course;

High nature amorous of the good,
But touch'd with no ascetic gloom;
And passion pure in snowy bloom
Thro' all the years of April blood;

A love of freedom rarely felt,
Of freedom in her regal seat
Of England; not the schoolboy heat,
The blind hysterics of the Celt;

And manhood fused with female grace
In such a sort, the child would twine
A trustful hand, unask'd, in thine,
And find his comfort in thy face;

All these have been, and thee mine eyes
Have look'd on: if they look'd in vain,
My shame is greater who remain,
Nor let thy wisdom make me wise.

CX

Thy converse drew us with delight,
The men of rathe and riper years:
The feeble soul, a haunt of fears,
Forgot his weakness in thy sight.

On thee the loyal-hearted hung,
The proud was half disarm'd of pride,
Nor cared the serpent at thy side
To flicker with his double tongue.

The stern were mild when thou wert by,
The flippant put himself to school
And heard thee, and the brazen fool
Was soften'd, and he knew not why;

While I, thy nearest, sat apart,
And felt thy triumph was as mine;
And loved them more, that they were thine,
The graceful tact, the Christian art;

Nor mine the sweetness or the skill,
But mine the love that will not tire,
And, born of love, the vague desire
That spurs an imitative will.

CXI

The churl in spirit, up or down
Along the scale of ranks, thro' all,
To him who grasps a golden ball,
By blood a king, at heart a clown;

The churl in spirit, howe'er he veil
His want in forms for fashion's sake,
Will let his coltish nature break
At seasons thro' the gilded pale:

For who can always act? but he,
To whom a thousand memories call,
Not being less but more than all
The gentleness he seem'd to be,

Best seem'd the thing he was, and join'd
Each office of the social hour
To noble manners, as the flower
And native growth of noble mind;

Nor ever narrowness or spite,
Or villain fancy fleeting by,
Drew in the expression of an eye,
Where God and Nature met in light;

And thus he bore without abuse
The grand old name of gentleman,
Defamed by every charlatan,
And soil'd with all ignoble use.

States of perfection

CXII

High wisdom holds my wisdom less,
That I, who gaze with temperate eyes
On glorious insufficiencies,
Set light by narrower perfectness.

But thou, that fillest all the room
Of all my love, art reason why
I seem to cast a careless eye
On souls, the lesser lords of doom.

For what wert thou? some novel power
Sprang up for ever at a touch,
And hope could never hope too much,
In watching thee from hour to hour,

Large elements in order brought,
And tracts of calm from tempest made,
And world-wide fluctuation sway'd
In vassal tides that follow'd thought.

CXIII

'Tis held that sorrow makes us wise;
Yet how much wisdom sleeps with thee
Which not alone had guided me,
But served the seasons that may rise;

For can I doubt, who knew thee keen
In intellect, with force and skill
To strive, to fashion, to fulfil—
I doubt not what thou wouldst have been:

A life in civic action warm,
A soul on highest mission sent,
A potent voice of Parliament,
A pillar steadfast in the storm,

Should licensed boldness gather force,
Becoming, when the time has birth,
A lever to uplift the earth
And roll it in another course,

With thousand shocks that come and go,
With agonies, with energies,
With overthrowings, and with cries,
And undulations to and fro.

CXIV

Who loves not Knowledge? Who shall rail
Against her beauty? May she mix
With men and prosper! Who shall fix
Her pillars? Let her work prevail.

But on her forehead sits a fire:
She sets her forward countenance
And leaps into the future chance,
Submitting all things to desire.

Half-grown as yet, a child, and vain—
She cannot fight the fear of death.
What is she, cut from love and faith,
But some wild Pallas from the brain

Of Demons? fiery-hot to burst
All barriers in her onward race
For power. Let her know her place;
She is the second, not the first.

A higher hand must make her mild,
If all be not in vain; and guide
Her footsteps, moving side by side
With wisdom, like the younger child:

For she is earthly of the mind,
But Wisdom heavenly of the soul.
O, friend, who camest to thy goal
So early, leaving me behind,

I would the great world grew like thee,
Who grewest not alone in power
And knowledge, but by year and hour
In reverence and in charity.

CXV

Now fades the last long streak of snow,
Now burgeons every maze of quick
About the flowering squares, and thick
By ashen roots the violets blow.

Now rings the woodland loud and long,
The distance takes a lovelier hue,
And drown'd in yonder living blue
The lark becomes a sightless song.

Now dance the lights on lawn and lea,
The flocks are whiter down the vale,
And milkier every milky sail
On winding stream or distant sea;

Where now the seamew pipes, or dives
In yonder greening gleam, and fly
The happy birds, that change their sky
To build and brood; that live their lives

From land to land; and in my breast
Spring wakens too; and my regret
Becomes an April violet,
And buds and blossoms like the rest.

CXVI

Is it, then, regret for buried time
That keenlier in sweet April wakes,
And meets the year, and gives and takes
The colours of the crescent prime?

Not all: the songs, the stirring air,
The life re-orient out of dust,
Cry thro' the sense to hearten trust
In that which made the world so fair.

Not all regret: the face will shine
Upon me, while I muse alone;
And that dear voice, I once have known,
Still speak to me of me and mine:

Yet less of sorrow lives in me
For days of happy commune dead;
Less yearning for the friendship fled,
Than some strong bond which is to be.

CXVII

O days and hours, your work is this
To hold me from my proper place,
A little while from his embrace,
For fuller gain of after bliss:

That out of distance might ensue
Desire of nearness doubly sweet;
And unto meeting when we meet,
Delight a hundredfold accrue,

For every grain of sand that runs,
And every span of shade that steals,
And every kiss of toothed wheels,
And all the courses of the suns.

CXVIII

Contemplate all this work of Time,
The giant labouring in his youth;
Nor dream of human love and truth,
As dying Nature's earth and lime;

But trust that those we call the dead
Are breathers of an ampler day
For ever nobler ends. They say,
The solid earth whereon we tread

In tracts of fluent heat began,
And grew to seeming-random forms,
The seeming prey of cyclic storms,
Till at the last arose the man;

Who throve and branch'd from clime to clime,
The herald of a higher race,
And of himself in higher place,
If so he type this work of time

Within himself, from more to more;
Or, crown'd with attributes of woe
Like glories, move his course, and show
That life is not as idle ore,

But iron dug from central gloom,
And heated hot with burning fears,
And dipt in baths of hissing tears,
And batter'd with the shocks of doom

To shape and use. Arise and fly
The reeling Faun, the sensual feast;
Move upward, working out the beast,
And let the ape and tiger die.

CXIX

Doors, where my heart was used to beat
So quickly, not as one that weeps
I come once more; the city sleeps;
I smell the meadow in the street;

I hear a chirp of birds; I see
Betwixt the black fronts long-withdrawn
A light-blue lane of early dawn,
And think of early days and thee,

And bless thee, for thy lips are bland,
And bright the friendship of thine eye;
And in my thoughts with scarce a sigh
I take the pressure of thine hand.

CXX

I trust I have not wasted breath:
I think we are not wholly brain,
Magnetic mockeries; not in vain,
Like Paul with beasts, I fought with Death;

Not only cunning casts in clay:
Let Science prove we are, and then
What matters Science unto men,
At least to me? I would not stay.

Let him, the wiser man who springs
Hereafter, up from childhood shape
His action like the greater ape,
But I was *born* to other things.

CXXI

Sad Hesper o'er the buried sun
And ready, thou, to die with him,
Thou watchest all things ever dim
And dimmer, and a glory done:

The team is loosen'd from the wain,
The boat is drawn upon the shore;
Thou listenest to the closing door,
And life is darken'd in the brain.

Bright Phosphor, fresher for the night,
By thee the world's great work is heard
Beginning, and the wakeful bird;
Behind thee comes the greater light:

The market boat is on the stream,
And voices hail it from the brink;
Thou hear'st the village hammer clink,
And see's the moving of the team.

Sweet Hesper-Phosphor, double name
For what is one, the first, the last,
Thou, like my present and my past,
Thy place is changed; thou art the same.

CXXII

Oh, wast thou with me, dearest, then,
While I rose up against my doom,
And yearn'd to burst the folded gloom,
To bare the eternal Heavens again,

To feel once more, in placid awe,
The strong imagination roll
A sphere of stars about my soul,
In all her motion one with law;

If thou wert with me, and the grave
Divide us not, be with me now,
And enter in at breast and brow,
Till all my blood, a fuller wave,

Be quicken'd with a livelier breath,
And like an inconsiderate boy,
As in the former flash of joy,
I slip the thoughts of life and death;

And all the breeze of Fancy blows,
And every dew-drop paints a bow,
The wizard lightnings deeply glow,
And every thought breaks out a rose.

CXXIII

There rolls the deep where grew the tree.
O earth, what changes hast thou seen!
There where the long street roars, hath been
The stillness of the central sea.

The hills are shadows, and they flow
From form to form, and nothing stands;
They melt like mist, the solid lands,
Like clouds they shape themselves and go.

But in my spirit will I dwell,
And dream my dream, and hold it true;
For tho' my lips may breathe adieu,
I cannot think the thing farewell.

CXXIV

That which we dare invoke to bless;
Our dearest faith; our ghastliest doubt,
He, They, One, All; within, without;
The Power in darkness whom we guess;

I found Him not in world or sun,
Or eagle's wing, or insect's eye;
Nor thro' the questions men may try,
The petty cobwebs we have spun:

If e'er when faith had fall'n asleep,
I heard a voice 'believe no more'
And heard an ever-breaking shore
That tumbled in the Godless deep;

A warmth within the breast would melt
The freezing reason's colder part,
And like a man in wrath the heart
Stood up and answer'd 'I have felt.'

No, like a child in doubt and fear:
But that blind clamour made me wise;
Then was I as a child that cries,
But, crying, knows his father near;

And what I am beheld again
What is, and no man understands;
And out of darkness came the hands
That reach thro' nature, moulding men.

CXXV

Whatever I have said or sung,
Some bitter notes my harp would give,
Yea, tho' there often seem'd to live
A contradiction on the tongue,

Yet Hope had never lost her youth;
She did but look through dimmer eyes;
Or Love but play'd with gracious lies,
Because he felt so fix'd in truth:

And if the song were full of care,
He breathed the spirit of the song;
And if the words were sweet and strong
He set his royal signet there;

Abiding with me till I sail
To seek thee on the mystic deeps,
And this electric force, that keeps
A thousand pulses dancing, fail.

CXXVI

Love is and was my Lord and King,
And in his presence I attend
To hear the tidings of my friend,
Which every hour his couriers bring.

Love is and was my King and Lord,
And will be, tho' as yet I keep
Within his court on earth, and sleep
Encompass'd by his faithful guard,

And hear at times a sentinel
Who moves about from place to place,
And whispers to the worlds of space,
In the deep night, that all is well.

CXXVII

And all is well, tho' faith and form
Be sunder'd in the night of fear;
Well roars the storm to those that hear
A deeper voice across the storm,

Proclaiming social truth shall spread,
And justice, ev'n tho' thrice again
The red fool-fury of the Seine
Should pile her barricades with dead.

But ill for him that wears a crown,
And him, the lazar, in his rags:
They tremble, the sustaining crags;
The spires of ice are toppled down,

And molten up, and roar in flood;
The fortress crashes from on high,
The brute earth lightens to the sky,
And the great Æon sinks in blood,

And compass'd by the fires of Hell;
While thou, dear spirit, happy star,
O'erlook'st the tumult from afar,
And smilest, knowing all is well.

CXXVIII

The love that rose on stronger wings,
Unpalsied when he met with Death,
Is comrade of the lesser faith
That sees the course of human things.

No doubt vast eddies in the flood
Of onward time shall yet be made,
And throned races may degrade;
Yet O ye mysteries of good,

Wild Hours that fly with Hope and Fear,
If all your office had to do
With old results that look like new;
If this were all your mission here,

To draw, to sheathe a useless sword,
To fool the crowd with glorious lies,
To cleave a creed in sects and cries,
To change the bearing of a word,

To shift an arbitrary power,
To cramp the student at his desk,
To make old bareness picturesque
And tuft with grass a feudal tower;

Why then my scorn might well descend
On you and yours. I see in part
That all, as in some piece of art,
Is toil coöperant to an end.

CXXIX

Dear friend, far off, my lost desire,
So far, so near in woe and weal;
O loved the most, when most I feel
There is a lower and a higher;

Known and unknown; human, divine;
Sweet human hand and lips and eye;
Dear heavenly friend that canst not die,
Mine, mine, for ever, ever mine;

Strange friend, past, present, and to be;
Loved deeplier, darklier understood;
Behold, I dream a dream of good,
And mingle all the world with thee.

CXXX

Thy voice is on the rolling air;
I hear thee where the waters run;
Thou standest in the rising sun,
And in the setting thou art fair.

What art thou then? I cannot guess;
But tho' I seem in star and flower
To feel thee some diffusive power,
I do not therefore love thee less:

My love involves the love before;
My love is vaster passion now;
Tho' mix'd with God and Nature thou,
I seem to love thee more and more.

Far off thou art, but ever nigh;
I have thee still, and I rejoice;
I prosper, circled with thy voice;
I shall not lose thee tho' I die.

CXXXI

O living will that shalt endure
When all that seems shall suffer shock,
Rise in the spiritual rock,
Flow thro' our deeds and make them pure,

That we may lift from out of dust
A voice as unto him that hears,
A cry above the conquer'd years
To one that with us works, and trust,

With faith that comes of self-control,
The truths that never can be proved
Until we close with all we loved,
And all we flow from, soul in soul.

O true and tried, so well and long,
Demand not thou a marriage lay;
In that it is thy marriage day
Is music more than any song.

Nor have I felt so much of bliss
Since first he told me that he loved
A daughter of our house; nor proved
Since that dark day a day like this;

Tho' I since then have number'd o'er
Some thrice three years: they went and came,
Remade the blood and changed the frame,
And yet is love not less, but more;

No longer caring to embalm
In dying songs a dead regret,
But like a statue solid-set,
And moulded in colossal calm.

Regret is dead, but love is more
Than in the summers that are flown,
For I myself with these have grown
To something greater than before;

Which makes appear the songs I made
As echoes out of weaker times,
As half but idle brawling rhymes,
The sport of random sun and shade.

But where is she, the bridal flower,
That must be made a wife ere noon?
She enters, glowing like the moon
Of Eden on its bridal bower:

On me she bends her blissful eyes
And then on thee; they meet thy look
And brighten like the star that shook
Betwixt the palms of paradise.

O when her life was yet in bud,
He too foretold the perfect rose.
For thee she grew, for thee she grows
For ever, and as fair as good.

And thou art worthy; full of power;
As gentle; liberal-minded, great,
Consistent; wearing all that weight
Of learning lightly like a flower.

But now set out: the noon is near,
And I must give away the bride;
She fears not, or with thee beside
And me behind her, will not fear.

For I that danced her on my knee,
That watch'd her on her nurse's arm,
That shielded all her life from harm
At last must part with her to thee;

Now waiting to be made a wife,
Her feet, my darling, on the dead;
Their pensive tablets round her head,
And the most living words of life

Breathed in her ear. The ring is on,
The 'wilt thou' answer'd, and again
The 'wilt thou' ask'd, till out of twain
Her sweet 'I will' has made you one.

Now sign your names, which shall be read,
Mute symbols of a joyful morn,
By village eyes as yet unborn;
The names are sign'd, and overhead

Begins the clash and clang that tells
The joy to every wandering breeze;
The blind wall rocks, and on the trees
The dead leaf trembles to the bells.

O happy hour, and happier hours
Await them. Many a merry face
Salutes them—maidens of the place,
That pelt us in the porch with flowers.

O happy hour, behold the bride
With him to whom her hand I gave.
They leave the porch, they pass the grave
That has to-day its sunny side.

To-day the grave is bright for me,
For them the light of life increased,
Who stay to share the morning feast,
Who rest to-night beside the sea.

Let all my genial spirits advance
To meet and greet a whiter sun;
My drooping memory will not shun
The foaming grape of eastern France.

It circles round, and fancy plays,
And hearts are warm'd and faces bloom,
As drinking health to bride and groom
We wish them store of happy days.

Nor count me all to blame if I
Conjecture of a stiller guest,
Perchance, perchance, among the rest,
And, tho' in silence, wishing joy.

But they must go, the time draws on,
And those white-favour'd horses wait;
They rise, but linger; it is late;
Farewell, we kiss, and they are gone.

A shade falls on us like the dark
From little cloudlets on the grass,
But sweeps away as out we pass
To range the woods, to roam the park,

Discussing how their courtship grew,
And talk of others that are wed,
And how she look'd, and what he said,
And back we come at fall of dew.

Again the feast, the speech, the glee,
The shade of passing thought, the wealth
Of words and wit, the double health,
The crowning cup, the three-times-three,

And last the dance;—till I retire:
Dumb is that tower which spake so loud,
And high in heaven the streaming cloud,
And on the downs a rising fire:

And rise, O moon, from yonder down,
Till over down and over dale
All night the shining vapour sail
And pass the silent-lighted town,

The white-faced halls, the glancing rills,
And catch at every mountain head,
And o'er the friths that branch and spread
Their sleeping silver thro' the hills;

And touch with shade the bridal doors,
With tender gloom the roof, the wall;
And breaking let the splendour fall
To spangle all the happy shores

By which they rest, and ocean sounds,
And, star and system rolling past,
A soul shall draw from out the vast
And strike his being into bounds,

And, moved thro' life of lower phase,
Result in man, be born and think,
And act and love, a closer link
Betwixt us and the crowning race

Of those that, eye to eye, shall look
On knowledge; under whose command
Is Earth and Earth's, and in their hand
Is Nature like an open book;

No longer half-akin to brute,
For all we thought and loved and did,
And hoped, and suffer'd, is but seed
Of what in them is flower and fruit;

Whereof the man, that with me trod
This planet, was a noble type
Appearing ere the times were ripe,
That friend of mine who lives in God,

That God, which ever lives and loves,
One God, one law, one element,
And one far-off divine event,
To which the whole creation moves.

[1850]

THE EAGLE

FRAGMENT

He clasps the crag with crooked hands;
Close to the sun in lonely lands,
Ring'd with the azure world, he stands.

The wrinkled sea beneath him crawls;
He watches from his mountain walls,
And like a thunderbolt he falls.

[1851]

COME NOT, WHEN I AM DEAD

Come not, when I am dead,
To drop thy foolish tears upon my grave,
To trample round my fallen head,
And vex the unhappy dust thou wouldst not save.
There let the wind sweep and the plover cry;
But thou, go by.

Child, if it were thine error or thy crime
I care no longer, being all unblest:
Wed whom thou wilt, but I am sick of Time,
And I desire to rest.
Pass on, weak heart, and leave me where I lie:
Go by, go by.

[1851]

ODE ON THE DEATH OF THE DUKE OF WELLINGTON

PUBLISHED IN 1852

I

Bury the Great Duke
With an empire's lamentation,
Let us bury the Great Duke
To the noise of the mourning of a mighty nation,
Mourning when their leaders fall,
Warriors carry the warrior's pall,
And sorrow darkens hamlet and hall.

II

Where shall we lay the man whom we deplore?
Here, in streaming London's central roar.
Let the sound of those he wrought for,
And the feet of those he fought for,
Echo round his bones for evermore.

III

Lead out the pageant: sad and slow,
As fits an universal woe,
Let the long long procession go,
And let the sorrowing crowd about it grow,
And let the mournful martial music blow;
The last great Englishman is low.

IV

Mourn, for to us he seems the last,
Remembering all his greatness in the Past.
No more in soldier fashion will he greet
With lifted hand the gazer in the street.
O friends, our chief state-oracle is mute:
Mourn for the man of long-enduring blood,
The statesman-warrior, moderate, resolute,
Whole in himself, a common good.
Mourn for the man of amplest influence,
Yet clearest of ambitious crime,
Our greatest yet with least pretence,
Great in council and great in war,
Foremost captain of his time,
Rich in saving common-sense,
And, as the greatest only are,
In his simplicity sublime.
O good gray head which all men knew,
O voice from which their omens all men drew,
O iron nerve to true occasion true,
O fall'n at length that tower of strength
Which stood four-square to all the winds that blew!
Such was he whom we deplore.
The long self-sacrifice of life is o'er.
The great World-victor's victor will be seen no more.

V

All is over and done:
Render thanks to the Giver,
England, for thy son.
Let the bell be toll'd.
Render thanks to the Giver,
And render him to the mould.
Under the cross of gold
That shines over city and river,
There he shall rest for ever
Among the wise and the bold.
Let the bell be toll'd:
And a reverent people behold
The towering car, the sable steeds:
Bright let it be with its blazon'd deeds,
Dark in its funeral fold.
Let the bell be toll'd:
And a deeper knell in the heart be knoll'd;
And the sound of the sorrowing anthem roll'd
Thro' the dome of the golden cross;
And the volleying cannon thunder his loss;
He knew their voices of old.
For many a time in many a clime
His captain's-ear has heard them boom
Bellowing victory, bellowing doom:
When he with those deep voices wrought,
Guarding realms and kings from shame;
With those deep voices our dead captain taught
The tyrant, and asserts his claim
In that dread sound to the great name,
Which he has worn so pure of blame,
In praise and in dispraise the same,
A man of well-attemper'd frame.
O civic muse, to such a name,
To such a name for ages long,
To such a name,
Preserve a broad approach of fame,
And ever-echoing avenues of song.

VI

Who is he that cometh, like an honour'd guest,
With banner and with music, with soldier and with priest,
With a nation weeping, and breaking on my rest?
Mighty Seaman, this is he
Was great by land as thou by sea.
Thine island loves thee well, thou famous man,
The greatest sailor since our world began.
Now, to the roll of muffled drums,
To thee the greatest soldier comes;
For this is he
Was great by land as thou by sea;
His foes were thine; he kept us free:
O give him welcome, this is he
Worthy of our gorgeous rites,
And worthy to be laid by thee;

For this is England's greatest son,
He that gain'd a hundred fights,
Nor ever lost an English gun;
This is he that far away
Against the myriads of Assaye
Clash'd with his fiery few and won;
And underneath another sun,
Warring on a later day,
Round affrighted Lisbon drew
The treble works, the vast designs
Of his labour'd rampart-lines,
Where he greatly stood at bay,
Whence he issued forth anew,
And ever great and greater grew,
Beating from the wasted vines
Back to France her banded swarms,
Back to France with countless blows,
Till o'er the hills her eagles flew
Beyond the Pyrenean pines,
Follow'd up in valley and glen
With blare of bugle, clamour of men,
Roll of cannon and clash of arms,
And England pouring on her foes.
Such a war had such a close.
Again their ravening eagle rose
In anger, wheel'd on Europe-shadowing wings,
And barking for the thrones of kings;
Till one that sought but Duty's iron crown
On that loud sabbath shook the spoiler down;
A day of onsets of despair!
Dash'd on every rocky square
Their surging charges foam'd themselves away;
Last, the Prussian trumpet blew;
Thro' the long-tormented air
Heaven flash'd a sudden jubilant ray,
And down we swept and charged and overthrew.
So great a soldier taught us there,
What long-enduring hearts could do
In that world-earthquake, Waterloo!
Mighty Seaman, tender and true,
And pure as he from taint of craven guile,
O saviour of the silver-coasted isle,
O shaker of the Baltic and the Nile,
If aught of things that here befall
Touch a spirit among things divine,
If love of country move thee there at all,
Be glad, because his bones are laid by thine!
And thro' the centuries let a people's voice
In full acclaim,
A people's voice,
The proof and echo of all human fame,
A people's voice, when they rejoice
At civic revel and pomp and game,
Attest their great commander's claim
With honour, honour, honour, honour to him,
Eternal honour to his name.

VII

A people's voice! we are a people yet.
Tho' all men else their nobler dreams forget,
Confused by brainless mobs and lawless Powers;
Thank Him who isled us here, and roughly set
His Briton in blown seas and storming showers,
We have a voice, with which to pay the debt
Of boundless love and reverence and regret
To those great men who fought, and kept it ours.
And keep it ours, O God, from brute control;
O Statesmen, guard us, guard the eye, the soul
Of Europe, keep our noble England whole,
And save the one true seed of freedom sown
Betwixt a people and their ancient throne,
That sober freedom out of which there springs
Our loyal passion for our temperate kings;
For, saving that, ye help to save mankind
Till public wrong be crumbled into dust,
And drill the raw world for the march of mind,
Till crowds at length be sane and crowns be just.
But wink no more in slothful overtrust.
Remember him who led your hosts;
He bade you guard the sacred coasts.
Your cannons moulder on the seaward wall;
His voice is silent in your council-hall
For ever; and whatever tempests lour
For ever silent; even if they broke
In thunder, silent; yet remember all
He spoke among you, and the Man who spoke;
Who never sold the truth to serve the hour,

Nor palter'd with Eternal God for power;
Who let the turbid streams of rumour flow
Thro' either babbling world of high and low;
Whose life was work, whose language rife
With rugged maxims hewn from life;
Who never spoke against a foe;
Whose eighty winters freeze with one rebuke
All great self-seekers trampling on the right:
Truth-teller was our England's Alfred named;
Truth-lover was our English Duke;
Whatever record leap to light
He never shall be shamed.

VIII

Lo, the leader in these glorious wars
Now to glorious burial slowly borne,
Follow'd by the brave of other lands,
He, on whom from both her open hands
Lavish Honour shower'd all her stars,
And affluent Fortune emptied all her horn.
Yea, let all good things await
Him who cares not to be great,
But as he saves or serves the state.
Not once or twice in our rough island-story,
The path of duty was the way to glory:
He that walks it, only thirsting
For the right, and learns to deaden
Love of self, before his journey closes,
He shall find the stubborn thistle bursting
Into glossy purples, which outredden
All voluptuous garden-roses.
Not once or twice in our fair island-story,
The path of duty was the way to glory:
He, that ever following her commands,
On with toil of heart and knees and hands,
Thro' the long gorge to the far light has won
His path upward, and prevail'd,
Shall find the toppling crags of Duty scaled
Are close upon the shining table-lands
To which our God Himself is moon and sun.
Such was he: his work is done.
But while the races of mankind endure,
Let his great example stand
Colossal, seen of every land,
And keep the soldier firm, the statesman pure:
Till in all lands and thro' all human story
The path of duty be the way to glory:
And let the land whose hearths he saved from shame
For many and many an age proclaim
At civic revel and pomp and game,
And when the long-illumined cities flame,
Their ever-loyal iron leader's fame,
With honour, honour, honour, honour to him,
Eternal honour to his name.

IX

Peace, his triumph will be sung
By some yet unmoulded tongue
Far on in summers that we shall not see:
Peace, it is a day of pain
For one about whose patriarchal knee
Late the little children clung:
O peace, it is a day of pain
For one, upon whose hand and heart and brain
Once the weight and fate of Europe hung.
Ours the pain, be his the gain!
More than is of man's degree
Must be with us, watching here
At this, our great solemnity.
Whom we see not we revere;
We revere, and we refrain
From talk of battles loud and vain,
And brawling memories all too free
For such a wise humility
As befits a solemn fane:
We revere, and while we hear
The tides of Music's golden sea
Setting toward eternity,
Uplifted high in heart and hope are we,
Until we doubt not that for one so true
There must be other nobler work to do
Than when he fought at Waterloo,
And Victor he must ever be.
For tho' the Giant Ages heave the hill
And break the shore, and evermore
Make and break, and work their will;
Tho' world on world in myriad myriads roll
Round us, each with different powers,
And other forms of life than ours,
What know we greater than the soul?
On God and Godlike men we build our trust.
Hush, the Dead March wails in the people's ears:

The dark crowd moves, and there are sobs and tears:
The black earth yawns: the mortal disappears;
Ashes to ashes, dust to dust;
He is gone who seem'd so great.—
Gone; but nothing can bereave him
Of the force he made his own
Being here, and we believe him
Something far advanced in State,
And that he wears a truer crown
Than any wreath that man can weave him.
Speak no more of his renown,
Lay your earthly fancies down,
And in the vast cathedral leave him.
God accept him, Christ receive him.

[1852]

MAUD; A MONODRAMA

PART I

I

I

I hate the dreadful hollow behind the little wood,
Its lips in the field above are dabbled with blood-red heath,
The red-ribb'd ledges drip with a silent horror of blood,
And Echo there, whatever is ask'd her, answers 'Death.'

II

For there in the ghastly pit long since a body was found,
His who had given me life—O father! O God! was it well?—
Mangled, and flatten'd, and crush'd, and dinted into the ground:
There yet lies the rock that fell with him when he fell.

III

Did he fling himself down? who knows? for a vast speculation had fail'd,
And ever he mutter'd and madden'd, and ever wann'd with despair,
And out he walk'd when the wind like a broken worldling wail'd,
And the flying gold of the ruin'd woodlands drove thro' the air.

IV

I remember the time, for the roots of my hair were stirr'd
By a shuffled step, by a dead weight trail'd, by a whisper'd fright,
And my pulses closed their gates with a shock on my heart as I heard
The shrill-edged shriek of a mother divide the shuddering night.

V

Villainy somewhere! whose? One says, we are villains all.
Not he: his honest fame should at least by me be maintained:
But that old man, now lord of the broad estate and the Hall,
Dropt off gorged from a scheme that had left us flaccid and drain'd.

VI

Why do they prate of the blessings of Peace? we have made them a curse,
Pickpockets, each hand lusting for all that is not its own;
And lust of gain, in the spirit of Cain, is it better or worse
Than the heart of the citizen hissing in war on his own hearthstone?

VII

But these are the days of advance, the works of the men of mind,
When who but a fool would have faith in a tradesman's ware or his word?
Is it peace or war? Civil war, as I think, and that of a kind
The viler, as underhand, not openly bearing the sword.

VIII

Sooner or later I too may passively take the print
Of the golden age—why not? I have neither hope nor trust;
May make my heart as a millstone, set my face as a flint,
Cheat and be cheated, and die: who knows? we are ashes and dust.

IX

Peace sitting under her olive, and slurring the days gone by,
When the poor are hovell'd and hustled together, each sex, like swine.
When only the ledger lives, and when only not all men lie;
Peace in her vineyard—yes!—but a company forges the wine.

X

And the vitriol madness flushes up in the ruffian's head,
Till the filthy by-lane rings to the yell of the trampled wife,
And chalk and alum and plaster are sold to the poor for bread,
And the spirit of murder works in the very means of life,

XI

And Sleep must lie down arm'd, for the villainous centre-bits
Grind on the wakeful ear in the hush of the moonless nights,
While another is cheating the sick of a few last gasps, as he sits
To pestle a poison'd poison behind his crimson lights.

XII

When a Mammonite mother kills her babe for a burial fee,
And Timour-Mammon grins on a pile of children's bones,
Is it peace or war? better, war! loud war by land and by sea,
War with a thousand battles, and shaking a hundred thrones.

XIII

For I trust if an enemy's fleet came yonder round by the hill,
And the rushing battle-bolt sang from the three-decker out of the foam,
That the smooth-faced snubnosed rogue would leap from his counter and till,
And strike, if he could, were it but his cheating yardwand, home.—

XIV

What! am I raging alone as my father raged in his mood?
Must *I* too creep to the hollow and dash myself down and die
Rather than hold by the law that I made, nevermore to brood
On a horror of shatter'd limbs and a wretched swindler's lie?

XV

Would there be sorrow for *me?* there was *love* in the passionate shriek,
Love for the silent thing that had made false haste to the grave—
Wrapt in a cloak, as I saw him, and thought he would rise and speak
And rave at the lie and the liar, ah God, as he used to rave.

XVI

I am sick of the Hall and the hill, I am sick of the moor and the main.
Why should I stay? can a sweeter chance ever come to me here?
O, having the nerves of motion as well as the nerves of pain,
Were it not wise if I fled from the place and the pit and the fear?

XVII

Workmen up at the Hall!—they are coming back from abroad;
The dark old place will be gilt by the touch of a millionaire:
I have heard, I know not whence, of the singular beauty of Maud;
I play'd with the girl when a child; she promised then to be fair.

XVIII

Maud with her venturous climbings and tumbles and childish escapes,
Maud the delight of the village, the ringing joy of the Hall,
Maud with her sweet purse-mouth when my father dangled the grapes,
Maud the beloved of my mother, the moon-faced darling of all,—

XIX

What is she now? My dreams are bad. She may bring me a curse.
No, there is fatter game on the moor; she will let me alone.
Thanks, for the fiend best knows whether woman or man be the worse.
I will bury myself in myself, and the Devil may pipe to his own.

II

Long have I sigh'd for a calm: God grant I may find it at last!
It will never be broken by Maud, she has neither savour nor salt,
But a cold and clear-cut face, as I found when her carriage past,
Perfectly beautiful: let it be granted her: where is the fault?
All that I saw (for her eyes were downcast, not to be seen)
Faultily faultless, icily regular, splendidly null,
Dead perfection, no more; nothing more, if it had not been
For a chance of travel, a paleness, an hour's defect of the rose,
Or an underlip, you may call it a little too ripe, too full,
Or the least little delicate aquiline curve in a sensitive nose,
From which I escaped heart-free, with the least little touch of spleen.

III

Cold and clear-cut face, why come you so cruelly meek,
Breaking a slumber in which all spleenful folly was drown'd,
Pale with the golden beam of an eyelash dead on the cheek,
Passionless, pale, cold face, star-sweet on a gloom profound;
Womanlike, taking revenge too deep for a transient wrong
Done but in thought to your beauty, and ever as pale as before
Growing and fading and growing upon me without a sound,
Luminous, gemlike, ghostlike, deathlike, half the night long
Growing and fading and growing, till I could bear it no more,
But arose, and all by myself in my own dark garden ground,
Listening now to the tide in its broad-flung shipwrecking roar,
Now to the scream of a madden'd beach dragg'd down by the wave,
Walk'd in a wintry wind by a ghastly glimmer, and found
The shining daffodil dead, and Orion low in his grave.

IV

I

A million emeralds break from the ruby-budded lime
In the little grove where I sit—ah, wherefore cannot I be
Like things of the season gay, like the bountiful season bland,
When the far-off sail is blown by the breeze of a softer clime,
Half-lost in the liquid azure bloom of a crescent of sea,
The silent sapphire-spangled marriage ring of the land?

II

Below me, there, is the village, and looks how quiet and small!
And yet bubbles o'er like a city, with gossip, scandal, and spite;
And Jack on his ale-house bench has as many lies as a Czar;
And here on the landward side, by a red rock, glimmers the Hall;
And up in the high Hall-garden I see her pass like a light;
But sorrow seize me if ever that light be my leading star!

III

When have I bow'd to her father, the wrinkled head of the race?
I met her to-day with her brother, but not to her brother I bow'd:
I bow'd to his lady-sister as she rode by on the moor;
But the fire of a foolish pride flash'd over her beautiful face.
O child, you wrong your beauty, believe it, in being so proud;
Your father has wealth well-gotten, and I am nameless and poor.

IV

I keep but a man and a maid, ever ready to slander and steal;
I know it, and smile a hard-set smile, like a stoic, or like
A wiser epicurean, and let the world have its way:
For nature is one with rapine, a harm no preacher can heal;
The Mayfly is torn by the swallow, the sparrow spear'd by the shrike,
And the whole little wood where I sit is a world of plunder and prey.

V

We are puppets, Man in his pride, and Beauty fair in her flower;
Do we move ourselves, or are moved by an unseen hand at a game
That pushes us off from the board, and others ever succeed?
Ah yet, we cannot be kind to each other here for an hour;
We whisper, and hint, and chuckle, and grin at a brother's shame;
However we brave it out, we men are a little breed.

VI

A monstrous eft was of old the Lord and Master of Earth,
For him did his high sun flame, and his river billowing ran,
And he felt himself in his force to be Nature's crowning race.
As nine months go to the shaping an infant ripe for his birth,
So many a million of ages have gone to the making of man:
He now is first, but is he the last? is he not too base?

VII

The man of science himself is fonder of glory, and vain,
An eye well-practised in nature, a spirit bounded and poor;
The passionate heart of the poet is whirl'd into folly and vice.

I would not marvel at either, but keep a temperate brain;
For not to desire or admire, if a man could learn it, were more
Than to walk all day like the sultan of old in a garden of spice.

VIII

For the drift of the Maker is dark, an Isis hid by the veil.
Who knows the ways of the world, how God will bring them about?
Our planet is one, the suns are many, the world is wide.
Shall I weep if a Poland fall? shall I shriek if a Hungary fail?
Or an infant civilisation be ruled with rod or with knout?
I have not made the world, and He that made it will guide.

IX

Be mine a philosopher's life in the quiet woodland ways,
Where if I cannot be gay let a passionless peace be my lot,
Far-off from the clamour of liars belied in the hubbub of lies;
From the long-neck'd geese of the world that are ever hissing dispraise
Because their natures are little, and, whether he heed it or not,
Where each man walks with his head in a cloud of poisonous flies.

X

And most of all would I flee from the cruel madness of love,
The honey of poison-flowers and all the measureless ill.
Ah Maud, you milkwhite fawn, you are all unmeet for a wife.
Your mother is mute in her grave as her image in marble above;
Your father is ever in London, you wander about at your will;
You have but fed on the roses and lain in the lilies of life.

V

I

A voice by the cedar tree
In the meadow under the Hall!
She is singing an air that is known to me,
A passionate ballad gallant and gay,
A martial song like a trumpet's call!
Singing alone in the morning of life,
In the happy morning of life and of May,
Singing of men that in battle array,
Ready in heart and ready in hand,
March with banner and bugle and fife
To the death, for their native land.

II

Maud with her exquisite face,
And wild voice pealing up to the sunny sky,
And feet like sunny gems on an English green,
Maud in the light of her youth and her grace,
Singing of Death, and of Honour that cannot die,
Till I well could weep for a time so sordid and mean,
And myself so languid and base.

III

Silence, beautiful voice!
Be still, for you only trouble the mind
With a joy in which I cannot rejoice,
A glory I shall not find.
Still! I will hear you no more,
For your sweetness hardly leaves me a choice
But to move to the meadow and fall before
Her feet on the meadow grass, and adore,
Not her, who is neither courtly nor kind,
Not her, not her, but a voice.

VI

I

Morning arises stormy and pale,
No sun, but a wannish glare
In fold upon fold of hueless cloud,
And the budded peaks of the wood are bow'd

Caught and cuff'd by the gale:
I had fancied it would be fair.

II

Whom but Maud should I meet
Last night, when the sunset burn'd
On the blossom'd gable-ends
At the head of the village street,
Whom but Maud should I meet?
And she touch'd my hand with a smile so sweet,
She made me divine amends
For a courtesy not return'd.

III

And thus a delicate spark
Of glowing and growing light
Thro' the livelong hours of the dark
Kept itself warm in the heart of my dreams,
Ready to burst in a colour'd flame;
Till at last when the morning came
In a cloud, it faded, and seems
But an ashen-gray delight.

IV

What if with her sunny hair,
And smile as sunny as cold,
She meant to weave me a snare
Of some coquettish deceit,
Cleopatra-like as of old
To entangle me when we met,
To have her lion roll in a silken net
And fawn at a victor's feet.

V

Ah, what shall I be at fifty
Should Nature keep me alive,
If I find the world so bitter
When I am but twenty-five?
Yet, if she were not a cheat,
If Maud were all that she seem'd,
And her smile were all that I dream'd,
Then the world were not so bitter
But a smile could make it sweet.

VI

What if tho' her eye seem'd full
Of a kind intent to me,
What if that dandy-despot, he,
That jewell'd mass of millinery,
That oil'd and curl'd Assyrian Bull
Smelling of musk and of insolence,
Her brother, from whom I keep aloof,
Who wants the finer politic sense
To mask, tho' but in his own behoof,
With a glassy smile his brutal scorn—
What if he had told her yestermorn
How prettily for his own sweet sake
A face of tenderness might be feign'd,
And a moist mirage in desert eyes,
That so, when the rotten hustings shake
In another month to his brazen lies,
A wretched vote may be gain'd.

VII

For a raven ever croaks, at my side,
Keep watch and ward, keep watch and ward,
Or thou wilt prove their tool.
Yea, too, myself from myself I guard,
For often a man's own angry pride
Is cap and bells for a fool.

VIII

Perhaps the smile and tender tone
Came out of her pitying womanhood,
For am I not, am I not, here alone
So many a summer since she died,
My mother, who was so gentle and good?
Living alone in an empty house,
Here half-hid in the gleaming wood,
Where I hear the dead at midday moan,
And the shrieking rush of the wainscot mouse,
And my own sad name in corners cried,
When the shiver of dancing leaves is thrown
About its echoing chambers wide,
Till a morbid hate and horror have grown
Of a world in which I have hardly mixt,
And a morbid eating lichen fixt
On a heart half-turn'd to stone.

IX

O heart of stone, are you flesh, and caught
By that you swore to withstand?
For what was it else within me wrought
But, I fear, the new strong wine of love,
That made my tongue so stammer and trip
When I saw the treasured splendour, her hand,
Come sliding out of her sacred glove,
And the sunlight broke from her lip?

X

I have play'd with her when a child;
She remembers it now we meet.
Ah well, well, well, I *may* be beguiled
By some coquettish deceit.
Yet, if she were not a cheat,
If Maud were all that she seem'd,
And her smile had all that I dream'd,
Then the world were not so bitter
But a smile could make it sweet.

VII

I

Did I hear it half in a doze
  Long since, I know not where?
Did I dream it an hour ago,
  When asleep in this arm-chair?

II

Men were drinking together,
  Drinking and talking of me;
'Well, if it prove a girl, the boy
  Will have plenty: so let it be.'

III

Is it an echo of something
  Read with a boy's delight,
Viziers nodding together
  In some Arabian night?

IV

Strange, that I hear two men,
  Somewhere, talking of me;
'Well, if it prove a girl, my boy
  Will have plenty: so let it be.'

VIII

She came to the village church,
And sat by a pillar alone;
An angel watching an urn
Wept over her, carved in stone;
And once, but once, she lifted her eyes,
And suddenly, sweetly, strangely blush'd
To find they were met by my own;
And suddenly, sweetly, my heart beat stronger
And thicker, until I heard no longer
The snowy-banded, dilettante,
Delicate-handed priest intone;
And thought, is it pride, and mused and sigh'd
'No surely, now it cannot be pride.'

IX

I was walking a mile,
More than a mile from the shore.
The sun look'd out with a smile
Betwixt the cloud and the moor
And riding at set of day
Over the dark moor land,
Rapidly riding far away,
She waved to me with her hand.
There were two at her side,
Something flash'd in the sun,
Down by the hill I saw them ride.
In a moment they were gone:
Like a sudden spark
Struck vainly in the night,
Then returns the dark
With no more hope of light.

X

I

Sick, am I sick of a jealous dread?
Was not one of the two at her side
This new-made lord, whose splendour plucks
The slavish hat from the villager's head?
Whose old grandfather has lately died,
Gone to a blacker pit, for whom
Grimy nakedness dragging his trucks
And laying his trams in a poison'd gloom
Wrought, till he crept from a gutted mine
Master of half a servile shire,
And left his coal all turn'd into gold
To a grandson, first of his noble line,
Rich in the grace all women desire,
Strong in the power that all men adore,
And simper and set their voices lower,
And soften as if to a girl, and hold
Awe-stricken breaths at a work divine,
Seeing his gewgaw castle shine,
New as his title, built last year,
There amid perky larches and pine,
And over the sullen-purple moor
(Look at it) pricking a cockney ear.

II

What, has he found my jewel out?
For one of the two that rode at her side
Bound for the Hall, I am sure was he:
Bound for the Hall, and I think for a bride.
Blithe would her brother's acceptance be.
Maud could be gracious too, no doubt

To a lord, a captain, a padded shape,
A bought commission, a waxen face,
A rabbit mouth that is ever agape—
Bought? what is it he cannot buy?
And therefore splenetic, personal, base,
A wounded thing with a rancorous cry,
At war with myself and a wretched race,
Sick, sick to the heart of life, am I.

III

Last week came one to the county town,
To preach our poor little army down,
And play the game of the despot kings,
Tho' the state has done it and thrice as well:
This broad-brimm'd hawker of holy things,
Whose ear is cramm'd with his cotton, and rings
Even in dreams to the chink of his pence,
This huckster put down war! can he tell
Whether war be a cause or a consequence?
Put down the passions that make earth Hell!
Down with ambition, avarice, pride,
Jealousy, down! cut off from the mind
The bitter springs of anger and fear;
Down too, down at your own fireside,
With the evil tongue and the evil ear,
For each is at war with mankind.

IV

I wish I could hear again
The chivalrous battle-song
That she warbled alone in her joy!
I might persuade myself then
She would not do herself this great wrong,
To take a wanton dissolute boy
For a man and leader of men.

V

Ah God, for a man with heart, head, hand,
Like some of the simple great ones gone
For ever and ever by,
One still strong man in a blatant land,
Whatever they call him, what care I,
Aristocrat, democrat, autocrat—one
Who can rule and dare not lie.

VI

And ah for a man to arise in me,
That the man I am may cease to be!

XI

I

O let the solid ground
Not fail beneath my feet
Before my life has found
What some have found so sweet;
Then let come what come may,
What matter if I go mad,
I shall have had my day.

II

Let the sweet heavens endure,
Not close and darken above me
Before I am quite quite sure
That there is one to love me;
Then let come what come may
To a life that has been so sad,
I shall have had my day.

XII

I

Birds in the high Hall-garden
When twilight was falling,
Maud, Maud, Maud, Maud,
They were crying and calling.

II

Where was Maud? in our wood;
And I, who else, was with her,
Gathering woodland lilies,
Myriads blow together.

III

Birds in our wood sang
Ringing thro' the valleys,
Maud is here, here, here
In among the lilies.

IV

I kiss'd her slender hand,
She took the kiss sedately;
Maud is not seventeen,
But she is tall and stately.

V

I to cry out on pride
Who have won her favour!
O Maud were sure of Heaven
If lowliness could save her.

VI

I know the way she went
Home with her maiden posy,
For her feet have touch'd the meadows
And left the daisies rosy.

VII

Birds in the high Hall-garden
Were crying and calling to her,
Where is Maud, Maud, Maud?
One is come to woo her.

VIII

Look, a horse at the door,
And little King Charley snarling,
Go back, my lord, across the moor,
You are not her darling.

XIII

I

Scorn'd, to be scorn'd by one that I scorn,
Is that a matter to make me fret?
That a calamity hard to be borne?
Well, he may live to hate me yet.
Fool that I am to be vext with his pride!
I past him, I was crossing his lands;
He stood on the path a little aside;
His face, as I grant, in spite of spite,
Has a broad-blown comeliness, red and white,
And six feet two, as I think, he stands;
But his essences turn'd the live air sick,
And barbarous opulence jewel-thick
Sunn'd itself on his breast and his hands.

II

Who shall call me ungentle, unfair,
I long'd so heartily then and there
To give him the grasp of fellowship;
But while I past he was humming an air,
Stopt, and then with a riding whip
Leisurely tapping a glossy boot,
And curving a contumelious lip,
Gorgonised me from head to foot
With a stony British stare.

III

Why sits he here in his father's chair?
That old man never comes to his place:
Shall I believe him ashamed to be seen?
For only once, in the village street,
Last year, I caught a glimpse of his face,
A gray old wolf and a lean.
Scarcely, now, would I call him a cheat;
For then, perhaps, as a child of deceit,
She might by a true descent be untrue;
And Maud is as true as Maud is sweet:
Tho' I fancy her sweetness only due
To the sweeter blood by the other side;
Her mother has been a thing complete,
However she came to be so allied.
And fair without, faithful within,
Maud to him is nothing akin:
Some peculiar mystic grace
Made her only the child of her mother,
And heap'd the whole inherited sin
On that huge scapegoat of the race,
All, all upon the brother.

IV

Peace, angry spirit, and let him be!
Has not his sister smiled on me?

XIV

I

Maud has a garden of roses
And lilies fair on a lawn;
There she walks in her state
And tends upon bed and bower,
And thither I climb'd at dawn
And stood by her garden-gate;
A lion ramps at the top,
He is claspt by a passion-flower.

II

Maud's own little oak-room
(Which Maud, like a precious stone
Set in the heart of the carven gloom,
Lights with herself, when alone
She sits by her music and books
And her brother lingers late
With a roystering company) looks
Upon Maud's own garden-gate:
And I thought as I stood, if a hand, as white
As ocean-foam in the moon, were laid
On the hasp of the window, and my Delight
Had a sudden desire, like a glorious ghost, to glide,
Like a beam of the seventh Heaven, down to my side,
There were but a step to be made.

III

The fancy flatter'd my mind,
And again seem'd overbold;
Now I thought that she cared for me,
Now I thought she was kind
Only because she was cold.

IV

I heard no sound where I stood
But the rivulet on from the lawn
Running down to my own dark wood;
Or the voice of the long sea-wave as it swell'd
Now and then in the dim-gray dawn;
But I look'd, and round, all round the house I beheld
The death-white curtain drawn;
Felt a horror over me creep,
Prickle my skin and catch my breath,
Knew that the death-white curtain meant but sleep,
Yet I shudder'd and thought like a fool of the sleep of death.

XV

So dark a mind within me dwells,
And I make myself such evil cheer,
That if *I* be dear to some one else,
Then some one else may have much to fear;
But if *I* be dear to some one else,
Then I should be to myself more dear.
Shall I not take care of all that I think,
Yea ev'n of wretched meat and drink,
If I be dear,
If I be dear to some one else.

XVI

I

This lump of earth has left his estate
The lighter by the loss of his weight;
And so that he find what he went to seek,
And fulsome Pleasure clog him, and drown
His heart in the gross mud-honey of town,
He may stay for a year who has gone for a week:
But this is the day when I must speak,
And I see my Oread coming down,
O this is the day!
O beautiful creature, what am I
That I dare to look her way;
Think I may hold dominion sweet,
Lord of the pulse that is lord of her breast,
And dream of her beauty with tender dread,
From the delicate Arab arch of her feet
To the grace that, bright and light as the crest
Of a peacock, sits on her shining head,
And she knows it not: O, if she knew it,
To know her beauty might half undo it.
I know it the one bright thing to save
My yet young life in the wilds of Time,
Perhaps from madness, perhaps from crime,
Perhaps from a selfish grave.

II

What, if she be fasten'd to this fool lord,
Dare I bid her abide by her word?
Should I love her so well if she
Had given her word to a thing so low?
Shall I love her as well if she
Can break her word were it even for me?
I trust that it is not so.

III

Catch not my breath, O clamorous heart,
Let not my tongue be a thrall to my eye,
For I must tell her before we part,
I must tell her, or die.

XVII

Go not, happy day,
From the shining fields,
Go not, happy day,
Till the maiden yields.
Rosy is the West,
Rosy is the South,
Roses are her cheeks,
And a rose her mouth
When the happy Yes
Falters from her lips,
Pass and blush the news
Over glowing ships;
Over blowing seas,
Over seas at rest,
Pass the happy news,
Blush it thro' the West;
Till the red man dance
By his red cedar-tree,
And the red man's babe
Leap, beyond the sea.

Maud's match is newly rich politician.

Blush from West to East,
Blush from East to West,
Till the West is East,
Blush it thro' the West.
Rosy is the West,
Rosy is the South,
Roses are her cheeks,
And a rose her mouth.

XVIII

I

I have led her home, my love, my only friend.
There is none like her, none.
And never yet so warmly ran my blood
And sweetly, on and on
Calming itself to the long-wish'd-for end,
Full to the banks, close on the promised good.

II

None like her, none.
Just now the dry-tongued laurels' pattering talk
Seem'd her light foot along the garden walk,
And shook my heart to think she comes once more;
But even then I heard her close the door,
The gates of Heaven are closed, and she is gone.

III

There is none like her, none.
Nor will be when our summers have deceased.
O, art thou sighing for Lebanon
In the long breeze that streams to thy delicious East,
Sighing for Lebanon,
Dark cedar, tho' thy limbs have here increased,
Upon a pastoral slope as fair,
And looking to the South, and fed
With honey'd rain and delicate air,
And haunted by the starry head
Of her whose gentle will has changed my fate,
And made my life a perfumed altar-flame;
And over whom thy darkness must have spread
With such delight as theirs of old, thy great
Forefathers of the thornless garden, there
Shadowing the snow-limb'd Eve from whom she came.

IV

Here will I lie while these long branches sway,
And you fair stars that crown a happy day
Go in and out as if at merry play,
Who am no more so all forlorn,
As when it seem'd far better to be born
To labour and the mattock-harden'd hand,
Than nursed at ease and brought to understand
A sad astrology, the boundless plan
That makes you tyrants in your iron skies,
Innumerable, pitiless, passionless eyes,
Cold fires, yet with power to burn and brand
His nothingness into man.

V

But now shine on, and what care I,
Who in this stormy gulf have found a pearl
The countercharm of space and hollow sky,
And do accept my madness, and would die
To save from some slight shame one simple girl.

VI

Would die; for sullen-seeming Death may give
More life to Love than is or ever was
In our low world, where yet 'tis sweet to live.
Let no one ask me how it came to pass;
It seems that I am happy, that to me
A livelier emerald twinkles in the grass,
A purer sapphire melts into the sea.

VII

Not die; but live a life of truest breath,
And teach true life to fight with mortal wrongs.
O, why should Love, like men in drinking-songs,
Spice his fair banquet with the dust of death?
Make answer, Maud my bliss,

Maud made my Maud by that long loving kiss,
Life of my life, wilt thou not answer this?
'The dusky strand of Death inwoven here
With dear Love's tie, makes Love himself more dear.'

VIII

Is that enchanted moan only the swell
Of the long waves that roll in yonder bay?
And hark the clock within, the silver knell
Of twelve sweet hours that past in bridal white,
And died to live, long as my pulses play;
But now by this my love has closed her sight
And given false death her hand, and stol'n away
To dreamful wastes where footless fancies dwell
Among the fragments of the golden day.
May nothing there her maiden grace affright!
Dear heart, I feel with thee the drowsy spell.
My bride to be, my evermore delight,
My own heart's heart, my ownest own, farewell;
It is but for a little space I go:
And ye meanwhile far over moor and fell
Beat to the noiseless music of the night!
Has our whole earth gone nearer to the glow
Of your soft splendours that you look so bright?
I have climb'd nearer out of lonely Hell.
Beat, happy stars, timing with things below,
Beat with my heart more blest than heart can tell,
Blest, but for some dark undercurrent woe
That seems to draw—but it shall not be so:
Let all be well, be well.

XIX

I

Her brother is coming back to-night,
Breaking up my dream of delight.

II

My dream? do I dream of bliss?
I have walk'd awake with Truth.
O when did a morning shine
So rich in atonement as this
For my dark-dawning youth,
Darken'd watching a mother decline
And that dead man at her heart and mine:
For who was left to watch her but I?
Yet so did I let my freshness die.

III

I trust that I did not talk
To gentle Maud in our walk
(For often in lonely wanderings
I have cursed him even to lifeless things)
But I trust that I did not talk,
Not touch on her father's sin:
I am sure I did but speak
Of my mother's faded cheek
When it slowly grew so thin,
That I felt she was slowly dying
Vext with lawyers and harass'd with debt:
For how often I caught her with eyes all wet,
Shaking her head at her son and sighing
A world of trouble within!

IV

And Maud too, Maud was moved
To speak of the mother she loved
As one scarce less forlorn,
Dying abroad and it seems apart
From him who had ceased to share her heart,
And ever mourning over the feud,
The household Fury sprinkled with blood
By which our houses are torn:
How strange was what she said,
When only Maud and the brother
Hung over her dying bed—
That Maud's dark father and mine
Had bound us one to the other,
Betrothed us over their wine,
On the day when Maud was born;
Seal'd her mine from her first sweet breath.
Mine, mine by a right, from birth till death.
Mine, mine—our fathers have sworn.

V

But the true blood spilt had in it a heat
To dissolve the precious seal on a bond,
That, if left uncancell'd, had been so sweet:
And none of us thought of a something beyond,

A desire that awoke in the heart of the child,
As it were a duty done to the tomb,
To be friends for her sake, to be reconciled;
And I was cursing them and my doom,
And letting a dangerous thought run wild
While often abroad in the fragrant gloom
Of foreign churches—I see her there,
Bright English lily, breathing a prayer
To be friends, to be reconciled!

VI

But then what a flint is he!
Abroad, at Florence, at Rome,
I find whenever she touch'd on me
This brother had laugh'd her down,
And at last, when each came home,
He had darken'd into a frown,
Chid her, and forbid her to speak
To me, her friend of the years before;
And this was what had redden'd her cheek
When I bow'd to her on the moor.

VII

Yet Maud, altho' not blind
To the faults of his heart and mind,
I see she cannot but love him,
And says he is rough but kind,
And wishes me to approve him,
And tells me, when she lay
Sick once, with a fear of worse,
That he left his wine and horses and play,
Sat with her, read to her, night and day,
And tended her like a nurse.

VIII

Kind? but the deathbed desire
Spurn'd by this heir of the liar—
Rough but kind? yet I know
He has plotted against me in this,
That he plots against me still.
Kind to Maud? that were not amiss.
Well, rough but kind; why let it be so:
For shall not Maud have her will?

IX

For, Maud, so tender and true,
As long as my life endures
I feel I shall owe you a debt,
That I never can hope to pay;
And if ever I should forget
That I owe this debt to you
And for your sweet sake to yours;
O then, what then shall I say?—
If ever I *should* forget,
May God make me more wretched
Than ever I have been yet!

X

So now I have sworn to bury
All this dead body of hate,
I feel so free and so clear
By the loss of that dead weight,
That I should grow light-headed, I fear,
Fantastically merry;
But that her brother comes, like a blight
On my fresh hope, to the Hall to-night.

XX

I

Strange, that I felt so gay,
Strange, that *I* tried to-day
To beguile her melancholy;
The sultan, as we name him,—
She did not wish to blame him—
But he vext her and perplext her
With his worldly talk and folly:
Was it gentle to reprove her
For stealing out of view
From a little lazy lover
Who but claims her as his due?
Or for chilling his caresses
By the coldness of her manners,
Nay, the plainness of her dresses?
Now I know her but in two,
Nor can pronounce upon it
If one should ask me whether
The habit, hat, and feather,
Or the frock and gipsy bonnet
Be the neater and completer;
For nothing can be sweeter
Than maiden Maud in either.

II

But to-morrow, if we live,
Our ponderous squire will give
A grand political dinner
To half the squirelings near;
And Maud will wear her jewels,
And the bird of prey will hover,
And the titmouse hope to win her
With his chirrup at her ear.

III

A grand political dinner
To the men of many acres,
A gathering of the Tory,
A dinner and then a dance
For the maids and marriage-makers,
And every eye but mine will glance
At Maud in all her glory.

IV

For I am not invited,
But, with the Sultan's pardon,
I am all as well delighted,
For I know her own rose-garden,
And mean to linger in it
Till the dancing will be over;
And then, oh then, come out to me
For a minute, but for a minute,
Come out to your own true lover,
That your true lover may see
Your glory also, and render
All homage to his own darling,
Queen Maud in all her splendour.

XXI

Rivulet crossing my ground,
And bringing me down from the Hall
This garden-rose that I found,
Forgetful of Maud and me,
And lost in trouble and moving round
Here at the head of a tinkling fall,
And trying to pass to the sea.
O Rivulet, born at the Hall,
My Maud has sent it by thee
(If I read her sweet will right)
On a blushing mission to me,
Saying in odour and colour, 'Ah, be
Among the roses to-night.'

XXII

I

Come into the garden, Maud,
  For the black bat, night, has flown,
Come into the garden, Maud,
  I am here at the gate alone;
And the woodbine spices are wafted abroad,
  And the musk of the rose is blown.

II

For a breeze of morning moves,
And the planet of Love is on high,
Beginning to faint in the light that she loves
  On a bed of daffodil sky,
To faint in the light of the sun she loves,
  To faint in his light, and to die.

III

All night have the roses heard
  The flute, violin, bassoon;
All night has the casement jessamine stirr'd
  To the dancers dancing in tune;
Till a silence fell with the waking bird,
  And a hush with the setting moon.

IV

I said to the lily, 'There is but one
  With whom she has heart to be gay.
When will the dancers leave her alone?
  She is weary of dance and play.'
Now half to the setting moon are gone,
  And half to the rising day;
Low on the sand and loud on the stone
  The last wheel echoes away.

V

I said to the rose, 'The brief night goes
  In babble and revel and wine.
O young lord-lover, what sighs are those,
  For one that will never be thine?
But mine, but mine,' so I sware to the rose,
  'For ever and ever, mine.'

VI

And the soul of the rose went into my blood,
  As the music clash'd in the hall;
And long by the garden lake I stood,
  For I heard your rivulet fall
From the lake to the meadow and on to the wood,
  Our wood, that is dearer than all;

VII

From the meadow your walks have left so sweet
  That whenever a March-wind sighs
He sets the jewel-print of your feet
  In violets blue as your eyes,
To the woody hollows in which we meet
  And the valleys of Paradise.

VIII

The slender acacia would not shake
One long milk-bloom on the tree;
The white lake-blossom fell into the lake
As the pimpernel dozed on the lea;
But the rose was awake all night for your sake,
Knowing your promise to me;
The lilies and roses were all awake,
They sigh'd for the dawn and thee.

IX

Queen rose of the rosebud garden of girls,
Come hither, the dances are done,
In gloss of satin and glimmer of pearls,
Queen lily and rose in one;
Shine out, little head, sunning over with curls,
To the flowers, and be their sun.

X

There has fallen a splendid tear
From the passion-flower at the gate.
She is coming, my dove, my dear;
She is coming, my life, my fate;
The red rose cries, 'She is near, she is near;'
And the white rose weeps, 'She is late;'
The larkspur listens, 'I hear, I hear;'
And the lily whispers, 'I wait.'

XI

She is coming, my own, my sweet;
Were it ever so airy a tread,
My heart would hear her and beat,
Were it earth in an earthy bed;
My dust would hear her and beat,
Had I lain for a century dead;
Would start and tremble under her feet,
And blossom in purple and red.

PART II

I

I

'The fault was mine, the fault was mine'—
Why am I sitting here so stunn'd and still,
Plucking the harmless wild-flower on the hill?—
It is this guilty hand!—
And there rises ever a passionate cry
From underneath in the darkening land—
What is it, that has been done?
O dawn of Eden bright over earth and sky,
The fires of Hell brake out of thy rising sun,
The fires of Hell and of Hate;
For she, sweet soul, had hardly spoken a word,
When her brother ran in his rage to the gate,
He came with the babe-faced lord;
Heap'd on her terms of disgrace,
And while she wept, and I strove to be cool,
He fiercely gave me the lie,
Till I with as fierce an anger spoke,
And he struck me, madman, over the face,
Struck me before the languid fool,
Who was gaping and grinning by:
Struck for himself an evil stroke;
Wrought for his house an irredeemable woe;
For front to front in an hour we stood,
And a million horrible bellowing echoes broke
From the red-ribb'd hollow behind the wood,
And thunder'd up into Heaven the Christless code,
That must have life for a blow.
Ever and ever afresh they seem'd to grow.
Was it he lay there with a fading eye?
'The fault was mine,' he whisper'd, 'fly!'
Then glided out of the joyous wood
The ghastly Wraith of one that I know;
And there rang on a sudden a passionate cry,
A cry for a brother's blood:
It will ring in my heart and my ears, till I die, till I die.

II

Is it gone? my pulses beat—
What was it? a lying trick of the brain?
Yet I thought I saw her stand,
A shadow there at my feet,
High over the shadowy land.
It is gone; and the heavens fall in a gentle rain,
When they should burst and drown with deluging storms
The feeble vassals of wine and anger and lust,
The little hearts that know not how to forgive:

Arise, my God, and strike, for we hold Thee just,
Strike dead the whole weak race of venomous worms,
That sting each other here in the dust;
We are not worthy to live.

II

I

See what a lovely shell,
Small and pure as a pearl,
Lying close to my foot,
Frail, but a work divine,
Made so fairily well
With delicate spire and whorl,
How exquisitely minute,
A miracle of design!

II

What is it? a learned man
Could give it a clumsy name.
Let him name it who can,
The beauty would be the same.

III

The tiny cell is forlorn,
Void of the little living will
That made it stir on the shore.
Did he stand at the diamond door
Of his house in a rainbow frill?
Did he push, when he was uncurl'd,
A golden foot or a fairy horn
Thro' his dim water-world?

IV

Slight, to be crush'd with a tap
Of my finger-nail on the sand,
Small, but a work divine,
Frail, but of force to withstand,
Year upon year, the shock
Of cataract seas that snap
The three-decker's oaken spine
Athwart the ledges of rock,
Here on the Breton strand!

V

Breton, not Briton; here
Like a shipwreck'd man on a coast
Of ancient fable and fear—
Plagued with a flitting to and fro,
A disease, a hard mechanic ghost
That never came from on high
Nor ever arose from below,
But only moves with the moving eye,
Flying along the land and the main—
Why should it look like Maud?
Am I to be overawed
By what I cannot but know
Is a juggle born of the brain?

VI

Back from the Breton coast,
Sick of a nameless fear,
Back to the dark sea-line
Looking, thinking of all I have lost;
An old song vexes my ear;
But that of Lamech is mine.

VII

For years, a measureless ill,
For years, for ever, to part—
But she, she would love me still;
And as long, O God, as she
Have a grain of love for me,
So long, no doubt, no doubt,
Shall I nurse in my dark heart,
However weary, a spark of will
Not to be trampled out.

VIII

Strange, that the mind, when fraught
With a passion so intense
One would think that it well
Might drown all life in the eye,—
That it should, by being so overwrought,
Suddenly strike on a sharper sense
For a shell, or a flower, little things
Which else would have been past by!
And now I remember, I,
When he lay dying there,
I noticed one of his many rings
(For he had many, poor worm) and thought
It is his mother's hair.

IX

Who knows if he be dead?
Whether I need have fled?
Am I guilty of blood?
However this may be,
Comfort her, comfort her, all things good,
While I am over the sea!
Let me and my passionate love go by,
But speak to her all things holy and high,
Whatever happen to me!
Me and my harmful love go by;

But come to her waking, find her asleep,
Powers of the height, Powers of the deep,
And comfort her tho' I die.

III

Courage, poor heart of stone!
I will not ask thee why
Thou canst not understand
That thou art left for ever alone:
Courage, poor stupid heart of stone.—
Or if I ask thee why,
Care not thou to reply:
She is but dead, and the time is at hand
When thou shalt more than die.

IV

I

O that 'twere possible
After long grief and pain
To find the arms of my true love
Round me once again!

II

When I was wont to meet her
In the silent woody places
By the home that gave me birth,
We stood tranced in long embraces
Mixt with kisses sweeter sweeter
Than anything on earth.

III

A shadow flits before me,
Not thou, but like to thee:
Ah Christ, that it were possible
For one short hour to see
The souls we loved, that they might tell us
What and where they be.

IV

It leads me forth at evening,
It lightly winds and steals
In a cold white robe before me,
When all my spirit reels
At the shouts, the leagues of lights,
And the roaring of the wheels.

V

Half the night I waste in sighs,
Half in dreams I sorrow after
The delight of early skies;
In a wakeful doze I sorrow
For the hand, the lips, the eyes,
For the meeting of the morrow,
The delight of happy laughter,
The delight of low replies.

VI

'Tis a morning pure and sweet,
And a dewy splendour falls
On the little flower that clings
To the turrets and the walls;
'Tis a morning pure and sweet,
And the light and shadow fleet;
She is walking in the meadow,
And the woodland echo rings;
In a moment we shall meet;
She is singing in the meadow
And the rivulet at her feet
Ripples on in light and shadow
To the ballad that she sings.

VII

Do I hear her sing as of old,
My bird with the shining head,
My own dove with the tender eye?
But there rings on a sudden a passionate
cry,
There is some one dying or dead,
And a sullen thunder is roll'd;
For a tumult shakes the city,
And I wake, my dream is fled;
In the shuddering dawn, behold,
Without knowledge, without pity,
By the curtains of my bed
That abiding phantom cold.

VIII

Get thee hence, nor come again,
Mix not memory with doubt,
Pass, thou deathlike type of pain,
Pass and cease to move about!
'Tis the blot upon the brain
That *will* show itself without.

IX

Then I rise, the eavedrops fall,
And the yellow vapours choke
The great city sounding wide;
The day comes, a dull red ball
Wrapt in drifts of lurid smoke
On the misty river-tide.

X

Thro' the hubbub of the market
I steal, a wasted frame,

It crosses here, it crosses there,
Thro' all that crowd confused and loud,
The shadow still the same;
And on my heavy eyelids
My anguish hangs like shame.

XI

Alas for her that met me,
That heard me softly call,
Came glimmering thro' the laurels
At the quiet evenfall,
In the garden by the turrets
Of the old manorial hall.

XII

Would the happy spirit descend,
From the realms of light and song,
In the chamber or the street,
As she looks among the blest,
Should I fear to greet my friend
Or to say 'Forgive the wrong,'
Or to ask her, 'Take me, sweet,
To the regions of thy rest'?

XIII

But the broad light glares and beats,
And the shadow flits and fleets
And will not let me be;
And I loathe the squares and streets,
And the faces that one meets,
Hearts with no love for me:
Always I long to creep
Into some still cavern deep,
There to weep, and weep, and weep
My whole soul out to thee.

V

I

Dead, long dead,
Long dead!
And my heart is a handful of dust,
And the wheels go over my head,
And my bones are shaken with pain,
For into a shallow grave they are thrust,
Only a yard beneath the street,
And the hoofs of the horses beat, beat,
The hoofs of the horses beat,
Beat into my scalp and my brain,
With never an end to the stream of passing feet,
Driving, hurrying, marrying, burying,
Clamour and rumble, and ringing and clatter,
And here beneath it is all as bad,
For I thought the dead had peace, but it is not so;
To have no peace in the grave, is that not sad?
But up and down and to and fro,
Ever about me the dead men go;
And then to hear a dead man chatter
Is enough to drive one mad.

II

Wretchedest age, since Time began,
They cannot even bury a man;
And tho' we paid our tithes in the days that are gone,
Not a bell was rung, not a prayer was read;
It is that which makes us loud in the world of the dead;
There is none that does his work, not one;
A touch of their office might have sufficed,
But the churchmen fain would kill their church,
As the churches have kill'd their Christ.

III

See, there is one of us sobbing,
No limit to his distress;
And another, a lord of all things, praying
To his own great self, as I guess;
And another, a statesman there, betraying
His party-secret, fool, to the press;
And yonder a vile physician, blabbing
The case of his patient—all for what?
To tickle the maggot born in an empty head,
And wheedle a world that loves him not,
For it is but a world of the dead.

IV

Nothing but idiot gabble!
For the prophecy given of old
And then not understood,
Has come to pass as foretold;
Not let any man think for the public good,
But babble, merely for babble.
For I never whisper'd a private affair
Within the hearing of cat or mouse,
No, not to myself in the closet alone,
But I heard it shouted at once from the top of the house;
Everything came to be known.
Who told *him* we were there?

V

Not that gray old wolf, for he came not back
From the wilderness, full of wolves, where he used to lie;
He has gather'd the bones for his o'ergrown whelp to crack;
Crack them now for yourself, and howl, and die.

VI

Prophet, curse me the blabbing lip,
And curse me the British vermin, the rat;
I know not whether he came in the Hanover ship,
But I know that he lies and listens mute
In an ancient mansion's crannies and holes:
Arsenic, arsenic, sure, would do it,
Except that now we poison our babes, poor souls!
It is all used up for that.

VII

Tell him now: she is standing here at my head;
Not beautiful now, not even kind;
He may take her now; for she never speaks her mind,
But is ever the one thing silent here.
She is not *of* us, as I divine;
She comes from another stiller world of the dead,
Stiller, not fairer than mine.

VIII

But I know where a garden grows,
Fairer than aught in the world beside,
All made up of the lily and rose
That blow by night, when the season is good,
To the sound of dancing music and flutes:
It is only flowers, they had no fruits,
And I almost fear they are not roses, but blood;
For the keeper was one, so full of pride,
He linkt a dead man there to a spectral bride;
For he, if he had not been a Sultan of brutes,
Would he have that hole in his side?

IX

But what will the old man say?
He laid a cruel snare in a pit
To catch a friend of mine one stormy day;
Yet now I could even weep to think of it;
For what will the old man say
When he comes to the second corpse in the pit?

X

Friend, to be struck by the public foe,
Then to strike him and lay him low,
That were a public merit, far,
Whatever the Quaker holds, from sin;
But the red life spilt for a private blow—
I swear to you, lawful and lawless war
Are scarcely even akin.

XI

O me, why have they not buried me deep enough?
Is it kind to have made me a grave so rough,
Me, that was never a quiet sleeper?
Maybe still I am but half-dead;
Then I cannot be wholly dumb;
I will cry to the steps above my head
And somebody, surely, some kind heart will come
To bury me, bury me
Deeper, ever so little deeper.

PART III

I

I

My life has crept so long on a broken wing
Thro' cells of madness, haunts of horror and fear,
That I come to be grateful at last for a little thing:
My mood is changed, for it fell at a time of year
When the face of night is fair on the dewy downs,
And the shining daffodil dies, and the Charioteer

And starry Gemini hang like glorious crowns
Over Orion's grave low down in the west,
That like a silent lightning under the stars
She seem'd to divide in a dream from a band of the blest,
And spoke of a hope for the world in the coming wars—
'And in that hope, dear soul, let trouble have rest,
Knowing I tarry for thee,' and pointed to Mars
As he glow'd like a ruddy shield on the Lion's breast.

II

And it was but a dream, yet it yielded a dear delight
To have look'd, tho' but in a dream, upon eyes so fair,
That had been in a weary world my one thing bright;
And it was but a dream, yet it lighten'd my despair
When I thought that a war would arise in defence of the right,
That an iron tyranny now should bend or cease,
The glory of manhood stand on his ancient height,
Nor Britain's one sole God be the millionaire:
No more shall commerce be all in all, and Peace
Pipe on her pastoral hillock a languid note,
And watch her harvest ripen, her herd increase,
Nor the cannon-bullet rust on a slothful shore,
And the cobweb woven across the cannon's throat
Shall shake its threaded tears in the wind no more.

III

And as months ran on and rumour of battle grew,
'It is time, it is time, O passionate heart,' said I
(For I cleaved to a cause that I felt to be pure and true),
'It is time, O passionate heart and morbid eye,
That old hysterical mock-disease should die.'
And I stood on a giant deck and mix'd my breath
With a loyal people shouting a battle cry,
Till I saw the dreary phantom arise and fly
Far into the North, and battle, and seas of death.

IV

Let it go or stay, so I wake to the higher aims
Of a land that has lost for a little her lust of gold,
And love of a peace that was full of wrongs and shames,
Horrible, hateful, monstrous, not to be told;
And hail once more to the banner of battle unroll'd!
Tho' many a light shall darken, and many shall weep
For those that are crush'd in the clash of jarring claims,
Yet God's just wrath shall be wreak'd on a giant liar;
And many a darkness into the light shall leap,
And shine in the sudden making of splendid names,
And noble thought be freër under the sun,
And the heart of a people beat with one desire;
For the peace, that I deem'd no peace, is over and done,
And now by the side of the Black and the Baltic deep,
And deathful-grinning mouths of the fortress, flames
The blood-red blossom of war with a heart of fire.

V

Let it flame or fade, and the war roll down like a wind,
We have proved we have hearts in a cause, we are noble still,
And myself have awaked, as it seems, to the better mind;
It is better to fight for the good than to rail at the ill;
I have felt with my native land, I am one with my kind,
I embrace the purpose of God, and the doom assign'd.

[1855]

NORTHERN FARMER

OLD STYLE

I

Wheer 'asta beän [1] saw long and meä liggin' [2] 'ere aloän?
Noorse? thourt nowt [3] o' a noorse: whoy, Doctor's abeän an' agoän:
Says that I moänt 'a naw moor aäle: but I beänt a fool:
Git ma my aäle, fur I beänt a-gawin' [4] to breäk my rule.

II

Doctors, they knaws nowt, fur a says what's nawways true:
Naw soort o' koind o' use to saäy the things that a do.
I've 'ed my point o' aäle ivry noight sin' I beän 'ere.
An' I've 'ed my quart ivry market-noight for foorty year.

III

Parson's a beän loikewoise, an' a sittin' 'ere o' my bed.
'The amoighty's a taäkin o' you [5] to 'issén,[6] my friend,' a said,
An' a towd ma my sins, an's toithe were due, an' I gied it in hond;
I done moy duty boy 'um, as I 'a done boy the lond.

IV

Larn'd a ma' beä. I reckons I 'annot sa mooch to larn.
But a cast oop,[7] thot a did, 'bout Bessy Marris's barne.[8]
Thaw a knaws I hallus voäted wi' Squoire an' choorch an' staäte,
An' i' the woost o' toimes I wur niver agin the raäte.[9]

V

An' I hallus coom'd to 's chooch afoor moy Sally wur deäd,
An' 'eärd 'um a bummin' awaäy loike a buzzard-clock [10] ower my 'eäd,
An' I niver knaw'd whot a meän'd but I thowt a 'ad summut to saäy,
An' I thowt a said whot a owt to 'a said an' I coom'd awaäy.

VI

Bessy Marris's barne! tha knaws she laäid it to meä.
Mowt a beän, mayhap, for she wur a bad un, sheä.
'Siver,[11] I kep 'um, I kep 'um, my lass, tha mun understond;
I done moy duty boy 'um as I 'a done boy the lond.

[1] Hast thou been.
[2] Lying.
[3] Nought.
[4] A-going.
[5] ou as in hour.
[6] Himself.
[7] Brought up.
[8] Child.
[9] A tax to maintain the poor.
[10] Cockchafer.
[11] However.

VII

But Parson a cooms an' a goäs, an' a says it eäsy an' freeä
'The amoighty's a taäkin o' you to 'issén, my friend,' says 'eä.
I weänt saäy men be loiars, thaw summun [12] said it in 'aäste:
But 'e reäds wonn sarmin a weeäk, an' I 'a stubb'd [13] Thurnaby waäste.

VIII

D'ya moind the waäste, my lass? naw, naw, tha was not born then;
Theer wur a boggle [14] in it, I often 'eärd 'um mysen;
Moäst loike a butter-bump,[15] fur I 'eärd 'um about an' about,
But I stubb'd 'um oop wi' the lot, an' raäved [16] an' rembled [17] 'um out.

IX

Keäper's [18] it wur; fo' they fun 'um theer a-laäid of 'is faäce
Down i' the woild 'enemies [19] afoor I coom'd to the plaäce.
Noäks or Thimbleby—toäner [20] 'ed shot 'um as deäd as a naäil.
Noäks wur 'ang'd for it oop at 'soize [21]—but git ma my aäle.

X

Dubbut [22] looök at the waäste: theer warn't not feeäd for a cow;
Nowt at all but bracken an' fuzz, an' looök at it now—
Warn't worth nowt a haäcre, an' now theer's lots o' feeäd,
Fourscoor [23] yows upon it an' some on it down i' seeäd.[24]

XI

Nobbut a bit on it's left, an' I meän'd to 'a stubb'd it at fall,
Done it ta-year [25] I meän'd, an' runn'd 'plow thruff it an' all,
If godamoighty an' parson 'ud nobbut let ma aloän,
Meä, wi' haäte hoonderd haäcre o' Squoire's, an' lond o' my oän.

XII

Do godamoighty knaw what a's doing a-taäkin' o' meä?
I beänt wonn as saws 'ere a beän an' yonder a peä;
An' Squoire 'ull be sa mad an' all—a' dear a' dear!
And I 'a managed for Squoire coom Michaelmas thutty year.

XIII

A mowt 'a taäen owd Joänes, as 'ant not a 'aäpoth [26] o' sense,
Or a mowt 'a taäen young Robins—a niver mended a fence:
But godamoighty a moost taäke meä an' taäke ma now
Wi' aäf the cows to cauve an' Thurnaby hoälms [27] to plow!

XIV

Looök 'ow quoloty [28] smoiles when they seeäs ma a passin' boy,
Says to thessén naw doubt 'what a man a beä sewer-loy!' [29]
Fur they knaws what I beän to Squoire sin fust a coom'd to the 'All;
I done moy duty by Squoire an' I done moy duty boy hall.

12 David (*Psalm* CXVI, 11)
13 Broken up.
14 Ghost.
15 Bittern.
16 Tore up.
17 Threw away.
18 Gamekeeper.
19 Anemones.
20 One or other.
21 Assize.
22 Do but.
23 ou as in hour.
24 Clover.
25 This year.
26 Halfpennyworth.
27 Flat hands.
28 Quality, gentry.
29 Surely.

XV

Squoire's i' Lunnon, an' summun I reckons 'ull 'a to wroite,
For whoä's to howd [30] the lond ater meä thot muddles ma quoit;
Sartin-sewer I beä, thot a weänt niver give it to Joänes,
Naw, nor a moänt to Robins—a niver rembles the stoäns.

XVI

But summun 'ull come ater meä mayhap wi' 'is kittle o' steäm [31]
Huzzin' [32] an' maäzin' the blessed feälds wi' the Divil's oän teäm.
Sin' I mun doy I mun doy, thaw loife they says is sweet,
But sin' I mun doy I mun doy, for I couldn abeär to see it.

XVII

What atta stannin' theer fur, an' doesn bring ma the aäle?
Doctor's a 'toättler,[33] lass, an a's hallus i' the owd taäle;
I weänt break rules fur Doctor, a knaws naw moor nor a floy;
Git ma my aäle I tell tha, an' if I mun doy I mun doy.

[1861] [1864]

NORTHERN FARMER

NEW STYLE

I

Doesn't thou 'ear my 'erse's legs, as they canters awaäy?
Proputty, proputty, proputty—that's what I 'ears 'em saäy.
Proputty, proputty, proputty—Sam, thou's an ass for thy paaïns:
Theer's moor sense i' one o' 'is legs nor in all thy braaïns.

II

Woä—theer's a craw [1] to pluck wi' tha, Sam: yon's parson's 'ouse—
Doesn't thou knaw that a man mun be eäther a man or a mouse?
Time to think on it then; for thou'll be twenty to weeäk.[2]
Proputty, proputty—woä then woä—let ma 'ear mysén [3] speäk.

III

Me an' thy muther, Sammy, 'as beän a-talkin' o' thee;
Thou's beän talkin' to muther, an' she beän a tellin' it me.
Thou'll not marry for munny—thou's sweet upo' parson's lass—
Noä—thou'll marry for luvv—an' we boäth on us thinks tha an ass.

IV

Seeä'd her todaäy goä by—Saäint's daäy they was ringing the bells.
She's a beauty thou thinks—an' soä is scoors o' gells,
Them as 'as munny an' all—wot's a beauty?—the flower as blaws.
But proputty, proputty sticks, an' proputty, proputty graws.

V

Do'ant be stunt: [4] taäke time: I knaws what maäkes tha sa mad.
Warn't I craäzed fur the lasses mysén when I wur a lad?

[30] Hold.
[31] Steam threshing-machine.
[32] Worrying.
[33] Teetotaler.

[1] Crow.
[2] This week.
[3] Myself.
[4] Obstinate.

But I knaw'd a Quaäker feller as often 'as towd ma this:
'Doänt thou marry for munny, but goä wheer munny is!'

VI

An' I went wheer munny war: an' thy muther coom to 'and,
Wi' lots o' munny laaïd by, an' a nicetish bit o' land.
Maäybe she warn't a beauty:—I niver giv it a thowt—
But warn't she as good to cuddle an' kiss as a lass as 'ant nowt?[5]

VII

Parson's lass ant nowt, an' she weänt 'a nowt when 'e's deäd,
Mun be a guvness, lad, or summut, and addle[6] her breäd:
Why? fur 'e's nobbut[7] a curate, an' weänt niver git hissen clear,
An' 'e maäde the bed as 'e ligs[8] on afoor 'e coom'd to the shere.

VIII

An' thin 'e coom'd to the parish wi' lots o' Varsity debt,
Stook to his taaïl they did, an' e' 'ant got shut[9] on 'em yet.
An' 'e ligs on 'is back i' the grip, wi' noän to lend 'im a shuvv,
Woorse nor a far-welter'd[10] yowe: fur, Sammy, 'e married fur luvv.

IX

Luvv? what's luvv? thou can luvv thy lass an' 'er munny too,
Maakin' 'em goä togither as they've good right to do.
Could'n I luvv thy muther by cause o' 'er munny laaïd by?
Naäy—fur I luvv'd 'er a vast sight moor fur it: reäson why.

X

Ay an' thy muther says thou wants to marry the lass,
Cooms of a gentleman burn: an' we boäth on us thinks tha an ass
Woä then, proputty, wiltha?—an ass as near as mays nowt[11]—
Woä then, wiltha? dangtha!—the bees is as fell as owt.[12]

XI

Breäk me a bit o' the esh[13] for his 'eäd, lad, out o' the fence!
Gentleman burn! what's gentleman burn? is it shillins an' pence?
Proputty, proputty's ivrything 'ere, an', Sammy, I'm blest
If it isn't the saäme oop yonder, fur them as 'as it's the best.

XII

Tis'n them as 'as munny as breäks into 'ouses an' steäls,
Them as 'as coäts to their backs an' taäkes their regular meäls.
Noä, but it's them as niver knaws wheer a meäl's to be 'ad.
Taäke my word for it, Sammy, the poor in a loomp is bad.

XIII

Them or thir feythers, tha sees, mun 'a beän a laäzy lot,
Fur work mun 'a gone to the gittin' whiniver munny was got.
Feyther 'ad ammost nowt; leästways 'is munny was 'id.
But 'e tued an' moil'd[14] issén deäd, an 'e died a good un, 'e did.

5 Has nothing.
6 Earn.
7 No more than.
8 Lies.
9 Rid.
10 Or fow-welter'd,—said of a sheep lying on its back.
11 Makes nothing.
12 The flies are as fierce as anything.
13 Ash.
14 Tugged and drudged.

XIV

Loook thou theer wheer Wrigglesby beck[15] cooms out by the 'ill!
Feyther run oop to the farm, an' I runs oop to the mill;
An' I'll run oop to the brig,[16] an' that thou'll live to see;
And if thou marries a good un I'll leäve the land to thee.

XV

Thim's my noätions, Sammy, wheerby I means to stick;
But if thou marries a bad un, I'll leäve the land to Dick.—
Coom oop, proputty, proputty—that's what I 'ears 'im saäy—
Proputty, proputty, proputty—canter an' canter awaäy.

[1869]

IN THE VALLEY OF CAUTERETZ

All along the valley, stream that flashest white,
Deepening thy voice with the deepening of the night,
All along the valley, where thy waters flow,
I walk'd with one I loved two and thirty years ago.
All along the valley, while I walk'd to-day,
The two and thirty years were a mist that rolls away;
For all along the valley, down thy rocky bed,
Thy living voice to me was as the voice of the dead,
And all along the valley, by rock and cave and tree,
The voice of the dead was a living voice to me.

[1861] [1864]

THE HIGHER PANTHEISM

The sun, the moon, the stars, the seas, the hills and the plains,—
Are not these, O Soul, the Vision of Him who reigns?

Is not the Vision He, though He be not that which He seems?
Dreams are true while they last, and do we not live in dreams?

Earth, these solid stars, this weight of body and limb,
Are they not sign and symbol of thy division from Him?

Dark is the world to thee; thyself art the reason why,
For is He not all but thou, that has power to feel 'I am I'?

Glory about thee, without thee; and thou fulfillest thy doom,
Making Him broken gleams and a stifled splendor and gloom.

Speak to Him, thou, for He hears, and Spirit with Spirit can meet—
Closer is He than breathing, and nearer than hands and feet.

God is law, say the wise; O Soul, and let us rejoice,
For if He thunder by law the thunder is yet His voice.

Law is God, say some; no God at all, says the fool,
For all we have power to see is a straight staff bent in a pool;

And the ear of man cannot hear, and the eye of man cannot see;
But if we could see and hear, this Vision—were it not He?

[1869]

15 Brook. 16 Bridge.

FLOWER IN THE CRANNIED WALL

Flower in the crannied wall,
I pluck you out of the crannies,
I hold you here, root and all, in my hand,
Little flower—but *if* I could understand
What you are, root and all, and all in all,
I should know what God and man is.

[1869]

IN THE GARDEN AT SWAINSTON

Nightingales warbled without,
Within was weeping for thee:
Shadows of three dead men
Walk'd in the walks with me,
Shadows of three dead men and thou wast one of the three.

Nightingales sang in his woods:
The Master was far away:
Nightingales warbled and sang
Of a passion that lasts but a day;
Still in the house in his coffin the Prince of courtesy lay.

Two dead men have I known
In courtesy like to thee:
Two dead men have I loved
With a love that ever will be:
Three dead men have I loved and thou art last of the three.

[1870] [1874]

IDYLLS OF THE KING

LANCELOT AND ELAINE

Elaine the fair, Elaine the loveable,
Elaine, the lily maid of Astolat,
High in her chamber up a tower to the east
Guarded the sacred shield of Lancelot;
Which first she placed where morning's earliest ray
Might strike it, and awake her with the gleam;
Then fearing rust or soilure fashion'd for it
A case of silk, and braided thereupon
All the devices blazon'd on the shield
In their own tinct, and added, of her wit,
A border fantasy of branch and flower,
And yellow-throated nestling in the nest.
Nor rested thus content, but day by day,
Leaving her household and good father, climb'd
That eastern tower, and entering barr'd her door,
Stript off the case, and read the naked shield,
Now guess'd a hidden meaning in his arms,
Now made a pretty history to herself
Of every dint a sword had beaten in it,
And every scratch a lance had made upon it,
Conjecturing when and where: this cut is fresh;
That ten years back; this dealt him at Caerlyle;
That at Caerleon; this at Camelot:
And ah God's mercy, what a stroke was there!
And here a thrust that might have kill'd, but God
Broke the strong lance, and roll'd his enemy down,
And saved him: so she lived in fantasy.

How came the lily maid by that good shield
Of Lancelot, she that knew not ev'n his name?
He left it with her, when he rode to tilt
For the great diamond in the diamond jousts,
Which Arthur had ordain'd, and by that name
Had named them, since a diamond was the prize.

For Arthur, long before they crown'd him King,
Roving the trackless realms of Lyonnesse,
Had found a glen, gray boulder and black tarn.
A horror lived about the tarn, and clave
Like its own mists to all the mountain side:
For here two brothers, one a king, had met
And fought together; but their names were lost;
And each had slain his brother at a blow;
And down they fell and made the glen abhorr'd:
And where they lay till all their bones were bleach'd,

And lichen'd into colour with the crags:
And he, that once was king, had on a crown
Of diamonds, one in front, and four aside.
And Arthur came, and labouring up the pass,
All in a misty moonshine, unawares
Had trodden that crown'd skeleton, and the skull
Brake from the nape, and from the skull the crown
Roll'd into light, and turning on its rims
Fled like a glittering rivulet to the tarn:
And down the shingly scaur he plunged, and caught,
And set it on his head, and in his heart
Heard murmurs, 'Lo, thou likewise shalt be King.'

Thereafter, when a King, he had the gems
Pluck'd from the crown, and show'd them to his knights,
Saying 'These jewels, whereupon I chanced
Divinely, are the kingdom's, not the King's—
For public use: henceforward let there be,
Once every year, a joust for one of these:
For so by nine years' proof we needs must learn
Which is our mightiest, and ourselves shall grow
In use of arms and manhood, till we drive
The heathen, who, some say, shall rule the land
Hereafter, which God hinder.' Thus he spoke:
And eight years past, eight jousts had been, and still
Had Lancelot won the diamond of the year,
With purpose to present them to the Queen,
When all were won; but meaning all at once
To snare her royal fancy with a boon
Worth half her realm, had never spoken word.

Now for the central diamond and the last
And largest, Arthur, holding then his court
Hard on the river nigh the place which now
Is this world's hugest, let proclaim a joust
At Camelot, and when the time drew nigh
Spake (for she had been sick) to Guinevere,
'Are you so sick, my Queen, you cannot move
To these fair jousts?' 'Yea, lord,' she said, 'ye know it.'
'Then will ye miss,' he answer'd, 'the great deeds
Of Lancelot, and his prowess in the lists,
A sight ye love to look on.' And the Queen
Lifted her eyes, and they dwelt languidly
On Lancelot, where he stood beside the King.
He thinking that he read her meaning there,
'Stay with me, I am sick; my love is more
Than many diamonds,' yielded; and a heart
Love-loyal to the least wish of the Queen
(However much he yearn'd to make complete
The tale of diamonds for his destined boon)
Urged him to speak against the truth, and say,
'Sir King, mine ancient wound is hardly whole,
And lets me from the saddle;' and the King
Glanced first at him, then her, and went his way.
No sooner gone than suddenly she began:

'To blame, my lord Sir Lancelot, much to blame!
Why go ye not to these fair jousts? the knights
Are half of them our enemies, and the crowd
Will murmur, "Lo the shameless ones, who take
Their pastime now the trustful King is gone!"'
Then Lancelot vext at having lied in vain:
'Are ye so wise? ye were not once so wise,
My Queen, that summer, when ye loved me first.
Then of the crowd ye took no more account
Than of the myriad cricket of the mead,
When its own voice clings to each blade of grass,
And every voice is nothing. As to knights,

Them surely can I silence with all ease.
But now my loyal worship is allow'd
Of all men: many a bard, without offence,
Has link'd our names together in his lay,
Lancelot, the flower of bravery, Guinevere,
The pearl of beauty: and our knights at feast
Have pledged us in this union, while the King
Would listen smiling. How then? is there more?
Has Arthur spoken aught? or would yourself,
Now weary of my service and devoir,
Henceforth be truer to your faultless lord?

She broke into a little scornful laugh:
'Arthur, my lord, Arthur, the faultless King,
That passionate perfection, my good lord—
But who can gaze upon the Sun in heaven?
He never spake word of reproach to me,
He never had a glimpse of mine untruth,
He cares not for me: only here to-day
There gleam'd a vague suspicion in his eyes:
Some meddling rogue has tamper'd with him—else
Rapt in this fancy of his Table Round,
And swearing men to vows impossible,
To make them like himself: but, friend, to me
He is all fault who hath no fault at all:
For who loves me must have a touch of earth;
The low sun makes the colour: I am yours,
Not Arthur's, as ye know, save by the bond.
And therefore hear my words: go to the jousts:
The tiny-trumpeting gnat can break our dream
When sweetest; and the vermin voices here
May buzz so loud—we scorn them, but they sting.'

Then answer'd Lancelot, the chief of knights:
'And with what face, after my pretext made,
Shall I appear, O Queen, at Camelot, I
Before a King who honours his own word,
As if it were his God's?'
'Yea,' said the Queen,
'A moral child without the craft to rule,
Else had he not lost me: but listen to me,
If I must find you wit: we hear it said
That men go down before your spear at a touch,
But knowing you are Lancelot; your great name,
This conquers: hide it therefore; go unknown:
Win! by this kiss you will: and our true King
Will then allow your pretext, O my knight,
As all for glory; for to speak him true,
Ye know right well, how meek soe'er he seem,
No keener hunter after glory breathes.
He loves it in his knights more than himself:
They prove to him his work: win and return.'

Then got Sir Lancelot suddenly to horse,
Wroth at himself. Not willing to be known,
He left the barren-beaten thoroughfare,
Chose the green path that show'd the rarer foot,
And there among the solitary downs,
Full often lost in fancy, lost his way;
Till as he traced a faintly-shadow'd track,
That all in loops and links among the dales
Ran to the Castle of Astolat, he saw
Fired from the west, far on a hill, the towers.
Thither he made, and blew the gateway horn.
Then came an old, dumb, myriad-wrinkled man,
Who let him into lodging and disarm'd.
And Lancelot marvell'd at the wordless man;
And issuing found the Lord of Astolat
With two strong sons, Sir Torre and Sir Lavaine,
Moving to meet him in the castle court;
And close behind them stept the lily maid
Elaine, his daughter: mother of the house
There was not: some light jest among them rose
With laughter dying down as the great knight
Approach'd them: then the Lord of Astolat:

'Whence comest thou, my guest, and by what name
Livest between the lips? for by thy state
And presence I might guess thee chief of those,
After the King, who eat in Arthur's halls.
Him have I seen: the rest, his Table Round,
Known as they are, to me they are unknown.'

Then answer'd Lancelot, the chief of knights:
'Known am I, and of Arthur's hall, and known,
What I by mere mischance have brought, my shield.
But since I go to joust as one unknown
At Camelot for the diamond, ask me not,
Hereafter ye shall know me—and the shield—
I pray you lend me one, if such you have,
Blank, or at least with some device not mine.'

Then said the Lord of Astolat, 'Here is Torre's:
Hurt in his first tilt was my son, Sir Torre.
And so, God wot, his shield is blank enough.
His ye can have.' Then added plain Sir Torre,
'Yea, since I cannot use it, ye may have it.'
Here laugh'd the father saying, 'Fie, Sir Churl,
Is that an answer for a noble knight?
Allow him! but Lavaine, my younger here,
He is so full of lustihood, he will ride,
Joust for it, and win, and bring it in an hour,
And set it in this damsel's golden hair,
To make her thrice as wilful as before.'

'Nay, father, nay good father, shame me not
Before this noble knight,' said young Lavaine,
'For nothing. Surely I but play'd on Torre:
He seem'd so sullen, vext he could not go:
A jest, no more! for, knight, the maiden dreamt
That some one put this diamond in her hand,
And that it was too slippery to be held,
And slipt and fell into some pool or stream,
The castle-well, belike; and then I said
That *if* I went and *if* I fought and won it
(But all was jest and joke among ourselves)
Then must she keep it safelier. All was jest.
But, father, give me leave, an if he will,
To ride to Camelot with this noble knight:
Win shall I not but do my best to win:
Young as I am, yet would I do my best.'

'So ye will grace me,' answer'd Lancelot,
Smiling a moment, 'with your fellowship
O'er these waste downs whereon I lost myself,
Then were I glad of you as guide and friend:
And you shall win this diamond,—as I hear
It is a fair large diamond,—if ye may,
And yield it to this maiden, if ye will.'
'A fair large diamond,' added plain Sir Torre,
'Such be for queens, and not for simple maids.'
Then she, who held her eyes upon the ground,
Elaine, and heard her name so tost about,
Flush'd slightly at the slight disparagement
Before the stranger knight, who, looking at her,
Full courtly, yet not falsely, thus return'd:
'If what is fair be but for what is fair,
And only queens are to be counted so,
Rash were my judgment then, who deem this maid
Might wear as fair a jewel as is on earth,
Not violating the bond of like to like.'

He spoke and ceased: the lily maid Elaine,
Won by the mellow voice before she look'd,
Lifted her eyes, and read his lineaments.
The great and guilty love he bare the Queen,
In battle with the love he bare his lord,
Had marr'd his face, and mark'd it ere his time.
Another sinning on such heights with one,
The flower of all the west and all the world,
Had been the sleeker for it: but in him

His mood was often like a fiend, and rose
And drove him into wastes and solitudes
For agony, who was yet a living soul.
Marr'd as he was, he seem'd the goodliest man
That ever among ladies ate in hall,
And noblest, when she lifted up her eyes.
However marr'd, of more than twice her years,
Seam'd with an ancient swordcut on the cheek,
And bruised and bronzed, she lifted up her eyes
And loved him, with that love which was her doom.

Then the great knight, the darling of the court,
Loved of the loveliest, into that rude hall
Stept with all grace, and not with half disdain
Hid under grace, as in a smaller time,
But kindly man moving among his kind:
Whom they with meats and vintage of their best
And talk and minstrel melody entertain'd.
And much they ask'd of court and Table Round,
And ever well and readily answer'd he:
But Lancelot, when they glanced at Guinevere,
Suddenly speaking of the wordless man,
Heard from the Baron that, ten years before,
The heathen caught and reft him of his tongue.
'He learnt and warn'd me of their fierce design
Against my house, and him they caught and maim'd;
But I, my sons, and little daughter fled
From bonds or death, and dwelt among the woods
By the great river in a boatman's hut.
Dull days were those, till our good Arthur broke
The Pagan yet once more on Badon hill.'

'O there, great lord, doubtless,' Lavaine said, rapt
By all the sweet and sudden passion of youth
Toward greatness in its elder, 'you have fought.
O tell us—for we live apart—you know
Of Arthur's glorious wars.' And Lancelot spoke
And answer'd him at full, as having been
With Arthur in the fight which all day long
Rang by the white mouth of the violent Glem;
And in the four loud battles by the shore
Of Duglas; that on Bassa; then the war
That thunder'd in and out the gloomy skirts
Of Celidon the forest; and again
By castle Gurnion, where the glorious King
Had on his cuirass worn our Lady's Head,
Carved of one emerald center'd in a sun
Of silver rays, that lighten'd as he breathed;
And at Caerleon had he help'd his lord,
When the strong neighings of the wild white Horse
Set every gilded parapet shuddering;
And up in Agned-Cathregonion too,
And down the waste sand-shores of Trath Treroit,
Where many a heathen fell; 'and on the mount
Of Badon I myself beheld the King
Charge at the head of all his Table Round,
And all his legions crying Christ and him,
And break them; and I saw him, after, stand
High on a heap of slain, from spur to plume
Red as the rising sun with heathen blood,
And seeing me, with a great voice he cried,
"They are broken, they are broken!" for the King,
However mild he seems at home, nor cares
For triumph in our mimic wars, the jousts—
For if his own knight cast him down, he laughs
Saying, his knights are better men than he—
Yet in this heathen war the fire of God
Fills him: I never saw his like: there lives
No greater leader.'

While he utter'd this,
Low to her own heart said the lily maid,
'Save your great self, fair lord;' and when he fell
From talk of war to traits of pleasantry—

Being mirthful he, but in a stately kind—
She still took note that when the living smile
Died from his lips, across him came a cloud
Of melancholy severe, from which again,
Whenever in her hovering to and fro
The lily maid had striven to make him cheer,
There brake a sudden-beaming tenderness
Of manners and of nature: and she thought
That all was nature, all, perchance, for her.
And all night long his face before her lived,
As when a painter, poring on a face,
Divinely thro' all hindrance finds the man
Behind it, and so paints him that his face,
The shape and colour of a mind and life,
Lives for his children, ever at its best
And fullest; so the face before her lived,
Dark-splendid, speaking in the silence, full
Of noble things, and held her from her sleep.
Till rathe she rose, half-cheated in the thought
She needs must bid farewell to sweet Lavaine.
First as in fear, step after step, she stole
Down the long tower-stairs, hesitating:
Anon, she heard Sir Lancelot cry in the court,
'This shield, my friend, where is it?' and Lavaine
Past inward, as she came from out the tower.
There to his proud horse Lancelot turn'd, and smooth'd
The glossy shoulder, humming to himself.
Half-envious of the flattering hand, she drew
Nearer and stood. He look'd, and more amazed
Than if seven men had set upon him, saw
The maiden standing in the dewy light.
He had not dream'd she was so beautiful.
Then came on him a sort of sacred fear,
For silent, tho' he greeted her, she stood
Rapt on his face as if it were a God's.
Suddenly flash'd on her a wild desire,
That he should wear her favour at the tilt.
She braved a riotous heart in asking for it.
'Fair lord, whose name I know not—noble it is,
I well believe, the noblest—will you wear
My favour at this tourney?' 'Nay,' said he,
'Fair lady, since I never yet have worn
Favour of any lady in the lists.
Such is my wont, as those, who know me, know.'
'Yea, so,' she answer'd; 'then in wearing mine
Needs must be lesser likelihood, noble lord,
That those who know should know you.' And he turn'd
Her counsel up and down within his mind,
And found it true, and answer'd, 'True, my child.
Well, I will wear it: fetch it out to me:
What is it?' and she told him 'A red sleeve
Broider'd with pearls,' and brought it: then he bound
Her token on his helmet, with a smile
Saying, 'I never yet have done so much
For any maiden living,' and the blood
Sprang to her face and fill'd her with delight;
But left her all the paler, when Lavaine
Returning brought the yet-unblazon'd shield,
His brother's; which he gave to Lancelot,
Who parted with his own to fair Elaine:
'Do me this grace, my child, to have my shield
In keeping till I come.' 'A grace to me,'
She answer'd, 'twice to-day. I am your squire!'
Whereat Lavaine said, laughing, 'Lily maid,
For fear our people call you lily maid
In earnest, let me bring your colour back;
Once, twice, and thrice: now get you hence to bed:'
So kiss'd her, and Sir Lancelot his own hand,
And thus they moved away: she stay'd a minute,
Then made a sudden step to the gate, and there—
Her bright hair blown about the serious face
Yet rosy-kindled with her brother's kiss—
Paused by the gateway, standing near the shield
In silence, while she watch'd their arms far-off
Sparkle, until they dipt below the downs.

Then to her tower she climb'd, and took the shield,
There kept it, and so lived in fantasy.

Meanwhile the new companions past away
Far o'er the long backs of the bushless downs,
To where Sir Lancelot knew there lived a knight
Not far from Camelot, now for forty years
A hermit, who had pray'd, labour'd and pray'd,
And ever labouring had scoop'd himself
In the white rock a chapel and a hall
On massive columns, like a shorecliff cave,
And cells and chambers: all were fair and dry;
The green light from the meadows underneath
Struck up and lived along the milky roofs;
And in the meadows tremulous aspen-trees
And poplars made a noise of falling showers.
And thither wending there that night they bode.

But when the next day broke from underground,
And shot red fire and shadows thro' the cave,
They rose, heard mass, broke fast, and rode away:
Then Lancelot saying. 'Hear, but hold my name
Hidden, you ride with Lancelot of the Lake.'
Abash'd Lavaine, whose instant reverence,
Dearer to true young hearts than their own praise,
But left him leave to stammer, 'Is it indeed?'
And after muttering 'The great Lancelot,'
At last he got his breath and answer'd, 'One,
One have I seen—that other, our liege lord,
The dread Pendragon, Britain's King of kings,
Of whom the people talk mysteriously,
He will be there—then were I stricken blind
That minute, I might say that I had seen.'

So spake Lavaine, and when they reach'd the lists
By Camelot in the meadow, let his eyes
Run thro' the peopled gallery which half round
Lay like a rainbow fall'n upon the grass,
Until they found the clear-faced King, who sat
Robed in red samite, easily to be known,
Since to his crown the golden dragon clung,
And down his robe the dragon writhed in gold,
And from the carven-work behind him crept
Two dragons gilded, sloping down to make
Arms for his chair, while all the rest of them
Thro' knots and loops and folds innumerable
Fled ever thro' the woodwork, till they found
The new design wherein they lost themselves,
Yet with all ease, so tender was the work:
And, in the costly canopy o'er him set,
Blazed the last diamond of the nameless king.

Then Lancelot answer'd young Lavaine and said,
'Me you call great: mine is the firmer seat,
The truer lance: but there is many a youth
Now crescent, who will come to all I am
And overcome it; and in me there dwells
No greatness, save it be some far-off touch
Of greatness to know well I am not great:
There is the man.' And Lavaine gaped upon him
As on a thing miraculous, and anon
The trumpets blew; and then did either side,
They that assail'd, and they that held the lists,
Set lance in rest, strike spur, suddenly move,
Meet in the midst, and there so furiously
Shock, that a man far-off might well perceive,
If any man that day were left afield,
The hard earth shake, and a low thunder of arms.
And Lancelot bode a little, till he saw

Which were the weaker; then he hurl'd into it
Against the stronger: little need to speak
Of Lancelot in his glory! King, duke, earl,
Count, baron—whom he smote, he overthrew.

But in the field were Lancelot's kith and kin,
Ranged with the Table Round that held the lists,
Strong men, and wrathful that a stranger knight
Should do and almost overdo the deeds
Of Lancelot; and one said to the other, 'Lo!
What is he? I do not mean the force alone—
The grace and versatility of the man!
Is it not Lancelot?' 'When has Lancelot worn
Favour of any lady in the lists?
Not such his wont, as we, that know him, know.'
'How then? who then?' a fury seized them all,
A fiery family passion for the name
Of Lancelot, and a glory one with theirs.
They couch'd their spears and prick'd their steeds, and thus,
Their plumes driv'n backward by the wind they made
In moving, all together down upon him
Bare, as a wild wave in the wide North-sea,
Green-glimmering toward the summit, bears, with all
Its stormy crests that smoke against the skies,
Down on a bark, and overbears the bark,
And him that helms it, so they overbore
Sir Lancelot and his charger, and a spear
Down-glancing lamed the charger, and a spear
Prick'd sharply his own cuirass, and the head
Pierced thro' his side, and there snapt, and remain'd.

Then Sir Lavaine did well and worshipfully;
He bore a knight of old repute to the earth,
And brought his horse to Lancelot where he lay.
He up the side, sweating with agony, got,
But thought to do while he might yet endure,
And being lustily holpen by the rest,
His party,—tho' it seem'd half-miracle
To those he fought with,—drave his kith and kin,
And all the Table Round that held the lists,
Back to the barrier; then the trumpets blew
Proclaiming his the prize, who wore the sleeve
Of scarlet, and the pearls; and all the knights,
His party, cried 'Advance and take thy prize
The diamond'; but he answer'd, 'Diamond me
No diamonds! for God's love, a little air!
Prize me no prizes, for my prize is death!
Hence will I, and I charge you, follow me not.'

He spoke, and vanish'd suddenly from the field
With young Lavaine into the poplar grove.
There from his charger down he slid, and sat,
Gasping to Sir Lavaine, 'Draw the lance-head:'
'Ah my sweet lord Sir Lancelot,' said Lavaine,
'I dread me, if I draw it, you will die.'
But he, 'I die already with it: draw—
Draw,'—and Lavaine drew, and Sir Lancelot gave
A marvellous great shriek and ghastly groan,
And half his blood burst forth, and down he sank
For the pure pain, and wholly swoon'd away.
Then came the hermit out and bare him in,
There stanch'd his wound; and there, in daily doubt
Whether to live or die, for many a week
Hid from the wide world's rumour by the grove
Of poplars with their noise of falling showers,
And ever-tremulous aspen-trees, he lay.

But on that day when Lancelot fled the lists,
His party, knights of utmost North and West,
Lords of waste marches, kings of desolate isles,
Came round their great Pendragon, saying to him,
'Lo, Sire, our knight, thro' whom we won the day,
Hath gone sore wounded, and hath left his prize
Untaken, crying that his prize is death.'
'Heaven hinder,' said the King, 'that such an one,
So great a knight as we have seen to-day—
He seem'd to me another Lancelot—
Yea, twenty times I thought him Lancelot—
He must not pass uncared for. Wherefore, rise,
O Gawain, and ride forth and find the knight.
Wounded and wearied needs must he be near.
I charge you that you get at once to horse.
And, knights and kings, there breathes not one of you
Will deem this prize of ours is rashly given:
His prowess was too wondrous. We will do him
No customary honour: since the knight
Came not to us, of us to claim the prize,
Ourselves will send it after. Rise and take
This diamond, and deliver it, and return,
And bring us where he is, and how he fares,
And cease not from your quest until ye find.'

So saying, from the carven flower above,
To which it made a restless heart, he took,
And gave, the diamond: then from where he sat
At Arthur's right, with smiling face arose,
With smiling face and frowning heart, a Prince
In the mid might and flourish of his May,
Gawain, surnamed The Courteous, fair and strong,
And after Lancelot, Tristram, and Geraint
And Gareth, a good knight, but therewithal
Sir Modred's brother, and the child of Lot,
Nor often loyal to his word, and now
Wroth that the King's command to sally forth
In quest of whom he knew not, made him leave
The banquet, and concourse of knights and kings.

So all in wrath he got to horse and went;
While Arthur to the banquet, dark in mood,
Past, thinking 'Is it Lancelot who hath come
Despite the wound he spake of, all for gain
Of glory, and hath added wound to wound,
And ridd'n away to die?' So fear'd the King,
And, after two days' tarriance there, return'd.
Then when he saw the Queen, embracing ask'd,
'Love, are you yet so sick?' 'Nay, lord,' she said.
'And where is Lancelot?' Then the Queen amazed,
'Was he not with you? won he not your prize?'
'Nay, but one like him.' 'Why that like was he.'
And when the King demanded how she knew,
Said, 'Lord, no sooner had ye parted from us,
Than Lancelot told me of a common talk
That men went down before his spear at a touch,
But knowing he was Lancelot; his great name
Conquer'd; and therefore would he hide his name
From all men, ev'n the King, and to this end
Had made the pretext of a hindering wound,
That he might joust unknown of all, and learn
If his old prowess were in aught decay'd;
And added, "Our true Arthur, when he learns,
Will well allow my pretext, as for gain
Of purer glory." '

Then replied the King:
'Far lovelier in our Lancelot had it been,
In lieu of idly dallying with the truth,
To have trusted me as he hath trusted thee.
Surely his King and most familiar friend
Might well have kept his secret. True, indeed,
Albeit I know my knights fantastical,
So fine a fear in our large Lancelot
Must needs have moved my laughter: now remains
But little cause for laughter: his own kin—
Ill news, my Queen, for all who love him, this!—
His kith and kin, not knowing, set upon him;
So that he went sore wounded from the field:
Yet good news too: for goodly hopes are mine
That Lancelot is no more a lonely heart.
He wore, against his wont, upon his helm
A sleeve of scarlet, broider'd with great pearls,
Some gentle maiden's gift.'

'Yea, lord,' she said,
'Thy hopes are mine,' and saying that, she choked,
And sharply turn'd about to hide her face,
Past to her chamber, and there flung herself
Down on the great King's couch, and writhed upon it,
And clench'd her fingers till they bit the palm,
And shriek'd out 'Traitor' to the unhearing wall,
Then flash'd into wild tears, and rose again,
And moved about her palace, proud and pale.

Gawain the while thro' all the region round
Rode with his diamond, wearied of the quest,
Touch'd at all points, except the poplar grove,
And came at last, tho' late, to Astolat:
Whom glittering in enamell'd arms the maid
Glanced at, and cried, 'What news from Camelot, lord?
What of the knight with the red sleeve?'
'He won.'
'I knew it,' she said. 'But parted from the jousts
Hurt in the side,' whereat she caught her breath;
Thro' her own side she felt the sharp lance go;
Thereon she smote her hand: wellnigh she swoon'd:
And, while he gazed wonderingly at her, came
The Lord of Astolat out, to whom the Prince
Reported who he was, and on what quest
Sent, that he bore the prize and could not find
The victor, but had ridd'n a random round
To seek him, and had wearied of the search.
To whom the Lord of Astolat, 'Bide with us,
And ride no more at random, noble Prince!
Here was the knight, and here he left a shield;
This will he send or come for: furthermore
Our son is with him; we shall hear anon,
Needs must we hear.' To this the courteous Prince
Accorded with his wonted courtesy,
Courtesy with a touch of traitor in it,
And stay'd; and cast his eyes on fair Elaine:
Where could be found face daintier? then her shape
From forehead down to foot, perfect—again
From foot to forehead exquisitely turn'd:
'Well—if I bide, lo! this wild flower for me!'
And oft they met among the garden yews,
And there he set himself to play upon her
With sallying wit, free flashes from a height
Above her, graces of the court, and songs,
Sighs, and slow smiles, and golden eloquence
And amorous adulation, till the maid
Rebell'd against it, saying to him, 'Prince,
O loyal nephew of our noble King,
Why ask you not to see the shield he left,

Whence you might learn his name? Why slight your King,
And lose the quest he sent you on, and prove
No surer than our falcon yesterday,
Who lost the hern we slipt her at, and went
To all the winds?' 'Nay, by mine head,' said he,
'I lose it, as we lose the lark in heaven,
O damsel, in the light of your blue eyes;
But an ye will it let me see the shield.'
And when the shield was brought, and Gawain saw
Sir Lancelot's azure lions, crown'd with gold,
Ramp in the field, he smote his thigh, and mock'd:
'Right was the King! our Lancelot! that true man!'
'And right was I,' she answer'd merrily, 'I,
Who dream'd my knight the greatest knight of all.'
'And if *I* dream'd,' said Gawain, 'that you love
This greatest knight, your pardon! lo, ye know it!
Speak therefore: shall I waste myself in vain?'
Full simple was her answer, 'What know I?
My brethren have been all my fellowship;
And I, when often they have talk'd of love,
Wish'd it had been my mother, for they talk'd,
Meseem'd, of what they knew not; so myself—
I know not if I know what true love is,
But if I know, then, if I love not him,
I know there is none other I can love.'
'Yea, by God's death,' said he, 'ye love him well,
But would not, knew ye what all others know,
And whom he loves.' 'So be it,' cried Elaine,
And lifted her fair face and moved away:
But he pursued her, calling, 'Stay a little!
One golden minute's grace! he wore your sleeve:
Would he break faith with one I may not name?
Must our true man change like a leaf at last?
Nay—like enow: why then, far be it from me
To cross our mighty Lancelot in his loves!
And, damsel, for I deem you know full well
Where your great knight is hidden, let me leave
My quest with you; the diamond also: here!
For if you love, it will be sweet to give it;
And if he love, it will be sweet to have it
From your own hand; and whether he love or not,
A diamond is a diamond. Fare you well
A thousand times!—a thousand times farewell!
Yet, if he love, and his love hold, we two
May meet at court hereafter: there, I think,
So ye will learn the courtesies of the court,
We two shall know each other.'

Then he gave,
And slightly kiss'd the hand to which he gave,
The diamond, and all wearied of the quest
Leapt on his horse, and carolling as he went
A true-love ballad, lightly rode away.

Thence to the court he past; there told the King
What the King knew, 'Sir Lancelot is the knight.'
And added, 'Sire, my liege, so much I learnt;
But fail'd to find him, tho' I rode all round
The region: but I lighted on the maid
Whose sleeve he wore; she loves him; and to her,
Deeming our courtesy is the truest law,
I gave the diamond: she will render it;
For by mine head she knows his hiding-place.'

The seldom-frowning King frown'd, and replied,
'Too courteous truly! ye shall go no more
On quest of mine, seeing that ye forget
Obedience is the courtesy due to kings.'

He spake and parted. Wroth, but all in awe,
For twenty strokes of the blood, without a word,
Linger'd that other, staring after him;
Then shook his hair, strode off, and buzz'd abroad
About the maid of Astolat, and her love.
All ears were prick'd at once, all tongues were loosed:
'The maid of Astolat loves Sir Lancelot,
Sir Lancelot loves the maid of Astolat.'
Some read the King's face, some the Queen's, and all
Had marvel what the maid might be, but most
Predoom'd her as unworthy. One old dame
Came suddenly on the Queen with the sharp news.
She, that had heard the noise of it before,
But sorrowing Lancelot should have stoop'd so low,
Marr'd her friend's aim with pale tranquillity.
So ran the tale like fire about the court,
Fire in dry stubble a nine-days' wonder flared:
Till ev'n the knights at banquet twice or thrice
Forgot to drink to Lancelot and the Queen,
And pledging Lancelot and the lily maid
Smiled at each other, while the Queen, who sat
With lips severely placid, felt the knot
Climb in her throat, and with her feet unseen
Crush'd the wild passion out against the floor
Beneath the banquet, where the meats became
As wormwood, and she hated all who pledged.

But far away the maid in Astolat,
Her guiltless rival, she that ever kept
The one-day-seen Sir Lancelot in her heart,
Crept to her father, while he mused alone,
Sat on his knee, stroked his gray face and said,
'Father, you call me wilful, and the fault
Is yours who let me have my will, and now,
Sweet father, will you let me lose my wits?'
'Nay,' said he, 'surely.' 'Wherefore, let me hence,'
She answer'd, 'and find out our dear Lavaine.'
'Ye will not lose your wits for dear Lavaine:
Bide,' answer'd he: 'we needs must hear anon
Of him, and of that other.' 'Ay,' she said,
'And of that other, for I needs must hence
And find that other, wheresoe'er he be,
And with mine own hand give his diamond to him,
Lest I be found as faithless in the quest
As yon proud prince who left the quest to me.
Sweet father, I behold him in my dreams
Gaunt as it were the skeleton of himself,
Death-pale, for lack of gentle maiden's aid.
The gentler-born the maiden, the more bound,
My father, to be sweet and serviceable
To noble knights in sickness, as ye know
When these have worn their tokens: let me hence
I pray you.' Then her father nodding said,
'Ay, ay, the diamond: wit ye well, my child,
Right fain were I to learn this knight were whole,
Being our greatest: yea, and you must give it—
And sure I think this fruit is hung too high
For any mouth to gape for save a queen's—
Nay, I mean nothing: so then, get you gone,
Being so very wilful you must go.'

Lightly, her suit allow'd, she slipt away,
And while she made her ready for her ride,
Her father's latest word humm'd in her ear,
'Being so very wilful you must go,'
And changed itself and echo'd in her heart,
'Being so very wilful you must die.'
But she was happy enough and shook it off,
As we shake off the bee that buzzes at us;
And in her heart she answer'd it and said;

'What matter, so I help him back to life?'
Then far away with good Sir Torre for guide
Rode o'er the long backs of the bushless downs
To Camelot, and before the city-gates
Came on her brother with a happy face
Making a roan horse caper and curvet
For pleasure all about a field of flowers:
Whom when she saw, 'Lavaine,' she cried, 'Lavaine,
How fares my lord Sir Lancelot?' He amazed,
'Torre and Elaine! why here? Sir Lancelot!
How know ye my lord's name is Lancelot?'
But when the maid had told him all her tale,
Then turn'd Sir Torre, and being in his moods
Left them, and under the strange-statued gate,
Where Arthur's wars were render'd mystically,
Past up the still rich city to his kin,
His own far blood, which dwelt at Camelot;
And her, Lavaine across the poplar grove
Led to the caves: there first she saw the casque
Of Lancelot on the wall: her scarlet sleeve,
Tho' carved and cut, and half the pearls away,
Stream'd from it still; and in her heart she laugh'd,
Because he had not loosed it from his helm,
But meant once more perchance to tourney in it.
And when they gain'd the cell wherein he slept,
His battle-writhen arms and mighty hands
Lay naked on the wolfskin, and a dream
Of dragging down his enemy made them move.
Then she that saw him lying unsleek, unshorn,
Gaunt as it were the skeleton of himself,
Utter'd a little tender dolorous cry.
The sound not wonted in a place so still
Woke the sick knight, and while he roll'd his eyes
Yet blank from sleep, she started to him, saying,
'Your prize the diamond sent you by the King:'
His eyes glisten'd: she fancied 'Is it for me?'
And when the maid had told him all the tale
Of King and Prince, the diamond sent, the quest
Assign'd to her not worthy of it, she knelt
Full lowly by the corners of his bed,
And laid the diamond in his open hand.
Her face was near, and as we kiss the child
That does the task assign'd, he kiss'd her face.
At once she slipt like water to the floor.
'Alas,' he said, 'your ride hath wearied you.
Rest must you have.' 'No rest for me,' she said;
'Nay, for near you, fair lord, I am at rest.'
What might she mean by that? his large black eyes,
Yet larger thro' his leanness, dwelt upon her,
Till all her heart's sad secret blazed itself
In the heart's colours on her simple face;
And Lancelot look'd and was perplext in mind,
And being weak in body said no more;
But did not love the colour; woman's love,
Save one, he not regarded, and so turn'd
Sighing, and feign'd a sleep until he slept.

Then rose Elaine and glided thro' the fields,
And past beneath the weirdly-sculptured gates
Far up the dim rich city to her kin;
There bode the night: but woke with dawn, and past
Down thro' the dim rich city to the fields,
Thence to the cave: so day by day she past
In either twilight ghost-like to and fro
Gliding, and every day she tended him,
And likewise many a night: and Lancelot
Would, tho' he call'd his wound a little hurt
Whereof he should be quickly whole, at times
Brain-feverous in his heat and agony, seem
Uncourteous, even he: but the meek maid
Sweetly forbore him ever, being to him
Meeker than any child to a rough nurse,
Milder than any mother to a sick child,

And never woman yet, since man's first fall,
Did kindlier unto man, but her deep love
Upbore her; till the hermit, skill'd in all
The simples and the science of that time,
Told him that her fine care had saved his life.
And the sick man forgot her simple blush,
Would call her friend and sister, sweet Elaine,
Would listen for her coming and regret
Her parting step, and held her tenderly,
And loved her with all love except the love
Of man and woman when they love their best,
Closest and sweetest, and had died the death
In any knightly fashion for her sake.
And peradventure had he seen her first
She might have made this and that other world
Another world for the sick man; but now
The shackles of an old love straiten'd him,
His honour rooted in dishonour stood,
And faith unfaithful kept him falsely true.

Yet the great knight in his mid-sickness made
Full many a holy vow and pure resolve.
These, as but born of sickness, could not live:
For when the blood ran lustier in him again,
Full often the bright image of one face,
Making a treacherous quiet in his heart,
Dispersed his resolution like a cloud.
Then if the maiden, while that ghostly grace
Beam'd on his fancy, spoke, he answer'd not,
Or short and coldly, and she knew right well
What the rough sickness meant, but what this meant
She knew not, and the sorrow dimm'd her sight,
And drave her ere her time across the fields
Far into the rich city, where alone
She murmur'd, 'Vain, in vain: it cannot be.
He will not love me: how then? must I die?'
Then as a little helpless innocent bird,
That has but one plain passage of few notes,
Will sing the simple passage o'er and o'er
For all an April morning, till the ear
Wearies to hear it, so the simple maid
Went half the night repeating, 'Must I die?'
And now to right she turn'd, and now to left,
And found no ease in turning or in rest;
And 'Him or death,' she mutter'd, 'death or him,'
Again and like a burthen, 'Him or death.'

But when Sir Lancelot's deadly hurt was whole,
To Astolat returning rode the three.
There morn by morn, arraying her sweet self
In that wherein she deem'd she look'd her best,
She came before Sir Lancelot, for she thought
'If I be loved, these are my festal robes,
If not, the victim's flowers before he fall.'
And Lancelot ever prest upon the maid
That she should ask some goodly gift of him
For her own self or hers; 'and do not shun
To speak the wish most near to your true heart;
Such service have ye done me, that I make
My will of yours, and Prince and Lord am I
In mine own land, and what I will I can.'
Then like a ghost she lifted up her face,
But like a ghost without the power to speak.
And Lancelot saw that she withheld her wish,
And bode among them yet a little space
Till he should learn it; and one morn it chanced
He found her in among the garden yews,
And said, 'Delay no longer, speak your wish,
Seeing I go to-day': then out she brake:
'Going? and we shall never see you more.
And I must die for want of one bold word.'
'Speak: that I live to hear,' he said, 'is yours.'
Then suddenly and passionately she spoke:
'I have gone mad. I love you: let me die.'
'Ah, sister,' answer'd Lancelot, 'what is this?'

And innocently extending her white arms,
'Your love,' she said, 'your love—to be your wife.'
And Lancelot answer'd, 'Had I chosen to wed,
I had been wedded earlier, sweet Elaine;
But now there never will be wife of mine.'
'No, no,' she cried, 'I care not to be wife,
But to be with you still, to see your face,
To serve you, and to follow you thro' the world.'
And Lancelot answer'd, 'Nay, the world, the world,
All ear and eye, with such a stupid heart
To interpret ear and eye, and such a tongue
To blare its own interpretation—nay,
Full ill then should I quit your brother's love,
And your good father's kindness.' And she said,
'Not to be with you, not to see your face—
Alas for me then, my good days are done.'
'Nay, noble maid,' he answer'd, 'ten times nay!
This is not love: but love's first flash in youth,
Most common: yea, I know it of mine own self:
And you yourself will smile at your own self
Hereafter, when you yield your flower of life
To one more fitly yours, not thrice your age:
And then will I, for true you are and sweet
Beyond mine old belief in womanhood,
More specially should your good knight be poor,
Endow you with broad land and territory
Even to the half my realm beyond the seas,
So that would make you happy: furthermore,
Ev'n to the death, as tho' ye were my blood,
In all your quarrels will I be your knight.
This will I do, dear damsel, for your sake,
And more than this I cannot.'

While he spoke
She neither blush'd nor shook, but deathly-pale
Stood grasping what was nearest, then replied:
'Of all this will I nothing'; and so fell,
And thus they bore her swooning to her tower.

Then spake, to whom thro' those black walls of yew
Their talk had pierced, her father: 'Ay, a flash,
I fear me, that will strike my blossom dead.
Too courteous are ye, fair Lord Lancelot.
I pray you, use some rough discourtesy
To blunt or break her passion.'

Lancelot said,
'That were against me: what I can I will';
And there that day remain'd, and toward even
Sent for his shield: full meekly rose the maid,
Stript off the case, and gave the naked shield;
Then, when she heard his horse upon the stones,
Unclasping flung the casement back, and look'd
Down on his helm, from which her sleeve had gone.
And Lancelot knew the little clinking sound;
And she by tact of love was well aware
That Lancelot knew that she was looking at him.
And yet he glanced not up, nor waved his hand,
Nor bad farewell, but sadly rode away.
This was the one discourtesy that he used.

So in her tower alone the maiden sat:
His very shield was gone; only the case,
Her own poor work, her empty labour, left.
But still she heard him, still his picture form'd
And grew between her and the pictured wall.
Then came her father, saying in low tones,
'Have comfort,' whom she greeted quietly.
Then came her brethren saying, 'Peace to thee,
Sweet sister,' whom she answer'd with all calm.
But when they left her to herself again,
Death, like a friend's voice from a distant field

Approaching thro' the darkness, call'd; the owls
Wailing had power upon her, and she mixt
Her fancies with the sallow-rifted glooms
Of evening, and the moanings of the wind.

And in those days she made a little song,
And call'd her song 'The Song of Love and Death,'
And sang it: sweetly could she make and sing.

'Sweet is true love tho' given in vain, in vain;
And sweet is death who puts an end to pain:
I know not which is sweeter, no, not I.

'Love, art thou sweet? then bitter death must be:
Love, thou art bitter; sweet is death to me.
O Love, if death be sweeter, let me die.

'Sweet love, that seems not made to fade away,
Sweet death, that seems to make us loveless clay,
I know not which is sweeter, no, not I.

'I fain would follow love, if that could be;
I needs must follow death, who calls for me;
Call and I follow, I follow! let me die.'

High with the last line scaled her voice, and this,
All in a fiery dawning wild with wind
That shook her tower, the brothers heard, and thought
With shuddering, 'Hark the Phantom of the house
That ever shrieks before a death,' and call'd
The father, and all three in hurry and fear
Ran to her, and lo! the blood-red light of dawn
Flared on her face, she shrilling, 'Let me die!'

As when we dwell upon a word we know,
Repeating, till the word we know so well
Becomes a wonder, and we know not why,
So dwelt the father on her face, and thought
'Is this Elaine?' till back the maiden fell,
Then gave a languid hand to each, and lay,
Speaking a still good-morrow with her eyes.
At last she said, 'Sweet brothers, yesternight
I seem'd a curious little maid again,
As happy as when we dwelt among the woods,
And when ye used to take me with the flood
Up the great river in the boatman's boat.
Only ye would not pass beyond the cape
That has the poplar on it: there ye fixt
Your limit, oft returning with the tide.
And yet I cried because ye would not pass
Beyond it, and far up the shining flood
Until we found the palace of the King.
And yet ye would not; but this night I dream'd
That I was all alone upon the flood,
And then I said, "Now shall I have my will:"
And there I woke, but still the wish remain'd.
So let me hence that I may pass at last
Beyond the poplar and far up the flood,
Until I find the palace of the King.
There will I enter in among them all,
And no man there will dare to mock at me;
But there the fine Gawain will wonder at me,
And there the great Sir Lancelot muse at me;
Gawain, who bad a thousand farewells to me,
Lancelot, who coldly went, nor bad me one:
And there the King will know me and my love,
And there the Queen herself will pity me,
And all the gentle court will welcome me,
And after my long voyage I shall rest!'

'Peace,' said her father, 'O my child, ye seem
Light-headed, for what force is yours to go
So far, being sick? and wherefore would ye look
On this proud fellow again, who scorns us all?'

Then the rough Torre began to heave and move,
And bluster into stormy sobs and say,
'I never loved him: an I meet with him,
I care not howsoever great he be,
Then will I strike at him and strike him down,
Give me good fortune, I will strike him dead,
For this discomfort he hath done the house.'

To whom the gentle sister made reply,
'Fret not yourself, dear brother, nor be wroth,
Seeing it is no more Sir Lancelot's fault
Not to love me, than it is mine to love
Him of all men who seems to me the highest.'

'Highest?' the father answer'd, echoing 'highest?'
(He meant to break the passion in her) 'nay,
Daughter, I know not what you call the highest;
But this I know, for all the people know it,
He loves the Queen, and in an open shame:
And she returns his love in open shame;
If this be high, what is it to be low?'

Then spake the lily maid of Astolat:
'Sweet father, all too faint and sick am I
For anger: these are slanders: never yet
Was noble man but made ignoble talk.
He makes no friend who never made a foe.
But now it is my glory to have loved
One peerless, without stain: so let me pass,
My father, howsoe'er I seem to you,
Not all unhappy, having loved God's best
And greatest, tho' my love had no return:
Yet, seeing you desire your child to live,
Thanks, but you work against your own desire;
For if I could believe the things you say
I should but die the sooner; wherefore cease,
Sweet father, and bid call the ghostly man
Hither, and let me shrive me clean, and die.'

So when the ghostly man had come and gone,
She with a face, bright as for sin forgiven,
Besought Lavaine to write as she devised
A letter, word for word; and when he ask'd
'Is it for Lancelot, is it for my dear lord?
Then will I bear it gladly;' she replied,
'For Lancelot and the Queen and all the world,
But I myself must bear it.' Then he wrote
The letter she devised; which being writ
And folded, 'O sweet father, tender and true,
Deny me not,' she said—'ye never yet
Denied my fancies—this, however strange,
My latest: lay the letter in my hand
A little ere I die, and close the hand
Upon it; I shall guard it even in death.
And when the heat is gone from out my heart,
Then take the little bed on which I died
For Lancelot's love, and deck it like the Queen's
For richness, and me also like the Queen
In all I have of rich, and lay me on it.
And let there be prepared a chariot-bier
To take me to the river, and a barge
Be ready on the river, clothed in black.
I go in state to court, to meet the Queen.
There surely I shall speak for mine own self,
And none of you can speak for me so well.
And therefore let our dumb old man alone
Go with me, he can steer and row, and he
Will guide me to that palace, to the doors.'

She ceased: her father promised; whereupon
She grew so cheerful that they deem'd her death
Was rather in the fantasy than the blood.
But ten slow mornings past, and on the eleventh
Her father laid the letter in her hand,
And closed the hand upon it, and she died.
So that day there was dole in Astolat.

But when the next sun brake from underground,
Then, those two brethren slowly with bent brows
Accompanying, the sad chariot-bier
Past like a shadow thro' the field, that shone

Full-summer, to that stream whereon the barge,
Pall'd all its length in blackest samite, lay.
There sat the lifelong creature of the house,
Loyal, the dumb old servitor, on deck,
Winking his eyes, and twisted all his face.
So those two brethren from the chariot took
And on the black decks laid her in her bed,
Set in her hand a lily, o'er her hung
The silken case with braided blazonings,
And kiss'd her quiet brows, and saying to her
'Sister, farewell for ever,' and again
'Farewell, sweet sister,' parted all in tears.
Then rose the dumb old servitor, and the dead,
Oar'd by the dumb, went upward with the flood—
In her right hand the lily, in her left
The letter—all her bright hair streaming down—
And all the coverlid was cloth of gold
Drawn to her waist, and she herself in white
All but her face, and that clear-featured face
Was lovely, for she did not seem as dead,
But fast asleep, and lay as tho' she smiled.

That day Sir Lancelot at the palace craved
Audience of Guinevere, to give at last
The price of half a realm, his costly gift,
Hard-won and hardly won with bruise and blow,
With deaths of others, and almost his own,
The nine-years-fought-for diamonds: for he saw
One of her house, and sent him to the Queen
Bearing his wish, whereto the Queen agreed
With such and so unmoved a majesty
She might have seem'd her statue, but that he,
Low-drooping till he wellnigh kiss'd her feet
For loyal awe, saw with a sidelong eye
The shadow of some piece of pointed lace,
In the Queen's shadow, vibrate on the walls,
And parted, laughing in his courtly heart.

All in an oriel on the summer side.
Vine-clad, of Arthur's palace toward the stream,
They met, and Lancelot kneeling utter'd, 'Queen,
Lady, my liege, in whom I have my joy,
Take, what I had not won except for you,
These jewels, and make me happy, making them
An armlet for the roundest arm on earth,
Or necklace for a neck to which the swan's
Is tawnier than her cygnet's: these are words:
Your beauty is your beauty, and I sin
In speaking, yet O grant my worship of it
Words, as we grant grief tears. Such sin in words
Perchance, we both can pardon: but, my Queen,
I hear of rumours flying thro' your court.
Our bond, as not the bond of man and wife,
Should have in it an absoluter trust
To make up that defect: let rumours be:
When did not rumours fly? these, as I trust
That you trust me in your own nobleness,
I may not well believe that you believe.'

While thus he spoke, half turn'd away, the Queen
Brake from the vast oriel-embowering vine
Leaf after leaf, and tore, and cast them off,
Till all the place whereon she stood was green;
Then, when he ceased, in one cold passive hand
Received at once and laid aside the gems
There on a table near her, and replied:

'It may be, I am quicker of belief
Than you believe me, Lancelot of the Lake.
Our bond is not the bond of man and wife.
This good is in it, whatsoe'er of ill,
It can be broken easier. I for you
This many a year have done despite and wrong
To one whom ever in my heart of hearts
I did acknowledge nobler. What are these?
Diamonds for me! they had been thrice their worth
Being your gift, had you not lost your own
To loyal hearts the value of all gifts
Must vary as the giver's. Not for me!
For her! for your new fancy. Only this

Grant me, I pray you: have your joys apart.
I doubt not that however changed, you keep
So much of what is graceful: and myself
Would shun to break those bounds of courtesy
In which as Arthur's Queen I move and rule:
So cannot speak my mind. An end to this!
A strange one! yet I take it with Amen.
So pray you, add my diamonds to her pearls;
Deck her with these; tell her, she shines me down:
An armlet for an arm to which the Queen's
Is haggard, or a necklace for a neck
O as much fairer—as a faith once fair
Was richer than these diamonds—hers not mine—
Nay, by the mother of our Lord himself,
Or hers or mine, mine now to work my will—
She shall not have them.'

Saying which she seized,
And, thro' the casement standing wide for heat,
Flung them, and down they flash'd, and smote the stream.
Then from the smitten surface flash'd, as it were,
Diamonds to meet them, and they past away.
Then while Sir Lancelot leant, in half disdain
At love, life, all things, on the window ledge,
Close underneath his eyes, and right across
Where these had fallen, slowly past the barge
Whereon the lily maid of Astolat
Lay smiling, like a star in blackest night.

But the wild Queen, who saw not, burst away
To weep and wail in secret; and the barge,
On to the palace-doorway sliding, paused.
There two stood arm'd, and kept the door; to whom,
All up the marble stair, tier over tier,
Were added mouths that gaped, and eyes that ask'd
'What is it?' but that oarsman's haggard face,
As hard and still as is the face that men
Shape to their fancy's eye from broken rocks
On some cliff-side, appall'd them, and they said,
'He is enchanted, cannot speak—and she,
Look how she sleeps—the Fairy Queen, so fair!
Yea, but how pale! what are they? flesh and blood?
Or come to take the King to Fairyland?
For some do hold our Arthur cannot die,
But that he passes into Fairyland.'

While thus they babbled of the King, the King
Came girt with knights: then turn'd the tongueless man
From the half-face to the full eye, and rose
And pointed to the damsel, and the doors.
So Arthur bad the meek Sir Percivale
And pure Sir Galahad to uplift the maid;
And reverently they bore her into hall.
Then came the fine Gawain and wonder'd at her,
And Lancelot later came and mused at her,
And last the Queen herself, and pitied her:
But Arthur spied the letter in her hand,
Stoopt, took, brake seal, and read it; this was all:

'Most noble lord, Sir Lancelot of the Lake,
I, sometime call'd the maid of Astolat,
Come, for you left me taking no farewell,
Hither, to take my last farewell of you.
I loved you, and my love had no return,
And therefore my true love has been my death.
And therefore to our Lady Guinevere.
And to all other ladies, I make moan:
Pray for my soul, and yield me burial.
Pray for my soul thou too, Sir Lancelot,
As thou art a knight peerless.'

Thus he read;
And ever in the reading, lords and dames
Wept, looking often from his face who read
To hers which lay so silent, and at times,

So touch'd were they, half-thinking that her lips,
Who had devised the letter, moved again.

Then freely spoke Sir Lancelot to them all:
'My lord liege Arthur, and all ye that hear,
Know that for this most gentle maiden's death
Right heavy am I; for good she was and true,
But loved me with a love beyond all love
In women, whomsoever I have known.
Yet to be loved makes not to love again;
Not at my years, however it hold in youth.
I swear by truth and knighthood that I gave
No cause, not willingly, for such a love:
To this I call my friends in testimony,
Her brethren, and her father, who himself
Besought me to be plain and blunt, and use,
To break her passion, some discourtesy
Against my nature: what I could, I did.
I left her and I bad her no farewell;
Tho', had I dreamt the damsel would have died,
I might have put my wits to some rough use,
And help'd her from herself.'

Then said the Queen
(Sea was her wrath, yet working after storm)
'Ye might at least have done her so much grace,
Fair lord, as would have help'd her from her death.'
He raised his head, their eyes met and hers fell,
He adding,
'Queen, she would not be content
Save that I wedded her, which could not be.
Then might she follow me thro' the world, she ask'd;
It could not be. I told her that her love
Was but the flash of youth, would darken down
To rise hereafter in a stiller flame
Toward one more worthy of her—then would I,
More specially were he, she wedded, poor,
Estate them with large land and territory
In mine own realm beyond the narrow seas,
To keep them in all joyance: more than this
I could not; this she would not, and she died.'

He pausing, Arthur answer'd, 'O my knight,
It will be to thy worship, as my knight,
And mine, as head of all our Table Round,
To see that she be buried worshipfully.'

So toward that shrine which then in all the realm
Was richest, Arthur leading, slowly went
The marshall'd Order of their Table Round,
And Lancelot sad beyond his wont, to see
The maiden buried, not as one unknown,
Nor meanly, but with gorgeous obsequies,
And mass, and rolling music, like a queen.
And when the knights had laid her comely head
Low in the dust of half-forgotten kings,
Then Arthur spake among them, 'Let her tomb
Be costly, and her image thereupon,
And let the shield of Lancelot at her feet
Be carven, and her lily in her hand.
And let the story of her dolorous voyage
For all true hearts be blazon'd on her tomb
In letters gold and azure!' which was wrought
Thereafter; but when now the lords and dames
And people, from the high door streaming, brake
Disorderly, as homeward each, the Queen,
Who mark'd Sir Lancelot where he moved apart,
Drew near, and sigh'd in passing, 'Lancelot,
Forgive me; mine was jealousy in love.'
He answer'd with his eyes upon the ground,
'That is love's curse; pass on, my Queen, forgiven.'
But Arthur, who beheld his cloudy brows,
Approach'd him, and with full affection said,

'Lancelot, my Lancelot, thou in whom I have
Most joy and most affiance, for I know

What thou hast been in battle by my side,
And many a time have watch'd thee at the tilt
Strike down the lusty and long practised knight,
And let the younger and unskill'd go by
To win his honour and to make his name,
And loved thy courtesies and thee, a man
Made to be loved; but now I would to God,
Seeing the homeless trouble in thine eyes,
Thou couldst have loved this maiden, shaped, it seems,
By God for thee alone, and from her face,
If one may judge the living by the dead,
Delicately pure and marvellously fair,
Who might have brought thee, now a lonely man
Wifeless and heirless, noble issue, sons
Born to the glory of thy name and fame,
My knight, the great Sir Lancelot of the Lake.'

Then answer'd Lancelot, 'Fair she was, my King,
Pure, as you ever wish your knights to be.
To doubt her fairness were to want an eye,
To doubt her pureness were to want a heart—
Yea, to be loved, if what is worthy love
Could bind him, but free love will not be bound.'
'Free love, so bound, were freëst,' said the King.
'Let love be free; free love is for the best:
And, after heaven, on our dull side of death,
What should be best, if not so pure a love
Clothed in so pure a loveliness? yet thee
She fail'd to find, tho' being, as I think,
Unbound as yet, and gentle, as I know.'

And Lancelot answer'd nothing, but he went,
And at the inrunning of a little brook
Sat by the river in a cove, and watch'd
The high reed wave, and lifted up his eyes
And saw the barge that brought her moving down,
Far-off, a blot upon the stream, and said
Low in himself, 'Ah simple heart and sweet,
Ye loved me, damsel, surely with a love
Far tenderer than my Queen's. Pray for thy soul?
Ay, that will I. Farewell too—now at last—
Farewell, fair lily. "Jealousy in love"?
Not rather dead love's harsh heir, jealous pride?
Queen, if I grant the jealousy as of love,
May not your crescent fear for name and fame
Speak, as it waxes, of a love that wanes?
Why did the King dwell on my name to me?
Mine own name shames me, seeming a reproach,
Lancelot, whom the Lady of the Lake
Caught from his mother's arms—the wondrous one
Who passes thro' the vision of the night—
She chanted snatches of mysterious hymns
Heard on the winding waters, eve and morn
She kiss'd me saying, "Thou art fair, my child,
As a king's son," and often in her arms
She bare me, pacing on the dusky mere.
Would she had drown'd me in it, where'er it be!
For what am I? what profits me my name
Of greatest knight? I fought for it, and have it:
Pleasure to have it, none; to lose it, pain;
Now grown a part of me: but what use in it?
To make men worse by making my sin known?
Or sin seem less, the sinner seeming great?
Alas for Arthur's greatest knight, a man
Not after Arthur's heart! I needs must break
These bonds that so defame me: not without
She wills it: would I, if she will'd it? nay,
Who knows? but if I would not, then may God,
I pray him, send a sudden Angel down
To seize me by the hair and bear me far,
And fling me deep in that forgotten mere,
Among the tumbled fragments of the hills.'

So groan'd Sir Lancelot in remorseful pain,
Not knowing he should die a holy man.

[1859]

THE HOLY GRAIL

From noiseful arms, and acts of prowess done
In tournament or tilt, Sir Percivale,
Whom Arthur and his knighthood call'd The Pure,
Had pass'd into the silent life of prayer,
Praise, fast, and alms; and leaving for the cowl
The helmet in an abbey far away
From Camelot, there, and not long after, died.

And one, a fellow-monk among the rest,
Ambrosius, loved him much beyond the rest,
And honour'd him, and wrought into his heart
A way by love that waken'd love within,
To answer that which came; and as they sat
Beneath a world-old yew-tree, darkening half
The cloisters, on a gustful April morn
That puff'd the swaying branches into smoke
Above them, ere the summer when he died,
The monk Ambrosius question'd Percivale:

'O brother, I have seen this yew-tree smoke,
Spring after spring, for half a hundred years:
For never have I known the world without,
Nor ever stray'd beyond the pale: but thee,
When first thou camest—such a courtesy
Spake thro' the limbs and in the voice—I knew
For one of those who eat in Arthur's hall;
For good ye are and bad, and like to coins,
Some true, some light, but every one of you
Stamp'd with the image of the King; and now
Tell me, what drove thee from the Table Round,
My brother? was it earthly passion crost?'

'Nay,' said the knight; 'for no such passion mine.
But the sweet vision of the Holy Grail
Drove me from all vainglories, rivalries,
And earthly heats that spring and sparkle out
Among us in the jousts, while women watch
Who wins, who falls; and waste the spiritual strength
Within us, better offer'd up to Heaven.'

To whom the monk: 'The Holy Grail!—I trust
We are green in Heaven's eyes; but here too much
We moulder—as to things without I mean—
Yet one of your own knights, a guest of ours,
Told us of this in our refectory,
But spake with such a sadness and so low
We heard not half of what he said. What is it?
The phantom of a cup that comes and goes?'

'Nay, monk! what phantom?' answer'd Percivale.
'The cup, the cup itself, from which our Lord
Drank at the last sad supper with his own.
This, from the blessed land of Aromat—
After the day of darkness, when the dead
Went wandering o'er Moriah—the good saint
Arimathæan Joseph, journeying brought
To Glastonbury, where the winter thorn
Blossoms at Christmas, mindful of our Lord.
And there awhile it bode; and if a man
Could touch or see it, he was heal'd at once,
By faith, of all his ills. But then the times
Grew to such evil that the holy cup
Was caught away to Heaven, and disappear'd.'

To whom the monk: 'From our old books I know
That Joseph came of old to Glastonbury,
And there the heathen Prince, Arviragus,
Gave him an isle of marsh whereon to build;
And there he built with wattles from the marsh
A little lonely church in days of yore,
For so they say, these books of ours, but seem
Mute of this miracle, far as I have read.
But who first saw the holy thing to-day?'

'A woman,' answer'd Percivale, 'a nun,
And one no further off in blood from me
Than sister; and if ever holy maid
With knees of adoration wore the stone,
A holy maid; tho' never maiden glow'd,
But that was in her earlier maidenhood,
With such a fervent flame of human love,
Which being rudely blunted, glanced and shot
Only to holy things; to prayer and praise
She gave herself, to fast and alms. And yet,
Nun as she was, the scandal of the Court,
Sin against Arthur and the Table Round,
And the strange sound of an adulterous race,
Across the iron grating of her cell
Beat, and she pray'd and fasted all the more.

'And he to whom she told her sins, or what
Her all but utter whiteness held for sin,
A man wellnigh a hundred winters old,
Spake often with her of the Holy Grail,
A legend handed down thro' five or six,
And each of these a hundred winters old,
From our Lord's time. And when King Arthur made
His Table Round, and all men's hearts became
Clean for a season, surely he had thought
That now the Holy Grail would come again;
But sin broke out. Ah, Christ, that it would come,
And heal the world of all their wickedness!
"O Father!" ask'd the maiden, "might it come
To me by prayer and fasting?" "Nay," said he,
"I know not, for thy heart is pure as snow."
And so she pray'd and fasted, till the sun
Shone, and the wind blew, thro' her, and I thought
She might have risen and floated when I saw her.

'For on a day she sent to speak with me.
And when she came to speak, behold her eyes
Beyond my knowing of them, beautiful,
Beyond all knowing of them, wonderful,
Beautiful in the light of holiness.
And "O my brother Percivale," she said,
"Sweet brother, I have seen the Holy Grail:
For, waked at dead of night, I heard a sound
As of a silver horn from o'er the hills
Blown, and I thought, 'It is not Arthur's use
To hunt by moonlight;' and the slender sound
As from a distance beyond distance grew
Coming upon me—O never harp nor horn,
Nor aught we blow with breath, or touch with hand,
Was like that music as it came; and then
Stream'd thro' my cell a cold and silver beam,
And down the long beam stole the Holy Grail,
Rose-red with beatings in it, as if alive,
Till all the white walls of my cell were dyed
With rosy colours leaping on the wall;
And then the music faded, and the Grail
Past, and the beam decay'd, and from the walls
The rosy quiverings died into the night.
So now the Holy Thing is here again
Among us, brother, fast thou too and pray,
And tell thy brother knights to fast and pray,
That so perchance the vision may be seen
By thee and those, and all the world be heal'd."

'Then leaving the pale nun, I spake of this
To all men; and myself fasted and pray'd
Always, and many among us many a week
Fasted and pray'd even to the uttermost,
Expectant of the wonder that would be.

'And one there was among us, ever moved
Among us in white armour, Galahad.
"God make thee good as thou art beautiful,"
Said Arthur, when he dubb'd him knight; and none,
In so young youth, was ever made a knight
Till Galahad; and this Galahad, when he heard
My sister's vision, fill'd me with amaze;
His eyes became so like her own, they seem'd
Hers, and himself her brother more than I.

'Sister or brother none had he; but some
Call'd him a son of Lancelot, and some said
Begotten by enchantment—chatterers they,
Like birds of passage piping up and down,
That gape for flies—we know not whence they come;
For when was Lancelot wanderingly lewd?

'But she, the wan sweet maiden, shore away
Clean from her forehead all that wealth of hair
Which made a silken mat-work for her feet;
And out of this she plaited broad and long
A strong sword-belt, and wove with silver thread
And crimson in the belt a strange device,
A crimson grail within a silver beam;
And saw the bright boy-knight, and bound it on him,
Saying, "My knight, my love, my knight of heaven,
O thou, my love, whose love is one with mine,
I, maiden, round thee, maiden, bind my belt.
Go forth, for thou shalt see what I have seen,
And break thro' all, till one will crown thee king
Far in the spiritual city:" and as she spake
She sent the deathless passion in her eyes
Thro' him, and made him hers, and laid her mind
On him, and he believed in her belief.

'Then came a year of miracle: O brother,
In our great hall there stood a vacant chair,
Fashion'd by Merlin ere he past away,
And carven with strange figures; and in and out
The figures, like a serpent, ran a scroll
Of letters in a tongue no man could read.
And Merlin call'd it "The Siege perilous,"
Perilous for good and ill: "for there," he said,
"No man could sit but he should lose himself:"
And once by misadvertence Merlin sat
In his own chair, and so was lost; but he,
Galahad, when he heard of Merlin's doom,
Cried, "If I lose myself, I save myself!"

'Then on a summer night it came to pass,
While the great banquet lay along the hall,
That Galahad would sit down in Merlin's chair.

'And all at once, as there we sat, we heard
A cracking and a riving of the roofs,
And rending, and a blast, and overhead
Thunder, and in the thunder was a cry.
And in the blast there smote along the hall
A beam of light seven times more clear than day:
And down the long beam stole the Holy Grail
All over cover'd with a luminous cloud,
And none might see who bare it, and it past.
But every knight beheld his fellow's face
As in a glory, and all the knights arose,
And staring each at other like dumb men
Stood, till I found a voice and sware a vow.

'I sware a vow before them all, that I,
Because I had not seen the Grail, would ride
A twelvemonth and a day in quest of it,
Until I found and saw it, as the nun
My sister saw it; and Galahad sware the vow,
And good Sir Bors, our Lancelot's cousin, sware,
And Lancelot sware, and many among the knights,
And Gawain sware, and louder than the rest.'

Then spake the monk Ambrosius, asking him,
'What said the King? Did Arthur take the vow?'

'Nay, for my lord,' said Percivale, 'the King,
Was not in hall: for early that same day,
Scaped thro' a cavern from a bandit hold,
An outraged maiden sprang into the hall
Crying on help: for all her shining hair
Was smear'd with earth, and either milky arm
Red-rent with hooks of bramble, and all she wore
Torn as a sail that leaves the rope is torn

In tempest: so the King arose and went
To smoke the scandalous hive of those wild bees
That made such honey in his realm. Howbeit
Some little of this marvel he too saw,
Returning o'er the plain that then began
To darken under Camelot; whence the King
Look'd up, calling aloud, "Lo, there! the roofs
Of our great hall are roll'd in thunder-smoke!
Pray Heaven, they be not smitten by the bolt."
For dear to Arthur was that hall of ours,
As having there so oft with all his knights
Feasted, and as the stateliest under heaven.

'O brother, had you known our mighty hall,
Which Merlin built for Arthur long ago!
For all the sacred mount of Camelot,
And all the dim rich city, roof by roof,
Tower after tower, spire beyond spire,
By grove, and garden-lawn, and rushing brook,
Climbs to the mighty hall that Merlin built.
And four great zones of sculpture, set betwixt
With many a mystic symbol, gird the hall:
And in the lowest beasts are slaying men,
And in the second men are slaying beasts,
And on the third are warriors, perfect men,
And on the fourth are men with growing wings,
And over all one statue in the mould
Of Arthur, made by Merlin, with a crown,
And peak'd wings pointed to the Northern Star.
And eastward fronts the statue, and the crown
And both the wings are made of gold, and flame
At sunrise till the people in far fields,
Wasted so often by the heathen hordes,
Behold it, crying, "We have still a King."

'And, brother, had you known our hall within,
Broader and higher than any in all the lands!
Where twelve great windows blazon Arthur's wars,
And all the light that falls upon the board
Streams thro' the twelve great battles of our King.
Nay, one there is, and at the eastern end,
Wealthy with wandering lines of mount and mere,
Where Arthur finds the brand Excalibur.
And also one to the west, and counter to it,
And blank: and who shall blazon it? when and how?—
O there, perchance, when all our wars are done,
The brand Excalibur will be cast away.

'So to this hall full quickly rode the King,
In horror lest the work by Merlin wrought,
Dreamlike, should on the sudden vanish, wrapt
In unremorseful folds of rolling fire.
And in he rode, and up I glanced, and saw
The golden dragon sparkling over all:
And many of those who burnt the hold, their arms
Hack'd and their foreheads grimed with smoke, and sear'd,
Follow'd, and in among bright faces, ours,
Full of the vision, prest: and then the King
Spake to me, being nearest, "Percivale,"
(Because the hall was all in tumult—some
Vowing, and some protesting), "what is this?"

'O brother, when I told him what had chanced,
My sister's vision, and the rest, his face
Darken'd, as I have seen it more than once,
When some brave deed seem'd to be done in vain,
Darken; and "Woe is me, my knights," he cried,
"Had I been here, ye had not sworn the vow."
Bold was mine answer, "Had thyself been here,
My King, thou wouldst have sworn."
"Yea, yea," said he,
"Art thou so bold and hast not seen the Grail?"

'"Nay, lord, I heard the sound, I saw the light,
But since I did not see the Holy Thing,
I sware a vow to follow it till I saw."

'Then when he ask'd us, knight by knight, if any
Had seen it, all their answers were as one:
"Nay, lord, and therefore have we sworn our vows."

' "Lo now," said Arthur, "have ye seen a cloud?
What go ye into the wilderness to see?"

'Then Galahad on the sudden, and in a voice
Shrilling along the hall to Arthur, call'd,
"But I, Sir Arthur, saw the Holy Grail,
I saw the Holy Grail and heard a cry—
'O Galahad, and O Galahad, follow me.' "

' "Ah, Galahad, Galahad," said the King, "for such
As thou art is the vision, not for these.
Thy holy nun and thou have seen a sign—
Holier is none, my Percivale, then she—
A sign to maim this Order which I made.
But ye, that follow but the leader's bell"
(Brother, the King was hard upon his knights)
"Taliessin is our fullest throat of song,
And one hath sung and all the dumb will sing.
Lancelot is Lancelot, and hath overborne
Five knights at once, and every younger knight,
Unproven, holds himself as Lancelot,
Till overborne by one, he learns—and ye,
What are ye? Galahads?—no, nor Percivales"
(For thus it pleased the King to range me close
After Sir Galahad); "nay," said he, "but men
With strength and will to right the wrong'd, of power
To lay the sudden heads of violence flat,
Knights that in twelve great battles splash'd and dyed
The strong White Horse in his own heathen blood—
But one hath seen, and all the blind will see.
Go, since your vows are sacred, being made:
Yet—for ye know the cries of all my realm
Pass thro' this hall—how often, O my knights,
Your places being vacant at my side,
This chance of noble deeds will come and go
Unchallenged, while ye follow wandering fires
Lost in the quagmire! Many of you, yea most,
Return no more: ye think I show myself
Too dark a prophet: come now, let us meet
The morrow morn once more in one full field
Of gracious pastime, that once more the King,
Before ye leave him for this Quest, may count
The yet-unbroken strength of all his knights,
Rejoicing in that Order which he made."

'So when the sun broke next from under ground,
All the great table of our Arthur closed
And clash'd in such a tourney and so full,
So many lances broken—never yet
Had Camelot seen the like, since Arthur came;
And I myself and Galahad, for a strength
Was in us from the vision, overthrew
So many knights that all the people cried,
And almost burst the barriers in their heat,
Shouting, "Sir Galahad and Sir Percivale!"

'But when the next day brake from under ground—
O brother, had you known our Camelot,
Built by old kings, age after age, so old
The King himself had fears that it would fall,
So strange, and rich, and dim; for where the roofs
Totter'd toward each other in the sky,
Met foreheads all along the street of those
Who watch'd us pass; and lower, and where the long
Rich galleries, lady-laden, weigh'd the necks
Of dragons clinging to the crazy walls,
Thicker than drops from thunder, showers of flowers
Fell as we past; and men and boys astride
On wyvern, lion, dragon, griffin, swan,
At all the corners, named us each by name,

Calling "God speed!" but in the ways below
The knights and ladies wept, and rich and poor
Wept, and the King himself could hardly speak
For grief, and all in middle street the Queen,
Who rode by Lancelot, wail'd and shriek'd aloud,
"This madness has come on us for our sins."
So to the Gate of the three Queens we came,
Where Arthur's wars are render'd mystically,
And thence departed every one his way.

'And I was lifted up in heart, and thought
Of all my late-shown prowess in the lists,
How my strong lance had beaten down the knights,
So many and famous names; and never yet
Had heaven appear'd so blue, nor earth so green,
For all my blood danced in me, and I knew
That I should light upon the Holy Grail.

'Thereafter, the dark warning of our King,
That most of us would follow wandering fires,
Came like a driving gloom across my mind.
Then every evil word I had spoken once,
And every evil thought I had thought of old,
And every evil deed I ever did,
Awoke and cried, "This Quest is not for thee."
And lifting up mine eyes, I found myself
Alone, and in a land of sand and thorns,
And I was thirsty even unto death;
And I, too, cried, "This Quest is not for thee."

'And on I rode, and when I thought my thirst
Would slay me, saw deep lawns, and then a brook,
With one sharp rapid, where the crisping white
Play'd ever back upon the sloping wave,
And took both ear and eye; and o'er the brook
Were apple-trees, and apples by the brook
Fallen, and on the lawns. "I will rest here,"
I said, "I am not worthy of the Quest;"
But even while I drank the brook, and ate
The goodly apples, all these things at once
Fell into dust, and I was left alone,
And thirsting, in a land of sand and thorns.

'And then behold a woman at a door
Spinning; and fair the house whereby she sat,
And kind the woman's eyes and innocent,
And all her bearing gracious; and she rose
Opening her arms to meet me, as who should say,
"Rest here;" but when I touch'd her, lo! she, too,
Fell into dust and nothing, and the house
Became no better than a broken shed,
And in it a dead babe; and also this
Fell into dust, and I was left alone.

'And on I rode, and greater was my thirst.
Then flash'd a yellow gleam across the world,
And where it smote the plowshare in the field,
The plowman left his plowing, and fell down
Before it; where it glitter'd on her pail,
The milkmaid left her milking, and fell down
Before it, and I knew not why, but thought
"The sun is rising," tho' the sun had risen.
Then was I ware of one that on me moved
In golden armour with a crown of gold
About a casque all jewels; and his horse
In golden armour jewell'd everywhere:
And on the splendour came, flashing me blind;
And seem'd to me the Lord of all the world,
Being so huge. But when I thought he meant
To crush me, moving on me, lo! he, too,
Open'd his arms to embrace me as he came,
And up I went and touch'd him, and he, too,
Fell into dust, and I was left alone
And wearying in a land of sand and thorns.

'And I rode on and found a mighty hill,
And on the top, a city wall'd: the spires
Prick'd with incredible pinnacles into heaven.
And by the gateway stirr'd a crowd; and these
Cried to me climbing, "Welcome, Percivale!
Thou mightiest and thou purest among men!"
And glad was I and clomb, but found at top
No man, nor any voice. And thence I past
Far thro' a ruinous city, and I saw
That man had once dwelt there; but there I found
Only one man of an exceeding age.
"Where is that goodly company," said I,
"That so cried out upon me?" and he had
Scarce any voice to answer, and yet gasp'd,
"Whence and what art thou?" and even as he spoke
Fell into dust, and disappear'd, and I
Was left alone once more, and cried in grief,
"Lo, if I find the Holy Grail itself
And touch it, it will crumble into dust."

'And thence I dropt into a lowly vale,
Low as the hill was high, and where the vale
Was lowest, found a chapel, and thereby
A holy hermit in a hermitage,
To whom I told my phantoms, and he said:

'"O son, thou hast not true humility,
The highest virtue, mother of them all;
For when the Lord of all things made Himself
Naked of glory for His mortal change,
'Take thou my robe,' she said, 'for all is thine,'
And all her form shone forth with sudden light
So that the angels were amazed, and she
Follow'd Him down, and like a flying star
Led on the gray-hair'd wisdom of the east;
But her thou hast not known: for what is this
Thou thoughtest of thy prowess and thy sins?
Thou hast not lost thyself to save thyself
As Galahad." When the hermit made an end,
In silver armour suddenly Galahad shone
Before us, and against the chapel door
Laid lance, and enter'd, and we knelt in prayer.
And there the hermit slaked my burning thirst,
And at the sacring of the mass I saw
The holy elements alone; but he,
"Saw ye no more? I, Galahad, saw the Grail,
The Holy Grail, descend upon the shrine:
I saw the fiery face as of a child
That smote itself into the bread, and went;
And hither am I come; and never yet
Hath what thy sister taught me first to see,
This Holy Thing, fail'd from my side, nor come
Cover'd, but moving with me night and day,
Fainter by day, but always in the night
Blood-red, and sliding down the blacken'd marsh
Blood-red, and on the naked mountain top
Blood-red, and in the sleeping mere below
Blood-red. And in the strength of this I rode,
Shattering all evil customs everywhere,
And past thro' Pagan realms, and made them mine,
And clash'd with Pagan hordes, and bore them down,
And broke thro' all, and in the strength of this
Come victor. But my time is hard at hand,
And hence I go; and one will crown me king
Far in the spiritual city; and come thou, too,
For thou shalt see the vision when I go."

'While thus he spake, his eye, dwelling on mine,
Drew me, with power upon me, till I grew
One with him, to believe as he believed.
Then, when the day began to wane, we went.

'There rose a hill that none but man could climb,
Scarr'd with a hundred wintry water-courses—
Storm at the top, and when we gain'd it, storm

Round us and death; for every moment glanced
His silver arms and gloom'd: so quick and thick
The lightnings here and there to left and right
Struck, till the dry old trunks about us, dead,
Yea, rotten with a hundred years of death,
Sprang into fire: and at the base we found
On either hand, as far as eye could see,
A great black swamp and of an evil smell,
Part black, part whiten'd with the bones of men,
Not to be crost, save that some ancient king
Had built a way, where, link'd with many a bridge,
A thousand piers ran into the great Sea.
And Galahad fled along them bridge by bridge,
And every bridge as quickly as he crost
Sprang into fire and vanish'd, tho' I yearn'd
To follow; and thrice above him all the heavens
Open'd and blazed with thunder such as seem'd
Shoutings of all the sons of God: and first
At once I saw him far on the great Sea,
In silver-shining armour starry-clear;
And o'er his head the Holy Vessel hung
Clothed in white samite or a luminous cloud.
And with exceeding swiftness ran the boat,
If boat it were—I saw not whence it came.
And when the heavens open'd and blazed again
Roaring, I saw him like a silver star—
And had he set the sail, or had the boat
Become a living creature clad with wings?
And o'er his head the Holy Vessel hung
Redder than any rose, a joy to me,
For now I knew the veil had been withdrawn.
Then in a moment when they blazed again
Opening, I saw the least of little stars
Down on the waste, and straight beyond the star
I saw the spiritual city and all her spires
And gateways in a glory like one pearl—
No larger, tho' the goal of all the saints—
Strike from the sea; and from the star there shot
A rose-red sparkle to the city, and there
Dwelt, and I knew it was the Holy Grail,
Which never eyes on earth again shall see.
Then fell the floods of heaven drowning the deep.
And how my feet recrost the deathful ridge
No memory in me lives; but that I touch'd
The chapel-doors as dawn I know; and thence
Taking my war-horse from the holy man,
Glad that no phantom vext me more, return'd
To whence I came, the gate of Arthur's wars.'

'O brother,' ask'd Ambrosius,—'for in sooth
These ancient books—and they would win thee—teem,
Only I find not there this Holy Grail,
With miracles and marvels like to these,
Not all unlike; which oftentime I read,
Who read but on my breviary with ease,
Till my head swims; and then go forth and pass
Down to the little thorpe that lies so close,
And almost plaster'd like a martin's nest
To these old walls—and mingle with our folk;
And knowing every honest face of theirs
As well as ever shepherd knew his sheep,
And every homely secret in their hearts,
Delight myself with gossip and old wives,
And ills and aches, and teethings, lyings-in,
And mirthful sayings, children of the place,
That have no meaning half a league away:
Or lulling random squabbles when they rise,
Chafferings and chatterings at the market-cross,
Rejoice, small man, in this small world of mine,
Yea, even in their hens and in their eggs—
O brother, saving this Sir Galahad,
Came ye on none but phantoms in your quest,
No man, no woman?'

Then Sir Percivale:
'All men, to one so bound by such a vow,
And women were as phantoms. O, my brother,
Why wilt thou shame me to confess to thee
How far I falter'd from my quest and vow?

For after I had lain so many nights,
A bedmate of the snail and eft and snake,
In grass and burdock, I was changed to wan
And meagre, and the vision had not come;
And then I chanced upon a goodly town
With one great dwelling in the middle of it;
Thither I made, and there was I disarm'd
By maidens each as fair as any flower:
But when they led me into hall, behold,
The Princess of that castle was the one,
Brother, and that one only, who had ever
Made my heart leap; for when I moved of old
A slender page about her father's hall,
And she a slender maiden, all my heart
Went after her with longing: yet we twain
Had never kiss'd a kiss, or vow'd a vow.
And now I came upon her once again,
And one had wedded her, and he was dead,
And all his land and wealth and state were hers.
And while I tarried, every day she set
A banquet richer than the day before
By me; for all her longing and her will
Was toward me as of old; till one fair morn,
I walking to and fro beside a stream
That flash'd across her orchard underneath
Her castle-walls, she stole upon my walk,
And calling me the greatest of all knights,
Embraced me, and so kiss'd me the first time,
And gave herself and all her wealth to me.
Then I remember'd Arthur's warning word,
That most of us would follow wandering fires,
And the Quest faded in my heart. Anon,
The heads of all her people drew to me,
With supplication both of knees and tongue:
"We have heard of thee: thou art our greatest knight,
Our Lady says it, and we well believe:
Wed thou our Lady, and rule over us,
And thou shalt be as Arthur in our land."
O me, my brother! but one night my vow
Burnt me within, so that I rose and fled,
But wail'd and wept, and hated mine own self,
And ev'n the Holy Quest, and all but her;
Then after I was join'd with Galahad
Cared not for her, nor anything upon earth.'

Then said the monk, 'Poor men, when yule is cold,
Must be content to sit by little fires.
And this am I, so that ye care for me
Ever so little; yea, and blest be Heaven
That brought thee here to this poor house of ours
Where all the brethren are so hard, to warm
My cold heart with a friend: but O the pity
To find thine own first love once more—to hold,
Hold her a wealthy bride within thine arms,
Or all but hold, and then—cast her aside,
Foregoing all her sweetness, like a weed.
For we that want the warmth of double life,
We that are plagued with dreams of something sweet
Beyond all sweetness in a life so rich,—
Ah, blessed Lord, I speak too earthlywise,
Seeing I never stray'd beyond the cell,
But live like an old badger in his earth,
With earth about him everywhere, despite
All fast and penance. Saw ye none beside,
None of your knights?'

'Yea so,' said Percivale:
'One night my pathway swerving east, I saw
The pelican on the casque of our Sir Bors
All in the middle of the rising moon:
And toward him spurr'd, and hail'd him, and he me,
And each made joy of either; then he ask'd,
"Where is he? hast thou seen him—Lancelot?—Once,"
Said good Sir Bors, "he dash'd across me—mad,
And maddening what he rode: and when I cried,
'Ridest thou then so hotly on a quest
So holy,' Lancelot shouted, 'Stay me not!
I have been the sluggard, and I ride apace,
For now there is a lion in the way.'
So vanish'd."

'Then Sir Bors had ridden on
Softly, and sorrowing for our Lancelot,
Because his former madness, once the talk
And scandal of our table, had return'd;
For Lancelot's kith and kin so worship him
That ill to him is ill to them; to Bors
Beyond the rest: he well had been content
Not to have seen, so Lancelot might have seen,
The Holy Cup of healing; and, indeed,
Being so clouded with his grief and love,
Small heart was his after the Holy Quest:
If God would send the vision, well: if not,
The Quest and he were in the hands of Heaven.

'And then, with small adventure met, Sir Bors
Rode to the lonest tract of all the realm,
And found a people there among their crags,
Our race and blood, a remnant that were left
Paynim amid their circles, and the stones
They pitch up straight to heaven: and their wise men
Were strong in that old magic which can trace
The wandering of the stars, and scoff'd at him
And this high Quest as at a simple thing:
Told him he follow'd—almost Arthur's words—
A mocking fire: "what other fire than he,
Whereby the blood beats, and the blossom blows,
And the sea rolls, and all the world is warm'd?"
And when his answer chafed them, the rough crowd,
Hearing he had a difference with their priests,
Seized him, and bound and plunged him into a cell
Of great piled stones; and lying bounden there
In darkness thro' innumerable hours
He heard the hollow-ringing heavens sweep
Over him till by miracle—what else?—
Heavy as it was, a great stone slipt and fell,
Such as no wind could move: and thro' the gap
Glimmer'd the streaming scud: then came a night
Still as the day was loud, and thro' the gap
The seven clear stars of Arthur's Table Round—
For, brother, so one night, because they roll
Thro' such a round in heaven, we named the stars,
Rejoicing in ourselves and in our King—
And these, like bright eyes of familiar friends,
In on him shone: "And then to me, to me,"
Said good Sir Bors, "beyond all hopes of mine,
Who scarce had pray'd or ask'd it for myself—
Across the seven clear stars—O grace to me—
In colour like the fingers of a hand
Before a burning taper, the sweet Grail
Glided and past, and close upon it peal'd
A sharp quick thunder." Afterwards, a maid,
Who kept our holy faith among her kin
In secret, entering, loosed and let him go.'

To whom the monk: 'And I remember now
That pelican on the casque: Sir Bors it was
Who spake so low and sadly at our board;
And mighty reverent at our grace was he:
A square-set man and honest; and his eyes,
An out-door sign of all the warmth within,
Smiled with his lips—a smile beneath a cloud,
But heaven had meant it for a sunny one:
Ay, ay, Sir Bors, who else? But when ye reach'd
The city, found ye all your knights return'd,
Or was there sooth in Arthur's prophecy,
Tell me, and what said each, and what the King?'

Then answer'd Percivale: 'And that can I,
Brother, and truly; since the living words
Of so great men as Lancelot and our King
Pass not from door to door and out again,
But sit within the house. O, when we reach'd

The city, our horses stumbling as they trode
On heaps of ruin, hornless unicorns,
Crack'd basilisks, and splinter'd cockatrices,
And shatter'd talbots, which had left the stones
Raw, that they fell from, brought us to the hall.

'And there sat Arthur on the daïs-throne,
And those that had gone out upon the Quest,
Wasted and worn, and but a tithe of them,
And those that had not, stood before the King,
Who, when he saw me, rose, and bad me hail,
Saying, "A welfare in thine eye reproves
Our fear of some disastrous chance for thee
On hill, or plain, at sea, or flooding ford.
So fierce a gale made havoc here of late
Among the strange devices of our kings;
Yea, shook this newer, stronger hall of ours,
And from the statue Merlin moulded for us
Half-wrench'd a golden wing; but now—the Quest,
This vision—hast thou seen the Holy Cup,
That Joseph brought of old to Glastonbury?"

'So when I told him all thyself hast heard,
Ambrosius, and my fresh but fixt resolve
To pass away into the quiet life,
He answer'd not, but, sharply turning, ask'd
Of Gawain, "Gawain, was this Quest for thee?"

'"Nay, lord," said Gawain, "not for such as I.
Therefore I communed with a saintly man,
Who made me sure the Quest was not for me;
For I was much awearied of the Quest:
But found a silk pavilion in a field,
And merry maidens in it; and then this gale
Tore my pavilion from the tenting-pin,
And blew my merry maidens all about
With all discomfort; yea, and but for this,
My twelvemonth and a day were pleasant to me."

'He ceased; and Arthur turn'd to whom at first
He saw not, for Sir Bors, on entering, push'd
Athwart the throng to Lancelot, caught his hand,
Held it, and there, half-hidden by him, stood,
Until the King espied him, saying to him,
"Hail, Bors! if ever loyal man and true
Could see it, thou hast seen the Grail"; and Bors,
"Ask me not, for I may not speak of it:
I saw it"; and the tears were in his eyes.

'Then there remain'd but Lancelot, for the rest
Spake but of sundry perils in the storm;
Perhaps, like him of Cana in Holy Writ,
Our Arthur kept his best until the last;
"Thou, too, my Lancelot," ask'd the King, "my friend,
Our mightiest, hath this Quest avail'd for thee?"

'"Our mightiest!" answer'd Lancelot, with a groan;
"O King!"—and when he paused, methought I spied
A dying fire of madness in his eyes—
"O King, my friend, if friend of thine I be,
Happier are those that welter in their sin,
Swine in the mud, that cannot see for slime,
Slime of the ditch: but in me lived a sin
So strange, of such a kind, that all of pure,
Noble, and knightly in me twined and clung
Round that one sin, until the wholesome flower
And poisonous grew together, each as each,
Not to be pluck'd asunder; and when thy knights
Sware, I sware with them only in the hope
That could I touch or see the Holy Grail
They might be pluck'd asunder. Then I spake
To one most holy saint, who wept and said,

That save they could be pluck'd asunder, all
My quest were but in vain; to whom I vow'd
That I would work according as he will'd.
And forth I went, and while I yearn'd and strove
To tear the twain asunder in my heart,
My madness came upon me as of old,
And whipt me into waste fields far away;
There was I beaten down by little men,
Mean knights, to whom the moving of my sword
And shadow of my spear had been enow
To scare them from me once; and then I came
All in my folly to the naked shore,
Wide flats, where nothing but coarse grasses grew;
But such a blast, my King, began to blow,
So loud a blast along the shore and sea,
Ye could not hear the waters for the blast,
Tho' heapt in mounds and ridges all the sea
Drove like a cataract, and all the sand
Swept like a river, and the clouded heavens
Were shaken with the motion and the sound.
And blackening in the sea-foam sway'd a boat,
Half-swallow'd in it, anchor'd with a chain;
And in my madness to myself I said,
'I will embark and I will lose myself,
And in the great sea wash away my sin.'
I burst the chain, I sprang into the boat.
Seven days I drove along the dreary deep,
And with me drove the moon and all the stars;
And the wind fell, and on the seventh night
I heard the shingle grinding in the surge,
And felt the boat shock earth, and looking up,
Behold, the enchanted towers of Carbonek,
A castle like a rock upon a rock,
With chasm-like portals open to the sea,
And steps that met the breaker! there was none
Stood near it but a lion on each side
That kept the entry, and the moon was full.
Then from the boat I leapt, and up the stairs.
There drew my sword. With sudden-flaring manes
Those two great beasts rose upright like a man,
Each gript a shoulder, and I stood between;
And, when I would have smitten them, heard a voice,
'Doubt not, go forward; if thou doubt, the beasts
Will tear thee piecemeal.' Then with violence
The sword was dash'd from out my hand, and fell.
And up into the sounding hall I past;
But nothing in the sounding hall I saw,
No bench nor table, painting on the wall
Or shield of knight; only the rounded moon
Thro' the tall oriel on the rolling sea.
But always in the quiet house I heard,
Clear as a lark, high o'er me as a lark,
A sweet voice singing in the topmost tower
To the eastward: up I climb'd a thousand steps
With pain: as in a dream I seem'd to climb
For ever: at the last I reach'd a door,
A light was in the crannies, and I heard,
'Glory and joy and honour to our Lord
And to the Holy Vessel of the Grail.'
Then in my madness I essay'd the door;
It gave; and thro' a stormy glare, a heat
As from a seventimes-heated furnace, I,
Blasted and burnt, and blinded as I was,
With such a fierceness that I swoon'd away—
O, yet methought I saw the Holy Grail,
All pall'd in crimson samite, and around
Great angels, awful shapes, and wings and eyes.
And but for all my madness and my sin,
And then my swooning, I had sworn I saw
That which I saw; but what I saw was veil'd
And cover'd; and this Quest was not for me."

'So speaking, and here ceasing, Lancelot left
The hall long silent, till Sir Gawain—nay,
Brother, I need not tell thee foolish words,—
A reckless and irreverent knight was he,
Now bolden'd by the silence of his King,—
Well, I will tell thee: "O King, my liege," he said,

"Hath Gawain fail'd in any quest of thine?
When have I stinted stroke in foughten field?
But as for thine, my good friend Percivale,
Thy holy nun and thou have driven men mad,
Yea, made our mightiest madder than our least.
But by mine eyes and by mine ears I swear,
I will be deafer than the blue-eyed cat,
And thrice as blind as any noonday owl,
To holy virgins in their ecstasies,
Henceforward."

'"Deafer," said the blameless King,
"Gawain, and blinder unto holy things
Hope not to make thyself by idle vows,
Being too blind to have desire to see.
But if indeed there came a sign from heaven,
Blessed are Bors, Lancelot and Percivale,
For these have seen according to their sight.
For every fiery prophet in old times,
And all the sacred madness of the bard,
When God made music thro' them, could but speak
His music by the framework and the chord;
And as ye saw it ye have spoken truth.

'"Nay—but thou errest, Lancelot: never yet
Could all of true and noble in knight and man
Twine round one sin, whatever it might be,
With such a closeness, but apart there grew,
Save that he were the swine thou spakest of,
Some root of knighthood and pure nobleness;
Whereto see thou, that it may bear its flower.

'"And spake I not too truly, O my knights?
Was I too dark a prophet when I said
To those who went upon the Holy Quest,
That most of them would follow wandering fires,
Lost in the quagmire?—lost to me and gone,
And left me gazing at a barren board,
And a lean Order—scarce return'd a tithe—
And out of those to whom the vision came
My greatest hardly will believe he saw;
Another hath beheld it afar off,
And leaving human wrongs to right themselves,
Cares but to pass into the silent life.
And one hath had the vision face to face,
And now his chair desires him here in vain,
However they may crown him otherwhere.

"And some among you held, that if the King
Had seen the sight he would have sworn the vow:
Not easily, seeing that the King must guard
That which he rules, and is but as the hind
To whom a space of land is given to plow.
Who may not wander from the allotted field
Before his work be done; but, being done,
Let visions of the night or of the day
Come, as they will; and many a time they come,
Until this earth he walks on seems not earth,
This light that strikes his eyeball is not light,
This air that smites his forehead is not air
But vision—yea, his very hand and foot—
In moments when he feels he cannot die,
And knows himself no vision to himself,
Nor the high God a vision, nor that One
Who rose again: ye have seen what ye have seen."

'So spake the King: I knew not all he meant.'

[1869]

THE LAST TOURNAMENT

Dagonet, the fool, whom Gawain in his mood
Had made mock-knight of Arthur's Table Round,
At Camelot, high above the yellowing woods,
Danced like a wither'd leaf before the hall.
And toward him from the hall, with harp in hand,
And from the crown thereof a carcanet

Of ruby swaying to and fro, the prize
Of Tristram in the jousts of yesterday,
Came Tristram, saying, 'Why skip ye so, Sir Fool?'

For Arthur and Sir Lancelot riding once
Far down beneath a winding wall of rock
Heard a child wail. A stump of oak half-dead,
From roots like some black coil of carven snakes,
Clutch'd at the crag, and started thro' mid air
Bearing an eagle's nest: and thro' the tree
Rush'd ever a rainy wind, and thro' the wind
Pierced ever a child's cry: and crag and tree
Scaling, Sir Lancelot from the perilous nest,
This ruby necklace thrice around her neck,
And all unscarr'd from beak or talon, brought
A maiden babe; which Arthur pitying took,
Then gave it to his Queen to rear: the Queen
But coldly acquiescing, in her white arms
Received, and after loved it tenderly,
And named it Nestling; so forgot herself
A moment, and her cares; till that young life
Being smitten in mid heaven with mortal cold
Past from her; and in time the carcanet
Vext her with plaintive memories of the child:
So she, delivering it to Arthur, said,
'Take thou the jewels of this dead innocence,
And make them, an thou wilt, a tourney-prize.'

To whom the King, 'Peace to thine eagle-borne
Dead nestling, and this honour after death,
Following thy will! but, O my Queen I muse
Why ye not wear on arm, or neck, or zone
Those diamonds that I rescued from the tarn,
And Lancelot won, methought, for thee to wear.'

'Would rather you had let them fall,' she cried,
'Plunge and be lost—ill-fated as they were,
A bitterness to me!—ye look amazed,
Not knowing they were lost as soon as given—
Slid from my hands, when I was leaning out
Above the river—that unhappy child
Past in her barge: but rosier luck will go
With these rich jewels, seeing that they came
Not from the skeleton of a brother-slayer,
But the sweet body of a maiden babe.
Perchance—who knows?—the purest of thy knights
May win them for the purest of my maids.'

She ended, and the cry of a great jousts
With trumpet-blowings ran on all the ways
From Camelot in among the faded fields
To furthest towers; and everywhere the knights
Arm'd for a day of glory before the King.

But on the hither side of that loud morn
Into the hall stagger'd, his visage ribb'd
From ear to ear with dogwhip-weals, his nose
Bridge-broken, one eye out, and one hand off,
And one with shatter'd fingers dangling lame,
A churl, to whom indignantly the King,

'My churl, for whom Christ died, what evil beast
Hath drawn his claws athwart thy face? or fiend
Man was it who marr'd heaven's image in thee thus?'

Then, sputtering thro' the hedge of splinter'd teeth,
Yet strangers to the tongue, and with blunt stump
Pitch-blacken'd sawing the air, said the maim'd churl,

'He took them and he drave them to his tower—
Some hold he was a table-knight of thine—
A hundred goodly ones—the Red Knight, he—

Lord, I was tending swine, and the Red Knight
Brake in upon me and drave them to his tower;
And when I call'd upon thy name as one
That doest right by gentle and by churl,
Maim'd me and maul'd, and would outright have slain,
Save that he sware me to a message, saying,
"Tell thou the King and all his liars, that I
Have founded my Round Table in the North,
And whatsoever his own knights have sworn
My knights have sworn the counter to it—and say
My tower is full of harlots, like his court,
But mine are worthier, seeing they profess
To be none other than themselves—and say
My knights are all adulterers like his own,
But mine are truer, seeing they profess
To be none other; and say his hour is come,
The heathen are upon him, his long lance
Broken, and his Excalibur a straw." '

Then Arthur turn'd to Kay the seneschal,
'Take thou my churl, and tend him curiously
Like a king's heir, till all his hurts be whole.
The heathen—but that ever-climbing wave,
Hurl'd back again so often in empty foam,
Hath lain for years at rest—and renegades,
Thieves, bandits, leavings of confusion, whom
The wholesome realm is purged of otherwhere,
Friends, thro' your manhood and your fealty,—now
Make their last head like Satan in the North.
My younger knights, new-made, in whom your flower
Waits to be solid fruit of golden deeds,
Move with me toward their quelling, which achieved,
The loneliest ways are safe from shore to shore.
But thou, Sir Lancelot, sitting in my place
Enchair'd to-morrow, arbitrate the field;
For wherefore shouldst thou care to mingle with it,
Only to yield my Queen her own again?
Speak, Lancelot, thou art silent: is it well?'

Thereto Sir Lancelot answer'd, 'It is well:
Yet better if the King abide, and leave
The leading of his younger knights to me.
Else, for the King has will'd it, it is well.'

Then Arthur rose and Lancelot follow'd him,
And while they stood without the doors, the King
Turn'd to him saying, 'Is it then so well?
Or mine the blame that oft I seem as he
Of whom was written, "A sound is in his ears"?
The foot that loiters, bidden go,—the glance
That only seems half-loyal to command,—
A manner somewhat fall'n from reverence—
Or have I dream'd the bearing of our knights
Tells of a manhood ever less and lower?
Or whence the fear lest this my realm, uprear'd,
By noble deeds at once with noble vows,
From flat confusion and brute violences,
Reel back into the beast, and be no more?'

He spoke, and taking all his younger knights,
Down the slope city rode, and sharply turn'd
North by the gate. In her high bower the Queen,
Working a tapestry, lifted up her head,
Watch'd her lord pass, and knew not that she sigh'd.
Then ran across her memory the strange rhyme
Of bygone Merlin, 'Where is he who knows?
From the great deep to the great deep he goes.'

But when the morning of a tournament,
By these in earnest those in mockery call'd
The Tournament of the Dead Innocence,
Brake with a wet wind blowing, Lancelot,
Round whose sick head all night, like birds of prey,
The words of Arthur flying shriek'd, arose,

And down a streetway hung with folds of pure
White samite, and by fountains running wine,
Where children sat in white with cups of gold,
Moved to the lists, and there, with slow sad steps
Ascending, fill'd his double-dragon'd chair.

He glanced and saw the stately galleries,
Dame, damsel, each thro' worship of their Queen
White-robed in honour of the stainless child,
And some with scatter'd jewels, like a bank
Of maiden snow mingled with sparks of fire.
He look'd but once, and vail'd his eyes again.

The sudden trumpet sounded as in a dream
To ears but half-awaked, then one low roll
Of Autumn thunder, and the jousts began:
And ever the wind blew, and yellowing leaf
And gloom and gleam, and shower and shorn plume
Went down it. Sighing weariedly, as one
Who sits and gazes on a faded fire,
When all the goodlier guests are past away,
Sat their great umpire, looking o'er the lists.
He saw the laws that ruled the tournament
Broken, but spake not; once, a knight cast down
Before his throne of arbitration cursed
The dead babe and the follies of the King;
And once the laces of a helmet crack'd,
And show'd him, like a vermin in its hole,
Modred, a narrow face: anon he heard
The voice that billow'd round the barriers roar
An ocean-sounding welcome to one knight,
But newly-enter'd, taller than the rest,
And armour'd all in forest green, whereon
There tript a hundred tiny silver deer,
And wearing but a holly-spray for crest,
With ever-scattering berries, and on shield
A spear, a harp, a bugle—Tristram—late
From overseas in Brittany return'd,
And marriage with a princess of that realm,
Isolt the White—Sir Tristram of the Woods—
Whom Lancelot knew, had held sometime with pain
His own against him, and now yearn'd to shake
The burthen off his heart in one full shock
With Tristram ev'n to death: his strong hands gript
And dinted the gilt dragons right and left,
Until he groan'd for wrath—so many of those,
That ware their ladies' colours on the casque,
Drew from before Sir Tristram to the bounds,
And there with gibes and flickering mockeries
Stood, while he mutter'd, 'Craven crests! O shame!
What faith have these in whom they sware to love?
The glory of our Round Table is no more.'

So Tristram won, and Lancelot gave, the gems,
Not speaking other word than 'Hast thou won?
Art thou the purest, brother? See, the hand
Wherewith thou takest this, is red!' to whom
Tristram, half plagued by Lancelot's languorous mood,
Made answer, 'Ay, but wherefore toss me this
Like a dry bone cast to some hungry hound?
Let be thy fair Queen's fantasy. Strength of heart
And might of limb, but mainly use and skill,
Are winners in this pastime of our King.
My hand—belike the lance hath dript upon it—
No blood of mine, I trow; but O chief knight,
Right arm of Arthur in the battlefield,
Great brother, thou nor I have made the world;
Be happy in thy fair Queen as I in mine.'

And Tristram round the gallery made his horse
Caracole; then bow'd his homage, bluntly saying,

'Fair damsels, each to him who worships each
Sole Queen of Beauty and of love, behold
This day my Queen of Beauty is not here.'
And most of these were mute, some anger'd, one
Murmuring, 'All courtesy is dead,' and one,
'The glory of our Round Table is no more.'

Then fell thick rain, plume droopt and mantle clung,
And pettish cries awoke, and the wan day
Went glooming down in wet and weariness:
But under her black brows a swarthy one
Laugh'd shrilly, crying, 'Praise the patient saints,
Our one white day of Innocence hath past,
Tho' somewhat draggled at the skirt. So be it.
The snowdrop only, flowering thro' the year,
Would make the world as blank as Winter-tide.
Come—let us gladden their sad eyes, our Queen's
And Lancelot's, at this night's solemnity
With all the kindlier colours of the field.'

So dame and damsel glitter'd at the feast
Variously gay: for he that tells the tale
Liken'd them, saying, as when an hour of cold
Falls on the mountain in midsummer snows,
And all the purple slopes of mountain flowers
Pass under white, till the warm hour returns
With veer of wind, and all are flowers again;
So dame and damsel cast the simple white,
And glowing in all colours, the live grass,
Rose-campion, bluebell, kingcup, poppy, glanced
About the revels, and with mirth so loud
Beyond all use, that, half-amazed, the Queen,
And wroth at Tristram and the lawless jousts,
Brake up their sports, then slowly to her bower
Parted, and in her bosom pain was lord.

And little Dagonet on the morrow morn,
High over all the yellowing Autumn-tide,
Danced like a wither'd leaf before the hall.
Then Tristram saying, 'Why skip ye so, Sir Fool?'
Wheel'd round on either heel, Dagonet replied,
'Belike for lack of wiser company;
Or being fool, and seeing too much wit
Makes the world rotten, why, belike I skip
To know myself the wisest knight of all.'
'Ay, fool,' said Tristram, 'but 'tis eating dry
To dance without a catch, a roundelay
To dance to.' Then he twangled on his harp,
And while he twangled little Dagonet stood
Quiet as any water-sodden log
Stay'd in the wandering warble of a brook;
But when the twangling ended, skipt again;
And being ask'd, 'Why skipt ye not, Sir Fool?'
Made answer, 'I had liefer twenty years
Skip to the broken music of my brains
Than any broken music thou canst make.'

Then Tristram, waiting for the quip to come,
'Good now, what music have I broken, fool?'
And little Dagonet, skipping, 'Arthur, the King's;
For when thou playest that air with Queen Isolt,
Thou makest broken music with thy bride,
Her daintier namesake down in Brittany—
And so thou breakest Arthur's music too.'
'Save for that broken music in thy brains,
Sir fool,' said Tristram, 'I would break thy head.
Fool, I came late, the heathen wars were o'er,
The life had flown, we sware but by the shell—
I am but a fool to reason with a fool—
Come, thou art crabb'd and sour: but lean me down,
Sir Dagonet, one of thy long asses' ears,
And harken if my music be not true.

' "Free love—free field—we love but while we may:
The woods are hush'd, their music is no more:
The leaf is dead, the yearning past away:
New leaf, new life—the days of frost are o'er:
New life, new love, to suit the newer day:
New loves are sweet as those that went before:
Free love—free field—we love but while we may."

'Ye might have moved slow-measure to my tune,
Not stood stockstill. I made it in the woods,
And heard it ring as true as tested gold.'

But Dagonet with one foot poised in his hand,
'Friend, did ye mark that fountain yesterday
Made to run wine?—but this had run itself
All out like a long life to a sour end—
And them that round it sat with golden cups
To hand the wine to whosoever came—
The twelve small damosels white as Innocence,
In honour of poor Innocence the babe,
Who left the gems which Innocence the Queen
Lent to the King, and Innocence the King
Gave for a prize—and one of those white slips
Handed her cup and piped, the pretty one,
"Drink, drink, Sir Fool," and thereupon I drank,
Spat—pish—the cup was gold, the draught was mud.'

And Tristram, 'Was it muddier than thy gibes?
Is all the laughter gone dead out of thee?—
Not marking how the knighthood mock thee, fool—
"Fear God: honour the King—his one true knight—
Sole follower of the vows"—for here be they
Who knew thee swine enow before I came,
Smuttier than blasted grain: but when the King
Had made thee fool, thy vanity so shot up
It frighted all free fool from out thy heart;
Which left thee less than fool, and less than swine,
A naked aught—yet swine I hold thee still,
For I have flung thee pearls and find thee swine.'

And little Dagonet mincing with his feet,
'Knight, an ye fling those rubies round my neck
In lieu of hers, I'll hold thou hast some touch
Of music, since I care not for thy pearls.
Swine? I have wallow'd, I have wash'd—the world
Is flesh and shadow—I have had my day.
The dirty nurse, Experience, in her kind
Hath foul'd me—an I wallow'd, then I wash'd—
I have had my day and my philosophies—
And thank the Lord I am King Arthur's fool.
Swine, say ye? swine, goats, asses, rams and geese
Troop'd round a Paynim harper once, who thrumm'd
On such a wire as musically as thou
Some such fine song—but never a king's fool.'

And Tristram, 'Then were swine, goats, asses, geese
The wiser fools, seeing thy Paynim bard
Had such a mastery of his mystery
That he could harp his wife up out of hell.'

Then Dagonet, turning on the ball of his foot,
'And whither harp'st thou thine? down! and thyself
Down! and two more: a helpful harper thou,
That harpest downward! Dost thou know the star
We call the harp of Arthur up in heaven?'

And Tristram, 'Ay, Sir Fool, for when our King
Was victor wellnigh day by day, the knights,
Glorying in each new glory, set his name
High on all hills, and in the signs of heaven.'

And Dagonet answer'd, 'Ay, and when the land
Was freed, and the Queen false, ye set yourself
To babble about him, all to show your wit—
And whether he were King by courtesy,
Or King by right—and so went harping down
The black king's highway, got so far, and grew
So witty that ye play'd at ducks and drakes
With Arthur's vows on the great lake of fire.
Tuwhoo! do ye see it? do ye see the star?'

'Nay, fool,' said Tristram, 'not in open day.'
And Dagonet, 'Nay, nor will: I see it and hear.
It makes a silent music up in heaven,
And I, and Arthur and the angels hear,
And then we skip.' 'Lo, fool,' he said, 'ye talk
Fool's treason: is the King thy brother fool?'
Then little Dagonet clapt his hands and shrill'd,
'Ay, ay, my brother fool, the king of fools!
Conceits himself as God that he can make
Figs out of thistles, silk from bristles, milk
From burning spurge, honey from hornet-combs,
And men from beasts—Long live the king of fools!'

And down the city Dagonet danced away;
But thro' the slowly-mellowing avenues
And solitary passes of the wood
Rode Tristram toward Lyonnesse and the west.
Before him fled the face of Queen Isolt
With ruby-circled neck, but evermore
Past, as a rustle or twitter in the wood
Made dull his inner, keen his outer eye
For all that walk'd, or crept, or perch'd, or flew.
Anon the face, as, when a gust hath blown,
Unruffling waters re-collect the shape
Of one that in them sees himself, return'd;
But at the slot or fewmets of a deer,
Or ev'n a fall'n feather, vanish'd again.

So on for all that day from lawn to lawn
Thro' many a league-long bower he rode. At length
A lodge of intertwisted beechen-boughs
Furze-cramm'd, and bracken-rooft, the which himself
Built for a summer day with Queen Isolt
Against a shower, dark in the golden grove
Appearing, sent his fancy back to where
She lived a moon in that low lodge with him:
Till Mark her lord had past, the Cornish King,
With six or seven, when Tristram was away,
And snatch'd her thence; yet dreading worse than shame
Her warrior Tristram, spake not any word,
But bode his hour, devising wretchedness.

And now that desert lodge to Tristram lookt
So sweet, that halting, in he past, and sank
Down on a drift of foliage random-blown;
But could not rest for musing how to smoothe
And sleek his marriage over to the Queen.
Perchance in lone Tintagil far from all
The tonguesters of the court she had not heard.
But then with folly had sent him overseas
After she left him lonely here? a name?
Was it the name of one in Brittany,
Isolt, the daughter of the King? 'Isolt
Of the white hands' they call'd her: the sweet name
Allured him first, and then the maid herself,
Who served him well with those white hands of hers,
And loved him well, until himself had thought
He loved her also, wedded easily,
But left her all as easily, and return'd.
The black-blue Irish hair and Irish eyes
Had drawn him home—what marvel? then he laid
His brows upon the drifted leaf and dream'd.

He seem'd to pace the strand of Brittany
Between Isolt of Britain and his bride,
And show'd them both the ruby-chain, and both

Began to struggle for it, till his Queen
Graspt it so hard, that all her hand was red.
Then cried the Breton, 'Look, her hand is red!
These be no rubies, this is frozen blood,
And melts within her hand—her hand is hot
With ill desires, but this I gave thee, look,
Is all as cool and white as any flower.'
Follow'd a rush of eagle's wings, and then
A whimpering of the spirit of the child,
Because the twain had spoil'd her carcanet.

He dream'd; but Arthur with a hundred spears
Rode far, till o'er the illimitable reed,
And many a glancing plash and sallowy isle,
The wide-wing'd sunset of the misty marsh
Glared on a huge machicolated tower
That stood with open doors, whereout was roll'd
A roar of riot, as from men secure
Amid their marshes, ruffians at their ease
Among their harlot-brides, an evil song.
'Lo there,' said one of Arthur's youth, for there,
High on a grim dead tree before the tower,
A goodly brother of the Table Round
Swung by the neck: and on the boughs a shield
Showing a shower of blood in a field noir,
And therebeside a horn, inflamed the knights
At that dishonour done the gilded spur,
Till each would clash the shield, and blow the horn.
But Arthur waved them back. Alone he rode.
Then at the dry harsh roar of the great horn,
That sent the face of all the marsh aloft
An ever upward-rushing storm and cloud
Of shriek and plume, the Red Knight heard, and all,
Even to tipmost lance and topmost helm,
In blood-red armour sallying, howl'd to the King,

The teeth of Hell flay bare and gnash thee flat!—
Lo! art thou not that eunuch-hearted King
Who fain had clipt free manhood from the world—
The woman-worshipper? Yea, God's curse, and I!
Slain was the brother of my paramour
By a knight of thine, and I that heard her whine
And snivel, being eunuch-hearted too,
Sware by the scorpion-worm that twists in hell,
And stings itself to everlasting death,
To hang whatever knight of thine I fought
And tumbled. Art thou King?—Look to thy life!'

He ended: Arthur knew the voice; the face
Wellnigh was helmet-hidden, and the name
Went wandering somewhere darkling in his mind.
And Arthur deign'd not use of word or sword,
But let the drunkard, as he stretch'd from horse
To strike him, overbalancing his bulk,
Down from the causeway heavily to the swamp
Fall, as the crest of some slow-arching wave,
Heard in dead night along that table-shore,
Drops flat, and after the great waters break
Whitening for half a league, and thin themselves,
Far over sands marbled with moon and cloud,
From less and less to nothing; thus he fell
Head-heavy; then the knights, who watch'd him, roar'd
And shouted and leapt down upon the fall'n;
There trampled out his face from being known,
And sank his head in mire, and slimed themselves:
Nor heard the King for their own cries, but sprang
Thro' open doors, and swording right and left
Men, women, on their sodden faces, hurl'd
The tables over and the wines, and slew
Till all the rafters rang with woman-yells,
And all the pavement stream'd with massacre:
Then, echoing yell with yell, they fired the tower,

Which half that autumn night, like the live North,
Red-pulsing up thro' Alioth and Alcor,
Made all above it, and a hundred meres
About it, as the water Moab saw
Came round by the East, and out beyond them flush'd
The long low dune, and lazy-plunging sea.

So all the ways were safe from shore to shore,
But in the heart of Arthur pain was lord.

Then, out of Tristram waking, the red dream
Fled with a shout, and that low lodge return'd,
Mid-forest, and the wind among the boughs.
He whistled his good warhorse left to graze
Among the forest greens, vaulted upon him,
And rode beneath an ever-showering leaf,
Till one lone woman, weeping near a cross,
Stay'd him. 'Why weep ye?' 'Lord,' she said, 'my man
Hath left me or is dead;' whereon he thought—
'What, if she hate me now? I would not this.
What, if she love me still? I would not that.
I know not what I would'—but said to her,
'Yet weep not thou, lest, if thy mate return,
He find thy favour changed and love thee not'—
Then pressing day by day thro' Lyonnesse
Last in a roky hollow, belling, heard
The hounds of Mark, and felt the goodly hounds
Yelp at his heart, but turning, past and gain'd
Tintagil, half in sea, and high on land,
A crown of towers.

Down in a casement sat,
A low sea-sunset glorying round her hair
And glossy-throated grace, Isolt the Queen.
And when she heard the feet of Tristram grind
The spiring stone that scaled about her tower,
Flush'd, started, met him at the doors, and there
Belted his body with her white embrace,
Crying aloud, 'Not Mark—not Mark, my soul!
The footstep flutter'd me at first: not he:
Catlike thro' his own castle steals my Mark,
But warrior-wise thou stridest thro' his halls
Who hates thee, as I him—ev'n to the death.
My soul, I felt my hatred for my Mark
Quicken within me, and knew that thou wert nigh.'
To whom Sir Tristram smiling, 'I am here.
Let be thy Mark, seeing he is not thine.'

And drawing somewhat backward she replied,
'Can he be wrong'd who is not ev'n his own,
But save for dread of thee had beaten me,
Scratch'd, bitten, blinded, marr'd me somehow—Mark?
What rights are his that dare not strike for them?
Not lift a hand—not, tho' he found me thus!
But harken! have ye met him? hence he went
To-day for three days' hunting—as he said—
And so returns belike within an hour.
Mark's way, my soul!—but eat not thou with Mark,
Because he hates thee even more than fears;
Nor drink: and when thou passest any wood
Close vizor, lest an arrow from the bush
Should leave me all alone with Mark and hell.
My God, the measure of my hate for Mark
Is as the measure of my love for thee.'

So, pluck'd one way by hate and one by love,
Drain'd of her force, again she sat, and spake
To Tristram, as he knelt before her, saying,
'O hunter, and O blower of the horn,
Harper, and thou hast been a rover too,
For, ere I mated with my shambling king,
Ye twain had fallen out about the bride
Of one—his name is out of me—the prize,
If prize she were—(what marvel—she could see)—
Thine, friend; and ever since my craven seeks

To wreck thee villainously: but, O Sir Knight,
What dame or damsel have ye kneel'd to last?'

And Tristram, 'Last to my Queen Paramount,
Here now to my Queen Paramount of love
And loveliness—ay, lovelier than when first
Her light feet fell on our rough Lyonnesse,
Sailing from Ireland.'

Softly laugh'd Isolt;
'Flatter me not, for hath not our great Queen
My dole of beauty trebled?' and he said,
'Her beauty is her beauty, and thine thine,
And thine is more to me—soft, gracious, kind—
Save when thy Mark is kindled on thy lips
Most gracious; but she, haughty, ev'n to him,
Lancelot; for I have seen him wan enow
To make one doubt if ever the great Queen
Have yielded him her love.'

To whom Isolt,
'Ah then, false hunter and false harper, thou
Who brakest thro' the scruple of my bond,
Calling me thy white hind, and saying to me
That Guinevere had sinn'd against the highest,
And I—misyoked with such a want of man—
That I could hardly sin against the lowest.'

He answer'd, 'O my soul, be comforted!
If this be sweet, to sin in leading-strings,
If here be comfort, and if ours be sin,
Crown'd warrant had we for the crowning sin
That made us happy: but how ye greet me—fear
And fault and doubt—no word of that fond tale—
Thy deep heart-yearnings, thy sweet memories
Of Tristram in that year he was away.'

And, saddening on the sudden, spake Isolt,
'I had forgotten all in my strong joy
To see thee—yearnings?—ay! for, hour by hour,
Here in the never-ended afternoon,
O sweeter than all memories of thee,
Deeper than any yearnings after thee
Seem'd those far-rolling, westward-smiling seas,
Watch'd from this tower. Isolt of Britain dash'd
Before Isolt of Brittany on the strand,
Would that have chill'd her bride-kiss? Wedded her?
Fought in her father's battles? wounded there?
The King was all fulfill'd with gratefulness,
And she, my namesake of the hands, that heal'd
Thy hurt and heart with unguent and caress—
Well—can I wish her any huger wrong
Than having known thee? her too hast thou left
To pine and waste in those sweet memories.
O were I not my Mark's, by whom all men
Are noble, I should hate thee more than love.'

And Tristram, fondling her light hands, replied,
'Grace, Queen, for being loved: she loved me well.
Did I love her? the name at least I loved.
Isolt?—I fought his battles, for Isolt!
The night was dark; the true star set. Isolt!
The name was ruler of the dark——Isolt?
Care not for her! patient, and prayerful, meek,
Pale-blooded, she will yield herself to God.'

And Isolt answer'd, 'Yea, and why not I?
Mine is the larger need, who am not meek,
Pale-blooded, prayerful. Let me tell thee now.
Here one black, mute midsummer night I sat,
Lonely, but musing on thee, wondering where,
Murmuring a light song I had heard thee sing,
And once or twice I spake thy name aloud.
Then flash'd a levin-brand; and near me stood,

In fuming sulphur blue and green, a fiend—
Mark's way to steal behind one in the dark—
For there was Mark: "He has wedded her," he said,
Not said, but hiss'd it: then this crown of towers
So shook to such a roar of all the sky,
That here in utter dark I swoon'd away,
And woke again in utter dark, and cried,
"I will flee hence and give myself to God"—
And thou wert lying in thy new leman's arms.'

Then Tristram, ever dallying with her hand,
'May God be with thee, sweet, when old and gray,
And past desire!' a saying that anger'd her.
'"May God be with thee, sweet, when thou art old,
And sweet no more to me!" I need Him now.
For when had Lancelot utter'd aught so gross
Ev'n to the swineherd's malkin in the mast?
The greater man, the greater courtesy.
Far other was the Tristram, Arthur's knight!
But thou, thro' ever harrying thy wild beasts—
Save that to touch a harp, tilt with a lance
Becomes thee well—art grown wild beast thyself.
How darest thou, if lover, push me even
In fancy from thy side, and set me far
In the gray distance, half a life away,
Her to be loved no more? Unsay it, unswear!
Flatter me rather, seeing me so weak,
Broken with Mark and hate and solitude,
Thy marriage and mine own, that I should suck
Lies like sweet wines: lie to me: I believe.
Will ye not lie? not swear, as there ye kneel,
And solemnly as when ye sware to him,
The man of men, our King—My God, the power
Was once in vows when men believed the King!
They lied not then, who sware, and thro' their vows
The King prevailing made his realm:—I say,
Swear to me thou wilt love me ev'n when old,
Gray-hair'd, and past desire, and in despair.'

Then Tristram, pacing moodily up and down,
'Vows! did you keep the vow you made to Mark
More than I mine? Lied, say ye? Nay, but learnt,
The vow that binds too strictly snaps itself—
My knighthood taught me this—ay, being snapt—
We run more counter to the soul thereof
Than had we never sworn. I swear no more.
I swore to the great King, and am forsworn.
For once—ev'n to the height—I honour'd him.
"Man, is he man at all?" methought, when first
I rode from our rough Lyonnesse, and beheld
That victor of the Pagan throned in hall—
His hair, a sun that ray'd from off a brow
Like hillsnow high in heaven, the steel-blue eyes,
The golden beard that clothed his lips with light—
Moreover, that weird legend of his birth,
With Merlin's mystic babble about his end
Amazed me; then, his foot was on a stool
Shaped as a dragon; he seem'd to me no man,
But Michaël trampling Satan; so I sware,
Being amazed: but this went by—The vows!
O ay—the wholesome madness of an hour—
They served their use, their time; for every knight
Believed himself a greater than himself,
And every follower eyed him as a God;
Till he, being lifted up beyond himself,
Did mightier deeds than elsewise he had done,
And so the realm was made; but then their vows—

First mainly thro' that sullying of our Queen—
Began to gall the knighthood, asking whence
Had Arthur right to bind them to himself?
Dropt down from heaven? wash'd up from out the deep?
They fail'd to trace him thro' the flesh and blood
Of our old kings: whence then? a doubtful lord
To bind them by inviolable vows,
Which flesh and blood perforce would violate:
For feel this arm of mine—the tide within
Red with free chase and heather-scented air,
Pulsing full man; can Arthur make me pure
As any maiden child? lock up my tongue
From uttering freely what I freely hear?
Bind me to one? The wide world laughs at it.
And worldling of the world am I, and know
The ptarmigan that whitens ere his hour
Woos his own end; we are not angels here
Nor shall be: vows—I am woodman of the woods,
And hear the garnet-headed yaffingale
Mock them: my soul, we love but while we may;
And therefore is my love so large for thee,
Seeing it is not bounded save by love.'

Here ending, he moved toward her, and she said,
'Good: an I turn'd away my love for thee
To some one thrice as courteous as thyself—
For courtesy wins woman all as well
As valour may, but he that closes both
Is perfect, he is Lancelot—taller indeed,
Rosier and comelier, thou—but say I loved
This knightliest of all knights, and cast thee back
Thine own small saw, "We love but while we may,"
Well then, what answer?'

He that while she spake,
Mindful of what he brought to adorn her with,
The jewels, had let one finger lightly touch
The warm white apple of her throat, replied,
'Press this a little closer, sweet, until—
Come, I am hunger'd and half-anger'd—meat,
Wine, wine—and I will love thee to the death,
And out beyond into the dream to come.'

So then, when both were brought to full accord,
She rose, and set before him all he will'd;
And after these had comforted the blood
With meats and wines, and satiated their hearts—
Now talking of their woodland paradise,
The deer, the dews, the fern, the founts, the lawns;
Now mocking at the much ungainliness,
And craven shifts, and long crane legs of Mark—
Then Tristram laughing caught the harp, and sang:

'Ay, ay, O ay—the winds that bend the brier!
A star in heaven, a star within the mere!
Ay, ay, O ay—a star was my desire,
And one was far apart, and one was near:
Ay, ay, O ay—the winds that bow the grass!
And one was water and one star was fire,
And one will ever shine and one will pass.
Ay, ay, O ay—the winds that move the mere.'

Then in the light's last glimmer Tristram show'd
And swung the ruby carcanet. She cried,
'The collar of some Order, which our King
Hath newly founded, all for thee, my soul,
For thee, to yield thee grace beyond thy peers.'

'Not so, my Queen,' he said, 'but the red fruit
Grown on a magic oak-tree in mid-heaven,
And won by Tristram as a tourney-prize,
And hither brought by Tristram for his last
Love-offering and peace-offering unto thee.

He spoke, he turn'd, then, flinging round her neck,
Claspt it, and cried 'Thine Order, O my Queen!'
But, while he bow'd to kiss the jewell'd throat,
Out of the dark, just as the lips had touch'd,
Behind him rose a shadow and a shriek—
'Mark's way,' said Mark, and clove him thro' the brain.

That night came Arthur home, and while he climb'd,
All in a death-dumb autumn-dripping gloom,
The stairway to the hall, and look'd and saw
The great Queen's bower was dark,—about his feet
A voice clung sobbing till he question'd it,
'What art thou?' and the voice about his feet
Sent up an answer, sobbing, 'I am thy fool,
And I shall never make thee smile again.'

[1871]

LUCRETIUS

Lucilia, wedded to Lucretius, found
Her master cold; for when the morning flush
Of passion and the first embrace had died
Between them, tho' he lov'd her none the less,
Yet often when the woman heard his foot
Return from pacings in the field, and ran
To greet him with a kiss, the master took
Small notice, or austerely, for—his mind
Half buried in some weightier argument,
Or fancy-borne perhaps upon the rise
And long roll of the Hexameter—he past
To turn and ponder those three hundred scrolls
Left by the Teacher, whom he held divine.
She brook'd it not; but wrathful, petulant,
Dreaming some rival, sought and found a witch
Who brew'd the philtre which had power, they said,
To lead an errant passion home again.
And this, at times, she mingled with his drink,
And this destroy'd him; for the wicked broth
Confused the chemic labour of the blood,
And tickling the brute brain within the man's
Made havock among those tender cells, and check'd
His power to shape: he loathed himself; and once
After a tempest woke upon a morn
That mock'd him with returning calm, and cried:

'Storm in the night! for thrice I heard the rain
Rushing; and once the flash of a thunder-bolt—
Methought I never saw so fierce a fork—
Struck out the streaming mountain-side, and show'd
A riotous confluence of watercourses
Blanching and billowing in a hollow of it,
Where all but yester-eve was dusty-dry.

'Storm, and what dreams, ye holy Gods, what dreams!
For thrice I waken'd after dreams. Perchance
We do but recollect the dreams that come
Just ere the waking: terrible! for it seem'd
A void was made in Nature; all her bonds
Crack'd; and I saw the flaring atom-streams
And torrents of her myriad universe,
Ruining along the illimitable inane,
Fly on to clash together again, and make
Another and another frame of things
For ever: that was mine, my dream, I knew it—
Of and belonging to me, as the dog
With inward yelp and restless forefoot plies
His function of the woodland: but the next!
I thought that all the blood by Sylla shed
Came driving rainlike down again on earth,
And where it dash'd the reddening meadow, sprang
No dragon warriors from Cadmean teeth,
For these I thought my dream would show to me,
But girls, Hetairai, curious in their art,
Hired animalisms, vile as those that made
The mulberry-faced Dictator's orgies worse

Than aught they fable of the quiet Gods.
And hands they mixt, and yell'd and round me drove
In narrowing circles till I yell'd again
Half-suffocated, and sprang up, and saw—
Was it the first beam of my latest day?

'Then, then, from utter gloom stood out the breasts,
The breasts of Helen, and hoveringly a sword
Now over and now under, now direct,
Pointed itself to pierce, but sank down shamed
At all that beauty; and as I stared, a fire,
The fire that left a roofless Ilion,
Shot out of them, and scorch'd me that I woke.

'Is this thy vengeance, holy Venus, thine,
Because I would not one of thine own doves,
Not ev'n a rose, were offer'd to thee? thine,
Forgetful how my rich prooemion makes
Thy glory fly along the Italian field,
In lays that will outlast thy Deity?

'Deity? nay, thy worshippers. My tongue
Trips, or I speak profanely. Which of these
Angers thee most, or angers thee at all?
Not if thou be'st of those who, far aloof
From envy, hate and pity, and spite and scorn,
Live the great life which all our greatest fain
Would follow, center'd in eternal calm.

'Nay, if thou canst, O Goddess, like ourselves
Touch, and be touch'd, then would I cry to thee
To kiss thy Mavors, roll thy tender arms
Round him, and keep him from the lust of blood
That makes a steaming slaughter-house of Rome.

'Ay, but I meant not thee; I meant not her,
Whom all the pines of Ida shook to see
Slide from that quiet heaven of hers, and tempt
The Trojan, while his neat-herds were abroad;
Nor her that o'er her wounded hunter wept
Her Deity false in human-amorous tears;
Nor whom her beardless apple-arbiter
Decided fairest. Rather, O ye Gods,
Poet-like, as the great Sicilian called
Calliope to grace his golden verse—
Ay, and this Kypris also—did I take
That popular name of thine to shadow forth
The all-generating powers and genial heat
Of Nature, when she strikes thro' the thick blood
Of cattle, and light is large, and lambs are glad
Nosing the mother's udder, and the bird
Makes his heart voice amid the blaze of flowers:
Which things appear the work of mighty Gods.

'The Gods! and if I go *my* work is left
Unfinish'd—*if* I go. The Gods, who haunt
The lucid interspace of world and world,
Where never creeps a cloud, or moves a wind,
Nor ever falls the least white star of snow,
Nor ever lowest roll of thunder moans,
Nor sound of human sorrow mounts to mar
Their sacred everlasting calm! and such,
Not all so fine, nor so divine a calm,
Not such, nor all unlike it, man may gain
Letting his own life go. The Gods, the Gods!
If all be atoms, how then should the Gods
Being atomic not be dissoluble,
Not follow the great law? My master held
That Gods there are, for all men so believe.
I prest my footsteps into his, and meant
Surely to lead my Memmius in a train
Of flowery clauses onward to the proof
That Gods these are, and deathless. Meant? I meant?
I have forgotten what I meant: my mind
Stumbles, and all my faculties are lamed.

'Look where another of our Gods, the Sun,
Apollo, Delius, or of older use
All-seeing Hyperion—what you will—
Has mounted yonder; since he never sware,

Except his wrath were wreak'd on wretched man,
That he would only shine among the dead
Hereafter; tales! for never yet on earth
Could dead flesh creep, or bits of roasting ox
Moan round the spit—nor knows he what he sees;
King of the East altho' he seem, and girt
With song and flame and fragrance, slowly lifts
His golden feet on those empurpled stairs
That climb into the windy halls of heaven:
And here he glances on an eye new-born,
And gets for greeting but a wail of pain;
And here he stays upon a freezing orb
That fain would gaze upon him to the last;
And here upon a yellow eyelid fall'n
And closed by those who mourn a friend in vain,
Not thankful that his troubles are no more.
And me, altho' his fire is on my face
Blinding, he sees not, nor at all can tell
Whether I mean this day to end myself,
Or lend an ear to Plato where he says,
That men like soldiers may not quit the post
Allotted by the Gods: but he that holds
The Gods are careless, wherefore need he care
Greatly for them, nor rather plunge at once,
Being troubled, wholly out of sight, and sink
Past earthquake—ay, and gout and stone, that break
Body toward death, and palsy, death-in-life,
And wretched age—and worst disease of all,
These prodigies of myriad nakednesses,
And twisted shapes of lust, unspeakable,
Abominable, strangers at my hearth
Not welcome, harpies miring every dish,
The phantom husks of something foully done,
And fleeting thro' the boundless universe,
And blasting the long quiet of my breast
With animal heat and dire insanity?

'How should the mind, except it loved them, clasp
These idols to herself? or do they fly
Now thinner, and now thicker, like the flakes
In a fall of snow, and so press in, perforce
Of multitude, as crowds that in an hour
Of civic tumult jam the doors, and bear
The keepers down, and throng, their rags and they
The basest, far into that council-hall
Where sit the best and stateliest of the land?

'Can I not fling this horror off me again,
Seeing with how great ease Nature can smile,
Balmier and nobler from her bath of storm,
At random ravage? and how easily
The mountain there has cast his cloudy slough,
Now towering o'er him in serenest air,
A mountain o'er a mountain,—ay, and within
All hollow as the hopes and fears of men?

'But who was he, that in the garden snared
Picus and Faunus, rustic Gods? a tale
To laugh at—more to laugh at in myself—
For look! what is it? there? yon arbutus
Totters; a noiseless riot underneath
Strikes through the wood, sets all the tops quivering—
The mountain quickens into Nymph and Faun;
And here an Oread—how the sun delights
To glance and shift about her slippery sides,
And rosy knees and supple roundedness,
And budded bosom-peaks—who this way runs
Before the rest—A satyr, a satyr, see,
Follows; but him I proved impossible;
Twy-natured is no nature: yet he draws
Nearer and nearer, and I scan him now
Beastlier than any phantom of his kind
That ever butted his rough brother-brute
For lust or lusty blood or provender:
I hate, abhor, spit, sicken at him; and she
Loathes him as well; such a precipitate heel,
Fledged as it were with Mercury's ankle-wing,

Whirls her to me: but will she fling herself,
Shameless upon me? Catch her, goatfoot: nay,
Hide, hide them, million-myrtled wilderness,
And cavern-shadowing laurels, hide! do I wish—
What?—that the bush were leafless? or to whelm
All of them in one massacre? O ye Gods,
I know you careless, yet, behold, to you
From childly wont and ancient use I call—
I thought I lived securely as yourselves—
No lewdness, narrowing envy, monkey-spite,
No madness of ambition, avarice, none:
No larger feast than under plane or pine
With neighbours laid along the grass, to take
Only such cups as left us friendly-warm,
Affirming each his own philosophy—
Nothing to mar the sober majesties
Of settled, sweet, Epicurean life.
But now it seems some unseen monster lays
His vast and filthy hands upon my will,
Wrenching it backward into his; and spoils
My bliss in being; and it was not great;
For save when shutting reasons up in rhythm,
Or Heliconian honey in living words,
To make a truth less harsh, I often grew
Tired of so much within our little life,
Or of so little in our little life—
Poor little life that toddles half an hour
Crown'd with a flower or two, and there an end—
And since the nobler pleasure seems to fade,
Why should I, beastlike as I find myself,
Not manlike end myself?—our privilege—
What beast has heart to do it? And what man,
What Roman would be dragg'd in triumph thus?
Not I; not he, who bears one name with her
Whose death-blow struck the dateless doom of kings,
When, brooking not the Tarquin in her veins,
She made her blood in sight of Collatine
And all his peers, flushing the guiltless air,
Spout from the maiden fountain in her heart.
And from it sprang the Commonwealth, which breaks
As I am breaking now!

'And therefore now
Let her, that is the womb and tomb of all,
Great Nature, take, and forcing far apart
Those blind beginnings that have made me man,
Dash them anew together at her will
Thro' all her cycles—into man once more,
Or beast or bird or fish, or opulent flower:
But till this cosmic order everywhere
Shatter'd into one earthquake in one day
Cracks all to pieces,—and that hour perhaps
Is not so far when momentary man
Shall seem no more a something to himself,
But he, his hopes and hates, his homes and fanes,
And even his bones long laid within the grave,
The very sides of the grave itself shall pass,
Vanishing, atom and void, atom and void,
Into the unseen for ever,—till that hour,
My golden work in which I told a truth
That stays the rolling Ixionian wheel,
And numbs the Fury's ringlet-snake, and plucks
The mortal soul from out immortal hell,
Shall stand: ay, surely: then it fails at last
And perishes as I must; for O Thou,
Passionless bride, divine Tranquillity,
Yearn'd after by the wisest of the wise,
Who fail to find thee, being as thou art
Without one pleasure and without one pain,
Howbeit I know thou surely must be mine
Or soon or late, yet out of season, thus
I woo thee roughly, for thou carest not
How roughly men may woo thee so they win—
Thus—thus: the soul flies out and dies in the air.'

With that he drove the knife into his side:
She heard him raging, heard him fall; ran in,
Beat breast, tore hair, cried out upon herself
As having fail'd in duty to him, shriek'd

That she but meant to win him back, fell on him,
Clasp'd, kiss'd him, wail'd: he answer'd, 'Care not thou!
Thy duty? What is duty? Fare thee well!'

[1865] [1868]

THE REVENGE

A BALLAD OF THE FLEET

I

At Flores in the Azores Sir Richard Grenville lay,
And a pinnace, like a flutter'd bird, came flying from far away:
'Spanish ships of war at sea! we have sighted fifty-three!'
Then sware Lord Thomas Howard: ''Fore God I am no coward;
But I cannot meet them here, for my ships are out of gear,
And the half my men are sick. I must fly, but follow quick.
We are six ships of the line; can we fight with fifty-three?'

II

Then spake Sir Richard Grenville: 'I know you are no coward;
You fly them for a moment to fight with them again.
But I've ninety men and more that are lying sick ashore.
I should count myself the coward if I left them, my Lord Howard,
To these Inquisition dogs and the devildoms of Spain.'

III

So Lord Howard past away with five ships of war that day,
Till he melted like a cloud in the silent summer heaven;
But Sir Richard bore in hand all his sick men from the land
Very carefully and slow,
Men of Bideford in Devon,
And we laid them on the ballast down below;
For we brought them all aboard,
And they blest him in their pain, that they were not left to Spain,
To the thumbscrew and the stake, for the glory of the Lord.

IV

He had only a hundred seamen to work the ship and to fight,
And he sailed away from Flores till the Spaniard came in sight,
With his huge sea-castles heaving upon the weather bow.
'Shall we fight or shall we fly?
Good Sir Richard, tell us now,
For to fight is but to die!
There'll be little of us left by the time this sun be set.'
And Sir Richard said again: 'We be all good English men.
Let us bang these dogs of Seville, the children of the devil,
For I never turn'd my back upon Don or devil yet.'

V

Sir Richard spoke and he laugh'd, and we roar'd a hurrah, and so
The little Revenge ran on sheer into the heart of the foe,
With her hundred fighters on deck, and her ninety sick below;
For half of their fleet to the right and half to the left were seen,
And the little Revenge ran on thro' the long sea-lane between.

VI

Thousands of their soldiers look'd down from their decks and laugh'd,
Thousands of their seamen made mock at the mad little craft
Running on and on, till delay'd
By their mountain-like San Philip that, of fifteen hundred tons,
And up-shadowing high above us with her yawning tiers of guns,
Took the breath from our sails, and we stay'd.

VII

And while now the great San Philip hung above us like a cloud
Whence the thunderbolt will fall
Long and loud,

Four galleons drew away
From the Spanish fleet that day,
And two upon the larboard and two upon the starboard lay,
And the battle-thunder broke from them all.

VIII

But anon the great San Philip, she bethought herself and went
Having that within her womb that had left her ill content;
And the rest they came aboard us, and they fought us hand to hand,
For a dozen times they came with their pikes and musqueteers,
And a dozen times we shook 'em off as a dog that shakes his ears
When he leaps from the water to the land.

IX

And the sun went down, and the stars came out far over the summer sea,
But never a moment ceased the fight of the one and the fifty-three.
Ship after ship, the whole night long, their high-built galleons came,
Ship after ship, the whole night long, with her battle-thunder and flame;
Ship after ship, the whole night long, drew back with her dead and her shame.
For some were sunk and many were shatter'd, and so could fight us no more—
God of battles, was ever a battle like this in the world before?

X

For he said 'Fight on! fight on!'
Tho' his vessel was all but a wreck;
And it chanced that, when half of the short summer night was gone,
With a grisly wound to be drest he had left the deck,
But a bullet struck him that was dressing it suddenly dead,
And himself he was wounded again in the side and the head,
And he said 'Fight on! fight on!'

XI

And the night went down, and the sun smiled out far over the summer sea,
And the Spanish fleet with broken sides lay round us all in a ring;
But they dared not touch us again, for they fear'd that we still could sting,
So they watch'd what the end would be.
And we had not fought them in vain,
But in perilous plight were we,
Seeing forty of our poor hundred were slain,
And half of the rest of us maim'd for life
In the crash of the cannonades and the desperate strife;
And the sick men down in the hold were most of them stark and cold,
And the pikes were all broken or bent, and the powder was all of it spent;
And the masts and the rigging were lying over the side;
But Sir Richard cried in his English pride,
'We have fought such a fight for a day and a night
As may never be fought again!
We have won great glory, my men!
And a day less or more
At sea or ashore,
We die—does it matter when?
Sink me the ship, Master Gunner—sink her, split her in twain!
Fall into the hands of God, not into the hands of Spain!'

XII

And the gunner said 'Ay, ay,' but the seamen made reply:
'We have children, we have wives,
And the Lord hath spared our lives.
We will make the Spaniard promise, if we yield, to let us go;
We shall live to fight again and to strike another blow.'
And the lion there lay dying, and they yielded to the foe.

XIII

And the stately Spanish men to their flagship bore him then,
Where they laid him by the mast, old Sir Richard caught at last,
And they praised him to his face with their courtly foreign grace;
But he rose upon their decks, and he cried:
'I have fought for Queen and Faith like a valiant man and true;

I have only done my duty as a man is bound to do:
With a joyful spirit I Sir Richard Grenville die!'
And he fell upon their decks, and he died.

XIV

And they stared at the dead that had been so valiant and true,
And had holden the power and glory of Spain so cheap
That he dared her with one little ship and his English few;
Was he devil or man? He was devil for aught they knew,
But they sank his body with honour down into the deep,
And they mann'd the Revenge with a swarthier alien crew,
And away she sail'd with her loss and long'd for her own;
When a wind from the lands they had ruin'd awoke from sleep,
And the water began to heave and the weather to moan,
And or ever that evening ended a great gale blew,
And a wave like the wave that is raised by an earthquake grew,
Till it smote on their hulls and their sails and their masts and their flags,
And the whole sea plunged and fell on the shot-shatter'd navy of Spain,
And the little Revenge herself went down by the island crags
To be lost evermore in the main.

[1873?] [1878]

'FRATER AVE ATQUE VALE'[1]

Row us out from Desenzano, to your Sirmione row!
So they row'd, and there we landed—'O venusta[2] Sirmio!'
There to me thro' all the groves of olive in the summer glow,
There beneath the Roman ruin where the purple flowers grow,
Came that 'Ave atque Vale' of the Poet's hopeless woe,
Tenderest of Roman poets nineteen-hundred years ago,
'Frater Ave atque Vale'—as we wander'd to and fro
Gazing at the Lydian laughter of the Garda Lake below
Sweet Catullus's all-but-island, olive-silvery Sirmio!

[1880] [1883]

[1] Hail, brother, and farewell.
[2] Lovely.

TO VIRGIL

WRITTEN AT THE REQUEST OF THE MANTUANS FOR THE NINETEENTH CENTENARY OF VIRGIL'S DEATH

I

Roman Virgil, thou that singest
Ilion's lofty temples robed in fire,
Ilion falling, Rome arising,
wars, and filial faith, and Dido's pyre;

II

Landscape-lover, lord of language
more than he that sang the Works and Days,
All the chosen coin of fancy
flashing out from many a golden phrase;

III

Thou that singest wheat and woodland,
tilth and vineyard, hive and horse and herd;
All the charm of all the Muses
often flowering in a lonely word;

IV

Poet of the happy Tityrus
piping underneath his beechen bowers;
Poet of the poet-satyr
whom the laughing shepherd bound with flowers;

V

Chanter of the Pollio, glorying
in the blissful years again to be, 9
Summers of the snakeless meadow,
unlaborious earth and oarless sea;

VI

Thou that seëst Universal Nature moved by Universal Mind;
Thou majestic in thy sadness at the doubtful doom of human kind;

VII

Light among the vanish'd ages; star that gildest yet this phantom shore;
Golden branch amid the shadows, kings and realms that pass to rise no more;

VIII

Now thy Forum roars no longer, fallen every purple Cæsar's dome—
Tho' thine ocean-roll of rhythm sound for ever of Imperial Rome—

IX

Now the Rome of slaves hath perish'd, and the Rome of freemen holds her place,
I, from out the Northern Island sunder'd once from all the human race,

X

I salute thee, Mantovano, I that loved thee since my day began,
Wielder of the stateliest measure ever moulded by the lips of man.

[1882]

LOCKSLEY HALL

SIXTY YEARS AFTER

Late, my grandson! half the morning have I paced these sandy tracts,
Watch'd again the hollow ridges roaring into cataracts,

Wander'd back to living boyhood while I heard the curlews call,
I myself so close on death, and death itself in Locksley Hall.

So—your happy suit was blasted—she the faultless, the divine;
And you liken—boyish babble—this boy-love of yours with mine.

I myself have often babbled doubtless of a foolish past;
Babble, babble; our old England may go down in babble at last.

'Curse him!' curse your fellow-victim? call him dotard in your rage?
Eyes that lured a doting boyhood well might fool a dotard's age.

Jilted for a wealthier! wealthier? yet perhaps she was not wise;
I remember how you kiss'd the miniature with those sweet eyes.

In the hall there hangs a painting—Amy's arms about my neck—
Happy children in a sunbeam sitting on the ribs of wreck.

In my life there was a picture, she that clasp'd my neck had flown;
I was left within the shadow sitting on the wreck alone.

Yours has been a slighter ailment, will you sicken for her sake?
You, not you! your modern amourist is of easier, earthlier make.

Amy loved me, Amy fail'd me, Amy was a timid child;
But your Judith—but your worldling—*she* had never driven me wild.

She that holds the diamond necklace dearer than the golden ring,
She that finds a winter sunset fairer than a morn of Spring.

She that in her heart is brooding on his briefer lease of life,
While she vows 'till death shall part us,' she the would-be-widow wife.

She the worldling born of worldlings—father, mother—be content,
Ev'n the homely farm can teach us there is something in descent.

Yonder in that chapel, slowly sinking now into the ground,
Lies the warrior, my forefather, with his feet upon the hound.

Cross'd! for once he sail'd the sea to crush the Moslem in his pride;
Dead the warrior, dead his glory, dead the cause in which he died.

Yet how often I and Amy in the mouldering aisle have stood,
Gazing for one pensive moment on that founder of our blood.

There again I stood to-day, and where of old we knelt in prayer,
Close beneath the casement crimson with the shield of Locksley—there,

All in white Italian marble, looking still as if she smiled,
Lies my Amy dead in child-birth, dead the mother, dead the child.

Dead—and sixty years ago, and dead her aged husband now—
I this old white-headed dreamer stoopt and kiss'd her marble brow.

Gone the fires of youth, the follies, furies, curses, passionate tears,
Gone like fires and floods and earthquakes of the planet's dawning years.

Fires that shook me once, but now to silent ashes fall'n away.
Cold upon the dead volcano sleeps the gleam of dying day.

Gone the tyrant of my youth, and mute below the chancel stones,
All his virtues—I forgive them—black in white above his bones.

Gone the comrades of my bivouac, some in fight against the foe,
Some thro' age and slow diseases, gone as all on earth will go.

Gone with whom for forty years my life in golden sequence ran,
She with all the charm of woman, she with all the breadth of man,

Strong in will and rich in wisdom, Edith, yet so lowly-sweet,
Woman to her inmost heart, and woman to her tender feet,

Very woman of very woman, nurse of ailing body and mind,
She that link'd again the broken chain that bound me to my kind.

Here to-day was Amy with me, while I wander'd down the coast,
Near us Edith's holy shadow, smiling at the slighter ghost.

Gone our sailor son thy father, Leonard early lost at sea;
Thou alone, my boy, of Amy's kin and mine art left to me.

Gone thy tender-natured mother, wearying to be left alone,
Pining for the stronger heart that once had beat beside her own.

Truth, for Truth is Truth, he worshipt, being true as he was brave;
Good, for Good is Good, he follow'd, yet he look'd beyond the grave,

Wiser there than you, that crowning barren Death as lord of all,
Deem this over-tragic drama's closing curtain is the pall!

Beautiful was death in him, who saw the death, but kept the deck,
Saving women and their babes, and sinking with the sinking wreck,

Gone for ever! Ever? no—for since our dying race began,
Ever, ever, and for ever was the leading light of man.

Those that at barbarian burials kill'd the slave, and slew the wife
Felt within themselves the sacred passion of the second life.

Indian warriors dream of ampler hunting grounds beyond the night;
Ev'n the black Australian dying hopes he shall return, a white.

Truth for truth, and good for good! The Good, the True, the Pure, the Just—
Take the charm 'For ever' from them, and they crumble into dust.

Gone the cry of 'Forward, Forward,' lost within a growing gloom;
Lost, or only heard in silence from the silence of a tomb.

Half the marvels of my morning, triumphs over time and space,
Staled by frequence, shrunk by usage into commonest commonplace!

'Forward' rang the voices then, and of the many mine was one.
Let us hush this cry of 'Forward' till ten thousand years have gone.

Far among the vanish'd races, old Assyrian kings would flay
Captives whom they caught in battle—iron-hearted victors they.

Ages after, while in Asia, he that lead the wild Moguls,
Timur built his ghastly tower of eighty thousand human skulls,

Then, and here in Edward's time, an age of noblest English names,
Christian conquerors took and flung the conquer'd Christian into flames.

Love your enemy, bless your haters, said the Greatest of the great;
Christian love among the Churches look'd the twin of heathen hate.

From the golden alms of Blessing man had coin'd himself a curse:
Rome of Cæsar, Rome of Peter, which was crueller? which was worse?

France had shown a light to all men, preach'd a Gospel, all men's good;
Celtic Demos rose a Demon, shriek'd and slaked the light with blood.

Hope was ever on her mountain, watching till the day begun—
Crown'd with sunlight—over darkness—from the still unrisen sun.

Have we grown at last beyond the passions of the primal clan?
'Kill your enemy, for you hate him,' still, 'your enemy' was a man.

Have we sunk below them? peasants maim the helpless horse, and drive
Innocent cattle under thatch, and burn the kindlier brutes alive.

Brutes, the brutes are not your wrongers—burnt at midnight, found at morn,
Twisted hard in mortal agony with their offspring, born-unborn,

Clinging to the silent mother! Are we devils? are we men?
Sweet St. Francis of Assisi, would that he were here again,

He that in his Catholic wholeness used to call the very flowers
Sisters, brothers—and the beasts—whose pains are hardly less than ours!

Chaos, Cosmos! Cosmos, Chaos! who can tell how all will end?
Read the wide world's annals, you, and take their wisdom for your friend.

Hope the best, but hold the Present fatal daughter of the Past,
Shape your heart to front the hour, but dream not that the hour will last.

Ay, if dynamite and revolver leave you courage to be wise:
When was age so cramm'd with menace? madness? written, spoken lies?

Envy wears the mask of Love, and, laughing sober fact to scorn,
Cries to Weakest as to Strongest, 'Ye are equals, equal-born.'

Equal-born? O yes, if yonder hill be level with the flat.
Charm us, Orator, till the Lion look no larger than the Cat,

Till the Cat thro' that mirage of overheated language loom
Larger than the Lion,—Demos end in working its own doom.

Russia bursts our Indian barrier, shall we fight her? shall we yield?
Pause! before you sound the trumpet, hear the voices from the field.

Those three hundred millions under one Imperial sceptre now,
Shall we hold them? shall we loose them? take the suffrage of the plow.

Nay, but these would feel and follow Truth if only you and you,
Rivals of realm-ruining party, when you speak were wholly true.

Plowmen, Shepherds, have I found, and more than once, and still could find
Sons of God, and kings of men in utter nobleness of mind,

Truthful, trustful, looking upward to the practised hustings-liar;
So the Higher wields the Lower, while the Lower is the Higher.

Here and there a cotter's babe is royal-born by right divine;
Here and there my lord is lower than his oxen or his swine.

Chaos, Cosmos! Cosmos, Chaos! once again the sickening game;
Freedom, free to slay herself, and dying while they shout her name,

Step by step we gain'd a freedom known to Europe, known to all;
Step by step we rose to greatness,—thro' the tonguesters we may fall.

You that woo the Voices—tell them 'old experience is a fool,'
Teach your flatter'd kings that only those who cannot read can rule.

Pluck the mighty from their seat, but set no meek ones in their place;
Pillory Wisdom in your markets, pelt your offal at her face.

Tumble Nature heel o'er head, and, yelling with the yelling street,
Set the feet above the brain and swear the brain is in the feet.

Bring the old dark ages back without the faith, without the hope,
Break the State, the Church, the Throne, and roll their ruins down the slope.

Authors—essayist, atheist, novelist, realist, rhymester, play your part,
Paint the mortal shame of nature with the living hues of Art.

Rip your brothers' vices open, strip your own foul passions bare;
Down with Reticence, down with Reverence—forward—naked—let them stare.

Feed the budding rose of boyhood with the drainage of your sewer;
Send the drain into the fountain, lest the stream should issue pure.

Set the maiden fancies wallowing in the troughs of Zolaism,—
Forward, forward, ay and backward, downward too into the abysm.

Do your best to charm the worst, to lower the rising race of men;
Have we risen from out the beast, then back into the beast again?

Only 'dust to dust' for me that sicken at your lawless din,
Dust in wholesome old-world dust before the newer world begin.

Heated am I? you—you wonder—well, it scarce becomes mine age—
Patience! let the dying actor mouth his last upon the stage.

Cries of unprogressive dotage ere the dotard fall asleep?
Noises of a current narrowing, not the music of a deep?

Ay, for doubtless I am old, and think gray thoughts, for I am gray:
After all the stormy changes shall we find a changeless May?

After madness, after massacre, Jacobinism and Jacquerie,
Some diviner force to guide us thro' the days I shall not see?

When the schemes and all the systems, Kingdoms and Republics fall,
Something kindlier, higher, holier—all for each and each for all?

All the full-brain, half-brain races, led by Justice, Love, and Truth;
All the millions one at length with all the visions of my youth?

All diseases quench'd by Science, no man halt, or deaf or blind;
Stronger ever born of weaker, lustier body, larger mind?

Earth at last a warless world, a single race, a single tongue—
I have seen her far away—for is not Earth as yet so young?—

Every tiger madness muzzled, every serpent passion kill'd,
Every grim ravine a garden, every blazing desert till'd,

Robed in universal harvest up to either pole she smiles,
Universal ocean softly washing all her warless Isles.

Warless? when her tens are thousands, and her thousands millions, then—
All her harvest all too narrow—who can fancy warless men?

Warless? war will die out late then. Will it ever? late or soon?
Can it, till this outworn earth be dead as yon dead world the moon?

Dead the new astronomy calls her. . . . On this day and at this hour,
In this gap between the sandhills, whence you see the Locksley tower,

Here we met, our latest meeting—Amy—sixty years ago—
She and I—the moon was falling greenish thro' a rosy glow,

Just above the gateway tower, and even where you see her now—
Here we stood and claspt each other, swore the seeming-deathless vow. . . .

Dead, but how her living glory lights the hall, the dune, the grass!
Yet the moonlight is the sunlight, and the sun himself will pass.

Venus near her! smiling downward at this earthlier earth of ours,
Closer on the Sun, perhaps a world of never fading flowers.

Hesper, whom the poet call'd the Bringer home of all good things.
All good things may move in Hesper, perfect peoples, perfect kings.

Hesper—Venus—were we native to that splendour or in Mars,
We should see the Globe we groan in, fairest of their evening stars.

Could we dream of wars and carnage, craft and madness, lust and spite,
Roaring London, raving Paris, in that point of peaceful light?

Might we not in glancing heavenward on a star so silver-fair,
Yearn, and clasp the hands and murmur, 'Would to God that we were there'?

Forward, backward, backward, forward, in the immeasurable sea,
Sway'd by vaster ebbs and flows than can be known to you or me.

All the suns—are these but symbols of innumerable man,
Man or Mind that sees a shadow of the planner or the plan?

Is there evil but on earth? or pain in every peopled sphere?
Well be grateful for the sounding watchword 'Evolution' here.

Evolution ever climbing after some ideal good,
And Reversion ever dragging Evolution in the mud.

What are men that He should heed us? cried the king of sacred song;
Insects of an hour, that hourly work their brother insect wrong,

While the silent Heavens roll, and Suns along their fiery way,
All their planets whirling round them, flash a million miles a day.

Many an Æon moulded earth before her highest, man, was born,
Many an Æon too may pass when earth is manless and forlorn,

Earth so huge, and yet so bounded—pools of salt, and plots of land—
Shallow skin of green and azure—chains of mountain, grains of sand!

Only That which made us, meant us to be mightier by and by,
Set the sphere of all the boundless Heavens within the human eye,

Sent the shadow of Himself, the boundless, thro' the human soul;
Boundless inward, in the atom, boundless outward, in the Whole.

* * * * * * *

Here is Locksley Hall, my grandson, here the lion-guarded gate.
Not to-night in Locksley Hall—to-morrow—you, you come so late.

Wreck'd—your train—or all but wreck'd? a shatter'd wheel? a vicious boy!
Good, this forward, you that preach it, is it well to wish you joy?

Is it well that while we range with Science, glorying in the Time,
City children soak and blacken soul and sense in city slime?

There among the glooming alleys Progress halts on palsied feet,
Crime and hunger cast our maidens by the thousand on the street.

There the Master scrimps his haggard sempstress of her daily bread,
There a single sordid attic holds the living and the dead.

There the smouldering fire of fever creeps across the rotted floor,
And the crowded couch of incest in the warrens of the poor.

Nay, your pardon, cry your 'forward,' yours are hope and youth, but I—
Eighty winters leave the dog too lame to follow with the cry,

Lame and old, and past his time, and passing now into the night;
Yet I would the rising race were half as eager for the light.

Light the fading gleam of Even? light the glimmer of the dawn?
Aged eyes may take the growing glimmer for the gleam withdrawn.

Far away beyond her myriad coming changes earth will be
Something other than the wildest modern guess of you and me.

Earth may reach her earthly-worst, or if she gain her earthly-best,
Would she find her human offspring this ideal man at rest?

Forward then, but still remember how the course of Time will swerve,
Crook and turn upon itself in many a backward streaming curve.

Not the Hall to-night, my grandson! Death and Silence hold their own.
Leave the Master in the first dark hour of his last sleep alone.

Worthier soul was he than I am, sound and honest, rustic Squire,
Kindly landlord, boon companion—youthful jealousy is a liar.

Cast the poison from your bosom, oust the madness from your brain.
Let the trampled serpent show you that you have not lived in vain.

Youthful! youth and age are scholars yet but in the lower school,
Nor is he the wisest man who never proved himself a fool.

Yonder lies our young sea-village—Art and Grace are less and less:
Science grows and Beauty dwindles—roofs of slated hideousness!

There is one old Hostel left us where they swing the Locksley shield,
Till the peasant cow shall butt the 'Lion passant' from his field.

Poor old Heraldry, poor old History, poor old Poetry, passing hence,
In the common deluge drowning old political common-sense!

Poor old voice of eighty crying after voices that have fled!
All I loved are vanish'd voices, all my steps are on the dead.

All the world is ghost to me, and as the phantom disappears,
Forward far and far from here is all the hope of eighty years.

* * * * * * *

In this Hostel—I remember—I repent it o'er his grave—
Like a clown—by chance he met me—I refused the hand he gave.

From that casement where the trailer mantles all the mouldering bricks—
I was then in early boyhood, Edith but a child of six—

While I shelter'd in this archway from a day of driving showers—
Peept the winsome face of Edith like a flower among the flowers.

Here to-night! the Hall to-morrow, when they toll the Chapel bell!
Shall I hear in one dark room a wailing, 'I have loved thee well.'

Then a peal that shakes the portal—one has come to claim his bride,
Her that shrank, and put me from her, shriek'd, and started from my side—

Silent echoes! You, my Leonard, use and not abuse your day,
Move among your people, know them, follow him who led the way,

Strove for sixty widow'd years to help his homelier brother men,
Served the poor, and built the cottage, raised the school, and drain'd the fen.

Hears he now the Voice that wrong'd him? who shall swear it cannot be?
Earth would never touch her worst, were one in fifty such as he.

Ere she gain her Heavenly-best, a God must mingle with the game:
Nay, there may be those about us whom we neither see nor name,

Felt within us as ourselves, the Powers of Good, the Powers of Ill,
Strowing balm, or shedding poison in the fountains of the Will.

Follow you the Star that lights a desert pathway, yours or mine.
Forward, till you see the highest Human Nature is divine.

Follow Light, and do the Right—for man can half-control his doom—
Till you find the deathless Angel seated in the vacant tomb.

Forward, let the stormy moment fly and mingle with the Past.
I that loathed, have come to love him. Love will conquer at the last.

Gone at eighty, mine own age, and I and you will bear the pall;
Then I leave thee Lord and Master, latest Lord of Locksley Hall.

[1886]

FAR—FAR—AWAY

(FOR MUSIC)

What sight so lured him thro' the fields he knew
As where earth's green stole into heaven's own hue,
Far—far—away?

What sound was dearest in his native dells?
The mellow lin-lan-lone of evening bells
Far—far—away.

What vague world-whisper, mystic pain or joy,
Thro' those three words would haunt him when a boy,
Far—far—away?

A whisper from his dawn of life? a breath
From some fair dawn beyond the doors of death
Far—far—away?

Far, far, how far? from o'er the gates of Birth,
The faint horizons, all the bounds of earth,
Far—far—away?

What charm in words, a charm no words could give?
O dying words, can Music make you live
Far—far—away?

[1888] [1889]

CROSSING THE BAR

Sunset and evening star,
And one clear call for me!
And may there be no moaning of the bar,
When I put out to sea,

But such a tide as moving seems asleep,
Too full for sound and foam,
When that which drew from out the boundless deep
Turns again home.

Twilight and evening bell,
And after that the dark!
And may there be no sadness of farewell,
When I embark;

For tho' from out our bourne of Time and Place
The flood may bear me far,
I hope to see my Pilot face to face
When I have crost the bar.

[1889] [1889]

1812-1889

ROBERT BROWNING

CHRONOLOGICAL TABLE

1812, May 7, born at Camberwell, a suburb of London, his father a prosperous employe of the Bank of England, and a collector of books and pictures, his mother a devout daughter of a Scottish ship-owner.

1820?–6 Attended private schools.

1828 For six months a student at the University of London.

1833 *Pauline* (anonymous).

1834 Journey to Russia.

1835 *Paracelsus.*

1837 *Strafford* (five performances, with Macready in the hero's role).

1838 First journey to Italy.

1840 *Sordello.*

1841–6 *Bells and Pomegranates* (in 8 parts).

1845–6 Courtship of Elizabeth Barrett; marriage on the 12 of September, 1846, followed at once by a "flight" to Italy.

1850 *Christmas Eve and Easter-Day.*

1855 *Men and Women.*

1856 A bequest of £11,000.

1861, June 29, Death of Elizabeth.

1864 *Dramatis Personae.*

1868–9 *The Ring and the Book.*

1871 *Balaustion's Adventure.*
Prince Hohenstiel-Schwangau, Saviour of Society.

1872 *Fifine at the Fair.*

1873 *Red Cotton Nightcap Country.*

1875 *Aristophanes' Apology.*
The Inn Album.

1876 *Pacchiarotto and How He Worked in Distemper, with Other Poems.*

1877 *Aeschylus' Agamemnon.*

1878 *La Saisiaz and the Two Poets of Croisic.*

1879–80 *Dramatic Idyls* (in 2 parts).

1881 Formation of the Browning Society in London.

1883 *Jocoseria.*

1884 *Ferishtah's Fancies.*

1887 *Parleyings with Certain People of Importance.*

1889 *Asolando.*
December 12, death in Venice, December 31, burial in Westminster Abbey.

Browning, the most original of the major Victorian poets, was for long an obscure and unconsidered writer. Not one copy of *Pauline* was sold; *Paracelsus* had a *succès d'estime; Strafford,* even with a great actor in the titular role, could not hold the boards; the unintelligibility of *Sordello* was a by-word and, as Mr. DeVane says, ruined whatever reputation Browning had acquired. Even at the price of sixpence, *Pippa Passes,* the first of the *Bells and Pomegranates,* sold slowly; and later parts of the series—even with such poems as "My Last Duchess," "The Bishop Orders His Tomb," and "The Laboratory"—fared no better. At the time of his marriage Browning's reputation was much narrower and much less secure than Elizabeth Barrett's. Even in *Men and Women,* where later readers have discerned the height of Browning's power in psychological analysis and vivid utterance, the public of 1855 took slight interest; after twenty-two years of writing and publishing poetry, Browning had won devout admirers especially among such younger readers as Swinburne, Rossetti and Morris, but he had almost entirely failed to win the attention and the shillings of the general reader of poetry. In deep discouragement he lapsed into a nine years' silence. In the course of those years his earlier collections and *Men and Women* slowly made their way; and when in 1864 he published *Dramatis Personae,* a second edition was required within a twelvemonth. His reputation was henceforth secure although as yet it was not very broadly based; even so vast and intricate a poem as *The Ring and the Book* was read not simply with admiration and respect but with enthusiasm.

Browning never again equalled the excellence of the three works which have just been named; but many of his later collections and experiments sold widely and were acclaimed. During the rest of his life he stood next to Tennyson in the opinion if not in the devotion of the general reader; and he had probably a larger circle of fanatical admirers than any other English poet of the century. *Asolando,* appearing on the day the poet died, ran rapidly through nine editions.

Browning's greatness is threefold: he is a great philosophical poet, a great psychological poet and a great artist in poetry. The union of his three kinds of power is most evident in the works of his middle years: *Men and Women, Dramatis Personae* and *The Ring and the Book.* In such pieces as *Abt Vogler* the art is triumphantly adequate to the expression of a philosophic doctrine so involved and so sublime as almost to resist expression: images of astonishing ingenuity and complete originality and rhythms of sweeping soaring contour never fail the poet. In such pieces as *Fra Lippo Lippi,* the psychological portrait is assisted by a great dramatist's mastery of speech and a great artist's mastery of imagery. Browning's psychological power was mature in some of the parts of *Bells and Pomegranates,* although he did not in them attempt complex fully rounded portraits; and its decline is already setting in in the seventies. His art, seldom altogether sure or perfectly sustained in poems of any length, underwent surprising fluctuations in the years following *The Ring and the Book.* Even in his latest poetry he could, however, burst into brief lyrics or toss off miniature portraits of perfect art. His prophetic power, so difficult for most readers of this age to appreciate at its true worth (which is high, if notably lower than some of his younger contemporaries believed), is best seen when, as in the Pope's monologue in *The Ring and the Book* it attempts a systematic exposition of thought in a frame of objective reference. In many passages in the latter part of that monologue the poet imparts to an ethical and metaphysical creed vitality and excitement such as most poets can impart only to the delineation of a personality or a mood, or the realization of a passionate experience.

JOHANNES AGRICOLA IN MEDITATION

There's Heaven above, and night by night
  I look right through its gorgeous roof;
No sun and moons though e'er so bright
  Avail to stop me; splendour-proof
I keep the broods of stars aloof;
For I intend to get to God,
  For 'tis to God I speed so fast,
For in God's breast, my own abode,
  Those shoals of dazzling glory past,
  I lay my spirit down at last.
I lie where I have always lain,
  God smiles as he has always smiled;
Ere suns and moons could wax and wane,
  Ere stars were thundergirt, or piled
The heavens, God thought on me his child;
Ordained a life for me, arrayed
  Its circumstances, every one
To the minutest; ay, God said
  This head this hand should rest upon
Thus, ere he fashioned star or sun.
And having thus created me,
  Thus rooted me, he bade me grow,
Guiltless for ever, like a tree
  That buds and blooms, nor seeks to know
  The law by which it prospers so:
But sure that thought and word and deed
  All go to swell his love for me,
Me, made because that love had need
  Of something irreversibly
Pledged solely its content to be.
Yes, yes, a tree which must ascend,
  No poison-gourd foredoomed to stoop!
I have God's warrant, could I blend
  All hideous sins, as in a cup,
To drink the mingled venoms up;
Secure my nature will convert
  The draught to blossoming gladness fast:
While sweet dews turn to the gourd's hurt,
  And bloat, and while they bloat it, blast,
As from the first its lot was cast.
For as I lie, smiled on, full fed
  By unexhausted power to bless,
I gaze below on Hell's fierce bed,
  And those its waves of flame oppress,
Swarming in ghastly wretchedness;
Whose life on earth aspired to be
  One altar-smoke, so pure!—to win
If not love like God's love for me,
  At least to keep his anger in;
And all their striving turned to sin.
  Priest, doctor, hermit, monk grown white
With prayer, the broken-hearted nun,
  The martyr, the wan acolyte,
The incense-swinging child,—undone
Before God fashioned star or sun!
God, whom I praise; how could I praise,
  If such as I might understand,
Make out, and reckon on his ways,
  And bargain for his love, and stand,
Paying a price, at his right hand?

[1834?] [1836]

PORPHYRIA'S LOVER

The rain set early in to-night
  The sullen wind was soon awake,
It tore the elm-tops down for spite,
  And did its worst to vex the lake:
I listened with heart fit to break.

When glided in Porphyria; straight
She shut the cold out and the storm,
And kneeled and made the cheerless grate
Blaze up, and all the cottage warm;
Which done, she rose, and from her form
Withdrew the dripping cloak and shawl,
And laid her soiled gloves by, untied
Her hat and let the damp hair fall,
And, last, she sate down by my side
And called me. When no voice replied,
She put my arm about her waist,
And made her smooth white shoulder bare,
And all her yellow hair displaced,
And, stooping, made my cheek lie there,
And spread, o'er all, her yellow hair,
Murmuring how she loved me—she
Too weak, for all her heart's endeavour,
To set its struggling passion free
From pride, and vainer ties dissever,
And give herself to me for ever.
But passion sometimes would prevail,
Nor could to-night's gay feast restrain
A sudden thought of one so pale
For love of her, and all in vain;
So, she was come through wind and rain.
Be sure I looked up at her eyes
Happy and proud; at last I knew
Porphyria worshipped me; surprise
Made my heart swell, and still it grew
While I debated what to do.
That moment she was mine, mine, fair,
Perfectly pure and good: I found
A think to do, and all her hair
In one long yellow string I wound
Three times her little throat around,
And strangled her. No pain felt she;
I am quite sure she felt no pain
As a shut bud that holds a bee,
I warily oped her lids: again
Laughed the blue eyes without a stain.
And I untightened next the tress
About her neck; her cheek once more
Blushed bright beneath my burning kiss:
I propped her head up as before,
Only, this time my shoulder bore
Her head, which droops upon it still:
The smiling rosy little head,
So glad it has its utmost will,
That all it scorned at once is fled,
And I, its love, am gained instead!
Porphyria's love: she guessed not how
Her darling one wish would be heard.
And thus we sit together now,
And all night long we have not stirred,
And yet God has not said a word!
[1834?] [1836]

CAVALIER TUNES

I.—MARCHING ALONG

I

Kentish Sir Byng stood for his King,
Bidding the crop-headed Parliament swing:
And, pressing a troop unable to stoop
And see the rogues flourish and honest folk droop,
Marched them along, fifty-score strong,
Great-hearted gentlemen, singing this song.

II

God for King Charles! Pym and such carles
To the Devil that prompts 'em their treasonous parles!
Cavaliers, up! Lips from the cup,
Hands from the pasty, nor bite take nor sup
Till you're
(CHORUS) *Marching along, fifty-score strong,*
Great-hearted gentlemen, singing this song.

III

Hampden to hell, and his obsequies' knell.
Serve Hazelrig, Fiennes, and young Harry as well!

England, good cheer! Rupert is near!
Kentish and loyalists, keep we not here
(CHORUS) *Marching along, fifty-score strong,*
Great-hearted gentlemen, singing this song?

IV

Then, God for King Charles! Pym and his snarls
To the Devil that pricks on such pestilent carles!
Hold by the right, you double your might;
So, onward to Nottingham, fresh for the fight,
(CHORUS) *March we along, fifty-score strong,*
Great-hearted gentlemen, singing this song!

II.—GIVE A ROUSE

I

King Charles, and who'll do him right now?
King Charles, and who's ripe for fight now?
Give a rouse: here's, in hell's despite now,
King Charles!

II

Who gave me the goods that went since?
Who raised me the house that sank once?
Who helped me to gold I spent since?
Who found me in wine you drank once?
(CHORUS) *King Charles, and who'll do him right now?*
King Charles, and who's ripe for fight now?
Give a rouse: here's, in hell's despite now,
King Charles!

III

To whom used my boy George quaff else,
By the old fool's side that begot him?
For whom did he cheer and laugh else,
While Noll's damned troopers shot him?
(CHORUS) *King Charles, and who'll do him right now?*
King Charles, and who's ripe for fight now?
Give a rouse: here's, in hell's despite now,
King Charles!

III.—BOOT AND SADDLE

I

Boot, saddle, to horse, and away!
Rescue my Castle, before the hot day
Brightens to blue from its silvery grey,
(CHORUS) *Boot, saddle, to horse, and away!*

II

Ride past the suburbs, asleep as you'd say;
Many's the friend there, will listen and pray
"God's luck to gallants that strike up the lay—
(CHORUS) *"Boot, saddle, to horse, and away!"*

III

Forty miles off, like a roebuck at bay,
Flouts Castle Brancepeth the Roundheads' array:
Who laughs, "Good fellows ere this, by my fay,
(CHORUS) *"Boot, saddle, to horse, and away!"*

IV

Who? My wife Gertrude; that, honest and gay,
Laughs when you talk of surrendering, "Nay!
"I've better counsellors; what counsel they?
(CHORUS) *"Boot, saddle, to horse, and away!"*

[1842]

MY LAST DUCHESS

FERRARA

That's my last Duchess painted on the wall,
Looking as if she were alive. I call
That piece a wonder, now: Frà Pandolf's hands
Worked busily a day, and there she stands.
Will't please you sit and look at her? I said
"Frà Pandolf" by design, for never read
Strangers like you that pictured countenance,
The depth and passion of its earnest glance,
But to myself they turned (since none puts by
The curtain I have drawn for you, but I)
And seemed as they would ask me, if they durst,
How such a glance came there; so, not the first
Are you to turn and ask thus. Sir, 'twas not
Her husband's presence only, called that spot
Of joy into the Duchess' cheek: perhaps
Frà Pandolf chanced to say "Her mantle laps
"Over my Lady's wrist too much," or "Paint
"Must never hope to reproduce the faint
"Half-flush that dies along her throat:" such stuff
Was courtesy, she thought, and cause enough
For calling up that spot of joy. She had
A heart—how shall I say?—too soon made glad,
Too easily impressed; she liked whate'er
She looked on, and her looks went everywhere.
Sir, 'twas all one! My favour at her breast,
The dropping of the daylight in the West,
The bough of cherries some officious fool
Broke in the orchard for her, the white mule
She rode with round the terrace—all and each
Would draw from her alike the approving speech,
Or blush, at least. She thanked men,—good! but thanked
Somehow—I know not how—as if she ranked
My gift of a nine hundred years old name
With anybody's gift. Who'd stoop to blame
This sort of trifling? Even had you skill
In speech—(which I have not)—to make your will
Quite clear to such an one, and say "Just this

"Or that in you disgusts me; here you miss,
"Or there exceed the mark"—and if she let
Herself be lessoned so, nor plainly set
Her wits to yours, forsooth, and made excuse,
—E'en then would be some stooping, and I choose
Never to stoop. Oh, Sir, she smiled, no doubt
Whene'er I passed her; but who passed without
Much the same smile? This grew; I gave commands;
Then all smiles stopped together. There she stands
As if alive. Will't please you rise? We'll meet
The company below, then. I repeat,
The Count your Master's known munificence
Is ample warrant that no just pretence
Of mine for dowry will be disallowed;
Though his fair daughter's self, as I avowed
At starting, is my object. Nay, we'll go
Together down, Sir! Notice Neptune, tho',
Taming a sea-horse, thought a rarity,
Which Claus of Innsbruck cast in bronze for me.

[1842]

SOLILOQUY OF THE SPANISH CLOISTER

I

Gr-r-r—there go, my heart's abhorrence!
  Water your damned flower-pots, do!
If hate killed men, Brother Lawrence,
  God's blood, would not mine kill you!
What? your myrtle-bush wants trimming?
  Oh, that rose has prior claims—
Needs its leaden vase filled brimming?
  Hell dry you up with its flames!

II

At the meal we sit together:
  Salve tibi! [1] I must hear
Wise talk of the kind of weather,
  Sort of season, time of year:
Not a plenteous cork-crop: scarcely
  Dare we hope oak-galls, I doubt:
What's the Latin name for "parsley"?
  What's the Greek name for Swine's
    Snout?

III

Whew! We'll have our platter burnished,
  Laid with care on our own shelf!
With a fire-new spoon we're furnished,
  And a goblet for ourself,
Rinsed like something sacrificial
  Ere 'tis fit to touch our chaps—
Marked with L. for our initial!
  (He—he! There his lily snaps!)

IV

Saint, forsooth! While brown Dolores
  Squats outside the Convent bank,
With Sanchicha, telling stories,
  Steeping tresses in the tank,
Blue-black, lustrous, thick like horsehairs,
  —Can't I see his dead eye glow,
Bright as 'twere a Barbary corsair's?
  (That is, if he'd let it show!)

V

When he finishes refection,
  Knife and fork he never lays
Cross-wise, to my recollection,
  As do I, in Jesu's praise.
I, the Trinity illustrate,
  Drinking watered orange-pulp—
In three sips the Arian frustrate;
  While he drains his at one gulp.

VI

Oh, those melons? If he's able
  We're to have a feast! so nice!
One goes to the Abbot's table,
  All of us get each a slice.
How go on your flowers? None double?
  Not one fruit-sort can you spy?
Strange!—And I, too, at such trouble,
  Keep them close-nipped on the sly!

1 Hail to you!

VII

There's a great text in Galatians,
  Once you trip on it, entails
Twenty-nine distinct damnations,
  One sure, if another fails.
If I trip him just a-dying,
  Sure of heaven as sure can be,
Spin him round and send him flying
  Off to hell, a Manichee?

VIII

Or, my scrofulous French novel,
  On grey paper with blunt type!
Simply glance at it, you grovel
  Hand and foot in Belial's gripe:
If I double down its pages
  At the woeful sixteenth print,
When he gathers his greengages,
  Ope a sieve and slip it in't?

IX

Or, there's Satan!—one might venture
  Pledge one's soul to him, yet leave
Such a flaw in the indenture
  As he'd miss till, past retrieve,
Blasted lay that rose-acacia
  We're so proud of! *Hy, Zy, Hine* . . .
'St, there's Vespers! *Plena gratiâ*
  Ave, Virgo! [1] Gr-r-r—you swine!

[1842]

IN A GONDOLA

He sings

I send my heart up to thee, all my heart
  In this my singing.
For the stars help me, and the sea bears part;
  The very night is clinging
Closer to Venice' streets to leave one space
  Above me, whence thy face
May light my joyous heart to thee its dwelling-place.

She speaks

Say after me, and try to say
My very words, as if each word
Came from you of your own accord,
In your own voice, in your own way:
"This woman's heart and soul and brain
"Are mine as much as this gold chain
"She bids me wear; which" (say again)
"I choose to make by cherishing
"A precious thing, or choose to fling
"Over the boat-side, ring by ring."
And yet once more say . . . no word more!
Since words are only words. Give o'er!
Unless you call me, all the same,
Familiarly by my pet-name
Which, if the Three should hear you call,
And me reply to, would proclaim
At once our secret to them all.
Ask of me, too, command me, blame—
Do, break down the partition-wall
'Twixt us, the daylight world beholds
Curtained in dusk and splendid folds!
What's left but—all of me to take?
I am the Three's: prevent them, slake
Your thirst! 'Tis said, the Arab sage
In practising with gems can loose
Their subtle spirit in his cruce
And leave but ashes: so, sweet mage,
Leave them my ashes when thy use
Sucks out my soul, thy heritage!

He sings

I

Past we glide, and past, and past!
  What's that poor Agnese doing
Where they make the shutters fast?
  Grey Zanobi's just a-wooing
To his couch the purchased bride:
  Past we glide!

II

Past we glide, and past, and past!
  Why's the Pucci Palace flaring
Like a beacon to the blast?
  Guests by hundreds, not one caring
If the dear host's neck were wried:
  Past we glide!

She sings

I

The moth's kiss, first!
Kiss me as if you made believe
You were not sure, this eve,
How my face, your flower, had pursed
Its petals up; so, here and there
You brush it, till I grow aware
Who wants me, and wide ope I burst.

II

The bee's kiss, now!
Kiss me as if you entered gay

1 Hail, Virgin, full of grace!

My heart at some noonday,
A bud that dares not disallow
The claim, so all is rendered up,
And passively its shattered cup
Over your head to sleep I bow.

He sings

I

What are we two?
I am a Jew,
And carry thee, farther than friends can pursue,
To a feast of our tribe;
Where they need thee to bribe
The devil that blasts them unless he imbibe
Thy . . . Scatter the vision for ever! And now,
As of old, I am I, thou art thou!

II

Say again, what we are?
The sprite of a star,
I lure thee above where the destinies bar
My plumes their full play
Till a ruddier ray
Than my pale one announce there is withering away
Some . . . Scatter the vision for ever! And now,
As of old, I am I, thou art thou!

He muses

Oh, which were best, to roam or rest?
The land's lap or the water's breast?
To sleep on yellow millet-sheaves,
Or swim in lucid shallows, just
Eluding water-lily leaves,
An inch from Death's black fingers, thrust
To lock you, whom release he must;
Which life were best on Summer eves?

He speaks, musing

Lie back; could thought of mine improve you?
From this shoulder let there spring
A wing; from this, another wing;
Wings, not legs and feet, shall move you!
Snow-white must they spring, to blend
With your flesh, but I intend
They shall deepen to the end,
Broader, into burning gold,
Till both wings crescent-wise enfold
Your perfect self, from 'neath your feet
To o'er your head, where, lo, they meet
As if a million sword-blades hurled
Defiance from you to the world!

Rescue me thou, the only real!
And scare away this mad ideal
That came, not motions to depart!
Thanks! Now, stay ever as thou art!

Still he muses

I

What if the Three should catch at last
Thy serenader? While there's cast
Paul's cloak about my head, and fast
Gian pinions me. Himself has passed
His stylet thro' my back; I reel;
And . . . is it thou I feel?

II

They trail me, these three godless knaves,
Past every church that sains and saves,
Nor stop till, where the cold sea raves
By Lido's wet accursed graves,
They scoop mine, roll me to its brink,
And . . . on thy breast I sink!

She replies, musing

Dip your arm o'er the boat-side, elbow-deep,
As I do: thus: were death so unlike sleep,
Caught this way? Death's to fear from flame, or steel,
Or poison doubtless; but from water—feel!

Go find the bottom! Would you stay me? There!
Now pluck a great blade of that ribbon-grass
To plait in where the foolish jewel was,
I flung away: since you have praised my hair,
'Tis proper to be choice in what I wear.

He speaks

Row home? must we row home? Too surely
Know I where its front 's demurely
Over the Giudecca piled;
Window just with window mating,
Door on door exactly waiting,
All's the set face of a child:
But behind it, where's a trace

Of the staidness and reserve,
And formal lines without a curve,
In the same child's playing-face?
No two windows look one way
O'er the small sea-water thread
Below them. Ah, the autumn day
I, passing, saw you overhead!
First, out a cloud of curtain blew,
Then, a sweet cry, and last, came you—
To catch your lory that must needs
Escape just then, of all times then,
To peck a tall plant's fleecy seeds,
And make me happiest of men.
I scarce could breathe to see you reach
So far back o'er the balcony
To catch him ere he climbed too high
Above you in the Smyrna peach
That quick the round smooth cord of gold,
This coiled hair on your head, unrolled,
Fell down you like a gorgeous snake
The Roman girls were wont, of old,
When Rome there was, for coolness' sake
To let lie curling o'er their bosoms.
Dear lory, may his beak retain
Ever its delicate rose stain
As if the wounded lotus-blossoms
Had marked their thief to know again!

Stay longer yet, for others' sake
Than mine! what should your chamber do?
—With all its rarities that ache
In silence while day lasts, but wake
At night-time and their life renew,
Suspended just to pleasure you
Who brought against their will together
These objects, and, while days last, weave
Around them such a magic tether
That dumb they look: your harp, believe,
With all the sensitive tight strings
That dare not speak, now to itself
Breathes slumberously as if some elf
Went in and out the chords, his wings
Make murmur wheresoe'er they graze,
As an angel may, between the maze
Of midnight palace-pillars, on
And on, to sow God's plagues have gone
Through guilty glorious Babylon.
And while such murmurs flow, the nymph
Bends o'er the harp-top from her shell
As the dry limpet for the lymph
Come with a tune he knows so well.
And how your statues' hearts must swell!
And how your pictures must descend
To see each other, friend with friend!
Oh, could you take them by surprise,
You'd find Schidone's eager Duke
Doing the quaintest courtesies
To that prim Saint by Haste-thee-Luke!
And, deeper into her rock den,
Bold Castelfranco's Magdalen
You'd find retreated from the ken
Of that robed counsel-keeping Ser—
As if the Tizian thinks of her,
And is not, rather, gravely bent
On seeing for himself what toys
Are these, his progeny invent,
What litter now the board employs
Whereon he signed a document
That got him murdered! Each enjoys
Its night so well, you cannot break
The sport up, so, indeed must make
More stay with me, for others' sake.

She speaks

I

To-morrow, if a harp-string, say,
Is used to tie the jasmine back
That overfloods my room with sweets,
Contrive your Zorzi somehow meets
My Zanze! if the ribbon's black,
The Three are watching; keep away.

II

Your gondola—let Zorzi wreathe
A mesh of water-weeds about
Its prow, as if he unaware
Had struck some quay or bridge-foot stair!
That I may throw a paper out
As you and he go underneath.

There's Zanze's vigilant taper; safe are we!
Only one minute more to-night with me?
Resume your past self of a month ago!
Be you the bashful gallant, I will be
The lady with the colder breast than snow:
Now bow you, as becomes, nor touch my hand
More than I touch yours when I step to land,
And say, "All thanks, Siora!"—

Heart to heart,
And lips to lips! Yet once more, ere we part,
Clasp me, and make me thine, as mine thou art!

He is surprised, and stabbed.

It was ordained to be so, sweet,—and best
Comes now, beneath thine eyes, and on thy breast.
Still kiss me! Care not for the cowards! Care
Only to put aside thy beauteous hair
My blood will hurt! The Three, I do not scorn
To death, because they never lived: but I
Have lived indeed, and so—(yet one more kiss)—can die!

[1842]

Spanish queen who marries Soldier

CRISTINA

I

She should never have looked at me,
  If she meant I should not love her!
There are plenty . . . men, you call such,
  I suppose . . . she may discover
All her soul to, if she pleases,
  And yet leave much as she found them:
But I'm not so, and she knew it
  When she fixed me, glancing round them.

II

What? To fix me thus meant nothing?
  But I can't tell (there's my weakness)
What her look said!—no vile cant, sure,
  About "need to strew the bleakness
"Of some lone shore with its pearl-seed,
  "That the sea feels"—no "strange yearning
"That such souls have, most to lavish
  "Where there's chance of least returning."

III

Oh, we're sunk enough here, God knows!
  But not quite so sunk that moments,
Sure tho' seldom, are denied us,
  When the spirit's true endowments
Stand out plainly from its false ones,
  And apprise it if pursuing
Or the right way or the wrong way,
  To its triumph or undoing.

IV

There are flashes struck from midnights,
  There are fire-flames noondays kindle,
Whereby piled-up honours perish,
  Whereby swollen ambitions dwindle,
While just this or that poor impulse,
  Which for once had play unstifled,
Seems the sole work of a life-time
  That away the rest have trifled.

V

Doubt you if, in some such moment,
  As she fixed me, she felt clearly,
Ages past the soul existed,
  Here an age 'tis resting merely,
And hence, fleets again for ages,
  While the true end, sole and single,
It stops here for is, this love-way,
  With some other soul to mingle?

VI

Else it loses what it lived for,
  And eternally must lose it;
Better ends may be in prospect,
  Deeper blisses (if you choose it)
But this life's end and this love-bliss
  Have been lost here. Doubt you whether
This she felt as, looking at me,
  Mine and her souls rushed together?

VII

Oh, observe! Of course, next moment,
  The world's honours, in derision,
Trampled out the light for ever:
  Never fear but there's provision
Of the devil's to quench knowledge
  Lest we walk the earth in rapture!
—Making those who catch God's secret
  Just so much more prize their capture.

VIII

Such am I: the secret's mine now!
  She has lost me, I have gained her!
Her soul's mine: and, thus, grown perfect,
  I shall pass my life's remainder.
Life will just hold out the proving
  Both our powers, alone and blended:
And then, come the next life quickly!
  This world's use will have been ended.

[1842]

THE LABORATORY

[ANCIEN RÉGIME]

I

Now that I, tying thy glass mask tightly,
May gaze thro' these faint smokes curling whitely,
As thou pliest thy trade in this devil's-smithy—
Which is the poison to poison her, prithee?

II

He is with her; and they know that I know
Where they are, what they do: they believe my tears flow
While they laugh, laugh at me, at me fled to the drear
Empty church, to pray God in, for them!—I am here.

III

Grind away, moisten and mash up thy paste,
Pound at thy powder,—I am not in haste!
Better sit thus, and observe thy strange things,
Than go where men wait me and dance at the King's.

IV

That in the mortar—you call it a gum?
Ah, the brave tree whence such gold oozings come!
And yonder soft phial, the exquisite blue,
Sure to taste sweetly,—is that poison too?

V

Had I but all of them, thee and thy treasures,
What a wild crowd of invisible pleasures!
To carry pure death in an earring, a casket,
A signet, a fan-mount, a filigree basket!

VI

Soon, at the King's, a mere lozenge to give
And Pauline should have just thirty minutes to live!
But to light a pastile, and Elise, with her head
And her breast and her arms and her hands, should drop dead!

VII

Quick—is it finished? The colour's too grim!
Why not soft like the phial's, enticing and dim?
Let it brighten her drink, let her turn it and stir,
And try it and taste, ere she fix and prefer!

VIII

What a drop! She's not little, no minion like me!
That's why she ensnared him: this never will free
The soul from those masculine eyes,—say, "no!"
To that pulse's magnificent come-and-go.

IX

For only last night, as they whispered, I brought
My own eyes to bear on her so, that I thought
Could I keep them one half minute fixed, she would fall,
Shrivelled; she fell not; yet this does it all!

X

Not that I bid you spare her the pain!
Let death be felt and the proof remain;
Brand, burn up, bite into its grace—
He is sure to remember her dying face!

XI

Is it done? Take my mask off! Nay, be not morose,
It kills her, and this prevents seeing it close:
The delicate droplet, my whole fortune's fee!
If it hurts her, beside, can it ever hurt me?

XII

Now, take all my jewels, gorge gold to your fill,
You may kiss me, old man, on my mouth if you will!
But brush this dust off me, lest horror it brings
Ere I know it—next moment I dance at the King's!

[1844]

THE BISHOP ORDERS HIS TOMB AT ST. PRAXED'S CHURCH

[ROME, 15—]

Vanity, saith the preacher, vanity!
Draw round my bed: is Anselm keeping back?
Nephews—sons mine . . . ah God, I know not! Well—
She, men would have to be your mother once,
Old Gandolf envied me, so fair she was!
What's done is done, and she is dead beside,
Dead long ago, and I am Bishop since,
And as she died so must we die ourselves,
And thence ye may perceive the world's a dream.
Life, how and what is it? As here I lie
In this state-chamber, dying by degrees,
Hours and long hours in the dead night, I ask
"Do I live, am I dead?" Peace, peace seems all.
Saint Praxed's ever was the church for peace;
And so, about this tomb of mine. I fought
With tooth and nail to save my niche, ye know:
—Old Gandolf cozened me, despite my care;
Shrewd was that snatch from out the corner South
He graced his carrion with, God curse the same!
Yet still my niche is not so cramped but thence
One sees the pulpit o' the epistle-side,
And somewhat of the choir, those silent seats,

And up into the aery dome where live
The angels, and a sunbeam's sure to lurk:
And I shall fill my slab of basalt there,
And 'neath my tabernacle take my rest,
With those nine columns round me, two and two,
The odd one at my feet where Anselm stands:
Peach-blossom marble all, the rare, the ripe
As fresh-poured red wine of a mighty pulse.
—Old Gandolf with his paltry onion-stone,
Put me where I may look at him! True peach,
Rosy and flawless: how I earned the prize!
Draw close: that conflagration of my church
—What then? So much was saved if aught were missed!
My sons, ye would not be my death? Go dig
The white-grape vineyard where the oil-press stood,
Drop water gently till the surface sinks,
And if ye find . . . Ah, God I know not, I! . . .
Bedded in store of rotten fig-leaves soft,
And corded up in a tight olive-frail,
Some lump, ah God, of *lapis lazuli,*
Big as a Jew's head cut off at the nape,
Blue as a vein o'er the Madonna's breast . . .
Sons, all have I bequeathed you, villas, all,
That brave Frascati villa with its bath,
So, let the blue lump poise between my knees,
Like God the Father's globe on both his hands
Ye worship in the Jesu Church so gay,
For Gandolf shall not choose but see and burst!
Swift as a weaver's shuttle fleet our years:
Man goeth to the grave, and where is he?
Did I say basalt for my slab, sons? Black—
'Twas ever antique-black I meant! How else
Shall ye contrast my frieze to come beneath?
The bas-relief in bronze ye promised me,
Those Pans and Nymphs ye wot of, and perchance
Some tripod, thyrsus, with a vase or so,
The Saviour at his sermon on the mount,
Saint Praxed in a glory, and one Pan
Ready to twitch the Nymph's last garment off,
And Moses with the tables . . . but I know
Ye mark me not! What do they whisper thee,
Child of my bowels, Anselm? Ah, ye hope
To revel down my villas while I gasp
Bricked o'er with beggar's mouldy travertine
Which Gandolf from his tomb-top chuckles at!
Nay, boys, ye love me—all of jasper, then!
'Tis jasper ye stand pledged to, lest I grieve
My bath must needs be left behind, alas!
One block, pure green as a pistachio-nut,
There's plenty jasper somewhere in the world—
And have I not Saint Praxed's ear to pray
Horses for ye, and brown Greek manuscripts,
And mistresses with great smooth marbly limbs?
—That's if ye carve my epitaph aright,

Choice Latin, picked phrase, Tully's every word,
No gaudy ware like Gandolf's second line—
Tully, my masters? Ulpian serves his need!
And then how I shall lie through centuries,
And hear the blessed mutter of the mass,
And see God made and eaten all day long,
And feel the steady candle-flame, and taste
Good strong thick stupefying incense-smoke!
For as I lie here, hours of the dead night,
Dying in state and by such slow degrees,
I fold my arms as if they clasped a crook,
And stretch my feet forth straight as stone can point,
And let the bedclothes, for a mortcloth, drop
Into great laps and folds of sculptor's-work:
And as yon tapers dwindle, and strange thoughts
Grow, with a certain humming in my ears,
About the life before I lived this life,
And this life too, popes, cardinals and priests,
Saint Praxed at his sermon on the mount,
Your tall pale mother with her talking eyes,
And new-found agate urns as fresh as day,
And marble's language, Latin pure, discreet,
—Aha, ELUCESCEBAT quoth our friend?
No Tully, said I, Ulpian at the best!
Evil and brief hath been my pilgrimage.
All *lapis,* all, sons! Else I give the Pope
My villas! Will ye ever eat my heart?
Ever your eyes were as a lizard's quick,
They glitter like your mother's for my soul,
Or ye would heighten my impoverished frieze,
Piece out its starved design, and fill my vase
With grapes, and add a vizor and a term,
And to the tripod ye would tie a lynx
That in his struggle throws the thyrsus down,
To comfort me on my entablature
Whereon I am to lie till I must ask
"Do I live, am I dead?" There, leave me, there!
For ye have stabbed me with ingratitude
To death—ye wish it—God, ye wish it! Stone—
Gritstone, a-crumble! Clammy squares which sweat
As if the corpse they keep were oozing through—
And no more *lapis* to delight the world!
Well, go! I bless ye. Fewer tapers there,
But in a row: and, going, turn your backs
—Ay, like departing altar-ministrants,
And leave me in my church, the church for peace,
That I may watch at leisure if he leers—
Old Gandolf, at me, from his onion-stone,
As still he envied me, so fair she was!

[1845]

"HOW THEY BROUGHT THE GOOD NEWS FROM GHENT TO AIX"

[16—]

I

I sprang to the stirrup, and Joris, and he;
I galloped, Dirck galloped, we galloped all three;
"Good speed!" cried the watch, as the gate-bolts undrew;
"Speed!" echoed the wall to us galloping through;
Behind shut the postern, the lights sank to rest,
And into the midnight we galloped abreast.

II

Not a word to each other; we kept the great pace
Neck by neck, stride by stride, never changing our place;
I turned in my saddle and made its girths tight,
Then shortened each stirrup, and set the pique right,
Rebuckled the cheek-strap, chained slacker the bit,
Nor galloped less steadily Roland a whit.

III

'Twas moonset at starting; but while we drew near
Lokern, the cocks crew and twilight dawned clear;
At Boom, a great yellow star came out to see;
At Düffeld, 'twas morning as plain as could be;
And from Mecheln church-steeple we heard the half-chime,
So Joris broke silence with, "Yet there is time!"

IV

At Aershot, up leaped of a sudden the sun,
And against him the cattle stood black every one,
To stare thro' the mist at us galloping past,
And I saw my stout galloper Roland at last,
With resolute shoulders, each butting away
The haze, as some bluff river headland its spray:

V

And his low head and crest, just one sharp ear bent back
For my voice, and the other pricked out on his track;
And one eye's black intelligence,—ever that glance
O'er its white edge at me, his own master, askance!
And the thick heavy spume-flakes which aye and anon
His fierce lips shook upwards in galloping on.

VI

By Hasselt, Dirck groaned; and cried Joris, "Stay spur!
"Your Roos galloped bravely, the fault's not in her,
"We'll remember at Aix"—for one heard the quick wheeze
Of her chest, saw the stretched neck and staggering knees,
And sunk tail, and horrible heave of the flank,
As down on her haunches she shuddered and sank.

VII

So we were left galloping, Joris and I,
Past Looz and past Tongres, no cloud in the sky;
The broad sun above laughed a pitiless laugh,
'Neath our feet broke the brittle bright stubble like chaff;
Till over by Dalhem a dome-spire sprang white,
And "Gallop," gasped Joris, "for Aix is in sight!"

VIII

"How they'll greet us!"—and all in a moment his roan
Rolled neck and croup over, lay dead as a stone;
And there was my Roland to bear the whole weight
Of the news which alone could save Aix from her fate,
With his nostrils like pits full of blood to the brim,
And with circles of red for his eye-sockets' rim.

IX

Then I cast loose my buffcoat, each holster let fall,
Shook off both my jack-boots, let go belt and all,
Stood up in the stirrup, leaned, patted his ear,
Called my Roland his pet-name, my horse without peer;
Clapped my hands, laughed and sang, any noise, bad or good,
Till at length into Aix Roland galloped and stood.

X

And all I remember is, friends flocking round
As I sate with his head 'twixt my knees on the ground,
And no voice but was praising this Roland of mine,
As I poured down his throat our last measure of wine,
Which (the burgesses voted by common consent)
Was no more than his due who brought good news from Ghent.

[1838? 1844?] [1845]

PICTOR IGNOTUS[1]

[FLORENCE, 15—]

I could have painted pictures like that youth's
  Ye praise so. How my soul springs up! No bar
Stayed me—ah, thought which saddens while it soothes!—
  Never did fate forbid me, star by star,
To outburst on your night with all my gift
  Of fires from God: nor would my flesh have shrunk
From seconding my soul, with eyes uplift
  And wide to heaven, or, straight like thunder, sunk
To the centre, of an instant; or around
  Turned calmly and inquisitive, to scan
The licence and the limit, space and bound,
  Allowed to truth made visible in Man.
And, like that youth ye praise so, all I saw,
  Over the canvas could my hand have flung,
Each face obedient to its passion's law,
  Each passion clear proclaimed without a tongue;
Whether Hope rose at once in all the blood,
  A tip-toe for the blessing of embrace,

[1] An unknown painter.

Or Rapture drooped the eyes, as when her brood
Pull down the nesting dove's heart to its place;
Or Confidence lit swift the forehead up,
And locked the mouth fast, like a castle braved,—
O human faces, hath it spilt, my cup?
What did ye give me that I have not saved?
Nor will I say I have not dreamed (how well!)
Of going—I, in each new picture,—forth,
As, making new hearts beat and bosoms swell,
To Pope or Kaiser, East, West, South, or North,
Bound for the calmly-satisfied great State,
Or glad aspiring little burgh, it went,
Flowers cast upon the car which bore the freight,
Through old streets named afresh from the event,
Till it reached home, where learned age should greet
My face, and youth, the star not yet distinct
Above his hair, lie learning at my feet!—
Oh, thus to live, I and my picture, linked
With love about, and praise, till life should end,
And then not go to Heaven, but linger here,
Here on my earth, earth's every man my friend,—
The thought grew frightful, 'twas so wildly dear!
But a voice changed it! Glimpses of such sights
Have scared me, like the revels through a door
Of some strange house of idols at its rites!
This world seemed not the world it was before:
Mixed with my loving trusting ones there trooped
. . . Who summoned those cold faces that begun
To press on me and judge me? Though I stooped
Shrinking, as from the soldiery a nun,
They drew me forth, and spite of me . . . enough!
These buy and sell our pictures, take and give,
Count them for garniture and household-stuff,
And where they live needs must our pictures live,
And see their faces, listen to their prate,
Partakers of their daily pettiness,
Discussed of—"This I love, or this I hate,
"This likes me more, and this affects me less!"
Wherefore I chose my portion. If at whiles
My heart sinks, as monotonous I paint
These endless cloisters and eternal aisles
With the same series, Virgin, Babe, and Saint,
With the same cold calm beautiful regard,—
At least no merchant traffics in my heart;
The sanctuary's gloom at least shall ward
Vain tongues from where my pictures stand apart:
Only prayer breaks the silence of the shrine
While, blackening in the daily candle-smoke,
They moulder on the damp wall's travertine,
'Mid echoes the light footstep never woke.
So die, my pictures! surely, gently die!
Oh, youth, men praise so,—holds their praise its worth?
Blown harshly, keeps the trump its golden cry?
Tastes sweet the water with such specks of earth?

[1845]

THE ITALIAN IN ENGLAND

That second time they hunted me
From hill to plain, from shore to sea,
And Austria, hounding far and wide
Her blood-hounds thro' the country-side,
Breathed hot and instant on my trace,—
I made six days a hiding-place
Of that dry green old aqueduct
Where I and Charles, when boys, have plucked
The fire-flies from the roof above,
Bright creeping thro' the moss they love:
—How long it seems since Charles was lost!
Six days the soldiers crossed and crossed
The country in my very sight;
And when that peril ceased at night,
The sky broke out in red dismay
With signal-fires; well, there I lay
Close covered o'er in my recess,
Up to the neck in ferns and cress,
Thinking on Metternich our friend,
And Charles's miserable end,
And much beside, two days; the third,
Hunger o'ercame me when I heard
The peasants from the village go
To work among the maize; you know,
With us in Lombardy, they bring
Provisions packed on mules, a string
With little bells that cheer their task,
And casks, and boughs on every cask
To keep the sun's heat from the wine;
These I let pass in jingling line,
And, close on them, dear noisy crew,
The peasants from the village, too;
For at the very rear would troop
Their wives and sisters in a group
To help, I knew: when these had passed,
I threw my glove to strike the last,
Taking the chance: she did not start,
Much less cry out, but stooped apart
One instant, rapidly glanced round,
And saw me beckon from the ground.
A wild bush grows and hides my crypt;
She picked my glove up while she stripped
A branch off, then rejoined the rest
With that; my glove lay in her breast.
Then I drew breath they disappeared:
It was for Italy I feared.

An hour, and she returned alone
Exactly where my glove was thrown.
Meanwhile came many thoughts: on me
Rested the hopes of Italy.
I had devised a certain tale
Which, when 'twas told her, could not fail
Persuade a peasant of its truth;
I meant to call a freak of youth
This hiding, and give hopes of pay,
And no temptation to betray.
But when I saw that woman's face,
Its calm simplicity of grace,
Our Italy's own attitude
In which she walked thus far, and stood,
Planting each naked foot so firm,
To crush the snake and spare the worm—
At first sight of her eyes, I said,
"I am that man upon whose head
"They fix the price, because I hate
"The Austrians over us: the State
"Will give you gold—oh, gold so much!—
"If you betray me to their clutch,
"And be your death, for aught I know,
"If once they find you saved their foe.
"Now, you must bring me food and drink,
"And also paper, pen and ink,
"And carry safe what I shall write
"To Padua, which you'll reach at night
"Before the duomo shuts; go in,
"And wait till Tenebræ begin;
"Walk to the third confessional,
"Between the pillar and the wall,
"And kneeling whisper, *Whence comes peace?*
"Say it a second time; then cease;
"And if the voice inside returns,
"From Christ and Freedom; what concerns
"The cause of Peace?—for answer, slip
"My letter where you placed your lip;
"Then come back happy we have done
"Our mother service — I, the son,
"As you the daughter of our land!"

Three mornings more, she took her stand
In the same place, with the same eyes:
I was no surer of sun-rise
Than of her coming. We conferred
Of her own prospects, and I heard
She had a lover — stout and tall,
She said — then let her eyelids fall,
"He could do much"—as if some doubt
Entered her heart,—then, passing out,
"She could not speak for others—who
"Had other thoughts; herself she knew:"
And so she brought me drink and food

After four days, the scouts pursued
Another path: at last arrived
The help my Paduan friends contrived
To furnish me: she brought the news.
For the first time I could not choose
But kiss her hand, and lay my own
Upon her head—"This faith was shown
"To Italy, our mother;—she
"Uses my hand and blesses thee!"
She followed down to the sea-shore;
I left and never saw her more.

How very long since I have thought
Concerning—much less wished for—aught
Beside the good of Italy,
For which I live and mean to die!
I never was in love; and since
Charles proved false, what shall now convince
My inmost heart I have a friend?
However, if I pleased to spend
Real wishes on myself—say, three—
I know at least what one should be.
I would grasp Metternich until
I felt his red wet throat distil
In blood thro' these two hands. And next,
—Nor much for that am I perplexed—
Charles, perjured traitor, for his part,
Should die slow of a broken heart
Under his new employers. Last
—Ah, there, what should I wish? For fast
Do I grow old and out of strength.
If I resolved to seek at length
My father's house again, how scared
They all would look, and unprepared!
My brothers live in Austria's pay
—Disowned me long ago, men say;
And all my early mates who used
To praise me so—perhaps induced
More than one early step of mine—
Are turning wise; while some opine
"Freedom grows license," some suspect
"Haste breeds delay," and recollect
They always said, such premature
Beginnings never could endure!
So, with a sullen "All's for best,"
The land seems settling to its rest.
I think, then, I should wish to stand
This evening in that dear, lost land,
Over the sea the thousand miles,
And know if yet that woman smiles
With the calm smile; some little farm
She lives in there, no doubt; what harm
If I sat on the door-side bench,
And, while her spindle made a trench
Fantastically in the dust,
Inquired of all her fortunes—just
Her children's ages and their names,
And what may be the husband's aims
For each of them. I'd talk this out,
And sit there, for an hour about,
Then kiss her hand once more, and lay
Mine on her head, and go my way.

So much for idle wishing—how
It steals the time! To business now.

[1845]

THE ENGLISHMAN IN ITALY

[PIANO DI SORRENTO] [1]

Fortù, Fortù, my beloved one,
Sit here by my side,
On my knees put up both little feet!
I was sure, if I tried,
I could make you laugh spite of Scirocco:
Now, open your eyes,
Let me keep you amused till he vanish
In black from the skies,
With telling my memories over
As you tell your beads;
All the Plain saw me gather, I garland
—The flowers or the weeds.

Time for rain! for your long hot dry Autumn
Had net-worked with brown
The white skin of each grape on the bunches,
Marked like a quail's crown,
Those creatures you make such account of,
Whose heads,—speckled with white
Over brown like a great spider's back,
As I told you last night,—
Your mother bites off for her supper.
Red-ripe as could be,
Pomegranates were chapping and splitting
In halves on the tree:
And betwixt the loose walls of great flintstone,
Or in the thick dust

[1] The plain of Sorrento.

On the path, or straight out of the rock-side,
Wherever could thrust
Some burnt sprig of bold hardy rock-flower
Its yellow face up,
For the prize were great butterflies fighting,
Some five for one cup.
So I guessed, ere I got up this morning,
What change was in store,
By the quick rustle-down of the quail-nets
Which woke me before
I could open my shutter, made fast
With a bough and a stone,
And look thro' the twisted dead vine-twigs,
Sole lattice that's known.
Quick and sharp rang the rings down the net-poles,
While, busy beneath,
Your priest and his brother tugged at them,
The rain in their teeth.
And out upon all the flat house-roofs
Where split figs lay drying,
The girls took the frails under cover:
Nor use seemed in trying
To get out the boats and go fishing,
For, under the cliff,
Fierce the black water frothed o'er the blind-rock.
No seeing our skiff
Arrive about noon from Amalfi,
—Our fisher arrive,
And pitch down his basket before us,
All trembling alive
With pink and grey jellies, your sea-fruit;
You touch the strange lumps,
And mouths gape there, eyes open, all manner
Of horns and of humps,
Which only the fisher looks grave at,
While round him like imps
Cling screaming the children as naked
And brown as his shrimps;
Himself too as bare to the middle
—You see round his neck
The string and its brass coin suspended,
That saves him from wreck.
But to-day not a boat reached Salerno,
So back, to a man,
Came our friends, with whose help in the vineyards
Grape-harvest began.
In the vat, half-way up in our house-side,
Like blood the juice spins,
While your brother all bare-legged is dancing
Till breathless he grins
Dead-beaten, in effort on effort
To keep the grapes under,
Since still when he seems all but master,
In pours the fresh plunder
From girls who keep coming and going
With basket on shoulder,
And eyes shut against the rain's driving;
Your girls that are older,—
For under the hedges of aloe,
And where, on its bed
Of the orchard's black mould, the love-apple
Lies pulpy and red,
All the young ones are kneeling and filling
Their laps with the snails
Tempted out by this first rainy weather,—
Your best of regales,
As to-night will be proved to my sorrow,
When, supping in state,
We shall feast our grape-gleaners (two dozen,
Three over one plate)
With lasagne so tempting to swallow
In slippery ropes,
And gourds fried in great purple slices,
That colour of popes.
Meantime, see the grape-bunch they've brought you:
The rain-water slips
O'er the heavy blue bloom on each globe
Which the wasp to your lips
Still follows with fretful persistence:
Nay, taste, while awake,
This half of a curd-white smooth cheese-ball,
That peels, flake by flake,
Like an onion's, each smoother and whiter;
Next, sip this weak wine
From the thin green glass flask, with its stopper,
A leaf of the vine;
And end with the prickly-pear's red flesh
That leaves thro' its juice

The stony black seeds on your pearl-teeth.
Scirocco is loose!
Hark! the quick, whistling pelt of the olives
Which, thick in one's track,
Tempt the stranger to pick up and bite them,
Tho' not yet half black!
How the old twisted olive trunks shudder,
The medlars let fall
Their hard fruit, and the brittle great fig-trees
Snap off, figs and all,—
For here comes the whole of the tempest!
No refuge, but creep
Back again to my side and my shoulder,
And listen or sleep.

O how will your country show next week,
When all the vine-boughs
Have been stripped of their foliage to pasture
The mules and the cows?
Last eve, I rode over the mountains;
Your brother, my guide,
Soon left me, to feast on the myrtles
That offered, each side,
Their fruit-balls, black, glossy, and luscious,—
Or strip from the sorbs
A treasure, or rosy and wondrous,
Those hairy gold orbs!
But my mule picked his sure sober path out,
Just stopping to neigh
When he recognized down in the valley
His mates on their way
With the faggots and barrels of water;
And soon we emerged
From the plain, where the woods could scarce follow;
And still as we urged
Our way, the woods wondered, and left us,
As up still we trudged
Though the wild path grew wilder each instant,
And place was e'en grudged
'Mid the rock-chasms, and piles of loose stones
Like the loose broken teeth
Of some monster which climbed there to die
From the ocean beneath—
Place was grudged to the silver-grey fume-weed
That clung to the path,
And dark rosemary, ever a-dying,
That, 'spite the wind's wrath,
So loves the salt rock's face to seaward,—
And lentisks as staunch
To the stone where they root and bear berries,—
And . . . what shows a branch
Coral-coloured, transparent, with circlets
Of pale seagreen leaves;
Over all trod my mule with the caution
Of gleaners o'er sheaves,
Still, foot after foot like a lady—
Till, round after round,
He climbed to the top of Calvano,
And God's own profound
Was above me, and round me the mountains,
And under, the sea,
And within me my heart to bear witness
What was and shall be!
Oh heaven, and the terrible crystal!
No rampart excludes
Your eye from the life to be lived
In the blue solitudes.
Oh, those mountains, their infinite movement!
Still moving with you—
For, ever some new head and breast of them
Thrusts into view
To observe the intruder; you see it
If quickly you turn
And, before they escape you, surprise them.
They grudge you should learn
How the soft plains they look on, lean over,
And love (they pretend)
—Cower beneath them; the flat sea-pine crouches,
The wild fruit-trees bend,
E'en the myrtle-leaves curl, shrink and shut:
All is silent and grave:
'Tis a sensual and timorous beauty,
How fair! but a slave.
So, I turned to the sea; and there slumbered
As greenly as ever
Those isles of the siren, your Galli;
No ages can sever

The Three, nor enable their sister
  To join them,—half way
On the voyage, she looked at Ulysses—
  No farther to-day;
Tho' the small one, just launched in the wave,
  Watches breast-high and steady
From under the rock, her bold sister
  Swum half-way already.
Fortù, shall we sail there together
  And see from the sides
Quite new rocks show their faces, new haunts
  Where the siren abides?
Shall we sail round and round them, close over
  The rocks, tho' unseen,
That ruffle the grey glassy water
  To glorious green?
Then scramble from splinter to splinter,
  Reach land and explore,
On the largest, the strange square black turret
  With never a door,
Just a loop to admit the quick lizards;
  Then, stand there and hear
The birds' quiet singing, that tells us
  What life is, so clear?
—The secret they sang to Ulysses,
  When, ages ago,
He heard and he knew this life's secret
  I hear and I know!

Ah, see! The sun breaks o'er Calvano;
  He strikes the great gloom
And flutters it o'er the mount's summit
  In airy gold fume.
All is over. Look out, see the gipsy,
  Our tinker and smith,
Has arrived, set up bellows and forge,
  And down-squatted forthwith
To his hammering, under the wall there;
  One eye keeps aloof
The urchins that itch to be putting
  His jews'-harps to proof,
While the other, thro' locks of curled wire,
  Is watching how sleek
Shines the hog, come to share in the windfall
  —Chew, abbot's own cheek!
All is over. Wake up and come out now,
  And down let us go,
And see the fine things got in order
  At church for the show
Of the Sacrament, set forth this evening.
  To-morrow's the Feast
Of the Rosary's Virgin, by no means
  Of Virgins the least,
As you'll hear in the off-hand discourse
  Which (all nature, no art)
The Dominican brother, these three weeks,
  Was getting by heart.
Not a post nor a pillar but is dizened
  With red and blue papers;
All the roof waves with ribbons, each altar
  A-blaze with long tapers;
But the great masterpiece is the scaffold
  Rigged glorious to hold
All the fiddlers and fifers and drummers,
  And trumpeters bold,
Not afraid of Bellini nor Auber,
  Who, when the priest's hoarse,
Will strike us up something that's brisk
  For the feast's second course.
And then will the flaxen-wigged Image
  Be carried in pomp
Thro' the plain, while in gallant procession
  The priests mean to stomp.
And all round the glad church lie old bottles
  With gunpowder stopped,
Which will be, when the Image re-enters,
  Religiously popped;
And at night from the crest of Calvano
  Great bonfires will hang,
On the plain will the trumpets join chorus,
  And more poppers bang.
At all events, come—to the garden,
  As far as the wall;
See me tap with a hoe on the plaster
  Till out there shall fall
A scorpion with wide angry nippers!

  —"Such trifles!" you say?
Fortù, in my England at home,
  Men meet gravely to-day
And debate, if abolishing Corn-laws
  Be righteous and wise
—If 't were proper, Scirocco should vanish
  In black from the skies!

[1845]

THE LOST LEADER

I

Just for a handful of silver he left us,
  Just for a riband to stick in his coat—
Found the one gift of which fortune bereft us,
  Lost all the others she lets us devote;
They, with the gold to give, doled him out silver,
  So much was theirs who so little allowed:
How all our copper had gone for his service!
  Rags—were they purple, his heart had been proud!
We that had loved him so, followed him, honoured him,
  Lived in his mild and magnificent eye,
Learned his great language, caught his clear accents,
  Made him our pattern to live and to die!
Shakespeare was of us, Milton was for us,
  Burns, Shelley, were with us,—they watch from their graves!
He alone breaks from the van and the freemen,
  —He alone sinks to the rear and the slaves!

II

We shall march prospering,—not thro' his presence;
  Songs may inspirit us,—not from his lyre;
Deeds will be done,—while he boasts his quiescence,
  Still bidding crouch whom the rest bade aspire:
Blot out his name, then, record one lost soul more,
  One task more declined, one more footpath untrod,
One more devils'-triumph, and sorrow for angels,
  One wrong more to man, one more insult to God!
Life's night begins: let him never come back to us!
  There would be doubt, hesitation and pain,
Forced praise on our part—the glimmer of twilight,
  Never glad confident morning again!
Best fight on well, for we taught him—strike gallantly,
  Menace our heart ere we master his own;
Then let him receive the new knowledge and wait us,
  Pardoned in heaven, the first by the throne!

[1845]

HOME-THOUGHTS, FROM ABROAD

I

Oh, to be in England
Now that April's there,
And whoever wakes in England
Sees, some morning, unaware,
That the lowest boughs and the brush wood sheaf
Round the elm-tree bole are in tiny leaf,
While the chaffinch sings on the orchard bough
In England—now!

II

And after April, when May follows,
And the whitethroat builds, and all the swallows!
Hark! where my blossomed pear-tree in the hedge
Leans to the field and scatters on the clover
Blossoms and dewdrops—at the bent spray's edge—
That's the wise thrush; he sings each song twice over,
Lest you should think he never could recapture

The first fine careless rapture!
And though the fields look rough with hoary dew,
All will be gay when noontide wakes anew
The buttercups, the little children's dower
—Far brighter than this gaudy melon-flower!

[1845]

"HERE'S TO NELSON'S MEMORY"

Here's to Nelson's memory!
'Tis the second time that I, at sea,
Right off Cape Trafalgar here,
Have drunk it deep in British beer:
Nelson for ever—any time
Am I his to command in prose or rhyme!
Give me of Nelson only a touch,
And I guard it, be it little or much;
Here's one the Captain gives, and so
Down at the word, by George, shall it go!
He says that at Greenwich they show the beholder
Nelson's coat, "still with tar on the shoulder,
"For he used to lean with one shoulder digging,
"Jigging, as it were, and zig-zag-zigging,
"Up against the mizen rigging!"

[1845–49]

HOME-THOUGHTS, FROM THE SEA

Nobly, nobly Cape Saint Vincent to the North-west died away;
Sunset ran, one glorious blood-red, reeking into Cadiz Bay;
Bluish mid the burning water, full in face Trafalgar lay;
In the dimmest North-east distance, dawned Gibraltar grand and gray;
"Here and here did England help me,—how can I help England?"—say,
Whoso turns as I, this evening, turn to God to praise and pray,
While Jove's planet rises yonder, silent over Africa.

[1845–49]

MEETING AT NIGHT

I

The grey sea and the long black land;
And the yellow half-moon large and low;
And the startled little waves that leap
In fiery ringlets from their sleep,
As I gain the cove with pushing prow,
And quench its speed i' the slushy sand.

II

Then a mile of warm sea-scented beach;
Three fields to cross till a farm appears;
A tap at the pane, the quick sharp scratch
And blue spurt of a lighted match,
And a voice less loud, thro' its joys and fears,
Than the two hearts beating each to each!

[1845]

PARTING AT MORNING

Round the cape of a sudden came the sea,
And the sun looked over the mountain's rim:
And straight was a path of gold for him,
And the need of a world of men for me.

[1845]

SAUL

I

Said Abner, "At last thou art come! Ere I tell, ere thou speak,
"Kiss my cheek, wish me well!" Then I wished it, and did kiss his cheek.
And he: "Since the King, O my friend, for thy countenance sent,
"Neither drunken nor eaten have we; nor until from his tent
"Thou return with the joyful assurance the King liveth yet,

"Shall our lip with the honey be bright, with the water be wet.
"For out of the black mid-tent's silence, a space of three days,
"Not a sound hath escaped to thy servants, of prayer nor of praise,
"To betoken that Saul and the Spirit have ended their strife,
"And that, faint in his triumph, the monarch sinks back upon life.

II

"Yet now my heart leaps, O beloved! God's child with his dew
"On thy gracious gold hair, and those lilies still living and blue
"Just broken to twine round thy harp-strings, as if no wild heat
"Were now raging to torture the desert!"

III

Then I, as was meet,
Knelt down to the God of my fathers, and rose on my feet,
And ran o'er the sand burnt to powder. The tent was unlooped;
I pulled up the spear that obstructed, and under I stooped;
Hands and knees on the slippery grass-patch, all withered and gone,
That extends to the second enclosure, I groped my way on
Till I felt where the foldskirts fly open. Then once more I prayed,
And opened the foldskirts and entered, and was not afraid
But spoke, "Here is David, thy servant!" And no voice replied.
At the first I saw nought but the blackness; but soon I descried
A something more black than the blackness—the vast, the upright
Main prop which sustains the pavilion: and slow into sight
Grew a figure against it, gigantic and blackest of all.
Then a sunbeam, that burst thro' the tent-roof, showed Saul.

IV

He stood as erect as that tent-prop, both arms stretched out wide
On the great cross-support in the centre, that goes to each side;
He relaxed not a muscle, but hung there as, caught in his pangs
And waiting his change, the king-serpent all heavily hangs,
Far away from his kind, in the pine, till deliverance come
With the spring-time,—so agonized Saul, drear and stark, blind and dumb.

V

Then I tuned my harp,—took off the lilies we twine round its chords
Lest they snap 'neath the stress of the noontide—those sunbeams like swords!
And I first played the tune all our sheep know, as, one after one,
So docile they come to the pen-door till folding be done.
They are white and untorn by the bushes, for lo, they had fed
Where the long grasses stifle the water within the stream's bed;
And now one after one seeks its lodging, as star follows star
Into eve and the blue far above us,—so blue and so far!

VI

—Then the tune, for which quails on the cornland will each leave his mate
To fly after the player; then, what makes the crickets elate
Till for boldness they fight one another; and then, what has weight
To set the quick jerboa a-musing outside his sand-house—
There are none such as he for a wonder, half bird and half mouse!
God made all the creatures and gave them our love and our fear,
To give sign, we and they are his children, one family here.

VII

Then I played the help-tune of our reapers, their wine-song, when hand
Grasps at hand, eye lights eye in good friendship, and great hearts expand
And grow one in the sense of this world's life.—And then, the last song
When the dead man is praised on his journey—"Bear, bear him along
"With his few faults shut up like dead flowerets! Are balm-seeds not here
"To console us? The land has none left such as he on the bier.
"Oh, would we might keep thee, my brother!"—And then, the glad chaunt
Of the marriage,—first go the young maidens, next, she whom we vaunt
As the beauty, the pride of our dwelling.—And then, the great march
Wherein man runs to man to assist him and buttress an arch
Nought can break; who shall harm them, our friends?—Then, the chorus intoned
As the Levites go up to the altar in glory enthroned.
But I stopped here: for here in the darkness Saul groaned.

VIII

And I paused, held my breath in such silence, and listened apart;
And the tent shook, for mighty Saul shuddered: and sparkles 'gan dart
From the jewels that woke in his turban, at once with a start,
All its lordly male-sapphires, and rubies courageous at heart.
So the head: but the body still moved not, still hung there erect.
And I bent once again to my playing, pursued it unchecked,
As I sang,—

IX

"Oh, our manhood's prime vigour! No spirit feels waste,
"Not a muscle is stopped in its playing nor sinew unbraced.
"Oh, the wild joys of living! the leaping from rock up to rock,
"The strong rending of boughs from the fir-tree, the cool silver shock
"Of the plunge in a pool's living water, the hunt of the bear,
"And the sultriness showing the lion is couched in his lair.
"And the meal, the rich dates yellowed over with gold dust divine,
"And the locust-flesh steeped in the pitcher, the full draught of wine,
"And the sleep in the dried river-channel where bulrushes tell
"That the water was wont to go warbling so softly and well.
"How good is man's life, the mere living! how fit to employ
"All the heart and the soul and the senses for ever in joy!
"Hast thou loved the white locks of thy father, whose sword thou didst guard
"When he trusted thee forth with the armies, for glorious reward?
"Didst thou see the thin hands of thy mother, held up as men sung
"The low song of the nearly-departed, and hear her faint tongue
"Joining in while it could to the witness, 'Let one more attest
"I have lived, seen God's hand through a lifetime, and all was for best?'
"Then they sung thro' their tears in strong triumph, not much, but the rest.
"And thy brothers, the help and the contest, the working whence grew
"Such result as, from seething grape-bundles, the spirit strained true:
"And the friends of thy boyhood—that boyhood of wonder and hope,
"Present promise and wealth of the future beyond the eye's scope,—
"Till lo, thou art grown to a monarch; a people is thine;
"And all gifts, which the world offers singly, on one head combine!
"On one head, all the beauty and strength, love and rage (like the throe
"That, a-work in the rock, helps its labour and lets the gold go),
"High ambition and deeds which surpass it, fame crowning them,—all
"Brought to blaze on the head of one creature—King Saul!"

X

And lo, with that leap of my spirit,—heart, hand, harp and voice,
Each lifting Saul's name out of sorrow, each bidding rejoice
Saul's fame in the light it was made for—as when, dare I say,
The Lord's army, in rapture of service, strains through its array,
And upsoareth the cherubim-chariot—"Saul!" cried I, and stopped,
And waited the thing that should follow. Then Saul, who hung propped
By the tent's cross-support in the centre, was struck by his name.
Have ye seen when Spring's arrowy summons goes right to the aim,
And some mountain, the last to withstand her, that held (he alone,
While the vale laughed in freedom and flowers) on a broad bust of stone
A year's snow bound about for a breastplate,—leaves grasp of the sheet?
Fold on fold all at once it crowds thunderously down to his feet,
And there fronts you, stark, black, but alive yet, your mountain of old,
With his rents, the successive bequeathings of ages untold—
Yea, each harm got in fighting your battles, each furrow and scar
Of his head thrust 'twixt you and the tempest—all hail, there they are!
—Now again to be softened with verdure, again hold the nest
Of the dove, tempt the goat and its young to the green on his crest
For their food in the ardours of summer. One long shudder thrilled
All the tent till the very air tingled, then sank and was stilled
At the King's self left standing before me, released and aware.
What was gone, what remained? All to traverse 'twixt hope and despair;
Death was past, life not come: so he waited. Awhile his right hand
Held the brow, helped the eyes left too vacant forthwith to remand
To their place what new objects should enter: 't was Saul as before.
I looked up, and dared gaze at those eyes, nor was hurt any more
Than by slow pallid sunsets in autumn, ye watch from the shore,
At their sad level gaze o'er the ocean—a sun's slow decline
Over hills which, resolved in stern silence, o'erlap and entwine
Base with base to knit strength more intensely: so, arm folded arm
O'er the chest whose slow heavings subsided.

XI

What spell or what charm,
(For, awhile there was trouble within me) what next should I urge
To sustain him where song had restored him?—Song filled to the verge
His cup with the wine of this life, pressing all that it yields
Of mere fruitage, the strength and the beauty: beyond, on what fields,
Glean a vintage more potent and perfect to brighten the eye
And bring blood to the lip, and commend them the cup they put by?
He saith, "It is good"; still he drinks not: he lets me praise life,
Gives assent, yet would die for his own part.

XII

Then fancies grew rife
Which had come long ago on the pasture, when round me the sheep
Fed in silence—above, the one eagle wheeled slow as in sleep;
And I lay in my hollow and mused on the world that might lie
'Neath his ken, though I saw but the strip 'twixt the hill and the sky:
And I laughed—"Since my days are ordained to be passed with my flocks,
"Let me people at least, with my fancies, the plains and the rocks,
"Dream the life I am never to mix with, and image the show
"Of mankind as they live in those fashions I hardly shall know!

"Schemes of life, its best rules and right uses, the courage that gains,
"And the prudence that keeps what men strive for." And now these old trains
Of vague thought came again; I grew surer; so once more the string
Of my harp made response to my spirit, as thus—

XIII

"Yea, my King,"
I began—"thou dost well in rejecting mere comforts that spring
"From the mere mortal life held in common by man and by brute:
"In our flesh grows the branch of this life, in our soul it bears fruit.
"Thou hast marked the slow rise of the tree,—how its stem trembled first
"Till it passed the kid's lip, the stag's antler; then safely outburst
"The fan-branches all round; and thou mindest when these too, in turn
"Broke a-bloom and the palm-tree seemed perfect: yet more was to learn,
"E'en the good that comes in with the palm-fruit. Our dates shall we slight,
"When their juice brings a cure for all sorrow? or care for the plight
"Of the palm's self whose slow growth produced them? Not so! stem and branch
"Shall decay, nor be known in their place, while the palm wine shall staunch
"Every wound of man's spirit in winter. I pour thee such wine.
"Leave the flesh to the fate it was fit for! the spirit be thine!
"By the spirit, when age shall o'ercome thee, thou still shalt enjoy
"More indeed, than at first when inconscious, the life of a boy.
"Crush that life, and behold its wine running! Each deed thou hast done
"Dies, revives, goes to work in the world; until e'en as the sun
"Looking down on the earth, though clouds spoil him, though tempests efface,
"Can find nothing his own deed produced not, must everywhere trace
"The results of his past summer-prime,—so, each ray of thy will,
"Every flash of thy passion and prowess, long over, shall thrill
"Thy whole people, the countless, with ardour, till they too give forth
"A like cheer to their sons; who in turn, fill the South and the North
"With the radiance thy deed was the germ of. Carouse in the past!
"But the license of age has its limit; thou diest at last:
"As the lion when age dims his eyeball, the rose at her height,
"So with man—so his power and his beauty for ever take flight.
"No! Again a long draught of my soul-wine! Look forth o'er the years!
"Thou hast done now with eyes for the actual; begin with the seer's!
"Is Saul dead? In the depth of the vale make his tomb—bid arise
"A gray mountain of marble heaped foursquare, till built to the skies,
"Let it mark where the great First King slumbers: whose fame would ye know?
"Up above see the rock's naked face, where the record shall go
"In great characters cut by the scribe,—Such was Saul, so he did;
"With the sages directing the work, by the populace chid,—
"For not half, they'll affirm, is comprised there! Which fault to amend,
"In the grove with his kind grows the cedar, whereon they shall spend
" (See, in tablets 't is level before them) their praise, and record
"With the gold of the graver, Saul's story,—the statesman's great word
"Side by side with the poet's sweet comment. The river's a-wave
"With smooth paper-reeds grazing each other when prophet-winds rave:
"So the pen gives unborn generations their due and their part
"In thy being! Then, first of the mighty, thank God that thou art!"

XIV

And behold while I sang . . . but O Thou who didst grant me that day,
And before it not seldom hast granted thy help to essay,

Carry on, and complete an adventure,—my shield and my sword
In that act where my soul was thy servant, thy word was my word,—
Still be with me, who then at the summit of human endeavour
And scaling the highest, man's thought could, gazed hopeless as ever
On the new stretch of heaven above me—till, mighty to save,
Just one lift of thy hand cleared that distance—God's throne from man's grave!
Let me tell out my tale to its ending—my voice to my heart
Which can scarce dare believe in what marvels last night I took part,
As this morning I gather the fragments, alone with my sheep,
And still fear lest the terrible glory evanish like sleep!
For I wake in the grey dewy covert, while Hebron upheaves
The dawn struggling with night on his shoulder, and Kidron retrieves
Slow the damage of yesterday's sunshine.

XV

I say then,—my song
While I sang thus, assuring the monarch, and, ever more strong,
Made a proffer of good to console him—he slowly resumed
His old motions and habitudes kingly. The right hand replumed
His black locks to their wonted composure, adjusted the swathes
Of his turban, and see—the huge sweat that his countenance bathes,
He wipes off with the robe; and he girds now his loins as of yore,
And feels slow for the armlets of price, with the clasp set before.
He is Saul, ye remember in glory,—ere error had bent
The broad brow from the daily communion; and still, though much spent
Be the life and the bearing that front you, the same, God did choose,
To receive what a man may waste, desecrate, never quite lose.
So sank he along by the tent-prop, till, stayed by the pile
Of his armour and war-cloak and garments, he leaned there awhile,
And sat out my singing,—one arm round the tent-prop, to raise
His bent head, and the other hung slack—till I touched on the praise
I foresaw from all men in all time, to the man patient there;
And thus ended, the harp falling forward. Then first I was 'ware
That he sat, as I say, with my head just above his vast knees
Which were thrust out on each side around me, like oak roots which please
To encircle a lamb when it slumbers. I looked up to know
If the best I could do had brought solace: he spoke not, but slow
Lifted up the hand slack at his side, till he laid it with care
Soft and grave, but in mild settled will, on my brow: thro' my hair
The large fingers were pushed, and he bent back my head, with kind power—
All my face back, intent to peruse it, as men do a flower.
Thus held he me there with his great eyes that scrutinized mine—
And oh, all my heart how it loved him! but where was the sign?
I yearned—"Could I help thee, my father, inventing a bliss,
"I would add, to that life of the past, both the future and this;
"I would give thee new life altogether, as good, ages hence,
As this moment,—had love but the warrant love's heart to dispense!"

XVI

Then the truth came upon me. No harp more—no song more! outbroke—

XVII

"I have gone the whole round of creation: I saw and I spoke:
"I, a work of God's hand for that purpose, received in my brain

"And pronounced on the rest of his handwork—returned him again
"His creation's approval or censure: I spoke as I saw,
"I report, as a man may of God's work—all's love, yet all's law.
"Now I lay down the judgeship he lent me. Each faculty tasked
"To perceive him has gained an abyss, where a dewdrop was asked.
"Have I knowledge? confounded it shrivels at Wisdom laid bare.
"Have I forethought? how purblind, how blank, to the Infinite Care!
"Do I task any faculty highest, to image success?
"I but open my eyes,—and perfection, no more and no less,
"In the kind I imagined, full-fronts me, and God is seen God
"In the star, in the stone, in the flesh, in the soul and the clod.
"And thus looking within and around me, I ever renew
"(With that stoop of the soul which in bending upraises it too)
"The submission of man's nothing-perfect to God's all-complete,
"As by each new obeisance in spirit, I climb to his feet.
"Yet with all this abounding experience, this deity known,
"I shall dare to discover some province, some gift of my own.
"There's a faculty pleasant to exercise, hard to hoodwink,
"I am fain to keep still in abeyance (I laugh as I think)
"Lest, insisting to claim and parade in it, wot ye, I worst
"E'en the Giver in one gift.—Behold! I could love if I durst!
"But I sink the pretension as fearing a man may o'ertake
"God's own speed in the one way of love: I abstain for love's sake.
"—What, my soul? see thus far and no farther? when doors, great and small,
"Nine-and-ninety flew ope at our touch, should the hundredth appal?
"In the least things have faith, yet distrust in the greatest of all?
"Do I find love so full in my nature, God's ultimate gift,
"That I doubt his own love can compete with it? Here, the parts shift?
"Here, the creature surpass the Creator,—the end, what Began?
"Would I fain in my impotent yearning do all for this man,
"And dare doubt he alone shall not help him, who yet alone can?
"Would it ever have entered my mind, the bare will, much less power,
"To bestow on this Saul what I sang of, the marvellous dower
"Of the life he was gifted and filled with? to make such a soul,
"Such a body, and then such an earth for insphering the whole?
"And doth it not enter my mind (as my warm tears attest),
"These good things being given, to go on, and give one more, the best?
"Ay, to save and redeem and restore him, maintain at the height
"This perfection,—succeed with life's day-spring, death's minute of night?
"Interpose at the difficult minute, snatch Saul the mistake,
"Saul the failure, the ruin he seems now,—and bid him awake
"From the dream, the probation, the prelude, to find himself set
"Clear and safe in new light and new life,—a new harmony yet
"To be run and continued, and ended—who knows?—or endure!
"The man taught enough by life's dream, of the rest to make sure;
"By the pain-throb, triumphantly winning intensified bliss,
"And the next world's reward and repose, by the struggles in this.

XVIII

"I believe it! 'Tis thou, God, that givest, 'tis I who receive:
"In the first is the last, in thy will is my power to believe.
"All's one gift: thou canst grant it moreover, as prompt to my prayer
"As I breathe out this breath, as I open these arms to the air.
"From thy will, stream the worlds, life and nature, thy dread Sabaoth:

"*I* will?—the mere atoms despise me! Why am I not loth
"To look that, even that in the face too? Why is it I dare
"Think but lightly of such impuissance? What stops my despair?
"This;—'tis not what man Does which exalts him, but what man Would do!
"See the King—I would help him but cannot, the wishes fall through.
"Could I wrestle to raise him from sorrow, grow poor to enrich,
"To fill up his life, starve my own out, I would—knowing which,
"I know that my service is perfect. Oh, speak through me now!
"Would I suffer for him that I love? So wouldst thou—so wilt thou!
"So shall crown thee the topmost, ineffablest, uttermost crown—
"And thy love fill infinitude wholly, nor leave up nor down
"One spot for the creature to stand in! It is by no breath,
"Turn of eye, wave of hand, that salvation joins issue with death!
"As thy Love is discovered almighty, almighty be proved
"Thy power, that exists with and for it, of being Beloved!
"He who did most, shall bear most; the strongest shall stand the most weak.
" 'Tis the weakness in strength, that I cry for! my flesh, that I seek
"In the Godhead! I seek and I find it. O Saul, it shall be
"A Face like my face that receives thee; a Man like to me,
"Thou shalt love and be loved by, for ever; a Hand like this hand
"Shall throw open the gates of new life to thee! See the Christ stand!"

XIX

I know not too well how I found my way home in the night.
There were witnesses, cohorts about me, to left and to right,
Angels, powers, the unuttered, unseen, the alive, the aware:
I repressed, I got through them as hardly, as strugglingly there,
As a runner beset by the populace famished for news—
Life or death. The whole earth was awakened, hell loosed with her crews;
And the stars of night beat with emotion, and tingled and shot
Out in fire the strong pain of pent knowledge: but I fainted not,
For the Hand still impelled me at once and supported, suppressed
All the tumult, and quenched it with quiet, and holy behest,
Till the rapture was shut in itself, and the earth sank to rest.
Anon at the dawn, all that trouble had withered from earth—
Not so much, but I saw it die out in the day's tender birth;
In the gathered intensity brought to the grey of the hills;
In the shuddering forests' held breath; in the sudden wind-thrills;
In the startled wild beasts that bore off, each with eye sidling still,
Though averted with wonder and dread; in the birds stiff and chill
That rose heavily as I approached them, made stupid with awe:
E'en the serpent that slid away silent,—he felt the new law.
The same stared in the white humid faces upturned by the flowers;
The same worked in the heart of the cedar and moved the vine-bowers:
And the little brooks witnessing murmured, persistent and low,
With their obstinate, all but hushed voices—"E'en so, it is so!"

[1845–53] [1855]

LOVE AMONG THE RUINS

Contrast of past + present

I

Where the quiet-coloured end of evening smiles
    Miles and miles
On the solitary pastures where our sheep
    Half-asleep
Tinkle homeward thro' the twilight, stray or stop
    As they crop—
Was the site once of a city great and gay,
    (So they say)
Of our country's very capital, its prince
    Ages since
Held his court in, gathered councils, wielding far
    Peace or war.

II

Now,—the country does not even boast a tree
    As you see,
To distinguish slopes of verdure, certain rills
    From the hills
Intersect and give a name to (else they run
    Into one)
Where the domed and daring palace shot its spires
    Up like fires
O'er the hundred-gated circuit of a wall
    Bounding all,
Made of marble, men might march on nor be pressed,
    Twelve abreast.

III

And such plenty and perfection, see, of grass
    Never was!
Such a carpet as, this summer-time, o'erspreads
    And embeds
Every vestige of the city, guessed alone,
    Stock or stone—
Where a multitude of men breathed joy and woe
    Long ago;
Lust of glory pricked their hearts up, dread of shame
    Struck them tame;
And that glory and that shame alike, the gold
    Bought and sold.

IV

Now,—the single little turret that remains
    On the plains,
By the caper overrooted, by the gourd
    Overscored,
While the patching houseleek's head of blossom winks
    Through the chinks—
Marks the basement whence a tower in ancient time
    Sprang sublime,

And a burning ring, all round, the chariots traced
    As they raced,
And the monarch and his minions and his dames
    Viewed the games.

V

And I know, while thus the quiet-coloured eve
    Smiles to leave
To their folding, all our many-tinkling fleece
    In such peace,
And the slopes and rills in undistinguished grey
    Melt away—
That a girl with eager eyes and yellow hair
    Waits me there
In the turret whence the charioteers caught soul
    For the goal,
When the king looked, where she looks now, breathless, dumb
    Till I come.

VI

But he looked upon the city, every side,
    Far and wide,
All the mountains topped with temples, all the glades'
    Colonnades,
All the causeys, bridges, aqueducts,—and then,
    All the men!
When I do come, she will speak not, she will stand,
    Either hand
On my shoulder, give her eyes the first embrace
    Of my face,
Ere we rush, ere we extinguish sight and speech
    Each on each.

VII

In one year they sent a million fighters forth
    South and north,
And they built their gods a brazen pillar high
    As the sky,
Yet reserved a thousand chariots in full force—
    Gold, of course.
Oh, heart! oh, blood that freezes, blood that burns!
    Earth's returns
For whole centuries of folly, noise and sin!
    Shut them in,
With their triumphs and their glories and the rest!
    Love is best.

[1855]

EVELYN HOPE

I

Beautiful Evelyn Hope is dead!
    Sit and watch by her side an hour.
That is her book-shelf, this her bed;

She plucked that piece of geranium-flower,
Beginning to die too, in the glass;
Little has yet been changed, I think:
The shutters are shut, no light may pass
Save two long rays thro' the hinge's chink.

II

Sixteen years old when she died!
Perhaps she had scarcely heard my name;
It was not her time to love; beside,
Her life had many a hope and aim,
Duties enough and little cares,
And now was quiet, now astir,
Till God's hand beckoned unawares,—
And the sweet white brow is all of her.

III

Is it too late then, Evelyn Hope?
What, your soul was pure and true,
The good stars met in your horoscope,
Made you of spirit, fire and dew—
And just because I was thrice as old,
And our paths in the world diverged so wide,
Each was nought to each, must I be told?
We were fellow mortals, nought beside?

IV

No, indeed! for God above
Is great to grant, as mighty to make,
And creates the love to reward the love:
I claim you still, for my own love's sake!
Delayed it may be for more lives yet,
Through worlds I shall traverse, not a few:
Much is to learn, much to forget
Ere the time be come for taking you.

V

But the time will come,—at last it will,
When, Evelyn Hope, what meant (I shall say)
In the lower earth, in the years long still,
That body and soul so pure and gay?
Why your hair was amber, I shall divine,
And your mouth of your own geranium's red—
And what you would do with me, in fine,
In the new life come in the old one's stead.

VI

I have lived (I shall say) so much since then,
Given up myself so many times,
Gained me the gains of various men,
Ransacked the ages, spoiled the climes;

Yet one thing, one, in my soul's full scope,
  Either I missed or itself missed me:
And I want and find you, Evelyn Hope!
  What is the issue? let us see!

VII

I loved you, Evelyn, all the while.
  My heart seemed full as it could hold?
There was place and to spare for the frank young smile,
  And the red young mouth and the hair's young gold.
So, hush,—I will give you this leaf to keep:
  See, I shut it inside the sweet cold hand!
There, that is our secret: go to sleep!
  You will wake, and remember, and understand.

[1855]

UP AT A VILLA—DOWN IN THE CITY

(AS DISTINGUISHED BY AN ITALIAN PERSON OF QUALITY)

I

Had I but plenty of money, money enough and to spare,
The house for me, no doubt, were a house in the city-square;
Ah, such a life, such a life, as one leads at the window there!

II

Something to see, by Bacchus, something to hear, at least!
There, the whole day long, one's life is a perfect feast;
While up at a villa one lives, I maintain it, no more than a beast.

III

Well, now, look at our villa! stuck like the horn of a bull
Just on a mountain-edge as bare as the creature's skull,
Save a mere shag of a bush with hardly a leaf to pull!
—I scratch my own, sometimes, to see if the hair's turned wool.

IV

But the city, oh the city—the square with the houses! Why?
They are stone-faced, white as a curd, there's something to take the eye!
Houses in four straight lines, not a single front awry;
You watch who crosses and gossips, who saunters, who hurries by;
Green blinds, as a matter of course, to draw when the sun gets high;
And the shops with fanciful signs which are painted properly.

V

What of a villa? Though winter be over in March by rights,
'Tis May perhaps ere the snow shall have withered well off the heights:
You've the brown ploughed land before, where the oxen steam and wheeze,
And the hills over-smoked behind by the faint grey olive trees.

VI

Is it better in May, I ask you? you've summer all at once;
In a day he leaps complete with a few strong April suns.
'Mid the sharp short emerald wheat, scarce risen three fingers well,
The wild tulip, at the end of its tube, blows out its great red bell,
Like a thin clear bubble of blood, for the children to pick and sell.

VII

Is it ever hot in the square? There's a fountain to spout and splash!
In the shade it sings and springs; in the shine such foam-bows flash
On the horses with curling fish-tails, that prance and paddle and pash
Round the lady atop in her conch—fifty gazers do not abash,
Though all that she wears is some weeds round her waist in a sort of sash!

VIII

All the year long at the villa, nothing to see though you linger,
Except yon cypress that points like death's lean lifted forefinger.
Some think fireflies pretty, when they mix i' the corn and mingle,
Or thrid the stinking hemp till the stalks of it seem a-tingle.
Late August or early September, the stunning cicala is shrill,
And the bees keep their tiresome whine round the resinous firs on the hill.
Enough of the seasons,—I spare you the months of the fever and chill.

IX

Ere opening your eyes in the city, the blessed church-bells begin:
No sooner the bells leave off, than the diligence rattles in:
You get the pick of the news, and it costs you never a pin.
By and by there's the traveling doctor gives pills, lets blood, draws teeth;
Or the Pulcinello-trumpet breaks up the market beneath.
At the post-office such a scene-picture—the new play, piping hot!
And a notice how, only this morning, three liberal thieves were shot.
Above it, behold the Archbishop's most fatherly of rebukes,
And beneath, with his crown and his lion, some little new law of the Duke's!
Or a sonnet with flowery marge, to the Reverend Don So-and-so
Who is Dante, Boccaccio, Petrarca, Saint Jerome, and Cicero,
"And moreover," (the sonnet goes rhyming,) "the skirts of St. Paul has reached,
Having preached us those six Lent-lectures more unctuous than ever he preached."
Noon strikes,—here sweeps the procession! our Lady borne smiling and smart
With a pink gauze gown all spangles, and seven swords stuck in her heart!
Bang—whang—whang goes the drum, *tootle-te-tootle* the fife;
No keeping one's haunches still: it's the greatest pleasure in life.

X

But bless you, it's dear—it's dear! fowls, wine, at double the rate.
They have clapped a new tax upon salt, and what oil pays passing the gate
It's a horror to think of. And so, the villa for me, not the city!
Beggars can scarcely be choosers: but still—ah, the pity, the pity!
Look, two and two go to the priests, then the monks with cowls and sandals,
And the penitents dressed in white shirts, a-holding the yellow candles;
One, he carries a flag up straight, and another a cross with handles,
And the Duke's guard brings up the rear, for the better prevention of scandals.
Bang—whang—whang goes the drum, *tootle-te-tootle* the fife.
Oh, a day in the city-square, there is no such pleasure in life!

[1850? 1853?] [1855]

A WOMAN'S LAST WORD

I

Let's contend no more, Love,
  Strive nor weep—
All be as before, Love,
  —Only sleep!

II

What so wild as words are?
  —I and thou
In debate, as birds are,
  Hawk on bough!

III

See the creature stalking
  While we speak
Hush and hide the talking,
  Cheek on cheek!

IV

What so false as truth is,
  False to thee?
Where the serpent's tooth is,
  Shun the tree–-

V

Where the apple reddens
  Never pry—
Lest we lose our Edens,
  Eve and I.

VI

Be a god and hold me
  With a charm!
Be a man and fold me
  With thine arm!

VII

Teach me, only teach, Love!
  As I ought
I will speak thy speech, Love,
  Think thy thought—

VIII

Meet, if thou require it,
  Both demands,
Laying flesh and spirit
  In thy hands!

IX

That shall be to-morrow
  Not to-night:
I must bury sorrow
  Out of sight:

X

—Must a little weep, Love,
  (Foolish me!)
And so fall asleep, Love,
  Loved by thee.

[1855]

FRA LIPPO LIPPI

cf. p. 241
Seized by guards

I am poor brother Lippo, by your leave!
You need not clap your torches to my face.
Zooks, what's to blame? you think you see a monk!
What, 'tis past midnight, and you go the rounds,
And here you catch me at an alley's end
Where sportive ladies leave their doors ajar.
The Carmine's my cloister: hunt it up,
Do,—harry out, if you must show your zeal,
Whatever rat, there, haps on his wrong hole,
And nip each softling of a wee white mouse,
Weke, weke, that's crept to keep him company!
Aha, you know your betters? Then, you'll take
Your hand away that's fiddling on my throat,
And please to know me likewise. Who am I?
Why, one, sir, who is lodging with a friend
Three streets off—he's a certain . . . how d'ye call?
Master—a . . . Cosimo of the Medici,
I' the house that caps the corner. Boh! you were best!
Remember and tell me, the day you're hanged,
How you affected such a gullet's-gripe

But you, sir, it concerns you that your knaves
Pick up a manner nor discredit you.
Zooks, are we pilchards, that they sweep the streets
And count fair prize what comes into their net?
He's Judas to a tittle, that man is!
Just such a face! why, sir, you make amends
Lord, I'm not angry! Bid your hangdogs go
Drink out this quarter-florin to the health
Of the munificent House that harbours me
(And many more beside, lads! more beside!)
And all's come square again. I'd like his face—
His, elbowing on his comrade in the door
With the pike and lantern,—for the slave that holds
John Baptist's head a-dangle by the hair
With one hand ("Look you, now," as who should say)
And his weapon in the other, yet unwiped!
It's not your chance to have a bit of chalk,
A wood-coal or the like? or you should see!
Yes, I'm the painter, since you style me so.
What, brother Lippo's doings, up and down,
You know them and they take you? like enough!
I saw the proper twinkle in your eye—
'Tell you I liked your looks at very first.
Let's sit and set things straight now, hip to haunch.
Here's spring come, and the nights one makes up bands
To roam the town and sing out carnival,
And I've been three weeks shut within my mew,
A-painting for the great man, saints and saints
And saints again. I could not paint all night—
Ouf! I leaned out of window for fresh air.
There came a hurry of feet and little feet,
A sweep of lute-strings, laughs, and whifts of song,—
Flower o' the broom,
Take away love, and our earth is a tomb!
Flower o' the quince,
I let Lisa go, and what good in life since?
Flower o' the thyme—and so on. Round they went.
Scarce had they turned the corner when a titter,
Like the skipping of rabbits by moonlight,—three slim shapes—
And a face that looked up . . . zooks, sir, flesh and blood,
That's all I'm made of! Into shreds it went,
Curtain and counterpane and coverlet,
All the bed-furniture—a dozen knots,
There was a ladder! Down I let myself,
Hands and feet, scrambling somehow, and so dropped,
And after them. I came up with the fun
Hard by Saint Laurence, hail fellow, well met,—
Flower o' the rose
If I've been merry, what matter who knows?
And so as I was stealing back again
To get to bed and have a bit of sleep
Ere I rise up to-morrow and go work
On Jerome knocking at his poor old breast
With his great round stone to subdue the flesh,
You snap me of the sudden. Ah. I see!

Though your eye twinkles still, you shake your head—
Mine's shaved,—a monk, you say—the sting's in that!
If Master Cosimo announced himself,
Mum's the word naturally; but a monk!
Come, what am I a beast for? tell us, now!
I was a baby when my mother died
And father died and left me in the street.
I starved there, God knows how, a year or two
On fig-skins, melon-parings, rinds and shucks,
Refuse and rubbish. One fine frosty day
My stomach being empty as your hat,
The wind doubled me up and down I went.
Old Aunt Lapaccia trussed me with one hand,
(Its fellow was a stinger as I knew)
And so along the wall, over the bridge,
By the straight cut to the convent. Six words there,
While I stood munching my first bread that month:
"So, boy, you're minded," quoth the good fat father
Wiping his own mouth, 't was refection-time,—
"To quit this very miserable world?
Will you renounce" . . . "The mouthful of bread?" thought I;
By no means! Brief, they made a monk of me;
I did renounce the world, its pride and greed,
Palace, farm, villa, shop and banking-house,
Trash, such as these poor devils of Medici
Have given their hearts to—all at eight years old.
Well, sir, I found in time, you may be sure,
'Twas not for nothing—the good bellyful,
The warm serge and the rope that goes all round,
And day-long blessed idleness beside!
"Let's see what the urchin's fit for"—that came next.
Not overmuch their way, I must confess.
Such a to-do! they tried me with their books:
Lord, they'd have taught me Latin in pure waste!
Flower o' the clove,
All the Latin I construe is, "amo" I love!
But, mind you, when a boy starves in the streets
Eight years together, as my fortune was,
Watching folk's faces to know who will fling
The bit of half-stripped grape-bunch he desires,
And who will curse or kick him for his pains,—
Which gentleman processional and fine,
Holding a candle to the Sacrament
Will wink and let him lift a plate and catch
The droppings of the wax to sell again,
Or holla for the Eight and have him whipped,—
How say I?—nay, which dog bites, which lets drop
His bone from the heap of offal in the street,—
Why, soul and sense of him grow sharp alike,
He learns the look of things, and none the less
For admonition from the hunger-pinch.
I had a store of such remarks, be sure,
Which, after I found leisure, turned to use.
I drew men's faces on my copy-books,
Scrawled them within the antiphonary's marge,

Joined legs and arms to the long music-notes,
Found nose and eyes and chin for As and Bs,
And made a string of pictures of the world
Betwixt the ins and outs of verb and noun,
On the wall, the bench, the door. The monks looked black.
"Nay," quoth the Prior, "turn him out, d'ye say?
In no wise. Lose a crow and catch a lark.
What if at last we get our man of parts,
We Carmelites, like those Camaldolese
And Preaching Friars, to do our church up fine
And put the front on it that ought to be!"
And hereupon they bade me daub away.
Thank you! my head being crammed, the walls a blank,
Never was such prompt disemburdening.
First, every sort of monk, the black and white,
I drew them, fat and lean: then, folk at church,
From good old gossips waiting to confess
Their cribs of barrel-droppings, candle-ends,—
To the breathless fellow at the altar-foot,
Fresh from his murder, safe and sitting there
With the little children round him in a row
Of admiration, half for his beard and half
For that white anger of his victim's son
Shaking a fist at him with one fierce arm,
Signing himself with the other because of Christ
(Whose sad face on the cross sees only this
After the passion of a thousand years)
Till some poor girl, her apron o'er her head,
(Which the intense eyes looked through) came at eve
On tip-toe, said a word, dropped in a loaf,
Her pair of earrings and a bunch of flowers
(The brute took growling), prayed, and so was gone.
I painted all, then cried " 'Tis ask and have;
"Choose, for more's ready!"—laid the ladder flat,
And showed my covered bit of cloister-wall.
The monks closed in a circle and praised loud
Till checked, taught what to see and not to see,
Being simple bodies,—"That's the very man!
"Look at the boy who stoops to pat the dog!
"That woman's like the Prior's niece who comes
"To care about his asthma: it's the life!"
But there my triumph's straw-fire flared and funked;
Their betters took their turn to see and say:
The Prior and the learned pulled a face
And stopped all that in no time. "How? what's here?
"Quite from the mark of painting, bless us all!
"Faces, arms, legs and bodies like the true
"As much as pea and pea! it's devil's game!
"Your business is not to catch men with show,
"With homage to the perishable clay,
"But lift them over it, ignore it all,
"Make them forget there's such a thing as flesh.
"Your business is to paint the souls of men—
"Man's soul, and it's a fire, smoke . . . no it's not . . .
"It's vapour done up like a new-born babe—

"(In that shape when you die it leaves your mouth)
"It's . . . well, what matters talking, it's the soul!
"Give us no more of body than shows soul!
"Here's Giotto, with his Saint a-praising God,
"That sets you praising,—why not stop with him?
"Why put all thoughts of praise out of our head
"With wonder at lines, colours, and what not?
"Paint the soul, never mind the legs and arms!
"Rub all out, try at it a second time.
"Oh, that white smallish female with the breasts,
"She's just my niece . . . Herodias, I would say,—
"Who went and danced and got men's heads cut off!
"Have it all out!" Now, is this sense, I ask?
A fine way to paint soul, by painting body
So ill, the eye can't stop there, must go further
And can't fare worse! Thus, yellow does for white
When what you put for yellow's simply black,
And any sort of meaning looks intense
When all beside itself means and looks nought.
Why can't a painter lift each foot in turn,
Left foot and right foot, go a double step,
Make his flesh liker and his soul more like,
Both in their order? Take the prettiest face,
The Prior's niece . . . patron-saint—is it so pretty
You can't discover if it means hope, fear,
Sorrow or joy? won't beauty go with these?
Suppose I've made her eyes all right and blue,
Can't I take breath and try to add life's flash
And then add soul and heighten them threefold?
Or say there's beauty with no soul at all—
(I never saw it—put the case the same—)
If you get simple beauty and nought else,
You get about the best thing God invents:
That's somewhat: and you'll find the soul you have missed,
Within yourself when you return him thanks!
"Rub all out!" well, well, there's my life, in short,
And so the thing has gone on ever since.
I'm grown a man no doubt, I've broken bounds—
You should not take a fellow eight years old
And make him swear to never kiss the girls.
I'm my own master, paint now as I please—
Having a friend, you see, in the Corner-house!
Lord, its fast holding by the rings in front—
Those great rings serve more purposes than just
To plant a flag in, or tie up a horse!
And yet the old schooling sticks—the old grave eyes
Are peeping o'er my shoulder as I work,
The heads shake still—"It's Art's decline, my son!
"You're not of the true painters, great and old;
"Brother Angelico's the man, you'll find:
"Brother Lorenzo stands his single peer.
Fag on at flesh, you'll never make the third!"
Flower o' the pine,
You keep your mistr . . . manners, and I'll stick to mine!
I'm not the third, then: bless us, they must know!

Don't you think they're the likeliest to know,
They, with their Latin? So I swallow my rage,
Clench my teeth, suck my lips in tight, and paint
To please them—sometimes do, and sometimes don't;
For, doing most, there's pretty sure to come
A turn, some warm eve finds me at my saints—
A laugh, a cry, the business of the world—
(*Flower o' the peach,*
Death for us all, and his own life for each!)
And my whole soul revolves, the cup runs over,
The world and life's too big to pass for a dream,
And I do these wild things in sheer despite,
And play the fooleries you catch me at,
In pure rage! The old mill-horse, out at grass
After hard years, throws up his stiff heels so,
Although the miller does not preach to him
The only good of grass is to make chaff.
What would men have? Do they like grass or no—
May they or mayn't they? all I want's the thing
Settled for ever one way. As it is,
You tell too many lies and hurt yourself:
You don't like what you only like too much,
You do like what, if given you at your word,
You find abundantly detestable.
For me, I think I speak as I was taught;
I always see the garden and God there
A-making man's wife—and, my lesson learned,
The value and significance of flesh,
I can't unlearn ten minutes afterward.

You understand me: I'm a beast, I know.
But see, now—why, I see as certainly
As that the morning-star's about to shine,
What will hap some day. We've a youngster here
Comes to our convent, studies what I do,
Slouches and stares and lets no atom drop:
His name is Guidi—he'll not mind the monks—
They call him Hulking Tom, he lets them talk—
He picks my practice up—he'll paint apace,
I hope so—though I never live so long,
I know what's sure to follow. You be judge!
You speak no Latin more than I, belike;
However, you're my man, you've seen the world
—The beauty and the wonder and the power,
The shapes of things, their colours, lights and shades,
Changes, surprises,—and God made it all!
—For what? do you feel thankful, ay or no,
For this fair town's face, yonder river's line,
The mountain round it and the sky above,
Much more the figures of man, woman, child,
These are the frame to? What's it all about?
To be passed over, despised? or dwelt upon,
Wondered at? oh, this last of course!—you say.
But why not do as well as say,—paint these
Just as they are, careless what comes of it?

God's works—paint any one, and count it crime
To let a truth slip. Don't object, "His works
"Are here already; nature is complete:
"Suppose you reproduce her—(which you can't)
"There's no advantage! you must beat her, then."
For, don't you mark, we're made so that we love
First when we see them painted, things we have passed
Perhaps a hundred times nor cared to see;
And so they are better, painted—better to us,
Which is the same thing. Art was given for that;
God uses us to help each other so,
Lending our minds out. Have you noticed, now,
Your cullion's hanging face? A bit of chalk,
And trust me but you should, though! How much more,
If I drew higher things with the same truth!
That were to take the Prior's pulpit-place,
Interpret God to all of you! Oh, oh,
It makes me mad to see what men shall do
And we in our graves! This world's no blot for us,
Nor blank—it means intensely, and means good:
To find its meaning is my meat and drink.
"Ay, but you don't so instigate to prayer!"
Strikes in the Prior: "when your meaning's plain
"It does not say to folks—remember matins,
"Or, mind you fast next Friday." Why, for this
What need of art at all? A skull and bones,
Two bits of stick nailed cross-wise, or, what's best,
A bell to chime the hour with, does as well.
I painted a Saint Laurence six months since
At Prato, splashed the fresco in fine style.
"How looks my painting, now the scaffold's down?"
I ask a brother: "Hugely," he returns—
"Already not one phiz of your three slaves
"Who turn the Deacon off his toasted side,
"But's scratched and prodded to our heart's content,
"The pious people have so eased their own
"With coming to say prayers there in a rage:
"We get on fast to see the bricks beneath.
"Expect another job this time next year,
"For pity and religion grow i' the crowd—
Your painting serves its purpose!" Hang the fools!

—That is—you'll not mistake an idle word
Spoke in a huff by a poor monk, God wot,
Tasting the air this spicy night which turns
The unaccustomed head like Chianti wine!
Oh, the church knows! don't misreport me, now!
It's natural a poor monk out of bounds
Should have his apt word to excuse himself:
And hearken how I plot to make amends.
I have bethought me: I shall paint a piece
. . . There's for you! Give me six months, then go, see
Something in Sant' Ambrogio's . . . Bless the nuns!
They want a cast o' my office. I shall paint
God in the midst, Madonna and her babe,

Ringed by a bowery, flowery angel-brood,
Lilies and vestments and white faces, sweet
As puff on puff of grated orris-root
When ladies crowd to church at midsummer.
And then i' the front, of course a saint or two—
Saint John, because he saves the Florentines,
Saint Ambrose, who puts down in black and white
The convent's friends and gives them a long day.
And Job, I must have him there past mistake,
The man of Uz, (and Us without the z,
Painters who need his patience). Well, all these
Secured at their devotion, up shall come
Out of a corner when you least expect,
As one by a dark stair into a great light,
Music and talking, who but Lippo! I!—
Mazed, motionless and moonstruck—I'm the man!
Back I shrink—what is this I see and hear?
I, caught up with my monk's things by mistake,
My old serge gown and rope that goes all round,
I, in this presence, this pure company!
Where's a hole, where's a corner for escape?
Then steps a sweet angelic slip of a thing
Forward, puts out a soft palm—"Not so fast!"
—Addresses the celestial presence, "nay—
"He made you and devised you, after all,
"Though he's none of you! Could Saint John there draw—
"His camel-hair make up a painting-brush?
"We come to brother Lippo for all that,
"Iste perfecit opus!" [1] So, all smile—
I shuffle sideways with my blushing face
Under the cover of a hundred wings
Thrown like a spread of kirtles when you're gay
And play hot cockles, all the doors being shut,
Till, wholly unexpected, in there pops
The hothead husband! Thus I scuttle off
To some safe bench behind, not letting go
The palm of her, the little lily thing
That spoke the good word for me in the nick,
Like the Prior's niece . . . Saint Lucy, I would say.
And so all's saved for me, and for the church
A pretty picture gained. Go, six months hence!
Your hand, sir, and good-bye: no lights, no lights!
The street's hushed, and I know my own way back—
Don't fear me! there's the grey beginning. Zooks!

[1855]

A TOCCATA OF GALUPPI'S

I

Oh, Galuppi, Baldassaro, this is very sad to find!
I can hardly misconceive you; it would prove me deaf and blind;
But although I take your meaning, 'tis with such a heavy mind!

[1] This man was the artist (performed the work).

II

Here you come with your old music, and here's all the good it brings.
What, they lived once thus at Venice where the merchants were the kings,
Where St. Mark's is, where the Doges used to wed the sea with rings?

III

Ay, because the sea's the street there; and 'tis arched by . . . what you call
. . . Shylock's bridge with houses on it, where they kept the carnival:
I was never out of England—it's as if I saw it all!

IV

Did young people take their pleasure when the sea was warm in May?
Balls and masks begun at midnight, burning ever to mid-day
When they made up fresh adventures for the morrow, do you say?

V

Was a lady such a lady, cheeks so round and lips so red,—
On her neck the small face buoyant, like a bell-flower on its bed,
O'er the breast's superb abundance where a man might base his head?

VI

Well, and it was graceful of them—they'd break talk off and afford
—She, to bite her mask's black velvet—he, to finger on his sword,
While you sat and played Toccatas, stately at the clavichord?

VII

What? Those lesser thirds so plaintive, sixths diminished, sigh on sigh,
Told them something? Those suspensions, those solutions—"Must we die?"
Those commiserating sevenths—"Life might last! we can but try!"

VIII

"Were you happy?"—"Yes."—"And are you still as happy?"—"Yes. And you?"
—"Then, more kisses!"—"Did *I* stop them, when a million seemed so few?"
Hark! the dominant's persistence, till it must be answered to!

IX

So an octave struck the answer. Oh, they praised you, I dare say!
"Brave Galuppi! that was music! good alike at grave and gay!
I can always leave off talking, when I hear a master play."

X

Then they left you for their pleasure: till in due time, one by one,
Some with lives that came to nothing, some with deeds as well undone,
Death came tacitly and took them where they never see the sun.

XI

But when I sit down to reason, think to take my stand nor swerve,
While I triumph o'er a secret wrung from nature's close reserve,
In you come with your cold music till I creep thro' every nerve.

XII

Yes, you, like a ghostly cricket, creaking where a house was burned:
"Dust and ashes, dead and done with, Venice spent what Venice earned.
The soul, doubtless, is immortal—where a soul can be discerned.

XIII

"Yours for instance, you know physics, something of geology,
"Mathematics are your pastime; souls shall rise in their degree;
"Butterflies may dread extinction,—you'll not die, it cannot be!

XIV

"As for Venice and her people, merely born to bloom and drop,
"Here on earth they bore their fruitage, mirth and folly were the crop:
"What of soul was left, I wonder, when the kissing had to stop?

XV

"Dust and ashes!" So you creak it, and I want the heart to scold.
Dear dead women, with such hair, too—what's become of all the gold
Used to hang and brush their bosoms? I feel chilly and grown old.

[1855]

AN EPISTLE

CONTAINING THE STRANGE MEDICAL EXPERIENCE OF KARSHISH, THE ARAB PHYSICIAN

Karshish, the picker-up of learning's crumbs,
The not-incurious in God's handiwork
(This man's-flesh he hath admirably made,
Blown like a bubble, kneaded like a paste,
To coop up and keep down on earth a space
That puff of vapour from his mouth, man's soul)
—To Abib, all-sagacious in our art,
Breeder in me of what poor skill I boast,
Like me inquisitive how pricks and cracks
Befall the flesh through too much stress and strain,
Whereby the wily vapour fain would slip
Back and rejoin its source before the term,—
And aptest in contrivance (under God)
To baffle it by deftly stopping such:—
The vagrant Scholar to his Sage at home
Sends greeting (health and knowledge, fame with peace)
Three samples of true snakestone—rarer still,
One of the other sort, the melon-shaped,
(But fitter, pounded fine, for charms than drugs)
And writeth now the twenty-second time.

My journeyings were brought to Jericho:
Thus I resume. Who studious in our art
Shall count a little labour unrepaid?
I have shed sweat enough, left flesh and bone
On many a flinty furlong of this land.
Also, the country-side is all on fire
With rumours of a marching hitherward:
Some say Vespasian cometh, some, his son.
A black lynx snarled and pricked a tufted ear;
Lust of my blood inflamed his yellow balls:
I cried and threw my staff and he was gone.
Twice have the robbers stripped and beaten me,
And once a town declared me for a spy;
But at the end, I reach Jerusalem,
Since this poor covert where I pass the night,
This Bethany, lies scarce the distance thence
A man with plague-sores at the third degree
Runs till he drops down dead. Thou laughest here!
'Sooth, it elates me, thus reposed and safe,
To void the stuffing of my travel-scrip
And share with thee whatever Jewry yields.
A viscid choler is observable
In tertians, I was nearly bold to say;
And falling-sickness hath a happier cure
Than our school wots of: there's a spider here

Weaves no web, watches on the ledge of tombs,
Sprinkled with mottles on an ash-grey back;
Take five and drop them . . . but who knows his mind,
The Syrian runagate I trust this to?
His service payeth me a sublimate
Blown up his nose to help the ailing eye.
Best wait: I reach Jerusalem at morn,
There set in order my experiences,
Gather what most deserves, and give thee all—
Or I might add, Judaea's gum-tragacanth
Scales off in purer flakes, shines clearer-grained,
Cracks 'twixt the pestle and the porphyry,
In fine exceeds our produce. Scalp-disease
Confounds me, crossing so with leprosy—
Thou hadst admired one sort I gained at Zoar—
But zeal outruns discretion. Here I end.

Yet stay: my Syrian blinketh gratefully,
Protesteth his devotion is my price—
Suppose I write what harms not, though he steal?
I half resolve to tell thee, yet I blush,
What set me off a-writing first of all.
An itch I had, a sting to write, a tang!
For, be it this town's barrenness—or else
The Man had something in the look of him—
His case has struck me far more than 'tis worth.
So, pardon it— (lest presently I lose
In the great press of novelty at hand
The care and pains this somehow stole from me)
I bid thee take the thing while fresh in mind,
Almost in sight—for, wilt thou have the truth?
The very man is gone from me but now,
Whose ailment is the subject of discourse.
Thus then, and let thy better wit help all!

'Tis but a case of mania—subinduced
By epilepsy, at the turning-point
Of trance prolonged unduly some three days:
When, by the exhibition of some drug
Or spell, exorcisation, stroke of art
Unknown to me and which 'twere well to know,
The evil thing out-breaking all at once
Left the man whole and sound of body indeed,—
But, flinging, so to speak, life's gates too wide,
Making a clear house of it too suddenly,
The first conceit that entered might inscribe
Whatever it was minded on the wall
So plainly at that vantage, as it were,
(First come, first served) that nothing subsequent
Attaineth to erase those fancy-scrawls
The just-returned and new-established soul
Hath gotten now so thoroughly by heart
That henceforth she will read or these or none.
And first—the man's own firm conviction rests
That he was dead (in fact they buried him)
—That he was dead and then restored to life
By a Nazarene physician of his tribe:
—'Sayeth, the same bade "Rise," and he did rise.
"Such cases are diurnal," thou wilt cry.
Not so this figment!—not, that such a fume,
Instead of giving way to time and health,
Should eat itself into the life of life,
As saffron tingeth flesh, blood, bones and all!
For see, how he takes up the after-life.
The man—it is one Lazarus a Jew,
Sanguine, proportioned, fifty years of age,
The body's habit wholly laudable,
As much, indeed, beyond the common health
As he were made and put aside to show.
Think, could we penetrate by any drug
And bathe the wearied soul and worried flesh,
And bring it clear and fair, by three days' sleep!
Whence has the man the balm that brightens all?
This grown man eyes the world now like a child.
Some elders of his tribe, I should premise,
Led in their friend, obedient as a sheep,
To bear my inquisition. While they spoke,

Now sharply, now with sorrow,—told the case,—
He listened not except I spoke to him,
But folded his two hands and let them talk,
Watching the flies that buzzed: and yet no fool.
And that's a sample how his years must go.
Look, if a beggar, in fixed middle-life,
Should find a treasure, can he use the same
With straitened habits and with tastes starved small
And take at once to his impoverished brain
The sudden element that changes things,
That sets the undreamed-of rapture at his hand,
And puts the cheap old joy in the scorned dust?
Is he not such an one as moves to mirth—
Warily parsimonious, when no need,
Wasteful as drunkenness at undue times,
All prudent counsel as to what befits
The golden mean, is lost on such an one:
The man's fantastic will is the man's law.
So here—we'll call the treasure knowledge, say,
Increased beyond the fleshly faculty—
Heaven opened to a soul while yet on earth,
Earth forced on a soul's use while seeing heaven.
The man is witless of the size, the sum,
The value in proportion of all things,
Or whether it be little or be much.
Discourse to him of prodigious armaments
Assembled to besiege his city now,
And of the passing of a mule with gourds—
'Tis one! Then take it on the other side,
Speak of some trifling fact—he will gaze rapt
With stupor at its very littleness,
(Far as I see) —as if in that indeed
He caught prodigious import, whole results;
And so will turn to us the bystanders
In ever the same stupor (note this point)
That we too see not with his opened eyes.
Wonder and doubt come wrongly into play,
Preposterously, at cross purposes.
Should his child sicken unto death—why, look
For scarce abatement of his cheerfulness,
Or pretermission of his daily craft!
While a word, gesture, glance, from that same child
At play or in the school or laid asleep,
Will startle him to an agony of fear,
Exasperation, just as like! Demand
The reason why—" 'tis but a word," object—
"A gesture"—he regards thee as our lord
Who lived there in the pyramid alone,
Looked at us (dost thou mind?) when, being young
We both would unadvisedly recite
Some charm's beginning, from that book of his,
Able to bid the sun throb wide and burst
All into stars, as suns grown old are wont.
Thou and the child have each a veil alike
Thrown o'er your heads, from under which ye both
Stretch your blind hands and trifle with a match
Over a mine of Greek fire, did ye know!
He holds on firmly to some thread of life—
(It is the life to lead perforcedly)
Which runs across some vast distracting orb
Of glory on either side that meagre thread,
Which, conscious of, he must not enter yet—
The spiritual life around the earthly life:
The law of that is known to him as this—
His heart and brain move there, his feet stay here.
So is the man perplext with impulses
Sudden to start off crosswise, not straight on,
Proclaiming what is right and wrong across,
And not along, this black thread through the blaze—
"It should be" baulked by "here it cannot be."
And oft the man's soul springs into his face
As if he saw again and heard again
His sage that bade him "Rise" and he did rise.
Something, a word, a tick o' the blood within
Admonishes—then back he sinks at once
To ashes, who was very fire before,

In sedulous recurrence to his trade
Whereby he earneth him the daily bread;
And studiously the humbler for that pride,
Professedly the faultier that he knows
God's secret, while he holds the thread of life.
Indeed the especial marking of the man
Is prone submission to the heavenly will—
Seeing it, what it is, and why it is.
'Sayeth, he will wait patient to the last
For that same death which must restore his being
To equilibrium, body loosening soul
Divorced even now by premature full growth:
He will live, nay, it pleaseth him to live
So long as God please, and just how God please.
He even seeketh not to please God more
(Which meaneth, otherwise) than as God please.
Hence, I perceive not he affects to preach
The doctrine of his sect whate'er it be,
Make proselytes as madmen thirst to do:
How can he give his neighbour the real ground,
His own conviction? Ardent as he is—
Call his great truth a lie, why, still the old
"Be it as God please" reassureth him.
I probed the sore as thy disciple should:
"How, beast," said I, "this stolid carelessness
"Sufficeth thee, when Rome is on her march
"To stamp out like a little spark thy town,
"Thy tribe, thy crazy tale and thee at once?"
He merely looked with his large eyes on me.
The man is apathetic, you deduce?
Contrariwise, he loves both old and young,
Able and weak—affects the very brutes
And birds—how say I? flowers of the field—
As a wise workman recognises tools
In a master's workshop, loving what they make.
Thus is the man as harmless as a lamb:
Only impatient, let him do his best,
At ignorance and carelessness and sin—
An indignation which is promptly curbed:
As when in certain travels I have feigned
To be an ignoramus in our art
According to some preconceived design,
And happed to hear the land's practitioners,
Steeped in conceit sublimed by ignorance,
Prattle fantastically on disease,
Its cause and cure—and I must hold my peace!

Thou wilt object—Why have I not ere this
Sought out the sage himself, the Nazarene
Who wrought this cure, inquiring at the source,
Conferring with the frankness that befits?
Alas! it grieveth me, the learned leech
Perished in a tumult many years ago,
Accused,—our learning's fate,—of wizardry,
Rebellion, to the setting up a rule
And creed prodigious as described to me.
His death which happened when the earthquake fell
(Prefiguring, as soon appeared, the loss
To occult learning in our lord the sage
Who lived there in the pyramid alone)
Was wrought by the mad people—that's their wont—
On vain recourse, as I conjecture it,
To his tried virtue, for miraculous help—
How could he stop the earthquake? That's their way!
The other imputations must be lies:
But take one, though I loathe to give it thee,
In mere respect to any good man's fame!
(And after all, our patient Lazarus
Is stark mad; should we count on what he says?
Perhaps not: though in writing to a leech
'Tis well to keep back nothing of a case.)
This man so cured regards the curer, then,
As—God forgive me! who but God himself,
Creator and sustainer of the world,
That came and dwelt in flesh on it awhile!
—'Sayeth that such an one was born and lived,
Taught, healed the sick, broke bread at his own house,
Then died, with Lazarus by, for aught I know,
And yet was . . . what I said nor choose repeat,
And must have so avouched himself, in fact,

In hearing of this very Lazarus
Who saith—but why all this of what he saith?
Why write of trivial matters, things of price
Calling at every moment for remark?
I noticed on the margin of a pool
Blue-flowering borage, the Aleppo sort,
Aboundeth, very nitrous. It is strange!

Thy pardon for this long and tedious case,
Which, now that I review it, needs must seem
Unduly dwelt on, prolixly set forth!
Nor I myself discern in what is writ
Good cause for the peculiar interest
And awe indeed this man has touched me with.
Perhaps the journey's end, the weariness
Had wrought upon me first. I met him thus:
I crossed a ridge of short sharp broken hills
Like an old lion's cheek-teeth. Out there came
A moon made like a face with certain spots
Multiform, manifold and menacing:
Then a wind rose behind me. So we met
In this old sleepy town at unaware,
The man and I. I send thee what is writ.
Regard it as a chance, a matter risked
To this ambiguous Syrian—he may lose,
Or steal, or give it thee with equal good.
Jerusalem's repose shall make amends
For time this letter wastes, thy time and mine;
Till when, once more thy pardon and farewell!

The very God! think, Abib; dost thou think?
So, the All-Great, were the All-Loving too—
So, through the thunder comes a human voice
Saying, "O heart I made, a heart beats here!
"Face, my hands fashioned, see it in myself.
"Thou hast no power nor mayst conceive of mine,
"But love I gave thee, with myself to love,
"And thou must love me who have died for thee!"
The madman saith He said so: it is strange.

[1855]

MY STAR

All that I know
Of a certain star,
Is, it can throw
(Like the angled spar)
Now a dart of red,
Now a dart of blue;
Till my friends have said
They would fain see, too,
My star that dartles the red and the blue!
Then it stops like a bird; like a flower, hangs furled:
They must solace themselves with the Saturn above it.
What matter to me if their star is a world?
Mine has opened its soul to me; therefore I love it.

[1855]

"CHILDE ROLAND TO THE DARK TOWER CAME"

(See Edgar's song in "Lear")

I

My first thought was, he lied in every word,
That hoary cripple, with malicious eye
Askance to watch the working of his lie
On mine, and mouth scarce able to afford
Suppression of the glee, that pursed and scored
Its edge, at one more victim gained thereby.

II

What else should he be set for, with his staff?
What, save to waylay with his lies, ensnare
All travellers that might find him posted there,
And ask the road? I guessed what skull-like laugh
Would break, what crutch 'gin write my epitaph
For pastime in the dusty thoroughfare,

III

If at his counsel I should turn aside
Into that ominous tract which, all agree,
Hides the Dark Tower. Yet acquiescingly
I did turn as he pointed: neither pride

Nor hope rekindling at the end descried,
  So much as gladness that some end might be.

IV

For, what with my whole world-wide wandering,
  What with my search drawn out thro' years, my hope
  Dwindled into a ghost not fit to cope
With that obstreperous joy success would bring,—
I hardly tried now to rebuke the spring
  My heart made, finding failure in its scope.

V

As when a sick man very near to death
  Seems dead indeed, and feels begin and end
  The tears and takes the farewell of each friend,
And hears one bid the other go, draw breath
Freelier outside, ("since all is o'er," he saith,
  "And the blow fallen no grieving can amend;")

VI

While some discuss if near the other graves
  Be room enough for this, and when a day
  Suits best for carrying the corpse away,
With care about the banners, scarves and staves:
And still the man hears all, and only craves
  He may not shame such tender love and stay.

VII

Thus, I had so long suffered in this quest,
  Heard failure prophesied so oft, been writ
  So many times among "The Band!"—to wit,
The knights who to the Dark Tower's search addressed
Their steps—that just to fail as they, seemed best.
  And all the doubt was now—should I be fit?

VIII

So, quiet as despair, I turned from him,
  That hateful cripple, out of his highway
  Into the path he pointed. All the day
Had been a dreary one at best, and dim
Was settling to its close, yet shot one grim
  Red leer to see the plain catch its estray.

IX

For mark! no sooner was I fairly found
  Pledged to the plain, after a pace or two,
  Than, pausing to throw backward a last view
O'er the safe road, 'twas gone; grey plain all round:
Nothing but plain to the horizon's bound.
  I might go on; nought else remained to do.

X

So, on I went. I think I never saw
  Such starved ignoble nature; nothing throve:
  For flowers—as well expect a cedar grove!
But cockle, spurge, according to their law
Might propagate their kind, with none to awe,
  You'd think; a burr had been a treasure-trove.

XI

No! penury, inertness and grimace,
  In some strange sort, were the land's portion. "See
  Or shut your eyes," said Nature peevishly,
"It nothing skills: I cannot help my case:
" 'Tis the Last Judgment's fire must cure this place,
  Calcine its clods and set my prisoners free."

XII

If there pushed any ragged thistle-stalk
  Above its mates, the head was chopped; the bents
  Were jealous else. What made those holes and rents
In the dock's harsh swarth leaves—bruised as to baulk
All hope of greenness? 'tis a brute must walk
  Pashing their life out, with a brute's intents.

XIII

As for the grass, it grew as scant as hair
  In leprosy; thin dry blades pricked the mud
  Which underneath looked kneaded up with blood.

One stiff blind horse, his every bone a-stare,
Stood stupefied, however he came there:
  Thrust out past service from the devil's stud!

XIV

Alive? he might be dead for aught I know,
  With that red, gaunt and colloped neck a-strain,
  And shut eyes underneath the rusty mane;
Seldom went such grotesqueness with such woe;
I never saw a brute I hated so;
  He must be wicked to deserve such pain.

XV

I shut my eyes and turned them on my heart.
  As a man calls for wine before he fights,
  I asked one draught of earlier, happier sights,
Ere fitly I could hope to play my part.
Think first, fight afterwards—the soldier's art:
  One taste of the old time sets all to rights.

XVI

Not it! I fancied Cuthbert's reddening face
  Beneath its garniture of curly gold,
  Dear fellow, till I almost felt him fold
An arm in mine to fix me to the place,
That way he used. Alas, one night's disgrace!
  Out went my heart's new fire and left it cold.

XVII

Giles, then, the soul of honour—there he stands
  Frank as ten years ago when knighted first.
  What honest men should dare (he said) he durst.
Good—but the scene shifts—faugh! what hangman's hands
Pin to his breast a parchment? His own bands
  Read it. Poor traitor, spit upon and curst!

XVIII

Better this present than a past like that;
  Back therefore to my darkening path again!
  No sound, no sight as far as eye could strain.
Will the night send a howlet or a bat?
I asked: when something on the dismal flat
  Came to arrest my thoughts and change their train.

XIX

A sudden little river crossed my path
  As unexpected as a serpent comes.
  No sluggish tide congenial to the glooms;
This, as it frothed by, might have been a bath
For the fiend's glowing hoof—to see the wrath
  Of its black eddy bespate with flakes and spumes.

XX

So petty yet so spiteful! All along,
  Low scrubby alders kneeled down over it;
  Drenched willows flung them headlong in a fit
Of mute despair, a suicidal throng:
The river which had done them all the wrong,
  Whate'er that was, rolled by, deterred no whit.

XXI

Which, while I forded,—good saints, how I feared
  To set my foot upon a dead man's cheek,
  Each step, or feel the spear I thrust to seek
For hollows, tangled in his hair or beard!
—It may have been a water-rat I speared,
  But, ugh! it sounded like a baby's shriek.

XXII

Glad was I when I reached the other bank.
  Now for a better country. Vain presage!
  Who were the strugglers, what war did they wage,
Whose savage trample thus could pad the dank
Soil to a plash? toads in a poisoned tank,
  Or wild cats in a red-hot iron cage—

XXIII

The fight must so have seemed in that fell cirque.
  What penned them there, with all the plain to choose?
  No foot-print leading to that horrid mews,

None out of it. Mad brewage set to work
Their brains, no doubt, like galley-slaves the Turk
  Pits for his pastime, Christians against Jews.

XXIV

And more than that—a furlong on—why, there!
  What bad use was that engine for, that wheel,
  Or brake, not wheel—that harrow fit to reel
Men's bodies out like silk? with all the air
Of Tophet's tool, on earth left unaware,
  Or brought to sharpen its rusty teeth of steel.

XXV

Then came a bit of stubbed ground, once a wood,
  Next a marsh, it would seem, and now mere earth
  Desperate and done with; (so a fool finds mirth,
Makes a thing and then mars it, till his mood
Changes and off he goes!) within a rood—
  Bog, clay and rubble, sand and stark black dearth.

XXVI

Now blotches rankling, coloured gay and grim,
  Now patches where some leanness of the soil's
  Broke into moss or substances like boils;
Then came some palsied oak, a cleft in him
Like a distorted mouth that splits its rim
  Gaping at death, and dies while it recoils.

XXVII

And just as far as ever from the end!
  Nought in the distance but the evening, nought
  To point my footstep further! At the thought,
A great black bird, Apollyon's bosom-friend,
Sailed past, nor beat his wide wing dragon-penned
  That brushed my cap—perchance the guide I sought.

XXVIII

For, looking up, aware I somehow grew,
  'Spite of the dusk, the plain had given place
  All round to mountains—with such name to grace
Mere ugly heights and heaps now stolen in view.
How thus they had surprised me,—solve it, you!
  How to get from them was no clearer case.

XXIX

Yet half I seemed to recognize some trick
  Of mischief happened to me, God knows when—
  In a bad dream perhaps. Here ended, then,
Progress this way. When, in the very nick
Of giving up, one time more, came a click
  As when a trap shuts—you're inside the den!

XXX

Burningly it came on me all at once,
  This was the place! those two hills on the right,
  Crouched like two bulls locked horn in horn in fight;
While to the left, a tall scalped mountain . . . Dunce,
Dotard, a-dozing at the very nonce,
  After a life spent training for the sight!

XXXI

What in the midst lay but the Tower itself?
  The round squat turret, blind as the fool's heart,
  Built of brown stone, without a counterpart
In the whole world. The tempest's mocking elf
Points to the shipman thus the unseen shelf
  He strikes on, only when the timbers start.

XXXII

Not see? because of night perhaps?—why, day
  Came back again for that! before it left,
  The dying sunset kindled through a cleft:
The hills, like giants at a hunting, lay,

Chin upon hand, to see the game at bay,—
"Now stab and end the creature—to the heft!"

XXXIII

Not hear? when noise was everywhere! it tolled
Increasing like a bell. Names in my ears,
Of all the lost adventurers my peers,—
How such a one was strong, and such was bold,
And such was fortunate, yet each of old
Lost, lost! one moment knelled the woe of years.

XXXIV

There they stood, ranged along the hill-sides, met
To view the last of me, a living frame
For one more picture! in a sheet of flame
I saw them and I knew them all. And yet
Dauntless the slug-horn to my lips I set,
And blew. *"Childe Roland to the Dark Tower came."*

[1852] [1855]

HOW IT STRIKES A CONTEMPORARY

I only knew one poet in my life:
And this, or something like it, was his way.

You saw go up and down Valladolid,
A man of mark, to know next time you saw.
His very serviceable suit of black
Was courtly once and conscientious still,
And many might have worn it, though none did:
The cloak, that somewhat shone and showed the threads,
Had purpose, and the ruff, significance.
He walked and tapped the pavement with his cane,
Scenting the world, looking it full in face,
An old dog, bald and blindish, at his heels.
They turned up, now, the alley by the church,
That leads nowhither; now, they breathed themselves
On the main promenade just at the wrong time:
You'd come upon his scrutinising hat,
Making a peaked shade blacker than itself
Against the single window spared some house
Intact yet with its mouldered Moorish work,—
Or else surprise the ferrel of his stick
Trying the mortar's temper 'tween the chinks
Of some new shop a-building, French and fine.
He stood and watched the cobbler at his trade,
The man who slices lemons into drink,
The coffee-roaster's brazier, and the boys
That volunteer to help him turn its winch.
He glanced o'er books on stalls with half an eye,
And fly-leaf ballads on the vendor's string,
And broad-edge bold-print posters by the wall.
He took such cognisance of men and things,
If any beat a horse, you felt he saw;
If any cursed a woman, he took note;
Yet stared at nobody,—you stared at him,
And found, less to your pleasure than surprise,
He seemed to know you and expect as much.
So, next time that a neighbour's tongue was loosed,
It marked the shameful and notorious fact,
We had among us, not so much a spy,
As a recording chief-inquisitor,
The town's true master if the town but knew!
We merely kept a governor for form,
While this man walked about and took account
Of all thought, said and acted, then went home,
And wrote it fully to our Lord the King
Who has an itch to know things, he knows why,
And reads them in his bedroom of a night.
Oh, you might smile! there wanted not a touch,
A tang of . . . well, it was not wholly ease
As back into your mind the man's look came.
Stricken in years a little,—such a brow
His eyes had to live under!—clear as flint
On either side the formidable nose
Curved, cut and coloured like an eagle's claw.
Had he to do with A.'s surprising fate?
When altogether old B. disappeared

And young C. got his mistress,—was't our friend,
His letter to the King, that did it all?
What paid the bloodless man for so much pains?
Our Lord the King has favourites manifold,
And shifts his ministry some once a month;
Our city gets new governors at whiles,—
But never word or sign, that I could hear,
Notified to this man about the streets
The King's approval of those letters conned
The last thing duly at the dead of night.
Did the man love his office? Frowned our Lord,
Exhorting when none heard—"Beseech me not!
"Too far above my people,—beneath me!
"I set the watch,—how should the people know?
"Forget them, keep me all the more in mind!"
Was some such understanding 'twixt the two?

I found no truth in one report at least—
That if you tracked him to his home, down lanes
Beyond the Jewry, and as clean to pace,
You found he ate his supper in a room
Blazing with lights, four Titians on the wall,
And twenty naked girls to change his plate!
Poor man, he lived another kind of life
In that new stuccoed third house by the bridge,
Fresh-painted, rather smart than otherwise!
The whole street might o'erlook him as he sat
Leg crossing leg, one foot on the dog's back,
Playing a decent cribbage with his maid
(Jacynth, you're sure her name was) o'er the cheese
And fruit, three red halves of starved winter-pears,
Or treat of radishes in April. Nine,
Ten, struck the church clock, straight to bed went he.

My father, like the man of sense he was,
Would point him out to me a dozen times;
" 'St—'St," he'd whisper, "the Corregidor!"
I had been used to think that personage
Was one with lacquered breeches, lustrous belt,
And feathers like a forest in his hat,
Who blew a trumpet and proclaimed the news,
Announced the bull-fights, gave each church its turn,
And memorised the miracle in vogue!
He had a great observance from us boys;
We were in error; that was not the man.

I'd like now, yet had haply been afraid,
To have just looked, when this man came to die,
And seen who lined the clean gay garret-sides
And stood about the neat low truckle-bed,
With the heavenly manner of relieving guard.
Here had been, mark, the general-in-chief,
Through a whole campaign of the world's life and death,
Doing the King's work all the dim day long,
In his old coat and up to knees in mud,
Smoked like a herring, dining on a crust,—
And, now the day was won, relieved at once!
No further show or need for that old coat,
You are sure, for one thing! Bless us, all the while
How sprucely we are dressed out, you and I!
A second, and the angels alter that.
Well, I could never write a verse,—could you?
Let's to the Prado and make the most of time.

[1851–52?] [1855]

BISHOP BLOUGRAM'S APOLOGY

No more wine? Then we'll push back chairs and talk.
A final glass for me, though; cool, i'faith!
We ought to have our Abbey back, you see.
It's different, preaching in basilicas,
And doing duty in some masterpiece
Like this of brother Pugin's, bless his heart!

I doubt if they're half baked, those chalk rosettes,
Ciphers and stucco-twiddlings everywhere;
It's just like breathing in a lime-kiln: eh?
These hot long ceremonies of our church
Cost us a little—oh, they pay the price,
You take me—amply pay it! Now, we'll talk.

So, you despise me, Mr. Gigadibs.
No deprecation,—nay, I beg you, sir!
Beside 'tis our engagement: don't you know,
I promised, if you'd watch a dinner out,
We'd see truth dawn together?—truth that peeps
Over the glasses' edge when dinner's done,
And body gets its sop and holds its noise
And leaves soul free a little. Now's the time—
'Tis break of day! You do despise me then.
And if I say, "despise me,"—never fear—
I know you do not in a certain sense—
Not in my arm-chair for example: here,
I well imagine you respect my place
(*Status, entourage,* worldly circumstance)
Quite to its value—very much indeed
—Are up to the protesting eyes of you
In pride at being seated here for once—
You'll turn it to such capital account!
When somebody, through years and years to come,
Hints of the bishop,—names me—that's enough—
"Blougram? I knew him"—(into it you slide)
"Dined with him once, a Corpus Christi Day,
"All alone, we two; he's a clever man:
"And after dinner,—why, the wine you know,—
"Oh, there was wine, and good!—what with the wine . . .
" 'Faith, we began upon all sorts of talk!
"He's no bad fellow, Blougram; he had seen
"Something of mine he relished, some review:
"He's quite above their humbug in his heart,
"Half-said as much, indeed—the thing's his trade.
"I warrant, Blougram's sceptical at times:
"How otherwise? I liked him, I confess!"
Che che,[1] my dear sir, as we say at Rome,
Don't you protest now! It's fair give and take;
You have had your turn and spoken your home-truths:
The hand's mine now, and here you follow suit.

Thus much conceded, still the first fact stays—
You do despise me; your ideal of life
Is not the bishop's: you would not be I.
You would like better to be Goethe, now,
Or Buonaparte—or, bless me, lower still,
Count D'Orsay,—so you did what you preferred,
Spoke as you thought, and, as you cannot help,
Believed or disbelieved, no matter what,
So long as on that point, whate'er it was,

[1] Come, come.

You loosed your mind, were whole and sole yourself.
—That, my ideal never can include,
Upon that element of truth and worth
Never be based! for say they make me Pope—
(They can't—suppose it for our argument!)
Why, there I'm at my tether's end, I've reached
My height, and not a height which pleases you:
An unbelieving Pope won't do, you say.
It's like those eerie stories nurses tell,
Of how some actor on a stage played Death
With pasteboard crown, sham orb, and tinselled dart,
And called himself the monarch of the world;
Then going in the tire-room afterward
Because the play was done, to shift himself,
Got touched upon the sleeve familiarly,
The moment he had shut the closet door
By Death himself. Thus God might touch a Pope
At unawares, ask what his baubles mean,
And whose part he presumed to play just now?
Best be yourself, imperial, plain and true!

So, drawing comfortable breath again,
You weigh and find, whatever more or less
I boast of my ideal realized
Is nothing in the balance when opposed
To your ideal, your grand simple life,
Of which you will not realize one jot.
I am much, you are nothing; you would be all,
I would be merely much: you beat me there.

No, friend, you do not beat me: hearken why!
The common problem, yours, mine, every one's,
Is not to fancy what were fair in life
Provided it could be,—but, finding first
What may be, then find how to make it fair
Up to our means: a very different thing!
No abstract intellectual plan of life
Quite irrespective of life's plainest laws,
But one, a man, who is man and nothing more,
May lead within a world which (by your leave)
Is Rome or London, not Fool's-paradise.
Embellish Rome, idealize away,
Make Paradise of London if you can,
You're welcome, nay, you're wise.

A simile!
We mortals cross the ocean of this world
Each in his average cabin of a life;
The best's not big, the worst yields elbow-room.
Now for our six months' voyage—how prepare?
You come on shipboard with a landsman's list
Of things he calls convenient: so they are!
An India screen is pretty furniture,
A piano-forte is a fine resource,

All Balzac's novels occupy one shelf,
The new edition fifty volumes long;
And little Greek books with the funny type
They get up well at Leipsic, fill the next:
Go on! slabbed marble, what a bath it makes!
And Parma's pride, the Jerome, let us add!
'Twere pleasant could Correggio's fleeting glow
Hang full in face of one where'er one roams,
Since he more than the others brings with him
Italy's self,—the marvellous Modenese!—
Yet 'twas not on your list before, perhaps.
—Alas, friend, here's the agent . . . is't the name?
The captain, or whoever's master here—
You see him screw his face up; what's his cry
Ere you set foot on shipboard? "Six feet square!"
If you won't understand what six feet mean,
Compute and purchase stores accordingly—
And if in pique because he overhauls
Your Jerome, piano and bath, you come on board
Bare—why you cut a figure at the first
While sympathetic landsmen see you off;
Not afterward, when, long ere half seas over,
You peep up from your utterly naked boards
Into some snug and well-appointed berth
Like mine, for instance (try the cooler jug—
Put back the other, but don't jog the ice!)
And mortified you mutter "Well and good;
"He sits enjoying his sea-furniture;
" 'Tis stout and proper, and there's store of it:
"Though I've the better notion, all agree,
"Of fitting rooms up. Hang the carpenter,
"Neat ship-shape fixings and contrivances—
"I would have brought my Jerome, frame and all!"
And meantime you bring nothing: never mind—
You've proved your artist-nature: what you don't,
You might bring, so despise me, as I say.

Now come, let's backward to the starting place.
See my way: we're two college friends, suppose.
Prepare together for our voyage, then;
Each note and check the other in his work,—
Here's mine, a bishop's outfit; criticise!
What's wrong? why won't you be a bishop too?

Why, first, you don't believe, you don't and can't,
(Not statedly, that is, and fixedly
And absolutely and exclusively)
In any revelation called divine.
No dogmas nail your faith; and what remains
But say so, like the honest man you are?
First, therefore, overhaul theology!
Nay, I too, not a fool, you please to think,
Must find believing every whit as hard:
And if I do not frankly say as much,
The ugly consequence is clear enough.

Now, wait, my friend: well, I do not believe—
If you'll accept no faith that is not fixed,
Absolute and exclusive, as you say.
You're wrong—I mean to prove it in due time.
Meanwhile, I know where difficulties lie
I could not, cannot solve, nor ever shall,
So give up hope accordingly to solve—
(To you, and over the wine). Our dogmas then
With both of us, though in unlike degree,
Missing full credence—overboard with them!
I mean to meet you on your own premise:
Good, there go mine in company with yours!

And now what are we? unbelievers both,
Calm and complete, determinately fixed
To-day, to-morrow, and for ever, pray?
You'll guarantee me that? Not so, I think.
In no-wise! all we've gained is, that belief,
As unbelief before, shakes us by fits,
Confounds us like its predecessor. Where's
The gain? how can we guard our unbelief,
Make it bear fruit to us?—the problem here.
Just when we are safest, there's a sunset-touch,
A fancy from a flower-bell, some one's death,
A chorus-ending from Euripides,—
And that's enough for fifty hopes and fears
As old and new at once as nature's self,
To rap and knock and enter in our soul,
Take hands and dance there, a fantastic ring,
Round the ancient idol, on his base again,—
The grand Perhaps! we look on helplessly.
There the old misgivings, crooked questions are—
This good God,—what he could do, if he would,
Would, if he could—then must have done long since:
If so, when, where, and how? some way must be,—
Once feel about, and soon or late you hit
Some sense, in which it might be, after all.
Why not, "The Way, the Truth, the Life?"
                                                            —That way
Over the mountain, which who stands upon
Is apt to doubt if it be meant for a road;
While, if he views it from the waste itself,
Up goes the line there, plain from base to brow,
Not vague, mistakeable! what's a break or two
Seen from the unbroken desert either side?
And then (to bring in fresh philosophy)
What if the breaks themselves should prove at last
The most consummate of contrivances
To train a man's eye, teach him what is faith?
And so we stumble at truth's very test!
All we have gained then by our unbelief
Is a life of doubt diversified by faith,
For one of faith diversified by doubt:
We called the chess-board white,—we call it black,

"Well," you rejoin, "the end's no worse, at least
"We've reason for both colours on the board.
"Why not confess, then, where I drop the faith
"And you the doubt, that I'm as right as you?"

Because, friend, in the next place, this being so,
And both things even,—faith and unbelief
Left to a man's choice,—we'll proceed a step,
Returning to our image, which I like.

A man's choice, yes—but a cabin-passenger's—
The man made for the special life o' the world—
Do you forget him? I remember though!
Consult our ship's conditions and you find
One and but one choice suitable to all,
The choice that you unluckily prefer
Turning things topsy-turvy—they or it
Going to the ground. Belief or unbelief
Bears upon life, determines its whole course,
Begins at its beginning. See the world
Such as it is,—you made it not, nor I;
I mean to take it as it is,—and you
Not so you'll take it,—though you get nought else.
I know the special kind of life I like,
What suits the most my idiosyncrasy,
Brings out the best of me and bears me fruit
In power, peace, pleasantness, and length of days.
I find that positive belief does this
For me, and unbelief, no whit of this.
—For you, it does, however?—that we'll try.
'Tis clear, I cannot lead my life, at least
Induce the world to let me peaceably,
Without declaring at the outset, "Friends,
"I absolutely and peremptorily
"Believe!"—I say faith is my waking life
One sleeps, indeed, and dreams at intervals,
We know, but waking's the main point with us,
And my provision's for life's waking part.
Accordingly, I use heart, head and hand
All day, I build, scheme, study and make friends;
And when night overtakes me, down I lie,
Sleep, dream a little, and get done with it,
The sooner the better, to begin afresh.
What's midnight's doubt before the dayspring's faith?
You, the philosopher, that disbelieve,
That recognize the night, give dreams their weight—
To be consistent you should keep your bed,
Abstain from healthy acts that prove you a man,
For fear you drowse perhaps at unawares!
And certainly at night you'll sleep and dream,
Live through the day and bustle as you please.
And so you live to sleep as I to wake,
To unbelieve as I to still believe?
Well, and the common sense o' the world calls you

Bed-ridden,—and its good things come to me.
Its estimation, which is half the fight,
That's the first cabin-comfort I secure—
The next . . . but you perceive with half an eye!
Come, come, it's best believing, if we may,
You can't but own that!
Next, concede again—
If once we choose belief, on all accounts
We can't be too decisive in our faith,
Conclusive and exclusive in its terms,
To suit the world which gives us the good things.
In every man's career are certain points
Whereon he dares not be indifferent;
The world detects him clearly, if he dare,
As baffled at the game, and losing life.
He may care little or he may care much
For riches, honour, pleasure, work, repose,
Since various theories of life and life's
Success are extant which might easily
Comport with either estimate of these,
And whoso chooses wealth or poverty,
Labour or quiet, is not judged a fool
Because his fellows would choose otherwise:
We let him choose upon his own account
So long as he's consistent with his choice.
But certain points, left wholly to himself,
When once a man has arbitrated on,
We say he must succeed there or go hang.
Thus, he should wed the woman he loves most
Or needs most, whatsoe'er the love or need—
For he can't wed twice. Then, he must avouch
Or follow, at the least, sufficiently,
The form of faith his conscience holds the best,
Whate'er the process of conviction was:
For nothing can compensate his mistake
On such a point, the man himself being judge:
He cannot wed twice, nor twice lose his soul.

Well now, there's one great form of Christian faith
I happened to be born in—which to teach
Was given me as I grew up, on all hands,
As best and readiest means of living by;
The same on examination being proved
The most pronounced moreover, fixed, precise
And absolute form of faith in the whole world—
Accordingly, most potent of all forms
For working on the world. Observe, my friend,
Such as you know me, I am free to say,
In these hard latter days which hamper one,
Myself—by no immoderate exercise
Of intellect and learning, but the tact
To let external forces work for me,
—Bid the street's stones be bread and they are bread;

Bid Peter's creed, or, rather, Hildebrand's,
Exalt me o'er my fellows in the world
And make my life an ease and joy and pride;
It does so,—which for me's a great point gained,
Who have a soul and body that exact
A comfortable care in many ways.
There's power in me and will to dominate
Which I must exercise, they hurt me else:
In many ways I need mankind's respect,
Obedience, and the love that's born of fear:
While at the same time, there's a taste I have,
A toy of soul, a titillating thing,
Refuses to digest these dainties crude.
The naked life is gross till clothed upon:
I must take what men offer, with a grace
As though I would not, could I help it, take!
A uniform to wear though over-rich—
Something imposed on me, no choice of mine;
No fancy-dress worn for pure fancy's sake
And despicable therefore! now folk kneel
And kiss my hand—of course the Church's hand.
Thus I am made, thus life is best for me,
And thus that it should be I have procured;
And thus it could not be another way,
I venture to imagine.

You'll reply—
So far my choice, no doubt, is a success;
But were I made of better elements,
With nobler instincts, purer tastes, like you,
I hardly would account the thing success
Though it did all for me I say.

But, friend,
We speak of what is; not of what might be.
And how 'twere better if 'twere otherwise.
I am the man you see here plain enough:
Grant I'm beast, why beasts must lead beasts' lives!
Suppose I own at once to tail and claws;
The tailless man exceeds me; but being tailed
I'll lash out lion-fashion, and leave apes
To dock their stump and dress their haunches up.
My business is not to remake myself,
But make the absolute best of what God made.
Or—our first simile—though you prove me doomed
To a viler berth still, to the steerage-hole,
The sheep-pen or the pig-stye, I should strive
To make what use of each were possible;
And as this cabin gets upholstery,
That hutch should rustle with sufficient straw.

But, friend, I don't acknowledge quite so fast
I fail of all your manhood's lofty tastes
Enumerated so complacently,

On the mere ground that you forsooth can find
In this particular life I choose to lead
No fit provision for them. Can you not?
Say you, my fault is I address myself
To grosser estimators than I should judge?
And that's no way of holding up the soul—
Which, nobler, needs men's praise perhaps, yet knows
One wise man's verdict outweighs all the fools',—
Would like the two, but, forced to choose, takes that.
I pine among my million imbeciles
(You think) aware some dozen men of sense
Eye me and know me, whether I believe
In the last winking Virgin, as I vow,
And am a fool, or disbelieve in her
And am a knave,—approve in neither case,
Withhold their voices though I look their way:
Like Verdi when, at his worst opera's end
(The thing they gave at Florence,—what's its name?)
While the mad houseful's plaudits near out-bang
His orchestra of salt-box, tongs and bones,
He looks through all the roaring and the wreaths
Where sits Rossini patient in his stall.

Nay, friend, I meet you with an answer here—
For even your prime men who appraise their kind
Are men still, catch a wheel within a wheel,
See more in a truth than the truth's simple self,
Confuse themselves. You see lads walk the street
Sixty the minute; what's to note in that?
You see one lad o'erstride a chimney-stack;
Him you must watch—he's sure to fall, yet stands!
Our interest's on the dangerous edge of things.
The honest thief, the tender murderer,
The superstitious atheist, demirep
That loves and saves her soul in new French books—
We watch while these in equilibrium keep
The giddy line midway: one step aside,
They're classed and done with. I, then, keep the line
Before your sages,—just the men to shrink
From the gross weights, coarse scales, and labels broad
You offer their refinement. Fool or knave?
Why needs a bishop be a fool or knave
When there's a thousand diamond weights between?
So I enlist them. Your picked twelve, you'll find,
Profess themselves indignant, scandalized
At thus being held unable to explain
How a superior man who disbelieves
May not believe as well: that's Schelling's way!
It's through my coming in the tail of time,
Nicking the minute with a happy tact.
Had I been born three hundred years ago
They'd say, "What's strange? Blougram of course believes;"
And, seventy years since, "disbelieves of course."
But now, "He may believe; and yet, and yet

How can he?"—All eyes turn with interest.
Whereas, step off the line on either side—
You, for example, clever to a fault,
The rough and ready man who write apace,
Read somewhat seldomer, think perhaps even less—
You disbelieve! Who wonders and who cares?
Lord So-and-So—his coat bedropped with wax,
All Peter's chains about his waist, his back
Brave with the needlework of Noodledom—
Believes! Again, who wonders and who cares?
But I, the man of sense and learning too,
The able to think yet act, the this, the that,
I, to believe at this late time of day!
Enough; you see, I need not fear contempt.

—Except it's yours! Admire me as these may,
You don't. But whom at least do you admire?
Present your own perfection, your ideal,
Your pattern man for a minute—oh, make haste,
Is it Napoleon you would have us grow?
Concede the means; allow his head and hand,
(A large concession, clever as you are)
Good!—In our common primal element
Of unbelief (we can't believe, you know—
We're still at that admission, recollect!)
Where do you find—apart from, towering o'er
The secondary temporary aims
Which satisfy the gross taste you despise—
Where do you find his star?—his crazy trust
God knows through what or in what? it's alive
And shines and leads him and that's all we want.
Have we aught in our sober night shall point
Such ends as his were, and direct the means
Of working out our purpose straight as his,
Nor bring a moment's trouble on success,
With after-care to justify the same?
—Be a Napoleon and yet disbelieve—
Why, the man's mad, friend, take his light away!
What's the vague good of the world for which you dare
With comfort to yourself blow millions up?
We neither of us see it! we do see
The blown-up millions—spatter of their brains
And writhing of their bowels and so forth,
In that bewildering entanglement
Of horrible eventualities
Past calculation to the end of time!
Can I mistake for some clear word of God
(Which were my ample warrant for it all)
His puff of hazy instincts, idle talk,
"The State, that's I," quack-nonsense about kings,
And (when one beats the man to his last hold)
The vague idea of setting things to rights,
Policing people efficaciously,
More to their profit, most of all to his own;

The whole to end that dismallest of ends
By an Austrian marriage, cant to us the Church,
And resurrection of the old *régime*?
Would I, who hope to live a dozen years,
Fight Austerlitz for reasons such and such?
No: for, concede me but the merest chance
Doubt may be wrong—there's judgment, life to come!
With just that chance, I dare not. Doubt proves right?
This present life is all? you offer me
Its dozen noisy years with not a chance
That wedding an archduchess, wearing lace,
And getting called by divers new-coined names,
Will drive off ugly thoughts and let me dine,
Sleep, read and chat in quiet as I like!
Therefore, I will not.

Take another case;
Fit up the cabin yet another way.
What say you to the poet? shall we write
Hamlet, Othello—make the world our own,
Without a risk to run of either sort?
I can't!—to put the strongest reason first.
"But try," you urge, "the trying shall suffice:
"The aim, if reached or not, makes great the life:
"Try to be Shakespeare, leave the rest to fate!"
Spare my self-knowledge—there's no fooling me!
If I prefer remaining my poor self,
I say so not in self-dispraise but praise.
If I'm a Shakespeare, let the well alone;
Why should I try to be what now I am?
If I'm no Shakespeare, as too probable,—
His power and consciousness and self-delight
And all we want in common, shall I find—
Trying for ever? while on points of taste
Wherewith, to speak it humbly, he and I
Are dowered alike—I'll ask you, I or he,
Which in our two lives realizes most?
Much, he imagined—somewhat, I possess.
He had the imagination; stick to that!
Let him say "In the face of my soul's works
"Your world is worthless and I touch it not
"Lest I should wrong them"—I'll withdraw my plea.
But does he say so? look upon his life!
Himself, who only can, gives judgment there.
He leaves his towers and gorgeous palaces
To build the trimmest house in Stratford town;
Saves money, spends it, owns the worth of things,
Giulio Romano's pictures, Dowland's lute;
Enjoys a show, respects the puppets, too,
And none more, had he seen its entry once,
Than "Pandulph, of fair Milan cardinal."
Why then should I who play that personage,
The very Pandulph Shakespeare's fancy made,
Be told that had the poet chanced to start

From where I stand now (some degree like mine
Being just the goal he ran his race to reach)
He would have run the whole race back, forsooth,
And left being Pandulph, to begin write plays?
Ah, the earth's best can be but the earth's best!
Did Shakespeare live, he could but sit at home
And get himself in dreams the Vatican,
Greek busts, Venetian paintings, Roman walls,
And English books, none equal to his own,
Which I read, bound in gold (he never did).
—Terni's fall, Naples' bay and Gothard's top—
Eh, friend? I could not fancy one of these—
But, as I pour this claret, there they are:
I've gained them—crossed St. Gothard last July
With ten mules to the carriage and a bed
Slung inside; is my hap the worse for that?
We want the same things, Shakespeare and myself,
And what I want, I have: he, gifted more,
Could fancy he too had them when he liked,
But not so thoroughly that, if fate allowed,
He would not have them also in my sense.
We play one game; I send the ball aloft
No less adroitly that of fifty strokes
Scarce five go o'er the wall so wide and high
Which sends them back to me: I wish and get.
He struck balls higher and with better skill,
But at a poor fence level with his head,
And hit—his Stratford house, a coat of arms,
Successful dealings in his grain and wool,—
While I receive heaven's incense in my nose
And style myself the cousin of Queen Bess.
Ask him, if this life's all, who wins the game?

Believe—and our whole argument breaks up.
Enthusiasm's the best thing, I repeat;
Only, we can't command it; fire and life
Are all, dead matter's nothing; we agree:
And be it a mad dream or God's very breath,
The fact's the same,—belief's fire, once in us,
Makes of all else mere stuff to show itself:
We penetrate our life with such a glow
As fire lends wood and iron—this turns steel,
That burns to ash—all's one, fire proves its power
For good or ill, since men call flare success.
But paint a fire, it will not therefore burn.
Light one in me, I'll find it food enough!
Why, to be Luther—that's a life to lead,
Incomparably better than my own.
He comes, reclaims God's earth for God, he says,
Sets up God's rule again by simple means,
Re-opens a shut book, and all is done.
He flared out in the flaring of mankind;
Such Luther's luck was—how shall such be mine?
If he succeeded, nothing's left to do:

And if he did not altogether—well,
Strauss is the next advance. All Strauss should be
I might be also. But to what result?
He looks upon no future: Luther did.
What can I gain on the denying side?
Ice makes no conflagration. State the facts,
Read the text right, emancipate the world—
The emancipated world enjoys itself
With scarce a thank-you: Blougram told it first
It could not owe a farthing,—not to him
More than St. Paul! 'twould press its pay, you think?
Then add there's still that plaguy hundredth chance
Strauss may be wrong. And so a risk is run—
For what gain? not for Luther's, who secured
A real heaven in his heart throughout his life,
Supposing death a little altered things!

"Ay, but since really I lack faith," you cry,
"I run the same risk really on all sides,
" In cool indifference as bold unbelief.
"As well be Strauss as swing 'twixt Paul and him.
"It's not worth having, such imperfect faith,
"Nor more available to do faith's work
Than unbelief like mine. Whole faith, or none!"

Softly, my friend! I must dispute that point.
Once own the use of faith, I'll find you faith.
We're back on Christian ground. You call for faith:
I show you doubt, to prove that faith exists.
The more of doubt, the stronger faith, I say,
If faith o'ercomes doubt. How I know it does?
By life and man's free will, God gave for that!
To mould life as we choose it, shows our choice:
That's our one act, the previous work's his own.
You criticize the soil? it reared this tree—
This broad life and whatever fruit it bears!
What matter though I doubt at every pore,
Head-doubts, heart-doubts, doubts at my fingers' ends,
Doubts in the trivial work of every day,
Doubts at the very bases of my soul
In the grand moments when she probes herself—
If finally I have a life to show,
The thing I did, brought out in evidence
Against the thing done to me underground
By hell and all its brood, for aught I know?
I say, whence sprang this? shows it faith or doubt?
All's doubt in me; where's break of faith in this?
It is the idea, the feeling and the love
God means mankind should strive for and show forth,
Whatever be the process to that end,—
And not historic knowledge, logic sound,
And metaphysical acumen, sure!
"What think ye of Christ," friend? when all's done and said,
You like this Christianity or not?

It may be false, but will you wish it true?
Has it your vote to be so if it can?
Trust you an instinct silenced long ago
That will break silence and enjoin you love
What mortified philosophy is hoarse,
And all in vain, with bidding you despise?
If you desire faith—then you've faith enough:
What else seeks God—nay, what else seek ourselves?
You form a notion of me, we'll suppose,
On hearsay; it's a favourable one:
"But still" (you add), "there was no such good man,
"Because of contradiction in the facts.
"One proves, for instance, he was born in Rome,
"This Blougram—yet throughout the tales of him
"I see he figures as an Englishman."
Well, the two things are reconcileable.
But would I rather you discovered that
Subjoining—"Still, what matter though they be?
"Blougram—concerns me naught, born here or there."

Pure faith indeed—you know not what you ask!
Naked belief in God the Omnipotent,
Omniscient, Omnipresent, sears too much
The sense of conscious creatures to be borne.
It were the seeing him, no flesh shall dare.
Some think, Creation's meant to show him forth:
I say, it's meant to hide him all it can,
And that's what all the blessed evil's for.
It's use in Time is to environ us,
Our breath, our drop of dew, with shield enough
Against that sight till we can bear its stress.
Under a vertical sun, the exposed brain
And lidless eye and disemprisoned heart
Less certainly would wither up at once
Than mind, confronted with the truth of him.
But time and earth case-harden us to live;
The feeblest sense is trusted most; the child
Feels God a moment, ichors o'er the place,
Plays on and grows to be a man like us.
With me, faith means perpetual unbelief
Kept quiet like the snake 'neath Michael's foot
Who stands calm just because he feels it writhe.
Or, if that's too ambitious,—here's my box—
I need the excitation of a pinch
Threatening the torpor of the inside-nose
Nigh on the imminent sneeze that never comes.
"Leave it in peace" advise the simple folk—
Make it aware of peace by itching-fits,
Say I—let doubt occasion still more faith!

You'll say, once all believed, man, woman, child,
In that dear middle-age these noodles praise.
How you'd exult if I could put you back
Six hundred years, blot out cosmogony,

Geology, ethnology, what not,
(Greek endings, each the little passing-bell
That signifies some faith's about to die),
And set you square with Genesis again,—
When such a traveller told you his last news,
He saw the ark a-top of Ararat
But did not climb there since 'twas getting dusk
And robber-bands infest the mountain's foot!
How should you feel, I ask, in such an age,
How act? As other people felt and did;
With soul more blank than this decanter's knob,
Believe—and yet lie, kill, rob, fornicate
Full in belief's face, like the beast you'd be!

No, when the fight begins within himself,
A man's worth something. God stoops o'er his head,
Satan looks up between his feet—both tug—
He's left, himself, i' the middle: the soul wakes
And grows. Prolong that battle through his life!
Never leave growing till the life to come!
Here, we've got callous to the Virgin's winks
That used to puzzle people wholesomely—
Men have outgrown the shame of being fools.
What are the laws of nature, not to bend
If the Church bid them? brother Newman asks.
Up with the Immaculate Conception, then—
On to the rack with faith!—is my advice!
Will not that hurry us upon our knees,
Knocking our breasts, "It can't be—yet it shall!
Who am I, the worm, to argue with my Pope?
Low things confound the high things!" and so forth.
That's better than acquitting God with grace
As some folks do. He's tried—no case is proved,
Philosophy is lenient—he may go!

You'll say—the old system's not so obsolete
But men believe still: ay, but who and where?
King Bomba's lazzaroni[1] foster yet
The sacred flame, so Antonelli writes;
But even of these, what ragamuffin-saint
Believes God watches him continually,
As he believes in fire that it will burn,
Or rain that it will drench him? Break fire's law,
Sin against rain, although the penalty
Be just singe or soaking? "No," he smiles;
"Those laws are laws that can enforce themselves."

The sum of all is—yes, my doubt is great,
My faith's still greater—then my faith's enough.
I have read much, thought much, experienced much,
Yet would die rather than avow my fear
The Naples' liquefaction may be false,

[1] Beggars, idle rogues.

When set to happen by the palace-clock
According to the clouds or dinner-time.
I hear you recommend, I might at least
Eliminate, decrassify my faith
Since I adopt it; keeping what I must
And leaving what I can—such points as this!
I won't—that is, I can't throw one away.
Supposing there's no truth in what I hold
About the need of trial to man's faith,
Still, when you bid me purify the same,
To such a process I discern no end,
Clearing off one excrescence to see two,
There's ever a next in size, now grown as big,
That meets the knife: I cut and cut again!
First cut the Liquefaction, what comes last
But Fichte's clever cut at God himself?
Experimentalize on sacred things?
I trust nor hand nor eye nor heart nor brain
To stop betimes: they all get drunk alike.
The first step, I am master not to take.

You'd find the cutting-process to your taste
As much as leaving growths of lies unpruned,
Nor see more danger in it,—you retort.
Your taste's worth mine; but my taste proves more wise
When we consider that the steadfast hold
On the extreme end of the chain of faith
Gives all the advantage, makes the difference,
With the rough purblind mass we seek to rule:
We are their lords, or they are free of us,
Just as we tighten or relax our hold.
So, other matters equal, we'll revert
To the first problem—which, if solved my way
And thrown into the balance, turns the scale—
How we may lead a comfortable life,
How suit our luggage to the cabin's size.

Of course you are remarking all this time
How narrowly and grossly I view life,
Respect the creature-comforts, care to rule
The masses, and regard complacently
"The cabin," in our old phrase! Well, I do.
I act for, talk for, live for this world now,
As this world calls for action, life and talk—
No prejudice to what next world may prove,
Whose new laws and requirements, my best pledge
To observe them, is that I observe these now,
Doing hereafter what I do meanwhile.
Let us concede (gratuitously though)
Next life relieves the soul of body, yields
Pure spiritual enjoyments: well, my friend,
Why lose this life i' the meantime, since its use
May be to make the next life more intense?

Do you know, I have often had a dream
(Work it up in your next month's article)
Of man's poor spirit in its progress, still
Losing true life for ever and a day
Through ever trying to be and ever being—
In the evolution of successive spheres—
Before its actual sphere and place of life,
Halfway into the next, which having reached,
It shoots with corresponding foolery
Halfway into the next still, on and off!
As when a traveller, bound from North to South,
Scouts fur in Russia: what's its use in France?
In France spurns flannel: where's its need in Spain?
In Spain drops cloth, too cumbrous for Algiers!
Linen goes next, and last the skin itself,
A superfluity at Timbuctoo.
When through his journey, was the fool at ease?
I'm at ease now, friend; worldly in this world,
I take and like its way of life; I think
My brothers, who administer the means,
Live better for my comfort—that's good too;
And God, if he pronounce upon it all,
Approves my service, which is better still.
If He keep silence,—why for you or me
Or that brute-beast pulled-up in to-day's "Times,"
What odds is't, save to ourselves, what life we lead?

You meet me at this issue: you declare,
All special pleading done with—truth is truth,
And justifies itself by undreamed ways.
You don't fear but it's better, if we doubt,
To say so, act up to our truth perceived
However feebly. Do then,—act away!
'Tis there I'm on the watch for you. How one acts
Is, both of us agree, our chief concern:
And how you'll act is what I fain would see
If, like the candid person you appear,
You dare to make the most of your life's scheme
As I of mine, live up to its full law
Since there's no higher law that counterchecks.
Put natural religion to the test
You've just demolished the revealed with—quick,
Down to the root of all that checks your will,
All prohibition to lie, kill and thieve
Or even to be an atheistic priest!
Suppose a pricking to incontinence—
Philosophers deduce you chastity
Or shame, from just the fact that at the first
Whoso embraced a woman in the field,
Threw club down, and forewent his brains beside,
So stood a ready victim in the reach
Of any brother-savage, club in hand;
Hence saw the use of going out of sight
In wood or cave to prosecute his loves:

I read this in a French book t'other day.
Does law so analysed coerce you much?
Oh, men spin clouds of fuzz where matters end,
But you who reach where the first thread begins,
You'll soon cut that!—which means you can, but won't
Through certain instincts, blind, unreasoned out,
You dare not set aside, you can't tell why,
But there they are, and so you let them rule.
Then, friend, you seem as much a slave as I,
A liar, conscious coward and hypocrite,
Without the good the slave expects to get,
Suppose he has a master after all!
You own your instincts—why what else do I,
Who want, am made for, and must have a God
Ere I can be aught, do aught?—no mere name
Want, but the true thing with what proves its truth,
To wit, a relation from that thing to me,
Touching from head to foot—which touch I feel,
And with it take the rest, this life of ours!
I live my life here; yours you dare not live.

Not as I state it, who (you please subjoin)
Disfigure such a life and call it names.
While, to your mind, remains another way
For simple men: knowledge and power have rights,
But ignorance and weakness have rights too.
There needs no crucial effort to find truth
If here or there or anywhere about:
We ought to turn each side, try hard and see,
And if we can't, be glad we've earned at least
The right, by one laborious proof the more,
To graze in peace earth's pleasant pasturage.
Men are not angels, neither are they brutes.
Something we may see, all we cannot see.
What need of lying? I say, I see all,
And swear to each detail the most minute
In what I think a Pan's face—you, mere cloud:
I swear I hear him speak and see him wink,
For fear, if once I drop the emphasis,
Mankind may doubt there's any cloud at all.
You take the simpler life—ready to see,
Willing to see (for no cloud's worth a face)
And leaving quiet what no strength can move,
And which, who bids you move? who has the right?
I bid you; but you are God's sheep, not mine—
"Pastor est tui Dominus." [1] You find
In this the pleasant pasture of our life
Much you may eat without the least offence,
Much you don't eat because your maw objects,
Much you would eat but that your fellow-flock
Open great eyes at you and even butt,
And thereupon you like your mates so well

[1] The Lord is thy Shepherd.

You cannot please yourself, offending them;
Though when they seem exorbitantly sheep,
You weigh your pleasure with their butts and bleats
And strike the balance. Sometimes certain fears
Restrain you, real checks since you find them so,
Sometimes you please yourself and nothing checks:
And thus you graze through life with not one lie,
And like it best.

But do you, in truth's name?
If so, you beat—which means you are not I—
Who needs must make earth mine and feed my fill
Not simply unbutted at, unbickered with,
But motioned to the velvet of the sward
By those obsequious wethers' very selves.
Look at me, sir; my age is double yours.
At yours, I knew beforehand, so enjoyed,
What now I should be—as, permit the word,
I pretty well imagine your whole range
And stretch of tether twenty years to come.
We both have minds and bodies much alike:
In truth's name, don't you want my bishopric,
My daily bread, my influence and my state?
You're young. I'm old; you must be old one day;
Will you find then, as I do hour by hour,
Women their lovers kneel to, who cut curls
From your fat lap-dog's ear to grace a brooch—
Dukes, who petition just to kiss your ring—
With much beside you know or may conceive?
Suppose we die to-night: well, here am I,
Such were my gains, life bore this fruit to me,
While writing all the same my articles
On music, poetry, the fictile vase
Found at Albano, chess, Anacreon's Greek.
But you—the highest honour in your life,
The thing you'll crown yourself with, all your days,
Is—dining here and drinking this last glass
I pour you out in sign of amity
Before we part for ever. Of your power
And social influence, worldly worth in short,
Judge what's my estimation by the fact,
I do not condescend to enjoin, beseech,
Hint secrecy on one of all these words!
You're shrewd and know that should you publish one
The world would brand the lie—my enemies first,
Who'd sneer—"the bishop's an arch-hypocrite,
"And knave perhaps, but not so frank a fool"
Whereas I should not dare for both my ears
Breathe one such syllable, smile one such smile,
Before the chaplain who reflects myself—
My shade's so much more potent than your flesh.
What's your reward, self-abnegating friend?
Stood you confessed of those exceptional
And privileged great natures that dwarf mine—

A zealot with a mad ideal in reach,
A poet just about to print his ode,
A statesman with a scheme to stop this war,
An artist whose religion is his art—
I should have nothing to object: such men
Carry the fire, all things grow warm to them,
Their drugget's worth my purple, they beat me.
But you,—you're just as little those as I—
You, Gigadibs, who, thirty years of age,
Write statedly for Blackwood's Magazine,
Believe you see two points in Hamlet's soul
Unseized by the Germans yet—which view you'll print—
Meantime the best you have to show being still
That lively lightsome article we took
Almost for the true Dickens,—what's its name?
"The Slum and Cellar—or Whitechapel life
"Limned after dark!" it made me laugh, I know,
And pleased a month and brought you in ten pounds.
—Success I recognize and compliment,
And therefore give you, if you choose, three words
(The card and pencil-scratch is quite enough)
Which whether here, in Dublin, or New York,
Will get you, prompt as at my eyebrow's wink,
Such terms as never you aspired to get
In all our own reviews and some not ours.
Go write your lively sketches! be the first
"Blougram, or The Eccentric Confidence"—
Or better simply say, "The Outward-bound."
Why, men as soon would throw it in my teeth
As copy and quote the infamy chalked broad
About me on the church-door opposite.
You will not wait for that experience though,
I fancy, howsoever you decide,
To discontinue—not detesting, not
Defaming, but at least—despising me!

Over his wine so smiled and talked his hour
Sylvester Blougram, styled *in partibus*
Episcopus, nec non—[1] (the deuce knows what
It's changed to by our novel hierarchy)
With Gigadibs the literary man,
Who played with spoons, explored his plate's design,
And ranged the olive stones about its edge,
While the great bishop rolled him out a mind.
Long crumpled, till creased consciousness lay smooth.

For Blougram, he believed, say, half he spoke.
The other portion, as he shaped it thus
For argumentatory purposes,
He felt his foe was foolish to dispute.
Some arbitrary accidental thoughts
That crossed his mind, amusing because new,

[1] Bishop in regions (of unbelievers) and . . .

He chose to represent as fixtures there,
Invariable convictions (such they seemed
Beside his interlocutor's loose cards
Flung daily down, and not the same way twice)
While certain hell-deep instincts, man's weak tongue
Is never bold to utter in their truth
Because styled hell-deep ('tis an old mistake
To place hell at the bottom of the earth)
He ignored these,—not having in readiness
Their nomenclature and philosophy:
He said true things, but called them by wrong names.
"On the whole," he thought, "I justify myself
"On every point where cavillers like this
"Oppugn my life: he tries one kind of fence,
"I close, he's worsted, that's enough for him.
"He's on the ground! if ground should break away
"I take my stand on, there's a firmer yet
"Beneath it, both of us may sink and reach.
"His ground was over mine and broke the first.
"So let him sit with me this many a year!"

He did not sit five minutes. Just a week
Sufficed his sudden healthy vehemence.
Something had struck him in the "Outward-bound"
Another way than Blougram's purpose was:
And having bought, not cabin-furniture
But settler's-implements (enough for three)
And started for Australia—there, I hope,
By this time he has tested his first plough,
And studied his last chapter of St. John.

[1855]

MEMORABILIA

I

Ah, did you once see Shelley plain,
And did he stop and speak to you?
And did you speak to him again?
How strange it seems, and new!

II

But you were living before that,
And you are living after,
And the memory I started at—
My starting moves your laughter!

III

I crossed a moor with a name of its own
And a use in the world no doubt,
Yet a hand's-breath of it shines alone
'Mid the blank miles round about—

IV

For there I picked up on the heather
And there I put inside my breast
A moulded feather, an eagle-feather—
Well, I forget the rest.

[1855]

ANDREA DEL SARTO

(CALLED 'THE FAULTLESS PAINTER')

But do not let us quarrel any more,
No, my Lucrezia; bear with me for once:
Sit down and all shall happen as you wish.
You turn your face, but does it bring your heart?
I'll work then for your friend's friend, never fear,
Treat his own subject after his own way,

Fix his own time, accept too his own price,
And shut the money into this small hand
When next it takes mine. Will it? tenderly?
Oh, I'll content him,—but to-morrow, Love!
I often am much wearier than you think,
This evening more than usual, and it seems
As if—forgive now—should you let me sit
Here by the window with your hand in mine
And look a half-hour forth on Fiesole,
Both of one mind, as married people use,
Quietly, quietly, the evening through,
I might get up to-morrow to my work
Cheerful and fresh as ever. Let us try.
To-morrow how you shall be glad for this!
Your soft hand is a woman of itself,
And mine the man's bared breast she curls inside.
Don't count the time lost, either; you must serve
For each of the five pictures we require—
It saves a model. So! keep looking so—
My serpentining beauty, rounds on rounds!
—How could you ever prick those perfect ears,
Even to put the pearl there! oh, so sweet—
My face, my moon, my everybody's moon,
Which everybody looks on and calls his,
And, I suppose, is looked on by in turn,
While she looks—no one's: very dear, no less!
You smile? why, there's my picture ready made,
There's what we painters call our harmony!
A common greyness silvers everything,—
All in a twilight, you and I alike
—You, at the point of your first pride in me
(That's gone, you know),—but I, at every point;
My youth, my hope, my art, being all toned down
To yonder sober pleasant Fiesole.
There's the bell clinking from the chapel-top;
That length of convent-wall across the way
Holds the trees safer, huddled more inside;
The lask monk leaves the garden; days decrease
And autumn grows, autumn in everything.
Eh? the whole seems to fall into a shape
As if I saw alike my work and self
And all that I was born to be and do,
A twilight-piece. Love, we are in God's hand.
How strange now, looks the life he makes us lead!
So free we seem, so fettered fast we are!
I feel He laid the fetter: let it lie!
This chamber for example—turn your head—
All that's behind us! you don't understand
Nor care to understand about my art,
But you can hear at least when people speak;
And that cartoon, the second from the door
—It is the thing, Love! so such things should be—
Behold Madonna, I am bold to say.
I can do with my pencil what I know,
What I see, what at bottom of my heart
I wish for, if I ever wish so deep—
Do easily, too—when I say, perfectly,
I do not boast, perhaps: yourself are judge
Who listened to the Legate's talk last week,
And just as much they used to say in France.
At any rate 'tis easy, all of it!
No sketches first, no studies, that's long past—
I do what many dream of all their lives
—Dream? strive to do, and agonize to do,
And fail in doing. I could count twenty such
On twice your fingers, and not leave this town,
Who strive—you don't know how the others strive
To paint a little thing like that you smeared
Carelessly passing with your robes afloat,—
Yet do much less, so much less, Someone says,
(I know his name, no matter) so much less!
Well, less is more, Lucrezia: I am judged.
There burns a truer light of God in them,
In their vexed, beating, stuffed and stopped-up brain,
Heart, or whate'er else, than goes on to prompt
This low-pulsed forthright craftsman's hand of mine.
Their works drop groundward, but themselves, I know,
Reach many a time a heaven that's shut to me,
Enter and take their place there sure enough,

Though they come back and cannot tell the world.
My works are nearer heaven, but I sit here.
The sudden blood of these men! at a word—
Praise them, it boils, or blame them, it boils too.
I, painting from myself and to myself,
Know what I do, am unmoved by men's blame
Or their praise either. Somebody remarks
Morello's outline there is wrongly traced,
His hue mistaken, what of that? or else,
Rightly traced and well ordered, what of that?
Speak as they please, what does the mountain care?
Ah, but a man's reach should exceed his grasp,
Or what's a heaven for? all is silver-grey
Placid and perfect with my art: the worse!
I know both what I want and what might gain,
And yet how profitless to know, to sigh
"Had I been two, another and myself.
"Our head would have o'erlooked the world!" No doubt.
Yonder's a work, now, of that famous youth,
The Urbinate who died five years ago.
('Tis copied, George Vasari sent it me.)
Well, I can fancy how he did it all,
Pouring his soul, with kings and popes to see,
Reaching, that Heaven might so replenish him,
Above and through his art—for it gives way;
That arm is wrongly put—and there again—
A fault to pardon in the drawing's lines,
Its body, so to speak: its soul is right,
He means right—that, a child may understand.
Still, what an arm! and I could alter it;
But all the play, the insight and the stretch
Out of me, out of me! And wherefore out?
Had you enjoined them on me, given me soul,
We might have risen to Rafael, I and you!
Nay, Love, you did give all I asked, I think—
More than I merit, yes, by many times.
But had you—oh, with the same perfect brow,
And perfect eyes, and more than perfect mouth,
And the low voice my soul hears, as a bird
The fowler's pipe, and follows to the snare—
Had you, with these the same, but brought a mind!
Some women do so. Had the mouth there urged
"God and the glory! never care for gain.
The present by the future, what is that?
Live for fame, side by side with Agnolo—
Rafael is waiting: up to God all three!"
I might have done it for you. So it seems:
Perhaps not. All is as God overrules.
Beside, incentives come from the soul's self;
The rest avail not. Why do I need you?
What wife had Rafael, or has Agnolo?
In this world, who can do a thing, will not;
And who would do it, cannot, I perceive:
Yet the will's somewhat—somewhat, too, the power—
And thus we half-men struggle. At the end,
God, I conclude, compensates, punishes.
'Tis safer for me, if the award be strict,
That I am something underrated here,
Poor this long while, despised, to speak the truth.
I dared not, do you know, leave home all day,
For fear of chancing on the Paris lords.
The best is when they pass and look aside;
But they speak sometimes; I must bear it all.
Well may they speak! That Francis, that first time,
And that long festal year at Fontainebleau!
I surely then could sometimes leave the ground,
Put on the glory, Rafael's daily wear,
In that humane great monarch's golden look,—
One finger in his beard or twisted curl
Over his mouth's good mark that made the smile,
One arm about my shoulder, round my neck,
The jingle of his gold chain in my ear,
I painting proudly with his breath on me,
All his court round him, seeing with his eyes,
Such frank French eyes, and such a fire of souls
Profuse, my hand kept plying by those hearts,—
And, best of all, this, this, this face beyond,

This in the background, waiting on my work,
To crown the issue with a last reward!
A good time, was it not, my kingly days?
And had you not grown restless . . . but I know—
'Tis done and past; 'twas right, my instinct said;
Too live the life grew, golden and not grey,
And I'm the weak-eyed bat no sun should tempt
Out of the grange whose four walls make his world.
How could it end in any other way?
You called me, and I came home to your heart.
The triumph was, reach and stay there; since if
I reached it ere the triumph, what is lost?
Let my hands frame your face in your hair's gold,
You beautiful Lucrezia that are mine!
"Rafael did this, Andrea painted that—
The Roman's is the better when you pray,
But still the other's Virgin was his wife—"
Men will excuse me. I am glad to judge
Both pictures in your presence; clearer grows
My better fortune, I resolve to think.
For, do you know, Lucrezia, as God lives,
Said one day Agnolo, his very self,
To Rafael . . . I have known it all these years . . .
(When the young man was flaming out his thoughts
Upon a palace-wall for Rome to see,
Too lifted up in heart because of it)
"Friend, there's a certain sorry little scrub
Goes up and down our Florence, none cares how,
Who, were he set to plan and execute
As you are, pricked on by your popes and kings,
Would bring the sweat into that brow of yours!"
To Rafael's!—And indeed the arm is wrong.
I hardly dare . . . yet, only you to see,
Give the chalk here—quick, thus the line should go!
Ay, but the soul! he's Rafael! rub it out!
Still, all I care for, if he spoke the truth,
(What he? why, who but Michel Agnolo?
Do you forget already words like those?)
If really there was such a chance, so lost,—
Is, whether you're—not grateful—but more pleased.
Well, let me think so. And you smile indeed!
This hour has been an hour! Another smile?
If you would sit thus by me every night
I should work better, do you comprehend?
I mean that I should earn more, give you more.
See, it is settled dusk now; there's a star;
Morello's gone, the watch-lights show the wall,
The cue-owls speak the name we call them by.
Come from the window, love,—come in, at last,
Inside the melancholy little house
We built to be so gay with. God is just.
King Francis may forgive me; oft at nights
When I look up from painting, eyes tired out,
The walls become illumined, brick from brick
Distinct, instead of mortar, fierce bright gold,
That gold of his I did cement them with!
Let us but love each other. Must you go?
That Cousin here again? he waits outside?
Must see you—you, and not with me? Those loans ?
More gaming debts to pay? you smiled for that?
Well, let smiles buy me! have you more to spend?
While hand and eye and something of a heart
Are left me, work's my ware, and what's it worth?
I'll pay my fancy. Only let me sit
The grey remainder of the evening out,
Idle, you call it, and muse perfectly
How I could paint, were I but back in France,
One picture, just one more—the Virgin's face,
Not yours this time! I want you at my side
To hear them—that is, Michel Agnolo—
Judge all I do and tell you of its worth.

Will you? To-morrow, satisfy your friend.
I take the subjects for his corridor,
Finish the portrait out of hand—there, there,
And throw him in another thing or two
If he demurs; the whole should prove enough
To pay for this same Cousin's freak. Beside,
What's better and what's all I care about,
Get you the thirteen scudi for the ruff.
Love, does that please you? Ah, but what does he,
The Cousin! what does he to please you more?

I am grown peaceful as old age to-night.
I regret little, I would change still less.
Since there my past life lies, why alter it?
The very wrong to Francis!—it is true
I took his coin, was tempted and complied,
And built this house and sinned, and all is said.
My father and my mother died of want.
Well, had I riches of my own? you see
How one gets rich! Let each one bear his lot.
They were born poor, lived poor, and poor they died:
And I have laboured somewhat in my time
And not been paid profusely. Some good son
Paint my two hundred pictures—let him try!
No doubt, there's something strikes a balance. Yes,
You loved me quite enough, it seems to-night.
This must suffice me here. What would one have?
In heaven, perhaps, new chances, one more chance—
Four great walls in the New Jerusalem
Meted on each side by the angel's reed,
For Leonard, Rafael, Agnolo and me
To cover—the three first without a wife,
While I have mine! So—still they overcome
Because there's still Lucrezia,—as I choose.

Again the Cousin's whistle! Go, my Love.

[1855]

"DE GUSTIBUS — "

I

Your ghost will walk, you lover of trees,
(If our loves remain)
In an English lane,
By a cornfield-side a-flutter with poppies.
Hark, those two in the hazel coppice—
A boy and a girl, if the good fates please,
Making love, say,—
The happier they!
Draw yourself up from the light of the moon,
And let them pass, as they will too soon,
With the beanflowers' boon,
And the blackbird's tune,
And May, and June!

II

What I love best in all the world,
Is a castle, precipice-encurled,
In a gash of the wind-grieved Apennine.
Or look for me, old fellow of mine,
(If I get my head from out the mouth
O' the grave, and loose my spirit's bands,
And come again to the land of lands) —
In a sea-side house to the farther South,
Where the baked cicala dies of drouth,
And one sharp tree—'tis a cypress—stands,
By the many hundred years red-rusted,
Rough iron-spiked, ripe fruit-o'ercrusted,
My sentinel to guard the sands
To the water's edge. For, what expands
Before the house, but the great opaque
Blue breadth of sea without a break?
While, in the house, for ever crumbles
Some fragment of the frescoed walls,
From blisters where a scorpion sprawls.
A girl bare-footed brings, and tumbles
Down on the pavement, green-flesh melons,
And says there's news to-day—the king
Was shot at, touched in the liver-wing,
Goes with his Bourbon arm in a sling:
—She hopes they have not caught the felons.
Italy, my Italy!
Queen Mary's saying serves for me—
(When fortune's malice
Lost her—Calais) —
Open my heart and you will see
Graved inside of it, "Italy."
Such lovers old are I and she:
So it always was, so shall ever be!

[1855]

CLEON

'As certain also of your own poets have said'—

Cleon the poet (from the sprinkled isles,
Lily on lily, that o'erlace the sea,
And laugh their pride when the light wave lisps 'Greece')—
To Protos in his Tyranny: much health!

They give thy letter to me, even now:
I read and seem as if I heard thee speak.
The master of thy galley still unlades
Gift after gift; they block my court at last
And pile themselves along its portico
Royal with sunset, like a thought of thee:
And one white she-slave from the group dispersed
Of black and white slaves (like the chequer-work
Pavement, at once my nation's work and gift,
Now covered with this settle-down of doves),
One lyric woman, in her crocus vest
Woven of sea-wools, with her two white hands
Commends to me the strainer and the cup
Thy lip hath bettered ere it blesses mine.

Well-counselled, king, in thy munificence!
For so shall men remark, in such an act
Of love for him whose song gives life its joy,
Thy recognition of the use of life;
Nor call thy spirit barely adequate
To help on life in straight ways, broad enough
For vulgar souls, by ruling and the rest.
Thou, in the daily building of thy tower,—
Whether in fierce and sudden spasms of toil,
Or through dim lulls of unapparent growth,
Or when the general work 'mid good acclaim
Climbed with the eye to cheer the architect,—
Didst ne'er engage in work for mere work's sake—
Hadst ever in thy heart the luring hope
Of some eventual rest a-top of it,
Whence, all the tumult of the building hushed,
Thou first of men mightst look out to the East:
The vulgar saw thy tower, thou sawest the sun.
For this, I promise on thy festival
To pour libation, looking o'er the sea,
Making this slave narrate thy fortunes, speak
Thy great words, and describe thy royal face—
Wishing thee wholly where Zeus lives the most,
Within the eventual element of calm.

Thy letter's first requirement meets me here.
It is as thou hast heard: in one short life
I, Cleon, have effected all those things
Thou wonderingly does enumerate.
That epos on thy hundred plates of gold
Is mine,—and also mine the little chant,
So sure to rise from every fishing-bark
When, lights at prow, the seamen haul their net.
The image of the sun-god on the phare
Men turn from the sun's self to see, is mine;
The Poecile, o'er-storied its whole length,
As thou didst hear, with painting, is mine too.
I know the true proportions of a man
And woman also, not observed before;
And I have written three books on the soul,
Proving absurd all written hitherto,
And putting us to ignorance again.
For music,—why, I have combined the moods,
Inventing one. In brief, all arts are mine;
Thus much the people know and recognize,
Throughout our seventeen islands. Marvel not.
We of these latter days, with greater mind
Than our forerunners, since more composite,
Look not so great, beside their simple way,
To a judge who only sees one way at once,
One mind-point, and no other at a time,—
Compares the small part of a man of us
With some whole man of the heroic age,
Great in his way—not ours, nor meant for ours;
And ours is greater, had we skill to know.

For, what we call this life of men on earth,
This sequence of the soul's achievements here,
Being, as I find much reason to conceive,
Intended to be viewed eventually
As a great whole, not analysed to parts,
But each part having reference to all,—
How shall a certain part, pronounced complete,
Endure effacement by another part?
Was the thing done?—then, what's to do again?
See, in the chequered pavement opposite,
Suppose the artist made a perfect rhomb,
And next a lozenge, then a trapezoid—
He did not overlay them, superimpose
The new upon the old and blot it out,
But laid them on a level in his work,
Making at last a picture; there it lies.
So, first the perfect separate forms were made,
The portions of mankind—and after, so,
Occurred the combination of the same.
Or where had been a progress, otherwise?
Mankind, made up of all the single men,—
In such a synthesis the labour ends.
Now, mark me—those divine men of old time
Have reached, thou sayest well, each at one point
The outside verge that rounds our faculty;
And where they reached, who can do more than reach?
It takes but little water just to touch
At some one point the inside of a sphere,
And, as we turn the sphere, touch all the rest
In due succession: but the finer air
Which not so palpably nor obviously,
Though no less universally, can touch
The whole circumference of that emptied sphere,
Fills it more fully than the water did;
Holds thrice the weight of water in itself
Resolved into a subtler element.
And yet the vulgar call the sphere first full
Up to the visible height—and after, void;
Not knowing air's more hidden properties.
And thus our soul, misknown, cries out to Zeus
To vindicate his purpose in our life:
Why stay we on the earth unless to grow?
Long since, I imaged, wrote the fiction out,
That he or other god, descended here
And, once for all, showed simultaneously
What, in its nature, never can be shown
Piecemeal or in succession;—showed, I say,
The worth both absolute and relative
Of all his children from the birth of time,
His instruments for all appointed work.
I now go on to image,—might we hear
The judgment which should give the due to each,
Show where the labour lay and where the ease,
And prove Zeus' self, the latent, everywhere!
This is a dream:—But no dream, let us hope,
That years and days, the summers and the springs
Follow each other with unwaning powers—
The grapes which dye thy wine, are richer far
Through culture, than the wild wealth of the rock;
The suave plum than the savage-tasted drupe;
The pastured honey-bee drops choicer sweet!
The flowers turn double, and the leaves turn flowers;
That young and tender crescent-moon, thy slave,
Sleeping above her robe as buoyed by clouds,
Refines upon the women of my youth.
What, and the soul alone deteriorates?
I have not chanted verse like Homer, no—
Nor swept string like Terpander, no—nor carved
And painted men like Phidias and his friend:
I am not great as they are, point by point:
But I have entered into sympathy
With these four, running these into one soul,
Who, separate, ignored each other's art.
Say, is it nothing that I know them all?
The wild flower was the larger—I have dashed
Rose-blood upon its petals, pricked its cup's
Honey with wine, and driven its seed to fruit,
And show a better flower if not so large.
I stand myself. Refer this to the gods
Whose gift alone it is! which, shall I dare
(All pride apart) upon the absurd pretext
That such a gift by chance lay in my hand,
Discourse of lightly or depreciate?

It might have fallen to another's hand: what then?
I pass too surely—let at least truth stay!

And next, of what thou followest on to ask.
This being with me as I declare, O king,
My works, in all these varicoloured kinds,
So done by me, accepted so by men—
Thou askest if (my soul thus in men's hearts)
I must not be accounted to attain
The very crown and proper end of life?
Inquiring thence how, now life closeth up,
I face death with success in my right hand:
Whether I fear death less than dost thyself
The fortunate of men. "For" (writest thou)
"Thou leavest much behind, while I leave nought.
Thy life stays in the poems men shall sing,
The pictures men shall study; while my life,
Complete and whole now in its power and joy.
Dies altogether with my brain and arm,
Is lost indeed; since, what survives myself?
The brazen statue to o'erlook my grave,
Set on the promontory which I named.
And that—some supple courtier of my heir
Shall use its robed and sceptred arm, perhaps,
To fix the rope to, which best drags it down.
I go, then: triumph thou, who dost not go!"

Nay, thou art worthy of hearing my whole mind.
Is this apparent, when thou turn'st to muse
Upon the scheme of earth and man in chief,
That admiration grows as knowledge grows?
That imperfection means perfection hid,
Reserved in part, to grace the after-time?
If, in the morning of philosophy,
Ere aught had been recorded, nay perceived,
Thou, with the light now in thee, couldst have looked
On all earth's tenantry, from worm to bird,
Ere man had yet appeared upon the stage—
Thou wouldst have seen them perfect, and deduced
The perfectness of others yet unseen.
Conceding which,—had Zeus then questioned thee
'Shall I go on a step, improve on this,
Do more for visible creatures than is done?'
Thou wouldst have answered, 'Ay, by making each
Grow conscious in himself—by that alone.
All's perfect else: the shell sucks fast the rock,
The fish strikes through the sea, the snake both swims
And slides, forth range the beasts, the birds take flight,
Till life's mechanics can no further go—
And all this joy in natural life is put
Like fire from off thy finger into each,
So exquisitely perfect is the same.
But 'tis pure fire—and they mere matter are;
It has them, not they it: and so I choose
For man, thy last premeditated work
(If I might add a glory to the scheme)
That a third thing should stand apart from both,
A quality arise within the soul,
Which, intro-active, made to supervise
And feel the force it has, may view itself,
And so be happy.' Man might live at first
The animal life: but is there nothing more?
In due time, let him critically learn
How he lives; and, the more he gets to know
Of his own life's adaptabilities,
The more joy-giving will his life become.
Thus man, who hath this quality, is best.

But thou, king, hadst more reasonably said:
"Let progress end at once,—man make no step
Beyond the natural man, the better beast,
Using his senses, not the sense of sense."
In man there's failure, only since he left
The lower and inconscious forms of life.
We called it an advance, the rendering plain
Man's spirit might grow conscious of man's life,
And, by new lore so added to the old,
Take each step higher over the brute's head.
This grew the only life, the pleasure-house,
Watch-tower and treasure-fortress of the soul,

Which whole surrounding flats of natural life
Seemed only fit to yield subsistence to;
A tower that crowns a country. But alas!
The soul now climbs it just to perish there!
For thence we have discovered ('tis no dream—
We know this, which we had not else perceived)
That there's a world of capability
For joy, spread round about us, meant for us,
Inviting us; and still the soul craves all,
And still the flesh replies, "Take no jot more
Than ere thou clombst the tower to look abroad!
Nay, so much less, as that fatigue has brought
Deduction to it." We struggle, fain to enlarge
Our bounded physical recipiency,
Increase our power, supply fresh oil to life,
Repair the waste of age and sickness; no,
It skills not!—life's inadequate to joy,
As the soul sees joy, tempting life to take.
They praise a fountain in my garden here
Wherein a Naiad sends the water-bow
Thin from her tube; she smiles to see it rise.
What if I told her, it is just a thread
From that great river which the hills shut up,
And mock her with my leave to take the same?
The artificer has given her one small tube
Past power to widen or exchange—what boots
To know she might spout oceans if she could?
She cannot lift beyond her first thin thread,
And so a man can use but a man's joy
While he sees God's. Is it for Zeus to boast,
"See, man, how happy I live, and despair—
That I may be still happier—for thy use!"
If this were so, we could not thank our lord,
As hearts beat on to doing: 'tis not so—
Malice it is not. Is it carelessness?
Still, no. If care—where is the sign, I ask,
And get no answer: and agree in sum,
O king, with thy profound discouragement,
Who seest the wider but to sigh the more.
Most progress is most failure: thou sayest well.

The last point now:—thou dost except a case—
Holding joy not impossible to one
With artist-gifts—to such a man as I
Who leave behind me living works indeed;
For, such a poem, such a painting lives.
What? dost thou verily trip upon a word,
Confound the accurate view of what joy is
(Caught somewhat clearer by my eyes than thine)
With feeling joy? confound the knowing how
And showing how to live (my faculty)
With actually living?—Otherwise
Where is the artist's vantage o'er the king?
Because in my great epos I display
How divers men young, strong, fair, wise, can act—
Is this as though I acted? if I paint,
Carve the young Phœbus, am I therefore young?
Methinks I'm older that I bowed myself
The many years of pain that taught me art!
Indeed, to know is something, and to prove
How all this beauty might be enjoyed, is more:
But, knowing nought, to enjoy is something too.
Yon rower, with the moulded muscles there,
Lowering the sail, is nearer it than I.
I can write love-odes: thy fair slave's an ode.
I get to sing of love, when grown too grey
For being beloved: she turns to that young man
The muscles all a-ripple on his back.
I know the joy of kingship: well—thou art king!

"But," sayest thou—(and I marvel, I repeat,
To find thee tripping on a mere word) "what
Thou writest, paintest, stays: that does not die:
Sappho survives, because we sing her songs,
And Æschylus, because we read his plays!"
Why, if they live still, let them come and take
Thy slave in my despite, drink from thy cup,

Speak in my place. Thou diest while I survive?
Say rather that my fate is deadlier still,—
In this, that every day my sense of joy
Grows more acute, my soul (intensified
By power and insight) more enlarged, more keen;
While every day my hairs fall more and more,
My hand shakes, and the heavy years increase—
The horror quickening still from year to year,
The consummation coming past escape
When I shall know most, and yet least enjoy—
When all my works wherein I prove my worth,
Being present still to mock me in men's mouths,
Alive still, in the praise of such as thou,
I, I, the feeling, thinking, acting man,
The man who loved his life so over-much,
Shall sleep in my urn. It is so horrible,
I dare at times imagine to my need
Some future state revealed to us by Zeus,
Unlimited in capability
For joy, as this is in desire for joy,
—To seek which, the joy-hunger forces us:
That, stung by straitness of our life, made strait
On purpose to make prized the life at large—
Freed by the throbbing impulse we call death
We burst there as the worm into the fly,
Who, while a worm still, wants his wings. But, no!
Zeus has not yet revealed it; and, alas,
He must have done so, were it possible!

Live long and happy, and in that thought die,
Glad for what was! Farewell. And for the rest,
I cannot tell thy messenger aright
Where to deliver what he bears of thine
To one called Paulus; we have heard his fame
Indeed, if Christus be not one with him—
I know not, nor am troubled much to know.
Thou canst not think a mere barbarian Jew,
As Paulus proves to be, one circumcized,
Hath access to a secret shut from us?
Thou wrongest our philosophy, O king,
In stooping to inquire of such an one,
As if his answer could impose at all!
He writeth, doth he? well, and he may write.
Oh, the Jew findeth scholars! certain slaves
Who touched on this same isle, preached him and Christ;
And (as I gathered from a bystander)
Their doctrine could be held by no sane man.

[1855]

A GRAMMARIAN'S FUNERAL

SHORTLY AFTER THE REVIVAL OF LEARNING IN EUROPE

Let us begin and carry up this corpse,
Singing together.
Leave we the common crofts, the vulgar thorpes,
Each in its tether
Sleeping safe in the bosom of the plain,
Cared-for till cock-crow:
Look out if yonder be not day again
Rimming the rock-row!
That's the appropriate country—there, man's thought,
Rarer, intenser,
Self-gathered for an outbreak, as it ought,
Chafes in the censer.
Leave we the unlettered plain its herd and crop;
Seek we sepulture
On a tall mountain, citied to the top,
Crowded with culture!

All the peaks soar, but one the rest excels;
    Clouds overcome it;
No! yonder sparkle is the citadel's
    Circling its summit.
Thither our path lies; wind we up the heights:
    Wait ye the warning?
Our low life was the level's and the night's;
    He's for the morning.
Step to a tune, square chests, erect each head,
    'Ware the beholders!
This is our master, famous calm and dead,
    Borne on our shoulders.

Sleep, crop and herd! sleep, darkling thorpe and croft,
    Safe from the weather!
He, whom we convoy to his grave aloft,
    Singing together,
He was a man born with thy face and throat,
    Lyric Apollo!
Long he lived nameless: how should spring take note
    Winter would follow?
Till lo, the little touch, and youth was gone!
    Cramped and diminished,
Moaned he, "New measures, other feet anon!
    My dance is finished?"
No, that's the world's way: (keep the mountain-side,
    Make for the city!)
He knew the signal, and stepped on with pride
    Over men's pity;
Left play for work, and grappled with the world
    Bent on escaping:
"What's in the scroll," quoth he, "thou keepest furled?
    "Show me their shaping,
"Theirs, who most studied man, the bard and sage,—
    "Give!"—So he gowned him,
Straight got by heart that book to its last page:
    Learned, we found him!
Yea, but we found him bald too, eyes like lead,
    Accents uncertain:
"Time to taste life," another would have said,
    "Up with the curtain!"
This man said rather, "Actual life comes next?
    "Patience a moment!
"Grant I have mastered learning's crabbed text,
    "Still, there's the comment.
"Let me know all! Prate not of most or least,
    "Painful or easy!
"Even to the crumbs I'd fain eat up the feast,
    "Ay, nor feel queasy."
Oh, such a life as he resolved to live,
    When he had learned it,
When he had gathered all books had to give!
    Sooner, he spurned it.

Image the whole, then execute the parts—
Fancy the fabric
Quite, ere you build, ere steel strike fire from quartz,
Ere mortar dab brick!

(Here's the town-gate reached: there's the market-place
Gaping before us.)
Yea, this in him was the peculiar grace
(Hearten our chorus!)
Still before living he'd learn how to live—
No end to learning:
Earn the means first—God surely will contrive
Use for our earning.
Others mistrust and say "But time escapes,
"Live now or never!"
He said, "What's Time? leave Now for dogs and apes!
"Man has Forever."
Back to his book then: deeper drooped his head:
Calculus racked him:
Leaden before, his eyes grew dross of lead:
Tussis attacked him.
"Now, master, take a little rest!"—not he!
(Caution redoubled,
Step two a-breast, the way winds narrowly!)
Not a whit troubled,
Back to his studies, fresher than at first,
Fierce as a dragon
He, (soul-hydroptic with a sacred thirst)
Sucked at the flagon.
Oh, if we draw a circle premature,
Heedless of far gain,
Greedy for quick returns of profit, sure,
Bad is our bargain!
Was it not great? did not he throw on God,
(He loves the burthen)—
God's task to make the heavenly period
Perfect the earthen?
Did not he magnify the mind, show clear
Just what it all meant?
He would not discount life, as fools do here,
Paid by instalment!
He ventured neck or nothing—heaven's success
Found, or earth's failure:
"Wilt thou trust death or not?" He answered "Yes.
"Hence with life's pale lure!"
That low man seeks a little thing to do,
Sees it and does it:
This high man, with a great thing to pursue,
Dies ere he knows it.
That low man goes on adding one to one,
His hundred's soon hit:
This high man, aiming at a million,
Misses an unit.

That, has the world here—should he need the next,
Let the world mind him!
This, throws himself on God, and unperplexed
Seeking shall find him.
So, with the throttling hands of death at strife,
Ground he at grammar;
Still, thro' the rattle, parts of speech were rife:
While he could stammer
He settled *Hoti's* business—let it be!—
Properly based *Oun*—
Gave us the doctrine of the enclitic *De,*
Dead from the waist down.
Well, here's the platform, here's the proper place:
Hail to your purlieus
All ye highfliers of the feathered race,
Swallows and curlews!
Here's the top-peak; the multitude below
Live, for they can, there:
This man decided not to Live but Know—
Bury this man there?
Here—here's his place, where meteors shoot, clouds form,
Lightnings are loosened,
Stars come and go! Let joy break with the storm,
Peace let the dew send!
Lofty designs must close in like effects:
Loftily lying,
Leave him—still loftier than the world suspects,
Living and dying.

[1855]

TWO IN THE CAMPAGNA

I

I wonder do you feel to-day
As I have felt, since, hand in hand,
We sat down on the grass, to stray
In spirit better through the land,
This morn of Rome and May?

II

For me, I touched a thought, I know,
Has tantalised me many times,
(Like turns of thread the spiders throw
Mocking across our path) for rhymes
To catch at and let go.

III

Help me to hold it! First it left
The yellowing fennel, run to seed
There, branching from the brickwork's cleft,
Some old tomb's ruin: yonder weed
Took up the floating weft,

IV

Where one small orange cup amassed
Five beetles,—blind and green they grope
Among the honey-meal: and last
Everywhere on the grassy slope
I traced it. Hold it fast!

V

The champaign with its endless fleece
Of feathery grasses everywhere!
Silence and passion, joy and peace,
An everlasting wash of air—
Rome's ghost since her decease.

VI

Such life there, through such lengths of hours,
Such miracles performed in play,
Such primal naked forms of flowers,
Such letting nature have her way
While heaven looks from its towers.

VII

How say you? Let us, O my dove,
  Let us be unashamed of soul,
As earth lies bare to heaven above!
  How is it under our control
To love or not to love?

VIII

I would that you were all to me,
  You that are just so much, no more —
Nor yours, nor mine, nor slave nor free!
  Where does the fault lie? what the core
Of the wound, since wound must be?

IX

I would I could adopt your will,
  See with your eyes, and set my heart
Beating by yours, and drink my fill
  At your soul's springs, — your part, my part
In life, for good and ill.

X

No. I yearn upward, touch you close,
  Then stand away. I kiss your cheek,
Catch your soul's warmth, — I pluck the rose
  And love it more than tongue can speak—
Then the good minute goes.

XI

Already how am I so far
  Out of that minute? Must I go
Still like the thistle-ball, no bar,
  Onward, whenever light winds blow,
Fixed by no friendly star?

XII

Just when I seemed about to learn!
  Where is the thread now? Off again!
The old trick! Only I discern —
  Infinite passion, and the pain
Of finite hearts that yearn.

[1854?] [1855]

ABT VOGLER

(AFTER HE HAS BEEN EXTEMPORIZING UPON THE MUSICAL INSTRUMENT OF HIS INVENTION)

I

Would that the structure brave, the manifold music I build,
  Bidding my organ obey, calling its keys to their work,
Claiming each slave of the sound, at a touch, as when Solomon willed
  Armies of angels that soar, legions of demons that lurk,
Man, brute, reptile, fly, — alien of end and of aim,
  Adverse, each from the other heaven-high, hell-deep removed,—
Should rush into sight at once as he named the ineffable Name,
  And pile him a palace straight, to pleasure the princess he loved!

II

Would it might tarry like his, the beautiful building of mine,
  This which my keys in a crowd pressed and importuned to raise!
Ah, one and all, how they helped, would dispart now and now combine,
  Zealous to hasten the work, heighten their master his praise!
And one would bury his brow with a blind plunge down to hell,
  Burrow awhile and build, broad on the roots of things,
Then up again swim into sight, having based me my palace well,
  Founded it, fearless of flame, flat on the nether springs.

III

And another would mount and march, like the excellent minion he was,
  Ay, another and yet another, one crowd but with many a crest,
Raising my rampired walls of gold as transparent as glass,
  Eager to do and die, yield each his place to the rest:

For higher still and higher (as a runner tips with fire,
When a great illumination surprises a festal night—
Outlining round and round Rome's dome from space to spire)
Up, the pinnacled glory reached, and the pride of my soul was in sight.

IV

In sight? Not half! for it seemed, it was certain, to match man's birth,
Nature in turn conceived, obeying an impulse as I;
And the emulous heaven yearned down, made effort to reach the earth,
As the earth had done her best, in my passion, to scale the sky:
Novel splendours burst forth, grew familiar and dwelt with mine,
Not a point nor peak but found and fixed its wandering star;
Meteor-moons, balls of blaze: and they did not pale nor pine,
For earth had attained to heaven, there was no more near nor far.

V

Nay more; for there wanted not who walked in the glare and glow,
Presences plain in the place; or, fresh from the Protoplast,
Furnished for ages to come, when a kindlier wind should blow,
Lured now to begin and live, in a house to their liking at last;
Or else the wonderful Dead who have passed through the body and gone,
But were back once more to breathe in an old world worth their new:
What never had been, was now; what was, as it shall be anon;
And what is,—shall I say, matched both? for I was made perfect too.

VI

All through my keys that gave their sounds to a wish of my soul,
All through my soul that praised as its wish flowed visibly forth,
All through music and me! For think, had I painted the whole,
Why, there it had stood, to see, nor the process so wonder-worth:
Had I written the same, made verse—still, effect proceeds from cause,
Ye know why the forms are fair, ye hear how the tale is told:
It is all triumphant art, but art in obedience to laws,
Painter and poet are proud in the artist-list enrolled:—

VII

But here is the finger of God, a flash of the will that can,
Existent behind all laws, that made them and, lo, they are!
And I know not if, save in this, such gift be allowed to man,
That out of three sounds he frame, not a fourth sound, but a star.
Consider it well: each tone of our scale in itself is nought;
It is everywhere in the world—loud, soft, and all is said:
Give it to me to use! I mix it with two in my thought:
And, there! Ye have heard and seen: consider and bow the head!

VIII

Well, it is gone at last, the palace of music I reared;
Gone! and the good tears start, the praises that come too slow;
For one is assured at first, one scarce can say that he feared,
That he even gave it a thought, the gone thing was to go.
Never to be again! But many more of the kind
As good, nay, better perchance: is this your comfort to me?
To me, who must be saved because I cling with my mind
To the same, same self, same love, same God: ay, what was shall be.

IX

Therefore to whom turn I but to Thee, the ineffable Name?
  Builder and maker, thou, of houses not made with hands!
What, have fear of change from thee who art ever the same?
  Doubt that thy power can fill the heart that thy power expands?
There shall never be one lost good! What was, shall live as before;
  The evil is null, is nought, is silence implying sound;
What was good, shall be good, with, for evil, so much good more;
  On the earth the broken arcs; in the heaven, a perfect round.

X

All we have willed or hoped or dreamed of good, shall exist;
  Not its semblance, but itself; no beauty, nor good, nor power
Whose voice has gone forth, but each survives for the melodist
  When eternity affirms the conception of an hour.
The high that proved too high, the heroic for earth too hard,
  The passion that left the ground to lose itself in the sky,
Are music sent up to God by the lover and the bard;
  Enough that he heard it once; we shall hear it by-and-by.

XI

And what is our failure here but a triumph's evidence
  For the fulness of the days? Have we withered or agonized?
Why else was the pause prolonged but that singing might issue thence?
  Why rushed the discords in, but that harmony should be prized?
Sorrow is hard to bear, and doubt is slow to clear,
  Each sufferer says his say, his scheme of the weal and woe:
But God has a few of us whom he whispers in the ear;
  The rest may reason and welcome: 'tis we musicians know.

XII

Well, it is earth with me; silence resumes her reign:
  I will be patient and proud, and soberly acquiesce.
Give me the keys. I feel for the common chord again,
  Sliding by semitones, till I sink to the minor,—yes,
And I blunt it into a ninth, and I stand on alien ground,
  Surveying a while the heights I rolled from into the deep;
Which, hark, I have dared and done, for my resting-place is found,
  The C Major of this life: so, now I will try to sleep.

[1864]

RABBI BEN EZRA

Grow old along with me!
The best is yet to be,
The last of life, for which the first was
    made:
Our times are in His hand
Who saith 'A whole I planned,
Youth shows but half; trust God: see all,
    nor be afraid!'

II

Not that, amassing flowers,
Youth sighed 'Which rose make ours,
Which lily leave and then as best recall?'
Not that, admiring stars,
It yearned 'Nor Jove, nor Mars;
Mine be some figured flame which blends,
    transcends them all!'

III

Not for such hopes and fears
Annulling youth's brief years,

Do I remonstrate: folly wide the mark!
Rather I prize the doubt
Low kinds exist without,
Finished and finite clods, untroubled by a spark.

IV

Poor vaunt of life indeed,
Were man but formed to feed
On joy, to solely seek and find and feast:
Such feasting ended, then
As sure an end to men;
Irks care the crop-full bird? Frets doubt the maw-crammed beast?

V

Rejoice we are allied
To That which doth provide
And not partake, effect and not receive!
A spark disturbs our clod;
Nearer we hold of God
Who gives, than of His tribes that take, I must believe.

VI

Then, welcome each rebuff
That turns earth's smoothness rough,
Each sting that bids nor sit nor stand but go!
Be our joys three-parts pain!
Strive, and hold cheap the strain;
Learn, nor account the pang; dare, never grudge the throe!

VII

For thence,—a paradox
Which comforts while it mocks,—
Shall life succeed in that it seems to fail:
What I aspired to be,
And was not, comforts me:
A brute I might have been, but would not sink i' the scale.

VIII

What is he but a brute
Whose flesh has soul to suit,
Whose spirit works lest arms and legs want play?
To man, propose this test—
Thy body at its best,
How far can that project thy soul on its lone way?

IX

Yet gifts should prove their use:
I own the Past profuse
Of power each side, perfection every turn:
Eyes, ears took in their dole,
Brain treasured up the whole;
Should not the heart beat once 'How good to live and learn?'

X

Not once beat 'Praise be Thine!
I see the whole design,
I, who saw power, see now love perfect too:
Perfect I call Thy plan:
Thanks that I was a man!
Maker, remake, complete,—I trust what Thou shalt do!'

XI

For pleasant is this flesh;
Our soul in its rose-mesh
Pulled ever to the earth, still yearns for rest:
Would we some prize might hold
To match those manifold
Possessions of the brute,—gain most, as we did best!

XII

Let us not always say
'Spite of this flesh to-day
I strove, made head, gained ground upon the whole!'
As the bird wings and sings,
Let us cry 'All good things
Are ours, nor soul helps flesh more, now, than flesh helps soul!'

XIII

Therefore I summon age
To grant youth's heritage,
Life's struggle having so far reached its term:
Thence shall I pass, approved
A man, for aye removed
From the developed brute; a god though in the germ.

XIV

And I shall thereupon
Take rest, ere I be gone
Once more on my adventure brave and new:

Fearless and unperplexed,
When I wage battle next,
What weapons to select, what armour to indue.

XV

Youth ended, I shall try
My gain or loss thereby;
Leave the fire ashes, what survives is gold:
And I shall weigh the same,
Give life its praise or blame:
Young, all lay in dispute; I shall know, being old.

XVI

For note, when evening shuts,
A certain moment cuts
The deed off, calls the glory from the grey:
A whisper from the west
Shoots—'Add this to the rest,
Take it and try its worth: here dies another day.'

XVII

So, still within this life,
Though lifted o'er its strife,
Let me discern, compare, pronounce at last,
'This rage was right i' the main,
That acquiescence vain:
The Future I may face now I have proved the Past.'

XVIII

For more is not reserved
To man, with soul just nerved
To act to-morrow what he learns to-day:
Here, work enough to watch
The Master work, and catch
Hints of the proper craft, tricks of the tool's true play.

XIX

As it was better, youth
Should strive, through acts uncouth,
Toward making, than repose on aught found made;
So, better, age, exempt
From strife, should know, than tempt
Further. Thou waitedest age; wait death nor be afraid!

XX

Enough now, if the Right
And Good and Infinite
Be named here, as thou callest thy hand thine own,
With knowledge absolute,
Subject to no dispute
From fools that crowded youth, nor let thee feel alone.

XXI

Be there, for once and all,
Severed great minds from small,
Announced to each his station in the Past!
Was I, the world arraigned,
Were they, my soul disdained,
Right? Let age speak the truth and give us peace at last!

XXII

Now, who shall arbitrate?
Ten men love what I hate,
Shun what I follow, slight what I receive;
Ten, who in ears and eyes
Match me: we all surmise,
They this thing, and I that: whom shall my soul believe?

XXIII

Not on the vulgar mass
Called 'work,' must sentence pass,
Things done, that took the eye and had the price;
O'er which, from level stand,
The low world laid its hand,
Found straightway to its mind, could value in a trice:

XXIV

But all, the world's coarse thumb
And finger failed to plumb,
So passed in making up the main account;
All instincts immature,
All purposes unsure,
That weighed not as his work, yet swelled the man's amount:

XXV

Thoughts hardly to be packed
Into a narrow act,
Fancies that broke through language and escaped;
All I could never be,
All, men ignored in me,
This, I was worth to God, whose wheel the pitcher shaped.

XXVI

Ay, note that Potter's wheel,
That metaphor! and feel
Why time spins fast, why passive lies our clay,—
Thou, to whom fools propound,
When the wine makes its round,
'Since life fleets, all is change; the Past gone, seize to-day!'

XXVII

Fool! All that is, at all,
Lasts ever, past recall;
Earth changes, but thy soul and God stand sure:
What entered into thee,
That was, is, and shall be:
Time's wheel runs back or stops; Potter and clay endure.

XXVIII

He fixed thee mid this dance
Of plastic circumstance,
This Present, thou, forsooth, wouldst fain arrest:
Machinery just meant
To give thy soul its bent,
Try thee and turn thee forth, sufficiently impressed.

XXIX

What though the earlier grooves
Which ran the laughing loves
Around thy base, no longer pause and press?
What though, about thy rim,
Skull-things in order grim
Grow out, in graver mood, obey the sterner stress?

XXX

Look not thou down but up!
To uses of a cup,
The festal board, lamp's flash and trumpet's peal,
The new wine's foaming flow,
The Master's lips aglow!
Thou, heaven's consummate cup, what need'st thou with earth's wheel?

XXXI

But I need, now as then,
Thee, God, who mouldest men;
And since, not even while the whirl was worst,
Did I,—to the wheel of life
With shapes and colours rife,
Bound dizzily,—mistake my end, to slake Thy thirst:

XXXII

So, take and use Thy work:
Amend what flaws may lurk,
What strain o' the stuff, what warpings past the aim!
My times be in Thy hand!
Perfect the cup as planned!
Let age approve of youth, and death complete the same!

[1864]

CALIBAN UPON SETEBOS;

OR, NATURAL THEOLOGY IN THE ISLAND

"Thou thoughtest that I was altogether such an one as thyself."

['Will sprawl, now that the heat of day is best,
Flat on his belly in the pit's much mire,
With elbows wide, fists clenched to prop his chin.
And, while he kicks both feet in the cool slush,
And feels about his spine small eft-things course,
Run in and out each arm, and make him laugh:
And while above his head a pompion-plant,
Coating the cave-top as a brow its eye,
Creeps down to touch and tickle hair and beard,
And now a flower drops with a bee inside,
And now a fruit to snap at, catch and crunch,—
He looks out o'er yon sea which sunbeams cross
And recross till they weave a spider-web,
(Meshes of fire, some great fish breaks at times)
And talks to his own self, howe'er he please,
Touching that other, whom his dam called God.

Because to talk about Him, vexes—ha,
Could He but know! and time to vex is now,
When talk is safer than in winter-time.
Moreover Prosper and Miranda sleep
In confidence he drudges at their task,
And it is good to cheat the pair, and gibe,
Letting the rank tongue blossom into speech.]

Setebos, Setebos, and Setebos!
'Thinketh, He dwelleth i' the cold o' the moon.

'Thinketh, He made it, with the sun to match,
But not the stars; the stars came otherwise;
Only made clouds, winds, meteors, such as that:
Also this isle, what lives and grows thereon,
And snaky sea which rounds and ends the same.

'Thinketh, it came of being ill at ease:
He hated that He cannot change His cold,
Nor cure its ache. 'Hath spied an icy fish
That longed to 'scape the rock-stream where she lived,
And throw herself within the lukewarm brine
O' the lazy sea her stream thrusts far amid,
A crystal spike 'twixt two warm walls of wave;
Only she ever sickened, found repulse
At the other kind of water, not her life,
(Green-dense and dim-delicious, bred o' the sun)
Flounced back from bliss she was not born to breathe,
And in her old bounds buried her despair,
Hating and loving warmth alike: so He.

'Thinketh, He made thereat the sun, this isle,
Trees and the fowls here, beast and creeping thing.
Yon otter, sleek-wet, black, lithe as a leech;
Yon auk, one fire-eye in a ball of foam,
That floats and feeds; a certain badger brown
He hath watched hunt with that slant white-wedge eye
By moonlight; and the pie with the long tongue
That pricks deep into oakwarts for a worm,
And says a plain word when she finds her prize,
But will not eat the ants; the ants themselves
That build a wall of seeds and settled stalks
About their hole—He made all these and more,
Made all we see, and us, in spite: how else?
He could not, Himself, make a second self
To be His mate; as well have made Himself.
He would not make what He mislikes or slights,
An eyesore to Him, or not worth His pains:
But did, in envy, listlessness or sport,
Make what Himself would fain, in a manner, be—
Weaker in most points, stronger in a few,
Worthy, and yet mere playthings all the while,
Things He admires and mocks too,—that is it.
Because, so brave, so better though they be,
It nothing skills if He begin to plague.
Look now, I melt a gourd-fruit into mash,
Add honeycomb and pods, I have perceived,
Which bite like finches when they bill and kiss,—
Then, when froth rises bladdery, drink up all,
Quick, quick, till maggots scamper through my brain;
And throw me on my back i' the seeded thyme,
And wanton, wishing I were born a bird.
Put case, unable to be what I wish,
I yet could make a live bird out of clay:
Would not I take clay, pinch my Caliban
Able to fly?—for, there, see, he hath wings,
And great comb like the hoopoe's to admire,
And there, a sting to do his foes offence,
There, and I will that he begin to live,
Fly to yon rock-top, nip me off the horns
Of grigs high up that make the merry din.

Saucy through their veined wings, and mind me not.
In which feat, if his leg snapped, brittle clay,
And he lay stupid-like,—why, I should laugh;
And if he, spying me, should fall to weep,
Beseech me to be good, repair his wrong,
Bid his poor leg smart less or grow again, —
Well, as the chance were, this might take or else
Not take my fancy: I might hear his cry,
And give the manikin three sound legs for one,
Or pluck the other off, leave him like an egg,
And lessoned he was mine and merely clay.
Were this no pleasure, lying in the thyme,
Drinking the mash, with brain become alive,
Making and marring clay at will? So He.

'Thinketh, such shows nor right nor wrong in Him,
Nor kind, nor cruel: He is strong and Lord.
'Am strong myself compared to yonder crabs
That march now from the mountain to the sea;
'Let twenty pass, and stone the twenty-first,
Loving not, hating not, just choosing so.
'Say, the first straggler that boasts purple spots
Shall join the file, one pincer twisted off;
'Say, this bruised fellow shall receive a worm,
And two worms he whose nippers end in red;
As it likes me each time, I do: so He.

Well then, 'supposeth He is good i' the main,
Placable if His mind and ways were guessed,
But rougher than His handiwork, be sure!
Oh, He hath made things worthier than Himself,
And envieth that, so helped, such things do more
Than He who made them! What consoles but this?
That they, unless through Him, do nought at all,
And must submit: what other use in things?
'Hath cut a pipe of pithless elder-joint
That, blown through, gives exact the scream o' the jay
When from her wing you twitch the feathers blue:
Sound this, and little birds that hate the jay
Flock within stone's throw, glad their foe is hurt:
Put case such pipe could prattle and boast forsooth
"I catch the birds, I am the crafty thing,
"I make the cry my maker cannot make
"With his great round mouth; he must blow through mine!"
Would not I smash it with my foot? So He.

But wherefore rough, why cold and ill at ease?
Aha, that is a question! Ask, for that,
What knows,—the something over Setebos
That made Him, or He, may be, found and fought,
Worsted, drove off and did to nothing, perchance.
There may be something quiet o'er His head,
Out of His reach, that feels nor joy nor grief,
Since both derive from weakness in some way.
I joy because the quails come; would not joy
Could I bring quails here when I have a mind:
This Quiet, all it hath a mind to, doth.
'Esteemeth stars the outposts of its couch.
But never spends much thought nor care that way.
It may look up, work up,—the worse for those
It works on! 'Careth but for Setebos
The many-handed as a cuttle-fish,
Who, making Himself feared through what He does,
Looks up, first, and perceives He cannot soar
To what is quiet and hath happy life;
Next looks down here, and out of very spite
Makes this a bauble-world to ape yon real,

These good things to match those as hips do grapes.
'Tis solace making baubles, ay, and sport.
Himself peeped late, eyed Prosper at his books
Careless and lofty, lord now of the isle:
Vexed, 'stitched a book of broad leaves, arrow-shaped,
Wrote thereon, he knows what, prodigious words;
Has peeled a wand and called it by a name;
Weareth at whiles for an enchanter's robe
The eyed skin of a supple ocelot;
And hath an ounce sleeker than youngling mole,
A four-legged serpent he makes cower and couch,
Now snarl, now hold its breath and mind his eye,
And saith she is Miranda and my wife:
'Keeps for his Ariel a tall pouch-bill crane
He bids go wade for fish and straight disgorge;
Also a sea-beast, lumpish, which he snared,
Blinded the eyes of, and brought somewhat tame,
And split its toe-webs, and now pens the drudge
In a hole o' the rock and calls him Caliban;
A bitter heart, that bides its time and bites.
'Plays thus at being Prosper in a way,
Taketh his mirth with make-believes: so He.

His dam held that the Quiet made all things
Which Setebos vexed only: 'holds not so.
Who made them weak, meant weakness He might vex.
Had He meant other, while His hand was in,
Why not make horny eyes no thorn could prick,
Or plate my scalp with bone against the snow,
Or overscale my flesh 'neath joint and joint,
Like an orc's armour? Ay,—so spoil His sport!
He is the One now: only He doth all.

'Saith, He may like, perchance, what profits him.
Ay, himself loves what does him good; but why?
'Gets good no otherwise. This blinded beast
Loves whoso places flesh-meat on his nose,
But, had he eyes, would want no help, but hate
Or love, just as it liked him: He hath eyes.
Also it pleaseth Setebos to work,
Use all His hands, and exercise much craft,
By no means for the love of what is worked.
'Tasteth, himself, no finer good i' the world
When all goes right, in this safe summer-time,
And he wants little, hungers, aches not much,
Than trying what to do with wit and strength.
'Falls to make something: 'piled yon pile of turfs,
And squared and stuck there squares of soft white chalk,
And, with a fish-tooth, scratched a moon on each,
And set up endwise certain spikes of tree,
And crowned the whole with a sloth's skull a-top,
Found dead i' the woods, too hard for one to kill.
No use at all i' the work, for work's sole sake;
'Shall some day knock it down again: so He.

'Saith he is terrible: watch His feats in proof!
One hurricane will spoil six good months' hope.
He hath a spite against me, that I know,
Just as He favours Prosper, who knows why?
So it is, all the same, as well I find.
'Wove wattles half the winter, fenced them firm
With stone and stake to stop she-tortoises
Crawling to lay their eggs here: well, one wave,
Feeling the foot of Him upon its neck,
Gaped as a snake does, lolled out its large tongue,

And licked the whole labour flat: so much for spite.
'Saw a ball flame down late (yonder it lies)
Where, half an hour before, I slept i' the shade:
Often they scatter sparkles: there is force!
'Dug up a newt He may have envied once
And turned to stone, shut up inside a stone.
Please Him and hinder this?—What Prosper does?
Aha, if He would tell me how! Not He!
There is the sport: discover how or die!
All need not die, for of the things o' the isle
Some flee afar, some dive, some run up trees;
Those at His mercy,—why, they please Him most
When . . . when . . . well, never try the same way twice!
Repeat what act has pleased, He may grow wroth.
You must not know His ways, and play Him off,
Sure of the issue. 'Doth the like himself:
'Spareth a squirrel that it nothing fears
But steals the nut from underneath my thumb,
And when I threat, bites stoutly in defence:
'Spareth an urchin that, contrariwise,
Curls up into a ball, pretending death
For fright at my approach: the two ways please.
But what would move my choler more than this,
That either creature counted on its life
To-morrow and next day and all days to come,
Saying forsooth in the inmost of its heart,
"Because he did so yesterday with me,
"And otherwise with such another brute,
"So must he do henceforth and always."—Ay?
'Would teach the reasoning couple what "must" means!
'Doth as he likes, or wherefore Lord? So He.

'Conceiveth all things will continue thus,
And we shall have to live in fear of Him
So long as He lives, keeps His strength: no change,
If He have done His best, make no new world
To please Him more, so leave off watching this,—
If He surprise not even the Quiet's self
Some strange day,—or, suppose, grow into it
As grubs grow butterflies: else, here are we,
And there is He, and nowhere help at all.

'Believeth with the life, the pain shall stop.
His dam held different, that after death
He both plagued enemies and feasted friends:
Idly! He doth His worst in this our life,
Giving just respite lest we die through pain,
Saving last pain for worst,—with which, an end.
Meanwhile the best way to escape His ire
Is, not to seem too happy. 'Sees, himself,
Yonder two flies, with purple films and pink,
Bask on the pompion-bell above: kills both.
'Sees two black painful beetles roll their ball
On head and tail as if to save their lives:
Moves them the stick away they strive to clear.

Even so, 'would have Him misconceive, suppose
This Caliban strives hard and ails no less,
And always, above all else, envies Him.
Wherefore he mainly dances on dark nights,
Moans in the sun, gets under holes to laugh,
And never speaks his mind save housed as now:
Outside, 'groans, curses. If He caught me here,
O'erheard this speech, and asked "What chucklest at?"
'Would, to appease Him, cut a finger off,
Or of my three kid yearlings burn the best,
Or let the toothsome apples rot on tree,
Or push my tame beast for the orc to taste:
While myself lit a fire, and made a song
And sung it, *"What I hate, be consecrate*
"To celebrate Thee and Thy state, no mate
"For Thee; what see for envy in poor me?"

Hoping the while, since evils sometimes mend,
Warts rub away and sores are cured with slime,
That some strange day, will either the Quiet catch
And conquer Setebos, or likelier He
Decrepit may doze, doze, as good as die.

[What, what? A curtain o'er the world at once!
Crickets stop hissing; not a bird—or, yes,
There scuds His raven that has told Him all!
It was fool's play, this prattling! Ha! The wind
Shoulders the pillared dust, death's house o' the move,
And fast invading fires begin! White blaze—
A tree's head snaps—and there, there, there, there, there, there,
His thunder follows! Fool to gibe at Him!
Lo! 'Lieth flat and loveth Setebos!
'Maketh his teeth meet through his upper lip,
Will let those quails fly, will not eat this month
One little mess of whelks, so he may 'scape!]

[1864]

CONFESSIONS

I

What is he buzzing in my ears?
'Now that I come to die,
Do I view the world as a vale of tears?'
Ah, reverend sir, not I!

II

What I viewed there once, what I view again
Where the physic bottles stand
On the table's edge,—is a suburb lane,
With a wall to my bedside hand.

III

That lane sloped, much as the bottles do,
From a house you could descry
O'er the garden-wall: is the curtain blue
Or green to a healthy eye?

IV

To mine, it serves for the old June weather
Blue above lane and wall;
And that farthest bottle labelled 'Ether'
Is the house o'er-topping all.

V

At a terrace, somewhat near the stopper,
There watched for me, one June,
A girl: I know, sir, it's improper,
My poor mind's out of tune.

VI

Only, there was a way . . . you crept
Close by the side, to dodge
Eyes in the house, two eyes except:
They styled their house 'The Lodge.'

VII

What right had a lounger up their lane?
But, by creeping very close,
With the good wall's help,—their eyes might strain
And stretch themselves to Oes,

VIII

Yet never catch her and me together,
As she left the attic, there,
By the rim of the bottle labelled 'Ether,'
And stole from stair to stair,

IX

And stood by the rose-wreathed gate. Alas,
We loved, sir—used to meet:
How sad and bad and mad it was—
But then, how it was sweet!

[1860] [1864]

YOUTH AND ART

I

It once might have been, once only:
We lodged in a street together,
You, a sparrow on the housetop lonely,
I, a lone she-bird of his feather.

II

Your trade was with sticks and clay,
You thumbed, thrust, patted and polished,
Then laughed "They will see some day
Smith made, and Gibson demolished."

III

My business was song, song, song;
  I chirped, cheeped, trilled and twittered,
"Kate Brown's on the boards ere long,
  And Grisi's existence embittered!"

IV

I earned no more by a warble
  Than you by a sketch in plaster;
You wanted a piece of marble,
  I needed a music-master.

V

We studied hard in our styles,
  Chipped each at a crust like Hindoos,
For air, looked out on the tiles,
  For fun, watched each other's windows.

VI

You lounged, like a boy of the South,
  Cap and blouse—nay, a bit of beard too;
Or you got it, rubbing your mouth
  With fingers the clay adhered to.

VII

And I—soon managed to find
  Weak points in the flower-fence facing,
Was forced to put up a blind
  And be safe in my corset-lacing.

VIII

No harm! It was not my fault
  If you never turned your eyes' tail up,
As I shook upon E *in alt,*
  Or ran the chromatic scale up:

IX

For spring bade the sparrows pair,
  And the boys and girls gave guesses,
And stalls in our street looked rare
  With bulrush and watercresses.

X

Why did not you pinch a flower
  In a pellet of clay and fling it?
Why did not I put a power
  Of thanks in a look, or sing it?

XI

I did look, sharp as a lynx,
  (And yet the memory rankles,)
When models arrived, some minx
  Tripped up-stairs, she and her ankles.

XII

But I think I gave you as good!
  "That foreign fellow,—who can know
How she pays, in a playful mood,
  For his tuning her that piano?"

XIII

Could you say so, and never say,
  "Suppose we join hands and fortunes,
And I fetch her from over the way,
  "Her, piano, and long tunes and short tunes?"

XIV

No, no: you would not be rash,
  Nor I rasher and something over:
You've to settle yet Gibson's hash,
  And Grisi yet lives in clover.

XV

But you meet the Prince at the Board,
  I'm queen myself at *bals-paré,*[1]
I've married a rich old lord,
  And you're dubbed knight and an R.A.

XVI

Each life unfulfilled, you see;
  It hangs still, patchy and scrappy:
We have not sighed deep, laughed free,
  Starved, feasted, despaired,—been happy.

XVII

And nobody calls you a dunce,
  And people suppose me clever:
This could but have happened once,
  And we missed it, lost it for ever.

[1861?] [1864]

[1] masquerades.

PROSPICE

Fear death?—to feel the fog in my throat,
  The mist in my face,
When the snows begin, and the blasts denote
  I am nearing the place,

The power of the night, the press of the storm,
  The post of the foe;
Where he stands, the Arch Fear in a visible form,
  Yet the strong man must go:
For the journey is done and the summit attained,
  And the barriers fall,
Though a battle 's to fight ere the guerdon be gained,
  The reward of it all.
I was ever a fighter, so—one fight more,
  The best and the last!
I would hate that death bandaged my eyes, and forbore,
  And bade me creep past.
No! let me taste the whole of it, fare like my peers
  The heroes of old,
Bear the brunt, in a minute pay glad life's arrears
  Of pain, darkness and cold.
For sudden the worst turns the best to the brave,
  The black minute 's at end,
And the elements' rage, the fiend-voices that rave,
  Shall dwindle, shall blend,
Shall change, shall become first a peace out of pain,
  Then a light, then thy breast,
O thou soul of my soul! I shall clasp thee again,
  And with God be the rest!

[1861?] [1864]

EPILOGUE

FIRST SPEAKER (*as David*)

I

On the first of the Feast of Feasts,
  The Dedication Day,
When the Levites joined the Priests
  At the Altar in robed array,
Gave signal to sound and say,—

II

When the thousands, rear and van,
  Swarming with one accord
Became as a single man
  (Look, gesture, thought and word)
In praising and thanking the Lord,—

III

When the singers lift up their voice,
  And the trumpets made endeavour,
Sounding, "In God rejoice!"
  Saying, "In Him rejoice
"Whose mercy endureth for ever!"—

IV

Then the Temple filled with a cloud,
  Even the House of the Lord;
Porch bent and pillar bowed:
  For the presence of the Lord,
In the glory of His cloud,
  Had filled the House of the Lord.

SECOND SPEAKER (*as Renan*)

Gone now! All gone across the dark so far,
  Sharpening fast, shuddering ever, shutting still,
Dwindling into the distance, dies that star
  Which came, stood, opened once! We gazed our fill
With upturned faces on as real a Face
  That, stooping from grave music and mild fire,
Took in our homage, made a visible place
  Through many a depth of glory, gyre on gyre,
For the dim human tribute. Was this true?
  Could man indeed avail, mere praise of his,
To help by rapture God's own rapture too,
  Thrill with a heart's red tinge that pure pale bliss?
Why did it end? Who failed to beat the breast,
  And shriek, and throw the arms protesting wide,
When a first shadow showed the star addressed
  Itself to motion, and on either side
The rims contracted as the rays retired;
  The music, like a fountain's sickening pulse,
Subsided on itself; awhile transpired
  Some vestige of a Face no pangs convulse,
No prayers retard; then even this was gone,
  Lost in the night at last. We, lone and left
Silent through centuries, ever and anon
  Venture to probe again the vault bereft
Of all now save the lesser lights, a mist
  Of multitudinous points, yet suns, men say—
And this leaps ruby, this lurks amethyst,
  But where may hide what came and loved our clay?
How shall the sage detect in yon expanse
  The star which chose to stoop and stay for us?
Unroll the records! Hailed ye such advance
  Indeed, and did your hope evanish thus?
Watchers of twilight, is the worst averred?
  We shall not look up, know ourselves are seen,
Speak, and be sure that we again are heard,
  Acting or suffering, have the disk's serene
Reflect our life, absorb an earthly flame,
  Nor doubt that, were mankind inert and numb,
Its core had never crimsoned all the same,
  Nor, missing ours, its music fallen dumb?
Oh, dread succession to a dizzy post,
  Sad sway of sceptre whose mere touch appals,
Ghastly dethronement, cursed by those the most
  On whose repugnant brow the crown next falls!

THIRD SPEAKER

I

Witless alike of will and way divine,
How heaven's high with earth's low should intertwine!
Friends, I have seen through your eyes: now use mine!

II

Take the least man of all mankind, as I;
Look at his head and heart, find how and why
He differs from his fellows utterly:

III

Then, like me, watch when nature by degrees
Grows alive round him, as in Arctic seas
(They said of old) the instinctive water flees

IV

Toward some elected point of central rock,
As though, for its sake only, roamed the flock
Of waves about the waste: awhile they mock

V

With radiance caught for the occasion,—hues
Of blackest hell now, now such reds and blues
As only heaven could fitly interfuse,—

VI

The mimic monarch of the whirlpool, king
O' the current for a minute: then they wring
Up by the roots and oversweep the thing,

VII

And hasten off, to play again elsewhere
The same part, choose another peak as bare,
They find and flatter, feast and finish there.

VIII

When you see what I tell you,—nature dance
About each man of us, retire, advance,
As though the pageant's end were to enhance

IX

His worth, and—once the life, his product, gained—
Roll away elsewhere, keep the strife sustained,
And show thus real, a thing the North but feigned—

X

When you acknowledge that one world could do
All the diverse work, old yet ever new,
Divide us, each from other, me from you,—

XI

Why, where's the need of Temple, when the walls
O' the world are that? What use of swells and falls
From Levites' choir, Priests' cries, and trumpet-calls?

XII

That one Face, far from vanish, rather grows,
Or decomposes but to recompose,
Become my universe that feels and knows.

[1863–64?] [1864]

THE RING AND THE BOOK

POMPILIA

I am just seventeen years and five months old,
And, if I lived one day more, three full weeks;
'Tis writ so in the church's register,
Lorenzo in Lucina, all my names
At length, so many names for one poor child,
—Francesca Camilla Vittoria Angela
Pompilia Comparini,—laughable!
Also 'tis writ that I was married there
Four years ago; and they will add, I hope,
When they insert my death, a word or two,—
Omitting all about the mode of death,—
This, in its place, this which one cares to know,
That I had been a mother of a son
Exactly two weeks. It will be through grace
O' the Curate, not through any claim I have;
Because the boy was born at, so baptized
Close to, the Villa, in the proper church:
A pretty church, I say no word against,
Yet stranger-like,—while this Lorenzo seems
My own particular place, I always say.
I used to wonder, when I stood scarce high
As the bed here, what the marble lion meant,
With half his body rushing from the wall,
Eating the figure of a prostrate man—
(To the right, it is, of entry by the door)
An ominous sign to one baptized like me,
Married, and to be buried there, I hope.
And they should add, to have my life complete,
He is a boy and Gaetan by name—
Gaetano, for a reason,—if the friar
Don Celestine will ask this grace for me
Of Curate Ottoboni: he it was
Baptized me: he remembers my whole life
As I do his grey hair.

All these few things
I know are true,—will you remember them?
Because time flies. The surgeon cared for me,

To count my wounds,—twenty-two dagger-wounds,
Five deadly, but I do not suffer much—
Or too much pain,—and am to die to-night.

Oh how good God is that my babe was born,
—Better than born, baptized and hid away
Before this happened, safe from being hurt!
That had been sin God could not well forgive:
He was too young to smile and save himself.
When they took, two days after he was born,
My babe away from me to be baptized
And hidden awhile, for fear his foe should find,—
The country-woman, used to nursing babes,
Said "Why take on so? where is the great loss?
"These next three weeks he will but sleep and feed,
"Only begin to smile at the month's end;
"He would not know you, if you kept him here,
"Sooner than that; so, spend three merry weeks
"Snug in the Villa, getting strong and stout,
"And then I bring him back to be your own,
"And both of you may steal to—we know where!"
The month—there wants of it two weeks this day!
Still, I half fancied when I heard the knock
At the Villa in the dusk, it might prove she—
Come to say "Since he smiles before the time,
"Why should I cheat you out of one good hour?
"Back I have brought him; speak to him and judge!"
Now I shall never see him; what is worse,
When he grows up and gets to be my age,
He will seem hardly more than a great boy;
And if he asks "What was my mother like?"
People may answer "Like girls of seventeen"—
And how can he but think of this and that,
Lucias, Marias, Sofias, who titter or blush
When he regards them as such boys may do?
Therefore I wish some one will please to say
I looked already old though I was young;
Do I not . . . say, if you are by to speak . . .
Look nearer twenty? No more like, at least,
Girls who look arch or redden when boys laugh,
Than the poor Virgin that I used to know
At our street-corner in a lonely niche,—
The babe, that sat upon her knees, broke off,—
Thin white glazed clay, you pitied her the more:
She, not the gay ones, always got my rose.

How happy those are who know how to write!
Such could write what their son should read in time,
Had they a whole day to live out like me.
Also my name is not a common name,
"Pompilia," and may help to keep apart
A little the thing I am from what girls are.
But then how far away, how hard to find
Will anything about me have become,

Even if the boy bethink himself and ask!
No father that he ever knew at all,
Nor ever had—no, never had, I say!
That is the truth,—nor any mother left,
Out of the little two weeks that she lived,
Fit for such memory as might assist:
As good too as no family, no name,
Not even poor old Pietro's name, nor hers,
Poor kind unwise Violante, since it seems
They must not be my parents any more.
That is why something put it in my head
To call the boy "Gaetano"—no old name
For sorrow's sake; I looked up to the sky
And took a new saint to begin anew.
One who has only been made saint—how long?
Twenty-five years: so, carefuller, perhaps,
To guard a namesake than those old saints grow,
Tired out by this time,—see my own five saints!

On second thoughts, I hope he will regard
The history of me as what someone dreamed,
And get to disbelieve it at the last:
Since to myself it dwindles fast to that,
Sheer dreaming and impossibility,—
Just in four days too! All the seventeen years,
Not once did a suspicion visit me
How very different a lot is mine
From any other woman's in the world.
The reason must be, 'twas by step and step
It got to grow so terrible and strange:
These strange woes stole on tiptoe, as it were,
Into my neighbourhood and privacy,
Sat down where I sat, laid them where I lay;
And I was found familiarized with fear,
When friends broke in, held up a torch and cried
"Why, you Pompilia in the cavern thus,
"How comes that arm of yours about a wolf?
"And the soft length,—lies in and out your feet
"And laps you round the knee,—a snake it is!"
And so on.

Well, and they are right enough,
By the torch they hold up now: for first, observe,
I never had a father,—no, nor yet
A mother: my own boy can say at least
"I had a mother whom I kept two weeks!"
Not I, who little used to doubt . . . *I* doubt
Good Pietro, kind Violante, gave me birth?
They loved me always as I love my babe
(—Nearly so, that is—quite so could not be—)
Did for me all I meant to do for him,
Till one surprising day, three years ago,
They both declared, at Rome, before some judge
In some court where the people flocked to hear,

That really I had never been their child,
Was a mere castaway, the careless crime
Of an unknown man, the crime and care too much
Of a woman known too well,—little to these,
Therefore, of whom I was the flesh and blood:
What then to Pietro and Violante, both
No more my relatives than you or you?
Nothing to them! You know what they declared.

So with my husband,—just such a surprise,
Such a mistake, in that relationship!
Everyone says that husbands love their wives,
Guard them and guide them, give them happiness;
'Tis duty, law, pleasure, religion: well,
You see how much of this comes true in mine!
People indeed would fain have somehow proved
He was no husband: but he did not hear,
Or would not wait, and so has killed us all.
Then there is . . . only let me name one more!
There is the friend,—men will not ask about,
But tell untruths of, and give nicknames to,
And think my lover, most surprise of all!
Do only hear, it is the priest they mean,
Giuseppe Caponsacchi: a priest—love,
And love me! Well, yet people think he did.
I am married, he has taken priestly vows,
They know that, and yet go on, say, the same,
"Yes, how he loves you!" "That was love"—they say,
When anything is answered that they ask:
Or else "No wonder you love him"—they say.
Then they shake heads, pity much, scarcely blame—
As if we neither of us lacked excuse,
And anyhow are punished to the full,
And downright love atones for everything!
Nay, I heard read-out in the public court
Before the judge, in presence of my friends,
Letters 'twas said the priest had sent to me,
And other letters sent him by myself,
We being lovers!

Listen what this is like!
When I was a mere child, my mother . . . that's
Violante, you must let me call her so
Nor waste time, trying to unlearn the word . . .
She brought a neighbour's child of my own age
To play with me of rainy afternoons;
And, since there hung a tapestry on the wall,
We two agreed to find each other out
Among the figures. "Tisbe, that is you,
"With half-moon on your hair-knot, spear in hand,
"Flying, but no wings, only the great scarf
"Blown to a bluish rainbow at your back:
"Call off your hound and leave the stag alone!"
"—And there are you, Pompilia, such green leaves

"Flourishing out of your five finger-ends,
"And all the rest of you so brown and rough:
"Why is it you are turned a sort of tree?"
You know the figures never were ourselves
Though we nicknamed them so. Thus, all my life,—
As well what was, as what, like this, was not,—
Looks old, fantastic and impossible:
I touch a fairy thing that fades and fades.
—Even to my babe! I thought, when he was born,
Something began for once that would not end,
Nor change into a laugh at me, but stay
For evermore, eternally quite mine.
Well, so he is,—but yet they bore him off,
The third day, lest my husband should lay traps
And catch him, and by means of him catch me.
Since they have saved him so, it was well done:
Yet thence comes such confusion of what was
With what will be,—that late seems long ago,
And, what years should bring round, already come,
Till even he withdraws into a dream
As the rest do: I fancy him grown great,
Strong, stern, a tall young man who tutors me,
Frowns with the others "Poor imprudent child!
"Why did you venture out of the safe street?
"Why go so far from help to that lone house?
"Why open at the whisper and the knock?"

Six days ago when it was New Year's-day,
We bent above the fire and talked of him,
What he should do when he was grown and great.
Violante, Pietro, each had given the arm
I leant on, to walk by, from couch to chair
And fireside,—laughed, as I lay safe at last,
"Pompilia's march from bed to board is made,
"Pompilia back again and with a babe,
"Shall one day lend his arm and help her walk!"
Then we all wished each other more New Years.
Pietro began to scheme—"Our cause is gained;
"The law is stronger than a wicked man:
"Let him henceforth go his way, leave us ours!
"We will avoid the city, tempt no more
"The greedy ones by feasting and parade,—
"Live at the other villa, we know where,
"Still farther off, and we can watch the babe
"Grow fast in the good air; and wood is cheap
"And wine sincere outside the city gate.
"I still have two or three old friends will grope
"Their way along the mere half-mile of road,
"With staff and lantern on a moonless night
"When one needs talk: they'll find me, never fear,
"And I'll find them a flask of the old sort yet!"
Violante said "You chatter like a crow:
"Pompilia tires o' the tattle, and shall to-bed:
"Do not too much the first day,—somewhat more

"To-morrow, and, the next, begin the cape
"And hood and coat! I have spun wool enough."
Oh what a happy friendly eve was that!

And, next day, about noon, out Pietro went—
He was so happy and would talk so much,
Until Violante pushed and laughed him forth
Sight-seeing in the cold,—"So much to see
"I' the churches! Swathe your throat three times!" she cried,
"And, above all, beware the slippery ways,
"And bring us all the news by supper-time!"
He came back late, laid by cloak, staff and hat,
Powdered so thick with snow it made us laugh,
Rolled a great log upon the ash o' the hearth,
And bade Violante treat us to a flask,
Because he had obeyed her faithfully,
Gone sight-see through the seven, and found no church
To his mind like San Giovanni—"There's the fold,
"And all the sheep together, big as cats!
"And such a shepherd, half the size of life,
"Starts up and hears the angel"—when, at the door,
A tap: we started up: you know the rest.

Pietro at least had done no harm, I know;
Nor even Violante, so much harm as makes
Such revenge lawful. Certainly she erred—
Did wrong, how shall I dare say otherwise?—
In telling that first falsehood, buying me
From my poor faulty mother at a price,
To pass off upon Pietro as his child:
If one should take my babe, give him a name,
Say he was not Gaetano and my own,
But that some other woman made his mouth
And hands and feet,—how very false were that!
No good could come of that; and all harm did.
Yet if a stranger were to represent
"Needs must you either give your babe to me
"And let me call him mine for ever more,
"Or let your husband get him"—ah, my God,
That were a trial I refuse to face!
Well, just so here: it proved wrong but seemed right
To poor Violante—for there lay, she said,
My poor real dying mother in her rags,
Who put me from her with the life and all,
Poverty, pain, shame and disease at once,
To die the easier by what price I fetched—
Also (I hope) because I should be spared
Sorrow and sin,—why may not that have helped?
My father,—he was no one, any one,—
The worse, the likelier,—call him,—he who came,
Was wicked for his pleasure, went his way,
And left no trace to track by; there remained
Nothing but me, the unnecessary life,
To catch up or left fall—and yet a thing

She could make happy, be made happy with,
This poor Violante,—who would frown thereat?

Well, God, you see! God plants us where we grow.
It is not that because a bud is born
At a wild briar's end, full i' the wild beast's way,
We ought to pluck and put it out of reach
On the oak-tree top,—say, "There the bud belongs!"
She thought, moreover, real lies were lies told
For harm's sake; whereas this had good at heart,
Good for my mother, good for me, and good
For Pietro who was meant to love a babe,
And needed one to make his life of use,
Receive his house and land when he should die.
Wrong, wrong and always wrong! how plainly wrong!
For see, this fault kept pricking, as faults do,
All the same at her heart: this falsehood hatched,
She could not let it go nor keep it fast.
She told me so,—the first time I was found
Locked in her arms once more after the pain,
When the nuns let me leave them and go home,
And both of us cried all the cares away,—
This it was set her on to make amends,
This brought about the marriage—simply this!
Do let me speak for her you blame so much!
When Paul, my husband's brother, found me out,
Heard there was wealth for who should marry me,
So, came and made a speech to ask my hand
For Guido,—she, instead of piercing straight
Through the pretence to the ignoble truth,
Fancied she saw God's very finger point,
Designate just the time for planting me,
(The wild briar-slip she plucked to love and wear)
In soil where I could strike real root, and grow,
And get to be the thing I called myself:
For, wife and husband are one flesh, God says,
And I, whose parents seemed such and were none,
Should in a husband have a husband now,
Find nothing, this time, but was what it seemed,
—All truth and no confusion any more.
I know she meant all good to me, all pain
To herself,—since how could it be aught but pain,
To give me up, so, from her very breast,
The wilding flower-tree-branch that, all those years,
She had got used to feel for and find fixed?
She meant well: has it been so ill i' the main?
That is but fair to ask: one cannot judge
Of what has been the ill or well of life,
The day that one is dying—sorrows change
Into not altogether sorrow-like;
I do see strangeness but scarce misery,
Now it is over, and no danger more.
My child is safe; there seems not so much pain.
It comes, most like, that I am just absolved,

Purged of the past, the foul in me, washed fair,—
One cannot both have and not have, you know,—
Being right now, I am happy and colour things.
Yes, every body that leaves life sees all
Softened and bettered: so with other sights:
To me at least was never evening yet
But seemed far beautifuller than its day,
For past is past.

There was a fancy came,
When somewhere, in the journey with my friend,
We stepped into a hovel to get food;
And there began a yelp here, a bark there,—
Misunderstanding creatures that were wroth
And vexed themselves and us till we retired.
The hovel is life: no matter what dogs bit
Or cats scratched in the hovel I break from,
All outside is lone field, moon and such peace—
Flowing in, filling up as with a sea
Whereon comes Someone, walks fast on the white,
Jesus Christ's self, Don Celestine declares,
To meet me and calm all things back again.

Beside, up to my marriage, thirteen years
Were, each day, happy as the day was long:
This may have made the change too terrible.
I know that when Violante told me first
The cavalier—she meant to bring next morn,
Whom I must also let take, kiss my hand—
Would be at San Lorenzo the same eve
And marry me,—which over, we should go
Home both of us without him as before,
And, till she bade speak, I must hold my tongue,
Such being the correct way with girl-brides,
From whom one word would make a father blush,—
I know, I say, that when she told me this,
—Well, I no more saw sense in what she said
Than a lamb does in people clipping wool;
Only lay down and let myself be clipped.
And when next day the cavalier who came
(Tisbe had told me that the slim young man
With wings at head, and wings at feet, and sword
Threatening a monster, in our tapestry,
Would eat a girl else,—was a cavalier)
When he proved Guido Franceschini,—old
And nothing like so tall as I myself,
Hook-nosed and yellow in a bush of beard,
Much like a thing I saw on a boy's wrist,
He called an owl and used for catching birds,—
And when he took my hand and made a smile—
Why, the uncomfortableness of it all
Seemed hardly more important in the case
Than,—when one gives you, say, a coin to spend,—
Its newness or its oldness; if the piece

Weigh properly and buy you what you wish,
No matter whether you get grime or glare!
Men take the coin, return you grapes and figs.
Here, marriage was the coin, a dirty piece
Would purchase me the praise of those I loved:
About what else should I concern myself?

So, hardly knowing what a husband meant,
I supposed this or any man would serve,
No whit the worse for being so uncouth:
For I was ill once and a doctor came
With a great ugly hat, no plume thereto,
Black jerkin and black buckles and black sword,
And white sharp beard over the ruff in front,
And oh so lean, so sour-faced and austere!—
Who felt my pulse, made me put out my tongue,
Then oped a phial, dripped a drop or two
Of a black bitter something,—I was cured!
What mattered the fierce beard or the grim face?
It was the physic beautified the man,
Master Malpichi,—never met his match
In Rome, they said,—so ugly all the same!

However, I was hurried through a storm,
Next dark eve of December's deadest day—
How it rained!—through our street and the Lion's-mouth
And the bit of Corso,—cloaked round, covered close,
I was like something strange or contraband,—
Into blank San Lorenzo, up the aisle,
My mother keeping hold of me so tight,
I fancied we were come to see a corpse
Before the altar which she pulled me toward.
There we found waiting an unpleasant priest
Who proved the brother, not our parish friend,
But one with mischief-making mouth and eye,
Paul, whom I know since to my cost. And then
I heard the heavy church-door lock out help
Behind us: for the customary warmth,
Two tapers shivered on the altar. "Quick—
"Lose no time!"—cried the priest. And straightway down
From . . . what's behind the altar where he hid—
Hawk-nose and yellowness and bush and all,
Stepped Guido, caught my hand, and there was I
O' the chancel, and the priest had opened book,
Read here and there, made me say that and this,
And after, told me I was now a wife,
Honoured indeed, since Christ thus weds the Church,
And therefore turned he water into wine,
To show I should obey my spouse like Christ.
Then the two slipped aside and talked apart,
And I, silent and scared, got down again
And joined my mother who was weeping now.
Nobody seemed to mind us any more,
And both of us on tiptoe found our way

To the door which was unlocked by this, and wide.
When we were in the street, the rain had stopped,
All things looked better. At our own house-door,
Violante whispered "No one syllable
"To Pietro! Girl-brides never breathe a word!"
" — Well treated to a wetting, draggle-tails!"
Laughed Pietro as he opened—"Very near
"You made me brave the gutter's roaring sea
"To carry off from roost old dove and young,
"Trussed up in church, the cote, by me, the kite!
"What do these priests mean, praying folk to death
"On stormy afternoons, with Christmas close
"To wash our sins off nor require the rain?"
Violante gave my hand a timely squeeze,
Madonna saved me from immodest speech,
I kissed him and was quiet, being a bride.

When I saw nothing more, the next three weeks,
Of Guido—"Nor the Church sees Christ" thought I:
"Nothing is changed however, wine is wine
"And water only water in our house.
"Nor did I see that ugly doctor since
"The cure of the illness: just as I was cured,
"I am married,—neither scarecrow will return."

Three weeks, I chuckled — "How would Giulia stare,
"And Tecla smile and Tisbe laugh outright,
"Were it not impudent for brides to talk!"—
Until one morning, as I sat and sang
At the broidery-frame alone i' the chamber,—loud
Voices, two, three together, sobbings too,
And my name, "Guido," "Paolo," flung like stones
From each to the other! In I ran to see.
There stood the very Guido and the priest
With sly face,—formal but nowise afraid,—
While Pietro seemed all red and angry, scarce
Able to stutter out his wrath in words;
And this it was that made my mother sob,
As he reproached her—"You have murdered us,
" Me and yourself and this our child beside!"
The Guido interposed "Murdered or not,
"Be it enough your child is now my wife!
"I claim and come to take her." Paul put in,
"Consider—kinsman, dare I term you so?—
" What is the good of your sagacity
"Except to counsel in a strait like this?
"I guarantee the parties man and wife
"Whether you like or loathe it, bless or ban.
"May spilt milk be put back within the bowl—
"The done thing, undone? You, it is, we look
"For counsel to, you fitliest will advise!
"Since milk, though spilt and spoilt, does marble good,
"Better we down on knees and scrub the floor,
"Than sigh, 'the waste would make a syllabub!'

"Help us so turn disaster to account,
"So predispose the groom, he needs shall grace
"The bride with favour from the very first,
"Not begin marriage an embittered man!"
He smiled,—the game so wholly in his hands!
While fast and faster sobbed Violante—"Ay,
"All of us murdered, past averting now!
"O my sin, O my secret!" and such like.

Then I began to half surmise the truth;
Something had happened, low, mean, underhand,
False, and my mother was to blame, and I
To pity, whom all spoke of, none addressed:
I was the chattel that had caused a crime.
I stood mute,—those who tangled must untie
The embroilment. Pietro cried "Withdraw, my child!
"She is not helpful to the sacrifice
"At this stage,—do you want the victim by
"While you discuss the value of her blood?
"For her sake, I consent to hear you talk:
"Go, child, and pray God help the innocent!"

I did go and was praying God, when came
Violante, with eyes swollen and red enough,
But movement on her mouth for make-believe
Matters were somehow getting right again.
She bade me sit down by her side and hear.
"You are too young and cannot understand,
"Nor did your father understand at first.
"I wished to benefit all three of us,
"And when he failed to take my meaning,—why,
"I tried to have my way at unaware—
"Obtained him the advantage he refused.
"As if I put before him wholesome food
"Instead of broken victual,—he finds change
"I' the viands, never cares to reason why,
"But falls to blaming me, would fling the plate
"From window, scandalize the neighborhood,
"Even while he smacks his lips,—men's way, my child!
"But either you have prayed him unperverse
"Or I have talked him back into his wits:
"And Paolo was a help in time of need,—
"Guido, not much—my child, the way of men!
"A priest is more a woman than a man,
"And Paul did wonders to persuade. In short,
"Yes, he was wrong, your father sees and says;
"My scheme was worth attempting: and bears fruit,
"Gives you a husband and a noble name,
"A palace and no end of pleasant things.
"What do you care about a handsome youth?
"They are so volatile, and tease their wives!
"This is the kind of man to keep the house.
"We lose no daughter,—gain a son, that's all:
"For 'tis arranged we never separate,

"Nor miss, in our grey time of life, the tints
"Of you that colour eve to match with morn.
"In good or ill, we share and share alike,
"And cast our lots into a common lap,
"And all three die together as we lived!
"Only, at Arezzo,—that's a Tuscan town,
"Not so large as this noisy Rome, no doubt,
"But older far and finer much, say folk,—
"In a great palace where you will be queen,
"Know the Archbishop and the Governor,
"And we see homage done you ere we die.
"Therefore, be good and pardon!"—"Pardon what?
"You know things, I am very ignorant:
"All is right if you only will not cry!"

And so an end! Because a blank begins
From when, at the word, she kissed me hard and hot,
And took me back to where my father leaned
Opposite Guido—who stood eyeing him,
As eyes the butcher the cast panting ox
That feels his fate is come, nor struggles more,—
While Paul looked archly on, pricked brow at whiles
With the pen-point as to punish triumph there,—
And said "Count Guido, take your lawful wife
"Until death part you!"

All since is one blank,
Over and ended; a terrific dream.
It is the good of dreams—so soon they go!
Wake in a horror of heart-beats, you may—
Cry, "The dread thing will never from my thoughts!"
Still, a few daylight doses of plain life,
Cock-crow and sparrow-chirp, or bleat and bell
Of goats that trot by, tinkling, to be milked;
And when you rub your eyes awake and wide,
Where is the harm o' the horror? Gone! So here,
I know I wake,—but from what? Blank, I say!
This is the note of evil: for good lasts.
Even when Don Celestine bade "Search and find!
"For your soul's sake, remember what is past,
"The better to forgive,"—all in vain!
What was fast getting indistinct before,
Vanished outright. By special grace perhaps,
Between that first calm and this last, four years
Vanish,—one quarter of my life, you know.
I am held up, amid the nothingness,
By one or two truths only—thence I hang,
And there I live,—the rest is death or dream,
All but those points of my support. I think
Of what I saw at Rome once in the Square
O' the Spaniards, opposite the Spanish House:
There was a foreigner had trained a goat,
A shuddering white woman of a beast,
To climb up, stand straight on a pile of sticks

Put close, which gave the creature room enough:
When she was settled there he, one by one,
Took away all the sticks, left just the four
Whereon the little hoofs did really rest,
There she kept firm, all underneath was air.
So, what I hold by, are my prayer to God,
My hope, that came in answer to the prayer,
Some hand would interpose and save me—hand
Which proved to be my friend's hand: and,—blest bliss,—
That fancy which began so faint at first,
That thrill of dawn's suffusion through my dark,
Which I perceive was promise of my child,
The light his unborn face sent long before,—
God's way of breaking the good news to flesh.
That is all left now of those four bad years.
Don Celestine urged "But remember more!
"Other men's faults may help me find your own.
"I need the cruelty exposed, explained,
"Or how can I advise you to forgive?"
He thought I could not properly forgive
Unless I ceased forgetting,—which is true:
For, bringing back reluctantly to mind
My husband's treatment of me,—by a light
That's later than my life-time, I review
And comprehend much and imagine more,
And have but little to forgive at last.
For now,—be fair and say,—is it not true
He was ill-used and cheated of his hope
To get enriched by marriage? Marriage gave
Me and no money, broke the compact so:
He had a right to ask me on those terms,
As Pietro and Violante to declare
They would not give me: so the bargain stood:
They broke it, and he felt himself aggrieved,
Became unkind with me to punish them.
They said 'twas he began deception first,
Nor, in one point whereto he pledged himself,
Kept promise: what of that, suppose it were?
Echoes die off, scarcely reverberate
For ever,—why should ill keep echoing ill,
And never let our ears have done with noise?
Then my poor parents took the violent way
To thwart him,—he must needs retaliate,—wrong,
Wrong, and all wrong,—better say, all blind!
As I myself was, that is sure, who else
Had understood the mystery: for his wife
Was bound in some sort to help somehow there.
It seems as if I might have interposed,
Blunted the edge of their resentment so,
Since he vexed me because they first vexed him;
"I will entreat them to desist, submit,
"Give him the money and be poor in peace,—
"Certainly not go tell the world: perhaps
"He will grow quiet with his gains."

Yes, say
Something to this effect and you do well!
But then you have to see first: I was blind.
That is the fruit of all such wormy ways,
The indirect, the unapproved of God:
You cannot find their author's end and aim,
Not even to substitute your good for bad,
Your open for the irregular; you stand
Stupefied, profitless, as cow or sheep
That miss a man's mind; anger him just twice
By trial at repairing the first fault.
Thus, when he blamed me, "You are a coquette,
"A lure-owl posturing to attract birds,
"You look love-lures at theatre and church,
"In walk, at window!"—that, I knew, was false:
But why he charged me falsely, whither sought
To drive me by such charge,—how could I know?
So, unaware, I only made things worse.
I tried to soothe him by abjuring walk,
Window, church, theatre, for good and all,
As if he had been in earnest: that, you know,
Was nothing like the object of his charge.
Yes, when I got my maid to supplicate
The priest, whose name she read when she would read
Those feigned false letters I was forced to hear
Though I could read no word of,—he should cease
Writing,—nay, if he minded prayer of mine,
Cease from so much as even pass the street
Whereon our house looked,—in my ignorance
I was just thwarting Guido's true intent;
Which was, to bring about a wicked change
Of sport to earnest, tempt a thoughtless man
To write indeed, and pass the house, and more,
Till both of us were taken in a crime.
He ought not to have wished me thus act lies,
Simulate folly:—but,—wrong or right, the wish,—
I failed to apprehend its drift. How plain
It follows,—if I fell into such fault,
He also may have overreached the mark,
Made mistake, by perversity of brain,
In the whole sad strange plot, the grotesque intrigue
To make me and my friend unself ourselves,
Be other man and woman than we were!
Think it out, you who have the time! for me,—
I cannot say less; more I will not say.
Leave it to God to cover and undo!
Only, my dulness should not prove too much!
—Not prove that in a certain other point
Wherein my husband blamed me,—and you blame,
If I interpret smiles and shakes of head,—
I was dull too. Oh, if I dared but speak!
Must I speak? I am blamed that I forwent
A way to make my husband's favour come.
That is true: I was firm, withstood, refused . . .
—Women as you are, how can I find the words?

I felt there was just one thing Guido claimed
I had no right to give nor he to take;
We being in estrangement, soul from soul:
Till, when I sought help, the Archbishop smiled,
Inquiring into privacies of life,
—Said I was blameable—(he stands for God)
Nowise entitled to exemption there.
Then I obeyed,—as surely had obeyed
Were the injunction "Since your husband bids,
"Swallow the burning coal he proffers you!"
But I did wrong, and he gave wrong advice
Though he were thrice Archbishop,—that, I know!—
Now I have got to die and see things clear.
Remember I was barely twelve years old—
A child at marriage: I was let alone
For weeks, I told you, lived my child-life still
Even at Arezzo, when I woke and found
First . . . but I need not think of that again—
Over and ended! Try and take the sense
Of what I signify, if it must be so.
After the first, my husband, for hate's sake,
Said one eve, when the simpler cruelty
Seemed somewhat dull at edge and fit to bear,
"We have been man and wife six months almost:
"How long is this your comedy to last?
"Go this night to my chamber, not your own!"
At which word, I did rush—most true the charge—
And gain the Archbishop's house—he stands for God—
And fall upon my knees and clasp his feet,
Praying him hinder what my estranged soul
Refused to bear, though patient of the rest:
"Place me within a convent," I implored—
"Let me henceforward lead the virgin life
"You praise in Her you bid me imitate!"
What did he answer? "Folly of ignorance!
"Know, daughter, circumstances make or mar
"Virginity,—'tis virtue or 'tis vice.
"That which was glory in the Mother of God
"Had been, for instance, damnable in Eve
"Created to be mother of mankind.
"Had Eve, in answer to her Maker's speech
" 'Be fruitful, multiply, replenish earth'—
"Pouted 'But I choose rather to remain
" 'Single'—why, she had spared herself forthwith
"Further probation by the apple and snake,
"Been pushed straight out of Paradise! For see—
"If motherhood be qualified impure,
"I catch you making God command Eve sin!
"—A blasphemy so like these Molinists',
"I must suspect you dip into their books."
Then he pursued " 'Twas in your covenant!"

No! There my husband never used deceit.
He never did by speech nor act imply
"Because of our souls' yearning that we meet

"And mix in soul through flesh, which yours and mine
"Wear and impress, and make their visible selves,
"—All which means, for the love of you and me,
"Let us become one flesh, being one soul!"
He only stipulated for the wealth;
Honest so far. But when he spoke as plain—
Dreadfully honest also—"Since our souls
"Stand each from each, a whole world's width between,
"Give me the fleshly vesture I can reach
"And rend and leave just fit for hell to burn!"—
Why, in God's name, for Guido's soul's own sake
Imperilled by polluting mine,—I say,
I did resist; would I had overcome!

My heart died out at the Archbishop's smile;
—It seemed so stale and worn a way o' the world,
As though 'twere nature frowning—"Here is Spring,
"The sun shines as he shone at Adam's fall,
"The earth requires that warmth reach everywhere:
"What, must your patch of snow be saved forsooth
"Because you rather fancy snow than flowers?"
Something in this style he began with me.
Last he said, savagely for a good man,
"This explains why you call your husband harsh,
"Harsh to you, harsh to whom you love. God's Bread!
"The poor Count has to manage a mere child
"Whose parents leave untaught the simplest things
"Their duty was and privilege to teach,—
"Goodwives' instruction, gossips' lore: they laugh
"And leave the Count the task,—or leave it me!"
Then I resolved to tell a frightful thing.
"I am not ignorant,—know what I say,
"Declaring this is sought for hate, not love.
"Sir, you may hear things like almighty God.
"I tell you that my housemate, yes—the priest
"My husband's brother, Canon Girolamo—
"Has taught me what depraved and misnamed love
"Means, and what outward signs denote the sin,
"For he solicits me and says he loves,
"The idle young priest with nought else to do.
"My husband sees this, knows this, and lets be.
"Is it your counsel I bear this beside?"
"—More scandal, and against a priest this time!
"What, 'tis the Canon now?"—less snappishly—
"Rise up, my child, for such a child you are,
" The rod were too advanced a punishment!
"Let's try the honeyed cake. A parable!
" 'Without a parable spake He not to them.'
"There was a ripe round long black toothsome fruit,
"Even a flower-fig, the prime boast of May:
"And, to the tree, said . . . either the spirit o' the fig,
"Or, if we bring in men, the gardener,
"Archbishop of the orchard—had I time
"To try o' the two which fits in best: indeed

"It might be the Creator's self, but then
"The tree should bear an apple, I suppose,—
"Well, anyhow, one with authority said
" 'Ripe fig, burst skin, regale the fig-pecker—
" 'The bird whereof thou art a perquisite!'
" 'Nay,' with a flounce, replied the restif fig,
" 'I much prefer to keep my pulp myself:
" 'He may go breakfastless and dinnerless,
" 'Supperless of one crimson seed, for me!'
"So, back she flopped into her bunch of leaves.
"He flew off, left her,—did the natural lord,—
"And lo, three hundred thousand bees and wasps
"Found her out, feasted on her to the shuck:
"Such gain the fig's that gave its bird no bite!
"The moral,—fools elude their proper lot,
"Tempt other fools, get ruined all alike.
"Therefore go home, embrace your husband quick!
"Which if his Canon brother chance to see,
"He will the sooner back to book again."

So, home I did go; so, the worst befell:
So, I had proof the Archbishop was just man,
And hardly that, and certainly no more.
For, miserable consequence to me,
My husband's hatred waxed nor waned at all,
His brother's boldness grew effrontery soon,
And my last stay and comfort in myself
Was forced from me: henceforth I looked to God
Only, nor cared my desecrated soul
Should have fair walls, gay windows for the world.
God's glimmer, that came through the ruin-top,
Was witness why all lights were quenched inside:
Henceforth I asked God counsel, not mankind.

So, when I made the effort, freed myself,
They said—"No care to save appearance here!
"How cynic,—when, how wanton, were enough!"
—Adding, it all came of my mother's life—
My own real mother, whom I never knew,
Who did wrong (if she needs must have done wrong)
Through being all her life, not my four years,
At mercy of the hateful: every beast
O' the field was wont to break that fountain-fence,
Trample the silver into mud so murk
Heaven could not find itself reflected there.
Now they cry "Out on her, who, plashy pool,
"Bequeathed turbidity and bitterness
"To the daughter-stream where Guido dipt and drank!"

Well, since she had to bear this brand—let me!
The rather do I understand her now,
From my experience of what hate calls love,—
Much love might be in what their love called hate.
If she sold . . . what they call, sold . . . me her child—

I shall believe she hoped in her poor heart
That I at least might try be good and pure,
Begin to live untempted, not go doomed
And done with ere once found in fault, as she.
Oh and, my mother, it all came to this?
Why should I trust those that speak ill of you,
When I mistrust who speaks even well of them?
Why, since all bound to do me good, did harm,
May not you, seeming as you harmed me most,
Have meant to do most good—and feed your child
From bramble-bush, whom not one orchard-tree
But drew bough back from, nor let one fruit fall?
This it was for you sacrificed your babe?
Gained just this, giving your heart's hope away
As I might give mine, loving it as you,
If . . . but that never could be asked of me!

There, enough! I have my support again,
Again the knowledge that my babe was, is,
Will be mine only. Him, by death, I give
Outright to God, without a further care,—
But not to any parent in the world,—
So to be safe: why is it we repine?
What guardianship were safer could we choose?
All human plans and projects come to nought,
My life, and what I know of other lives,
Prove that: no plan nor project! God shall care!

And now you are not tired? How patient then
All of you,—Oh yes, patient this long while
Listening, and understanding, I am sure!
Four days ago, when I was sound and well
And like to live, no one would understand.
People were kind, but smiled "And what of him,
"Your friend, whose tonsure, the rich dark-brown hides?
"There, there!—your lover, do we dream he was?
"A priest too—never were such naughtiness!
"Still, he thinks many a long think, never fear,
"After the shy pale lady,—lay so light
"For a moment in his arms, the lucky one!"
And so on: wherefore should I blame you much?
So we are made, such difference in minds,
Such difference too in eyes that see the minds!
That man, you misinterpret and misprise—
The glory of his nature, I had thought,
Shot itself out in white light, blazed the truth
Through every atom of his act with me:
Yet where I point you, through the crystal shrine,
Purity in quintessence, one dew-drop,
You all descry a spider in the midst.
One says, "The head of it is plain to see,"
And one, "They are the feet by which I judge,"
All say, "Those films were spun by nothing else."

Then, I must lay my babe away with God,
Nor think of him again, for gratitude.
Yes, my last breath shall wholly spend itself
In one attempt more to disperse the stain,
The mist from other breath fond mouths have made,
About a lustrous and pellucid soul:
So that, when I am gone but sorrow stays,
And people need assurance in their doubt
If God yet have a servant, man a friend,
The weak a saviour and the vile a foe,—
Let him be present, by the name invoked,
Giuseppe-Maria Caponsacchi!

There,
Strength comes already with the utterance!
I will remember once more for his sake
The sorrow: for he lives and is belied.
Could he be here, how he would speak for me!

I had been miserable three drear years
In that dread palace and lay passive now,
When I first learned there could be such a man.
Thus it fell: I was at a public play,
In the last days of Carnival last March,
Brought there I knew not why, but now know well.
My husband put me where I sat, in front;
Then crouched down, breathed cold through me from behind,
Stationed i' the shadow,—none in front could see,—
I, it was, faced the stranger-throng beneath,
The crowd with upturned faces, eyes one stare,
Voices one buzz. I looked but to the stage,
Whereon two lovers sang and interchanged
"True life is only love, love only bliss:
"I love thee—thee I love!" then they embraced.
I looked thence to the ceiling and the walls,—
Over the crowd, those voices and those eyes,—
My thoughts went through the roof and out, to Rome
On wings of music, waft of measured words,—
Set me down there, a happy child again,
Sure that to-morrow would be festa-day,[1]
Hearing my parents praise past festas more,
And seeing they were old if I was young,
Yet wondering why they still would end discourse
With "We must soon go, you abide your time,
"And,—might we haply see the proper friend
"Throw his arm over you and make you safe!"

Sudden I saw him; into my lap there fell
A foolish twist of comfits, broke my dream
And brought me from the air and laid me low,
As ruined as the soaring bee that's reached
(So Pietro told me at the Villa once)

[1] feast day, holiday.

By the dust-handful. There the comfits lay:
I looked to see who flung them, and I faced
This Caponsacchi, looking up in turn.
Ere I could reason out why, I felt sure,
Whoever flung them, his was not the hand,—
Up rose the round face and good-natured grin
Of him who, in effect, had played the prank,
From covert close beside the earnest face,—
Fat waggish Conti, friend of all the world.
He was my husband's cousin, privileged
To throw the thing: the other, silent, grave,
Solemn almost, saw me, as I saw him.

There is a psalm Don Celestine recites,
"Had I a dove's wings, how I fain would flee!"
The psalm runs not "I hope, I pray for wings,"—
Not "If wings fall from heaven, I fix them fast,"—
Simply "How good it were to fly and rest,
"Have hope now, and one day expect content!
"How well to do what I shall never do!"
So I said "Had there been a man like that,
"To lift me with his strength out of all strife
"Into the calm, how I could fly and rest!
"I have a keeper in the garden here
"Whose sole employment is to strike me low
"If ever I, for solace, seek the sun.
"Life means with me successful feigning death,
"Lying stone-like, eluding notice so,
"Forgoing here the turf and there the sky.
"Suppose that man had been instead of this!"

Presently Conti laughed into my ear,
—Had tripped up to the raised place where I sat—
"Cousin, I flung them brutishly and hard!
"Because you must be hurt, to look austere
"As Caponsacchi yonder, my tall friend
"A-gazing now. Ah, Guido, you so close?
"Keep on your knees, do! Beg her to forgive!
"My cornet battered like a cannon-ball.
"Good bye, I'm gone!"—nor waited the reply.

That night at supper, out my husband broke,
"Why was that throwing, that buffoonery?
"Do you think I am your dupe? What man would dare
"Throw comfits in a stranger lady's lap?
"'Twas knowledge of you bred such insolence
"In Caponsacchi; he dared shoot the bolt,
"Using that Conti for his stalking-horse.
"How could you see him this once and no more,
"When he is always haunting hereabout
"At the street-corner or the palace-side,
"Publishing my shame and your impudence?
"You are a wanton,—I a dupe, you think?
"O Christ, what hinders that I kill her quick?"

Whereat he drew his sword and feigned a thrust.
All this, now,—being not so strange to me,
Used to such misconception day by day
And broken-in to bear,—I bore, this time,
More quietly than woman should perhaps:
Repeated the mere truth and held my tongue.

Then he said, "Since you play the ignorant,
"I shall instruct you. This armour,—commenced
"Or finished or midway in act, all's one,—
" 'Tis the town-talk; so my revenge shall be.
"Does he presume because he is a priest?
"I warn him that the sword I wear shall pink
"His lily-scented cassock through and through,
"Next time I catch him underneath your eaves!"
But he had threatened with the sword so oft
And, after all, not kept his promise. All
I said was, "Let God save the innocent!
"Moreover, death is far from a bad fate.
"I shall go pray for you and me, not him;
"And then I look to sleep, come death or, worse,
"Life." So, I slept.

There may have elapsed a week,
When Margherita,—called my waiting-maid,
Whom it is said my husband found too fair—
Who stood and heard the charge and the reply,
Who never once would let the matter rest
From that night forward, but rang changes still
On this the thrust and that the shame, and how
Good cause for jealousy cures jealous fools,
And what a paragon was this same priest
She talked about until I stopped my ears,—
She said, "A week is gone; you comb your hair,
"Then go mope in a corner, cheek on palm,
"Till night comes round again,—so, waste a week
"As if your husband menaced you in sport.
"Have not I some acquaintance with his tricks?
"Oh no, he did not stab the serving-man
"Who made and sang the rhymes about me once!
"For why? They sent him to the wars next day.
"Nor poisoned he the foreigner, my friend,
"Who wagered on the whiteness of my breast,—
"The swarth skins of our city in dispute:
"For, though he paid me proper compliment,
"The Count well knew he was besotted with
"Somebody else, a skin as black as ink,
" (As all the town knew save my foreigner)
"He found and wedded presently,—'Why need
" 'Better revenge?'—the Count asked. But what's here?
"A priest, that does not fight, and cannot wed,
"Yet must be dealt with! If the Count took fire
"For the poor pastime of a minute,—me—
"What were the conflagration for yourself,

"Countess and lady-wife and all the rest?
"The priest will perish; you will grieve too late:
"So shall the city-ladies' handsomest,
"Frankest and liberalest gentleman
"Die for you, to appease a scurvy dog
"Hanging's too good for. Is there no escape?
"Were it not simple Christian charity
"To warn the priest be on his guard,—save him
"Assured death, save yourself from causing it?
"I meet him in the street. Give me a glove,
"A ring to show for token! Mum's the word!"

I answered, "If you were, as styled, my maid,
"I would command you: as you are, you say,
"My husband's intimate,—assist his wife
"Who can do nothing but entreat 'Be still!'
"Even if you speak truth and a crime is planned,
"Leave help to God as I am forced to do!
"There is no other course, or we should craze,
"Seeing such evil with no human cure.
"Reflect that God, who makes the storm desist,
"Can make an angry violent heart subside.
"Why should we venture teach Him governance?
"Never address me on this subject more!"

Next night she said, "But I went, all the same,
"—Ay, saw your Caponsacchi in his house,
"And come back stuffed with news I must outpour.
"I told him, 'Sir, my mistress is a stone:
" 'Why should you harm her for no good you get?
" 'For you do harm her—prowl about our place
" 'With the Count never distant half the street,
" 'Lurking at every corner, would you look!
" ''Tis certain she has witched you with a spell.
" 'Are there not other beauties at your back?
" 'We all know, Donna This and Monna That
" 'Die for a glance of yours, yet here you gaze!
" 'Go make them grateful, leave the stone its cold!'
"And he—oh, he turned first white and then red,
"And then—'To her behest I bow myself,
" 'Whom I love with my body and my soul:
" 'Only, a word i' the bowing! See, I write
" 'One little word, no harm to see or hear!
" 'Then, fear no further!' This is what he wrote.
"I know you cannot read,—therefore, let me!
" '*My idol!*' " . . .

But I took it from her hand
And tore it into shreds. "Why join the rest
"Who harm me? Have I ever done you wrong?
"People have told me 'tis you wrong myself:
"Let it suffice I either feel no wrong
"Or else forgive it,—yet you turn my foe!
"The others hunt me and you throw a noose!"

She muttered, "Have your wilful way!" I slept.

Whereupon . . . no, I leave my husband out!
It is not to do him more hurt, I speak.
Let it suffice, when misery was most,
One day, I swooned and got a respite so.
She stooped as I was slowly coming to,
This Margherita, ever on my trace,
And whispered—"Caponsacchi!"

If I drowned,
But woke afloat i' the wave with upturned eyes,
And found their first sight was a star! I turned—
For the first time, I let her have her will,
Heard passively,—"The imposthume at such head,
"One touch, one lancet-puncture would relieve,—
"And still no glance the good physician's way
"Who rids you of the torment in a trice!
"Still he writes letters you refuse to hear.
"He may prevent your husband, kill himself,
"So desperate and all fordone is he!
"Just hear the pretty verse he made to-day!
"A sonnet from Mirtillo. *'Peerless fair . . .'*
"All poetry is difficult to read,
"—The sense of it is, anyhow, he seeks
"Leave to contrive you an escape from hell,
"And for that purpose asks an interview.
"I can write, I can grant it in your name,
"Or, what is better, lead you to his house.
"Your husband dashes you against the stones;
"This man would place each fragment in a shrine:
"You hate him, love your husband!"

I returned,
"It is not true I love my husband,—no,
"Nor hate this man. I listen while you speak,
"—Assured that what you say is false, the same:
"Much as when once, to me a little child,
"A rough gaunt man in rags, with eyes on fire,
" A crowd of boys and idlers at his heels,
"Rushed as I crossed the Square, and held my head
"In his two hands, 'Here's she will let me speak!
" 'You little girl, whose eyes do good to mine,
" 'I am the Pope, am Sextus, now the Sixth;
" 'And that Twelfth Innocent, proclaimed to-day,
" 'Is Lucifer disguised in human flesh!
" 'The angels, met in conclave, crowned me!'—thus
"He gibbered and I listened; but I knew
"All was delusion, ere folks interposed
" 'Unfasten him, the maniac!' Thus I know
"All your report of Caponsacchi false,
"Folly or dreaming; I have seen so much
"By that adventure at the spectacle,
"The face I fronted that one first, last time:

"He would belie it by such words and thoughts.
"Therefore while you profess to show him me,
"I ever see his own face. Get you gone!"

"—That will I, nor once open mouth again,—
"No, by Saint Joseph and the Holy Ghost!
"On your head be the damage, so adieu!"

And so more days, more deeds I must forget,
Till . . . what a strange thing now is to declare!
Since I say anything, say all if true!
And how my life seems lengthened as to serve!
It may be idle or inopportune,
But, true?—why, what was all I said but truth,
Even when I found that such as are untrue
Could only take the truth in through a lie?
Now—I am speaking truth to the Truth's self:
God will lend credit to my words this time.

It had got half through April. I arose
One vivid daybreak,—who had gone to bed
In the old way my wont those last three years,
Careless until, the cup drained, I should die.
The last sound in my ear, the over-night,
Had been a something let drop on the sly
In prattle by Margherita, "Soon enough
"Gaieties end, now Easter's past: a week,
"And the Archbishop gets him back to Rome,—
"Everyone leaves the town for Rome, this Spring,—
"Even Caponsacchi, out of heart and hope,
"Resigns himself and follows with the flock."
I heard this drop and drop like rain outside
Fast-falling through the darkness while she spoke:
So had I heard with like indifference,
"And Michael's pair of wings will arrive first
"At Rome to introduce the company,
"Will bear him from our picture where he fights
"Satan,—expect to have that dragon loose
"And never a defender!"—my sole thought
Being still, as night came, "Done, another day!
"How good to sleep and so get nearer death!"—
When, what, first thing at daybreak, pierced the sleep
With a summons to me? Up I sprang alive,
Light in me, light without me, everywhere
Change! A broad yellow sun-beam was let fall
From heaven to earth,—a sudden drawbridge lay,
Along which marched a myriad merry motes,
Mocking the flies that crossed them and recrossed
In rival dance, companions new-born too.
On the house-eaves, a dripping shag of weed
Shook diamonds on each dull grey lattice-square,
As first one, then another bird leapt by,
And light was off, and lo was back again,
Always with one voice,—where are two such joys?—

The blessed building-sparrow! I stepped forth,
Stood on the terrace,—o'er the roofs, such sky!
My heart sang, "I too am to go away,
"I too have something I must care about,
"Carry away with me to Rome, to Rome!
"The bird brings hither sticks and hairs and wool,
"And nowhere else i' the world; what fly breaks rank,
"Falls out of the procession that befits,
"From window here to window there, with all
"The world to choose,—so well he knows his course?
"I have my purpose and my motive too,
"My march to Rome, like any bird or fly!
"Had I been dead! How right to be alive!
"Last night I almost prayed for leave to die,
"Wished Guido all his pleasure with the sword
"Or the poison,—poison, sword, was but a trick,
"Harmless, may God forgive him the poor jest!
"My life is charmed, will last till I reach Rome!
"Yesterday, but for the sin,—ah, nameless be
"The deed I could have dared against myself!
"Now—see if I will touch an unripe fruit,
"And risk the health I want to have and use!
"Not to live, now, would be the wickedness,—
"For life means to make haste and go to Rome
"And leave Arezzo, leave all woes at once!"

Now, understand here, by no means mistake!
Long ago had I tried to leave that house
When it seemed such procedure would stop sin;
And still failed more the more I tried—at first
The Archbishop, as I told you,—next, our lord
The Governor,—indeed I found my way,
I went to the great palace where he rules,
Though I knew well 'twas he who,—when I gave
A jewel or two, themselves had given me,
Back to my parents,—since they wanted bread,
They who had never let me want a nosegay,—he
Spoke of the jail for felons, if they kept
What was first theirs, then mine, so doubly theirs,
Though all the while my husband's most of all!
I knew well who had spoke the word wrought this:
Yet, being in extremity, I fled
To the Governor, as I say,—scarce opened lip
When—the cold cruel snicker close behind—
Guido was on my trace, already there,
Exchanging nod and wink for shrug and smile,
And I—pushed back to him and, for my pains,
Paid with . . . but why remember what is past?
I sought out a poor friar the people call
The Roman, and confessed my sin which came
Of their sin,—that fact could not be repressed,—
The frightfulness of my despair in God:
And, feeling, through the grate, his horror shake,
Implored him, "Write for me who cannot write,

"Apprise my parents, make them rescue me!
"You bid me be courageous and trust God:
"Do you in turn dare somewhat, trust and write
" 'Dear friends, who used to be my parents once,
" 'And now declare you have no part in me,
" 'This is some riddle I want wit to solve,
" 'Since you must love me with no difference.
" 'Even suppose you altered,—there's your hate,
" 'To ask for: hate of you two dearest ones
" 'I shall find liker love than love found here,
" 'If husbands love their wives. Take me away
" 'And hate me as you do the gnats and fleas,
" 'Even the scorpions! How I shall rejoice!'
"Write that and save me!" And he promised—wrote
Or did not write; things never changed at all:
He was not like the Augustinian here!
Last, in a desperation I appealed
To friends, whoever wished me better days,
To Guillichini, that's of kin,—"What, I—
"Travel to Rome with you? A flying gout
"Bids me deny my heart and mind my leg!"
Then I tried Conti, used to brave—laugh back
The louring thunder when his cousin scowled
At me protected by his presence: "You—
"Who well know what you cannot save me from,—
"Carry me off! What frightens you, a priest?"
He shook his head, looked grave—"Above my strength!
"Guido has claws that scratch, shows feline teeth;
"A formidabler foe than I dare fret:
"Give me a dog to deal with, twice the size!
"Of course I am a priest and Canon too,
"But . . by the bye . . though both, not quite so bold
"As he, my fellow-Canon, brother-priest,
"The personage in such ill odour here
"Because of the reports—pure birth o' the brain!
"Our Caponsacchi, he's your true Saint George
"To slay the monster, set the Princess free,
"And have the whole High-Altar to himself:
"I always think so when I see that piece
"I' the Pieve, that's his church and mine, you know:
"Though you drop eyes at mention of his name!"

That name had got to take a half-grotesque
Half-ominous, wholly enigmatic sense,
Like any by-word, broken bit of song
Born with a meaning, changed by mouth and mouth
That mix it in a sneer or smile, as chance
Bids, till it now means nought but ugliness
And perhaps shame.

—All this intends to say,
That, over-night, the notion of escape
Had seemed distemper, dreaming; and the name,—
Not the man, but the name of him, thus made

Into a mockery and disgrace,—why, she
Who uttered it persistently, had laughed,
"I name his name, and there you start and wince
"As criminal from the red tongs' touch!"—yet now,
Now, as I stood letting morn bathe me bright,
Choosing which butterfly should bear my news,—
The white, the brown one, or that tinier blue,—
The Margherita, I detested so,
In she came—"The fine day, the good Spring time!
"What, up and out at window? That is best.
"No thought of Caponsacchi?—who stood there
"All night on one leg, like the sentry crane,
"Under the pelting of your water-spout—
"Looked last look at your lattice ere he leave
"Our city, bury his dead hope at Rome?
"Ay, go to looking-glass and make you fine,
"While he may die ere touch one least loose hair
"You drag at with the comb in such a rage!"

I turned—"Tell Caponsacchi he may come!"

"Tell him to come? Ah, but, for charity,
"A truce to fooling! Come? What,—come this eve?
"Peter and Paul! But I see through the trick—
"Yes, come, and take a flower-pot on his head,
"Flung from your terrace! No joke, sincere truth?"

How plainly I perceived hell flash and fade
O' the face of her,—the doubt that first paled joy,
Then, final reassurance I indeed
Was caught now, never to be free again!
What did I care?—who felt myself of force
To play with the silk, and spurn the horsehair-springe.

"But—do you know that I have bade him come,
"And in your own name? I presumed so much,
"Knowing the thing you needed in your heart.
"But somehow—what had I to show in proof?
"He would not come: half-promised, that was all,
"And wrote the letters you refused to read.
"What is the message that shall move him now?

"After the Ave Maria, at first dark,
"I will be standing on the terrace, say!

"I would I had a good long lock of hair
"Should prove I was not lying! Never mind!"

Off she went—"May he not refuse, that's all—
"Fearing a trick!"

I answered, "He will come."
And, all day, I sent prayer like incense up
To God the strong, God the beneficent,

God ever mindful in all strife and strait,
Who, for our own good, makes the need extreme,
Till at the last He puts forth might and saves.
An old rhyme came into my head and rang
Of how a virgin, for the faith of God,
Hid herself, from the Paynims that pursued,
In a cave's heart; until a thunderstone,
Wrapped in a flame, revealed the couch and prey:
And they laughed—"Thanks to lightning, ours at last!"
And she cried "Wrath of God, assert His love!
"Servant of God, thou fire, befriend His child!"
And lo, the fire she grasped at, fixed its flash,
Lay in her hand a calm cold dreadful sword
She brandished till pursuers strewed the ground,
So did the souls within them die away,
As o'er the prostrate bodies, sworded, safe,
She walked forth to the solitudes and Christ:
So should I grasp the lightning and be saved!

And still, as the day wore, the trouble grew
Whereby I guessed there would be born a star,
Until at an intense throe of the dusk,
I started up, was pushed, I dare to say,
Out on the terrace, leaned and looked at last
Where the deliverer waited me: the same
Silent and solemn face, I first descried
At the spectacle, confronted mine once more.

So was that minute twice vouchsafed me, so
The manhood, wasted then, was still at watch
To save me yet a second time: no change
Here, though all else changed in the changing world!

I spoke on the instant as my duty bade,
In some such sense as this, whatever the phrase.

"Friend, foolish words were borne from you to me;
"Your soul behind them is the pure strong wind,
"Not dust and feathers which its breath may bear:
"These to the witless seem the wind itself,
"Since proving thus the first of it they feel.
"If by mischance you blew offence my way,
"The straws are dropt, the wind desists no whit,
"And how such strays were caught up in the street
"And took a motion from you, why inquire?
"I speak to the strong soul, no weak disguise.
"If it be truth,—why should I doubt it truth?—
"You serve God specially, as priests are bound,
"And care about me, stranger as I am,
"So far as wish my good,—that miracle
"I take to intimate He wills you serve
"By saving me,—what else can He direct?
"Here is the service. Since a long while now,
"I am in course of being put to death:

"While death concerned nothing but me, I bowed
"The head and bade, in heart, my husband strike.
"Now I imperil something more, it seems,
"Something that's truelier me than this myself,
"Something I trust in God and you to save.
"You go to Rome, they tell me: take me there,
"Put me back with my people!"

He replied—
The first word I heard ever from his lips,
All himself in it,—an eternity
Of speech, to match the immeasurable depths
O' the soul that then broke silence—"I am yours."

So did the star rise, soon to lead my step,
Lead on, not pause before it should stand still
Above the House o' the Babe,—my babe to be,
That knew me first and thus made me know him,
That had his right of life and claim on mine,
And would not let me die till he was born,
But pricked me at the heart to save us both,
Saying "Have you the will? Leave God the way!"
And the way was Caponsacchi—"mine," thank God!
He was mine, he is mine, he will be mine.

No pause i' the leading and the light! I know,
Next night there was a cloud came, and not he:
But I prayed through the darkness till it broke
And let him shine. The second night, he came.

"The plan is rash; the project desperate:
"In such a flight needs must I risk your life,
"Give food for falsehood, folly or mistake,
"Ground for your husband's rancour and revenge"—
So he began again, with the same face.
I felt that, the same loyalty—one star
Turning now red that was so white before—
One service apprehended newly: just
A word of mine and there the white was back!

"No, friend, for you will take me! 'Tis yourself
"Risk all, not I,—who let you, for I trust
"In the compensating great God: enough!
"I know you: when is it that you will come?"

"To-morrow at the day's dawn." Then I heard
What I should do: how to prepare for flight
And where to fly.

That night my husband bade
"—You, whom I loathe, beware you break my sleep
"This whole night! Couch beside me like the corpse
"I would you were!" The rest you know, I think—
How I found Caponsacchi and escaped.

And this man, men call sinner? Jesus Christ!
Of whom men said, with mouths Thyself mad'st once,
"He hath a devil"—say he was Thy saint,
My Caponsacchi! Shield and show—unshroud
In Thine own time the glory of the soul
If aught obscure,—if ink-spot, from vile pens
Scribbling a charge against him—(I was glad
Then, for the first time, that I could not write)—
Flirted his way, have flecked the blaze!

For me,
'Tis otherwise: let men take, sift my thoughts
—Thoughts I throw like the flax for sun to bleach!
I did pray, do pray, in the prayer shall die,
"Oh, to have Caponsacchi for my guide!"
Ever the face upturned to mine, the hand
Holding my hand across the world,—a sense
That reads, as only such can read, the mark
God sets on woman, signifying so
She should—shall peradventure—be divine;
Yet 'ware, the while, how weakness mars the print
And makes confusion, leaves the thing men see,
—Not this man,—who from his own soul, re-writes
The obliterated charter,—love and strength
Mending what's marred: "So kneels a votarist,
"Weeds some poor waste traditionary plot
"Where shrine once was, where temple yet may be,
"Purging the place but worshipping the while,
"By faith and not by sight, sight clearest so,—
"Such way the saints work,"—says Don Celestine.
But I, not privileged to see a saint
Of old when such walked earth with crown and palm,
If I call "saint" what saints call something else—
The saints must bear with me, impute the fault
To a soul i' the bud, so starved by ignorance,
Stinted of warmth, it will not blow this year
Nor recognise the orb which Spring-flowers know.
But if meanwhile some insect with a heart
Worth floods of lazy music, spendthrift joy—
Some fire-fly renounced Spring for my dwarfed cup,
Crept close to me with lustre for the dark,
Comfort against the cold,—what though excess
Of comfort should miscall the creature—sun?
What did the sun to hinder while harsh hands
Petal by petal, crude and colourless,
Tore me? This one heart brought me all the Spring!

Is all told? There's the journey: and where's time
To tell you how that heart burst out in shine?
Yet certain points do press on me too hard.
Each place must have a name, though I forget:
How strange it was—there where the plain begins
And the small river mitigates its flow—

When eve was fading fast, and my soul sank,
And he divined what surge of bitterness,
In overtaking me, would float me back
Whence I was carried by the striding day—
So,—"This grey place was famous once," said he—
And he began that legend of the place
As if in answer to the unspoken fear,
And told me all about a brave man dead,
Which lifted me and let my soul go on!
How did he know too,—at that town's approach
By the rock-side,—that in coming near the signs,
Of life, the house-roofs and the church and tower,
I saw the old boundary and wall o' the world
Rise plain as ever round me, hard and cold,
As if the broken circlet joined again,
Tightened itself about me with no break,—
As if the town would turn Arezzo's self,—
The husband there,—the friends my enemies,
All ranged against me, not an avenue
I try, but would be blocked and drive me back
On him,—this other, . . . oh the heart in that!
Did not he find, bring, put into my arms
A new-born babe?—and I saw faces beam
Of the young mother proud to teach me joy,
And gossips round expecting my surprise
At the sudden hole through earth that lets in heaven.
I could believe himself by his strong will
Had woven around me what I thought the world
We went along in, every circumstance,
Towns, flowers and faces, all things helped so well!
For, through the journey, was it natural
Such comfort should arise from first to last?
As I look back, all is one milky way;
Still bettered more, the more remembered, so
Do new stars bud while I but search for old,
And fill all gaps i' the glory, and grow him—
Him I now see make the shine everywhere.
Even at the last when the bewildered flesh,
The cloud of weariness about my soul
Clogging too heavily, sucked down all sense,—
Still its last voice was, "He will watch and care;
"Let the strength go, I am content: he stays!"
I doubt not he did stay and care for all—
From that sick minute when the head swam round,
And the eyes looked their last and died on him,
As in his arms he caught me and, you say,
Carried me in, that tragical red eve,
And laid me where I next returned to life
In the other red of morning, two red plates
That crushed together, crushed the time between,
And are since then a solid fire to me,—
When in, my dreadful husband and the world
Broke,—and I saw him, master, by hell's right,
And saw my angel helplessly held back

By guards that helped the malice—the lamb prone,
The serpent towering and triumphant—then
Came all the strength back in a sudden swell,
I did for once see right, do right, give tongue
The adequate protest: for a worm must turn
If it would have its wrong observed by God.
I did spring up, attempt to thrust aside
That ice-block 'twixt the sun and me, lay low
The neutralizer of all good and truth.
If I sinned so,—never obey voice more
O' the Just and Terrible, who bids us—"Bear!"
Not—"Stand by, bear to see my angels bear!"
I am clear it was on impulse to serve God
Not save myself,—no—nor my child unborn!
Had I else waited patiently till now?—
Who saw my old kind parents, silly-sooth
And too much trustful, for their worst of faults,
Cheated, brow-beaten, stripped and starved, cast out
Into the kennel: I remonstrated,
Then sank to silence, for,—their woes at end,
Themselves gone,—only I was left to plague.
If only I was threatened and belied,
What matter? I could bear it and did bear;
It was a comfort, still one lot for all:
They were not persecuted for my sake
And I, estranged, the single happy one.
But when at last, all by myself I stood
Obeying the clear voice which bade me rise,
Not for my own sake but my babe unborn,
And take the angel's hand was sent to help—
And found the old adversary athwart the path—
Not my hand simply struck from the angel's but
The very angel's self made foul i' the face
By the fiend who struck there,—that I would not bear,
That only I resisted! So, my first
And last resistance was invincible.
Prayers move God; threats, and nothing else, move men!
I must have prayed a man as he were God
When I implored the Governor to right
My parents' wrongs: the answer was a smile.
The Archbishop,—did I clasp his feet enough,
Hide my face hotly on them, while I told
More than I dared make my own mother know?
The profit was—compassion and a jest.
This time, the foolish prayers were done with, right
Used might, and solemnized the sport at once.
All was against the combat: vantage, mine?
The runaway avowed, the accomplice-wife,
In company with the plan-contriving priest?
Yet, shame thus rank and patent, I struck, bare,
At foe from head to foot in magic mail,
And off it withered, cobweb-armoury
Against the lightning! 'Twas truth singed the lies
And saved me, not the vain sword nor weak speech!

You see, I will not have the service fail!
I say, the angel saved me: I am safe!
Others may want and wish, I wish nor want
One point o' the circle plainer, where I stand
Traced round about with white to front the world.
What of the calumny I came across,
What o' the way to the end?—the end crowns all.
The judges judged aright i' the main, gave me
The uttermost of my heart's desire, a truce
From torture and Arezzo, balm for hurt
With the quiet nuns,—God recompense the good!
Who said and sang away the ugly past.
And, when my final fortune was revealed,
What safety while, amid my parents' arms,
My babe was given me! Yes, he saved my babe:
It would not have peeped forth, the bird-like thing,
Through that Arezzo noise and trouble: back
Had it returned nor ever let me see!
But the sweet peace cured all, and let me live
And give my bird the life among the leaves
God meant him! Weeks and months of quietude,
I could lie in such peace and learn so much—
Begin the task, I see how needful now,
Of understanding somewhat of my past,—
Know life a little, I should leave so soon.
Therefore, because this man restored my soul,
All has been right; I have gained my gain, enjoyed
As well as suffered,—nay, got foretaste too
Of better life beginning where this ends—
All through the breathing-while allowed me thus,
Which let good premonitions reach my soul
Unthwarted, and benignant influence flow
And interpenetrate and change my heart,
Uncrossed by what was wicked,—nay, unkind.
For, as the weakness of my time drew nigh,
Nobody did me one disservice more,
Spoke coldly or looked strangely, broke the love
I lay in the arms of, till my boy was born,
Born all in love, with nought to spoil the bliss
A whole long fortnight: in a life like mine
A fortnight filled with bliss is long and much.
All women are not mothers of a boy,
Though they live twice the length of my whole life,
And, as they fancy, happily all the same.
There I lay, then, all my great fortnight long,
As if it would continue, broaden out
Happily more and more, and lead to heaven:
Christmas before me,—was not that a chance?
I never realized God's birth before—
How he grew likest God in being born.
This time I felt like Mary, had my babe
Lying a little on my breast like hers.
So all went on till, just four days ago—
The night and the tap.

Oh it shall be success
To the whole of our poor family! My friends
. . . Nay, father and mother,—give me back my word!
They have been rudely stripped of life, disgraced
Like children who must needs go clothed too fine,
Carry the garb of Carnival in Lent:
If they too much affected frippery,
They have been punished and submit themselves,
Say no word: all is over, they see God
Who will not be extreme to mark their fault
Or he had granted respite: they are safe.

For that most woeful man my husband once,
Who, needing respite, still draws vital breath,
I—pardon him? So far as lies in me,
I give him for his good the life he takes,
Praying the world will therefore acquiesce.
Let him make God amends,—none, none to me
Who thank him rather that, whereas strange fate
Mockingly styled him husband and me wife,
Himself this way at least pronounced divorce,
Blotted the marriage-bond: this blood of mine
Flies forth exultingly at any door,
Washes the parchment white, and thanks the blow.
We shall not meet in this world nor the next,
But where will God be absent? In His face
Is light, but in His shadow healing too:
Let Guido touch the shadow and be healed!
And as my presence was importunate,—
My earthly good, temptation and a snare,—
Nothing about me but drew somehow down
His hate upon me,—somewhat so excused
Therefore, since hate was thus the truth of him,—
May my evanishment for evermore
Help further to relieve the heart that cast
Such object of its natural loathing forth!
So he was made; he nowise made himself:
I could not love him, but his mother did.
His soul has never lain beside my soul;
But for the unresisting body,—thanks!
He burned that garment spotted by the flesh!
Whatever he touched is rightly ruined: plague
It caught, and disinfection it had craved
Still but for Guido; I am saved through him
So as by fire; to him—thanks and farewell!

Even for my babe, my boy, there's safety thence—
From the sudden death of me, I mean: we poor
Weak souls, how we endeavour to be strong!
I was already using up my life,—
This portion, now, should do him such a good,
This other go to keep off such an ill!
The great life; see, a breath and it is gone!
So is detached, so left all by itself

The little life, the fact which means so much.
Shall not God stoop the kindlier to His work,
His marvel of creation, foot would crush,
Now that the hand He trusted to receive
And hold it, lets the treasure fall perforce?
The better; He shall have in orphanage
His own way all the clearlier: if my babe
Outlived the hour—and he has lived two weeks—
It is through God who knows I am not by.
Who is it makes the soft gold hair turn black,
And sets the tongue, might lie so long at rest,
Trying to talk? Let us leave God alone!
Why should I doubt He will explain in time
What I feel now, but fail to find the words?
My babe nor was, nor is, nor yet shall be
Count Guido Franceschini's child at all—
Only his mother's, born of love not hate!
So shall I have my rights in after-time.
It seems absurd, impossible to-day;
So seems so much else, not explained but known!
Ah! Friends, I thank and bless you every one!
No more now: I withdraw from earth and man
To my own soul, compose myself for God.

Well, and there is more! Yes, my end of breath
Shall bear away my soul in being true!
He is still here, not outside with the world,
Here, here, I have him in his rightful place!
'Tis now, when I am most upon the move,
I feel for what I verily find—again
The face, again the eyes, again, through all,
The heart and its immeasurable love
Of my one friend, my only, all my own,
Who put his breast between the spears and me.
Ever with Caponsacchi! Otherwise
Here alone would be failure, loss to me—
How much more loss to him, with life debarred
From giving life, love locked from love's display,
The day-star stopped its task that makes night morn!
O lover of my life, O soldier-saint,
No work begun shall ever pause for death!
Love will be helpful to me more and more
I' the coming course, the new path I must tread,
My weak hand in thy strong hand, strong for that!
Tell him that if I seem without him now,
That's the world's insight! Oh, he understands!
He is at Civita—do I once doubt
The world again is holding us apart?
He had been here, displayed in my behalf
The broad brow that reverberates the truth,
And flashed the word God gave him, back to man!
I know where the free soul is flown! My fate
Will have been hard for even him to bear:
Let it confirm him in the trust of God,

Showing how holily he dared the deed!
And, for the rest,—say, from the deed, no touch
Of harm came, but all good, all happiness,
Not one faint fleck of failure! Why explain?
What I see, oh, he sees and how much more!
Tell him,—I know not wherefore the true word
Should fade and fall unuttered at the last—
It was the name of him I sprang to meet
When came the knock, the summons and the end.
"My great heart, my strong hand are back again!"
I would have sprung to these, beckoning across
Murder and hell gigantic and distinct
O' the threshold, posted to exclude me heaven:
He is ordained to call and I to come!
Do not the dead wear flowers when dressed for God?
Say,—I am all in flowers from head to foot!
Say,—not one flower of all he said and did,
Might seem to flit unnoticed, fade unknown,
But dropped a seed has grown a balsam-tree
Whereof the blossoming perfumes the place
At this supreme of moments! He is a priest;
He cannot marry therefore, which is right:
I think he would not marry if he could.
Marriage on earth seems such a counterfeit,
Mere imitation of the inimitable:
In heaven we have the real and true and sure.
'Tis there they neither marry nor are given
In marriage but are as the angels: right,
Oh how right that is, how like Jesus Christ
To say that! Marriage-making for the earth,
With gold so much,—birth, power, repute so much,
Or beauty, youth so much, in lack of these!
Be as the angels rather, who, apart,
Know themselves into one, are found at length
Married, but marry never, no, nor give
In marriage; they are man and wife at once
When the true time is: here we have to wait
Not so long neither! Could we by a wish
Have what we will and get the future now,
Would we wish aught done undone in the past?
So, let him wait God's instant men call years;
Meantime hold hard by truth and his great soul,
Do out the duty! Through such souls alone
God stooping shows sufficient of His light
For us i' the dark to rise by. And I rise.

[1869]

THE POPE

Like to Ahasuerus, that shrewd prince,
I will begin,—as is, these seven years now,
My daily wont,—and read a History
(Written by one whose deft right hand was dust

To the last digit, ages ere my birth)
Of all my predecessors, Popes of Rome:
For though mine ancient early dropped the pen,
Yet others picked it up and wrote it dry,
Since of the making books there is no end.
And so I have the Papacy complete
From Peter first to Alexander last;
Can question each and take instruction so.
Have I to dare,—I ask, how dared this Pope?
To suffer?—Suchanone, how suffered he?
Being about to judge, as now, I seek
How judged once, well or ill, some other Pope;
Study some signal judgment that subsists
To blaze on, or else blot, the page which seals
The sum up of what gain or loss to God
Came of His one more Vicar in the world.
So, do I find example, rule of life;
So, square and set in order the next page,
Shall be stretched smooth o'er my own funeral cyst.

Eight hundred years exact before the year
I was made Pope, men made Formosus Pope,
Say Sigebert and other chroniclers.
Ere I confirm or quash the Trial here
Of Guido Franceschini and his friends,
Read,—how there was a ghastly Trial once
Of a dead man by a live man, and both, Popes:
Thus—in the antique penman's very phrase.

"Then Stephen, Pope and seventh of the name,
"Cried out, in synod as he sat in state,
"While choler quivered on his brow and beard,
" 'Come into court, Formosus, thou lost wretch,
" 'That claimedst to be late Pope as even I!'

"And at the word, the great door of the church
"Flew wide, and in they brought Formosus' self,
"The body of him, dead, even as embalmed
"And buried duly in the Vatican
"Eight months before, exhumed thus for the nonce.
"They set it, that dead body of a Pope,
"Clothed in pontific vesture now again,
"Upright on Peter's chair as if alive.

"And Stephen, springing up, cried furiously
" 'Bishop of Porto, wherefore didst presume
" 'To leave that see and take this Roman see,
" 'Exchange the lesser for the greater see,
" '—A thing against the canons of the Church?'

"Then one (a Deacon who, observing forms,
"Was placed by Stephen to repel the charge,
"Be advocate and mouthpiece of the corpse)
"Spoke as he dared, set stammeringly forth
"With white lips and dry tongue,—as but a youth,

"For frightful was the corpse-face to behold,—
"How nowise lacked there precedent for this.
"But when, for his last precedent of all,
"Emboldened by the Spirit, out he blurts
" 'And, Holy Father, didst not thou thyself
" 'Vacate the lesser for the greater see,
" 'Half a year since change Arago for Rome?'
" '—Ye have the sin's defence now, Synod mine!'
"Shrieks Stephen in a beastly froth of rage:
" 'Judge now betwixt him dead and me alive!
" 'Hath he intruded or do I pretend?
" 'Judge, judge!'—breaks wavelike one whole foam of wrath.

"Whereupon they, being friends and followers,
"Said 'Ay, thou art Christ's Vicar, and not he!
" 'Away with what is frightful to behold!
" 'This act was uncanonic and a fault.'

"Then, swallowed up in rage, Stephen exclaimed
" 'So, guilty! So, remains I punish guilt!
" 'He is unpoped, and all he did I damn:
" 'The Bishop, that ordained him, I degrade:
" 'Depose to laics those he raised to priests:
" 'What they have wrought is mischief nor shall stand,
" 'It is confusion, let it vex no more!
" 'Since I revoke, annul and abrogate
" 'All his decrees in all kinds: they are void!
" 'In token whereof and warning to the world,
" 'Strip me yon miscreant of those robes usurped,
" 'And clothe him with vile serge befitting such!
" 'Then hale the carrion to the market-place;
" 'Let the town-hangman chop from his right hand
" 'Those same three fingers which he blessed withal;
" 'Next cut the head off, once was crowned forsooth:
" 'And last go fling all, fingers, head and trunk,
" 'To Tiber that my Christian fish may sup!'
"—Either because of ΙΧΘΥΣ which means Fish
"And very aptly symbolizes Christ,
"Or else because the Pope is Fisherman
"And seals with Fisher's-signet.

"Anyway,
"So said, so done: himself, to see it done,
"Followed the corpse they trailed from street to street
"Till into Tiber wave they threw the thing.
"The people, crowded on the banks to see,
"Were loud or mute, wept or laughed, cursed or jeered,
"According as the deed addressed their sense;
"A scandal verily: and out spake a Jew

" 'Wot ye your Christ had vexed our Herod thus?'
"Now when, Formosus being dead a year,
"His judge Pope Stephen tasted death in turn,
"Made captive by the mob and strangled straight,

"Romanus, his successor for a month,
"Did make protest Formosus was with God,
"Holy, just, true in thought and word and deed.
"Next Theodore, who reigned but twenty days,
"Therein convoked a synod, whose decree
"Did reinstate, repope the late unpoped,
"And do away with Stephen as accursed.
"So that when presently certain fisher-folk
" (As if the queasy river could not hold
"Its swallowed Jonas, but discharged the meal)
"Produced the timely product of their nets,
"The mutilated man, Formosus,—saved
"From putrefaction by the embalmer's spice,
"Or, as some said, by sanctity of flesh,—
" 'Why, lay the body again' bade Theodore
" 'Among his predecessors, in the church
" 'And burial-place of Peter!' which was done.
" 'And' addeth Luitprand 'many of repute,
" 'Pious and still alive, avouch to me
" 'That as they bore the body up the aisle
" 'The saints in imaged row bowed each his head
" 'For welcome to a brother-saint come back.'
"As for Romanus and this Theodore,
"These two Popes, through the brief reign granted each,
"Could but initiate what John came to close
"And give the final stamp to: he it was,
"Ninth of the name, (I follow the best guides)
"Who,—in full synod at Ravenna held
"With Bishops seventy-four, and present too
"Eude King of France with his Archbishopry,—
"Did condemn Stephen, anathematise
"The disinterment, and make all blots blank.
" 'For,' argueth here Auxilius in a place
"*De Ordinationibus,* 'precedents
" 'Had been, no lack, before Formosus long,
" 'Of Bishops so transferred from see to see,—
" 'Marinus, for example': read the tract.

"But, after John, came Sergius, reaffirmed
"The right of Stephen, cursed Formosus, nay
"Cast out, some say, his corpse a second time.
"And here,—because the matter went to ground,
"Fretted by new griefs, other cares of the age,—
"Here is the last pronouncing of the Church,
"Her sentence that subsists unto this day.
"Yet constantly opinion hath prevailed
"I' the Church, Formosus was a holy man."

Which of the judgments was infallible?
Which of my predecessors spoke for God?
And what availed Formosus that this cursed,
That blessed, and then this other cursed again?
"Fear ye not those whose power can kill the body
"And not the soul," saith Christ "but rather those

"Can cast both soul and body into hell!"
John judged thus in Eight Hundred Ninety Eight,
Exact eight hundred years ago to-day
When, sitting in his stead, Vice-gerent here,
I must give judgment on my own behoof.
So worked the predecessor: now, my turn!

In God's name! Once more on this earth of God's,
While twilight lasts and time wherein to work,
I take His staff with my uncertain hand,
And stay my six and fourscore years, my due
Labour and sorrow, on His judgment-seat,
And forthwith think, speak, act, in place of Him—
The Pope for Christ. Once more appeal is made
From man's assize to mine: I sit and see
Another poor weak trembling human wretch
Pushed by his fellows, who pretend the right,
Up to the gulf which, where I gaze, begins
From this world to the next,—gives way and way,
Just on the edge over the awful dark:
With nothing to arrest him but my feet.
He catches at me with convulsive face,
Cries "Leave to live the natural minute more!"
While hollowly the avengers echo "Leave?
"None! So has he exceeded man's due share
"In man's fit licence, wrung by Adam's fall,
"To sin and yet not surely die,—that we,
"All of us sinful, all with need of grace,
"All chary of our life,—the minute more
"Or minute less of grace which saves a soul,—
"Bound to make common cause with who craves time,
"—We yet protest against the exorbitance
"Of sin in this one sinner, and demand
"That his poor sole remaining piece of time
"Be plucked from out his clutch: put him to death!
"Punish him now! As for the weal or woe
"Hereafter, God grant mercy! Man be just,
"Nor let the felon boast he went scot-free!"
And I am bound, the solitary judge,
To weigh the worth, decide upon the plea,
And either hold a hand out, or withdraw
A foot and let the wretch drift to the fall.
Ay, and while thus I dally, dare perchance
Put fancies for a comfort 'twixt this calm
And yonder passion that I have to bear,—
As if reprieve were possible for both
Prisoner and Pope,—how easy were reprieve!
A touch o' the hand-bell here, a hasty word
To those who wait, and wonder they wait long,
I' the passage there, and I should gain the life!—
Yea, though I flatter me with fancy thus,
I know it is but nature's craven-trick.
The case is over, judgment at an end,
And all things done now and irrevocable:

A mere dead man is Franceschini here,
Even as Formosus centuries ago.
I have worn through this sombre wintry day,
With winter in my soul beyond the world's,
Over these dismalest of documents
Which drew night down on me ere eve befell,—
Pleadings and counter-pleadings, figure of fact
Beside fact's self, these summaries to wit,—
How certain three were slain by certain five:
I read here why it was, and how it went,
And how the chief o' the five preferred excuse,
And how law rather chose defence should lie,—
What argument he urged by wary word
When free to play off wile, start subterfuge,
And what the unguarded groan told, torture's feat
When law grew brutal, outbroke, overbore
And glutted hunger on the truth, at last,—
No matter for the flesh and blood between.
All's a clear rede and no more riddle now.
Truth, nowhere, lies yet everyhere in these—
Not absolutely in a portion, yet
Evolvable from the whole: evolved at last
Painfully, held tenaciously by me.
Therefore there is not any doubt to clear
When I shall write the brief word presently
And chink the hand-bell, which I pause to do.
Irresolute? Not I more than the mound
With the pine-trees on it yonder! Some surmise,
Perchance, that since man's wit is fallible,
Mine may fail here? Suppose it so,—what then?
Say,—Guido, I count guilty, there's no babe
So guiltless, for I misconceive the man!
What's in the chance should move me from my mind?
If, as I walk in a rough country-side,
Peasants of mine cry "Thou art he can help,
"Lord of the land and counted wise to boot:
"Look at our brother, strangling in his foam,
"He fell so where we find him,—prove thy worth!"
I may presume, pronounce, "A frenzy-fit,
"A falling-sickness or a fever-stroke!
"Breathe a vein, copiously let blood at once!"
So perishes the patient, and anon
I hear my peasants—"All was error, lord!
"Our story, thy prescription: for there crawled
"In due time from our hapless brother's breast
"The serpent which had stung him: bleeding slew
"Whom a prompt cordial had restored to health."
What other should I say than "God so willed:
"Mankind is ignorant, a man am I:
"Call ignorance my sorrow, not my sin!"
So and not otherwise, in after-time,
If some acuter wit, fresh probing, sound
This multifarious mass of words and deeds
Deeper, and reach through guilt to innocence,

I shall face Guido's ghost nor blench a jot.
"God who set me to judge thee, meted out
"So much of judging faculty, no more:
"Ask Him if I was slack in use thereof!"
I hold a heavier fault imputable
Inasmuch as I changed a chaplain once,
For no cause,—no, if I must bare my heart,—
Save that he snuffled somewhat saying mass.
For I am ware it is the seed of act,
God holds appraising in His hollow palm,
Not act grown great thence on the world below,
Leafage and branchage, vulgar eyes admire.
Therefore I stand on my integrity,
Not fear at all: and if I hesitate,
It is because I need to breathe awhile,
Rest, as the human right allows, review,
Intent the little seeds of act, my tree,—
The thought, to clothe in deed, and give the world
At chink of bell and push of arrased door.

O pale departure, dim disgrace of day!
Winter's in wane, his vengeful worst art thou,
To dash the boldness of advancing March!
Thy chill persistent rain has purged our streets
Of gossipry; pert tongue and idle ear
By this, consort 'neath archway, portico.
But wheresoe'er Rome gathers in the grey,
Two names now snap and flash from mouth to mouth—
(Sparks, flint and steel strike) Guido and the Pope.
By this same hour to-morrow eve—aha,
How do they call him?—the sagacious Swede—
Who finds by figures how the chances prove,
Why one comes rather than another thing,
As, say, such dots turn up by throw of dice,
Or, if we dip in Virgil here and there
And prick for such a verse, when such shall point.
Take this Swede, tell him, hiding name and rank,
Two men are in our city this dull eve;
One doomed to death,—but hundreds in such plight
Slip aside, clean escape by leave of law
Which leans to mercy in this latter time;
Moreover in the plenitude of life
Is he, with strength of limb and brain adroit,
Presumably of service here: beside,
The man is noble, backed by nobler friends:
Nay, for who wish him well, the city's self
Makes common cause with who—house-magistrate,
Patron of hearth and home, domestic lord
Who ruled his own, let aliens cavil. Die?
He'll bribe a gaoler or break prison first!
Nay, a sedition may be helpful, give
Hint to the mob to batter wall, burn gate,
And bid the favourite malefactor march.
Calculate now these chances of escape!

"It is not probable, but well may be."
Again, there is another man, weighed now
By twice eight years beyond the seven-times-ten,
Appointed overweight to break our branch.
And this man's loaded branch lifts, more than snow,
All the world's cark and care, though a bird's nest
Were a superfluous burthen: notably
Hath he been pressed, as if his age were youth,
From to-day's dawn till now that day departs,
Trying one question with true sweat of soul
"Shall the said doomed man fitlier die or live?"
When a straw swallowed in his posset, stool
Stumbled on where his path lies, any puff
That's incident to such a smoking flax,
Hurries the natural end and quenches him!
Now calculate, thou sage, the chances here,
Say, which shall die the sooner, this or that?
"That, possibly, this in all likelihood."
I thought so: yet thou tripp'st, my foreign friend!
No, it will be quite otherwise,—to-day
Is Guido's last: my term is yet to run.

But say the Swede were right, and I forthwith
Acknowledge a prompt summons and lie dead:
Why, then I stand already in God's face
And hear "Since by its fruit a tree is judged,
"Show me thy fruit, the latest act of thine!
"For in the last is summed the first and all,—
"What thy life last put heart and soul into,
"There shall I taste thy product." I must plead
This condemnation of a man to-day.

No so! Expect nor question nor reply
At what we figure as God's judgment-bar!
None of this vile way by the barren words
Which, more than any deed, characterize
Man as made subject to a curse: no speech—
That still bursts o'er some lie which lurks inside,
As the split skin across the coppery snake,
And most denotes man! since, in all beside,
In hate or lust or guile or unbelief,
Out of some core of truth the excrescence comes,
And, in the last resort, the man may urge
"So was I made, a weak thing that gave way
"To truth, to impulse only strong since true,
"And hated, lusted, used guile, forwent faith."
But when man walks the garden of this world
For his own solace, and, unchecked by law,
Speaks or keeps silence as himself sees fit,
Without the least incumbency to lie,
—Why, can he tell you what a rose is like,
Or how the birds fly, and not slip to false
Though truth serve better? Man must tell his mate
Of you, me and himself, knowing he lies,

Knowing his fellow knows the same,—will think
"He lies, it is the method of a man!"
And yet will speak for answer "It is truth"
To him who shall rejoin "Again a lie!"
Therefore this filthy rags of speech, this coil
Of statement, comment, query and response,
Tatters all too contaminate for use,
Have no renewing: He, the Truth, is, too,
The Word. We men, in our degree, may know
There, simply, instantaneously, as here
After long time and amid many lies,
Whatever we dare think we know indeed
—That I am I, as He is He,—what else?
But be man's method for man's life at least!
Wherefore, Antonio Pignatelli, thou
My ancient self, who wast no Pope so long
But studiedst God and man, the many years
I' the school, i' the cloister, in the diocese
Domestic, legate-rule in foreign lands,—
Thou other force in those old busy days
Than this grey ultimate decrepitude,—
Yet sensible of fires that more and more
Visit a soul, in passage to the sky,
Left nakeder than when flesh-robe was new—
Thou, not Pope but the mere old man o' the world,
Supposed inquisitive and dispassionate,
Wilt thou, the one whose speech I somewhat trust,
Question the after-me, this self now Pope,
Hear his procedure, criticize his work?
Wise in its generation is the world.

This is why Guido is found reprobate.
I see him furnished forth for his career,
On starting for the life-chance in our world,
With nearly all we count sufficient help:
Body and mind in balance, a sound frame,
A solid intellect: the wit to seek,
Wisdom to choose, and courage wherewithal
To deal with whatsoever circumstance
Should minister to man, make life succeed.
Oh, and much drawback! what were earth without?
Is this our ultimate stage, or starting-place
To try man's foot, if it will creep or climb,
'Mid obstacles in seeming, points that prove
Advantage for who vaults from low to high
And makes the stumbling-block a stepping-stone?
So, Guido, born with appetite, lacks food,
Is poor, who yet could deftly play-off wealth,
Straitened, whose limbs are restless till at large.
He, as he eyes each outlet of the cirque,
And narrow penfold for probation, pines
After the good things just outside its grate,
With less monition, fainter conscience-twitch,
Rarer instinctive qualm at the first feel
Of greed unseemly prompting grasp undue,

Than nature furnishes her main mankind,—
Making it harder to do wrong than right
The first time, careful lest the common ear
Break measure, miss the outstep of life's march.
Wherein I see a trial fair and fit
For one else too unfairly fenced about,
Set above sin, beyond his fellows here,
Guarded from the arch-tempter all must fight,
By a great birth, traditionary name,
Diligent culture, choice companionship,
Above all, conversancy with the faith
Which puts forth for its base of doctrine just
"Man is born nowise to content himself
"But please God." He accepted such a rule,
Recognized man's obedience; and the Church,
Which simply is such rule's embodiment,
He clave to, he held on by,—nay, indeed,
Near pushed inside of, deep as layman durst,
Professed so much of priesthood as might sue
For priest's-exemption where the layman sinned,—
Got his arm frocked which, bare, the law would bruise.
Hence, at this moment, what's his last resource,
His extreme stay and utmost stretch of hope
But that,—convicted of such crime as law
Wipes not away save with a worldling's blood,—
Guido, the three-parts consecrate, may 'scape?
Nay, the portentous brothers of the man
Are veritably priests, protected each
May do his murder in the Church's pale,
Abate Paul, Canon Girolamo!
This is the man proves irreligiousest
Of all mankind, religion's parasite!
This may forsooth plead dinned ear, jaded sense,
The vice o' the watcher who bides near the bell,
Sleeps sound because the clock is vigilant,
And cares not whether it be shade or shine,
Doling out day and night to all men else!
Why was the choice o' the man to niche himself
Perversely 'neath the tower where Time's own tongue
Thus undertakes to sermonize the world?
Why, but because the solemn is safe too,
The belfry proves a fortress of a sort,
Has other uses than to teach the hour,
Turns sunscreen, paravent and ombrifuge
To whoso seeks a shelter in its pale,
—Ay, and attractive to unwary folk
Who gaze at storied portal, statued spire,
And go home with full head but empty purse
Nor dare suspect the sacristan the thief!
Shall Judas,—hard upon the donor's heel,
To filch the fragments of the basket,—plead
He was too near the preacher's mouth, nor sat
Attent with fifties in a company?
No,—closer to promulgated decree,
Clearer the censure of default. Proceed!

I find him bound, then, to begin life well;
Fortified by propitious circumstance,
Great birth, good breeding, with the Church for guide.
How lives he? Cased thus in a coat of proof,
Mailed like a man-at-arms, though all the while
A puny starveling,—does the breast pant big,
The limb swell to the limit, emptiness
Strive to become solidity indeed?
Rather, he shrinks up like the ambiguous fish,
Detaches flesh from shell and outside show,
And steals my moonlight (I have seen the thing)
In and out, now to prey and now to skulk.
Armour he boasts when a wave breaks on beach,
Or bird stoops for the prize: with peril nigh,—
The man of rank, the much-befriended man,
The man almost affiliate to the Church,
Such is to deal with, let the world beware!
Does the world recognize, pass prudently?
Do tides abate and sea-fowl hunt i' the deep?
Already is the slug from out its mew,
Ignobly faring with all loose and free,
Sand-fly and slush-worm at their garbage-feast,
A naked blotch no better than they all:
Guido has dropped nobility, slipped the Church,
Plays trickster if not cut-purse, body and soul
Prostrate among the filthy feeders—faugh!
And when Law takes him by surprise at last,
Catches the foul thing on its carrion-prey,
Behold, he points to shell left high and dry,
Pleads "But the case out yonder is myself!"
Nay, it is thou, Law prongs amid thy peers,
Congenial vermin; that was none of thee,
Thine outside,—give it to the soldier-crab!

For I find this black mark impinge the man,
That he believes in just the vile of life.
Low instinct, base pretension, are these truth?
Then, that aforesaid armour, probity
He figures in, is falsehood scale on scale;
Honour and faith,—a lie and a disguise,
Probably for all livers in this world,
Certainly for himself! All say good words
To who will hear, all do thereby bad deeds
To who must undergo; so thrive mankind!
See this habitual creed exemplified
Most in the last deliberate act; as last,
So, very sum and substance of the soul
Of him that planned and leaves one perfect piece,
The sin brought under jurisdiction now,
Even the marriage of the man: this act
I sever from his life as sample, show
For Guido's self, intend to test him by,
As, from a cup filled fairly at the fount,
By the components we decide enough
Or to let flow as late, or staunch the source.

He purposes this marriage, I remark,
On no one motive that should prompt thereto—
Farthest, by consequence, from ends alleged
Appropriate to the action; so they were:
The best, he knew and feigned, the worst he took.
Not one permissible impulse moves the man,
From the mere liking of the eye and ear,
To the true longing of the heart that loves,
No trace of these: but all to instigate,
Is what sinks man past level of the brute,
Whose appetite if brutish is a truth.
All is the lust for money: to get gold,—
Why, lie, rob, if it must be, murder! Make
Body and soul wring gold out, lured within
The clutch of hate by love, the trap's pretence!
What good else get from bodies and from souls?
This got, there were some life to lead thereby,
—What, where or how, appreciate those who tell
How the toad lives: it lives,—enough for me!
To get this good,—with but a groan or so,
Then, silence of the victims,—were the feat.
He foresaw, made a picture in his mind,—
Of father and mother stunned and echoless
To the blow, as they lie staring at fate's jaws
Their folly danced into, till the woe fell;
Edged in a month by strenuous cruelty
From even the poor nook whence they watched the wolf
Feast on their heart, the lamb-like child his prey;
Plundered to the last remnant of their wealth,
(What daily pittance pleased the plunderer dole)
Hunted forth to go hide head, starve and die,
And leave the pale awe-stricken wife, past hope
Of help i' th world now, mute and motionless,
His slave, his chattel, to use, then destroy:
All this, he bent mind how to bring about,
Put this in act and life, as painted plain,
So have success, reach crown of earthly good,
In this particular enterprise of man,
By marriage—undertaken in God's face
With all those lies so opposite God's truth,
For ends so other than man's end.

Thus schemes
Guido, and thus would carry out his scheme:
But when an obstacle first blocks the path,
When he finds none may boast monopoly
Of lies and trick i' the tricking lying world,—
That sorry timid natures, even this sort
O' the Comparini, want nor trick nor lie
Proper to the kind,—that as the gor-crow treats
The bramble-finch so treats the finch the moth,
And the great Guido is minutely matched
By this same couple,—whether true or false
The revelation of Pompilia's birth,
Which in a moment brings his scheme to nought,—

Then, he is piqued, advances yet a stage,
Leaves the low region to the finch and fly,
Soars to the zenith whence the fiercer fowl
May dare the inimitable swoop. I see.
He draws now on the curious crime, the fine
Felicity and flower of wickedness;
Determines, by the utmost exercise
Of violence, made safe and sure by craft,
To satiate malice, pluck one last arch-pang
From the parents, else would triumph out of reach,
By punishing their child, within reach yet,
Who thought, word or deed, could nowise wrong
I' the matter that now moves him. So plans he,
Always subordinating (note the point!)
Revenge, the manlier sin, to interest
The meaner,—would pluck pang forth, but unclench
No gripe in the act, let fall no money-piece.
Hence a plan for so plaguing, body and soul,
His wife, so putting, day by day, hour by hour,
The untried torture to the untouched place,
As must precipitate an end foreseen,
Goad her into some plain revolt, most like
Plunge upon patent suicidal shame,
Death to herself, damnation by rebound
To those whose hearts he, holding hers, holds still:
Such a plan as, in its bad completeness, shall
Ruin the three together and alike,
Yet leave himself in luck and liberty,
No claim renounced, no right a forfeiture,
His person unendangered, his good fame
Without a flaw, his pristine worth intact,—
While they, with all their claims and rights that cling,
Shall forthwith crumble off him every side,
Scorched into dust, a plaything for the winds.
As when, in our Campagna, there is fired
The nest-like work that overruns a hut;
And, as the thatch burns here, there, everywhere,
Even to the ivy and wild vine, that bound
And blessed the home where men were happy once,
There rises gradual, black amid the blaze,
Some grim and unscathed nucleus of the nest,—
Some old malicious tower, some obscene tomb
They thought a temple in their ignorance,
And clung about and thought to lean upon—
There laughs it o'er their ravage,—where are they?
So did his cruelty burn life about,
And lay the ruin bare in dreadfulness,
Try the persistency of torment so
O' the wife, that, at some fierce extremity,
Some crisis brought about by fire and flame,
The patient frenzy stung must needs break loose,
Fly anyhow, find refuge anywhere,
Even in the arms of who might front her first,
No monster but a man—while nature shrieked

"Or thus escape, or die!" The spasm arrived,
Not the escape by way of sin,—O God,
Who shall pluck sheep Thou holdest, from Thy hand?
Therefore she lay resigned to die,—so far
The simple cruelty was foiled. Why then,
Craft to the rescue, let craft supplement
Cruelty and show hell a masterpiece!
Hence this consummate lie, this love-intrigue,
Unmanly simulation of a sin,
With place and time and circumstance to suit—
These letters false beyond all forgery—
Not just handwriting and mere authorship,
But false to body and soul they figure forth—
As though the man had cut out shape and shape
From fancies of that other Aretine,
To paste below—incorporate the filth
With cherub faces on a missal-page!

Whereby the man so far attains his end
That strange temptation is permitted,—see!
Pompilia wife, and Caponsacchi priest,
Are brought together as nor priest nor wife
Should stand, and there is passion in th' place,
Power in the air for evil as for good,
Promptings from heaven and hell, as if the stars
Fought in their courses for a fate to be.
Thus stand the wife and priest, a spectacle,
I doubt not, to unseen assemblage there.
No lamp will mark that window for a shrine,
No tablet signalize the terrace, teach
New generations which succeed the old,
The pavement of the street is holy ground;
No bard describe in verse how Christ prevailed
And Satan fell like lightning! Why repine?
What does the world, told truth, but lie the more?

A second time the plot is foiled; nor, now,
By corresponding sin for countercheck,
No wile and trick to baffle trick and wile,—
The play o' the parents! Here the blot is blanched
By God's gift of a purity of soul
That will not take pollution, ermine-like
Armed from dishonour by its own soft snow.
Such was this gift of God who showed for once
How He would have the world go white: it seems
As a new attribute were born of each
Champion of truth, the priest and wife I praise,—
As a new safeguard sprang up in defence
Of their new noble nature: so a thorn
Comes to the aid of and completes the rose—
Courage to-wit, no woman's gift nor priest's,
I' the crisis; might leaps vindicating right.
See how the strong aggressor, bad and bold,
With every vantage, preconcerts surprise,

Leaps of a sudden at his victim's throat
In a byeway,—how fares he when face to face
With Caponsacchi? Who fights, who fears now?
There quails Count Guido, armed to the chattering teeth,
Cowers at the steadfast eye and quiet word
O' the Canon at the Pieve! There skulks crime
Behind law called in to back cowardice:
While out of the poor trampled worm the wife,
Springs up a serpent!

But anon of these!
Him I judge now,—of him proceed to note,
Failing the first, a second chance befriends
Guido, gives pause ere punishment arrive.
The law he called, comes, hears, adjudicates,
Nor does amiss i' the main,—secludes the wife
From the husband, respites the oppressed one, grants
Probation to the oppressor, could he know
The mercy of a minute's fiery purge!
The furnace-coals alike of public scorn,
Private remorse, heaped glowing on his head,
What if,—the force and guile, the ore's alloy,
Eliminate, his baser soul refined—
The lost be saved even yet, so as by fire?
Let him, rebuked, go softly all his days
And, when no graver musings claim their due,
Meditate on a man's immense mistake
Who, fashioned to use feet and walk, deigns crawl—
Takes the unmanly means—ay, though to ends
Man scarce should make for, would but reach thro' wrong,—
May sin, but nowise needs shame manhood so:
Since fowlers hawk, shoot, nay and snare the game,
And yet eschew vile practice, nor find sport
In torch-light treachery or the luring owl.

But how hunts Guido? Why, the fraudful trap—
Late spurned to ruin by the indignant feet
Of fellows in the chase who loved fair play—
Here he picks up the fragments to the least,
Lades him and hies to the old lurking-place
Where haply he may patch again, refit
The mischief, file its blunted teeth anew,
Make sure, next time, first snap shall break the bone.
Craft, greed and violence complot revenge:
Craft, for its quota, schemes to bring about
And seize occasion and be safe withal:
Greed craves its act may work both far and near,
Crush the tree, branch and trunk and root, beside.
Whichever twig or leaf arrests a streak
Of possible sunshine else would coin itself,
And drop down one more gold piece in the path:
Violence stipulates "Advantage proved,
"And safety sure, be pain the overplus!
"Murder with jagged knife! Cut but tear too!
"Foiled oft, starved long, glut malice for amends!"

And what craft's scheme?—scheme sorrowful and strange
As though the elements, whom mercy checked,
Had mustered hate for one eruption more,
One final deluge to surprise the Ark
Cradled and sleeping on its mountain-top:
The outbreak-signal—what but the dove's coos
Back with the olive in her bill for news
Sorrow was over? 'Tis an infant's birth,
Guido's first born, his son and heir, that gives
The occasion: other men cut free their souls
From care in such a case, fly up in thanks
To God, reach, recognize His love for once:
Guido cries "Soul, at last the mire is thine!
"Lie there in likeness of a money-bag,
"This babe's birth so pins down past moving now,
"That I dare cut adrift the lives I late
"Scrupled to touch lest thou escape with them!
"These parents and their child my wife,—touch one
"Lose all! Their rights determined on a head
"I could but hate, not harm, since from each hair
"Dangled a hope for me: now—chance and change!
"No right was in their child but passes plain
"To that child's child and through such child to me.
"I am a father now,—come what, come will,
"I represent my child; he comes between—
"Cuts sudden off the sunshine of this life
"From those three: why, the gold is in his curls!
"Not with old Pietro's, Violante's head,
"Not his grey horror, her more hideous black—
"Go these, devoted to the knife!"

'Tis done:
Wherefore should mind misgive, heart hesitate?
He calls to counsel, fashions certain four
Colourless natures counted clean till now,
—Rustic simplicity, uncorrupted youth,
Ignorant virtue! Here's the gold o' the prime
When Saturn ruled, shall shock our leaden day—
The clown abash the courtier! Mark it, bards!
The courtier tries his hand on clownship here,
Speaks a word, names a crime, appoints a price,—
Just breathes on what, suffused with all himself,
Is red-hot henceforth past distinction now
I' the common glow of hell. And thus they break
And blaze on us at Rome, Christ's birthnight-eve!
Oh angels that sang erst "On the earth, peace!
"To man, good will!"—such peace finds earth to-day!
After the seventeen hundred years, so man
Wills good to man, so Guido makes complete
His murder! what is it I said?—cuts loose
Three lives that hitherto he suffered cling,
Simply because each served to nail secure,
By a corner of the money-bag, his soul,—
Therefore, lives sacred till the babe's first breath
O'erweights them in the balance,—off they fly!

So is the murder managed, sin conceived
To the full: and why not crowned with triumph too?
Why must the sin, conceived thus, bring forth death?
I note how, within hair's-breadth of escape,
Impunity and the thing supposed success,
Guido is found when the check comes, the change,
The monitory touch o' the tether—felt
By few, not marked by many, named by none
At the moment, only recognized aright
I' the fulness of the days, for God's, lest sin
Exceed the service, leap the line: such check—
A secret which this life finds hard to keep,
And, often guessed, is never quite revealed—
Needs must trip Guido on a stumbling-block
Too vulgar, too absurdly plain i' the path!
Study this single oversight of care,
This hebetude that marred sagacity,
Forgetfulness of all the man best knew!
Here is a stranger who, with need to fly,
Needs but to ask and have the means of flight.
Why, the first urchin tells you, to leave Rome,
Get horses, you must show the warrant, just
The banal scrap, clerk's scribble, a fair word buys,
Or foul one, if a ducat sweeten word,—
And straight authority will back demand,
Give you the pick o' the post-house!—how should he,
Then, resident at Rome for thirty years,
Guido, instruct a stranger! And himself
Forgets just this poor paper scrap, wherewith
Armed, every door he knocks at opens wide
To save him: horsed and manned, with such advance
O' the hunt behind, why 'twere the easy task
Of hours told on the fingers of one hand,
To reach the Tuscan Frontier, laugh at-home,
Light-hearted with his fellows of the place,—
Prepared by that strange shameful judgment, that
Satire upon a sentence just pronounced
By the Rota and confirmed by the Granduke,—
Ready in a circle to receive their peer,
Appreciate his good story how, when Rome,
The Pope-King and the populace of priests
Made common cause with their confederate
The other priestling who seduced his wife,
He, all unaided, wiped out the affront
With decent bloodshed and could face his friends,
Frolic it in the world's eye. Ay, such tale
Missed such applause, and by such oversight!
So, tired and footsore, those blood-flustered five
Went reeling on the road through dark and cold,
The few permissible miles, to sink at length,
Wallow and sleep in the first wayside straw,
As the other herd quenched, i' the wash o' the wave,
—Each swine, the devil inside him: so slept they,
And so were caught and caged—all through one trip,

Touch of the fool in Guido the astute!
He curses the omission, I surmise,
More than the murder. Why, thou fool and blind,
It is the mercy-stroke that stops thy fate,
Hamstrings and holds thee to thy hurt,—but how?
On the edge o' the precipice! One minute more,
Thou hadst gone farther and fared worse, my son,
Fathoms down on the flint and fire beneath!
Thy comrades each and all were of one mind
Thy murder done, to straightway murder thee
In turn, because of promised pay withheld.
So, to the last, greed found itself at odds
With craft in thee, and, proving conqueror,
Had sent thee, the same night that crowned thy hope,
Thither where, this same day, I see thee not,
Nor, through God's mercy, need, to-morrow, see.

Such I find Guido, midmost blotch of black
Discernible in this group of clustered crimes
Huddling together in the cave they call
Their palace, outraged day thus penetrates.
Around him ranged, now close and now remote,
Prominent or obscure to meet the needs
O' the mage and master, I detect each shape
Subsidiary i' the scene nor loathed the less,
All alike coloured, all descried akin
By one and the same pitchy furnace stirred
At the centre: see, they lick the master's hand,—
This fox-faced horrible priest, this brother-brute
The Abate,—why, mere wolfishness looks well,
Guido stands honest in the red o' the flame,
Beside this yellow that would pass for white,
This Guido, all craft but no violence,
This copier of the mien and gait and garb
Of Peter and Paul, that he may go disguised,
Rob halt and lame, sick folk i' the temple-porch!
Armed with religion, fortified by law,
A man of peace, who trims the midnight lamp
And turns the classic page—and all for craft,
All to work harm with, yet incur no scratch!
While Guido brings the struggle to a close,
Paul steps back the due distance, clear o' the trap
He builds and baits. Guido I catch and judge;
Paul is past reach in this world and my time:
That is a case reserved. Pass to the next,
The boy of the brood, the young Girolamo
Priest, Canon, and what more? nor wolf nor fox,
But hybrid, neither craft nor violence
Wholly, part violence part craft: such cross
Tempts speculation—will both blend one day,
And prove hell's better product? Or subside
And let the simple quality emerge,
Go on with Satan's service the old way?
Meanwhile, what promise,—what performance too!

For there's a new distinctive touch, I see,
Lust—lacking in the two—hell's own blue tint
That gives a character and marks the man
More than a match for yellow and red. Once more,
A case reserved: why should I doubt? Then comes
The gaunt grey nightmare in the furthest smoke,
The hag that gave these three abortions birth,
Unmotherly mother and unwomanly
Woman, that near turns motherhood to shame,
Womanliness to loathing: no one word,
No gesture to curb cruelty a whit
More than the she-pard thwarts her playsome whelps
Trying their milk-teeth on the soft o' the throat
O' the first fawn, flung, with those beseeching eyes,
Flat in the covert! How should she but couch,
Lick the dry lips, unsheath the blunted claw,
Catch 'twixt her placid eyewinks at what chance
Old bloody half-forgotten dream may flit,
Born when herself was novice to the taste,
The while she lets youth take its pleasure. Last,
These God-abandoned wretched lumps of life,
These four companions,—country-folk this time,
Not tainted by the unwholesome civic breath,
Much less the curse o' the Court! Mere striplings too,
Fit to do human nature justice still!
Surely when impudence in Guido's shape
Shall propose crime and proffer money's-worth
To these stout tall bright-eyed black-haired boys,
The blood shall bound in answer to each cheek
Before the indignant outcry break from lip!
Are these i' the mood to murder, hardly loosed
From healthy autumn-finish of ploughed glebe,
Grapes in the barrel, work at happy end,
And winter come with rest and Christmas play?
How greet they Guido with his final task—
(As if he but proposed "One vineyard more
"To dig, ere frost come, then relax indeed!")
"Anywhere, anyhow and anywhy,
"Murder me some three people, old and young,
"Ye never heard the names of,—and be paid
"So much!" And the whole four accede at once.
Demur? Do cattle bidden march or halt?
Is it some lingering habit, old fond faith
I' the lord of the land, instructs them,—birthright-badge
Of feudal tenure claims its slaves again?
Not so at all, thou noble human heart!
All is done purely for the pay,—which, earned,
And not forthcoming at the instant, makes
Religion heresy, and the lord o' the land
Fit subject for a murder in his turn.
The patron with cut throat and rifled purse,
Deposited i' the roadside-ditch, his due,
Nought hinders each good fellow trudging home
The heavier by a piece or two in poke,

And so with new zest to the common life,
Mattock and spade, plough-tail and waggon-shaft,
Till some such other piece of luck betide,
Who knows? Since this is a mere start in life,
And none of them exceeds the twentieth year.
Nay, more i' the background, yet? Unnoticed forms
Claim to be classed, subordinately vile?
Complacent lookers-on that laugh,—perchance
Shake head as their friend's horse-play grows too rough
With the mere child he manages amiss—
But would not interfere and make bad worse
For twice the fractious tears and prayers: thou know'st
Civility better, Marzi-Medici,
Governor for thy kinsman the Granduke!
Fit representative of law, man's lamp
I' the magistrate's grasp full-flare, no rushlight-end
Sputtering 'twixt thumb and finger of the priest!
Whose answer to the couple's cry for help
Is a threat,—whose remedy of Pompilia's wrong
A shrug o' the shoulder, and facetious word
Or wink, traditional with Tuscan wits,
To Guido in the doorway. Laud to law!
The wife is pushed back to the husband, he
Who knows how these home-squabblings persecute
People who have the public good to mind,
And work best with a silence in the court!

Ah, but I save my word at least for thee,
Archbishop, who art under me i' the Church,
As I am under God,—thou, chosen by both
To do the shepherd's office, feed the sheep—
How of this lamb that panted at thy foot
While the wolf pressed on her within crook's reach?
Wast thou the hireling that did turn and flee?
With thee at least anon the little word!

Such denizens o' the cave now cluster round
And heat the furnace sevenfold: time indeed
A bolt from heaven should cleave roof and clear place,
Transfix and show the world, suspiring flame,
The main offender, scar and brand the rest
Hurrying, each miscreant to his hole: then flood
And purify the scene with outside day—
Which yet, in the absolutest drench of dark,
Ne'er wants a witness, some stray beauty-beam
To the despair of hell.

First of the first,
Such I pronounce Pompilia, then as now
Perfect in whiteness: stoop thou down, my child,
Give one good moment to the poor old Pope
Heart-sick at having all his world to blame—
Let me look at thee in the flesh as erst,
Let me enjoy the old clean linen garb,

Not the new splendid vesture! Armed and crowned,
Would Michael, yonder, be, nor crowned nor armed,
The less pre-eminent angel? Everywhere
I see in the world the intellect of man,
That sword, the energy his subtle spear,
The knowledge which defends him like a shield—
Everywhere; but they make not up, I think,
The marvel of a soul like thine, earth's flower
She holds up to the softened gaze of God!
It was not given Pompilia to know much,
Speak much, to write a book, to move mankind,
Be memorized by who records my time.
Yet if in purity and patience, if
In faith held fast despite the plucking fiend,
Safe like the signet-stone with the new name
That saints are known by,—if in right returned
For wrong, most pardon for worst injury,
If there be any virtue, any praise,—
Then will this woman-child have proved—who knows?—
Just the one prize vouchsafed unworthy me,
Seven years a gardener of the untoward ground,
I till,—this earth, my sweat and blood manure
All the long day that barrenly grows dusk:
At least one blossom makes me proud at eve
Born 'mid the briers of my enclosure! Still
(Oh, here as elsewhere, nothingness of man!)
Those be the plants, imbedded yonder South
To mellow in the morning, those made fat
By the master's eye, that yield such timid leaf,
Uncertain bud, as product of his pains!
While—see how this mere chance-sown, cleft-nursed seed,
That sprang up by the wayside 'neath the foot
Of the enemy, this breaks all into blaze,
Spreads itself, one wide glory of desire
To incorporate the whole great sun it loves
From the inch-height whence it looks and longs! My flower,
My rose, I gather for the breast of God,
This I praise most in thee, where all I praise,
That having been obedient to the end
According to the light allotted, law
Prescribed thy life, still tried, still standing test,—
Dutiful to the foolish parents first,
Submissive next to the bad husband,—nay,
Tolerant of those meaner miserable
That did his hests, eked out the dole of pain,—
Thou, patient thus, couldst rise from law to law,
The old to the new, promoted at one cry
O' the trump of God to the new service, not
To longer bear, but henceforth fight, be found
Sublime in new impatience with the foe!
Endure man and obey God: plant firm foot
On neck of man, tread man into the hell
Meet for him, and obey God all the more!
Oh child that didst despise thy life so much

When it seemed only thine to keep or lose,
How the fine ear felt fall the first low word
"Value life, and preserve life for My sake!"
Thou didst . . . how shall I say? . . . receive so long
The standing ordinance of God on earth,
What wonder if the novel claim had clashed
With old requirement, seemed to supersede
Too much the customary law? But, brave,
Thou at first prompting of what I call God,
And fools call Nature, didst hear, comprehend,
Accept the obligation laid on thee,
Mother elect, to save the unborn child,
As brute and bird do, reptile and the fly,
Ay and, I nothing doubt, even tree, shrub, plant
And flower o' the field, all in a common pact
To worthily defend the trust of trusts,
Life from the Ever Living:—didst resist—
Anticipate the office that is mine—
And with his own sword stay the upraised arm,
The endeavour of the wicked, and defend
Him who,—again in my default,—was there
For visible providence: one less true than thou
To touch, i' the past, less practised in the right,
Approved less far in all docility
To all instruction,—how had such an one
Made scruple "Is this motion a decree?"
It was authentic to the experienced ear
O' the good and faithful servant. Go past me
And get thy praise,—and be not far to seek
Presently when I follow if I may!

And surely not so very much apart
Need I place thee, my warrior-priest,—in whom
What if I gain the other rose, the gold,
We grave to imitate God's miracle,
Greet monarchs with, good rose in its degree?
Irregular noble 'scapegrace—son the same!
Faulty—and peradventure ours the fault
Who still misteach, mislead, throw hook and line
Thinking to land leviathan forsooth,
Tame the scaled neck, play with him as a bird,
And bind him for our maidens! Better bear
The King of Pride go wantoning awhile,
Unplagued by cord in nose and thorn in jaw,
Through deep to deep, followed by all that shine,
Churning the blackness hoary: He who made
The comely terror, He shall make the sword
To match that piece of netherstone his heart,
Ay, nor miss praise thereby; who else shut fire
I' the stone, to leap from mouth at sword's first stroke,
In lamps of love and faith, the chivalry
That dares the right and disregards alike
The yea and nay o' the world? Self-sacrifice,—
What if an idol took it? Ask the Church

Why she was wont to turn each Venus here,—
Poor Rome perversely lingered round, despite
Instruction, for the sake of purblind love,—
Into Madonna's shape, and waste no whit
Of aught so rare on earth as gratitude!
All this sweet savour was not ours but thine,
Nard of the rock, a natural wealth we name
Incense, and treasure up as food for saints,
When flung to us—whose function was to give
Not find the costly perfume. Do I smile?
Nay, Caponsacchi, much I find amiss,
Blameworthy, punishable in this freak
Of thine, this youth prolonged though age was ripe,
This masquerade in sober day, with change
Of motley too,—now hypocrite's disguise,
Now fool's-costume: which lie was least like truth,
Which the ungainlier, more discordant garb
With that symmetric soul inside my son,
The churchman's or the worldling's,—let him judge,
Our adversary who enjoys the task!
I rather chronicle the healthy rage,—
When the first moan broke from the martyr-maid
At that uncaging of the beasts,—made bare
My athlete on the instant, gave such good
Great undisguised leap over post and pale
Right into the mid-cirque, free fighting-place.
There may have been rash stripping—every rag
Went to the winds,—infringement manifold
Of laws prescribed pudicity, I fear,
In this impulsive and prompt self-display!
Ever such tax comes of the foolish youth;
Men mulct the wiser manhood, and suspect
No veritable star swims out of cloud:
Bear thou such imputation, undergo
The penalty I nowise dare relax,—
Conventional chastisement and rebuke.
But for the outcome, the brave starry birth
Conciliating earth with all that cloud,
Thank heaven as I do! Ay, such championship
Of God at first blush, such prompt cherry thud
Of glove on ground that answers ringingly
The challenge of the false knight,—watch we long,
And wait we vainly for its gallant like
From those appointed to the service, sworn
His body-guard with pay and privilege—
White-cinct, because in white walks sanctity,
Red-socked, how else proclaim fine scorn of flesh,
Unchariness of blood when blood faith begs?
Where are the men-at-arms with cross on coat?
Aloof, bewraying their attire: whilst thou
In mask and motley, pledged to dance not fight,
Sprang'st forth the hero! In thought, word and deed,
How throughout all thy warfare thou wast pure,
I find it easy to believe: and if

At any fateful moment of the strange
Adventure, the strong passion of that strait,
Fear and surprise, may have revealed too much,—
As when a thundrous midnight, with black air
That burns, rain-drops that blister, breaks a spell,
Draws out the excessive virtue of some sheathed
Shut unsuspected flower that hoards and hides
Immensity of sweetness,—so, perchance,
Might the surprise and fear release too much
The perfect beauty of the body and soul
Thou savedst in thy passion for God's sake,
He who is Pity: was the trial sore?
Temptation sharp? Thank God a second time!
Why comes temptation but for man to meet
And master and make crouch beneath his foot,
And so be pedestaled in triumph? Pray
"Lead us into no such temptations, Lord!"
Yea, but, O Thou whose servants are the bold,
Lead such temptations by the head and hair,
Reluctant dragons, up to who dares fight,
That so he may do battle and have praise!
Do I not see the praise?—that while thy mates
Bound to deserve i' the matter, prove at need
Unprofitable through the very pains
We gave to train them well and start them fair,—
Are found too stiff, with standing ranked and ranged,
For onset in good earnest, too obtuse
Of ear, through iteration of command,
For catching quick the sense of the real cry,—
Thou, whose sword-hand was used to strike the lute,
Whose sentry-station graced some wanton's gate,
Thou didst push forward and show mettle, shame
The laggards, and retrieve the day. Well done!
Be glad thou hast let light into the world,
Through that irregular breach o' the boundary,—see
The same upon thy path and march assured,
Learning anew the use of soldiership,
Self-abnegation, freedom from all fear,
Loyalty to the life's end! Ruminate,
Deserve the initiatory spasm,—once more
Work, be unhappy but bear life, my son!

And troop you, somewhere 'twixt the best and worst,
Where crowd the indifferent product, all too poor
Makeshift, starved samples of humanity!
Father and mother, huddle there and hide!
A gracious eye may find you! Foul and fair,
Sadly mixed natures: self-indulgent,—yet
Self-sacrificing too: how the love soars,
How the craft, avarice, vanity and spite
Sink again! So they keep the middle course,
Slide into silly crime at unaware,
Slip back upon the stupid virtue, stay
Nowhere enough for being classed, I hope

And fear. Accept the swift and rueful death,
Taught, somewhat sternlier than is wont, what waits
The ambiguous creature,—how the one black tuft
Steadies the aim of the arrow just as well
As the wide faultless white on the bird's breast.
Nay, you were punished in the very part
That looked most pure of speck,—the honest love
Betrayed you,—did love seem most worthy pains,
Challenge such purging, since ordained survive
When all the rest of you was done with? Go!
Never again elude the choice of tints!
White shall not neutralize the black, nor good
Compensate bad in man, absolve him so:
Life's business being just the terrible choice.

So do I see, pronounce on all and some
Grouped for my judgment now,—profess no doubt
While I pronounce: dark, difficult enough
The human sphere, yet eyes grow sharp by use,
I find the truth, dispart the shine from shade,
As a mere man may, with no special touch
O' the lynx-gift in each ordinary orb:
Nay, if the popular notion class me right,
One of well-nigh decayed intelligence,—
What of that? Through hard labour and good will,
And habitude that gives a blind man sight
At the practised finger-ends of him, I do
Discern, and dare decree in consequence,
Whatever prove the peril of mistake.
Whence, then, this quite new quick cold thrill,—cloud-like,
This keen dread creeping from a quarter scarce
Suspected in the skies I nightly scan?
What slacks the tense nerve, saps the wound-up spring
Of the act that should and shall be, sends the mount
And mass o' the whole man's-strength,—conglobed so late—
Shudderingly into dust, a moment's work?
While I stand firm, go fearless, in this world,
For this life recognize and arbitrate,
Touch and let stay, or else remove a thing,
Judge "This is right, this object out of place,"
Candle in hand that helps me and to spare,—
What if a voice deride me, "Perk and pry!
"Brighten each nook with thine intelligence!
"Play the good householder, ply man and maid
"With tasks prolonged into the midnight, test
"Their work and nowise stint of the due wage
"Each worthy worker: but with gyves and whip
"Pay thou misprision of a single point
"Plain to thy happy self who lift'st the light,
"Lament's the darkling,—bold to all beneath!
"What if thyself adventure, now the place
"Is purged so well? Leave pavement and mount roof,
"Look round thee for the light of the upper sky,
"The fire which lit thy fire which finds default

"In Guido Franceschini to his cost!
"What if, above in the domain of light,
"Thou miss the accustomed signs, remark eclipse?
"Shalt thou still gaze on ground nor lift a lid,—
"Steady in thy superb prerogative,
"Thy inch of inkling,—nor once face the doubt
"I' the sphere above thee, darkness to be felt?"

Yet my poor spark had for its source, the sun;
Thither I sent the great looks which compel
Light from its fount: all that I do and am
Comes from the truth, or seen or else surmised,
Remembered or divined, as mere man may:
I know just so, nor otherwise. As I know,
I speak,—what should I know, then, and how speak
Were there a wild mistake of eye or brain
As to recorded governance above?
If my own breath, only, blew coal alight
I called celestial and the morning-star?
I, who in this world act resolvedly,
Dispose of men, their bodies and their souls,
As they acknowledge or gainsay the light
I show them,—shall I too lack courage?—leave
I, too, the post of me, like those I blame?
Refuse, with kindred inconsistency,
Grapple with danger whereby souls grow strong?
I am near the end; but still not at the end;
All till the very end is trial in life:
At this stage is the trial of my soul
Danger to face, or danger to refuse?
Shall I dare try the doubt now, or not dare?

O Thou,—as represented here to me
In such conception as my soul allows,—
Under Thy measureless my atom width!—
Man's mind—what is it but a convex glass
Wherein are gathered all the scattered points
Picked out of the immensity of sky,
To reunite there, be our heaven for earth,
Our known unknown, our God revealed to man?
Existent somewhere, somehow, as a whole;
Here, as a whole proportioned to our sense,—
There, (which is nowhere, speech must babble thus!)
In the absolute immensity, the whole
Appreciable solely by Thyself,—
Here, by the little mind of man, reduced
To littleness that suits his faculty,
In the degree appreciable too;
Between Thee and ourselves—nay even, again,
Below us, to the extreme of the minute,
Appreciable by how many and what diverse
Modes of the life Thou madest be! (why live
Except for love,—how love unless they know?)
Each of them, only filling to the edge,

Insect or angel, his just length and breadth,
Due facet of reflection,—full, no less,
Angel or insect, as Thou framedst things,—
I it is who have been appointed here
To represent Thee, in my turn, on earth,
Just as, if new philosophy know aught,
This one earth, out of all the multitude
Of peopled worlds, as stars are now supposed,—
Was chosen, and no sun-star of the swarm,
For stage and scene of Thy transcendent act
Beside which even the creation fades
Into a puny exercise of power.
Choice of the world, choice of the thing I am,
Both emanate alike from Thy dread play
Of operation outside this our sphere
Where things are classed and counted small or great,—
Incomprehensibly the choice is Thine!
I therefore bow my head and take Thy place.
There is, beside the works, a tale of Thee
In the world's mouth which I find credible:
I love it with my heart: unsatisfied,
I try it with my reason, nor discept
From any point I probe and pronounce sound.
Mind is not matter nor from matter, but
Above,—leave matter then, proceed with mind!
Man's be the mind recognized at the height,—
Leave the inferior minds and look at man!
Is he the strong, intelligent and good
Up to his own conceivable height? No wise.
Enough o' the low,—soar the conceivable height,
Find cause to match the effect in evidence,
The work i' the world, not man's but God's; leave man!
Conjecture of the worker by the work:
Is there strength there?—enough: intelligence?
Ample: but goodness in a like degree?
Not to the human eye in the present state,
An isoscele deficient in the base.
What lacks, then, of perfection fit for God
But just the instance which this tale supplies
Of love without a limit? So is strength,
So is intelligence; let love be so,
Unlimited in its self-sacrifice,
Then is the tale true and God shows complete.
Beyond the tale, I reach into the dark,
Feel what I cannot see, and still faith stands:
I can believe this dread machinery
Of sin and sorrow, would confound me else,
Devised,—all pain, at most expenditure
Of pain by Who devised pain,—to evolve,
By new machinery in counterpart,
The moral qualities of man—how else?—
To make him love in turn and be beloved,
Creative and self-sacrificing too,
And thus eventually God-like, (ay,

"I have said ye are Gods"—shall it be said for nought?)
Enable man to wring, from out all pain,
All pleasure for a common heritage
To all eternity: this may be surmised,
The other is revealed,—whether a fact,
Absolute, abstract, independent truth,
Historic, not reduced to suit man's mind,—
Or only truth reverberate, changed, made pass
A spectrum into mind, the narrow eye,—
The same and not the same, else unconceived—
Though quite conceivable to the next grade
Above it in intelligence,—as truth
Easy to man were blindness to the beast
By parity of procedure,—the same truth
In a new form, but changed in either case:
What matter so the intelligence be filled?
To the child, the sea is angry, for it roars;
Frost bites, else why the tooth-like fret on face?
Man makes acoustics deal with the sea's wrath,
Explains the choppy cheek by chymic law,—
To man and child, remains the same effect
On drum of ear and root of nose, change cause
Never so thoroughly: so our heart be struck,
What care I,—by God's gloved hand or the bare?
Nor do I much perplex me with aught hard,
Dubious in the transmitting of the tale,—
No, nor with certain riddles set to solve.
This life is training and a passage; pass,—
Still, we march over some flat obstacle
We made give way before us; solid truth
In front of it, what motion for the world?
The moral sense grows but by exercise.
'Tis even as man grew probatively
Initiated in Godship, set to make
A fairer moral world than this he finds,
Guess now what shall be known hereafter. Deal
Thus with the present problem: as we see,
A faultless creature is destroyed, and sin
Has had its way i' the world where God should rule.
Ay, but for this irrelevant circumstance
Of inquisition after blood, we see
Pompilia lost and Guido saved: how long?
For his whole life: how much is that whole life?
We are not babes, but know the minute's worth,
And feel that life is large and the world small,
So, wait till life have passed from out the world.
Neither does this astonish at the end,
That, whereas I can so receive and trust,
Other men, made with hearts and souls the same,
Reject and disbelieve,—subordinate
The future to the present,—sin, nor fear.
This I refer still to the foremost fact,
Life is probation and the earth no goal
But starting-point of man: compel him strive,

Which means, in man, as good as reach the goal,—
Why institute that race, his life, at all?
But this does overwhelm me with surprise,
Touch me to terror,—not that faith, the pearl,
Should be let lie by fishers wanting food,—
Nor, seen and handled by a certain few
Critical and contemptuous, straight consigned
To shore and shingle for the pebble it proves,—
But that, when haply found and known and named
By the residue made rich for evermore,
These,—that these favoured ones, should in a trice
Turn, and with double zest go dredge for whelks,
Mud-worms that make the savoury soup! Enough
O' the disbelievers, see the faithful few!
How do the Christians here deport them, keep
Their robes of white unspotted by the world?
What is this Aretine Archbishop, this
Man under me as I am under God,
This champion of the faith, I armed and decked,
Pushed forward, put upon a pinnacle,
To show the enemy his victor,—see!
What's the best fighting when the couple close?
Pompilia cries, "Protect me from the wolf!"
"No, thy Guido is rough heady, strong,
"Dangerous to disquiet: let him bide!
"He needs some bone to mumble, help amuse
"The darkness of his den with: so, the fawn
"Which limps up bleeding to my foot and lies,
"—Come to me, daughter!—thus I throw him back!"
Have we misjudged here, over-armed our knight,
Given gold and silk where the plain steel serves best,
Enfeebled whom we sought to fortify,
Made an archbishop and undone a saint?
Well then, descend these heights, this pride of life,
Sit in the ashes with a barefoot monk
Who long ago stamped out the worldly sparks.
By fasting, watching, stone cell and wire scourge,
—No such indulgence as unknits the strength—
These breed the tight nerve and touch cuticle,
And the world's praise or blame runs rillet-wise
Off the broad back and brawny breast, we know!
He meets the first cold sprinkle of the world
And shudders to the marrow. "Save this child?
"Oh, my superiors, oh, the Archbishop's self!
"Who was it dared lay hand upon the ark
"His betters saw fall nor put finger forth?
"Great ones could help yet help not: why should small?
"I break my promise: let her break her heart!"
These are the Christians not the worldlings, not
The sceptics, who thus battle for the faith!
If foolish virgins disobey and sleep,
What wonder? But, this time the wise that watch,
Sell lamps and buy lutes, exchange oil for wine,
The mystic Spouse betrays the Bridegroom here.

To our last resource, then! Since all flesh is weak,
Blind weaknesses together, we get strength:
The individual weighed, found wanting, try
Some institution, honest artifice
Whereby the units grow compact and firm!
Each props the other, and so stand is made
By our embodied cowards that grow brave.
The Monastery called of Convertites,
Meant to help women because these helped Christ,—
A thing existent only while it acts,
Does as designed, else a nonentity,
For what is an idea unrealized?—
Pompilia is consigned to these for help.
They do help; they are prompt to testify
To her pure life and saintly dying days.
She dies, and lo, who seemed so poor, proves rich.
What does the body that lives through helpfulness
To women for Christ's sake? The kiss turns bite,
The dove's note changes to the crow's cry; judge!
"Seeing that this our Convent claims of right
"What goods belong to those we succour, be
"The same proved women of dishonest life,—
"And seeing that this Trial made appear
"Pompilia was in such predicament,—
"The Convent hereupon pretends to said
"Succession of Pompilia, issues writ,
"And takes possession by the Fisc's advice."
Such is their attestation to the cause
Of Christ, who had one saint at least, they hoped:
But, is a title-deed to filch, a corpse
To slander, and an infant-heir to cheat?
Christ must give up his gains then! They unsay
All the fine speeches,—who was saint is whore.
Why, scripture yields no parallel for this!
The soldiers only threw dice for Christ's coat;
We want another legend of the Twelve
Disputing if it was Christ's coat at all,
Claiming as prize the woof of price—for why?
The Master was a thief, purloined the same,
Or paid for it out of the common bag!
Can it be this is end and outcome, all
I take with me to show as stewardship's fruit,
The best yield of the latest time, this year
The seventeenth-hundredth since God died for man?
Is such effect proportionate to cause?
And still the terror keeps on the increase
When I perceive . . . how can I blink the fact?
That the fault, the obduracy to good,
Lies not with the impracticable stuff
Whence man is made, his very nature's fault,
As if it were of ice, the moon may gild
Not melt, or stone 'twas meant the sun should warm
Not make bear flowers,—nor ice nor stone to blame:
But it can melt, that ice, can bloom, that stone,

Impassible to rule of day and night!
This terrifies me, thus compelled perceive
Whatever love and faith we looked should spring
At advent of the authoritative star,
Which yet lie sluggish, curdled at the source,—
These have leapt forth profusely in old time,
These still respond with promptitude to-day,
At challenge of—what unacknowledged powers
O' the air, what uncommissioned meteors, warmth
By law, and light by rule should supersede?
For see this priest, this Caponsacchi, stung
At the first summons,—"Help for honour's sake,
"Play the man, pity the oppressed!"—no pause,
How does he lay about him in the midst,
Strike any foe, right wrong at any risk,
All blindness, bravery and obedience!—blind?
Ay, as a man would be inside the sun,
Delirious with the plenitude of light
Should interfuse him to the finger-ends—
Let him rush straight, and how shall he go wrong?
Where are the Christians in their panoply?
The loins we girt about with truth, the breasts
Righteousness plated round, the shield of faith,
The helmet of salvation, and that sword
O' the Spirit, even the word of God,—where these?
Slunk into corners! Oh, I hear at once
Hubbub of protestation! "What, we monks
"We friars, of such an order, such a rule,
"Have not we fought, bled, left our martyr-mark
"At every point along the boundary-line
" 'Twixt true and false, religion and the world,
"Where this or the other dogma of our Church
"Called for defence?" And I, despite myself,
How can I but speak loud what truth speaks low,
"Or better than the best, or nothing serves!
"What boots deed, I can cap and cover straight
"With such another doughtiness to match,
"Done at an instinct of the natural man?"
Immolate body, sacrifice soul too,—
Do not these publicans the same? Outstrip!
Or else stop race, you boast runs neck and neck,
You with the wings, they with the feet,—for shame!
Oh, I remark your diligence and zeal!
Five years long, now, rounds faith into my ears,
"Help thou, or Christendom is done to death!"
Five years since, in the Province of To-kien,
Which is in China as some people know,
Maigrot, my Vicar Apostolic there,
Having a great qualm, issues a decree.
Alack, the converts use as God's name, not
Tien-chu but plain *Tien* or else mere *Shang-ti,*
As Jesuits please to fancy politic,
While, say Dominicans, it calls down fire,—
For *Tien* means heaven, and *Shang-ti,* supreme prince,

While *Tien-chu* means the lord of heaven: all cry,
"There is no business urgent for despatch
"As that thou send a legate, specially
"Cardinal Tournon, straight to Pekin, there
"To settle and compose the difference!"
So have I seen a potentate all fume
For some infringement of his realm's just right,
Some menace to a mud-built straw-thatched farm
O' the frontier, while inside the mainland lie,
Quite undisputed-for in solitude,
Whole cities plague may waste or famine sap:
What if the sun crumble, the sands encroach,
While he looks on sublimely at his ease?
How does their ruin touch the empire's bound?

And is this little all that was to be?
Where is the gloriously-decisive change,
Metamorphosis the immeasurable
Of human clay to divine gold, we looked
Should, in some poor sort, justify its price?
Had an adept of the mere Rosy Cross
Spent his life to consummate the Great Work,
Would not we start to see the stuff it touched
Yield not a grain more than the vulgar got
By the old smelting-process years ago?
If this were sad to see in just the sage
Who should profess so much, perform no more,
What is it when suspected in that Power
Who undertook to make and made the world,
Devised and did effect man, body and soul,
Ordained salvation for them both, and yet . . .
Well, is the thing we see, salvation?

I

Put no such dreadful question to myself,
Within whose circle of experience burns
The central truth, Power, Wisdom, Goodness,—God:
I must outlive a thing ere know it dead:
When I outlive the faith there is a sun,
When I lie, ashes to the very soul,—
Someone, not I, must wail above the heap,
"He died in dark whence never morn arose."
While I see day succeed the deepest night—
How can I speak but as I know?—my speech
Must be, throughout the darkness, "It will end:
"The light that did burn, will burn!" Clouds obscure—
But for which obscuration all were bright?
Too hastily concluded! Sun-suffused,
A cloud may soothe the eye made blind by blaze,—
Better the very clarity of heaven:
The soft streaks are the beautiful and dear.
What but the weakness in a faith supplies
The incentive to humanity, no strength

Absolute, irresistible, comports?
How can man love but what he yearns to help?
And that which men think weakness within strength,
But angels know for strength and stronger yet—
What were it else but the first things made new,
But repetition of the miracle,
The divine instance of self-sacrifice
That never ends and aye begins for man?
So, never I miss footing in the maze,
No,—I have light nor fear the dark at all.

But are mankind not real, who pace outside
My petty circle, world that's measured me?
And when they stumble even as I stand,
Have I a right to stop ear when they cry,
As they were phantoms who took clouds for crags,
Tripped and fell, where man's march might safely move?
Beside, the cry is other than a ghost's,
When out of the old time there pleads some bard,
Philosopher, or both and—whispers not,
But words it boldly. "The inward work and worth
"Of any mind, what other mind may judge
"Save God who only knows the thing He made,
"The veritable service He exacts?
"It is the outward product men appraise.
"Behold, an engine hoists a tower aloft:
" 'I looked that it should move the mountain too!'
"Or else 'Had just a turret toppled down,
"Success enough!'—may say the Machinist
"Who knows what less or more result might be:
"But we, who see that done we cannot do,
" 'A feat beyond man's force,' we men must say.
"Regard me and that shake I gave the world!
"I was born, not so long before Christ's birth,
"As Christ's birth haply did precede thy day,—
"But many a watch before the star of dawn:
"Therefore I lived,—it is thy creed affirms,
"Pope Innocent, who art to answer me!—
"Under conditions, nowise to escape,
"Whereby salvation was impossible.
"Each impulse to achieve the good and fair,
"Each aspiration to the pure and true,
"Being without a warrant or an aim,
"Was just as sterile a felicity
"As if the insect, born to spend his life
"Soaring his circles, stopped them to describe
" (Painfully motionless in the mid-air)
"Some word of weighty counsel for man's sake,
"Some 'Know thyself' or 'Take the golden mean!'
"—Forwent his happy dance and the glad ray,
"Died half an hour the sooner and was dust.
"I, born to perish like the brutes, or worse,
"Why not live brutishly, obey brutes' law?
"But I, of body as of soul complete,

"A gymnast at the games, philosopher
"I' the schools, who painted, and made music,—all
"Glories that met upon the tragic stage
"When the Third Poet's tread surprised the Two,—
"Whose lot fell in a land where life was great
"And sense went free and beauty lay profuse,
"I, untouched by one adverse circumstance,
"Adopted virtue as my rule of life,
"Waived all reward, loved but for loving's sake,
"And, what my heart taught me, I taught the world,
"And have been teaching now two thousand years.
"Witness my work,—plays that should please, forsooth!
" 'They might please, they may displease, they shall teach,
" 'For truth's sake,' so I said, and did, and do.
"Five hundred years ere Paul spoke, Felix heard,—
"How much of temperance and righteousness,
"Judgment to come, did I find reason for,
"Corroborate with my strong style that spared
"No sin, nor swerved the more from branding brow
"Because the sinner was called Zeus and God?
"How nearly did I guess at that Paul knew?
"How closely come, in what I represent
"As duty, to his doctrine yet a blank?
"And as that limner not untruly limns
"Who draws an object round or square, which square
"Or round seems to the unassisted eye,
"Though Galileo's tube display the same
"Oval or oblong,—so, who controverts
"I rendered rightly what proves wrongly wrought
"Beside Paul's picture? Mine was true for me.
"I saw that there are, first and above all,
"The hidden forces, blind necessities,
"Named Nature, but the thing's self unconceived:
"Then follow,—how dependent upon these,
"We know not, how imposed above ourselves,
"We well know,—what I name the gods, a power
"Various or one; for great and strong and good
"Is there, and little, weak and bad there too,
"Wisdom and folly: say, these make no God,—
"What is it else that rules outside man's self?
"A fact then,—always, to the naked eye,—
"And so, the one revealment possible
"Of what were unimagined else by man.
"Therefore, what gods do, man may criticize,
"Applaud, condemn,—how should he fear the truth?
"But likewise have in awe because of power,
"Venerate for the main munificence,
"And give the doubtful deed its due excuse
"From the acknowledged creature of a day
"To the Eternal and Divine. Thus, bold
"Yet self-mistrusting, should man bear himself,
"Most assured on what now concerns him most—
"The law of his own life, the path he prints,—
"Which law is virtue and not vice, I say,—

"And least inquisitive where search least skills,
"I' the nature we best give the clouds to keep.
"What could I paint beyond a scheme like this
"Out of the fragmentary truths where light
"Lay fitful in a tenebrific time?
"You have the sunrise now, joins truth to truth,
"Shoots life and substance into death and void;
"Themselves compose the whole we made before:
"The forces and necessity grow God,—
"The beings so contrarious that seemed gods,
"Prove just His operation manifold
"And multiform, translated, as must be,
"Into intelligible shape so far
"As suits our sense and sets us free to feel.
"What if I let a child think, childhood-long,
"That lightning, I would have him spare his eye,
"Is a real arrow shot at naked orb?
"The man knows more, but shuts his lids the same:
"Lightning's cause comprehends nor man nor child.
"Why then, my scheme, your better knowledge broke,
"Presently readjusts itself, the small
"Proportioned largelier, parts and whole named new:
"So much, no more two thousand years have done!
"Pope, dost thou dare pretend to punish me,
"For not descrying sunshine at midnight,
"Me who crept all-fours, found my way so far—
"While thou rewardest teachers of the truth,
"Who miss the plain way in the blaze of noon,—
"Though just a word from that strong style of mine,
"Grasped honestly in hand as guiding-staff,
"Had pricked them a sure path across the bog,
"That mire of cowardice and slush of lies
"Wherein I find them wallow in wide day?"

How should I answer this Euripides?
Paul,—'tis a legend,—answered Seneca,
But that was in the day-spring; noon is now:
We have got too familiar with the light.
Shall I wish back once more that thrill of dawn?
When the whole truth-touched man burned up, one fire?
—Assured the trial, fiery, fierce, but fleet,
Would, from his little heap of ashes, lend
Wings to the conflagration of the world
Which Christ awaits ere He make all things new:
So should the frail become the perfect, rapt
From glory of pain to glory of joy; and so,
Even in the end,—the act renouncing earth,
Lands, houses, husbands, wives and children here,—
Begin that other act which finds all, lost,
Regained, in this time even, a hundredfold,
And, in the next time, feels the finite love
Blent and embalmed with the eternal life.
So does the sun ghastlily seem to sink
In those north parts, lean all but out of life,

Desist a dread mere breathing-stop, then slow
Re-assert day, begin the endless rise.
Was this too easy for our after-stage?
Was such a lighting-up of faith, in life,
Only allowed initiate, set man's step
In the true way by help of the great glow?
A way wherein it is ordained he walk,
Bearing to see the light from heaven still more
And more encroached on by the light of earth,
Tentatives earth puts forth to rival heaven,
Earthly incitements that mankind serve God
For man's sole sake, not God's and therefore man's.
Till at last, who distinguishes the sun
From a mere Druid fire on a far mount?
More praise to him who with his subtle prism
Shall decompose both beams and name the true.
In such sense, who is last proves first indeed;
For how could saints and martyrs fail see truth
Streak the night's blackness? Who is faithful now,
Who untwists heaven's white from the yellow flare
O' the world's gross torch, without night's foil that helped
Produce the Christian act so possible
When in the way stood Nero's cross and stake,—
So hard now when the world smiles "Right and wise!
"Faith points the politic, the thrifty way,
"Will make who plods it in the end returns
"Beyond mere fool's-sport and improvidence.
"We fools dance thro' the cornfield of this life,
"Pluck ears to left and right and swallow raw,
"—Nay, tread, at pleasure, a sheaf underfoot,
"To get the better at some poppy-flower,—
"Well aware we shall have so much less wheat
"In the eventual harvest: you meantime
"Waste not a spike,—the richlier will you reap!
"What then? There will be always garnered meal
"Sufficient for our comfortable loaf,
"While you enjoy the undiminished sack!"
Is it not this ignoble confidence,
Cowardly hardihood, that dulls and damps,
Makes the old heroism impossible?
Unless . . . what whispers me of times to come?
What if it be the mission of that age
My death will usher into life, to shake
This torpor of assurance from our creed,
Re-introduce the doubt discarded, bring
That formidable danger back, we drove
Long ago to the distance and the dark?
No wild beast now prowls round the infant camp:
We have built wall and sleep in city safe:
But if some earthquake try the towers that laugh
To think they once saw lions rule outside,
And man stand out again, pale, resolute,
Prepared to die,—which means, alive at last?
As we broke up that old faith of the world,

Have we, next age, to break up this the new—
Faith, in the thing, grown faith in the report—
Whence need to bravely disbelieve report
Through increased faith i' the thing reports belie?
Must we deny,—do they, these Molinists,
At peril of their body and their soul,—
Recognized truths, obedient to some truth
Unrecognized yet, but perceptible?—
Correct the portrait by the living face,
Man's God, by God's God in the mind of man?
Then, for the few that rise to the new height,
The many that must sink to the old depth,
The multitude found fall away! A few,
E'en ere new law speak clear, may keep the old,
Preserve the Christian level, call good good
And evil evil, (even though razed and blank
The old titles,) helped by custom, habitude,
And all else they mistake for finer sense
O' the fact that reason warrants,—as before,
They hope perhaps, fear not impossibly.
At least some one Pompilia left the world
Will say "I know the right place by foot's feel,
"I took it and tread firm there; wherefore change?"
But what a multitude will surely fall
Quite through the crumbling truth, late subjacent,
Sink to the next discoverable base,
Rest upon human nature, settle there
On what is firm, the lust and pride of life!
A mass of men, whose very souls even now
Seem to need re-creating,—so they slink
Worm-like into the mud, light now lays bare,—
Whose future we dispose of with shut eyes
And whisper—"They are grafted, barren twigs,
"Into the living stock of Christ: may bear
"One day, till when they lie death-like, not dead,"

Those who with all the aid of Christ succumb,
How, without Christ, shall they, unaided, sink?
Whither but to this gulf before my eyes?
Do not we end, the century and I?
The impatient antimasque treads close on kibe
O' the very masque's self it will mock,—on me,
Last lingering personage, the impatient mime
Pushes already,—will I block the way?
Will my slow trail of garments ne'er leave space
For pantaloon, sock, plume and castanet?
Here comes the first experimentalist
In the new order of things,—he plays a priest;
Does he take inspiration from the Church,
Directly make her rule his law of life?
Not he: his own mere impulse guides the man—
Happily sometimes, since ourselves allow
He has danced, in gaiety of heart, i' the main
The right step through the maze we bade him foot.

But if his heart had prompted him break loose
And mar the measure? Why, we must submit,
And thank the chance that brought him safe so far.
Will he repeat the prodigy? Perhaps.
Can he teach others how to quit themselves,
Show why this step was right while that were wrong?
How should he? "Ask your hearts as I asked mine,
"And get discreetly through the morrice too;
"If your hearts misdirect you,—quit the stage,
"And make amends,—be there amends to make!"
Such is, for the Augustin that was once,
This Canon Caponsacchi we see now.
"But my heart answers to another tune,"
Puts in the Abate, second in the suite,
"I have my taste too, and tread no such step!
"You choose the glorious life, and may, for me!
"I like the lowest of life's appetites,—
"So you judge,—but the very truth of joy
"To my own apprehension which decides.
"Call me knave and you get yourself called fool!
"I live for greed, ambition, lust, revenge;
"Attain these ends by force, guile: hypocrite,
"To-day, perchance to-morrow recognized
"The rational man, the type of commonsense."
There's Loyola adapted to our time!
Under such guidance Guido plays his part,
He also influencing in the due turn
These last clods where I track intelligence
By any glimmer, these four at his beck
Ready to murder any, and, at their own,
As ready to murder him,—such make the world!
And, first effect of the new cause of things,
There they lie also duly,—the old pair
Of the weak head and not so wicked heart,
And the one Christian mother, wife and girl,
—Which three gifts seem to make an angel up,—
The world's first foot o' the dance is on their heads!
Still, I stand here, not off the stage though close
On the exit: and my last act, as my first,
I owe the scene, and Him who armed me thus
With Paul's sword as with Peter's key. I smite
With my whole strength once more, ere end my part,
Ending, so far as man may, this offence.
And when I raise my arm, who plucks my sleeve?
Who stops me in the righteous function,—foe
Or friend? O, still as ever, friends are they
Who, in the interest of outraged truth
Deprecate such rough handling of a lie!
The facts being proved and incontestable,
What is the last word I must listen to?
Is it "Spare yet a term this barren stock,
"We pray thee dig about and dung and dress
"Till he repent and bring forth fruit even yet!"
Perchance—"So poor and swift a punishment

"Shall throw him out of life with all that sin:
"Let mercy rather pile up pain on pain
"Till the flesh expiate what the soul pays else!"
Nowise! Remonstrants on each side commence
Instructing, there's a new tribunal now
Higher than God's,—the educated man's!
Nice sense of honour in the human breast
Supersedes here the old coarse oracle—
Confirming none the less a point or so
Wherein blind predecessors worked aright
By rule of thumb: as when Christ said,—when, where?
Enough, I find it pleaded in a place,—
"All other wrongs done, patiently I take:
"But touch my honour and the case is changed!
"I feel the due resentment,—*nemini*
"*Honorem trado*,[1] is my quick retort."
Right of Him, just as if pronounced to-day!
Still, should the old authority be mute,
Or doubtful, or in speaking clash with new,
The younger takes permission to decide.
At last we have the instinct of the world
Ruling its household without tutelage,
And while the two laws, human and divine,
Have busied finger with this tangled case,
In pushes the brisk junior, cuts the knot,
Pronounces for acquittal. How it trips
Silverly o'er the tongue! "Remit the death!
"Forgive . . . well, in the old way, if thou please,
"Decency and the relics of routine
"Respected,—let the Count go free as air!
"Since he may plead a priest's immunity,—
"The minor orders help enough for that,
"With Farinacci's licence,—who decides
"That the mere implication of such man,
"So privileged, in any cause, before
"Whatever court except the Spiritual,
"Straight quashes law-procedure,—quash it, then!
"Remains a pretty loophole of escape
"Moreover, that, beside the patent fact
"O' the law's allowance, there's involved the weal
"O' the Popedom: a son's privilege at stake,
"Thou wilt pretend the Church's interest,
"Ignore all finer reasons to forgive!
"But herein lies the crowning cogency—
" (Let thy friends teach thee while thou tellest beads)
"That in this case the spirit of culture speaks,
"Civilization is imperative.
"To her shall we remand all delicate points
"Henceforth, nor take irregular advice
"O' the sly, as heretofore: she used to hint
"Remonstrances, when law was out of sorts
"Because a saucy tongue was put to rest,

[1] I give my glory into no one's keeping.

"An eye that roved was cured of arrogance:
"But why be forced to mumble under breath
"What soon shall be acknowledged as plain fact,
"Outspoken, say, in thy successor's time?
"Methinks we see the golden age return!
"Civilization and the Emperor
"Succeed to Christianity and Pope.
"One Emperor then, as one Pope now: meanwhile,
"Anticipate a little! We tell thee 'Take
" 'Guido's life, sapped society shall crash,
" 'Whereof the main prop was, is, and shall be
" '—Supremacy of husband over wife!'
"Does the man rule i' the house, and may his mate
"Because of any plea dispute the same?
"Oh, pleas of all sorts shall abound, be sure,
"One but allowed validity,—for, harsh
"And savage, for, inept and silly-sooth,
"For, this and that, will the ingenious sex
"Demonstrate the best master e'er graced slave:
"And there's but one short way to end the coil,—
"Acknowledge right and reason steadily
"I' the man and master: then the wife submits
"To plain truth broadly stated. Does the time
"Advise we shift—a pillar? nay, a stake
"Out of its place i' the social tenement?
"One touch may send a shudder through the heap
"And bring it toppling on our children's heads!
"Moreover, if ours breed a qualm in thee,
"Give thine own better feeling play for once!
"Thou, whose own life winks o'er the socket-edge,
"Wouldst thou it went out in such ugly snuff
"As dooming sons dead, e'en though justice prompt?
"Why, on a certain feast, Barabbas' self
"Was set free, not to cloud the general cheer:
"Neither shalt thou pollute thy Sabbath close!
"Mercy is safe and graceful. How one hears
"The howl begin, scarce the three little taps
"O' the silver mallet silent on thy brow,—
" 'His last act was to sacrifice a Count
" 'And thereby screen a scandal of the Church!
" 'Guido condemned, the Canon justified
" 'Of course,—delinquents of his cloth go free!'
"And so the Luthers chuckle, Calvins scowl,
"So thy hand helps Molinos to the chair
"Whence he may hold forth till doom's day on just
"These *petit-maître* priestlings,—in the choir,
"Sanctus et Benedictus,[2] with a brush
"Of soft guitar-strings that obey the thumb,
"Touched by the bedside, for accompaniment!
"Does this give umbrage to a husband? Death
"To the fool, and to the priest impunity!
"But no impunity to any friend
"So simply over-loyal as these four

[2] Holy and blessed.

"Who made religion of their patron's cause,
"Believed in him and did his bidding straight,
"Asked not one question but laid down the lives
"This Pope took,—all four lives together make
"Just his own length of days,—so, dead they lie,
"As these were times when loyalty's a drug,
"And zeal in a subordinate too cheap
"And common to be saved when we spend life!
"Come, 'tis too much good breath we waste in words:
"The pardon, Holy Father! Spare grimace,
"Shrugs and reluctance! Are not we the world,
"Art thou not Priam? let soft culture plead
"Hecuba-like, *'non tali'* (Virgil serves)
"*'Auxilio,'* [3] and the rest! Enough, it works!
"The Pope relaxes, and the Prince is loth,
"The father's bowels yearn, the man's will bends,
"Reply is apt. Our tears on tremble, hearts
"Big with a benediction, wait the word
"Shall circulate thro' the city in a trice,
"Set every window flaring, give each man
"O' the mob his torch to wave for gratitude.
"Pronounce it, for our breath and patience fail!"

I will, Sirs: for a voice other than yours
Quickens my spirit. *"Quis pro Domino?*
"Who is upon the Lord's side?" asked the Count.
I, who write—
"On receipt of this command,
"Acquaint Count Guido and his fellows four
"They die to-morrow: could it be to-night,
"The better, but the work to do, takes time.
"Set with all diligence a scaffold up,
"Not in the customary place, by Bridge
"Saint Angelo, where die the common sort;
"But since the man is noble, and his peers
"By predilection haunt the People's Square,
"There let him be beheaded in the midst,
"And his companions hanged on either side:
"So shall the quality see, fear, and learn.
"All which work takes time: till to-morrow, then,
"Let there be prayer incessant for the five!"

For the main criminal I have no hope
Except in such a suddenness of fate.
I stood at Naples once, a night so dark
I could have scarce conjectured there was earth
Anywhere, sky or sea or world at all:
But the night's black was burst through by a blaze—
Thunder struck blow on blow, earth groaned and bore,
Through her whole length of mountain visible:
There lay the city thick and plain with spires,
And, like a ghost disshrouded, white the sea.

[3] Not by such aid.

So may the truth be flashed out by one blow,
And Guido see, one instant, and be saved.
Else I avert my face, nor follow him
Into that sad obscure sequestered state
Where God unmakes but to remake the soul
He else made first in vain; which must not be.
Enough, for I may die this very night
And how should I dare die, this man let live?

Carry this forthwith to the Governor!

[1869]

HOUSE

I

Shall I sonnet-sing you about myself?
  Do I live in a house you would like to see?
Is it scant of gear, has it store of pelf?
  "Unlock my heart with a sonnet-key?"

II

Invite the world, as my betters have done?
  "Take notice: this building remains on view,
Its suites of reception every one,
  Its private apartment and bedroom too;

III

"For a ticket, apply to the Publisher."
  No: thanking the public, I must decline.
A peep through my window, if folk prefer;
  But, please you, no foot over threshold of mine!

IV

I have mixed with a crowd and heard free talk
  In a foreign land where an earthquake chanced:
And a house stood gaping, nought to baulk
  Man's eye wherever he gazed or glanced.

V

The whole of the frontage shaven sheer,
  The inside gaped: exposed to day,
Right and wrong and common and queer,
  Bare, as the palm of your hand, it lay.

VI

The owner? Oh, he had been crushed, no doubt!
  "Odd tables and chairs for a man of wealth!
What a parcel of musty old books about!
  He smoked,—no wonder he lost his health!

VII

"I doubt if he bathed before he dressed.
  A brasier?—the pagan, he burned perfumes!
You see it is proved, what the neighbours guessed:
  His wife and himself had separate rooms."

VIII

Friends, the goodman of the house at least
  Kept house to himself till an earthquake came:
'T is the fall of its frontage permits you feast
  On the inside arrangement you praise or blame.

IX

Outside should suffice for evidence:
  And whoso desires to penetrate
Deeper, must dive by the spirit-sense—
  No optics like yours, at any rate!

X

"Hoity toity! A street to explore,
  Your house the exception! *'With this same key*
Shakespeare unlocked his heart,' once more!"
  Did Shakespeare? If so, the less Shakespeare he!

[1874] [1876]

SHOP

I

So, friend, your shop was all your house!
  Its front, astonishing the street,
Invited view from man and mouse
  To what diversity of treat
  Behind its glass—the single sheet!

II

What gimcracks, genuine Japanese:
  Gape-jaw and goggle-eye, the frog;
Dragons, owls, monkeys, beetles, geese;
  Some crush-nosed human-hearted dog:
  Queer names, too, such a catalogue!

III

I thought "And he who owns the wealth
  Which blocks the window's vastitude,
—Ah, could I peep at him by stealth
  Behind his ware, pass shop, intrude
  On house itself, what scenes were viewed!

IV

"If wide and showy thus the shop,
  What must the habitation prove?
The true house with no name a-top—
  The mansion, distant one remove,
  Once get him off his traffic-groove!

V

"Pictures he likes, or books perhaps;
  And as for buying most and best,

Commend me to these City chaps!
  Or else he's social, takes his rest
  On Sundays, with a Lord for guest.

VI

"Some suburb-palace, parked about
  And gated grandly, built last year:
The four-mile walk to keep off gout;
  Or big seat sold by bankrupt peer:
  But then he takes the rail, that's clear.

VII

"Or, stop! I wager, taste selects
  Some out o' the way, some all-unknown
Retreat: the neighbourhood suspects
  Little that he who rambles lone
  Makes Rothschild tremble on his throne!"

VIII

Nowise! Nor Mayfair residence
  Fit to receive and entertain,—
Nor Hampstead villa's kind defence
  From noise and crowd, from dust and drain,—
  Nor country-box was soul's domain!

IX

Nowise! At back of all that spread
  Of merchandize, woe's me, I find
A hole i' the wall where, heels by head,
  The owner couched, his ware behind,
  —In cupboard suited to his mind.

X

For why? He saw no use of life
  But, while he drove a roaring trade,
To chuckle "Customers are rife!"
  To chafe "So much hard cash outlaid
  Yet zero in my profits made!

XI

"This novelty costs pains, but—takes?
  Cumbers my counter! Stock no more!
This article, no such great shakes,
  Fizzes like wildfire? Underscore
  The cheap thing—thousands to the fore!"

XII

'T was lodging best to live most nigh
  (Cramp, coffinlike as crib might be)
Receipt of Custom; ear and eye
  Wanted no outworld: "Hear and see
  The bustle in the shop!" quoth he.

XIII

My fancy of a merchant-prince
 Was different. Through his wares we groped
Our darkling way to—not to mince
 The matter—no black den where moped
 The master if we interloped!

XIV

Shop was shop only: household-stuff?
 What did he want with comforts there?
"Walls, ceiling, floor, stay blank and rough,
 So goods on sale show rich and rare!
 'Sell and scud home' be shop's affair!"

XV

What might he deal in? Gems, suppose!
 Since somehow business must be done
At cost of trouble,—see, he throws
 You choice of jewels, everyone,
 Good, better, best, star, moon and sun!

XVI

Which lies within your power of purse?
 This ruby that would tip aright
Solomon's sceptre? Oh, your nurse
 Wants simply coral, the delight
 Of teething baby,—stuff to bite!

XVII

Howe'er your choice fell, straight you took
 Your purchase, prompt your money rang
On counter,—scarce the man forsook
 His study of the "Times," just swang
 Till-ward his hand that stopped the clang,—

XVIII

Then off made buyer with a prize,
 Then seller to his "Times" returned,
And so did day wear, wear, till eyes
 Brightened apace, for rest was earned:
 He locked door long ere candle burned.

XIX

And whither went he? Ask himself,
 Not me! To change of scene, I think.
Once sold the ware and pursed the pelf,
 Chaffer was scarce his meat and drink,
 Nor all his music—money-chink.

XX

Because a man has shop to mind
 In time and place, since flesh must live,

Need spirit lack all life behind,
All stray thoughts, fancies fugitive,
All loves except what trade can give?

XXI

I want to know a butcher paints,
A baker rhymes for his pursuit,
Candlestick-maker much acquaints
His soul with song, or, haply mute,
Blows out his brains upon the flute!

XXII

But—shop each day and all day long!
Friend, your good angel slept, your star
Suffered eclipse, fate did you wrong!
From where these sorts of treasures are,
There should our hearts be—Christ, how far!
[1874] [1876]

ECHETLOS

Here is a story shall stir you! Stand up, Greeks dead and gone,
Who breasted, beat Barbarians, stemmed Persia rolling on,
Did the deed and saved the world, for the day was Marathon!

No man but did his manliest, kept rank and fought away
In his tribe and file: up, back, out, down—was the spear-arm play:
Like a wind-whipt branchy wood, all spear-arms a-swing that day!

But one man kept no rank and his sole arm plied no spear,
As a flashing came and went, and a form i' the van, the rear,
Brightened the battle up, for he blazed now there, now here.

Nor helmed nor shielded, he! but a goat-skin all his wear,
Like a tiller of the soil, with a clown's limbs broad and bare,
Went he ploughing on and on: he pushed with a ploughman's share.

Did the weak mid-line give way, as tunnies on whom the shark
Precipitates his bulk? Did the right wing halt when, stark
On his heap of slain lay stretched Kallimachos Polemarch?

Did the steady phalanx falter? To the rescue, at the need,
The clown was ploughing Persia, clearing Greek earth of weed,
As he routed through the Sakian and rooted up the Mede.

But the deed done, battle won,—nowhere to be descried
On the meadow, by the stream, at the marsh,—look far and wide
From the foot of the mountain, no, to the last blood-plashed seaside,—

Not anywhere on view blazed the large limbs thonged and brown,
Shearing and clearing still with the share before which—down
To the dust went Persia's pomp, as he ploughed for Greece, that clown!

How spake the Oracle? "Care for no name at all!
Say but just this: 'We praise one helpful whom we call
The Holder of the Ploughshare.' The great deed ne'er grows small."

Not the great name! Sing—woe for the great name Míltiadés
And its end at Paros isle! Woe for Themistokles
—Satrap in Sardis court! Name not the clown like these!

[1880] [1880]

NEVER THE TIME AND THE PLACE

Never the time and the place
And the loved one all together!
This path—how soft to pace!
This May—what magic weather!
Where is the loved one's face?
In a dream that loved one's face meets mine,
But the house is narrow, the place is bleak
Where, outside, rain and wind combine
With a furtive ear, if I strive to speak,
With a hostile eye at my flushing cheek,
With a malice that marks each word, each sign!
O enemy sly and serpentine,
Uncoil thee from the waking man!
Do I hold the Past
Thus firm and fast
Yet doubt if the Future hold I can?
This path so soft to pace shall lead
Through the magic of May to herself indeed!
Or narrow if needs the house must be,
Outside are the storms and strangers: we—
Oh, close, safe, warm, sleep I and she,
—I and she!

[1883]

PROLOGUE TO "ASOLANDO"

"The Poet's age is sad: for why?
In youth, the natural world could show
No common object but his eye
At once involved with alien glow—
His own soul's iris-bow.

"And now a flower is just a flower:
Man, bird, beast are but beast, bird, man—
Simply themselves, uncinct by dower
Of dyes which, when life's day began,
Round each in glory ran."

Friend, did you need an optic glass,
Which were your choice? A lens to drape
In ruby, emerald, chrysopras,
Each object—or reveal its shape
Clear outlined, past escape,

The naked very thing?—so clear
That, when you had the chance to gaze,
You found its inmost self appear
Through outer seeming—truth ablaze,
Not falsehood's fancy haze?

How many a year, my Asolo,
Since—one step just from sea to land—
I found you, loved yet feared you so—
For natural objects seemed to stand
Palpably fire-clothed! No—

No mastery of mine o'er these!
Terror with beauty, like the Bush
Burning but unconsumed. Bend knees,
Drop eyes to earthward! Language? Tush!
Silence 'tis awe decrees.

And now? The lambent flame is—where?
Lost from the naked world: earth, sky,
Hill, vale, tree, flower,—Italia's rare
O'er-running beauty crowds the eye—
But flame? The Bush is bare.

Hill, vale, tree, flower—they stand distinct,
Nature to know and name. What then?
A Voice spoke thence which straight unlinked
Fancy from fact: see, all's in ken:
Has once my eyelid winked?

No, for the purged ear apprehends
Earth's import, not the eye late dazed:
The Voice said "Call my works thy friends!
At Nature dost thou shrink amazed?
God is it who transcends."

[1889] [1889]

DUBIETY

I will be happy if but for once:
  Only help me, Autumn weather,
Me and my cares to screen, ensconce
  In luxury's sofa-lap of leather!

Sleep? Nay, comfort—with just a cloud
  Suffering day too clear and bright:
Eve's essence, the single drop allowed
  To sully, like milk, Noon's water-white.

Let gauziness shade, not shroud,—adjust,
  Dim and not deaden,—somehow sheathe
Aught sharp in the rough world's busy thrust,
  If it reach me through dreaming's vapour-wreath.

Be life so, all things ever the same!
  For, what has disarmed the world? Outside,
Quiet and peace: inside, nor blame
  Nor want, nor wish whate'er betide.

What is it like that has happened before?
  A dream? No dream, more real by much.
A vision? But fanciful days of yore
  Brought many: mere musing seems not such.

Perhaps but a memory, after all!
  —Of what came once when a woman leant
To feel for my brow where her kiss might fall.
  Truth ever, truth only the excellent!

[1889]

EPILOGUE TO "ASOLANDO"

At the midnight in the silence of the sleep-time,
  When you set your fancies free,
Will they pass to where—by death, fools think, imprisoned—
Low he lies who once so loved you, whom you loved so,
  —Pity me?

Oh to love so, be so loved, yet so mistaken!
  What had I on earth to do
With the slothful, with the mawkish, the unmanly?
Like the aimless, helpless, hopeless, did I drivel
  —Being—who?

[1889]

One who never turned his back but marched breast forward,
  Never doubted clouds would break,
Never dreamed, though right were worsted, wrong would triumph,
Held we fall to rise, are baffled to fight better,
  Sleep to wake.

No, at noonday in the bustle of man's work-time
  Greet the unseen with a cheer!
Bid him forward, breast and back as either should be,
"Strive and thrive!" cry "Speed,—fight on, fare ever
  There as here!"

[1889]

ELIZABETH BARRETT BROWNING

CHRONOLOGICAL TABLE

1806 Born March 6, at Coxhoe Hall in Durham, her father a capitalist with interests in West Indian slave plantations. Educated at home (Hope End, Herefordshire) with aid in reading Greek from an amateur instructor.

1820 *The Battle of Marathon* (fifty copies privately printed at her father's command).

1826 *An Essay on Mind and Other Poems.*

1833 *Prometheus Bound and Miscellaneous Poems.* Miss Barrett attempted to remove this work from circulation because of her dissatisfaction with the title piece, a translation from Aeschylus.

1835 Removal of the family of the Barretts to London.

1838 *The Seraphim and Other Poems.* About this time, for no single cause, her health rapidly deteriorated and she became (and continued for eight years to be) an invalid.

1842 Contributed several essays to *The Athenaeum* on Greek Christian poets and English poets.

1844 *Poems.*

1845 First meeting with Robert Browning.

1846, September 12, marriage, followed by "flight" to Pisa.

1847 Choice of Florence as a permanent home.

1848 Renting of an unfurnished apartment in the Palazzo Guidi, in Florence, in which, when not travelling, the Brownings lived until Mrs. Browning died.

1850 *Poems* (a collected edition containing *Sonnets from the Portuguese*).

1851 *Casa Guidi Windows.*

1856 *Aurora Leigh.*

1860 *Poems before Congress* (a pamphlet).

1861 Died at Florence, June 29, buried in the English cemetery.

No other Victorian poet of comparable talent has suffered so steep a decline in public admiration or critical interest. When in 1844 Miss Barrett published her *Poems* she stood next to Tennyson in the opinion of cultivated readers and orthodox critics. As long as she lived her reputation eclipsed her husband's in England and rivalled it in America. The spread of her fame was aided by knowledge (or half-knowledge) of the circumstances of her life: her precocity, exemplified in the philosophical poetry of the *Essay on Mind* (published when she was twenty) and in the classical scholarship, impressive if not exact, shown in the *Prometheus Bound* and other pieces; her retired life from which, even in London, all literary persons were excluded unless they knocked and knocked again; her long-drawn-out illness which appeared to point to an early death; her marriage, followed by a breach with her father which was never in the least measure healed and by her flight to a remote country from which she seldom and briefly returned. She was a legend even in her lifetime. However, even if her life had been prosaic, there were qualities enough in her poetry to win the admiration of her contemporaries. It combines with intensity of emotion, a constant reflection of clearly Christian morality and humanitarian and liberal sympathies, and a warm delight in nature. Here and there she offended against standards of subject: there were those who found indelicacy in *Aurora Leigh* and there were many who disliked the exalted liberal enthusiasm which marks the *Poems before Congress.* Her carelessness of form found then, as it finds now, strong objectors: she herself was aware that her form was careless, that, as she says, she *spluttered* forth the truth, and defended her method by claiming that only so could *she* achieve the perfect spontaneity which in art, as in life, she valued so much. The peculiarities of her style cannot be defended as can the oddities of Robert Browning's: her style, unlike his, is thin and monotonous. But spontaneity, in an extreme degree it does possess: the temper of Mrs. Browning fully dominates her poetry. Since, notably in the years after she met Browning, she was a woman of her special time, the dominance of her temper has in the end done her poetry a disservice. Christina Rossetti's quieter expression of feeling, her quieter technique, her less peculiar and less contemporary nature have slowly revealed themselves to have deeper meaning and deeper pleasure for another age.

COWPER'S GRAVE

I

It is a place where poets crowned may feel the heart's decaying;
It is a place where happy saints may weep amid their praying.
Yet let the grief and humbleness, as low as silence, languish!
Earth surely now may give her calm to whom she gave her anguish.

II

O poets, from a maniac's tongue was poured the deathless singing!
O Christians, at your cross of hope, a hopeless hand was clinging!
O men, this man in brotherhood your weary paths beguiling,
Groaned inly while he taught you peace, and died while ye were smiling!

III

And now, what time ye all may read through dimming tears his story,
How discord on the music fell and darkness on the glory,
And how when, one by one, sweet sounds and wandering lights departed,
He wore no less a loving face because so broken-hearted,

IV

He shall be strong to sanctify the poet's high vocation,
And bow the meekest Christian down in meeker adoration;
Nor ever shall he be, in praise, by wise or good forsaken,
Named softly as the household name of one whom God hath taken.

V

With quiet sadness and no gloom I learn to think upon him,—
With meekness that is gratefulness to God whose heaven hath won him,
Who suffered once the madness-cloud to His own love to blind him,
But gently led the blind along where breath and bird could find him;

VI

And wrought within his shattered brain such quick poetic senses
As hills have language for, and stars, harmonious influences.
The pulse of dew upon the grass, kept his within its number,
And silent shadows from the trees refreshed him like a slumber.

VII

Wild timid hares were drawn from woods to share his home-caresses,
Uplooking to his human eyes with sylvan tendernesses;
The very world, by God's constraint, from falsehood's ways removing,
Its women and its men became, beside him, true and loving.

VIII

And though, in blindness, he remained unconscious of that guiding,
And things provided came without the sweet sense of providing,
He testified this solemn truth, while frenzy desolated,
—Nor man nor nature satisfies whom only God created.

IX

Like a sick child that knoweth not his mother while she blesses
And drops upon his burning brow the coolness of her kisses,—
That turns his fevered eyes around—'My mother! where's my mother?'—
As if such tender words and deeds could come from any other!—

X

The fever gone, with leaps of heart he sees her bending o'er him,
Her face all pale from watchful love, the unweary love she bore him!—
Thus woke the poet from the dream his life's long fever gave him,
Beneath those deep pathetic Eyes which closed in death to save him.

XI

Thus? oh, not *thus!* No type of earth can imagine that awaking,
Wherein he scarcely heard the chant of seraphs, round him breaking,
Or felt the new immortal throb of soul from body parted,
But felt those eyes alone, and knew—'*My* Saviour! *not* deserted!'

XII

Deserted! Who hath dreamt that when the cross in darkness rested,
Upon the Victim's hidden face no love was manifested?
What frantic hands outstretched have e'er the atoning drops averted?
What tears have washed them from the soul, that *one* should be deserted?

XIII

Deserted! God could separate from his own essence rather;
And Adam's sins *have* swept between the righteous Son and Father.
Yea, once, Immanuel's orphaned cry his universe hath shaken—
It went up single, echoless, 'My God, I am forsaken!'

XIV

It went up from the Holy's lips amid his lost creation,
That of the lost, no son should use those words of desolation!
That Earth's worst frenzies, marring hope, should mar not hope's fruition,
And I, on Cowper's grave, should see his rapture in a vision.

[1838]

THE CRY OF THE CHILDREN

Φεῦ, φεῦ. τί προσδερκεσθέ μ' ὄμμασιν τεκνα:

Medea[1]

I

Do ye hear the children weeping, O my brothers,
Ere the sorrow comes with years?
They are leaning their young heads against their mothers,
And *that* cannot stop their tears.
The young lambs are bleating in the meadows,
The young birds are chirping in the nest,
The young fawns are playing with the shadows,
The young flowers are blowing toward the west—
But the young, young children, O my brothers,
They are weeping bitterly!
They are weeping in the playtime of the others,
In the country of the free.

[1]Alas, alas, why do you gaze at me with your eyes, my children?

II

Do you question the young children in the sorrow
Why their tears are falling so?
The old man may weep for his to-morrow
Which is lost in Long Ago;
The old tree is leafless in the forest,
The old year is ending in the frost,
The old wound, if stricken, is the sorest,
The old hope is hardest to be lost:
But the young, young children, O my brothers,
Do you ask them why they stand
Weeping before the bosoms of their mothers,
In our happy Fatherland?

III

They look up with their pale and sunken faces,
And their looks are sad to see,
For the man's hoary anguish draws and presses
Down the cheeks of infancy.
'Your old earth,' they say, 'is very dreary;
Our young feet,' they say, 'are very weak!
Few paces have we taken, yet are weary—
Our grave-rest is very far to seek.
Ask the aged why they weep, and not the children;
For the outside earth is cold;
And we young ones stand without, in our bewildering,
And the graves are for the old.'

IV

'True,' say the children, 'it may happen
That we die before our time;
Little Alice died last year—her grave is shapen
Like a snowball, in the rime.
We looked into the pit prepared to take her:
Was no room for any work in the close clay!
From the sleep wherein she lieth none will wake her,
Crying, "Get up, little Alice! it is day."
If you listen by that grave, in sun and shower,
With your ear down, little Alice never cries;
Could we see her face, be sure we should not know her.
For the smile has time for growing in her eyes:
And merry go her moments, lulled and stilled in
The shroud by the kirk-chime.
'It is good when it happens,' say the children,
'That we die before our time.'

V

Alas, alas, the children! they are seeking
Death in life, as best to have;
They are binding up their hearts away from breaking,
With a cerement from the grave.
Go out, children, from the mine and from the city,
Sing out, children, as the little thrushes do;

Pluck your handfuls of the meadow-cowslips pretty,
Laugh aloud, to feel your fingers let them through!
But they answer, 'Are your cowslips of the meadows
Like our weeds anear the mine?
Leave us quiet in the dark of the coal-shadows,
From your pleasures fair and fine!

VI

'For oh,' say the children, we are weary,
And we cannot run or leap;
If we cared for any meadows, it were merely
To drop down in them and sleep.
Our knees tremble sorely in the stooping,
We fall upon our faces, trying to go;
And, underneath our heavy eyelids drooping
The reddest flower would look as pale as snow.
For, all day, we drag our burden tiring
Through the coal-dark, underground;
Or, all day, we drive the wheels of iron
In the factories, round and round.

VII

'For all day the wheels are droning, turning,—
Their wind comes in our faces,—
Till our hearts turn,—our heads with pulses burning,
And the walls turn in their places:
Turns the sky in the high window, blank and reeling
Turns the long light that drops adown the wall,
Turn the black flies that crawl along the ceiling:
All are turning, all the day, and we with all.
And all day the iron wheels are droning,
And sometimes we could pray,
"O ye wheels" (breaking out in a mad moaning).
"Stop! be silent for to-day!" '

VIII

Aye! be silent! Let them hear each other breathing
For a moment, mouth to mouth!
Let them touch each other's hands, in a fresh wreathing
Of their tender human youth!
Let them feel that this cold metallic motion
Is not all the life God fashions or reveals:
Let them prove their living souls against the notion
That they live in you, or under you, O wheels!
Still, all day, the iron wheels go onward,
Grinding life down from its mark;
And the children's souls, which God is calling sunward,
Spin on blindly in the dark.

IX

Now tell the poor young children, O my brothers,
To look up to Him and pray;
So the blessèd One who blesseth all the others,
Will bless them another day.

They answer, 'Who is God that He should hear us,
  While the rushing of the iron wheels is stirred?
When we sob aloud, the human creatures near us
  Pass by, hearing not, or answer not a word.
And *we* hear not (for the wheels in their resounding)
    Strangers speaking at the door:
Is it likely God, with angels singing round Him,
    Hears our weeping any more?

X

'Two words, indeed, of praying we remember,
    And at midnight's hour of harm,
"Our Father," looking upward in the chamber,
    We say softly for a charm.
We know no other words, except "Our Father,"
  And we think that, in some pause of angels' song,
God may pluck them with the silence sweet to gather,
  And hold both within His right hand which is strong.
"Our Father!" If He heard us, He would surely
    (For they call Him good and mild)
Answer, smiling down the steep world very purely,
    "Come and rest with me, my child."

XI

'But no!' say the children, weeping faster,
    'He is speechless as a stone;
And they tell us, of His image is the master
    Who commands us to work on.
Go to!' say the children,—'up in Heaven,
    Dark, wheel-like, turning clouds are all we find.
Do not mock us; grief has made us unbelieving—
  We look up for God, but tears have made us blind.'
Do you hear the children weeping and disproving,
    O my brothers, what ye preach?
For God's possible is taught by His world's loving,
    And the children doubt of each.

XII

And well may the children weep before you!
    They are weary ere they run;
They have never seen the sunshine, nor the glory
    Which is brighter than the sun.
They know the grief of man, without its wisdom;
  They sink in man's despair, without its calm;
Are slaves, without the liberty in Christdom,
  Are martyrs, by the pang without the palm,—
Are worn as if with age, yet unretrievingly
    The harvest of its memories cannot reap,—
Are orphans of the earthly love and heavenly.
    Let them weep! let them weep!

XIII

They look up with their pale and sunken faces,
    And their look is dread to see,

For they mind you of their angels in high places,
With eyes turned on Deity.
'How long,' they say, 'how long, O cruel nation,
Will you stand, to move the world, on a child's heart,—
Stifle down with a mailed heel its palpitation,
And tread onward to your throne amid the mart?
Our blood splashes upward, O gold-heaper,
And your purple shows your path!
But the child's sob in the silence curses deeper
Than the strong man in his wrath.'

[1843]

GRIEF

I tell you, hopeless grief is passionless;
That only men incredulous of despair,
Half-taught in anguish, through the midnight air
Beat upward to God's throne in loud access
Of shrieking and reproach. Full desertness,
In souls as countries, lieth silent-bare
Under the blanching, vertical eye-glare
Of the absolute Heavens. Deep-hearted man, express
Grief for thy Dead in silence like to death:—
Most like a monumental statue set
In everlasting watch and moveless woe
Till itself crumble to the dust beneath.
Touch it; the marble eyelids are not wet;
If it could weep, it could arise and go.

[1844]

THE DEAD PAN

I

Gods of Hellas, gods of Hellas,
Can ye listen in your silence?
Can your mystic voices tell us
Where ye hide? In floating islands,
With a wind that evermore
Keeps you out of sight of shore?
Pan, Pan is dead.

II

In what revels are ye sunken,
In old Aethiopia?
Have the Pygmies made you drunken,
Bathing in mandragora
Your divine pale lips that shiver
Like the lotus in the river?
Pan, Pan is dead.

III

Do ye sit there still in slumber,
In gigantic Alpine rows?
The black poppies out of number
Nodding, dripping from your brows
To the red lees of your wine,
And so kept alive and fine?
Pan, Pan is dead.

IV

Or lie crushed your stagnant corses
Where the silver spheres roll on,
Stung to life by centric forces
Thrown like rays out from the sun?—
While the smoke of your old altars
Is the shroud that round you welters?
Great Pan is dead.

V

'Gods of Hellas, gods of Hellas,'
Said the old Hellenic tongue!
Said the hero-oaths, as well as
Poets' songs the sweetest sung!
Have ye grown deaf in a day?
Can ye speak not yea or nay—
Since Pan is dead?

VI

Do ye leave your rivers flowing
All alone, O Naiades,
While your drenched locks dry slow in
This cold feeble sun and breeze?—
Not a word the Naiads say,
Though the rivers run for ay.
For Pan is dead.

VII

From the gloaming of the oak-wood,
O ye Dryads, could ye flee?
At the rushing thunderstroke, would
No sob tremble through the tree?—

Not a word the Dryads say,
Though the forests wave for ay.
For Pan is dead.

VIII

Have ye left the mountain places,
Oreads wild for other tryst?
Shall we see no sudden faces
Strike a glory through the mist?
Not a sound the silence thrills
Of the everlasting hills.
Pan, Pan is dead.

IX

O twelve gods of Plato's vision,
Crowned to starry wanderings,—
With your chariots in procession,
And your silver clash of wings!
Very pale ye seem to rise,
Ghosts of Grecian deities,—
Now Pan is dead!

X

Jove, that right hand is unloaded,
Whence the thunder did prevail,
While in idiocy of godhead
Thou art staring the stars pale!
And thine eagle, blind and old,
Roughs his feathers in the cold.
Pan, Pan is dead.

XI

Where, O Juno, is the glory
Of thy regal look and tread?
Will they lay, for evermore, thee
On thy dim, straight, golden bed?
Will thy queendom all lie hid
Meekly under either lid?
Pan, Pan is dead.

XII

Ha, Apollo! floats his golden
Hair all mist-like where he stands,
While the Muses hang enfolding
Knee and foot with faint wild hands?
'Neath the clanging of thy bow,
Niobe looked lost as thou!
Pan, Pan is dead.

XIII

Shall the casque with its brown iron
Pallas' broad blue eyes eclipse,
And no hero take inspiring
From the god-Greek of her lips?
'Neath her olive dost thou sit,
Mars the mighty, cursing it?
Pan, Pan is dead.

XIV

Bacchus, Bacchus! on the panther
He swoons,—bound with his own vines;
And his Mænads slowly saunter,
Head aside, among the pines,
While they murmur dreamingly
"Evohe—ah—evohe—!
Ah, Pan is dead!"

XV

Neptune lies beside the trident,
Dull and senseless as a stone;
And old Pluto deaf and silent
Is cast out into the sun:
Ceres smileth stern thereat,
"We *all* now are desolate—
Now Pan is dead."

XVI

Aphrodite! dead and driven
As thy native foam thou art;
With the cestus long done heaving
On the white calm of thine heart!
Ai[1] *Adonis!* at that shriek
Not a tear runs down her cheek—
Pan, Pan is dead.

XVII

And the Loves, we used to know from
One another, huddled lie,
Frore as taken in a snow-storm,
Close beside her tenderly;
As if each had weakly tried
Once to kiss her as he died.
Pan, Pan is dead.

XVIII

What, and Hermes? Time enthralleth
All thy cunning, Hermes, thus,—
And the ivy blindly crawleth
Round thy brave caduceus?
Hast thou no new message for us,
Full of thunder and Jove-glories?
Nay, Pan is dead.

[1] Alas.

XIX

Crownèd Cybele's great turret
Rocks and crumbles on her head;
Roar the lions of her chariot
Toward the wilderness, unfed:
Scornful children are not mute,—
'Mother, mother, walk afoot,
Since Pan is dead!'

XX

In the fiery-hearted centre
Of the solemn universe,
Ancient Vesta,—who could enter
To consume thee with this curse?
Drop thy grey chin on thy knee,
O thou palsied Mystery!
For Pan is dead.

XXI

Gods, we vainly do adjure you,—
Ye return nor voice nor sign!
Not a votary could secure you
Even a grave for your Divine!
Not a grave, to show thereby
Here these grey old gods do lie.
Pan, Pan is dead.

XXII

Even that Greece who took your wages
Calls the obolus outworn;
And the hoarse, deep-throated ages
Laugh your godships unto scorn;
And the poets do disclaim you,
Or grow colder if they name you—
And Pan is dead.

XXIII

Gods bereavèd, gods belated,
With your purples rent asunder!
Gods discrowned and desecrated,
Disinherited of thunder!
Now, the goats may climb and crop
The soft grass on Ida's top—
Now Pan is dead.

XXIV

Calm, of old, the bark went onward,
When a cry more loud than wind
Rose up, deepened, and swept sunward
From the pilèd Dark behind;
And the sun shrank and grew pale,
Breathed against by the great wail—
'Pan, Pan is dead.'

XXV

And the rowers from the benches
Fell,—each shuddering on his face,—
While departing Influences
Struck a cold back through the place;
And the shadow of the ship
Reeled along the passive deep—
'Pan, Pan is dead.'

XXVI

And that dismal cry rose slowly
And sank slowly through the air,
Full of spirit's melancholy
And eternity's despair!
And they heard the words it said—
'Pan is dead—Great Pan is dead—
Pan, Pan is dead.'

XXVII

'Twas the hour when One in Sion
Hung for love's sake on a cross;
When His brow was chill with dying
And His soul was faint with loss;
When His priestly blood dropped downward
And His kingly eyes looked throneward—
Then, Pan was dead.

XXVIII

By the love, He stood alone in,
His sole Godhead rose complete,
And the false gods fell down moaning
Each from off his golden seat;
All the false gods with a cry
Rendered up their deity—
Pan, Pan was dead.

XXIX

Wailing wide across the islands,
They rent, vest-like, their Divine;
And a darkness and a silence
Quenched the light of every shrine;
And Dodona's oak swang lonely
Henceforth, to the tempest only:
Pan, Pan was dead.

XXX

Pythia staggered, feeling o'er her,
Her lost god's forsaking look;
Straight her eyeballs filmed with horror
And her crispy fillets shook
And her lips gasped through their foam
For a word that did not come.
Pan, Pan was dead.

XXXI

O ye vain false gods of Hellas,
Ye are silent evermore!
And I dash down this old chalice
Whence libations ran of yore.
See, the wine crawls in the dust
Wormlike—as your glories must,
Since Pan is dead.

XXXII

Get to dust, as common mortals,
By a common doom and track!
Let no Schiller from the portals
Of that Hades call you back,
Or instruct us to weep all
At your antique funeral.
Pan, Pan is dead.

XXXIII

So your beauty, which confesses
Some chief Beauty conquering you,—
By our grand heroic guesses,
Through your falsehood, at the True,—
We will weep *not* . . . ! earth shall roll
Heir to each god's aureole—
And Pan is dead.

XXXIV

Earth outgrows the mythic fancies
Sung beside her in her youth;
And those debonair romances
Sound but dull beside the truth.
Phoebus' chariot-course is run:
Look up, poets, to the sun!
Pan, Pan is dead.

XXXV

Christ hath sent us down the angels;
And the whole earth and the skies
Are illumed by altar-candles
Lit for blessèd mysteries;
And a Priest's hand through creation,
Waveth calm and consecration—
And Pan is dead.

XXXVI

Truth is fair: should we forgo it?
Can we sigh right for a wrong?
God Himself is the best Poet,
And the Real is His song.
Sing His truth out fair and full,
And secure His beautiful.
Let Pan be dead.

XXXVII

Truth is large. Our aspiration
Scarce embraces half we be:
Shame, to stand in His creation,
And doubt truth's sufficiency!—
To think God's song unexcelling
The poor tales of our own telling—
When Pan is dead.

XXXVIII

What is true and just and honest,
What is lovely, what is pure—
All of praise that hath admonisht,
All of virtue shall endure,—
These are themes for poets' uses,
Stirring nobler than the Muses,
Ere Pan was dead.

XXXIX

O brave poets, keep back nothing,
Nor mix falsehood with the whole:
Look up Godward; speak the truth in
Worthy song from earnest soul!
Hold in high poetic duty,
Truest Truth the fairest Beauty.
Pan, Pan is dead.

[1844]

SONNETS FROM THE PORTUGUESE

I

I thought once how Theocritus had sung
Of the sweet years, the dear and wished-for years,
Who each one in a gracious hand appears
To bear a gift for mortals, old or young:
And, as I mused it in his antique tongue,
I saw, in gradual vision through my tears,
The sweet, sad years, the melancholy years,
Those of my own life, who by turns had flung
A shadow across me. Straightway I was 'ware,
So weeping, how a mystic Shape did move
Behind me, and drew me backward by the hair, 11
And a voice said in mastery, while I strove,—
'Guess now who holds thee?'—'Death,' I said. But, there,
The silver answer rang, . . 'Not Death, but Love.'

III

Unlike are we, unlike, O princely Heart!
Unlike our uses and our destinies.
Our ministering two angels look surprise
On one another, as they strike athwart
Their wings in passing. Thou, bethink thee, art
A guest for queens to social pageantries,—
With gages from a hundred brighter eyes
Than tears even can make mine, to play thy part
Of chief musician. What hast *thou* to do
With looking from the lattice-lights at me,
A poor, tired, wandering singer, . . singing through
The dark, and leaning up a cypress tree?
The chrism is on thine head,—on mine, the dew,—
And Death must dig the level where these agree.

V

I lift my heavy heart up solemnly,
As once Electra her sepulchral urn,
And looking in thine eyes, I overturn
The ashes at thy feet. Behold and see
What a great heap of grief lay hid in me,
And how the red wild sparkles dimly burn
Through the ashen grayness. If thy foot in scorn
Could tread them out to darkness utterly,
It might be well perhaps. But if instead
Thou wait beside me for the wind to blow
The gray dust up, . . those laurels on thine head,
O my Belovèd, will not shield thee so,
That none of all the fires shall scorch and shred
The hair beneath. Stand farther off then! go.

VI

Go from me. Yet I feel that I shall stand
Henceforward in thy shadow. Nevermore
Alone upon the threshold of my door
Of individual life, I shall command
The uses of my soul, nor lift my hand
Serenely in the sunshine as before,
Without the sense of that which I forbore, . .
Thy touch upon the palm. The widest land
Doom takes to part us, leaves thy heart in mine
With pulses that beat double. What I do
And what I dream include thee, as the wine
Must taste of its own grapes. And when I sue
God for myself, He hears that name of thine,
And sees within my eyes the tears of two.

VII

The face of all the world is changed, I think,
Since first I heard the footsteps of thy soul
Move still, oh, still, beside me, as they stole
Betwixt me and the dreadful outer brink
Of obvious death, where I, who thought to sink,
Was caught up into love, and taught the whole
Of life in a new rhythm. The cup of dole
God gave for baptism, I am fain to drink,
And praise its sweetness, Sweet, with thee anear.
The names of country, heaven, are changed away
For where thou art or shalt be, there or here;
And this . . . this lute and song . . . loved yesterday,
(The singing angels know) are only dear
Because thy name moves right in what they say.

VIII

What can I give thee back, O liberal
And princely giver, who hast brought the gold
And purple of thine heart, unstained, untold,
And laid them on the outside of the wall
For such as I to take or leave withal,
In unexpected largesse? am I cold,
Ungrateful, that for these most manifold
High gifts, I render nothing back at all?
Not so; not cold,—but very poor instead.
Ask God who knows. For frequent tears have run
The colours from my life, and left so dead
And pale a stuff, it were not fitly done
To give the same as pillow to thy head.
Go farther! let it serve to trample on.

XIV

If thou must love me, let it be for nought
Except for love's sake only. Do not say

'I love her for her smile . . . her look . . . her way
Of speaking gently, . . for a trick of thought
That falls in well with mine, and certes brought
A sense of pleasant ease on such a day'—
For these things in themselves, Belovèd, may
Be changed, or change for thee,—and love, so wrought,
May be unwrought so. Neither love me for
Thine own dear pity's wiping my cheeks dry,—
A creature might forget to weep, who bore
Thy comfort long, and lose thy love thereby!
But love me for love's sake, that evermore
Thou mayst love on, through love's eternity.

XVI

And yet, because thou overcomest so,
Because thou art more noble and like a king,
Thou canst prevail against my fears and fling
Thy purple round me, till my heart shall grow
Too close against thine heart, henceforth to know
How it shook when alone. Why, conquering
May prove as lordly and complete a thing
In lifting upward, as in crushing low!
And as a vanquished soldier yields his sword
To one who lifts him from the bloody earth,—
Even so, Belovèd, I at last record,
Here ends my strife. If *thou* invite me forth,
I rise above abasement at the word.
Make thy love larger to enlarge my worth.

XX

Belovèd, my Belovèd, when I think
That thou wast in the world a year ago,
What time I sat alone here in the snow
And saw no footprint, heard the silence sink
No moment at thy voice, . . but, link by link,
Went counting all my chains as if that so
They never could fall off at any blow
Struck by thy possible hand . . . why, thus I drink
Of life's great cup of wonder! Wonderful,
Never to feel thee thrill the day or night
With personal act or speech,—nor ever cull
Some prescience of thee with the blossoms white
Thou sawest growing! Atheists are as dull,
Who cannot guess God's presence out of sight.

XXI

Say over again, and yet once over again,
That thou dost love me. Though the word repeated
Should seem "a cuckoo-song," as thou dost treat it,
Remember, never to the hill or plain,
Valley and wood, without her cuckoo-strain
Comes the fresh Spring in all her green completed.
Belovèd, I, amid the darkness greeted
By a doubtful spirit-voice, in that doubt's pain
Cry . . . 'Speak once more . . . thou lovest!' Who can fear
Too many stars, though each in heaven shall roll—
Too many flowers, though each shall crown the year?
Say thou dost love me, love me, love me—toll
The silver iterance—only minding, dear,
To love me also in silence, with thy soul.

XXII

When our two souls stand up erect and strong,
Face to face, silent, drawing nigh and nigher,
Until the lengthening wings break into fire
At either curvèd point,—what bitter wrong
Can the earth do to us, that we should not long
Be here contented? Think. In mounting higher,
The angels would press on us and aspire
To drop some golden orb of perfect song
Into our deep, dear silence. Let us stay
Rather on earth, Belovèd,—where the unfit
Contrarious moods of men recoil away
And isolate pure spirits, and permit
A place to stand and love in for a day,
With darkness and the death-hour rounding it.

XXVI

I lived with visions for my company
Instead of men and women, years ago,
And found them gentle mates, nor thought to know
A sweeter music than they played to me.
But soon their trailing purple was not free
Of this world's dust, their lutes did silent grow,
And I myself grew faint and blind below
Their vanishing eyes. Then thou didst come . . . to be,
Belovèd, what they seemed. Their shining fronts,
Their songs, their splendours (better, yet the same,
As river-water hallowed into fonts),
Met in thee, and from out thee overcame
My soul with satisfaction of all wants:
Because God's gifts put man's best dreams to shame.

XXVIII

My letters! all dead paper, . . mute and white!—
And yet they seem alive and quivering
Against my tremulous hands which loose the string
And let them drop down on my knee to-night.
This said, . . he wished to have me in his sight
Once, as a friend: this fixed a day in spring
To come and touch my hand . . . a simple thing,
Yet I wept for it!—this, . . the paper's light . . .
Said, *Dear, I love thee;* and I sank and quailed
As if God's future thundered on my past.
This said, *I am thine*—and so its ink has paled
With lying at my heart that beat too fast.
And this . . . O Love, thy words have ill availed
If, what this said, I dared repeat at last!

XXXII

The first time that the sun rose on thine oath
To love me, I looked forward to the moon
To slacken all those bonds which seemed too soon
And quickly tied to make a lasting troth.
Quick-loving hearts, I thought, may quickly loathe;
And, looking on myself, I seemed not one
For such man's love!—more like an out-of-tune
Worn viol, a good singer would be wroth
To spoil his song with, and which, snatched in haste,
Is laid down at the first ill-sounding note.
I did not wrong myself so, but I placed
A wrong on *thee.* For perfect strains may float
'Neath master-hands, from instruments defaced,—
And great souls, at one stroke, may do and doat.

XXXV

If I leave all for thee, wilt thou exchange
And be all to me? Shall I never miss
Home-talk and blessing and the common kiss
That comes to each in turn, nor count it strange,
When I look up, to drop on a new range
Of walls and floors . . . another home than this?
Nay, wilt thou fill that place by me which is
Filled by dead eyes too tender to know change?
That's hardest. If to conquer love, has tried,
To conquer grief, tries more . . . as all things prove;
For grief indeed is love and grief beside.
Alas, I have grieved so I am hard to love.
Yet love me—wilt thou? Open thine heart wide,
And fold within, the wet wings of thy dove.

XXXVIII

First time he kissed me, he but only kissed
The fingers of this hand wherewith I write;
And ever since, it grew more clean and white, . . .
Slow to world-greetings . . . quick with its 'Oh, list,'
When the angels speak. A ring of amethyst
I could not wear here, plainer to my sight,
Than that first kiss. The second passed in height
The first, and sought the forehead, and half missed,

Half falling on the hair. O beyond meed!
That was the chrism of love, which love's own crown,
With sanctifying sweetness, did precede.
The third upon my lips was folded down
In perfect, purple state; since when, indeed,
I have been proud and said, 'My love, my own.'

XLI

I thank all who have loved me in their hearts,
With thanks and love from mine. Deep thanks to all
Who paused a little near the prison-wall
To hear my music in its louder parts
Ere they went onward, each one to the mart's
Or temple's occupation, beyond call.
But thou, who, in my voice's sink and fall
When the sob took it, thy divinest Art's
Own instrument didst drop down at thy foot
To hearken what I said between my tears, . .
Instruct me how to thank thee!—Oh, to shoot
My soul's full meaning into future years,
That *they* should lend it utterance, and salute
Love that endures, from Life that disappears!

XLIII

How do I love thee? Let me count the ways.
I love thee to the depth and breadth and height
My soul can reach, when feeling out of sight
For the ends of Being and ideal Grace.
I love thee to the level of every day's
Most quiet need, by sun and candlelight.
I love thee freely, as men strive for Right;
I love thee purely, as they turn from Praise.
I love thee with the passion put to use
In my old griefs, and with my childhood's faith.
I love thee with a love I seemed to lose
With my lost saints,—I love thee with the breath,
Smiles, tears, of all my life!—and, if God choose,
I shall but love thee better after death.

XLIV

Belovèd, thou hast brought me many flowers
Plucked in the garden, all the summer through
And winter, and it seemed as if they grew
In this close room, nor missed the sun and showers.
So, in the like name of that love of ours,
Take back those thoughts which here unfolded too,
And which on warm and cold days I withdrew
From my heart's ground. Indeed, those beds and bowers
Be overgrown with bitter weeds and rue,
And wait thy weeding; yet here's eglantine,
Here's ivy!—take them as I used to do
Thy flowers, and keep them where they shall not pine.
Instruct thine eyes to keep their colours true,
And tell thy soul their roots are left in mine.

[1850]

A MUSICAL INSTRUMENT

I

What was he doing, the great god Pan,
Down in the reeds by the river?
Spreading ruin and scattering ban,
Splashing and paddling with hoofs of a goat,
And breaking the golden lilies afloat
With the dragon-fly on the river.

II

He tore out a reed, the great god Pan,
From the deep cool bed of the river:
The limpid water turbidly ran,
And the broken lilies a-dying lay,
And the dragon-fly had fled away,
Ere he brought it out of the river.

III

High on the shore sat the great god Pan
While turbidly flowed the river;
And hacked and hewed as a great god can,
With his hard bleak steel at the patient reed,
Till there was not a sign of the leaf indeed
To prove it fresh from the river.

IV

He cut it short, did the great god Pan,
(How tall it stood in the river!)
Then drew the pith, like the heart of a man,
Steadily from the outside ring,
And notched the poor dry empty thing
In holes, as he sate by the river.

V

'This is the way,' laughed the great god Pan
(Laughed while he sate by the river),
'The only way, since gods began
To make sweet music, they could succeed.'
Then, dropping his mouth to a hole in the reed,
He blew in power by the river.

VI

Sweet, sweet, sweet, O Pan!
Piercing sweet by the river!
Blinding sweet, O great god Pan!
The sun on the hill forgot to die,
And the lilies revived, and the dragon-fly
Came back to dream on the river.

VII

Yet half a beast is the great god Pan,
To laugh as he sits by the river,
Making a poet out of a man:
The true gods sigh for the cost and pain,—
For the reed which grows nevermore again
As a reed with the reeds in the river.

[1860]

BIANCA AMONG THE NIGHTINGALES

I

The cypress stood up like a church
That night we felt our love would hold,
And saintly moonlight seemed to search
And wash the whole world clean as gold;
The olives crystallized the vales'
Broad slopes until the hills grew strong:
The fireflies and the nightingales
Throbbed each to either, flame and song.
The nightingales, the nightingales.

II

Upon the angle of its shade
The cypress stood, self-balanced high;
Half up, half down, as double-made,
Along the ground, against the sky.
And *we*, too! from such soul-height went
Such leaps of blood, so blindly driven,
We scarce knew if our nature meant
Most passionate earth or intense heaven.
The nightingales, the nightingales.

III

We paled with love, we shook with love,
We kissed so close we could not vow;
Till Giulio whispered, 'Sweet, above
God's Ever guarantees this Now.'
And through his words the nightingales
Drove straight and full their long clear call,
Like arrows through heroic mails,
And love was awful in it all.
The nightingales, the nightingales.

IV

O cold white moonlight of the north,
Refresh these pulses, quench this hell!
O coverture of death drawn forth
Across this garden-chamber . . well!
But what have nightingales to do
In gloomy England called the free . .
(Yes, free to die in! . .) when we two
Are sundered, singing still to me?
And still they sing, the nightingales.

V

I think I hear him, how he cried
'My own soul's life' between their notes.
Each man has but one soul supplied,
And that's immortal. Though his throat's
On fire with passion now, to *her*
He can't say what to me he said!
And yet he moves her, they aver.
The nightingales sing through my head,
The nightingales, the nightingales.

VI

He says to *her* what moves her most.
He would not name his soul within
Her hearing,—rather pays her cost
With praises to her lips and chin.
Man has but one soul, 'tis ordained,
And each soul but one love, I add;
Yet souls are damned and love's profaned.
These nightingales will sing me mad!
The nightingales, the nightingales.

VII

I marvel how the birds can sing.
There's little difference, in their view,
Betwixt our Tuscan trees that spring
As vital flames into the blue,

And dull round blots of foliage meant
  Like saturated sponges here
To suck the fogs up. As content
  Is *he* too in this land, 'tis clear.
And still they sing, the nightingales.

VIII

My native Florence! dear, forgone!
  I see across the Alpine ridge
How the last feast-day of Saint John
  Shot rockets from Carraia bridge.
The luminous city, tall with fire,
  Trod deep down in that river of ours,
While many a boat with lamp and choir
  Skimmed birdlike over glittering towers.
I will not hear these nightingales.

IX

I seem to float, *we* seem to float
  Down Arno's stream in festive guise;
A boat strikes flame into our boat,
  And up that lady seems to rise
As then she rose. The shock had flashed
  A vision on us! What a head,
What leaping eyeballs!—beauty dashed
  To splendour by a sudden dread.
And still they sing, the nightingales.

X

Too bold to sin, too weak to die;
  Such women are so. As for me,
I would we had drowned there, he and I,
  That moment, loving perfectly.
He had not caught her, with her loosed
  Gold ringlets . . rarer in the south . .
Nor heard the 'Grazie tanto' [1] bruised
  To sweetness by her English mouth.
And still they sing, the nightingales.

XI

She had not reached him at my heart
  With her fine tongue, as snakes indeed
Kill flies; nor had I, for my part,
  Yearned after, in my desperate need,
And followed him as he did her
  To coasts left bitter by the tide,
Whose very nightingales, elsewhere
  Delighting, torture and deride!
For still they sing, the nightingales.

XII

A worthless woman, mere cold clay
  As all false things are! but so fair,
She takes the breath of men away
  Who gaze upon her unaware.
I would not play her larcenous tricks
  To have her looks! She lied and stole,
And spat into my love's pure pyx
  The rank saliva of her soul.
And still they sing, the nightingales.

XIII

I would not for her white and pink,
  Though such he likes—her grace of limb,
Though such he has praised—nor yet, I
    think,
  For life itself, though spent with him,
Commit such sacrilege, affront
  God's nature which is love, intrude
'Twixt two affianced souls, and hunt
  Like spiders, in the altar's wood.
I cannot bear these nightingales.

XIV

If she chose sin, some gentler guise
  She might have sinned in, so it seems:
She might have pricked out both my eyes,
  And I still seen him in my dreams!
—Or drugged me in my soup or wine,
  Nor left me angry afterward:
To die here with his hand in mine
  His breath upon me, were not hard.
(Our Lady hush these nightingales!)

XV

But set a springe for *him*, 'mio ben,' [2]
  My only good, my first last love!—
Though Christ knows well what sin is, when
  He sees some things done they must move
Himself to wonder. Let her pass.
  I think of her by night and day.
Must *I* too join her . . out alas! . .
  With Giulio, in each word I say!
And evermore the nightingales!

XVI

Giulio, my Giulio!—sing they so,
  And you be silent? Do I speak,
And you not hear? An arm you throw
  Round some one, and I feel so weak?
—Oh, owl-like birds! They sing for spite,
  They sing for hate, they sing for doom!
They'll sing through death who sing
    through night,
  They'll sing and stun me in the tomb—
The nightingales, the nightingales!

[1860]

[1] Many thanks.

[2] My dear.

EDWARD FITZGERALD

CHRONOLOGICAL TABLE

1809, March 31, born at the White House, Bredfield, near Woodbridge, his father a squire and M.P. for Seaford, his mother, Mary FitzGerald, descended from the earls of Kildare.

1818 His father, John Purcell, on the death of Mary FitzGerald's father takes the name FitzGerald.

1821– Attended King Edward's School, at Bury St. Edmunds.

1826–30 At Trinity College, Cambridge, where he formed lasting friendships with Tennyson and Thackeray.

1830 Left Cambridge with a degree.

1831 His first poem published in *Hone's Year Book* ("The Meadows in Spring").

1842 Beginning of his friendship with Carlyle.

1846 Met E. B. Cowell, later Professor of Sanskrit at Cambridge, who subsequently sent him the manuscript of the *Rubáiyát.*

1849 *Selections from the Poems and Letters of Bernard Barton.*

1851 *Euphranor.*

1852 *Polonius: A Collection of Wise Saws and Modern Instances.*

1853 *Six Dramas of Calderon* (translations).

1856 *Salaman and Absal* (a translation from the Persian of Jami).
Married to Bernard Barton's daughter.

1857 Separated from his wife (without legal proceedings).

1859 *The Rubáiyát of Omar Khayyám.*

1865 *The Mighty Magician* and *Such Stuff as Dreams are made of* (translations of two more plays of Calderon, printed for private circulation).
Agamemnon (translation, privately printed).

1868 *The Rubáiyát* (revised).

1872 *The Rubáiyát* (again revised).

1876 *Agamemnon.*
Readings in Crabbe (Part I; privately printed).

1880–1 *Oedipus* (translations).

1882–3 *Readings in Crabbe.*

1883 Died June 13–14 at Merton Rectory, buried at Boulge.

Only one of FitzGerald's productions in verse sustains a reputation which is nevertheless secure. His original poems do not rise above the level of accomplished verse; and apart from his one great performance his translations (which would be more exactly termed free-and-easy adaptations) were conceived on mistaken principles and executed with but wavering skill. He translated from Greek, Spanish and Persian. None of these languages was perfectly known to him; nor was his spirit specially attuned to the authors from whom he translated, to the complicated elegance of Calderon, to the bleak grandeur of Aeschylus.

The *Rubáiyát* alone are exempt from such a severity of estimate. His friend E. B. Cowell, a fervent orientalist, instructed him in the Persian language, sent to him a manuscript of Omar, answered a multitude of queries about idiom and customs. The translation of the *Rubáiyát* rested, then, upon a fairly sound scholarly knowledge, although this knowledge was not FitzGerald's. Besides FitzGerald had already familiarized himself with the problem of translating from Persian in his version of the *Salaman and Absal* of the poet Jami. The manuscript sent by Cowell contained one hundred and fifty-eight quatrains of which FitzGerald has given a description as "independent stanzas, consisting each of four lines of equal, though varied, Prosody; sometimes all rhyming, but oftener (as here imitated) the third line a blank. . . . As usual with such kind of Oriental Verse, the Rubáiyát follow one another according to Alphabetic Rhyme—a strange succession of Grave and Gay." It should be added that occasionally three or more of the quatrains are related; and that the succession of grave and gay is not systematic and invariable.

Through Cowell's zeal, FitzGerald came to know other works of the physicist, mathematician, astronomer and metaphysician who lived in twelfth-century Persia. He was engaged for many months in his desultory way in imposing a unity and a development on his discontinuous material, in introducing phrases and even ideas from other Persian writers, in inserting, occasionally, entire stanzas which were original with him, and expressed the sensibility of his own age, in suppressing whatever in Omar displeased him. Four versions of the poem appeared. In the first there were seventy-five quatrains, in the second one hundred and ten, in the third and fourth one hundred and one; besides revising the extent of the poem FitzGerald corrected (often with unhappy results) the language.

The first edition of a poem which was to be one of the most widely diffused of the century ran to no more than two hundred and fifty copies. Although many of these were given away by the author, it was eight years before a second edition was required. The fortune of the poem was made not by FitzGerald himself, nor by his intimates such as Tennyson, but by a younger generation of poets, notably Rossetti and Swinburne, who found in the *Rubáiyát* at once a view of human life with which in certain moods at least they sympathized and an idiom whose biting phrases and sumptuous imagery delighted their ears and fired their imaginations.

RUBÁIYÁT OF OMAR KHAYYÁM OF NAISHÁPÚR

I

Wake! For the Sun who scattered into flight
The Stars before him from the Field of Night,
  Drives Night along with them from Heav'n, and strikes
The Sultán's Turret with a Shaft of Light.

II

Before the phantom of False morning died,
Methought a Voice within the Tavern cried,
  "When all the Temple is prepared within,
Why nods the drowsy Worshipper outside?"

III

And, as the Cock crew, those who stood before
The Tavern shouted—"Open then the door!
  You know how little while we have to stay,
And, once departed, may return no more."

IV

Now the New Year reviving old Desires,
The thoughtful Soul to Solitude retires,
  Where the WHITE HAND OF MOSES on the Bough
Puts out, and Jesus from the Ground suspires.

V

Iram indeed is gone with all his Rose,
And Jamshyd's Sev'n-ringed Cup where no one knows;
  But still a Ruby kindles in the Vine,
And many a Garden by the Water blows.

VI

And David's lips are lockt; but in divine
High-piping Pehleví, with "Wine! Wine! Wine!
  Red Wine!"—the Nightingale cries to the Rose
That sallow cheek of hers to 'incarnadine.

VII

Come, fill the Cup, and in the fire of Spring
Your Winter-garment of Repentance fling:
  The Bird of Time has but a little way
To flutter—and the Bird is on the Wing.

VIII

Whether at Naishápúr or Babylon,
Whether the Cup with sweet or bitter run,
  The Wine of Life keeps oozing drop by drop,
The Leaves of Life keep falling one by one.

IX

Each Morn a thousand Roses brings, you say;
Yes, but where leaves the Rose of Yesterday?
  And this first Summer month that brings the Rose
Shall take Jamshyd and Kaikobád away.

X

Well, let it take them! What have we to do
With Kaikobád the Great, or Kaikhosrú?
  Let Zál and Rustum bluster as they will,
Or Hátim call to Supper—heed not you.

XI

With me along the strip of Herbage strown
That just divides the desert from the sown,
  Where name of Slave and Sultán is forgot—
And Peace to Mahmúd on his golden Throne!

XII

A Book of Verses underneath the Bough,
A Jug of Wine, a Loaf of Bread—and Thou
  Beside me singing in the Wilderness—
Oh, Wilderness were Paradise enow!

XIII

Some for the Glories of This World; and some
Sigh for the Prophet's Paradise to come;
  Ah, take the Cash, and let the Credit go,
Nor heed the rumble of a distant Drum!

XIV

Look to the blowing Rose about us—"Lo,
Laughing," she says, "into the world I blow,
  At once the silken tassel of my Purse
Tear, and its Treasure on the Garden throw."

XV

And those who husbanded the Golden grain,
And those who flung it to the winds like Rain,
  Alike to no such aureate Earth are turned
As, buried once, Men want dug up again.

XVI

The Worldly Hope men set their Hearts upon
Turns Ashes—or it prospers; and anon,
  Like Snow upon the Desert's dusty Face,
Lighting a little hour or two—is gone.

XVII

Think, in this battered Caravanserai
Whose Portals are alternate Night and Day,
  How Sultán after Sultán with his Pomp
Abode his destined Hour, and went his way.

XVIII

They say the Lion and the Lizard keep
The Courts where Jamshyd gloried and drank deep:
  And Bahrám, that great Hunter—the Wild Ass
Stamps o'er his Head, but cannot break his Sleep.

XIX

I sometimes think that never blows so red
The Rose as where some buried Cæsar bled;
  That every Hyacinth the Garden wears
Dropt in her Lap from some once lovely Head.

XX

And this reviving Herb whose tender Green
Fledges the River-Lip on which we lean—
  Ah, lean upon it lightly! for who knows
From what once lovely Lip it springs unseen!

XXI

Ah, my Belovéd, fill the cup that clears
TO-DAY of past Regrets and future Fears:
  To-morrow!—Why, To-morrow I may be
Myself with Yesterday's Sev'n thousand Years.

XXII

For some we loved, the loveliest and the best
That from his Vintage rolling Time hath prest,
  Have drunk their Cup a Round or two before,
And one by one crept silently to rest.

XXIII

And we, that now make merry in the Room
They left, and Summer dresses in new bloom,
  Ourselves must we beneath the Couch of Earth
Descend—ourselves to make a Couch—for whom?

XXIV

Ah, make the most of what we yet may spend,
Before we too into the Dust descend;
  Dust into Dust, and under Dust, to lie,
Sans [1] Wine, sans Song, sans Singer, and—sans End!

XXV

Alike for those who for TO-DAY prepare,
And those that after some TO-MORROW stare,
  A Muezzín from the Tower of Darkness cries,
"Fools! your Reward is neither Here nor There."

[1] Without.

XXVI

Why, all the Saints and Sages who discussed
Of the Two Worlds so wisely—they are thrust
Like foolish Prophets forth; their Words to Scorn
Are scatter'd, and their Mouths are stopt with Dust.

XXVII

Myself when young did eagerly frequent
Doctor and Saint, and heard great argument
About it and about: but evermore
Came out by the same door where in I went.

XXVIII

With them the seed of Wisdom did I sow,
And with mine own hand wrought to make it grow;
And this as all the Harvest that I reap'd—
"I came like Water, and like Wind I go."

XXIX

Into this Universe, and *Why* not knowing,
Nor *Whence*, like Water willy-nilly flowing;
And out of it, as Wind along the Waste,
I know not *Whither*, willy-nilly blowing.

XXX

What, without asking, hither hurried *Whence?*
And, without asking, *Whither* hurried hence!
Oh, many a Cup of this forbidden Wine
Must drown the memory of that insolence!

XXXI

Up from Earth's Centre through the Seventh Gate
I rose, and on the Throne of Saturn sate;
And many a Knot unravel'd by the Road;
But not the Master-knot of Human Fate.

XXXII

There was the Door to which I found no Key;
There was the Veil through which I might not see:
Some little talk awhile of ME AND THEE
There was—and then no more of THEE and ME.

XXXIII

Earth could not answer; nor the Seas that mourn
In flowing Purple, of their Lord forlorn;
Nor rolling Heaven, with all his Signs revealed
And hidden by the sleeve of Night and Morn.

XXXIV

Then of the THEE IN ME who works behind
The Veil, I lifted up my hands to find
A Lamp amid the Darkness; and I heard,
As from Without—"THE ME WITHIN THEE BLIND!"

XXXV

Then to the Lip of this poor earthen Urn
I lean'd, the Secret of my Life to learn:
  And Lip to Lip it murmur'd—"While you live,
Drink!—for, once dead, you never shall return."

XXXVI

I think the Vessel, that with fugitive
Articulation answer'd, once did live,
  And drink; and Ah! the passive Lip I kiss'd,
How many Kisses might it take—and give!

XXXVII

For I remember stopping by the way
To watch a Potter thumping his wet Clay:
  And with its all-obliterated Tongue
It murmured—"Gently, Brother, gently pray!"

XXXVIII

And has not such a Story from of Old
Down Man's successive generations roll'd,
  Of such a clod of saturated Earth
Cast by the Maker into Human mould?

XXXIX

And not a drop that from our Cups we throw
For Earth to drink of, but may steal below
  To quench the fire of Anguish in some Eye
There hidden—far beneath, and long ago.

XL

As then the Tulip for her morning sup
Of Heav'nly Vintage from the soil looks up,
  Do you devoutly do the like, till Heav'n
To Earth invert you—like an empty Cup.

XLI

Perplext no more with Human or Divine,
To-morrow's tangle to the winds resign,
  And lose your fingers in the tresses of
The Cypress-slender Minister of Wine.

XLII

And if the Wine you drink, the Lip you press,
End in what All begins and ends in—Yes;
  Think then you are TO-DAY what YESTERDAY
You were—TO-MORROW you shall not be less.

XLIII

So when the Angel of the darker Drink
At last shall find you by the river-brink,
  And, offering his Cup, invite your Soul
Forth to your Lips to quaff—you shall not shrink.

XLIV

Why, if the Soul can fling the Dust aside,
And naked on the Air of Heaven ride,
  Were't not a Shame—were't not a Shame for him
In this clay carcase crippled to abide?

XLV

'Tis but a Tent where takes his one-day's rest
A Sultán to the realm of Death addrest;
  The Sultán rises, and the dark Ferrásh [1]
Strikes, and prepares it for another Guest.

XLVI

And fear not lest Existence closing your
Account, and mine, should know the like no more;
  The Eternal Sákí [2] from that Bowl has pour'd
Millions of Bubbles like us, and will pour.

XLVII

When You and I behind the Veil are past,
Oh but the long, long while the World shall last,
  Which of our Coming and Departure heeds
As the SEA'S SELF should heed a pebble-cast.

XLVIII

A Moment's Halt—a momentary taste
Of BEING from the Well amid the Waste—
  And Lo!—the phantom Caravan has reach'd
The NOTHING it set out from—Oh, make haste!

XLIX

Would you that spangle of Existence spend
About THE SECRET—quick about it, Friend!
  A Hair perhaps divides the False and True—
And upon what, prithee, may Life depend?

L

A Hair perhaps divides the False and True;
Yes; and a single Alif were the clue—
  Could you but find it—to the Treasure-house,
And peradventure to THE MASTER too;

LI

Whose secret Presence, through Creation's veins
Running Quicksilver-like eludes your pains;
  Taking all shapes from Máh [3] to Máhi; and
They change and perish all—but He remains;

LII

A moment guess'd—then back behind the Fold
Immerst of Darkness round the Drama roll'd
  Which, for the Pastime of Eternity,
He does Himself contrive, enact, behold.

[1] Servitor. [2] Wine-bearer. [3] From fish to moon.

LIII

But if in vain, down on the stubborn floor
Of Earth, and up to Heav'n's unopening door,
You gaze TO-DAY, while You are You—how then
TO-MORROW, You when shall be You no more?

LIV

Waste not your Hour, nor in the vain pursuit
Of This and That endeavour and dispute;
Better be jocund with the fruitful Grape
Then sadden after none, or bitter, Fruit.

LV

You know, my Friends, with what a brave Carouse
I made a Second Marriage in my house;
Divorced old barren Reason from my Bed,
And took the Daughter of the Vine to Spouse.

LVI

For "Is" and "IS-NOT" though with Rule and Line,
And "UP-AND-DOWN" by Logic I define,
Of all that one should care to fathom, I
Was never deep in anything but—Wine.

LVII

Ah, but my Computations, People say,
Reduced the Year to better reckoning?—Nay,
'Twas only striking from the Calendar
Unborn To-morrow, and dead Yesterday.

LVIII

And lately, by the Tavern Door agape,
Came shining through the Dusk an Angel Shape
Bearing a Vessel on his Shoulder; and
He bid me taste of it; and 'twas—the Grape!

LIX

The Grape that can with Logic absolute
The Two-and-Seventy jarring Sects confute:
The sovereign Alchemist that in a trice
Life's leaden metal into Gold transmute:

LX

The mighty Mahmúd, Allah-breathing Lord,
That all the misbelieving and black Horde
Of Fears and Sorrows that infest the Soul
Scatters before him with his whirlwind Sword.

LXI

Why, be this Juice the growth of God, who dare
Blaspheme the twisted tendril as a Snare?
A Blessing, we should use it, should we not?
And if a Curse—why, then, Who set it there?

LXII

I must abjure the Balm of Life, I must,
Scared by some After-reckoning ta'en on trust,
  Or lured with Hope of some Diviner Drink,
To fill the Cup—when crumbled into Dust!

LXIII

O threats of Hell and Hopes of Paradise!
One thing at least is certain,—*This* Life flies;
  One thing is certain and the rest is Lies;
The Flower that once has blown for ever dies.

LXIV

Strange, is it not? that of the myriads who
Before us passed the door of Darkness through
  Not one returns to tell us of the Road
Which to discover we must travel too.

LXV

The Revelations of Devout and Learn'd
Who rose before us, and as Prophets burn'd,
  Are all but Stories, which, awoke from Sleep
They told their fellows, and to Sleep return'd.

LXVI

I sent my Soul through the Invisible,
Some letter of that After-life to spell:
  And by and by my Soul return'd to me,
And answered "I Myself am Heav'n and Hell":

LXVII

Heav'n but the Vision of fulfill'd Desire,
And Hell the Shadow from a Soul on fire,
  Cast on the Darkness into which Ourselves,
So late emerged from, shall so soon expire.

LXVIII

We are no other than a moving row
Of Magic Shadow-shapes that come and go
  Round with this Sun-illumined Lantern held
In Midnight by the Master of the Show;

LXIX

But helpless Pieces of the Game He plays
Upon this Chequer-board of Nights and Days;
  Hither and thither moves, and checks, and slays,
And one by one back in the Closet lays.

LXX

The Ball no question makes of Ayes and Noes,
But Here or There as strikes the Player goes;
  And He that tossed you down into the Field,
He knows about it all—HE knows—HE knows!

LXXI

The Moving Finger writes; and, having writ,
Moves on: nor all your Piety nor Wit
  Shall lure it back to cancel half a Line,
Nor all your Tears wash out a Word of it.

LXXII

And that inverted Bowl they call the Sky,
Whereunder crawling coop'd we live and die,
  Lift not your hands to *It* for help—for It
As impotently rolls as you or I.

LXXIII

With Earth's first Clay They did the Last Man knead,
And there of the Last Harvest sowed the Seed:
  And the first Morning of Creation wrote
What the Last Dawn of Reckoning shall read.

LXXIV

YESTERDAY *This* Day's Madness did prepare;
TO-MORROW's Silence, Triumph, or Despair:
  Drink! for you know not whence you came, nor why:
Drink! for you know not why you go, nor where.

LXXV

I tell you this—When, started from the Goal,
Over the flaming shoulders of the Foal
  Of Heav'n Parwin and Mushtarí [1] they flung,
In my predestined Plot of Dust and Soul

LXXVI

The Vine had struck a fibre: which about
If clings my Being—let the Dervish flout;
  Of my Base metal may be filed a Key,
That shall unlock the Door he howls without.

LXXVII

And this I know: whether the one True Light
Kindle to Love, or Wrath-consume me quite,
  One Flash of It within the Tavern caught
Better than in the Temple lost outright.

LXXVIII

What! out of senseless Nothing to provoke
A conscious Something to resent the yoke
  Of unpermitted Pleasure, under pain
Of Everlasting Penalties, if broke!

LXXIX

What, from his helpless Creature be repaid
Pure Gold for what he lent him dross-allayed—
  Sue for a Debt we never did contract,
And cannot answer—Oh the sorry trade!

[1] The Pleïades and Jupiter.

LXXX

Oh Thou, who didst with pitfall and with gin
Beset the Road I was to wander in,
  Thou wilt not with Predestined Evil round
Enmesh, and then impute my Fall to Sin!

LXXXI

Oh, Thou, who Man of baser Earth didst make
And ev'n with Paradise devise the Snake:
  For all the Sin wherewith the Face of Man
Is blacken'd—Man's Forgiveness give—and take!

. . . .

LXXXII

As under cover of departing Day
Slunk hunger-stricken Ramazán away,
  Once more within the Potter's house alone
I stood, surrounded by the Shapes of Clay.

LXXXIII

Shapes of all Sorts and Sizes, great and small,
That stood along the floor and by the wall;
  And some loquacious Vessels were; and some
Listen'd perhaps, but never talk'd at all.

LXXXIV

Said one among them—"Surely not in vain
My substance of the common Earth was ta'en
  And to this Figure moulded, to be broke,
Or trampled back to shapeless Earth again."

LXXXV

Then said a Second—"Ne'er a peevish Boy
Would break the Bowl from which he drank in joy;
  And He that with his hand the Vessel made
Will surely not in after Wrath destroy."

LXXXVI

After a momentary silence spake
Some Vessel of a more ungainly Make;
  "They sneer at me for leaning all awry:
What! did the Hand then of the Potter shake?"

LXXXVII

Whereat some one of the loquacious Lot—
I think a Súfi pipkin—waxing hot—
  "All this of Pot and Potter—Tell me then,
Who is the Potter, pray, and who the Pot?"

LXXXVIII

"Why," said another, "Some there are who tell
Of one who threatens he will toss to Hell
  The luckless Pots he marr'd in making—Pish!
He's a Good Fellow, and 'twill all be well."

LXXXIX

"Well," murmur'd one, "Let whoso make or buy,
My Clay with long Oblivion is gone dry:
  But fill me with the old familiar Juice,
Methinks I might recover by and by."

XC

So while the Vessels one by one were speaking,
The little Moon look'd in that all were seeking:
  And then they jogg'd each other, "Brother! Brother!
Now for the Porter's shoulder-knot a-creaking!"

. . . . .

XCI

Ah, with the Grape my fading Life provide,
And wash the Body whence the Life has died,
  And lay me, shrouded in the living Leaf,
By some not unfrequented Garden-side.

XCII

That ev'n my buried Ashes such a snare
Of Vintage shall fling up into the Air
  As not a True-believer passing by
But shall be overtaken unaware.

XCIII

Indeed the Idols I have loved so long
Have done my credit in this world much wrong:
  Have drown'd my Glory in a shallow Cup,
And sold my Reputation for a Song.

XCIV

Indeed, indeed, Repentance oft before
I swore—but was I sober when I swore?
  And then and then came Spring, and Rose-in-hand
My thread-bare Penitence apieces tore.

XCV

And much as Wine has play'd the Infidel,
And robb'd me of my Robe of Honour—Well,
  I wonder often what the Vintners buy
One half so precious as the stuff they sell.

XCVI

Yet Ah, that Spring should vanish with the Rose!
That Youth's sweet-scented manuscript should close!
  The Nightingale that in the branches sang,
Ah whence, and whither flown again, who knows!

XCVII

Would but the Desert of the Fountain yield
One glimpse—if dimly, yet indeed, reveal'd,
  To which the fainting Traveller might spring,
As springs the trampled herbage of the field!

XCVIII

Would but some wingèd Angel ere too late
Arrest the yet unfolded Roll of Fate,
  And make the stern Recorder otherwise
Enregister, or quite obliterate!

XCIX

Ah Love! could you and I with Him conspire
To grasp this sorry Scheme of Things entire,
  Would not we shatter it to bits—and then
Re-mould it nearer to the Heart's Desire!

. . . . .

C

Yon rising Moon that looks for us again—
How oft hereafter will she wax and wane;
  How oft hereafter rising look for us
Through this same Garden—and for *one* in vain!

CI

And when like her, oh Sákí, you shall pass
Among the Guests Star-scatter'd on the Grass,
  And in your joyous errand reach the spot
Where I made One—turn down an empty Glass!

TAMÁM

[1859, '68, '72, '79]

ARTHUR HUGH CLOUGH

CHRONOLOGICAL TABLE

1819, January 1, born at Liverpool, his father a cotton merchant, his mother the daughter of a banker.

1823–8 Lived with his family on the East Bay, Charleston, South Carolina.

1828–9 Returned to England and attended a preparatory school at Chester.

1829–37 At Rugby, of which Dr. Thomas Arnold had become headmaster in 1828.

1837–41 At Balliol College, Oxford, graduating with second class honours in *litterae humaniores.*

1841–8 Fellow and Tutor of Oriel College.

1848 Resigns his tutorship and fellowship, partly in protest against obligation to subscribe to the Thirty-Nine articles of the Church of England, partly in dissatisfaction with life in the university.
Travels to Paris where he witnesses the Revolution.
The Bothie of Tober-na-Vuolich.

1849–52 At University College, London, first as Head of University Hall (a residence), later also as Professor of English.

1849 Writes *Amours de Voyage,* in Venice.
Ambarvalia (in collaboration with T. Burbidge).

1850 Writes *Dipsychus* (published in 1869)

1852–3 In Boston and Cambridge, tutoring, translating, writing articles.

1853 Returns to England.

1853–60 In the Education Office.

1854 Marriage to Blanche Smith.

1858 *Amours de Voyage.*

1859 *Plutarch's Lives* (a translation).

1860–1 Writes *Mari Magno, or Tales on Board* (published 1862).

1861 In broken health goes to Italy, where, at Florence, he died on November 13, and was buried in the Protestant cemetery.

In the *English Men of Letters* series, which now runs to about a hundred volumes, there is no study of Clough: FitzGerald has been distinguished by a volume and Christina Rossetti, but Clough remains excluded. He may well be judged a figure important in the development of English culture and English thought, broadly conceived, rather than in the development of English poetry. Expectations awakened by his first book, *The Bothie of Tober-na-Vuolich,* were almost entirely disappointed. In that charming, stimulating pastoral, a fresh flexible manner and a firm sense of character were fused with an original power in formulating ideas and relating them to real situations. It was reasonable to expect that the author of *The Bothie* might become a rival of Browning, endowed with a sharper awareness of contemporary realities and a greater power in projecting normal character. In his last writing, *Mari Magno,* he returned to the kind of poetry exemplified in *The Bothie,* but the glory had departed.

In the interim his main expression was in the intellectual lyric, in which his uncertainties of form were painfully evident. The austerity of his manner and the severe intellectualism of his substance robbed his poetry—apart from *The Bothie*—of any general currency: it has been read by few, and if these few have read it with enthusiasm, they have done so for reasons not poetic. Criticism of Clough has accepted the position taken by Lowell—that in his poetry can be found the best expression of the intellectual and spiritual anxieties of the mid-Victorian elite. The personality of the man was clearly greater—more profound, more luminous, more vital—than any of its expressions, whether in literature or in action, and the poems are best approached as so many windows to that significant personality.

IN A LECTURE-ROOM

Away, haunt thou not me,
Thou vain Philosophy!
Little hast thou bestead,
Save to perplex the head,
And leave the spirit dead.
Unto thy broken cisterns wherefore go,
While from the secret treasure-depths below,
Fed by the skiey shower,
And clouds that sink and rest on hill-tops high,
Wisdom at once, and Power,
Are welling, bubbling forth, unseen, incessantly?
Why labour at the dull mechanic oar,
When the fresh breeze is blowing,
And the strong current flowing,
Right onward to the Eternal Shore?

[1840] [1849]

Τὸ Καλόν

I have seen higher holier things than these,
And therefore must to these refuse my heart,
Yet am I panting for a little ease;
I'll take, and so depart.

Ah hold! the heart is prone to fall away,
Her high and cherished visions to forget,
And if thou takest, how wilt thou repay
So vast, so dread a debt?

How will the heart, which now thou trustest, then
Corrupt, yet in corruption mindful yet,
Turn with sharp stings upon itself! Again,
Bethink thee of the debt!

—Hast thou seen higher holier things than these,
And therefore must to these thy heart refuse?
With the true best, alack, how ill agrees,
That best that thou wouldst choose!

The Summum Pulchrum rests in heaven above;
Do thou, as best thou may'st, thy duty do;
Amid the things allowed thee live and love;
Some day thou shalt it view.

[1841] [1849]

QUA CURSUM VENTUS

As ships, becalmed at eve, that lay
With canvass droopings, side by side,
Two towers of sail at dawn of day
Are scarce long leagues apart descried;

When fell the night, upsprung the breeze,
And all the darkling hours they plied,
Nor dreamt but each the self-same seas
By each was cleaving, side by side:

E'en so—but why the tale reveal
Of those, whom year by year unchanged,
Brief absence joined anew to feel,
Astounded, soul from soul estranged.

At dead of night their sails were filled,
And onward each rejoicing steered—
Ah, neither blame, for neither willed,
Or wist, what first with dawn appeared!

To veer, how vain! On, onward strain,
Brave barks! In light, in darkness too,
Through winds and tides one compass guides—
To that, and your own selves, be true.

But O blithe breeze! and O great seas,
Though ne'er, that earliest parting past,
On your wide plain they join again,
Together lead them home at last.

One port, methought, alike, they sought,
One purpose hold where'er they fare,—
O bounding breeze, O rushing seas!
At last, at last, unite them there!

[1849]

THE NEW SINAI

Lo, here is God, and there is God!
Believe it not, O man;
In such vain sort to this and that
The ancient heathen ran:
Though old Religion shake her head,
And say in bitter grief,
The day behold, at first foretold,
Of atheist unbelief;
Take better part, with manly heart,
Thine adult spirit can;
Receive it not, believe it not,
Believe it not, O Man!

As men at dead of night awaked
With cries, 'The king is here,'
Rush forth and greet whome'er they meet,
Whoe'er shall first appear;
And still repeat, to all the street,
' 'Tis he,—the king is here;'
The long procession moveth on,
Each nobler form they see,
With changeful suit they still salute,
And cry, ' 'Tis he, 'tis he!'

So, even so, when men were young,
And earth and heaven were new,
And His immediate presence He
From human hearts withdrew,
The soul perplexed and daily vexed
With sensuous False and True,
Amazed, bereaved, no less believed,
And fain would see Him too:
'He is!' the prophet-tongues proclaimed;
In joy and hasty fear,
'He is!' aloud replied the crowd,
'Is here, and here, and here.'

'He is! They are!' in distance seen
On yon Olympus high,
In those Avernian woods abide,
And walk this azure sky:
'They are! They are!' to every show
Its eyes the baby turned,
And blazes sacrificial, tall,
On thousand altars burned:
'They are! They are!'—On Sinai's top
Far seen the lightnings shone,
The thunder broke, a trumpet spoke,
And God said, 'I am One.'

God spake it out, 'I, God, am One;'
The unheeding ages ran,
And baby-thoughts again, again,
Have dogged the growing man:
And as of old from Sinai's top
God said that God is One,
By Science strict so speaks He now
To tell us, There is None!
Earth goes by chemic forces; Heaven's
A Mécanique Céleste!
And heart and mind of human kind
A watch-work as the rest!

Is this a Voice, as was the Voice
Whose speaking told abroad,
When thunder pealed, and mountain reeled,
The ancient Truth of God?
Ah, not the Voice; 'tis but the cloud,
The cloud of darkness dense,
Where image none, nor e'er was seen
Similitude of sense.
'Tis but the cloudy darkness dense
That wrapt the Mount around;
While in dull amaze the people stays,
To hear the Coming Sound.

Is there no prophet-soul the while
To dare, sublimely meek,
Within the shroud of blackest cloud
The Deity to seek:
'Midst atheistic systems dark,
And darker hearts' despair
That soul has heard perchance His word,
And on the dusky air
His skirts, as passed He by, to see
Hath strained on their behalf,
Who on the plain, with dance amain,
Adore the Golden Calf.

'Tis but the cloudy darkness dense;
Though blank the tale it tells,
No God, no Truth! yet He, in sooth,
Is there—within it dwells;

Within the sceptic darkness deep
He dwells that none may see,
Till idol forms and idol thoughts
Have passed and ceased to be:
No God, no Truth! ah though, in sooth,
So stand the doctrine's half;
On Egypt's track return not back,
Nor own the Golden Calf.

Take better part, with manlier heart,
Thine adult spirit can;
No God, no Truth, receive it ne'er—
Believe it ne'er—O Man!
But turn not then to seek again
What first the ill began;
No God, it saith; ah, wait in faith
God's self-completing plan;
Receive it not, but leave it not,
And wait it out, O Man!

'The Man that went the cloud within
Is gone and vanished quite;
He cometh not,' the people cries,
'Nor bringeth God to sight:
Lo these thy gods, that safety give,
Adore and keep the feast!'
Deluding and deluded cries
The Prophet's brother-Priest:
And Israel all bows down to fall
Before the gilded beast.

Devout indeed! that priestly creed,
O Man, reject as sin;
The clouded hill attend thou still,
And him that went within.
He yet shall bring some worthy thing
For waiting souls to see;
Some sacred word that he hath heard
Their light and life shall be;
Some lofty part, than which the heart
Adopt no nobler can,
Thou shalt receive, thou shalt believe,
And thou shalt do, O Man!

[1845] [1849]

THE LATEST DECALOGUE

Thou shalt have one God only; who
Would be at the expense of two?
No graven images may be
Worshipped, except the currency;
Swear not at all; for, for thy curse
Thine enemy is none the worse:
At church on Sunday to attend
Will serve to keep the world thy friend:
Honour thy parents; that is, all
From whom advancement may befall;
Thou shalt not kill; but need'st not strive
Officiously to keep alive:
Do not adultery commit;
Advantage rarely comes of it:
Thou shalt not steal; an empty feat,
When it's so lucrative to cheat:
Bear not false witness; let the lie
Have time on its own wings to fly:
Thou shalt not covet, but tradition
Approves all forms of competition.

[1847] [1862]

AT VENICE

ON THE LIDO

On her still lake the city sits
While bark and boat beside her flits,
Nor hears, her soft siesta taking,
The Adriatic billows breaking.

IN THE PIAZZA AT NIGHT

O beautiful beneath the magic moon
To walk the watery way of palaces;
O beautiful, o'er-vaulted with gemmed blue
This spacious court; with colour and with gold,
With cupolas, and pinnacles, and points,
And crosses multiplex, and tips, and balls,
(Wherewith the bright stars unreproving mix,

Nor scorn by hasty eyes to be confused;)
Fantastically perfect this lone pile
Of oriental glory; these long ranges
Of classic chiselling; this gay flickering crowd,
And the calm Campanile.—Beautiful!
O beautiful!

My mind is in her rest; my heart at home
In all around; my soul secure in place,
And the vext needle perfect to her poles.
Aimless and hopeless in my life, I seemed
To thread the winding byeways of the town,
Bewildered, baffled, hurried hence and thence,
All at cross purpose ever with myself,
Unknowing whence, or whither. Then, at once,
At a step, I crown the Campanile's top,
And view all mapped below. Islands, lagoon,
An hundred steeples, and a million roofs,
The fruitful champaign, and the cloud-capt Alps,
And the broad Adriatic.

Come, leave your Gothic worn-out story,
San Giorgio and the Redentore,
I from no building gay or solemn
Can spare the shapely Grecian column.
'Tis not, these centuries four, for nought,
Our European world of thought
Hath made familiar to its home
The classic mind of Greece and Rome;
In all new work that would look forth
To more than antiquarian worth,
Palladio's pediments and bases,
Or something such, will find their places;
Maturer optics don't delight
In childish dim religious light;
In evanescent vague effects
That shirk, not face one's intellects;
They love not fancies just betrayed,
And artful tricks of light and shade,
But pure form nakedly displayed
And all things absolutely made.

[1847] [1862]

PESCHIERA

What voice did on my spirit fall,
Peschiera, when thy bridge I crost?
' 'Tis better to have fought and lost,
Than never to have fought at all.'

The tricolor—a trampled rag
Lies dirt and dust; the lines I track
By sentry boxes yellow-black,
Lead up to no Italian flag.

I see the Croat soldier stand
Upon the grass of your redoubts;
The eagle with his black wings flouts
The breath and beauty of your land.

Yet not in vain, although in vain,
O men of Brescia, on the day

Of loss past hope, I heard you say
Your welcome to the noble pain.

You say, 'Since so it is,—good-bye
Sweet life, high hope; but whatsoe'er
May be, or must, no tongue shall dare
To tell, "The Lombard feared to die!"

You said (there shall be answer fit),
'And if our children must obey,
They must; but thinking on this day
'Twill less debase them to submit.'

You said (Oh not in vain you said),
'Haste, brothers, haste, while yet we may;
The hours ebb fast of this one day
When blood may yet be nobly shed.'

Ah! not for idle hatred, not
For honour, fame, nor self-applause,
But for the glory of the cause,
You did, what will not be forgot.

And though the stranger stand, 'tis true,
By force and fortune's right he stands;
By fortune, which is in God's hands,
And strength which yet shall spring in you.

This voice did on my spirit fall,
Peschiera, when thy bridge I crost,
' 'Tis better to have fought and lost,
Than never to have fought at all.'

[1849]

QUI LABORAT, ORAT

O only Source of all our light and life,
  Whom as our truth, our strength, we see and feel,
But whom the hours of mortal moral strife
  Alone aright reveal!

Mine inmost soul, before Thee inly brought,
  Thy presence owns ineffable, divine;
Chastised each rebel self-encentered thought,
  My will adoreth Thine.

With eye down-dropt, if then this earthly mind
  Speechless remain, or speechless e'en depart;
Nor seek to see—for what of earthly kind
  Can see Thee as Thou art?—

If sure-assured 'tis but profanely bold
  In thought's abstractest forms to seem to see,
It dare not dare the dread communion hold
  In ways unworthy Thee.

O not unowned, Thou shalt unnamed forgive,
  In worldly walks the prayerless heart prepare;
And if in work its life it seem to live,
  Shalt make that work be prayer.

Nor times shall lack, when while the work it plies,
  Unsummoned powers the blinding film shall part,
And scarce by happy tears made dim, the eyes
  In recognition start.

As wills Thy will, or give or e'en forbear
  The beatific supersensual sight,
So, with Thy blessing blest, that humbler prayer
  Approach Thee morn and night.

[1849]

"WITH WHOM IS NO VARIABLENESS, NEITHER SHADOW OF TURNING"

It fortifies my soul to know
That, though I perish, Truth is so:
That, howsoe'er I stray and range,
Whate'er I do, Thou dost not change.
I steadier step when I recall
That, if I slip, Thou dost not fall.

[1862]

SAY NOT, THE STRUGGLE NOUGHT AVAILETH

Say not, the struggle nought availeth,
The labour and the wounds are vain,
The enemy faints not, nor faileth,
And as things have been they remain.

If hopes were dupes, fears may be liars;
It may be, in yon smoke concealed,
Your comrades chase e'en now the fliers,
And, but for you, possess the field.

For while the tired waves, vainly breaking,
Seem here no painful inch to gain,
Far back, through creeks and inlets making,
Comes silent, flooding in, the main,

And not by eastern windows only,
When daylight comes, comes in the light,
In front, the sun climbs slow, how slowly,
But westward, look, the land is bright.

[1849] [1862]

WHERE LIES THE LAND TO WHICH THE SHIP WOULD GO?

Where lies the land to which the ship would go?
Far, far ahead, is all her seamen know.
And where the land she travels from? Away,
Far, far behind, is all that they can say.

On sunny noons upon the deck's smooth face,
Linked arm in arm, how pleasant here to pace;
Or, o'er the stern reclining, watch below
The foaming wake far widening as we go.

On stormy nights when wild north-westers rave,
How proud a thing to fight with wind and wave!
The dripping sailor on the reeling mast
Exults to bear, and scorns to wish it past.

Where lies the land to which the ship would go?
Far, far ahead, is all her seamen know.
And where the land she travels from? Away,
Far, far behind, is all that they can say.

[1852] [1862]

MATTHEW ARNOLD

CHRONOLOGICAL TABLE

1822, December 24, born at Laleham near Staines, son of Thomas Arnold, subsequently headmaster of Rugby school and Regius Professor of Modern History at Oxford, and of Mary Penrose Arnold.
Attended his uncle's preparatory school at Laleham, Marlborough, and Rugby.

1841–4 Balliol College, Oxford.

1843 Won Newdigate prize for poetry.

1844 Degree in *Literae Humaniores,* with second class honours.

1845 Elected a fellow of Oriel College, Oxford.

1847–51 Private Secretary to Lord Lansdowne, Lord President of the Council (in whose charge were all the educational undertakings of the government).

1849 *The Strayed Reveller and other Poems* (by "A.")

1851 Married Lucy, daughter of Mr. Justice Wightman.
Appointed an inspector of schools.

1852 *Empedocles on Etna.*

1853 *Poems.*

1855 *Poems, Second Series.*

1857 Elected Professor of Poetry at Oxford, the first layman to hold the chair.

1858 *Merope.*

1861 *On Translating Homer* (lectures delivered from the Oxford chair).

1864 *A French Eton* (the result of an official mission to examine education on the continent.

1865 *Essays in Criticism* (first series)

1867 *On the Study of Celtic Literature* (Oxford lectures).
New Poems.
End of tenure of the Oxford chair.

1868 *Schools and Universities on the Continent* (the result of another mission).

1869 *Culture and Anarchy.*

1870 *St. Paul and Protestantism.*

1871 *Friendship's Garland.*

1873 *Literature and Dogma.*

1875 *God and the Bible.*

1877 *Last Essays on Church and Religion.*

1879 *Mixed Essays.*

1882 *Irish Essays and Others.*

1883 *Isaiah of Jerusalem.*

1883–4 Lecture tour in America.

1885 *Discourses in America.*

1886 Retired as inspector.

1888 April 15, died at Liverpool, buried at Laleham.
Essays in Criticism, Second Series.

1889 *Civilization in the United States.*

It is an old conception that in his youth Matthew Arnold was a poet and that he subsequently put childish things away to become a critic. No generalization so bold as this should be expected to attain absolute truth; but despite recent attempts to weaken it, this one requires but slight correction. At twenty-six Arnold published his first collection of verse, a volume signed merely "A" and withdrawn from circulation almost as soon as it had been published. In the following six years, three other collections appeared; and by thirty-two his work as a poet was practically completed although his work as a prose writer had no more than begun.

In the second half of his life—he lived to be sixty-five—he published almost twenty volumes of prose, in verse only *Merope,* his arid play, and the important but slim collection *New Poems* which came out when he was forty-four. After *New Poems,* his writings in verse were in his opinion too few or too slight to merit collecting. That one of the greatest of the Victorian poets should have abandoned poetry for prose at an age at which neither Browning nor Tennyson had reached great popularity or received general acclaim from criticism is a problem of deep interest. No reader of Arnold will believe that as a poet he was on a false track, and that his true destiny was to write about poetry rather than to write poetry.

However Arnold's central ambition was to be not a poet but a sage, to be what he said that Marcus Aurelius had been, a friend and aider of those who would live in the spirit. It is significant that among modern writers his deepest respect was for Goethe; he respected Goethe so highly because he thought him uniquely wise. No other words of Arnold's throw so sharp a shaft of light upon his own aim as these in which he is speaking of Goethe:

It is by no means as the greatest of poets that Goethe deserves the pride and praise of his German countrymen. It is as the clearest, the largest, the most helpful thinker of our modern times. . . . Goethe is the greatest poet of modern times not because he is one of the half dozen human beings who in the history of our race have shown the most signal gift for poetry, but, because having a very considerable gift for poetry, he was at the same time, in the width, depth and richness of his criticism of life, by far our greatest modern man.

Arnold aspired to be the clearest, largest, most helpful thinker of his time and place; this is what links his poetry and his prose. If he could realize such an aspiration it would matter little whether he did so in prose or poetry.

Quite soon he recognized certain impediments to his success in poetry. He recognized that it was not easy, perhaps not possible, to write great poetry in the interstices of his busy inspector's life, a life which for many years condemned him to traveling the length and breadth of England, at the mercy of slow and comfortless trains, and cold dismal hotels. He became more and more devoted to his task as a reformer of education, more and more aware of the need to see the problems of education in the context of the entire national life, more and more persuaded that reform in education must go hand in hand with reform in religion, politics and morality. Caught in so rich a complex of intellectual problems, he must have felt himself somewhat disqualified for the writing of great poetry. And he did not much care to write poetry which would be less than great. He recognized another impediment in the romanticism which lingered in his temperament long after he had expelled it from his intelligence. His poetry tended to express the melancholy, the anxiety, the loneliness which made so large a part of his personal life. Such purely personal lamentation did not seem to him great poetry: great poetry, he thought, could not be written about gloomy personal moods, however intense.

Great poetry, he believed, should be objective: it should be epic or dramatic rather than lyric. His one finished drama, *Merope,* was a failure; his *Lucretius* remained no more than disjointed fragments; and although, among his epic fragments, *Sohrab and Rustum* met with acclaim, the apathy towards *Balder Dead* discouraged him. He appears never to have attempted a full length epic; and it was only in such a work that he could perhaps have risen to the level of what he would have regarded as really great achievement in poetry. He may properly be said to have retired from the writing of poetry, but to have indulged himself with occasional returns to his instrument.

It is not on *Sohrab and Rustum,* despite its moving presentation of a dramatic conflict, its brilliance of language, and its richness of tone, that his reputation primarily depends. It depends primarily on the poetry which he somewhat undervalued; on such lyrics as "Yes, in the sea of life enisled," *The Future,* and *A Summer Night,* on such elegies as *Thyrsis,* and *The Scholar Gipsy*—substantially an elegy, although the gipsy is not conceived as dead. In such poems as these deep personal emotion, and deep thinking about human nature and the nineteenth century mind in particular are expressed with an art which mingles in exquisite proportions the austere and the elegiac tones.

MYCERINUS

'Not by justice that my father spurn'd,
Not for the thousands whom my father slew,
Altars unfed and temples overturn'd,
Cold hearts and thankless tongues, where thanks are due;
Fell this dread voice from lips that cannot lie,
Stern sentence of the Powers of Destiny.

'I will unfold my sentence and my crime.
My crime—that, rapt in reverential awe,
I sate obedient, in the fiery prime
Of youth, self-govern'd, at the feet of Law;
Ennobling this dull pomp, the life of kings,
By contemplation of diviner things.

'My father lov'd injustice, and lived long;
Crown'd with grey hairs he died, and full of sway.
I lov'd the good he scorn'd, and hated wrong—

The Gods declare my recompence to-day.
I look'd for life more lasting, rule more high;
And when six years are measured, lo, I die!

'Yet surely, O my people, did I deem
Man's justice from the all-just Gods was given;
A light that from some upper fount did beam,
Some better archetype, whose seat was heaven;
A light that, shining from the blest abodes,
Did shadow somewhat of the life of Gods.

'Mere phantoms of man's self-tormenting heart,
Which on the sweets that woo it dares not feed!
Vain dreams, which quench our pleasures, then depart,
When the duped soul, self-master'd, claims its meed;
When, on the strenuous just man, Heaven bestows,
Crown of his struggling life, an unjust close!

'Seems it so light a thing then, austere Powers,
To spurn man's common lure, life's pleasant things?
Seems there no joy in dances crown'd with flowers,
Love, free to range, and regal banquetings?
Bend ye on these, indeed, an unmoved eye,
Not Gods but ghosts, in frozen apathy?

'Or is it that some Force, too wise, too strong,
Even for yourselves to conquer or beguile,
Sweeps earth, and heaven, and men, and gods along,
Like the broad volume of the insurgent Nile?
And the great powers we serve, themselves may be
Slaves of a tyrannous necessity?

'Or in mid-heaven, perhaps, your golden cars,
Where earthly voice climbs never, wing their flight,
And in wild hunt, through mazy tracts of stars,
Sweep in the sounding stillness of the night?
Or in deaf ease, on thrones of dazzling sheen,
Drinking deep draughts of joy, ye dwell serene.

'Oh, wherefore cheat our youth, if thus it be,
Of one short joy, one lust, one pleasant dream?
Stringing vain words of powers we cannot see,
Blind divinations of a will supreme;
Lost labour! when the circumambient gloom
But hides, if Gods, Gods careless of our doom?

'The rest I give to joy. Even while I speak
My sand runs short; and—as yon star-shot ray,
Hemm'd by two banks of cloud, peers pale and weak,
Now, as the barrier closes, dies away—
Even so do past and future intertwine,
Blotting this six years' space, which yet is mine.

'Six years—six little years—six drops of time—
Yet suns shall rise, and many moons shall wane,

And old men die, and young men pass their prime,
And languid pleasure fade and flower again,
And the dull Gods behold, ere these are flown,
Revels more deep, joy keener than their own.

'Into the silence of the groves and woods
I will go forth; though something would I say—
Something—yet what I know not: for the Gods
The doom they pass revoke not, nor delay;
And prayers, and gifts, and tears, are fruitless all,
And the night waxes, and the shadows fall.

'Ye men of Egypt, ye have heard your king.
I go, and I return not. But the will
Of the great Gods is plain; and ye must bring
Ill deeds, ill passions, zealous to fulfil
Their pleasure, to their feet; and reap their praise,
The praise of Gods, rich boon! and length of days.'

—So spake he, half in anger, half in scorn;
And one loud cry of grief and of amaze
Broke from his sorrowing people: so he spake;
And turning, left them there; and with brief pause,
Girt with a throng of revellers, bent his way
To the cool region of the groves he loved.
There by the river banks he wander'd on,
From palm-grove on to palm-grove, happy trees,
Their smooth tops shining sunwards, and beneath
Burying their unsunn'd stems in grass and flowers:
Where in one dream the feverish time of youth
Might fade in slumber, and the feet of joy
Might wander all day long and never tire.
Here came the king, holding high feast, at morn
Rose-crown'd; and ever, when the sun went down,
A hundred lamps beam'd in the tranquil gloom,
From tree to tree, all through the twinkling grove,
Revealing all the tumult of the feast,
Flush'd guests, and golden goblets, foam'd with wine;
While the deep-burnish'd foliage overhead
Splinter'd the silver arrows of the moon.
It may be that sometimes his wondering soul
From the loud joyful laughter of his lips
Might shrink half startled, like a guilty man
Who wrestles with his dream; as some pale Shape,
Gliding half hidden through the dusky stems,
Would thrust a hand before the lifted bowl,
Whispering, *'A little space, and thou art mine!'*
It may be on that joyless feast his eye
Dwelt with mere outward seeming; he, within,
Took measure of his soul, and knew its strength,
And by that silent knowledge, day by day,
Was calm'd, ennobled, comforted, sustain'd.
It may be; but not less his brow was smooth,
And his clear laugh fled ringing through the gloom,

And his mirth quail'd not at the mild reproof
Sigh'd out by winter's sad tranquillity;
Nor, pall'd with its own fulness, ebb'd and died
In the rich languor of long summer days;
Nor wither'd, when the palm-tree plumes, that roof'd
With their mild dark his grassy banquet-hall,
Bent to the cold winds of the showerless spring;
No, nor grew dark when autumn brought the clouds.
So six long years he revell'd, night and day;
And when the mirth wax'd loudest, with dull sound
Sometimes from the grove's centre echoes came,
To tell his wondering people of their king;
In the still night, across the steaming flats,
Mix'd with the murmur of the moving Nile.

[1849]

THE STRAYED REVELLER

The portico of Circe's Palace. Evening

A YOUTH. CIRCE

THE YOUTH

Faster, faster,
O Circe, Goddess,
Let the wild, thronging train,
The bright procession
Of eddying forms,
Sweep through my soul!

Thou standest, smiling
Down on me! thy right arm,
Lean'd up against the column there,
Props thy soft cheek;
Thy left holds, hanging loosely,
The deep cup, ivy-cinctured,
I held but now.

Is it then evening
So soon? I see, the night-dews,
Cluster'd in thick beads, dim
The agate brooch-stones
On thy white shoulder;
The cool night-wind, too,
Blows through the portico,
Stirs thy hair, Goddess,
Waves thy white robe.

CIRCE

Whence art thou, sleeper?

THE YOUTH

When the white dawn first
Through the rough fir-planks
Of my hut, by the chestnuts,
Up at the valley-head,
Came breaking, Goddess!
I sprang up, I threw round me
My dappled fawn-skin;
Passing out, from the wet turf,
Where they lay, by the hut door,
I snatch'd up my vine-crown, my fir-staff,
All drench'd in dew—
Came swift down to join
The rout early gather'd
In the town, round the temple,
Iacchus' white fane
On yonder hill.

Quick I pass'd, following
The wood-cutters' cart-track
Down the dark valley;—I saw
On my left, through the beeches,
Thy palace, Goddess,
Smokeless, empty!
Trembling, I enter'd; beheld
The court all silent,
The lions sleeping,
On the altar this bowl.
I drank, Goddess!
And sunk down here, sleeping,
On the steps of thy portico.

CIRCE

Foolish boy! Why tremblest thou?
Thou lovest it, then, my wine?
Wouldst more of it? See, how glows,
Through the delicate flush'd marble,
The red, creaming liquor,
Strown with dark seeds!
Drink, then! I chide thee not,

Deny thee not my bowl.
Come, stretch forth thy hand, then—so!
Drink—drink again!

THE YOUTH

Thanks gracious one!
Ah, the sweet fumes again!
More soft, ah me,
More subtle-winding
Than Pan's flute-music!
Faint—faint! Ah me,
Again the sweet sleep!

CIRCE

Hist! Thou—within there!
Come forth, Ulysses!
Art tired with hunting?
While we range the woodland,
See what the day brings.

ULYSSES

Ever new magic!
Hast thou then lur'd hither,
Wonderful Goddess, by thy art,
The young, languid-eyed Ampelus,
Iacchus' darling—
Or some youth beloved of Pan,
Of Pan and the Nymphs?
That he sits, bending downward
His white, delicate neck
To the ivy-wreathed marge
Of thy cup; the bright, glancing vine-leaves
That crown his hair,
Falling forwards, mingling
With the dark ivy-plants—
His fawn-skin, half untied,
Smear'd with red wine-stains? Who is he,
That he sits, overweigh'd
By fumes of wine and sleep,
So late, in thy portico?
What youth, Goddess,—what guest
Of Gods or mortals?

CIRCE

Hist! he wakes!
I lur'd him not hither, Ulysses.
Nay, ask him!

THE YOUTH

Who speaks? Ah! Who comes forth
To thy side, Goddess, from within?
How shall I name him?
This spare, dark-featured,
Quick-eyed stranger?
Ah! and I see too
His sailor's bonnet,
His short coat, travel-tarnish'd,
With one arm bare!—
Art thou not he, whom fame
This long time rumours
The favour'd guest of Circe, brought by the waves?
Art thou he, stranger?
The wise Ulysses,
Laertes' son?

ULYSSES

I am Ulysses.
And thou, too, sleeper?
Thy voice is sweet.
It may be that thou hast follow'd
Through the islands some divine bard,
By age taught many things,
Age and the Muses;
And heard him delighting
The chiefs and people
In the banquet, and learn'd his songs,
Of Gods and Heroes,
Of war and arts,
And peopled cities
Inland, or built
By the grey sea.—If so, then hail!
I honour and welcome thee.

THE YOUTH

The Gods are happy,
They turn on all sides
Their shining eyes:
And see, below them,
The earth, and men.

They see Tiresias
Sitting, staff in hand,
On the warm, grassy
Asopus bank:
His robe drawn over
His old, sightless head,
Revolving inly
The doom of Thebes.

They see the Centaurs
In the upper glens
Of Pelion, in the streams,
Where red-berried ashes fringe
The clear-brown shallow pools,
With streaming flanks, and heads
Rear'd proudly, snuffing
The mountain wind.

They see the Indian
Drifting, knife in hand,
His frail boat moor'd to
A floating isle thick-matted
With large-leav'd, low-creeping melon-plants,
And the dark cucumber.
He reaps, and stows them,
Drifting—drifting;—round him,
Round his green harvest-plot,
Flow the cool lake-waves,
The mountains ring them.

They see the Scythian
On the wide stepp, unharnessing
His wheel'd house at noon.
He tethers his beast down, and makes his meal—
Mares' milk, and bread
Baked on the embers;—all around
The boundless waving grass-plains stretch, thick-starr'd
With saffron and the yellow hollyhock
And flag-leav'd iris flowers.
Sitting in his cart
He makes his meal; before him, for long miles,
Alive with bright green lizards,
And the springing bustard fowl,
The track, a straight black line,
Furrows the rich soil; here and there
Clusters of lonely mounds
Topp'd with rough-hewn
Grey, rain-blear'd statues, overpeer
The sunny waste.

They see the ferry
On the broad, clay-laden
Lone Chorasmian stream;—thereon
With snort and strain,
Two horses, strongly swimming, tow
The ferry boat, with woven ropes
To either bow
Firm-harness'd by the mane; a chief,
With shout and shaken spear,
Stands at the prow, and guides them; but astern
The cowering merchants, in long robes,
Sit pale beside their wealth
Of silk-bales and of balsam-drops,
Of gold and ivory,
Of turquoise-earth and amethyst,
Jasper and chalcedony,
And milk-barr'd onyx stones.
The loaded boat swings groaning
In the yellow eddies;
The Gods behold them.

They see the Heroes
Sitting in the dark ship
On the foamless, long-heaving,
Violet sea,
At sunset nearing
The Happy Islands.

These things, Ulysses,
The wise bards also
Behold and sing.
But oh, what labour!
O prince, what pain!

They too can see
Tiresias;—but the Gods,
Who give them vision,
Added this law:
That they should bear too
His groping blindness,
His dark foreboding,
His scorn'd white hairs;
Bear Hera's anger
Through a life lengthen'd
To seven ages.

They see the Centaurs
On Pelion;—then they feel,
They too, the maddening wine
Swell their large veins to bursting; in wild pain
They feel the biting spears
Of the grim Lapithæ, and Theseus, drive,
Drive crashing through their bones; they feel
High on a jutting rock in the red stream
Alcmena's dreadful son
Ply his bow;—such a price
The Gods exact for song:
To become what we sing.

They see the Indian
On his mountain lake; but squalls
Make their skiff reel, and worms
In the unkind spring have gnawn
Their melon-harvest to the heart.—They see
The Scythian; but long frosts
Parch them in winter-time on the bare stepp,
Till they too fade like grass; they crawl
Like shadows forth in spring.

They see the Merchants
On the Oxus stream;—but care
Must visit first them too, and make them pale.
Whether, through whirling sand,
A cloud of desert robber-horse has burst
Upon their caravan; or greedy kings,
In the wall'd cities the way passes through,
Crush'd them with tolls; or fever-airs,
On some great river's marge,
Mown them down, far from home.

They see the Heroes
Near harbour;—but they share
Their lives, and former violent toil, in Thebes,
Seven-gated Thebes, or Troy;
Or where the echoing oars
Of Argo first,
Startled the unknown sea.

The old Silenus
Came, lolling in the sunshine,
From the dewy forest coverts,
This way, at noon.
Sitting by me, while his Fauns
Down at the water-side
Sprinkled and smooth'd
His drooping garland,
He told me these things.

But I, Ulysses,
Sitting on the warm steps,
Looking over the valley,
All day long, have seen,
Without pain, without labour,
Sometimes a wild-hair'd Mænad,—
Sometimes a Faun with torches,—
And sometimes, for a moment,
Passing through the dark stems
Flowing-robed, the beloved,
The desired, the divine,
Beloved Iacchus.

Ah cool night-wind, tremulous stars!
Ah glimmering water,
Fitful earth-murmur,
Dreaming woods!
Ah golden-hair'd, strangely-smiling Goddess,
And thou, proved much enduring,
Wave-toss'd Wanderer!
Who can stand still?
Ye fade, ye swim, ye waver before me—
The cup again!

Faster, faster,
O Circe, Goddess,
Let the wild, thronging train,
The bright procession
Of eddying forms,
Sweep through my soul!

[1849]

TO A FRIEND

Who prop, thou ask'st, in these bad days, my mind?—
He much, the old man, who, clearest-soul'd of men,
Saw The Wide Prospect, and the Asian Fen,
And Tmolus' hill, and Smyrna bay, though blind.

What keeps spirit up? Ans.: Greek Literat.

Much he, whose friendship I not long since won,
That halting slave, who in Nicopolis
Taught Arrian, when Vespasian's brutal son
Clear'd Rome of what most shamed him. But be his

My special thanks, whose even-balanced soul,
From first youth tested up to extreme old age,
Business could not make dull, nor passion wild:

Who saw life steadily, and saw it whole;
The mellow glory of the Attic stage;
Singer of sweet Colonus, and its child.

[1848?] [1849]

SHAKESPEARE

Others abide our question. Thou art free.
We ask and ask—Thou smilest and art still,
Out-topping knowledge. For the loftiest hill,
Who to the stars uncrowns his majesty,

Planting his stedfast footsteps in the sea,
Making the heaven of heavens his dwelling-place,
Spares but the cloudy border of his base
To the foil'd searching of mortality;

And thou, who didst the stars and sunbeams know,
Self-school'd, selfscann'd, self-honour'd, self-secure,
Didst walk on earth unguess'd at.—Better so!

All pains the immortal spirit must endure,
All weakness which impairs, all griefs which bow,
Find their sole voice in that victorious brow.

[1844] [1849]

THE FORSAKEN MERMAN

Come, dear children, let us away;
Down and away below!
Now my brothers call from the bay;
Now the great winds shoreward blow,
Now the salt tides seaward flow;
Now the wild white horses play,
Champ and chafe and toss in the spray.
Children dear, let us away.
This way, this way.

Call her once before you go—
Call once yet!
In a voice that she will know:
'Margaret! Margaret!'
Children's voices should be dear
(Call once more) to a mother's ear;
Children's voices, wild with pain—
Surely she will come again!
Call her once and come away;
This way, this way!
'Mother dear, we cannot stay!
The wild white horses foam and fret,
Margaret! Margaret!

Come, dear children, come away down;
Call no more!
One last look at the white-wall'd town,
And the little grey church on the windy shore;
Then come down!
She will not come though you call all day;
Come away, come away!

Children dear, was it yesterday
We heard the sweet bells over the bay?
In the caverns where we lay,
Through the surf and through the swell
The far-off sound of a silver bell?
Sand-strewn caverns, cool and deep,
Where the winds are all asleep;
Where the spent lights quiver and gleam,
Where the salt weed sways in the stream,
Where the sea-beasts, ranged all round,
Feed in the ooze of their pasture-ground;
Where the sea-snakes coil and twine,
Dry their mail and bask in the brine;
Where great whales come sailing by,
Sail and sail, with unshut eye,
Round the world for ever and aye?
When did music come this way?
Children dear, was it yesterday?

Children dear, was it yesterday
(Call yet once) that she went away?
Once she sate with you and me,
On a red gold throne in the heart of the sea,
And the youngest sate on her knee.
She comb'd its bright hair, and she tended it well,
When down swung the sound of a far-off bell.
She sigh'd, she look'd up through the clear green sea.
She said; 'I must go, for my kinsfolk pray
In the little grey church on the shore to-day.
'Twill be Easter-time in the world—ah me!
And I lose my poor soul, Merman! here with thee.'
I said; 'Go up, dear heart, through the waves;
Say thy prayer, and come back to the kind sea-caves.'
She smiled, she went up through the surf in the bay.
Children dear, was it yesterday?

Children dear, were we long alone?
'The sea grows stormy, the little ones moan;
Long prayers,' I said, 'in the world they say;
Come!' I said, and we rose through the surf in the bay.
We went up the beach, by the sandy down
Where the sea-stocks bloom, to the white-wall'd town;
Through the narrow paved streets, where all was still,
To the little grey church on the windy hill.
From the church came a murmur of folk at their prayers,
But we stood without in the cold blowing airs.
We climb'd on the graves, on the stones worn with rains,
And we gazed up the aisle through the small leaded panes.
She sate by the pillar; we saw her clear:
'Margaret, hist! come quick, we are here!
Dear heart,' I said, 'we are long alone;
The sea grows stormy, the little ones moan.'
But, ah, she gave me never a look,
For her eyes were seal'd to the holy book!

'Loud prays the priest; shut stands the door.'
Come away, children, call no more!
Come away, come down, call no more!

Down, down, down!
Down to the depths of the sea!
She sits at her wheel in the humming town,
Singing most joyfully.
Hark, what she sings; 'O joy, O joy,
For the humming street, and the child with its toy!
For the priest, and the bell, and the holy well;
For the wheel where I spun,
And the blessed light of the sun!'
And so she sings her fill,
Singing most joyfully,
Till the spindle drops from her hand,
And the whizzing wheel stands still.
She steals to the window, and looks at the sand,
And over the sand at the sea;
And her eyes are set in a stare;
And anon there breaks a sigh,
And anon there drops a tear,
From a sorrow-clouded eye,
And a heart sorrow-laden,
A long, long sigh.
For the cold strange eyes of a little Mermaiden,
And the gleam of her golden hair.

Come away, away children.
Come children, come down.
The hoarse wind blows coldly;
Lights shine in the town.
She will start from her slumber
When gusts shake the door;
She will hear the winds howling,
Will hear the waves roar.
We shall see, while above us
The waves roar and whirl,
A ceiling of amber,
A pavement of pearl.
Singing, 'Here came a mortal,
But faithless was she!
And alone dwell for ever
The kings of the sea.'

But, children, at midnight,
When soft the winds blow,
When clear falls the moonlight,
When spring-tides are low;
When sweet airs come seaward
From heaths starr'd with broom,
And high rocks throw mildly
On the blanch'd sands a gloom:
Up the still, glistening beaches,

Up the creeks we will hie,
Over banks of bright seaweed
The ebb-tide leaves dry.
We will gaze, from the sand-hills,
At the white, sleeping town;
At the church on the hill-side—
And then come back down.
Singing, 'There dwells a loved one,
But cruel is she!
She left lonely for ever
The kings of the sea.'

[1849]

MEMORIAL VERSES

APRIL, 1850

Goethe in Weimar sleeps, and Greece,
Long since, saw Byron's struggle cease.
But one such death remain'd to come.
The last poetic verse is dumb—
We stand to-day by Wordsworth's tomb.

When Byron's eyes were shut in death,
We bow'd our head and held our breath.
He taught us little; but our soul
Had *felt* him like the thunder's roll.
With shivering heart the strife we saw
Of passion with eternal law;
And yet with reverential awe
We watch'd the fount of fiery life
Which serv'd for that Titanic strife.

When Goethe's death was told, we said:
Sunk, then, is Europe's sagest head.
Physician of the iron age
Goethe has done his pilgrimage.
He took the suffering human race,
He read each wound, each weakness clear;
And struck his finger on the place,
And said—*Thou ailest here, and here!*
He look'd on Europe's dying hour
Of fitful dream and feverish power;
His eye plunged down the weltering strife,
The turmoil of expiring life—
He said: *The end is everywhere,*
Art still has truth, take refuge there!
And he was happy, if to know
Causes of things, and far below
His feet to see the lurid flow
Of terror, and insane distress,
And headlong fate, be happiness.

And Wordsworth!—Ah, pale ghosts, rejoice!
For never has such soothing voice
Been to your shadowy world convey'd,
Since erst, at morn, some wandering shade
Heard the clear song of Orpheus come
Through Hades, and the mournful gloom.
Wordsworth is gone from us—and ye,
Ah, may ye feel his voice as we!
He too upon a wintry clime
Had fallen—on this iron time
Of doubts, disputes, distractions, fears.
He found us when the age had bound
Our souls in its benumbing round;
He spoke, and loosed our heart in tears.
He laid us as we lay at birth
On the cool flowery lap of earth,
Smiles broke from us and we had ease;
The hills were round us, and the breeze
Went o'er the sun-lit fields again;
Our foreheads felt the wind and rain.
Our youth return'd; for there was shed
On spirits that had long been dead,
Spirits dried up and closely furl'd,
The freshness of the early world.

Ah! since dark days still bring to light
Man's prudence and man's fiery might,
Time may restore us in his course
Goethe's sage mind and Byron's force;
But where will Europe's latter hour
Again find Wordsworth's healing power?
Others will teach us how to dare,
And against fear our breast to steel;
Others will strengthen us to bear—
But who, ah! who, will make us feel?
The cloud of mortal destiny,
Others will front it fearlessly—
But who, like him, will put it by?

Keep fresh the grass upon his grave,
O Rotha, with thy living wave!
Sing him thy best! for few or none
Hears thy voice right, now he is gone.

[1850]

CADMUS AND HARMONIA

Far, far from here,
The Adriatic breaks in a warm bay
Among the green Illyrian hills; and there
The sunshine in the happy glens is fair,
And by the sea, and in the brakes.
The grass is cool, the sea-side air
Buoyant and fresh, the mountain flowers
As virginal and sweet as ours.
And there, they say, two bright and agèd snakes,
Who once were Cadmus and Harmonia,
Bask in the glens or on the warm sea-shore,
In breathless quiet, after all their ills.
Nor do they see their country, nor the place
Where the Sphinx lived among the frowning hills,
Nor the unhappy palace of their race,
Nor Thebes, nor the Ismenus, any more.

There those two live, far in the Illyrian brakes.
They had staid long enough to see,
In Thebes, the billow of calamity
Over their own dear children roll'd,
Curse upon curse, pang upon pang,
For years, they sitting helpless in their home,
A grey old man and woman; yet of old
The gods had to their marriage come,
And at the banquet all the Muses sang.

Therefore they did not end their days
In sight of blood; but were rapt, far away,
To where the west wind plays,
And murmurs of the Adriatic come
To those untrodden mountain lawns: and there
Placed safely in changed forms, the Pair
Wholly forget their first sad life, and home,
And all that Theban woe, and stray
For ever through the glens, placid and dumb.

[1852]

APOLLO

Through the black, rushing smoke-bursts,
Quick breaks the red flame;
All Etna heaves fiercely
Her forest-clothed frame.

Not here, O Apollo!
Are haunts meet for thee.
But, where Helicon breaks down
In cliff to the sea,

Where the moon-silver'd inlets
Send far their light voice
Up the still vale of Thisbe,
O speed, and rejoice!

On the sward at the cliff-top
Lie strewn the white flocks,
On the cliff-side the pigeons
Roost deep in the rocks.

In the moonlight the shepherds,
Soft lull'd by the rills,
Lie wrapt in their blankets,
Asleep on the hills.

—What forms are these coming
So white through the gloom?
What garments out-glistening
The gold-flower'd broom?

What sweet-breathing presence
Out-perfumes the thyme?
What voices enrapture
The night's balmy prime?—

'Tis Apollo comes leading
His choir, The Nine.
—The leader is fairest,
But all are divine.

They are lost in the hollows!
They stream up again!
What seeks on this mountain
The glorified train?—

They bathe on this mountain,
In the spring by their road;
Then on to Olympus,
Their endless abode!

—Whose praise do they mention?
Of what is it told?—
What will be for ever;
What was from of old.

First hymn they the Father
Of all things; and then
The rest of immortals,
The action of men.

The day in his hotness,
The strife with the palm;
The night in her silence,
The stars in their calm.

[1852]

TO MARGUERITE

Yes! in the sea of life enisled,
With echoing straits between us thrown,
Dotting the shoreless watery wild,
We mortal millions live *alone.*
The islands feel the enclasping flow,
And then their endless bounds they know.

But when the moon their hollows lights,
And they are swept by balms of spring,
And in their glens, on starry nights,
The nightingales divinely sing;
And lovely notes, from shore to shore,
Across the sounds and channels pour—

Oh! then a longing like despair
Is to their farthest caverns sent;
For surely once, they feel, we were
Parts of a single continent!
Now round us spreads the watery plain—
Oh might our marges meet again!

Who order'd, that their longing's fire
Should be, as soon as kindled, cool'd?
Who renders vain their deep desire?—
A God, a God their severance ruled!
And bade betwixt their shores to be
The unplumb'd, salt, estranging sea.

[1852]

TRISTRAM AND ISEULT

I

TRISTRAM

TRISTRAM

Is she not come? The messenger was sure.
Prop me upon the pillows once again—
Raise me, my page: this cannot long endure.
—Christ! what a night! how the sleet whips the pane!
What lights will those out to the northward be?

THE PAGE

The lanterns of the fishing-boats at sea.

TRISTRAM

Soft—who is that stands by the dying fire?

THE PAGE

Iseult.

TRISTRAM

Ah! not the Iseult I desire.

. . . .

What Knight is this, so weak and pale,
Though the locks are yet brown on his noble head,
Propt on pillows in his bed,
Gazing seaward for the light
Of some ship that fights the gale
On this wild December night?
Over the sick man's feet is spread
A dark green forest dress;
A gold harp leans against the bed,

Ruddy in the fire's light.
—I know him by his harp of gold,
Famous in Arthur's court of old;
I know him by his forest dress—
—The peerless hunter, harper, knight,
Tristram of Lyoness.

What Lady is this, whose silk attire
Gleams so rich in the light of the fire?
The ringlets on her shoulders lying
In their flitting lustre vying
With the clasp of burnish'd gold
Which her heavy robe doth hold.
Her looks are mild, her fingers slight
As the driven snow are white;
And her cheeks are sunk and pale.
Is it that the bleak sea-gale
Beating from the Atlantic sea
On this coast of Brittany,
Nips too keenly the sweet flower?
Is it that a deep fatigue
Hath come on her, a chilly fear,
Passing all her youthful hour
Spinning with her maidens here,
Listlessly through the window-bars
Gazing seawards many a league
From her lonely shore-built tower,
While the knights are at the wars?
Or, perhaps, has her young heart
Felt already some deeper smart,
Of those that in secret the heart-strings rive,
Leaving her sunk and pale, though fair?
Who is this snowdrop by the sea?—
I know her by her mildness rare,
Her snow-white hands, her golden hair;
I know her by her rich silk dress,
And her fragile loveliness—
The sweetest Christian soul alive,
Iseult of Brittany.

Iseult of Brittany?—but where
Is that other Iseult fair,
That proud, first Iseult, Cornwall's queen?
She, whom Tristram's ship of yore
From Ireland to Cornwall bore,
To Tyntagel, to the side
Of King Marc, to be his bride?
She who, as they voyaged, quaff'd
With Tristram that spiced magic draught,
Which since then for ever rolls
Through their blood, and binds their souls,
Working love, but working teen?—
There were two Iseults who did sway
Each her hour of Tristram's day;

But one possess'd his waning time,
The other his resplendent prime,
Behold her here, the patient flower,
Who possess'd his darker hour!
Iseult of the Snow-White Hand
Watches pale by Tristram's bed.
She is here who had his gloom,
Where art thou who hadst his bloom?
One such kiss as those of yore
Might thy dying knight restore!
Does the love-draught work no more?
Art thou cold, or false, or dead,
Iseult of Ireland?

. . . .

Loud howls the wind, sharp patters the rain,
And the knight sinks back on his pillows again.
He is weak with fever and pain,
And his spirit is not clear:
Hark! he mutters in his sleep,
As he wanders far from here,
Changes place and time of year,
And his closèd eye doth sweep
O'er some fair unwintry sea,
Not this fierce Atlantic deep,
As he mutters brokenly:—

TRISTRAM

The calm sea shines, loose hang the vessel's sails;
Before us are the sweet green fields of Wales,
And overhead the cloudless sky of May.—
'Ah, would I were in those green fields at play,
Not pent on ship-board this delicious day!
Tristram, I pray thee, of thy courtesy,
Reach me my golden cup that stands by thee,
And pledge me in it first for courtesy.—'
Ha! dost thou start? are thy lips blanch'd like mine?
Child, 'tis no true draught, 'tis poison'd wine!
Iseult! . . .

. . . .

Ah, sweet angels, let him dream!
Keep his eyelids! let him seem
Not this fever-wasted wight
Thinn'd and paled before his time,
But the brilliant youthful knight
In the glory of his prime,
Sitting in the gilded barge,
At thy side, thou lovely charge,
Bending gaily o'er thy hand,
Iseult of Ireland!
And she too, that princess fair,
If her bloom be now less rare,
Let her have her youth again—
Let her be as she was then!

Let her have her proud dark eyes,
And her petulant quick replies—
Let her sweep her dazzling hand
With its gesture of command,
And shake back her raven hair
With the old imperious air!
As of old, so let her be,
That first Iseult, princess bright
Chatting with her youthful knight
As he steers her o'er the sea,
Quitting at her father's will
The green isle where she was bred,
And her bower in Ireland,
For the surge-beat Cornish strand,
Where the prince whom she must wed
Dwells on loud Tyntagel's hill,
High above the sounding sea.
And that potion rare her mother
Gave her, that her future lord,
Gave her, that King Marc and she
Might drink it on their marriage-day,
And for ever love each other—
Let her, as she sits on board,
Ah, sweet saints, unwittingly!
See it shine, and take it up,
And to Tristram laughing say:
'Sir Tristram, of thy courtesy
Pledge me in my golden cup!'
Let them drink it—let their hands
Tremble, and their cheeks be flame,
As they feel the fatal bands
Of a love they dare not name,
With a wild delicious pain,
Twine about their hearts again.
Let the early summer be
Once more round them, and the sea
Blue, and o'er its mirror kind
Let the breath of the May-wind,
Wandering through their drooping sails,
Die on the green fields of Wales!
Let a dream like this restore
What his eye must see no more.

TRISTRAM

Chill blows the wind, the pleasaunce walks are drear—
Madcap, what jest was this, to meet me here?
Were feet like those made for so wild a way?
The southern winter-parlour, by my fay,
Had been the likeliest trysting place to-day.
'Tristram!—nay, nay—thou must not take my hand!—
Tristram!—sweet love!—we are betray'd—out-plann'd.
Fly—save thyself—save me!—I dare not stay.'—
One last kiss first!—' 'Tis vain—to horse—away!'

. . . .

Ah, sweet saints, his dream doth move
Faster surely than it should,
From the fever in his blood!
All the spring-time of his love
Is already gone and past,
And instead thereof is seen
Its winter, which endureth still—
Tyntagel on its surge-beat hill,
The pleasaunce walks, the weeping queen,
The flying leaves, the straining blast,
And that long, wild kiss—their last.
And this rough December night
And his burning fever-pain,
Mingle with his hurrying dream,
Till they rule it, till he seem
The press'd fugitive again,
The love-desperate banish'd knight
With a fire in his brain
Flying o'er the stormy main.
—Whither does he wander now?
Haply in his dreams the wind
Wafts him here, and lets him find
The lovely orphan child again
In her castle by the coast;
The youngest, fairest chatelaine,
Whom this realm of France can boast,
Our snowdrop by the Atlantic sea,
Iseult of Brittany.
And—for through the haggard air,
The stain'd arms, the matted hair
Of that stranger knight ill-starr'd,
There gleam'd something which recall'd
The Tristram who in better days
Was Launcelot's guest at Joyous Gard—
Welcomed here, and here install'd,
Tended of his fever here,
Haply he seems again to move
His young guardian's heart with love;
In his exiled loneliness,
In his stately, deep distress,
Without a word, without a tear.
—Ah, 'tis well he should retrace
His tranquil life in this lone place;
His gentle bearing at the side
Of his timid youthful bride;
His long rambles by the shore
On winter evenings, when the roar
Of the near waves came, sadly grand,
Through the dark, up the drown'd sand,
Or his endless reveries
In the woods, where the gleams play
On the grass under the trees,
Passing the long summer's day
Idle as a mossy stone

In the forest depths alone,
The chase neglected, and his hound
Couch'd beside him on the ground.
—Ah, what trouble's on his brow?
Hither let him wander now,
Hither, to the quiet hours
Pass'd among these heaths of ours
By the grey Atlantic sea;
Hours, if not of ecstasy,
From violent anguish surely free!

TRISTRAM

All red with blood the whirling river flows,
The wide plain rings, the dazed air throbs with blows.
Upon us are the chivalry of Rome—
Their spears are down, their steeds are bathed in foam.
'Up, Tristram, up,' men cry, 'thou moonstruck knight!
What foul fiend rides thee? On into the fight!'
—Above the din her voice is in my ears;
I see her form glide through the crossing spears.—
Iseult! . . .

. . . .

Ah, he wanders forth again;
We cannot keep him; now as then,
There's a secret in his breast
That will never let him rest.
These musing fits in the green wood
They cloud the brain, they dull the blood!
—His sword is sharp, his horse is good;
Beyond the mountains will he see
The famous towns of Italy,
And label with the blessed sign
The heathen Saxons on the Rhine.
At Arthur's side he fights once more
With the Roman Emperor.
There's many a gay knight where he goes
Will help him to forget his care;
The march, the leaguer, Heaven's blithe air,
The neighing steeds, the ringing blows—
Sick pining comes not where these are.
Ah! what boots it, that the jest
Lightens every other brow,
What, that every other breast
Dances as the trumpets blow,
If one's own heart beats not light
On the waves of the toss'd fight,
If oneself cannot get free
From the clog of misery?
Thy lovely youthful wife grows pale
Watching by the salt sea-tide
With her children at her side
For the gleam of thy white sail.

Home, Tristram, to thy halls again!
To our lonely sea complain,
To our forests tell thy pain!

TRISTRAM

All round the forest sweeps off, black in shade,
But it is moonlight in the open glade;
And in the bottom of the glade shine clear
The forest chapel and the fountain near.
—I think, I have a fever in my blood;
Come, let me leave the shadow of this wood,
Ride down, and bathe my hot brow in the flood.
—Mild shines the cold spring in the moon's clear light;
God! 'tis *her* face plays in the waters bright.
'Fair love,' she says, 'canst thou forget so soon,
At this soft hour, under this sweet moon?'—
Iseult! . . .

. . . .

Ah poor soul, if this be so,
Only death can balm thy woe.
The solitudes of the green wood
Had no medicine for thy mood.
The rushing battle clear'd thy blood
As little as did solitude.
—Ah, his eyelids slowly break
Their hot seals, and let him wake;
What new change shall we now see?
A happier? Worse it cannot be.

TRISTRAM

Is my page here? Come, turn me to the fire.
Upon the window-panes the moon shines bright;
The wind is down—but she'll not come to-night.
Ah no! she is asleep in Cornwall now,
Far hence; her dreams are fair—smooth is her brow;
Of me she recks not, nor my vain desire.
—I have had dreams, I have had dreams, my page,
Would take a score years from a strong man's age;
And with a blood like mine, will leave, I fear,
Scant leisure for a second messenger.
—My princess, art thou there? Sweet, do not wait!
To bed, and sleep! my fever is gone by;
To-night my page shall keep me company.
Where do the children sleep? kiss them for me!
Poor child, thou art almost as pale as I;
This comes of nursing long and watching late.
To bed—good-night!

. . . .

She left the gleam-lit fireplace,
She came to the bed-side;
She took his hands in hers—her tears
Down on his wasted fingers rain'd.
She raised her eyes upon his face—

Nor with a look of wounded pride,
A look as if the heart complain'd—
Her look was like a sad embrace;
The gaze of one who can divine
A grief, and sympathise.
Sweet flower! thy children's eyes
Are not more innocent than thine.
But they sleep in shelter'd rest,
Like helpless birds in the warm nest,
On the castle's southern side;
Where feebly comes the mournful roar
Of buffeting wind and surging tide
Through many a room and corridor.
—Full on their window the moon's ray
Makes their chamber as bright as day.
It shines upon the blank white walls,
And on the snowy pillow falls,
And on two angel-heads doth play
Turn'd to each other—the eyes closed,
The lashes on the cheeks reposed.
Round each sweet brow the cap close-set
Hardly lets peep the golden hair;
Through the soft-open'd lips the air
Scarcely moves the coverlet.
One little wandering arm is thrown
At random on the counterpane,
And often the fingers close in haste
As if their baby owner chased
The butterflies again.
This stir they have and this alone;
But else they are so still!
—Ah, tired madcaps, you lie still;
But were you at the window now,
To look forth on the fairy sight
Of your illumin'd haunts by night,
To see the park-glades where you play
Far lovelier than they are by day,
To see the sparkle on the eaves,
And upon every giant bough
Of those old oaks, whose wet red leaves
Are jewell'd with bright drops of rain—
How would your voices run again!
And far beyond the sparkling trees
Of the castle park one sees
The bare heaths spreading, clear as day,
Moor behind moor, far, far away,
Into the heart of Brittany.
And here and there, lock'd by the land,
Long inlets of smooth glittering sea,
And many a stretch of watery sand
All shining in the white moon-beams—
But you see fairer in your dreams.

What voices are these on the clear night air?
What lights in the court—what steps on the stair?

II

ISEULT OF IRELAND

TRISTRAM

Raise the light, my page! that I may see her.—
    Thou art come at last then, haughty Queen!
Long I've waited, long I've fought my fever;
    Late thou comest, cruel that hast been.

ISEULT

Blame me not, poor sufferer! that I tarried;
    I was bound, I could not break the band.
Chide not with the past, but feel the present!
    I am here—we meet—I hold thy hand.

TRISTRAM

Thou art come, indeed—thou hast rejoin'd me;
    Thou hast dared it: but too late to save.
Fear not now that men should tax thy honour.
    I am dying: build— (thou may'st) —my grave!

ISEULT

Tristram, for the love of Heaven, speak kindly!
    What, I hear these bitter words from thee?
Sick with grief I am, and faint with travel—
    Take my hand—dear Tristram, look on me!

TRISTRAM

I forgot, thou comest from thy voyage—
    Yes, the spray is on thy cloak and hair.
But thy dark eyes are not dimm'd, proud Iseult!
    And thy beauty never was more fair.

ISEULT

Ah, harsh flatterer! let alone my beauty.
    I, like thee, have left my youth afar.
Take my hand, and touch these wasted fingers—
    See my cheek and lips, how white they are!

TRISTRAM

Thou art paler—but thy sweet charm, Iseult!
    Would not fade with the dull years away.
Ah, how fair thou standest in the moonlight!
    I forgive thee, Iseult!—thou wilt stay?

ISEULT

Fear me not, I will be always with thee;
    I will watch thee, tend thee, soothe thy pain;
Sing thee tales of true long-parted lovers,
    Join'd at evening of their days again.

TRISTRAM

No, thou shalt not speak; I should be finding
    Something alter'd in thy courtly tone.
Sit—sit by me: I will think, we've lived so
    In the greenwood, all our lives, alone.

ISEULT

Alter'd, Tristram? Not in courts, believe me,
Love like mine is alter'd in the breast;
Courtly life is light and cannot reach it—
Ah, it lives, because so deep suppress'd!

What, thou think'st men speak in courtly chambers
Words by which the wretched are consoled?
What, thou think'st this aching brow was cooler,
Circled, Tristram, by a band of gold?

Royal state with Marc, my deep-wrong'd husband—
That was bliss to make my sorrows flee!
Silken courtiers whispering honied nothings—
Those were friends to make me false to thee!

Ah, on which, if both our lots were balanced,
Was indeed the heaviest burden thrown—
Thee, a pining exile in thy forest,
Me, a smiling queen upon my throne?

Vain and strange debate, where both have suffer'd,
Both have pass'd a youth consumed and sad,
Both have brought their anxious day to evening,
And have now short space for being glad.

Join'd we are henceforth; nor will thy people,
Nor thy younger Iseult take it ill
That an ancient rival shares her office,
When she sees her humbled, pale, and still.

I, a faded watcher by thy pillow,
I, a statue on thy chapel floor,
Pour'd in grief before the Virgin Mother,
Rouse no anger, make no rivals more.

She will cry—'Is this the foe I dreaded?
This his idol? this that royal bride?
Ah, an hour of health would purge his eyesight!
Stay, pale queen! for ever by my side.'

Hush, no words! that smile, I see, forgives me.
I am now thy nurse, I bid thee sleep.
Close thine eyes—this flooding moonlight blinds them!
Nay, all's well again! thou must not weep.

TRISTRAM

I am happy: yet I feel, there's something
Swells my heart, and takes my breath away.
Through a mist I see thee; near!—come nearer!
Bend—bend down!—I yet have much to say.

ISEULT

Heaven! his head sinks back upon the pillow—
Tristram! Tristram! let thy heart not fail.

Call on God and on the holy angels!
What, love, courage!—Christ! he is so pale.

TRISTRAM

Hush, 'tis vain, I feel my end approaching!
This is what my mother said should be,
When the fierce pains took her in the forest,
The deep draughts of death, in bearing me.

'Son,' she said, 'thy name shall be of sorrow;
Tristram art thou call'd for my death's sake.'
So she said, and died in the drear forest.
Grief since then his home with me doth make.

I am dying.—Start not, nor look wildly!
Me, thy living friend, thou canst not save.
But, since living we were ununited,
Go not far, O Iseult! from my grave.

Rise, go hence, and seek the princess Iseult;
Speak her fair, she is of royal blood!
Say, I willed so that thou stay beside me—
She will grant it; she is kind and good.

Now to sail the seas of death I leave thee—
One last kiss upon the living shore!

ISEULT

Tristram!—Tristram!—stay—receive me with thee!
Iseult leaves thee, Tristram! never more.

. . . .

You see them clear—the moon shines bright.
Slow, slow and softly, where she stood,
She sinks upon the ground;—her hood
Had fallen back; her arms outspread
Still hold her lover's hand; her head
Is bow'd, half-buried, on the bed.
O'er the blanch'd sheet her raven hair
Lies in disorder'd streams; and there,
Strung like white stars, the pearls still are,
And the golden bracelets, heavy and rare,
Flash on her white arms still.
The very same which yesternight
Flash'd in the silver sconces' light,
When the feast was gay and the laughter loud
In Tyntagel's palace proud.
But then they deck'd a restless ghost
With hot-flush'd cheeks and brilliant eyes
And quivering lips on which the tide
Of courtly speech abruptly died,
And a glance which over the crowded floor,
The dancers, and the festive host,
Flew ever to the door.
That the knights eyed her in surprise,

And the dames whisper'd scoffingly—
'Her moods, good lack, they pass like showers!
But yesternight and she would be
As pale and still as wither'd flowers,
And now to-night she laughs and speaks
And has a colour in her cheeks.
Christ keep us from such fantasy!'—

Yes, now the longing is o'erpast,
Which, dogg'd by fear and fought by shame,
Shook her weak bosom day and night,
Consumed her beauty like a flame,
And dimm'd it like the desert-blast.
And though the bed-clothes hide her face,
Yet were it lifted to the light,
The sweet expression of her brow
Would charm the gazer, till his thought
Erased the ravages of time,
Fill'd up the hollow cheek, and brought
A freshness back, as of her prime—
So healing is her quiet now.
So perfectly the lines express
A tranquil, settled loveliness,
Her younger rival's purest grace.

The air of the December night
Steals coldly around the chamber bright,
Where those lifeless lovers be;
Swinging with it, in the light
Flaps the ghostlike tapestry.
And on the arras wrought you see
A stately Huntsman, clad in green,
And round him a fresh forest-scene.
On that clear forest-knoll he stays,
With his pack round him, and delays.
He stares and stares, with troubled face,
At this huge, gleam-lit fireplace,
At that bright, iron-figured door,
And those blown rushes on the floor.
He gazes down into the room
With heated cheeks and flurried air,
And to himself he seems to say—
'What place is this, and who are they?
Who is that kneeling Lady fair?
And on his pillows that pale Knight
Who seems of marble on a tomb?
How comes it here, this chamber bright,
Through whose mullion'd windows clear
The castle-court all wet with rain,
The drawbridge and the moat appear,
And then the beach, and, mark'd with spray,
The sunken reefs, and far away
The unquiet bright Atlantic plain?
—What, has some glamour made me sleep,

And sent me with my dogs to sweep,
By night, with boisterous bugle-peal,
Through some old, sea-side, knightly hall,
Not in the free green wood at all?
That Knight's asleep, and at her prayer
That Lady by the bed doth kneel:
Then hush, thou boisterous bugle-peal!'
—The wild boar rustles in his lair;
The fierce hounds snuff the tainted air;
But lord and hounds keep rooted there.

Cheer, cheer thy dogs into the brake,
O Hunter! and without a fear
Thy golden-tassell'd bugle blow,
And through the glades thy pastime take—
For thou wilt rouse no sleepers here!
For these thou seest are unmoved;
Cold, cold as those who lived and loved
A thousand years ago.

III

ISEULT OF BRITTANY

A year had flown, and o'er the sea away,
In Cornwall, Tristram and Queen Iseult lay;
In King Marc's chapel, in Tyntagel old—
There in a ship they bore those lovers cold.

The young surviving Iseult, one bright day,
Had wander'd forth: her children were at play
In a green circular hollow in the heath
Which borders the sea-shore; a country path
Creeps over it from the till'd fields behind.
The hollow's grassy banks are soft-inclined,
And to one standing on them, far and near
The lone unbroken view spreads bright and clear
Over the waste. This cirque of open ground
Is light and green; the heather, which all round
Creeps thickly, grows not here; but the pale grass
Is strewn with rocks, and many a shiver'd mass
Of vein'd white-gleaming quartz, and here and there
Dotted with holly trees and juniper.
In the smooth centre of the opening stood
Three hollies side by side, and made a screen,
Warm with the winter sun, of burnish'd green,
With scarlet berries gemm'd, the fell-fare's food.
Under the glittering hollies Iseult stands
Watching her children play: their little hands
Are busy gathering spars of quartz, and streams
Of stagshorn for their hats: anon, with screams
Of mad delight they drop their spoils, and bound
Among the holly clumps and broken ground,
Racing full speed, and startling in their rush

The fell-fares and the speckled missel-thrush
Out of their glossy coverts;—but when now
Their cheeks were flush'd, and over each hot brow
Under the feather'd hats of the sweet pair
In blinding masses shower'd the golden hair—
Then Iseult call'd them to her, and the three
Cluster'd under the holly screen, and she
Told them an old-world Breton history.

Warm in their mantles wrapt, the three stood there,
Under the hollies, in the clear still air—
Mantles with those rich furs deep glistering
Which Venice ships do from swart Egypt bring.
Long they staid still—then, pacing at their ease,
Moved up and down under the glossy trees.
But still as they pursued their warm dry road
From Iseult's lips the unbroken story flow'd,
And still the children listen'd, their blue eyes
Fix'd on their mother's face in wide surprise;
Nor did their looks stray once to the sea-side,
Nor to the brown heaths round them, bright and wide,
Nor to the snow which, though 'twas all away
From the open heath, still by the hedgerows lay,
Nor to the shining sea-fowl that with screams
Bore up from where the bright Atlantic gleams,
Swooping to landward; nor to where, quite clear,
The fell-fares settled on the thickets near.
And they would still have listen'd, till dark night
Came keen and chill down on the heather bright;
But, when the red glow on the sea grew cold,
And the grey turrets of the castle old
Look'd sternly through the frosty evening-air,
Then Iseult took by the hand those children fair,
And brought her tale to an end, and found the path,
And led them home over the darkening heath.

And is she happy? Does she see unmoved
The days in which she might have lived and loved
Slip without bringing bliss slowly away,
One after one, to-morrow like to-day?
Joy has not found her yet, nor ever will—
Is it this thought that makes her mien so still,
Her features so fatigued, her eyes, though sweet,
So sunk, so rarely lifted save to meet
Her children's? She moves slow: her voice alone
Has yet an infantine and silver tone,
But even that comes languidly: in truth,
She seems one dying in a mask of youth.
And now she will go home, and softly lay
Her laughing children in their beds, and play
Awhile with them before they sleep; and then
She'll light her silver lamp, which fishermen
Dragging their nets through the rough waves, afar,

Along this iron coast, know like a star,
And take her broidery frame, and there she'll sit
Hour after hour, her gold curls sweeping it;
Lifting her soft-bent head only to mind
Her children, or to listen to the wind.
And when the clock peals midnight, she will move
Her work away, and let her fingers rove
Across the shaggy brows of Tristram's hound
Who lies, guarding her feet, along the ground;
Or else she will fall musing, her blue eyes
Fix'd, her slight hands clasp'd on her lap; then rise,
And at her prie-dieu kneel, until she have told
Her rosary-beads of ebony tipp'd with gold,
Then to her soft sleep and to-morrow'll be
To-day's exact repeated effigy.

Yes, it is lonely for her in her hall.
The children, and the grey-hair'd seneschal,
Her women, and Sir Tristram's aged hound,
Are there the sole companions to be found.
But these she loves; and noisier life than this
She would find ill to bear, weak as she is:
She has her children too, and night and day
Is with them; and the wide heaths where they play,
The hollies, and the cliff, and the sea-shore,
The sand, the sea-birds, and the distant sails,
These are to her dear as to them; the tales
With which this day the children she beguiled
She gleaned from Breton grandames when a child
In every hut along this sea-coast wild.
She herself loves them still, and when they are told,
Can forget all to hear them, as of old.

Dear saints, it is not sorrow, as I hear,
Not suffering, which shuts up eye and ear
To all that has delighted them before,
And lets us be what we were once no more.
No, we may suffer deeply, yet retain
Power to be moved and soothed, for all our pain,
By what of old pleased us, and will again.
No, 'tis the gradual furnace of the world,
In whose hot air our spirits are upcurl'd
Until they crumble, or else grow like steel—
Which kills in us the bloom, the youth, the spring—
Which leaves the fierce necessity to feel,
But takes away the power—this can avail,
By drying up our joy in everything,
To make our former pleasures all seem stale.
This, or some tyrannous single thought, some fit
Of passion, which subdues our souls to it,
Till for its sake alone we live and move—
Call it ambition, or remorse, or love—
This too can change us wholly, and make seem
All that we did before, shadow and dream.

And yet, I swear, it angers me to see
How this fool passion gulls men potently;
Being in truth but a diseased unrest
And an unnatural overheat at best.
How they are full of languor and distress
Not having it; which when they do possess
They straightway are burnt up with fume and care,
And spend their lives in posting here and there
Where this plague drives them; and have little ease,
Are fretful with themselves and hard to please.
Like that bald Cæsar, the fam'd Roman wight,
Who wept at reading of a Grecian knight
Who made a name at younger years than he;
Or that renown'd mirror of chivalry,
Prince Alexander, Philip's peerless son,
Who carried the great war from Macedon
Into the Soudan's realm, and thunder'd on
To die at thirty-five in Babylon.

What tale did Iseult to the children say,
Under the hollies, that bright winter's day?

She told them of the fairy-haunted land
Away the other side of Brittany,
Beyond the heaths, edged by the lonely sea;
Of the deep forest-glades of Broce-liande,
Through whose green boughs the golden sunshine creeps
Where Merlin by the enchanted thorn-tree sleeps.
For here he came with the fay Vivian,
One April, when the warm days first began;
He was on foot, and that false fay, his friend,
On her white palfrey; here he met his end,
In these lone sylvan glades, that April-day.
This tale of Merlin and the lovely fay
Was the one Iseult chose, and she brought clear
Before the children's fancy him and her.

Blowing between the stems the forest air
Had loosen'd the brown locks of Vivian's hair,
Which play'd on her flush'd cheek, and her blue eyes
Sparkled with mocking glee and exercise.
Her palfrey's flanks were mired and bathed in sweat,
For they had travell'd far and not stopp'd yet.
A brier in that tangled wilderness
Had scored her white right hand, which she allows
To rest ungloved on her green riding-dress;
The other warded off the drooping boughs.
But still she chatted on, with her blue eyes
Fix'd full on Merlin's face, her stately prize.
Her 'haviour had the morning's fresh clear grace,
The spirit of the woods was in her face.
She look'd so witching fair, that learned wight
Forgot his craft, and his best wits took flight;
And he grew fond, and eager to obey
His mistress, use her empire as she may.

They came to where the brushwood ceased, and day
Peer'd 'twixt the stems; and the ground broke away
In a sloped sward down to a brawling brook;
And up as high as where they stood to look
On the brook's farther side was clear; but then
The underwood and trees began again.
This open glen was studded thick with thorns
Then white with blossom; and you saw the horns,
Through last year's fern, of the shy fallow-deer
Which come at noon down to the water here.
You saw the bright-eyed squirrels dart along
Under the thorns on the green sward; and strong
The blackbird whistled from the dingles near,
And the weird chipping of the woodpecker
Rang lonelily and sharp: the sky was fair,
And a fresh breath of spring stirr'd everywhere.
Merlin and Vivian stopp'd on the slope's brow
To gaze on the light sea of leaf and bough
Which glistering plays all round them, lone and mild,
As if to itself the quiet forest smiled.
Upon the brow-top grew a thorn, and here
The grass was dry and moss'd, and you saw clear
Across the hollow; white anemonies
Starr'd the cool turf, and clumps of primroses
Ran out from the dark underwood behind.
No fairer resting-place a man could find.
'Here let us halt,' said Merlin then; and she
Nodded, and tied her palfrey to a tree.

They sate them down together, and a sleep
Fell upon Merlin, more like death, so deep.
Her finger on her lips, then Vivian rose,
And from her brown-lock'd head the wimple throws,
And takes it in her hand, and waves it over
The blossom'd thorn-tree and her sleeping lover.
Nine times she waved the fluttering wimple round,
And made a little plot of magic ground.
And in that daisied circle, as men say,
Is Merlin prisoner till the judgment-day,
But she herself whither she will can rove—
For she was passing weary of his love.

[1852]

A SUMMER NIGHT

In the deserted moon-blanch'd street
How lonely rings the echo of my feet!
Those windows, which I gaze at, frown,
Silent and white, unopening down,
Repellent as the world;—but see,
A break between the housetops shows
The moon! and, lost behind her, fading dim
Into the dewy dark obscurity
Down at the far horizon's rim,
Doth a whole tract of heaven disclose.

And to my mind the thought
Is on a sudden brought
Of a past night, and a far different scene.
Headlands stood out into the moon-lit deep
As clearly as at noon;
The spring-tide's brimming flow
Heaved dazzlingly between;
Houses with long white sweep
Girdled the glistening bay;
Behind, through the soft air,
The blue haze-cradled mountains spread away.
That night was far more fair—
But the same restless pacings to and fro,
And the same vainly throbbing heart was there,
And the same bright, calm moon.

And the calm moonlight seems to say:
Hast thou then still the old unquiet breast,
Which neither deadens into rest,
Nor ever feels the fiery glow
That whirls the spirit from itself away,
But fluctuates to and fro,
Never by passion quite possess'd
And never quite benumb'd by the world's sway?—
And I, I know not if to pray
Still to be what I am, or yield and be
Like all the other men I see.
For most men in a brazen prison live,
Where in the sun's hot eye,
With heads bent o'er their toil, they languidly
Their lives to some unmeaning taskwork give,
Dreaming of nought beyond their prison wall.
And as, year after year,
Fresh products of their barren labour fall
From their tired hands, and rest
Never yet comes more near,
Gloom settles slowly down over their breast;
And while they try to stem
The waves of mournful thought by which they are prest,
Death in their prison reaches them
Unfreed, having seen nothing, still unblest.

And the rest, a few,
Escape their prison, and depart
On the wide ocean of life anew.
There the freed prisoner, where'er his heart
Listeth, will sail;
Nor does he know how there prevail,
Despotic on that sea,
Trade-winds that cross it from eternity.
Awhile he holds some false way, undebarr'd
By thwarting signs, and braves
The freshening wind and blackening waves.
And then the tempest strikes him; and between

The lightning bursts is seen
Only a driving wreck,
And the pale master on his spar-strewn deck
With anguish'd face and flying hair
Grasping the rudder hard,
Still bent to make some port he knows not where,
Still standing for some false impossible shore.
And sterner comes the roar
Of sea and wind, and through the deepening gloom
Fainter and fainter wreck and helmsman loom,
And he too disappears, and comes no more.

Is there no life, but these alone?
Madman or slave, must man be one?

Plainness and clearness without shadow of stain!
Clearness divine!
Ye heavens, whose pure dark regions have no sign
Of languor, though so calm, and, though so great,
Are yet untroubled and unpassionate;
Who, though so noble, share in the world's toil,
And though so task'd, keep free from dust and soil!
I will not say that your mild deeps retain
A tinge, it may be, of their silent pain
Who have long'd deeply once, and long'd in vain—
But I will rather say that you remain
A world above man's head, to let him see
How boundless might his soul's horizons be,
How vast, yet of what clear transparency!
How it were good to abide there, and breathe free;
How fair a lot to fill
Is left to each man still!

[1852]

THE BURIED LIFE

Light flows our war of mocking words, and yet,
Behold, with tears my eyes are wet!
I feel a nameless sadness o'er me roll.
Yes, yes, we know that we can jest,
We know, we know that we can smile!
But there's a something in this breast
To which thy light words bring no rest,
And thy gay smiles no anodyne.
Give me thy hand, and hush awhile,
And turn those limpid eyes on mine,
And let me read there, love! thy inmost soul.

Alas, is even love too weak
To unlock the heart and let it speak?
Are even lovers powerless to reveal
To one another what indeed they feel?
I knew the mass of men conceal'd
Their thoughts, for fear that if reveal'd

They would by other men be met
With blank indifference, or with blame reproved;
I knew they lived and moved
Trick'd in disguises, alien to the rest
Of men, and alien to themselves—and yet
  The same heart beats in every human breast!

But we, my love!—doth a like spell benumb
Our hearts, our voices?—must we too be dumb?

Ah, well for us, if even we,
Even for a moment, can get free
Our heart, and have our lips unchain'd;
For that which seals them hath been deep ordain'd.

Fate, which foresaw
How frivolous a baby man would be—
By what distractions he would be possess'd,
How he would pour himself in every strife,
And well-nigh change his own identity—
That it might keep from his capricious play
His genuine self, and force him to obey
Even in his own despite his being's law,
Bade, through the deep recesses of our breast,
The unregarded river of our life
Pursue with indiscernible flow its way;
And that we should not see
The buried stream, and seem to be
Eddying about in blind uncertainty,
Though driving on with it eternally.

But often, in the world's most crowded streets,
But often, in the din of strife,
There rises an unspeakable desire
After knowledge of our buried life;
A thirst to spend our fire and restless force
In tracking out our true, original course;
A longing to inquire
Into the mystery of this heart that beats
So wild, so deep in us—to know
Whence our thoughts come and where they go.
And many a man in his own breast then delves,
But deep enough, alas! none ever mines.
And we have been on many thousand lines,
And we have shown, on each, spirit and power,
But hardly have we, for one little hour,
Been on our own line, have we been ourselves
Hardly had skill to utter one of all
The nameless feelings that course through our breast,
But they course on for ever unexpress'd.
And long we try in vain to speak and act
Our hidden self, and what we say and do
Is eloquent, is well—but 'tis not true!
And then we will no more be rack'd

With inward striving, and demand
Of all the thousand nothings of the hour
Their stupefying power;
Ah yes, and they benumb us at our call!
Yet still, from time to time, vague and forlorn,
From the soul's subterranean depth upborne
As from an infinitely distant land,
Come airs, and floating echoes, and convey
A melancholy into all our day.

Only—but this is rare—
When a belovéd hand is laid in ours,
When, jaded with the rush and glare
Of the interminable hours,
Our eyes can in another's eyes read clear,
When our world-deafen'd ear
Is by the tones of a loved voice caress'd—
A bolt is shot back somewhere in our breast
And a lost pulse of feeling stirs again.
The eye sinks inward, and the heart lies plain,
And what we mean, we say, and what we would, we know.
A man becomes aware of his life's flow
And hears its winding murmur, and he sees
The meadows where it glides, the sun, the breeze.

And there arrives a lull in the hot race
Wherein he doth for ever chase
That flying and elusive shadow, rest.
An air of coolness plays upon his face,
And an unwonted calm pervades his breast.
And then he thinks he knows
The hills where his life rose,
And the sea where it goes.

[1852]

STANZAS IN MEMORY OF THE AUTHOR OF "OBERMANN"

NOVEMBER, 1849

In front the awful Alpine track
Crawls up its rocky stair;
The autumn storm-winds drive the rack,
Close o'er it, in the air.

Behind are the abandon'd baths
Mute in their meadows lone;
The leaves are on the valley paths;
The mists are on the Rhone—

The white mists rolling like a sea!
I hear the torrents roar.
—Yes, Obermann, all speaks of thee;
I feel thee near once more!

I turn thy leaves! I feel their breath
Once more upon me roll;
That air of languor, cold, and death,
Which brooded o'er thy soul.

Fly hence, poor wretch, whoe'er thou art,
Condemn'd to cast about,
All shipwreck in thy own weak heart,
For comfort from without!

A fever in these pages burns
Beneath the calm they feign;
A wounded human spirit turns,
Here, on its bed of pain.

Yes, though the virgin mountain air
Fresh through these pages blows;
Though to these leaves the glaciers spare
The soul of their white snows,

Though here a mountain murmur swells
Of many a dark-bough'd pine;
Though, as you read, you hear the bells
Of the high-pasturing kine—

Yet, through the hum of torrent lone,
And brooding mountain-bee,
There sobs I know not what ground-tone
Of human agony.

Is it for this, because the sound
Is fraught too deep with pain,
That, Obermann! the world around
So little loves thy strain?

Some secrets may the poet tell,
For the world loves new ways;
To tell too deep ones is not well—
It knows not what he says.

Yet of the spirits who have reign'd
In this our troubled day,
I know but two, who have attain'd,
Save thee, to see their way.

By England's lakes, in grey old age,
His quiet home one keeps;
And one, the strong much-toiling sage,
In German Weimar sleeps.

But Wordsworth's eyes avert their ken
From half of human fate;
And Goethe's course few sons of men
May think to emulate.

For he pursued a lonely road,
His eyes on Nature's plan;
Neither made man too much a God,
Nor God too much a man.

Strong was he, with a spirit free
From mists, and sane, and clear;
Clearer, how much! than ours—yet we
Have a worse course to steer.

For though his manhood bore the blast
Of Europe's stormiest time,
Yet in a tranquil world was pass'd
His tenderer youthful prime.

But we, brought forth and rear'd in hours
Of change, alarm, surprise—
What shelter to grow ripe is ours?
What leisure to grow wise?

Like children bathing on the shore,
Buried a wave beneath,
The second wave succeeds, before
We have had time to breathe.

Too fast we live, too much are tried,
Too harass'd to attain
Wordsworth's sweet calm, or Goethe's wide
And luminous view to gain.

And then we turn, thou sadder sage!
To thee! we feel thy spell!
The hopeless tangle of our age,
Thou too hast scann'd it well!

Immoveable thou sittest, still
As death, composed to bear!
Thy head is clear, thy feeling chill,
And icy thy despair.

Yes, as the Son of Thetis said,
I hear thee saying now:
Greater by far than thou are dead;
Strive not! die also thou!

Ah! Two desires toss about
The poet's feverish blood.
One drives him to the world without,
And one to solitude.

The glow, he cries, *the thrill of life,*
Where, where do these abound?
Not in the world, not in the strife
Of men, shall they be found.

He who hath watch'd, not shared, the strife,
Knows how the day hath gone;
He only lives with the world's life
Who hath renounced his own.

To thee we come, then! Clouds are roll'd
Where thou, O seer, art set;
Thy realm of thought is drear and cold—
The world is colder yet!

And thou hast pleasures, too, to share
With those who come to thee—
Balms floating on thy mountain-air,
And healing sights to see.

How often, where the slopes are green
On Jaman, hast thou sate
By some high chalet-door, and seen
The summer-day grow late,

And darkness steal o'er the wet grass
With the pale crocus starr'd,
And reach that glimmering sheet of glass
Beneath the piny sward,

Lake Leman's waters, far below!
And watch'd the rosy light
Fade from the distant peaks of snow;
And on the air of night

Heard accents of the eternal tongue
Through the pine branches play—
Listen'd, and felt thyself grow young!
Listen'd and wept—Away!

Away the dreams that but deceive!
And thou, sad guide, adieu!
I go, fate drives me; but I leave
Half of my life with you.

We, in some unknown Power's employ,
Move on a rigorous line;
Can neither, when we will, enjoy,
Nor, when we will, resign.

I in the world must live; but thou,
Thou melancholy shade!
Wilt not, if thou can'st see me now,
Condemn me, nor upbraid.

For thou art gone away from earth,
And place with those dost claim,
The Children of the Second Birth,
Whom the world could not tame;

And with that small, transfigured Band,
Whom many a different way
Conducted to their common land,
Thou learn'st to think as they.

Christian and pagan, king and slave,
Soldier and anchorite,
Distinctions we esteem so grave,
Are nothing in their sight.

They do not ask, who pined unseen,
Who was on action hurl'd,
Whose one bond is, that all have been
Unspotted by the world.

There without anger thou wilt see
Him who obeys thy spell
No more, so he but rest, like thee,
Unsoil'd! and so, Farewell.

Farewell!—Whether thou now liest near
That much-loved inland sea,
The ripples of whose blue waves cheer
Vevey and Meillerie;

And in that gracious region bland,
Where with clear-rustling wave
The scented pines of Switzerland
Stand dark round thy green grave,

Between the dusty vineyard walls
Issuing on that green place
The early peasant still recalls
The pensive stranger's face,

And stoops to clear thy moss-grown date
Ere he plods on again;—
Or whether, by maligner fate,
Among the swarms of men,

Where between granite terraces
The blue Seine rolls her wave
The Capital of Pleasure sees
Thy hardly-heard-of grave;—

Farewell! Under the sky we part,
In this stern Alpine dell.
O unstrung will! O broken heart!
A last, a last farewell!

[1849] [1852]

CONSOLATION

Mist clogs the sunshine.
Smoky dwarf houses
Hem me round everywhere;
A vague dejection
Weighs down my soul.

Yet, while I languish,
Everywhere countless
Prospects unroll themselves,
And countless beings
Pass countless moods.

Far hence, in Asia,
On the smooth convent-roofs,
On the gold terraces

Of holy Lassa,
Bright shines the sun.

Grey time-worn marbles
Hold the pure Muses;
In their cool gallery,
By yellow Tiber,
They still look fair.

Strange unlov'd uproar [1]
Shrills round their portal;
Yet not on Helicon
Kept they more cloudless
Their noble calm.

Through sun-proof alleys,
In a lone, sand-hemm'd
City of Africa,
A blind, led beggar,
Age-bow'd, asks alms.

No bolder robber
Erst abode ambush'd
Deep in the sandy waste;
No clearer eyesight
Spied prey afar.

Saharan sand-winds
Sear'd his keen eyeballs;
Spent is the spoil he won.
For him the present
Holds only pain.

Two young, fair lovers,
Where the warm June-wind,
Fresh from the summer fields,
Plays fondly, round them,
Stand, tranced in joy.

With sweet, join'd voices,
And with eyes brimming—
'Ah,' they cry, 'Destiny,
Prolong the present!
Time, stand still here!'

The prompt stern Goddess
Shakes her head, frowning;
Time gives his hour-glass
Its due reversal;
Their hour is gone.

[1] Written during the siege of Rome by the French.

With weak indulgence
Did the just Goddess
Lengthen their happiness,
She lengthened also
Distress elsewhere.

The hour, whose happy
Unalloy'd moments
I would eternalise,
Ten thousand mourners
Well pleased see end.

The bleak stern hour,
Whose severe moments
I would annihilate,
Is pass'd by others
In warmth, light, joy.

Time, so complain'd of,
Who to no one man
Shows partiality,
Brings round to all men
Some undimm'd hours.
[1849?] [1852]

LINES WRITTEN IN KENSINGTON GARDENS

In this lone, open glade I lie,
Screen'd by deep boughs on either hand;
And at its end, to stay the eye,
Those black-crown'd, red-boled pine-trees stand!

Birds here make song, each bird has his,
Across the girdling city's hum.
How green under the boughs it is!
How thick the tremulous sheep-cries come!

Sometimes a child will cross the glade
To take his nurse his broken toy;
Sometimes a thrush flit overhead
Deep in her unknown day's employ.

Here at my feet what wonders pass,
What endless, active life is here!
What blowing daisies, fragrant grass!
An air-stirred forest, fresh and clear.

Scarce fresher is the mountain-sod
Where the tired angler lies, stretch'd out,
And, eased of basket and of rod,
Counts his day's spoil, the spotted trout.

In the huge world which roars hard by
Be others happy, if they can!
But in my helpless cradle I
Was breathed on by the rural Pan.

I, on men's impious uproar hurl'd,
Think often, as I hear them rave,
That peace has left the upper world,
And now keeps only in the grave.

Yet here is peace for ever new!
When I, who watch them, am away
Still all things in this glade go through
The changes of their quiet day.

Then to their happy rest they pass!
The flowers upclose, the birds are fed,
The night comes down upon the grass,
The child sleeps warmly in his bed.

Calm soul of all things! make it mine
To feel, amid the city's jar,
That there abides a peace of thine,
Man did not make, and cannot mar.

The will to neither strive nor cry,
The power to feel with others give!
Calm, calm me more! nor let me die
Before I have begun to live.

[1852]

THE FUTURE

A wanderer is man from his birth.
He was born in a ship
On the breast of the river of Time;
Brimming with wonder and joy
He spreads out his arms to the light,
Rivets his gaze on the banks of the stream.

As what he sees is, so have his thoughts been.
Whether he wakes
Where the snowy mountainous pass
Echoing the screams of the eagles
Hems in its gorges the bed
Of the new-born clear-flowing stream;
Whether he first sees light
Where the river in gleaming rings
Sluggishly winds through the plain;
Whether in sound of the swallowing sea—
As is the world on the banks,
So is the mind of the man.

Vainly does each, as he glides,
Fable and dream
Of the lands which the river of Time
Had left ere he woke on its breast,
Or shall reach when his eyes have been closed.
Only the tract where he sails
He wots of; only the thoughts,
Raised by the objects he passes, are his.

Who can see the green earth any more
As she was by the sources of Time?
Who imagines her fields as they lay
In the sunshine, unworn by the plough?
Who thinks as they thought,
The tribes who then roam'd on her breast,
Her vigorous primitive sons?

What girl
Now reads in her bosom as clear
As Rebekah read, when she sate
At eve by the palm-shaded well?
Who guards in her breast
As deep, as pellucid a spring
Of feeling, as tranquil, as sure?

What Bard,
At the height of his vision, can deem
Of God, of the world, of the soul,
With a plainness as near,
As flashing as Moses felt,
When he lay in the night by his flock
On the starlit Arabian waste?
Can rise and obey
The beck of the Spirit like him?

This tract which the river of Time
Now flows through with us, is the plain.
Gone is the calm of its earlier shore.
Border'd by cities and hoarse
With a thousand cries is its stream.
And we on its breast, our minds
Are confused as the cries which we hear,
Changing and shot as the sights which we see.

And we say that repose has fled
For ever the course of the river of Time.
That cities will crowd to its edge
In a blacker incessanter line;
That the din will be more on its banks,
Denser the trade on its stream,

Flatter the plain where it flows,
Fiercer the sun overhead.
That never will those on its breast
See an ennobling sight,
Drink of the feeling of quiet again.

But what was before us we know not,
And we know not what shall succeed.

Haply, the river of Time—
As it grows, as the towns on its marge
Fling their wavering lights
On a wider, statelier stream—
May acquire, if not the calm
Of its early mountainous shore,
Yet a solemn peace of its own.

And the width of the waters, the hush
Of the grey expanse where he floats,
Freshening its current and spotted with foam
As it draws to the Ocean, may strike
Peace to the soul of the man on its breast—
As the pale Waste widens around him,
As the banks fade dimmer away,
As the stars come out, and the night-wind
Brings up the stream
Murmurs and scents of the infinite sea.

[1852]

MORALITY

We cannot kindle when we will
The fire that in the heart resides;
The spirit bloweth and is still,
In mystery our soul abides.
  But tasks in hours of insight will'd
  Can be through hours of gloom fulfill'd.

With aching hands and bleeding feet
We dig and heap, lay stone on stone;
We bear the burden and the heat
Of the long day, and wish 'twere done.
  Not till the hours of light return
  All we have built do we discern.

Then, when the clouds are off the soul,
When thou dost bask in Nature's eye,
Ask, how *she* view'd thy self-control,
Thy struggling task'd morality—
  Nature, whose free, light, cheerful air,
  Oft made thee, in thy gloom, despair.

And she, whose censure thou dost dread,
Whose eyes thou wast afraid to seek,
See, on her face a glow is spread,
A strong emotion on her cheek!
  'Ah child!' she cries, 'that strife divine,
  Whence was it, for it is not mine?

'There is no effort on *my* brow—
I do not strive, I do not weep;
I rush with the swift spheres, and glow
In joy, and, when I will, I sleep.—
  Yet that severe, that earnest air,
  I saw, I felt it once—but where?

'I knew not yet the gauge of time,
Nor wore the manacles of space;

I felt it in some other clime,
I saw it in some other place.
'Twas when the heavenly house I trod.
And lay upon the breast of God.'

[1852]

SOHRAB AND RUSTUM

AN EPISODE

And the first grey of morning fill'd the east,
And the fog rose out of the Oxus stream.
But all the Tartar camp along the stream
Was hush'd, and still the men were plunged in sleep;
Sohrab alone, he slept not; all night long
He had lain wakeful, tossing on his bed;
But when the grey dawn stole into his tent,
He rose, and clad himself, and girt his sword,
And took his horseman's cloak, and left his tent,
And went abroad into the cold wet fog,
Through the dim camp to Peran-Wisa's tent.
Through the black Tartar tents he pass'd, which stood
Clustering like bee-hives on the low flat strand
Of Oxus, where the summer floods o'erflow
When the sun melts the snows in high Pamere;
Through the black tents he pass'd, o'er that low strand,
And to a hillock came, a little back
From the stream's brink—the spot where first a boat,
Crossing the stream in summer, scrapes the land.
The men of former times had crown'd the top
With a clay fort; but that was fall'n, and now
The Tartars built there Peran-Wisa's tent,
A dome of laths, and o'er it felts were spread.
And Sohrab came there, and went in, and stood
Upon the thick piled carpets in the tent,
And found the old man sleeping on his bed
Of rugs and felts, and near him lay his arms.
And Peran-Wisa heard him, though the step
Was dull'd; for he slept light, an old man's sleep;
And he rose quickly on one arm, and said:—
'Who art thou? for it is not yet clear dawn.
Speak! is there news, or any night alarm?'
But Sohrab came to the bedside, and said:—
'Thou know'st me, Peran-Wisa! it is I.
The sun is not yet risen, and the foe
Sleep; but I sleep not; all night long I lie
Tossing and wakeful, and I come to thee.
For so did King Afrasiab bid me seek
Thy counsel, and to heed thee as thy son,
In Samarcand, before the army march'd;
And I will tell thee what my heart desires.
Thou know'st if, since from Ader-baijan first
I came among the Tartars, and bore arms,

I have still served Afrasiab well, and shown,
At my boy's years, the courage of a man.
This too thou know'st, that, while I still bear on
The conquering Tartar ensigns through the world,
And beat the Persians back on every field,
I seek one man, one man, and one alone—
Rustum, my father; who, I hoped, should greet,
Should one day greet, upon some well-fought field
His not unworthy, not inglorious son.
So I long hoped, but him I never find.
Come then, hear now, and grant me what I ask.
Let the two armies rest to-day; but I
Will challenge forth the bravest Persian lords
To meet me, man to man: if I prevail,
Rustum will surely hear it; if I fall—
Old man, the dead need no one, claim no kin.
Dim is the rumour of a common fight,
Where host meets host, and many names are sunk;
But of a single combat fame speaks clear.'
  He spoke: and Peran-Wisa took the hand
Of the young man in his, and sigh'd, and said:—
  'O Sohrab, an unquiet heart is thine!
Canst thou not rest among the Tartar chiefs,
And share the battle's common chance with us
Who love thee, but must press for ever first,
In single fight incurring single risk,
To find a father thou hast never seen?
That were far best, my son, to stay with us
Unmurmuring; in our tents, while it is war,
And when 'tis truce, then in Afrasiab's towns.
But, if this one desire indeed rules all,
To seek out Rustum—seek him not through fight!
Seek him in peace, and carry to his arms,
O Sohrab, carry an unwounded son!
But far hence seek him, for he is not here.
For now it is not as when I was young,
When Rustum was in front of every fray;
But now he keeps apart, and sits at home,
In Seistan, with Zal, his father old.
Whether that his own mighty strength at last
Feels the abhorr'd approaches of old age,
Or in some quarrel with the Persian King.
There go!—Thou wilt not? Yet my heart forebodes
Danger or death awaits thee on this field.
Fain would I know thee safe and well, though lost
To us; fain therefore send thee hence, in peace
To seek thy father, not seek single fights
In vain;—but who can keep the lion's cub
From ravening? and who govern Rustum's son?
Go: I will grant thee what thy heart desires.'
  So said he, and dropp'd Sohrab's hand, and left
His bed, and the warm rugs whereon he lay,
And o'er his chilly limbs his woollen coat
He pass'd, and tied his sandals on his feet,

And threw a white cloak round him, and he took
In his right hand a ruler's staff, no sword;
And on his head he set his sheep-skin cap,
Black, glossy, curl'd, the fleece of Kara-Kul;
And rais'd the curtain of his tent, and call'd
His herald to his side, and went abroad.
  The sun, by this, had risen, and clear'd the fog
From the broad Oxus and the glittering sands.
And from their tents the Tartar horsemen filed
Into the open plain; so Haman bade—
Haman, who next to Peran-Wisa ruled
The host, and still was in his lusty prime.
From their black tents, long files of horse, they stream'd;
As when, some grey November morn, the files,
In marching order spread, of long-neck'd cranes,
Stream over Casbin, and the southern slopes
Of Elburz, from the Aralian estuaries,
Or some frore Caspian reed-bed, southward bound
For the warm Persian sea-board—so they stream'd.
The Tartars of the Oxus, the King's guard,
First with black sheep-skin caps and with long spears;
Large men, large steeds; who from Bokhara come
And Khiva, and ferment the milk of mares.
Next the more temperate Toorkmuns of the south,
The Tukas, and the lances of Salore,
And those from Attruck and the Caspian sands;
Light men, and on light steeds, who only drink
The acrid milk of camels, and their wells.
And then a swarm of wandering horse, who came
From far, and a more doubtful service own'd;
The Tartars of Ferghana, from the banks
Of the Jaxartes, men with scanty beards
And close-set skull-caps; and those wilder hordes
Who roam o'er Kipchak and the northern waste,
Kalmuks and unkemp'd Kuzzaks, tribes who stray
Nearest the Pole, and wandering Kirghizzes,
Who come on shaggy ponies from Pamere;
These all filed out from camp into the plain.
And on the other side the Persians form'd:
First a light cloud of horse, Tartars they seem'd,
The Ilyats of Khorassan; and behind,
The royal troops of Persia, horse and foot,
Marshall'd battalions bright in burnish'd steel.
But Peran-Wisa with his herald came
Threading the Tartar squadrons to the front,
And with his staff kept back the foremost ranks.
And when Ferood, who led the Persians, saw
That Peran-Wisa kept the Tartars back,
He took his spear, and to the front he came,
And check'd his ranks, and fix'd them where they stood.
And the old Tartar came upon the sand
Betwixt the silent hosts, and spake, and said:—
  'Ferood, and ye, Persians and Tartars, hear!
Let there be truce between the hosts to-day.

But choose a champion from the Persian lords
To fight our champion Sohrab, man to man.'
  As, in the country, on a morn in June,
When the dew glistens on the pearled ears,
A shiver runs through the deep corn for joy—
So, when they heard what Peran-Wisa said,
A thrill through all the Tartar squadrons ran
Of pride and hope for Sohrab, whom they loved.
  But as a troop of pedlars, from Cabool,
Cross underneath the Indian Caucasus,
That vast sky-neighbouring mountain of milk snow;
Winding so high, that, as they mount, they pass
Long flocks of travelling birds dead on the snow,
Choked by the air, and scarce can they themselves
Slake their parch'd throats with sugar'd mulberries—
In single file they move, and stop their breath,
For fear they should dislodge the o'erhanging snows—
So the pale Persians held their breath with fear.
  And to Ferood his brother chiefs came up
To counsel: Gudurz and Zoarrah came,
And Feraburz, who ruled the Persian host
Second, and was the uncle of the King;
These came and counsell'd, and then Gudurz said:—
  'Ferood, shame bids us take their challenge up,
Yet champion have we none to match this youth.
He has the wild stag's foot, the lion's heart.
But Rustum came last night; aloof he sits
And sullen, and has pitch'd his tents apart:
Him will I seek, and carry to his ear
The Tartar challenge, and this young man's name.
Haply he will forget his wrath, and fight.
Stand forth the while, and take their challenge up.'
  So spake he; and Ferood stood forth and said:—
'Old man, be it agreed as thou hast said.
Let Sohrab arm, and we will find a man.'
  He spake; and Peran-Wisa turn'd, and strode
Back through the opening squadrons to his tent.
But through the anxious Persians Gudurz ran,
And cross'd the camp which lay behind, and reach'd,
Out on the sands beyond it, Rustum's tents.
Of scarlet cloth they were, and glittering gay,
Just pitch'd: the high pavilion in the midst
Was Rustum's, and his men lay camp'd around.
And Gudurz enter'd Rustum's tent, and found
Rustum; his morning meal was done, but still
The table stood before him, charged with food;
A side of roasted sheep, and cakes of bread,
And dark green melons; and there Rustum sate
Listless, and held a falcon on his wrist,
And play'd with it; but Gudurz came and stood
Before him; and he look'd, and saw him stand,
And with a cry sprang up, and dropp'd the bird,
And greeted Gudurz with both hands, and said:—

'Welcome! these eyes could see no better sight.
What news? but sit down first, and eat and drink.'
But Gudurz stood in the tent-door, and said:—
'Not now! a time will come to eat and drink,
But not to-day; to-day has other needs.
The armies are drawn out, and stand at gaze;
For from the Tartars is a challenge brought
To pick a champion from the Persian lords
To fight their champion—and thou know'st his name—
Sohrab men call him, but his birth is hid.
O Rustum, like thy might is this young man's!
He has the wild stag's foot, the lion's heart;
And he is young, and Iran's chiefs are old,
Or else too weak; and all eyes turn to thee.
Come down and help us, Rustum, or we lose!'
He spoke: but Rustum answer'd with a smile:—
'Go to! if Iran's chiefs are old, then I
Am older: if the young are weak, the King
Errs strangely; for the King, for Kai Khosroo,
Himself is young, and honours younger men,
And lets the aged moulder to their graves.
Rustum he loves no more, but loves the young—
The young may rise at Sohrab's vaunts, not I.
For what care I, though all speak Sohrab's fame?
For would that I myself had such a son,
And not that one slight helpless girl I have,
A son so famed, so brave, to send to war,
And I to tarry with the snow-hair'd Zal,
My father, whom the robber Afghans vex,
And clip his borders short, and drive his herds,
And he has none to guard his weak old age.
There would I go, and hang my armour up,
And with my great name fence that weak old man,
And spend the goodly treasures I have got,
And rest my age, and hear of Sohrab's fame,
And leave to death the hosts of thankless kings,
And with these slaughterous hands draw sword no more.'
He spoke, and smiled; and Gudurz made reply:—
'What then, O Rustum, will men say to this,
When Sohrab dares our bravest forth, and seeks
Thee most of all, and thou whom most he seeks,
Hidest thy face? Take heed, that men should say,
Like some old miser, Rustum hoards his fame,
And shuns to peril it with younger men.'
And, greatly moved, then Rustum made reply:—
'O Gudurz, wherefore dost thou say such words?
Thou knowest better words than this to say.
What is one more, one less, obscure or famed,
Valiant or craven, young or old, to me?
Are not they mortal, am not I myself?
But who for men of nought would do great deeds?
Come, thou shalt see how Rustum hoards his fame!
But I will fight unknown, and in plain arms;

Let not men say of Rustum, he was match'd
In single fight with any mortal man.'
  He spoke, and frown'd; and Gudurz turn'd and ran
Back quickly through the camp in fear and joy,
Fear at his wrath, but joy that Rustum came.
But Rustum strode to his tent door, and call'd
His followers in, and bade them bring his arms,
And clad himself in steel: the arms he chose
Were plain, and on his shield was no device,
Only his helm was rich, inlaid with gold,
And, from the fluted spine atop, a plume
Of horsehair waved, a scarlet horsehair plume.
So arm'd he issued forth; and Ruksh, his horse,
Follow'd him, like a faithful hound, at heel—
Ruksh, whose renown was noised through all the earth,
The horse, whom Rustum on a foray once
Did in Bokhara by the river find
A colt beneath its dam, and drove him home,
And rear'd him; a bright bay, with lofty crest;
Dight with a saddle-cloth of broider'd green
Crusted with gold, and on the ground were work'd
All beasts of chase, all beasts which hunters know.
So follow'd, Rustum left his tents, and cross'd
The camp, and to the Persian host appear'd.
And all the Persians knew him, and with shouts
Hail'd; but the Tartars knew not who he was.
And dear as the wet diver to the eyes
Of his pale wife who waits and weeps on shore,
By sandy Bahrein, in the Persian Gulf,
Plunging all day in the blue waves, at night,
Having made up his tale of precious pearls,
Rejoins her in their hut upon the sands—
So dear to the pale Persians Rustum came.
  And Rustum to the Persian front advanced,
And Sohrab arm'd in Haman's tent, and came.
And as afield the reapers cut a swath
Down through the middle of a rich man's corn,
And on each side are squares of standing corn,
And in the midst a stubble, short and bare—
So on each side were squares of men, with spears
Bristling, and in the midst, the open sand.
And Rustum came upon the sand, and cast
His eyes towards the Tartar tents, and saw
Sohrab come forth, and eyed him as he came.
  As some rich woman, on a winter's morn,
Eyes through her silken curtains the poor drudge
Who with numb blacken'd fingers makes her fire—
At cock-crow, on a starlit winter's morn,
When the frost flowers the whiten'd window panes—
And wonders how she lives, and what the thoughts
Of that poor drudge may be; so Rustum eyed
The unknown adventurous youth, who from afar
Came seeking Rustum, and defying forth
All the most valiant chiefs: long he perused

His spirited air, and wonder'd who he was.
For very young he seem'd, tenderly rear'd;
Like some young cypress, tall, and dark, and straight,
Which in a queen's secluded garden throws
Its slight dark shadow on the moonlit turf,
By midnight, to a bubbling fountain's sound—
So slender Sohrab seem'd, so softly rear'd.
And a deep pity enter'd Rustum's soul
As he beheld him coming; and he stood,
And beckon'd to him with his hand, and said:—
'O thou young man, the air of Heaven is soft,
And warm, and pleasant; but the grave is cold!
Heaven's air is better than the cold dead grave.
Behold me! I am vast, and clad in iron,
And tried; and I have stood on many a field
Of blood, and I have fought with many a foe—
Never was that field lost, or that foe saved.
O Sohrab, wherefore wilt thou rush on death?
Be govern'd: quit the Tartar host, and come
To Iran, and be as my son to me,
And fight beneath my banner till I die!
There are no youths in Iran brave as thou.'
So he spake, mildly: Sohrab heard his voice,
The mighty voice of Rustum, and he saw
His giant figure planted on the sand,
Sole, like some single tower, which a chief
Hath builded on the waste in former years
Against the robbers; and he saw that head,
Streak'd with its first grey hairs—hope fill'd his soul,
And he ran forward and embraced his knees,
And clasp'd his hand within his own and said:—
'Oh, by thy father's head! by thine own soul!
Art thou not Rustum? speak! art thou not he?'
But Rustum eyed askance the kneeling youth,
And turn'd away, and spake to his own soul:—
'Ah me, I muse what this young fox may mean.
False, wily, boastful, are these Tartar boys.
For if I now confess this thing he asks,
And hide it not, but say: *Rustum is here!*
He will not yield indeed, nor quit our foes,
But he will find some pretext not to fight,
And praise my fame, and proffer courteous gifts,
A belt or sword perhaps, and go his way.
And on a feast-tide, in Afrasiab's hall,
In Samarcand, he will arise and cry:
"I challenged once, when the two armies camp'd
Beside the Oxus, all the Persian lords
To cope with me in single fight; but they
Shrank, only Rustum dared; then he and I
Changed gifts, and went on equal terms away."
So will he speak, perhaps, while men applaud.
Then were the chiefs of Iran shamed through me.'
And then he turn'd, and sternly spake aloud:—
'Rise! wherefore dost thou vainly question thus

Of Rustum? I am here, whom thou hast call'd
By challenge forth; make good thy vaunt, or yield!
Is it with Rustum only thou wouldst fight?
Rash boy, men look on Rustum's face and flee.
For well I know, that did great Rustum stand
Before thy face this day, and were reveal'd
There would be then no talk of fighting more.
But being what I am, I tell thee this—
Do thou record it in thine inmost soul:
Either thou shalt renounce thy vaunt, and yield;
Or else thy bones shall strew this sand, till winds
Bleach them, or Oxus with his summer floods,
Oxus in summer wash them all away.'
He spoke; and Sohrab answer'd, on his feet:—
'Art thou so fierce? Thou wilt not fright me so!
I am no girl, to be made pale by words.
Yet this thou hast said well, did Rustum stand
Here on this field, there were no fighting then.
But Rustum is far hence, and we stand here.
Begin! thou are more vast, more dread than I,
And thou art proved, I know, and I am young—
But yet success sways with the breath of Heaven.
And though thou thinkest that thou knowest sure
Thy victory, yet thou canst not surely know.
For we are all, like swimmers in the sea,
Poised on the top of a huge wave of fate,
Which hangs uncertain to which side to fall.
And whether it will heave us up to land,
Or whether it will roll us out to sea,
Back out to sea, to the deep waves of death,
We know not, and no search will make us know;
Only the event will teach us in its hour.'
He spoke; and Rustum answer'd not, but hurl'd
His spear; down from the shoulder, down it came,
As on some partridge in the corn a hawk
That long has tower'd in the airy clouds
Drops like a plummet; Sohrab saw it come,
And sprang aside, quick as a flash; the spear
Hiss'd, and went quivering down into the sand,
Which it sent flying wide;—then Sohrab threw
In turn, and full struck Rustum's shield; sharp rang,
The iron plates rang sharp, but turn'd the spear.
And Rustum seized his club, which none but he
Could wield; an unlopp'd trunk it was, and huge,
Still rough—like those which men in treeless plains
To build them boats fish from the flooded rivers,
Hyphasis or Hydaspes, when, high up
By their dark springs, the wind in winter-time
Has made in Himalayan forests wrack,
And strewn the channels with torn boughs—so huge
The club which Rustum lifted now, and struck
One stroke; but again Sohrab sprang aside
Lithe as the glancing snake, and the club came
Thundering to earth, and leapt from Rustum's hand.

And Rustum follow'd his own blow, and fell
To his knees, and with his fingers clutch'd the sand;
And now might Sohrab have unsheathed his sword,
And pierced the mighty Rustum while he lay
Dizzy, and on his knees, and choked with sand;
But he look'd on, and smiled, nor bared his sword,
But courteously drew back, and spoke, and said:—
'Thou strik'st too hard: that club of thine will float
Upon the summer floods, and not my bones.
But rise, and be not wroth! not wroth am I;
No, when I see thee, wrath forsakes my soul.
Thou say'st, thou are not Rustum; be it so!
Who art thou then, that canst so touch my soul?
Boy as I am, I have seen battles too—
Have waded foremost in their bloody waves,
And heard their hollow roar of dying men;
But never was my heart thus touch'd before.
Are they from Heaven, these softenings of the heart?
O thou old warrior, let us yield to Heaven!
Come, plant we here in earth our angry spears,
And make a truce, and sit upon this sand,
And pledge each other in red wine, like friends,
And thou shalt talk to me of Rustum's deeds.
There are enough foes in the Persian host
Whom I may meet, and strike, and feel no pang;
Champions enough Afrasiab has, whom thou
Mayst fight; fight *them,* when they confront thy spear!
But oh, let there be peace 'twixt thee and me!'
He ceased: but while he spake, Rustum had risen,
And stood erect, trembling with rage; his club
He left to lie, but had regain'd his spear,
Whose fiery point now in his mail'd right-hand
Blazed bright and baleful, like that autumn-star,
The baleful sign of fevers; dust had soil'd
His stately crest, and dimm'd his glittering arms.
His breast heaved; his lips foam'd; and twice his voice
Was choked with rage: at last these words broke way:—
'Girl! nimble with thy feet, not with thy hands!
Curl'd minion, dancer, coiner of sweet words!
Fight, let me hear thy hateful voice no more!
Thou art not in Afrasiab's gardens now
With Tartar girls, with whom thou art wont to dance;
But on the Oxus-sands, and in the dance
Of battle, and with me, who make no play
Of war; I fight it out, and hand to hand.
Speak not to me of truce, and pledge, and wine!
Remember all thy valour; try thy feints
And cunning! all the pity I had is gone;
Because thou hast shamed me before both the hosts
With thy light skipping tricks, and thy girl's wiles.'
He spoke; and Sohrab kindled at his taunts,
And he too drew his sword: at once they rush'd
Together, as two eagles on one prey
Come rushing down together from the clouds,

One from the east, one from the west; their shields
Dash'd with a clang together, and a din
Rose, such as that the sinewy woodcutters
Make often in the forest's heart at morn,
Of hewing axes, crashing trees—such blows
Rustum and Sohrab on each other hail'd.
And you would say that sun and stars took part
In that unnatural conflict; for a cloud
Grew suddenly in Heaven, and dark'd the sun
Over the fighters' heads; and a wind rose
Under their feet, and moaning swept the plain,
And in a sandy whirlwind wrapp'd the pair.
In gloom they twain were wrapp'd, and they alone;
For both the on-looking hosts on either hand
Stood in broad daylight, and the sky was pure,
And the sun sparkled on the Oxus stream.
But in the gloom they fought, with bloodshot eyes
And labouring breath; first Rustum struck the shield
Which Sohrab held stiff out; the steel-spiked spear
Rent the tough plates, but fail'd to reach the skin,
And Rustum pluck'd it back with angry groan.
Then Sohrab with his sword smote Rustum's helm,
Nor clove its steel quite through; but all the crest
He shore away, and that proud horsehair plume,
Never till now defiled, sank to the dust;
And Rustum bow'd his head; but then the gloom
Grew blacker, thunder rumbled in the air,
And lightnings rent the cloud; and Ruksh, the horse,
Who stood at hand, utter'd a dreadful cry;—
No horse's cry was that, most like the roar
Of some pain'd desert lion, who all day
Hath trail'd the hunter's javelin in his side,
And comes at night to die upon the sand.
The two hosts heard that cry, and quaked for fear,
And Oxus curdled as it cross'd his stream.
But Sohrab heard, and quail'd not, but rush'd on,
And struck again; and again Rustum bow'd
His head; but this time all the blade, like glass,
Sprang in a thousand shivers on the helm,
And in his hand the hilt remain'd alone.
Then Rustum raised his head; his dreadful eyes
Glared, and he shook on high his menacing spear,
And shouted: *Rustum!*—Sohrab heard that shout,
And shrank amazed; back he recoil'd one step,
And scann'd with blinking eyes the advancing form;
And then he stood bewilder'd; and he dropp'd
His covering shield, and the spear pierced his side.
He reel'd, and staggering back, sank to the ground.
And then the gloom dispersed, and the wind fell,
And the bright sun broke forth, and melted all
The cloud; and the two armies saw the pair—
Saw Rustum standing, safe upon his feet,
And Sohrab, wounded, on the bloody sand.

Then, with a bitter smile, Rustum began:—
'Sohrab, thou thoughtest in thy mind to kill
A Persian lord this day, and strip his corpse,
And bear thy trophies to Afrasiab's tent.
Or else that the great Rustum would come down
Himself to fight, and that thy wiles would move
His heart to take a gift, and let thee go.
And then that all the Tartar host would praise
Thy courage or thy craft, and spread thy fame,
To glad thy father in his weak old age.
Fool! thou art slain, and by an unknown man!
Dearer to the red jackals shalt thou be,
Than to thy friends, and to thy father old.'
And with a fearless mien Sohrab replied:—
'Unknown thou art; yet thy fierce vaunt is vain.
Thou dost not slay me, proud and boastful man!
No! Rustum slays me, and this filial heart.
For were I match'd with ten such men as thee,
And I were he who till to-day I was,
They should be lying here, I standing there.
But that belovéd name unnerved my arm—
That name, and something, I confess, in thee,
Which troubles all my heart, and made my shield
Fall; and thy spear transfix'd an unarm'd foe.
And now thou boastest, and insult'st my fate.
But hear thou this, fierce man, tremble to hear:
The mighty Rustum shall avenge my death!
My father, whom I seek through all the world,
He shall avenge my death, and punish thee!'
As when some hunter in the spring hath found
A breeding eagle sitting on her nest,
Upon the craggy isle of a hill-lake,
And pierced her with an arrow as she rose,
And follow'd her to find her where she fell
Far off;—anon her mate comes winging back
From hunting, and a great way off descries
His huddling young left sole; at that, he checks
His pinion, and with short uneasy sweeps
Circles above his eyry, with loud screams
Chiding his mate back to her nest; but she
Lies dying, with the arrow in her side,
In some far stony gorge out of his ken,
A heap of fluttering feathers—never more
Shall the lake glass her, flying over it;
Never the black and dripping precipices
Echo her stormy scream as she sails by—
As that poor bird flies home, nor knows his loss,
So Rustum knew not his own loss, but stood
Over his dying son, and knew him not.
But with a cold, incredulous voice, he said:—
'What prate is this of fathers and revenge?
The mighty Rustum never had a son.'
And, with a failing voice, Sohrab replied:—
'Ah yes, he had! and that lost son am I.

Surely the news will one day reach his ear,
Reach Rustum, where he sits, and tarries long,
Somewhere, I know not where, but far from here;
And pierce him like a stab, and make him leap
To arms, and cry for vengeance upon thee.
Fierce man, bethink thee, for an only son!
What will that grief, what will that vengeance be!
Oh, could I live, till I that grief had seen!
Yet him I pity not so much, but her,
My mother, who in Ader-baijan dwells
With that old King, her father, who grows grey
With age, and rules over the valiant Koords.
Her most I pity, who no more will see
Sohrab returning from the Tartar camp,
With spoils and honour, when the war is done.
But a dark rumour will be bruited up,
From tribe to tribe, until it reach her ear;
And then will that defenceless woman learn
That Sohrab will rejoice her sight no more,
But that in battle with a nameless foe,
By the far distant Oxus, he is slain.'
He spoke; and as he ceas'd he wept aloud,
Thinking of her he left, and his own death.
He spoke; but Rustum listen'd, plunged in thought.
Nor did he yet believe it was his son
Who spoke, although he call'd back names he knew;
For he had had sure tidings that the babe,
Which was in Ader-baijan born to him,
Had been a puny girl, no boy at all—
So that sad mother sent him word, for fear
Rustum should take the boy, to train in arms.
And so he deem'd that either Sohrab took,
By a false boast, the style of Rustum's son;
Or that men gave it him, to swell his fame.
So deem'd he; yet he listen'd, plunged in thought:
And his soul set to grief, as the vast tide
Of the bright rocking Ocean sets to shore
At the full moon; tears gather'd in his eyes;
For he remember'd his own early youth,
And all its bounding rapture; as, at dawn,
The shepherd from his mountain-lodge descries
A far bright city, smitten by the sun,
Through many rolling clouds—so Rustum saw
His youth; saw Sohrab's mother, in her bloom;
And that old king, her father, who loved well
His wandering guest, and gave him his fair child
With joy; and all the pleasant life they led,
They three, in that long-distant summer-time—
The castle, and the dewy woods, and hunt
And hound, and morn on those delightful hills
In Ader-baijan. And he saw that Youth,
Of age and looks to be his own dear son,
Piteous and lovely, lying on the sand,
Like some rich hyacinth, which by the scythe

Of an unskilful gardener has been cut,
Mowing the garden grass-plots near its bed,
And lies, a fragrant tower of purple bloom,
On the mown, dying grass—so Sohrab lay,
Lovely in death, upon the common sand.
And Rustum gazed on him with grief, and said:—
'O Sohrab, thou indeed art such a son
Whom Rustum, wert thou his, might well have loved!
Yet here thou errest, Sohrab, or else men
Have told thee false—thou art not Rustum's son.
For Rustum had no son; one child he had—
But one—a girl; who with her mother now
Plies some light female task, nor dreams of us—
Of us she dreams not, nor of wounds, nor war.'
But Sohrab answer'd him in wrath: for now
The anguish of the deep-fix'd spear grew fierce,
And he desired to draw forth the steel,
And let the blood flow free, and so to die—
But first he would convince his stubborn foe;
And, rising sternly on one arm, he said:—
'Man, who art thou who dost deny my words?
Truth sits upon the lips of dying men,
And falsehood, while I liv'd, was far from mine.
I tell thee, prick'd upon this arm I bear
That seal which Rustum to my mother gave,
That she might prick it on the babe she bore.'
He spoke: and all the blood left Rustum's cheeks,
And his knees totter'd, and he smote his hand,
Against his breast, his heavy mailed hand,
That the hard iron corslet clank'd aloud;
And to his heart he press'd the other hand,
And in a hollow voice he spake, and said:—
'Sohrab, that were a proof which could not lie!
If thou show this, then art thou Rustum's son.'
Then, with weak hasty fingers, Sohrab loosed
His belt, and near the shoulder bared his arm,
And show'd a sign in faint vermilion points
Prick'd: as a cunning workman, in Pekin,
Pricks with vermilion some clear porcelain vase,
An emperor's gift—at early morn he paints,
And all day long, and, when night comes, the lamp
Lights up his studious forehead and thin hands—
So delicately prick'd the sign appear'd
On Sohrab's arm, the sign of Rustum's seal.
It was that griffin, which of old rear'd Zal,
Rustum's great father, whom they left to die,
A helpless babe, among the mountain rocks;
Him that kind creature found, and rear'd, and loved—
Then Rustum took it for his glorious sign.
And Sohrab bared that image on his arm,
And himself scann'd it long with mournful eyes,
And then he touch'd it with his hand and said:—
'How say'st thou? Is that sign the proper sign
Of Rustum's son, or of some other man's?'

He spoke; but Rustum gazed, and gazed, and stood
Speechless; and then he utter'd one sharp cry:
O boy—thy father!—and his voice choked there.
And then a dark cloud pass'd before his eyes,
And his head swam, and he sank down to earth.
But Sohrab crawl'd to where he lay, and cast
His arms about his neck, and kiss'd his lips,
And with fond faltering fingers stroked his cheeks,
Trying to call him back to life; and life
Came to Rustum, and he oped his eyes,
And they stood wide with horror; and he seized
In both his hands the dust which lay around,
And threw it on his head, and smirch'd his hair,—
His hair, and face, and beard, and glittering arms;
And strong convulsive groanings shook his breast,
And his sobs choked him; and he clutch'd his sword,
To draw it, and for ever let life out.
But Sohrab saw his thought, and held his hands,
And with a soothing voice he spoke, and said:—
'Father, forbear: for I but meet to-day
The doom that at my birth was written down
In Heaven, and thou art Heaven's unconscious hand.
Surely my heart cried out that it was thou,
When first I saw thee; and thy heart spoke too,
I know it: but fate trod those promptings down
Under its iron heel; fate, fate engaged
The strife, and hurl'd me on my father's spear.
But let us speak no more of this! I find
My father; let me feel that I have found!
Come, sit beside me on this sand, and take
My head betwixt thy hands, and kiss my cheeks,
And wash them with thy tears, and say: *My Son!*
Quick! quick! for number'd are my sands of life,
And swift; for like the lightning to this field
I came, and like the wind I go away—
Sudden, and swift, and like a passing wind.
But it was writ in Heaven that this should be.'
So said he, and his voice released the heart
Of Rustum, and his tears broke forth; he cast
His arms round his son's neck, and wept aloud,
And kiss'd him. And awe fell on both the hosts
When they saw Rustum's grief; and Ruksh, the horse,
With his head bowing to the ground, and mane
Sweeping the dust, came near, and in mute woe
First to the one then to the other moved
His head, as if enquiring what their grief
Might mean; and from his dark, compassionate eyes,
The big warm tears roll'd down, and caked the sand.
But Rustum chid him with stern voice, and said:—
'Ruksh, now thou grievest; but, O Ruksh, thy feet
Should then have rotted on their nimble joints,
Or ere they brought thy master to this field!'
But Sohrab look'd upon the horse and said:—
'Is this, then, Ruksh? How often, in past days,

My mother told me of thee, thou brave steed,
My terrible father's terrible horse! and said,
That I should one day find thy lord and thee.
Come, let me lay my hand upon thy mane!
O Ruksh, thou art more fortunate than I;
For thou hast gone where I shall never go,
And snuff'd the breezes of my father's home.
And thou hast trod the sands of Seistan,
And seen the River of Helmund, and the Lake
Of Zirrah; and the aged Zal himself
Has often stroked thy neck, and given thee food,
Corn in a golden platter soak'd with wine,
And said—*O Ruksh! bear Rustum well!*—but I
Have never known my grandsire's furrow'd face,
Nor seen his lofty house in Seistan,
Nor slaked my thirst at the clear Helmund stream;
But lodged among my father's foes, and seen
Afrasiab's cities only, Samarcand,
Bokhara, and lone Khiva in the waste,
And the black Toorkmun tents; and only drunk
The desert rivers, Moorghab and Tejend,
Kohik, and where the Kalmuks feed their sheep,
The northern Sir; and this great Oxus stream,
The yellow Oxus, by whose brink I die.'
  And, with a heavy groan, Rustum bewailed:—
'Oh that its waves were flowing over me!
Oh that I saw its grains of yellow silt
Roll tumbling in the current o'er my head!'
  And, with a grave mild voice, Sohrab replied:—
'Desire not that, my father! thou must live.
For some are born to do great deeds, and live,
As some are born to be obscured, and die.
Do thou the deeds I die too young to do,
And reap a second glory in thine age;
Thou art my father, and thy gain is mine.
But come! thou seest this great host of men
Which follow me; I pray thee, slay not these!
Let me entreat for them; what have they done?
They follow'd me, my hope, my fame, my star.
Let them all cross the Oxus back in peace.
But me thou must bear hence, not send with them,
But carry me with thee to Seistan,
And place me on a bed, and mourn for me,
Thou, and the snow-hair'd Zal, and all thy friends.
And thou must lay me in that lovely earth,
And heap a stately mound above my bones,
And plant a far-seen pillar over all.
That so the passing horseman on the waste
May see my tomb a great way off, and cry:
Sohrab, the mighty Rustum's son, lies there,
Whom his great father did in ignorance kill!
And I be not forgotten in my grave.'
  And, with a mournful voice, Rustum replied:—
'Fear not! as thou hast said, Sohrab, my son,

So shall it be; for I will burn my tents,
And quit the host, and bear thee hence with me,
And carry thee away to Seistan,
And place thee on a bed, and mourn for thee,
With the snow-headed Zal, and all my friends.
And I will lay thee in that lovely earth,
And heap a stately mound above thy bones,
And plant a far-seen pillar over all,
And men shall not forget thee in thy grave.
And I will spare thy host; yea, let them go!
Let them all cross the Oxus back in peace!
What should I do with slaying any more?
For would that all whom I have ever slain
Might be once more alive; my bitterest foes,
And they who were call'd champions in their time,
And through whose death I won that fame I have—
And I were nothing but a common man,
A poor, mean soldier, and without renown,
So thou mightest live too, my son, my son!
Or rather would that I, even I myself,
Might now be lying on this bloody sand,
Near death, and by an ignorant stroke of thine,
Not thou of mine; and I might die, not thou;
And I, not thou, be borne to Seistan;
And Zal might weep above my grave, not thine;
And say: *O son, I weep thee not too sore,*
For willingly, I know, thou met'st thine end!
But now in blood and battles was my youth,
And full of blood and battles is my age;
And I shall never end this life of blood.'
  Then, at the point of death, Sohrab replied:—
'A life of blood indeed, thou dreadful man!
But thou shalt yet have peace; only not now;
Not yet! but thou shalt have it on that day,
When thou shalt sail in a high-masted ship,
Thou and the other peers of Kai-Khosroo,
Returning home over the salt blue sea,
From laying thy dear master in his grave.'
  And Rustum gazed in Sohrab's face, and said:—
'Soon be that day, my Son, and deep that sea!
Till then, if fate so wills, let me endure.'
  He spoke; and Sohrab smiled on him, and took
The spear, and drew it from his side, and eased
His wound's imperious anguish; but the blood
Came welling from the open gash, and life
Flow'd with the stream;—all down his cold white side
The crimson torrent ran, dim now, and soil'd,
Like the soil'd tissue of white violets
Left, freshly gather'd, on their native bank,
By children, whom their nurses call with haste
Indoors from the sun's eye; his head droop'd low,
His limbs grew slack; motionless, white, he lay—
White, with eyes closed; only when heavy gasps,
Deep, heavy gasps, quivering through all his frame,

Convulsed him back to life, he open'd them,
And fix'd them feebly on his father's face;
Till now all strength was ebb'd, and from his limbs
Unwillingly the spirit fled away,
Regretting the warm mansion which it left,
And youth and bloom, and this delightful world.
  So, on the bloody sand, Sohrab lay dead;
And the great Rustum drew his horseman's cloak
Down o'er his face, and sate by his dead son.
As those black granite pillars, once high-rear'd
By Jemshid in Persepolis, to bear
His house, now, mid their broken flights of steps,
Lie prone, enormous, down the mountain side—
So in the sand lay Rustum by his son.
  And night came down over the solemn waste,
And the two gazing hosts, and that sole pair,
And darken'd all; and a cold fog, with night,
Crept from the Oxus. Soon a hum arose,
As of a great assembly loosed, and fires
Began to twinkle through the fog; for now
Both armies moved to camp, and took their meal;
The Persians took it on the open sands
Southward, the Tartars by the river marge;
And Rustum and his son were left alone.
  But the majestic river floated on,
Out of the mist and hum of that low land,
Into the frosty starlight, and there moved,
Rejoicing, through the hush'd Chorasmian waste,
Under the solitary moon: he flow'd
Right for the polar star, past Orgunjé,
Brimming, and bright, and large; then sands begin
To hem his watery march, and dam his streams,
And split his currents; that for many a league
The shorn and parcell'd Oxus strains along
Through beds of sand and matted rushy isles—
Oxus, forgetting the bright speed he had
In his high mountain cradle in Pamere,
A foil'd circuitous wanderer—till at last
The long'd-for dash of waves is heard, and wide
His luminous home of waters opens, bright
And tranquil, from whose floor the new-bathed stars
Emerge, and shine upon the Aral Sea.

[1853] [1853]

PHILOMELA

Hark! ah, the nightingale—
The tawny-throated!
Hark, from that moonlit cedar what a burst!
What triumph! hark!—what pain!

O wanderer from a Grecian shore,
Still, after many years, in distant lands,
Still nourishing in thy bewilder'd brain
That wild, unquench'd, deep-sunken, old-world pain—
Say, will it never heal?
And can this fragrant lawn
With its cool trees, and night,
And the sweet, tranquil Thames,
And moonshine, and the dew,
To thy rack'd heart and brain
Afford no balm?

Dost thou to-night behold
Here, through the moonlight on this English grass,
The unfriendly palace in the Thracian wild?
Dost thou again peruse
With hot cheeks and sear'd eyes
The too clear web, and thy dumb sister's shame?

Dost thou once more assay
Thy flight, and feel come over thee,
Poor fugitive, the feathery change
Once more, and once more seem to make resound
With love and hate, triumph and agony,
Lone Daulis, and the high Cephissian vale?
Listen, Eugenia—
How thick the bursts come crowding through the leaves!
Again—thou hearest?
Eternal Passion!
Eternal Pain!

[1853]

REQUIESCAT

Strew on her roses, roses,
And never a spray of yew!
In quiet she reposes:
Ah! would that I did too!

Her mirth the world required:
She bathed it in smiles of glee.
But her heart was tired, tired,
And now they let her be.

Her life was turning, turning,
In mazes of heat and sound.
But for peace her soul was yearning,
And now peace laps her round.

Her cabin'd, ample spirit,
It flutter'd and fail'd for breath.
To-night it doth inherit
The vasty hall of death.

[1853]

THE SCHOLAR GIPSY

Go, for they call you, shepherd, from the hill;
Go, shepherd, and untie the wattled cotes!
No longer leave thy wistful flock unfed,
Nor let thy bawling fellows rack their throats,
Nor the cropp'd herbage shoot another head.
But when the fields are still,
And the tired men and dogs all gone to rest,
And only the white sheep are sometimes seen
Cross and recross the strips of moon-blanch'd green,
Come, shepherd, and again begin the quest.

Here, where the reaper was at work of late—
In this high field's dark corner, where he leaves
His coat, his basket, and his earthen cruse,
And in the sun all morning binds the sheaves,
Then here, at noon, comes back his stores to use—
Here will I sit and wait,
While to my ear from uplands far away
The bleating of the folded flocks is borne,
With distant cries of reapers in the corn—
All the live murmur of a summer's day.

Screen'd in this nook o'er the high, half-reap'd field,
And here till sun-down, shepherd! will I be.
Through the thick corn the scarlet poppies peep
And round green roots and yellowing stalks I see

Pale blue convolvulus in tendrils creep;
And air-swept lindens yield
Their scent, and rustle down their perfumed showers
Of bloom on the bent grass where I am laid,
And bower me from the August sun with shade;
And the eye travels down to Oxford's towers:

And near me on the grass lies Glanvil's book—
Come, let me read the oft-read tale again!
The story of that Oxford scholar poor
Of pregnant parts and quick inventive brain,
Who, tired of knocking at preferment's door,
One summer morn forsook
His friends, and went to learn the gipsy-lore,
And roam'd the world with that wild brotherhood,
And came, as most men deem'd, to little good,
But came to Oxford and his friends no more.

But once, years after, in the country lanes,
Two scholars whom at college erst he knew
Met him, and of his way of life enquired.
Whereat he answer'd, that the gipsy-crew,
His mates, had arts to rule as they desired
The workings of men's brains,
And they can bind them to what thoughts they will.
'And I,' he said, 'the secret of their art,
When fully learn'd, will to the world impart;
But it needs heaven-sent moments for this skill.'

This said, he left them, and return'd no more.—
But rumours hung about the country-side
That the lost Scholar long was seen to stray,
Seen by rare glimpses, pensive and tongue-tied,
In hat of antique shape, and cloak of grey,
The same the Gipsies wore.
Shepherds had met him on the Hurst in spring;
At some lone alehouse in the Berkshire moors,
On the warm ingle-bench, the smock-frock'd boors
Had found him seated at their entering.

But, 'mid their drink and clatter, he would fly.
And I myself seem half to know thy looks,
And put the shepherds, wanderer, on thy trace;
And boys who in lone wheatfields scare the rooks
I ask if thou hast pass'd their quiet place;
Or in my boat I lie
Moor'd to the cool bank in the summer-heats,
Mid wide grass meadows which the sunshine fills,
And watch the warm green-muffled Cumner hills,
And wonder if thou haunt'st their shy retreats.

For most, I know, thou lov'st retired ground!
Thee, at the ferry, Oxford riders blithe,
Returning home on summer nights, have met

Crossing the stripling Thames at Bab-lock-hithe,
Trailing in the cool stream thy fingers wet,
As the punt's rope chops round;
And leaning backwards in a pensive dream,
And fostering in thy lap a heap of flowers
Pluck'd in shy fields and distant Wychwood bowers,
And thine eyes resting on the moonlit stream:

And then they land, and thou art seen no more!—
Maidens who from the distant hamlets come
To dance around the Fyfield elm in May,
Oft through the darkening fields have seen thee roam,
Or cross a stile into the public way.
Oft thou hast given them store
Of flowers—the frail-leaf'd, white anemony,
Dark bluebells drench'd with dews of summer eves,
And purple orchises with spotted leaves—
But none hath words she can report of thee.

And, above Godstow Bridge, when hay-time's here
In June, and many a scythe in sunshine flames,
Men who through those wide fields of breezy grass
Where black-wing'd swallows haunt the glittering Thames,
To bathe in the abandon'd lasher pass,
Have often pass'd thee near
Sitting upon the river bank o'ergrown;
Mark'd thine outlandish garb, thy figure spare,
Thy dark vague eyes, and soft abstracted air—
But, when they came from bathing, thou wast gone!

At some lone homestead in the Cumner hills,
Where at her open door the housewife darns,
Thou hast been seen, or hanging on a gate
To watch the threshers in the mossy barns.
Children, who early range these slopes and late
For cresses from the rills,
Have known thee eyeing, all an April day,
The springing pastures and the feeding kine;
And mark'd thee, when the stars come out and shine,
Through the long dewy grass move slow away.

In Autumn, on the skirts of Bagley Wood—
Where most the Gipsies by the turf-edged way
Pitch their smoked tents, and every bush you see
With scarlet patches tagg'd and shreds of grey,
Above the forest ground call'd Thessaly—
The blackbird, picking food,
Sees thee, nor stops his meal, nor fears at all;
So often has he known thee past him stray,
Rapt, twirling in thy hand a wither'd spray,
And waiting for the spark from heaven to fall.

And once, in winter, on the causeway chill
Where home through flooded fields foot-travellers go,

Have I not pass'd thee on the wooden bridge,
Wrapt in thy cloak and battling with the snow,
Thy face tow'rd Hinksey and its wintry ridge?
And thou hast climb'd the hill
And gain'd the white brow of the Cumner range;
Turn'd once to watch, while thick the snowflakes fall,
The line of festal light in Christ-Church hall—
Then sought thy straw in some sequester'd grange.

But what—I dream! Two hundred years are flown
Since first thy story ran through Oxford halls,
And the grave Glanvil did the tale inscribe
That thou wert wander'd from the studious walls
To learn strange arts, and join a gipsy-tribe:
And thou from earth art gone
Long since, and in some quiet churchyard laid—
Some country nook, where o'er thy unknown grave
Tall grasses and white flowering nettles wave,
Under a dark, red-fruited yew-tree's shade.

—No, no, thou hast not felt the lapse of hours!
For what wears out the life of mortal men?
'Tis that from change to change their being rolls;
'Tis that repeated shocks, again, again,
Exhaust the energy of strongest souls,
And numb the elastic powers.
Till having used our nerves with bliss and teen,
And tired upon a thousand schemes our wit,
To the just-pausing Genius we remit
Our worn-out life, and are—what we have been.

Thou hast not lived, why should'st thou perish, so?
Thou hadst *one* aim, *one* business, *one* desire;
Else wert thou long since number'd with the dead!
Else hadst thou spent, like other men, thy fire!
The generations of thy peers are fled,
And we ourselves shall go;
But thou possessest an immortal lot,
And we imagine thee exempt from age
And living as thou liv'st on Glanvil's page,
Because thou hadst—what we, alas! have not.

For early didst thou leave the world, with powers
Fresh, undiverted to the world without,
Firm to their mark, not spent on other things;
Free from the sick fatigue, the languid doubt,
Which much to have tried, in much been baffled, brings.
O life unlike to ours!
Who fluctuate idly without term or scope,
Of whom each strives, nor knows for what he strives,
And each half lives a hundred different lives;
Who wait like thee, but not, like thee, in hope.

Thou waitest for the spark from heaven! and we,
Light half-believers of our casual creeds,
Who never deeply felt, nor clearly will'd,
Whose insight never has borne fruit in deeds,
Whose vague resolves never have been fulfill'd;
For whom each year we see
Breeds new beginnings, disappointments new;
Who hesitate and falter life away,
And lose to-morrow the ground won to-day—
Ah! do not we, wanderer! await it too?

Yes, we await it!—but it still delays,
And then we suffer; and amongst us one,
Who most has suffer'd, takes dejectedly
His seat upon the intellectual throne;
And all his store of sad experience he
Lays bare of wretched days;
Tells us his misery's birth and growth and signs,
And how the dying spark of hope was fed,
And how the breast was soothed, and how the head,
And all his hourly varied anodynes.

This for our wisest! and we others pine,
And wish the long unhappy dream would end,
And waive all claim to bliss, and try to bear;
With close-lipp'd patience for our only friend,
Sad patience, too near neighbour to despair—
But none has hope like thine!
Thou through the fields and through the woods dost stray,
Roaming the country side, a truant boy,
Nursing thy project in unclouded joy,
And every doubt long blown by time away.

O born in days when wits were fresh and clear,
And life ran gaily as the sparkling Thames;
Before this strange disease of modern life,
With its sick hurry, its divided aims,
Its heads o'ertax'd, its palsied hearts, was rife—
Fly hence, our contact fear!
Still fly, plunge deeper in the bowering wood!
Averse, as Dido did with gesture stern
From her false friend's approach in Hades turn,
Wave us away, and keep thy solitude.

Still nursing the unconquerable hope,
Still clutching the inviolable shade,
With a free, onward impulse brushing through,
By night, the silver'd branches of the glade—
Far on the forest skirts, where none pursue,
On some mild pastoral slope
Emerge, and resting on the moonlit pales,
Freshen thy flowers, as in former years
With dew, or listen with enchanted ears,
From the dark dingles, to the nightingales.

But fly our paths, our feverish contact fly!
For strong the infection of our mental strife,
Which, though it gives no bliss, yet spoils for rest;
And we should win thee from thy own fair life,
Like us distracted, and like us unblest.
Soon, soon thy cheer would die,
Thy hopes grow timorous, and unfix'd thy powers,
And thy clear aims be cross and shifting made:
And then thy glad perennial youth would fade,
Fade, and grow old at last, and die like ours.

Then fly our greetings, fly our speech and smiles!
—As some grave Tyrian trader, from the sea,
Descried at sunrise an emerging prow
Lifting the cool-hair'd creepers stealthily,
The fringes of a southward-facing brow
Among the Ægean isles;
And saw the merry Grecian coaster come,
Freighted with amber grapes, and Chian wine,
Green bursting figs, and tunnies steep'd in brine—
And knew the intruders on his ancient home,

The young light-hearted masters of the waves—
And snatch'd his rudder, and shook out more sail,
And day and night held on indignantly
O'er the blue Midland waters with the gale,
Betwixt the Syrtes and soft Sicily,
To where the Atlantic raves
Outside the western straits; and unbent sails
There, where down cloudy cliffs, through sheets of foam,
Shy traffickers, the dark Iberians come;
And on the beach undid his corded bales.

[1853]

STANZAS FROM THE GRANDE CHARTREUSE

Through Alpine meadows soft-suffused
With rain, where thick the crocus blows,
Past the dark forges long disused,
The mule-track from Saint Laurent goes.
The bridge is cross'd, and slow we ride,
Through forest, up the mountain-side.

The autumnal evening darkens round,
The wind is up, and drives the rain;
While, hark! far down, with strangled sound
Doth the Dead Guier's stream complain,
Where that wet smoke, among the woods,
Over his boiling cauldron broods.

Swift rush the spectral vapours white
Past limestone scars with ragged pines,
Showing—then blotting from our sight!—
Halt—through the cloud-drift something shines!
High in the valley, wet and drear,
The huts of Courrerie appear.

Strike leftward! cries our guide; and higher
Mounts up the stony forest-way.
At last the encircling trees retire;
Look! through the showery twilight grey
What pointed roofs are these advance?—
A palace of the Kings of France?

Approach, for what we seek is here!
Alight, and sparely sup, and wait
For rest in this outbuilding near;
Then cross the sward and reach that gate.
Knock; pass the wicket! Thou art come
To the Carthusians' world-famed home.

The silent courts, where night and day
Into their stone-carved basins cold
The splashing icy fountains play—
The humid corridors behold!
Where, ghostlike in the deepening night,
Cowl'd forms brush by in gleaming white.

The chapel, where no organ's peal
Invests the stern and naked prayer—
With penitential cries they kneel
And wrestle; rising then, with bare
And white uplifted faces stand,
Passing the Host from hand to hand;

Each takes, and then his visage wan
Is buried in his cowl once more.
The cells!—the suffering Son of Man
Upon the wall—the knee-worn floor—
And where they sleep, that wooden bed,
Which shall their coffin be, when dead!

The library, where tract and tome
Not to feed priestly pride are there,
To hymn the conquering march of Rome,
Nor yet to amuse, as ours are!
They paint of souls the inner strife,
Their drops of blood, their death in life.

The garden, overgrown—yet mild,
See, fragrant herbs are flowering there!
Strong children of the Alpine wild
Whose culture is the brethren's care;
Of human tasks their only one,
And cheerful works beneath the sun.

Those halls, too, destined to contain
Each its own pilgrim-host of old,
From England, Germany, or Spain—
All are before me! I behold
The House, the Brotherhood austere!
—And what am I, that I am here?

For rigorous teachers seized my youth,
And purged its faith, and trimm'd its fire,
Show'd me the high white star of Truth,
There bade me gaze, and there aspire;
Even now their whispers pierce the gloom:
What dost thou in this living tomb?

Forgive me, masters of the mind!
At whose behest I long ago
So much unlearnt, so much resign'd—
I come not here to be your foe!
I seek these anchorites, not in ruth,
To curse and to deny your truth;

Not as their friend, or child, I speak!
But as, on some far northern strand,
Thinking of his own Gods, a Greek
In pity and mournful awe might stand
Before some fallen Runic stone—
For both were faiths, and both are gone.

Wandering between two worlds, one dead,
The other powerless to be born,
With nowhere yet to rest my head,
Like these, on earth I wait forlorn.
Their faith, my tears, the world deride—
I come to shed them at their side.

Oh, hide me in your gloom profound,
Ye solemn seats of holy pain!
Take me, cowl'd forms, and fence me round,
Till I possess my soul again;
Till free my thoughts before me roll;
Not chafed by hourly false control!

For the world cries your faith is now
But a dead time's exploded dream;
My melancholy, sciolists say,
Is a pass'd mode, an outworn theme—
As if the world had ever had
A faith, or sciolists been sad!

Ah, if it *be* pass'd, take away,
At least, the restlessness, the pain;
Be man henceforth no more a prey
To these out-dated stings again!
The nobleness of grief is gone—
Ah, leave us not the fret alone!

But—if you cannot give us ease
Last of the race of them who grieve
Here leave us to die out with these
Last of the people who believe!
Silent, while years engrave the brow;
Silent—the best are silent now.

Achilles ponders in his tent,
The kings of modern thought are dumb;
Silent they are, though not content,
And wait to see the future come.
They have the grief men had of yore,
But they contend and cry no more.

Our fathers water'd with their tears
This sea of time whereon we sail,

Their voices were in all men's ears
Who pass'd within their puissant hail.
Still the same ocean round us raves,
But we stand mute, and watch the waves.

For what avail'd it, all the noise
And outcry of the former men?—
Say, have their sons achieved more joys,
Say, is life lighter now than then?
The sufferers died, they left their pain—
The pangs which tortured them remain.

What helps it now, that Byron bore,
With haughty scorn which mock'd the smart,
Through Europe to the Ætolian shore
The pageant of his bleeding heart?
That thousands counted every groan,
And Europe made his woe her own?

What boots it, Shelley! that the breeze
Carried thy lovely wail away,
Musical through Italian trees
Which fringe thy soft blue Spezzian bay?
Inheritors of thy distress
Have restless hearts one throb the less?

Or are we easier, to have read,
O Obermann! the sad, stern page,
Which tells us how thou hidd'st thy head
From the fierce tempest of thine age
In the lone brakes of Fontainebleau,
Or chalets near the Alpine snow?

Ye slumber in your silent grave!—
The world, which for an idle day
Grace to your mood of sadness gave,
Long since hath flung her weeds away.
The eternal trifler breaks your spell;
But we—we learnt your lore too well!

Years hence, perhaps, may dawn an age,
More fortunate, alas! than we,
Which without hardness will be sage,
And gay without frivolity,
Sons of the world, ho, speed those years;
But, while we wait, allow our tears!

Allow them! We admire with awe
The exulting thunder of your race;
You give the universe your law,
You triumph over time and space!
Your pride of life, your tireless powers,
We laud them, but they are not ours.

We are like children rear'd in shade
Beneath some old-world abbey wall,
Forgotten in a forest-glade,
And secret from the eyes of all.
Deep, deep the greenwood round them waves,
Their abbey, and its close of graves!

But, where the road runs near the stream,
Oft through the trees they catch a glance
Of passing troops in the sun's beam—
Pennon, and plume, and flashing lance!
Forth to the world those soldiers fare,
To life, to cities, and to war!

And through the wood, another way,
Faint bugle-notes from far are borne,
Where hunters gather, staghounds bay,
Round some fair forest-lodge at morn.
Gay dames are there, in sylvan green;
Laughter and cries—those notes between!

The banners flashing through the trees
Make their blood dance and chain their eyes;
That bugle-music on the breeze
Arrests them with a charm'd surprise.
Banner by turns and bugle woo:
Ye shy recluses, follow too!

O children, what do ye reply?—
'Action and pleasure, will ye roam
Through these secluded dells to cry
And call us?—but too late ye come!
Too late for us your call ye blow,
Whose bent was taken long ago.

'Long since we pace this shadow'd nave,
We watch those yellow tapers shine,
Emblems of hope over the grave,
In the high altar's depth divine;
The organ carries to our ear
Its accents of another sphere.

'Fenced early in this cloistral round
Of reverie, of shade, of prayer,
How should we grow in other ground?
How can we flower in foreign air?
Pass, banners, pass, and bugles, cease,
And leave our desert to its peace!'

[1855]

A SOUTHERN NIGHT

The sandy spits, the shorelock'd lakes,
Melt into open, moonlit sea;
The soft Mediterranean breaks
At my feet, free.

Dotting the fields of corn and vine,
Like ghosts, the huge, gnarl'd olives stand.
Behind, that lovely mountain-line!
While, by the strand,

Cette, with its glistening houses white,
Curves with the curving beach away
To where the lighthouse beacons bright
Far in the bay.

Ah! such a night, so soft, so lone,
So moonlit, saw me once of yore
Wander unquiet, and my own
Vext heart deplore.

But now that trouble is forgot;
Thy memory, thy pain, to-night,
My brother! and thine early lot,
Possess me quite.

The murmur of this Midland deep,
Is heard to-night around thy grave,
There, where Gibraltar's cannon'd steep
O'erfrowns the wave.

For there, with bodily anguish keen,
With Indian heats at last fordone,
With public toil and private teen—
Thou sank'st, alone.

Slow to a stop, at morning grey,
I see the smoke-crown'd vessel come;
Slow round her paddles dies away
The seething foam.

A boat is lower'd from her side;
Ah, gently place him on the bench!
That spirit—if all have not yet died—
A breath might quench.

Is this the eye, the footstep fast,
The mien of youth we used to see,
Poor gallant boy! for such thou wast,
Still art, to me.

The limbs their wonted tasks refuse;
The eyes are glazed, thou canst not speak;
And whiter than thy white burnous
That wasted cheek!

Enough! The boat, with quiet shock,
Unto its haven coming nigh,
Touches, and on Gibraltar's rock
Lands thee, to die.

Ah me! Gibraltar's strand is far,
But farther yet across the brine
Thy dear wife's ashes buried are,
Remote from thine.

For there, where morning's sacred fount
Its golden rain on earth confers,
The snowy Himalayan Mount
O'ershadows hers.

Strange irony of fate, alas,
Which, for two jaded English, saves,
When from their dusty life they pass,
Such peaceful graves!

In cities should we English lie,
Where cries are rising ever new,
And men's incessant stream goes by—
We who pursue

Our business with unslackening stride,
Travers in troops, with care-fill'd breast,
The soft Mediterranean side,
The Nile, the East,

And see all sights from pole to pole,
And glance, and nod, and bustle by;
And never once possess our soul
Before we die.

Not by those hoary Indian hills,
Not by this gracious Midland sea
Whose floor to-night sweet moonshine fills,
Should our graves be.

Some sage, to whom the world was dead,
And men were specks, and life a play;
Who made the roots of trees his bed,
And once a day

With staff and gourd his way did bend
To villages and homes of man,
For food to keep him till he end
His mortal span

And the pure goal of being reach;
Hoar-headed, wrinkled, clad in white,
Without companion, without speech,
By day and night

Pondering God's mysteries untold,
  And tranquil as the glacier-snows—
He by those Indian Mountains old
    Might well repose!

Some grey crusading knight austere,
  Who bore Saint Louis company,
And came home hurt to death, and here
    Landed to die;

Some youthful troubadour, whose tongue
  Fill'd Europe once with his love-pain,
Who here outworn had sunk, and sung
    His dying strain;

Some girl, who here, from castle-bower,
  With furtive step and cheek of flame,
'Twixt myrtle-hedges all in flower
    By moonlight came

To meet her pirate-lover's ship;
  And from the wave-kiss'd marble stair
Beckon'd him on, with quivering lip
    And floating hair;

And lived some moons in happy trance,
  Then learnt his death and pined away—
Such by these waters of romance
    'Twas meet to lay!

But *you*—a grave for knight or sage,
  Romantic, solitary, still,
Oh, spent ones of a work-day age!
    Befits you ill.

So sang I; but the midnight breeze,
  Down to the brimm'd moon-charmed main
Comes softly through the olive-trees,
    And checks my strain.

I think of her, whose gentle tongue
  All plaint in her own cause controll'd;
Of thee I think, my brother! young
    In heart, high-soul'd—

That comely face, that cluster'd brow,
  That cordial hand, that bearing free,
I see them still, I see them now,
    Shall always see!

And what, but gentleness untired,
  And what, but noble feeling warm,
Wherever shown, howe'er inspired,
    Is grace, is charm?

What else is all these waters are,
  What else is steep'd in lucent sheen,
What else is bright, what else is fair,
    What else serene?

Mild o'er her grave, ye mountains, shine!
  Gently by his, ye waters, glide!
To that in you which is divine
    They were allied.

[1859] [1861]

THYRSIS

A MONODY, *to commemorate the author's friend,* Arthur Hugh Clough, *who died at Florence,* 1861

Thus yesterday, to-day, to-morrow come,
They hustle one another and they pass;
But all our hustling morrows only make
The smooth to-day of God.

From *Lucretius, An unpublished Tragedy.*

How changed is here each spot man makes or fills!
  In the two Hinkseys nothing keeps the same;
    The village-street its haunted mansion lacks,
  And from the sign is gone Sibylla's name,
    And from the roofs the twisted chimney-stacks—
      Are ye too changed, ye hills?
  See, 'tis no foot of unfamiliar men
    To-night from Oxford up your pathway strays!
    Here came I often, often, in old days—
  Thyrsis and I; we still had Thrysis then.

Runs it not here, the track by Childsworth Farm,
Past the high wood, to where the elm-tree crowns
The hill behind whose ridge the sunset flames?
The signal-elm, that looks on Ilsley Downs,
The Vale, the three lone weirs, the youthful Thames?—
This winter-eve is warm,
Humid the air! leafless, yet soft as spring,
The tender purple spray on copse and briers!
And that sweet city with her dreaming spires,
She needs not June for beauty's heightening,

Lovely all times she lies, lovely to-night!—
Only, methinks, some loss of habit's power
Befalls me wandering through this upland dim.
Once pass'd I blindfold here, at any hour;
Now seldom come I, since I came with him.
That single elm-tree bright
Against the west—I miss it! is it gone?
We prized it dearly; while it stood, we said,
Our friend, the Gipsy Scholar, was not dead;
While the tree lived, he in these fields lived on.

Too rare, too rare, grow now my visits here,
But once I knew each field, each flower, each stick;
And with the country-folk acquaintance made
By barn in threshing-time, by new-built rick.
Here, too, our shepherd-pipes we first assay'd.
Ah me! this many a year
My pipe is lost, my shepherd's-holiday!
Needs must I lose them, needs with heavy heart
Into the world and wave of men depart;
But Thyrsis of his own will went away.

It irk'd him to be here, he could not rest.
He loved each simple joy the country yields,
He loved his mates; but yet he could not keep,
For that a shadow lour'd on the fields,
Here with the shepherds and the silly sheep.
Some life of men unblest
He knew, which made him droop, and fill'd his head.
He went; his piping took a troubled sound
Of storms that rage outside our happy ground;
He could not wait their passing, he is dead.

So, some tempestuous morn in early June,
When the year's primal burst of bloom is o'er,
Before the roses and the longest day—
When garden-walks and all the grassy floor,
With blossoms red and white of fallen May,
And chestnut-flowers are strewn—
So have I heard the cuckoo's parting cry,
From the wet field, through the vext garden-trees,
Come with the volleying rain and tossing breeze:
The bloom is gone, and with the bloom go I!

Too quick despairer, wherefore wilt thou go?
Soon will the high Midsummer pomps come on,
Soon will the musk carnations break and swell,
Soon shall we have gold-dusted snapdragon,
Sweet-William with his homely cottage-smell,
And stocks in fragrant blow;
Roses that down the alleys shine afar,
And open, jasmine-muffled lattices,
And groups under the dreaming garden-trees,
And the full moon, and the white evening-star.

He hearkens not! light comer, he is flown!
What matters it? next year he will return,
And we shall have him in the sweet spring-days,
With whitening hedges, and uncrumpling fern,
And blue-bells trembling by the forest-ways,
And scent of hay new-mown.
But Thyrsis never more we swains shall see;
See him come back, and cut a smoother reed,
And blow a strain the world at last shall heed—
For Time, not Corydon, hath conquer'd thee.

Alack, for Corydon no rival now!—
But when Sicilian shepherds lost a mate,
Some good survivor with his flute would go,
Piping a ditty sad for Bion's fate,
And cross the unpermitted ferry's flow,
And relax Pluto's brow,
And make leap up with joy the beauteous head
Of Proserpine, among whose crowned hair
Are flowers, first open'd on Sicilian air;
And flute his friend, like Orpheus, from the dead.

O easy access to the hearer's grace,
When Dorian shepherds sang to Proserpine!
For she herself had trod Sicilian fields,
She knew the Dorian water's gush divine,
She knew each lily white which Enna yields,
Each rose with blushing face;
She loved the Dorian pipe, the Dorian strain.
But ah, of our poor Thames she never heard!
Her foot the Cumner cowslips never stirr'd;
And we should tease her with our plaint in vain!

Well! wind-dispersed and vain the words will be,
Yet, Thyrsis, let me give my grief its hour
In the old haunt, and find our tree-topp'd hill!
Who, if not I, for questing here hath power?
I know the wood which hides the daffodil,
I know the Fyfield tree,
I know what white, what purple fritillaries
The grassy harvest of the river-fields,
Above by Ensham, down by Sandford, yields,
And what sedged brooks are Thames's tributaries;

I know these slopes; who knows them if not I?—
But many a dingle on the loved hill-side,
With thorns once studded, old, white-blossom'd trees,
Where thick the cowslips grew, and, far descried
High tower'd the spikes of purple orchises,
Hath since our day put by
The coronals of that forgotten time;
Down each green bank hath gone the ploughboy's team,
And only in the hidden brookside gleam
Primroses, orphans of the flowery prime.

Where is the girl, who, by the boatman's door,
Above the locks, above the boating throng,
Unmoor'd our skiff, when, through the Wytham flats,
Red loosestrife and blond meadow-sweet among,
And darting swallows, and light water-gnats,
We track'd the shy Thames shore?
Where are the mowers, who, as the tiny swell
Of our boat passing heaved the river-grass,
Stood with suspended scythe to see us pass?—
They all are gone, and thou art gone as well.

Yes, thou art gone! and round me too the night
In ever-nearing circle weaves her shade.
I see her veil draw soft across the day,
I feel her slowly chilling breath invade
The cheek grown thin, the brown hair sprent with grey;
I feel her finger light
Laid pausefully upon life's headlong train;—
The foot less prompt to meet the morning dew,
The heart less bounding at emotion new,
And hope, once crush'd, less quick to spring again.

And long the way appears, which seem'd so short
To the less practised eye of sanguine youth;
And high the mountain-tops, in cloudy air,
The mountain-tops where is the throne of Truth,
Tops in life's morning-sun so bright and bare.
Unbreachable the fort
Of the long-batter'd world uplifts its wall;
And strange and vain the earthly turmoil grows,
And near and real the charm of thy repose,
And night as welcome as a friend would fall.

But hush! the upland hath a sudden loss
Of quiet!—Look, adown the dusk hill-side,
A troop of Oxford hunters going home,
As in old days, jovial and talking, ride!
From hunting with the Berkshire hounds they come.
Quick! let me fly, and cross
Into yon farther field!—'Tis done; and see,
Back'd by the sunset, which doth glorify
The orange and pale violet evening-sky,
Bare on its lonely ridge, the Tree! the Tree!

I take the omen! Eve lets down her veil,
The white fog creeps from bush to bush about,
The west unflushes, the high stars grow bright,
And in the scatter'd farms the lights come out.
I cannot reach the signal-tree to-night,
Yet, happy omen, hail!
Hear it from thy broad lucent Arno-vale
(For there thine earth-forgetting eyelids keep
The morningless and unawakening sleep
Under the flowery oleanders pale),

Hear it, O Thyrsis, still our tree is there!—
Ah, vain! These English fields, this upland dim,
These brambles pale with mist engarlanded,
That lone, sky-pointing tree, are not for him.
To a boon southern country he is fled,
And now in happier air,
Wandering with the great Mother's train divine
(And purer or more subtle soul than thee,
I trow, the mighty Mother doth not see!)
Within a folding of the Apennine,

Thou hearest the immortal chants of old!—
Putting his sickle to the perilous grain,
In the hot cornfield of the Phrygian king,
For thee the Lityerses song again
Young Daphnis with his silver voice doth sing;
Sings his Sicilian fold,
His sheep, his hapless love, his blinded eyes—
And how a call celestial round him rang,
And heavenward from the fountain-brink he sprang,
And all the marvel of the golden skies.

There thou art gone, and me thou leavest here
Sole in these fields! yet will I not despair;
Despair I will not, while I yet descry
'Neath the mild canopy of English air
That lonely tree against the western sky.
Still, still these slopes, 'tis clear,
Our Gipsy-Scholar haunts, outliving thee!
Fields where soft sheep from cages pull the hay,
Woods with anemonies in flower till May,
Know him a wanderer still; then why not me?

A fugitive and gracious light he seeks,
Shy to illumine; and I seek it too.
This does not come with houses or with gold,
With place, with honour, and a flattering crew;
'Tis not in the world's market bought and sold—
But the smooth-slipping weeks
Drop by, and leave its seeker still untired;
Out of the heed of mortals he is gone,
He wends unfollow'd, he must house alone;
Yet on he fares, by his own heart inspired.

Thou too, O Thyrsis, on like quest wast bound,
Thou wanderedst with me for a little hour!
Men gave thee nothing; but this happy quest,
If men esteem'd thee feeble, gave thee power,
If men procured thee trouble, gave thee rest.
And this rude Cumner ground,
Its fir-topped Hurst, its farms, its quiet fields,
Here cam'st thou in thy jocund youthful time,
Here was thine height of strength, thy golden prime!
And still the haunt beloved a virtue yields.

What though the music of thy rustic flute
Kept not for long its happy, country tone;
Lost it too soon, and learnt a stormy note
Of men contention-tost, of men who groan,
Which task'd thy pipe too sore, and tired thy throat—
It fail'd, and thou wast mute!
Yet hadst thou alway visions of our light,
And long with men of care thou couldst not stay,
And soon thy foot resumed its wandering way,
Left human haunt, and on alone till night.

Too rare, too rare, grow now my visits here!
'Mid city-noise, not, as with thee of yore,
Thyrsis! in reach of sheep-bells is my home.
—Then through the great town's harsh, heart-wearying roar,
Let in thy voice a whisper often come,
To chase fatigue and fear:
Why faintest thou? I wander'd till I died.
Roam on! the light we sought is shining still.
Dost thou ask proof? Our tree yet crowns the hill,
Our Scholar travels yet the loved hill-side.

[1866] [1866]

DOVER BEACH

The sea is calm to-night.
The tide is full, the moon lies fair
Upon the straits;—on the French coast, the light
Gleams, and is gone; the cliffs of England stand,
Glimmering and vast, out in the tranquil bay.
Come to the window, sweet is the night air!
Only, from the lone line of spray
Where the sea meets the moon-blanch'd land,
Listen! you hear the grating roar
Of pebbles which the waves draw back, and fling,
At their return, up the high strand,
Begin, and cease, and then again begin,
With tremulous cadence slow, and bring
The eternal note of sadness in.

Sophocles long ago
Heard it on the Ægæan, and it brought
Into his mind the turbid ebb and flow
Of human misery; we
Find also in the sound a thought,
Hearing it by this distant northern sea.

The Sea of Faith
Was once, too, at the full, and round earth's shore
Lay like the folds of a bright girdle furl'd.
But now I only hear
Its melancholy, long, withdrawing roar,
Retreating, to the breath

Of the night-wind down the vast edges drear
And naked shingles of the world.

Ah, love, let us be true
To one another! for the world, which seems
To lie before us like a land of dreams,
So various, so beautiful, so new,
Hath really neither joy, nor love, nor light,
Nor certitude, nor peace, nor help for pain;
And we are here as on a darkling plain
Swept with confused alarms of struggle and flight,
Where ignorant armies clash by night.

[1851–2?] [1867]

THE LAST WORD

Creep into thy narrow bed,
Creep, and let no more be said!
Vain thy onset! all stands fast;
Thou thyself must break at last.

Let the long contention cease!
Geese are swans and swans are geese.
Let them have it how they will!
Thou art tired; best be still!

They out-talked thee, hissed thee, tore thee.
Better men fared thus before thee;
Fired their ringing shot and passed,
Hotly charged—and broke at last.

Charge once more, then, and be dumb!
Let the victors, when they come,
When the forts of folly fall,
Find thy body by the wall.

[1867]

RUGBY CHAPEL

NOVEMBER, 1857

Coldly, sadly descends
The autumn evening. The Field
Strewn with its dank yellow drifts
Of wither'd leaves, and the elms,
Fade into dimness apace,
Silent;—hardly a shout
From a few boys late at their play!
The lights come out in the street,
In the school-room windows;—but cold,
Solemn, unlighted, austere,
Through the gathering darkness, arise
The chapel-walls, in whose bound
Thou, my father! art laid.

There thou dost lie, in the gloom
Of the autumn evening. But ah!
That word, *gloom,* to my mind
Brings thee back in the light
Of thy radiant vigour again;
In the gloom of November we pass'd
Days not dark at thy side;
Seasons impair'd not the ray
Of thy buoyant cheerfulness clear.
Such thou wast! and I stand
In the autumn evening, and think
Of bygone autumns with thee.

Fifteen years have gone round
Since thou arosest to tread,
In the summer morning, the road
Of death, at a call unforeseen,
Sudden. For fifteen years,
We who till then in thy shade
Rested as under the boughs
Of a mighty oak, have endured
Sunshine and rain as we might,
Bare, unshaded, alone,
Lacking the shelter of thee.

O strong soul, by what shore
Tarriest thou now? For that force,
Surely, has not been left vain!
Somewhere, surely, afar,
In the sounding labour-house vast
Of being, is practised that strength,
Zealous, beneficent, firm!

Yes, in some far-shining sphere,
Conscious or not of the past,
Still thou performest the word
Of the Spirit in whom thou dost live—
Prompt, unwearied, as here!
Still thou upraisest with zeal
The humble good from the ground,
Sternly repressest the bad!
Still, like a trumpet, dost rouse
Those who with half-open eyes
Tread the border-land dim
'Twixt vice and virtue; reviv'st,
Succourest!—this was thy work,
This was thy life upon earth.

What is the course of the life
Of mortal men on the earth?—

Most men eddy about
Here and there—eat and drink,
Chatter and love and hate,
Gather and squander, are raised
Aloft, are hurl'd in the dust,
Striving blindly, achieving
Nothing, and then they die—
Perish;—and no one asks
Who or what they have been,
More than he asks what waves
In the moonlit solitudes mild
Of the midmost Ocean, have swell'd,
Foam'd for a moment, and gone.

And there are some, whom a thirst
Ardent, unquenchable, fires,
Not with the crowd to be spent,
Not without aim to go round
In an eddy of purposeless dust,
Effort unmeaning and vain.
Ah yes! some of us strive
Not without action to die
Fruitless, but something to snatch
From dull oblivion, nor all
Glut the devouring grave!
We, we have chosen our path—
Path to a clear-purposed goal,
Path of advance!—but it leads
A long, steep journey, through sunk
Gorges, o'er mountains in snow.
Cheerful, with friends, we set forth—
Then, on the height, comes the storm.

Thunder crashes from rock
To rock, the cataracts reply,
Lightnings dazzle our eyes.
Roaring torrents have breach'd
The track, the stream-bed descends
In the place where the wayfarer once
Planted his footstep—the spray
Boils o'er its borders! aloft
The unseen snow-beds dislodge
Their hanging ruin; alas,
Havoc is made in our train!
Friends who set forth at our side
Falter, are lost in the storm.
We, we only, are left!
With frowning foreheads, with lips
Sternly compress'd, we strain on,
On—and at nightfall at last
Come to the end of our way,
To the lonely inn 'mid the rocks;
Where the gaunt and taciturn host
Stands on the threshold, the wind
Shaking his thin white hairs—
Holds his lantern to scan
Our storm-beat figures, and asks:
Whom in our party we bring?
Whom we have left in the snow?

Sadly we answer: We bring
Only ourselves! we lost
Sight of the rest in the storm.
Hardly ourselves we fought through,
Stripp'd, without friends, as we are.
Friends, companions, and train
The avalanche swept from our side.

But thou would'st not *alone*
Be saved, my father! *alone*
Conquer and come to thy goal,
Leaving the rest in the wild.
We were weary, and we
Fearful, and we, in our march,
Fain to drop down and to die.
Still thou turnedst, and still
Beckonedst the trembler, and still
Gavest the weary thy hand.

If, in the paths of the world,
Stones might have wounded thy feet,
Toil or dejection have tried
Thy spirit, of that we saw
Nothing—to us thou wast still
Cheerful, and helpful, and firm!
Therefore to thee it was given
Many to save with thyself;
And, at the end of thy day,
O faithful shepherd! to come,
Bringing thy sheep in thy hand.

And through thee I believe
In the noble and great who are gone;
Pure souls honour'd and blest
By former ages, who else—

Such, so soulless, so poor,
Is the race of men whom I see—
Seem'd but a dream of the heart,
Seem'd but a cry of desire.

Yes! I believe that there lived
Others like thee in the past,
Not like the men of the crowd
Who all round me to-day
Bluster or cringe, and make life
Hideous, and arid, and vile;
But souls temper'd with fire,

Fervent, heroic, and good,
Helpers and friends of mankind.

Servants of God!—or sons
Shall I not call you? because
Not as servants ye knew
Your Father's innermost mind,
His, who unwillingly sees
One of his little ones lost—
Yours is the praise, if mankind
Hath not as yet in its march
Fainted, and fallen, and died!

See! in the rocks of the world
Marches the host of mankind,
A feeble, wavering line.
Where are they tending?—A God
Marshall'd them, gave them their goal.
Ah, but the way is so long!
Years they have been in the wild!
Sore thirst plagues them, the rocks,
Rising all round, overawe;
Factions divide them; their host
Threatens to break, to dissolve.
Ah, keep, keep them combined!
Else, of the myriads who fill
That army, not one shall arrive;
Sole they shall stray; in the rocks
Labour for ever in vain,
Die one by one in the waste.

Then, in such hour of need
Of your fainting, dispirited race,
Ye, like angels, appear,
Radiant with ardour divine!
Beacons of hope, ye appear!
Languor is not in your heart,
Weakness is not in your word,
Weariness not on your brow.
Ye alight in our van! at your voice,
Panic, despair, flee away.
Ye move through the ranks, recall
The stragglers, refresh the outworn,
Praise, re-inspire the brave!
Order, courage, return.
Eyes rekindling, and prayers,
Follow your steps as ye go.
Ye fill up the gaps in our files,
Strengthen the wavering line,
Stablish, continue our march,
On, to the bound of the waste,
On, to the City of God.

[1858?] [1867]

WESTMINSTER ABBEY

JULY 25, 1881

(*The Day of Burial, in the Abbey, of* Arthur Penrhyn Stanley, *Dean of Westminster.*)

What! for a term so scant
Our shining visitant
Cheer'd us, and now is pass'd into the night?
Couldst thou no better keep, O Abbey old,
The boon thy dedication-sign foretold,
The presence of that gracious inmate, light?—
A child of light appear'd;
Hither he came, late-born and long-desired,
And to men's hearts this ancient place endear'd;
What, is the happy glow so soon expired?

—Rough was the winter eve;
Their craft the fishes leave,
And down over the Thames the darkness drew.
One still lags last, and turns, and eyes the Pile
Huge in the gloom, across in Thorney Isle,

King Sebert's work, the wondrous Minster new.
—'Tis Lambeth now, where then

They moor'd their boats among the bulrush stems;
  And that new Minster in the matted fen
The world-famed Abbey by the westering Thames.

  His mates are gone, and he
  For mist can scarcely see
A strange wayfarer coming to his side—
  Who bade him loose his boat, and fix his oar,
  And row him straightway to the further shore,
And wait while he did there a space abide.
  The fisher awed obeys,
That voice had note so clear of sweet command;
  Through pouring tide he pulls, and drizzling haze,
And sets his freight ashore on Thorney strand.

  The Minster's outlined mass
  Rose dim from the morass,
And thitherward the stranger took his way.
  Lo, on a sudden all the Pile is bright!
  Nave, choir and transept glorified with light,
While tongues of fire on coign and carving play!
  And heavenly odours fair
Come streaming with the floods of glory in,
  And carols float along the happy air,
As if the reign of joy did now begin.

  Then all again is dark;
  And by the fisher's bark
The unknown passenger returning stands.
  O Saxon fisher! thou hast had with thee
  The fisher from the Lake of Galilee—
So saith he, blessing him with outspread hands;
  Then fades, but speaks the while:
At dawn thou to King Sebert shalt relate
  How his St. Peter's Church in Thorney Isle
Peter, his friend, with light did consecrate.

  Twelve hundred years and more
  Along the holy floor
Pageants have pass'd, and tombs of mighty kings
  Efface the humbler graves of Sebert's line,
  And, as years sped, the minster-aisles divine
Grew used to the approach of Glory's wings.
  Arts came, and arms, and law,
And majesty, and sacred form and fear;
  Only that primal guest the fisher saw,
Light, only light, was slow to reappear.

  The Saviour's happy light,
  Wherein at first was dight
His boon of life and immortality,
  In desert ice of subtleties was spent
  Or drown'd in mists of childish wonderment,

Fond fancies here, there false philosophy!
And harsh the temper grew
Of men with mind thus darken'd and astray;
And scarce the boon of life could struggle through,
For want of light which should the boon convey.

Yet in this latter time
The promise of the prime
Seem'd to come true at last, O Abbey old!
It seem'd a child of light did bring the dower
Foreshown thee in thy consecration-hour,
And in thy courts his shining freight unroll'd:
Bright wits, and instincts sure,
And goodness warm, and truth without alloy,
And temper sweet, and love of all things pure,
And joy in light, and power to spread the joy.

And on that countenance bright
Shone oft so high a light,
That to my mind there came how, long ago
Lay on the hearth, amid a fiery ring,
The charm'd babe of the Eleusinian king—
His nurse, the Mighty Mother, will'd it so.
Warm in her breast, by day,
He slumber'd, and ambrosia balm'd the child;
But all night long amid the flames he lay,
Upon the hearth, and play'd with them, and smiled.

But once, at midnight deep,
His mother woke from sleep,
And saw her babe amidst the fire, and scream'd
A sigh the Goddess gave, and with a frown
Pluck'd from the fire the child, and laid him down;
Then raised her face, and glory round her stream'd.
The mourning-stole no more
Mantled her form, no more her head was bow'd;
But raiment of celestial sheen she wore,
And beauty fill'd her, and she spake aloud:—

"O ignorant race of man!
Achieve your good who can,
If your own hands the good begun undo?
Had human cry not marr'd the work divine,
Immortal had I made this boy of mine;
But now his head to death again is due
And I have now no power
Unto this pious household to repay
Their kindness shown me in my wandering hour."
—She spake, and from the portal pass'd away.

The Boy his nurse forgot,
And bore a mortal lot.

Long since, his name is heard on earth no more.
In some chance battle on Cithaeron-side
The nursling of the Mighty Mother died,
And went where all his fathers went before.
—On thee too, in thy day
Of Childhood, Arthur! did some check have power.
That, radiant though thou wert, thou couldst
but stay,
Bringer of heavenly light, a human hour?

Therefore our happy guest
Knew care, and knew unrest,
And weakness warn'd him, and he fear'd decline.
And in the grave he laid a cherish'd wife,
And men ignoble harass'd him with strife,
And deadly airs his strength did undermine.
Then from his Abbey fades
The sound beloved of his victorious breath;
And light's fair nursling stupor first invades,
And next the crowning impotence of death.

But hush! This mournful strain,
Which would of death complain,
The oracle forbade, not ill-inspired.—
That Pair, whose head did plan, whose hands did
forge
The Temple in the pure Parnassian gorge,
Finish'd their work, and then a meed required.
"Seven days," the God replied,
"Live happy, then expect your perfect meed!"
Quiet in sleep, the seventh night, they died.
Death, death was judged the boon supreme indeed.

And truly he who here
Hath run his bright career,
And served men nobly, and acceptance found,
And borne to light and right his witness high,
What could he better wish than then to die,
And wait the issue, sleeping underground?
Why should he pray to range
Down the long age of truth that ripens slow;
And break his heart with all the baffling change,
And all the tedious tossing to and fro?

For this and that way swings
The flux of mortal things,
Though moving inly to one far-set goal.—
What had our Arthur gain'd, to stop and see,
After light's term, a term of cecity,
A Church once large and then grown strait in soul?
To live, and see arise,
Alternating with wisdom's too short reign,
Folly revived, re-furbish'd sophistries,
And pullulating rites externe and vain?

Ay me! 'Tis deaf, that ear
Which joy'd my voice to hear;
Yet would I not disturb thee from thy tomb,
Thus sleeping in thine Abbey's friendly shade,
And the rough waves of life for ever laid!
I would not break thy rest, nor change thy doom.
Even as my father, thou—
Even as that loved, that well-recorded friend—
Hast thy commission done; ye both may now
Wait for the leaven to work, the let to end.

And thou, O Abbey grey!
Predestined to the ray
By this dear guest over thy precinct shed—
Fear not but that thy light once more shall burn,
Once more thine immemorial gleam return,
Though sunk be now this bright, this gracious head!
Let but the light appear
And thy transfigured walls be touch'd with flame—
Our Arthur will again be present here,
Again from lip to lip will pass his name.

[1882]

DANTE GABRIEL ROSSETTI

CHRONOLOGICAL TABLE

1828, May 12, born in London, his father a Neapolitan political exile, subsequently professor of Italian at King's College, University of London, his mother a former governess, half-English, half-Italian.

1837–42 Attended King's College School.

1842–6 Attended Cary's Academy (of Art).

1846 Entered Antique School of the British Academy.

1848 Formation of the Pre-Raphaelite Brotherhood, in which the dominant spirits were Rossetti, Millais and Hunt.

1849 Exhibited for the first time (The Girlhood of the Virgin).

1849–50 *The Germ* (two numbers) followed by *Art and Poetry* (two numbers). Appearance of the first version of "The Blessed Damozel."

1854 Patronage from Ruskin.

1856 *Oxford and Cambridge Magazine* (with second version of the "Blessed Damozel").

1860 Marriage to Elizabeth Siddal, after ten years of intimacy, during most of which he had been engaged to her.

1861 *The Early Italian Poets* (translations).

1862 Death of his wife.

1869 Disinterment of the poems buried with his wife.

1870 *Poems.*

1871 Bitterly assailed by Robert Buchanan in "The Fleshly School of Poetry."

1874 *Dante and His Circle* (a rearrangement of the translations of 1861).

1881 *Poems.*
Ballads and Sonnets.

1882 Died April 14, and buried at Birchington.

To Morris poetry was one of many arts; to Rossetti it was, more dangerously, the lesser of two. What education he received—and it was meagre and haphazard—was a painter's; during his formative years his associates were painters and sculptors; his reputation as a painter long preceded any recognition, beyond a very narrow circle, as a poet. His determination to make the most of his poetic gift had to wait upon the disturbance of his sight and his terror of blindness. The preference he gave to painting over poetry is readily explained: he was strangely sensitive to visual impressions which made a large part of his life, as of his poetry; and what he had to express in artistic form had, he thought, been many times uttered by poets, never by painters.

His first collection of verse appeared when he was forty-two; and at forty-two he was physically and spiritually a broken man. Prior to its appearance, some lyrics which had come out in magazines—notably in the two Pre-Raphaelite organs, *The Germ* and the *Oxford and Cambridge Magazine*—had led to recognition within the Brotherhood and among their enthusiastic camp-followers as a poet of some distinction. That was all; that was as much as poems as perfect as "The Blessed Damozel" had been able to realize. The collection of 1870 was, to the somewhat larger public it could reach, the first expression in another art of a mind which thanks to Ruskin's advocacy had been accepted as that of one of the master-painters of the time. Apart from its technical excellence and its Italianate traits, the collection was such poetry as one might expect a great painter to write. Tennyson had revealed an unprecedented power in combining the accurate and the richly suggestive in his rendering of specific objects and persons; Rossetti went notably beyond him and strove to make words perform what only colours had performed before. It was also clear to anyone who was well read in poetry that the author of the collection was steeped in Dante and the poets of his age. Rossetti loved the rich soft music of serious Italian poetry; and he contrived to produce effects reminiscent of the Italian with the rougher, more varied English idiom. At times his sweetness was rich to suffocation; painter as he was, his pictures in words were too often blurred by the verbal music in which he enfolded them. He was Italianate also in his mode of dealing with love, or at any rate he was alien to the English temperament. Watts-Dunton was to say in an admirable formula that he had removed asceticism from mysticism. He was a mystic of love; his mysticism insisted on the contribution of fleshly love to the life of the spirit and insisted upon it heavily. Whether in so doing he betrayed the doctrine of Dante and his colleagues in thirteenth- and twelfth-century Italy has been sharply debated; but this at least may be said—his poetry of love would not have puzzled and frightened his readers if they had been Italian. About human life apart from love he had little to say, and that little was not deeply felt or deeply thought. He had escaped from the bookish life of his father, and rejected along with erudition the whole range of political and economic ideas. Ruskin's *Unto This Last*, to so many Victorians a crucial moment in their development, he dismissed as unreadable bosh. Life at first hand he knew but slightly: he kept to painters and connoisseurs and beautiful women.

The collection of 1870 was moderately popular. However a year after its publication an insignificant critic, to gratify a spite, directed against it one of the bitterest attacks of the time. Rossetti was tragically dejected. Most of his life he had managed to keep his works sheltered from such public verdicts. After the very first years of his career as a painter, he seldom exhibited his pictures: usually they passed immediately from his studio to the walls of a purchaser, who usually had been kept fuming for them months or even years. His original verse had appeared in magazines of limited circulation, commonly unsigned. Now morbidly exaggerating the effectiveness of an attack which had included Morris's and Swinburne's as well as his own work, his feelings were intensified, since in the assailed collection he had printed the poems in which he had so intimately celebrated his love for his wife, the poems he had buried with her and then seven years later, with the Home Secretary's authorization, disinterred. During the decade of life that remained to him, he was haunted by delusions of persecution: he broke with almost all his friends, saw attacks on himself in words, spoken or written, which had nothing to do with him, heard voices gibing at him when he was by himself, and on at least one evening, alone in his room, sought to take his life with an overdose of laudanum.

Nevertheless he continued to paint and to write. Many of his greatest paintings belong to the last shattered decade of his life; and to this period belong also some of his greatest poems, notably the greatest of his ballads in which there is an intensity of hallucinated terror in which Coleridge alone surpassed him. These and other poems he collected in the year before he died, revealing in the new poems a wider range of power, if less perfect performance, than in the collection of 1870. In comparison with the great Victorian poets Rossetti was narrow and strained; but within his own range he makes a contribution to poetry which is, despite impassable limits and evident defects, irreplaceable.

THE BLESSED DAMOZEL

The blessed damozel leaned out
  From the gold bar of Heaven;
Her eyes were deeper than the depth
  Of waters stilled at even;
She had three lilies in her hand,
  And the stars in her hair were seven.

Her robe, ungirt from clasp to hem,
  No wrought flowers did adorn,
But a white rose of Mary's gift,
  For service meetly worn;
Her hair that lay along her back
  Was yellow like ripe corn.

Herseemed she scarce had been a day
  One of God's choristers;
The wonder was not yet quite gone
  From that still look of hers;
Albeit, to them she left, her day
  Had counted as ten years.

(To one, it is ten years of years.
  . . . Yet now, and in this place,
Surely she leaned o'er me—her hair
  Fell all about my face. . . .
Nothing: the autumn fall of leaves.
  The whole year sets apace.)

It was the rampart of God's house
  That she was standing on;
By God built over the sheer depth
  The which is Space begun;
So high, that looking downward thence
  She scarce could see the sun.

It lies in Heaven, across the flood
  Of ether, as a bridge.
Beneath, the tides of day and night
  With flame and darkness ridge
The void, as low as where this earth
  Spins like a fretful midge.

Around her, lovers, newly met
  'Mid deathless love's acclaims,

Spoke evermore among themselves
  Their heart-remembered names;
And the souls mounting up to God
  Went by her like thin flames.

And still she bowed herself and stooped
  Out of the circling charm;
Until her bosom must have made
  The bar she leaned on warm,
And the lilies lay as if asleep
  Along her bended arm.

From the fixed place of Heaven she saw
  Time like a pulse shake fierce
Through all the worlds. Her gaze still strove
  Within the gulf to pierce
Its path; and now she spoke as when
  The stars sang in their spheres.

The sun was gone now; the curled moon
  Was like a little feather
Fluttering far down the gulf; and now
  She spoke through the still weather.
Her voice was like the voice the stars
  Had when they sang together.

(Ah sweet! Even now, in that bird's song,
  Strove not her accents there,
Fain to be hearkened? When those bells
  Possessed the mid-day air,
Strove not her steps to reach my side
  Down all the echoing stair?)

'I wish that he were come to me,
  For he will come,' she said.
'Have I not prayed in Heaven?—on earth;
  Lord, Lord, has he not pray'd?
Are not two prayers a perfect strength?
  And shall I feel afraid?

'When round his head the aureole clings,
  And he is clothed in white,
I'll take his hand and go with him
  To the deep wells of light;
We will step down as to a stream,
  And bathe there in God's sight.

'We two will stand beside that shrine,
  Occult, withheld, untrod,
Whose lamps are stirred continually
  With prayer sent up to God;
And see our old prayers, granted, melt
  Each like a little cloud.

'We two will lie i' the shadow of
  That living mystic tree
Within whose secret growth the Dove
  Is sometimes felt to be,
While every leaf that His plumes touch
  Saith His Name audibly.

'And I myself will teach to him,
  I myself, lying so,
The songs I sing here; which his voice
  Shall pause in, hushed and slow,
And find some knowledge at each pause,
  Or some new thing to know.'

(Alas! We two, we two, thou say'st!
  Yea, one wast thou with me
That once of old. But shall God lift
  To endless unity
The soul whose likeness with thy soul
  Was but its love for thee?)

'We two,' she said, 'will seek the groves
  Where the lady Mary is,
With her five handmaidens, whose names
  Are five sweet symphonies,
Cecily, Gertrude, Magdalen,
  Margaret and Rosalys.

'Circlewise sit they, with bound locks
  And foreheads garlanded;
Into the fine cloth white like flame
  Weaving the golden thread,
To fashion the birth-robes for them
  Who are just born, being dead.

'He shall fear, haply, and be dumb:
  Then will I lay my cheek
To his, and tell about our love,
  Not once abashed or weak:
And the dear Mother will approve
  My pride, and let me speak.

'Herself shall bring us, hand in hand,
  To Him round whom all souls
Kneel, the clear-ranged unnumbered heads
  Bowed with their aureoles:
And angels meeting us shall sing
  To their citherns and citoles.

'There will I ask of Christ the Lord
  Thus much for him and me:—
Only to live as once on earth
  With Love,—only to be,
As then awhile, for ever now
  Together, I and he.'

She gazed and listened and then said,
Less sad of speech than mild,—
'All this is when he comes.' She ceased.
The light thrilled towards her, fill'd
With angels in strong level flight.
Her eyes prayed, and she smil'd.

(I saw her smile.) But soon their path
Was vague in distant spheres;
And then she cast her arms along
The golden barriers,
And laid her face between her hands,
And wept. (I heard her tears.)

[1847] [1850]

MY SISTER'S SLEEP

She fell asleep on Christmas Eve:
At length the long-ungranted shade
Of weary eyelids overweigh'd
The pain nought else might yet relieve.

Our mother, who had leaned all day
Over the bed from chime to chime,
Then raised herself for the first time,
And as she sat her down, did pray.

Her little work-table was spread
With work to finish. For the glare
Made by her candle, she had care
To work some distance from the bed.

Without, there was a cold moon up,
Of winter radiance sheer and thin;
The hollow halo it was in
Was like an icy crystal cup.

Through the small room, with subtle sound
Of flame, by vents the fireshine drove
And reddened. In its dim alcove
The mirror shed a clearness round.

I had been sitting up some nights,
And my tired mind felt weak and blank;
Like a sharp strengthening wine it drank
The stillness and the broken lights.

Twelve struck. That sound, by dwindling years
Heard in each hour, crept off; and then
The ruffled silence spread again,
Like water that a pebble stirs.

Our mother rose from where she sat:
Her needles, as she laid them down,
Met lightly, and her silken gown
Settled: no other noise than that.

'Glory unto the Newly Born!'
So, as said angels, she did say;
Because we were in Christmas Day,
Though it would still be long till morn.

Just then in the room over us
There was a pushing back of chairs,
As some who had sat unawares
So late, now heard the hour, and rose.

With anxious softly-stepping haste
Our mother went where Margaret lay,
Fearing the sounds o'erhead—should they
Have broken her long watched-for rest!

She stooped an instant, calm, and turned;
But suddenly turned back again;
And all her features seemed in pain
With woe, and her eyes gazed and yearned.

For my part, I but hid my face,
And held my breath, and spoke no word:
There was none spoken; but I heard
The silence for a little space.

Our mother bowed herself and wept:
And both my arms fell, and I said,
'God knows I knew that she was dead.'
And there, all white, my sister slept.

Then kneeling, upon Christmas morn
A little after twelve o'clock
We said, ere the first quarter struck,
'Christ's blessing on the newly born!'

[1847] [1850]

THE PORTRAIT

This is her picture as she was:
It seems a thing to wonder on,
As though mine image in the glass
Should tarry when myself am gone.
I gaze until she seems to stir,—
Until mine eyes almost aver
That now, even now, the sweet lips part
To breathe the words of the sweet heart:—
And yet the earth is over her.

Alas! even such the thin-drawn ray
That makes the prison-depths more rude,—
The drip of water night and day
Giving a tongue to solitude.
Yet only this, of love's whole prize,
Remains; save what in mournful guise
Takes counsel with my soul alone,—
Save what is secret and unknown,
Below the earth, above the skies.

In painting her I shrined her face
'Mid mystic trees, where light falls in
Hardly at all; a covert place
Where you might think to find a din
Of doubtful talk, and a live flame
Wandering, and many a shape whose name
Not itself knoweth, and old dew,
And your own footsteps meeting you,
And all things going as they came.

A deep dim wood; and there she stands
As in that wood that day: for so
Was the still movement of her hands
And such the pure line's gracious flow.
And passing fair the type must seem,
Unknown the presence and the dream.
'Tis she: though of herself, alas!
Less than her shadow on the grass
Or than her image in the stream.

That day we met there, I and she
One with the other all alone;
And we were blithe; yet memory
Saddens those hours, as when the moon
Looks upon daylight. And with her
I stooped to drink the spring-water,
Athirst where other waters sprang:
And where the echo is, she sang,—
My soul another echo there.

But when that hour my soul won strength
For words whose silence wastes and kills,
Dull raindrops smote us, and at length
Thundered the heat within the hills.
That eve I spoke those words again
Beside the pelted window-pane;
And there she hearkened what I said,
With under-glances that surveyed
The empty pastures blind with rain.

Next day the memories of these things,
Like leaves through which a bird has flown,
Still vibrated with Love's warm wings;
Till I must make them all my own
And paint this picture. So, 'twixt ease
Of talk and sweet long silences,
She stood among the plants in bloom
At windows of a summer room,
To feign the shadow of the trees.

And as I wrought, while all above
And all around was fragrant air,
In the sick burthen of my love
It seemed each sun-thrilled blossom there
Beat like a heart among the leaves.
O heart that never beats nor heaves,
In that one darkness lying still,
What now to thee my love's great will,
Or the fine web the sunshine weaves?

For now doth daylight disavow
Those days—nought left to see or hear.
Only in solemn whispers now
At night-time these things reach mine ear;
When the leaf-shadows at a breath
Shrink in the road, and all the heath,
Forest and water, far and wide,
In limpid starlight glorified,
Lie like the mystery of death.

Last night at last I could have slept,
And yet delayed my sleep till dawn,
Still wandering. Then it was I wept:
For unawares I came upon
Those glades where once she walked with me:
And as I stood there suddenly,
All wan with traversing the night,
Upon the desolate verge of light
Yearned loud the iron-bosomed sea.

Even so, where Heaven holds breath and hears
The beating heart of Love's own breast,—
Where round the secret of all spheres
All angels lay their wings to rest,—
How shall my soul stand rapt and awed,
When, by the new birth borne abroad
Throughout the music of the suns,
It enters in her soul at once
And knows the silence there for God!

Here with her face doth memory sit
Meanwhile, and wait the day's decline,
Till other eyes shall look from it,
Eyes of the spirit's Palestine,

Even than the old gaze tenderer:
While hopes and aims long lost with her
Stand round her image side by side,
Like tombs of pilgrims that have died
About the Holy Sepulchre.

[1847] [1870]

JENNY

'Vengeance of Jenny's case! Fie on her! Never name her, child!'—(*Mrs. Quickly*.)

Lazy laughing languid Jenny,
Fond of a kiss and fond of a guinea,
Whose head upon my knee to-night
Rests for a while, as if grown light
With all our dances and the sound
To which the wild tunes spun you round:
Fair Jenny mine, the thoughtless queen
Of kisses which the blush between
Could hardly make much daintier;
Whose eyes are as blue skies, whose hair
Is countless gold incomparable:
Fresh flower, scarce touched with signs that tell
Of Love's exuberant hotbed:—Nay,
Poor flower left torn since yesterday
Until to-morrow leave you bare;
Poor handful of bright spring-water
Flung in the whirlpool's shrieking face,
Poor shameful Jenny, full of grace
Thus with your head upon my knee;—
Whose person or whose purse may be
The lodestar of your reverie?

This room of yours, my Jenny, looks
A change from mine so full of books,
Whose serried ranks hold fast, forsooth,
So many captive hours of youth,—
The hours they thieve from day and night
To make one's cherished work come right,
And leave it wrong for all their theft,
Even as to-night my work was left:
Until I vowed that since my brain
And eyes of dancing seemed so fain,
My feet should have some dancing too:—
And thus it was I met with you.
Well, I suppose 'twas hard to part,
For here I am. And now, sweetheart,
You seem too tired to get to bed.

It was a careless life I led
When rooms like this were scarce so strange
Not long ago. What breeds the change,—
The many aims or the few years?
Because to-night it all appears
Something I do not know again.

The cloud's not danced out of my brain,—
The cloud that made it turn and swim
While hour by hour the books grew dim.
Why, Jenny, as I watch you there,—
For all your wealth of loosened hair,
Your silk ungirdled and unlac'd
And warm sweets open to the waist,
All golden in the lamplight's gleam,—
You know not what a book you seem,
Half-read by lightning in a dream!
How should you know, my Jenny? Nay,
And I should be ashamed to say:—
Poor beauty, so well worth a kiss!
But while my thought runs on like this
With wasteful whims more than enough,
I wonder what you're thinking of.

If of myself you think at all,
What is the thought?—conjectural
On sorry matters best unsolved?—
Or inly is each grace revolved
To fit me with a lure?—or (sad
To think!) perhaps you're merely glad
That I'm not drunk or ruffianly
And let you rest upon my knee.

For sometimes, were the truth confess'd,
You're thankful for a little rest,—
Glad from the crush to rest within,
From the heart-sickness and the din
Where envy's voice at virtue's pitch
Mocks you because your gown is rich;
And from the pale girl's dumb rebuke,
Whose ill-clad grace and toil-worn look
Proclaim the strength that keeps her weak
And other nights than yours bespeak;
And from the wise unchildish elf,
To schoolmate lesser than himself
Pointing you out, what thing you are:—
Yes, from the daily jeer and jar,
From shame and shame's outbraving too,
Is rest not sometimes sweet to you?—
But most from the hatefulness of man
Who spares not to end what he began,
Whose acts are ill and his speech ill,
Who, having used you at his will,
Thrusts you aside, as when I dine
I serve the dishes and the wine.

Well, handsome Jenny mine, sit up,
I've filled our glasses, let us sup,
And do not let me think of you,
Lest shame of yours suffice for two.
What, still so tired? Well, well then, keep
Your head there, so you do not sleep;
But that the weariness may pass
And leave you merry, take this glass.
Ah! lazy lily hand, more bless'd
If ne'er in rings it had been dress'd
Nor ever by a glove conceal'd!

Behold the lilies of the field,
They toil not neither do they spin;
(So doth the ancient text begin,—
Not of such rest as one of these
Can share.) Another rest and ease.
Along each summer-sated path
From its new lord the garden hath,
Than that whose spring in blessings ran
Which praised the bounteous husbandman,
Ere yet, in days of hankering breath,
The lilies sickened unto death.

What, Jenny, are your lilies dead?
Aye, and the snow-white leaves are spread
Like winter on the garden-bed.
But you had roses left in May,—
They were not gone too. Jenny, nay,
But must your roses die, and those
Their purified buds that should unclose?
Even so; the leaves are curled apart,
Still red as from the broken heart,
And here's the naked stem of thorns.

Nay, nay, mere words. Here nothing warns
As yet of winter. Sickness here
Or want alone could waken fear,—
Nothing but passion wrings a tear.
Except when there may rise unsought
Haply at times a passing thought
Of the old days which seem to be
Much older than any history
That is written in any book;
When she would lie in fields and look
Along the ground through the blown grass,
And wonder where the city was,
Far out of sight, whose broil and bale
They told her then for a child's tale.

Jenny, you know the city now,
A child can tell the tale there, how
Some things which are not yet enroll'd
In market-lists are bought and sold
Even till the early Sunday light,
When Saturday night is market-night
Everywhere, be it dry or wet,
And market-night in the Haymarket.
Our learned London children know,
Poor Jenny, all your pride and woe;
Have seen your lifted silken skirt
Advertise dainties through the dirt;
Have seen your coach-wheels splash rebuke
On virtue; and have learned your look
When, wealth and health slipped past, you stare
Along the streets alone, and there,
Round the long park, across the bridge,
The cold lamps at the pavement's edge
Wind on together and apart,
A fiery serpent for your heart.

Let the thoughts pass, an empty cloud!
Suppose I were to think aloud,—
What if to her all this were said?
Why, as a volume seldom read
Being opened halfway shuts again,
So might the pages of her brain
Be parted at such words, and thence
Close back upon the dusty sense.
For is there hue or shape defin'd
In Jenny's desecrated mind,
Where all contagious currents meet,
A Lethe of the middle street?
Nay, it reflects not any face,
Nor sound is in its sluggish pace,
But as they coil those eddies clot,
And night and day remember not.

Why, Jenny, you're asleep at last!—
Asleep, poor Jenny, hard and fast,—
So young and soft and tired; so fair,
With chin thus nestled in your hair,
Mouth quiet, eyelids almost blue
As if some sky of dreams shone through!

Just as another woman sleeps!
Enough to throw one's thoughts in heaps
Of doubt and horror,—what to say
Or think,—this awful secret sway,
The potter's power over the clay!
Of the same lump (it has been said)
For honour and dishonour made,
Two sister vessels. Here is one.

My cousin Nell is fond of fun,
And fond of dress, and change, and praise,

So mere a woman in her ways:
And if her sweet eyes rich in youth
Are like her lips that tell the truth,
My cousin Nell is fond of love.
And she's the girl I'm proudest of.
Who does not prize her, guard her well?
The love of change, in cousin Nell,
Shall find the best and hold it dear:
The unconquered mirth turn quieter
Not through her own, through others' woe:
The conscious pride of beauty glow
Beside another's pride in her,
One little part of all they share.
For Love himself shall ripen these
In a kind of soil to just increase
Through years of fertilizing peace.

Of the same lump (as it is said)
For honour and dishonour made,
Two sister vessels. Here is one.

It makes a goblin of the sun.

So pure,—so fall'n! How dare to think
Of the first common kindred link?
Yet, Jenny, till the world shall burn
It seems that all things take their turn;
And who shall say but this fair tree
May need, in changes that may be,
Your children's children's charity?
Scorned then, no doubt, as you are scorn'd!
Shall no man hold his pride forewarn'd
Till in the end, the Day of Days,
At Judgement, one of his own race,
As frail and lost as you, shall rise,—
His daughter, with his mother's eyes?

How Jenny's clock ticks on the shelf!
Might not the dial scorn itself
That has such hours to register?
Yet as to me, even so to her
Are golden sun and silver moon,
In daily largesse of earth's boon,
Counted for life-coins to one tune.
And if, as blindfold fates are toss'd,
Through some one man this life be lost,
Shall soul not somehow pay for soul?

Fair shines the gilded aureole
In which our highest painters place
Some living woman's simple face.
And the stilled features thus descried
As Jenny's long throat droops aside,—
The shadows where the cheeks are thin,
And pure wide curve from ear to chin,—
With Raffael's or Da Vinci's hand
To show them to men's souls, might stand,
Whole ages long, the whole world through,
For preachings of what God can do.
What has man done here? How atone,
Great God, for this which man has done?
And for the body and soul which by
Man's pitiless doom must now comply
With lifelong hell, what lullaby
Of sweet forgetful second birth
Remains? All dark. No sign on earth
What measure of God's rest endows
The many mansions of his house.

If but a woman's heart might see
Such erring heart unerringly
For once! But that can never be.

Like a rose shut in a book
In which pure women may not look,
For its base pages claim control
To crush the flower within the soul;
Where through each dead rose-leaf that clings,
Pale as transparent psyche-wings,
To the vile text, are traced such things
As might make lady's cheek indeed
More than a living rose to read;
So nought save foolish foulness may
Watch with hard eyes the sure decay;
And so the life-blood of this rose,
Puddled with shameful knowledge, flows
Through leaves no chaste hand may unclose:
Yet still it keeps such faded show
Of when 'twas gathered long ago,
That the crushed petals' lovely grain,
The sweetness of the sanguine stain,
Seen of a woman's eyes, must make
Her pitiful heart, so prone to ache,
Love roses better for its sake:—
Only that this can never be:—
Even so unto her sex is she.

Yet, Jenny, looking long at you,
The woman almost fades from view.
A cipher of man's changeless sum
Of lust, past, present, and to come,
Is left. A riddle that one shrinks
To challenge from the scornful sphinx.

Like a toad within a stone
Seated while Time crumbles on;

Which sits there since the earth was curs'd
For Man's transgression at the first;
Which, living through all centuries,
Not once has seen the sun arise;
Whose life, to its cold circle charmed,
The earth's whole summers have not warmed;
Which always—whitherso the stone
Be flung—sits there, deaf, blind, alone;—
Aye, and shall not be driven out
Till that which shuts him round about
Break at the very Master's stroke,
And the dust thereof vanish as smoke,
And the seed of Man vanish as dust:—
Even so within this world is Lust.

Come, come, what use in thoughts like this?
Poor little Jenny, good to kiss,—
You'd not believe by what strange roads
Thought travels, when your beauty goads
A man to-night to think of toads!
Jenny, wake up. . . . Why, there's the dawn!

And there's an early waggon drawn
To market, and some sheep that jog
Bleating before a barking dog;
And the old streets come peering through
Another night that London knew;
And all as ghostlike as the lamps.

So on the wings of day decamps
My last night's frolic. Glooms begin
To shiver off as lights creep in
Past the gauze curtains half drawn-to,
And the lamp's doubled shade grows blue,—
Your lamp, my Jenny, kept alight,
Like a wise virgin's, all one night!
And in the alcove coolly spread
Glimmers with dawn your empty bed;
And yonder your fair face I see
Reflected lying on my knee,
Where teems with first foreshadowings
Your pier-glass scrawled with diamond rings.

And now without, as if some word
Had called upon them that they heard,
The London sparrows far and nigh
Clamour together suddenly;
And Jenny's cage-bird grown awake
Here in their song his part must take,
Because here too the day doth break.

And somehow in myself the dawn
Among stirred clouds and veils withdrawn
Strikes greyly on her. Let her sleep.
But will it wake her if I heap
These cushions thus beneath her head
Where my knee was? No,—there's your bed,
My Jenny, while you dream. And there
I lay among your golden hair
Perhaps the subject of your dreams,
These golden coins.

For still one deems
That Jenny's flattering sleep confers
New magic on the magic purse,—
Grim web, how clogged with shrivelled flies!
Between the threads fine fumes arise
And shape their pictures in the brain.
There roll no streets in glare and rain,
Nor flagrant man-swine whets his tusk;
But delicately sighs in musk
The homage of the dim boudoir;
Or like a palpitating star
Thrilled into song, the opera-night
Breathes faint in the quick pulse of light;
Or at the carriage-window shine
Rich wares for choice; or, free to dine,
Whirls through its hour of health (divine
For her) the concourse of the Park.
And though in the discounted dark
Her functions there and here are one,
Beneath the lamps and in the sun
There reigns at least the acknowledged belle
Apparelled beyond parallel.
Ah Jenny, yes, we know your dreams.

For even the Paphian Venus seems
A goddess o'er the realms of love,
When silver-shrined in shadowy grove:
Aye, or let offerings nicely placed
But hide Priapus to the waist,
And whoso looks on him shall see
An eligible deity.

Why, Jenny, waking here alone
May help you to remember one,
Though all the memory's long outworn
Of many a double-pillowed morn.
I think I see you when you wake,
And rub your eyes for me, and shake
My gold, in rising, from your hair,
A Danaë for a moment there.

Jenny, my love rang true! for still
Love at first sight is vague, until
That tinkling makes him audible.

And must I mock you to the last,
Ashamed of my own shame,—aghast
Because some thoughts not born amiss
Rose at a poor fair face like this?
Well, of such thoughts so much I know:
In my life, as in hers, they show,
By a far gleam which I may near,
A dark path I can strive to clear.

Only one kiss. Good-bye, my dear.
[1848] [1870]

THE CARD-DEALER

Could you not drink her gaze like wine?
Yet though its splendour swoon
Into the silence languidly
As a tune into a tune,
Those eyes unravel the coiled night
And know the stars at noon.

The gold that's heaped beside her hand,
In truth rich prize it were;
And rich the dreams that wreathe her brows
With magic stillness there;
And he were rich who should unwind
That woven golden hair.

Around her, where she sits, the dance
Now breathes its eager heat;
And not more lightly or more true
Fall there the dancers' feet
Than fall her cards on the bright board
As 'twere a heart that beat.

Her fingers let them softly through,
Smooth polished silent things;
And each one as it falls reflects
In swift light-shadowings,
Blood-red and purple, green and blue,
The great eyes of her rings.

Whom plays she with? With thee, who lov'st
Those gems upon her hand;
With me, who search her secret brows;
With all men, bless'd or bann'd.
We play together, she and we,
Within a vain strange land:

A land without any order,—
Day even as night, (one saith,)—
Where who lieth down ariseth not
Nor the sleeper awakeneth;
A land of darkness as darkness itself
And of the shadow of death.

What be her cards, you ask? Even these:—
The heart, that doth but crave
More, having fed; the diamond
Skilled to make base seem brave;
The club, for smiting in the dark;
The spade, to dig a grave.

And do you ask what game she plays?
With me 'tis lost or won;
With thee it is playing still; with him
It is not well begun;
But 'tis a game she plays with all
Beneath the sway o' the sun.

Thou seest the card that falls,—she knows
The card that followeth:
Her game in thy tongue is called Life,
As ebbs thy daily breath:
When she shall speak, thou'lt learn her tongue
And know she calls it Death.
[1849] [1870]

SISTER HELEN

'Why did you melt your waxen man,
Sister Helen?
To-day is the third since you began.'
'The time was long, yet the time ran,
Little brother.'
(O Mother, Mary Mother,
Three days to-day, between Hell and Heaven!)

'But if you have done your work aright,
Sister Helen,
You'll let me play, for you said I might.'
'Be very still in your play to-night,
Little brother.'
(O Mother, Mary Mother,
Third night, to-night, between Hell and Heaven!)

'You said it must melt ere vesper-bell,
Sister Helen;
If now it be molten, all is well.'
'Even so,—nay, peace! you cannot tell,
Little brother.'
(O Mother, Mary Mother,
What is this, between Hell and Heaven?)

'Oh the waxen knave was plump to-day,
Sister Helen;
How like dead folk he has dropped away!'
'Nay now, of the dead what can you say,
Little brother?'
(O Mother, Mary Mother,
What of the dead, between Hell and Heaven?)

'See, see, the sunken pile of wood,
Sister Helen,
Shines through the thinned wax red as blood!'
'Nay now, when looked you yet on blood,
Little brother?'
(O Mother, Mary Mother,
How pale she is, between Hell and Heaven!)

'Now close your eyes, for they're sick and sore,
Sister Helen,
And I'll play without the gallery door.'
'Aye, let me rest,—I'll lie on the floor,
Little brother.'
(O Mother, Mary Mother,
What rest to-night between Hell and Heaven?)

'Here high up in the balcony,
Sister Helen,
The moon flies face to face with me.'
'Aye, look and say whatever you see,
Little brother.'
(O Mother, Mary Mother,
What sight to-night, between Hell and Heaven?)

'Outside it's merry in the wind's wake,
Sister Helen;
In the shaken trees the chill stars shake.'
'Hush, heard you a horse-tread as you spake,
Little brother?'
(O Mother, Mary Mother,
What sound to-night, between Hell and Heaven?)

'I hear a horse-tread, and I see,
Sister Helen,
Three horsemen that ride terribly.'
'Little brother, whence come the three,
Little brother?'
(O Mother, Mary Mother,
Whence should they come, between Hell and Heaven?)

'They come by the hill-verge from Boyne Bar,
Sister Helen,
And one draws nigh, but two are afar.'
'Look, look, do you know them who they are,
Little brother?'
(O Mother, Mary Mother,
Who should they be, between Hell and Heaven?)

'Oh, it's Keith of Eastholm rides so fast,
Sister Helen,
For I know the white mane on the blast.'
'The hour has come, has come at last,
Little brother!'
(O Mother, Mary Mother,
Her hour at last, between Hell and Heaven!)

'He has made a sign and called Halloo!
Sister Helen,
And he says that he would speak with you.'
'Oh tell him I fear the frozen dew,
Little brother.'
(O Mother, Mary Mother,
Why laughs she thus, between Hell and Heaven?)

'The wind is loud, but I hear him cry,
Sister Helen,
That Keith of Ewern's like to die.'
'And he and thou, and thou and I,
Little brother.'
(O Mother, Mary Mother,
And they and we, between Hell and Heaven!)

'Three days ago, on his marriage-morn,
Sister Helen,
He sickened, and lies since then forlorn.'
'For bridegroom's side is the bride a thorn,
Little brother?'

(*O Mother, Mary Mother,*
Cold bridal cheer, between Hell and Heaven!)

'Three days and nights he has lain abed,
Sister Helen,
And he prays in torment to be dead.'
'The thing may chance, if he have prayed,
Little brother!'
(*O Mother, Mary Mother,*
If he have prayed, between Hell and Heaven!)

'But he has not ceased to cry to-day,
Sister Helen,
That you should take your curse away.'
'*My* prayer was heard,—he need but pray,
Little brother!'
(*O Mother, Mary Mother,*
Shall God not hear, between Hell and Heaven?)

'But he says, till you take back your ban,
Sister Helen,
His soul would pass, yet never can.'
'Nay then, shall I slay a living man,
Little brother?'
(*O Mother, Mary Mother,*
A living soul, between Hell and Heaven!)

'But he calls for ever on your name,
Sister Helen,
And says that he melts before a flame.'
'My heart for his pleasure fared the same,
Little brother.'
(*O Mother, Mary Mother,*
Fire at the heart, between Hell and Heaven!)

'Here's Keith of Westholm riding fast,
Sister Helen,
For I know the white plume on the blast.'
'The hour, the sweet hour I forecast,
Little brother!'
(*O Mother, Mary Mother,*
Is the hour sweet, between Hell and Heaven?)

'He stops to speak, and he stills his horse,
Sister Helen;
But his words are drowned in the wind's course.'
'Nay hear, nay hear, you must hear perforce,
Little brother!'
(*O Mother, Mary Mother,*
What word now heard, between Hell and Heaven?)

'Oh he says that Keith of Ewern's cry,
Sister Helen,
Is ever to see you ere he die.'
'In all that his soul sees, there am I,
Little brother!'
(*O Mother, Mary Mother,*
The soul's one sight, between Hell and Heaven!)

'He sends a ring and a broken coin,
Sister Helen,
And bids you mind the banks of Boyne.'
'What else he broke will he ever join,
Little brother?'
(*O Mother, Mary Mother,*
No, never joined, between Hell and Heaven!)

'He yields you these and craves full fain,
Sister Helen,
You pardon him in his mortal pain.'
'What else he took will he give again,
Little brother?'
(*O Mother, Mary Mother,*
Not twice to give, between Hell and Heaven!)

'He calls your name in an agony,
Sister Helen,
That even dead Love must weep to see.'
'Hate, born of Love, is blind as he,
Little brother!'
(*O Mother, Mary Mother,*
Love turned to hate, between Hell and Heaven!)

'Oh it's Keith of Keith now that rides fast,
Sister Helen,
For I know the white hair on the blast.'
'The short, short hour will soon be past,
Little brother!'
(*O Mother, Mary Mother,*
Will soon be past, between Hell and Heaven!)

'He looks at me and he tries to speak,
Sister Helen,
But oh! his voice is sad and weak!'
'What here should the mighty Baron seek,
Little brother?'
(O Mother, Mary Mother,
Is this the end, between Hell and Heaven?)

'Oh his son still cries, if you forgive,
Sister Helen,
The body dies, but the soul shall live.'
'Fire shall forgive me as I forgive,
Little brother!'
(O Mother, Mary Mother,
As she forgives, between Hell and Heaven!)

'Oh he prays you, as his heart would rive,
Sister Helen,
To save his dear son's soul alive.'
'Fire cannot slay it, it shall thrive,
Little brother!'
(O Mother, Mary Mother,
Alas, alas, between Hell and Heaven!)

'He cries to you, kneeling in the road,
Sister Helen,
To go with him for the love of God!'
'The way is long to his son's abode,
Little brother?'
(O Mother, Mary Mother,
The way is long, between Hell and Heaven!)

'A lady's here, by a dark steed brought,
Sister Helen,
So darkly clad, I saw her not.'
'See her now or never see aught,
Little brother!'
(O Mother, Mary Mother,
What more to see, between Hell and Heaven!)

'Her hood falls back, and the moon shines fair,
Sister Helen,
On the lady of Ewern's golden hair.'
'Blest hour of my power and her despair,
Little brother!'
(O Mother, Mary Mother,
Hour blest and bann'd, between Hell and Heaven!)

'Pale, pale her cheeks, that in pride did glow,
Sister Helen,
'Neath the bridal-wreath three days ago.'
'One morn for pride and three days for woe,
Little brother!'
(O Mother, Mary Mother,
Three days, three nights, between Hell and Heaven!)

'Her clasped hands stretch from her bending head,
Sister Helen;
With the loud wind's wail her sobs are wed.'
'What wedding-strains hath her bridal-bed,
Little brother?'
(O Mother, Mary Mother,
What strain but death's between Hell and Heaven?)

'She may not speak, she sinks in a swoon,
Sister Helen,—
She lifts her lips and gasps on the moon.'
'Oh! might I but hear her soul's blithe tune,
Little brother!'
(O Mother, Mary Mother,
Her woe's dumb cry, between Hell and Heaven!)

'They've caught her to Westholm's saddle-bow,
Sister Helen,
And her moonlit hair gleams white in its flow.'
'Let it turn whiter than winter snow,
Little brother!'
(O Mother, Mary Mother,
Woe-withered gold, between Hell and Heaven!)

'O Sister Helen, you heard the bell,
Sister Helen!
More loud than the vesper-chime it fell.'
'No vesper-chime, but a dying knell,
Little brother!'
(O Mother, Mary Mother,
His dying knell, between Hell and Heaven!)

'Alas! but I fear the heavy sound,
Sister Helen;
Is it in the sky or in the ground?'

'Say, have they turned their horses round,
Little brother?'
*(O Mother, Mary Mother,
What would she more, between Hell and Heaven?)*

'They have raised the old man from his knee,
Sister Helen,
And they ride in silence hastily.'
'More fast the naked soul doth flee,
Little brother!'
*(O Mother, Mary Mother,
The naked soul, between Hell and Heaven!)*

'Flank to flank are the three steeds gone,
Sister Helen,
But the lady's dark steed goes alone.'
'And lonely her bridegroom's soul hath flown,
Little brother.'
*(O Mother, Mary Mother,
The lonely ghost, between Hell and Heaven!)*

'Oh the wind is sad in the iron chill,
Sister Helen,
And weary sad they look by the hill.'
'But he and I are sadder still,
Little brother!'
*(O Mother, Mary Mother,
Most sad of all, between Hell and Heaven!)*

'See, see, the wax has dropped from its place,
Sister Helen,
And the flames are winning up apace!'
'Yet here they burn but for a space,
Little brother!'
*(O Mother, Mary Mother,
Here for a space, between Hell and Heaven!)*

'Ah! what white thing at the door has cross'd,
Sister Helen,
Ah! what is this that sighs in the frost?'
'A soul that's lost as mine is lost,
Little brother!'
*(O Mother, Mary Mother,
Lost, lost, all lost, between Hell and Heaven!)*

[1854, 1880]

TROY TOWN

Heavenborn Helen, Sparta's queen,
(*O Troy Town!*)
Had two breasts of heavenly sheen,
The sun and moon of the heart's desire:
All Love's lordship lay between.
(*O Troy's down,
Tall Troy's on fire!*)

Helen knelt at Venus' shrine,
(*O Troy Town!*)
Saying, 'A little gift is mine,
A little gift for heart's desire.
Hear me speak and make me a sign!
(*O Troy's down,
Tall Troy's on fire!*)

'Look, I bring thee a carven cup;
(*O Troy Town!*)
See it here as I hold it up,—
Shaped it is to the heart's desire,
Fit to fill when the gods would sup.
(*O Troy's down,
Tall Troy's on fire!*)

'It was moulded like my breast;
(*O Troy Town!*)
He that sees it may not rest,
Rest at all for his heart's desire.
O give ear to my heart's behest!
(*O Troy's down,
Tall Troy's on fire!*)

'See my breast, how like it is;
(*O Troy Town!*)
See it bare for the air to kiss!
Is the cup to thy heart's desire?
O for the breast, O make it his!
(*O Troy's down,
Tall Troy's on fire!*)

'Yea, for my bosom here I sue;
(*O Troy Town!*)
Thou must give it where 'tis due,
Give it there to the heart's desire.
Whom do I give my bosom to?
(*O Troy's down,
Tall Troy's on fire!*)

'Each twin breast is an apple sweet.
(*O Troy Town!*)
Once an apple stirred the beat
Of thy heart with the heart's desire:—

Say, who brought it then to thy feet?
(O Troy's down,
Tall Troy's on fire!)

'They that claimed it then were three:
(O Troy Town!)
For thy sake two hearts did he
Make forlorn of the heart's desire.
Do for him as he did for thee!
(O Troy's down,
Tall Troy's on fire!)

'Mine are apples grown to the south,
(O Troy Town!)
Grown to taste in the days of drouth,
Taste and waste to the heart's desire:
Mine are apples meet for his mouth.'
(O Troy's down,
Tall Troy's on fire!)

Venus looked on Helen's gift,
(O Troy Town!)
Looked and smiled with subtle drift,
Saw the work of her heart's desire:—
'There thou kneel'st for Love to lift!'
(O Troy's down,
Tall Troy's on fire!)

Venus looked in Helen's face,
(O Troy Town!)
Knew far off an hour and place,
And fire lit from the heart's desire;
Laughed and said, 'Thy gift hath grace!'
(O Troy's down,
Tall Troy's on fire!)

Cupid looked on Helen's breast,
(O Troy Town!)
Saw the heart within its nest,
Saw the flame of the heart's desire,—
Marked his arrow's burning crest.
(O Troy's down,
Tall Troy's on fire!)

Cupid took another dart,
(O Troy Town!)
Fledged it for another heart,
Winged the shaft with the heart's desire,
Drew the string and said, 'Depart!'
(O Troy's down,
Tall Troy's on fire!)

Paris turned upon his bed,
(O Troy Town!)
Turned upon his bed and said,
Dead at heart with the heart's desire,—
'O to clasp her golden head!'
(O Troy's down,
Tall Troy's on fire!)

[1870]

AVE

Mother of the Fair Delight,
Thou handmaid perfect in God's sight,
Now sitting fourth beside the Three,
Thyself a woman-Trinity,—
Being a daughter borne to God,
Mother of Christ from stall to rood,
And wife unto the Holy Ghost:—
Oh when our need is uttermost,
Think that to such as death may strike
Thou once wert sister sisterlike!
Thou headstone of humanity,
Groundstone of the great Mystery,
Fashioned like us, yet more than we!

Mind'st thou not (when June's heavy breath
Warmed the long days in Nazareth,)
That eve thou didst go forth to give
Thy flowers some drink that they might live
One faint night more amid the sands?
Far off the trees were as pale wands
Against the fervid sky; the sea
Sighed further off eternally
As human sorrow sighs in sleep.
Then suddenly the awe grew deep,
As of a day to which all days
Were footsteps in God's secret ways:
Until a folding sense, like prayer,
Which is, as God is, everywhere,
Gathered about thee; and a voice
Spake to thee without any noise,
Being of the silence:—'Hail,' it said,
'Thou that are highly favourèd;
The Lord is with thee here and now;
Blessed among all women thou.'

Ah! knew'st thou of the end, when first
That Babe was on thy bosom nurs'd?—
Or when He tottered round thy knee
Did thy great sorrow dawn on thee?—
And through His boyhood, year by year
Eating with Him the Passover,
Didst thou discern confusedly
That holier sacrament, when He,
The bitter cup about to quaff,

Should break the bread and eat thereof?—
Or came not yet the knowledge, even
Till on some day forecast in Heaven
His feet passed through thy door to press
Upon His Father's business?—
Or still was God's high secret kept?

Nay, but I think the whisper crept
Like growth through childhood. Work and play,
Things common to the course of day,
Awed thee with meanings unfulfill'd;
And all through girlhood, something still'd
Thy senses like the birth of light,
When thou hast trimmed thy lamp at night
Or washed thy garments in the stream;
To whose white bed had come the dream
That He was thine and thou wast His
Who feeds among the field-lilies.
O solemn shadow of the end
In that wise spirit long contain'd!
O awful end! and those unsaid
Long years when It was Finishèd!

Mind'st thou not (when the twilight gone
Left darkness in the house of John,)
Between the naked window-bars
That spacious vigil of the stars?—
For thou, a watcher even as they,
Wouldst rise from where throughout the day
Thou wroughtest raiment for His poor;
And, finding the fixed terms endure
Of day and night which never brought
Sounds of His coming chariot,
Wouldst lift through cloud-waste unexplor'd
Those eyes which said, 'How long, O Lord?'
Then that disciple whom He loved,
Well heeding, haply would be moved
To ask thy blessing in His name;
And that one thought in both, the same
Though silent, then would clasp ye round
To weep together,—tears long bound,
Sick tears of patience, dumb and slow.
Yet, 'Surely I come quickly,'—so
He said, from life and death gone home.
Amen: even so, Lord Jesus, come!

But oh! what human tongue can speak
That day when death was sent to break
From the tir'd spirit, like a veil,
Its covenant with Gabriel
Endured at length unto the end?
What human thought can apprehend
That mystery of motherhood
When thy Beloved at length renew'd
The sweet communion severèd,—
His left hand underneath thine head
And His right hand embracing thee?—
Lo! He was thine, and this is He!

Soul, is it Faith, or Love, or Hope,
That lets me see her standing up
Where the light of the Throne is bright?
Unto the left, unto the right,
The cherubim, arrayed, conjoint,
Float inward to a golden point,
And from between the seraphim
The glory issues for a hymn.
O Mary Mother, be not loth
To listen,—thou whom the stars clothe,
Who seëst and mayst not be seen!
Hear us at last, O Mary Queen!
Into our shadow bend thy face,
Bowing thee from the secret place,
O Mary Virgin, full of grace!

[1870]

THE HOUSE OF LIFE

THE SONNET

A sonnet is a moment's monument,—
Memorial from the Soul's eternity
To one dead deathless hour. Look that it be,
Whether for lustral rite or dire portent,
Of its own arduous fulness reverent:
Carve it in ivory or in ebony,
As Day or Night may rule; and let Time see
Its flowering crest impearled and orient.

A Sonnet is a coin: its face reveals
The soul,—its converse, to what Power 't is due:—
Whether for tribute to the august appeals
Of Life, or dower in Love's high retinue,
It serve; or, 'mid the dark wharf's cavernous breath,
In Charon's palm it pay the toll to Death.

[1880] [1881]

PART ONE: YOUTH AND CHANGE

I. LOVE ENTHRONED

I marked all kindred Powers the heart finds fair:—
Truth, with awed lips; and Hope, with eyes upcast;
And Fame, whose loud wings fan the ashen Past
To signal-fires, Oblivion's flight to scare;
And Youth, with still some single golden hair
Unto his shoulder clinging, since the last
Embrace wherein two sweet arms held him fast;
And Life, still wreathing flowers for Death to wear.

Love's throne was not with these; but far above
All passionate wind of welcome and farewell
He sat in breathless bowers they dream not of;
Though Truth foreknow Love's heart, and Hope foretell,
And fame be for Love's sake desirable,
And Youth be dear, and Life be sweet to Love.

[1881]

II. BRIDAL BIRTH [I]

As when desire, long darkling, dawns, and first
The mother looks upon the newborn child,
Even so my Lady stood at gaze and smiled
When her soul knew at length the Love it nurs'd.
Born with her life, creature of poignant thirst
And exquisite hunger, at her heart Love lay
Quickening in darkness, till a voice that day
Cried on him, and the bonds of birth were burst.

Now, shadowed by his wings, our faces yearn
Together, as his full-grown feet now range
The grove, and his warm hands our couch prepare
Till to his song our bodiless souls in turn
Be born his children, when Death's nuptial change
Leaves us for light the halo of his hair.

[1870]

III [II]

O thou who at Love's hour ecstatically
Upon my heart dost evermore present,
Clothed with his fire, thy heart his testament,
Whom I have neared and felt thy breath to be
The inmost incense of his sanctuary;
Who without speech hast owned him, and, intent
Upon his will, thy life with mine hast blent,
And murmured, "I am thine, thou'rt one with me!"

O what from thee the grace, to me the prize,
And what to Love the glory,—when the whole
Of the deep stair thou tread'st to the dim shoal

And weary water of the place of sighs,
And there dost work deliverance, as thine eyes
  Draw up my prison spirit to thy soul.

[1870]

IV. LOVESIGHT [III]

When do I see thee most, beloved one?
  When in the light the spirits of mine eyes
  Before thy face, their altar, solemnize
The worship of that Love through thee made known?
Or when in the dusk hours, (we two alone,)
  Close-kissed and eloquent of still replies
  Thy twilight-hidden glimmering visage lies,
And my soul only sees thy soul its own?

O love, my love! if I no more should see
Thyself, nor on the earth the shadow of thee,
  Nor image of thine eyes in any spring,—
How then should sound upon Life's darkening slope
The ground-whirl of the perished leaves of Hope,
  The wind of Death's imperishable wing?

[1870]

V. HEART'S HOPE

By what word's power, the key of paths untrod,
  Shall I the difficult deeps of Love explore,
  Till parted waves of Song yield up the shore
Even as that sea which Israel crossed dryshod?
For lo! in some poor rhythmic period,
  Lady, I fain would tell how evermore
  Thy soul I know not from thy body, nor
Thee from myself, neither our love from God.

Yea, in God's name, and Love's, and thine would I
  Draw from one loving heart such evidence
As to all hearts all things shall signify;
  Tender as dawn's first hill-fire, and intense
  As instantaneous penetrating sense,
In Spring's birth-hour, of other Springs gone by.

[1881]

VI [IV]

What smouldering senses in death's sick delay
  Or seizure of malign vicissitude
  Can rob this body of honour, or denude
This soul of wedding-rainment worn to-day?
For lo! even now my lady's lips did play
  With these my lips such consonant interlude
  As laurelled Orpheus longed for when he wooed
The half-drawn hungering face with that last lay.

I was a child beneath her touch,—a man
When breast to breast we clung, even I and she,—
A spirit when her spirit looked through me,—
A god when all our life-breath met to fan
Our life-blood, till love's emulous ardours ran,
Fire within fire, desire in deity.

[1870]

VI A. NUPTIAL SLEEP [V]

At length their long kiss severed, with sweet smart:
And as the last slow sudden drops are shed
From sparkling eaves when all the storm has fled,
So singly flagged the pulses of each heart.
Their bosoms sundered, with the opening start
Of married flowers to either side outspread
From the knit stem; yet still their mouths, burnt red,
Fawned on each other where they lay apart.

Sleep sank them lower than the tide of dreams,
And their dreams watched them sink, and slid away.
Slowly their souls swam up again, through gleams
Of watered light and dull drowned waifs of day;
Till from some wonder of new woods and streams
He woke, and wondered more: for there she lay.

[1870]

VII. SUPREME SURRENDER [VI]

To all the spirits of love that wander by
Along the love-sown harvest-field of sleep
My Lady lies apparent; and the deep
Calls to the deep; and no man sees but I.
The bliss so long afar, at length so nigh,
Rests there attained. Methinks proud Love must weep
When Fate's control doth from his harvest reap
The sacred hour for which the years did sigh.

First touched, the hand now warm around my neck
Taught memory long to mock desire: and lo!
Across my breast the abandoned hair doth flow,
Where one shorn tress long stirred the longing ache:
And next the heart that trembled for its sake
Lies the queen-heart in sovereign overthrow.

[1870]

VIII. LOVE'S LOVERS [VII]

Some ladies love the jewels in Love's zone
And gold-tipped darts he hath for painless play
In idle scornful hours he flings away;
And some that listen to his lute's soft tone
Do love to vaunt the silver praise their own;
Some prize his blindfold sight; and there be they
Who kissed his wings which brought him yesterday
And thank his wings to-day that he is flown.

My lady only loves the heart of Love:
  Therefore Love's heart, my lady, hath for thee
  His bower of unimagined flower and tree:
There kneels he now, and all-anhungered of
Thine eyes gray-lit in shadowing hair above,
  Seals with thy mouth his immortality.

[1870]

IX. PASSION AND WORSHIP [VIII]

One flame-winged brought a white-winged harp-player
  Even where my lady and I lay all alone;
  Saying: "Behold, this minstrel is unknown;
Bid him depart, for I am minstrel here:
Only my strains are to Love's dear ones dear."
  Then said I: "Through thine hautboy's rapturous tone
  Unto my lady still this harp makes moan,
And still she deems the cadence deep and clear."

Then said my lady: "Thou art Passion of Love,
  And this Love's Worship: both he plights to me.
  Thy mastering music walks the sunlit sea:
But where wan water trembles in the grove
And the wan moon is all the light thereof,
  This harp still makes my name its voluntary."

[1870]

X. THE PORTRAIT [IX]

O Lord of all compassionate control,
  O Love! let this my lady's picture glow
  Under my hand to praise her name, and show
Even of her inner self the perfect whole:
That he who seeks her beauty's furthest goal,
  Beyond the light that the sweet glances throw
  And refluent wave of the sweet smile, may know
The very sky and sea-line of her soul.

Lo! it is done. Above the enthroning throat
  The mouth's mould testifies of voice and kiss,
  The shadowed eyes remember and foresee.
Her face is made her shrine. Let all men note
  That in all years (O Love, thy gift is this!)
    They that would look on her must come to me.

[1870]

XI. THE LOVE-LETTER [X]

Warmed by her hand and shadowed by her hair
  As close she leaned and poured her heart through thee,
  Whereof the articulate throbs accompany
The smooth black stream that makes thy whiteness fair,—
Sweet fluttering sheet, even of her breath aware,—
  Oh let thy silent song disclose to me
  That soul wherewith her lips and eyes agree
Like married music in Love's answering air.

Fain had I watched her when, at some fond thought,
Her bosom to the writing closelier press'd,
And her breast's secrets peered into her breast;
When, through eyes raised an instant, her soul sought
My soul and from the sudden confluence caught
The words that made her love the loveliest.

[1870]

XII. THE LOVERS' WALK

Sweet twining hedgeflowers wind-stirred in no wise
On this June day; and hand that clings in hand:—
Still glades; and meeting faces scarcely fann'd:—
An osier-odoured stream that draws the skies
Deep to its heart; and mirrored eyes in eyes:—
Fresh hourly wonder o'er the Summer land
Of light and cloud; and two souls softly spann'd
With one o'erarching heaven of smiles and sighs:—

Even such their path, whose bodies lean unto
Each other's visible sweetness amorously,—
Whose passionate hearts lean by Love's high decree
Together on his heart for ever true,
As the cloud-foaming firmamental blue
Rests on the blue line of a foamless sea.

[1871] [1881]

XIII. YOUTH'S ANTIPHONY

"I love you, sweet: how can you ever learn
How much I love you?" "You I love even so,
And so I learn it." "Sweet, you cannot know
How fair you are." "If fair enough to earn
Your love, so much is all my love's concern."
"My love grows hourly, sweet." "Mine too doth grow,
Yet love seemed full so many hours ago!"
Thus lovers speak, till kisses claim their turn.

Ah! happy they to whom such words as these
In youth have served for speech the whole day long,
Hour after hour, remote from the world's throng,
Work, contest, fame, all life's confederate pleas,—
What while Love breathed in sighs and silences
Through two blent souls one rapturous undersong.

[1881]

XIV. YOUTH'S SPRING-TRIBUTE

On this sweet bank your head thrice sweet and dear
I lay, and spread your hair on either side,
And see the newborn woodflowers bashful-eyed
Look through the golden tresses here and there.
On these debateable borders of the year
Spring's foot half falters; scarce she yet may know
The leafless blackthorn-blossom from the snow;
And through her bowers the wind's way still is clear.

But April's sun strikes down the glades to-day;
So shut your eyes upturned, and feel my kiss
Creep, as the Spring now thrills through every spray,
Up your warm throat to your warm lips: for this
Is even the hour of Love's sworn suitservice,
With whom cold hearts are counted castaway.

[1881]

XV. THE BIRTH-BOND [XI]

Have you not noted, in some family
Where two were born of a first marriage-bed,
How still they own their gracious bond, though fed
And nursed on the forgotten breast and knee?—
How to their father's children they shall be
In act and thought of one goodwill; but each
Shall for the other have, in silence speech,
And in a word complete community?

Even so, when first I saw you, seemed it, love,
That among souls allied to mine was yet
One nearer kindred than life hinted of.
O born with me somewhere that men forget,
And though in years of sight and sound unmet,
Known for my soul's birth-partner well enough!

[1854] [1870]

XVI. A DAY OF LOVE [XII]

Those envied places which do know her well,
And are so scornful of this lonely place,
Even now for once are emptied of her grace:
Nowhere but here she is: and while Love's spell
From his predominant presence doth compel
All alien hours, an outworn populace,
The hours of Love fill full the echoing space
With sweet confederate music favorable.

Now many memories make solicitous
The delicate love-lines of her mouth, till, lit
With quivering fire, the words take wing from it;
As here between our kisses we sit thus
Speaking of things remembered, and so sit
Speechless while things forgotten call to us.

[1870]

XVII. BEAUTY'S PAGEANT

What dawn-pulse at the heart of heaven, or last
Incarnate flower of culminating day,—
What marshalled marvels on the skirts of May,
Or song full-quired, sweet June's encomiast;
What glory of change by nature's hand amass'd
Can vie with all those moods of varying grace
Which o'er one loveliest woman's form and face
Within this hour, within this room, have pass'd?

Love's very vesture and elect disguise
  Was each fine movement,—wonder new-begot
  Of lily or swan or swan-stemmed galiot;
Joy to his sight who now the sadlier sighs.
Parted again; and sorrow yet for eyes
  Unborn, that read these words and saw her not.

[1881]

XVIII. GENIUS IN BEAUTY

Beauty like hers is genius. Not the call
  Of Homer's or of Dante's heart sublime,—
  Not Michael's hand furrowing the zones of time,—
Is more with compassed mysteries musical;
Nay, not in Spring's or Summer's sweet footfall
  More gathered gifts exuberant Life bequeaths
  Than doth this sovereign face, whose love-spell breathes
Even from its shadowed contour on the wall.

As many men are poets in their youth,
  But for one sweet-strung soul the wires prolong
  Even through all change the indomitable song;
So in likewise the envenomed years, whose tooth
Rends shallower grace with ruin void of ruth,
  Upon this beauty's power shall wreak no wrong.

[1881]

XIX. SILENT NOON

Your hands lie open in the long fresh grass,—
  The finger-points look through like rosy blooms:
  Your eyes smile peace. The pasture gleams and glooms
'Neath billowing skies that scatter and amass.
All around our nest, far as the eye can pass,
  Are golden kingcup-fields with silver edge
  Where the cow-parsley skirts the hawthorn-hedge.
'T is visible silence, still as the hour-glass.

Deep in the sun-searched growths the dragon-fly
Hangs like a blue thread loosened from the sky:—
  So this wing'd hour is dropt to us from above.
Oh! clasp we to our hearts, for deathless dower,
This close-companioned inarticulate hour
  When twofold silence was the song of love.

[1881]

XX. GRACIOUS MOONLIGHT

Even as the moon grows queenlier in mid-space
  When the sky darkens, and her cloud-rapt car
  Thrills with intenser radiance from afar,—
So lambent, lady, beams thy sovereign grace
When the drear soul desires thee. Of that face
  What shall be said,—which, like a governing star,
  Gathers and garners from all things that are
Their silent penetrative loveliness?

O'er water-daisies and wild waifs of Spring,
There where the iris rears its gold-crowned sheaf
With flowering rush and sceptred arrow-leaf,
So have I marked Queen Dian, in bright ring
Of cloud above and wave below, take wing
And chase night's gloom, as thou the spirit's grief.

[1881]

XXI. LOVE-SWEETNESS [XIII]

Sweet dimness of her loosened hair's downfall
About thy face; her sweet hands round thy head
In gracious fostering union garlanded;
Her tremulous smiles; her glances' sweet recall
Of love; her murmuring sighs memorial;
Her mouth's culled sweetness by thy kisses shed
On cheeks and neck and eyelids, and so led
Back to her mouth which answers there for all:—

What sweeter than these things, except the thing
In lacking which all these would lose their sweet:—
The confident heart's still fervor: the swift beat
And soft subsidence of the spirit's wing,
Then when it feels, in cloud-girt wayfaring,
The breath of kindred plumes against its feet?

[1870]

XXII. HEART'S HAVEN

Sometimes she is a child within mine arms,
Cowering beneath dark wings that love must chase,—
With still tears showering and averted face,
Inexplicably filled with faint alarms:
And oft from mine own spirit's hurtling harms
I crave the refuge of her deep embrace,—
Against all ills the fortified strong place
And sweet reserve of sovereign counter-charms.

And Love, our light at night and shade at noon,
Lulls us to rest with songs, and turns away
All shafts of shelterless tumultuous day.
Like the moon's growth, his face gleams through his tune;
And as soft waters warble to the moon,
Our answering spirits chime one roundelay.

[1871] [1881]

XXIII. LOVE'S BAUBLES [XIV]

I stood where Love in brimming armfuls bore
Slight wanton flowers and foolish toys of fruit:
And round him ladies thronged in warm pursuit,
Fingered and lipped and proffered the strange store.
And from one hand the petal and the core
Savoured of sleep; and cluster and curled shoot
Gifts that I felt my cheek was blushing for.
Seemed from another hand like shame's salute,—

At last Love bade my Lady give the same:
And as I looked, the dew was light thereon;
And as I took them, at her touch they shone
With inmost heaven-hue of the heart of flame.
And then Love said: "Lo! when the hand is hers,
Follies of love are love's true ministers."

[1870]

XXIV. PRIDE OF YOUTH

Even as a child, of sorrow that we give
The dead, but little in his heart can find,
Since without need of thought to his clear mind
Their turn it is to die and his to live:—
Even so the winged New Love smiles to receive
Along his eddying plumes the auroral wind,
Nor, forward glorying, casts one look behind
Where night-rack shrouds the Old Love fugitive.

There is a change in every hour's recall,
And the last cowslip in the fields we see
On the same day with the first corn-poppy.
Alas for hourly change! Alas for all
The loves that from his hand proud Youth lets fall,
Even as the beads of a told rosary!

[1880] [1881]

XXV. WINGED HOURS [XV]

Each hour until we meet is as a bird
That wings from far his gradual way along
The rustling covert of my soul,—his song
Still loudlier trilled through leaves more deeply stirr'd:
But at the hour of meeting, a clear word
Is every note he sings, in Love's own tongue;
Yet, Love, thou know'st the sweet strain suffers wrong,
Full oft through our contending joys unheard.

What of that hour at last, when for her sake
No wing may fly to me nor song may flow;
When, wandering round my life unleaved, I know
The bloodied feathers scattered in the brake,
And think how she, far from me, with like eyes
Sees through the untuneful bough the wingless skies?

[1869]

XXVI. MID-RAPTURE

Thou lovely and beloved, thou my love;
Whose kiss seems still the first; whose summoning eyes,
Even now, as for our love-world's new sunrise,
Shed very dawn; whose voice, attuned above
All modulation of the deep-bowered dove,
Is like a hand laid softly on the soul;
Whose hand is like a sweet voice to control
Those worn tired brows it hath the keeping of:—

What word can answer to thy word,—what gaze
To thine, which now absorbs within its sphere
My worshiping face, till I am mirrored there
Light-circled in a heaven of deep-drawn rays?
What clasp, what kiss mine inmost heart can prove
O lovely and beloved, O my love?

[1869? 1881]

XXVII. HEART'S COMPASS

Sometimes thou seem'st not as thyself alone,
But as the meaning of all things that are;
A breathless wonder, shadowing forth afar
Some heavenly solstice hushed and halcyon;
Whose unstirred lips are music's visible tone;
Whose eyes the sun-gate of the soul unbar,
Being of its furthest fires oracular;—
The evident heart of all life sown and mown.

Even such Love is; and is not thy name Love?
Yea, by thy hand the Love-god rends apart
All gathering clouds of Night's ambiguous art;
Flings them far down, and sets thine eyes above;
And simply, as some gage of flower or glove,
Stakes with a smile the world against thy heart.

[1881]

XXVIII. SOUL-LIGHT

What other woman could be loved like you,
Or how of you should love possess his fill?
After the fulness of all rapture, still,—
As at the end of some deep avenue
A tender glamour of day,—there comes to view
Far in your eyes a yet more hungering thrill,—
Such fire as Love's soul-winnowing hands distil
Even from his inmost ark of light and dew.

And as the traveller triumphs with the sun,
Glorying in heat's mid-height, yet startide brings
Wonder new-born, and still fresh transport springs
From limpid lambent hours of day begun;—
Even so, through eyes and voice, your soul doth move
My soul with changeful light of infinite love.

[1881]

XXIX. THE MOONSTAR

Lady, I thank thee for thy loveliness,
Because my lady is more lovely still.
Glorying I gaze, and yield with glad goodwill
To thee thy tribute; by whose sweet-spun dress
Of delicate life Love labours to assess
My lady's absolute queendom; saying, "Lo!
How high this beauty is, which yet doth show
But as that beauty's sovereign votaress."

Lady, I saw thee with her, side by side;
  And as, when night's fair fires their queen surround,
An emulous star too near the moon will ride,—
  Even so thy rays within her luminous bound
  Were traced no more; and by the light so drown'd,
Lady, not thou but she was glorified.

[1881]

XXX. LAST FIRE

Love, through your spirit and mine what summer eve
  Now glows with glory of all things possess'd,
  Since this day's sun of rapture filled the west
And the light sweetened as the fire took leave?
Awhile now softlier let your bosom heave,
  As in Love's harbour, even that loving breast,
  All care takes refuge while we sink to rest,
And mutual dreams the bygone bliss retrieve.

Many the days that Winter keeps in store,
  Sunless throughout, or whose brief sun-glimpses
  Scarce shed the heaped snow through the naked trees.
This day at least was Summer's paramour,
Sun-coloured to the imperishable core
With sweet well-being of love and full heart's ease.

[1881]

XXXI. HER GIFTS

High grace, the dower of queens; and therewithal
  Some wood-born wonder's sweet simplicity;
  A glance like water brimming with the sky
Or hyacinth-light where forest-shadows fall;
Such thrilling pallor of cheek as doth enthral
  The heart; a mouth whose passionate forms imply
  All music and all silence held thereby;
Deep golden locks, her sovereign coronal;

A round reared neck, meet column of Love's shrine
  To cling to when the heart takes sanctuary;
  Hands which for ever at Love's bidding be,
And soft-stirred feet still answering to his sign:—
  These are her gifts, as tongue may tell them o'er.
  Breathe low her name, my soul; for that means more.

[1881]

XXXII. EQUAL TROTH

Not by one measure mayst thou mete our love;
  For how should I be loved as I love thee?—
  I, graceless, joyless, lacking absolutely
All gifts that with thy queenship best behove;—
Thou, throned in every heart's elect alcove,
  And crowned with garlands culled from every tree,
  Which for no head but thine, by Love's decree,
All beauties and all mysteries interwove

But here thine eyes and lips yield soft rebuke:—
"Then only" (say'st thou) "could I love thee less,
When thou couldst doubt my love's equality."
Peace, sweet! If not to sum but worth we look,—
Thy heart's transcendence, not my heart's excess,—
Then more a thousandfold thou lov'st than I.

[1881]

XXXIII. VENUS VICTRIX [1]

Could Juno's self more sovereign presence wear
Than thou, 'mid other ladies throned in grace?—
Or Pallas, when thou bend'st with soul-stilled face
O'er poet's page gold-shadowed in thy hair?
Dost thou than Venus seem less heavenly fair
When o'er the sea of love's tumultuous trance
Hovers thy smile, and mingles with thy glance
That sweet voice like the last wave murmuring there?

Before such triune loveliness divine
Awestruck I ask, which goddess here most claims
The prize that, howsoe'er adjudged, is thine?
Then Love breathes low the sweetest of thy names;
And Venus Victrix to my heart doth bring
Herself, the Helen of thy guerdoning.

[1881]

XXXIV. THE DARK GLASS

Not I myself know all my love for thee:
How should I reach so far, who cannot weigh
To-morrow's dower by gage of yesterday?
Shall birth and death, and all dark names that be
As doors and windows bared to some loud sea,
Lash deaf mine ears and blind my face with spray;
And shall my sense pierce love,—the last relay
And ultimate outpost of eternity?

Lo! what am I to Love, the lord of all?
One murmuring shell he gathers from the sand,—
One little heart-flame sheltered in his hand
Yet through thine eyes he grants me clearest call
And veriest touch of powers primordial
That any hour-girt life may understand.

[1871] [1881]

XXXV. THE LAMP'S SHRINE

Sometimes I fain would find in thee some fault,
That I might love thee still in spite of it:
Yet how should our Lord Love curtail one whit
Thy perfect praise whom most he would exalt?
Alas! he can but make my heart's low vault

[1] Victorious Venus.

Even in men's sight unworthier, being lit
By thee, who thereby show'st more exquisite
Like fiery chrysoprase in deep basalt.

Yet will I nowise shrink; but at Love's shrine
Myself within the beams his brow doth dart
Will set the flashing jewel of thy heart
In that dull chamber where it deigns to shine:
For lo! in honour of thine excellencies
My heart takes pride to show how poor it is.

[1881]

XXXVI. LIFE-IN-LOVE [XVI]

Not in thy body is thy life at all
But in this lady's lips and hands and eyes;
Through these she yields thee life that vivifies
What else were sorrow's servant and death's thrall.
Look on thyself without her, and recall
The waste remembrance and forlorn surmise
That lived but in a dead-drawn breath of sighs
O'er vanished hours and hours eventual.

Even so much life hath the poor tress of hair
Which, stored apart, is all love hath to show
For heart-beats and for fire-heats long ago;
Even so much life endures unknown, even where,
'Mid change the changeless night environeth,
Lies all that golden hair undimmed in death.

[1870]

XXXVII. THE LOVE-MOON [XVII]

"When that dead face, bowered in the furthest years,
Which once was all the life years held for thee,
Can now scarce bid the tides of memory
Cast on thy soul a little spray of tears,—
How canst thou gaze into these eyes of hers
Whom now thy heart delights in, and not see
Within each orb Love's philtred euphrasy
Make them of buried troth remembrancers?"

"Nay, pitiful Love, nay, loving Pity! Well
Thou knowest that in these twain I have confess'd
Two very voices of thy summoning bell.
Nay, Master, shall not Death make manifest
In these the culminant changes which approve
The love-moon that must light my soul to Love?"

[1870]

XXXVIII. THE MORROW'S MESSAGE [XVIII]

"Thou Ghost," I said, "and is thy name To-day?—
Yesterday's son, with such an abject brow!—
And can To-morrow be more pale than thou?"

While yet I spoke, the silence answered: "Yea,
Henceforth our issue is all grieved and grey,
And each beforehand makes such poor avow
As of old leaves beneath the budding bough
Or night-drift that the sundawn shreds away."

Then cried I: "Mother of many malisons,
O Earth, receive me to thy dusty bed!"
But therewithal the tremulous silence said:
"Lo! Love yet bids thy lady greet thee once:—
Yea, twice,—whereby thy life is still the sun's;
And thrice,—whereby the shadow of death is dead."

[1870]

XXXIX. SLEEPLESS DREAMS [XIX]

Girt in dark growths, yet glimmering with one star,
O night desirous as the nights of youth!
Why should my heart within thy spell, forsooth,
Now beat, as the bride's finger-pulses are
Quickened within the girdling golden bar?
What wings are these that fan my pillow smooth?
And why does Sleep, waved back by Joy and Ruth,
Tread softly round and gaze at me from far?

Nay, night deep-leaved! And would Love feign in thee
Some shadowy palpitating grove that bears
Rest for man's eyes and music for his ears?
O lonely night! art thou not known to me,
A thicket hung with masks of mockery
And watered with the wasteful warmth of tears?

[1869]

XL. SEVERED SELVES

Two separate divided silences,
Which, brought together, would find loving voice;
Two glances which together would rejoice
In love, now lost like stars beyond dark trees;
Two hands apart whose touch alone gives ease;
Two bosoms which, heart-shrined with mutual flame,
Would, meeting in one clasp, be made the same;
Two souls, the shores wave-mocked of sundering seas:—

Such are we now. Ah! may our hope forecast
Indeed one hour again, when on this stream
Of darkened love once more the light shall gleam?—
An hour how slow to come, how quickly past,—
Which blooms and fades, and only leaves at last
Faint as shed flowers, the attenuated dream.

[1881]

XLI. THROUGH DEATH TO LOVE

Like labour-laden moonclouds faint to flee
From winds that sweep the winter-bitten wold,—
Like multiform circumfluence manifold
Of night's flood-tide,—like terrors that agree
Of hoarse-tongued fire and inarticulate sea,—
Even such, within some glass dimmed by our breath,
Our hearts discern wild images of Death,
Shadows and shoals that edge eternity.

Howbeit athwart Death's imminent shade doth soar
One Power, than flow of stream or flight of dove
Sweeter to glide around, to brood above.
Tell me, my heart,—what angel-greeted door
Or threshold of wing-winnowed threshing-floor
Hath guest fire-fledged as thine, whose lord is Love?

[1871] [1881]

XLII. HOPE OVERTAKEN

I deemed thy garments, O my Hope, were grey,
So far I viewed thee. Now the space between
Is passed at length; and garmented in green
Even as in days of yore thou stand'st to-day.
Ah God! and but for lingering dull dismay,
On all that road our footsteps erst had been
Even thus commingled, and our shadows seen
Blent on the hedgerows and the water-way.

O Hope of mine whose eyes are living love,
No eyes but hers,—O Love and Hope the Same!—
Lean close to me, for now the sinking sun
That warmed our feet scarce gilds our hair above.
O hers thy voice and very hers thy name!
Alas, cling round me, for the day is done!

[1881]

XLIII. LOVE AND HOPE

Bless love and hope. Full many a withered year
Whirled past us, eddying to its chill doomsday;
And clasped together where the blown leaves lay,
We long have knelt and wept full many a tear.
Yet lo! one hour at last, the Spring's compeer,
Flutes softly to us from some green byeway:
Those years, those tears are dead, but only they:—
Bless love and hope, true soul; for we are here.

Cling heart to heart; nor of this hour demand
Whether in very truth, when we are dead,
Our hearts shall wake to know Love's golden head,
Sole sunshine of the imperishable land;
Or but discern, through night's unfeatured scope,
Scorn-fired at length the illusive eyes of Hope.

[1881]

XLIV. CLOUD AND WIND

Love, should I fear death most for you or me?
  Yet if you die, can I not follow you,
  Forcing the straits of change? Alas! but who
Shall wrest a bond from night's inveteracy,
Ere yet my hazardous soul put forth, to be
  Her warrant against all her haste might rue?—
  Ah! in your eyes so reached what dumb adieu,
What unsunned gyres of waste eternity?

And if I die the first, shall death be then
  A lampless watchtower whence I see you weep?—
  Or (woe is me!) a bed wherein my sleep
Ne'er notes (as death's dear cup at last you drain)
The hour when you too learn that all is vain
  And that Hope sows what Love shall never reap?

[1881]

XLV. SECRET PARTING [XX]

Because our talk was of the cloud-control
  And moon-track of the journeying face of Fate,
  Her tremulous kisses faltered at love's gate
And her eyes dreamed against a distant goal:
But soon, remembering her how brief the whole
  Of joy, which its own hours annihilate,
  Her set gaze gathered, thirstier than of late,
And as she kissed, her mouth became her soul.

Thence in what ways we wandered, and how strove
  To build with fire-tried vows the piteous home
  Which memory haunts and whither sleep may roam,—
They only know for whom the roof of Love
Is the still-seated secret of the grove,
  Nor spire may rise nor bell be heard therefrom.

[1870]

XLVI. PARTED LOVE [XXI]

What shall be said of this embattled day
  And armèd occupation of this night
  By all thy foes beleaguered,—now when sight
Nor sound denotes the loved one far away?
Of these thy vanquished hours what shalt thou say,—
  As every sense to which she dealt delight
  Now labours lonely o'er the stark noon-height
To reach the sunset's desolate disarray?

Stand still, fond fettered wretch! while Memory's art
  Parades the Past before thy face, and lures
  Thy spirit to her passionate portraitures:
Till the tempestuous tide-gates flung apart
Flood with wild will the hollows of thy heart,
  And thy heart rends thee, and thy body endures.

[1869] [1870]

XLVII. BROKEN MUSIC [XXII]

The mother will not turn, who thinks she hears
  Her nursling's speech first grow articulate;
  But breathless with averted eyes elate
She sits, with open lips and open ears,
That it may call her twice. 'Mid doubts and fears
  Thus oft my soul has hearkened; till the song,
  A central moan for days, at length found tongue.
And the sweet music welled and the sweet tears.

But now, whatever while the soul is fain
  To list that wonted murmur, as it were
The speech-bound sea-shell's low importunate strain,—
  No breath of song, thy voice alone is there,
O bitterly beloved! and all her gain
  Is but the pang of unpermitted prayer.
[1869]

XLVIII. DEATH-IN-LOVE

There came an image in Life's retinue
  That had Love's wings and bore his gonfalon:
  Fair was the web, and nobly wrought thereon,
O soul-sequestered face, thy form and hue!
Bewildering sounds, such as Spring wakens to,
  Shook in its folds; and through my heart its power
  Sped trackless as the immemorable hour
When birth's dark portal groaned and all was new.

But a veiled woman followed, and she caught
  The banner round its staff, to furl and cling,—
  Then plucked a feather from the bearer's wing,
And held it to his lips that stirred it not,
  And said to me, "Behold, there is no breath:
  I and this Love are one, and I am Death."
[1869] [1870]

XLIX-LII. WILLOWWOOD [XXIV-XXVII]

I

I sat with Love upon a woodside well,
  Leaning across the water, I and he;
  Nor ever did he speak nor looked at me,
But touched his lute wherein was audible
The certain secret thing he had to tell:
  Only our mirrored eyes met silently
  In the low wave; and that sound came to be
The passionate voice I knew; and my tears fell.

And at their fall, his eyes beneath grew hers;
And with his foot and with his wing-feathers
  He swept the spring that watered my heart's drouth.
Then the dark ripples spread to waving hair,

And as I stooped, her own lips rising there
  Bubbled with brimming kisses at my mouth.
[1868] [1869]

II

And now Love sang: but his was such a song,
  So meshed with half-remembrance hard to free,
  As souls disused in death's sterility
May sing when the new birthday tarries long.
And I was made aware of a dumb throng
  That stood aloof, one form by every tree,
  All mournful forms, for each was I or she,
The shades of those our days that had no tongue.

They looked on us, and knew us and were known;
  While fast together, alive from the abyss,
  Clung the soul-wrung implacable close kiss;
And pity of self through all made broken moan
Which said, "For once, for once, for once alone!"
  And still Love sang, and what he sang was this:—
[1868] [1869]

III

"O ye, all ye that walk in Willowwood,
  That walk with hollow faces burning white;
What fathom-depth of soul-struck widowhood,
  What long, what longer hours, one lifelong night,
Ere ye again, who so in vain have wooed
  Your last hope lost, who so in vain invite
Your lips to that their unforgotten food,
  Ere ye, ere ye again shall see the light!

Alas! the bitter banks in Willowwood,
  With tear-spurge wan, with blood-wort burning red:
Alas! if ever such a pillow could
  Steep deep the soul in sleep till she were dead,—
Better all life forget her than this thing,
That Willowwood should hold her wandering!"
[1868] [1869]

IV

So sang he: and as meeting rose and rose
  Together cling through the wind's wellaway
  Nor change at once, yet near the end of day
The leaves drop loosened where the heart-stain glows,—
So when the song died did the kiss unclose;
  And her face fell back drowned, and was as grey
  As its grey eyes; and if it ever may
Meet mine again I know not if Love knows.

Only I know that I leaned low and drank
A long draught from the water where she sank,
  Her breath and all her tears and all her soul:

And as I leaned, I know I felt Love's face
Pressed on my neck with moan of pity and grace,
Till both our heads were in his aureole.
[1868] [1869]

LIII. WITHOUT HER

What of her glass without her? The blank gray
There where the pool is blind of the moon's face.
Her dress without her? The tossed empty space
Of cloud-rack whence the moon has passed away.
Her paths without her? Day's appointed sway
Usurped by desolate night. Her pillowed place
Without her? Tears, ah me! for love's good grace
And cold forgetfulness of night or day.

What of the heart without her? Nay, poor heart,
Of thee what word remains ere speech be still?
A wayfarer by barren ways and chill,
Steep ways and weary, without her thou art,
Where the long cloud, the long wood's counterpart,
Sheds doubled darkness up the labouring hill.
[1881]

LIV. LOVE'S FATALITY

Sweet Love,—but oh! most dread Desire of Love
Life-thwarted. Linked in gyves I saw them stand,
Love shackled with Vain-longing, hand to hand:
And one was eyed as the blue vault above:
But hope tempestuous like a fire-cloud hove
I' the other's gaze, even as in his whose wand
Vainly all night with spell-wrought power has spann'd
The unyielding caves of some deep treasure-trove.

Also his lips, two writhen flakes of flame,
Made moan: "Alas O Love, thus leashed with me!
Wing-footed thou, wing-shouldered, once born free,
And I, thy cowering self, in chains grown tame,—
Bound to thy body and soul, named with thy name,—
Life's iron heart, even Love's Fatality."
[1881]

LV. STILLBORN LOVE [XXVIII]

The hour which might have been yet might not be,
Which man's and woman's heart conceived and bore
Yet whereof life was barren,—on what shore
Bides it the breaking of Time's weary sea?
Bondchild of all consummate joys set free,
It somewhere sighs and serves, and mute before
The house of Love, hears through the echoing door
His hours elect in choral consonancy.

But lo! what wedded souls now hand in hand
Together tread at last the immortal strand
With eyes where burning memory lights love home?
Lo! how the little outcast hour has turned
And leaped to them and in their faces yearned:—
"I am your child: O parents, ye have come!"

[1870]

LVI-LVIII. TRUE WOMAN

I. HERSELF

To be a sweetness more desired than Spring;
A bodily beauty more acceptable
Than the wild rose-tree's arch that crowns the fell;
To be an essence more environing
Than wine's drained juice; a music ravishing
More than the passionate pulse of Philomel;—
To be all this 'neath one soft bosom's swell
That is the flower of life:—how strange a thing!

How strange a thing to be what Man can know
But as a sacred secret! Heaven's own screen
Hides her soul's purest depth and loveliest glow;
Closely withheld, as all things most unseen,—
The wave-bowered pearl,—the heart-shaped seal of green
That flecks the snowdrop underneath the snow.

[1881]

II. HER LOVE

She loves him; for her infinite soul is Love,
And he her lodestar. Passion in her is
A glass facing his fire, where the bright bliss
Is mirrored, and the heat returned. Yet move
That glass, a stranger's amorous flame to prove,
And it shall turn, by instant contraries,
Ice to the moon; while her pure fire to his
For whom it burns, clings close i' the heart's alcove.

Lo! they are one. With wifely breast to breast
And circling arms, she welcomes all command
Of love,—her soul to answering ardours fann'd:
Yet as morn springs or twilight sinks to rest,
Ah! who shall say she deems not loveliest
The hour of sisterly sweet hand-in-hand?

[1881]

TRUE WOMAN

III. HER HEAVEN

If to grow old in Heaven is to grow young,
(As the Seer saw and said,) then blest were he
With youth for evermore, whose heaven should be

True woman, she whom these weak notes have sung.
Here and hereafter,—choir-strains of her tongue,—
  Sky-spaces of her eyes,—sweet signs that flee
  About her soul's immediate sanctuary,—
Were Paradise all uttermost worlds among.

The sunrise blooms and withers on the hill
  Like any hillflower; and the noblest troth
  Dies here to dust. Yet shall Heaven's promise clothe
Even yet those lovers who have cherished still
  This test for love:—in every kiss sealed fast
  To feel the first kiss and forbode the last.

[1881]

LIX. LOVE'S LAST GIFT

Love to his singer held a glistening leaf,
  And said: "The rose-tree and the apple-tree
  Have fruits to vaunt or flowers to lure the bee;
And golden shafts are in the feathered sheaf
Of the great harvest-marshal, the year's chief,
  Victorious Summer; aye, and 'neath warm sea
  Strange secret grasses lurk inviolably
Between the filtering channels of sunk reef.

All are my blooms; and all sweet blooms of love
  To thee I gave while Spring and Summer sang;
  But Autumn stops to listen, with some pang
From those worse things the wind is moaning of.
  Only this laurel dreads no winter days:
  Take my last gift; thy heart hath sung my praise."

[1881]

PART TWO: CHANGE AND FATE

LX. TRANSFIGURED LIFE

As growth of form or momentary glance
  In a child's features will recall to mind
  The father's with the mother's face combin'd,—
Sweet interchange that memories still enhance:
And yet, as childhood's years and youth's advance,
  The gradual mouldings leave one stamp behind,
  Till in the blended likeness now we find
A separate man's or woman's countenance:—

So in the Song, the singer's Joy and Pain,
  Its very parents, evermore expand
To bid the passion's fullgrown birth remain,
  By Art's transfiguring essense subtly spann'd;
  And from that song-cloud shaped as a man's hand
There comes the sound as of abundant rain.

[1881]

LXI. THE SONG-THROE

By thine own tears thy song must tears beget,
O Singer! Magic mirror thou hast none
Except thy manifest heart; and save thine own
Anguish or ardour, else no amulet.
Cisterned in Pride, verse is the feathery jet
Of soulless air-flung fountains; nay, more dry
Than the Dead Sea for throats that thirst and sigh,
That song o'er which no singer's lids grew wet.

The Song-god—He the Sun-god—is no slave
Of thine: thy Hunter he, who for thy soul
Fledges his shaft: to no august control
Of thy skilled hand his quivered store he gave:
But if thy lips' loud cry leap to his smart,
The inspir'd recoil shall pierce thy brother's heart.

[1880] [1881]

LXII. THE SOUL'S SPHERE

Some prisoned moon in steep cloud-fastnesses,—
Throned queen and thralled; some dying sun whose pyre
Blazed with momentous memorable fire;—
Who hath not yearned and fed his heart with these?
Who, sleepless, hath not anguished to appease
Tragical shadow's realm of sound and sight
Conjectured in the lamentable night? . . .
Lo! the soul's sphere of infinite images!

What sense shall count them? Whether it forecast
The rose-winged hours that flutter in the van
Of Love's unquestioning unrevealèd span,—
Visions of golden futures: or that last
Wild pageant of the accumulated past
That clangs and flashes for a drowning man.

[1881]

LXIII. INCLUSIVENESS [XXIX]

The changing guests, each in a different mood,
Sit at the roadside table and arise:
And every life among them in likewise
Is a soul's board set daily with new food.
What man has bent o'er his son's sleep, to brood
How that face shall watch his when cold it lies?—
Or thought, as his own mother kissed his eyes,
Of what her kiss was when his father wooed?

May not this ancient room thou sit'tst in dwell
In separate living souls for joy or pain?
Nay, all its corners may be painted plain
Where Heaven shows pictures of some life spent well;
And may be stamped, a memory all in vain,
Upon the sight of lidless eyes in Hell.

[1870]

LXIV. ARDOUR AND MEMORY

The cuckoo-throb, the heartbeat of the Spring;
The rosebud's blush that leaves it as it grows
Into the full-eyed fair unblushing rose;
The summer clouds that visit every wing
With fires of sunrise and of sunsetting;
The furtive flickering streams to light re-born
'Mid airs new-fledged and valorous lusts of morn,
While all the daughters of the daybreak sing:—

These ardour loves, and memory: and when flown
All joys, and through dark forest-boughs in flight
The wind swoops onward brandishing the light,
Even yet the rose-tree's verdure left alone
Will flush all ruddy though the rose be gone;
With ditties and with dirges infinite.

[1879] [1881]

LXV. KNOWN IN VAIN [XXX]

As two whose love, first foolish, widening scope,
Knows suddenly, to music high and soft,
The Holy of holies; who because they scoff'd
Are now amazed with shame, nor dare to cope
With the whole truth aloud, lest heaven should ope;
Yet, at their meetings, laugh not as they laugh'd
In speech; nor speak, at length; but sitting oft
Together, within hopeless sight of hope
For hours are silent:—So it happeneth
When Work and Will awake too late, to gaze
After their life sailed by, and hold their breath.
Ah! who shall dare to search through what sad maze
Thenceforth their incommunicable ways
Follow the desultory feet of Death?

[1869]

LXVI. THE HEART OF THE NIGHT

From child to youth; from youth to arduous man;
From lethargy to fever of the heart;
From faithful life to dream-dowered days apart;
From trust to doubt; from doubt to brink of ban;—
Thus much of change in one swift cycle ran
Till now. Alas, the soul!—how soon must she
Accept her primal immortality,—
The flesh resume its dust whence it began?

O Lord of work and peace! O Lord of life!
O Lord, the awful Lord of will! though late,
Even yet renew this soul with duteous breath:
That when the peace is garnered in from strife,
The work retrieved, the will regenerate,
This soul may see thy face, O Lord of death!

[1881]

LXVII. THE LANDMARK [XXXI]

Was *that* the landmark? What,—the foolish well
Whose wave, low down, I did not stoop to drink,
But sat and flung the pebbles from its brink
In sport to send its imaged skies pell-mell,
(And mine own image, had I noted well!)—
Was that my point of turning?—I had thought
The stations of my course should rise unsought,
As altar-stone or ensigned citadel.

But lo! the path is missed, I must go back,
And thirst to drink when next I reach the spring
Which once I stained, which since may have grown black.
Yet though no light be left nor bird now sing
As here I turn, I'll thank God, hastening,
That the same goal is still on the same track.

[1869]

LXVIII. A DARK DAY [XXXII]

The gloom that breathes upon me with these airs
Is like the drops which strike the traveller's brow
Who knows not, darkling, if they bring him now
Fresh storm, or be old rain the covert bears.
Ah! bodes this hour some harvest of new tares,
Or hath but memory of the day whose plough
Sowed hunger once,—the night at length when thou,
O prayer found vain, didst fall from out my prayers?

How prickly were the growths which yet how smooth,
Along the hedgerows of this journey shed,
Lie by Time's grace till night and sleep may soothe!
Even as the thistledown from pathsides dead
Gleaned by a girl in autumns of her youth,
Which one new year makes soft her marriage-bed.

[1855] [1869]

LXIX. AUTUMN IDLENESS [1]

This sunlight shames November where he grieves
In dead red leaves, and will not let him shun
The day, though bough with bough be over-run.
But with a blessing every glade receives
High salutation; while from hillock-eaves
The deer gaze calling, dappled white and dun,
As if, being foresters of old, the sun
Had marked them with the shade of forest-leaves.

Here dawn to-day unveiled her magic glass;
Here noon now gives the thirst and takes the dew;

[1] Although this sonnet appeared in the collection of 1870 it was not incorporated in *The House of Life* until 1881.

Till eve bring rest when other good things pass.
And here the lost hours the lost hours renew
While I still lead my shadow o'er the grass,
Nor know, for longing, that which I should do.
[1850?] [1870]

LXX. THE HILL SUMMIT [XXXIII]

This feast-day of the sun, his altar there
In the broad west has blazed for vesper-song;
And I have loitered in the vale too long
And gaze now a belated worshipper.
Yet may I not forget that I was 'ware,
So journeying, of his face at intervals
Transfigured where the fringed horizon falls,—
A fiery bush with coruscating hair.

And now that I have climbed and won this height,
I must tread downward through the sloping shade
And travel the bewildered tracks till night.
Yet for this hour I still may here be stayed
And see the gold air and the silver fade
And the last bird fly into the last light.
[1853] [1870]

LXXI-LXXIII. THE CHOICE—I [XXXV-XXXVII]

Eat thou and drink; to-morrow thou shalt die.
Surely the earth, that's wise being very old,
Needs not our help. Then loose me, love, and hold
Thy sultry hair up from my face; that I
May pour for thee this golden wine, brim-high,
Till round the glass thy fingers glow like gold.
We'll drown all hours: thy song, while hours are toll'd,
Shall leap, as fountains veil the changing sky.

Now kiss, and think that there are really those,
My own high-bosomed beauty, who increase
Vain gold, vain lore, and yet might choose our way!
Through many years they toil; then on a day
They die not,—for their life was death,—but cease;
And round their narrow lips the mould falls close.
[1847–8] [1870]

THE CHOICE—II

Watch thou and fear; tomorrow thou shalt die.
O art thou sure thou shalt have time for death?
Is not the day which God's word promiseth
To come man knows not when? In yonder sky,
Now while we speak, the sun speeds forth: can I
Or thou assure him of his goal? God's breath
Even at this moment haply quickeneth
The air to a flame; till spirits, always nigh

Though screened and hid, shall walk the daylight here.
And dost thou prate of all that man shall do?
Canst thou, who hast but plagues, presume to be
Glad in his gladness that comes after thee?
Will *his* strength slay *thy* worm in Hell? Go to:
Cover thy countenance, and watch, and fear.
[1847–8] [1870]

THE CHOICE—III

Think thou and act; to-morrow thou shalt die.
Outstretched in the sun's warmth upon the shore,
Thou say'st: "Man's measured path is all gone o'er:
Up all his years, steeply, with strain and sigh,
Man clomb until he touched the truth; and I,
Even I, am he whom it was destined for."
How should this be? Art thou then so much more
Than they who sowed, that thou shouldst reap thereby?

Nay, come up hither. From this wave-washed mound
Unto the furthest flood-brim look with me;
Then reach on with thy thought till it be drown'd.
Miles and miles distant though the last line be,
And though thy soul sail leagues and leagues beyond,—
Still, leagues beyond those leagues, there is more sea.
[1847–8] [1870]

LXXIV, LXXV, LXXVI. OLD AND NEW ART

I. ST. LUKE THE PAINTER [2]

Give honour unto Luke Evangelist;
For he it was (the aged legends say)
Who first taught Art to fold her hands and pray.
Scarcely at once she dared to rend the mist
Of devious symbols: but soon having wist
How sky-breadth and field-silence and this day
Are symbols also in some deeper way,
She looked through these to God and was God's priest.

And if, past noon, her toil began to irk,
And she sought talismans, and turned in vain
To soulless self-reflections of man's skill,—
Yet now, in this the twilight, she might still
Kneel in the latter grass to pray again,
Ere the night cometh and she may not work.
[1849] [1881]

OLD AND NEW ART

II. NOT AS THESE

"I am not as these are," the poet saith
In youth's pride, and the painter, among men
At bay, where never pencil comes nor pen,

[2] Although this sonnet appeared in the collection of 1870 it was not incorporated in *The House of Life* until 1881.

And shut about with his own frozen breath.
To others, for whom only rhyme wins faith
As poets,—only paint as painter,—then
He turns in the cold silence; and again
Shrinking, "I am not as these are," he saith.

And say that this is so, what follows it?
For were thine eyes set backwards in thine head,
Such words were well, but they see on, and far.
Unto the lights of the great Past, new-lit
Fair for the Future's track, look thou instead,—
Say thou instead, "I am not as *these* are."
[1849] [1881]

OLD AND NEW ART

III. THE HUSBANDMAN

Though God, as one that is an householder,
Called these to labour in His vineyard first,
Before the husk of darkness was well burst
Bidding them grope their way out and bestir,
(Who, questioned of their wages, answered, "Sir,
Unto each man a penny":) though the worst
Burthen of heat was theirs and the dry thirst:
Though God hath since found none such as these were

To do their work like them:—Because of this
Stand not ye idle in the market-place.
Which of ye knoweth *he* is not that last
Who may be first by faith and will?—yea, his
The hand which after the appointed days
And hours shall give a Future to their Past?
[1849] [1881]

LXXVII. SOUL'S BEAUTY [3]

Under the arch of Life, where love and death,
Terror and mystery, guard her shrine, I saw
Beauty enthroned; and though her gaze struck awe,
I drew it in as simply as my breath.
Hers are the eyes which, over and beneath,
The sky and sea bend on thee,—which can draw,
By sea or sky or woman, to one law,
The allotted bondman of her palm and wreath.

This is that Lady Beauty, in whose praise
Thy voice and hand shake still,—long known to thee
By flying hair and fluttering hem,—the beat
Following her daily of thy heart and feet,
How passionately and irretrievably,
In what fond flight, how many ways and days!
[1868]

[3] After appearing as a pamphlet *Notes on the Royal Academy Exhibition,* in 1868, this sonnet was reprinted in the collection of 1870 but was not incorporated in *The House of Life* until 1881.

LXXVIII. BODY'S BEAUTY [4]

Of Adam's first wife, Lilith, it is told
(The witch he loved before the gift of Eve,)
That, ere the snake's, her sweet tongue could deceive,
And her enchanted hair was the first gold.
And still she sits, young while the earth is old,
And, subtly of herself contemplative,
Draws men to watch the bright web she can weave,
Till heart and body and life are in its hold.

The rose and poppy are her flowers; for where
Is he not found, O Lilith, whom shed scent
And soft-shed kisses and soft sleep shall snare?
Lo! as that youth's eyes burned at thine, so went
Thy spell through him, and left his straight neck bent
And round his heart one strangling golden hair.

[1868]

LXXIX. THE MONOCHORD [5]

Is it this sky's vast vault or ocean's sound
That is Life's self and draws my life from me,
And by instinct ineffable decree
Holds my breath quailing on the bitter bound?
Nay, is it Life or Death, thus thunder-crowned,
That 'mid the tide of all emergency
Now notes my separate wave, and to what sea
Its difficult eddies labour in the ground?

Oh! what is this that knows the road I came,
The flame turned cloud, the cloud returned to flame,
The lifted shifted steeps and all the way?—
That draws round me at last this wind-warm space,
And in regenerate rapture turns my face
Upon the devious coverts of dismay?

[1870]

LXXX. FROM DAWN TO NOON

As the child knows not if his mother's face
Be fair; nor of his elders yet can deem
What each most is; but as of hill or stream
At dawn, all glimmering life surrounds his place:
Who yet, tow'rd noon of his half-weary race,
Pausing awhile beneath the high sun-beam
And gazing steadily back,—as through a dream,
In things long past new features now can trace:—

Even so the thought that is at length fullgrown
Turns back to note the sun-smit paths, all grey

[4] See the note on the preceding sonnet.
[5] See the note on sonnet LXXVII.

And marvellous once, where first it walked alone;
And haply doubts, amid the unblenching day,
Which most or least impelled its onward way,—
Those unknown things or these things overknown.

[1881]

LXXXI. MEMORIAL THRESHOLDS

What place so strange,—though unrevealèd snow
With unimaginable fires arise
At the earth's end,—what passion of surprise
Like frost-bound fire-girt scenes of long ago?
Lo! this is none but I this hour; and lo!
This is the very place which to mine eyes
Those mortal hours in vain immortalize,
'Mid hurrying crowds, with what alone I know.

City, of thine a single simple door,
By some new Power reduplicate, must be
Even yet my life-porch in eternity,
Even with one presence filled, as once of yore:
Or mocking winds whirl round a chaff-strown floor
Thee and thy years and these my words and me.

[1881]

LXXXII. HOARDED JOY [XXXVIII]

I said: "Nay, pluck not,—let the first fruit be:
Even as thou sayest, it is sweet and red,
But let it ripen still. The tree's bent head
Sees in the stream its own fecundity
And bides the day of fulness. Shall not we
At the sun's hour that day possess the shade,
And claim our fruit before its ripeness fade,
And eat it from the branch and praise the tree?"

I say: "Alas! our fruit hath wooed the sun
Too long,—'tis fallen and floats adown the stream.
Lo, the last clusters! Pluck them every one,
And let us sup with summer; ere the gleam
Of autumn set the year's pent sorrow free,
And the woods wail like echoes from the sea."

[1870]

LXXXIII. BARREN SPRING [XXXIV]

Once more the changed year's turning wheel returns:
And as a girl sails balanced in the wind,
And now before and now again behind
Stoops as it swoops, with cheek that laughs and burns,—
So Spring comes merry towards me here, but earns
No answering smile from me, whose life is twin'd
With the dead boughs that winter still must bind,
And whom to-day the Spring no more concerns.

Behold, this crocus is a withering flame;
  This snowdrop, snow; this apple-blossom's part
  To breed the fruit that breeds the serpent's art.
Nay, for these Spring-flowers, turn thy face from them,
  Nor gaze till on the year's last lily-stem
  The white cup shrivels round the golden heart.
[1870]

LXXXIV. FAREWELL TO THE GLEN

Sweet stream-fed glen, why say "farewell" to thee
  Who far'st so well and find'st for ever smooth
  The brow of Time where man may read no ruth?
Nay, do thou rather say "farewell" to me,
Who now fare forth in bitterer fantasy
  Than erst was mine where other shade might soothe
  By other streams, what while in fragrant youth
The bliss of being sad made melancholy.

And yet, farewell! For better shalt thou fare
  When children bathe sweet faces in thy flow
And happy lovers blend sweet shadows there
  In hours to come, than when an hour ago
Thine echoes had but one man's sighs to bear
  And thy trees whispered what he feared to know.
[1869] [1881]

LXXXV. VAIN VIRTUES [XXXIX]

What is the sorriest thing that enters Hell?
  None of the sins,—but this and that fair deed
  Which a soul's sin at length could supersede.
These yet are virgins, whom death's timely knell
Might once have sainted; whom the fiends compel
  Together now, in snake-bound shuddering sheaves
  Of anguish, while the pits' pollution leaves
Their refuse maidenhood abominable.

Night sucks them down, the tribute of the pit,
  Whose names, half entered in the book of Life,
    Were God's desire at noon. And as their hair
And eyes sink last, the Torturer deigns no whit
  To gaze, but, yearning, waits his destined wife,
    The Sin still blithe on earth that sent them there.
[1869] [1870]

LXXXVI. LOST DAYS [XL]

The lost days of my life until to-day,
  What were they, could I see them on the street
  Lie as they fell? Would they be ears of wheat
Sown once for food but trodden into clay?
Or golden coins squandered and still to pay?
  Or drops of blood dabbling the guilty feet?
  Or such spilt water as in dreams must cheat
The undying throats of Hell, athirst alway?

I do not see them here; but after death
God knows I know the faces I shall see,
Each one a murdered self, with low last breath.
"I am thyself,—what has thou done to me?"
"And I—and I—thyself," (lo! each one saith,)
"And thou thyself to all eternity!"

[1869]

LXXXVII. DEATH'S SONGSTERS [XLI]

When first that horse, within whose populous womb
The birth was death, o'ershadowed Troy with fate,
Her elders, dubious of its Grecian freight,
Brought Helen there to sing the songs of home:
She whispered, "Friends, I am alone; come, come!"
Then, crouched within, Ulysses waxed afraid,
And on his comrades' quivering mouths he laid
His hands, and held them till the voice was dumb.

The same was he who, lashed to his own mast,
There where the sea-flowers screen the charnel-caves,
Beside the sirens' singing island pass'd,
Till sweetness failed along the inveterate waves. . .
Say, soul,—are songs of Death no heaven to thee,
Nor shames her lip the cheek of Victory?

[1870]

LXXXVIII. HERO'S LAMP

That lamp thou fill'st in Eros' name to-night,
O Hero, shall the Sestian augurs take
To-morrow, and for drowned Leander's sake
To Anteros its fireless lip shall plight.
Aye, waft the unspoken vow: yet dawn's first light
On ebbing storm and life twice ebb'd must break;
While 'neath no sunrise, by the Avernian Lake,
Lo where Love walks, Death's pallid neophyte.

That lamp within Anteros' shadowy shrine
Shall stand unlit (for so the gods decree)
Till some one man the happy issue see
Of a life's love, and bid its flame to shine:
Which still may rest unfir'd; for, theirs or thine,
O brother, what brought love to them or thee?

[1881]

LXXXIX. THE TREES OF THE GARDEN

Ye who have passed Death's haggard hills; and ye
Whom trees that knew your sires shall cease to know
And still stand silent:—is it all a show,—
A wisp that laughs upon the wall?—decree
Of some inexorable supremacy
Which ever, as man strains his blind surmise
From depth to ominous depth, looks past his eyes,
Sphinx-faced with unabashèd augury?

Nay, rather question the Earth's self. Invoke
The storm-felled forest-trees moss-grown to-day
Whose roots are hillocks where the children play;
Or ask the silver sapling 'neath what yoke
Those stars, his spray-crown's clustering gems, shall wage
Their journey still when his boughs shrink with age.

[1881]

XC. "RETRO ME, SATHANA!" [XLII]

Get thee behind me. Even as, heavy-curled,
Stooping against the wind, a charioteer
Is snatched from out his chariot by the hair,
So shall Time be; and as the void car, hurled
Abroad by reinless steeds, even so the world:
Yea, even as chariot-dust upon the air,
It shall be sought and not found anywhere.
Get thee behind me, Satan. Oft unfurled,

Thy perilous wings can beat and break like lath
Much mightiness of men to win thee praise.
Leave these weak feet to tread in narrow ways.
Thou still, upon the broad vine-sheltered path,
Mayst wait the turning of the phials of wrath
For certain years, for certain months and days.

[1847] [1870]

XCI. LOST ON BOTH SIDES [XLIII]

As when two men have loved a woman well,
Each hating each, through Love's and Death's deceit;
Since not for either this stark marriage-sheet
And the long pauses of this wedding-bell;
Yet o'er her grave the night and day dispel
At last their feud forlorn, with cold and heat;
Nor other than dear friends to death may fleet
The two lives left that most of her can tell:—

So separate hopes, which in a soul had wooed
The one same Peace, strove with each other long,
And Peace before their faces perished since:
So through that soul, in restless brotherhood,
They roam together now, and wind among
Its bye-streets, knocking at the dusty inns.

[1854] [1869]

XCII-III. THE SUN'S SHAME [XLIV-V]

I

Beholding youth and hope in mockery caught
From life; and mocking pulses that remain
When the soul's death of bodily death is fain;
Honour unknown, and honour known unsought;
And penury's sedulous self-torturing thought

On gold, whose master therewith buys his bane;
And longed-for woman longing all in vain
For lonely man with love's desire distraught;

And wealth, and strength, and power, and pleasantness,
Given unto bodies of whose soul's men say,
None poor and weak, slavish and foul, as they:—
Beholding these things, I behold no less
The blushing morn and blushing eve confess
The shame that loads the intolerable day.

[1870]

XCIII

II

As some true chief of men, bowed down with stress
Of life's disastrous eld, on blossoming youth
May gaze, and murmur with self-pity and ruth,—
"Might I thy fruitless treasure but possess,
Such blessing of mine all coming years should bless;"—
Then sends one sigh forth to the unknown goal,
And bitterly feels breathe against his soul
The hour swift-winged of nearer nothingness:—

Even so the World's grey Soul to the green World
Perchance one hour must cry: "Woe's me, for whom
Inveteracy of ill portends the doom.—
Whose heart's old fire in shadow of shame is furl'd:
While thou even as of yore art journeying,
All soulless now, yet merry with the Spring!"

[1881]

XCIV. MICHELANGELO'S KISS

Great Michelangelo, with age grown bleak
And uttermost labours, having once o'ersaid
All grievous memories on his long life shed,
This worst regret to one true heart could speak:—
That when, with sorrowing love and reverence meek,
He stooped o'er sweet Colonna's dying bed,
His Muse and dominant Lady, spirit-wed,—
Her hand he kissed, but not her brow or cheek.

O Buonarroti—good at Art's fire-wheels
To urge her chariot!—even thus the Soul,
Touching at length some sorely-chastened goal,
Earns oftenest but a little: her appeals
Were deep and mute,—lowly her claim. Let be:
What holds for her Death's garner, And for thee?

[1881] [1881]

XCV. THE VASE OF LIFE [XLV]

Around the vase of Life at your slow pace
He has not crept, but turned it with his hands,
And all its sides already understands.

There, girt, one breathes alert for some great race;
Whose road runs far by sands and fruitful space;
  Who laughs, yet through the jolly throng has pass'd;
  Who weeps, nor stays for weeping; who at last,
A youth, stands somewhere crowned, with silent face.

And he has filled this vase with wine for blood,
  With blood for tears, with spice for burning vow,
    With watered flowers for buried love most fit;
And would have cast it shattered to the flood,
  Yet in Fate's name has kept it whole; which now
    Stands empty till his ashes fall in it.

[1869]

XCVI. LIFE THE BELOVED

As thy friend's face, with shadow of soul o'erspread
  Somewhile unto thy sight perchance hath been
  Ghastly and strange, yet never so is seen
In thought, but to all fortunate favour wed;
As thy love's death-bound features never dead
  To memory's glass return, but contravene
  Frail fugitive days, and alway keep, I ween,
Than all new life a livelier lovelihead:—

So Life herself, thy spirit's friend and love,
  Even still as Spring's authentic harbinger
  Glows with fresh hours for hope to glorify;
Though pale she lay when in the winter grove
  Her funeral flowers were snow-flakes shed on her
    And the red wings of frost-fire rent the sky.

[1881]

XCVII. A SUPERSCRIPTION [XLVI]

Look in my face; my name is Might-have-been;
  I am also called No-more, Too-late, Fare-well;
  Unto thine ear I hold the dead-sea shell
Cast up thy Life's foam-fretted feet between:
Unto thine eyes the glass where that is seen
  Which had Life's form and Love's, but by my spell
  Is now a shaken shadow intolerable,
Of ultimate things unuttered the frail screen.

Mark me, how still I am! But should there dart
  One moment through thy soul the soft surprise
  Of that winged Peace which lulls the breath of sighs,—
Then shalt thou see me smile, and turn apart
Thy visage to mine ambush at thy heart
  Sleepless with cold commemorative eyes.

[1869] [1869]

XCVIII. HE AND I [XLVII]

Whence came his feet into my field, and why?
  How is it that he sees it all so drear?
  How do I see his seeing, and how hear
The name his bitter silence knows it by?
This was the little fold of separate sky
  Whose pasturing clouds in the soul's atmosphere
  Drew living light from one continual year:
How should he find it lifeless? He, or I?

Lo! this new Self now wanders round my field,
  With plaints for every flower, and for each tree
  A moan, the sighing wind's auxiliary:
And o'er sweet waters of my life, that yield
Unto his lips no draught but tears unseal'd,
  Even in my place he weeps. Even I, not he.

[1870]

XCIX-C. NEWBORN DEATH [XLVIII-XLIX]

I

To-day Death seems to me an infant child
  Which her worn mother Life upon my knee
  Has set to grow my friend and play with me;
If haply so my heart might be beguil'd
To find no terrors in a face so mild,—
  If haply so my weary heart might be
  Unto the newborn milky eyes of thee,
O Death, before resentment reconcil'd.

How long, O Death? And shall thy feet depart
  Still a young child's with mine, or wilt thou stand
Fullgrown the helpful daughter of my heart,
  What time with thee indeed I reach the strand
Of the pale wave which knows thee what thou art,
  And drink it in the hollow of thy hand?

[1868?] [1869]

II

And thou, O Life, the lady of all bliss,
  With whom, when our first heart beat full and fast,
  I wandered till the haunts of men were pass'd,
And in fair places found all bowers amiss
Till only woods and waves might hear our kiss,
  While to the winds all thought of Death we cast:—
  Ah, Life! and must I have from thee at last
No smile to greet me and no babe but this?

Lo! Love, the child once ours; and Song, whose hair
  Blew like a flame and blossomed like a wreath;
And Art, whose eyes were worlds by God found fair:
  These o'er the book of Nature mixed their breath

With neck-twined arms, as oft we watched them there;
  And did these die that thou mightst bear me Death?

[1868?] [1869]

CI. THE ONE HOPE [L]

When vain desire at last and vain regret
  Go hand in hand to death, and all is vain,
  What shall assuage the unforgotten pain
And teach the unforgetful to forget?
Shall Peace be still a sunk stream long unmet,—
  Or may the soul at once in a green plain
  Stoop through the spray of some sweet life-fountain
And cull the dew-drenched flowering amulet?

Ah! when the wan soul in that golden air
  Between the scriptured petals softly blown
  Peers breathless for the gift of grace unknown,—
Ah! let none other alien spell soe'er
But only the one Hope's one name be there,—
  Not less nor more, but even that word alone.

[1870]

THE KING'S TRAGEDY

JAMES I OF SCOTS
20TH FEBRUARY, 1437

I Catherine am a Douglas born,
  A name to all Scots dear;
And Kate Barlass they've called me now
  Through many a waning year.

This old arm's withered now. 'T was once
  Most deft 'mong maidens all
To rein the steed, to wing the shaft,
  To smite the palm-play ball.

In hall adown the close-linked dance
  It has shone most white and fair;
It has been the rest for a true lord's head,
And many a sweet babe's nursing-bed,
  And the bar to a King's chambère.

Aye, lasses, draw round Kate Barlass,
  And hark with bated breath
How good King James, King Robert's son,
  Was foully done to death.

Through all the days of his gallant youth
  The princely James was pent,
By his friends at first and then by his foes,
  In long imprisonment.

For the elder Prince, the kingdom's heir,
  By treason's murderous brood
Was slain; and the father quaked for the child
  With the royal mortal blood.

I' the Bass Rock fort, by his father's care,
  Was his childhood's life assured;
And Henry the subtle Bolingbroke,
Proud England's King, 'neath the southron yoke
  His youth for long years immured.

Yet in all things meet for a kingly man
  Himself did he approve;
And the nightingale through his prison-wall
  Taught him both lore and love.

For once, when the bird's song drew him close
  To the opened window-pane,
In her bower beneath a lady stood,
A light of life to his sorrowful mood,
  Like a lily amid the rain.

And for her sake, to the sweet bird's note,
  He framed a sweeter Song,
More sweet than ever a poet's heart
  Gave yet to the English tongue.

She was a lady of royal blood;
  And when, past sorrow and teen,
He stood where still through his crownless years
  His Scotish realm had been,
At Scone were the happy lovers crowned,
  A heart-wed King and Queen.

But the bird may fall from the bough of youth,
  And song be turned to moan,
And Love's storm-cloud be the shadow of Hate,
When the tempest-waves of a troubled State
  Are beating against a throne.

Yet well they loved; and the god of Love,
  Whom well the King had sung,
Might find on the earth no truer hearts
  His lowliest swains among.

From the days when first she rode abroad
  With Scotish maids in her train,
I Catherine Douglas won the trust
  Of my mistress sweet Queen Jane.

And oft she sighed, "To be born a King!"
  And oft along the way
When she saw the homely lovers pass
  She has said, "Alack the day!"

Years waned,—the loving and toiling years:
  Till England's wrong renewed
Drove James, by outrage cast on his crown,
  To the open field of feud.

'T was when the King and his host were met
  At the leaguer of Roxbro' hold,
The Queen o' the sudden sought his camp
  With a tale of dread to be told.

And she showed him a secret letter writ
  That spoke of treasonous strife,
And how a band of his noblest lords
  Were sworn to take his life.

"And it may be here or it may be there,
  In the camp or the court," she said:
"But for my sake come to your people's arms
  And guard your royal head."

Quoth he, "'T is the fifteenth day of the siege,
  And the castle's night to yield."
"O face your foes on your throne," she cried,
  "And show the power you wield;
And under your Scotish people's love
  You shall sit as under your shield."

At the fair Queen's side I stood that day
  When he bade them raise the siege,
And back to his Court he sped to know
  How the lords would meet their Liege.

But when he summoned his Parliament,
  The louring brows hung round,
Like clouds that circle the mountain-head
  Ere the first low thunders sound.

For he had tamed the nobles' lust
  And curbed their power and pride,
And reached out an arm to right the poor
  Through Scotland far and wide;
And many a lordly wrong-doer
  By the headsman's axe had died.

'T was then upspoke Sir Robert Græme,
  The bold o'ermastering man:—
"O King, in the name of your Three Estates
  I set you under their ban!

"For, as your lords made oath to you
  Of service and fealty,
Even in like wise you pledged your oath
  Their faithful sire to be:—

"Yet all we here that are nobly sprung
  Have mourned dear kith and kin
Since first for the Scotish Barons' curse
  Did your bloody rule begin."

With that he laid his hands on his King:—
  "Is this not so, my lords?"
But of all who had sworn to league with him
  Not one spake back to his words.

Quoth the King:—"Thou speak'st but for one Estate,
  Nor doth it avow thy gage.
Let my liege lords hale this traitor hence!"
  The Græme fired dark with rage:—

"Who works for lesser men than himself,
He earns but a witless wage!"

But soon from the dungeon where he lay
He won by privy plots,
And forth he fled with a price on his head
To the country of the Wild Scots.

And word there came from Sir Robert Græme
To the King at Edinbro':—
"No Liege of mine thou art; but I see
From this day forth alone in thee
God's creature, my mortal foe.

"Through thee are my wife and children lost,
My heritage and lands;
And when my God shall show me a way,
Thyself my mortal foe will I slay
With these my proper hands."

Against the coming of Christmastide
That year the King bade call
I' the Black Friars' Charterhouse of Perth
A solemn festival.

And we of his household rode with him
In a close-ranked company;
But not till the sun had sunk from his throne
Did we reach the Scotish Sea.

That eve was clenched for a boding storm,
'Neath a toilsome moon half seen;
The cloud stooped low and the surf rose high;
And where there was a line of the sky,
Wild wings loomed dark between.

And on a rock of the black beach-side
By the veiled moon dimly lit,
There was something seemed to heave with life
As the King drew nigh to it.

And was it only the tossing furze
Or brake of the waste sea-wold?
Or was it an eagle bent to the blast?
When near we came, we knew it at last
For a woman tattered and old.

But it seemed as though by a fire within
Her writhen limbs were wrung;
And as soon as the King was close to her,
She stood up gaunt and strong.

'T was then the moon sailed clear of the rack
On high in her hollow dome;
And still as aloft with hoary crest
Each clamorous wave rang home,
Like fire in snow the moonlight blazed
Amid the champing foam.

And the woman held his eyes with her eyes:—
"O King, thou art come at last;
But thy wraith has haunted the Scotish Sea
To my sight for four years past.

"Four years it is since first I met,
'Twixt the Duchray and the Dhu,
A shape whose feet clung close in a shroud,
And that shape for thine I knew.

"A year again, and on Inchkeith Isle
I saw thee pass in the breeze,
With the cerecloth risen above thy feet
And wound about thy knees.

"And yet a year, in the Links of Forth,
As a wanderer without rest,
Thou cam'st with both thine arms i' the shroud
That clung high up thy breast.

"And in this hour I find thee here,
And well mine eyes may note
That the winding-sheet hath passed thy breast
And risen around thy throat.

"And when I meet thee again, O King,
That of death hast such sore drouth,—
Except thou turn again on this shore,—
The winding-sheet shall have moved once more
And covered thine eyes and mouth.

"O King, whom poor men bless for their King,
Of thy fate be not so fain;
But these my words for God's message take,
And turn thy steed, O King, for her sake
Who rides beside thy rein!"

While the woman spoke, the King's horse reared
  As if it would breast the sea,
And the Queen turned pale as she heard on the gale
  The voice die dolorously.

When the woman ceased, the steed was still,
  But the King gazed on her yet,
And in silence save for the wail of the sea
  His eyes and her eyes met.

At last he said:—"God's ways are His own;
  Man is but shadow and dust.
Last night I prayed by His altar-stone;
To-night I wend to the Feast of His Son;
  And in Him I set my trust.

"I have held my people in sacred charge,
  And have not feared the sting
Of proud men's hate,—to His will resign'd
Who has but one same death for a hind
  And one same death for a King.

"And if God in His wisdom have brought close
  The day when I must die,
That day by water or fire or air
My feet shall fall in the destined snare
  Wherever my road may lie.

"What man can say but the Fiend hath set
  Thy sorcery on my path,
My heart with the fear of death to fill,
And turn me against God's very will
  To sink in His burning wrath?"

The woman stood as the train rode past,
  And moved nor limb nor eye;
And when we were shipped, we saw her there
  Still standing against the sky.

As the ship made way, the moon once more
  Sank slow in her rising pall;
And I thought of the shrouded wraith of the King,
  And I said, "The Heavens know all."

And now, ye lasses, must ye hear
  How my name is Kate Barlass:—
But a little thing, when all the tale
  It told of the weary mass
Of crime and woe which in Scotland's realm
  God's will let come to pass.

'T was in the Charterhouse of Perth
  That the King and all his Court
Were met, the Christmas Feast being done,
  For solace and disport.

'T was a wind-wild eve in February,
  And against the casement-pane
The branches smote like summoning hands
  And muttered the driving rain.

And when the wind swooped over the lift
  And made the whole heaven frown,
It seemed a grip was laid on the walls
  To tug the housetop down.

And the Queen was there, more stately fair
  Than a lily in garden set;
And the King was loth to stir from her side;
For as on the day when she was his bride,
  Even so he loved her yet.

And the Earl of Athole, the King's false friend,
  Sat with him at the board;
And Robert Stuart the chamberlain
  Who had sold his sovereign Lord.

Yet the traitor Christopher Chaumber there
  Would fain have told him all,
And vainly four times that night he strove
  To reach the King through the hall.

But the wine is bright at the goblet's brim
  Though the poison lurk beneath;
And the apples still are red on the tree
Within whose shade may the adder be
  That shall turn thy life to death.

There was a knight of the King's fast friends
  Whom he called the King of Love;
And to such bright cheer and courtesy
  That name might best behove.

And the King and Queen both loved him well
  For his gentle knightliness;

And with him the King, as that eve wore on,
Was playing at the chess.

And the King said, (for he thought to jest
And soothe the Queen thereby;) —
"In a book 't is writ that this same year
A King shall in Scotland die.

"And I have pondered the matter o'er,
And this have I found, Sir Hugh,—
There are but two Kings on Scotish ground,
And those Kings are I and you.

"And I have a wife and a newborn heir,
And you are yourself alone;
So stand you stark at my side with me
To guard our double throne.

"For here sit I and my wife and child,
As well your heart shall approve,
In full surrender and soothfastness,
Beneath your Kingdom of Love."

And the Knight laughed, and the Queen too smiled:
But I knew her heavy thought,
And I strove to find in the good King's jest
What cheer might thence be wrought.

And I said, "My Liege, for the Queen's dear love
Now sing the song that of old
You made, when a captive Prince you lay,
And the nightingale sang sweet on the spray,
In Windsor's castle-hold."

Then he smiled the smile I knew so well
When he thought to please the Queen;
The smile which under all bitter frowns
Of hate that rose between,
For ever dwelt at the poet's heart
Like the bird of love unseen.

And he kissed her hand and took his harp,
And the music sweetly rang;
And when the song burst forth, it seemed
'T was the nightingale that sang.

"Worship, ye lovers, on this May:
Of bliss your kalends are begun:
Sing with us, Away, Winter, away!
Come, Summer, the sweet season and sun!
Awake for shame,—your heaven is won,—
And amorously your heads lift all:
Thank Love, that you to his grace doth call!"

But when he bent to the Queen, and sang
The speech whose praise was hers,
It seemed his voice was the voice of the Spring
And the voice of the bygone years.

"The fairest and the freshest flower
That ever I saw before that hour,
The which o' the sudden made to start
The blood of my body to my heart.

* * * *

Ah sweet, are ye a worldly creature
Or heavenly thing in form of nature?"

And the song was long, and richly stored
With wonder and beauteous things;
And the harp was tuned to every change
Of minstrel ministerings;
But when he spoke of the Queen at the last,
Its strings were his own heart-strings.

"Unworthy but only of her grace,
Upon Love's rock that's easy and sure,
In guerdon of all my lovè's space
She took me her humble creäture.
Thus fell my blissful aventure
In youth of love that from day to day
Flowereth aye new, and further I say.

"To reckon all the circumstance
As it happened when lessen gan my sore,
Of my rancor and woful chance,
It were too long,—I have done therefor.
And of this flower I say no more
But unto my help her heart hath tended
And even from death her man defended."

"Aye, even from death," to myself I said;
For I thought of the day when she
Had borne him the news, at Roxbro' siege,
Of the fell confederacy.

But Death even then took aim as he sang
With an arrow deadly bright;
And the grinning skull lurked grimly aloof,
And the wings were spread far over the roof
More dark than the winter night.

Yet truly along the amorous song
Of Love's high pomp and state,
There were words of Fortune's trackless doom
And the dreadful face of Fate.

And oft have I heard again in dreams
The voice of dire appeal
In which the King then sang of the pit
That is under Fortune's wheel.

"And under the wheel beheld I there
An ugly Pit as deep as hell,
That to behold I quaked for fear:
And this I heard, that who therein fell
Came no more up, tidings to tell:
Whereat, astound of the fearful sight,
I wist not what to do for fright."

And oft has my thought called up again
These words of the changeful song:—
"Wist thou thy pain and thy travàil
To come, well might'st thou weep and wail!"
And our wail, O God! is long.

But the song's end was all of his love;
And well his heart was grac'd
With her smiling lips and her tear-bright eyes
As his arm went round her waist.

And on the swell of her long fair throat
Close clung the necklet-chain
As he bent her pearl-tir'd head aside,
And in the warmth of his love and pride
He kissed her lips full fain.

And her true face was a rosy red,
The very red of the rose
That, couched on the happy garden-bed,
In the summer sunlight glows.

And all the wondrous things of love
That sang so sweet through the song
Were in the look that met in their eyes,
And the look was deep and long.

'T was then a knock came at the outer gate,
And the usher sought the King.
"The woman you met by the Scottish Sea,
My Liege, would tell you a thing;
And she says that her present need for speech
Will bear no gainsaying."

And the King said: "The hour is late;
To-morrow will serve, I ween."
Then he charged the usher strictly, and said:
"No word of this to the Queen."

But the usher came again to the King.
"Shall I call her back?" quoth he:
"For as she went on her way, she cried,
'Woe! Woe! then the thing must be!' "

And the King paused, but he did not speak.
Then he called for the Voidee-cup:
And as we heard the twelfth hour strike,
There by true lips and false lips alike
Was the draught of trust drained up.

So with reverence meet to King and Queen,
To bed went all from the board;
And the last to leave of the courtly train
Was Robert Stuart the chamberlain
Who had sold his sovereign lord.

And all the locks of the chamber door
Had the traitor riven and brast;
And that Fate might win sure way from afar,
He had drawn out every bolt and bar
That made the entrance fast.

And now at midnight he stole his way
To the moat of the outer wall,
And laid strong hurdles closely across
Where the traitors' tread should fall.

But we that were the Queen's bower-maids
Alone were left behind;
And with heed we drew the curtains close
Against the winter wind.

And now that all was still through the hall,
More clearly we heard the rain
That clamored ever against the glass
And the boughs that beat on the pane.

But the fire was bright in the ingle-nook,
And through empty space around
The shadows cast on the arras'd wall
'Mid the pictured kings stood sudden and tall
Like spectres sprung from the ground.

And the bed was dight in a deep alcove;
And as he stood by the fire
The king was still in talk with the Queen
While he doffed his goodly attire.

And the song had brought the image back
Of many a bygone year;
And many a loving word they said
With hand in hand and head laid to head;
And none of us went anear.

But Love was weeping outside the house,
A child in the piteous rain;
And as he watched the arrow of Death,
He wailed for his own shafts close in the sheath
That never should fly again.

And now beneath the window arose
A wild voice suddenly:
And the King reared straight, but the Queen fell back
As for bitter dule to dree;
And all of us knew the woman's voice
Who spoke by the Scottish Sea.

"O King," she cried, "in an evil hour
They drove me from thy gate;
And yet my voice must rise to thine ears;
But alas! it comes too late!

"Last night at mid-watch, by Aberdour,
When the moon was dead in the skies,
O King, in a death-light of thine own
I saw thy shape arise.

"And in full season, as erst I said,
The doom had gained its growth;
And the shroud had risen above thy neck
And covered thine eyes and mouth.

"And no moon woke, but the pale dawn broke,
And still thy soul stood there;
And I thought its silence cried to my soul
As the first rays crowned its hair.

"Since then have I journeyed fast and fain
In very despite of Fate,
Lest Hope might still be found in God's will:
But they drove me from thy gate.

"For every man on God's ground, O King,
His death grows up from his birth
In a shadow-plant perpetually;
And thine towers high, a black yew-tree,
O'er the Charterhouse of Perth!"

That room was built far out from the house;
And none but we in the room
Might hear the voice that rose beneath,
Nor the tread of the coming doom.

For now there came a torchlight-glare,
And a clang of arms there came;
And not a soul in that space but thought
Of the foe Sir Robert Græme.

Yea, from the country of the Wild Scots,
O'er mountain, valley, and glen,
He had brought with him in murderous league
Three hundred armèd men.

The King knew all in an instant's flash;
And like a King did he stand;
But there was no armour in all the room,
Nor weapon lay to his hand.

And all we women flew to the door
And thought to have made it fast;
But the bolts were gone and the bars were gone
And the locks were riven and brast.

And he caught the pale pale Queen in his arms
As the iron footsteps fell,—
Then loosed her, standing alone, and said,
"Our bliss was our farewell!"

And 'twixt his lips he murmured a prayer,
And he crossed his brow and breast;
And proudly in royal hardihood
Even so with folded arms he stood,—
The prize of the bloody quest.

Then on me leaped the Queen like a deer:—
"O Catherine, help!" she cried.
And low at his feet we clasped his knees
Together side by side.
"Oh! even a King, for his people's sake,
From treasonous death must hide!"

"For *her* sake most!" I cried, and I marked
The pang that my words could wring.
And the iron tongs from the chimney-nook
I snatched and held to the king:—
"Wrench up the plank! and the vault beneath
Shall yield safe harbouring."

With brows low-bent, from my eager hand
The heavy heft did he take;
And the plank at his feet he wrenched and tore;
And as he frowned through the open floor,
Again I said, "For her sake!"

Then he cried to the Queen, "God's will be done!"
For her hands were clasped in prayer.
And down he sprang to the inner crypt;
And straight we closed the plank he had ripp'd
And toiled to smoothe it fair.

(Alas! in that vault a gap once was
Wherethro' the King might have fled;
But three days since close-walled had it been
By his will; for the ball would roll therein
When without at the palm he play'd.)

Then the Queen cried, "Catherine, keep the door
And I to this will suffice!"
At her word I rose all dazed to my feet,
And my heart was fire and ice.

And louder ever the voices grew,
And the tramp of men in mail;
Until to my brain it seemed to be
As though I tossed on a ship at sea
In the teeth of a crashing gale.

Then back I flew to the rest; and hard
We strove with sinews knit
To force the table against the door;
But we might not compass it.

Then my wild gaze sped far down the hall
To the place of the hearthstone-sill;
And the Queen bent ever above the floor,
For the plank was rising still.

And now the rush was heard on the stair,
And "God, what help?" was our cry.
And was I frenzied or was I bold?
I looked at each empty stanchion-hold,
And no bar but my arm had I!

Like iron felt my arm, as through
The staple I made it pass:—
Alack! it was flesh and bone—no more!
'T was Catherine Douglas sprang to the door,
But I fell back Kate Barlass.

With that they all thronged into the hall,
Half dim to my failing ken;
And the space that was but a void before
Was a crowd of wrathful men.

Behind the door I had fall'n and lay,
Yet my sense was wildly aware,
And for all the pain of my shattered arm
I never fainted there.

Even as I fell, my eyes were cast
Where the King leaped down to the pit;
And lo! the plank was smooth in its place,
And the Queen stood far from it.

And under the litters and through the bed
And within the presses all
The traitors sought for the King, and pierced
The arras around the wall.

And through the chamber they ramped and stormed
Like lions loose in the lair,
And scarce could trust to their very eyes,—
For behold! no King was there.

Then one of them seized the Queen, and cried,—
"Now tell us, where is thy lord?"
And he held the sharp point over her heart:
She dropped not her eyes nor did she start,
But she answered never a word.

Then the sword half pierced the true true breast:
But it was the Græme's own son
Cried, "This is a woman,—we seek a man!"
And away from her girdle-zone
He struck the point of the murderous steel;
And that foul deed was not done.

And forth flowed all the throng like a sea,
And 't was empty space once more;
And my eyes sought out the wounded Queen
As I lay behind the door.

And I said: "Dear Lady, leave me here,
For I cannot help you now;
But fly while you may, and none shall reck
Of my place here lying low."

And she said, "My Catherine, God help thee!"
Then she looked to the distant floor,
And clasping her hands, "O God help *him*,"
She sobbed, "for we can no more!"

But God He knows what help may mean,
If it mean to live or to die;
And what sore sorrow and mighty moan
On earth it may cost ere yet a throne
Be filled in His house on high.

And now the ladies fled with the Queen;
And through the open door
The night-wind wailed round the empty room
And the rushes shook on the floor.

And the bed drooped low in the dark recess
Whence the arras was rent away;
And the firelight still shone over the space
Where our hidden secret lay.

And the rain had ceased, and the moon-beams lit
The window high in the wall,—
Bright beams that on the plank that I knew
Through the painted pane did fall
And gleamed with the splendour of Scotland's crown
And shield armorial.

But then a great wind swept up the skies,
And the climbing moon fell back;
And the royal blazon fled from the floor,
And nought remained on its track;
And high in the darkened window-pane
The shield and the crown were black.

And what I say next I partly saw
And partly I heard in sooth,
And partly since from the murderers' lips
The torture wrung the truth.

For now again came the armèd tread,
And fast through the hall it fell;
But the throng was less: and ere I saw,
By the voice without I could tell
That Robert Stuart had come with them
Who knew that chamber well.

And over the space the Græme strode dark
With his mantle round him flung;
And in his eye was a flaming light
But not a word on his tongue.

And Stuart held a torch to the floor,
And he found the thing he sought;
And they slashed the plank away with their swords;
And O God! I fainted not!

And the traitor held his torch in the gap,
All smoking and smouldering;
And through the vapour and fire, beneath
In the dark crypt's narrow ring,
With a shout that pealed to the room's high roof
They saw their naked King.

Half naked he stood, but stood as one
Who yet could do and dare:
With the crown, the King was stript away,—
The Knight was 'reft of his battle-array,—
But still the Man was there.

From the rout then stepped a villain forth,—
Sir John Hall was his name;
With a knife unsheathed he leapt to the vault
Beneath the torchlight-flame.

Of his person and stature was the King
A man right manly strong,
And mightily by the shoulder-blades
His foe to his feet he flung.

Then the traitor's brother, Sir Thomas Hall,
Sprang down to work his worst;
And the King caught the second man by the neck
And flung him above the first.

And he smote and trampled them under him;
And a long month thence they bare
All black their throats with the grip of his hands
When the hangman's hand came there.

And sore he strove to have had their knives,
But the sharp blades gashed his hands.
Oh James! so armed, thou hadst battled there
Till help had come of thy bands;
And oh! once more thou hadst held our throne
And ruled thy Scotish lands!

But while the King o'er his foes still raged
With a heart that nought could tame,
Another man sprang down to the crypt;
And with his sword in his hand hard-gripp'd,
There stood Sir Robert Græme.

(Now shame on the recreant traitor's heart
Who durst not face his King
Till the body unarmed was wearied out
With two-fold combating!

Ah! well might the people sing and say,
As oft ye have heard aright:—
"O Robert Græme, O Robert Græme,
Who slew our King, God give thee shame!"
For he slew him not as a knight.)

And the naked King turned round at bay,
But his strength had passed the goal,
And he could but gasp:—"Mine hour is come;
But oh! to succour thine own soul's doom,
Let a priest now shrive my soul!"

And the traitor looked on the King's spent strength
And said:—"Have I kept my word?—
Yea, King, the mortal pledge that I gave?
No black friar's shrift thy soul shall save,
But the shrift of this red sword!"

With that he smote his King through the breast;
And all they three in the pen
Fell on him and stabbed and stabbed him there
Like merciless murderous men.

Yet seemed it now that Sir Robert Græme,
Ere the King's last breath was o'er,
Turned sick at heart with the deadly sight
And would have done no more.

But a cry came from the troop above:—
"If him thou do not slay,
The price of his life that thou dost spare
Thy forfeit life shall pay!"

O God! what more did I hear or see,
Or how should I tell the rest?
But there at length our King lay slain
With sixteen wounds in his breast.

O God! and now did a bell boom forth,
And the murderers turned and fled;—
Too late, too late, O God, did it sound!—
And I heard the true men mustering round,
And the cries and the coming tread.

But ere they came, to the black death-gap
Somewise did I creep and steal;
And lo! or ever I swooned away,
Through the dusk I saw where the white face lay
In the Pit of Fortune's Wheel.

And now, ye Scotish maids who have heard
Dread things of the days grown old,—
Even at the last, of true Queen Jane
May somewhat yet be told,
And how she dealt for her dear lord's sake
Dire vengeance manifold.

'T was in the Charterhouse of Perth,
In the fair-lit Death-chapelle,
That the slain King's corpse on bier was laid
With chaunt and requiem-knell.

And all with royal wealth of balm
Was the body purified;
And none could trace on the brow and lips
The death that he had died.

In his robes of state he lay asleep
With orb and sceptre in hand;
And by the crown he wore on his throne
Was his kingly forehead spann'd.

And, girls, 't was a sweet sad thing to see
How the curling golden hair,
As in the day of the poet's youth,
From the King's crown clustered there.

And if all had come to pass in the brain
That throbbed beneath those curls,
Then Scots had said in the days to come
That this their soil was a different home
And a different Scotland, girls!

And the Queen sat by him night and day,
And oft she knelt in prayer,
All wan and pale in the widow's veil
That shrouded her shining hair.

And I had got good help of my hurt:
And only to me some sign
She made; and save the priests that were there
No face would she see but mine.

And the month of March wore on apace;
And now fresh couriers fared
Still from the country of the Wild Scots
With news of the traitors snared.

And still as I told her day by day,
Her pallor changed to sight,
And the frost grew to a furnace-flame
That burnt her visage white.

And evermore as I brought her word,
She bent to her dead King James,
And in the cold ear with fire-drawn breath
She spoke the traitors' names.

But when the name of Sir Robert Græme
Was the one she had to give,
I ran to hold her up from the floor;
For the froth was on her lips, and sore
I feared that she could not live.

And the month of March wore nigh to its end,
And still was the death-pall spread;
For she would not bury her slaughtered lord
Till his slayers all were dead.

And now of their dooms dread tidings came,
And of torments fierce and dire;
And nought she spake,—she had ceased to speak,—
But her eyes were a soul on fire.

But when I told her the bitter end
Of the stern and just award,
She leaned o'er the bier, and thrice three times
She kissed the lips of her lord.

And then she said,—"My King, they are dead!"
And she knelt on the chapel-floor,
And whispered low with a strange proud smile,—
"James, James, they suffered more!"

Last she stood up to her queenly height.
But she shook like an autumn leaf,
As though the fire wherein she burned
Then left her body, and all were turned
To winter of life-long grief.

And "O James!" she said,—"My James!" she said,—
Alas for the woful thing,
That a poet true and a friend of man,
In desperate days of bale and ban,
Should needs be born a King!"

[1881] [1881]

CHRISTINA ROSSETTI

CHRONOLOGICAL TABLE

1830, December 5, born in London, her father a Neapolitan political exile, subsequently professor of Italian at King's College, University of London, her mother a former governess, half-English, half-Italian. Educated at home.

1847 At her grandfather's private press a small collection of her poems was privately printed.

1848 First poem published, in *The Athenaeum*.

1849–50 Engaged to James Collinson, one of the Pre-Raphaelites. The engagement was terminated by Christina Rossetti on religious grounds.

1850 Contributed to the Pre-Raphaelite organ, *The Germ*.

1861 Poems published in *Macmillan's Magazine*.

1862 *Goblin Market and Other Poems.*

1866 Terminated her engagement to Charles Bagot Cayley, for religious reasons. *The Prince's Progress and Other Poems.*

1870 *Commonplace and Other Short Stories.*

1872 *Sing Song.*

1874 *Annus Domini.* *Speaking Likenesses.*

1879 *Seek and Find.*

1881 *A Pageant and Other Poems.* *Called to be Saints.*

1883 *Letter and Spirit.*

1885 *Time Flies.*

1892 *The Face of the Deep.*

1893 *Verses.*

1894 Died at London, December 29, buried at Highgate.

The dominant strain in the poetry of Christina Rossetti, as in her life, was religious. In her treatment of profane subjects the preoccupation with religion is often plain and almost always discernible. Many of her most moving lyrics and the whole of the sonnet sequence *Monna Innominata* reflect her feelings of love, curbed by religious scruples: great as is the grief expressed in such poetry, it is not altogether like the grief which secular poets such as Arnold (in the Marguerite lyrics) or Swinburne (in "The Triumph of Time") voice in their moments of disappointment in love. Whenever Christina Rossetti presents natural pictures of any fullness the note of devotion and estrangement from the life of the senses is present. Only in her nonsense verses or in her multitude of poems for children, does she throw off her religious intensity, her moral gravity.

Less than almost any other Victorian poet does she "date." Her poetry in diction, stanza form, mood and substance is as timeless as lyric poetry can be. Much of it might be supposed to have been written by a contemporary of George Herbert rather than by a contemporary of Dante Rossetti. Against much of it the charge of colorlessness and thinness can properly be urged; such defects were inevitable in the work of a poet who was productive, incapable of self-criticism and devoted to an ideal of economical, unemphatic, exquisite simplicity.

DREAM LAND

Where sunless rivers weep
Their waves into the deep,
She sleeps a charmèd sleep:
  Awake her not.
Led by a single star,
She came from very far
To seek where shadows are
  Her pleasant lot.

She left the rosy morn,
She left the fields of corn,
For twilight cold and lorn
  And water springs.
Through sleep, as through a veil,

She sees the sky look pale,
And hears the nightingale
  That sadly sings.

Rest, rest, a perfect rest
Shed over brow and breast;
Her face is toward the west,
  The purple land.
She cannot see the grain
Ripening on hill and plain;
She cannot feel the rain
  Upon her hand.

Rest, rest, for evermore
Upon a mossy shore;
Rest, rest at the heart's core
  Till time shall cease:
Sleep that no pain shall wake,
Night that no morn shall break
Till joy shall overtake
  Her perfect peace.
[1849, 1850]

SONG (OH ROSES FOR THE FLUSH OF YOUTH)

Oh roses for the flush of youth,
  And laurel for the perfect prime;
But pluck an ivy branch for me
  Grown old before my time.

Oh violets for the grave of youth,
  And bay for those dead in their prime;
Give me the withered leaves I chose
  Before in the old time.
[1849] [1850]

UP-HILL

Does the road wind up-hill all the way?
  Yes, to the very end.
Will the day's journey take the whole long day?
  From morn to night, my friend.

But is there for the night a resting-place?
  A roof for when the slow dark hours begin.
May not the darkness hide it from my face?
  You cannot miss that inn.

Shall I meet other wayfarers at night?
  Those who have gone before.
Then must I knock, or call when just in sight?
  They will not keep you standing at that door.

Shall I find comfort, travel-sore and weak?
  Of labour you shall find the sum.
Will there be beds for me and all who seek?
  Yea, beds for all who come.
[1858] [1861]

A BIRTHDAY

My heart is like a singing bird
  Whose nest is in a watered shoot;
My heart is like an apple-tree
  Whose boughs are bent with thickset fruit;
My heart is like a rainbow shell
  That paddles in a halcyon sea;
My heart is gladder than all these
  Because my love is come to me.

Raise me a dais of silk and down;
  Hang it with vair and purple dyes;
Carve it in doves, and pomegranates,
  And peacocks with a hundred eyes;
Work it in gold and silver grapes,
  In leaves, and silver fleurs-de-lys;
Because the birthday of my life
  Is come, my love is come to me.
[1857] [1861]

SONG (WHEN I AM DEAD, MY DEAREST)

When I am dead, my dearest,
  Sing no sad songs for me;
Plant thou no roses at my head,
  Nor shady cypress tree:
Be the green grass above me
  With showers and dewdrops wet:
And if thou wilt, remember,
  And if thou wilt, forget.

I shall not see the shadows,
  I shall not feel the rain;
I shall not hear the nightingale
  Sing on as if in pain:
And dreaming through the twilight
  That doth not rise nor set,
Haply I may remember,
  And haply may forget.
[1848] [1862]

REMEMBER

Remember me when I am gone away,
  Gone far away into the silent land;
  When you can no more hold me by the hand,
Nor I half turn to go yet turning stay.
Remember me when no more day by day
  You tell me of our future that you plann'd:
  Only remember me; you understand
It will be late to counsel then or pray.
Yet if you should forget me for a while
  And afterwards remember, do not grieve:
  For if the darkness and corruption leave
  A vestige of the thoughts that once I had,
Better by far you should forget and smile
  Than that you should remember and be sad.

[1849] [1862]

THE THREE ENEMIES

[1862]

THE FLESH

'Sweet, thou art pale.'
  'More pale to see
Christ hung upon the cruel tree
And bore His Father's wrath for me.'

'Sweet, thou art sad.'
  'Beneath a rod
More heavy, Christ for my sake trod
The winepress of the wrath of God.'

'Sweet, thou art weary.'
  'Not so Christ:
Whose mighty love of me sufficed
For Strength, Salvation, Eucharist.'

'Sweet, thou art footsore.'
  'If I bleed,
His feet have bled: yea, in my need
His Heart once bled for mine indeed.'

THE WORLD

'Sweet, thou art young.'
  'So He was young
Who for my sake in silence hung
Upon the Cross with Passion wrung.'

'Look, thou art fair.'
  'He was more fair
Than men, Who deigned for me to wear
A visage marred beyond compare.'

'And thou hast riches.'
  'Daily bread:
All else is His; Who living, dead,
For me lacked where to lay His Head.'

'And life is sweet.'
  'It was not so
To Him, Whose Cup did overflow
With mine unutterable woe.'

THE DEVIL

'Thou drinkest deep.'
  'When Christ would sup
He drained the dregs from out my cup:
So how should I be lifted up?'

'Thou shalt win Glory.'
  'In the skies,
Lord Jesus, cover up mine eyes
Lest they should look on vanities.'

'Thou shalt have Knowledge.'
  'Helpless dust!
In Thee, O Lord, I put my trust:
Answer Thou for me, Wise and Just.'

'And Might.'—
  'Get thee behind me. Lord,
Who hast redeemed and not abhorred
My soul, oh keep it by Thy Word.'

[1851] [1862]

ECHO

Come to me in the silence of the night;
  Come in the speaking silence of a dream;
Come with soft rounded cheeks and eyes as bright
  As sunlight on a stream;
    Come back in tears,
O memory, hope, love of finished years.

O dream how sweet, too sweet, too bitter sweet,
  Whose wakening should have been in Paradise,
Where souls brimfull of love abide and meet;

Where thirsty longing eyes
Watch the slow door
That opening, letting in, lets out no more.

Yet come to me in dreams, that I may live
My very life again though cold in death:
Come back to me in dreams, that I may give
Pulse for pulse, breath for breath:
Speak low, lean low,
As long ago, my love, how long ago!
[1854] [1862]

GOBLIN MARKET

Morning and evening
Maids heard the goblins cry:
'Come buy our orchard fruits,
Come buy, come buy:
Apples and quinces,
Lemons and oranges,
Plump unpecked cherries,
Melons and raspberries,
Bloom-down-cheeked peaches,
Swart-headed mulberries,
Wild free-born cranberries,
Crab-apples, dewberries,
Pine-apples, blackberries,
Apricots, strawberries;—
All ripe together
In summer weather,—
Morns that pass by,
Fair eves that fly;
Come buy, come buy:
Our grapes fresh from the vine,
Pomegranates full and fine,
Dates and sharp bullaces,
Rare pears and greengages,
Damsons and bilberries,
Taste them and try:
Currants and gooseberries,
Bright-fire-like barberries,
Figs to fill your mouth,
Citrons from the South,
Sweet to tongue and sound to eye;
Come buy, come buy.'

Evening by evening
Among the brookside rushes,
Laura bowed her head to hear,
Lizzie veiled her blushes:
Crouching close together
In the cooling weather,
With clasping arms and cautioning lips,
With tingling cheeks and finger tips.
'Lie close,' Laura said,
Pricking up her golden head:
'We must not look at goblin men,
We must not buy their fruits:
Who knows upon what soil they fed
Their hungry thirsty roots?'
'Come buy,' call the goblins
Hobbling down the glen.
'Oh,' cried Lizzie, 'Laura, Laura,
You should not peep at goblin men.
Lizzie covered up her eyes,
Covered close lest they should look;
Laura reared her glossy head,
And whispered like the restless brook:
'Look, Lizzie, look, Lizzie,
Down the glen tramp little men.
One hauls a basket,
One bears a plate,
One lugs a golden dish
Of many pounds weight.
How fair the vine must grow
Whose grapes are so luscious;
How warm the wind must blow
Through those fruit bushes.'
'No,' said Lizzie: 'No, no, no;
Their offers should not charm us,
Their evil gifts would harm us.'
She thrust a dimpled finger
In each ear, shut eyes and ran:
Curious Laura chose to linger
Wondering at each merchant man.
One had a cat's face,
One whisked a tail,
One tramped at a rat's pace,
One crawled like a snail,
One like a wombat prowled obtuse and furry,
One like a ratel tumbled hurry skurry.
She heard a voice like voice of doves
Cooing all together:
They sounded kind and full of loves
In the pleasant weather.

Laura stretched her gleaming neck
Like a rush-imbedded swan,
Like a lily from the beck,
Like a moonlit poplar branch,
Like a vessel at the launch
When its last restraint is gone.

Backwards up the mossy glen
Turned and trooped the goblin men,
With their shrill repeated cry,
'Come buy, come buy.'

When they reached where Laura was
They stood stock still upon the moss,
Leering at each other,
Brother with queer brother;
Signalling each other,
Brother with sly brother.
One set his basket down,
One reared his plate;
One began to weave a crown
Of tendrils, leaves, and rough nuts brown
(Men sell not such in any town);
One heaved the golden weight
Of dish and fruit to offer her:
'Come buy, come buy,' was still their cry.
Laura stared but did not stir,
Longed but had no money:
The whisk-tailed merchant bade her taste
In tones as smooth as honey,
The cat-faced purr'd,
The rat-paced spoke a word
Of welcome, and the snail-paced even was heard;
One parrot-voiced and jolly
Cried 'Pretty Goblin' still for 'Pretty Polly;'—
One whistled like a bird.

But sweet-tooth Laura spoke in haste:
'Good folk, I have no coin;
To take were to purloin:
I have no copper in my purse,
I have no silver either,
And all my gold is on the furze
That shakes in windy weather
Above the rusty heather.'
'You have much gold upon your head,'
They answered all together:
'Buy from us with a golden curl.'
She clipped a precious golden lock,
She dropped a tear more rare than pearl,
Then sucked their fruit globes fair or red:
Sweeter than honey from the rock,
Stronger than man-rejoicing wine,
Clearer than water flowed that juice;
She never tasted such before,
How should it cloy with length of use?
She sucked and sucked and sucked the more
Fruits which that unknown orchard bore;
She sucked until her lips were sore;
Then flung the emptied rinds away
But gathered up one kernel stone,
And knew not was it night or day
As she turned home alone.

Lizzie met her at the gate
Full of wise upbraidings:
'Dear, you should not stay so late,
Twilight is not good for maidens;
Should not loiter in the glen
In the haunts of goblin men.
Do you not remember Jeanie,
How she met them in the moonlight,
Took their gifts both choice and many,
Ate their fruits and wore their flowers
Plucked from bowers
Where summer ripens at all hours?
But ever in the noonlight
She pined and pined away;
Sought them by night and day,
Found them no more but dwindled and grew grey;
Then fell with the first snow,
While to this day no grass will grow
Where she lies low:
I planted daisies there a year ago
That never blow.
You should not loiter so.'
'Nay, hush,' said Laura:
'Nay, hush, my sister:
I ate and ate my fill,
Yet my mouth waters still;
To-morrow night I will
Buy more:' and kissed her:
'Have done with sorrow;
I'll bring you plums to-morrow
Fresh on their mother twigs,
Cherries worth getting;
You cannot think what figs
My teeth have met in,
What melons icy-cold
Piled on a dish of gold
Too huge for me to hold,
What peaches with a velvet nap,
Pellucid grapes without one seed:
Odorous indeed must be the mead
Whereon they grow, and pure the wave they drink
With lilies at the brink,
And sugar-sweet their sap.'

Golden head by golden head,
Like two pigeons in one nest
Folded in each other's wings,
They lay down in their curtained bed:
Like two blossoms on one stem,
Like two flakes of new-fall'n snow,
Like two wands of ivory
Tipped with gold for awful kings.

Moon and stars gazed in at them,
Wind sang to them lullaby,
Lumbering owls forbore to fly,
Not a bat flapped to and fro
Round their nest:
Cheek to cheek and breast to breast
Locked together in one nest.

Early in the morning
When the first cock crowed his warning,
Neat like bees, as sweet and busy,
Laura rose with Lizzie:
Fetched in honey, milked the cows,
Aired and set to rights the house,
Kneaded cakes of whitest wheat,
Cakes for dainty mouths to eat,
Next churned butter, whipped up cream,
Fed their poultry, sat and sewed;
Talked as modest maidens should:
Lizzie with an open heart,
Laura in an absent dream,
One content, one sick in part;
One warbling for the mere bright day's delight,
One longing for the night.

At length slow evening came:
They went with pitchers to the reedy brook;
Lizzie most placid in her look,
Laura most like a leaping flame.
They drew the gurgling water from its deep;
Lizzie plucked purple and rich golden flags,
Then turning homewards said: 'The sunset flushes
Those furthest loftiest crags;
Come, Laura, not another maiden lags,
No wilful squirrel wags,
The beasts and birds are fast asleep.'
But Laura loitered still among the rushes
And said the bank was steep.

And said the hour was early still,
The dew not fall'n, the wind not chill:
Listening ever, but not catching
The customary cry,
'Come buy, come buy,'
With its iterated jingle
Of sugar-baited words:
Not for all her watching
Once discerning even one goblin
Racing, whisking, tumbling, hobbling;
Let alone the herds
That used to tramp along the glen,
In groups or single,
Of brisk fruit-merchant men.

Till Lizzie urged, 'O Laura, come;
I hear the fruit-call but I dare not look:
You should not loiter longer at this brook:
Come with me home.
The stars rise, the moon bends her arc,
Each glowworm winks her spark,
Let us get home before the night grows dark:
For clouds may gather
Though this is summer weather,
Put out the lights and drench us through;
Then if we lost our way what should we do?'

Laura turned cold as stone
To find her sister heard that cry alone,
That goblin cry,
'Come buy our fruits, come buy.'
Must she then buy no more such dainty fruit?
Must she no more such succous pasture find,
Gone deaf and blind?
Her tree of life drooped from the root:
She said not one word in her heart's sore ache;
But peering thro' the dimness, nought discerning,
Trudged home, her pitcher dripping all the way;
So crept to bed, and lay
Silent till Lizzie slept;
Then sat up in a passionate yearning,
And gnashed her teeth for baulked desire, and wept
As if her heart would break.

Day after day, night after night,
Laura kept watch in vain
In sullen silence of exceeding pain.
She never caught again the goblin cry:
'Come buy, come buy;'—
She never spied the goblin men
Hawking their fruits along the glen:
But when the noon waxed bright
Her hair grew thin and grey;
She dwindled, as the fair full moon doth turn
To swift decay and burn
Her fire away.

One day remembering her kernel-stone
She set it by a wall that faced the south;
Dewed it with tears, hoped for a root,
Watched for a waxing shoot,
But there came none;
It never saw the sun,
It never felt the trickling moisture run:
While with sunk eyes and faded mouth
She dreamed of melons, as a traveller sees
False waves in desert drouth
With shade of leaf-crowned trees,
And burns the thirstier in the sandful breeze.

She no more swept the house,
Tended the fowls or cows,
Fetched honey, kneaded cakes of wheat,
Brought water from the brook,
But sat down listless in the chimney-nook
And would not eat.

Tender Lizzie could not bear
To watch her sister's cankerous care
Yet not to share.
She night and morning
Caught the goblins' cry:
'Come buy our orchard fruits,
Come buy, come buy;'—
Beside the brook, along the glen,
She heard the tramp of goblin men,
The voice and stir
Poor Laura could not hear;
Longed to buy fruit to comfort her
But feared to pay too dear.
She thought of Jeanie in her grave,
Who should have been a bride;
But who for joys brides hope to have
Fell sick and died
In her gay prime,
In earliest Winter time,
With the first glazing rime,
With the first snow-fall of crisp Winter time.

Till Laura dwindling
Seemed knocking at Death's door:
Then Lizzie weighed no more
Better and worse;
But put a silver penny in her purse,
Kissed Laura, crossed the heath with clumps of furze
At twilight, halted by the brook:
And for the first time in her life
Began to listen and look.

Laughed every goblin
When they spied her peeping:
Came towards her hobbling,
Flying, running, leaping,
Puffing and blowing,
Chuckling, clapping, crowing,
Clucking and gobbling,
Mopping and mowing,
Full of airs and graces,
Pulling wry faces,
Demure grimaces,
Cat-like and rat-like,
Ratel- and wombat-like,
Snail-paced in a hurry,
Parrot-voiced and whistler,
Helter skelter, hurry skurry,
Chattering like magpies,
Fluttering like pigeons,
Gliding like fishes,—
Hugged her and kissed her:
Squeezed and caressed her:
Stretched up their dishes,
Panniers, and plates:
'Look at our apples
Russet and dun,
Bob at our cherries,
Bite at our peaches,
Citrons and dates,
Grapes for the asking,
Pears red with basking
Out in the sun,
Plums on their twigs;
Pluck them and suck them,
Pomegranates, figs.'—

'Good folk,' said Lizzie,
Mindful of Jeanie:
'Give me much and many:'—
Held out her apron,
Tossed them her penny.
'Nay, take a seat with us,
Honour and eat with us,'
They answered grinning:
'Our feast is but beginning.
Night yet is early,
Warm and dew-pearly,
Wakeful and starry:
Such fruits as these
No man can carry;
Half their bloom would fly,
Half their dew would dry,
Half their flavour would pass by.
Sit down and feast with us,
Be welcome guest with us,

Cheer you, and rest with us.'—
'Thank you,' said Lizzie: 'But one waits
At home alone for me:
So without further parleying,
If you will not sell me any
Of your fruits though much and many,
Give me back my silver penny
I tossed you for a fee.'—
They began to scratch their pates,
No longer wagging, purring,
But visibly demurring,
Grunting and snarling.
One called her proud,
Cross-grained, uncivil;
Their tones waxed loud,
Their looks were evil.
Lashing their tails
They trod and hustled her,
Elbowed and jostled her,
Clawed with their nails,
Barking, mewing, hissing, mocking,
Tore her gown and soiled her stocking,
Twitched her hair out by the roots,
Stamped upon her tender feet,
Held her hands and squeezed their fruits
Against her mouth to make her eat.

White and golden Lizzie stood,
Like a lily in a flood,—
Like a rock of blue-veined stone
Lashed by tides obstreperously,—
Like a beacon left alone
In a hoary roaring sea,
Sending up a golden fire,—
Like a fruit-crowned orange-tree
White with blossoms honey-sweet
Sore beset by wasp and bee,—
Like a royal virgin town
Topped with gilded dome and spire
Close beleaguered by a fleet
Mad to tug her standard down.

One may lead a horse to water,
Twenty cannot make him drink.
Though the goblins cuffed and caught her,
Coaxed and fought her,
Bullied and besought her,
Scratched her, pinched her black as ink,
Kicked and knocked her,
Mauled and mocked her,
Lizzie uttered not a word;
Would not open lip from lip
Lest they should cram a mouthful in:
But laughed in heart to feel the drip
Of juice that syrupped all her face,
And lodged in dimples of her chin,
And streaked her neck which quaked like
curd.
At last the evil people
Worn out by her resistance
Flung back her penny, kicked their fruit
Along whichever road they took,
Not leaving root or stone or shoot;
Some writhed into the ground,
Some dived into the brook
With ring and ripple,
Some scudded on the gale without a sound,
Some vanished in the distance.

In a smart, ache, tingle,
Lizzie went her way;
Knew not was it night or day;
Sprang up the bank, tore thro' the furze,
Threaded copse and dingle,
And heard her penny jingle
Bouncing in her purse,—
Its bounce was music to her ear.
She ran and ran
As if she feared some goblin man
Dogged her with gibe or curse
Or something worse:
But not one goblin skurried after,
Nor was she pricked by fear;
The kind heart made her windy-paced
That urged her home quite out of breath
with haste
And inward laughter.

She cried 'Laura,' up the garden,
'Did you miss me?
Come and kiss me.
Never mind my bruises,
Hug me, kiss me, suck my juices
Squeezed from goblin fruits for you,
Goblin pulp and goblin dew.
Eat me, drink me, love me;
Laura, make much of me:
For your sake I have braved the glen
And had to do with goblin merchant men.'

Laura started from her chair,
Flung her arms up in the air,
Clutched her hair:
'Lizzie, Lizzie, have you tasted
For my sake the fruit forbidden?
Must your light like mine be hidden,
Your young life like mine be wasted,
Undone in mine undoing

And ruined in my ruin,
Thirsty, cankered, goblin-ridden?'—
She clung about her sister,
Kissed and kissed and kissed her:
Tears once again
Refreshed her shrunken eyes,
Dropping like rain
After long sultry drouth;
Shaking with aguish fear, and pain,
She kissed and kissed her with a hungry mouth.

Her lips began to scorch,
That juice was wormwood to her tongue,
She loathed the feast:
Writhing as one possessed she leaped and sung,
Rent all her robe, and wrung
Her hands in lamentable haste,
And beat her breast.
Her locks streamed like the torch
Borne by a racer at full speed,
Or like the mane of horses in their flight,
Or like an eagle when she stems the light
Straight toward the sun,
Or like a caged thing freed,
Or like a flying flag when armies run.

Swift fire spread through her veins, knocked at her heart,
Met the fire smouldering there
And overbore its lesser flame;
She gorged on bitterness without a name:
Ah! fool, to choose such part
Of soul-consuming care!
Sense failed in the mortal strife:
Like the watch-tower of a town
Which an earthquake shatters down,
Like a lightning-stricken mast,
Like a wind-uprooted tree
Spun about,
Like a foam-topped waterspout
Cast down headlong in the sea,
She fell at last;
Pleasure past and anguish past,
Is it death or is it life?

Life out of death.
That night long Lizzie watched by her,
Counted her pulse's flagging stir,
Felt for her breath,
Held water to her lips, and cooled her face
With tears and fanning leaves:
But when the first birds chirped about their eaves,
And early reapers plodded to the place
Of golden sheaves,
And dew-wet grass
Bowed in the morning winds so brisk to pass,
And new buds with new day
Opened of cup-like lilies on the stream,
Laura awoke as from a dream,
Laughed in the innocent old way,
Hugged Lizzie but not twice or thrice;
Her gleaming locks showed not one thread of grey,
Her breath was sweet as May
And light danced in her eyes.

Days, weeks, months, years
Afterwards, when both were wives
With children of their own
Their mother-hearts beset with fears,
Their lives bound up in tender lives;
Laura would call the little ones
And tell them of her early prime,
Those pleasant days long gone
Of not-returning time:
Would talk about the haunted glen,
The wicked, quaint fruit-merchant men,
Their fruits like honey to the throat
But poisons in the blood;
(Men sell not such in any town:)
Would tell them how her sister stood
In deadly peril to do her good,
And win the fiery antidote:
Then joining hands to little hands
Would bid them cling together,
'For there is no friend like a sister
In calm or stormy weather;
To cheer one on the tedious way,
To fetch one if one goes astray,
To lift one if one totters down,
To strengthen whilst one stands.'

[1859] [1862]

A BETTER RESURRECTION

I have no wit, no words, no tears;
My heart within me like a stone
Is numbed too much for hopes or fears;
Look right, look left, I dwell alone;
I lift mine eyes, but dimmed with grief
No everlasting hills I see;
My life is in the falling leaf:
O Jesus, quicken me.

My life is like a faded leaf,
My harvest dwindled to a husk;
Truly my life is void and brief
And tedious in the barren dusk:
My life is like a frozen thing,
No bud nor greenness can I see:
Yet rise it shall—the sap of Spring;
O Jesus, rise in me.

My life is like a broken bowl,
A broken bowl that cannot hold
One drop of water for my soul
Or cordial in the searching cold;
Cast in the fire the perished thing,
Melt and remould it, till it be
A royal cup for Him my King:
O Jesus, drink of me.
[1859] [1862]

PASSING AWAY, SAITH THE WORLD

Passing away, saith the World, passing away:
Chances, beauty and youth sapped day by day:
Thy life never continueth in one stay.
Is the eye waxen dim, is the dark hair changing to grey
That hath won neither laurel nor bay?
I shall clothe myself in Spring and bud in May:
Thou, root-stricken, shalt not rebuild thy decay
On my bosom for aye.
Then I answered: Yea.

Passing away, saith my Soul, passing away:
With its burden of fear and hope, of labour and play;
Hearken what the past doth witness and say:
Rust in thy gold, a moth is in thine array,
A canker is in thy bud, thy leaf must decay,
At midnight, at cockcrow, at morning, one certain day
Lo, the Bridegroom shall come and shall not delay:
Watch thou and pray.
Then I answered: Yea.

Passing away, saith my God, passing away:
Winter passeth after the long delay:
New grapes on the vine, new figs on the tender spray,
Turtle calleth turtle in Heaven's May.
Though I tarry wait for me, trust Me, watch and pray.
Arise, come away, night is past and lo it is day,
My love, My sister, My spouse, thou shalt hear Me say.
Then I answered: Yea.
[1860] [1862]

WIFE TO HUSBAND

Pardon the faults in me,
For the love of years ago:
Good by.
I must drift across the sea,
I must sink into the snow,
I must die.

You can bask in this sun,
You can drink wine, and eat:
Good by.
I must gird myself and run,
Though with unready feet:
I must die.

Blank sea to sail upon,
Cold bed to sleep in:
Good by.
While you clasp, I must be gone
For all your weeping:
I must die.

A kiss for one friend,
And a word for two,—
Good by:—
A lock that you must send,
A kindness you must do:
I must die.

Not a word for you,
Not a lock or kiss,
Good by.
We, one, must part in two:
Verily death is this:
I must die.
[1861] [1862]

AMOR MUNDI

'Oh, where are you going with your lovelocks flowing,
On the west wind blowing along this valley track?'
'The downhill path is easy, come with me an' it please ye,
We shall escape the uphill by never turning back.'

So they two went together in glowing August weather,
The honey-breathing heather lay to their left and right;
And dear she was to doat on, her swift feet seemed to float on
The air like soft twin pigeons too sportive to alight.

'Oh, what is that in heaven where grey cloudflakes are seven,
Where blackest clouds hang riven just at the rainy skirt?'
'Oh, that's a meteor sent us, a message dumb, portentous,
An undecipher'd solemn signal of help or hurt.'

'Oh, what is that glides quickly where velvet flowers grow thickly,
Their scent comes rich and sickly?' 'A scaled and hooded worm.'
'Oh, what's that in the hollow, so pale I quake to follow?'
'Oh, that's a thin dead body which waits the eternal term.'

'Turn again, O my sweetest,—turn again, false and fleetest:
This beaten way thou beatest I fear is hell's own track.'
'Nay, too steep for hill-mounting; nay, too late for cost counting:
This downhill path is easy, but there's no turning back.'

[1865]

PARADISE: IN A DREAM

Once in a dream I saw the flowers
That bud and bloom in Paradise;
More fair they are than waking eyes
Have seen in all this world of ours.
And faint the perfume-bearing rose,
And faint the lily on its stem,
And faint the perfect violet
Compared with them.

I heard the songs of Paradise:
Each bird sat singing in his place;
A tender song so full of grace
It soared like incense to the skies.
Each bird sat singing to his mate
Soft cooing notes among the trees:
The nightingale herself were cold
To such as these.

I saw the fourfold River flow,
And deep it was, with golden sand;
It flowed between a mossy land
Which murmured music grave and low.
It hath refreshment for all thirst,
For fainting spirits strength and rest;
Earth holds not such a draught as this
From east to west.

The Tree of Life stood budding there,
Abundant with its twelvefold fruits;
Eternal sap sustains its roots,
Its shadowing branches fill the air.
Its leaves are healing for the world,
Its fruit the hungry world can feed.
Sweeter than honey to the taste
And balm indeed.

I saw the gate called Beautiful;
And looked, but scarce could look, within;
I saw the golden streets begin,
And outskirts of the glassy pool.
Oh harps, oh crowns of plenteous stars,
Oh green palm-branches many-leaved—
Eye hath not seen, nor ear hath heard,
Nor heart conceived.

I hope to see these things again,
But not as once in dreams by night;
To see them with my very sight,

And touch, and handle, and attain:
To have all Heaven beneath my feet
For narrow way that once they trod;
To have my part with all the saints,
And with my God.

[1854] [1865]

SOMEWHERE OR OTHER

Somewhere or other there must surely be
The face not seen, the voice not heard,
The heart that not yet—never yet—ah me!
Made answer to my word.

Somewhere or other, may be near or far;
Past land and sea, clean out of sight;
Beyond the wandering moon, beyond the star
That tracks her night by night.

Somewhere or other, may be far or near;
With just a wall, a hedge, between;
With just the last leaves of the dying year
Fallen on a turf grown green.

[1863] [1866]

WEARY IN WELL-DOING

I would have gone; God bade me stay:
I would have worked; God bade me rest.
He broke my will from day to day,
He read my yearnings unexprest,
And said them nay.

Now I would stay; God bids me go:
Now I would rest; God bids me work.
He breaks my heart tost to and fro,
My soul is wrung with doubts that lurk
And vex it so.

I go, Lord, where Thou sendest me;
Day after day I plod and moil:
But, Christ my God, when will it be
That I may let alone my toil
And rest with Thee?

[1864] [1866]

THE LOWEST PLACE

Give me the lowest place; not that I dare
Ask for that lowest place, but Thou hast died
That I might live and share
Thy glory by Thy side.

Give me the lowest place: or if for me
That lowest place too high, make one more low
Where I may sit and see
My God and love Thee so.

[1863] [1866]

A DIRGE

Why were you born when the snow was falling?
You should have come to the cuckoo's calling,
Or when grapes are green in the cluster,
Or at least when lithe swallows muster
From their far off flying
From summer dying.

Why did you die when the lambs were cropping?
You should have died at the apples' dropping,
When the grasshopper comes to trouble,
And the wheat-fields are sodden stubble,
And all winds go sighing
For sweet things dying.

[1865] [1875]

BIRD RAPTURES

The sunrise wakes the lark to sing,
The moonrise wakes the nightingale.
Come, darkness, moonrise, everything
That is so silent, sweet, and pale,
Come, so ye wake the nightingale.

Make haste to mount, thou wistful moon,
Make haste to wake the nightingale:
Let silence set the world in tune,
To hearken to that wordless tale
Which warbles from the nightingale.

O herald skylark, stay thy flight
One moment, for a nightingale
Floods us with sorrow and delight.
To-morrow thou shalt hoist the sail;
Leave us to-night the nightingale.

[1875]

MONNA INNOMINATA

A SONNET OF SONNETS

I

'Lo dì che han detto a' dolci amici addio.'
—DANTE.[1]
'Amor, con quanto sforzo oggi mi vinci!'
—PETRARCA.[2]

Come back to me, who wait and watch for you:—
Or come not yet, for it is over then,
And long it is before you come again,
So far between my pleasures are and few.
While, when you come not, what I do I do
Thinking 'Now when he comes,' my sweetest 'when':
For one man is my world of all the men
This wide world holds; O love, my world is you.
Howbeit, to meet you grows almost a pang
Because the pang of parting comes so soon;
My hope hangs waning, waxing, like a moon
Between the heavenly days on which we meet:
Ah me, but where are now the songs I sang
When life was sweet because you called them sweet?

II

'Era già l'ora che volge il desio.'—DANTE.[3]
'Ricorro al tempo ch' io vi vidi prima.'
—PETRARCA.[4]

I wish I could remember that first day,
First hour, first moment of your meeting me,
If bright or dim the season, it might be
Summer or Winter for aught I can say;
So unrecorded did it slip away,
So blind was I to see and to foresee,
So dull to mark the budding of my tree
That would not blossom yet for many a May.
If only I could recollect it, such
A day of days! I let it come and go
As traceless as a thaw of bygone snow;
It seemed to mean so little, meant so much;
If only now I could recall that touch,
First touch of hand in hand—Did one but know!

III

'O ombre vane, fuor che ne l'aspetto!'—DANTE.[5]
'Immaginata guida la conduce.'—PETRARCA.[6]

I dream of you, to wake: would that I might
Dream of you and not wake but slumber on;
Nor find with dreams the dear companion gone,
As, Summer ended, Summer birds take flight.
In happy dreams I hold you full in sight,
I blush again who waking look so wan;
Brighter than sunniest day that ever shone,
In happy dreams your smile makes day of night.
Thus only in a dream we are at one,
Thus only in a dream we give and take
The faith that maketh rich who take or give;
If thus to sleep is sweeter than to wake,
To die were surely sweeter than to live,
Though there be nothing new beneath the sun.

IV

'Poca favilla gran fiamma seconda.'—DANTE.[7]
'Ogni altra cosa, ogni pensier va fore,
E sol ivi con voi rimansi amore.'—PETRARCA.[8]

I loved you first: but afterwards your love,
Outsoaring mine, sang such a loftier song
As drowned the friendly cooings of my dove.
Which owes the other most? My love was long,
And yours one moment seemed to wax more strong;
I loved and guessed at you, you construed me
And loved me for what might or might not be—
Nay, weights and measures do us both a wrong.
For verily love knows not 'mine' or 'thine';

[1] The day that to their sweet friends they have said good-bye.

[2] Love, with how great force to-day thou dost conquer me!

[3] It was already the hour which turns back desire.

[4] I return to the time that I first saw thee.

[5] Oh shades, empty save in semblance!

[6] An imagined guide conducts her.

[7] A little spark fosters a great flame.

[8] Every other thing, every thought goes away, and only love remains there with you.

With separate 'I' and 'thou' free love has done,
For one is both and both are one in love:
Rich love knows nought of 'thine that is not mine';
Both have the strength and both the length thereof,
Both of us, of the love which makes us one.

V

'Amor che a nullo amato amar perdona.'
—DANTE.[9]
'Amor m'addusse in sì gioiosa spene.'
PETRARCA.[10]

O my heart's heart, and you who are to me
More than myself myself, God be with you,
Keep you in strong obedience leal and true
To Him whose noble service setteth free;
Give you all good we see or can foresee,
Make your joys many and your sorrows few,
Bless you in what you bear and what you do,
Yea, perfect you as He would have you be.
So much for you; but what for me, dear friend?
To love you without stint and all I can,
To-day, to-morrow, world without an end;
To love you much and yet to love you more,
As Jordan at his flood sweeps either shore;
Since woman is the helpmeet made for man.

VI

'Or puoi la quantitate
Comprender de l'amor che a te mi scalda.'
—DANTE.[11]
'Non vo' che da tal nodo amor mi scioglia.'
—PETRARCA.[12]

Trust me, I have not earned your dear rebuke,—
I love, as you would have me, God the most;
Would lose not Him, but you, must one be lost,
Nor with Lot's wife cast back a faithless look,
Unready to forego what I forsook;
This say I, having counted up the cost,
This, though I be the feeblest of God's host,
The sorriest sheep Christ shepherds with His crook.
Yet while I love my God the most, I deem
That I can never love you overmuch;
I love Him more so let me love you too;
Yea, as I apprehend it, love is such
I cannot love you if I love not Him,
I cannot love Him if I love not you.

VII

'Qui primavera sempre ed ogni frutto.'
—DANTE.[13]
'Ragionando con meco ed io con lui.'
—PETRARCA.[14]

'Love me, for I love you'—and answer me,
'Love me, for I love you': so shall we stand
As happy equals in the flowering land
Of love, that knows not a dividing sea.
Love builds the house on rock and not on sand,
Love laughs what while the winds rave desperately;
And who hath found love's citadel unmanned?
And who hath held in bonds love's liberty?—
My heart's a coward though my words are brave—
We meet so seldom, yet we surely part
So often; there's a problem for your art!
Still I find comfort in his Book who saith,
Though jealousy be cruel as the grave,
And death be strong, yet love is strong as death.

VIII

'Come dicesse a Dio, D'altro non calme.'
—DANTE.[15]
'Spero trovar pietà non che perdono.'
—PETRARCA.[16]

'I, if I perish, perish'—Esther spake:
And, bride of life or death, she made her fair

[9] Love who excuses no beloved from loving.
[10] Love brought me to such joyous hope.
[11] Now canst thou understand the greatness of the love which burns in me for thee.
[12] I do not wish love to release me from such a tie.
[13] Here is always spring and every fruit.
[14] Conversing with me, and I with him.
[15] As if he were to say to God, I care for nothing else.
[16] I hope to find pity, not only pardon.

In all the lustre of her perfumed hair
And smiles that kindle longing but to slake.
She put on pomp of loveliness, to take
Her husband through his eyes at unaware;
She spread abroad her beauty for a snare,
Harmless as doves and subtle as a snake.
She trapped him with one mesh of silken hair,
She vanquished him by wisdom of her wit,
And built her people's house that it should stand:— 109
If I might take my life so in my hand,
And for my love to Love put up my prayer,
And for love's sake by Love be granted it!

IX

'O dignitosa coscienza e netta!'—DANTE.[17]
'Spirto piu acceso di virtuti ardenti.'
—PETRARCA.[18]

Thinking of you, and all that was, and all
That might have been and now can never be,
I feel your honoured excellence, and see
Myself unworthy of the happier call:
For woe is me who walk so apt to fall,
So apt to shrink afraid, so apt to flee,
Apt to lie down and die, (ah woe is me!)
Faithless and hopeless turning to the wall.
And yet not hopeless quite nor faithless quite, 121
Because not loveless; love may toil all night,
But take at morning; wrestle till the break
Of day, but then wield power with God and man:—
So take I heart of grace as best I can,
Ready to spend and be spent for your sake.

X

'Con miglior corso e con migliore stella.'
—DANTE.[19]
'La vita fugge e non s'arresta un' ora.'
—PETRARCA.[20]

Time flies, hope flags, life plies a wearied wing;
Death following hard on life gains ground apace;
Faith runs with each and rears an eager face,
Outruns the rest, makes light of everything,
Spurns earth, and still finds breath to pray and sing; 131
While love ahead of all uplifts his praise,
Still asks for grace and still gives thanks for grace,
Content with all day brings and night will bring.
Life wanes; and when love folds his wings above
Tired hope, and less we feel his conscious pulse,
Let us go fall asleep, dear friend, in peace:
A little while, and age and sorrow cease;
A little while, and life reborn annuls 139
Loss and decay and death, and all is love.

XI

'Vien dietro a me e lascia dir le genti.'
—DANTE.[21]
'Contando i casi della vita nostra.'—PETRARCA.[22]

Many in aftertimes will say of you
'He loved her'—while of me what will they say?
Not that I loved you more than just in play,
For fashion's sake as idle women do.
Even let them prate; who know not what we knew
Of love and parting in exceeding pain,
Of parting hopeless here to meet again,
Hopeless on earth, and heaven is out of view.
But by my heart of love laid bare to you,
My love that you can make not void nor vain, 150
Love that foregoes you but to claim anew
Beyond this passage of the gate of death,
I charge you at the Judgment make it plain
My love of you was life and not a breath.

XII

'Amor che ne la mente mi ragiona.'—DANTE.[23]
'Amor vien nel bel viso di costei.'—PETRARCA.[24]

If there be any one can take my place
And make you happy whom I grieve to grieve,

[17] Oh worthy and pure conscience!
[18] Spirit more fired with burning virtues.
[19] With better course and better star.
[20] Life fleets and stays not for an hour.
[21] Come after me and leave people to talk.
[22] Relating the casualties of our life.
[23] Love who speaks to me within my mind.
[24] Love comes in the fair face of this lady.

Think not that I can grudge it, but believe
I do commend you to that nobler grace,
That readier wit than mine, that sweeter face;
Yea, since your riches make me rich, conceive
I too am crowned, while bridal crowns I weave,
And thread the bridal dance with jocund pace.
For if I did not love you, it might be
That I should grudge you some one dear delight;
But since the heart is yours that was mine own,
Your pleasure is my pleasure, right my right,
Your honourable freedom makes me free,
And you companioned I am not alone.

XIII

'E drizzeremo gli occhi al Primo Amore.'
—DANTE.[25]
'Ma trovo peso non da le mie braccia.'
—PETRARCA.[26]

If I could trust mine own self with your fate,
Shall I not rather trust it in God's hand?
Without Whose Will one lily doth not stand,
Nor sparrow fall at his appointed date;
Who numbereth the innumerable sand,
Who weighs the wind and water with a weight,
To Whom the world is neither small nor great,
Whose knowledge foreknew every plan we planned.
Searching my heart for all that touches you,
I find there only love and love's goodwill
Helpless to help and impotent to do,
Of understanding dull, of sight most dim;
And therefore I commend you back to Him
Whose love your love's capacity can fill.

XIV

'E la Sua Voluntade è nostra pace.'—DANTE.[27]
'Sol con questi pensier, con altre chiome.'
—PETRARCA.[28]

Youth gone, and beauty gone if ever there
Dwelt beauty in so poor a face as this;
Youth gone and beauty, what remains of bliss?
I will not bind fresh roses in my hair,
To shame a cheek at best but little fair,—
Leave youth his roses, who can bear a thorn,—
I will not seek for blossoms anywhere,
Except such common flowers as blow with corn.
Youth gone and beauty gone, what doth remain?
The longing of a heart pent up forlorn,
A silent heart whose silence loves and longs;
The silence of a heart which sang its songs
While youth and beauty made a summer morn,
Silence of love that cannot sing again.

[1881]

[25] And we will direct our eyes to the First Love.

[26] But I find a burden too great for my arms.

[27] And His Will is our peace.

[28] Only with these thoughts, with other locks.

GEORGE MEREDITH

CHRONOLOGICAL TABLE

1828, Born February 12, at Portsmouth, his grandfather, Melchizedek Meredith, a naval outfitter and tailor, his father a ne'er-do-well.

1836–42 Attended schools at Portsmouth and Southsea.

1842–4 Attended a Moravian school at Neuwied on the Rhine.

1846 Articled to a solicitor in London.

1849 Married Mary Peacock Nicolls, daughter of the poet and novelist T. L. Peacock, and widow of a marine officer.

1851 *Poems.*

1855 *The Shaving of Shagpat* (a fantasy in prose).

1857 *Farina: a Legend of Cologne.*

1858 Mrs. Meredith separates from her husband.

1859 *The Ordeal of Richard Feverel.*

1860 Marriage of Janet Duff-Gordon, whom Meredith loved, to a banker in Alexandria.

1861 *Evan Harrington.*
Death of Mrs. Meredith.

1862 *Modern Love and Poems of the English Roadside.*

1864 *Emilia in England* (later renamed *Sandra Belloni*).
Married Marie Vulliamy, daughter of a Huguenot manufacturer, living in England.

1865 *Rhoda Fleming.*

1866 War correspondent for the *Morning Post* in Italy.

1867 *Vittoria.*
Established himself at Flint Cottage, Box Hill, in Surrey.

1871 *The Adventures of Harry Richmond.*

1875 *Beauchamp's Career.*

1877 *On the Idea of Comedy and the Uses of the Comic Spirit* (a lecture at the London Institution, printed in the *New Quarterly*).

1879 *The Egoist.*

1880 *The Tragic Comedians.*

1883 *Poems and Lyrics of the Joy of Earth.*

1884 Death of the second Mrs. Meredith.

1885 *Diana of the Crossways.*

1887 *Ballads and Poems of Tragic Life.*

1888 *A Reading of Earth.*

1891 *One of Our Conquerors.*

1892 *Jump to Glory Jane.*
Poems.
President of the Society of Authors.

1894 *Lord Ormont and his Aminta.*
The Tale of Chloe, The House on the Beach, The Case of General Ople and Lady Camper.

1895 *The Amazing Marriage.*

1898 *Odes in Contribution to the Song of French History.*

1905 Awarded the Order of Merit.

1906 *The Poetry and Philosophy of George Meredith,* by G. M. Trevelyan.

1909 *Last Poems.*
Died, at Box Hill, May 18, buried in Dorking Cemetery.

Writing in 1906, the most understanding interpreter Meredith's poetry has ever had remarked that the poet was fortunate in living to a great age, surviving to receive from the men of Mr. Trevelyan's generation the homage due from their grandfathers. It is true that both as novelist and as poet Meredith had to wait long for appreciation; and the poet had the longer wait. It is not surprising that Meredith's poetry was not widely hailed at the beginning of his career. His first collection, the *Poems* of 1851, is full of obscure suggestion and studded with such a bewildering richness of detail as to dazzle—uncomfortably—any ordinary lover of poetry. Such richness of detail and such obscure suggestion were always to be characteristic of Meredith, both in poetry and in prose, but in later years his substance was more solid and his details more precious in beauty; and readers of poetry did not so inevitably grow impatient of the difficulties which lay between them and the pleasures which the poems concealed. Many of the notices even of the first collection divined in its author a poet from whom uncommon achievement might come.

Meredith was, however, more than testy about the failure of his collection to make its way to immediate glory. He did not publish his second until he had made a name for himself, at least among an elite, with such novels as *The Ordeal of Richard Feverel* and *Evan Harrington.* Eleven years had elapsed when in 1862 he brought out a collection in which the longest and most prominent work was the sonnet-sequence *Modern Love.* Most of the later Victorian poets had to encounter at one time or another an angered critical opinion: *Modern Love* was bitterly attacked. Unlike the scandals over Hardy's *Jude* and over Swinburne's *Poems and Ballads,* the attack on *Modern Love* was essentially an affair among critics. The poem was much too difficult for popular success; it is indeed one of the deepest psychological soundings made in the Victorian age, comparing favorably as an interpretation of feeling and personality with the most elaborate achievements of the Victorian novel.

Twenty years passed before Meredith published another volume of poems. By that time he had taken his place as one of the chief (if not among the most popular) novelists of his time; but the critics of his poetry were not really disarmed. Nor did the deepened thought or the occasional passages of immediately exciting beauty, of phrase, image or music, suffice to disarm them. For English criticism Meredith was unpardonably obscure and mannered; and annoyance at his obscurity and manneredness, justified in itself, was allowed to affect almost fatally the perception of his great beauties and his even greater wisdom. So unreasonable did Meredith think the severity of his reviews that when in 1888 he publishd *A Reading of Earth* he forbade the issuance of review copies. Even in his last years, when young men and, even more, young women, were revering him as a sage, when Mr. Trevelyan was composing his tribute, the general critical opinion was not fundamentally changed. Critics were aware that, by reason of his novels, Meredith was one of the masters of contemporary writing: they dealt with his verse more respectfully, sometimes regretting their censures even as they expressed them, but at heart they were unreconciled to the crabbedness of the style, the saltatory method of thought, the incomprehensibly subtle twistings of emotion. Later criticism has confirmed many of the hesitations of these reviewers: but it has perceived in more than a few of his poems, strong evidence of depth of mind, sensibility amazingly intense, a style, which, whatever at its worst it may be, is at its best one of the most subtle and vigorous instruments for transmitting thought and feeling in the whole range of English poetry.

LOVE IN THE VALLEY

Under yonder beech-tree single on the green-sward,
  Couched with her arms behind her golden head,
Knees and tresses folded to slip and ripple idly,
  Lies my young love sleeping in the shade.
Had I the heart to slide an arm beneath her,
  Press her parting lips as her waist I gather slow,
Waking in amazement she could not but embrace me:
  Then would she hold me and never let me go?

. . . . . .

Shy as the squirrel and wayward as the swallow,
  Swift as the swallow along the river's light
Circleting the surface to meet his mirrored winglets,
  Fleeter she seems in her stay than in her flight.
Shy as the squirrel that leaps among the pine-tops,
  Wayward as the swallow overhead at set of sun,
She whom I love is hard to catch and conquer,
  Hard, but O the glory of the winning were she won!

When her mother tends her before the laughing mirror,
  Tying up her laces, looping up her hair,
Often she thinks, were this wild thing wedded,
  More love should I have, and much less care.
When her mother tends her before the lighted mirror,
  Loosening her laces, combing down her curls,

Often she thinks, were this wild thing wedded,
  I should miss but one for many boys and girls.

. . . . .

Heartless she is as the shadow in the meadows
  Flying to the hills on a blue and breezy noon.
No, she is athirst and drinking up her wonder:
  Earth to her is young as the slip of the new moon.
Deals she an unkindness, 't is but her rapid measure,
  Even as in a dance; and her smile can heal no less:
Like the swinging May-cloud that pelts the flowers with hailstones
  Off a sunny border, she was made to bruise and bless.

Lovely are the curves of the white owl sweeping
  Wavy in the dusk lit by one large star.
Lone on the fir-branch, his rattle-note unvaried,
  Brooding o'er the gloom, spins the brown evejar.
Darker grows the valley, more and more forgetting:
  So were it with me if forgetting could be willed.
Tell the grassy hollow that holds the bubbling well-spring,
  Tell it to forget the source that keeps it filled.

. . . . .

Stepping down the hill with her fair companions,
  Arm in arm, all against the raying West,
Boldly she sings, to the merry tune she marches,
  Brave is her shape, and sweeter unpossessed.
Sweeter, for she is what my heart first awakening
  Whispered the world was; morning light is she.
Love that so desires would fain keep her changeless;
  Fain would fling the net, and fain have her free.

Happy happy time, when the white star hovers
  Low over dim fields fresh with bloomy dew,
Near the face of dawn, that draws athwart the darkness,
  Threading it with colour, like yewberries the yew.
Thicker crowd the shades as the grave East deepens
  Glowing, and with crimson a long cloud swells.
Maiden still the morn is; and strange she is, and secret;
  Strange her eyes; her cheeks are cold as cold sea-shells.

. . . . .

Sunrays, leaning on our southern hills and lighting
  Wild cloud-mountains that drag the hills along,
Oft ends the day of your shifting brilliant laughter
  Chill as a dull face frowning on a song.
Ay, but shows the South-West a ripple-feathered bosom
  Blown to silver while the clouds are shaken and ascend
Scaling the mid-heavens as they stream, there comes a sunset
  Rich, deep like love in beauty without end.

When at dawn she sighs, and like an infant to the window
  Turns grave eyes craving light, released from dreams,

Beautiful she looks, like a white water-lily
  Bursting out of bud in havens of the streams.
When from bed she rises clothed from neck to ankle
  In her long nightgown sweet as boughs of May,
Beautiful she looks, like a tall garden lily
  Pure from the night, and splendid for the day.

. . . . .

Mother of the dews, dark eye-lashed twilight,
  Low-lidded twilight, o'er the valley's brim,
Rounding on thy breast sings the dew-delighted skylark,
  Clear as though the dewdrops had their voice in him.
Hidden where the rose-flush drinks the rayless planet,
  Fountain-full he pours the spraying fountain-showers.
Let me hear her laughter, I would have her ever
  Cool as dew in twilight, the lark above the flowers.

All the girls are out with their baskets for the primrose;
  Up lanes, woods through, they troop in joyful bands.
My sweet leads: she knows not why, but now she loiters,
  Eyes the bent anemones, and hangs her hands.
Such a look will tell that the violets are peeping,
  Coming the rose: and unaware a cry
Springs in her bosom for odours and for colour,
  Covert and the nightingale; she knows not why.

. . . .

Kerchiefed head and chin she darts between her tulips,
  Streaming like a willow grey in arrowy rain:
Some bend beaten cheek to gravel, and their angel
  She will be; she lifts them, and on she speeds again.
Black the driving raincloud breasts the iron gateway:
  She is forth to cheer a neighbour lacking mirth.
So when sky and grass met rolling dumb for thunder
  Saw I once a white dove, sole light of earth.

Prim little scholars are the flowers of her garden,
  Trained to stand in rows, and asking if they please.
I might love them well but for loving more the wild ones:
  O my wild ones! they tell me more than these.
You, my wild one, you tell of honied field-rose,
  Violet, blushing eglantine in life; and even as they,
They by the wayside are earnest of your goodness,
  You are of life's, on the banks that line the way.

. . . .

Peering at her chamber the white crowns the red rose,
  Jasmine winds the porch with stars two and three.
Parted is the window; she sleeps; the starry jasmine
  Breathes a falling breath that carries thoughts of me,
Sweeter unpossessed, have I said of her my sweetest?
  Not while she sleeps: while she sleeps the jasmine breathes,
Luring her to love; she sleeps; the starry jasmine
  Bears me to her pillow under white rose-wreaths.

Yellow with birdfoot-trefoil are the grass-glades;
  Yellow with cinquefoil of the dew-grey leaf;
Yellow with stonecrop; the moss-mounds are yellow;
  Blue-necked the wheat sways, yellowing to the sheaf.
Green-yellow bursts from the copse the laughing yaffle;
  Sharp as a sickle is the edge of shade and shine:
Earth in her heart laughs looking at the heavens,
  Thinking of the harvest: I look and think of mine.

. . . . . .

This I may know: her dressing and undressing
  Such a change of light shows as when the skies in sport
Shift from cloud to moonlight; or edging over thunder
  Slips a ray of sun; or sweeping into port
White sails furl; or on the ocean borders
  White sails lean along the waves leaping green.
Visions of her shower before me, but from eyesight
  Guarded she would be like the sun were she seen.

Front door and back of the mossed old farmhouse
  Open with the morn, and in a breezy link
Freshly sparkles garden to stripe-shadowed orchard,
  Green across a rill where on sand the minnows wink.
Busy in the grass the early sun of summer
  Swarms, and the blackbird's mellow fluting notes
Call my darling up with round and roguish challenge:
  Quaintest, richest carol of all the singing throats!

. . . . . .

Cool was the woodside; cool as her white dairy
  Keeping sweet the cream-pan; and there the boys from school,
Cricketing below, rushed brown and red with sunshine;
  O the dark translucence of the deep-eyed cool!
Spying from the farm, herself she fetched a pitcher
  Full of milk, and tilted for each in turn the beak.
Then a little fellow, mouth up and on tiptoe,
  Said, 'I will kiss you'; she laughed and leaned her cheek.

Doves of the fir-wood walling high our red roof
  Through the long noon coo, crooning through the coo.
Loose droop the leaves, and down the sleepy roadway
  Sometimes pipes a chaffinch; loose droops the blue.
Cows flap a slow tail knee-deep in the river,
  Breathless, given up to sun and gnat and fly.
Nowhere is she seen; and if I see her nowhere,
Lightning may come, straight rains and tiger sky.

O the golden sheaf, the rustling treasure-armful!
  O the nutbrown tresses nodding interlaced!
O the treasure-tresses one another over
  Nodding! O the girdle slack about the waist!
Slain are the poppies that shot their random scarlet
  Quick amid the wheatears: wound about the waist,
Gathered, see these brides of Earth one blush of ripeness!
  O the nutbrown tresses nodding interlaced!

Large and smoky red the sun's cold disk drops,
  Clipped by naked hills, on violet shaded snow:
Eastward large and still lights up a bower of moonrise,
  Whence at her leisure steps the moon aglow.
Nightlong on black print-branches our beech-tree
  Gazes in this whiteness; nightlong could I.
Here may life on death or death on life be painted.
  Let me clasp her soul to know she cannot die!

. . . . . .

Gossips count her faults: they scour a narrow chamber
  Where there is no window, read not heaven or her.
'When she was a tiny,' one aged woman quavers,
  Plucks at my heart and leads me by the ear.
Faults she had once as she learnt to run and tumbled:
  Faults of feature some see, beauty not complete.
Yet, good gossips, beauty that makes holy
  Earth and air, may have faults from head to feet.

Hither she comes; she comes to me; she lingers,
  Deepens her brown eyebrows, while in new surprise
High rise the lashes in wonder of a stranger;
  Yet am I the light and living of her eyes.
Something friends have told her fills her heart to brimming,
  Nets her in her blushes, and wounds her, and tames.—
Sure of her haven, O like a dove alighting,
  Arms up, she dropped: our souls were in our names.

. . . . . .

Soon will she lie like a white frost sunrise.
  Yellow oats and brown wheat, barley pale as rye,
Long since your sheaves have yielded to the thresher,
  Felt the girdle loosened, seen the tresses fly.
Soon will she lie like a blood-red sunset.
  Swift with the to-morrow, green-winged Spring!
Sing from the South-West, bring her back the truants,
  Nightingale and swallow, song and dipping wing.

Soft new beech-leaves, up to beamy April
  Spreading bough on bough a primrose mountain, you
Lucid in the moon, raise lilies to the skyfields,
  Youngest green transfused in silver shining through:
Fairer than the lily, than the wild white cherry:
  Fair as in image my seraph love appears
Borne to me by dreams when dawn is at my eyelids:
  Fair as in the flesh she swims to me on tears.

. . . . . .

Could I find a place to be alone with heaven,
  I would speak my heart out: heaven is my need.
Every woodland tree is flushing like the dogwood,
  Flashing like the whitebeam, swaying like the reed.
Flushing like the dogwood crimson in October;
  Streaming like the flag-reed South-West blown;
Flashing as in gusts the sudden-lighted whitebeam:
  All seem to know what is for heaven alone.

[1851, 1878]

JUGGLING JERRY

I

Pitch here the tent, while the old horse grazes:
By the old hedge-side we'll halt a stage.
It's nigh my last above the daisies:
My next leaf'll be man's blank page.
Yes, my old girl! and it's no use crying:
Juggler, constable, king, must bow.
One that outjuggles all's been spying
Long to have me, and he has me now.

II

We've travelled times to this old common:
Often we've hung our pots in the gorse.
We've had a stirring life, old woman!
You, and I, and the old grey horse.
Races, and fairs, and royal occasions,
Found us coming to their call:
Now they'll miss us at our stations:
There's a Juggler outjuggles all!

III

Up goes the lark, as if all were jolly!
Over the duck-pond the willow shakes.
Easy to think that grieving's folly,
When the hand's firm as driven stakes!
Ay, when we're strong, and braced, and manful,
Life's a sweet fiddle: but we're a batch
Born to become the Great Juggler's han'ful:
Balls he shies up, and is safe to catch.

IV

Here's where the lads of the village cricket:
I was a lad not wide from here:
Could'nt I whip off the bale from the wicket?
Like an old world those days appear!
Donkey, sheep, geese, and thatched ale-house—I know them!
They are old friends of my halts, and seem,
Somehow, as if kind thanks I owe them:
Juggling don't hinder the heart's esteem.

V

Juggling's no sin, for we must have victual:
Nature allows us to bait for the fool.
Holding one's own makes us juggle no little;
But, to increase it, hard juggling's the rule.
You that are sneering at my profession,
Haven't you juggled a vast amount?
There's the Prime Minister, in one Session,
Juggles more games than my sins'll count.

VI

I've murdered insects with mock thunder:
Conscience, for that, in men don't quail.
I've made bread from the bump of wonder:
That's my business, and there's my tale.
Fashion and rank all praised the professor:
Ay! and I've had my smile from the Queen:
Bravo, Jerry! she meant: God bless her!
Ain't this a sermon on that scene?

VII

I've studied men from my topsy-turvy
Close, and, I reckon, rather true.
Some are fine fellows: some, right scurvy:
Most, a dash between the two.
But it's a woman, old girl, that makes me
Think more kindly of the race:
And it's a woman, old girl, that shakes me
When the Great Juggler I must face.

VIII

We two were married, due and legal:
Honest we've lived since we've been one.
Lord! I could then jump like an eagle:
You danced bright as a bit o' the sun.
Birds in a May-bush we were! right merry!
All night we kiss'd, we juggled all day.
Joy was the heart of Juggling Jerry!
Now from his old girl he's juggled away.

IX

It's past parsons to console us:
No, nor no doctor fetch for me:
I can die without my bolus;
Two of a trade, lass, never agree!
Parson and Doctor!—don't they love rarely,
Fighting the devil in other men's fields!
Stand up yourself and match him fairly:
Then see how the rascal yields!

X

I, lass, have lived no gipsy, flaunting
Finery while his poor helpmate grubs:
Coin I've stored, and you won't be wanting:
You sha'n't beg from the troughs and tubs.
Nobly you've stuck to me, though in his kitchen

Many a Marquis would hail you Cook!
Palaces you could have ruled and grown rich in,
But your old Jerry you never forsook.

XI

Hand up the chirper! ripe ale winks in it;
Let's have comfort and be at peace.
Once a stout draught made me light as a linnet.
Cheer up! the Lord must have his lease.
May be—for none see in that black hollow—
It's just a place where we're held in pawn,
And, when the Great Juggler makes as to swallow,
It's just the sword trick—I ain't quite gone!

XII

Yonder came smells of the gorse, so nutty,
Gold-like and warm: it's the prime of May.
Better than mortar, brick and putty,
Is God's house on a blowing day.
Lean me more up the mound; now I feel it:
All the old heath-smells! Ain't it strange?
There's the world laughing, as if to conceal it,
But He's by us, juggling the change.

XIII

I mind it well, by the sea-beach lying,
Once—it's long gone—when two gulls we beheld,
Which, as the moon got up, were flying
Down a big wave that sparked and swelled.
Crack, went a gun: one fell: the second
Wheeled round him twice, and was off for new luck:
There in the dark her white wing beckon'd:—
Drop me a kiss—I'm the bird deadstruck!

[1859]

MODERN LOVE

THE PROMISE IN DISTURBANCE

How low when angels fall their black descent,
Our primal thunder tells: known is the pain
Of music, that nigh throning wisdom went,
And one false note cast wailful to the insane.
Now seems the language heard of Love as rain
To make a mire where fruitfulness was meant.
The golden harp gives out a jangled strain,
Too like revolt from heaven's Omnipotent.
But listen in the thought; so may there come
Conception of a newly-added chord,
Commanding space beyond where ear has home.
In labour of the trouble at its fount,
Leads Life to an intelligible Lord
The rebel discords up the sacred mount.

[1892]

I

By this he knew she wept with waking eyes:
That, at his hand's light quiver by her head,
The strange low sobs that shook their common bed,
Were called into her with a sharp surprise,
And strangled mute, like little gaping snakes,
Dreadfully venomous to him. She lay
Stone-still, and the long darkness flowed away

With muffled pulses. Then, as midnight makes
Her giant heart of Memory and Tears
Drink the pale drug of silence, and so beat
Sleep's heavy measure, they from head to feet
Were moveless, looking through their dead black years,
By vain regret scrawled over the blank wall.
Like sculptured effigies they might be seen
Upon their marriage-tomb, the sword between;
Each wishing for the sword that severs all.

II

It ended, and the morrow brought the task.
Her eyes were guilty gates, that let him in
By shutting all too zealous for their sin:
Each sucked a secret, and each wore a mask.
But, oh, the bitter taste her beauty had!
He sickened as at breath of poison-flowers:
A languid humour stole among the hours,
And if their smiles encountered, he went mad,
And raged deep inward, till the light was brown
Before his vision, and the world, forgot,
Looked wicked as some old dull murder-spot.
A star with lurid beams, she seemed to crown
The pit of infamy: and then again
He fainted on his vengefulness, and strove
To ape the magnanimity of love,
And smote himself, a shuddering heap of pain.

III

This was the woman; what now of the man?
But pass him. If he comes beneath a heel,
He shall be crushed until he cannot feel,
Or, being callous, haply till he can.
But he is nothing:—nothing? Only mark
The rich light striking out from her on him!
Ha! what a sense it is when her eyes swim
Across the man she singles, leaving dark
All else! Lord God, who mad'st the thing so fair,
See that I am drawn to her even now!
It cannot be such harm on her cool brow
To put a kiss? Yet if I meet him there!
But she is mine! Ah, no! I know too well
I claim a star whose light is overcast:
I claim a phantom-woman in the Past.
The hour has struck, though I heard not the bell!

IV

All other joys of life he strove to warm,
And magnify, and catch them to his lip:
But they had suffered shipwreck with the ship,
And gazed upon him sallow from the storm.
Or if Delusion came, 't was but to show

The coming minute mock the one that went.
Cold as a mountain in its star-pitched tent,
Stood high Philosophy, less friend than foe:
Whom self-caged Passion, from its prison-bars,
Is always watching with a wondering hate.
Not till the fire is dying in the grate,
Look we for any kinship with the stars.
Oh, wisdom never comes when it is gold,
And the great price we pay for it full worth:
We have it only when we are half earth.
Little avails that coinage to the old!

V

A message from her set his brain aflame.
A world of household matters filled her mind,
Wherein he saw hypocrisy designed:
She treated him as something that is tame,
And but at other provocation bites.
Familiar was her shoulder in the glass,
Through that dark rain: yet it may come to pass
That a changed eye finds such familiar sights
More keenly tempting than new loveliness.
The 'What has been' a moment seemed his own:
The splendours, mysteries, dearer because known,
Nor less divine: Love's inmost sacredness,
Called to him, 'Come!'—In his restraining start,
Eyes nurtured to be looked at, scarce could see
A wave of the great waves of Destiny
Convulsed at a checked impulse of the heart.

VI

It chanced his lips did meet her forehead cool.
She had no blush, but slanted down her eye.
Shamed nature, then, confesses love can die:
And most she punishes the tender fool
Who will believe what honours her the most!
Dead! is it dead? She has a pulse, and flow
Of tears, the price of blood-drops, as I know,
For whom the midnight sobs around Love's ghost,
Since then I heard her, and so will sob on.
The love is here; it has but changed its aim.
O bitter barren woman! what's the name?
The name, the name, the new name thou hast won?
Behold me striking the world's coward stroke!
That will I not do, though the sting is dire.
—Beneath the surface this, while by the fire
They sat, she laughing at a quiet joke.

VII

She issues radiant from her dressing-room,
Like one prepared to scale an upper sphere:
—By stirring up a lower, much I fear!

How deftly that oiled barber lays his bloom!
That long-shanked dapper Cupid with frisked curls,
Can make known women torturingly fair;
The gold-eyed serpent dwelling in rich hair,
Awakes beneath his magic whisks and twirls.
His art can take the eyes from out my head,
Until I see with eyes of other men;
While deeper knowledge crouches in its den,
And sends a spark up:—is it true we are wed?
Yea! filthiness of body is most vile,
But faithlessness of heart I do hold worse.
The former, it were not so great a curse
To read on the steel-mirror of her smile.

VIII

Yet it was plain she struggled, and that salt
Of righteous feeling made her pitiful.
Poor twisting worm, so queenly beautiful!
Where came the cleft between us? whose the fault
My tears are on thee, that have rarely dropped
As balm for any bitter wound of mine:
My breast will open for thee at a sign!
But, no: we are two reed-pipes, coarsely stopped:
The God once filled them with his mellow breath;
And they were music till he flung them down,
Used! used! Hear now the discord-loving clown
Puff his gross spirit in them, worse than death!
I do not know myself without thee more:
In this unholy battle I grow base:
If the same soul be under the same face,
Speak, and a taste of that old time restore!

IX

He felt the wild beast in him betweenwhiles
So masterfully rude, that he would grieve
To see the helpless delicate thing receive
His guardianship through certain dark defiles.
Had he not teeth to rend, and hunger too?
But still he spared her. Once: 'Have you no fear?'
He said: 't was dusk; she in his grasp; none near
She laughed: 'No, surely; am I not with you?'
And uttering that soft starry 'you,' she leaned
Her gentle body near him, looking up;
And from her eyes, as from a poison-cup,
He drank until the flittering eyelids screened.
Devilish malignant witch! and oh, young beam
Of heaven's circle-glory! Here thy shape
To squeeze like an intoxicating grape—
I might, and yet thou goest safe, supreme.

X

But where began the change; and what's my crime?
The wretch condemned, who has not been arraigned
Chafes at his sentence. Shall I, unsustained,
Drag on Love's nerveless body thro' all time?
I must have slept, since now I wake. Prepare,
You lovers, to know Love a thing of moods:
Not like hard life, of laws. In Love's deep woods,
I dreamt of loyal Life:—the offence is there!
Love's jealous woods about the sun are curled;
At least, the sun far brighter there did beam.—
My crime is, that the puppet of a dream,
I plotted to be worthy of the world.
Oh, had I with my darling helped to mince
The facts of life, you still had seen me go
With hindward feather and with forward toe,
Her much-adored delightful Fairy Prince!

XI

Out in the yellow meadows, where the bee
Hums by us with the honey of the Spring,
And showers of sweet notes from the larks on wing,
Are dropping like a noon-dew, wander we.
Or is it now? or was it then? for now,
As then, the larks from running rings pour showers:
The golden foot of May is on the flowers,
And friendly shadows dance upon her brow.
What's this, when Nature swears there is no change
To challenge eyesight? Now, as then, the grace
Of heaven seems holding earth in its embrace.
Nor eyes, nor heart, has she to feel it strange?
Look, woman, in the West. There wilt thou see
An amber cradle near the sun's decline:
Within it, featured even in death divine,
Is lying a dead infant, slain by thee.

XII

Not solely that the Future she destroys,
And the fair life which in the distance lies
For all men, beckoning out from dim rich skies:
Nor that the passing hour's supporting joys
Have lost the keen-edged flavour, which begat
Distinction in old times, and still should breed
Sweet Memory, and Hope,—earth's modest seed,
And heaven's high-prompting: not that the world is flat
Since that soft-luring creature I embraced
Among the children of Illusion went:
Methinks with all this loss I were content,
If the mad Past, on which my foot is based,
Were firm, or might be blotted: but the whole
Of life is mixed: the mocking Past will stay:
And if I drink oblivion of a day,
So shorten I the stature of my soul.

XIII

'I play for Seasons; not Eternities!'
Says Nature, laughing on her way. 'So must
All those whose stake is nothing more than dust!'
And lo, she wins, and of her harmonies
She is full sure! Upon her dying rose
She drops a look of fondness, and goes by,
Scarce any retrospection in her eye;
For she the laws of growth most deeply knows,
Whose hands bear, here, a seed-bag—there, an urn.
Pledged she herself to aught, 't would mark her end!
This lesson of our only visible friend,
Can we not teach our foolish hearts to learn?
Yes! yes!—but, oh, our human rose is fair
Surpassingly! Lose calmly Love's great bliss,
When the renewed for ever of a kiss
Whirls life within the shower of loosened hair!

XIV

What soul would bargain for a cure that brings
Contempt the nobler agony to kill?
Rather let me bear on the bitter ill,
And strike this rusty bosom with new stings!
It seems there is another veering fit,
Since on a gold-haired lady's eyeballs pure,
I looked with little prospect of a cure,
The while her mouth's red bow loosed shafts of wit.
Just heaven! can it be true that jealousy
Has decked the woman thus? and does her head
Swim somewhat for possessions forfeited?
Madam, you teach me many things that be.
I open an old book, and there I find,
That 'Women still may love whom they deceive.'
Such love I prize not, madam: by your leave,
The game you play at is not to my mind.

XV

I think she sleeps: it must be sleep, when low
Hangs that abandoned arm toward the floor;
The face turned with it. Now make fast the door.
Sleep on: it is your husband, not your foe.
The Poet's black stage-lion of wronged love,
Frights not our modern dames:—well if he did!
Now will I pour new light upon that lid,
Full-sloping like the breasts beneath. 'Sweet dove,
Your sleep is pure. Nay, pardon: I disturb.
I do not? good!' Her waking infant-stare
Grows woman to the burden my hands bear:
Her own handwriting to me when no curb
Was left on Passion's tongue. She trembles through;
A woman's tremble—the whole instrument:—
I show another letter lately sent.
The words are very like: the name is new.

XVI

In our old shipwrecked days there was an hour,
When in the firelight steadily aglow,
Joined slackly, we beheld the red chasm grow
Among the clicking coals. Our library-bower
That eve was left to us: and hushed we sat
As lovers to whom Time is whispering.
From sudden-opened doors we heard them sing:
The nodding elders mixed good wine with chat.
Well knew we that Life's greatest treasure lay
With us, and of it was our talk. 'Ah, yes!
Love dies!' I said: I never thought it less.
She yearned to me that sentence to unsay.
Then when the fire domed blackening, I found
Her cheek was salt against my kiss, and swift
Up the sharp scale of sobs her breast did lift:—
Now am I haunted by that taste! that sound!

XVII

At dinner, she is hostess, I am host.
Went the feast ever cheerfuller? She keeps
The Topic over intellectual deeps
In buoyancy afloat. They see no ghost.
With sparkling surface-eyes we ply the ball:
It is in truth a most contagious game:
HIDING THE SKELETON, shall be its name.
Such play as this the devils might appal!
But here's the greater wonder; in that we
Enamoured of an acting nought can tire,
Each other, like true hypocrites, admire;
Warm-lighted looks, Love's ephemeriae,
Shoot gaily o'er the dishes and the wine.
We waken envy of our happy lot.
Fast, sweet, and golden, shows the marriage-knot.
Dear guests, you now have seen Love's corpse-light shine.

XVIII

Here Jack and Tom are paired with Moll and Meg.
Curved open to the river-reach is seen
A country merry-making on the green.
Fair space for signal shakings of the leg.
That little screwy fiddler from his booth,
Whence flows one nut-brown stream, commands the joints
Of all who caper here at various points.
I have known rustic revels in my youth:
The May-fly pleasures of a mind at ease.
An early goddess was a county lass:
A charmed Amphion-oak she tripped the grass.
What life was that I lived? The life of these?
Heaven keep them happy! Nature they seem near
They must, I think, be wiser than I am;
They have the secret of the bull and lamb.
'Tis true that when we trace its source, 'tis beer.

XIX

No state is enviable. To the luck alone
Of some few favoured men I would put claim.
I bleed, but her who wounds I will not blame.
Have I not felt her heart as 'twere my own
Beat thro' me? could I hurt her? heaven and hell!
But I could hurt her cruelly! Can I let
My Love's old time-piece to another set,
Swear it can't stop, and must for ever swell?
Sure, that's one way Love drifts into the mart
Where goat-legged buyers throng. I see not plain:—
My meaning is, it must not be again.
Great God! the maddest gambler throws his heart.
If any state be enviable on earth,
'Tis yon born idiot's, who, as days go by,
Still rubs his hands before him, like a fly,
In a queer sort of meditative mirth.

XX

I am not of those miserable males
Who sniff at vice, and daring not to snap,
Do therefore hope for heaven. I take the hap
Of all my deeds. The wind that fills my sails
Propels; but I am helmsman. Am I wrecked,
I know the devil has sufficient weight
To bear: I lay it not on him, or fate.
Besides, he's damned. That man I do suspect
A coward, who would burden the poor deuce
With what ensues from his own slipperiness.
I have just found a wanton-scented tress
In an old desk, dusty for lack of use.
Of days and nights it is demonstrative,
That, like some aged star, gleam luridly
If for those times I must ask charity.
Have I not any charity to give?

XXI

We three are on the cedar-shadowed lawn;
My friend being third. He who at love once laughed
Is in the weak rib by a fatal shaft
Struck through, and tells his passion's bashful dawn
And radiant culmination, glorious crown,
When 'this' she said: went 'thus': most wondrous she.
Our eyes grow white, encountering: that we are three,
Forgetful; then together we look down.
But he demands our blessing; is convinced
That words of wedded lovers must bring good.
We question; if we dare! or if we should!
And pat him, with light laugh. We have not winced.
Next, she has fallen. Fainting points the sign
To happy things in wedlock. When she wakes,
She looks the star that thro' the cedar shakes:
Her lost moist hand clings mortally to mine.

XXII

What may the woman labour to confess?
There is about her mouth a nervous twitch.
'Tis something to be told, or hidden:—which?
I get a glimpse of hell in this mild guess.
She has desires of touch, as if to feel
That all the household things are things she knew.
She stops before the glass. What sight in view?
A face that seems the latest to reveal!
For she turns from it hastily, and tossed
Irresolute, steals shadow-like to where
I stand; and wavering pale before me there,
Her tears fall still as oak-leaves after frost.
She will not speak. I will not ask. We are
League-sundered by the silent gulf between.
You burly lovers on the village green,
Yours is a lower, and a happier star!

XXIII

'Tis Christmas weather, and a country house
Receives us: rooms are full: we can but get
An attic-crib. Such lovers will not fret
At that, it is half-said. The great carouse
Knocks hard upon the midnight's hollow door,
But when I knock at hers, I see the pit.
Why did I come here in that dullard fit?
I enter, and lie couched upon the floor.
Passing, I caught the coverlet's quick beat:—
Come, Shame, burn to my soul! and Pride, and Pain—
Foul demons that have tortured me, enchain!
Out in the freezing darkness the lambs bleat.
The small bird stiffens in the low starlight.
I know not how, but shuddering as I slept,
I dreamed a banished angel to me crept:
My feet were nourished on her breasts all night.

XXIV

The misery is greater, as I live!
To know her flesh so pure, so keen her sense,
That she does penance now for no offence,
Save against Love. The less can I forgive!
The less can I forgive, though I adore
That cruel lovely pallor which surrounds
Her footsteps; and the low vibrating sounds
That come on me, as from a magic shore.
Low are they, but most subtle to find out
The shrinking soul. Madam, 'tis understood
When women play upon their womanhood,
It means, a Season gone. And yet I doubt
But I am duped. That nun-like look waylays
My fancy. Oh! I do but wait a sign!
Pluck out the eyes of pride! thy mouth to mine
Never! though I die thirsting. Go thy ways.

XXV

You like not that French novel? Tell me why.
You think it quite unnatural. Let us see.
The actors are, it seems, the usual three:
Husband, and wife and lover. She—but fie!
In England we'll not hear of it. Edmond,
The lover, her devout chagrin doth share;
Blanc-mange and absinthe are his penitent fare,
Till his pale aspect makes her over-fond:
So, to preclude fresh sin, he tries rosbif.
Meantime the husband is no more abused:
Auguste forgives her ere the tear is used.
Then hangeth all on one tremendous IF:—
If she will choose between them. She does choose;
And takes her husband, like a proper wife.
Unnatural? My dear, these things are life:
And life, some think, is worthy of the Muse.

XXVI

Love ere he bleeds, an eagle in high skies,
Has earth beneath his wings: from reddened eve
He views the rosy dawn. In vain they weave
The fatal web below while far he flies.
But when the arrow strikes him, there's a change.
He moves but in the track of his spent pain,
Whose red drops are the links of a harsh chain,
Binding him to the ground, with narrow range.
A subtle serpent then has Love become.
I had the eagle in my bosom erst:
Henceforward with the serpent I am cursed.
I can interpret where the mouth is dumb.
Speak, and I see the side-lie of a truth.
Perchance my heart may pardon you this deed:
But be no coward:—you that made Love bleed,
You must bear all the venom of his tooth!

XXVII

Distraction is the panacea, Sir!
I hear my oracle of Medicine say.
Doctor! that same specific yesterday
I tried, and the result will not deter
A second trial. Is the devil's line
Of golden hair, or raven black, composed?
And does a cheek, like any sea-shell rosed,
Or clear as widowed sky, seem most divine?
No matter, so I taste forgetfulness.
And if the devil snare me, body and mind,
Here gratefully I score:—he seemëd kind,
When not a soul would comfort my distress!
O sweet new world, in which I rise new made!
O Lady, once I gave love: now I take!
Lady, I must be flattered. Shouldst thou wake
The passion of a demon, be not afraid.

XXVIII

I must be flattered. The imperious
Desire speaks out. Lady, I am content
To play with you the game of Sentiment,
And with you enter on paths perilous;
But if across your beauty I throw light,
To make it threefold, it must be all mine.
First secret; then avowed. For I must shine
Envied,—I, lessened in my proper sight!
Be watchful of your beauty, Lady dear!
How much hangs on that lamp you cannot tell.
Most earnestly I pray you, tend it well:
And men shall see me as a burning sphere;
And men shall mark you eying me, and groan
To be the God of such a grand sunflower!
I feel the promptings of Satanic power,
While you do homage unto me alone.

XXIX

Am I failing? For no longer can I cast
A glory round about this head of gold.
Glory she wears, but springing from the mould;
Not like the consecration of the Past!
Is my soul beggared? Something more than earth
I cry for still: I cannot be at peace
In having Love upon a mortal lease.
I cannot take the woman at her worth!
Where is the ancient wealth wherewith I clothed
Our human nakedness, and could endow
With spiritual splendour a white brow
That else had grinned at me the fact I loathed?
A kiss is but a kiss now! and no wave
Of a great flood that whirls me to the sea.
But, as you will! we'll sit contentedly,
And eat our pot of honey on the grave.

XXX

What are we first? First, animals; and next
Intelligences at a leap, on whom
Pale lies the distant shadow of the tomb,
And all that draweth on the tomb for text.
Into which state comes Love, the crowning sun:
Beneath whose light the shadow loses form.
We are the lords of life, and life is warm.
Intelligence and instinct now are one.
But nature says: 'My children most they seem
When they least know me: therefore I decree
That they shall suffer.' Swift doth young Love flee,
And we stand wakened, shivering from our dream.
Then if we study Nature we are wise.
Thus do the few who live but with the day:
The scientific animals are they.—
Lady, this is my sonnet to your eyes.

XXXI

This golden head has wit in it. I live
Again, and a far higher life, near her,
Some women like a young philosopher;
Perchance because he is diminutive.
For woman's manly god must not exceed
Proportions of the natural nursing size.
Great poets and great sages draw no prize
With women: but the little lap-dog breed,
Who can be hugged, or on a mantel-piece
Perched up for adoration, these obtain
Her homage. And of this we men are vain?
Of this! 'Tis ordered for the world's increase!
Small flattery! Yet she has that rare gift
To beauty, Common Sense. I am approved.
It is not half so nice as being loved,
And yet I do prefer it. What's my drift?

XXXII

Full faith I have she holds that rarest gift
To beauty, Common Sense. To see her lie
With her fair visage an inverted sky
Bloom-covered, while the underlids uplift,
Would almost wreck the faith; but when her mouth
(Can it kiss sweetly? sweetly!) would address
The inner me that thirsts for her no less,
And has so long been languishing in drouth,
I feel that I am matched; that I am man!
One restless corner of my heart or head,
That holds a dying something never dead,
Still frets, though Nature giveth all she can.
It means, that woman is not, I opine,
Her sex's antidote. Who seeks the asp
For serpents' bites? 'Twould calm me could I clasp
Shrieking Bacchantes with their souls of wine!

XXXIII

'In Paris, at the Louvre, there have I seen
The sumptuously-feathered angel pierce
Prone Lucifer, descending. Looked he fierce,
Showing the fight a fair one? Too serene!
The young Pharsalians did not disarray
Less willingly their locks of floating silk:
That suckling mouth of his, upon the milk
Of heaven might still be feasting through the fray.
Oh, Raphael! when men the Fiend do fight,
They conquer not upon such easy terms.
Half serpent in the struggle grow these worms.
And does he grow half human, all is right.'
This to my Lady in a distant spot,
Upon the theme: *While mind is mastering clay,*
Gross clay invades it. If the spy you play,
My wife, read this! Strange love-talk, is it not?

XXXIV

Madam would speak with me. So, now it comes:
The Deluge or else Fire! She's well; she thanks
My husbandship. Our chain on silence clanks.
Time leers between, above his twiddling thumbs.
Am I quite well? Most excellent in health!
The journals, too, I diligently peruse.
Vesuvius is expected to give news:
Niagara is no noisier. By stealth
Our eyes dart scrutinizing snakes. She's glad
I'm happy, says her quivering under-lip.
'And are not you?' 'How can I be?' 'Take ship!
For happiness is somewhere to be had.'
'Nowhere for me!' Her voice is barely heard.
I am not melted, and make no pretence.
With commonplace I freeze her, tongue and sense.
Niagara or Vesuvius is deferred.

XXXV

It is no vulgar nature I have wived.
Secretive, sensitive, she takes a wound
Deep to her soul, as if the sense had swooned,
And not a thought of vengeance had survived.
No confidences has she: but relief
Must come to one whose suffering is acute.
O have a care of natures that are mute!
They punish you in acts: their steps are brief.
What is she doing? What does she demand
From Providence or me? She is not one
Long to endure this torpidly, and shun
The drugs that crowd about a woman's hand.
At Forfeits during snow we played, and I
Must kiss her. 'Well performed!' I said: then she:
' 'Tis hardly worth the money, you agree?'
Save her? What for? To act this wedded lie!

XXXVI

My Lady unto Madam makes her bow.
The charm of women is, that even while
You're probed by them for tears, you yet may smile,
Nay, laugh outright, as I have done just now.
The interview was gracious: they anoint
(To me aside) each other with fine praise:
Discriminating compliments they raise,
That hit with wondrous aim on the weak point:
My Lady's nose of Nature might complain.
It is not fashioned aptly to express
Her character of large-browed steadfastness.
But Madam says: Thereof she may be vain!
Now, Madam's faulty feature is a glazed
And inaccessible eye, that has soft fires,
Wide gates, at love-time only. This admires
My Lady. At the two I stand amazed.

XXXVII

Along the garden terrace, under which
A purple valley (lighted at its edge
By smoky torch-flame on the long cloud-ledge
Whereunder dropped the chariot), glimmers rich,
A quiet company we pace, and wait
The dinner-bell in prae-digestive calm.
So sweet up violet banks the Southern balm
Breathes round, we care not if the bell be late:
Though here and there grey seniors question Time
In irritable coughings. With slow foot
The low rosed moon, the face of Music mute,
Begins among her silent bars to climb.
As in and out, in silvery dusk, we thread,
I hear the laugh of Madam, and discern
My Lady's heel before me at each turn.
Our tragedy, is it alive or dead?

XXXVIII

Give to imagination some pure light
In human form to fix it, or you shame
The devils with that hideous human game:—
Imagination urging appetite!
Thus fallen have earth's greatest Gogmagogs,
Who dazzle us, whom we can not revere:
Imagination is the charioteer
That, in default of better, drives the hogs.
So, therefore, my dear Lady, let me love!
My soul is arrowy to the light in you.
You know me that I never can renew
The bond that woman broke: what would you have?
'Tis Love, or Vileness! not a choice between,
Save petrifaction! What does Pity here?
She killed a thing, and now it's dead, 'tis dear.
Oh, when you counsel me, think what you mean!

XXXIX

She yields: my Lady in her noblest mood
Has yielded: she, my golden-crownëd rose!
The bride of every sense! more sweet than those
Who breathe the violet breath of maidenhood.
O visage of still music in the sky!
Soft moon! I feel thy song, my fairest friend!
True harmony within can apprehend
Dumb harmony without. And hark! 'tis nigh!
Belief has struck the note of sound: a gleam
Of living silver shows me where she shook
Her long white fingers down the shadowy brook,
That sings her song, half waking, half in dream.
What two come here to mar this heavenly tune?
A man is one: the woman bears my name,
And honour. Their hands touch! Am I still tame?
God, what a dancing spectre seems the moon!

XL

I bade my Lady think what she might mean.
Know I my meaning, I? Can I love one,
And yet be jealous of another? None
Commits such folly. Terrible Love, I ween,
Has might, even dead, half sighing to upheave
The lightless seas of selfishness amain:
Seas that in a man's heart have no rain
To fall and still them. Peace can I achieve,
By turning to this fountain-source of woe,
This woman, who's to Love as fire to wood?
She breathed the violet breath of maidenhood
Against my kisses once! but I say, No!
The thing is mocked at! Helplessly afloat,
I know not what I do, where to I strive,
The dread that my old love may be alive
Has seized my nursling new love by the throat.

XLI

How many a thing which we cast to the ground,
When others pick it up becomes a gem!
We grasp at all the wealth it is to them;
And by reflected light its worth is found.
Yet for us still 'tis nothing! and that zeal
Of false appreciating quickly fades.
This truth is little known to human shades,
How rare from their own instinct 'tis to feel!
They waste the soul with spurious desire,
That is not the ripe flame upon the bough.
We two have taken up a lifeless vow
To rob a living passion: dust for fire!
Madam is grave, and eyes the clock that tells
Approaching midnight. We have struck despair
Into two hearts. O, look we like a pair
Who for fresh nuptials joyfully yield all else?

XLII

I am to follow her. There is much grace
In woman when thus bent on martyrdom.
They think that dignity of soul may come,
Perchance, with dignity of body. Base!
But I was taken by that air of cold
And statuesque sedateness, when she said
'I'm going'; lit a taper, bowed her head,
And went, as with the stride of Pallas bold.
Fleshly indifference horrible! The hands
Of Time now signal: O, she's safe from me!
Within those secret walls what do I see?
Where first she set the taper down she stands:
Not Pallas: Hebe shamed! Thoughts black as death,
Like a stirred pool in sunshine break. Her wrists
I catch: she faltering, as she half resists,
'You love . . . ? love . . . ? love . . . ?' all on an indrawn breath.

XLIII

Mark where the pressing wind shoots javelin-like,
Its skeleton shadow on the broad-backed wave!
Here is a fitting spot to dig Love's grave;
Here where the ponderous breakers plunge and strike,
And dart their hissing tongues high up the sand:
In hearing of the ocean, and in sight
Of those ribbed wind-streaks running into white.
If I the death of Love had deeply planned,
I never could have made it half so sure,
As by the unblest kisses which upbraid
The full-waked sense; or failing that, degrade!
'Tis morning: but no morning can restore
What we have forfeited. I see no sin:
The wrong is mixed. In tragic life, God wot,
No villain need be! Passions spin the plot:
We are betrayed by what is false within.

XLIV

They say, that Pity in Love's service dwells,
A porter at the rosy temple's gate.
I missed him going: but it is my fate
To come upon him now beside his wells;
Whereby I know that I Love's temple leave,
And that the purple doors have closed behind.
Poor soul! if in those early days unkind,
The power to sting had been but power to grieve,
We now might with an equal spirit meet,
And not be matched like innocence and vice.
She for the Temple's worship has paid price,
And takes the coin of Pity as a cheat.
She sees through simulation to the bone:
What's best in her impels her to the worst:
Never, she cries, shall Pity soothe Love's thirst,
Or foul hypocrisy for truth atone!

XLV

It is the season of the sweet wild rose,
My Lady's emblem in the heart of me!
So golden-crownëd shines she gloriously
And with that softest dream of blood she glows:
Mild as an evening heaven round Hesper bright!
I pluck the flower, and smell it, and revive
The time when in her eyes I stood alive.
I seem to look upon it out of Night.
Here's Madam, stepping hastily. Her whims
Bid her demand the flower, which I let drop.
As I proceed, I feel her sharply stop,
And crush it under heel with trembling limbs.
She joins me in a cat-like way, and talks
Of company, and even condescends
To utter laughing scandal of old friends.
These are the summer days, and these our walks.

XLVI

At last we parley: we so strangely dumb
In such a close communion! It befell
About the sounding of the Matin-bell,
And lo! her place was vacant, and the hum
Of loneliness was round me. Then I rose,
And my disordered brain did guide my foot
To that old wood where our first love-salute
Was interchanged: the source of many throes!
There did I see her, not alone. I moved
Toward her, and made proffer of my arm.
She took it simply, with no rude alarm;
And that disturbing shadow passed reproved.
I felt the pained speech coming, and declared
My firm belief in her, ere she could speak.
A ghastly morning came into her cheek,
While with a widening soul on me she stared.

XLVII

We saw the swallows gathering in the sky,
And in the osier-isle we heard them noise.
We had not to look back on summer joys,
Or forward to a summer of bright dye:
But in the largeness of the evening earth
Our spirits grew as we went side by side.
The hour became her husband and my bride.
Love that had robbed us so, thus blessed our dearth!
The pilgrims of the year waxed very loud
In multitudinous chatterings, as the flood
Full brown came from the West, and like pale blood
Expanded to the upper crimson cloud.
Love that had robbed us of immortal things,
This little moment mercifully gave,
Where I have seen across the twilight wave
The swan sail with her young beneath her wings.

XLVIII

Their sense is with their senses all mixed in,
Destroyed by subtleties these women are!
More brain, O Lord, more brain! or we shall mar
Utterly this fair garden we might win.
Behold! I looked for peace, and thought it near.
Our inmost hearts had opened, each to each.
We drank the pure daylight of honest speech.
Alas! that was the fatal draught, I fear.
For when of my lost Lady came the word,
This woman, O this agony of flesh!
Jealous devotion bade her break the mesh,
That I might seek that other like a bird.
I do adore the nobleness! despise
The act! She has gone forth, I know not where.
Will the hard world my sentience of her share?
I feel the truth; so let the world surmise.

XLIX

He found her by the ocean's moaning verge,
Nor any wicked change in her discerned;
And she believed his old love had returned,
Which was her exultation, and her scourge.
She took his hand, and walked with him, and seemed
The wife he sought, though shadow-like and dry.
She had one terror, lest her heart should sigh,
And tell her loudly she no longer dreamed.
She dared not say, 'This is my breast: look in.'
But there's a strength to help the desperate weak.
That night he learned how silence best can speak
The awful things when Pity pleads for Sin.
About the middle of the night her call
Was heard, and he came wondering to the bed.
'Now kiss me, dear! it may be, now!' she said.
Lethe had passed those lips, and he knew all.

L

Thus piteously Love closed what he begat:
The union of this ever-diverse pair!
These two were rapid falcons in a snare,
Condemned to do the flitting of the bat.
Lovers beneath the singing sky of May,
They wandered once; clear as the dew on flowers:
But they fed not on the advancing hours:
Their hearts held cravings for the buried day.
Then each applied to each that fatal knife,
Deep questioning, which probes to endless dole.
Ah, what a dusty answer gets the soul
When hot for certainties in this our life!—
In tragic hints here see what evermore
Moves dark as yonder midnight ocean's force,
Thundering like ramping hosts of warrior horse,
To throw that faint thin line upon the shore!

[1862]

THE WOODS OF WESTERMAIN

I

Enter these enchanted woods,
You who dare.
Nothing harms beneath the leaves
More than waves a swimmer cleaves.
Toss your heart up with the lark,
Foot at peace with mouse and worm,
Fair you fare.
Only at a dread of dark
Quaver, and they quit their form:
Thousand eyeballs under hoods
Have you by the hair.
Enter these enchanted woods,
You who dare.

II

Here the snake across your path
Stretches in his golden bath:
Mossy-footed squirrels leap
Soft as winnowing plumes of Sleep:
Yaffles on a chuckle skim
Low to laugh from branches dim:
Up the pine, where sits the star,
Rattles deep the moth-winged jar.
Each has business of his own;
But should you distrust a tone,
Then beware.

Shudder all the haunted roods,
All the eyeballs under hoods
    Shroud you in their glare.
Enter these enchanted woods,
    You who dare.

III

Open hither, open hence,
Scarce a bramble weaves a fence,
Where the strawberry runs red,
With white star-flower overhead;
Cumbered by dry twig and cone,
Shredded husks of seedlings flown,
Mine of mole and spotted flint:
Of dire wizardry no hint,
Save mayhap the print that shows
Hasty outward-tripping toes,
Heels to terror, on the mould.
These, the woods of Westermain,
Are as others to behold,
Rich of wreathing sun and rain;
Foliage lustreful around
Shadowed leagues of slumbering sound.
Wavy tree-tops, yellow whins,
Shelter eager minikins,
Myriads, free to peck and pipe:
Would you better? would you worse?
You with them may gather ripe
Pleasures flowing not from purse.
Quick and far as Colour flies
Taking the delighted eyes,
You of any well that springs
May unfold the heaven of things;
Have it homely and within,
And thereof its likeness win,
Will you so in soul's desire:
This do sages grant t' the lyre.
This is being bird and more,
More than glad musician this;
Granaries you will have a store
Past the world of woe and bliss;
Sharing still its bliss and woe;
Harnessed to its hungers, no.
On the throne Success usurps,
You shall seat the joy you feel
Where a race of water chirps,
Twisting hues of flourished steel:
Or where light is caught in hoop
Up a clearing's leafy rise,
Where the crossing deerherds troop
Classic splendours, knightly dyes.
Or, where old-eyed oxen chew
Speculation with the cud,
Read their pool of vision through,
Back to hours when mind was mud;
Nigh the knot, which did untwine
Timelessly to drowsy suns;
Seeing Earth a slimy spine,
Heaven a space for winging tons.
Farther, deeper, may you read,
Have you sight for things afield,
Where peeps she, the Nurse of seed,
Cloaked, but in the peep revealed;
Showing a kind face and sweet:
Look you with the soul you see 't.
Glory narrowing to grace,
Grace to glory magnified,
Following that will you embrace
Close in arms or aëry wide.
Banished is the white Foam-born
Not from here, nor under ban
Phœbus lyrist, Phœbe's horn,
Pipings of the reedy Pan.
Loved of Earth of old they were,
Loving did interpret her;
And the sterner worship bars
None whom Song has made her stars.
You have seen the huntress moon
Radiantly facing dawn,
Dusky meads between them strewn
Glimmering like downy awn:
Argent Westward glows the hunt,
East the blush about to climb;
One another fair they front,
Transient, yet outshine the time;
Even as dewlight off the rose
In the mind a jewel sows.
Thus opposing grandeurs live
Here if Beauty be their dower:
Doth she of her spirit give,
Fleetingness will spare her flower.
This is in the tune we play,
Which no spring of strength would quell;
In subduing does not slay;
Guides the channel, guards the well:
Tempered holds the young blood-heat,
Yet through measured grave accord,
Hears the heart of wildness beat
Like a centaur's hoof on sward.
Drink the sense the notes infuse,
You a larger self will find:
Sweetest fellowship ensues
With the creatures of your kind.
Ay, and Love, if Love it be
Flaming over *I* and *ME*,
Love meet they who do not shove
Cravings in the van of Love.
Courtly dames are here to woo,

Knowing love if it be true.
Reverence the blossom-shoot
Fervently, they are the fruit.
Mark them stepping, hear them talk,
Goddess, is no myth inane,
You will say of those who walk
In the woods of Westermain.
Waters that from throat and thigh
Dart the sun his arrows back;
Leaves that on a woodland sigh
Chat of secret things no lack;
Shadowy branch-leaves, waters clear,
Bare or veiled they move sincere;
Not by slavish terrors tripped;
Being anew in nature dipped,
Growths of what they step on, these;
With the roots the grace of trees.
Casket-breasts they give, nor hide,
For a tyrant's flattered pride,
Mind, which nourished not by light,
Lurks the shuffling trickster sprite:
Whereof are strange tales to tell;
Some in blood writ, tombed in bell.
Here the ancient battle ends,
Joining two astonished friends,
Who the kiss can give and take
With more warmth than in that world
Where the tiger claws the snake,
Snake her tiger clasps infurled,
And the issue of their fight
Peoples lands in snarling plight.
Here her splendid beast she leads
Silken-leashed and decked with weeds
Wild as he, but breathing faint
Sweetness of unfelt constraint.
Love, the great volcano, flings
Fires of lower Earth to sky;
Love, the sole permitted, sings
Sovereignly of *ME* and *I*.
Bowers he has of sacred shade,
Spaces of superb parade,
Voiceful . . . But bring you a note
Wrangling, howsoe'er remote,
Discords out of discord spin
Round and round derisive din:
Sudden will a pallor pant
Chill at screeches miscreant;
Owls or spectres, thick they flee;
Nightmare upon horror broods;
Hooded laughter, monkish glee,
    Gaps the vital air.
Enter these enchanted woods
    You who dare.

IV

You must love the light so well
That no darkness will seem fell.
Love it so you could accost
Fellowly a livid ghost.
Whish! the phantom wisps away,
Owns him smoke to cocks of day.
In your breast the light must burn
Fed of you, like corn in quern
Ever plumping while the wheel
Speeds the mill and drains the meal.
Light to light sees little strange,
Only features heavenly new;
Then you touch the nerve of Change,
Then of Earth you have the clue;
Then her two-sexed meanings melt
Through you, wed the thought and felt.
Sameness locks no scurfy pond
Here for Custom, crazy-fond:
Change is on the wing to bud
Rose in brain from rose in blood.
Wisdom, throbbing shall you see
Central in complexity;
From her pasture 'mid the beasts
Rise to her ethereal feasts,
Not, though lightnings track your wit
Starward, scorning them you quit:
For be sure the bravest wing
Preens it in our common spring,
Thence along the vault to soar,
You with others, gathering more,
Glad of more, till you reject
Your proud title of elect,
Perilous even here while few
Roam the arched greenwood with you.
    Heed that snare.
Muffled by his cavern-cowl
Squats the scaly Dragon-fowl,
Who was lord ere light you drank,
And lest blood of knightly rank
Stream, let not your fair princess
Stray: he holds the leagues in stress,
    Watches keenly there.
Oft has he been riven; slain
Is no force in Westermain.
Wait, and we shall forge him curbs,
Put his fangs to uses, tame,
Teach him, quick as cunning herbs,
How to cure him sick and lame.
Much restricted, much enringed,
Much he frets, the hooked and winged,
    Never known to spare.
'T is enough: the name of Sage
Hits no thing in nature, nought;

Man the least, save when grave Age
From yon Dragon guards his thought.
Eye him when you hearken dumb
To what words from Wisdom come.
When she says how few are by
Listening to her, eye his eye.
  Self, his name declare.
Him shall Change, transforming late,
Wonderously renovate.
Hug himself the creature may:
What he hugs is loathed decay.
Crying, slip thy scales, and slough!
Change will strip his armour off;
Make of him who was all maw,
Inly only thrilling-shrewd,
Such a servant as none saw
Through his days of dragonhood.
Days when growling o'er his bone,
Sharpened he for mine and thine;
Sensitive within alone;
Scaly as in clefts of pine.
Change, the strongest son of Life,
Has the Spirit here to wife.
Lo, their young of vivid breed,
Bear the lights that onward speed,
Threading thickets, mounting glades,
Up the verdurous colonnades,
Round the fluttered curves, and down,
Out of sight of Earth's blue crown,
Whither, in her central space,
Spouts the Fount and Lure o' the chase.
Fount unresting, Lure divine!
There meet all: too late look most.
Fire in water hued as wine,
Springs amid a shadowy host;
Circled: one close-headed mob,
Breathless, scanning divers heaps
Where a Heart begins to throb,
Where it ceases, slow, with leaps.
And 't is very strange, 't is said,
How you spy in each of them
Semblance of that Dragon red,
As the oak in bracken-stem.
And, 't is said, how each and each:
Which commences, which subsides:
First my Dragon! doth beseech
Her who food for all provides.
And she answers with no sign;
Utters neither yea nor nay;
Fires the water hued as wine;
Kneads another spark in clay.
Terror is about her hid;
Silence of the thunders locked;
Lightnings lining the shut lid;
Fixity on quaking rocked.
Lo, you look at Flow and Drought
Interflashed and interwrought:
Ended is begun, begun
Ended, quick as torrents run.
Young Impulsion spouts to sink;
Luridness and lustre link;
'T is your come and go of breath;
Mirrored pants the Life, the Death;
Each of either reaped and sown:
Rosiest rosy wanes to crone.
See you so? your senses drift;
'T is a shuttle weaving swift.
Look with spirit past the sense,
Spirit shines in permanence.
That is She, the view of whom
Is the dust within the tomb,
Is the inner blush above,
Look to loathe, or look to love;
Think her Lump, or know her Flame;
Dread her scourge, or read her aim;
Shoot your hungers from their nerve;
Or, in her example, serve.
Some have found her sitting grave;
Laughing, some; or, browed with sweat,
Hurling dust of fool and knave
In a hissing smithy's jet.
More it were not well to speak;
Burn to see, you need but seek.
Once beheld she gives the key
Airing every doorway, she.
Little can you stop or steer
Ere of her you are the seër.
On the surface she will witch,
Rendering Beauty yours, but gaze
Under, and the soul is rich
Past computing, past amaze.
Then is courage that endures
Even her awful tremble yours.
Then, the reflex of that Fount
Spied below, will Reason mount
Lordly and a quenchless force,
Lighting Pain to its mad source,
Scaring Fear till Fear escapes,
Shot through all its phantom shapes.
Then your spirit will perceive
Fleshly seed of fleshly sins;
Where the passions interweave,
How the serpent tangle spins
Of the sense of Earth misprised,
Brainlessly unrecognized;
She being Spirit in her clods,
Footway to the God of Gods.
Then for you are pleasures pure,

Sureties as the stars are sure:
Not the wanton beckoning flags
Which, of flattery and delight,
Wax to the grim Habit-Hags
Riding souls of men to night:
Pleasures that through blood run sane,
Quickening spirit from the brain.
Each of each in sequent birth,
Blood and brain and spirit, three
(Say the deepest gnomes of Earth),
Join for true felicity.
Are they parted, then expect
Some one sailing will be wrecked:
Separate hunting are they sped,
Scan the morsel coveted.
Earth that Triad is: she hides
Joy from him who that divides;
Showers it when the three are one
Glassing her in union.
Earth your haven, Earth your helm,
You command a double realm:
Labouring here to pay your debt,
Till your little sun shall set;
Leaving her the future task:
Loving her too well to ask.
Eglantine that climbs the yew,
She her darkest wreathes for those
Knowing her the Ever-new,
And themselves the kin o' the rose.
Life, the chisel, axe and sword,
Wield who have her depths explored:
Life, the dream, shall be their robe,
Large as air about the globe;
Life, the question, hear its cry
Echoed with concordant Why;
Life, the small self-dragon ramped,
Thrill for service to be stamped.
Ay, and over every height
Life for them shall wave a wand:
That, the last, where sits affright,
Homely shows the stream beyond.
Love the light and be its lynx,
You will track her and attain;
Read her as no cruel Sphinx
In the woods of Westermain.
Daily fresh the woods are ranged;
Glooms which otherwhere appal,
Sounded: here, their worths exchanged,
Urban joins with pastoral:
Little lost, save what may drop
Husk-like, and the mind preserves.
Natural overgrowths they lop,
Yet from nature neither swerves,
Trained or savage: for this cause:
Of our Earth they ply the laws,
Have in Earth their feeding root,
Mind of man and bent of brute.
Hear that song; both wild and ruled.
Hear it: is it wail or mirth?
Ordered, bubbled, quite unschooled?
None, and all: it springs of Earth.
O but hear it! 't is the mind;
Mind that with deep Earth unites,
Round the solid trunk to wind
Rings of clasping parasites.
Music have you there to feed
Simplest and most soaring need.
Free to wind, and in desire
Winding, they to her attached
Feel the trunk a spring of fire,
And ascend to heights unmatched,
Whence the tidal world is viewed
As a sea of windy wheat,
Momently black, barren, rude;
Golden-brown, for harvest meet;
Dragon-reaped from folly-sown;
Bride-like to the sickle-blade:
Quick it varies, while the moan,
Moan of a sad creature strayed,
Chiefly is its voice. So flesh
Conjures tempest-flails to thresh
Good from worthless. Some clear lamps
Light it; more of dead marsh-damps.
Monster is it still, and blind,
Fit but to be led by Pain.
Glance we at the paths behind,
Fruitful sight has Westermain.
There we laboured, and in turn
Forward our blown lamps discern,
As you see on the dark deep
Far the loftier billows leap,
        Foam for beacon bear.
Hither, hither, if you will,
Drink instruction, or instil,
Run the woods like vernal sap,
Crying, hail to luminousness!
        But have care.
In yourself may lurk the trap:
On conditions they caress.
Here you meet the light invoked:
Here is never secret cloaked.
Doubt you with the monster's fry
All his orbit may exclude;
Are you of the stiff, the dry,
Cursing the not understood;
Grasp you with the monster's claws;
Govern with his truncheon-saws;
Hate, the shadow of a grain;

You are lost in Westermain:
Earthward swoops a vulture sun,
Nighted upon carrion:
Straightway venom winecups shout
Toasts to One whose eyes are out:
Flowers along the reeling floor
Drip henbane and hellebore:
Beauty, of her tresses shorn,
Shrieks as nature's maniac:
Hideousness on hoof and horn
Tumbles, yapping in her track:
Haggard Wisdom, stately once,
Leers fantastical and trips:
Allegory drums the sconce,
Impiousness nibblenips.
Imp that dances, imp that flits,
Imp o' the demon-growing girl,
Maddest! whirl with imp o' the pits
Round you, and with them you whirl
Fast where pours the fountain-rout
Out of Him whose eyes are out:
Multitudes on multitudes,
Drenched in wallowing devilry:
And you ask where you may be,
  In what reek of a lair
Given to bones and ogre-broods:
  And they yell you Where.
Enter these enchanted woods,
  You who dare.

[1883]

EARTH AND MAN

I

On her great venture, Man,
Earth gazes while her fingers dint the breast
Which is his well of strength, his home of rest,
And fair to scan.

II

More aid than that embrace,
That nourishment, she cannot give: his heart
Involves his fate; and she who urged the start
Abides the race.

III

For he is in the lists
Contentious with the elements, whose dower
First sprang him; for swift vultures to devour
If he desists.

IV

His breath of instant thirst
Is warning of a creature matched with strife,
To meet it as a bride, or let fall life
On life's accursed.

V

No longer forth he bounds
The lusty animal, afield to roam,
But peering in Earth's entrails, where the gnome
Strange themes propounds.

VI

By hunger sharply sped
To grasp at weapons ere he learns their use,
In each new ring he bears a giant's thews,
An infant's head.

VII

And ever that old task
Of reading what he is and whence he came,
Whither to go, finds wilder letters flame
Across her mask.

VIII

She hears his wailful prayer,
When now to the Invisible he raves
To rend him from her, now of his mother craves
Her calm, her care.

IX

The thing that shudders most
Within him is the burden of his cry.
Seen of his dread, she is to his blank eye
The eyeless Ghost.

X

Or sometimes she will seem
Heavenly, but her blush, soon wearing white,
Veils like a gorsebush in a web of blight,
With gold-buds dim.

XI

Once worshiped Prime of Powers,
She still was the Implacable: as a beast,
She struck him down and dragged him from the feast
She crowned with flowers.

XII

Her pomp of glorious hues,
Her revelries of ripeness, her kind smile,
Her songs, her peeping faces, lure awhile
With symbol-clues.

XIII

The mystery she holds
For him, inveterately he strains to see,
And sight of his obtuseness is the key
Among those folds.

XIV

He may entreat, aspire,
He may despair, and she has never heed.
She drinking his warm sweat will soothe his need,
Not his desire.

XV

She prompts him to rejoice,
Yet scares him on the threshold with the shroud.
He deems her cherishing of her best-endowed
A wanton's choice.

XVI

Albeit thereof he has found
Firm roadway between lustfulness and pain;
Has half transferred the battle to his brain,
From bloody ground;

XVII

He will not read her good,
Or wise, but with the passion Self obscures;
Through that old devil of the thousand lures,
Through that dense hood:

XVIII

Through terror, through distrust;
The greed to touch, to view, to have, to live:
Through all that makes of him a sensitive
Abhorring dust.

XIX

Behold his wormy home!
And he the wind-whipped, anywhither wave
Crazily tumbled on a shingle-grave
To waste in foam.

XX

Therefore the wretch inclines
Afresh to the Invisible, who, he saith,
Can raise him high: with vows of living faith
For little signs.

XXI

Some signs he must demand,
Some proofs of slaughtered nature; some prized few,
To satisfy the senses it is true,
And in his hand,

XXII

This miracle which saves
Himself, himself doth from extinction clutch,
By virtue of his worth, contrasting much
With brutes and knaves.

XXIII

From dust, of him abhorred,
He would be snatched by Grace discovering worth.
'Sever me from the hollowness of earth!
Me take, dear Lord!'

XXIV

She hears him. Him she owes
For half her loveliness a love well won
By work that lights the shapeless and the dun,
Their common foes.

XXV

He builds the soaring spires,
That sing his soul in stone: of her he draws,
Though blind to her, by spelling at her laws,
Her purest fires.

XXVI

Through him hath she exchanged,
For the gold harvest-robes, the mural crown,
Her haggard quarry-features and thick frown
Where monsters ranged.

XXVII

And order, high discourse,
And decency, than which is life less dear,

She has of him: the lyre of language clear,
Love's tongue and source.

XXVIII

She hears him, and can hear
With glory in his gains by work achieved:
With grief for grief that is the unperceived
In her so near.

XXIX

If he aloft for aid
Imploring storms, her essence is the spur.
His cry to heaven is a cry to her
He would evade.

XXX

Not elsewhere can he tend.
Those are her rules which bid him wash foul sins;
Those her revulsions from the skull that grins
To ape his end.

XXXI

And her desires are those
For happiness, for lastingness, for light.
'Tis she who kindles in his haunting night
The hoped dawn-rose.

XXXII

Fair fountains of the dark
Daily she waves him, that his inner dream
May clasp amid the glooms a springing beam,
A quivering lark:

XXXIII

This life and her to know
For Spirit: with awakenedness of glee
To feel stern joy her origin: not he
The child of woe.

XXXIV

But that the senses still
Usurp the station of their issue mind,
He would have burst the chrysalis of the blind:
As yet he will;

XXXV

As yet he will, she prays,
Yet will when his distempered devil of Self;—
The glutton for her fruits, the wily elf
In shifting rays;—

XXXVI

That captain of the scorned;
The coveter of life in soul and shell,
The fratricide, the thief, the infidel,
The hoofed and horned;—

XXXVII

He singularly doomed
To what he execrates and writhes to shun;—
When fire has passed him vapour to the sun
And sun relumed,

XXXVIII

Then shall the horrid pall
Be lifted, and a spirit nigh divine,
'Live in thy offspring as I live in mine,'
Will hear her call.

XXXIX

Whence looks he on a land
Whereon his labour is a carven page;
And forth from heritage to heritage
Nought writ on sand.

XL

His fables of the Above,
And his gapped readings of the crown and sword,
The hell detested and the heaven adored,
The hate, the love,

XLI

The bright wing, the black hoof,
He shall peruse, from Reason not disjoined,
And never unfaith clamouring to be coined
To faith by proof.

XLII

She her just Lord may view,
Not he, her creature, till his soul has yearned
With all her gifts to reach the light discerned
Her spirit through.

XLIII

Then in him time shall run
As in the hour that to young sunlight crows;
And—"If thou has good faith it can repose,"
She tells her son.

XLIV

Meanwhile on him, her chief
Expression, her great word of life, looks she;
Twi-minded of him, as the waxing tree,
Or dated leaf.

[1883]

LUCIFER IN STARLIGHT

On a starred night Prince Lucifer uprose
Tired of his dark dominion swung the fiend
Above the rolling ball in cloud part screened,
Where sinners hugged their spectre of repose.
Poor prey to his hot fit of pride were those.
And now upon his western wing he leaned,
Now his huge bulk o'er Afric's sands careened,
Now the black planet shadowed Arctic snows.
Soaring through wider zones that pricked his scars
With memory of the old revolt from Awe,
He reached a middle height, and at the stars,
Which are the brain of heaven, he looked, and sank.
Around the ancient track marched, rank on rank,
The army of unalterable law.

[1883]

THE SPIRIT OF SHAKESPEARE

Thy greatest knew thee, Mother Earth; unsoured
He knew thy sons. He probed from hell to hell
Of human passions, but of love deflowered
His wisdom was not, for he knew thee well.
Thence came the honeyed corner at his lips,
The conquering smile wherein his spirit sails
Calm as the God who the white sea-wave whips,
Yet full of speech and intershifting tales,
Close mirrors of us: thence had he the laugh
We feel is thine: broad as ten thousand beeves
At pasture! thence thy songs, that winnow chaff
From grain, bid sick Philosophy's last leaves
Whirl, if they have no response—they enforced
To fatten Earth when from her soul divorced.

THE SPIRIT OF SHAKESPEARE

(*Continued*)

How smiles he at a generation ranked
In gloomy noddings over life! They pass.
Not he to feed upon a breast unthanked,
Or eye a beauteous face in a cracked glass.
But he can spy that little twist of brain
Which moved some weighty leader of the blind,
Unwitting 't was the goad of personal pain,
To view in curst eclipse our Mother's mind,
And show us of some rigid harridan
The wretched bondmen till the end of time.
O lived the Master now to paint us Man,
That little twist of brain would ring a chime
Of whence it came and what it caused, to start
Thunders of laughter, clearing air and heart.

[1883]

WILLIAM MORRIS

CHRONOLOGICAL TABLE

1834, March 24, born at Clay Hill Walthamstow, his father a discount broker who made a fortune in tin.
1848–51 Attended Marlborough College.
1851–3 Study with a private tutor.
1853–5 Exeter College, Oxford.
1853 Meeting with Edward Burne-Jones.
1854 First journey abroad: to Belgium and northern France with Burne-Jones.
1855 Coming of age, assured an income of almost £1000 a year.
Wrote his first poetry, and his first prose romances.
B.A. degree in *Litterae humaniores.*
1856 *Oxford and Cambridge Magazine,* financed by Morris.
Articled to an architect in Oxford.
1857 Study of painting in London.
1858 *The Defence of Guenevere and other Poems.*
1859 Married to Jane Burden.
1861 Foundation of Morris, Marshall, Faulkner and Co.
1867 *The Life and Death of Jason.*
1868–70 *The Earthly Paradise.*
1871 First journey to Iceland.
1872 *Love is Enough.*
1873 Second journey to Iceland.
1875 *The Aeneids* (a translation).
1876 *Sigurd the Volsung.*
1877 Foundation of the Society for the Protection of Ancient buildings ("Anti-Scrape").
1882 Enrolled as member of the Democratic Federation.
1884 Resigned.
1885 Joins in founding the Socialist League, founding and editing its journal *The Commonweal.*
1887 *The Odyssey* (a translation).
A play, *The Tables Turned or Nupkins Awakened,* performed, with the author in the role of Archbishop of Canterbury.
1888 *A Dream of John Ball.*
Signs of Change.
The House of the Wolfings.
1889 *The Roots of the Mountains.*
Removed from editorship of *The Commonweal.*
1890 Resigned from the Socialist League.
News from Nowhere.
1891 *The Story of the Glittering Plain.*
Poems by the Way.
1893 *Socialism, its Growth and Outcome* (With E. B. Bax).
1894 *The Wood beyond the World.*
1895 *Beowulf* (a translation, with A. J. Wyatt).
1896 Completion of the Kelmscott Chaucer, the principal production of Morris's press.
The Sundering Flood.
October 3, died at Kelmscott House, October 6, buried in Kelmscott Churchyard.

Large and varied as Morris's body of poetry is, poetry was never for very long the mastering occupation of his life. It is noteworthy that he was more than twenty before he made his first experiments in verse; and that for long periods in his maturity he refrained almost entirely from poetic composition. The first art in which he tried to find adequate expression was architecture; and he had turned from it to painting before he published his first volume of poetry. *The Defence of Guenevere,* coolly received, did not persuade its author that he should abandon all for poetry. Shortly after its appearance Morris at last found his way to the field in which he was to make his most original and most satisfying artistic achievements: the field of what he himself called the lesser arts, the arts of decoration. The decisive moment in his development is that of the founding of Morris and Co. in 1861. Twenty years afterwards the activities of that unique company were listed in one of its circulars as: painted glass windows, arras tapestry woven on the high-warp loom, carpets, embroidery, tiles, furniture, general house decoration, printed cotton goods, paper hangings, figured woven stuffs, furniture velvets and cloths, upholstery. In each of the company's activities Morris took a part: he wove and dyed and designed. Later he gave much of his time to the making of fine books; and it would be hard to say whether the deeper artistic pleasure came from writing a book or from printing, hand-lettering and illustrating it.

For Morris poetry was but one of many arts. Yet his poetry is so fully original as to be irreplaceable. No other Pre-Raphaelite has the secrets of the trembling rhythms and sharp phrases, of the strange moods of terror and passion, which went into the making of the early lyrics and narratives. In *The Life and Death of Jason,* his second publication in verse, and a work so popular as to require eight editions within fifteen years, he explored the possibilities of quite another mood and manner—a sweet serenity in which the spirit of Chaucer and the milder qualities of the romantics were united. In *The Earthly Paradise,* the note of *Jason* is struck again; and there are other notes which were later to be struck with greater power of execution and greater purity of tone. In *Sigurd the Volsung,* writing in a period subtly and confidently civilized, he was able to regain much of the spirit and manner of primitive epic poetry, to write of heroes and perils belonging to the dark spaces of the north, to move easily among the beings and objects of a legendary and infinitely remote past. His conversion to militant socialism resulted in a number of poems of combat and exhortation, in which for the first time his style was denuded of beauty.

The poetic career of Morris is one of perpetual experiment: it is impossible to say that one of his many manners is more authentic than others. It is a career without a climax. In the perspective available to readers of to-day, it is easily seen that *The Defence of Guenevere* is one of the three or four principal expressions of Pre-Raphaelitism in poetry; that *The Life and Death of Jason,* weak in character portrayal as it is, remains one of the most beautiful and one of the best conducted narrative poems in modern literature; that some of the parts of *The Earthly Paradise* are in their slighter way the glorious satellites if not the equals of *Jason;* and that *Sigurd the Volsung,* in language, incident, character, and manner is a triumphant realization of the ideal of objective poetry for which Matthew Arnold had contended.

RIDING TOGETHER

For many, many days together
  The wind blew steady from the East;
For many days hot grew the weather,
  About the time of our Lady's Feast.

For many days we rode together,
  Yet met we neither friend nor foe;
Hotter and clearer grew the weather,
  Steadily did the East wind blow.

We saw the trees in the hot, bright weather,
  Clear-cut, with shadows very black,
As freely we rode on together
  With helms unlaced and bridles slack.

And often, as we rode together,
  We, looking down the green-bank'd stream,
Saw flowers in the sunny weather,
  And saw the bubble-making bream.

And in the night lay down together,
  And hung above our heads the rood,
Or watch'd night-long in the dewy weather,
  The while the moon did watch the wood.

Our spears stood bright and thick together,
  Straight out the banners stream'd behind,
As we gallop'd on in the sunny weather,
  With faces turn'd towards the wind.

Down sank our threescore spears together,
  As thick we saw the pagans ride;
His eager face in the clear fresh weather,
  Shone out that last time by my side.

Up the sweep of the bridge we dash'd together,
  It rock'd to the crash of the meeting spears,
Down rain'd the buds of the dear spring weather,
  The elm-tree flowers fell like tears.

There, as we roll'd and writhed together,
  I threw my arms above my head,
For close by my side, in the lovely weather,
  I saw him reel and fall back dead.

I and the slayer met together,
  He waited the death-stroke there in his place,
With thoughts of death, in the lovely weather,
  Gapingly mazed at my madden'd face.

Madly I fought as we fought together;
  In vain: the little Christian band

The pagans drown'd, as in stormy weather,
  The river drowns low-lying land.

They bound my blood-stain'd hands together,
  They bound his corpse to nod by my side:
Then on we rode, in the bright March weather,
  With clash of cymbals did we ride.

We ride no more, no more together;
  My prison-bars are thick and strong,
I take no heed of any weather,
  The sweet Saints grant I live not long.

[1856]

THE CHAPEL IN LYONESS

SIR OZANA LE CURE HARDY. SIR GALAHAD. SIR BORS DE GANYS.

Sir Ozana

All day long and every day,
From Christmas-Eve to Whit-Sunday,
Within that Chapel-aisle I lay,
  And no man came a-near.

Naked to the waist was I.
And deep within my breast did lie,
Though no man any blood could spy,
  The truncheon of a spear.

No meat did ever pass my lips.
Those days—(Alas! the sunlight slips
From off the gilded parclose, dips,
  And night comes on apace.)

My arms lay back behind my head;
Over my raised-up knees was spread
A samite cloth of white and red;
  A rose lay on my face.

Many a time I tried to shout;
But as in dream of battle-rout,
My frozen speech would not well out;
  I could not even weep.

With inward sigh I see the sun
Fade off the pillars one by one,
My heart faints when the day is done,
  Because I cannot sleep.

Sometimes strange thoughts pass through my head;
Not like a tomb is this my bed,
Yet oft I think that I am dead;
  That round my tomb is writ,

"Ozana of the hardy heart,
Knight of the Table Round,
Pray for his soul, lords, of your part;
  A true knight he was found."
Ah! me, I cannot fathom it.

[*He sleeps.*

Sir Galahad

All day long and every day,
Till his madness pass'd away,
I watch'd Ozana as he lay
  Within the gilded screen.

All my singing moved him not;
As I sung my heart grew hot,
With the thought of Launcelot
  Far away, I ween.

So I went a little space
From out the chapel, bathed my face
In the stream that runs apace
  By the churchyard wall.

There I pluck'd a faint wild rose,
Hard by where the linden grows,
Sighing over silver rows
  Of the lilies tall.

I laid the flower across his mouth;
The sparkling drops seem'd good for drouth;
He smiled, turn'd round toward the south,
  Held up a golden tress.

The light smote on it from the west:
He drew the covering from his breast,
Against his heart that hair he prest;
  Death him soon will bless.

Sir Bors

I enter'd by the western door;
  I saw a knight's helm lying there:
I raised my eyes from off the floor,
  And caught the gleaming of his hair.

I stept full softly up to him;
  I laid my chin upon his head;
I felt him smile; my eyes did swim,
  I was so glad he was not dead.

I heard Ozana murmur low,
  "There comes no sleep nor any love."
But Galahad stoop'd and kiss'd his brow:
  He shiver'd; I saw his pale lips move.

SIR OZANA

There comes no sleep nor any love;
  Ah me! I shiver with delight.
I am so weak I cannot move;
  God move me to thee, dear, to-night!
Christ help! I have but little wit:
My life went wrong; I see it writ,

"Ozana of the hardy heart,
  Knight of the Table Round,
Pray for his soul, lords, on your part;
  A good knight he was found."
Now I begin to fathom it.

[*He dies.*

SIR BORS

Galahad sits dreamily:
What strange things may his eyes see,
Great blue eyes fix'd full on me?
On his soul, Lord, have mercy.

SIR GALAHAD

Ozana, shall I pray for thee?
  Her cheek is laid to thine;
No long time hence, also I see
  Thy wasted fingers twine

Within the tresses of her hair
  That shineth gloriously,
Thinly outspread in the clear air
  Against the jasper sea.

[1856]

SUMMER DAWN

Pray but one prayer for me 'twixt thy closed lips,
  Think but one thought of me up in the stars.
The summer night waneth, the morning light slips,
  Faint and grey 'twixt the leaves of the aspen, betwixt the cloud-bars,
That are patiently waiting there for the dawn:
  Patient and colourless, though Heaven's gold
Waits to float through them along with the sun.
Far out in the meadows, above the young corn,
  The heavy elms wait, and restless and cold
The uneasy wind rises; the roses are dun;
Through the long twilight they pray for the dawn,
Round the lone house in the midst of the corn.
  Speak but one word to me over the corn,
  Over the tender, bow'd locks of the corn.

[1856]

THE DEFENCE OF GUENEVERE

But, knowing now that they would have her speak,
She threw her wet hair backward from her brow,
Her hand close to her mouth touching her cheek,

As though she had had there a shameful blow,
And feeling it shameful to feel ought but shame
All through her heart, yet felt her cheek burned so,

She must a little touch it; like one lame
She walked away from Gauwaine, with her head
Still lifted up; and on her cheek of flame

The tears dried quick; she stopped at last and said:
"O knights and lords, it seems but little skill
To talk of well-known things past now and dead.

"God wot I ought to say, I have done ill,
And pray you all forgiveness heartily!
Because you must be right such great lords—still

"Listen, suppose your time were come to die,
And you were quite alone and very weak;
Yea, laid a dying while very mightily

"The wind was ruffling up the narrow streak
Of river through your broad lands running well:
Suppose a hush should come, then some one speak:

" 'One of these cloths is heaven, and one is hell,
Now choose one cloth for ever, which they be,
I will not tell you, you must somehow tell

" 'Of your strength and mightiness; here, see!'
Yea, yea, my lord, and you to ope your eyes,
At foot of your familiar bed to see

"A great God's angel standing, with such dyes,
Not known on earth, on his great wings, and hands,
Held out two ways, light from the inner skies

"Showing him well, and making his commands
Seem to be God's commands, moreover, too,
Holding within his hands the cloths on wands;

"And one of these strange choosing cloths was blue,
Wavy and long, and one cut short and red;
No man could tell the better of the two.

"After a shivering half-hour you said,
'God help! heaven's colour, the blue;' and he said, 'hell.'
Perhaps you then would roll upon your bed,

"And cry to all good men that loved you well,
'Ah Christ! if only I had known, known, known';
Launcelot went away, then I could tell,

"Like wisest man how all things would be, moan,
And roll and hurt myself, and long to die,
And yet fear much to die for what was sown.

"Nevertheless you, O Sir Gauwaine, lie,
Whatever may have happened through these years,
God knows I speak truth, saying that you lie."

Her voice was low at first, being full of tears,
But as it cleared, it grew full loud and shrill,
Growing a windy shriek in all men's ears,

A ringing in their startled brains, until
She said that Gauwaine lied, then her voice sunk,
And her great eyes began again to fill,

Though still she stood right up, and never shrunk,
But spoke on bravely, glorious lady fair!
Whatever tears her full lips may have drunk,

She stood, and seemed to think, and wrung her hair,
Spoke out at last with no more trace of shame,
With passionate twisting of her body there:

"It chanced upon a day that Launcelot came
To dwell at Arthur's court: at Christmas-time
This happened; when the heralds sung his name,

" 'Son of King Ban of Benwick,' seemed to chime
Along with all the bells that rang that day,
O'er the white roofs, with little change of rhyme.

"Christmas and whitened winter passed away,
And over me the April sunshine came,
Made very awful with black hail-clouds, yea

"And in the Summer I grew white with flame,
And bowed my head down—Autumn, and the sick
Sure knowledge things would never be the same,

"However often Spring might be most thick
Of blossoms and buds, smote on me, and I grew
Careless of most things, let the clock tick, tick,

"To my unhappy pulse, that beat right through
My eager body; while I laughed out loud,
And let my lips curl up at false or true,

"Seemed cold and shallow without any cloud.
Behold my judges, then the cloths were brought:
While I was dizzied thus, old thoughts would crowd,

"Belonging to the time ere I was bought
By Arthur's great name and his little love,
Must I give up for ever then, I thought,

"That which I deemed would ever round me move
Glorifying all things; for a little word,
Scarce ever meant at all, must I now prove

"Stone-cold for ever? Pray you, does the Lord
Will that all folks should be quite happy and good?
I love God now a little, if this cord

"Were broken, once for all what striving could
Make me love anything in earth or heaven.
So day by day it grew, as if one should

"Slip slowly down some path worn smooth and even,
Down to a cool sea on a summer day;
Yet still in slipping was there some small leaven

"Of stretched hands catching small stones by the way,
Until one surely reached the sea at last,
And felt strange new joy as the worn head lay

"Back, with the hair like sea-weed; yea all past
Sweat of the forehead, dryness of the lips,
Washed utterly out by the dear waves o'ercast

"In the lone sea, far off from any ships!
Do I not know now of a day in Spring?
No minute of that wild day ever slips

"From out my memory; I hear thrushes sing,
And wheresoever I may be, straightway
Thoughts of it all come up with most fresh sting;

"I was half mad with beauty on that day,
And went without my ladies all alone,
In a quiet garden walled round every way;

"I was right joyful of that wall of stone,
That shut the flowers and trees up with the sky,
And trebled all the beauty: to the bone,

"Yea right through to my heart, grown very shy
With weary thoughts, it pierced, and made me glad;
Exceedingly glad, and I knew verily,

"A little thing just then had made me mad;
I dared not think, as I was wont to do,
Sometimes, upon my beauty; if I had

"Held out my long hand up against the blue,
And, looking on the tenderly darken'd fingers,
Thought that by rights one ought to see quite through,

"There, see you, where the soft still light yet lingers,
Round by the edges; what should I have done,
If this had joined with yellow spotted singers,

"And startling green drawn upward by the sun?
But shouting, loosed out, see now! all my hair,
And trancedly stood watching the west wind run

"With faintest half-heard breathing sound—why there
I lose my head e'en now in doing this;
But shortly listen—In that garden fair

"Came Launcelot walking; this is true, the kiss
Wherewith we kissed in meeting that spring day,
I scarce dare talk of the remember'd bliss.

"When both our mouths went wandering in one way,
And aching sorely, met among the leaves;
Our hands being left behind strained far away.

"Never within a yard of my bright sleeves
Had Launcelot come before—and now, so nigh!
After that day why is it Guenevere grieves?

"Nevertheless you, O Sir Gauwaine, lie,
Whatever happened on through all those years,
God knows I speak truth, saying that you lie.

"Being such a lady could I weep these tears
If this were true? A great queen such as I
Having sinn'd this way, straight her conscience sears;

"And afterwards she liveth hatefully,
Slaying and poisoning, certes never weeps,—
Gauwaine be friends now, speak me lovingly.

"Do I not see how God's dear pity creeps
All through your frame, and trembles in your mouth?
Remember in what grave your mother sleeps,

"Buried in some place far down in the south,
Men are forgetting as I speak to you;
By her head sever'd in that awful drouth

"Of pity that drew Agravaine's fell blow,
I pray your pity! let me not scream out
For ever after, when the shrill winds blow

"Through half your castle-locks! let me not shout
For ever after in the winter night
When you ride out alone! in battle-rout

"Let not my rusting tears make your sword light!
Ah! God of mercy how he turns away!
So, ever must I dress me to the fight,

"So—let God's justice work! Gauwaine, I say,
See me hew down your proofs: yea all men know
Even as you said how Mellyagraunce one day,

"One bitter day in *la Fausse Garde,* for so
All good knights held it after, saw—
Yea, sirs, by cursed unknightly outrage; though

"You, Gauwaine, held his word without a flaw,
This Mellyagraunce saw blood upon my bed—
Whose blood then pray you? is there any law

"To make a queen say why some spots of red
Lie on her coverlet? or will you say,
'Your hands are white, lady, as when you wed,

" 'Where did you bleed?' and must I stammer out—'Nay,
I blush indeed, fair lord, only to rend
My sleeve up to my shoulder, where there lay

" 'A knife-point last night': so must I defend
The honour of the Lady Guenevere?
Not so, fair lords, even if the world should end

"This very day, and you were judges here
Instead of God. Did you see Mellyagraunce
When Launcelot stood by him? what white fear

"Curdled his blood, and how his teeth did dance,
His side sink in? as my knight cried and said,
'Slayer of unarm'd men, here is a chance!

" 'Setter of traps, I pray you guard your head,
By God I am so glad to fight with you,
Stripper of ladies, that my hand feels lead

" 'For driving weight; hurrah now! draw and do,
For all my wounds are moving in my breast,
And I am getting mad with waiting so.'

"He struck his hands together o'er the beast,
Who fell down flat, and grovell'd at his feet,
And groan'd at being slain so young—'at least.'

"My knight said, 'Rise you, sir, who are so fleet
At catching ladies, half-arm'd will I fight,
My left side all uncovered!' then, I weet,

"Up sprang Sir Mellyagraunce with great delight
Upon his knave's face; not until just then
Did I quite hate him, as I saw my knight

"Along the lists look to my stake and pen
With such a joyous smile, it made me sigh
From agony beneath my waist-chain, when

"The fight began, and to me they drew nigh;
Ever Sir Launcelot kept him on the right,
And traversed warily, and ever high

"And fast leapt caitiff's sword, until my knight
Sudden threw up his sword to his left hand,
Caught it, and swung it; that was all the fight.

"Except a spout of blood on the hot land;
For it was hottest summer; and I know
I wonder'd how the fire, while I should stand,

"And burn, against the heat, would quiver so,
Yards above my head; thus these matters went;
Which things were only warnings of the woe

"That fell on me. Yet Mellyagraunce was shent,
For Mellyagraunce had fought against the Lord;
Therefore, my lords, take heed lest you be blent

"With all this wickedness say no rash word
Against me, being so beautiful; my eyes,
Wept all away to grey, may bring some sword

"To drown you in your blood; see my breast rise,
Like waves of purple sea, as here I stand;
And how my arms are moved in wonderful wise,

"Yea also at my full heart's strong command,
See through my long throat how the words go up
In ripples to my mouth; how in my hand

"The shadow lies like wine within a cup
Of marvellously colour'd gold; yea now
This little wind is rising, look you up,

"And wonder how the light is falling so
Within my moving tresses: will you dare,
When you have looked a little on my brow,

"To say this thing is vile or will you care
For any plausible lies of cunning woof,
When you can see my face with no lie there

"For ever? am I not a gracious proof—
'But in your chamber Launcelot was found'—
Is there a good knight then would stand aloof,

"When a queen says with gentle queenly sound:
'O true as steel come now and talk with me,
I love to see your step upon the ground

" 'Unwavering, also well I love to see
That gracious smile light up your face, and hear
Your wonderful words, that all mean verily

" 'The thing they seem to mean: good friend, so dear
To me in everything, come here to-night,
Or else the hours will pass most dull and drear;

" 'If you come not, I fear this time I might
Get thinking over much of times gone by,
When I was young, and green hope was in sight;

" 'For no man cares now to know why I sigh;
And no man comes to sing me pleasant songs,
Nor any brings me the sweet flowers that lie

" 'So thick in the gardens; therefore one so longs
To see you, Launcelot; that we may be
Like children once again, free from all wrongs

" 'Just for one night.' Did he not come to me?
What thing could keep true Launcelot away
If I said 'come'? there was one less than three

"In my quiet room that night, and we were gay;
Till sudden I rose up, weak, pale, and sick,
Because a bawling broke our dream up, yea

"I looked at Launcelot's face and could not speak,
For he looked helpless too, for a little while;
Then I remember how I tried to shriek,

"And could not, but fell down; from tile to tile
The stones they threw up rattled o'er my head,
And made me dizzier; till within a while

"My maids were all about me, and my head
On Launcelot's breast was being soothed away
From its white chattering, until Launcelot said—

"By God! I will not tell you more to-day,
Judge any way you will—what matters it?
You know quite well the story of that fray,

"How Launcelot still'd their bawling, the mad fit
That caught up Gauwaine—all, all, verily,
But just that which would save me; these things flit.

"Nevertheless you, O Sir Gauwaine, lie,
Whatever may have happen'd these long years,
God knows I speak truth, saying that you lie!

"All I have said is truth, by Christ's dear tears."
She would not speak another word, but stood
Turn'd sideways; listening, like a man who hears

His brother's trumpet sounding through the wood
Of his foes' lances. She lean'd eagerly,
And gave a slight spring sometimes, as she could

At last hear something really; joyfully
Her cheek grew crimson, as the headlong speed
Of the roan charger drew all men to see,
The knight who came was Launcelot at good need.

[1858]

CONCERNING GEFFRAY TESTE NOIRE

And if you meet the Canon of Chimay,
  As going to Ortaise you well may do,
Greet him from John of Castel Neuf, and say,
  All that I tell you, for all this is true.

This Geffray Teste Noire was a Gascon thief,
  Who, under shadow of the English name,
Pilled all such towns and countries as were lief
  To King Charles and St. Dennis; thought it blame

If anything escaped him; so my lord,
  The Duke of Berry, sent Sir John Bonne Lance,
And other knights, good players with the sword,
  To check this thief, and give the land a chance.

Therefore we set our bastides round the tower
  That Geffray held, the strong thief! like a king,
High perch'd upon the rock of Ventadour,
  Hopelessly strong by Christ! it was mid spring,

When first I joined the little army there
  With ten good spears; Auvergne is hot, each day
We sweated armed before the barrier,
  Good feats of arms were done there often—eh?

Your brother was slain there? I mind me now
  A right, good man-at-arms, God pardon him!
I think 'twas Geffray smote him on the brow
  With some spiked axe, and while he totter'd, dim

About the eyes, the spear of Alleyne Roux
  Slipped through his camaille and his throat; well, well!
Alleyne is paid now; your name Alleyne too?
  Mary! how strange—but this tale I would tell—

For spite of all our bastides, damned blackhead
  Would ride abroad whene'er he chose to ride,
We could not stop him; many a burgher bled
  Dear gold all round his girdle; far and wide

The villaynes dwelt in utter misery
  'Twixt us and thief Sir Geffray; hauled this way
By Sir Bonne Lance at one time, he gone by,
  Down comes this Teste Noire on another day.

And therefore they dig up the stone, grind corn,
  Hew wood, draw water, yea, they lived, in short,
As I said just now, utterly forlorn,
  Till this our knave and blackhead was out-fought.

So Bonne Lance fretted, thinking of some trap
  Day after day, till on a time he said;
"John of Newcastle, if we have good hap,
  We catch our thief in two days." "How?" I said.

"Why, Sir, to-day he rideth out again,
  Hoping to take well certain sumpter mules
From Carcassonne, going with little train,
  Because, forsooth, he thinketh us mere fools;

"But if we set an ambush in some wood,
He is but dead: So, Sir, take thirty spears
To Verville forest, if it seem you good."
Then felt I like the horse in Job, who hears

The dancing trumpet sound, and we went forth;
And my red lion on the spear-head flapped,
As faster than the cool wind we rode North,
Towards the wood of Verville; thus it happed.

We rode a soft space on that day while spies
Got news about Sir Geffray; the red wine
Under the road-side bush was clear; the flies,
The dragon-flies I mind me most, did shine

In brighter arms than ever I put on;
So—"Geffray," said our spies, "would pass that way
Next day at sundown;" then he must be won;
And so we enter'd Verville wood next day,

In the afternoon; through it the highway runs,
'Twixt copses of green hazel, very thick,
And underneath, with glimmering of suns,
The primroses are happy; the dews lick

The soft green moss. "Put cloths about your arms,
Lest they should glitter; surely they will go
In a long thin line, watchful for alarms,
With all their carriages of booty, so—

"Lay down my pennon in the grass—Lord God!
What have we lying here? will they be cold,
I wonder, being so bare, above the sod,
Instead of under? This was a knight too, fold

"Lying on fold of ancient rusted mail;
No plate at all, gold rowels to the spurs,
And see the quiet gleam of turquoise pale
Along the ceinture; but the long time blurs

"Even the tinder of his coat to nought,
Except these scraps of leather; see how white
The skull is, loose within the coif! He fought
A good fight, maybe, ere he was slain quite.

"No armour on the legs too; strange in faith—
A little skeleton for a knight though—ah!
This one is bigger, truly without scathe
His enemies escaped not—ribs driven out far,—

"That must have reach'd the heart, I doubt—how now,
What say you, Aldovrand—a woman? why?"
"Under the coif a gold wreath on the brow,
Yea, see the hair not gone to powder, lie,

"Golden, no doubt, once—yea, and very small—
  This for a knight; but for a dame, my lord,
These loose-hung bones seem shapely still, and tall,—
  Didst ever see a woman's bones, my lord?"

Often, God help me! I remember when
  I was a simple boy, fifteen years old,
The Jacquerie froze up the blood of men
  With their fell deeds, not fit now to be told:

God help again! we enter'd Beauvais town,
  Slaying them fast, whereto I help'd, mere boy
As I was then; we gentles cut them down,
  These burners and defilers, with great joy.

Reason for that, too, in the great church there
  These fiends had lit a fire, that soon went out,
The church at Beauvais being so great and fair—
  My father, who was by me, gave a shout

Between a beast's howl and a woman's scream,
  Then, panting, chuckled to me: "John, look! look!
Count the dames' skeletons!" From some bad dream
  Like a man just awaked, my father shook;

And I, being faint with smelling the burnt bones,
  And very hot with fighting down the street,
And sick of such a life, fell down, with groans
  My head went weakly nodding to my feet.—

—An arrow had gone through her tender throat,
  And her right wrist was broken; then I saw
The reason why she had on that war-coat,
  Their story came out clear without a flaw;

For when he knew that they were being waylaid,
  He threw it over her, yea, hood and all;
Whereby he was much hack'd, while they were stay'd
  By those their murderers; many an one did fall

Beneath his arm, no doubt, so that he clear'd
  Their circle, bore his death-wound out of it;
But as they rode, some archer least afear'd
  Drew a strong bow, and thereby she was hit.

Still as he rode he knew not she was dead,
  Thought her but fainted from her broken wrist,
He bound with his great leathern belt—she bled?
  Who knows! he bled too, neither was there miss'd

The beating of her heart, his heart beat well
  For both of them, till here, within this wood,
He died scarce sorry; easy this to tell;
  After these years the flowers forget their blood.—

How could it be? never before that day,
  However much a soldier I might be,
Could I look on a skeleton and say
  I care not for it, shudder not—now see,

Over those bones I sat and pored for hours,
  And thought, and dream'd, and still I scarce could see
The small white bones that lay upon the flowers,
  But evermore I saw the lady; she

With her dear gentle walking leading in,
  By a chain of silver twined about her wrists,
Her loving knight, mounted and arm'd to win
  Great honour for her, fighting in the lists.

O most pale face, that brings such joy and sorrow
  Into men's hearts—yea, too, so piercing sharp
That joy is, that it marcheth nigh to sorrow
  For ever—like an overwinded harp.

Your face must hurt me always; pray you now,
  Doth it not hurt you too? seemeth some pain
To hold you always, pain to hold your brow
  So smooth, unwrinkled ever; yea again,

Your long eyes where the lids seem like to drop,
  Would you not, lady, were they shut fast, feel
Far merrier? there so high they will not stop,
  They are most sly to glide forth and to steal

Into my heart; *I kiss their soft lids there,*
  And in green gardens scarce can stop my lips
From wandering on your face, but that your hair
  Falls down and tangles me, back my face slips.

Or say your mouth—I saw you drink red wine
  Once at a feast; how slowly it sank in,
As though you fear'd that some wild fate might twine
  Within that cup, and slay you for a sin.

And when you talk your lips do arch and move
  In such wise that a language new I know
Besides their sound; they quiver, too, with love
  When you are standing silent; know this, too

I saw you kissing once, like a curved sword
  That bites with all its edge, did your lips lie,
Curled gently, slowly, long time could afford
  For caught-up breathings: like a dying sigh

They gather'd up their lines and went away,
  And still kept twitching with a sort of smile,
As likely to be weeping presently,—
  Your hands too—how I watch'd them all the while!

"Cry out St. Peter now," quoth Aldovrand;
I cried, "St. Peter," broke out from the wood
With all my spears; we met them hand to hand,
And shortly slew them; natheless, by the rood,

We caught not blackhead then, or any day;
Months after that he died at last in bed,
From a wound pick'd up at a barrier-fray;
That same year's end a steel bolt in the head,

And much bad living kill'd Teste Noire at last;
John Froissart knoweth he is dead by now,
No doubt, but knoweth not this tale just past;
Perchance then you can tell him what I show

In my new castle, down beside the Eure,
There is a little chapel of squared stone,
Painted inside and out; in green nook pure
There did I lay them, every wearied bone;

And over it they lay, with stone-white hands
Clasped fast together, hair made bright with gold
This Jaques Picard, known through many lands,
Wrought cunningly; he's dead now—I am old.

[1858]

OLD LOVE

"You must be very old, Sir Giles,"
I said; he said: "Yea, very old":
Whereat the mournfullest of smiles
Creased his dry skin with many a fold.

"They hammer'd out my basnet point
Into a round salade," he said,
"The basnet being quite out of joint,
Natheless the salade rasps my head."

He gazed at the great fire awhile:
"And you are getting old, Sir John";
(He said this with that cunning smile
That was most sad;) "we both wear on,

"Knights come to court and look at me,
With eyebrows up, except my lord,
And my dear lady, none I see
That know the ways of my old sword."

(My lady! at that word no pang
Stopp'd all my blood.) "But tell me, John
Is it quite true that pagans hang
So thick about the east, that on

"The eastern sea no Venice flag
Can fly unpaid for?" "True," I said,
"And in such way the miscreants drag
Christ's cross upon the ground, I dread

"That Constantine must fall this year."
Within my heart; "These things are small;
This is not small, that things outwear
I thought were made for ever, yea, all,

"All things go soon or late"; I said—
I saw the duke in court next day;
Just as before, his grand great head
Above his gold robes dreaming lay,

Only his face was paler; there
I saw his duchess sit by him;
And she—she was changed more; her hair
Before my eyes that used to swim,

And make me dizzy with great bliss
Once, when I used to watch her sit—
Her hair is bright still, yet it is
As though some dust were thrown on it.

Her eyes are shallower, as though
Some grey glass were behind; her brow

And cheeks the straining bones show through,
Are not so good for kissing now.

Her lips are drier now she is
A great duke's wife these many years,
They will not shudder with a kiss
As once they did, being moist with tears.

Also her hands have lost that way
Of clinging that they used to have;
They look'd quite easy, as they lay
Upon the silken cushions brave

With broidery of the apples green
My Lord Duke bears upon his shield.
Her face, alas! that I have seen
Look fresher than an April field,

This is all gone now; gone also
Her tender walking; when she walks
She is most queenly I well know,
And she is fair still:—as the stalks

Of faded summer-lilies are,
So is she grown now unto me
This spring-time, when the flowers star
The meadows, birds sing wonderfully.

I warrant once she used to cling
About his neck, and kiss'd him so,
And then his coming step would ring
Joy-bells for her,—some time ago.

Ah! sometimes like an idle dream
That hinders true life overmuch,
Sometimes like a lost heaven, these seem—
This love is not so hard to smutch.

[1858]

THE GILLIFLOWER OF GOLD

A Golden gilliflower to-day
I wore upon my helm alway,
And won the prize of this tourney.
Hah! hah! la belle jaune giroflée.[1]

However well Sir Giles might sit,
His sun was weak to wither it,
Lord Miles's blood was dew on it;
Hah! hah! la belle jaune giroflée.

Although my spear in splinters flew,
From John's steel-coat my eye was true;
I wheel'd about, and cried for you,
Hah! hah! la belle jaune giroflée.

Yea, do not doubt my heart was good,
Though my sword flew like rotten wood,
To shout, although I scarcely stood,
Hah! hah! la belle jaune giroflée.

My hand was steady too, to take
My axe from round my neck, and break
John's steel-coat up for my love's sake.
Hah! hah! la belle jaune giroflée.

When I stood in my tent again,
Arming afresh, I felt a pain
Take hold of me, I was so fain—
Hah! hah! la belle jaune giroflée.

To hear: *"Honneur aux fils des preux!"*[2]
Right in my ears again, and shew
The gilliflower blossom'd new.
Hah! hah! la belle jaune giroflée.

The Sieur Guillaume against me came,
His tabard bore three points of flame
From a red heart: with little blame—
Hah! hah! la belle jaune giroflée.

Our tough spears crackled up like straw;
He was the first to turn and draw
His sword, that had nor speck nor flaw,—
Hah! hah! la belle jaune giroflée.

But I felt weaker than a maid,
And my brain, dizzied and afraid,
Within my helm a fierce tune play'd,—
Hah! hah! la belle jaune giroflée.

Until I thought of your dear head,
Bow'd to the gilliflower bed,
The yellow flowers stain'd with red;—
Hah! hah! la belle jaune giroflée.

Crash! how the swords met, *"giroflée!"*
The fierce tune in my helm would play,
"La belle! la belle! jaune giroflée!"
Hah! hah! la belle jaune giroflée.

Once more the great swords met again,
"La belle! la belle!" but who fell then?

[1] The beautiful yellow gilliflower.

[2] Honor to the sons of the brave!

Le Sieur Guillaume, who struck down ten;—
Hah! hah! la belle jaune giroflée.

And as with mazed and unarm'd face,
Toward my own crown and the Queen's place,
They led me at a gentle pace—
Hah! hah! la belle jaune giroflée.

I almost saw your quiet head
Bow'd o'er the gilliflower bed,
The yellow flowers stain'd with red—
Hah! hah! la belle jaune giroflée.

[1858]

SHAMEFUL DEATH

There were four of us about that bed;
The mass-priest knelt at the side,
I and his mother stood at the head,
Over his feet lay the bride;
We were quite sure that he was dead,
Though his eyes were open wide.

He did not die in the night,
He did not die in the day,
But in the morning twilight
His spirit pass'd away,
When neither sun nor moon was bright,
And the trees were merely grey.

He was not slain with the sword,
Knight's axe, or the knightly spear,
Yet spoke he never a word
After he came in here;
I cut away the cord
From the neck of my brother dear.

He did not strike one blow,
For the recreants came behind,
In a place where the hornbeams grow,
A path right hard to find,
For the hornbeam boughs swing so,
That the twilight makes it blind.

They lighted a great torch then,
When his arms were pinion'd fast,
Sir John the knight of the Fen,
Sir Guy of the Dolorous Blast,
With knights threescore and ten,
Hung brave Lord Hugh at last.

I am threescore and ten,
And my hair is all turn'd grey,
But I met Sir John of the Fen
Long ago on a summer day,
And am glad to think of the moment when
I took his life away.

I am threescore and ten,
And my strength is mostly pass'd,
But long ago I and my men,
When the sky was overcast,
And the smoke roll'd over the reeds of the fen,
Slew Guy of the Dolorous Blast.

And now, knights all of you,
I pray you pray for Sir Hugh,
A good knight and a true,
And for Alice, his wife, pray too.

[1858]

THE EVE OF CRECY

Gold on her head, and gold on her feet,
And gold where the hems of her kirtle meet,
And a golden girdle round my sweet;—
Ah! qu'elle est belle La Marguerite.[1]

Margaret's maids are fair to see,
Freshly dress'd and pleasantly;
Margaret's hair falls down to her knee;—
Ah! qu'elle est belle La Marguerite.

If I were rich I would kiss her feet,
I would kiss the place where the gold hems meet,

[1] Oh, how beautiful is Margaret.

And the golden girdle round my sweet—
Ah! qu'elle est belle La Marguerite.

Ah me! I have never touch'd her hand;
When the arriere-ban goes through the land,
Six basnets under my pennon stand;—
Ah! qu'elle est belle La Marguerite.

And many an one grins under his hood:
"Sir Lambert de Bois, with all his men good,
Has neither food nor firewood;"—
Ah! qu'elle est belle La Marguerite.

If I were rich I would kiss her feet,
And the golden girdle of my sweet,
And thereabouts where the gold hems meet;—
Ah! qu'elle est belle La Marguerite.

Yet even now it is good to think,
While my few poor varlets grumble and drink
In my desolate hall, where the fires sink,—
Ah! qu'elle est belle La Marguerite.

Of Margaret sitting glorious there,
In glory of gold and glory of hair,
And glory of glorious face most fair;—
Ah! qu'elle est belle La Marguerite.

Likewise to-night I make good cheer,
Because this battle draweth near:
For what have I to lose or fear?—
Ah! qu'elle est belle La Marguerite.

For, look you, my horse is good to prance
A right fair measure in this war-dance,
Before the eyes of Philip of France;—
Ah! qu'elle est belle La Marguerite.

And sometime it may hap, perdie,
While my new towers stand up three and three,
And my hall gets painted fair to see—
Ah! qu'elle est belle La Marguerite.

That folks may say: "Times change, by the rood,
For Lambert, banneret of the wood,
Has heaps of food and firewood;—
Ah! qu'elle est belle La Marguerite.

"And wonderful eyes, too, under the hood
Of a damsel of right noble blood:"
St. Ives, for Lambert of the wood!—
Ah! qu'elle est belle La Marguerite.

[1858]

THE BLUE CLOSET

THE DAMOZELS

Lady Alice, Lady Louise,
Between the wash of the tumbling seas
We are ready to sing, if so ye please;
So lay your long hands on the keys;
Sing, "*Laudate pueri.*" [1]

And ever the great bell overhead
Boom'd in the wind a knell for the dead,
Though no one toll'd it, a knell for the dead.

LADY LOUISE

Sister, let the measure swell
Not too loud; for you sing not well
If you drown the faint boom of the bell;
He is weary, so am I.

And ever the chevron overhead
Flapp'd on the banner of the dead;
(Was he asleep, or was he dead?)

LADY ALICE

Alice the Queen, and Louise the Queen,
Two damozels wearing purple and green,
Four lone ladies dwelling here
From day to day and year to year;
And there is none to let us go;
To break the locks of the doors below,
Or shovel away the heaped-up snow;
And when we die no man will know
That we are dead; but they give us leave,
Once every year on Christmas-eve,
To sing in the Closet Blue one song;
And we should be so long, so long,
If we dared, in singing; for dream on dream,
They float on in a happy stream;
Float from the gold strings, float from the keys,
Float from the open'd lips of Louise;
But, alas! the sea-salt oozes through
The chinks of the tiles of the Closet Blue;
And ever the great bell overhead
Booms in the wind a knell for the dead,
The wind plays on it a knell for the dead.

[*They sing all together.*]

How long ago was it, how long ago,
He came to this tower with hands full of snow?

[1] Praise, children.

"Kneel down, O love Louise, kneel down," he said,
And sprinkled the dusty snow over my head.

He watch'd the snow melting, it ran through my hair,
Ran over my shoulders, white shoulders and bare.

"I cannot weep for thee, poor love Louise,
For my tears are all hidden deep under the seas;

"In a gold and blue casket she keeps all my tears,
But my eyes are no longer blue, as in old years;

"Yea, they grow grey with time, grow small and dry,
I am so feeble now, would I might die."

And in truth the great bell overhead
Left off his pealing for the dead,
Perchance, because the wind was dead.

Will he come back again, or is he dead?
O! is he sleeping, my scarf round his head?

Or did they strangle him as he lay there,
With the long scarlet scarf I used to wear?

Only I pray thee, Lord, let him come here!
Both his soul and his body to me are most dear.

Dear Lord, that loves me, I wait to receive
Either body or spirit this wild Christmas-eve.

Through the floor shot up a lily red,
With a patch of earth from the land of the dead,
For he was strong in the land of the dead.

What matter that his cheeks were pale,
His kind kiss'd lips all grey?
"O, love Louise, have you waited long?"
"O, my lord Arthur, yea."

What if his hair that brush'd her cheek
Was stiff with frozen rime?
His eyes were grown quite blue again,
As in the happy time.

"O, love Louise, this is the key
Of the happy golden land!
O, sisters, cross the bridge with me,
My eyes are full of sand.
What matter that I cannot see,
If ye take me by the hand?"

And ever the great bell overhead,
And the tumbling seas mourn'd for the dead;
For their song ceased, and they were dead.

[1858]

THE HAYSTACK IN THE FLOODS

Had she come all the way for this,
To part at last without a kiss?
Yea, had she borne the dirt and rain
That her own eyes might see him slain
Beside the haystack in the floods?

Along the dripping leafless woods,
The stirrup touching either shoe,
She rode astride as troopers do;
With kirtle kilted to her knee,
To which the mud splash'd wretchedly;
And the wet dripp'd from every tree
Upon her head and heavy hair,
And on her eyelids broad and fair;
The tears and rain ran down her face.

By fits and starts they rode apace,
And very often was his place
Far off from her; he had to ride
Ahead, to see what might betide
When the roads cross'd; and sometimes, when
There rose a murmuring from his men,
Had to turn back with promises;
Ah me! she had but little ease;
And often for pure doubt and dread
She sobb'd, made giddy in the head
By the swift riding; while, for cold,
Her slender fingers scarce could hold
The wet reins: yea, and scarcely, too,
She felt the foot within her shoe
Against the stirrup: all for this,
To part at last without a kiss
Beside the haystack in the floods.

For when they near'd that old soak'd hay,
They saw across the only way
That Judas, Godmar, and the three
Red running lions dismally
Grinn'd from his pennon, under which,
In one straight line along the ditch,
They counted thirty heads.

So then,
While Robert turn'd round to his men,
She saw at once the wretched end,
And, stooping down, tried hard to rend
Her coif the wrong way from her head,
And hid her eyes; while Robert said:
"Nay, love, 'tis scarcely two to one,
At Poictiers where we made them run
So fast—why, sweet my love, good cheer,
The Gascon frontier is so near,
Nought after this."

But, "O," she said,
"My God! my God! I have to tread
The long way back without you; then
The court at Paris; those six men;
The gratings of the Chatelet;
The swift Seine on some rainy day
Like this, and people standing by,
And laughing, while my weak hands try
To recollect how strong men swim.
All this, or else a life with him,
For which I should be damned at last,
Would God that this next hour were past!"

He answer'd not, but cried his cry,
"St. George for Marny!" cheerily;
And laid his hand upon her rein.
Alas! no man of all his train
Gave back that cheery cry again;
And, while for rage his thumb beat fast
Upon his sword-hilt, some one cast
About his neck a kerchief long,
And bound him.

Then they went along
To Godmar; who said: "Now, Jehane,
Your lover's life is on the wane
So fast, that, if this very hour
You yield not as my paramour,
He will not see the rain leave off—
Nay, keep your tongue from gibe and scoff,
Sir Robert, or I slay you now."

She laid her hand upon her brow,
Then gazed upon the palm, as though
She thought her forehead bled, and—"No."
She said, and turn'd her head away,
As there were nothing else to say,
And everything were settled: red
Grew Godmar's face from chin to head:
"Jehane, on yonder hill there stands
My castle, guarding well my lands:
What hinders me from taking you,
And doing that I list to do
To your fair wilful body, while
Your knight lies dead?"

A wicked smile
Wrinkled her face, her lips grew thin,
A long way out she thrust her chin:
"You know that I should strangle you

While you were sleeping; or bite through
Your throat, by God's help—ah!" she said,
"Lord Jesus, pity your poor maid!
For in such wise they hem me in,
I cannot choose but sin and sin,
Whatever happens: yet I think
They could not make me eat or drink,
And so should I just reach my rest."
"Nay, if you do not my behest,
O Jehane! though I love you well,"
Said Godmar, " would I fail to tell
All that I know." "Foul lies," she said.
"Eh? lies my Jehane? by God's head,
At Paris folks would deem them true!
Do you know, Jehane, they cry for you,
'Jehane the brown! Jehane the brown!
Give us Jehane to burn or drown!'—
Eh—gag me Robert!—sweet my friend,
This were indeed a piteous end
For those long fingers, and long feet,
And long neck, and smooth shoulders sweet:
An end that few men would forget
That saw it—So, an hour yet:
Consider, Jehane, which to take
Of life or death!"

So, scarce awake,
Dismounting, did she leave that place,
And totter some yards: with her face
Turn'd upward to the sky she lay,
Her head on a wet heap of hay,
And fell asleep: and while she slept
And did not dream, the minutes crept
Round to the twelve again; but she,
Being waked at last, sigh'd quietly,
And strangely childlike came, and said:
"I will not." Straightway Godmar's head,
As though it hung on strong wires, turn'd
Most sharply round, and his face burn'd.

For Robert—both his eyes were dry,
He could not weep, but gloomily
He seem'd to watch the rain; yea, too,
His lips were firm; he tried once more
To touch her lips; she reach'd out, sore
And vain desire so tortured them,
The poor grey lips, and now the hem
Of his sleeve brush'd them.

With a start
Up Godmar rose, thrust them apart;
From Robert's throat he loosed the bands
Of silk and mail; with empty hands
Held out, she stood and gazed, and saw,
The long bright blade without a flaw
Glide out from Godmar's sheath, his hand
In Robert's hair; she saw him bend
Back Robert's head; she saw him send
The thin steel down; the blow told well,
Right backward the knight Robert fell,
And moan'd as dogs do, being half dead,
Unwitting, as I deem: so then
Godmar turn'd grinning to his men,
Who ran, some five or six, and beat
His head to pieces at their feet.

Then Godmar turn'd again and said:
"So, Jehane, the first fitte is read!
Take note, my lady, that your way
Lies backward to the Chatelet!"
She shook her head and gazed awhile
At her cold hands with a rueful smile,
As though this thing had made her mad.

This was the parting that they had
Beside the haystack in the floods.

[1858]

SIR GILES' WAR-SONG

Ho! is there any will ride with me,
Sir Giles, le bon des barrières? [1]

The clink of arms is good to hear,
The flap of pennons fair to see;
Ho! is there any will ride with me,
Sir Giles, le bon des barrières?

The leopards and lilies are fair to see,
"St. George Guienne" right good to hear:
Ho! is there any will ride with me,
Sir Giles, le bon des barrières?

I stood by the barrier,
My coat being blazon'd fair to see;
Ho! is there any will ride with me,
Sir Giles, le bon des barrières?

Clisson put out his head to see,
And lifted his basnet up to hear;
I pull'd him through the bars to ME,
Sir Giles, le bon des barrières?

[1858]

[1] good at assaults.

PRAISE OF MY LADY

My lady seems of ivory
Forehead, straight nose, and cheeks that be
Hollow'd a little mournfully.
Beata mea Domina! [1]

Her forehead, overshadow'd much
By bows of hair, has a wave such
As God was good to make for me.
Beata mea Domina!

Nor greatly long my lady's hair,
Nor yet with yellow colour fair,
But thick and crisped wonderfully:
Beata mea Domina!

Heavy to make the pale face sad,
And dark, but dead as though it had
Been forged by God most wonderfully
—Beata mea Domina!—

Of some strange metal, thread by thread,
To stand out from my lady's head,
Not moving much to tangle me.
Beata mea Domina!

Beneath her brows the lids fall slow,
The lashes a clear shadow throw
Where I would wish my lips to be.
Beata mea Domina!

Her great eyes, standing far apart,
Draw up some memory from her heart,
And gaze out very mournfully;
—Beata mea Domina!—

So beautiful and kind they are,
But most times looking out afar,
Waiting for something, not for me.
Beata mea Domina!

I wonder if the lashes long
Are those that do her bright eyes wrong,
For always half tears seem to be
—Beata mea Domina!—

Lurking below the underlid,
Darkening the place where they lie hid—
If they should rise and flow for me!
Beata mea Domina!

Her full lips being made to kiss,
Curl'd up and pensive each one is;
This makes me faint to stand and see.
Beata mea Domina!

Her lips are not contented now,
Because the hours pass so slow
Towards a sweet time: (pray for me),
—Beata mea Domina!—

Nay, hold thy peace! for who can tell;
But this at least I know full well,
Her lips are parted longingly,
—Beata mea Domina!—

So passionate and swift to move,
To pluck at any flying love,
That I grow faint to stand and see.
Beata mea Domina!

Yea! there beneath them is her chin,
So fine and round, it were a sin
To feel no weaker when I see
—Beata mea Domina!—

God's dealings; for with so much care
And troublous, faint lines wrought in there,
He finishes her face for me.
Beata mea Domina!

Of her long neck what shall I say?
What things about her body's sway,
Like a knight's pennon or slim tree
—Beata mea Domina!—

Set gently waving in the wind;
Or her long hands that I may find
On some day sweet to move o'er me?
Beata mea Domina!

God pity me though, if I miss'd
The telling, how along her wrist
The veins creep, dying languidly
—Beata mea Domina!—

Inside her tender palm and thin.
Now give me pardon, dear, wherein
My voice is weak and vexes thee.
Beata mea Domina!

All men that see her any time,
I charge you straightly in this rhyme,
What, and wherever you may be,
—Beata mea Domina!—

[1] My blessed lady!

To kneel before her; as for me,
I choke and grow quite faint to see
My lady moving graciously.
Beata mea Domina!

[1858]

SONGS FROM *THE LIFE AND DEATH OF JASON*

"I KNOW A LITTLE GARDEN CLOSE"

I know a little garden close
Set thick with lily and red rose,
Where I would wander if I might
From dewy dawn to dewy night,
And have one with me wandering.
And though within it no birds sing,
And though no pillared house is there,
And though the apple boughs are bare
Of fruit and blossom, would to God,
Her feet upon the green grass trod,
And I beheld them as before.
There comes a murmur from the shore,
And in the place two fair streams are,
Drawn from the purple hills afar,
Drawn down unto the restless sea;
The hills whose flowers ne'er fed the bee,
The shore no ship has ever seen,
Still beaten by the billows green,
Whose murmur comes unceasingly
Unto the place for which I cry.
For which I cry both day and night,
For which I let slip all delight,
That maketh me both deaf and blind,
Careless to win, unskilled to find,
And quick to lose what all men seek.
Yet tottering as I am, and weak,
Still have I left a little breath
To seek within the jaws of death
An entrance to that happy place,
To seek the unforgotten face
Once seen, once kissed, once reft from me
Anigh the murmuring of the sea.

[1867]

"O DEATH, THAT MAKETH LIFE SO SWEET"

O death, that maketh life so sweet,
O fear, with mirth before thy feet,
What have ye yet in store for us,
The conquerors, the glorious?
Men say: 'For fear that thou shouldst die
To-morrow, let to-day pass by
Flower-crowned and singing'; yet have we
Passed our to-day upon the sea,
Or in a poisonous unknown land,
With fear and death on either hand,
And listless when the day was done
Have scarcely hoped to see the sun
Dawn on the morrow of the earth,
Nor in our hearts have thought of mirth.
And while the world lasts, scarce again
Shall any sons of men bear pain
Like we have borne, yet be alive.
So surely not in vain we strive
Like other men for our reward;
Sweet peace and deep, the chequered sward
Beneath the ancient mulberry-trees,
The smooth-paved gilded palaces,
Where the shy thin-clad damsels sweet
Make music with their gold-ringed feet.
The fountain court amidst of it,
Where the short-haired slave maidens sit,
While on the veined pavement lie
The honied things and spicery
Their arms have borne from out of the town.
The dancers on the thymy down
In summer twilight, when the earth
Is still of all things but their mirth,
And echoes borne upon the wind
Of others in like way entwined.
The merchant towns' fair market-place,
Where over many a changing face
The pigeons of the temple flit,
And still the outland merchants sit
Like kings above their merchandise,
Lying to foolish men and wise.
Ah! if they heard that we were come
Into the bay, and bringing home
That which all men have talked about,
Some men with rage, and some with doubt,
Some with desire, and some with praise,
Then would the people throng the ways,
Nor heed the outland merchandise,
Nor any talk, from fools or wise,
But tales of our accomplished quest.
What soul within the house shall rest
When we come home? The wily king
Shall leave his throne to see the thing;
No man shall keep the landward gate,
The hurried traveller shall wait
Until our bulwarks graze the quay,
Unslain the milk-white bull shall be
Beside the quivering altar-flame;
Scarce shall the maiden clasp for shame

Over her breast the raiment thin
The morn that Argo cometh in.
  Then cometh happy life again
That payeth well our toil and pain
In that sweet hour, when all our woe
But as a pensive tale we know,
Nor yet remember deadly fear;
For surely now if death be near,
Unthought-of is it, and unseen
When sweet is, that hath bitter been.

[1867]

THE EARTHLY PARADISE

AN APOLOGY

Of Heaven or Hell I have no power to sing,
I cannot ease the burden of your fears,
Or make quick-coming death a little thing,
Or bring again the pleasure of past years,
Nor for my words shall ye forget your tears,
Or hope again for aught that I can say,
The idle singer of an empty day.

But rather, when aweary of your mirth,
From full hearts still unsatisfied ye sigh,
And, feeling kindly unto all the earth,
Grudge every minute as it passes by,
Made the more mindful that the sweet days die—
Remember me a little then, I pray,
The idle singer of an empty day.

The heavy trouble, the bewildering care
That weighs us down who live and earn our bread,
These idle verses have no power to bear;
So let me sing of names remembered,
Because they, living not, can ne'er be dead,
Or long time take their memory quite away
From us poor singers of an empty day.

Dreamer of dreams, born out of my due time,
Why should I strive to set the crooked straight?
Let it suffice me that my murmuring rhyme
Beats with light wing against the ivory gate,
Telling a tale not too importunate
To those who in the sleepy region stay,
Lulled by the singer of an empty day.

Folk say, a wizard to a northern king
At Christmas-tide such wondrous things did show,
That through one window men beheld the spring,
And through another saw the summer glow,
And through a third the fruited vines arow,
While still, unheard, but in its wonted way,
Piped the drear wind of that December day.

So with this Earthly Paradise it is,
If ye will read aright and pardon me,
Who strive to build a shadowy isle of bliss
Midmost the beating of the steely sea,
Where tossed about all hearts of men must be;
Whose ravening monsters mighty men shall slay,
Not the poor singer of an empty day.

[1868]

INTRODUCTION

Forget six countries overhung with smoke,
Forget the snorting steam and piston stroke,
Forget the spreading of the hideous town;
Think rather of the pack-horse on the down,
And dream of London, small, and white, and clean,
The clear Thames bordered by its gardens green;
Think, that below bridge the green lapping waves
Smite some few keels that bear Levantine staves
Cut from the yew wood on the burnt-up hill,
And pointed jars that Greek hands toiled to fill,
And treasured scanty spice from some far sea,

Florence gold cloth, and Ypres napery,
And cloth of Bruges, and hogsheads of Guienne;
While nigh the thronged wharf Geoffrey Chaucer's pen
Moves over bills of lading—mid such times
Shall dwell the hollow puppets of my rhymes.

[1868]

ATALANTA'S RACE

Through thick Arcadian woods a hunter went,
Following the beasts up, on a fresh spring day;
But since his horn-tipped bow but seldom bent,
Now at the noontide nought had happed to slay,
Within a vale he called his hounds away,
Hearkening the echoes of his lone voice cling
About the cliffs and through the beech-trees ring.

But when they ended, still awhile he stood,
And but the sweet familiar thrush could hear,
And all the day-long noises of the wood,
And o'er the dry leaves of the vanished year
His hound's feet pattering as they drew anear,
And heavy breathing from their heads low hung,
To see the mighty cornel bow unstrung.

Then smiling did he turn to leave the place,
But with his first step some new fleeting thought
A shadow cast across his sun-burnt face;
I think the golden net that April brought
From some warm world his wavering soul had caught;
For, sunk in vague sweet longing, did he go
Betwixt the trees with doubtful steps and slow.

Yet howsoever slow he went, at last
The trees grew sparser, and the wood was done;
Whereon one farewell, backward look he cast,
Then, turning round to see what place was won,
With shaded eyes looked underneath the sun,
And o'er green meads and new-turned furrows brown
Beheld the gleaming of King Schœneus' town.

So thitherward he turned, and on each side
The folk were busy on the teeming land,
And man and maid from the brown furrows cried,
Or midst the newly-blossomed vines did stand,
And as the rustic weapon pressed the hand
Thought of the nodding of the well-filled ear,
Or how the knife the heavy bunch should shear.

Merry it was: about him sung the birds,
The spring flowers bloomed along the firm dry road,
The sleek-skinned mothers of the sharp-horned herds
Now for the barefoot milking-maidens lowed;

While from the freshness of his blue abode,
Glad his death-bearing arrows to forget,
The broad sun blazed, nor scattered plagues as yet.

Through such fair things unto the gates he came,
And found them open, as though peace were there;
Wherethrough, unquestioned of his race or name,
He entered, and along the streets 'gan fare,
Which at the first of folk were well-nigh bare;
But pressing on, and going more hastily,
Men hurrying too he 'gan at last to see.

Following the last of these, he still pressed on,
Until an open space he came unto,
Where wreaths of fame had oft been lost and won,
For feats of strength folk there were wont to do.
And now our hunter looked for something new,
Because the whole wide space was bare, and stilled
The high seats were, with eager people filled.

There with the others to a seat he gat,
Whence he beheld a broidered canopy,
'Neath which in fair array King Schœneus sat
Upon his throne with councillors thereby;
And underneath his well-wrought seat and high,
He saw a golden image of the sun,
A silver image of the Fleet-foot One.

A brazen altar stood beneath their feet
Whereon a thin flame flickered in the wind;
Nigh this a herald clad in raiment meet
Made ready even now his horn to wind,
By whom a huge man held a sword, entwined
With yellow flowers; these stood a little space
From off the altar, nigh the starting place.

And there two runners did the sign abide
Foot set to foot,—a young man slim and fair,
Crisp-haired, well knit, with firm limbs often tried
In places where no man his strength may spare;
Dainty his thin coat was, and on his hair
A golden circlet of renown he wore,
And in his hand an olive garland bore.

But on this day with whom shall he contend?
A maid stood by him like Diana clad
When in the woods she lists her bow to bend,
Too fair for one to look on and be glad,
Who scarcely yet has thirty summers had,
If he must still behold her from afar;
Too fair to let the world live free from war.

She seemed all earthly matters to forget;
Of all tormenting lines her face was clear,

Her wide grey eyes upon the goal were set
Calm and unmoved as though no soul were near,
But her foe trembled as a man in fear,
Nor from her loveliness one moment turned
His anxious face with fierce desire that burned.

Now through the hush there broke the trumpet's clang
Just as the setting sun made eventide.
Then from light feet a spurt of dust there sprang,
And swiftly were they running side by side;
But silent did the thronging folk abide
Until the turning-post was reached at last,
And round about it still abreast they passed.

But when the people saw how close they ran,
When halfway to the starting-point they were,
A cry of joy broke forth, whereat the man
Headed the white-foot runner, and drew near
Unto the very end of all his fear;
And scarce his straining feet the ground could feel,
And bliss unhoped for o'er his heart 'gan steal.

But midst the loud victorious shouts he heard
Her footsteps drawing nearer, and the sound
Of fluttering raiment, and thereat afeard
His flushed and eager face he turned around,
And even then he felt her past him bound
Fleet as the wind, but scarcely saw her there
Till on the goal she laid her fingers fair.

There stood she breathing like a little child
Amid some warlike clamour laid asleep,
For no victorious joy her red lips smiled,
Her cheek its wonted freshness did but keep;
No glance lit up her clear grey eyes and deep,
Though some divine thought softened all her face
As once more rang the trumpet through the place.

But her late foe stopped short amidst his course,
One moment gazed upon her piteously,
Then with a groan his lingering feet did force
To leave the spot whence he her eyes could see;
And, changed like one who knows his time must be
But short and bitter, without any word
He knelt before the bearer of the sword;

Then high rose up the gleaming deadly blade,
Bared of its flowers, and through the crowded place
Was silence now, and midst of it the maid
Went by the poor wretch at a gentle pace,
And he to hers upturned his sad white face:
Nor did his eyes behold another sight
Ere on his soul there fell eternal night.

So was the pageant ended, and all folk
Talking of this and that familiar thing
In little groups from that sad concourse broke,
For now the shrill bats were upon the wing,
And soon dark night would slay the evening,
And in dark gardens sang the nightingale
Her little-heeded, oft-repeated tale.

And with the last of all the hunter went,
Who, wondering at the strange sight he had seen,
Prayed an old man to tell him what it meant,
Both why the vanquished man so slain had been,
And if the maiden were an earthly queen,
Or rather what much more she seemed to be,
No sharer in the world's mortality.

"Stranger," said he, "I pray she soon may die
Whose lovely youth has slain so many an one!
King Schœneus' daughter is she verily,
Who when her eyes first looked upon the sun
Was fain to end her life but new begun,
For he had vowed to leave but men alone
Sprung from his loins when he from earth was gone.

"Therefore he bade one leave her in the wood,
And let wild things deal with her as they might,
But this being done, some cruel god thought good
To save her beauty in the world's despite:
Folk say that her, so delicate and white
As now she is, a rough root-grubbing bear
Amidst her shapeless cubs at first did rear.

"In course of time the woodfolk slew her nurse,
And to their rude abode the youngling brought,
And reared her up to be a kingdom's curse,
Who grown a woman, of no kingdom thought,
But armed and swift, 'mid beasts destruction wrought,
Nor spared two shaggy centaur kings to slay
To whom her body seemed an easy prey.

"So to this city, led by fate, she came
Whom known by signs, whereof I cannot tell,
King Schœneus for his child at last did claim,
Nor otherwhere since that day doth she dwell
Sending too many a noble soul to hell—
What! thine eyes glisten! what then, thinkest thou
Her shining head unto the yoke to bow?

"Listen, my son, and love some other maid,
For she the saffron gown will never wear,
And on no flower-strewn couch shall she be laid,
Nor shall her voice make glad a lover's eye:
Yet if of Death thou hast not any fear,
Yea, rather, if thou lovest him utterly,
Thou still may'st woo her ere thou com'st to die,

"Like him that on this day thou sawest lie dead;
For, fearing as I deem the sea-born one,
The maid has vowed e'en such a man to wed
As in the course her swift feet can outrun,
But whoso fails herein, his days are done:
He came the nighest that was slain to-day,
Althought with him I deem she did but play.

"Behold, such mercy Atalanta gives
To those that long to win her loveliness;
Be wise! be sure that many a maid there lives
Gentler than she, of beauty little less,
Whose swimming eyes thy loving words shall bless,
When in some garden, knee set close to knee,
Thou sing'st the song that love may teach to thee."

So to the hunter spake that ancient man,
And left him for his own home presently:
But he turned round, and through the moonlight wan
Reached the thick wood, and there 'twixt tree and tree
Distraught he passed the long night feverishly,
'Twixt sleep and waking, and at dawn arose
To wage hot war against his speechless foes.

There to the hart's flank seemed his shaft to grow
As panting down the broad green glades he flew,
There by his horn the Dryads well might know
His thrust against the bear's heart had been true,
And there Adonis' bane his javelin slew,
But still in vain through rough and smooth he went
For none the more his restlessness was spent.

So wandering, he to Argive cities came,
And in the lists with valiant men he stood,
And by great deeds he won him praise and fame,
And heaps of wealth for little-valued blood;
But none of all these things, or life, seemed good
Unto his heart, where still unsatisfied
A ravenous longing warred with fear and pride.

Therefore it happed when but a month had gone
Since he had left King Schœneus' city old,
In hunting-gear again, again alone
The forest-bordered meads did he behold,
Where still mid thoughts of August's quivering gold
Folk hoed the wheat, and clipped the vine in trust
Of faint October's purple-foaming must.

And once again he passed the peaceful gate,
While to his beating heart his lips did lie,
That owning not victorious love and fate,
Said, half aloud, "And here too must I try,
To win of alien men the mastery,
And gather for my head fresh meed of fame
And cast new glory on my father's name."

In spite of that, how beat his heart when first
Folk said to him, "And art thou come to see
That which still makes our city's name accurst
Among all mothers for its cruelty?
Then know indeed that fate is good to thee
Because to-morrow a new luckless one
Against the whitefoot maid is pledged to run."

So on the morrow with no curious eyes
As once he did, that piteous sight he saw,
Nor did that wonder in his heart arise
As toward the goal the conquering maid 'gan draw,
Nor did he gaze upon her eyes with awe,
Too full the pain of longing filled his heart
For fear or wonder there to have a part.

But O, how long the night was ere it went!
How long it was before the dawn begun
Showed to the wakening birds the sun's intent
That not in darkness should the world be done!
And then, and then, how long before the sun
Bade silently the toilers of the earth
Get forth to fruitless cares or empty mirth!

And long it seemed that in the market-place
He stood and saw the chaffering folk go by,
Ere from the ivory throne King Schœneus' face
Looked down upon the murmur royally,
But then came trembling that the time was nigh
When he midst pitying looks his love must claim,
And jeering voices must salute his name.

But as the throng he pierced to gain the throne,
His alien face distraught and anxious told
What hopeless errand he was bound upon,
And, each to each, folk whispered to behold
His godlike limbs; nay, and one woman old
As he went by must pluck him by the sleeve
And pray him yet that wretched love to leave.

For sidling up she said, "Canst thou live twice,
Fair son? canst thou have joyful youth again,
That thus thou goest to the sacrifice
Thyself the victim? nay then, all in vain
Thy mother bore her longing and her pain
And one more maiden on the earth must dwell
Hopeless of joy, nor fearing death and hell.

"O, fool, thou knowest not the compact then
That with the threeformed goddess she has made
To keep her from the loving lips of men,
And in no saffron gown to be arrayed,
And therewithal with glory to be paid,
And love of her the moonlit river sees
White 'gainst the shadow of the formless trees.

"Come back, and I myself will pray for thee
Unto the sea-born framer of delights,
To give thee her who on the earth may be
The fairest stirrer up to death and fights,
To quench with hopeful days and joyous nights
The flame that doth thy youthful heart consume:
Come back, nor give thy beauty to the tomb."

How should he listen to her earnest speech?
Words, such as he not once or twice had said
Unto himself, whose meaning scarce could reach
The firm abode of that sad hardihead—
He turned about, and through the marketstead
Swiftly he passed, until before the throne
In the cleared space he stood at last alone.

Then said the King, "Stranger, what dost thou here?
Have any of my folk done ill to thee?
Or art thou of the forest men in fear?
Or art thou of the sad fraternity
Who still will strive my daughter's mates to be,
Staking their lives to win to earthly bliss
The lonely maid, the friend of Artemis?"

"O King," he said, "thou sayest the word indeed;
Nor will I quit the strife till I have won
My sweet delight, or death to end my need.
And know that I am called Milanion,
Of King Amphidamas the well-loved son:
So fear not that to thy old name, O King,
Much loss or shame my victory will bring."

"Nay, Prince," said Schœneus, "welcome to this land
Thou wert indeed, if thou wert here to try
Thy strength 'gainst some one mighty of his hand;
Nor would we grudge thee well-won mastery.
But now, why wilt thou come to me to die,
And at my door lay down thy luckless head,
Swelling the band of the unhappy dead,

"Whose curses even now my heart doth fear?
Lo, I am old, and know what life can be,
And what a bitter thing is death anear.
O Son! be wise, and hearken unto me,
And if no other can be dear to thee,
At least as now, yet is the world full wide,
And bliss in seeming hopeless hearts may hide:

"But if thou losest life, then all is lost."
"Nay, King," Milanion said, "thy words are vain.
Doubt not that I have counted well the cost.
But say, on what day wilt thou that I gain
Fulfilled delight, or death to end my pain?
Right glad were I if it could be to-day,
And all my doubts at rest for ever lay."

"Nay," said King Schœneus, "thus it shall not be,
But rather shalt thou let a month go by,
And weary with thy prayers for victory
What god thou know'st the kindest and most nigh.
So doing, still perchance thou shalt not die:
And with my goodwill wouldst thou have the maid,
For of the equal gods I grow afraid.

"And until then, O Prince, be thou my guest,
And all these troublous things awhile forget."
"Nay," said he, "couldst thou give my soul good rest,
And on mine head a sleepy garland set,
Then had I 'scaped the meshes of the net,
Nor shouldst thou hear from me another word;
But now, make sharp thy fearful heading sword.

"Yet will I do what son of man may do,
And promise all the gods may most desire,
That to myself I may at least be true;
And on that day my heart and limbs so tire,
With utmost strain and measureless desire,
That, at the worst, I may but fall asleep
When in the sunlight round that sword shall sweep."

He went with that, nor anywhere would bide,
But unto Argos restlessly did wend;
And there, as one who lays all hope aside,
Because the leech has said his life must end,
Silent farewell he bade to foe and friend,
And took his way unto the restless sea,
For there he deemed his rest and help might be.

Upon the shore of Argolis there stands
A temple to the goddess that he sought,
That, turned unto the lion-bearing lands,
Fenced from the east, of cold winds hath no thought,
Though to no homestead there the sheaves are brought,
No groaning press torments the close-clipped murk,
Lonely the fane stands, far from all men's work.

Pass through a close, set thick with myrtle-trees,
Through the brass doors that guard the holy place,
And entering, hear the washing of the seas
That twice a day rise high above the base,
And with the south-west urging them, embrace
The marble feet of her that standeth there
That shrink not, naked though they be and fair.

Small is the fane through which the seawind sings
About Queen Venus' well-wrought image white,
But hung around are many precious things,
The gifts of those who, longing for delight,
Have hung them there within the goddess' sight,

And in return have taken at her hands
The living treasures of the Grecian lands.

And thither now has come Milanion,
And showed unto the priests' wide open eyes
Gifts fairer than all those that there have shone,
Silk cloths, inwrought with Indian fantasies,
And bowls inscribed with sayings of the wise
Above the deeds of foolish living things,
And mirrors fit to be the gifts of kings.

And now before the Sea-born One he stands,
By the sweet veiling smoke made dim and soft,
And while the incense trickles from his hands,
And while the odorous smoke-wreaths hang aloft,
Thus doth he pray to her: "O Thou, who oft
Hast holpen man and maid in their distress,
Despise me not for this my wretchedness!

"O goddess, among us who dwell below,
Kings and great men, great for a little while,
Have pity on the lowly heads that bow,
Nor hate the hearts that love them without guile;
Wilt thou be worse than these, and is thy smile
A vain device of him who set thee here,
An empty dream of some artificer?

"O, great one, some men love, and are ashamed,
Some men are weary of the bonds of love;
Yea, and by some men lightly art thou blamed,
That from thy toils their lives they cannot move,
And 'mid the ranks of men their manhood prove.
Alas! O goddess, if thou slayest me
What new immortal can I serve but thee?

"Think then, will it bring honour to thy head
If folk say, 'Everything aside he cast
And to all fame and honour was he dead,
And to his one hope now is dead at last,
Since all unholpen he is gone and past:
Ah, the gods love not man, for certainly,
He to his helper did not cease to cry.'

"Nay, but thou wilt help; they who died before
Not single-hearted as I deem came here,
Therefore unthanked they had their gifts before
Thy stainless feet, still shivering with their fear,
Lest in their eyes their true thought might appear,
Who sought to be the lords of that fair town,
Dreaded of men and winners of renown.

"O Queen, thou knowest I pray not for this:
O set us down together in some place
Where not a voice can break our heaven of bliss,

Where nought but rocks and I can see her face,
Softening beneath the marvel of thy grace,
Where not a foot our vanished steps can track—
The golden age, the golden age come back!

"O fairest, hear me now who do thy will,
Plead for thy rebel that he be not slain,
But live and love and be thy servant still;
Ah, give her joy and take away my pain,
And thus two long-enduring servants gain.
An easy thing this is to do for me,
What need of my vain words to weary thee!

"But none the less, this place will I not leave
Until I needs must go my death to meet,
Or at thy hands some happy sign receive
That in great joy we twain may one day greet
Thy presence here and kiss thy silver feet,
Such as we deem thee, fair beyond all words,
Victorious o'er our servants and our lords."

Then from the altar back a space he drew,
But from the Queen turned not his face away,
But 'gainst a pillar leaned, until the blue
That arched the sky, at ending of the day,
Was turned to ruddy gold and changing grey,
And clear, but low, the nigh-ebbed windless sea
In the still evening murmured ceaselessly.

And there he stood when all the sun was down,
Nor had he moved when the dim golden light,
Like a far lustre of a godlike town,
Had left the world to seeming hopeless night,
Nor would he move the more when wan moonlight
Streamed through the pillars for a little while,
And lighted up the white Queen's changeless smile.

Nought noted he the shallow flowing sea
As step by step it set the wrack a-swim,
The yellow torchlight nothing noted he
Wherein with fluttering gown and half-bared limb
The temple damsels sung their midnight hymn,
And nought the doubled stillness of the fane
When they were gone and all was hushed again.

But when the waves had touched the marble base,
And steps the fish swim over twice a-day,
The dawn beheld him sunken in his place
Upon the floor; and sleeping there he lay,
Not heeding aught the little jets of spray
The roughened sea brought nigh, across him cast,
For as one dead all thought from him had passed.

Yet long before the sun had showed his head,
Long ere the varied hangings on the wall
Had gained once more their blue and green and red,
He rose as one some well-known sign doth call
When war upon the city's gates doth fall,
And scarce like one fresh risen out of sleep,
He 'gan again his broken watch to keep.

Then he turned round; not for the sea-gull's cry
That wheeled above the temple in his flight,
Not for the fresh south wind that lovingly
Breathed on the new-born day and dying night,
But some strange hope 'twixt fear and great delight
Drew round his face, now flushed, now pale and wan,
And still constrained his eyes the sea to scan.

Now a faint light lit up the southern sky,
Not sun or moon, for all the world was grey,
But this a bright cloud seemed, that drew anigh,
Lighting the dull waves that beneath it lay
As toward the temple still it took its way,
And still grew greater, till Milanion
Saw nought for dazzling light that round him shone.

But as he staggered with his arms outspread,
Delicious unnamed odours breathed around.
For languid happiness he bowed his head,
And with wet eyes sank down upon the ground,
Nor wished for aught, nor any dream he found
To give him reason for that happiness,
Or make him ask more knowledge of his bliss.

At last his eyes were cleared, and he could see
Through happy tears the goddess face to face
With that faint image of Divinity,
Whose well-wrought smile and dainty changeless grace
Until that morn so gladdened all the place;
Then he unwitting cried aloud her name
And covered up his eyes for fear and shame.

But through the stillness he her voice could hear
Piercing his heart with joy scarce bearable,
That said, "Milanion, wherefore dost thou fear,
I am not hard to those who love me well;
List to what I a second time will tell,
And thou mayest hear perchance, and live to save
The cruel maiden from a loveless grave.

"See, by my feet three golden apples lie—
Such fruit among the heavy roses falls,
Such fruit my watchful damsels carefully
Store up within the best loved of my walls,
Ancient Damascus, here the lover calls,
Above my unseen head, and faint and light
The rose-leaves flutter round me in the night.

"And note, that these are not alone most fair
With heavenly gold, but longing strange they bring
Unto the hearts of men, who will not care,
Beholding these, for any once-loved thing
Till round the shining sides their fingers cling.
And thou shalt see thy well-girt swiftfoot maid
By sight of these amid her glory stayed.

"For bearing these within a scrip with thee,
When first she heads thee from the starting-place
Cast down the first one for her eyes to see,
And when she turns aside make on apace,
And if again she heads thee in the race
Spare not the other two to cast aside
If she not long enough behind will bide.

"Farewell, and when has come the happy time
That she Diana's raiment must unbind
And all the world seems blessed with Saturn's clime,
And thou with eager arms about her twined
Beholdest first her grey eyes growing kind,
Surely, O trembler, thou shalt scarcely then
Forget the Helper of unhappy men."

Milanion raised his head at this last word,
For now so soft and kind she seemed to be
No longer of her Godhead was he feared;
Too late he looked, for nothing could he see
But the white image glimmering doubtfully
In the departing twilight cold and grey,
And those three apples on the steps that lay.

These then he caught up quivering with delight,
Yet fearful lest it all might be a dream,
And though aweary with the watchful night,
And sleepless nights of longing, still did deem
He could not sleep; but yet the first sunbeam
That smote the fane across the heaving deep
Shone on him laid in calm untroubled sleep.

But little ere the noontide did he rise,
And why he felt so happy scarce could tell
Until the gleaming apples met his eyes.
Then leaving the fair place where this befell
Oft he looked back as one who loved it well,
Then homeward to the haunts of men 'gan wend
To bring all things unto a happy end.

Now has the lingering month at last gone by,
Again are all folk round the running place,
Nor other seems the dismal pageantry
Than heretofore, but that another face
Looks o'er the smooth course ready for the race,

For now, beheld of all, Milanion
Stands on the spot he twice has looked upon.

But yet—what change is this that holds the maid?
Does she indeed see in his glittering eye
More than disdain of the sharp shearing blade,
Some happy hope of help and victory?
The others seemed to say, "We come to die,
Look down upon us for a little while,
That dead, we may bethink us of thy smile."

But he—what look of mastery was this
He cast on her? why were his lips so red?
Why was his face so flushed with happiness?
So looks not one who deems himself but dead,
E'en if to death he bows a willing head;
So rather looks a god well pleased to find
Some earthly damsel fashioned to his mind.

Why must she drop her lids before his gaze,
And even as she casts adown her eyes
Redden to note his eager glance of praise,
And wish that she were clad in other guise?
Why must the memory to her heart arise
Of things unnoticed when they first were heard,
Some lover's song, some answering maiden's word?

What makes these longings, vague, without a name,
And this vain pity never felt before,
This sudden languor, this contempt of fame,
This tender sorrow for the time past o'er,
These doubts that grow each minute more and more?
Why does she tremble as the time grows near,
And weak defeat and woeful victory fear?

Now while she seemed to hear her beating heart,
Above their heads the trumpet blast rang out
And forth they sprang; and she must play her part.
Then flew her white feet, knowing not a doubt,
Though slackening once, she turned her head about,
But then she cried aloud and faster fled
Than e'er before, and all men deemed him dead.

But with no sound he raised aloft his hand,
And thence what seemed a ray of light there flew
And past the maid rolled on along the sand;
Then trembling she her feet together drew
And in her heart a strong desire there grew
To have the toy; some god she thought had given
That gift to her, to make of earth a heaven.

Then from the course with eager steps she ran,
And in her odorous bosom laid the gold.
But when she turned again, the great-limbed man

Now well ahead she failed not to behold,
And mindful of her glory waxing cold,
Sprang up and followed him in hot pursuit,
Though with one hand she touched the golden fruit.

Note too, the bow that she was wont to bear
She laid aside to grasp the glittering prize,
And o'er her shoulder from the quiver fair
Three arrows fell and lay before her eyes
Unnoticed, as amidst the people's cries
She sprang to head the strong Milanion,
Who now the turning-post had well-nigh won.

But as he set his mighty hand on it
White fingers underneath his own were laid,
And white limbs from his dazzled eyes did flit,
Then he the second fruit cast by the maid,
But she ran on awhile, then as one afraid
Wavered and stopped, and turned and made no stay,
Until the globe with its bright fellow lay.

Then, as a troubled glance she cast around
Now far ahead the Argive could she see,
And in her garment's hem one hand she wound
To keep the double prize, and strenuously
Sped o'er the course, and little doubt had she
To win the day, though now but scanty space
Was left betwixt him and the winning place.

Short was the way unto such winged feet,
Quickly she gained upon him till at last
He turned about her eager eyes to meet
And from his hand the third fair apple cast.
She wavered not, but turned and ran so fast
After the prize that should her bliss fulfil,
That in her hand it lay ere it was still.

Nor did she rest, but turned about to win
Once more, an unblest woeful victory—
And yet—and yet—why does her breath begin
To fail her, and her feet drag heavily?
Why fails she now to see if far or nigh
The goal is? why do her grey eyes grow dim?
Why do these tremors run through every limb?

She spreads her arms abroad some stay to find
Else must she fall, indeed, and findeth this,
A strong man's arms about her body twined,
Nor may she shudder now to feel his kiss,
So wrapped she is in new unbroken bliss:
Made happy that the foe the prize hath won.
She weeps glad tears for all her glory done.

Shatter the trumpet, hew adown the posts!
Upon the brazen altar break the sword,
And scatter incense to appease the ghosts
Of those who died here by their own award.
Bring forth the image of the mighty Lord,
And her who unseen o'er the runners hung,
And did a deed for ever to be sung.

Here are the gathered folk, make no delay,
Open King Schœneus' well-filled treasury,
Bring out the gifts long hid from light of day,
The golden bowls o'erwrought with imagery,
Gold chains, and unguents brought from over sea,
The saffron gown the old Phœnician brought,
Within the temple of the Goddess wrought.

O ye, O damsels, who shall never see
Her, that Love's servant bringeth now to you,
Returning from another victory,
In some cool bower do all that now is due!
Since she in token of her service new
Shall give to Venus offerings rich enow,
Her maiden zone, her arrows, and her bow.

[1868]

FEBRUARY

Noon—and the north-west sweeps the empty road,
The rain-washed fields from hedge to hedge are bare;
Beneath the leafless elms some hind's abode
Looks small and void, and no smoke meets the air
From its poor hearth: one lonely rook doth dare
The gale, and beats above the unseen corn,
Then turns, and whirling down the wind is borne.

Shall it not hap that on some dawn of May
Thou shalt awake, and thinking of days dead,
See nothing clear but this same dreary day,
Of all the days that have passed o'er thine head?
Shalt thou not wonder, looking from thy bed,
Through green leaves on the windless east a-fire,
That this day too thine heart doth still desire?

Shalt thou not wonder that it liveth yet,
The useless hope, the useless craving pain,
That made thy face, that lonely noontide, wet
With more than beating of the chilly rain?
Shalt thou not hope for joy new born again,
Since no grief ever born can ever die
Through changeless change of seasons passing by?

JUNE

O June, O June, that we desired so,
Wilt thou not make us happy on this day?
Across the river thy soft breezes blow
Sweet with the scent of beanfields far away,
Above our heads rustle the aspens grey,
Calm is the sky with harmless clouds beset,
No thought of storm the morning vexes yet.

See, we have left our hopes and fears behind
To give our very hearts up unto thee;
What better place than this then could we find
By this sweet stream that knows not of the sea,
That guesses not the city's misery,
This little stream whose hamlets scarce have names,
This far-off lonely mother of the Thames?

Here then, O June, thy kindness will we take;
And if indeed but pensive men we seem,
What should we do? thou wouldst not have us wake
From out the arms of this rare happy dream
And wish to leave the murmur of the stream,
The rustling boughs, the twitter of the birds,
And all thy thousand peaceful happy words.

NOVEMBER

Are thine eyes weary? is thy heart too sick
To struggle any more with doubt and thought,
Whose formless veil draws darkening now and thick
Across thee, e'en as smoke-tinged mist-wreaths brought
Down a fair dale to make it blind and nought?
Art thou so weary that no world there seems
Beyond these four walls, hung with pain and dreams?

Look out upon the real world, where the moon,
Half-way 'twixt root and crown of these high trees,
Turns the dead midnight into dreamy noon,
Silent and full of wonders, for the breeze
Died at the sunset, and no images,
No hopes of day, are left in sky or earth—
Is it not fair, and of most wondrous worth?

Yea, I have looked, and seen November there;
The changeless seal of change it seemed to be,
Fair death of things that living once were fair;
Bright sign of loneliness too great for me,
Strange image of the dread eternity,
In whose void patience how can these have part,
These outstretched feverish hands, this restless heart?

[1868–70]

L'ENVOI

Here are we for the last time face to face,
Thou and I, Book, before I bid thee speed
Upon thy perilous journey to that place
For which I have done on thee pilgrim's weed,
Striving to get thee all things for thy need—
—I love thee, whatso time or men may say
Of the poor singer of an empty day.

Good reason why I love thee, e'en if thou
Be mocked or clean forgot as time wears on;
Forever as thy fashioning did grow,
Kind word and praise because of thee I won
From those without whom were my world all gone,
My hope fallen dead, my singing cast away,
And I set soothly in an empty day.

I love thee; yet this last time must it be
That thou must hold thy peace and I must speak,
Lest if thou babble I begin to see
Thy gear too thin, thy limbs and heart too weak,
To find the land thou goest forth to seek—
—Though what harm if thou die upon the way,
Thou idle singer of an empty day?

But though this land desired thou never reach,
Yet folk who know it mayst thou meet, or death;
Therefore a word unto thee would I teach
To answer these, who, noting thy weak breath,
Thy wandering eyes, thy heart of little faith,
May make thy fond desire a sport and play,
Mocking the singer of an empty day.

That land's name, say'st thou? and the road thereto?
Nay, Book, thou mockest, saying thou know'st it not;
Surely no book of verse I ever knew
But ever was the heart within him hot
To gain the Land of Matters Unforgot—
—There, now we both laugh—as the whole world may,
At us poor singers of an empty day.

Nay, let it pass, and hearken! Hast thou heard
That therein I believe I have a friend,
Of whom for love I may not be afeard?
It is to him indeed I bid thee wend;
Yea, he perchance may meet thee ere thou end,
Dying so far off from the hedge of bay,
Thou idle singer of an empty day!

Well, think of him, I bid thee, on the road,
And if it hap that midst of thy defeat,
Fainting beneath thy follies' heavy load,
My Master, GEOFFRY CHAUCER, thou do meet,
Then shalt thou win a space of rest full sweet;
Then be thou bold, and speak the words I say,
The idle singer of an empty day!

"O Master, O thou great of heart and tongue
Thou well mayst ask me why I wander here,
In raiment rent of stories oft besung!
But of thy gentleness draw thou anear,
And then the heart of one who held thee dear
Mayst thou behold! So near as that I lay
Unto the singer of an empty day.

"For this he ever said, who sent me forth
To seek a place amid thy company;
That howsoever little was my worth,
Yet was he worth e'en just so much as I;
He said that rime hath little skill to lie;
Nor feigned to cast his worser part away;
In idle singing for an empty day.

"I have beheld him tremble oft enough
At things he could not choose but trust to me,
Although he knew the world was wise and rough:
And never did he fail to let me see
His love,—his folly and faithlessness, maybe;
And still in turn I gave him voice to pray
Such prayers as cling about an empty day.

"Thou, keen-eyed, reading me, mayst read him through,
For surely little is there left behind;
No power great deeds unnameable to do;
No knowledge for which words he may not find,
No love of things as vague as autumn wind—
—Earth of the earth lies hidden by my clay,
The idle singer of an empty day!

"Children we twain are, saith he, late made wise
In love, but in all else most childish still,
And seeking still the pleasure of our eyes,
And what our ears with sweetest sounds may fill;
Not fearing Love, lest these things he should kill;
Howe'er his pain by pleasure doth he lay,
Making a strange tale of an empty day.

"Death have we hated, knowing not what it meant;
Life have we loved, through green leaf and through sere,
Though still the less we knew of its intent:
The Earth and Heaven through countless year on year,
Slow changing, were to us but curtains fair,
Hung round about a little room, where play
Weeping and laughter of man's empty day.

"O Master, if thine heart could love us yet,
Spite of things left undone, and wrongly done,
Some place in loving hearts then should we get,
For thou, sweet-souled, didst never stand alone,
But knew'st the joy and woe of many an one—
—By lovers dead, who live through thee, we pray,
Help thou us singers of an empty day!"

Fearest thou, Book, what answer thou mayst gain
Lest he should scorn thee and thereof thou die?
Nay, it shall not be.—Thou mayst toil in vain,
And never draw the House of Fame anigh;
Yet he and his shall know whereof we cry,
Shall call it not ill done to strive to lay
The ghosts that crowd about life's empty day.

Then let the others go! and if indeed
In some old garden thou and I have wrought,
And made fresh flowers spring up from hoarded seed,
And fragrance of old days and deeds have brought
Back to folk weary; all was not for nought.
—No little part it was for me to play—
The idle single of an empty day.

[1870]

SIGURD THE VOLSUNG

[GUNNAR IN THE PIT OF ADDERS]

Then was Gunnar silent a little, and the shout in the hall had died,
And he spoke as a man awakening, and turned on Atli's pride.
"Thou all-rich King of the Eastlands, e'en such a man might I be
That I might utter a word, and the heart should be glad in thee,
And I should live and be sorry; for I, I only am left
To tell of the ransom of Odin, and the wealth from the toiler reft.
Lo, once it lay in the water, hid, deep adown it lay,
Till the gods were grieved and lacking, and men saw it and the day:
Let it lie in the water once more, let the gods be rich and in peace!
But I at least in the world from the words and the babble shall cease."

So he spake and Atli beheld him, and before his eyes he shrank;
Still deep of the cup of desire the mighty Atli drank,

And to overcome seemed little if the Gold he might not have,
And his hard heart craved for a while to hold the King for a slave,
A bondman blind and guarded in his glorious house and great:
But he thought of the overbold, and of kings who have dallied with fate,
And died bemocked and smitten; and he deemed it worser than well
While the last of the sons of Giuki hangeth back from his journey to Hell:
So he turneth away from the stranger, and beholdeth Gudrun his wife,
Not glad nor sorry by seeming, no stirrer nor stayer of strife:
Then he looked at his living earl-folk, and thought of his groves of war,
And his realm and the kindred nations, and his measureless guarded store:
And he thought: Shall Atli perish, shall his name be cast to the dead,
Though the feeble folk go wailing? Then he cried aloud and said:
"Why tarry ye, Sons of the Morning? The wain for the bondman is dight;
And the folk that are waiting his body have need of no sunshine to smite.
Go forth 'neath the stars and night-wind; go forth by the cloud and the moon,
And come back with the word in the dawning, that my house may be merry at noon!"

Then the sword-folk rise round Gunnar, round the fettered and bound they throng,
As men in the bitter battle round the God-kin over-strong;
They bore him away to the doorway, and the winds were awake in the night,
And the wood of the thorns of battle in the moon shone sharp and bright;
But Gunnar looked to the heavens, and blessed the promise of rain,
And the windy drift of the clouds, and the dew on the builded wain:
And the sword-folk tarried a little, and the sons of the wise were there,
And beheld his face o'er the war-helms, and the wavy night of his hair.
Then they feared for the weal of Atli, and the Niblung's harp they brought,
And they dealt with the thralls of the sword, and commanded and besought,
Till men loosened the gyves of Gunnar, and laid the harp by his side.
Then the yoke-beasts lowed in the forecourt, and the wheels of the wagon cried,
And the war-thorns clashed in the night, and the men went dark on their way,
And the city was silent before them; on the roofs the white moon lay.

Now they left the gate and the highway, and came to a lonely place,
Where the sun all day had been shining on the desert's empty face;
Then the moon ran forth from a cloud, the grey light shone and showed
The pit of King Atli's adders in the land without a road,
Digged deep adown in the desert with shining walls and smooth
For the Serpents' habitation, and the folk that know not ruth.
Therein they thrust King Gunnar, and he bare of his kingly weed,
But they gave his harp to the Niblung, and his hands of the gyves they freed;
They stood around in their war-gear to note what next should befall
For the comfort of King Atli, and the glee of the Eastland hall.

Still hot was that close with the sun, and thronged with the coiling folk,
And about the feet of Gunnar their hissing mouths awoke;
But he heeded them not nor beheld them, and his hands in the harp-strings ran,
As he sat down in the midmost on a sun-scorched rock and wan:
And he sighed as one who resteth on a flowery bank by the way
When the wind is in the blossoms at the eventide of day.
But his harp was murmuring low, and he mused: Am I come to the death,
And I, who was Gunnar the Niblung? Nay, nay, how I draw my breath,
And love my life as the living! and so I ever shall do,
Though wrack be loosed in the heavens and the world be fashioned anew.

But the worms were beholding their prey, and they drew around and nigher,
Smooth coil, and flickering tongue, and eyes as the gold in the fire;
And he looked and beheld them and spake, nor stilled his harp meanwhile:
"What will ye, O thralls of Atli, O images of guile?"

Then he rose at once to his feet, and smote the harp with his hand,
And it rang as if with a cry in the dream of a lonely land;
Then he fondled its wail as it faded, and orderly over the strings
Went the marvelous sound of its sweetness, like the march of Odin's kings
New-risen for play in the morning when o'er meadows of God-home they wend,
And hero playeth with hero, that their hands may be deft in the end.
But the crests of the worms were uplifted, though coil on coil was stayed,
And they moved but as dark-green rushes by the summer river swayed.

Then uprose the Song of Gunnar, and sang o'er his crafty hands,
And told of the World of Aforetime, unshapen, void of lands;
Yet it wrought, for its memory bideth, and it died and abode its doom;
It shaped, and the Upper-Heavens, and the hope came forth from its womb.
Great then grew the voice of Gunnar, and his speech was sweet on the wild,
And the moon on his harp was shining, and the hands of the Niblung child:

"So perished the Gap of the Gaping, and the cold sea swayed and sang.
And the wind came down on the waters, and the beaten rock-walls rang;
Then the Sun from the south came shining, and the Starry Host stood round,
And the wandering Moon of the heavens his habitation found;
And they knew not why they were gathered, nor the deeds of their shaping they knew:
But lo, Mid-Earth the Noble 'neath their might and their glory grew,
And the grass spread over its face, and the Night and the Day were born,
And it cried on the Death in the even, and it cried on the Life in the morn:
Yet it waxed and waxed, and knew not, and it lived and had not learned;
And where were the Framers that framed, and the Soul and the Might that had yearned?

"On the Thrones are the Powers that fashioned, and they name the Night and the Day,
And the tide of the Moon's increasing, and the tide of his waning away:
And they name the years for the story; and the Lands they change and change,
The great and the mean and the little, that this unto that may be strange:
They met, and they fashioned dwellings, and the House of Glory they built;
They met, and they fashioned the Dwarf-kind, and the Gold and the Gifts and the Guilt.

"There were twain, and they went upon earth, and were speechless unmighty and wan;
They were hopeless, deathless, lifeless, and the Mighty named them Man.
Then they gave them speech and power, and they gave them colour and breath;
And deeds and the hope they gave them, and they gave them Life and Death;
Yea, hope, as the hope of the Framers; yea, might, as the Fashioners had,
Till they wrought, and rejoiced in their bodies, and saw their sons and were glad;
And they changed their lives and departed, and came back as the leaves of the trees
Come back and increase in the summer:—and I, I, I am of these;
And I know of Them that have fashioned, and the deeds that have blossomed and grow;
But naught of the Gods' repentance, or the Gods' undoing I know."

Then falleth the speech of Gunnar, and his lips the word forget,
But his crafty hands are busy, and the harp is murmuring yet.

And the crests of the worms have fallen, and their flickering tongues are still,
The Roller and the Coiler, and Greyback, lord of ill,
Grave-groper and Death-swaddler, the Slumberer of the Heath,
Gold-wallower, Venom-smiter, lie still, forgetting death,
And loose are coils of Long-back; yea, all as soft are laid
As the kine in midmost summer about the elmy glade;
—All save the Grey and Ancient, that holds his crest aloft,
Light-wavering as the flame-tongue when the evening wind is soft:
For he comes of the kin of the Serpent once wrought all wrong to nurse,
The bond of earthly evil, and Midworld's ancient curse.

But Gunnar looked and considered, and wise and wary he grew,
And the dark of night was waning and chill in the dawning it grew;
But his hands were strong and mighty and the fainting harp he woke,
And cried in the deadly desert, and the song from his soul out-broke:

"O Hearken, Kindreds and Nations, and all Kings of the plenteous earth,
Heed, ye that shall come hereafter, and are far and far from birth!
I have dwelt in the world aforetime, and I called it the garden of God;
I have stayed my heart with its sweetness, and fair on its freshness I trod;
I have seen its tempest and wondered, I have cowered adown from its rain,
And desired the brightening sunshine, and seen it and been fain;
I have waked, time was, in its dawning; its noon and its even I wore;
I have slept unafraid of its darkness, and the days have been many and more:
I have dwelt with the deeds of the mighty; I have woven the web of the sword;
I have borne up the guilt nor repented; I have sorrowed nor spoken the word;
And I fought and was glad in the morning, and I sing in the night and the end:
So let him stand forth, the Accuser, and do on the death-shoon to wend;
For not here on the earth shall I hearken, nor on earth for the dooming shall stay,
Nor stretch out mine hand for the pleading; for I see the spring of the day
Round the doors of the golden Valhall, and I see the mighty arise,
And I hearken the voice of Odin, and his mouth on Gunnar cries,
And he nameth the Son of Giuki, and cries on deeds long done,
And the fathers of my fathers, and the sons of yore agone.

"O Odin, I see, and I hearken; but, lo thou, the bonds on my feet,
And the walls of the wilderness round me, ere the light of thy land I meet!
I crave and I weary, Allfather, and long and dark is the road;
And the feet of the mighty are weakened, and the back is bent with the load."

Then fainted the song of Gunnar, and the harp from his hand fell down,
And he cried: "Ah, what hath betided? for cold the world hath grown,
And cold is the heart within me, and my hand is heavy and strange;
What voice is the voice I hearken in the chill and the dusk and the change?
Where art thou, God of the war-fain? for this is the death indeed;
And I unsworded, unshielded, in the Day of the Niblungs' Need!"

He fell to the earth as he spake, and life left Gunnar the King,
For his heart was chilled forever by the sleepless serpent's sting,
The grey Worm, Great and Ancient—and day in the East began,
And the moon was low in the heavens, and the light clouds over him ran.

[1876]

THE DAY IS COMING

Come hither, lads, and hearken, for a tale there is to tell,
Of the wonderful days a-coming, when all shall be better than well.

And the tale shall be told of a country, a land in the midst of the sea,
And folk shall call it England in the days that are going to be.

There more than one in a thousand in the days that are yet to come,
Shall have some hope of the morrow, some joy of the ancient home.

For then, laugh not, but listen to this strange tale of mine,
All folk that are in England shall be better lodged than swine.

Then a man shall work and bethink him, and rejoice in the deeds of his hand,
Nor yet come home in the even too faint and weary to stand.

Men in that time a-coming shall work and have no fear
For to-morrow's lack of earning and the hunger-wolf anear.

I tell you this for a wonder, that no man then shall be glad
Of his fellow's fall and mishap to snatch at the work he had.

For that which the worker winneth shall then be his indeed,
Nor shall half be reaped for nothing by him that sowed no seed.

O strange new wonderful justice! But for whom shall we gather the gain?
For ourselves and for each of our fellows, and no hand shall labour in vain.

Then all Mine and all Thine shall be Ours, and no more shall any man crave
For riches that serve for nothing but to fetter a friend for a slave.

And what wealth then shall be left us when none shall gather gold
To buy his friend in the market, and pinch and pine the sold?

Nay, what save the lovely city, and the little house on the hill,
And the wastes and the woodland beauty, and the happy fields we till;

And the homes of ancient stories, the tombs of the mighty dead;
And the wise men seeking out marvels, and the poet's teeming head;

And the painter's hand of wonder; and the marvelous fiddle-bow,
And the banded choirs of music: all those that do and know.

For all these shall be ours and all men's, nor shall any lack a share
Of the toil and the gain of living in the days when the world grows fair.

Ah! such are the days that shall be! But what are the deeds of to-day,
In the days of the years we dwell in, that wear our lives away?

Why, then, and for what are we waiting? There are three words to speak;
WE WILL IT, and what is the foeman but the dream-strong wakened and weak?

O why and for what are we waiting? while our brothers droop and die,
And on every wind of the heavens a wasted life goes by.

How long shall they reproach us where crowd on crowd they dwell,
Poor ghosts of the wicked city, the gold-crushed hungry hell?

Through squalid life they laboured, in sordid grief they died,
Those sons of a mighty mother, those props of England's pride.

They are gone; there is none can undo it, nor save our souls from the curse;
But many a million cometh, and shall they be better or worse?

It is we must answer and hasten, and open wide the door
For the rich man's hurrying terror, and the slow-foot hope of the poor.

Yea, the voiceless wrath of the wretched, and their unlearned discontent.
We must give it voice and wisdom till the waiting-tide be spent.

Come, then, since all things call us, the living and the dead,
And o'er the weltering tangle a glimmering light is shed.

Come, then, let us cast off fooling, and put by ease and rest,
For the Cause alone is worthy till the good days bring the best.

Come, join in the only battle wherein no man can fail,
Where whoso fadeth and dieth, yet his deed shall still prevail.

Ah! come, cast off all fooling, for this, at least, we know:
That the Dawn and the Day is coming, and forth the Banners go.

[1884]

A. C. SWINBURNE

CHRONOLOGICAL TABLE

1837, April 6, born in London, his father an admiral, his mother a daughter of the Earl of Ashburnham.
Lived at home, on the Isle of Wight, until 1849.

1849–53 Attended Eton.

1856–9 Attended Balliol College, Oxford.

1856 An original member of the Old Mortality Club (which included A. V. Dicey and John Nichol, and subsequently Pater, T. H. Green and Bryce).

1859 Left Oxford without a degree.

1860 Began to live in London.
The Queen Mother and Rosamond.

1862 Met Jane Faulkner with whom he fell in love and who rejected him.
Contributed prose and verse to *The Spectator.*

1865 *Atalanta in Calydon.*
Chastelard.

1866 *Poems and Ballads* [First Series].
Notes on Poems and Reviews (a pamphlet).

1867 Began to write for *The Fortnightly Review.*
A Song of Italy.

1868 *William Blake.*

1871 *Songs before Sunrise.*

1872 *Under the Microscope* (a pamphlet).
First met Theodore Watts (subsequently Watts-Dunton) a solicitor from Huntingdonshire).

1874 *Bothwell.*

1875 *Songs of Two Nations.*
Essays and Studies.

1876 *Erechtheus.*
His health began to give alarm partly because of excesses of many sorts and partly because of nervous tension.

1877 *A Note on Charlotte Bronte* (a volume, not an opuscule as the title suggests).

1878 *Poems and Ballads, Second Series.*

1879 In extreme ill health and nervous disorder, removed by Watts to his villa in Putney which was Swinburne's home for the rest of his life.

1880 *A Study of Shakespeare.*
The Heptalogia; or the Seven against Sense (parodies published anonymously).
Songs of the Springtides.
Studies in Song.

1881 *Mary Stuart.*

1882 *Tristram of Lyonesse and Other Poems.*
Presented to Victor Hugo in Paris.

1883 *A Century of Roundels.*

1884 *A Midsummer Holiday.*

1885 *Marino Faliero.*

1886 *A Study of Victor Hugo.*
Miscellanies.

1887 *Locrine.*
Gathered Songs.

1888 *The Whippingham Papers* (anonymous).

1889 *A Study of Ben Jonson.*
Poems and Ballads, Third Series.

1892 *The Sisters.*

1894 *Astrophel and Other Poems.*
Studies in Prose and Poetry.

1896 *The Tale of Balen.*

1899 *Rosamund, Queen of the Lombards.*

1904 *A Channel Passage and Other Poems.*

1905 *Love's Cross-Currents* (published anonymously in the *Tatler* in 1877, as *A Year's Letters*).

1908 *The Duke of Gandia.*
The Age of Shakespeare.

1909 *Three Plays of Shakespeare.*
Shakespeare.
Died at Putney, April 10, buried at Bonchurch in the Isle of Wight.

In the year in which he went up to Eton a twelve year old boy Swinburne composed a tragedy on the Elizabethan model into which—and it remained a fragment—he crammed two murders, four executions, a suicide and a rape. Violence was always to be a part of his distinctive and excellent writing whether in poetry or in prose, violence of passion as in *Poems and Ballads,* violence in political and philosophical ideas as in *Songs before Sunrise,* violence of vituperation or of eulogy in his critical essays, violence of feeling about nature or even about babies as in the lyrics of his superficially sobered age. Throughout all his best poetry he maintains a style which likewise may be called violent: strong, resonant, energetic, abounding in repetition and exulting in its own copiousness. Violence is his unique contribution to Victorian poetry.

Swinburne's first volume contained two plays richly Elizabethan; and not unnaturally it passed unobserved. It was not till, in 1865, he published *Atalanta in Calydon* that he attracted attention. All who cared for rhythm found in this play the evidence of a new mastery; but the bold repudiation of Christian conceptions implicit in the treatment of the theme stirred many of Swinburne's readers to concern or indignation. But bold as his theology in *Atalanta* had been and deep as was the resentment he had aroused, the reception of this work was tranquil compared with what was to befall his first collection of lyrics. *Poems and Ballads* was a conscious defiance of Victorian reticence; and not until Hardy published *Jude the Obscure* thirty years later did the Victorians greet another work with such screaming of abuse. Its publisher declined to handle his edition; and another publisher, none too reputable, took over the sheets. The scandal was inevitable; not only did Swinburne deal with passion with an integrity and intensity going beyond the most daring passages of Byron, but the passion he dealt with had abnormal aspects. Doubtless few of his critics clearly perceived the sadism which lay thinly disguised within many of the most powerful lyrics; but it is probable that they could recognize that there was some alien and formidable emotion shaping this rebel's presentation of love. It is noteworthy that many of those who most fiercely assailed the volume were aware of the splendor and force of the poet's temperament and style.

Swinburne never again struck with such power the note which resounded through *Poems and Ballads.* He became an intimate of Mazzini and his interest suddenly shifted to a less personal aspect of the problem of pain. He especially devoted himself to the cause of Italian freedom; but wherever in Europe the victim of oppression could be found, Swinburne flamed into angry and prophetic verse against the oppressor. Hugo, whom he had revered ever since his boyhood, now became his exemplar. In *Songs before Sunrise* he displays an awareness of the main problems of European politics which none of his contemporaries in England could match. He became a European man. Mingled with his political utterances in that collection were lyrics such as "Hertha" in which he expressed his adherence to naturalism in philosophy, his repudiation of a personal God, his adoration of humanity. Again the reviews abounded in hostility: Swinburne was denounced as a promoter of the Revolution.

The poet's private life had become extremely irregular. Towards the end of the seventies his health was undermined. Living by himself in a London apartment, drawn to strange and depraved people, eager to satisfy his abnormal tastes, always delighted with the extreme and the violent, he seemed close to a total breakdown, if not to death. He was rescued by a solicitor with literary ambition who already had undertaken to protect his interests as an author. Theodore Watts, subsequently Watts-Dunton, took the poet to live with him in a villa at Putney. Here in suburban quiet, his life devotedly watched over by a timid and ultra-respectable friend, the most tumultuous spirit of his time in poetry spent his last thirty years.

The splendor had departed. Now and then in his poems about nature, in his literary estimates in prose or verse, in his outbursts of patriotic poetry, fire and brilliance appeared. But the second half of Swinburne's poetic career was an anticlimax. The life which was good for him as a man was ruin to him as a poet. Victorian England never forgave *Poems and Ballads;* a great Victorian liberal, Lord Morley, had written the most savage review of that book when it appeared and when in 1891 the death of Tennyson left the laureateship vacant, another great Victorian liberal, Lord Acton, prevented the offer of the honour to Swinburne by his emphasis on the unconventionalities of the same book. Recently an attempt has been made to present Swinburne as a precursor of the twentieth century lost among the Victorians; among the Victorians he was indeed lost but rather as Shelley or Byron would have been. His life and his poetry relate him with the young romantic poets of the doomed second generation.

ATALANTA IN CALYDON

CHIEF HUNTSMAN

Maiden, and mistress of the months and stars
Now folded in the flowerless fields of heaven,
Goddess whom all gods love with threefold heart,
Being treble in thy divided deity,
A light for dead men and dark hours, a foot

Swift on the hills as morning, and a hand
To all things fierce and fleet that roar and range
Mortal, with gentler shafts than snow or sleep;
Hear now and help and lift no violent hand,
But favourable and fair as thine eye's beam
Hidden and shown in heaven; for I all night
Amid the king's hounds and the hunting men
Have wrought and worshipped toward thee; nor shall man
See goodlier hounds or deadlier edge of spears;
But for the end, that lies unreached at yet
Between the hands and on the knees of gods.
O fair-faced sun, killing the stars and dews
And dreams and desolation of the night!
Rise up, shine, stretch thine hand out, with thy bow
Touch the most dimmest height of trembling heaven,
And burn and break the dark about thy ways,
Shot through and through with arrows; let thine hair
Lighten as flame above the flameless shell
Which was the moon, and thine eyes fill the world
And thy lips kindle with swift beams; let earth
Laugh, and the long sea fiery from thy feet
Through all the roar and ripple of streaming springs
And foam in reddening flakes and flying flowers
Shaken from hands and blown from lips of nymphs
Whose hair or breast divides the wandering wave
With salt close tresses cleaving lock to lock,
All gold, or shuddering and unfurrowed snow;
And all the winds about thee with their wings,
And fountain-heads of all the watered world;
Each horn of Acheloüs, and the green
Euenus, wedded with the straitening sea.
For in fair time thou comest; come also thou,
Twin-born with him, and virgin, Artemis,
And give our spears their spoil, the wild boar's hide,
Sent in thine anger against us for sin done
And bloodless altars without wine or fire.
Him now consume thou; for thy sacrifice
With sanguine-shining steam divides the dawn,
And one, the maiden rose of all thy maids,
Arcadian Atalanta, snowy-souled,
Fair as the snow and footed as the wind,
From Ladon and well-wooded Mænalus
Over the firm hills and the fleeting sea
Hast thou drawn hither, and many an armèd king,
Heroes, the crown of men, like gods in fight.
Moreover out of all the Ætolian land,
From the full-flowered Lelantian pasturage
To what of fruitful field the son of Zeus
Won from the roaring river and labouring sea
When the wild god shrank in his horn and fled
And foamed and lessened through his wrathful fords,
Leaving clear lands that steamed with sudden sun,
These virgins with the lightening of the day
Bring thee fresh wreaths and their own sweeter hair,

Luxurious locks and flower-like mixed with flowers,
Clean offering, and chaste hymns; but he the time
Divides from these things; whom do thou not less
Help and give honour, and to mine hounds good speed,
And edge to spears, and luck to each man's hand.

CHORUS

When the hounds of spring are on winter's traces,
  The mother of months in meadow or plain
Fills the shadows and windy places
  With lisp of leaves and ripple of rain;
And the brown bright nightingale amorous
Is half assuaged for Itylus,
For the Thracian ships and the foreign faces,
  The tongueless vigil, and all the pain.

Come with bows bent and with emptying of quivers,
  Maiden most perfect, lady of light,
With a noise of winds and many rivers,
  With a clamour of waters, and with might;
Bind on thy sandals, O thou most fleet,
Over the splendour and speed of thy feet;
For the faint east quickens, the wan west shivers,
  Round the feet of the day and the feet of the night.

Where shall we find her, how shall we sing to her,
  Fold our hands round her knees, and cling?
O that man's heart were as fire and could spring to her,
  Fire, or the strength of the streams that spring!
For the stars and the winds are unto her
As raiment, as songs of the harp-player;
For the risen stars and the fallen cling to her,
  And the southwest-wind and the west-wind sing.

For winter's rains and ruins are over,
  And all the season of snows and sins;
The days dividing lover and lover,
  The light that loses, the night that wins;
And time remembered is grief forgotten,
And frosts are slain and flowers begotten,
And in green underwood and cover
  Blossom by blossom the spring begins.

The full streams feed on flower of rushes,
  Ripe grasses trammel a travelling foot,
The faint fresh flame of the young year flushes
  From leaf to flower and flower to fruit;
And fruit and leaf are as gold and fire,
And the oat is heard above the lyre,
And the hoofèd heel of a satyr crushes
  The chestnut-husk at the chestnut-root

And Pan by noon and Bacchus by night,
  Fleeter of foot than the fleet-foot kid,

Follows with dancing and fills with delight
  The Mænad and the Bassarid;
And soft as lips that laugh and hide
The laughing leaves of the trees divide,
And screen from seeing and leave in sight
  The god pursuing, the maiden hid.

The ivy falls with the Bacchanal's hair
  Over her eyebrows hiding her eyes;
The wild vine slipping down leaves bare
  Her bright breast shortening into sighs;
The wild vine slips with the weight of its leaves,
But the berried ivy catches and cleaves
To the limbs that glitter, the feet that scare
  The wolf that follows, the fawn that flies.

ALTHÆA

What do ye singing? what is this ye sing?

CHORUS

Flowers bring we, and pure lips that please the gods,
And raiment meet for service: lest the day
Turn sharp with all its honey in our lips.

ALTHÆA

Night, a black hound, follows that white fawn day,
Swifter than dreams the white flown feet of sleep;
Will ye pray back the night with any prayers?
And though the spring put back a little while
Winter, and snows that plague all men for sin,
And the iron time of cursing, yet I know
Spring shall be ruined with the rain, and storm
Eat up like fire the ashen autumn days.
I marvel what men do with prayers awake
Who dream and die with dreaming; any god,
Yea the least god of all things called divine,
Is more than sleep and waking; yet we say,
Perchance by praying a man shall match his god.
For if sleep have no mercy, and man's dreams
Bite to the blood and burn into the bone,
What shall this man do waking? By the gods,
He shall not pray to dream sweet things to-night,
Having dreamt once more bitter things than death.

CHORUS

Queen, but what is it that hath burnt thine heart?
For thy speech flickers like a blown-out flame.

ALTHÆA

Look, ye say well, and know not what ye say;
For all my sleep is turned into a fire,
And all my dreams to stuff that kindles it.

CHORUS

Yet one doth well being patient of the gods.

ALTHÆA

Yea, lest they smite us with some four-foot plague.

CHORUS

But when time spreads find out some herb for it.

ALTHÆA

And with their healing herbs infect our blood.

CHORUS

What ails thee to be jealous of their ways?

ALTHÆA

What if they give us poisonous drinks for wine?

CHORUS

They have their will; much talking mends it not.

ALTHÆA

And gall for milk, and cursing for a prayer?

CHORUS

Have they not given life, and the end of life?

ALTHÆA

Lo, where they heal, they help not; thus they do,
They mock us with a little piteousness,
And we say prayers and weep; but at the last,
Sparing awhile, they smite and spare no whit.

CHORUS

Small praise man gets dispraising the high gods:
What have they done that thou dishonourest them?

ALTHÆA

First Artemis for all this harried land
I praise not, and for wasting of the boar
That mars with tooth and tusk and fiery feet
Green pasturage and the grace of standing corn
And meadow and marsh with springs and unblown leaves,
Flocks and swift herds and all that bite sweet grass,
I praise her not; what things are these to praise?

CHORUS

But when the king did sacrifice, and gave
Each god fair dues of wheat and blood and wine,
Her not with bloodshed nor burnt-offering
Revered he, nor with salt or cloven cake;
Wherefore being wroth she plagued the land: but now

Takes off from us fate and her heavy things.
Which deed of these twain were not good to praise?
For a just deed looks always either way
With blameless eyes, and mercy is no fault.

ALTHÆA

Yea, but a curse she hath sent above all these
To hurt us where she healed us; and hath lit
Fire where the old fire went out, and where the wind
Slackened, hath blown on us with deadlier air.

CHORUS

What storm is this that tightens all our sail?

ALTHÆA

Love, a thwart sea-wind full of rain and foam.

CHORUS

Whence blown, and born under what stormier star?

ALTHÆA

Southward across Euenus from the sea.

CHORUS

Thy speech turns toward Arcadia like blown wind.

ALTHÆA

Sharp as the north sets when the snows are out.

CHORUS

Nay, for this maiden hath no touch of love.

ALTHÆA

I would she had sought in some cold gulf of sea
Love, or in dens where strange beasts lurk, or fire,
Or snows on the extreme hills, or iron land
Where no spring is; I would she had sought therein
And found, or ever love had found her here.

CHORUS

She is holier than all holy days or things,
The sprinkled water or fume of perfect fire;
Chaste, dedicated to pure prayers, and filled
With higher thoughts than heaven; a maiden clean,
Pure iron, fashioned for a sword; and man
She loves not; what should one such do with love?

ALTHÆA

Look you, I speak not as one light of wit,
But as a queen speaks, being heart-vexed; for oft
I hear my brothers wrangling in mid hall,
And am not moved; and my son chiding them,
And these things nowise move me, but I know

Foolish and wise men must be to the end,
And feed myself with patience; but this most,
This moves me, that for wise men as for fools
Love is one thing, an evil thing, and turns
Choice words and wisdom into fire and air.
And in the end shall no joy come, but grief,
Sharp words and soul's division and fresh tears
Flower-wise upon the old root of tears brought forth,
Fruit-wise upon the old flower of tears sprung up,
Pitiful sighs, and much regrafted pain.
These things are in my presage, and myself
Am part of them and know not; but in dreams
The gods are heavy on me, and all the fates
Shed fire across my eyelids mixed with night,
And burn me blind, and disilluminate
My sense of seeing, and my perspicuous soul
Darken with vision; seeing I see not, hear
And hearing am not holpen, but mine eyes
Stain many tender broideries in the bed
Drawn up about my face that I may weep
And the king wake not; and my brows and lips
Tremble and sob in sleeping, like swift flames
That tremble, or water when it sobs with heat
Kindled from under; and my tears fill my breast
And speck the fair dyed pillows round the king
With barren showers and salter than the sea,
Such dreams divide me dreaming; for long since
I dreamed that out of this my womb had sprung
Fire and a firebrand; this was ere my son,
Meleager, a goodly flower in fields of fight,
Felt the light touch him coming forth, and wailed
Childlike; but yet he was not; and in time
I bare him, and my heart was great; for yet
So royally was never strong man born,
Nor queen so nobly bore as noble a thing
As this my son was: such a birth God sent
And such a grace to bear it. Then came in
Three weaving women, and span each a thread,
Saying This for strength and That for luck, and one
Saying Till the brand upon the hearth burn down,
So long shall this man see good days and live.
And I with gathered raiment from the bed
Sprang, and drew forth the brand, and cast on it
Water, and trod the flame bare-foot, and crushed
With naked hand spark beaten out of spark
And blew against and quenched it; for I said,
These are the most high Fates that dwell with us,
And we find favour a little in their sight,
A little, and more we miss of, and much time
Foils us; howbeit they have pitied me, O son,
And thee most piteous, thee a tenderer thing
Than any flower of freshly seed alive.
Wherefore I kissed and hid him with my hands,
And covered under arms and hair, and wept,

And feared to touch him with my tears, and laughed;
So light a thing was this man, grown so great
Men cast their heads back, seeing against the sun
Blaze the armed man carven on his shield, and hear
The laughter of little bells along the brace
Ring, as birds singing or flutes blown, and watch,
High up, the cloven shadow of either plume
Divide the bright line of the brass, and make
His helmet as a windy and wintering moon
Seen through blown cloud and plume-like drift, when ships
Drive, and men strive with all the sea, and oars
Break, and the beaks dip under, drinking death;
Yet was he then but a span long, and moaned
With inarticulate mouth inseparate words,
And with blind lips and fingers wrung my breast
Hard, and thrust out with foolish hands and feet,
Murmuring; but those grey women with bound hair
Who fright the gods frighted not him; he laughed
Seeing them, and pushed out hands to feel and haul
Distaff and thread, intangible; but they
Passed, and I hid the brand, and in my heart
Laughed likewise, having all my will of heaven.
But now I know not if to left or right
The gods have drawn us hither; for again
I dreamt, and saw the black brand burst on fire
As a branch bursts in flower, and saw the flame
Fade flower-wise, and Death came and with dry lips
Blew the charred ash into my breast; and Love
Trampled the ember and crushed it with swift feet.
This I have also at heart; that not for me,
Not for me only or son of mine, O girls,
The gods have wrought life, and desire of life,
Heart's love and heart's division; but for all
There shines one sun and one wind blows till night,
And when night comes the wind sinks and the sun,
And there is no light after, and no storm,
But sleep and much forgetfulness of things.
In such wise I gat knowledge of the gods
Years hence and heard high sayings of one most wise,
Eurythemis my mother, who beheld
With eyes alive and spake with lips of these
As one on earth disfleshed and disallied
From breath or blood corruptible; such gifts
Time gave her, and an equal soul to these
And equal face to all things; thus she said.
But whatsoever intolerable or glad
The swift hours weave and unweave, I go hence
Full of mine own soul, perfect of myself,
Toward mine and me sufficient; and what chance
The gods cast lots for and shake out on us,
That shall we take, and that much bear withal.
And now, before these gather to the hunt,
I will go arm my son and bring him forth,
Lest love or some man's anger work him harm.

CHORUS

Before the beginning of years
  There came to the making or man
Time, with a gift of tears;
  Grief, with a glass that ran;
Pleasure, with pain for leaven;
  Summer, with flowers that fell;
Remembrance fallen from heaven,
  And madness risen from hell;
Strength without hands to smite;
  Love that endures for a breath:
Night, the shadow of light,
  And life, the shadow of death.

And the high gods took in hand
  Fire, and the falling of tears,
And a measure of sliding sand
  From under the feet of the years;
And froth and drift of the sea;
  And dust of the labouring earth;
And bodies of things to be
  In the houses of death and of birth;
And wrought with weeping and laughter,
  And fashioned with loathing and love
With life before and after
  And death beneath and above
For a day and a night and a morrow,
  That his strength might endure for a span
With travail and heavy sorrow,
  The holy spirit of man.

From the winds of the north and the south
  They gathered as unto strife;
They breathed upon his mouth,
  They filled his body with life;
Eyesight and speech they wrought
  For the veils of the soul therein,
A time for labour and thought,
  A time to serve and to sin;
They gave him light in his ways,
  And love, and a space for delight,
And beauty and length of days,
  And night, and sleep in the night.
His speech is a burning fire;
  With his lips he travaileth;
In his heart is a blind desire,
  In his eyes foreknowledge of death;
He weaves, and is clothed with derision;
  Sows, and he shall not reap;
His life is a watch or a vision
  Between a sleep and a sleep.

MELEAGER

O sweet new heaven and air without a star,
Fair day, be fair and welcome, as to men
With deeds to do and praise to pluck from thee.
Come forth a child, born with clear sound and light,
With laughter and swift limbs and prosperous looks;
That this great hunt with heroes for the hounds
May leave thee memorable and us well sped.

ALTHÆA

Son, first I praise thy prayer, then bid thee speed;
But the gods hear men's hands before their lips,
And heed beyond all crying and sacrifice
Light of things done and noise of labouring men.
But thou, being armed and perfect for the deed,
Abide; for like rain-flakes in a wind they grow,
The men thy fellows, and the choice of the world,
Bound to root out the tuskèd plague, and leave
Thanks and safe days and peace in Calydon.

MELEAGER

For the whole city and all the low-lying land
Flames, and the soft air sounds with them that come;
The gods give all these fruit of all their works.

ALTHÆA

Set thine eye thither and fix thy spirit and say
Whom there thou knowest; for sharp mixed shadow and wind
Blown up between the morning and the mist
With steam of steeds and flash of bridle or wheel,
And fire, and parcels of the broken dawn,
And dust divided by hard light, and spears
That shine and shift as the edge of wild beasts' eyes,
Smite upon mine; so fiery their blind edge
Burns, and bright points break up and baffle day.

MELEAGER

The first, for many I know not, being far off,
Peleus the Larissæan, couched with whom
Sleeps the white sea-bred wife and silver-shod,
Fair as fled foam, a goddess; and their son
Most swift and splendid of men's children born,
Most like a god, full of the future fame.

ALTHÆA

Who are these shining like one sundered star?

MELEAGER

Thy sister's sons, a double flower of men.

ALTHÆA

O sweetest kin to me in all the world,
O twin-born blood of Leda, gracious heads
Like kindled lights in untempestuous heaven,

Fair flower-like stars on the iron foam of fight,
With what glad heart and kindliness of soul,
Even to the staining of both eyes with tears
And kindling of warm eyelids with desire,
A great way off I greet you, and rejoice
Seeing you so fair, and moulded like as gods.
Far off ye come, and least in years of these,
But lordliest, but worth love to look upon.

MELEAGER

Even such (for sailing hither I saw far hence,
And where Eurotas hollows his moist rock
Nigh Sparta with a strenuous-hearted stream)
Even such I saw their sisters; one swan-white,
The little Helen, and less fair than she
Fair Clytæmnestra, grave as pasturing fawns
Who feed and fear some arrow; but at whiles,
As one smitten with love or wrung with joy,
She laughs and lightens with her eyes, and then
Weeps; whereat Helen, having laughed, weeps too,
And the other chides her, and she being chid speaks nought,
But cheeks and lips and eyelids kisses her,
Laughing; so fare they, as in their bloomless bud
And full of unblown life, the blood of gods.

ALTHÆA

Sweet days befall them and good loves and lords,
And tender and temperate honours of the hearth,
Peace, and a perfect life and blameless bed.
But who shows next an eagle wrought in gold,
That flames and beats broad wings against the sun
And with void mouth gapes after emptier prey?

MELEAGER

Know by that sign the reign of Telamon
Between the fierce mouths of the encountering brine
On the strait reefs of twice-washed Salamis.

ALTHÆA

For like one great of hand he bears himself,
Vine-chapleted, with savours of the sea,
Glittering as wine and moving as a wave.
But who girt round there roughly follows him?

MELEAGER

Ancæus, great of hand, an iron bulk,
Two-edged for fight as the axe against his arm,
Who drives against the surge of stormy spears
Full-sailed; him Cepheus follows, his twin-born,
Chief name next his of all Arcadian men.

ALTHÆA

Praise be with men abroad; chaste lives with us,
Home-keeping days and household reverences.

MELEAGER

Next by the left unsandalled foot know thou
The sail and oar of this Ætolian land,
Thy brethren, Toxeus and the violent-souled
Plexippus, over-swift with hand and tongue;
For hands are fruitful, but the ignorant mouth
Blows and corrupts their work with barren breath.

ALTHÆA

Speech too bears fruit, being worth; and air blows down
Things poisonous, and high-seated violences,
And with charmed words and songs have men put out
Wild evil, and the fire of tyrannies.

MELEAGER

Yea, all things have they, save the gods and love.

ALTHÆA

Love thou the law and cleave to things ordained.

MELEAGER

Law lives upon their lips whom these applaud.

ALTHÆA

How sayest thou these? what god applauds new things?

MELEAGER

Zeus, who hath fear and custom under foot.

ALTHÆA

But loves not laws thrown down and lives awry.

MELEAGER

Yet is not less himself than his own law.

ALTHÆA

Nor shifts and shuffles old things up and down.

MELEAGER

But what he will remoulds and discreates.

ALTHÆA

Much, but not this, that each thing live its life.

MELEAGER

Nor only live, but lighten and lift up higher.

ALTHÆA

Pride breaks itself, and too much gained is gone.

MELEAGER

Things gained are gone, but great things done endure.

ALTHÆA

Child, if a man serve law through all his life
And with his whole heart worship, him all gods
Praise; but who loves it only with his lips,
And not in heart and deed desiring it
Hides a perverse will with obsequious words,
Him heaven infatuates and his twin-born fate
Tracks, and gains on him, scenting sins far off,
And the swift hounds of violent death devour.
Be man at one with equal-minded gods,
So shall he prosper; not through laws torn up,
Violated rule and a new face of things.
A woman armed makes war upon herself,
Unwomanlike, and treads down use and wont
And the sweet common honour that she hath,
Love, and the cry of children, and the hand
Trothplight and mutual mouth of marriages.
This doth she, being unloved; whom if one love,
Not fire nor iron and the wide-mouthed wars
Are deadlier than her lips or braided hair.
For of the one comes poison, and a curse
Falls from the other and burns the lives of men.
But thou, son, be not filled with evil dreams,
Nor with desire of these things; for with time
Blind love burns out; but if one feed it full
Till some discolouring stain dyes all his life,
He shall keep nothing praiseworthy, nor die
The sweet wise death of old men honourable,
Who have lived out all the length of all their years
Blameless, and seen well-pleased the face of gods,
And without shame and without fear have wrought
Things memorable, and while their days held out
In sight of all men and the sun's great light
Have gat them glory and given of their own praise
To the earth that bare them and the day that bred,
Home friends and far-off hospitalities,
And filled with gracious and memorial fame
Lands loved of summer or washed by violent seas,
Towns populous and many unfooted ways,
And alien lips and native with their own.
But when white age and venerable death
Mow down the strength and life within their limbs,
Drain out the blood and darken their clear eyes,
Immortal honour is on them, having past
Through splendid life and death desirable
To the clear seat and remote throne of souls,
Lands indiscoverable in the unheard-of west,
Round which the strong stream of a sacred sea
Rolls without wind for ever, and the snow
There shows not her white wings and windy feet,
Nor thunder nor swift rain saith anything,
Nor the sun burns, but all things rest and thrive;
And these, filled full of days, divine and dead,
Sages and singers fiery from the god,

And such as loved their land and all things good
And, best beloved of best men, liberty,
Free lives and lips, free hands of men free-born,
And whatsoever on earth was honourable
And whosoever of all the ephemeral seed,
Live there a life no liker to the gods
But nearer than their life of terrene days.
Love thou such life and look for such a death.
But from the light and fiery dreams of love
Spring heavy sorrows and a sleepless life,
Visions not dreams, whose lids no charm shall close
Nor song assuage them waking; and swift death
Crushes with sterile feet the unripening ear,
Treads out the timeless vintage; whom do thou
Eschewing embrace the luck of this thy life,
Not without honour; and it shall bear to thee
Such fruit as men reap from spent hours and wear,
Few men, but happy; of whom be thou, O son,
Happiest, if thou submit thy soul to fate,
And set thine eyes and heart on hopes high-born
And divine deeds and abstinence divine.
So shalt thou be toward all men all thy days
As light and might communicable, and burn
From heaven among the stars above the hours,
And break not as a man breaks nor burn down:
For to whom other of all heroic names
Have the gods given his life in hand as thine?
And gloriously hast thou lived, and made thy life
To me that bare thee and to all men born
Thankworthy, a praise for ever; and hast won fame
When wild wars broke all round thy father's house,
And the mad people of windy mountain ways
Laid spears against us like a sea, and all
Ætolia thundered with Thessalian hoofs;
Yet these, as wind baffles the foam, and beats
Straight back the relaxed ripple, didst thou break
And loosen all their lances, till undone
And man from man they fell; for ye twain stood
God against god, Ares and Artemis,
And thou the mightier; wherefore she unleashed
A sharp-toothed curse thou too shalt overcome;
For in the greener blossom of thy life
Ere the full blade caught flower, and when time gave
Respite, thou didst not slacken soul nor sleep,
But with great hand and heart seek praise of men
Out of sharp straits and many a grievous thing,
Seeing the strange foam of undivided seas
On channels never sailed in, and by shores
Where the old winds cease not blowing, and all the night
Thunders, and day is no delight to men.

CHORUS

Meleager, a noble wisdom and fair words
The gods have given this woman; hear thou these.

MELEAGER

O mother, I am not fain to strive in speech
Nor set my mouth against thee, who art wise
Even as they say and full of sacred words.
But one thing I know surely, and cleave to this;
That though I be not subtle of wit as thou
Nor womanlike to weave sweet words, and melt
Mutable minds of wise men as with fire,
I too, doing justly and reverencing the gods,
Shall not want wit to see what things be right.
For whom they love and whom reject, being gods,
There is no man but seeth, and in good time
Submits himself, refraining all his heart.
And I too as thou sayest have seen great things;
Seen otherwhere, but chiefly when the sail
First caught between stretched ropes the roaring west,
And all our oars smote eastward, and the wind
First flung round faces of seafaring men
White splendid snow-flakes of the sundering foam,
And the first furrow in virginal green sea
Followed the plunging ploughshare of hewn pine,
And closed, as when deep sleep subdues man's breath
Lips close and heart subsides; and closing, shone
Sunlike with many a Nereid's hair, and moved
Round many a trembling mouth of doubtful gods,
Risen out of sunless and sonorous gulfs
Through waning water and into shallow light,
That watched us; and when flying the dove was snared
As with men's hands, but we shot after and sped
Clear through the irremeable Symplegades;
And chiefliest when hoar beach and herbless cliff
Stood out ahead from Colchis, and we heard
Clefts hoarse with wind, and saw through narrowing reefs
The lightning of the intolerable wave
Flash, and the white wet flame of breakers burn
Far under a kindling south-wind, as a lamp
Burns and bends all its blowing flame one way;
Wild heights untravelled of the wind, and vales
Cloven seaward by their violent streams, and white
With bitter flowers and bright salt scurf of brine;
Heard sweep their sharp swift gales, and bowing birdwise
Shriek with birds' voices, and with furious feet
Tread loose the long skirts of a storm; and saw
The whole white Euxine clash together and fall
Full-mouthed, and thunderous from a thousand throats:
Yet we drew thither and won the fleece and won
Medea, deadlier than the sea; but there
Seeing many a wonder and fearful things to men
I saw not one thing like this one seen here,
Most fair and fearful, feminine, a god,
Faultless; whom I that love not, being unlike,
Fear, and give honour, and choose from all the gods.

ŒNEUS

Lady, the daughter of Thestius, and thou, son,
Not ignorant of your strife nor light of wit,
Scared with vain dreams and fluttering like spent fire,
I come to judge between you, but a king
Full of past days and wise from years endured.
Nor thee I praise, who are fain to undo things done:
Nor thee, who art swift to esteem them overmuch.
For what the hours have given is given, and this
Changeless; howbeit these change, and in good time
Devise new things and good, not one thing still.
Us have they sent now at our need for help
Among men armed a woman, foreign born,
Virgin, not like the natural flower of things
That grows and bears and brings forth fruit and dies;
Unlovable, no light for a husband's house,
Espoused; a glory among unwedded girls,
And chosen of gods who reverence maidenhood.
These too we honour in honouring her; but thou,
Abstain thy feet from following, and thine eyes
From amorous touch; nor set toward hers thine heart,
Son, lest hate bear no deadlier fruit than love.

ALTHÆA

O king, thou art wise, but wisdom halts; and just,
But the gods love not justice more than fate,
And smite the righteous and the violent mouth,
And mix with insolent blood the reverent man's,
And bruise the holier as the lying lips.
Enough; for wise words fail me, and my heart
Takes fire and trembles flamewise, O my son,
O child, for thine head's sake; mine eyes wax thick,
Turning toward thee, so goodly a weaponed man,
So glorious; and for love of thine own eyes
They are darkened, and tears burn them, fierce as fire,
And my lips pause and my soul sinks with love.
But by thine hand, by thy sweet life and eyes,
By thy great heart and these clasped knees, O son,
I pray thee that thou slay me not with thee.
For there was never a mother woman-born
Loved her sons better; and never a queen of men
More perfect in her heart toward whom she loved.
For what lies light on many and they forget,
Small things and transitory as a wind o' the sea.
I forget never; I have seen thee all thine years
A man in arms, strong and a joy to men
Seeing thine head glitter and thine hand burn its way
Through a heavy and iron furrow of sundering spears;
But always also a flower of three suns old,
The small one thing that lying drew down my life
To lie with thee and feed thee; a child and weak,
Mine, a delight to no man, sweet to me.
Who then sought to thee? who gat help? who knew

If thou wert goodly? nay, no man at all.
Or what sea saw thee, or sounded with thine oar,
Child? or what strange land shone with war through thee?
But fair for me thou wert, O little life,
Fruitless, the fruit of mine own flesh, and blind,
More than much gold, ungrown, a foolish flower.
For silver nor bright snow nor feather of foam
Was whiter, and no gold yellower than thine hair,
O child, my child; and now thou art lordlier grown,
Not lovelier, nor a new thing in mine eyes,
I charge thee by thy soul and this my breast,
Fear thou the gods and me and thine own heart,
Lest all these turn against thee; for who knows
What wind upon what wave of altering time
Shall speak a storm and blow calamity?
And there is nothing stabile in the world
But the gods break it; yet not less, fair son,
If but one thing be stronger, if one endure,
Surely the bitter and the rooted love
That burns between us, going from me to thee,
Shall more endure than all things. What dost thou,
Following strange loves? why wilt thou kill mine heart?
Lo, I talk wild and windy words, and fall
From my clear wits, and seem of mine own self
Dethroned, dispraised, disseated; and my mind,
That was my crown, breaks, and mine heart is gone,
And I am naked of my soul, and stand
Ashamed, as a mean woman; take thou thought:
Live if thou wilt, and if thou wilt not, look,
The gods have given thee life to lose or keep,
Thou shalt not die as men die, but thine end
Fallen upon thee shall break me unaware.

MELEAGER

Queen, my whole heart is molten with thy tears,
And my limbs yearn with pity of thee, and love
Compels with grief mine eyes and labouring breath;
For what thou art I know thee, and this thy breast
And thy fair eyes I worship, and am bound
Toward thee in spirit and love thee in all my soul.
For there is nothing terribler to men
Than the sweet face of mothers, and the might.
But what shall be let be; for us the day
Once only lives a little, and is not found.
Time and the fruitful hour are more than we,
And these lay hold upon us; but thou, God,
Zeus, the sole steersman of the helm of things,
Father, be swift to see us, and as thou wilt
Help: of if adverse, as thou wilt, refrain.

CHORUS

We have seen thee, O Love, thou art fair; thou art goodly, O Love;
Thy wings make light in the air as the wings of a dove.
Thy feet are as winds that divide the stream of the sea;

Earth is thy covering to hide thee, the garment of thee.
Thou art swift and subtle and blind as a flame of fire;
Before thee the laughter, behind thee the tears of desire;
And twain go forth beside thee, a man with a maid;
Her eyes are the eyes of a bride whom delight makes afraid;
As the breath in the buds that stir is her bridal breath:
But Fate is the name of her; and his name is Death.

For an evil blossom was born
  Of sea-foam and the frothing of blood,
    Blood-red and bitter of fruit,
      And the seed of it laughter and tears,
And the leaves of it madness and scorn;
  A bitter flower from the bud,
    Sprung of the sea without root,
      Sprung without graft from the years.

The weft of the world was untorn
  That is woven of the day on the night,
  The hair of the hours was not white
Nor the raiment of time overworn,
  When a wonder, a world's delight,
A perilous goddess was born;
  And the waves of the sea as she came
Clove, and the foam at her feet,
    Fawning, rejoiced to bring forth
  A fleshly blossom, a flame
Filling the heavens with heat
    To the cold white ends of the north.

And in air the clamorous birds,
  And men upon earth that hear
Sweet articulate words
    Sweetly divided apart,
  And in shallow and channel and mere
The rapid and footless herds,
  Rejoiced, being foolish of heart.

For all they said upon earth,
  She is fair, she is white like a dove,
    And the life of the world in her breath
Breathes, and is born at her birth;
  For they knew thee for mother of love,
    And knew thee not mother of death.
What hadst thou to do being born,
  Mother, when winds were at ease,
As a flower of the springtime of corn,
  A flower of the foam of the seas?
For bitter thou wast from thy birth,
  Aphrodite, a mother of strife;
For before thee some rest was on earth,
    A little respite from tears,
  A little pleasure of life;
For life was not then as thou art,
    But as one that waxeth in years

Sweet-spoken, a fruitful wife;
Earth had no thorn, and desire
No sting, neither death any dart;
What hadst thou to do among these,
Thou, clothed with a burning fire,
Thou, girt with sorrow of heart,
Thou, sprung of the seed of the seas
As an ear from a seed of corn,
As a brand plucked forth of a pyre,
As a ray shed forth of the morn,
For division of soul and disease,
For a dart and a sting and a thorn?
What ailed thee then to be born?

Was there not evil enough,
Mother, and anguish on earth
Born with a man at his birth,
Wastes underfoot, and above
Storm out of heaven, and dearth
Shaken down from the shining thereof,
Wrecks from afar overseas
And peril of shallow and firth,
And tears that spring and increase
In the barren places of mirth,
That thou, having wings as a dove,
Being girt with desire for a girth,
That thou must come after these,
That thou must lay on him love?

Thou shouldst not so have been born:
But death should have risen with thee,
Mother, and visible fear,
Grief, and the wringing of hands,
And noise of many that mourn;
The smitten bosom, the knee
Bowed, and in each man's ear
A cry as of perishing lands,
A moan as of people in prison,
A tumult of infinite griefs;
And thunder of storm on the sands,
And wailing of wives on the shore;
And under thee newly arisen
Loud shoals and shipwrecking reefs,
Fierce air and violent light;
Sail rent and sundering oar,
Darkness, and noises of night;
Clashing of streams in the sea,
Wave against wave as a sword,
Clamour of currents, and foam;
Rains making ruin on earth,
Winds that wax ravenous and roam
As wolves in a wolfish horde;
Fruits growing faint in the tree,
And blind things dead in their birth;

Famine, and blighting of corn,
When thy time was come to be born.

All these we know of; but thee
Who shall discern or declare?
In the uttermost ends of the sea
The light of thine eyelids and hair,
The light of thy bosom as fire
Between the wheel of the sun
And the flying flames of the air?
Wilt thou turn thee not yet nor have pity,
But abide with despair and desire
And the crying of armies undone,
Lamentation of one with another
And breaking of city by city;
The dividing of friend against friend,
The severing of brother and brother;
Wilt thou utterly bring to an end?
Have mercy, mother!

For against all men from of old
Thou hast set thine hand as a curse,
And cast out gods from their places.
These things are spoken of thee.
Strong kings and goodly with gold
Thou hast found out arrows to pierce,
And made their kingdoms and races
As dust and surf of the sea.
All these, overburdened with woes
And with length of their days waxen weak,
Thou slewest; and sentest moreover
Upon Tyro an evil thing,
Rent hair and a fetter and blows
Making bloody the flower of the cheek,
Though she lay by a god as a lover,
Though fair, and the seed of a king.
For of gold, being full of thy fire,
She endured not longer to wear
On her bosom a saffron vest,
On her shoulder an ashwood quiver;
Being mixed and made one through desire
With Enipeus, and all her hair
Made moist with his mouth, and her breast
Filled full of the foam of the river.

ATALANTA

Sun, and clear light among green hills, and day
Late risen and long sought after, and you just gods
Whose hands divide anguish and recompense,
But first the sun's white sister, a maid in heaven,
On earth of all maids worshipped—hail, and hear,
And witness with me if not without sign sent,
Not without rule and reverence, I a maid
Hallowed, and huntress holy as whom I serve,

Here in your sight and eyeshot of these men
Stand, girt as they toward hunting, and my shafts
Drawn; wherefore all ye stand up on my side,
If I be pure and all ye righteous gods,
Lest one revile me, a woman, yet no wife,
That bear a spear for spindle, and this bow strung
For a web woven; and with pure lips salute
Heaven, and the face of all the gods, and dawn
Filling with maiden flames and maiden flowers
The starless fold o' the stars, and making sweet
The warm wan heights of the air, moon-trodden ways
And breathless gates and extreme hills of heaven.
Whom, having offered water and bloodless gifts,
Flowers, and a golden circlet of pure hair,
Next Artemis I bid be favourable
And make this day all golden, hers and ours,
Gracious and good and white to the unblamed end.
But thou, O well-beloved, of all my days
Bid it be fruitful, and a crown for all,
To bring forth leaves and bind round all my hair
With perfect chaplets woven for thine of thee.
For not without the word of thy chaste mouth,
For not without law given and clean command,
Across the white straits of the running sea
From Elis even to the Acheloïan horn,
I with clear winds came hither and gentle gods,
Far off my father's house, and left uncheered
Iasius, and uncheered the Arcadian hills
And all their green-haired waters, and all woods
Disconsolate, to hear no horn of mine
Blown, and behold no flash of swift white feet.

MELEAGER

For thy name's sake and awe toward thy chaste head,
O holiest Atalanta, no man dares
Praise thee, though fairer than whom all men praise,
And godlike for thy grace of hallowed hair
And holy habit of thine eyes, and feet
That make the blown foam neither swift nor white
Though the wind winnow and whirl it; yet we praise
Gods, found because of thee adorable
And for thy sake praiseworthiest from all men:
Thee therefore we praise also, thee as these,
Pure, and a light lit at the hands of gods.

TOXEUS

How long will ye whet spears with eloquence,
Fight, and kill beasts dry-handed with sweet words?
Cease, or talk still and slay thy boars at home.

PLEXIPPUS

Why, if she ride among us for a man,
Sit thou for her and spin; a man grown girl
Is worth a woman weaponed; sit thou here.

MELEAGER

Peace, and be wise; no gods love idle speech.

PLEXIPPUS

Nor any man a man's mouth woman-tongued.

MELEAGER

For my lips bite not sharper than mine hands.

PLEXIPPUS

Nay, both bite soft, but no whit softly mine.

MELEAGER

Keep thine hands clean; they have time enough to stain.

PLEXIPPUS

For thine shall rest and wax not red to-day.

MELEAGER

Have all thy will of words; talk out thine heart.

ALTHÆA

Refrain your lips, O brethren, and my son,
Lest words turn snakes and bite you uttering them.

TOXEUS

Except she give her blood before the gods,
What profit shall a maid be among men?

PLEXIPPUS

Let her come crowned and stretch her throat for a knife,
Bleat out her spirit and die, and so shall men
Through her too prosper and through prosperous gods;
But nowise through her living; shall she live
A flower-bud of the flower-bed, or sweet fruit
For kisses and the honey-making mouth,
And play the shield for strong men and the spear?
Then shall the heifer and her mate lock horns,
And the bride overbear the groom, and men
Gods! for no less division sunders these;
Since all things made are seasonable in time,
But if one alter unseasonable are all.
But thou, O Zeus, hear me that I may slay
This beast before thee and no man halve with me
Nor woman, lest these mock thee, though a god,
Who hast made men strong, and thou being wise be held
Foolish; for wise is that thing which endures.

ATALANTA

Men, and the chosen of all this people, and thou,
King, I beseech you a little bear with me.
For if my life be shameful that I live,
Let the gods witness and their wrath; but these

Cast no such word against me. Thou, O mine,
O holy, O happy goddess, if I sin
Changing the words of women and the works
For spears and the strange men's faces, hast not thou
One shaft of all thy sudden seven that pierced
Seven through the bosom or shining throat or side,
All couched about one mother's loosening knees,
All holy born, engraffed of Tantalus?
But if toward any of you I am overbold
That take thus much upon me, let him think
How I, for all my forest holiness,
Fame, and this armed and iron maidenhood,
Pay thus much also; I shall have no man's love
For ever, and no face of children born
Or feeding lips upon me or fastening eyes
For ever, nor being dead shall kings my sons
Mourn me and bury, and tears on daughters' cheeks
Burn; but a cold and sacred life, but strange;
But far from dances and the back-blowing torch,
Far off from flowers or any bed of man,
Shall my life be for ever: me the snows
That face the first o' the morning, and cold hills
Full of the land-wind and sea-travelling storms
And many a wandering wing of noisy nights
That know the thunder and hear the thickening wolves—
Me the utmost pine and footless frost of woods
That talk with many winds and gods, the hours
Re-risen, and white divisions of the dawn,
Springs thousand-tongued with the intermitting reed
And streams that murmur of the mother snow—
Me these allure, and know me; but no man
Knows, and my goddess only. Lo now, see
If one of all you these things vex at all.
Would God that any of you had all the praise
And I no manner of memory when I die,
So might I show before her perfect eyes
Pure, whom I follow, a maiden to my death.
But for the rest let all have all they will;
For is it a grief to you that I have part,
Being woman merely, in your male might and deeds
Done by main strength? yet in my body is throned
As great a heart, and in my spirit, O men,
I have not less of godlike. Evil it were
That one a coward should mix with you, one hand
Fearful, one eye abase itself; and these
Well might ye hate and well revile, not me.
For not the difference of the several flesh
Being vile or noble or beautiful or base
Makes praiseworthy, but purer spirit and heart
Higher than these meaner mouths and limbs, that feed,
Rise, rest, and are and are not; and for me,
What should I say? but by the gods of the world
And this my maiden body, by all oaths
That bind the tongue of men and the evil will,

I am not might-minded, nor desire
Crowns, nor the spoil of slain things nor the fame;
Feed ye on these, eat and wax fat; cry out,
Laugh, having eaten, and leap without a lyre,
Sing, mix the wind with clamour, smite and shake
Sonorous timbrels and tumultuous hair,
And fill the dance up with tempestuous feet,
For I will note; but having prayed my prayers
And made thank-offering for prosperities,
I shall go hence and no man see me more.
What thing is this for you to shout me down,
What, for a man to grudge me this my life
As it were envious of all yours, and I
A thief of reputations? nay, for now,
If there be any highest in heaven, a god
Above all thrones and thunders of the gods
Throned, and the wheel of the world roll under him,
Judge he between me and all of you, and see
If I transgress at all: but ye, refrain
Transgressing hands and reinless mouths, and keep
Silence, lest by much foam of violent words
And proper poison of your lips ye die.

ŒNEUS

O flower of Tegea, maiden, fleetest foot
And holiest head of women, have good cheer
Of thy good words: but ye, depart with her
In peace and reverence, each with blameless eye
Following his fate; exalt your hands and hearts,
Strike, cease not, arrow on arrow and wound on wound,
And go with gods and with the gods return.

CHORUS

Who hath given man speech? or who hath set therein
A thorn for peril and a snare for sin?
For in the word his life is and his breath,
  And in the word his death,
That madness and the infatuate heart may breed
  From the word's womb the deed
And life bring one thing forth ere all pass by,
Even one thing which is ours yet cannot die—
Death. Hast thou seen him ever anywhere,
Time's twin-born brother, imperishable as he
Is perishable and plaintive, clothed with care
  And mutable as sand,
But death is strong and full of blood and fair
And perdurable and like a lord of land?
Nay, time thou seest not, death thou wilt not see
Till life's right hand be loosened from thine hand
  And thy life-days from thee.
For the gods very subtly fashion
  Madness with sadness upon earth:
Not knowing in any wise compassion,
  Nor holding pity of any worth;

And many things they have given and taken,
  And wrought and ruined many things;
The firm land have they loosed and shaken,
  And sealed the sea with all her springs;
They have wearied time with heavy burdens
  And vexed the lips of life with breath:
Set men to labour and given them guerdons,
  Death, and great darkness after death:
Put moans into the bridal measure
  And on the bridal wools a stain
And circled pain about with pleasure,
  And girdled pleasure about with pain;
And strewed one marriage-bed with tears and fire
For extreme loathing and supreme desire.

What shall be done with all these tears of ours?
  Shall they make watersprings in the fair heaven
To bathe the brows of morning? or like flowers
Be shed and shine before the starriest hours,
  Or made the raiment of the weeping Seven?
Or rather, O our masters, shall they be
Food for the famine of the grievous sea,
  A great well-head of lamentation
Satiating the sad gods? or fall and flow
Among the years and seasons to and fro,
  And wash their feet with tribulation
And fill them full with grieving ere they go?
  Alas, our lords, and yet alas again,
Seeing all your iron heaven is gilt as gold
  But all we smite thereat in vain;
Smite the gates barred with groanings manifold,
  But all the floors are paven with our pain.
Yea, and with weariness of lips and eyes,
With breaking of the bosom, and with sighs,
  We labour, and are clad and fed with grief
And filled with days we would not fain behold
And nights we would not hear of; we wax old,
  All we wax old and wither like a leaf.
We are outcast, strayed between bright sun and moon;
  Our light and darkness are as leaves of flowers,
Black flowers and white, that perish; and the noon
  As midnight, and the night as daylight hours.
  A little fruit a little while is ours,
      And the worm finds it soon,

But up in heaven the high gods one by one
  Lay hands upon the draught that quickeneth,
Fulfilled with all tears shed and all things done,
  And stir with soft imperishable breath
  The bubbling bitterness of life and death,
And hold it to our lips and laugh; but they
Preserve their lips from tasting night or day,
  Lest they too change and sleep, the fates that spun,

The lips that made us and the hands that slay;
Lest all these change, and heaven bow down to none,
Change and be subject to the secular sway
And terrene revolution of the sun.
Therefore they thrust it from them, putting time away.

I would the wine of time, made sharp and sweet
With multitudinous days and nights and tears
And many mixing savours of strange years,
Were no more trodden of them under feet,
Cast out and spilt about their holy places:
That life were given them as a fruit to eat
And death to drink as water; that the light
Might ebb, drawn backward from their eyes, and night
Hide for one hour the imperishable faces.
That they might rise up sad in heaven, and know
Sorrow and sleep, one paler than young snow,
One cold as blight of dew and ruinous rain;
Rise up and rest and suffer a little, and be
Awhile as all things born with us and we,
And grieve as men, and like slain men be slain.

For now we know not of them; but one saith
The gods are gracious, praising God; and one,
When hast thou seen? or hast thou felt his breath
Touch, nor consume thine eyelids as the sun,
Nor fill thee to the lips with fiery death?
None hath beheld him, none
Seen above other gods and shapes of things,
Swift without feet and flying without wings,
Intolerable, not clad with death or life,
Insatiable, nor known of night or day,
The lord of love and loathing and of strife
Who gives a star and takes a sun away;
Who shapes the soul, and makes her a barren wife
To the earthly body and grievous growth of clay;
Who turns the large limbs to a little flame
And binds the great sea with a little sand;
Who makes desire, and slays desire with shame;
Who shakes the heaven as ashes in his hand;
Who seeing the light and shadow for the same,
Bids days waste night as fire devours a brand,
Smites without sword, and scourges without rod;
The supreme evil, God.

Yea, with thine hate, O God, thou hast covered us,
One saith, and hidden our eyes away from sight,
And made us transitory and hazardous,
Light things and slight;
Yet have men praised thee, saying, He hath made man thus,
And he doeth right.
Thou hast kissed us, and hast smitten; thou hast laid
Upon us with thy left hand life, and said,
Live: and again thou hast said, Yield up your breath,

And with thy right hand laid upon us death.
Thou hast sent us sleep, and stricken sleep with dreams,
  Saying, Joy is not, but love of joy shall be;
Thou hast made sweet springs for all the pleasant streams,
  In the end thou hast made them bitter with the sea.
Thou hast fed one rose with dust of many men;
  Thou hast marred one face with fire of many tears;
Thou hast taken love, and given us sorrow again;
  With pain thou hast filled us full to the eyes and ears.
Therefore because thou art strong, our father, and we
  Feeble; and thou art against us, and thine hand
Constrains us in the shallows of the sea
  And breaks us at the limits of the land;
Because thou hast bent thy lightnings as a bow,
  And loosed the hours like arrows; and let fall
Sins and wild words and many a wingèd woe
  And wars among us, and one end of all;
Because thou hast made the thunder, and thy feet
  Are as a rushing water when the skies
Break, but thy face as an exceeding heat
  And flames of fire the eyelids of thine eyes;
Because thou art over all who are over us;
  Because thy name is life and our name death;
Because thou art cruel and men are piteous,
  And our hands labour and thine hand scattereth;
Lo, with hearts rent and knees made tremulous,
  Lo, with ephemeral lips and casual breath,
    At least we witness of thee ere we die
That these things are not otherwise, but thus;
  That each man in his heart sigheth, and saith,
    That all men even as I,
All we are against thee, against thee, O God most high.
  But ye, keep ye on earth
  Your lips from over-speech,
Loud words and longing are so little worth;
  And the end is hard to reach.
For silence after grievous things is good,
  And reverence, and the fear that makes men whole,
And shame, and righteous governance of blood,
  And lordship of the soul.
But from sharp words and wits men pluck no fruit,
And gathering thorns they shake the tree at root;
For words divide and rend;
But silence is most noble till the end.

ALTHÆA

I heard within the house a cry of news
And came forth eastward hither, where the dawn
Cheers first these warder gods that face the sun
And next our eyes unrisen; for unaware
Came clashes of swift hoofs and trampling feet
And through the windy pillared corridor
Light sharper than the frequent flames of day
That daily fill it from the fiery dawn;

Gleams, and a thunder of people that cried out,
And dust and hurrying horsemen; lo their chief,
That rode with Œneus rein by rein, returned.
What cheer, O herald of my lord the king?

HERALD

Lady, good cheer and great; the boar is slain.

CHORUS

Praised be all gods that look toward Calydon.

ALTHÆA

Good news and brief; but by whose happier hand?

HERALD

A maiden's and a prophet's and thy son's.

ALTHÆA

Well fare the spear that severed him and life.

HERALD

Thine own, and not an alien, hast thou blest.

ALTHÆA

Twice be thou too for my sake blest and his.

HERALD

At the king's word I rode afoam for thine.

ALTHÆA

Thou sayest he tarrieth till they bring the spoil?

HERALD

Hard by the quarry, where they breathe, O Queen.

ALTHÆA

Speak thou their chance; but some bring flowers and crown
These gods and all the lintel, and shed wine,
Fetch sacrifice and slay; for heaven is good.

HERALD

Some furlongs northward where the brakes begin
West of that narrowing range of warrior hills
Whose brooks have bled with battle when thy son
Smote Acarnania, there all they made halt,
And with keen eye took note of spear and hound,
Royally ranked; Laertes island-born,
The young Gerenian Nestor, Panopeus,
And Cepheus and Ancæus, mightiest thewed,
Arcadians; next, and evil-eyed of these,
Arcadian Atalanta, with twain hounds
Lengthening the leash, and under nose and brow
Glittering with lipless tooth and fire-swift eye;
But from her white braced shoulder the plumed shafts

Rang, and the bow shone from her side; next her
Meleager, like a sun in spring that strikes
Branch into leaf and bloom into the world,
A glory among men meaner: Iphicles,
And following him that slew the biform bull
Pirithous, and divine Eurytion,
And, bride-bound to the gods, Æacides.
Then Telamon his brother, and Argive-born
The seer and sayer of visions and of truth,
Amphiaraus; and a four-fold strength,
Thine, even thy mother's and thy sister's sons.
And recent from the roar of foreign foam
Jason, and Dryas twin-begot with war,
A blossom of bright battle, sword and man
Shining; and Idas, and the keenest eye
Of Lynceus, and Admetus twice-espoused,
And Hippasus and Hyleus, great in heart.
These having halted bade blow horns, and rode
Through woods and waste lands cleft by stormy streams,
Past yew-trees and the heavy hair of pines,
And where the dew is thickest under oaks,
This way and that; but questing up and down
They saw no trail nor scented; and one said,
Plexippus, Help, or help not, Artemis,
And we will flay thy boarskin with male hands;
But saying, he ceased and said not that he would,
Seeing where the green ooze of a sun-struck marsh
Shook with a thousand reeds untunable,
And in their moist and multitudinous flower
Slept no soft sleep, with violent visions fed,
The blind bulk of the immeasurable beast.
And seeing, he shuddered with sharp lust of praise
Through all his limbs, and launched a double dart.
And missed; for much desire divided him,
Too hot of spirit and feebler than his will,
That his hand failed, though fervent; and the shaft,
Sundering the rushes, in a tamarisk stem
Shook, and stuck fast; then all abode save one,
The Arcadian Atalanta; from her side
Sprang her hounds, labouring at the leash, and slipped,
And plashed ear-deep with plunging feet; but she
Saying, Speed it as I send it for thy sake,
Goddess, drew bow and loosed; the sudden string
Rang, and sprang inward, and the waterish air
Hissed, and the moist plumes of the songless reeds
Moved as a wave which the wind moves no more.
But the boar heaved half out of ooze and slime
His tense flank trembling round the barbèd wound,
Hateful; and fiery with invasive eyes
And bristling with intolerable hair
Plunged, and the hounds clung, and green flowers and white
Reddened and broke all round them where they came.
And charging with sheer tusk he drove, and smote
Hyleus; and sharp death caught his sudden soul,

And violent sleep shed night upon his eyes.
Then Peleus, with strong strain of hand and heart,
Shot; but the sidelong arrow slid, and slew
His comrade born and loving countryman,
Under the left arm smitten, as he no less
Poised a like arrow; and bright blood brake afoam,
And falling, and weighed back by clamourous arms,
Sharp rang the dead limbs of Eurytion.
Then one shot happier, the Cadmean seer,
Amphiaraus; for his sacred shaft
Pierced the red circlet of one ravening eye
Beneath the brute brows of the sanguine boar,
Now bloodier from one slain; but he so galled
Sprang straight, and rearing cried no lesser cry
Than thunder and the roar of wintering streams
That mix their own foam with the yellower sea;
And as a tower that falls by fire in fight
With ruin of walls and all its archery,
And breaks the iron flower of war beneath,
Crushing charred limbs and molten arms of men;
So through crushed branches and the reddening brake
Clamoured and crashed the fervour of his feet,
And trampled, springing sideways from the tusk,
Too tardy a moving mould of heavy strength,
Ancæus; and as flakes of weak-winged snow
Break, all the hard thews of his heaving limbs
Broke, and rent flesh fell every way, and blood
Flew, and fierce fragments of no more a man.
Then all the heroes drew sharp breath, and gazed,
And smote not; but Meleager, but thy son,
Right in the wild way of the coming curse
Rock-rooted, fair with fierce and fastened lips,
Clear eyes, and springing muscle and shortening limb—
With chin aslant indrawn to a tightening throat,
Grave, and with gathered sinews, like a god,—
Aimed on the left side his well-handled spear
Grasped where the ash was knottiest hewn, and smote;
And with no missile wound, the monstrous boar
Right in the hairiest hollow of his hide
Under the last rib, sheer through bulk and bone,
Deep in; and deeply smitten, and to death,
The heavy horror with his hanging shafts
Leapt, and fell furiously, and from raging lips
Foamed out the latest wrath of all his life.
And all they praised the gods with mightier heart,
Zeus and all gods, but chiefliest Artemis,
Seeing; but Meleager bade whet knives and flay,
Strip and stretch out the splendour of the spoil;
And hot and horrid from the work all these
Sat, and drew breath and drank and made great cheer
And washed the hard sweat off their calmer brows.
For much sweet grass grew higher than grew the reed,
And good for slumber, and every holier herb,
Narcissus, and the low-lying melilote,

And all of goodliest blade and bloom that springs
Where, hid by heavier hyacinth, violet buds
Blossom and burn; and fire of yellower flowers
And light of crescent lilies, and such leaves
As fear the Faun's and know the Dryad's foot;
Olive and ivy and poplar dedicate,
And many a well-spring overwatched of these.
There now they rest; but me the king bade bear
Good tidings to rejoice this town and thee.
Wherefore be glad, and all ye give much thanks,
For fallen is all the trouble of Calydon.

ALTHÆA

Laud ye the gods; for this they have given is good,
And what shall be they hide until their time.
Much good and somewhat grievous hast thou said,
And either well; but let all sad things be,
Till all have made before the prosperous gods
Burnt-offering, and poured out the floral wine.
Look fair, O gods, and favourable; for we
Praise you with no false heart or flattering mouth,
Being merciful, but with pure souls and prayer.

HERALD

Thou hast prayed well; for whoso fears not these,
But once being prosperous waxes huge of heart,
Him shall some new thing unaware destroy.

CHORUS

O that I now, I too were
By deep wells and water-floods,
Streams of ancient hills, and where
All the wan green places bear
Blossoms cleaving to the sod,
Fruitless fruit, and grasses fair,
Or such darkest ivy-buds
As divide thy yellow hair,
Bacchus, and their leaves that nod
Round thy fawnskin brush the bare
Snow-soft shoulders of a god;
There the year is sweet, and there
Earth is full of secret springs,
And the fervent rose-cheeked hours,
Those that marry dawn and noon,
There are sunless, there look pale
In dim leaves and hidden air,
Pale as grass or latter flowers
Or the wild vine's wan wet rings
Full of dew beneath the moon,
And all day the nightingale
Sleeps, and all night sings;
There in cold remote recesses
That nor alien eyes assail,

Feet, nor imminence of wings,
Nor a wind nor any tune,
Thou, O queen and holiest,
Flower the whitest of all things,
With reluctant lengthening tresses
And with sudden splendid breast
Save of maidens unbeholden,
There art wont to enter, there
Thy divine swift limbs and golden
Maiden growth of unbound hair,
Bathed in waters white,
Shine, and many a maid's by thee
In moist woodland or the hilly
Flowerless brakes where wells abound
Out of all men's sight;
Or in lower pools that see
All their marges clothed all round
With the innumerable lily,
Whence the golden-girdled bee
Flits through flowering rush to fret
White or duskier violet,
Fair as those that in far years
With their buds left luminous
And their little leaves made wet,
From the warmer dew of tears,
Mother's tears in extreme need,
Hid the limbs of Iamus,
Of thy brother's seed;
For his heart was piteous
Toward him, even as thine heart now
Pitiful toward us;
Thine, O goddess, turning hither
A benignant blameless brow;
Seeing enough of evil done
And lives withered as leaves wither
In the blasting of the sun;
Seeing enough of hunters dead,
Ruin enough of all our year,
Herds and harvests slain and shed,
Herdsmen stricken many an one,
Fruits and flocks consumed together,
And great length of deadly days.
Yet with reverent lips and fear
Turn we toward thee, turn and praise
For this lightening of clear weather
And prosperities begun.
For not seldom, when all air
As bright water without breath
Shines, and when men fear not, fate
Without thunder unaware
Breaks, and brings down death.
Joy with grief ye great gods give,
Good with bad, and overbear
All the pride of us that live,

All the high estate,
As ye long since overbore,
As in old time long before,
Many a strong man and a great,
All that were.
But do thou, sweet, otherwise,
Having heed of all our prayer,
Taking note of all our sighs;
We beseech thee by thy light,
By thy bow, and thy sweet eyes,
And the kingdom of the night,
Be thou favourable and fair;
By thine arrows and thy might
And Orion overthrown;
By the maiden thy delight,
By the indissoluble zone
And the sacred hair.

MESSENGER

Maidens, if ye will sing now, shift your song,
Bow down, cry, wail for pity; is this a time
For singing? nay, for strewing of dust and ash,
Rent raiment, and bruising of the breast.

CHORUS

What new thing wolf-like lurks behind thy words?
What snake's tongue in thy lips? what fire in the eyes?

MESSENGER

Bring me before the queen and I will speak.

CHORUS

Lo, she comes forth as from thank-offering made.

MESSENGER

A barren offering for a bitter gift.

ALTHÆA

What are these borne on branches, and the face
Covered? no mean men living, but now slain
Such honour have they, if any dwell with death.

MESSENGER

Queen, thy twain brethren and thy mother's sons.

ALTHÆA

Lay down your dead till I behold their blood
If it be mine indeed, and I will weep.

MESSENGER

Weep if thou wilt, for these men shall no more.

ALTHÆA

O brethren, O my father's sons, of me
Well loved and well reputed, I should weep
Tears dearer than the dear blood drawn from you
But that I know you not uncomforted,
Sleeping no shameful sleep, however slain,
For my son surely hath avenged you dead.

MESSENGER

Nay, should thine own seed slay himself, O queen?

ALTHÆA

Thy double word brings forth a double death.

MESSENGER

Know this then singly, by one hand they fell.

ALTHÆA

What mutterest thou with thine ambiguous mouth?

MESSENGER

Slain by thy son's hand; is that saying so hard?

ALTHÆA

Our time is come upon us: it is here.

CHORUS

O miserable, and spoiled at thine own hand.

ALTHÆA

Wert thou not called Meleager from this womb?

CHORUS

A grievous huntsman hath it bred to thee.

ALTHÆA

Wert thou born fire, and shalt thou not devour?

CHORUS

The fire thou madest, will it consume even thee?

ALTHÆA

My dreams are fallen upon me; burn thou too.

CHORUS

Not without God are visions born and die.

ALTHÆA

The gods are many about me; I am one.

CHORUS

She groans as men wrestling with heavier gods.

ALTHÆA

They rend me, they divide me, they destroy.

CHORUS

Or one labouring in travail of strange births.

ALTHÆA

They are strong, they are strong; I am broken, and these prevail.

CHORUS

The god is great against her; she will die.

ALTHÆA

Yea, but not now; for my heart too is great.
I would I were not here in sight of the sun.
But thou, speak all thou sawest, and I will die.

MESSENGER

O queen, for queenlike hast thou borne thyself,
A little word may hold so great mischance.
For in division of the sanguine spoil
These men thy brethren wrangling bade yield up
The boar's head and the horror of the hide
That this might stand a wonder in Calydon,
Hallowed; and some drew toward them; but thy son
With great hands grasping all that weight of hair
Cast down the dead heap clanging and collapsed
At female feet, saying This thy spoil not mine,
Maiden, thine own hand for thyself hath reaped,
And all this praise God gives thee: she thereat
Laughed, as when dawn touches the sacred night
The sky sees laugh and redden and divide
Dim lips and eyelids virgin of the sun,
Hers, and the warm slow breasts of morning heave,
Fruitful, and flushed with flame from lamp-lit hours,
And maiden undulation of clear hair
Colour the clouds; so laughed she from pure heart,
Lit with a low blush to the braided hair,
And rose-coloured and cold like very dawn,
Golden and godlike, chastely with chaste lips,
A faint grave laugh; and all they held their peace,
And she passed by them. Then one cried Lo now,
Shall not the Arcadian shoot out lips at us,
Saying all we were despoiled by this one girl?
And all they rode against her violently
And cast the fresh crown from her hair, and now
They had rent her spoil away, dishonouring her,
Save that Meleager, as a tame lion chafed,
Bore on them, broke them, and as fire cleaves wood
So clove and drove them, smitten in twain; but she
Smote not nor heaved up hand; and this man first
Plexippus, crying out This for love's sake, sweet,
Drove at Meleager, who with spear straightening

Pierced his cheek through; then Toxeus made for him,
Dumb, but his spear spake; vain and violent words,
Fruitless; for him too stricken through both sides
The earth felt falling, and his horse's foam
Blanched thy son's face, his slayer; and these being slain,
None moved nor spake; but Œneus bade bear hence
These made of heaven infatuate in their deaths,
Foolish; for these would baffle fate, and fell.
And they passed on, and all men honoured her,
Being honourable, as one revered of heaven.

ALTHÆA

What say you, women? is all this not well done?

CHORUS

No man doth well but God hath part in him.

ALTHÆA

But no part here; for these my brethren born
Ye have no part in, these ye know not of
As I that was their sister, a sacrifice
Slain in their slaying. I would I had died for these;
For this man dead walked with me, child by child,
And made a weak staff for my feebler feet
With his own tender wrist and hand, and held
And led me softly and shewed me gold and steel
And shining shapes of mirror and bright crown
And all things fair; and threw light spears, and brought
Young hounds to huddle at my feet and thrust
Tame heads against my little maiden breasts
And please me with great eyes; and those days went
And these are bitter and I a barren queen
And sister miserable, a grievous thing
And mother of many curses; and she too,
My sister Leda, sitting overseas
With fair fruits round her, and her faultless lord,
Shall curse me, saying A sorrow and not a son,
Sister, thou barest, even a burning fire,
A brand consuming thine own soul and me.
But ye now, sons of Thestius, make good cheer,
For ye shall have such wood to funeral fire
As no king hath; and flame that once burnt down
Oil shall not quicken or breath relume or wine
Refresh again; much costlier than fine gold,
And more than many lives of wandering men.

CHORUS

O queen, thou hast yet with thee love-worthy things,
Thine husband, and the great strength of thy son.

ALTHÆA

Who shall get brothers for me while I live?
Who bear them? who bring forth in lieu of these?

Are not our fathers and our brethren one,
And no man like them? are not mine here slain?
Have we not hung together, he and I,
Flowerwise feeding as the feeding bees,
With mother-milk for honey? and this man too,
Dead, with my son's spear thrust between his sides,
Hath he not seen us, later born than he,
Laugh with lips filled, and laughed again for love?
There were no sons then in the world, nor spears,
Nor deadly births of women; but the gods
Allowed us, and our days were clear of these.
I would I had died unwedded, and brought forth
No swords to vex the world; for these that spake
Sweet words long since and loved me will not speak
Nor love nor look upon me; and all my life
I shall not hear nor see them living men.
But I too living, how shall I now live?
What life shall this be with my son, to know
What hath been and desire what will not be,
Look for dead eyes and listen for dead lips,
And kill mine own heart with remembering them,
And with those eyes that see their slayer alive
Weep, and wring hands that clasp him by the hand?
How shall I bear my dreams of them, to hear
False voices, feel the kisses of false mouths
And footless sound of perished feet, and then
Wake and hear only it may be their own hounds
Whine masterless in miserable sleep,
And see their boar-spears and their beds and seats
And all the gear and housings of their lives
And not the men? shall hounds and horses mourn,
Pine with strange eyes, and prick up hungry ears,
Famish and fail at heart for their dear lords,
And I not heed at all? and those blind things
Fall off from life for love's sake, and I live?
Surely some death is better than some life,
Better one death for him and these and me
For if the gods had slain them it may be
I had endured it; if they had fallen by war
Or by the nets and knives of privy death
And by hired hands while sleeping, this thing too
I had set my soul to suffer; or this hunt,
Had this despatched them, under tusk or tooth
Torn, sanguine, trodden, broken; for all deaths
Or honourable or with facile feet avenged
And hands of swift gods following, all save this,
Are bearable; but not for their sweet land
Fighting, but not a sacrifice, lo these
Dead; for I had not then shed all mine heart
Out at mine eyes: then either with good speed,
Being just, I had slain their slayer atoningly,
Or strewn with flowers their fire and on their tombs
Hung crowns, and over them a song, and seen
Their praise outflame their ashes: for all men,

All maidens, had come thither, and from pure lips
Shed songs upon them, from heroic eyes
Tears; and their death had been a deathless life;
But now, by no man hired nor alien sword,
By their own kindred are they fallen, in peace,
After much peril, friendless among friends,
By hateful hands they loved; and how shall mine
Touch these returning red and not from war,
These fatal from the vintage of men's veins,
Dead men my brethren? how shall these wash off
No festal stains of undelightful wine,
How mix the blood, my blood on them, with me,
Holding mine hand? or how shall I say, son,
That am no sister? but by night and day
Shall we not sit and hate each other, and think
Things hate-worthy? not live with shamefast eyes,
Brow-beaten, treading soft with fearful feet,
Each unupbraided, each without rebuke
Convicted, and without a word reviled
Each of another? and I shall let thee live
And see thee strong and hear men for thy sake
Praise me, but these thou wouldest not let live
No man shall praise for ever? these shall lie
Dead, unbeloved, unholpen, all through thee.
Sweet were they toward me living, and mine heart
Desired them, but was then well satsified,
That now is as men hungered; and these dead
I shall want always to the day I die.
For all things else and all men may renew;
Yea, son for son the gods may give and take,
But never a brother or sister any more.

CHORUS

Nay, for the son lies close about thine heart,
Full of thy milk, warm from thy womb, and drains
Life and the blood of life and all thy fruit,
Eats thee and drinks thee as who breaks bread and eats,
Treads wine and drinks, thyself, a sect of thee;
And if he feed not, shall not thy flesh faint?
Or drink not, are not thy lips dead for thirst?
This thing moves more than all things, even thy son,
That thou cleave to him; and he shall honour thee,
Thy womb that bare him and the breasts he knew,
Reverencing most for thy sake all his gods.

ALTHÆA

But these the gods too gave me, and these my son,
Not reverencing his gods nor mine own heart
Nor the old sweet years nor all venerable things,
But cruel, and in his ravin like a beast,
Hath taken away to slay them: yea, and she
She the strange woman, she the flower, the sword,
Red from spilt blood, a mortal flower to men,

Adorable, detestable—even she
Saw with strange eyes and with strange lips rejoiced,
Seeing these mine own slain of mine own, and me
Made miserable above all miseries made,
A grief among all women in the world,
A name to be washed out with all men's tears.

CHORUS

Strengthen thy spirit; is this not also a god,
Chance, and the wheel of all necessities?
Hard things have fallen upon us from harsh gods,
Whom lest worse hap rebuke we not for these.

ALTHÆA

My spirit is strong against itself, and I
For these things' sake cry out on mine own soul
That it endures outrage, and dolorous days,
And life, and this inexpiable impotence.
Weak am I, weak and shameful; my breath drawn
Shames me, and monstrous things and violent gods.
What shall atone? what heal me? what bring back
Strength to the foot, light to the face? what herb
Assuage me? what restore me? what release?
What strange thing eaten or drunken, O great gods,
Make me as you or as the beasts that feed,
Slay and divide and cherish their own hearts?
For these ye show us; and we less than these
Have not wherewith to live as all these things
Which all their lives fare after their own kind
As who doth well rejoicing; but we ill,
Weeping or laughing, we whom eyesight fails,
Knowledge and light of face and perfect heart,
And hands we lack, and wit; and all our days
Sin, and have hunger, and die infatuated.
For madness have ye given us and not health,
And sins whereof we know not; and for these
Death, and sudden destruction unaware.
What shall we say now? what thing comes of us?

CHORUS

Alas, for all this all men undergo.

ALTHÆA

Wherefore I will not that these twain, O gods,
Die as a dog dies, eaten of creeping things,
Abominable, a loathing; but though dead
Shall they have honour and such funereal flame
As strews men's ashes in their enemies' face
And blinds their eyes who hate them: lest men say,
'Lo how they lie, and living had great kin,
And none of these hath pity of them, and none
Regards them lying, and none is wrung at heart,
None moved in spirit for them, naked and slain,
Abhorred, abased, and no tears comfort them:'

And in the dark this grieve Eurythemis,
Hearing how these her sons come down to her
Unburied, unavenged, as kinless men,
And had a queen their sister. That were shame
Worse than this grief. Yet how to atone at all
I know not; seeing the love of my born son,
A new-made mother's new-born love, that grows
From the soft child to the strong man, now soft
Now strong as either, and still one sole same love,
Strives with me, no light thing to strive withal;
This love is deep, and natural to man's blood,
And ineffaceable with many tears.
Yet shall not these rebuke me though I die,
Nor she in that waste world with all her dead,
My mother, among the pale flocks fallen as leaves,
Folds of dead people, and alien from the sun;
Nor lack some bitter comfort, some poor praise,
Being queen, to have borne her daughter like a queen,
Righteous; and though mine own fire burn me too,
She shall have honour and these her sons, though dead.
But all the gods will, all they do, and we
Not all we would, yet somewhat; and one choice
We have, to live and do just deeds and die.

CHORUS

Terrible words she communes with, and turns
Swift fiery eyes in doubt against herself,
And murmurs as who talks in dreams with death.

ALTHÆA

For the unjust also dieth, and him all men
Hate, and himself abhors the unrighteousness,
And seeth his own dishonour intolerable.
But I being just, doing right upon myself,
Slay mine own soul, and no man born shames me.
For none constrains nor shall rebuke, being done,
What none compelled me doing; thus these things fare.
Ah, ah, that such things should so fare; ah me,
That I am found to do them and endure,
Chosen and constrained to choose, and bear myself
Mine own wound through mine own flesh to the heart
Violently stricken, a spoiler and a spoil,
A ruin ruinous, fallen on mine own son.
Ah, ah, for me too as for these; alas,
For that is done that shall be, and mine hand
Full of the deed, and full of blood mine eyes,
That shall see never nor touch anything
Save blood unstanched and fire unquenchable.

CHORUS

What wilt thou do? what ails thee? for the house
Shakes ruinously; wilt thou bring fire for it?

ALTHÆA

Fire in the roofs, and on the lintels fire.
Lo ye, who stand and weave, between the doors,
There; and blood drips from hand and thread, and stains
Threshold and raiment and me passing in
Flecked with the sudden sanguine drops of death.

CHORUS

Alas that time is stronger than strong men,
Fate than all gods: and these are fallen on us.

ALTHÆA

A little since and I was glad; and now
I never shall be glad or sad again.

CHORUS

Between two joys a grief grows unaware.

ALTHÆA

A little while and I shall laugh; and then
I shall weep never and laugh not any more.

CHORUS

What shall be said? for words are thorns to grief.
Withhold thyself a little and fear the gods.

ALTHÆA

Fear died when these were slain; and I am as dead,
And fear is of the living; these fear none.

CHORUS

Have pity upon all people for their sake.

ALTHÆA

It is done now; shall I put back my day?

CHORUS

An end is come, an end; this is of God.

ALTHÆA

I am fire, and burn myself; keep clear of fire.

CHORUS

The house is broken, is broken; it shall not stand.

ALTHÆA

Woe, woe for him that breaketh; and a rod
Smote it of old, and now the axe is here.

CHORUS

Not as with sundering of the earth
Nor as with cleaving of the sea

Nor fierce foreshadowings of a birth
  Nor flying dreams of death to be
Nor loosening of the large world's girth
And quickening of the body of night,
  And sound of thunder in men's ears
And fire of lightning in men's sight,
  Fate, mother of desires and fears,
  Bore unto men the law of tears;
But sudden, an unfathered flame,
  And broken out of night, she shone,
She, without body, without name,
  In days forgotten and foregone;
And heaven rang round her as she came
Like smitten cymbals, and lay bare;
  Clouds and great stars, thunders and snows,
The blue sad fields and folds of air,
  The life that breathes, the life that grows,
  All wind, all fire, that burns or blows,
Even all these knew her: for she is great;
  The daughter of doom, the mother of death,
The sister of sorrow; a lifelong weight
  That no man's finger lighteneth,
Nor any god can lighten fate;
A landmark seen across the way
  Where one race treads as the other trod;
An evil sceptre, an evil stay,
  Wrought for a staff, wrought for a rod,
  The bitter jealousy of God.
For death is deep as the sea,
  And fate as the waves thereof.
Shall the waves take pity on thee
  Or the southwind offer thee love?
Wilt thou take the night for thy day
Or the darkness for light on thy way,
  Till thou say in thine heart Enough?
Behold, Thou art over fair, thou art over wise;
The sweetness of spring in thine hair, and the light in thine eyes.
The light of the spring in thine eyes, and the sound in thine ears;
Yet thine heart shall wax heavy with sighs and thine eyelids with tears.
Wilt thou cover thine hair with gold, and with silver thy feet?
Hast thou taken the purple to fold thee, and made thy mouth sweet?
Behold, when thy face is made bare, he that loved thee shall hate;
Thy face shall be no more fair at the fall of thy fate.
For thy life shall fall as a leaf and be shed as the rain;
And the veil of thine head shall be grief; and the crown shall be pain.

ALTHÆA

Ho, ye that wail, and ye that sing, make way
Till I be come among you. Hide your tears,
Ye little weepers, and your laughing lips,
Ye laughers for a little; lo mine eyes
That outweep heaven at rainiest, and my mouth
That laughs as gods laugh at us. Fate's are we,

Yet fate is ours a breathing-space; yea, mine,
Fate is made mine for ever; he is my son,
My bedfellow, my brother. You strong gods,
Give place unto me; I am as any of you,
To give life and to take life. Thou, old earth,
That hast made man and unmade; thou whose mouth
Looks red from the eaten fruits of thine own womb;
Behold me with what lips upon what food
I feed and fill my body; even with flesh
Made of my body. Lo, the fire I lit
I burn with fire to quench it; yea, with flame
I burn up even the dust and ash thereof.

CHORUS

Woman, what fire is this thou burnest with?

ALTHÆA

Yea to the bone, yea to the blood and all.

CHORUS

For this thy face and hair are as one fire.

ALTHÆA

A tongue that licks and beats upon the dust.

CHORUS

And in thine eyes are hollow light and heat.

ALTHÆA

Of flame not fed with hand or frankincense.

CHORUS

I fear thee for the trembling of thine eyes.

ALTHÆA

Neither with love they tremble nor for fear.

CHORUS

And thy mouth shuddering like a shot bird.

ALTHÆA

Not as the bride's mouth when man kisses it.

CHORUS

Nay, but what thing is this thing thou hast done?

ALTHÆA

Look, I am silent, speak your eyes for me.

CHORUS

I see a faint fire lightening from the hall.

ALTHÆA

Gaze, stretch your eyes, strain till the lids drop off.

CHORUS

Flushed pillars down the flickering vestibule.

ALTHÆA

Stretch with your necks like birds: cry, chirp as they.

CHORUS

And a long brand that blackens: and white dust.

ALTHÆA

O children, what is this ye see? your eyes
Are blinder than night's face at fall of moon.
That is my son, my flesh, my fruit of life,
My travail, and the year's weight of my womb.
Meleager, a fire enkindled of mine hands
And of mine hands extinguished; this is he.

CHORUS

O gods, what word has flown out at thy mouth?

ALTHÆA

I did this and I say this and I die.

CHORUS

Death stands upon the doorway of thy lips,
And in thy mouth has death set up his house.

ALTHÆA

O death, a little, a little while, sweet death,
Until I see the brand burnt down and die.

CHORUS

She reels as any reed under the wind,
And cleaves unto the ground with staggering feet.

ALTHÆA

Girls, one thing will I say and hold my peace.
I that did this will weep nor cry out,
Cry ye and weep: I will not call on gods,
Call ye on them; I will not pity man,
Shew ye your pity. I know not if I live;
Save that I feel the fire upon my face
And on my cheek the burning of a brand.
Yea the smoke bites me, yea I drink the steam
With nostril and with eyelid and with lip
Insatiate and intolerant; and mine hands
Burn, and fire feeds upon mine eyes; I reel
As one made drunk with living, whence he draws
Drunken delight; yet I, though mad for joy,
Loathe my long living and am waxen red
As with the shadow of shed blood; behold,
I am kindled with the flames that fade in him,
I am swollen with subsiding of his veins,

I am flooded with his ebbing; my lit eyes
Flame with the falling fire that leaves his lids
Bloodless; my cheek is luminous with blood
Because his face is ashen. Yet, O Child,
Son, first-born, fairest—O sweet mouth, sweet eyes,
That drew my life out through my suckling breast,
That shone and clove mine heart through—O soft knees
Clinging, O tender treadings of soft feet,
Cheeks warm with little kissings—O child, child,
What have we made each other? Lo, I felt
Thy weight cleave to me, a burden of beauty, O son,
Thy cradled brows and loveliest loving lips,
The floral hair, the little lightening eyes,
And all thy goodly glory; with mine hands
Delicately I fed thee, with my tongue
Tenderly spake, saying, Verily in God's time,
For all the little likeness of thy limbs,
Son, I shall make thee a kingly man to fight,
A lordly leader; and hear before I die,
'She bore the goodliest sword of all the world.'
Oh! oh! For all my life turns round on me;
I am severed from myself, my name is gone,
My name that was a healing, it is changed,
My name is a consuming. From this time,
Though mine eyes reach to the end of all these things,
My lips shall not unfasten till I die.

SEMICHORUS

She has filled with sighing the city,
  And the ways thereof with tears;
She arose, she girdled her sides,
She set her face as a bride's;
She wept, and she had no pity;
  Trembled, and felt no fears.

SEMICHORUS

Her eyes were clear as the sun,
  Her brows were fresh as the day;
She girdled herself with gold,
Her robes were manifold;
But the days of her worship are done,
  Her praise is taken away.

SEMICHORUS

For she set her hand to the fire,
  With her mouth she kindled the same;
As the mouth of a flute-player,
So was the mouth of her;
With the might of her strong desire
  She blew the breath of the flame.

SEMICHORUS

She set her hand to the wood,
  She took the fire in her hand;

As one who is nigh to death,
She panted with strange breath;
She opened her lips unto blood,
She breathed and kindled the brand.

SEMICHORUS

As a wood-dove newly shot,
She sobbed and lifted her breast;
She sighed and covered her eyes,
Filling her lips with sighs;
She sighed, she withdrew herself not,
She refrained not, taking not rest;

SEMICHORUS

But as the wind which is drouth,
And as the air which is death,
As storm that severeth ships,
Her breath severing her lips,
Her breath came forth of her mouth
And the fire came forth of her breath.

SECOND MESSENGER

Queen, and you maidens, there is come on us
A thing more deadly than the face of death;
Meleager the good lord is as one slain.

SEMICHORUS

Without sword, without sword is he stricken;
Slain, and slain without hand.

SECOND MESSENGER

For as keen ice divided of the sun
His limbs divide, and as thawed snow the flesh
Thaws from off all his body to the hair.

SEMICHORUS

He wastes as the embers quicken;
With the brand he fades as a brand.

SECOND MESSENGER

Even while they sang and all drew hither and he
Lifted both hands to crown the Arcadian's hair
And fix the looser leaves, both hands fell down.

SEMICHORUS

With rending of cheek and of hair
Lament ye, mourn for him, weep.

SECOND MESSENGER

Straightway the crown slid off and smote on earth,
First fallen; and he, grasping his own hair, groaned
And cast his raiment round his face and fell.

SEMICHORUS

Alas for visions that were,
And soothsayings spoken in sleep.

SECOND MESSENGER

But the king twitched his reins in and leapt down
And caught him, crying out twice 'O child' and thrice,
So that men's eyelids thickened with their tears.

SEMICHORUS

Lament with a long lamentation,
Cry, for an end is at hand.

SECOND MESSENGER

O son, he said, son, lift thine eyes, draw breath,
Pity me; but Meleager with sharp lips
Grasped, and his face waxed like as sunburnt grass.

SEMICHORUS

Cry aloud, O thou kingdom, O nation,
O stricken, a ruinous land.

SECOND MESSENGER

Whereat king Œneus, straightening feeble knees,
With feeble hands heaved up a lessening weight,
And laid him sadly in strange hands, and wept.

SEMICHORUS

Thou art smitten, her lord, her desire,
Thy dear blood wasted as rain.

SECOND MESSENGER

And they with tears and rendings of the beard
Bear hither a breathing body, wept upon
And lightening at each footfall, sick to death.

SEMICHORUS

Thou madest thy sword as a fire,
With fire for a sword thou art slain.

SECOND MESSENGER

And lo, the feast turned funeral, and the crowns
Fallen; and the huntress and the hunter trapped;
And weeping and changed faces and veiled hair.

MELEAGER

Let your hands meet
Round the weight of my head;
Lift ye my feet
As the feet of the dead;
For the flesh of my body is molten, the limbs of it molten as lead.

CHORUS

O thy luminous face.
Thine imperious eyes!
O the grief, O the grace,
As of day when it dies!
Who is this bending over thee, lord, with tears and suppression of sighs?

MELEAGER

Is a bride so fair?
Is a maid so meek?
With unchapleted hair,
With unfilleted cheek,
Atalanta, the pure among women, whose name is as blessing to speak.

ATALANTA

I would that with feet
Unsandalled, unshod,
Overbold, overfleet,
I had swum not nor trod
From Arcadia to Calydon northward, a blast of the envy of God.

MELEAGER

Unto each man his fate;
Unto each as he saith
In whose fingers the weight
Of the world is as breath;
Yet I would that in clamour of battle mine hands had laid hold upon death.

CHORUS

Not with cleaving of shields
And their clash in thine ear,
When the lord of fought fields
Breaketh spearshaft from spear,
Thou art broken, our lord, thou art broken, with travail and labour and fear.

MELEAGER

Would God he had found me
Beneath fresh boughs!
Would God he had bound me
Unawares in mine house,
With light in mine eyes, and songs in my lips, and a crown on my brows!

CHORUS

Whence art thou sent from us?
Whither thy goal?
How art thou rent from us,
Thou that wert whole,
As with severing of eyelids and eyes, as with sundering of body and soul!

MELEAGER

My heart is within me
As an ash in the fire;
Whosoever hath seen me,
Without lute, without lyre,
Shall sing of me grievous things, even things that were ill to desire.

CHORUS

Who shall raise thee
From the house of the dead?
Or what man praise thee
That thy praise may be said?
Alas thy beauty! alas thy body! alas thine head!

MELEAGER

But thou, O mother,
The dreamer of dreams,
Wilt thou bring forth another
To feel the sun's beams
When I move among shadows a shadow, and wail by impassable streams?

ŒNEUS

What thing wilt thou leave me
Now this thing is done?
A man wilt thou give me,
A son for my son,
For the light of mine eyes, the desire of my life, the desirable one?

CHORUS

Thou wert glad above others,
Yea, fair beyond word;
Thou were glad among mothers;
For each man that heard
Of thee, praise there was added unto thee, as wings to the feet of a bird.

ŒNEUS

Who shall give back
Thy face of old years,
With travail made black,
Grown grey among fears,
Mother of sorrow, mother of cursing, mother of tears?

MELEAGER

Though thou art as fire
Fed with fuel in vain,
My delight, my desire,
Is more chaste than the rain,
More pure than the dewfall, more holy than stars are that live without stain.

ATALANTA

I would that as water
My life's blood had thawn,
Or as winter's wan daughter
Leaves lowland and lawn
Spring-stricken, or ever mine eyes had beheld thee made dark in thy dawn.

CHORUS

When thou dravest the men
Of the chosen of Thrace,
None turned him again
Nor endured he thy face
Clothed round with the blush of the battle, with light from a terrible place.

ŒNEUS

Thou shouldst die as he dies
For whom none sheddeth tears;
Filling thine eyes
And fulfilling thine ears
With the brilliance of battle, the bloom and the beauty, the splendour of spears.

CHORUS

In the ears of the world
It is sung, it is told,
And the light thereof hurled
And the noise thereof rolled
From the Acroceraunian snow to the ford of the fleece of gold.

MELEAGER

Would God ye could carry me
Forth of all these;
Heap sand and bury me
By the Chersonese
Where the thundering Bosphorus answers the thunder of Pontic seas.

ŒNEUS

Dost thou mock at our praise
And the singing begun
And the men of strange days
Praising my son
In the folds of the hills of home, high places of Calydon?

MELEAGER

For the dead man no home is;
Ah, better to be
What the flower of the foam is
In fields of the sea,
That the sea-waves might be as my raiment, the gulf-stream a garment for me.

CHORUS

Who shall seek thee and bring
And restore thee thy day,
When the dove dipt her wing
And the oars won their way
Where the narrowing Symplegades whitened the straits of Propontis with spray?

MELEAGER

Will ye crown me my tomb
Or exalt me my name,
Now my spirits consume,
Now my flesh is a flame?
Let the sea slake it once, and men speak of me sleeping to praise me or shame.

CHORUS

Turn back now, turn thee,
As who turns him to wake;
Though the life in thee burn thee,
Couldst thou bathe it and slake
Where the sea-ridge of Helle hangs heavier, and east upon west waters break?

MELEAGER

Would the winds blow me back
Or the waves hurl me home?
Ah, to touch in the track
Where the pine learnt to roam
Cold girdles and crowns of the sea-gods, cool blossoms of water and foam!

CHORUS

The gods may release
That they made fast;
Thy soul shall have ease
In thy limbs at the last;
But what shall they give thee for life, sweet life that is overpast?

MELEAGER

Not the life of men's veins,
Not of flesh that conceives;
But the grace that remains,
The fair beauty that cleaves
To the life of the rains in the grasses, the life of the dews on the leaves.

CHORUS

Thou wert helmsman and chief;
Wilt thou turn in an hour,
Thy limbs to the leaf,
Thy face to the flower,
Thy blood to the water, thy soul to the gods who divide and devour?

MELEAGER

The years are hungry,
They wail all their days;
The gods wax angry
And weary of praise;
And who shall bridle their lips? and who shall straiten their ways?

CHORUS

The gods guard over us
With sword and with rod;
Weaving shadow to cover us,
Heaping the sod,
That law may fulfil herself wholly, to darken man's face before God.

MELEAGER

O holy head of Œneus; lo thy son
Guiltless, yet red from alien guilt, yet foul
With kinship of contaminated lives,
Lo, for their blood I die; and mine own blood
For bloodshedding of mine is mixed therewith,
That death may not discern me from my kin.
Yet with clean heart I die and faultless hand,
Not shamefully; thou therefore of thy love
Salute me, and bid fare among the dead
Well, as the dead fare; for the best man dead
Fares sadly; nathless I now faring well

Pass without fear where nothing is to fear
Having thy love about me and thy goodwill,
O father, among dark places and men dead.

ŒNEUS

Child, I salute thee with sad heart and tears,
And bid thee comfort, being a perfect man
In fight, and honourable in the house of peace.
The gods give thee fair wage and dues of death,
And me brief days and ways to come at thee.

MELEAGER

Pray thou thy days be long before thy death,
And full of ease and kingdom; seeing in death
There is no comfort and none aftergrowth,
Nor shall one thence look up and see day's dawn
Nor light upon the land whither I go.
Live thou and take thy fill of days and die
When thy day comes; and make not much of death
Lest ere thy day thou reap an evil thing.
Thou too, the bitter mother and mother-plague
Of this my weary body—thou too, queen,
The source and end, the sower and the scythe,
The rain that ripens and the drought that slays,
The sand that swallows and the spring that feeds,
To make me and unmake me—thou, I say,
Althæa, since my father's ploughshare, drawn
Through fatal seedland of a female field,
Furrowed thy body, whence a wheaten ear
Strong from the sun and fragrant from the rains
I sprang and cleft the closure of thy womb,
Mother, I dying with unforgetful tongue
Hail thee as holy and worship thee as just
Who art unjust and unholy; and with my knees
Would worship, but thy fire and subtlety,
Dissundering them, devour me; for these limbs
Are as light dust and crumblings from mine urn
Before the fire has touched them, and my face
As a dead leaf or dead foot's mark on snow,
And all this body a broken barren tree
That was so strong, and all this flower of life
Disbranched and desecrated miserably,
And minished all that god-like muscle and might
And lesser than a man's: for all my veins
Fail me, and all mine ashen life burns down.
I would thou hadst let me live; but gods averse,
But fortune, and the fiery feet of change,
And time, these would not, these tread out my life,
These and not thou; me too thou hast loved, and I
Thee; but this death was mixed with all my life,
Mine end with my beginning: and this law,
This only, slays me, and not my mother at all.
And let no brother or sister grieve too sore,
Nor melt their hearts out on me with their tears,

Since extreme love and sorrowing overmuch
Vex the great gods, and overloving men
Slay and are slain for love's sake; and this house
Shall bear much better children; why should these
Weep? but in patience let them live their lives
And mine pass by forgotten: thou alone,
Mother, thou sole and only, thou not these,
Keep me in mind a little when I die
Because I was thy first-born; let thy soul
Pity me, pity even me gone hence and dead,
Though thou wert wroth, and though thou bear again
Much happier sons, and all men later born
Exceedingly excel me; yet do thou
Forget not, nor think shame; I was thy son.
Time was I did not shame thee; and time was
I thought to live and make thee honourable
With deeds as great as these men's; but they live,
These, and I die; and what thing should have been
Surely I know not; yet I charge thee, seeing
I am dead already, love me not the less,
Me, O my mother; I charge thee by these gods,
My father's, and that holier breast of thine,
By these that see me dying, and that which nursed,
Love me not less, thy first-born: though grief come,
Grief only, of me, and of all these great joy,
And shall come always to thee; for thou knowest,
O mother, O breasts that bare me, for ye know
O sweet head of my mother, sacred eyes,
Ye know my soul albeit I sinned, ye know
Albeit I kneel not neither touch thy knees,
But with my lips I kneel, and with my heart
I fall about thy feet and worship thee.
And ye farewell now, all my friends; and ye,
Kinsmen, much younger and glorious more than I,
Sons of my mother's sister; and all farewell
That were in Colchis with me, and bare down
The waves and wars that met us: and though times
Change, and though now I be not anything,
Forget not me among you, what I did
In my good time; for even by all those days,
Those days and this, and your own living souls,
And by the light and luck of you that live,
And by this miserable spoil, and me
Dying, I beseech you, let my name not die.
But thou, dear, touch me with thy rose-like hands,
And fasten up mine eyelids with thy mouth,
A bitter kiss; and grasp me with thine arms,
Printing with heavy lips my light waste flesh,
Made light and thin by heavy-handed fate,
And with thine holy maiden eyes drop dew,
Drop tears for dew upon me who am dead,
Me who have loved thee; seeing without sin done
I am gone down to the empty weary house
Where no flesh is nor beauty nor swift eyes

Nor sound of mouth nor might of hands and feet.
But thou, dear, hide my body with thy veil,
And with thy raiment cover foot and head,
And stretch thyself upon me and touch hands
With hands and lips with lips: be pitiful
As thou art maiden perfect; let no man
Defile me to despise me, saying, This man
Died woman-wise, a woman's offering, slain
Through female fingers in his woof of life,
Dishonourable; for thou hast honoured me.
And now for God's sake kiss me once and twice
And let me go; for the night gathers me,
And in the night shall no man gather fruit.

ATALANTA

Hail thou: but I with heavy face and feet
Turn homeward and am gone out of thine eyes.

CHORUS

Who shall contend with his lords
  Or cross them or do them wrong?
Who shall bind them as with cords?
  Who shall tame them as with song?
Who shall smite them as with swords?
  For the hands of their kingdom are strong.

[1865]

DEDICATION

To Poems and Ballads

[FIRST SERIES]

The sea gives her shells to the shingle,
  The earth gives her streams to the sea:
They are many, but my gift is single,
  My verses, the firstfruits of me.
Let the wind take the green and the grey leaf
  Cast forth without fruit upon air;
Take rose-leaf and vine-leaf and bay-leaf
  Blown loose from the hair.

The night shakes them round me in legions,
  Dawn drives them before her like dreams;
Time sheds them like snows on strange regions,
  Swept shoreward on infinite streams;
Leaves pallid and sombre and ruddy,
  Dead fruits of the fugitive years;
Some stained as with wine and made bloody,
  And some as with tears.

Some scattered in seven years' traces,
  As they fell from the boy that was then;
Long left among idle green places,
  Or gathered but now among men;
On seas full of wonder and peril,
  Blown white round the capes of the north;
Or in islands where myrtles are sterile
  And loves bring not forth.

O daughters of dreams and of stories
  That life is not wearied of yet,
Faustine, Fragoletta, Dolores,
  Félise and Yolande and Juliette,
Shall I find you not still, shall I miss you,
  When sleep, that is true or that seems,
Comes back to me hopeless to kiss you,
  O daughters of dreams?

They are past as a slumber that passes,
  As the dew of a dawn of old time;
More frail than the shadows on glasses,
  More fleet than a wave or a rhyme.
As the waves after ebb drawing seaward,
  When their hallows are full of the night,
So the birds that flew singing to me-ward
  Recede out of sight.

The songs of dead seasons, that wander
On wings of articulate words;
Lost leaves that the shore-wind may squander,
Light flocks of untameable birds;
Some sang to me dreaming in class-time
And truant in hand as in tongue;
For the youngest were born of boy's pastime,
The eldest are young.

Is there shelter while life in them lingers,
Is there hearing for songs that recede,
Tunes touched from a harp with man's fingers
Or blown with boy's mouth in a reed?
Is there place in the land of your labour,
Is there room in your world of delight,
Where change has not sorrow for neighbour
And day has not night?

In their wings though the sea-wind yet quivers
Will you spare not a space for them there
Made green with the running of rivers
And gracious with temperate air;
In the fields and the turreted cities,
That cover from sunshine and rain
Fair passions and bountiful pities
And loves without stain?

In a land of clear colours and stories,
In a region of shadowless hours.
Where earth has a garment of glories
And a murmur of musical flowers;
In the woods where the spring half uncovers
The flush of her amorous face,
By the waters that listen for lovers,
For these is there place?

For the song-birds of sorrow, that muffle
Their music as clouds do their fire:
For the storm-birds of passion, that ruffle
Wild wings in a wind of desire;
In the stream of the storm as it settles
Blown seaward, borne far from the sun,
Shaken loose on the darkness like petals
Dropt one after one?

Though the world of your hands be more gracious
And the lovelier in lordship of things
Clothed round by sweet art with the spacious
Warm heaven of her imminent wings,
Let them enter, unfledged and nigh fainting,
For the love of old loves and lost times;
And receive in your palace of painting
This revel of rhymes.

Though the seasons of man full of losses
Make empty the years full of youth,
If but one thing be constant in crosses,
Change lays not her hand upon truth;
Hopes die, and their tombs are for token
That the grief as the joy of them ends
Ere time that breaks all men has broken
The faith between friends.

Though the many lights dwindle to one light,
There is help if the heaven has one;
Though the skies be discrowned of the sunlight
And the earth dispossessed of the sun,
They have moonlight and sleep for repayment,
When, refreshed as a bride and set free,
With stars and sea-winds in her raiment,
Night sinks on the sea.

[1865] [1866]

THE TRIUMPH OF TIME

Before our lives divide for ever,
While time is with us and hands are free,
(Time, swift to fasten and swift to sever
Hand from hand, as we stand by the sea)
I will say no word that a man might say
Whose whole life's love goes down in a day;
For this could never have been; and never,
Though the gods and the years relent, shall be.

Is it worth a tear, is it worth an hour,
To think of things that are well outworn?
Of fruitless husk and fugitive flower,
The dream foregone and the deed forborne?
Though joy be done with and grief be vain,

Time shall not sever us wholly in twain;
Earth is not spoilt for a single shower;
But the rain has ruined the ungrown corn.
It will grow not again, this fruit of my heart,
Smitten with sunbeams, ruined with rain.
The singing seasons divide and depart,
Winter and summer depart in twain.
It will grow not again, it is ruined at root,
The bloodlike blossom, the dull red fruit;
Though the heart yet sickens, the lips yet smart,
With sullen savour of poisonous pain.

I have given no man of my fruit to eat;
I trod the grapes, I have drunken the wine.
Had you eaten and drunken and found it sweet,
This wild new growth of the corn and vine,
This wine and bread without lees or leaven,
We had grown as gods, as the gods in heaven,
Souls fair to look upon, goodly to greet,
One splendid spirit, your soul and mine.

In the change of years, in the coil of things,
In the clamour and rumour of life to be,
We, drinking love at the furthest springs,
Covered with love as a covering tree,
We had grown as gods, as the gods above,
Filled from the heart to the lips with love,
Held fast in his hands, clothed warm with his wings,
O love, my love, had you loved but me!

We had stood as the sure stars stand, and moved
As the moon moves, loving the world; and seen
Grief collapse as a thing disproved,
Death consume as a thing unclean.
Twain halves of a perfect heart, made fast
Soul to soul while the years fell past;
Had you loved me once, as you have not loved;
Had the chance been with us that has not been.

I have put my days and dreams out of mind,
Days that are over, dreams that are done.
Though we seek life through, we shall surely find
There is none of them clear to us now, not one.
But clear are these things; the grass and the sand,
Where, sure as the eyes reach, ever at hand,
With lips wide open and face burnt blind,
The strong sea-daisies feast on the sun.

The low downs lean to the sea; the stream,
One loose thin pulseless tremulous vein,
Rapid and vivid and dumb as a dream,
Works downward, sick of the sun and the rain;
No wind is rough with the rank rare flowers;
The sweet sea, mother of loves and hours,
Shudders and shines as the grey winds gleam,
Turning her smile to a fugitive pain.

Mother of loves that are swift to fade,
Mother of mutable winds and hours,
A barren mother, a mother-maid,
Cold and clean as her faint salt flowers.
I would we twain were even as she,
Lost in the night and the light of the sea,
Where faint sounds falter and wan beams wade,
Break, and are broken, and shed into showers.

The loves and hours of the life of a man,
They are swift and sad, being born of the sea.
Hours that rejoice and regret for a span,
Born with a man's breath, mortal as he;
Loves that are lost ere they come to birth,
Weeds of the wave, without fruit upon earth.
I lose what I long for, save what I can,
My love, my love, and no love for me!

It is not much that a man can save
On the sands of life, in the straits of time,

Who swims in sight of the great third wave
That never a swimmer shall cross or climb,
Some waif washed up with the strays and spars
That ebb-tide shows to the shore and the stars;
Weed from the water, grass from a grave,
A broken blossom, a ruined rhyme.

There will no man do for your sake, I think,
What I would have done for the least word said.
I had wrung life dry for your lips to drink,
Broken it up for your daily bread:
Body for body and blood for blood,
As the flow of the full sea risen to flood
That yearns and trembles before it sink,
I had given, and lain down for you, glad and dead.

Yea, hope at highest and all her fruit,
And time at fullest and all his dower,
I had given you surely, and life to boot,
Were we once made one for a single hour.
But now, you are twain, you are cloven apart,
Flesh of his flesh, but heart of my heart;
And deep in one is the bitter root,
And sweet for one is the lifelong flower.

To have died if you cared I should die for you, clung
To my life if you bade me, played my part
As it pleased you—these were the thoughts that stung,
The dream that smote with a keener dart
Than shafts of love or arrows of death;
These were but as fire is, dust, or breath,
Or poisonous foam on the tender tongue
Of the little snakes that eat my heart.

I wish we were dead together to-day,
Lost sight of, hidden away out of sight,
Clasped and clothed in the cloven clay,
Out of the world's way, out of the light,
Out of the ages of worldly weather,
Forgotten of all men altogether,
As the world's first dead, taken wholly away,
Made one with death, filled full of the night.

How we should slumber, how we should sleep,
Far in the dark with the dreams and the dews!
And dreaming, grow to each other, and weep,
Laugh low, live softly, murmur and muse;
Yea, and it may be, struck through by the dream,
Feel the dust quicken and quiver, and seem
Alive as of old to the lips, and leap
Spirit to spirit as lovers use.

Sick dreams and sad of a dull delight;
For what shall it profit when men are dead
To have dreamed, to have loved with the whole soul's might,
To have looked for day when the day was fled?
Let come what will, there is one thing worth,
To have had fair love in the life upon earth:
To have held love safe till the day grew night,
While skies had colour and lips were red.

Would I lose you now? would I take you then,
If I lose you now that my heart has need?
And come what may after death to men,
What thing worth this will the dead years breed?
Lose life, lose all: but at least I know,
O sweet life's love, having loved you so,
Had I reached you on earth, I should lose not again,
In death nor life, nor in dream or deed.

Yea, I know this well: were you once sealed mine,
Mine in the blood's beat, mine in the breath,
Mixed into me as honey in wine,
Not time, that sayeth and gainsayeth,

Nor all strong things had severed us then;
Not wrath of gods, nor wisdom of men,
Nor all things earthly, nor all divine,
Nor joy nor sorrow, nor life nor death.

I had grown pure as the dawn and the dew,
You had grown strong as the sun or the sea.
But none shall triumph a whole life through:
For death is one, and the fates are three.
At the door of life, by the gate of breath,
There are worse things waiting for men than death;
Death could not sever my soul and you,
As these have severed your soul from me.

You have chosen and clung to the chance they sent you,
Life sweet as perfume and pure as prayer.
But will it not one day in heaven repent you?
Will they solace you wholly, the days that were?
Will you lift up your eyes between sadness and bliss,
Meet mine, and see where the great love is,
And tremble and turn and be changed? Content you;
The gate is strait; I shall not be there.

But you, had you chosen, had you stretched hand,
Had you seen good such a thing were done,
I too might have stood with the souls that stand
In the sun's sight, clothed with the light of the sun;
But who now on earth need care how I live?
Have the high gods anything left to give,
Save dust and laurels and gold and sand?
Which gifts are goodly; but I will none.

O all fair lovers about the world,
There is none of you, none, that shall comfort me.
My thoughts are as dead things, wrecked and whirled
Round and round in a gulf of the sea;
And still, through the sound and the straining stream,
Through the coil and chafe, they gleam in a dream,
The bright fine lips so cruelly curled,
And strange swift eyes where the soul sits free.

Free, without pity, withheld from woe,
Ignorant; fair as the eyes are fair.
Would I have you change now, change at a blow,
Startled and stricken, awake and aware?
Yea, if I could, would I have you see
My very love of you filling me,
And know my soul to the quick, as I know
The likeness and look of your throat and hair?

I shall not change you. Nay, though I might,
Would I change my sweet one love with a word?
I had rather your hair should change in a night,
Clear now as the plume of a black bright bird;
Your face fail suddenly, cease, turn grey,
Die as a leaf that dies in a day.
I will keep my soul in a place out of sight,
Far off, where the pulse of it is not heard.

Far off it walks, in a bleak blown space,
Full of the sound of the sorrow of years.
I have woven a veil for the weeping face,
Whose lips have drunken the wine of tears;
I have found a way for the failing feet,
A place for slumber and sorrow to meet;
There is no rumour about the place,
Nor light, nor any that sees or hears.

I have hidden my soul out of sight, and said
"Let none take pity upon thee, none
Comfort thy crying: for lo, thou art dead,
Lie still now, safe out of sight of the sun.
Have I not built thee a grave, and wrought
Thy grave-clothes on thee of grievous thought,
With soft spun verses and tears unshed,
And sweet light visions of things undone?

"I have given thee garments and balm and myrrh,
And gold, and beautiful burial things.
But thou, be at peace now, make no stir;
Is not thy grave as a royal king's?
Fret not thyself though the end were sore;
Sleep, be patient, vex me no more.
Sleep, what hast thou to do with her?
The eyes that weep, with the mouth that sings?"

Where the dead red leaves of the years lie rotten,
The cold old crimes and the deeds thrown by,
The misconceived and the misbegotten,
I would find a sin to do ere I die,
Sure to dissolve and destroy me all through,
That would set you higher in heaven, serve you
And leave you happy, when clean forgotten,
As a dead man out of mind, am I.

Your lithe hands draw me, your face burns through me,
I am swift to follow you, keen to see;
But love lacks might to redeem or undo me;
As I have been, I know I shall surely be;
"What should such fellows as I do?" Nay,
My part were worse if I chose to play;
For the worst is this after all; if they knew me,
Not a soul upon earth would pity me.

And I play not for pity of these; but you,
If you saw with your soul what man am I,
You would praise me at least that my soul all through
Clove to you, loathing the lives that lie;
The souls and lips that are bought and sold,
The smiles of silver and kisses of gold,
The lapdog loves that whine as they chew,
The little lovers that curse and cry.

There are fairer women, I hear; that may be;
But I, that I love you and find you fair,
Who are more than fair in my eyes if they be,
Do the high gods know or the great gods care?
Though the swords in my heart for one were seven,
Should the iron hollow of doubtful heaven,
That knows not itself whether night-time or day be,
Reverberate words and a foolish prayer?

I will go back to the great sweet mother,
Mother and lover of men, the sea.
I will go down to her, I and none other,
Close with her, kiss her and mix her with me;
Cling to her, strive with her, hold her fast:
O fair white mother, in days long past
Born without sister, born without brother,
Set free my soul as thy soul is free.

O fair green-girdled mother of mine,
Sea, that art clothed with the sun and the rain,
Thy sweet hard kisses are strong like wine,
Thy large embraces are keen like pain.
Save me and hide me with all thy waves,
Find me one grave of thy thousand graves,
Those pure cold populous graves of thine
Wrought without hand in a world without stain.

I shall sleep, and move with the moving ships,
Change as the winds change, veer in the tide;
My lips will feast on the foam of thy lips,
I shall rise with thy rising, with thee subside;
Sleep, and not know if she be, if she were,
Filled full with life to the eyes and hair,
As a rose is fulfilled to the roseleaf tips
With splendid summer and perfume and pride.

This woven raiment of nights and days,
Were it once cast off and unwound from me,
Naked and glad would I walk in thy ways,
Alive and aware of thy ways and thee;
Clear of the whole world, hidden at home,
Clothed with the green and crowned with the foam,
A pulse of the life of thy straits and bays,
A vein in the heart of the streams of the sea.

Fair mother, fed with the lives of men,
Thou art subtle and cruel of heart, men say.
Thou hast taken, and shalt not render again;
Thou art full of thy dead, and cold as they.
But death is the worst that comes of thee;
Thou art fed with our dead, O mother, O sea,
But when hast thou fed on our hearts? or when,
Having given us love, hast thou taken away?

O tender-hearted, O perfect lover,
Thy lips are bitter, and sweet thine heart.
The hopes that hurt and the dreams that hover,
Shall they not vanish away and apart?
But thou, thou art older than earth;
Thou art strong for death and fruitful of birth;
Thy depths conceal and thy gulfs discover;
From the first thou wert; in the end thou art.

And grief shall endure not for ever, I know.
As things that are not shall these things be;
We shall live through seasons of sun and of snow,
And none be grievous as this to me.
We shall hear, as one in a trance that hears,
The sound of time, the rhyme of the years;
Wrecked hope and passionate pain will grow
As tender things of a spring-tide sea.

Sea-fruit that swings in the waves that hiss,
Drowned gold and purple and royal rings.
And all time past, was it all for this?
Times unforgotten, and treasures of things?
Swift years of liking and sweet long laughter,
That wist not well of the years thereafter
Till love woke, smitten at heart by a kiss,
With lips that trembled and trailing wings?

There lived a singer in France of old
By the tideless dolorous midland sea.
In a land of sand and ruin and gold
There shone one woman, and none but she.
And finding life for her love's sake fail,
Being fain to see her, he bade set sail,
Touched land, and saw her as life grew cold,
And praised God, seeing; and so died he.

Died, praising God for his gift and grace:
For she bowed down to him weeping, and said
"Live;" and her tears were shed on his face
Or ever the life in his face was shed.
The sharp tears fell through her hair, and stung
Once, and her close lips touched him and clung
Once, and grew one with his lips for a space;
And so drew back, and the man was dead.

O brother, the gods were good to you.
Sleep, and be glad while the world endures.
Be well content as the years wear through;
Give thanks for life, and the loves and lures;
Give thanks for life, O brother, and death,
For the sweet last sound of her feet, her breath,
For gifts she gave you, gracious and few,
Tears and kisses, that lady of yours.

Rest, and be glad of the gods; but I,
How shall I praise them, or how take rest?
There is not room under all the sky
For me that know not of worst or best,
Dream or desire of the days before,
Sweet things or bitterness, any more.
Love will not come to me now though I die,
As love came close to you, breast to breast.

I shall never be friends again with roses;
I shall loathe sweet tunes, where a note grown strong

Relents and recoils, and climbs and closes,
As a wave of the sea turned back by song.
There are sounds where the soul's delight takes fire,
Face to face with its own desire;
A delight that rebels, a desire that reposes;
I shall hate sweet music my whole life long.

The pulse of war and passion of wonder,
The heavens that murmur, the sounds that shine,
The stars that sing and the loves that thunder,
The music burning at heart like wine,
An armed archangel whose hands raise up
All senses mixed in the spirit's cup
Till flesh and spirit are molten in sunder—
These things are over, and no more mine.

These were a part of the playing I heard
Once, ere my love and my heart were at strife;
Love that sings and hath wings as a bird,
Balm of the wound and heft of the knife.
Fairer than earth is the sea, and sleep
Than overwatching of eyes that weep,
Now time has done with his one sweet word,
The wine and leaven of lovely life.

I shall go my ways, tread out my measure,
Fill the days of my daily breath
With fugitive things not good to treasure,
Do as the world doth, say as it saith;
But if we had loved each other—O sweet,
Had you felt, lying under the palms of your feet,
The heart of my heart, beating harder with pleasure
To feel you tread it to dust and death—

Ah, had I not taken my life up and given
All that life gives and the years let go,
The wine and honey, the balm and leaven,
The dreams reared high and the hopes brought low?
Come life, come death, not a word be said;
Should I lose you living, and vex you dead?
I never shall tell you on earth; and in heaven,
If I cry to you then, will you hear or know?

[1863] [1866]

ITYLUS

Swallow, my sister, O sister swallow,
How can thine heart be full of the spring?
A thousand summers are over and dead.
What hast thou found in the spring to follow?
What hast thou found in thine heart to sing?
What wilt thou do when the summer is shed?

O swallow sister, O fair swift swallow,
Why wilt thou fly after spring to the south,
The soft south whither thine heart is set?
Shall not the grief of the old time follow?
Shall not the song thereof cleave to thy mouth?
Hast thou forgotten ere I forget?

Sister, my sister, O fleet sweet swallow,
Thy way is long to the sun and the south;
But I, fulfilled of my heart's desire,
Shedding my song upon height, upon hollow,
From tawny body and sweet small mouth
Feed the heart of the night with fire.

I the nightingale all spring through,
O swallow, sister, O changing swallow,
All spring through till the spring be done,
Clothed with the light of the night on the dew,
Sing, while the hours and the wild birds follow,
Take flight and follow and find the sun.

Sister, my sister, O soft light swallow,
Though all things feast in the spring's guest-chamber,
How hast thou heart to be glad thereof yet?
For where thou fliest I shall not follow,
Till life forget and death remember,
Till thou remember and I forget.

Swallow, my sister, O singing swallow,
I know not how thou hast heart to sing.
Hast thou the heart? is it all past over?
Thy lord the summer is good to follow,
And fair the feet of thy lover the spring:
But what wilt thou say to the spring thy lover?

O swallow, sister, O fleeting swallow,
My heart in me is a molten ember
And over my head the waves have met.
But thou wouldst tarry or I would follow,
Could I forget or thou remember,
Couldst thou remember and I forget.

O sweet stray sister, O shifting swallow,
The heart's division divideth us.
Thy heart is light as a leaf of a tree;
But mine goes forth among sea-gulfs hollow
To the place of the slaying of Itylus,
The feast of Daulis, the Thracian sea.

O swallow, sister, O rapid swallow,
I pray thee sing not a little space.
Are not the roofs and the lintels wet?
The woven web that was plain to follow,
The small slain body, the flowerlike face,
Can I remember if thou forget?

O sister, sister, thy first-begotten!
The hands that cling and the feet that follow,
The voice of the child's blood crying yet
Who hath remembered me? who hath forgotten?
Thou hast forgotten, O summer swallow,
But the world shall end when I forget.

[1864] [1866]

HYMN TO PROSERPINE

(AFTER THE PROCLAMATION IN ROME OF THE CHRISTIAN FAITH)

VICISTI, GALILÆE.

I have lived long enough, having seen one thing, that love hath an end;
Goddess and maiden and queen, be near me now and befriend.
Thou art more than the day or the morrow, the seasons that laugh or that weep;
For these give joy and sorrow; but thou, Proserpina, sleep.
Sweet is the treading of wine, and sweet the feet of the dove;
But a goodlier gift is thine than foam of the grapes or love.
Yea, is not even Apollo, with hair and harpstring of gold,
A bitter God to follow, a beautiful God to behold?
I am sick of singing; the bays burn deep and chafe: I am fain
To rest a little from praise and grievous pleasure and pain.
For the Gods we know not of, who give us our daily breath,
We know they are cruel as love or life, and lovely as death.
O Gods dethroned and deceased, cast forth, wiped out in a day!
From your wrath is the world released, redeemed from your chains, men say.
New Gods are crowned in the city; their flowers have broken your rods;
They are merciful, clothed with pity, the young compassionate Gods.
But for me their new device is barren, the days are bare;
Things long past over suffice, and men forgotten that were.

Time and the Gods are at strife; ye dwell in the midst thereof,
Draining a little life from the barren breasts of love.
I say to you, cease, take rest; yea, I say to you all, be at peace,
Till the bitter milk of her breast and the barren bosom shall cease.
Wilt thou yet take all, Galilean? but these thou shalt not take,
The laurel, the palms and the pæan, the breasts of the nymphs in the brake;
Breasts more soft than a dove's, that tremble with tenderer breath;
And all the wings of the Loves, and all the joy before death;
All the feet of the hours that sound as a single lyre,
Dropped and deep in the flowers, with strings that flicker like fire.
More than these wilt thou give, things fairer than all these things?
Nay, for a little we live, and life hath mutable wings.
A little while and we die; shall life not thrive as it may?
For no man under the sky lives twice, outliving his day.
And grief is a grievous thing, and a man hath enough of his tears:
Why should he labour, and bring fresh grief to blacken his years?
Thou hast conquered, O pale Galilean; the world has grown grey from thy breath;
We have drunken of things Lethean, and fed on the fullness of death.
Laurel is green for a season, and love is sweet for a day;
But love grows bitter with treason, and laurel outlives not May.
Sleep, shall we sleep after all? for the world is not sweet in the end;
For the old faiths loosen and fall, the new years ruin and rend.
Fate is a sea without shore, and the soul is a rock that abides;
But her ears are vexed with the roar and her face with the foam of the tides.
O lips that the live blood faints in, the leavings of racks and rods!
O ghastly glories of saints, dead limbs of gibbeted Gods!
Though all men abase them before you in spirit, and all knees bend,
I kneel not neither adore you, but standing, look to the end.
All delicate days and pleasant, all spirits and sorrows are cast
Far out with the foam of the present that sweeps to the surf of the past:
Where beyond the extreme sea-wall, and between the remote sea-gates,
Waste water washes, and tall ships founder, and deep death waits:
Where, mighty with deepening sides, clad about with the seas as with wings,
And impelled of invisible tides, and fulfilled of unspeakable things,
White-eyed and poisonous-finned, shark-toothed and serpentine-curled,
Rolls, under the whitening wind of the future, the wave of the world.
The depths stand naked in sunder behind it, the storms flee away;
In the hollow before it the thunder is taken and snared as a prey;
In its sides is the north-wind bound: and its salt is of all men's tears;
With light of ruin, and sound of changes, and pulse of years:
With travail of day after day, and with trouble of hour upon hour;
And bitter as blood is the spray; and the crests are as fangs that devour:
And its vapour and storm of its steam as the sighing of spirits to be;
And its noise as the noise in a dream; and its depth as the roots of the sea:
And the height of its heads as the height of the utmost stars of the air:
And the ends of the earth at the might thereof tremble, and time is made bare.
Will ye bridle the deep sea with reins, will ye chasten the high sea with rods?
Will ye take her to chain her with chains, who is older than all ye Gods?
All ye as a wind shall go by, as a fire shall ye pass and be past;
Ye are Gods, and behold, ye shall die, and the waves be upon you at last.
In the darkness of time, in the deeps of the years, in the changes of things,
Ye shall sleep as a slain man sleeps, and the world shall forget you for kings.
Though the feet of thine high priests tread where thy lords and our forefathers trod,
Though these that were Gods are dead, and thou being dead art a God,

Though before thee the throned Cytherean be fallen, and hidden her head,
Yet thy kingdom shall pass, Galilean, thy dead shall go down to thee dead.
Of the maiden thy mother men sing as a goddess with grace clad around;
Thou art throned where another was king; where another was queen she is crowned.
Yea, once we had sight of another: but now she is queen, say these.
Not as thine, not as thine was our mother, a blossom of flowering seas,
Clothed round with the world's desire as with raiment, and fair as the foam,
And fleeter than kindled fire, and a goddess, and mother of Rome.
For thine came pale and a maiden, and sister to sorrow; but ours,
Her deep hair heavily laden with odour and colour of flowers,
White rose of the rose-white water, a silver splendour, a flame,
Bent down unto us that besought her, and earth grew sweet with her name.
For thine came weeping, a slave among slaves, and rejected; but she
Came flushed from the full-flushed wave, and imperial, her foot on the sea.
And the wonderful waters knew her, the winds and the viewless ways,
And the roses grew rosier, and bluer the sea-blue stream of the bays.
Ye are fallen, our lords, by what token? we wist that ye should not fall.
Ye were all so fair that are broken; and one more fair than ye all.
But I turn to her still, having seen she shall surely abide in the end;
Goddess and maiden and queen, be near me now and befriend.
O daughter of earth, of my mother, her crown and blossom of birth,
I am also, I also, thy brother; I go as I came unto earth.
In the night where thine eyes are as moons are in heaven, the night where thou art,
Where the silence is more than all tunes, where sleep overflows from the heart,
Where the poppies are sweet as the rose in our world, and the red rose is white,
And the wind falls faint as it blows with the fume of the flowers of the night,
And the murmur of spirits that sleep in the shadow of Gods from afar
Grows dim in thine ears and deep as the deep dim soul of a star,
In the sweet low light of thy face, under heavens untrod by the sun,
Let my soul with their souls find place, and forget what is done and undone.
Thou art more than the Gods who number the days of our temporal breath;
For these give labour and slumber; but thou, Proserpina, death.
Therefore now at thy feet I abide for a season in silence. I know
I shall die as my fathers died, and sleep as they sleep; even so.
For the glass of the years is brittle wherein we gaze for a span;
A little soul for a little bears up this corpse which is man.
So long I endure, no longer; and laugh not again, neither weep.
For there is no God found stronger than death; and death is a sleep.

[1862] [1866]

FAUSTINE

AVE FAUSTINA IMPERATRIX,
MORITURI TE SALUTANT [1]

Lean back, and get some minutes' peace;
Let your head lean
Back to the shoulder with its fleece
Of locks, Faustine.

The shapely silver shoulder stoops,
Weighed over clean
With state of splendid hair that droops
Each side, Faustine.

Let me go over your good gifts
That crown you queen;
A queen whose kingdom ebbs and shifts
Each week, Faustine.

Bright heavy brow well gathered up:
White gloss and sheen;

[1] "Hail, Empress, Faustina; they who are about to die, salute you."

Carved lips that make my lips a cup
  To drink, Faustine.

Wine and rank poison, milk and blood,
  Being mixed therein
Since first the devil threw dice with God
  For you, Faustine.

Your naked new-born soul, their stake,
  Stood blind between;
God said "let him that wins her take
  And keep Faustine."

But this time Satan throve, no doubt;
  Long since, I ween,
God's part in you was battered out;
  Long since, Faustine.

The die rang sideways as it fell,
  Rang cracked and thin,
Like a man's laughter heard in hell
  Far down, Faustine.

A shadow of laughter like a sigh,
  Dead sorrow's kin;
So rang, thrown down, the devil's die
  That won Faustine.

A suckling of his breed you were,
  One hard to wean;
But God, who lost you, left you fair,
  We see, Faustine.

You have the face that suits a woman
  For her soul's screen—
The sort of beauty that's called human
  In hell, Faustine.

You could do all things but be good
  Or chaste of mien;
And that you would not if you could,
  We know, Faustine.

Even he who cast seven devils out
  Of Magdalene
Could hardly do as much, I doubt,
  For you, Faustine.

Did Satan make you to spite God?
  Or did God mean
To scourge with scorpions for a rod
  Our sins, Faustine?

I know what queen at first you were,
  As though I had seen
Red gold and black imperious hair
  Twice crown Faustine.

As if your fed sarcophagus
  Spared flesh and skin,
You come back face to face with us,
  The same Faustine.

She loved the games men played with death,
  Where death must win;
As though the slain man's blood and breath
  Revived Faustine.

Nets caught the pike, pikes tore the net;
  Lithe limbs and lean
From drained-out pores dripped thick red sweat
  To soothe Faustine.

She drank the steaming drift and dust
  Blown off the scene;
Blood could not ease the bitter lust
  That galled Faustine.

All round the foul fat furrows reeked,
  Where blood sank in;
The circus splashed and seethed and shrieked
  All round Faustine.

But these are gone now: years entomb
  The dust and din;
Yea, even the bath's fierce reek and fume
  That slew Faustine.

Was life worth living then? and now
  Is life worth sin?
Where are the imperial years? and how
  Are you, Faustine?

Your soul forgot her joys, forgot
  Her times of teen;
Yea, this life likewise will you not
  Forget, Faustine?

For in the time we know not of
  Did fate begin
Weaving the web of days that wove
  Your doom, Faustine.

The threads were wet with wine, and all
Were smooth to spin;
They wove you like a Bacchanal,
The first Faustine.

And Bacchus cast your mates and you
Wild grapes to glean;
Your flower-like lips were dashed with dew
From his, Faustine.

Your drenched loose hands were stretched to hold
The vine's wet green,
Long ere they coined in Roman gold
Your face, Faustine.

Then after change of soaring feather
And winnowing fin,
You woke in weeks of feverish weather,
A new Faustine.

A star upon your birthday burned,
Whose fierce serene
Red pulseless planet never yearned
In heaven, Faustine.

Stray breaths of Sapphic song that blew
Through Mitylene
Shook the fierce quivering blood in you
By night, Faustine.

The shameless nameless love that makes
Hell's iron gin
Shut on you like a trap that breaks
The soul, Faustine.

And when your veins were void and dead,
What ghosts unclean
Swarmed round the straitened barren bed
That hid Faustine?

What sterile growths of sexless root
Or epicene?
What flower of kisses without fruit
Of love, Faustine?

What adders came to shed their coats?
What coiled obscene
Small serpents with soft stretching throats
Caressed Faustine?

But the time came of famished hours,
Maimed loves and mean,
This ghastly thin-faced time of ours,
To spoil Faustine.

You seem a thing that hinges hold,
A love-machine
With clockwork joints of supple gold—
No more, Faustine.

Not Godless, for you serve one God,
The Lampsacene,
Who metes the gardens with his rod;
Your lord, Faustine.

If one should love you with real love
(Such things have been,
Things your fair face knows nothing of,
It seems, Faustine);

That clear hair heavily bound back,
The lights wherein
Shift from dead blue to burnt-up black;
Your throat, Faustine,

Strong, heavy, throwing out the face
And hard bright chin
And shameful scornful lips that grace
Their shame, Faustine,

Curled lips, long since half kissed away,
Still sweet and keen;
You'd give him—poison shall we say?
Or what, Faustine?

[1862] [1866]

DOLORES

NOTRE-DAME DES SEPT DOULEURS [1]

Cold eyelids that hide like a jewel
Hard eyes that grow soft for an hour;
The heavy white limbs, and the cruel
Red mouth like a venomous flower;
When these are gone by with their glories,
What shall rest of thee then, what remain,
O mystic and sombre Dolores,
Our Lady of Pain?

Seven sorrows the priests give their Virgin;
But thy sins, which are seventy times seven,

[1] "Our Lady of the seven sorrows."

Seven ages would fail thee to purge in,
And then they would haunt thee in heaven:
Fierce midnights and famishing morrows,
And the loves that complete and control
All the joys of the flesh, all the sorrows
That wear out the soul.

O garment not golden but gilded,
O garden where all men may dwell,
O tower not of ivory, but builded
By hands that reach heaven from hell;
O mystical rose of the mire,
O house not of gold but of gain,
O house of unquenchable fire,
Our Lady of Pain!

O lips full of lust and of laughter,
Curled snakes that are fed from my breast,
Bite hard, lest remembrance come after
And press with new lips where you pressed.
For my heart too springs up at the pressure,
Mine eyelids too moisten and burn;
Ah, feed me and fill me with pleasure,
Ere pain come in turn.

In yesterday's reach and to-morrow's,
Out of sight though they lie of to-day,
There have been and there yet shall be sorrows
That smite not and bite not in play.
The life and the love thou despisest,
These hurt us indeed, and in vain,
O wise among women, and wisest,
Our Lady of Pain.

Who gave thee thy wisdom? what stories
That stung thee, what visions that smote?
Wert thou pure and a maiden, Dolores,
When desire took thee first by the throat?
What bud was the shell of a blossom
That all men may smell to and pluck?
What milk fed thee first at what bosom?
What sins gave thee suck?

We shift and bedeck and bedrape us,
Thou art noble and nude and antique;
Libitina thy mother, Priapus
Thy father, a Tuscan and Greek.
We play with light loves in the portal,
And wince and relent and refrain;
Loves die, and we know thee immortal,
Our Lady of Pain.

Fruits fail and love dies and time ranges;
Thou art fed with perpetual breath,
And alive after infinite changes,
And fresh from the kisses of death;
Of languors rekindled and rallied,
Of barren delights and unclean,
Things monstrous and fruitless, a pallid
And poisonous queen.

Could you hurt me, sweet lips, though I hurt you?
Men touch them, and change in a trice
The lilies and languors of virtue
For the raptures and roses of vice;
Those lie where thy foot on the floor is,
These crown and caress thee and chain,
O splendid and sterile Dolores,
Our Lady of Pain.

There are sins it may be to discover,
There are deeds it may be to delight.
What new work wilt thou find for thy lover,
What new passions for daytime or night?
What spells that they know not a word of
Whose lives are as leaves overblown?
What tortures undreamt of, unheard of,
Unwritten, unknown?

Ah, beautiful passionate body
That never has ached with a heart!
On thy mouth though the kisses are bloody,
Though they sting till it shudder and smart,
More kind than the love we adore is,
They hurt not the heart or the brain,
O bitter and tender Dolores,
Our Lady of Pain.

As our kisses relax and redouble,
From the lips and the foam and the fangs
Shall no new sin be born for men's trouble,
No dream of impossible pangs?
With the sweet of the sins of old ages
Wilt thou satiate thy soul as of yore?
Too sweet is the rind, say the sages,
Too bitter the core.

Hast thou told all thy secrets the last time,
And bared all thy beauties to one?
Ah, where shall we go then for pastime,
If the worst that can be has been done?
But sweet as the rind was the core is;
We are fain of thee still, we are fain,
O sanguine and subtle Dolores,
Our Lady of Pain.

By the hunger of change and emotion,
By the thirst of unbearable things,
By despair, the twin-born of devotion,
By the pleasure that winces and stings,
The delight that consumes the desire,
The desire that outruns the delight,
By the cruelty deaf as a fire
And blind as the night,

By the ravenous teeth that have smitten
Through the kisses that blossom and bud,
By the lips intertwisted and bitten
Till the foam has a savour of blood,
By the pulse as it rises and falters,
By the hands as they slacken and strain,
I adjure thee, respond from thine altars,
Our Lady of Pain.

Wilt thou smile as a woman disdaining
The light fire in the veins of a boy?
But he comes to thee sad, without feigning,
Who has wearied of sorrow and joy;
Less careful of labour and glory
Than the elders whose hair has uncurled;
And young, but with fancies as hoary
And grey as the world.

I have passed from the outermost portal
To the shrine where a sin is a prayer;
What care though the service be mortal?
O our Lady of Torture, what care?
All thine the last wine that I pour is,
The last in the chalice we drain,
O fierce and luxurious Dolores,
Our Lady of Pain.

All thine the new wine of desire,
The fruit of four lips as they clung
Till the hair and the eyelids took fire,
The foam of a serpentine tongue,
The froth of the serpents of pleasure,
More salt than the foam of the sea,
Now felt as a flame, now at leisure
As wine shed for me.

Ah, thy people, thy children, thy chosen,
Marked cross from the womb and perverse!
They have found out the secret to cozen
The gods that constrain us and curse;
They alone, they are wise, and none other;
Give me place, even me, in their train,
O my sister, my spouse, and my mother,
Our Lady of Pain.

For the crown of our life as it closes
Is darkness, the fruit thereof dust;
No thorns go as deep as a rose's,
And love is more cruel than lust.
Time turns the old days to derision,
Our loves into corpses or wives;
And marriage and death and division
Make barren our lives.

And pale from the past we draw nigh thee,
And satiate with comfortless hours;
And we know thee, how all men belie thee,
And we gather the fruit of thy flowers;
The passion that slays and recovers,
The pangs and the kisses that rain
On the lips and the limbs of thy lovers,
Our Lady of Pain.

The desire of thy furious embraces
Is more than the wisdom of years,
On the blossom though blood lie in traces,
Though the foliage be sodden with tears.
For the lords in whose keeping the door is
That opens on all who draw breath
Gave the cypress to love, my Dolores,
The myrtle to death.

And they laughed, changing hands in the measure,
And they mixed and made peace after strife;
Pain melted in tears, and was pleasure;
Death tingled with blood and was life.
Like lovers they melted and tingled,
In the dusk of thine innermost fane;
In the darkness they murmured and mingled,
Our Lady of Pain.

In a twilight where virtues are vices,
In thy chapels, unknown of the sun,

To a tune that enthralls and entices,
They were wed, and the twain were as one.
For the tune from thine altar hath sounded
Since God bade the world's work begin,
And the fume of thine incense abounded,
To sweeten the sin.

Love listens, and paler than ashes,
Through his curls as the crown on them slips,
Lifts languid wet eyelids and lashes,
And laughs with insatiable lips.
Thou shalt hush him with heavy caresses,
With music that scares the profane;
Thou shalt darken his eyes with thy tresses,
Our Lady of Pain.

Thou shalt bind his bright eyes though he wrestle,
Thou shalt strain his light limbs though he strive;
In his lips all thy serpents shall nestle,
In his hands all thy cruelties thrive.
In the daytime thy voice shall go through him,
In his dreams he shall feel thee and ache;
Thou shalt kindle by night and subdue him
Asleep and awake.

Thou shalt touch and make redder his roses
With juice not of fruit nor of bud;
When the sense in the spirit reposes,
Thou shalt quicken the soul through the blood.
Thine, thine, the one grace we implore is,
Who would live, and not languish or feign,
O sleepless and deadly Dolores,
Our Lady of Pain.

Dost thou dream in a respite of slumber,
In a lull of the fires of thy life,
Of the days without name, without number,
When thy will stung the world into strife;
When, a goddess, the pulse of thy passion
Smote kings as they revelled in Rome;
And they hailed thee re-risen, O Thalassian,
Foam-white from the foam?

When thy lips had such lovers to flatter;
When the city lay red from thy rods,
And thine hands were as arrows to scatter
The children of change and their gods;
When the blood of thy foemen made fervent
A sand never moist from the main,
As one smote them, their lord and thy servant,
Our Lady of Pain.

On sands by the storm never shaken,
Nor wet from the washing of tides;
Nor by foam of the waves overtaken,
Nor winds that the thunder bestrides;
But red from the print of thy paces,
Made smooth for the world and its lords,
Ringed round with a flame of fair faces,
And splendid with swords.

There the gladiator, pale for thy pleasure,
Drew bitter and perilous breath;
There torments laid hold on the treasure
Of limbs too delicious for death;
When thy gardens were lit with live torches;
When the world was a steed for thy rein;
When the nations lay prone in thy porches,
Our Lady of Pain.

When with flame all around him aspirant,
Stood flushed as a harp-player stands,
The implacable beautiful tyrant,
Rose-crowned, having death in his hands;
And a sound as the sound of loud water
Smote far through the flight of the fires,
And mixed with the lightning of slaughter
A thunder of lyres.

Dost thou dream of what was and no more is
The old kingdoms of earth and the kings?
Dost thou hunger for these things, Dolores,
For these, in a world of new things?
But thy bosom no fasts could emaciate,
No hunger compel to complain

Those lips that no bloodshed could satiate,
Our Lady of Pain.

As of old when the world's heart was lighter,
Through thy garments the grace of thee glows,
The white wealth of thy body made whiter
By the blushes of amorous blows,
And seamed with sharp lips and fierce fingers,
And branded by kisses that bruise;
When all shall be gone that now lingers,
Ah, what shall we lose?

Thou wert fair in the fearless old fashion,
And thy limbs are as melodies yet,
And move to the music of passion
With lithe and lascivious regret.
What ailed us, O gods, to desert you
For creeds that refuse and restrain?
Come down and redeem us from virtue,
Our Lady of Pain.

All shrines that were Vestal are flameless,
But the flame has not fallen from this;
Though obscure be the god and though nameless
The eyes and the hair that we kiss;
Low fires that love sits by and forges
Fresh heads for his arrows and thine;
Hair loosened and soiled in mid orgies
With kisses and wine.

Thy skin changes country and colour,
And shrivels or swells to a snake's.
Let it brighten and bloat and grow duller,
We know it, the flames and the flakes,
Red brands on it smitten and bitten,
Round skies where a star is a stain,
And the leaves with thy litanies written
Our Lady of Pain.

On thy bosom though many a kiss be,
There are none such as knew it of old.
Was it Alciphron once or Arisbe,
Male ringlets or feminine gold
That thy lips met with under the statue,
Whence a look shot out sharp after thieves
From the eyes of the garden god at you
Across the fig-leaves?

Then still, through dry seasons and moister,
One god had a wreath to his shrine;
Then love was the pearl of his oyster,
And Venus rose red out of wine.
We have all done amiss, choosing rather
Such loves as the wise gods disdain;
Intercede for us thou with thy father
Our Lady of Pain.

In spring he had crowns of his garden,
Red corn in the heat of the year,
Then hoary green olives that harden
When the grape-blossom freezes with fear;
And milk-budded myrtles with Venus
And vine-leaves with Bacchus he trod;
And ye said, "We have seen, he hath seen us,
A visible god."

What broke off the garlands that girt you?
What sundered you spirit and clay?
Weak sins yet alive are as virtue
To the strength of the sins of that day.
For dried is the blood of thy lover,
Ipsithilla, contracted the vein;
Cry aloud, "Will he rise and recover,
Our Lady of Pain?"

Cry aloud; for the old world is broken.
Cry out; for the Phrygian is priest,
And rears not the bountiful token
And spreads not the fatherly feast.
From the midmost of Ida, from shady
Recesses that murmur at morn,
They have brought and baptized her, Our Lady,
A goddess new-born.

And the chaplets of old are above us,
And the oyster-bed teems out of reach;
Old poets outsing and outlove us,
And Catullus makes mouths at our speech.
Who shall kiss, in thy father's own city,
With such lips as he sang with, again?
Intecede for us all of thy pity,
Our Lady of Pain.

Out of Dindymus heavily laden
Her lions draw bound and unfed
A mother, a mortal, a maiden,
A queen over death and the dead.
She is cold, and her habit is lowly,
Her temple of branches and sods;

Most fruitful and virginal, holy,
A mother of gods.

She hath wasted with fire thine high places,
She hath hidden and marred and made sad
The fair limbs of the Loves, the fair faces
Of gods that were goodly and glad.
She slays, and her hands are not bloody;
She moves as a moon in the wane,
White-robed, and thy raiment is ruddy,
Our Lady of Pain.

They shall pass and their places be taken,
The gods and the priests that are pure.
They shall pass, and shalt thou not be shaken?
They shall perish, and shalt thou endure?
Death laughs, breathing close and relentless
In the nostrils and eyelids of lust,
With a pinch in his fingers of scentless
And delicate dust.

But the worm shall revive thee with kisses;
Thou shalt change and transmute as a god,
As the rod to a serpent that hisses,
As the serpent again to a rod.
Thy life shall not cease though thou doff it;
Thou shalt live until evil be slain,
And good shall die first, said thy phophet,
Our Lady of Pain.

Did he lie? did he laugh? does he know it,
Now he lies out of reach, out of breath,
Thy prophet, thy preacher, thy poet,
Sin's child by incestuous Death?
Did he find out in fire at his waking,
Or discern as his eyelids lost light,
When the bands of the body were breaking
And all came in sight?

Who has known all the evil before us,
Or the tyrannous secrets of time?
Though we match not the dead men that bore us
At a song, at a kiss, at a crime—
Though the heathen outface and outlive us,
And our lives and our longings are twain—
Ah, forgive us our virtues, forgive us,
Our Lady of Pain.

Who are we that embalm and embrace thee
With spices and savours of song?
What is time, that his children should face thee?
What am I, that my lips do thee wrong?
I could hurt thee—but pain would delight thee;
Or caress thee—but love would repel;
And the lovers whose lips would excite thee
Are serpents in hell.

Who now shall content thee as they did,
Thy lovers, when temples were built
And the hair of the sacrifice braided
And the blood of the sacrifice spilt,
In Lampsacus fervent with faces,
In Aphaca red from thy reign,
Who embraced thee with awful embraces,
Our Lady of Pain?

Where are they, Cotytto or Venus,
Astarte or Ashtaroth, where?
Do their hands as we touch come between us?
Is the breath of them hot in thy hair?
From their lips have thy lips taken fever,
With the blood of their bodies grown red?
Hast thou left upon earth a believer
If these men are dead?

They were purple of raiment and golden,
Filled full of thee, fiery with wine,
Thy lovers, in haunts unbeholden,
In marvelous chambers of thine.
They are fled, and their footprints escape us,
Who appraise thee, adore, and abstain,
O daughter of Death and Priapus,
Our Lady of Pain.

What ails us to fear overmeasure,
To praise thee with timorous breath,
O mistress and mother of pleasure,
The one thing as certain as death?
We shall change as the things that we cherish,
Shall fade as they faded before,
As foam upon water shall perish,
As sand upon shore.

We shall know what the darkness discovers,
  If the grave-pit be shallow or deep;
And our fathers of old, and our lovers,
  We shall know if they sleep not or sleep.
We shall see whether hell be not heaven,
  Find out whether tares be not grain,
And the joys of thee seventy times seven,
  Our Lady of Pain.

[1865] [1866]

THE GARDEN OF PROSERPINE

Here, where the world is quiet;
  Here, where all trouble seems
Dead winds' and spent waves' riot
  In doubtful dreams of dreams;
I watch the green field growing
For reaping folk and sowing,
For harvest-time and mowing,
  A sleepy world of streams.

I am tired of tears and laughter,
  And men that laugh and weep;
Of what may come hereafter
  For men that sow to reap:
I am weary of days and hours,
Blown buds of barren flowers,
Desires and dreams and powers
  And everything but sleep.

Here life has death for neighbour,
  And far from eye or ear
Wan waves and wet winds labour,
  Weak ships and spirits steer;
They drive adrift, and whither
They wot not who make thither;
But no such winds blow hither,
  And no such things grow here.

No growth of moor or coppice,
  No heather-flower or vine,
But bloomless buds of poppies,
  Green grapes of Proserpine,
Pale beds of blowing rushes
Where no leaf blooms or blushes
Save this whereout she crushes
  For dead men deadly wine.

Pale, without name or number,
  In fruitless fields of corn,
They bow themselves and slumber
  All night till light is born;
And like a soul belated,
In hell and heaven unmated,
By cloud and mist abated
  Comes out of darkness morn.

Though one were strong as seven,
  He too with death shall dwell,
Nor wake with wings in heaven,
  Nor weep for pains in hell;
Though one were fair as roses,
His beauty clouds and closes;
And well though love reposes,
  In the end it is not well.

Pale, beyond porch and portal,
  Crowned with calm leaves, she stands
Who gathers all things mortal
  With cold immortal hands;
Her languid lips are sweeter
Than love's who fears to greet her
To men that mix and meet her
  From many times and lands.

She waits for each and other,
  She waits for all men born;
Forgets the earth her mother,
  The life of fruits and corn;
And spring and seed and swallow
Take wing for her and follow
Where summer song rings hollow
  And flowers are put to scorn.

There go the loves that wither,
  The old loves with wearier wings;
And all dead years draw thither,
  And all disastrous things;
Dead dreams of days forsaken,
Blind buds that snows have shaken,
Wild leaves that winds have taken
  Red strays of ruined springs.

We are not sure of sorrow,
  And joy was never sure;
To-day will die to-morrow;
  Time stoops to no man's lure;
And love, grown faint and fretful,
With lips but half regretful
Sighs, and with eyes forgetful
  Weeps that no loves endure.

From too much love of living,
  From hope and fear set free,

We thank with brief thanksgiving
Whatever gods may be
That no life lives for ever;
That dead men rise up never;
That even the weariest river
Winds somewhere safe to sea.

Then star nor sun shall waken,
Nor any change of light:
Nor sound of waters shaken,
Nor any sound or sight:
Nor wintry leaves nor vernal,
Nor days nor things diurnal;
Only the sleep eternal
In an eternal night.

[1866]

SAPPHICS

All the night sleep came not upon my eyelids,
Shed not dew, nor shook nor unclosed a feather,
Yet with lips shut close and with eyes of iron
Stood and beheld me.

Then to me so lying awake a vision
Came without sleep over the seas and touched me,
Softly touched mine eyelids and lips; and I too,
Full of the vision,

Saw the white implacable Aphrodite,
Saw the hair unbound and the feet unsandalled
Shine as fire of sunset on western waters;
Saw the reluctant

Feet, the straining plumes of the doves that drew her,
Looking always, looking with necks reverted,
Back to Lesbos, back to the hills whereunder
Shone Mitylene;

Heard the flying feet of the Loves behind her
Make a sudden thunder upon the waters,
As the thunder flung from the strong unclosing
Wings of a great wind.

So the goddess fled from her place, with awful
Sound of feet and thunder of wings around her;
While behind a clamour of singing women
Severed the twilight.

Ah the singing, ah the delight, the passion!
All the Loves wept, listening; sick with anguish,
Stood the crowned nine Muses about Apollo;
Fear was upon them,

While the tenth sang wonderful things they knew not.
Ah the tenth, the Lesbian! the nine were silent,
None endured the sound of her song for weeping;
Laurel by laurel,

Faded all their crowns; but about her forehead,
Round her woven tresses and ashen temples
White as dead snow, paler than grass in summer,
Ravaged with kisses,

Shone a light of fire as a crown for ever.
Yea, almost the implacable Aphrodite
Paused, and almost wept; such a song was that song.
Yea, by her name too

Called her, saying, "Turn to me, O my Sappho;"
Yet she turned her face from the Loves, she saw not
Tears for laughter darken immortal eyelids,
Heard not about her

Fearful fitful wings of the doves departing,
Saw not how the bosom of Aphrodite
Shook with weeping, saw not her shaken raiment,
Saw not her hands wrung;

Saw the Lesbians kissing across their smitten
Lutes with lips more sweet than the sound of lute-strings,
Mouth to mouth and hand upon hand, her chosen,
Fairer than all men;

Only saw the beautiful lips and fingers,
Full of songs and kisses and little whispers,
Full of music; only beheld among them
Soar, as a bird soars

Newly fledged, her visible song, a marvel,
Made of perfect sound and exceeding passion,
Sweetly shapen, terrible, full of thunders,
Clothed with the wind's wings.

Then rejoiced she, laughing with love, and scattered
Roses, awful roses of holy blossom;
Then the Loves thronged sadly with hidden faces
Round Aphrodite,

Then the Muses, stricken at heart, were silent;
Yea, the gods waxed pale; such a song was that song.
All reluctant, all with a fresh repulsion,
Fled from before her.

All withdrew long since, and the land was barren,
Full of fruitless women and music only.
Now perchance, when winds are assuaged at sunset,
Lulled at the dewfall,

By the grey sea-side, unassuaged, unheardof,
Unbeloved, unseen in the ebb of twilight,
Ghosts of outcast women return lamenting,
Purged not in Lethe,

Clothed about with flame and with tears, and singing
Songs that move the heart of the shaken heaven,
Songs that break the heart of the earth with pity,
Hearing, to hear them.

[1866]

PRELUDE TO SONGS BEFORE SUNRISE

Between the green bud and the red
Youth sat and sang by Time, and shed
From eyes and tresses flowers and tears,
From heart and spirit hopes and fears,
Upon the hollow stream whose bed
Is channeled by the foamless years;
And with the white the gold-haired head
Mixed running locks, and in Time's ears
Youth's dreams hung singing, and Time's truth
Was half not harsh in the ears of Youth.

Between the bud and the blown flower
Youth talked with joy and grief an hour,
With footless joy and wingless grief
And twin-born faith and disbelief
Who share the seasons to devour;
And long ere these made up their sheaf
Felt the winds round him shake and shower
The rose-red and the blood-red leaf,
Delight whose germ never grew grain,
And passion dyed in its own pain.

Then he stood up and trod to dust
Fear and desire, mistrust and trust,
And dreams of bitter sleep and sweet,
And bound for sandals on his feet
Knowledge and patience of what must
And what things may be, in the heat
And cold of years that rot and rust
And alter; and his spirit's meat
Was freedom, and his staff was wrought
Of strength, and his cloak woven of thought.

For what has he whose will sees clear
To do with doubt and faith and fear,
Swift hopes and slow despondencies?
His heart is equal with the sea's
And with the sea-wind's, and his ear
Is level to the speech of these,
And his soul communes and takes cheer
With the actual earth's equalities,
Air, light, and night, hills, winds, and streams,
And seeks not strength from strengthless dreams.

His soul is even with the sun
Whose spirit and whose eyes are one,
Who seeks not stars by day nor light
And heavy heat of day by night.
Him can no God cast down, whom none
Can lift in hope beyond the height
Of fate and nature and things done
By the calm rule of might and right
That bids men be and bear and do,
And die beneath blind skies or blue.

To him the lights of even and morn
Speak no vain things of love or scorn,
  Fancies and passions miscreate
  By man in things dispassionate.
Nor holds he fellowship forlorn
  With souls that pray and hope and hate,
And doubt they had better not been born,
  And fain would lure or scare off fate
And charm their doomsman from their doom
And make fear dig its own false tomb.

He builds not half of doubts and half
Of dreams his own soul's cenotaph
  Whence hopes and fears with helpless eyes,
  Wrapped loose in cast-off cerecloths, rise
And dance and wring their hands and laugh,
  And weep thin tears and sigh light sighs,
And without living lips would quaff
  The living spring in man that lies,
And drain his soul of faith and strength
It might have lived on a life's length.

He hath given himself and hath not sold
To God for heaven or man for gold,
  Or grief for comfort that it gives,
  Or joy for grief's restoratives,
He hath given himself to time, whose fold
  Shuts in the mortal flock that lives
On its plain pasture's heat and cold
  And the equal year's alternatives.
Earth, heaven, and time, death, life, and he,
Endure while they shall be to be.

"Yet between death and life are hours
To flush with love and hide in flowers;
  What profit save in these?" men cry:
  "Ah, see, between soft earth and sky,
What only good things here are ours!"
  They say, "what better wouldst thou try,
What sweeter sing of? or what powers
  Serve, that will give thee ere thou die
More joy to sing and be less sad,
More heart to play and grow more glad?"

Play then and sing; we too have played,
We likewise, in that subtle shade.
  We too have twisted through our hair
  Such tendrils as the wild Loves wear,
And heard what mirth the Mænads made,
  Till the wind blew our garlands bare
And left their roses disarrayed,
  And smote the summer with strange air,
And disengirdled and discrowned
The limbs and locks that vine-wreaths bound.

We too have tracked by star-proof trees
The tempest of the Thyiades
  Scare the loud night on hills that hid
  The blood-feasts of the Bassarid,
Heard their song's iron cadences
  Fright the wolf hungering from the kid,
Outroar the lion-throated seas,
  Outchide the north-wind if it chid,
And hush the torrent-tongued ravines
With thunders of their tambourines.

But the fierce flute whose notes acclaim
Dim goddesses of fiery fame,
  Cymbal and clamorous kettledrum,
  Timbrels and tabrets, all are dumb
That turned the high chill air to flame;
  The singing tongues of fire are numb
That called on Cotys by her name
  Edonian, till they felt her come
And maddened, and her mystic face
Lightened along the streams of Thrace.

For Pleasure slumberless and pale,
And Passion with rejected veil,
  Pass, and the tempest-footed throng
  Of hours that follow them with song
Till their feet flag and voices fail,
  And lips that were so loud so long
Learn silence, or a wearier wail;
  So keen is change, and time so strong,
To weave the robes of life and rend
And weave again till life have end.

But weak is change, but strengthless time,
To take the light from heaven or climb
  The hills of heaven with wasting feet.
  Songs they can stop that earth found meet,
But the stars keep their ageless rime;
  Flowers they can slay that spring thought sweet,
But the stars keep their spring sublime;
  Passions and pleasures can defeat,
Actions and agonies control,
And life and death, but not the soul.

Because man's soul is man's God still,
What wind soever waft his will
Across the waves of day and night
To port or shipwreck, left or right,
By shores and shoals of good and ill;
And still its flame at mainmast height
Through the rent air that foam-flakes fill
Sustains the indomitable light
Whence only man hath strength to steer
Or helm to handle without fear.

Save his own soul's light overhead,
None leads him, and none ever led,
Across birth's hidden harbour-bar,
Past youth where shoreward shallows are,
Through age that drives on toward the red
Vast void of sunset hailed from far,
To the equal waters of the dead;
Save his own soul he hath no star,
And sinks, except his own soul guide,
Helmless in middle turn of tide.

No blast of air or fire of sun
Puts out the light whereby we run
With girded loins our lamplit race,
And each from each takes heart of grace
And spirit till his turn be done,
And light of face from each man's face
In whom the light of trust is one;
Since only souls that keep their place
By their own light, and watch things roll,
And stand, have light for any soul.

A little time we gain from time
To set our seasons in some chime,
For harsh or sweet or loud or low,
With seasons played out long ago
And souls that in their time and prime
Took part with summer or with snow,
Lived abject lives out or sublime,
And had their chance of seed to sow
For service or disservice done
To those days dead and this their son.

A little time that we may fill
Or with such good works or such ill
As loose the bonds or make them strong
Wherein all manhood suffers wrong,
By rose-hung river and light-foot rill
There are who rest not; who think long
Till they discern as from a hill
At the sun's hour of morning song,
Known of souls only, and those souls free,
The sacred spaces of the sea.

[1871]

SUPER FLUMINA BABYLONIS

By the waters of Babylon we sat down and wept,
Remembering thee,
That for ages of agony hast endured and slept,
And wouldst not see.

By the waters of Babylon we stood up and sang,
Considering thee,
That a blast of deliverance in the darkness rang,
To set thee free.

And with trumpets and thunderings and with morning song
Came up the light;
And thy spirit uplifted thee to forget thy wrong
As day doth night.

And thy sons were dejected not any more, as then
When thou wast shamed;
When thy lovers went heavily without heart, as men
Whose life was maimed.

In the desolate distances, with a great desire
For thy love's sake,

With our hearts going back to thee, they were filled with fire,
Were nigh to break.

It was said to us: "Verily ye are great of heart,
But ye shall bend;
Ye are bondmen and bondwomen, to be scourged and smart,
To toil and tend."

And with harrows men harrowed us, and subdued with spears,
And crushed with shame;
And the summer and winter was, and the length of years,
And no change came.

By the rivers of Italy, by the dry streams' beds,
By town, by tower,
There was feasting with revelling, there was sleep with dreams,
Until thine hour.

And they slept and they rioted on their rose-hung beds,
With mouths on flame,
And with love-locks vine-chapleted, and with rose-crowned heads
And robes of shame.

And they knew not their forefathers, nor the hills and streams
And words of power,
Nor the gods that were good to them, but with songs and dreams
Filled up their hour.

By the rivers of Italy, by the dry streams' beds,
When thy time came,
There was casting of crowns from them, from their young men's heads,
The crowns of shame.

By the horn of Eridanus, by the Tiber mouth,
As the day rose,
They arose up and girded them to the north and south,
By seas, by snows.

As a water in January the frost confines,
Thy kings bound thee;
As a water in April is, in the new-blown vines,
Thy sons made free.

And thy lovers that looked for thee, and that mourned from far,
For thy sake dead,
We rejoiced in the light of thee, in the signal star
Above thine head.

In thy grief had we followed thee, in thy passion loved,
Loved in thy loss;
In thy shame we stood fast to thee, with thy pangs were moved,
Clung to thy cross.

By the hillside of Calvary we beheld thy blood,
Thy bloodred tears,

As a mother's in bitterness, an unebbing flood,
    Years upon years.

And the north was Gethsemane, without leaf or bloom,
    A garden sealed;
And the south was Aceldama, for a sanguine fume
    Hid all the field.

By the stone of the sepulchre we returned to weep,
    From far, from prison;
And the guards by it keeping it we beheld asleep,
    But thou wast risen.

And an angel's similitude by the unsealed grave,
    And by the stone:
And the voice was angelical, to whose words God gave
    Strength like his own.

"Lo, the graveclothes of Italy that are folded up
    In the grave's gloom!
And the guards as men wrought upon with a charmèd cup,
    By the open tomb.

"And her body most beautiful, and her shining head,
    These are not here;
For your mother, for Italy, is not surely dead:
    Have ye no fear.

"As of old time she spake to you, and you hardly heard,
    Hardly took heed,
So now also she saith to you, yet another word,
    Who is risen indeed.

"By my saying she saith to you, in your ears she saith,
    Who hear these things,
Put no trust in men's royalties, nor in great men's breath,
    Nor words of kings.

"For the life of them vanishes and is no more seen,
    Nor no more known;
Nor shall any remember him if a crown hath been,
    Or where a throne.

"Unto each man his handiwork, unto each his crown,
    The just Fate gives;
Whoso takes the world's life on him and his own lays down,
    He, dying so, lives.

"Whoso bears the whole heaviness of the wronged world's weight
    And puts it by,
It is well with him suffering, though he face man's fate;
    How should he die?

"Seeing death has no part in him any more, no power
    Upon his head;

He has bought his eternity with a little hour,
And is not dead.

"For an hour, if ye look for him, he is no more found,
For one hour's space;
Then lift ye up your eyes to him and behold him crowned,
A deathless face

"On the mountains of memory, by the world's well-springs,
In all men's eyes,
Where the light of the life of him is on all past things,
Death only dies.

"Not the light that was quenched for us, nor the deeds that were,
Nor the ancient days,
Nor the sorrows not sorrowful, nor the face most fair
Of perfect praise."

So the angel of Italy's resurrection said,
So yet he saith;
So the son of her suffering, that from breasts nigh dead
Drew life, not death.

That the pavement of Golgotha should be white as snow,
Not red but white;
That the waters of Babylon should no longer flow,
And men see light.

[1869] [1871]

HERTHA

I am that which began;
Out of me the years roll;
Out of me God and man;
I am equal and whole;
God changes, and man, and the form of them bodily; I am the soul.

Before ever land was,
Before ever the sea,
Or soft hair of the grass,
Or fair limbs of the tree,
Or the flesh-coloured fruit of my branches, I was, and thy soul was in me.

First life on my sources
First drifted and swam;
Out of me are the forces
That save it or damn;
Out of me man and woman, and wild-beast and bird; before God was, I am.

Beside or above me
Nought is there to go;
Love or unlove me,
Unknow me or know,
I am that which unloves me and loves; I am stricken, and I am the blow.

I the mark that is missed
And the arrows that miss,
I the mouth that is kissed
And the breath in the kiss,
The search, and the sought, and the seeker, the soul and the body that is.

I am that thing which blesses
My spirit elate;
That which caresses
With hands uncreate
My limbs unbegotten that measure the length of the measure of fate.

But what thing dost thou now,
Looking Godward, to cry
"I am I, thou art thou,
I am low, thou art high"?
I am thou, whom thou seekest to find him; find thou but thyself, thou art I.

I the grain and the furrow,
The plough-cloven clod
And the ploughshare drawn thorough,
The germ and the sod,
The deed and the doer, the seed and the sower, the dust which is God.

Hast thou known how I fashioned thee,
Child, underground?
Fire that impassioned thee,
Iron that bound,
Dim changes of water, what thing of all these hast thou known of or found?

Canst thou say in thine heart
Thou hast seen with thine eyes
With what cunning of art
Thou wast wrought in what wise,
By what force of what stuff thou wast shapen, and shown on my breast to the skies?

Who hath given, who hath sold it thee,
Knowledge of me?
Hath the wilderness told it thee?
Hast thou learnt of the sea?
Hast thou communed in spirit with night? have the winds taken counsel with thee?

Have I set such a star
To show light on thy brow
That thou sawest from afar
What I show to thee now?
Have ye spoken as brethren together, the sun and the mountains and thou?

What is here, dost thou know it?
What was, hast thou known?
Prophet nor poet
Nor tripod nor throne
Nor spirit nor flesh can make answer, but only thy mother alone.

Mother, not maker,
Born, and not made;
Though her children forsake her,
Allured or afraid,
Praying prayers to the God of their fashion, she stirs not for all that have prayed.

A creed is a rod,
And a crown is of night;
But this thing is God,
To be man with thy might,
To grow straight in the strength of thy spirit, and live out thy life as the light.

I am in thee to save thee,
As my soul in thee saith;
Give thou as I gave thee,
Thy life-blood and breath,
Green leaves of thy labour, white flowers of thy thought, and red fruit of thy death.

Be the ways of thy giving
As mine were to thee;
The free life of thy living,
Be the gift of it free;
Not as servant to lord, nor as master to slave, shalt thou give thee to me.

O children of banishment,
Souls overcast,
Were the lights ye see vanish meant
Alway to last,
Ye would know not the sun overshining the shadows and stars overpast.

I that saw where ye trod
The dim paths of the night
Set the shadow called God
In your skies to give light;
But the morning of manhood is risen, and the shadowless soul is in sight.

The tree many-rooted
That swells to the sky
With frondage red-fruited,
The life-tree am I;
In the buds of your lives is the sap of my leaves: ye shall live and not die.

But the Gods of your fashion
That take and that give
In their pity and passion
That scourge and forgive,
They are worms that are bred in the bark that falls off; they shall die and not live.

My own blood is what stanches
The wounds in my bark;
Stars caught in my branches
Make day of the dark,
And are worshipped as suns till the sunrise shall tread out their fires as a spark.

Where dead ages hide under
The live roots of the tree,
In my darkness the thunder
Makes utterance of me;
In the clash of my boughs with each other ye hear the waves sound of the sea.

That noise is of Time,
As his feathers are spread
And his feet set to climb
Through the boughs overhead,
And my foliage rings round him and rustles, and branches are bent with his tread.

The storm-winds of ages
Blow through me and cease,
The war-wind that rages,
The spring-wind of peace,
Ere the breath of them roughen my tresses, ere one of my blossoms increase.

All sounds of all changes,
All shadows and lights
On the world's mountain-ranges
And stream-riven heights,
Whose tongue is the wind's tongue and language of storm-clouds on earth-shaking nights;

All forms of all faces,
All works of all hands
In unsearchable places
Of time-stricken lands,
All death and all life, and all reigns and all ruins, drop through me as sands.

Though sore be my burden
And more than ye know,
And my growth have no guerdon
But only to grow,
Yet I fail not of growing for lightnings above me or deathworms below.

These too have their part in me,
As I too in these;
Such fire is at heart in me,
Such sap is this tree's,
Which hath in it all sounds and all secrets of infinite lands and of seas.

In the spring-coloured hours
When my mind was as May's,
There brake forth of me flowers
By centuries of days,
Strong blossoms with perfume of manhood, shot out from my spirit as rays.

And the sound of them springing
And smell of their shoots
Were as warmth and sweet singing
And strength to my roots;
And the lives of my children made perfect with freedom of soul were my fruits.

I bid you but be;
  I have need not of prayer;
I have need of you free
  As your mouths of mine air;
That my heart may be greater within me, beholding the fruits of me fair.

More fair than strange fruit is
  Of faiths ye espouse;
In me only the root is
  That blooms in your boughs;
Behold now your God that ye made you, to feed him with faith of your vows.

In the darkening and whitening
  Abysses adored,
With dayspring and lightning
  For lamp and for sword,
God thunders in heaven, and his angels are red with the wrath of the Lord.

O my sons, O too dutiful
  Towards Gods not of me,
Was not I enough beautiful?
  Was it hard to be free?
For behold, I am with you, am in you and of you; look forth now and see.

Lo, winged with world's wonders,
  With miracles shod,
With the fires of his thunders
  For raiment and rod,
God trembles in heaven, and his angels are white with the terror of God.

For his twilight is come on him,
  His anguish is here;
And his spirits gaze dumb on him,
  Grown grey from his fear;
And his hour taketh hold on him stricken, the last of his infinite year.

Thought made him and breaks him,
  Truth slays and forgives;
But to you, as time takes him,
  This new thing it gives,
Even love, the beloved Republic, that feeds upon freedom and lives.

For truth only is living,
  Truth only is whole,
And the love of his giving
  Man's polestar and pole;
Man, pulse of my centre, and fruit of my body, and seed of my soul.

One birth of my bosom;
  One beam of mine eye;
One topmost blossom
  That scales the sky;
Man, equal and one with me, man that is made of me, man that is I.

[1871]

TO WALT WHITMAN IN AMERICA

Send but a song oversea for us,
Heart of their hearts who are free,
Heart of their singer, to be for us
More than our singing can be;
Ours, in the tempest at error,
With no light but the twilight of terror;
Send us a song oversea!

Sweet-smelling of pine leaves and grasses,
And blown as a tree through and through
With the winds of the keen mountain-passes,
And tender as sun-smitten dew;
Sharp-tongued as the winter that shakes
The wastes of your limitless lakes,
Wide-eyed as the sea-line's blue.

O strong-winged soul with prophetic
Lips hot with the bloodbeats of song,
With tremor of heartstrings magnetic,
With thoughts as thunders in throng,
With consonant ardours of chords
That pierce men's souls as with swords
And hale them hearing along.

Make us, too, music, to be with us
As a word from a world's heart warm,
To sail the dark as a sea with us,
Full-sailed, outsinging the storm,
A song to put fire in our ears
Whose burning shall burn up tears,
Whose sign bid battle reform;

A note in the ranks of a clarion,
A word in the wind of cheer,
To consume as with lightning the carrion
That makes time foul for us here;
In the air that our dead things infest
A blast of the breath of the west,
Till east way as west way is clear.

Out of the sun beyond sunset,
From the evening whence morning shall be,
With the rollers in measureless onset,
With the van of the storming sea,
With the world-wide wind, with the breath
That breaks ships driven upon death,
With the passion of all things free,
With the sea-steeds footless and frantic,
White myriads for death to bestride
In the charge of the ruining Atlantic
Where deaths by regiments ride,
With clouds and clamours of waters,
With a long note shriller than slaughter's
On the furrowless fields world-wide,

With terror, with ardour and wonder,
With the soul of the season that wakes
When the weight of a whole year's thunder
In the tidestream of autumn breaks,
Let the flight of the wide-winged word
Come over, come in and be heard,
Take form and fire for our sakes.

For a continent bloodless with travail
Here toils and brawls as it can,
And the web of it who shall unravel
Of all that peer on the plan;
Would fain grow men, but they grow not,
And fain be free, but they know not
One name for freedom and man?

One name, not twain for division;
One thing, not twain, from the birth;
Spirit and substance and vision,
Worth more than worship is worth;
Unbeheld, unadored, undivined,
The cause, the centre, the mind,
The secret and sense of the earth.

Here as a weakling in irons,
Here as a weanling in bands,
As a prey that the stake-net environs,
Our life that we looked for stands;
And the man-child naked and dear,
Democracy, turns on us here
Eyes trembling with tremulous hands.

It sees not what season shall bring to it
Sweet fruit of its bitter desire;
Few voices it hears yet sing to it,
Few pulses of hearts reaspire;
Foresees not time, nor forehears
The noises of imminent years,
Earthquake, and thunder, and fire:

When crowned and weaponed and curbless
It shall walk without helm or shield
The bare burnt furrows and herbless
Of war's last flame-stricken field,
Till godlike, equal with time,

It stand in the sun sublime,
  In the godhead of man revealed.

Round your people and over them
  Light like raiment is drawn,
Close as a garment to cover them
  Wrought not of mail nor of lawn;
Here, with hope hardly to wear,
Naked nations and bare
  Swim, sing, strike out for the dawn.

Chains are here, and a prison,
  Kings, and subjects, and shame.
If the God upon you be arisen,
  How should our songs be the same?
How, in confusion of change,
How shall we sing, in a strange
  Land, songs praising his name?

God is buried and dead to us,
  Even the spirit of earth,
Freedom; so have they said to us,
  Some with mocking and mirth,
Some with heartbreak and tears;
And a God without eyes, without ears,
  Who shall sing of him, dead in the birth?

The earth-god Freedom, the lonely
  Face lightening, the footprint unshod,
Not as one man crucified only
  Nor scourged with but one life's rod;
The soul that is substance of nations,
Reincarnate with fresh generations;
  The great god Man, which is God.

But in weariest of years and obscurest
  Doth it live not at heart of all things,
The one God and one spirit, a purest
  Life, fed from unstanchable springs?
Within love, within hatred it is,
And its seed in the stripe as the kiss,
  And in slaves is the germ, and in kings.

Freedom we call it, for holier
  Name of the soul's there is none;
Surelier its labours, if slowlier,
  Than the metres of star or of sun;
Slowlier than life unto breath,
Surelier than time unto death,
  It moves till its labour be done.

Till the motion be done and the measure
  Circling through season and clime.
Slumber and sorrow and pleasure,
  Vision of virtue and crime;
Till consummate with conquering eyes,
A soul disembodied, it rise
  From the body transfigured of time.

Till it rise and remain and take station
  With the stars of the worlds that rejoice;
Till the voice of its heart's exultation
  Be as theirs an invariable voice;
By no discord of evil estranged,
By no pause, by no breach in it changed,
  By no clash in the chord of its choice.

It is one with the world's generations,
  With the spirit, the star, and the sod;
With the kingless and king-stricken nations,
  With the cross, and the chain, and the
      rod;
The most high, the most secret, most lonely,
The earth-soul Freedom, that only
  Lives, and that only is God.

[1870] [1871]

SIENA

Inside this northern summer's fold
The fields are full of naked gold,
Broadcast from heaven on lands it loves;
The green veiled air is full of doves;
Soft leaves that sift the sunbeams let
Light on the small warm grasses wet
Fall in short broken kisses sweet,
And break again like waves that beat
Round the sun's feet.

But I, for all this English mirth
Of golden-shod and dancing days,
And the old green-girt sweet-hearted earth,
Desire what here no spells can raise.
Far hence, with holier heavens above,
The lovely city of my love
Bathes deep in the sun-satiate air
That flows round no fair thing more fair
Her beauty bare.

There the utter sky is holier, there
More pure the intense white height of air,
More clear men's eyes that mine would
  meet,
And the sweet springs of things more sweet.
There for this one warm note of doves
A clamour of a thousand loves

Storms the night's ear, the day's assails,
From the tempestuous nightingales,
And fills, and fails.

O gracious city well-beloved,
Italian, and a maiden crowned,
Siena, my feet are no more moved
Toward thy strange-shapen mountain-bound:
But my heart in me turns and moves,
O lady loveliest of my loves,
Toward thee, to lie before thy feet
And gaze from thy fair fountain-seat
Up the sheer street;

And the house midway hanging see
That saw Saint Catherine bodily,
Felt on its floors her sweet feet move,
And the live light of fiery love
Burn from her beautiful strange face,
As in the sanguine sacred place
Where in pure hands she took the head
Severed, and with pure lips still red
Kissed the lips dead.

For years through, sweetest of the saints,
In quiet without cease she wrought,
Till cries of men and fierce complaints
From outward moved her maiden thought;
And prayers she heard and sighs toward France,
"God, send us back deliverance,
Send back thy servant, lest we die!"
With an exceeding bitter cry
They smote the sky.

Then in her sacred saving hands
She took the sorrows of the lands,
With maiden palms she lifted up
The sick time's blood-embittered cup
And in her virgin garment furled
The faint limbs of a wounded world.
Clothed with calm love and clear desire,
She went forth in her soul's attire,
A missive fire.

Across the might of men that strove
It shone, and over heads of kings;
And molten in red flames of love
Were swords and many monstrous things;
And shields were lowered, and snapt were spears,
And sweeter-tuned the clamorous years;
And faith came back, and peace, that were
Fled; for she bade, saying, "Thou, God's heir,
Hast thou no care?

"Lo, men lay waste thine heritage
Still, and much heathen people rage
Against thee, and devise vain things.
What comfort in the face of kings,
What counsel is there? Turn thine eyes
And thine heart from them in like wise;
Turn thee unto thine holy place
To help us that of God for grace
Require thy face.

"For who shall hear us if not thou
In a strange land? what doest thou there?
Thy sheep are spoiled, and the ploughers plough
Upon us; why hast thou no care
For all this, and beyond strange hills
Liest unregardful what snow chills
Thy foldless flock, or what rains beat?
Lo, in thine ears, before thy feet,
Thy lost sheep bleat.

"And strange men feed on faultless lives,
And there is blood, and men put knives,
Shepherd, unto the young lamb's throat;
And one hath eaten, and one smote,
And one had hunger and is fed
Full of the flesh of these, and red
With blood of these as who drinks wine
And God knoweth, who hath sent thee a sign,
If these were thine."

But the Pope's heart within him burned,
So that he rose up, seeing the sign,
And came among them; but she turned
Back to her daily way divine,
And fed her faith with silent things,
And lived her life with curbed white wings,
And mixed herself with heaven and died:
And now on the sheer city-side
Smiles like a bride.

You see her in the fresh clear gloom,
Where walls shut out the flame and bloom
Of full-breathed summer, and the roof
Keeps the keen ardent air aloof
And sweet weight of the violent sky:
There bodily beheld on high,
She seems as one hearing in tune

Heaven within heaven, at heaven's full noon,
In sacred swoon:

A solemn swoon of sense that aches
With imminent blind heat of heaven,
While all the wide-eyed spirit wakes,
Vigilant of the supreme Seven,
Whose choral flames in God's sight move,
Made unendurable with love,
That without wind or blast of breath
Compels all things through life and death
Whither God saith.

There on the dim side-chapel wall
Thy mighty touch memorial,
Razzi, raised up, for ages dead,
And fixed for us her heavenly head:
And, rent with plaited thorn and rod,
Bared the live likeness of her God
To men's eyes turning from strange lands,
Where, pale from thine immortal hands,
Christ wounded stands;

And the blood blots his holy hair
And white brows over hungering eyes
That plead against us, and the fair
Mute lips forlorn of words or sighs
In the great torment that bends down
His bruised head with the bloomless crown,
White as the unfruitful thorn-flower,
A God beheld in dreams that were
Beheld of her.

In vain on all these sins and years
Falls the sad blood, fall the slow tears;
In vain poured forth as watersprings,
Priests, on your altars, and ye, kings,
About your seats of sanguine gold;
Still your God, spat upon and sold,
Bleeds at your hands; but now is gone
All his flock from him saving one;
Judas alone.

Surely your race it was that he,
O men signed backward with his name,
Beholding in Gethsemane
Bled the red bitter sweat of shame,
Knowing how the word of Christian should
Mean to men evil and not good,
Seem to men shameful for your sake,
Whose lips, for all the prayers they make,
Man's blood must slake.

But blood nor tears ye love not, you
That my love leads my longing to,
Fair as the world's old faith of flowers,
O golden goddesses of ours!
From what Idalian rose-pleasance
Hath Aphrodite bidden glance
The lovelier lightnings of your feet?
From what sweet Paphian sward or seat
Led you more sweet?

O white three sisters, three as one,
With flowerlike arms for flowery bands
Your linked limbs glitter like the sun,
And time lies beaten at your hands.
Time and wild years and wars and men
Pass, and ye care not whence or when;
With calm lips over sweet for scorn,
Ye watch night pass, O children born
Of the old-world morn.

Ah, in this strange and shrineless place,
What doth a goddess, what a Grace,
Where no Greek worships her shrined limbs
With wreaths and Cytherean hymns?
Where no lute makes luxurious
The adoring airs in Amathus,
Till the maid, knowing her mother near,
Sobs with love, aching with sweet fear?
What do ye here?

For the outer land is sad, and wears
A raiment of a flaming fire;
And the fierce fruitless mountain stairs
Climb, yet seem wroth and loth to aspire,
Climb, and break, and are broken down,
And through their clefts and crests the town
Looks west and sees the dead sun lie,
In sanguine death that stains the sky
With angry dye.

And from the war-worn wastes without
In twilight, in the time of doubt,
One sound comes of one whisper, where
Moved with low motions of slow air
The great trees nigh the castle swing
In the sad coloured evening;
"*Ricorditi di me, che son*
La Pia" [1]—that small sweet word alone
Is not yet gone.

[1] Remember me, who am Pia.

"Ricorditi di me"—the sound
  Sole out of deep dumb days remote
Across the fiery and fatal ground
  Comes tender as a hurt bird's note
To where, a ghost with empty hands,
A woe-worn ghost, her palace stands
In the mid city, where the strong
Bells turn the sunset air to song,
And the towers throng.

With other face, with speech the same,
A mightier maiden's likeness came
Late among mourning men that slept,
A sacred ghost that went and wept,
White as the passion-wounded Lamb,
Saying, "Ah, remember me, that am
Italia." (From deep sea to sea
Earth heard, earth knew her, that this was
  she.)
"Ricorditi.

"Love made me of all things fairest thing,
  And Hate unmade me; this knows he
Who with God's sacerdotal ring
  Enringed mine hand, espousing me."
Yea, in thy myriad-mooded woe,
Yea, Mother, hast thou not said so?
Have not our hearts within us stirred,
O thou most holiest, at thy word?
Have we not heard?

As this dead tragic land that she
Found deadly, such was time to thee;
Years passed thee withering in the red
Maremma, years that deemed thee dead,
Ages that sorrowed or that scorned;
And all this while though all they mourned
Thou sawest the end of things unclean,
And the unborn that should see thee a
  queen.
Have we not seen?

The weary poet, thy sad son,
  Upon thy soil, under thy skies,
Saw all Italian things save one—
  Italia; this thing missed his eyes;
The old mother-might, the breast, the face,
That reared, that lit the Roman race;
This not Leopardi saw; but we,
What is it, Mother, that we see,
What if not thee?

Look thou from Siena southward home,
Where the priest's pall hangs rent on Rome,
And through the red rent swaddling-bands
Towards thine she strains her labouring
  hands.
Look thou and listen, and let be
All the dead quick, all the bond free;
In the blind eyes let there be sight;
In the eighteen centuries of the night
Let there be light.

Bow down the beauty of thine head,
  Sweet, and with lips of living breath
Kiss thy sons sleeping and thy dead,
  That there be no more sleep or death.
Give us thy light, thy might, thy love,
Whom thy face seen afar above
Drew to thy feet; and when, being free,
Thou hast blest thy children born to thee,
Bless also me.

Me that when others played or slept
Sat still under thy cross and wept;
Me who so early and unaware
Felt fall on bent bared brows and hair
(Thin drops of the overflowing flood!)
The bitter blessing of thy blood;
The sacred shadow of thy pain,
Thine, the true maiden-mother, slain
And raised again.

Me consecrated, if I might,
  To praise thee, or to love at least,
O mother of all men's dear delight,
  Thou madest a choral-souled boy-priest,
Before my lips had leave to sing,
Or my hands hardly strength to cling
About the intolerable tree
Whereto they had nailed my heart and thee
And said, "Let be."

For to thee too the high Fates gave
Grace to be sacrificed and save,
That being arisen, in the equal sun,
God and the People should be one;
By those red roads thy footprints trod,
Man more divine, more human God,
Saviour; that where no light was known
But darkness, and a daytime flown,
Light should be shown.

Let there be light, O Italy!
  For our feet falter in the night.
O lamp of living years to be,
  O light of God, let there be light!
Fill with a love keener than flame

Men sealed in spirit with thy name,
The cities and the Roman skies,
Where men with other than man's eyes
Saw thy sun rise.

For theirs thou wast and thine were they
Whose names outshine thy very day;
For they are thine and theirs thou art
Whose blood beats living in man's heart,
Remembering ages fled and dead
Wherein for thy sake these men bled;
They that saw Trebia, they that see
Mentana, they in years to be
That shall see thee.

For thine are all of us, and ours
Thou; till the seasons bring to birth
A perfect people, and all the powers
Be with them that bear fruit on earth;
Till the inner heart of man be one
With freedom, and the sovereign sun;
And Time, in likeness of a guide,
Lead the Republic as a bride
Up to God's side.

[1868]

COR CORDIUM[1]

O heart of hearts, the chalice of love's fire,
Hid round with flowers and all the bounty of bloom;
O wonderful and perfect heart, for whom
The lyrist liberty made life a lyre;
O heavenly heart, at whose most dear desire
Dead love, living and singing, cleft his tomb,
And with him risen and regent in death's room
All day thy choral pulses rang full choir;
O heart whose beating blood was running song,
O sole thing sweeter than thine own songs were,
Help us for thy free love's sake to be free,
True for thy truth's sake, for thy strength's sake strong,
Till very liberty make clean and fair
The nursing earth as the sepulchral sea.

[1869] [1871]

[1] Heart of hearts.

MESSIDOR

Put in the sickles and reap;
For the morning of harvest is red,
And the long large ranks of the corn
Coloured and clothed as the morn
Stand thick in the fields and deep
For them that faint to be fed.
Let all that hunger and weep
Come hither, and who would have bread
Put in the sickles and reap.

Coloured and clothed as the morn
The grain grows ruddier than gold,
And the good strong sun is alight
In the mists of the day-dawn white,
And the crescent, a faint sharp horn,
In the fear of his face turns cold
As the snakes of the night-time that creep
From the flag of our faith unrolled.
Put in the sickles and reap.

In the mists of the day-dawn white
That roll round the morning star,
The large flame lightens and grows
Till the red-gold harvest-rows,
Full-grown, are full of the light
As the spirits of strong men are,
Crying, Who shall slumber or sleep?
Who put back morning or mar?
Put in the sickles and reap.

Till the red-gold harvest-rows
For miles through shudder and shine
In the wind's breath, fed with the sun,
A thousand spear-heads as one
Bowed as for battle to close
Line in rank against line
With place and station to keep
Till all men's hands at a sign
Put in the sickles and reap.

A thousand spear-heads as one
Wave as with swing of the sea
When the mid tide sways at its height
For the hour is for harvest or fight
In face of the just calm sun,
As the signal in season may be
And the lot in the helm may leap
When chance shall shake it; but ye,
Put in the sickles and reap.

For the hour is for harvest or fight
To clothe with raiment of red;
O men sore stricken of hours,
Lo, this one, is not it ours
To glean, to gather, to smite?
Let none make risk of his head
Within reach of the clean scythe-sweep,
When the people that lay as the dead
Put in the sickles and reap.

Lo, this one, is not it ours,
Now the ruins of dead things rattle
As dead men's bones in the pit,
Now the kings wax lean as they sit
Girt round with memories of powers,
With musters counted as cattle
And armies folded as sheep
Till the red blind husbandman battle
Put in the sickles and reap.

Now the kings wax lean as they sit,
The people grow strong to stand;
The men they trod on and spat,
The dumb dread people that sat
As corpses cast in a pit,
Rise up with God at their hand,
And thrones are hurled on a heap,
And strong men, sons of the land,
Put in the sickles and reap.

The dumb dread people that sat
All night without screen for the night,
All day without food for the day,
They shall not give their harvest away,
They shall eat of its fruit and wax fat:
They shall see the desire of their sight,
Though the ways of the seasons be steep,
They shall climb with face to the light,
Put in the sickles and reap. 81

[1871]

A FORSAKEN GARDEN

In a coign of the cliff between lowland and highland,
At the sea-down's edge between windward and lee,
Walled round with rocks as an inland island,
The ghost of a garden fronts the sea.
A girdle of brushwood and thorn encloses
The steep square slope of the blossomless bed
Where the weeds that grew green from the graves of its roses
Now lie dead.

The fields fall southward, abrupt and broken,
To the low last edge of the long lone land.
If a step should sound or a word be spoken,
Would a ghost not rise at the strange guest's hand?
So long have the grey bare walks lain guestless,
Through branches and briars if a man make way,
He shall find no life but the sea-wind's, restless
Night and day.

The dense hard passage is blind and stifled,
That crawls by a track none turn to climb
To the strait waste place that the years have rifled
Of all but the thorns that are touched not of time.
The thorns he spares when the rose is taken;
The rocks are left when he wastes the plain.
The wind that wanders, the weeds windshaken,
These remain.

Not a flower to be pressed of the foot that falls not;
As the heart of a dead man the seedplots are dry;

From the thicket of thorns whence the nightingale calls not,
  Could she call, there were never a rose to reply.
Over the meadows that blossom and wither
  Rings but the note of a sea-bird's song;
Only the sun and the rain come hither
    All year long.

The sun burns sere and the rain dishevels
  One gaunt bleak blossom of scentless breath.
Only the wind here hovers and revels
  In a round where life seems barren as death.
Here there was laughing of old, there was weeping,
  Haply, of lovers none ever will know,
Whose eyes went seaward a hundred sleeping
    Years ago.

Heart handfast in heart as they stood, "Look thither,"
  Did he whisper? "look forth from the flowers to the sea;
For the foam-flowers endure when the rose-blossoms wither,
  And men that love lightly may die—but we?"
And the same wind sang and the same waves whitened,
  And or ever the garden's last petals were shed,
In the lips that had whispered, the eyes that had lightened,
    Love was dead.

Or they loved their life through, and then went whither?
  And were one to the end—but what end who knows?
Love deep as the sea as a rose must wither,
  As the rose-red seaweed that mocks the rose.
Shall the dead take thought for the dead to love them?
  What love was ever as deep as a grave?
They are loveless now as the grass above them
    Or the wave.

All are at one now, roses and lovers,
  Not known of the cliffs and the fields and the sea.
Not a breath of the time that has been hovers
  In the air now soft with a summer to be.
Not a breath shall there sweeten the seasons hereafter
  Of the flowers or the lovers that laugh now or weep,
When as they that are free now of weeping and laughter,
    We shall sleep.

Here death may deal not again for ever;
  Here change may come not till all change end.
From the graves they have made they shall rise up never,
  Who have left nought living to ravage and rend.
Earth, stones, and thorns of the wild ground growing,
  While the sun and the rain live, these shall be:
Till a last wind's breath upon all these blowing
    Roll the sea.

Till the slow sea rise and the sheer cliff crumble,
  Till terrace and meadow the deep gulfs drink,

Till the strength of the waves of the high tides humble
  The fields that lessen, the rocks that shrink,
Here now in his triumph where all things falter,
  Stretched out on the spoils that his own hand spread,
As a god self-slain on his own strange altar,
    Death lies dead.

[1876] [1878]

FOR THE FEAST OF GIORDANO BRUNO

PHILOSOPHER AND MARTYR

I

Son of the lightning and the light that glows
  Beyond the lightning's or the morning's light,
  Soul splendid with all-righteous love of right,
In whose keen fire all hopes and fears and woes
Were clean consumed, and from their ashes rose
  Transfigured, and intolerable to sight
  Save of purged eyes whose lids had cast off night,
In love's and wisdom's likeness when they close,
Embracing, and between them truth stands fast,
  Embraced of either; thou whose feet were set
  On English earth, while this was England yet,
Our friend that art, our Sidney's friend that wast,
Heart hardier found and higher than all men's past,
  Shall we not praise thee though thine own forget?

II

Lift up thy light on us and on thine own,
  O soul whose spirit on earth was as a rod
  To scourge off priests, a sword to pierce their God,
A staff for man's free thought to walk alone,
A lamp to lead him far from shrine and throne
  On ways untrodden where his fathers trod
  Ere earth's heart withered at a high priest's nod
And all men's mouths that made not prayer made moan.
From bonds and torments and the ravening flame
  Surely thy spirit of sense rose up to greet
  Lucretius where such only spirits meet,
And walk with him apart till Shelley came
  To make the heaven of heavens more heavenly sweet
And mix with yours a third incorporate name.

[1878]

THE HIGHER PANTHEISM IN A NUTSHELL

One, who is not, we see: but one, whom we see not, is:
Surely this is not that: but that is assuredly this.

What, and wherefore, and whence? for under is over and under:
If thunder could be without lightning, lightning could be without thunder.

Doubt is faith, in the main: but faith, on the whole, is doubt.
We cannot believe by proof: but could we believe without?

Why, and whither, and how? for barley and rye are not clover:
Neither are straight lines curves: yet over is under and over.

Two and two may be four: but four and four are not eight:
Fate and God may be twain: but God is the same thing as fate.

Ask a man what he thinks, and get from a man what he feels:
God, once caught in the fact, shows you a fair pair of heels.

Body and spirit are twins: God only knows which is which:
The soul squats down in the flesh, like a tinker drunk in a ditch.

More is the whole than a part: but half is more than the whole:
Clearly, the soul is the body: but is not the body the soul?

One and two are not one: but one and nothing is two:
Truth can hardly be false, if falsehood cannot be true.

Once the mastodon was: pterodactyls were common as cocks.
Then the mammoth was God: now is He a prize ox.

Parallels all things are: yet many of these are askew:
You are certainly I: but certainly I am not you.

Springs the rock from the plain, shoots the stream from the rock:
Cocks exist for the hen: but hens exist for the cock.

God, whom we see not, is: and God, who is not, we see:
Fiddle, we know, is diddle: and diddle, we take it, is dee.

[1880]

NEPHELIDIA

From the depth of the dreamy decline of the dawn through a notable nimbus of nebulous noonshine,
Pallid and pink as the palm of the flag-flower that flickers with fear of the flies as they float,
Are they looks of our lovers that lustrously lean from a marvel of mystic miraculous moonshine,
These that we feel in the blood of our blushes that thicken and threaten with throbs through the throat?
Thicken and thrill as a theatre thronged at appeal of an actor's appalled agitation,
Fainter with fear of the fires of the future that pale with the promise of pride in the past;
Flushed with the famishing fullness of fever that reddens with radiance of rathe recreation,
Gaunt as the ghastliest of glimpses that gleam through the gloom of the gloaming when ghosts go aghast?
Nay, for the nick of the tick of the time is a tremulous touch on the temples of terror,
Strained as the sinews yet strenuous with strife of the dead who is dumb as the dust-heaps of death:

Surely no soul is it, sweet as the spasm of erotic emotional exquisite error,
Bathed in the balms of beatified bliss, beatific itself by beatitudes' breath.
Surely no spirit or sense of a soul that was soft to the spirit and soul of our senses
Sweetens the stress of suspiring suspicion that sobs in the semblance and sound of a sigh;
Only this oracle opens Olympian, in mystical moods and triangular tenses—
"Life is the lust of a lamp for the light that is dark till the dawn of the day when we die."
Mild is the mirk and monotonous music of memory, melodiously mute as it may be,
While the hope in the heart of a hero is bruised by the breach of men's rapiers, resigned to the rod;
Made meek as a mother whose bosom-beats bound with the bliss-bringing bulk of a balm-breathing baby,
As they grope through the grave-yard of creeds, under skies growing green at a groan for the grimness of God.
Blank is the book of his bounty beholden of old, and its binding is blacker than bluer:
Out of blue into black is the scheme of the skies, and their dews are the wine of the bloodshed of things;
Till the darkling desire of delight shall be free as a fawn that is freed from the fangs that pursue her,
Till the heart-beats of hell shall be hushed by a hymn from the hunt that has harried the kennel of kings.

[1880]

AFTER LOOKING INTO CARLYLE'S REMINISCENCES

I

Three men lived yet when this dead man was young
Whose names and words endure for ever: one
Whose eyes grew dim with straining toward the sun,
And his wings weakened and his angel's tongue
Lost half the sweetest song was ever sung,
But like the strain half uttered earth hears none,
Nor shall man hear till all man's songs are done:
One whose clear spirit like an eagle hung
Between the mountains hallowed by his love
And the sky stainless as his soul above:
And one the sweetest heart that ever spake
The brightest words wherein sweet wisdom smiled.
These deathless names by this dead snake defiled
Bid memory spit upon him for their sake.

II

Sweet heart, forgive me for thine own sweet sake,
Whose kind blithe soul such seas of sorrow swam,
And for my love's sake, powerless as I am
For love to praise thee, or like thee to make
Music of mirth where hearts less pure would break,
Less pure than thine, our life-unspotted Lamb,
Things hatefullest thou hadst not heart to damn,
Nor wouldst have set thy heel on this dead snake.
Let worms consume its memory with its tongue,

The fang that stabbed fair Truth, the lip that stung
Men's memories uncorroded with its breath.
Forgive me that with bitter words like his
I mix the gentlest English name that is,
The tenderest held of all that know not death.
[1883] [1883]

NEAP-TIDE

Far off is the sea, and the land is afar:
The low banks reach at the sky,
Seen hence, and are heavenward high;
Though light for the leap of a boy they are,
And the far sea late was nigh.

The fair wild fields and the circling downs,
The bright sweet marshes and meads
All glorious with flowerlike weeds,
The great gray churches, the sea-washed towns,
Recede as a dream recedes.

The world draws back, and the world's light wanes,
As a dream dies down and is dead;
And the clouds and the gleams overhead
Change, and change; and the sea remains,
A shadow of dreamlike dread.

Wild, and woeful, and pale, and grey,
A shadow of sleepless fear,
A corpse with the night for bier,
The fairest thing that beholds the day
Lies haggard and hopeless here.

And the wind's wings, broken and spent, subside;
And the dumb waste world is hoar,
And strange as the sea the shore;
And shadows of shapeless dreams abide
Where life may abide no more.

A sail to seaward, a sound from shoreward,
And the spell were broken that seems
To reign in a world of dreams
Where vainly the dreamer's feet make forward
And vainly the low sky gleams.

The sea-forsaken forlorn deep-wrinkled
Salt slanting stretches of sand
That slope to the seaward hand,
Were they fain of the ripples that flashed and twinkled
And laughed as they struck the strand?

As bells on the reins of the fairies ring
The ripples that kissed them rang,
The light from the sundawn sprang,
And the sweetest of songs that the world may sing
Was theirs when the full sea sang.

Now no light is in heaven; and now
Not a note of the sea-wind's tune
Rings hither: the bleak sky's boon
Grants hardly sight of a grey sun's brow—
A sun more sad than the moon.

More sad than a moon that clouds beleaguer
And storm is a scourge to smite,
The sick sun's shadowlike light
Grows faint as the clouds and the waves wax eager,
And withers away from sight.

The day's heart cowers, and the night's heart quickens:
Full fain would the day be dead
And the stark night reign in his stead:
The sea falls dumb as the sea-fog thickens
And the sunset dies for dread.

Outside of the range of time, whose breath
Is keen as the manslayer's knife
And his peace but a truce for strife,
Who knows if haply the shadow of death
May be not the light of life?

For the storm and the rain and the darkness borrow
But an hour from the suns to be,
But a strange swift passage, that we
May rejoice, who have mourned not to-day, to-morrow,
In the sun and the wind and the sea.
[1889]

ENGLAND: AN ODE

I

Sea and strand, and a lordlier land than sea-tides rolling and rising sun
Clasp and lighten in climes that brighten with day when day that was here is done,
Call aloud on their children, proud with trust that future and past are one.

Far and near from the swan's nest here the stormbirds bred of her fair white breast,
Sons whose home was the sea-wave's foam, have borne the fame of her east and west;
North and south has the storm-wind's mouth rung praise of England and England's quest.

Fame, wherever her flag flew, never forbore to fly with an equal wing:
France and Spain with their warrior train bowed down before her as thrall to king;
India knelt at her feet, and felt her sway more fruitful of life than spring.

Darkness round them as iron bound fell off from races of elder name,
Slain at sight of her eyes, whose light bids freedom lighten and burn as flame;
Night endures not the touch that cures of kingship tyrants, and slaves of shame.

All the terror of time, where error and fear were lords of a world of slaves,
Age on age in resurgent rage and anguish darkening as waves on waves,
Fell or fled from a face that shed such grace as quickens the dust of graves.

Things of night at her glance took flight: the strengths of darkness recoiled and sank:
Sank the fires of the murderous pyres whereon wild agony writhed and shrank:
Rose the light of the reign of right from gulfs of years that the darkness drank.

Yet the might of her wings in flight, whence glory lightens and music rings,
Loud and bright as the dawn's, shall smite and still the discord of evil things,
Yet not slain by her radiant reign, but darkened now by her sail-stretched wings.

II

Music made of change and conquest, glory born of evil slain,
Stilled the discord, slew the darkness, bade the lights of tempest wane,
Where the deathless dawn of England rose in sign that right should reign.

Mercy, where the tiger wallowed mad and blind with blood and lust,
Justice, where the jackal yelped and fed, and slaves allowed it just,
Rose as England's light on Asia rose, and smote them down to dust.

Justice bright as mercy, mercy girt by justice with her sword,
Smote and saved and raised and ruined, till the tyrant-ridden horde
Saw the lightning fade from heaven and knew the sun for God and lord.

Where the footfall sounds of England, where the smile of England shines,
Rings the tread and laughs the face of freedom, fair as hope divines
Days to be, more brave than ours and lit by lordlier stars for signs.

All our past acclaims our future: Shakespeare's voice and Nelson's hand,
Milton's faith and Wordsworth's trust in this our chosen and chainless land,
Bear us witness: come the world against her, England yet shall stand.

Earth and sea bear England witness if he lied who said it; he
Whom the winds that ward her, waves that clasp, and herb and flower and tree
Fed with English dews and sunbeams, hail as more than man may be.

No man ever spake as he that bade our England be but true,
Keep but faith with England fast and firm, and none should bid her rue;
None may speak as he: but all may know the sign that Shakespeare knew.

III

From the springs of the dawn, from the depths of the noon, from the heights of the night that shine,
Hope, faith, and remembrance of glory that found but in England her throne and her shrine,
Speak louder than song may proclaim them that here is the seal of them set for a sign.

And loud as the sea's voice thunders applause of the land that is one with the sea
Speaks Time in the ear of the people that never at heart was not inly free
The word of command that assures us of life, if we will but that life shall be;

If the race that is first of the races of men who behold unashamed the sun
Stand fast and forget not the sign that is given of the years and the wars that are done,
The token that all who are born of its blood should in heart as in blood be one.

The word of remembrance that lightens as fire from the steeps of the storm-lit past
Bids only the faith of our fathers endure in us, firm as they held it fast:
That the glory which was from the first upon England alone may endure to the last.

That the love and the hate may change not, the faith may not fade, nor the wrath nor scorn,
That shines for her sons and that burns for her foemen as fire of the night or the morn:
That the births of her womb may forget not the sign of the glory wherein they were born.

A light that is more than the sunlight, an air that is brighter than morning's breath,
Clothes England about as the strong sea clasps her, and answers the word that it saith;
The word that assures her of life if she change not, and choose not the ways of death.

Change darkens and lightens around her, alternate in hope and in fear to be:
Hope knows not if fear speak truth, nor fear whether hope be not blind as she:
But the sun is in heaven that beholds her immortal, and girdled with life by the sea.

[1894]

THOMAS HARDY

CHRONOLOGICAL TABLE

1840, June 2, born at Higher Bockhampton, near Dorchester, in Dorset, his father a builder.
1848–55 Attended schools in Bockhampton and Dorchester.
1855–61 Articled to an architect in Dorchester.
1861 Went to London to continue study and practice of architecture under Sir Arthur Blomfield.
1865 Published his first story: "How I Built Myself a House" (*Chambers Journal*).
1867 Ailing in health returned to work as an architect in his native district.
1868 Despaired of a poetic career and abandoned verse for fiction.
Submitted a novel *The Poor Man and the Lady* to Chapman and Hall: it was so judged by their reader, Meredith, that Hardy withdrew it (and subsequently destroyed the ms.).
1871 *Desperate Remedies* (anonymous).
1872 *Under the Greenwood Tree* (anonymous).
Ceased to work as an architect.
1873 *A Pair of Blue Eyes.*
1874 *Far From the Madding Crowd.*
Married to Emma Lavinia Gifford, daughter of a Plymouth solicitor.
1876 *The Hand of Ethelberta.*
1878 *The Return of the Native.*
1880 *The Trumpet Major.*
1881 *A Laodicean.*
1882 *Two on a Tower.*
1883 *The Romantic Adventures of a Milkmaid.*
1885 Established himself in Max Gate, a house built according to his own designs, near Dorchester.
1886 *The Mayor of Casterbridge.*
1887 *The Woodlanders.*
1888 *Wessex Tales.*
1890 *A Group of Noble Dames.*
1891 *Tess of the D'Urbervilles.*
1892 *The Well-Beloved.*
1894 *Life's Little Ironies.*
1896 *Jude the Obscure.*
The outcry following this novel was such that Hardy resolved against writing another.
1898 *Wessex Poems, and Other Verses,* the first collection of his poems.
1901 *Poems of the Past and the Present.*
1903–8 *The Dynasts* (in three parts).
1909 *Time's Laughingstocks.*
1910 Awarded the Order of Merit.
1912 Death of his wife.
1914 *Satires of Circumstance.*
Married Florence Emily Dugdale, author of books for children.
1917 *Moments of Vision.*
1922 *Late Lyrics and Earlier.*
1923 *The Famous Tragedy of the Queen of Cornwall.*
1925 *Human Shows, Far Phantasies.*
1928 Died at Max Gate, January 11, his heart buried with his first wife in the graveyard of Stinstock Church, near Bockhampton, his body in Westminster Abbey.
Winter Words (posthumous).

The solidest reputations established in fiction in the last third of the nineteenth century were those of two men who each valued far above any skill in the novel the capacity to write poetry. Meredith was disheartened by the reception in 1851 of his first volume of verse, which was also his first book, and again in 1862 by the uncomprehending vituperation and the coarse witticisms encountered by his intimate sonnet-sequence *Modern Love.* From 1862 till almost the end of his career he was perforce primarily a novelist. Hardy from his earliest years of literary activity wrote poetry; but he withheld it from publication until in 1898, almost sixty years of age, he had finished with the novel forever. For his long silence as a poet, and for his uncompromising repudiation of fiction for poetry in his age, many reasons have been advanced, some by Hardy himself, none of them seeming entirely adequate.

The problem of his decisive shift from fiction to poetry is the simpler of the two. At all times, even in his last venerated decade, Hardy was extremely sensitive to bludgeoning criticism; and the outcry which began in 1894–5, when *Jude the Obscure* was passing through serial publication, and continued long after its appearance as a book in 1896, saddened and stung him. He saw that it was extremely dangerous to affront popular susceptibilities in the novel; and he may well have seen also that those susceptibilities are not so dangerous to the poet, whose audience is almost inevitably much more limited. It must be remembered too that by the time *Jude* was published Hardy's income was large enough, and seemed secure enough, for him to devote himself to poetry, with an unconcern as to its remunerativeness which he could not have shown in the sixties. The problem is, however, not in his decision to publish some poetry, but in his never once returning, during the thirty years of life that remained, to the novel, in which he had won successses not only resounding at the moment, but continuing to resound more and more deeply every year. He was a classical novelist in his own life time and yet for thirty years he seemed to show not the slightest inclination to return to the novel. Incomplete as any explanation of such a phenomenon must be, three remarks may be made. First, Hardy was wounded by the outcry over *Jude* far more deeply and permanently than it is possible for us to conceive; second he disliked the new tendencies in fiction, which seemed to him to be destroying its narrative and architectural beauties; third, he appears never to have found in fiction as adequate a mode of aesthetic expression as he found in poetry, and he did not find it easy to create in both forms in the same years.

Hardy's decision not to publish the poetry he was writing, a decision adhered to for over thirty years, is more bewildering. It has been said that he felt his poetry was out of harmony with what other poets were writing in the sixties and seventies, and therefore would not find an audience. But his poetry was not out of harmony with Browning's in form, nor with some of the pessimists of the younger generations in feeling. His poetry is essentially, if not completely, Victorian. It has to do with many of the great problems which weighed so heavily upon the Victorians: immortality, the existence and nature of God, the degree of freedom possessed by the human will, the pains and ecstasies of complex love and friendship. Other elements in his substance, if not to be found in other great Victorians, were not unlike the Victorian anxieties: his insistence upon the role of chance in life, his alarm at the existence of pain, his horror of spiritual waste. There is nothing in his substance which a cultivated Victorian might not have respected. In so far as his form is rough and hoarse—"wheezy" is Sir Herbert Grierson's expressive word for it—it may be antithetical to Tennyson's, but it is clearly akin to Browning's and Meredith's. The prevailing mood may be more grey and depressed than that of other Victorians, but its gravity and sincerity the Victorians would also have respected. One is driven to the belief that Hardy felt he must choose between fiction and poetry, confining himself to one alone; and in the sixties he could not have afforded to confine himself to poetry.

Victorian as his poetry is, readers of the first quarter of the present century did not repudiate it with the works of the other great Victorians. In its rigid honesty, its transparent simplicity, its rich and moving humanity, and also in its persistent emphasis on the darker aspects of personal and universal life, it was profoundly attractive. Hardy's most enthusiastic readers have indeed commonly exalted his poetry at the expense of his fiction, a judgment which it is difficult to believe that time will confirm.

HAP

If but some vengeful god would call to me
From up the sky, and laugh: "Thou suffering thing,
Know that thy sorrow is my ecstasy,
That thy love's loss is my hate's profiting!"
Then would I bear it, clench myself, and die,
Steeled by the sense of ire unmerited;
Half-eased in that a Powerfuller than I
Had willed and meted me the tears I shed.

But not so. How arrives it joy lies slain,
And why unblooms the best hope ever sown?
—Crass Casualty obstructs the sun and rain,
And dicing Time for gladness casts a moan. . . .
These purblind Doomsters had as readily stown
Blisses about my pilgrimage as pain.

[1866] [1898]

NATURE'S QUESTIONING

When I look forth at dawning, pool,
Field, flock, and lonely tree,
All seem to gaze at me
Like chastened children sitting silent in a school;

Their faces dulled, constrained, and worn,
As though the master's ways
Through the long teaching days
Had cowed them till their early zest was overborne.

Upon them stirs in lippings mere
(As if once clear in call,
But now scarce breathed at all)—
"We wonder, ever wonder, why we find us here!

"Has some Vast Imbecility,
Mighty to build and blend,
But impotent to tend,
Framed us in jest, and left us now to hazardry?

"Or come we of an Automaton
Unconscious of our pains? . . .
Or are we live remains
Of Godhead dying downwards, brain and eye now gone?

"Or is it that some high Plan betides,
As yet not understood,
Of Evil stormed by Good,
We the Forlorn Hope over which Achievement strides?"

Thus things around. No answerer I . . .
Meanwhile the winds, and rains,
And Earth's old glooms and pains
Are still the same, and Life and Death are neighbours nigh.

[1898]

THE IMPERCIPIENT

(AT A CATHEDRAL SERVICE)

That with this bright believing band
I have no claim to be,
That faiths by which my comrades stand
Seem fantasies to me,
And mirage-mists their Shining Land,
Is a strange destiny.

Why thus my soul should be consigned
To infelicity,
Why always I must feel as blind
To sights my brethren see,
Why joys they've found I cannot find,
Abides a mystery.

Since heart of mine knows not that ease
Which they know; since it be
That He who breathes All's Well to these
Breathes no All's-Well to me,
My lack might move their sympathies
And Christian charity!

I am like a gazer who should mark
An inland company
Standing upfingered, with, "Hark! hark!
The glorious distant sea!"
And feel, "Alas, 'tis but yon dark
And wind-swept pine to me!"

Yet I would bear my shortcomings
With meet tranquillity,
But for the charge that blessed things
I'd liefer not have be.
O, doth a bird deprived of wings
Go earthbound wilfully!

. . . .

Enough. As yet disquiet clings
About us. Rest shall we.

[1898]

DRUMMER HODGE

I

They throw in Drummer Hodge, to rest
Uncoffined,—just as found:
His landmark is a kopje-crest
That breaks the veldt around;
And foreign constellations west
Each night above his mound.

II

Young Hodge the Drummer never knew—
Fresh from his Wessex home—
The meaning of the broad Karoo,
The Bush, the dusty loam,
And why uprose to nightly view
Strange stars amid the gloam.

III

Yet portion of that unknown plain
Will Hodge for ever be;
His homely Northern breast and brain
Grow to some Southern tree,
And strange-eyed constellations reign
His stars eternally.

[1899 ?] [1902]

LAUSANNE

IN GIBBON'S OLD GARDEN: 11–12 P.M.

June 27, 1897

(*The 110th anniversary of the completion of the "Decline and Fall" at the same hour and place*)

A spirit seems to pass,
Formal in pose, but grave withal and grand:
He contemplates a volume in his hand,
And far lamps fleck him through the thin acacias.

Anon the book is closed,
With "It is finished!" And at the alley's end
He turns, and when on me his glances bend
As from the Past comes speech—small, muted, yet composed.

"How fares the Truth now?—Ill?
—Do pens but slily further her advance?
May one not speed her but in phrase askance?
Do scribes aver the Comic to be Reverend still?

"Still rule those minds on earth
At whom sage Milton's wormwood words were hurled:
'Truth like a bastard comes into the world
Never without ill-fame to him who gives her birth'?"

[1902]

"I SAID TO LOVE"

I said to Love,
"It is not now as in old days
When men adored thee and thy ways
All else above;
Named thee the Boy, the Bright, the One
Who spread a heaven beneath the sun,"
I said to Love.

I said to him,
"We now know more of thee than then;
We were but weak in judgment when,
With hearts abrim,
We clamoured thee that thou would'st please
Inflict on us thine agonies,"
I said to him.

I said to Love,
"Thou art not young, thou art not fair,
No elfin darts, no cherub air,
Nor swan, nor dove
Are thine; but features pitiless,
And iron daggers of distress,"
I said to Love.

"Depart then, Love! . . .
—Man's race shall perish, threatenest thou,
Without thy kindling coupling-vow?
The age to come the man of now
Know nothing of?—
We fear not such a threat from thee;
We are too old in apathy!
Mankind shall cease.—So let it be,"
I said to Love.

[1902]

BY THE EARTH'S CORPSE

I

"O Lord, why grievest Thou?—
Since Life has ceased to be
Upon this globe now cold
As lunar land and sea,
And humankind, and fowl, and fur
Are gone eternally,
All is the same to Thee as ere
They knew mortality."

II

"O Time," replied the Lord,
"Thou readest me ill, I ween;
Were all *the same,* I should not grieve
At that late earthly scene,
Now blestly past—though planned by me
With interest close and keen!—
Nay, nay: things now are *not* the same
As they have earlier been.

III

"Written indelibly
On my eternal mind
Are all the wrongs endured
By Earth's poor patient kind,
Which my too oft unconscious hand
Let enter undesigned.
No god can cancel deeds foredone,
Or thy old coils unwind!

IV

"As when in Noë's days,
I whelmed the plains with sea
So at this last, when flesh
And herb but fossils be,
And all extinct, their piteous dust
Revolves obliviously,
That I made Earth, and life, and man,
It still repenteth me!"

[1902]

MUTE OPINION

I

I traversed a dominion
Whose spokesmen spake out strong
Their purpose and opinion
Through pulpit, press, and song.
I scarce had means to note there
A large-eyed few, and dumb,
Who thought not as those thought there
That stirred the heat and hum.

II

When, grown a Shade, beholding
That land in lifetime trode,
To learn if its unfolding
Fulfilled its clamoured code,
I saw, in web unbroken,
Its history outwrought
Not as the loud had spoken,
But as the mute had thought.

[1902]

A BROKEN APPOINTMENT

You did not come,
And marching Time drew on, and wore me numb.—
Yet less for loss of your dear presence there
Than that I thus found lacking in your make
That high compassion which can overbear
Reluctance for pure lovingkindness' sake
Grieved I, when, as the hope-hour stroked its sum,
You did not come.

You love not me,
And love alone can lend you loyalty;
—I know and knew it. But, unto the store
Of human deeds divine in all but name,
Was it not worth a little hour or more
To add yet this: Once you, a woman, came
To soothe a time-torn man; even though it be
You love not me?

[1902]

THE DARKLING THRUSH

I leant upon a coppice gate
  When Frost was spectre-gray,
And Winter's dregs made desolate
  The weakening eye of day.
The tangled bine-stems scored the sky
  Like strings of broken lyres,
And all mankind that haunted nigh
  Had sought their household fires.

The land's sharp features seemed to be
  The Century's corpse outleant,
His crypt the cloudy canopy,
  The wind his death-lament.
The ancient pulse of germ and birth
  Was shrunken hard and dry,
And every spirit upon earth
  Seemed fervourless as I.

At once a voice arose among
  The bleak twigs overhead
In a full-hearted evensong
  Of joy illimited;
An aged thrush, frail, gaunt, and small,
  In blast-beruffled plume,
Had chosen thus to fling his soul
  Upon the growing gloom.

So little cause for carolings
  Of such ecstatic sound
Was written on terrestrial things
  Afar or nigh around,
That I could think there trembled through
  His happy good-night air
Some blessed Hope, whereof he knew
  And I was unaware.

31 December 1900 [1902]

IN TENEBRIS

I

"Percussus sum sicut foenum, et aruit cor meum."[1]
—*Ps.* ci.

  Wintertime nighs;
But my bereavement-pain
It cannot bring again:
  Twice no one dies.

  Flower-petals flee;
But, since it once hath been,
No more that severing scene
  Can harrow me.

  Birds faint in dread:
I shall not lose old strength
In the lone frost's black length:
  Strength long since fled!

  Leaves freeze to dun;
But friends can not turn cold
This season as of old
  For him with none.

  Tempests may scath;
But love cannot make smart
Again this year his heart
  Who no heart hath.

  Black is night's cope;
But death will not appal
One who, past doubtings all,
  Waits in unhope.

[1] My heart is smitten and withered like grass.

IN TENEBRIS

II

"Considerabam ad dexteram, et videbam; et non erat qui cognosceret me. . . . Non est qui requirat animam meam,"—*Ps.* cxli.[1]

When the clouds' swoln bosoms echo back the shouts of the many and strong
That things are all as they best may be, save a few to be right ere long,
And my eyes have not the vision in them to discern what to these is so clear,
The blot seems straightway in me alone; one better he were not here.

[1] I looked on my right hand, and beheld, but there was no man that would know me . . . no man cared for my soul.

The stout upstanders say, All's well with us: ruers have nought to rue!
And what the potent say so oft, can it fail to be somewhat true?
Breezily go they, breezily come; their dust smokes around their career,
Till I think I am one born out of due time, who has no calling here.

Their dawns bring lusty joys, it seems; their evenings all that is sweet;
Our times are blessed times, they cry: Life shapes it as is most meet,
And nothing is much the matter; there are many smiles to a tear;
Then what is the matter is I, I say. Why should such an one be here? . . .

Let him in whose ears the low-voiced Best is killed by the clash of the First,
Who holds that if way to the Better there be, it exacts a full look at the Worst,
Who feels that delight is a delicate growth cramped by crookedness, custom, and fear,
Get him up and be gone as one shaped awry; he disturbs the order here.

[1895–6]

IN TENEBRIS

III

"Heu mihi, quia incolatus meus prolongatus est! Habitavi cum habitantibus Cedar; multum incola fuit anima mea."—*Ps.* cxix.[1]

There have been times when I well might have passed and the ending have come—
Points on my path when the dark might have stolen on me, artless, unrueing—
Ere I had learnt that the world was a welter of futile doing!
Such had been times when I well might have passed, and the ending have come!

Say, on the noon when the half-sunny hours told that April was nigh,
And I upgathered and cast forth the snow from the crocus-border,
Fashioned and furbished the soil into a summer-seeming order,
Glowing in gladsome faith that I quickened the year thereby.

Or on that loneliest of eves when afar and benighted we stood,
She who upheld me and I, in the midmost of Egdon together,
Confident I in her watching and ward through the blackening heather,
Deeming her matchless in might and with measureless scope endued.

Or on that winter-wild night when, reclined by the chimney-nook quoin,
Slowly a drowse overgat me, the smallest and feeblest of folk there,
Weak from my baptism of pain; when at times and anon I awoke there—
Heard of a world wheeling on, with no listing or longing to join.
Even then! while unweeting that vision could vex or that knowledge could numb,
That sweets to the mouth in the belly are bitter, and tart, and untoward,
Then on some dim-coloured scene should my briefly raised curtain have lowered,
Then might the Voice that is law have said "Cease!" and the ending have come.

[1896] [1902]

[1] Woe is me that I sojourn (in Mesech), that I dwell in the tents of Kedar. My soul hath long dwelt with him that hateth peace.

WHEN I SET OUT FOR LYONNESSE

(1870)

When I set out for Lyonnesse,
  A hundred miles away,
  The rime was on the spray,
And starlight lit my lonesomeness
When I set out for Lyonnesse
  A hundred miles away.

What would bechance at Lyonnesse
  While I should sojourn there
  No prophet durst declare,
Nor did the wisest wizard guess
What would bechance at Lyonnesse
  While I should sojourn there.

When I came back from Lyonnesse
  With magic in my eyes,
  All marked with mute surmise
My radiance rare and fathomless,
When I came back from Lyonnesse
  With magic in my eyes.

[1870] [1914]

GERARD MANLEY HOPKINS

CHRONOLOGICAL TABLE

1844, Born June 11, at Stratford (Essex), his father Consul General for the Hawaiian Islands in Great Britain, his mother the cultivated daughter of a London physician.

1854–63 Attended Grammar School at Highgate, a suburb of London, where among his teachers was the poet Richard Watson Dixon, later one of his intimates.

1863 Entered Balliol College, Oxford, with an Exhibition.

1866 Received into the Roman Catholic church, after establishing a relation with John Henry Newman.

1867 B.A. with first class in *literae humaniores.*

1868 Entered Jesuit Novitiate at Roehampton.

1874 Began theological studies at St. Beuno's College, in North Wales.

1875 Wrote *The Wreck of the Deutschland.*

1877 Ordained to the priesthood.

1879 Became a preacher at St. Francis Xavier's Church, Liverpool.

1882 Taught Classics at Stonyhurst College, a Jesuit foundation at Oxford.

1884–9 Professor of Greek in the Royal University, Dublin.

1889, June 8, died at Dublin, buried in the Jesuit burial-ground at Glasnevin.

1918 Robert Bridges edited the *Poems of Gerard Manley Hopkins.*

The reputation and influence of Gerard Hopkins is essentially a growth of the past twenty years. On his death, in 1889, his poems became a trust of Robert Bridges; most of the poems had gone to Bridges as they were composed; very few had appeared in print or circulated in manuscript beyond an exceedingly small group of poetic friends. Bridges, dubious of the appreciation the poems would meet, contented himself, up to 1918, with printing a few in anthologies, without attempting to direct much attention towards even these; in that year finally, convinced that poetic taste was moving into a phase in which Hopkins's art would be impressive, he gave a closely annotated edition to the world. The volume made its way slowly and surely. The audience created for metrical innovation and "difficult lonely music" by such masters as Eliot, Pound, and other new figures assured Hopkins a perceptive and enthusiastic reception.

Full justice has been done to the beauty and originality of his forms. Critics have vied with one another in pointing out their charm, and their root in older English fashions. The substance, often repellent to Bridges himself, has been less warmly esteemed, and Hopkins has too often been acclaimed as no more than a master technician. The substance of his best work is often profound and intense. The delights and agonies of the spiritual life have rarely been recorded with such authenticity; nature has seldom been celebrated with such lingering delight in her aspects, such rapture in her simple beauties; common human character has in some of the poems found a presentation at once highly realistic and full of suggestion of depth.

THE WINDHOVER

TO CHRIST OUR LORD

I caught this morning morning's minion, king-
    dom of daylight's dauphin, dapple-dawn-drawn Falcon, in his riding
  Of the rolling level underneath him steady air, and striding
High there, how he rung upon the rein of a wimpling wing

In his ecstasy! then off, off forth on swing,
  As a skate's heel sweeps smooth on a bow-bend; the hurl and gliding
  Rebuffed the big wind. My heart in hiding
Stirred for a bird,—the achieve of, the mastery of the thing!

Brute beauty and valour and act, oh, air, pride, plume, here
  Buckle! AND the fire that breaks from thee then, a billion
Times told lovelier, more dangerous, O my chevalier!

No wonder of it: shéer plód makes plough down sillion
Shine, and blue-bleak embers, ah my dear,
Fall, gall themselves, and gash gold-vermilion.

[1877] [1918]

PIED BEAUTY

Glory be to God for dappled things—
  For skies of couple-colour as a brinded cow;
    For rose-moles all in stipple upon trout that swim;
Fresh-firecoal chestnut falls; finches' wings;
  Landscape plotted and pieced—fold, fallow, and plough;
    And áll trádes, their gear and tackle and trim.
All things counter, original, spare, strange;
  Whatever is fickle, freckled (who knows how?)
    With swift, slow; sweet, sour; adazzle, dim;
He fathers-forth whose beauty is past change:
          Praise him.

[1877] [1918]

FELIX RANDAL

Felix Randal, the farrier, O he is dead then? my duty all ended,
Who have watched his mould of man, big-boned and hardy-handsome
Pining, pining, till time when reason rambled in it and some
Four fatal disorders, fleshed there, all contended?

Sickness broke him. Impatient he cursed at first, but mended
Being anointed and all; though a heavenlier heart began some
Months earlier, since I had our sweet reprieve and ransom
Tendered to him. Ah well, God rest him all road ever he offended!

This seeing the sick endears them to us, us too it endears.
My tongue had taught thee comfort, touch had quenched thy tears,
Thy tears that touched my heart, child, Felix, poor Felix Randal;

How far from then forethought of, all thy more boisterous years,
When thou at the random grim forge, powerful amidst peers,
Didst fettle for the great grey drayhorse his bright and battering sandal!

[1880] [1918]

THE LEADEN ECHO AND THE GOLDEN ECHO

(Maidens' song from St. Winefred's Well)

THE LEADEN ECHO

How to kéep—is there ány any, is there none such, nowhere known some, bow or brooch or braid or brace, láce, latch or catch or key to keep
Back beauty, keep it, beauty, beauty, beauty, . . . from vanishing away?
Ó is there no frowning of these wrinkles, ranked wrinkles deep,
Dówn? no waving off of these most mournful messengers, still messengers, sad and stealing messengers of grey?
No there's none, there's none, O no there's none,
Nor can you long be, what you now are, called fair,
Do what you may do, what, do what you may,
And wisdom is early to despair:
Be beginning; since, no, nothing can be done
To keep at bay
Age and age's evils, hoar hair,
Ruck and wrinkle, drooping, dying, death's worst, winding sheets, tombs and worms and tumbling to decay;
So be beginning, be beginning to despair.
O there's none; no no no there's none:
Be beginning to despair, to despair,
Despair, despair, despair, despair.

THE GOLDEN ECHO

Spare!
There ís one, yes I have one (Hush there!) ;
Only not within seeing of the sun,
Not within the singeing of the strong sun,
Tall sun's tingeing, or treacherous the tainting of the earth's air,
Somewhere elsewhere there is ah well where! one,
Óne. Yes I can tell such a key, I do know such a place,
Where whatever's prized and passes of us, everything that's fresh and fast flying of us, seems to us sweet of us and swiftly away with, done away with, undone,
Undone, done with, soon done with, and yet dearly and dangerously sweet
Of us, the wimpled-water-dimpled, not-by-morning-matched face,
The flower of beauty, fleece of beauty, too too apt to, ah! to fleet,
Never fleets more, fastened with the tenderest truth
To its own best being and its loveliness of youth: it is an everlastingness of, O it is an all youth!
Come then, your ways and airs and looks, locks, maiden gear, gallantry and gaiety and grace,
Winning ways, airs innocent, maiden manners, sweet looks, loose locks, long locks, love-locks, gaygear, going gallant, girlgrace—
Resign them sign them, seal them, send them, motion them with breath,
And with sighs soaring, soaring sighs deliver
Them; beauty-in-the-ghost, deliver it, early now, long before death
Give beauty back, beauty, beauty, beauty, back to God, beauty's self and beauty's giver.
See; not a hair is, not an eyelash, not the least lash lost; every hair
Is, hair of the head, numbered.
Nay, what we had lighthanded left in surly the mere mould
Will have waked and have waxed and have walked with the wind what while we slept,
This side, that side hurling a heavyheaded hundredfold

What while we, while we slumbered.
O then, weary then whý should we tread? O why are we so haggard at the heart, so
care-coiled, care-killed, so fagged, so fashed, so cogged, so cumbered,
When the thing we freely fórfeit is kept with fonder a care,
Fonder a care kept than we could have kept it, kept
Far with fonder a care (and we, we should have lost it) finer, fonder
A care kept.—Where kept? Do but tell us where kept, where.—
Yonder.—What high as that! We follow, now we follow.—
Yonder, yes yonder, yonder,
Yonder.

[1882] [1918]

CARRION COMFORT

Not, I'll not, carrion comfort, Despair, not feast on thee;
Not untwist—slack they may be—these last strands of man
In me, or, most weary, cry *I can no more*. I can;
Can something, hope, wish day come, not choose not to be.
But ah, but O thou terrible, why wouldst thou rude on me
Thy wring-world right foot rock? lay a lionlimb against me? scan
With darksome devouring eyes my bruisèd bones? and fan,
O in turns of tempest, me heaped there; me frantic to avoid thee and flee?
Why? That my chaff might fly; my grain lie, sheer and clear.
Nay in all that toil, that coil, since (seems) I kissed the rod,
Hand rather, my heart lo! lapped strength, stole joy, would laugh, chéer.
Cheer whom though? the hero whose heaven-handling flung me, fóot tród
Me? or me that fought him? O which one? is it each one? That night, that year
Of now done darkness I wretch lay wrestling with (my God!) my God.

[1885?] [1918]

A. E. HOUSMAN

CHRONOLOGICAL TABLE

1859, Born, March 26, at The Valley House, Fockbury, Worcestershire (close to the border of Shropshire), his father a solicitor and inventor.

1870 Foundation Scholar at the Bromsgrove School in Worcestershire.

1877–81 Attended St. John's College, Oxford.

1879 Awarded a first class standing at the intermediate examination (Moderations) in the school of *Literae humaniores*.

1881 Failed at the final examination in that school.

1882 Awarded a pass degree (B.A.) at Oxford.

1882–92 Employed in the Patents Office of the British Government. During these years he published a number of papers (chiefly relating to textual criticism) in classical journals.

1892 Appointed to the chair of Latin at University College, London. [His inaugural, entitled *Introductory Lecture* privately printed by the College, published in 1937.]

1896 *A Shropshire Lad.*

1903 *Manilius, Book I.* (an edition of a Latin poet).

1905 *Juvenal* (another edition).

1911 Appointed to the chair of Latin Philology at the University of Cambridge.

1912 *Manilius, Book II.*

1916 *Manilius, Book III.*

1920 *Manilius, Book IV.*

1922 *Last Poems.*

1926 *Lucan* (another edition of a Latin poet).

1930 *Manilius, Book V* (the edition was now completed).

1933 *The Name and Nature of Poetry* (the Leslie Stephen lecture for 1933).

1936 Died at Cambridge, April 30.
More Poems.

Housman published two collections of verse: *A Shropshire Lad,* brought out when he was thirty-seven, and *Last Poems,* a characteristically sombre title for a work appearing when the author still had fourteen years to live. Between them the two volumes, separated by a little more than a quarter century, contain one hundred and five poems and a little more than two thousand lines. A third collection containing forty-nine poems, many of them fragments, and substantially less than a thousand lines appeared a few months after Housman's death. Much of this last collection is markedly inferior to the level maintained almost without a swerve in the books given us by Housman himself.

Slight as Housman's poetry is in bulk, it is no less limited in range. He had little to say: death is the end of all; life is cruel and inadequate but it is also delightful; youth passes; love and friendship are chequered with deception, misunderstanding and misfortune; the present and the past are fundamentally the same; nature is indifferent but beautiful. But if his themes are few they are great. A perfect, if limited technician, he developed his ideas and feelings again and again in the same contexts and with the same comments. His small body of verse is surprisingly uniform in manner, so much so that it may be found monotonous. Neither in diction nor in rhythm nor in stanzaic form does it vary notably. If it is untrue to say that Housman had but one style—he could be colloquial, or lapidary, or rhetorical—it is true that his lines are almost always brief, his stanzas simple, his rhythm unwaveringly emphatic, his sonorous monosyllables and dissyllables following one another in the simplest of successions.

The uniformity or near-uniformity in substance and style flows from a constancy of mood. Writing little in verse, Housman drew only from the deepest wells, recording no ordinary or trivial feelings but only the crises which shook a nature which under a grim severity hid an intensity of emotion no less quivering than Shelley's.

A SHROPSHIRE LAD

I

(1887)

From Clee to Heaven the beacon burns,
  The shires have seen it plain,
From north and south the sign returns
  And beacons burn again.

Look left, look right, the hills are bright,
  The dales are light between,
Because 'tis fifty years to-night
  That God has saved the Queen.

Now, when the flame they watch not towers
  About the soil they trod,
Lads, we'll remember friends of ours
  Who shared the work with God.

To skies that knit their heartstrings, right,
  To fields that bred them brave,
The Saviours come not home to-night
  Themselves they could not save.

It dawns in Asia, tombstones show
  And Shropshire names are read;
And the Nile spills his overflow
  Beside the Severn's dead.

We pledge in peace by farm and town
  The Queen they served in war,
And fire the beacons up and down
  The land they perished for.

'God save the Queen' we living sing,
  From height to height 'tis heard;
And with the rest your voices ring,
  Lads of the Fifty-third.

Oh, God will save her, fear you not:
  Be you the men you've been,
Get you the sons your fathers got,
  And God will save the Queen.

[1896]

II

Loveliest of trees, the cherry now
Is hung with bloom along the bough,
And stands about the woodland ride,
Wearing white for Eastertide.

Now, of my threescore years and ten,
Twenty will not come again,
And take from seventy springs a score,
It only leaves me fifty more.

And since to look at things in bloom
Fifty springs are little room,
About the woodlands I will go
To see the cherry hung with snow.

[1896]

IV

REVEILLE

Wake: the silver dusk returning
  Up the beach of darkness brims,
And the ship of sunrise burning
  Strands upon the eastern rims.

Wake: the vaulted shadow shatters,
  Trampled to the floor it spanned,
And the tent of night in tatters
  Straws the sky-pavilioned land.

Up, lad, up, 'tis late for lying:
  Hear the drums of morning play;
Hark, the empty highways crying
  'Who'll beyond the hills away?'

Towns and countries woo together,
  Forelands beacon, belfries call;
Never lad that trod on leather
  Lived to feast his heart with all.

Up, lads: thews that lie and cumber
  Sunlit pallets never thrive;
Morns abed and daylight slumber
  Were not meant for man alive.

Clay lies still, but blood's a rover;
  Breath's a ware that will not keep
Up, lad: when the journey's over
  There'll be time enough to sleep.

[1895] [1896]

VI

When the lad for longing sighs,
  Mute and dull of cheer and pale,
If at death's own door he lies,
  Maiden, you can heal his ail.

Lovers' ills are all to buy:
  The wan look, the hollow tone,
The hung head, the sunken eye—
  You can have them for your own.

Buy them, buy them: eve and morn
  Lovers' ills are all to sell.
Then you can lie down forlorn;
  But the lover will be well.

[1896]

XII

When I watch the living meet,
  And the moving pageant file
Warm and breathing through the street
  Where I lodge a little while,

If the heats of hate and lust
  In the house of flesh are strong,
Let me mind the house of dust
  Where my sojourn shall be long.

In the nation that is not
  Nothing stands that stood before;
There revenges are forgot,
  And the hater hates no more;

Lovers lying two and two
  Ask not whom they sleep beside,
And the bridegroom all night through
  Never turns him to the bride.

[1896]

XIV

There pass the careless people
  That call their souls their own:
Here by the road I loiter,
  How idle and alone.

Ah, past the plunge of plummet,
  In seas I cannot sound,
My heart and soul and senses,
  World without end, are drowned.

His folly has not fellow
  Beneath the blue of day
That gives to man or woman
  His heart and soul away.

There flowers no balm to sain him
  From east of earth to west
That's lost for everlasting
  The heart out of his breast.

Here by the labouring highway
  With empty hands I stroll:
Sea-deep, till doomsday morning,
  Lie lost my heart and soul.

[1896]

XVIII

Oh, when I was in love with you,
  Then I was clean and brave,
And miles around the wonder grew
  How well did I behave.

And now the fancy passes by,
  And nothing will remain,
And miles around they'll say that I
  Am quite myself again.

[1895] [1896]

XIX

TO AN ATHLETE DYING YOUNG

The time you won your town the race
We chaired you through the market-place;
Man and boy stood cheering by,
And home we brought you shoulder-high.

To-day, the road all runners come,
Shoulder-high we bring you home,
And set you at your threshold down,
Townsman of a stiller town.

Smart lad, to slip betimes away
From fields where glory does not stay
And early though the laurel grows
It withers quicker than the rose.

Eyes the shady night has shut
Cannot see the record cut,
And silence sounds no worse than cheers
After earth has stopped the ears:

Now you will not swell the rout
Of lads that wore their honours out,
Runners whom renown outran
And the name died before the man.

So set, before its echoes fade,
The fleet foot on the sill of shade,
And hold to the low lintel up
The still-defended challenge-cup.

And round that early-laurelled head
Will flock to gaze the strengthless dead,
And find unwithered on its curls
The garland briefer than a girl's.

[1896]

XXI

BREDON * HILL

In summertime on Bredon
  The bells they sound so clear;
Round both the shires they ring them
  In steeples far and near,
  A happy noise to hear.

Here of a Sunday morning
  My love and I would lie,
And see the coloured counties,
  And hear the larks so high
  About us in the sky.

The bells would ring to call her
  In valleys miles away:
"Come all to church, good people;
  Good people, come and pray."
  But here my love would stay.

And I would turn and answer
  Among the springing thyme,
"Oh, peal upon our wedding,
  And we will hear the chime,
  And come to church in time."

But when the snows at Christmas
  On Bredon top were strown,
My love rose up so early
  And stole out unbeknown
  And went to church alone.

They tolled the one bell only,
  Groom there was none to see,
The mourners followed after,
  And so to church went she,
  And would not wait for me.

The bells they sound on Bredon,
  And still the steeples hum.
"Come all to church, good people,"—
  Oh, noisy bells, be dumb;
  I hear you, I will come.

[1891] [1896]

XXVI

Along the field as we came by
A year ago, my love and I,
The aspen over stile and stone
Was talking to itself alone.
'Oh who are these that kiss and pass?
A country lover and his lass;
Two lovers looking to be wed;
And time shall put them both to bed,
But she shall lie with earth above,
And he beside another love.'

And sure enough beneath the tree
There walks another love with me,
And overhead the aspen heaves
Its rainy-sounding silver leaves;
And I spell nothing in their stir,
But now perhaps they speak to her,
And plain for her to understand
They talk about a time at hand
When I shall sleep with clover clad,
And she beside another lad.

[1895?] [1896]

* Pronounced Breedon.

XXVII

'Is my team ploughing,
  That I was used to drive
And hear the harness jingle
  When I was man alive?'

Ay, the horses trample,
  The harness jingles now;
No change though you lie under
  The land you used to plough.

'Is football playing
  Along the river shore,
With lads to chase the leather,
  Now I stand up no more?'

Ay, the ball is flying,
  The lads play heart and soul;
The goal stands up, the keeper
  Stands up to keep the goal.

'Is my girl happy,
  That I thought hard to leave,
And has she tired of weeping
  As she lies down at eve?'

Ay, she lies down lightly,
  She lies not down to weep:
Your girl is well contented.
  Be still, my lad, and sleep.

'Is my friend hearty,
  Now I am thin and pine,
And has he found to sleep in
  A better bed than mine?'

Yes, lad, I lie easy,
I lie as lads would choose;
I cheer a dead man's sweetheart,
Never ask me whose.

[1896]

XXVIII

THE WELSH MARCHES

High the vanes of Shrewsbury gleam
Islanded in Severn stream;
The bridges from the steepled crest
Cross the water east and west.

The flag of morn in conqueror's state
Enters at the English gate;
The vanquished eve, as night prevails,
Bleeds upon the road to Wales.

Ages since the vanquished bled
Round my mother's marriage-bed;
There the ravens feasted far
About the open house of war.

When Severn down to Buildwas ran,
Coloured with the death of man,
Couched upon her brother's grave
The Saxon got me on the slave.

The sound of fight is silent long
That began the ancient wrong;
Long the voice of tears is still
That wept of old the endless ill.

In my heart it has not died,
The war that sleeps on Severn side;
They cease not fighting, east and west,
On the marches of my breast.

Here the truceless armies yet
Trample, rolled in blood and sweat;
They kill and kill and never die;
And I think that each is I.

None will part us, none undo
The knot that makes one flesh of two,
Sick with hatred, sick with pain,
Strangling—When shall we be slain?

When shall I be dead and rid
Of the wrong my father did?
How long, how long, till spade and hearse
Put to sleep my mother's curse?

[1895] [1896]

XXXI

On Wenlock Edge the wood's in trouble;
His forest fleece the Wrekin heaves;
The gale, it plies the saplings double,
And thick on Severn snow the leaves.

'Twould blow like this through holt and hanger
When Uricon the city stood;
'Tis the old wind in the old anger,
But then it threshed another wood.

Then, 'twas before my time, the Roman
At yonder heaving hill would stare;
The blood that warms an English yeoman,
The thoughts that hurt him, they were there.

There, like the wind through woods in riot,
Through him the gale of life blew high;
The tree of man was never quiet—
Then 'twas the Roman, now 'tis I.

The gale, it plies the saplings double;
It blows so hard, 'twill soon be gone.
Today the Roman and his trouble
Are ashes under Uricon.

[1896]

XXXII

From far, from eve and morning
And yon twelve-winded sky,
The stuff of life to knit me
Blew hither: here am I.

Now—for a breath I tarry
Nor yet disperse apart—
Take my hand quick and tell me,
What have you in your heart.

Speak now, and I will answer;
How shall I help you, say;
Ere to the wind's twelve quarters
I take my endless way.

[1896]

XL

Into my heart an air that kills
From yon far country blows:
What are those blue remembered hills,
What spires, what farms are those?

That is the land of lost content,
  I see it shining plain,
The happy highways where I went
  And cannot come again.

[1896]

XLII

THE MERRY GUIDE

Once in the wind of morning
  I ranged the thymy wold;
The world-wide air was azure,
  And all the brooks ran gold.

There through the dews beside me,
  Behold a youth that trod,
With feathered cap on forehead,
  And poised a golden rod.

With mien to match the morning
  And gay delightful guise
And friendly brows and laughter,
  He looked me in the eyes.

Oh, whence, I asked, and whither?
  He smiled and would not say,
And looked at me and beckoned,
  And laughed and led the way.

And with kind looks and laughter
  And nought to say beside,
We two went on together,
  I and my happy guide.

Across the glittering pastures
  And empty upland still
And solitude of shepherds
  High in the folded hill,

By hanging woods and hamlets
  That gaze through orchards down
On many a windmill turning
  And far-discovered town,

With gay regards of promise
  And sure unslackened stride
And smiles and nothing spoken,
  Led on my merry guide.

By blowing realms of woodland
  With sunstruck vanes afield
And cloud-led shadows sailing
  About the windy weald,

By valley-guarded granges
  And silver waters wide,
Content at heart I followed
  With my delightful guide.

And like the cloudy shadows
  Across the country blown,
We two fare on forever,
  But not we two alone.

With the great gale we journey
  That breathes from gardens thinned,
Borne in the drift of blossoms
  Whose petals throng the wind;

Buoyed on the heaven-heard whisper
  Of dancing leaflets whirled
From all the woods that autumn
  Bereaves in all the world.

And midst the fluttering legion
  Of all that ever died
I follow, and before us
  Goes the delightful guide,

With lips that brim with laughter
  But never once respond,
And feet that fly on feathers,
  And serpent-circled wand.

[1890] [1896]

L

Clunton and Clunbury,
  Clungunford and Clun,
Are the quietest places
  Under the sun.

In valleys of springs of rivers,
  By Ony and Teme and Clun,
The country for easy livers,
  The quietest under the sun,

We still had sorrows to lighten,
  One could not be always glad,
And lads knew trouble at Knighton
  When I was a Knighton lad.

By bridges that Thames runs under,
  In London, the town built ill,
'Tis sure small matter for wonder
  If sorrow is with one still.

And if as a lad grows older
  The troubles he bears are more,
He carries his griefs on a shoulder
  That handselled them long before.

Where shall one halt to deliver
  This luggage I'd lief set down?
Not Thames, not Teme is the river,
  Nor London nor Knighton the town:

'Tis a long way further than Knighton,
  A quieter place than Clun,
Where doomsday may thunder and lighten
  And little 'twill matter to one.

[1896]

LII

Far in a western brookland
  That bred me long ago
The poplars stand and tremble
  By pools I used to know.

There, in the windless night-time,
  The wanderer, marvelling why,
Halts on the bridge to hearken
  How soft the poplars sigh.

He hears: long since forgotten
  In fields where I was known,
Here I lie down in London
  And turn to rest alone.

There, by the starlit fences,
  The wanderer halts and hears
My soul that lingers sighing
  About the glimmering weirs.

[1891–2] [1896]

LIV

With rue my heart is laden
  For golden friends I had,
For many a rose-lipt maiden
  And many a lightfoot lad.

By brooks too broad for leaping
  The lightfoot boys are laid;
The rose-lipt girls are sleeping
  In fields where roses fade.

[1893] [1896]

LXI

HUGHLEY STEEPLE

The vane on Hughley steeple
  Veers bright, a far-known sign,
And there lie Hughley people,
  And there lie friends of mine.
Tall in their midst the tower
  Divides the shade and sun,
And the clock strikes the hour
  And tells the time to none.

To south the headstones cluster,
  The sunny mounds lie thick;
The dead are more in muster
  At Hughley than the quick.
North, for a soon-told number,
  Chill graves the sexton delves,
And steeple-shadowed slumber
  The slayers of themselves.

To north, to south, lie parted,
  With Hughley tower above,
The kind, the single-hearted,
  The lads I used to love.
And, south or north, 'tis only
  A choice of friends one knows,
And I shall ne'er be lonely
  Asleep with these or those.

[1896]

LXII

'Terence, this is stupid stuff:
You eat your victuals fast enough;
There can't be much amiss, 'tis clear,
To see the rate you drink your beer.
But oh, good Lord, the verse you make,
It gives a chap the belly-ache.
The cow, the old cow, she is dead;
It sleeps well, the horned head:
We poor lads, 'tis our turn now
To hear such tunes as killed the cow.
Pretty friendship 'tis to rhyme
Your friends to death before their time
Moping melancholy mad:
Come, pipe a tune to dance to, lad.'

  Why, if 'tis dancing you would be,
There's brisker pipes than poetry.
Say for what were hop-yards meant,
Or why was Burton built on Trent?
Oh many a peer of England brews
Livelier liquor than the Muse,

And malt does more than Milton can
To justify God's ways to man.
Ale, man, ale's the stuff to drink
For fellows whom it hurts to think:
Look into the pewter pot
To see the world as the world's not.
And faith 'tis pleasant till 'tis past:
The mischief is that 'twill not last.
Oh I have been to Ludlow fair
And left my necktie God knows where,
And carried halfway home, or near,
Pints and quarts of Ludlow beer:
Then the world seemed none so bad,
And I myself a sterling lad;
And down in lovely muck I've lain,
Happy till I woke again.
Then I saw the morning sky:
Heigho, the tale was all a lie;
The world it was the old world yet,
I was I, my things were wet,
And nothing now remained to do
But begin the game anew.

Therefore, since the world has still
Much good, but much less good than ill,
And while the sun and moon endure
Luck's a chance but trouble's sure,
I'd face it as a wise man would,
And train for ill and not for good.
'Tis true, the stuff I bring for sale
Is not so brisk a brew as ale:
Out of a stem that scored the hand
I wrung it in a weary land.
But take it: if the smack is sour,
The better for the embittered hour;
It should do good to heart and head
When your soul is in my soul's stead;
And I will friend you, if I may,
In the dark and cloudy day.

There was a king reigned in the East:
There, when kings will sit to feast,
They get their fill before they think
With poisoned meat and poisoned drink.
He gathered all that springs to birth
From the many-venomed earth;
First a little, thence to more,
He sampled all her killing store;
And easy, smiling, seasoned sound,
Sate the king when healths went round.
They put arsenic in his meat
And stared aghast to watch him eat;
They poured strychnine in his cup
And shook to see him drink it up:
They shook, they stared as white's their shirt:
Them it was their poison hurt.
—I tell the tale that I heard told.
Mithridates, he died old.

[1896]

LXIII

I hoed and trenched and weeded,
And took the flowers to fair:
I brought them home unheeded;
The hue was not the wear.

So up and down I sow them
For lads like me to find,
When I shall lie below them,
A dead man out of mind.

Some seed the birds devour,
And some the season mars,
But here and there will flower
The solitary stars,

And fields will yearly bear them
As light-leaved spring comes on,
And luckless lads will wear them
When I am dead and gone.

[1896]

LAST POEMS

IX

The chestnut casts his flambeaux, and the flowers
Stream from the hawthorn on the wind away,
The doors clap to, the pane is blind with showers.
Pass me the can, lad; there's an end of May.

There's one spoilt spring to scant our mortal lot,
One season ruined of our little store.
May will be fine next year as like as not:
Oh ay, but then we shall be twenty-four.

We for a certainty are not the first
Have sat in taverns while the tempest hurled
Their hopeful plans to emptiness, and cursed
Whatever brute and blackguard made the world.

It is in truth iniquity on high
  To cheat our sentenced souls of aught they crave,
And mar the merriment as you and I
  Fare on our long fool's-errand to the grave.

Iniquity it is; but pass the can.
  My lad, no pair of kings our mothers bore;
Our only portion is the estate of man:
  We want the moon, but we shall get no more.

If here to-day the cloud of thunder lours
  To-morrow it will hie on far behests;
The flesh will grieve on other bones than ours
  Soon, and the soul will mourn in other breasts.

The troubles of our proud and angry dust
  Are from eternity and shall not fail.
Bear them we can, and if we can we must.
  Shoulder the sky, my lad, and drink your ale.

[1896] [1922]

GENERAL BIBLIOGRAPHY

The works in the following strictly selective list should be consulted prior to the study of each of the poets represented in this collection. The entries are not repeated.

I. BOOKS

BEACH, J. W.: *The Concept of Nature in Nineteenth Century English Poetry*, Macmillan, 1936.

BUSH, D.: *Mythology and the Romantic Tradition in English Poetry*, Harvard, 1937.

CAZAMIAN, L.: *History of English Literature*, 1660–1914, Macmillan, 1927.

CHESTERTON, G. K.: *The Victorian Age in Literature*, Williams and Norgate (London), 1913.

DRINKWATER, J.: *Victorian Poetry*, Hodder, 1923.

ELTON, O.: *A Survey of English Literature*, 1830–1880, Arnold, 1920.

EVANS, B. I.: *English Poetry in the Later Nineteenth Century*, Methuen, 1933.

GRIERSON, SIR HERBERT: *Lyrical Poetry from Blake to Hardy*, Hogarth, 1928.

ROUTH, H. V.: *Towards the Twentieth Century*, Cambridge, 1937.

SAINTSBURY, G.: *A History of Nineteenth Century Literature*, Macmillan, 1896.

STEVENSON, L.: *Darwin Among the Poets*, Chicago, 1932.

WALKER, H.: *The Age of Tennyson, 1830–1870*, Bell, 1900.

WALKER, H.: *The Greater Victorian Poets* (Tennyson, Browning, Arnold), Sonnenschein, 1895.

II. ESSAYS IN BOOKS

CAZAMIAN, L.: "Parallelism in the Recent Development of English and French Literature" in *Criticism in the Making*, Macmillan, 1929.

DRINKWATER, J.: "The Poetry of the Seventies" in *The Eighteen-Seventies* (ed. by H. Granville-Barker), Cambridge, 1929.

ELTON, O.: "Poetic Romancers after 1850" in *Proceedings of the British Academy*, Oxford, 1914.

GRANVILLE-BARKER, H.: "Tennyson, Swinburne and Meredith and the Theatre" in *The Eighteen-Seventies* (ed. by the same), Cambridge, 1929.

MACCALLUM, SIR M. W.: "The Dramatic Monologue in the Victorian Period" in *Proceedings of the British Academy*, Oxford, 1925.

SYMONDS, J. A.: "A Comparison of Elizabethan and Victorian Poetry" in *Essays Speculative and Suggestive*, Chapman, 1890.

BIBLIOGRAPHY

TENNYSON

I. EDITIONS

Works, 6 vols., annotated by Alfred Lord Tennyson, ed. by Hallam, Lord Tennyson, Macmillan, 1908.
Works, with notes by the author, ed. with a memoir by Hallam, Lord Tennyson, Macmillan, 1913.
Poems, ed. by Henry Van Dyke and D. L. Chambers, Ginn (Athenaeum Press Series), 1903.
Selections, ed. by W. C. DeVane and M. P. DeVane, Crofts, 1940.
Selections from the Poems, ed. by Myra Reynolds, Scott, 1913.
The Best of Tennyson, ed. by Walter Graham, Nelson, 1930.
In Memoriam, The Princess, and Maud, ed. by J. Churton Collins, Methuen, 1902.
The Early Poems, ed. by J. Churton Collins, Methuen, 1900.

II. BIOGRAPHY AND LETTERS

BENSON, A. C.: *Alfred Tennyson*, Methuen, 1904.
FAUSSET, H. I'A.: *Tennyson*, Selwyn, 1923, Cape (Traveller's Library), 1929.
LANG, A.: *Alfred Tennyson*, Blackwood, 1901.
LOUNSBURY, T. R.: *The Life and Times of Tennyson*, Yale, 1915.
LYALL, SIR A. C.: *Tennyson*, Macmillan, 1902.
RAWNSLEY, H. D.: *Memories of the Tennysons*, Maclehose, 1900.
RITCHIE, ANNE T.: *Records of Tennyson, Ruskin, and the Brownings*, Harper, 1892.
TENNYSON, HALLAM, LORD: *Alfred Lord Tennyson, a Memoir*, 2 vols., Macmillan, 1897.
TENNYSON, HALLAM, LORD: *Tennyson and His Friends*, Macmillan, 1902.
WAUGH, A.: *Alfred Lord Tennyson, A Study of His Life and Work*, Heinemann, 1892.

III. CRITICISM

I. MONOGRAPHS

ALDEN, R. M.: *Tennyson, How to Know Him*, Bobbs-Merrill, 1917.
BAKER, A. E.: *A Concordance to the Poetical and Dramatic Works of Alfred Lord Tennyson*, Macmillan, 1914.
BAKER, A. E.: *A Tennyson Dictionary*, Macmillan, 1916.
BRADLEY, A. C.: *A Commentary on Tennyson's 'In Memoriam,'* Macmillan, 1901, revised 1902.
GENUNG, J. F.: *Tennyson's 'In Memoriam' its Purpose and Structure*, Houghton, 1884.
GORDON, W. C.: *The Social Ideals of Alfred Tennyson, as Related to his Time*, Univ. of Chicago, 1906.
MACCALLUM, SIR M. W.: *Tennyson's 'Idylls of the King' and Arthurian Story*, Maclehose, 1894.
MUSTARD, W. P.: *Classical Echoes in Tennyson*, Macmillan, 1904.
NICOLSON, H.: *Tennyson, Aspects of his Life, Character and Poetry*, Constable, 1923.
PYRE, J. F. A.: *The Formation of Tennyson's Style*, University of Wisconsin Studies, 1921.
SNEATH, E. H.: *The Mind of Tennyson*, Scribner, 1900.
THOMSON, J. C.: *Bibliography of the Writings of Alfred, Lord Tennyson*, Stechert, 1905.
WISE, T. J.: *A Bibliography of the Writings of Alfred, Lord Tennyson*, 2 vols., Clay (London), 1908.

II. ESSAYS IN BOOKS

BAGEHOT, W.: "Wordsworth, Tennyson, and Browning" in *Literary Studies*, 3 vols., Longmans, 1895.
BRADLEY, A. C.: "The Reaction against Tennyson" in *A Miscellany*, Macmillan, 1929.
BRIMLEY, GEORGE: "Tennyson's Poems" in *Essays*, Parker, 1855.
CHAUVET, P.: "Tennyson" in *Sept essais de littérature anglaise*, Figuiere, 1931.
DOWDEN, E.: "Mr. Tennyson and Mr. Browning" in *Studies in Literature*, Paul, 1882.
ELIOT, T. S.: " 'In Memoriam' " in *Essays Ancient and Modern*, Faber, 1935.
ELTON, O.: "Tennyson, an Inaugural Lecture" in *Modern Studies*, Arnold, 1907.

Gates, L.: "Nature in Tennyson's Poetry" and "Tennyson in Relation to Modern Life" in *Studies and Appreciations*, Macmillan, 1900.
Gingerich, S.: *Wordsworth, Tennyson and Browning*, Wahr, 1911.
Hallam, A. H.: "On Some Characteristics of Modern Poetry and on the Lyrical Poems of Alfred Tennyson" in *Literary Remains*, Ticknor, 1863.
Harrison, F.: "Tennyson" in *Tennyson, Ruskin, Mill, and Other Literary Estimates*, Macmillan, 1900.
Hutton, R. H.: "Tennyson" in *Literary Essays*, Macmillan, 1888.
Jones, Sir Henry: "Tennyson" in *Proceedings of the British Academy*, IV, 1909.
Ker, W. P.: "Tennyson" in *Collected Essays*, 2 vols., Macmillan, 1925.
Mackail, J. W.: "Tennyson" in *Studies of English Poets*, Longmans, 1926.
Mill, J. S.: "Tennyson's Early Poems," in *Early Essays*, Bell, 1895.
Noyes, A.: "Tennyson and Some Recent Critics" in *Some Aspects of Modern Poetry*, Hodder, 1924.
Palgrave, F. T.: "The Landscape of Alfred, Lord Tennyson" in *Landscape in Poetry*, Macmillan, 1897.
Royce, J.: "Tennyson and Pessimism" in *Studies of Good and Evil*, Appleton, 1898.
Saintsbury, G.: "Tennyson" in *Corrected Impressions*, 1895.
Swinburne, A. C.: "Tennyson and Musset" in *Miscellanies*, Chatto, 1886.
Warren, Sir Herbert: " 'In Memoriam' after Fifty Years," "Virgil and Tennyson," and "Tennyson and Dante" in *Essays of Poets and Poetry, Ancient and Modern*, Murray, 1909.
Wilson, John (Christopher North): "Tennyson's Poems" in *Essays Critical and Imaginative*, 4 vols., Blackwood, 1856–7.

III. Articles in Periodicals

Cross, T. P.: "Alfred Tennyson as a Celticist" in *Modern Philology*, January, 1921.
Faguet, E.: "Centenary of Tennyson" in *Quarterly Review*, April, 1909.
Lockhart, J. G.: "Tennyson's Poems" in *Quarterly Review*, April, 1833.
Milsand, J.: "La poésie anglaise depuis Lord Byron: Alfred Tennyson" in *Revue des deux mondes*, July 15, 1851.
Thomas, G.: "Tennyson and the Georgians" in *London Quarterly Review*, July, 1923.
Ward, W.: "Tennyson's Religious Poetry" in *Dublin Review*, October, 1909.

NOTES AND COMMENTS

2. CLARIBEL

This poem first appeared in the collection of 1830, *Poems chiefly Lyrical.* The name occurs in the *Faerie Queene* and in the *Tempest.* In 1830 and in 1842 the poem was one unbroken stanza.

2, 11. In 1830 for *wild bee hummeth*, stood *bee low-hummeth.*

2, 15. *lintwhite*, linnet.

2, 16. *mavis*, thrush.

2, 17. In 1830 and up to 1851 for *callow* stood fledgling.

2, 19. *runnel*, brook.

2. MARIANA

This poem first appeared in the collection of 1830, *Poems chiefly Lyrical.* It was in part suggested by *Measure for Measure*, III, i, "at the moated grange resides the dejected Mariana."

3, 40. *marish*, marshy or marsh.

3, 43. Up to 1843 *dark* had stood for *mark.*

3, 80. In 1830 this line had the extremely elaborate form: "Downsloped was westering in his bower."

3. THE POET

This poem first appeared in the collection of 1830, *Poems chiefly Lyrical.*

It is Tennyson's first notable expression of opinion on the nature and function of his art.

4, 45–47. The first version of these lines was much more mannered:

> And in the bordure of her robe was writ
> Wisdom, a name to shake
> Hoar anarchies as with a thunderfit.

4. TO J. M. K.

This poem first appeared in the collection of 1830, *Poems chiefly Lyrical.* It was addressed to John Mitchell Kemble, an intimate of Tennyson's at Cambridge. Kemble did not take holy orders as Tennyson expected.

4. THE LADY OF SHALOTT

First appeared in the *Poems* of 1833. F. T. Palgrave asserts its source to have been an Italian romance on the Donna di Scalotta. Shalott is a variant form of Astolat; and Churton Collins points to the likelihood that the poem is a treatment, in another mood and tone, of the theme subsequently used in Lancelot and Elaine, the maid of Astolat. He also (*Early Poems of Tennyson*, 43) gives a likely Italian source.

This is one of the many poems in the collection of 1833 which underwent a severe revision before republication in 1842. Only a very few of the variants can be cited here.

5. *Camelot:* a city in Cornwall, the seat of King Arthur's court.

6–9. In the first edition:

> The yellow leavèd water lily,
> The green sheathed daffodilly,
> Tremble in the water chilly,
> Round about Shalott.

7. *blow:* blossom.

4, 10–11.

> Willows whiten, aspens shiver
> The sunbeam-showers break and quiver.

Note the transposition of the final words.

5, 45–52.
She lives with little joy or fear
Over the water running near,
The sheep-bell tinkles in her ear,
Before her hangs a mirror clear
  Reflecting towered Camelot.
And as the mazy web she whirls,
She sees the surly village-churls.

Note how the later version contributes to the idea of the poem with clarity and power not even adumbrated in the first version.

5, 56. *pad:* palfrey.
5, 84. *galaxy:* milky way.
127–143. These two stanzas replace three in the first version.

6, 163–171.
They crossed themselves, their stars they blest
Knight, minstrel, abbot, squire and guest,
There lay a parchment on her breast,
That puzzled more than all the rest,
  The well-fed wits at Camelot.
"*The web was woven curiously,*
The charm is broken utterly,
Draw near and fear not — this is I,
  The Lady of Shalott."

Note the dramatic significance in assigning, in the second version, the closing lines to Lancelot and the alteration in the effect produced by the poem when the parchment is excluded.

Tennyson proffered the following explanation of the poem: "The new-born love for something, for some one in the wide world from which she has been so long excluded, takes her out of the region of shadows into that of realities."

6. ŒNONE

This poem first appeared in the *Poems* of 1833. It was begun in 1830 when Tennyson was in Spain and a part was written in that valley in the Pyrenees which the poet was later to evoke in the brief piece "In the Valley of Cauteretz." The natural setting of the poem is not Trojan but Spanish in its general quality. Bush (*Mythology and the Romantic Tradition*, 203) describes the handling of the old story of the judgment of Paris as "freely original"; and points out fully the affinities in the general texture of the poem between Tennyson and Theocritus.

Œnone underwent very notable revisions before its republication in 1842. The descriptive passages became clearer without losing anything really sound in their sensuous richness; the famous speech of Pallas, 145–167 became more direct and weighty. The versions should be compared in detail.

6, 1. *Ida:* a mountain near Troy.
6, 2. *Ionian:* belonging to Ionia, an area in Asia Minor.
6, 10. *Gargarus:* the highest peak of Ida.
6, 13. *Troas:* the region of which Troy was the capital.
Ilion: Troy.
6, 17. *Paris once her playmate:* Paris was the husband of Œnone, seduced from her love by the goddess Aphrodite, as described below.
7, 38. *a River-God:* she was the daughter of Cebrenus, god of the river Cebren nearby.
7, 40–41. *yonder walls rose slowly to a music:* the walls of Ilion were believed to have risen to the music of Apollo's lyre.
7, 52. *Simois:* a river.
7, 66. *fruit of pure Hesperian gold:* the Hesperides, daughters of Hesperus (Atlas) were thought to guard in their western island apples of gold.
7, 67. *ambrosially:* like ambrosia, a food of the gods.
7, 74. *Oread:* mountain nymph.
7, 81. *Peleus:* a grandson of Jupiter, at whose marriage to Thetis, a nymph, all the gods attended.
7, 83. *Iris:* a messenger of the gods, and herself goddess of the rainbow.
7, 85. *Here:* Juno, the wife of Jupiter.
7, 86. *Pallas:* Minerva, goddess of wisdom.
Aphrodite: Venus, goddess of love and beauty.

7, 97. *amaracus:* marjoram.

8, 104. *peacock:* this was one of the most frequent accompaniments of Juno in classical representations of her.

8, 128. *king-born:* Paris was the son of Priam, king of Troy.

8, 153. *sequel of guerdon:* the meaning of this condensed expression is that if the goddess were to reward Paris so that in consequence he should name her fairest. . . .

8, 174. *Idalian:* belonging to Idalium, a town in the island of Cyprus, where the goddess was specially worshipped, in a grove at the foot of a mountain.

8, 175. *Paphian:* belonging to Paphos, another town in the same island, where Aphrodite was also worshipped.

8, 177–178. In the first version Tennyson represented Aphrodite as dark:

> From her warm brow and bosom her dark hair
> Fragrant and thick. . . .

9, 208. *they:* men from Troy, desiring timber.

9, 224. *the Abominable:* Eris, goddess of discord.

9, 225. *Peleian:* belonging to Peleus.

10, 251. *purpose:* Œnone, to whom Paris later came to be healed of a wound, refused to heal him, suffered him to die and then killed herself.

10, 261. *The Greek woman:* Helen, wife of Menelaus, king of Sparta, given to Paris by the power of Aphrodite.

10, 263. *the wild Cassandra:* a daughter of Priam, gifted with the power of prophecy but unheeded because she was deemed mad.

10, 264–265. The prophecy is of the Trojan war, provoked by the loss of Helen to Paris.

10. THE PALACE OF ART

This poem first appeared in the *Poems* of 1833. In 1890 Tennyson stated the impulse behind the poem: "Trench [an early friend, later Archbishop of Dublin] said to me when we were at Trinity together, 'Tennyson, we cannot live in art.' "The Palace of Art" is the embodiment of my own belief that the Godlike life is with man and for man, that

> Beauty, Good and Knowledge are three sisters,
> That never can be sunder'd without tears.
> And he that shuts out Love, in turn shall be
> Shut out from Love, and on her threshold lie
> Howling in outer darkness. (*Memoir*, I, 119.)

Like "Œnone," this poem underwent many and important revisions before republication in 1842.

10, 15–16. "The shadow of Saturn thrown upon the bright ring that surrounds the planet appears motionless, though the body of the planet revolves" (Rowe and Webb).

11, 54. *grateful:* pleasant.

11, 65–68. This, one of Tennyson's most suggestive pictures, had in 1833 been a quite commonplace passage:

> Some were all dark and red, a glimmering land
> Lit with a low round moon,
> Among brown rocks a man upon the sand
> Went weeping all alone.

11, 69–76. Added in 1842.

11, 95. *Sardonyx:* an onyx, with alternate white and orange layers.

11, 96. In 1833 a footnote was appended to this stanza, and led to revelry among the critics: "When I first conceived the plan of the "Palace of Art," I intended to have introduced both sculptures and paintings into it; but it is the most difficult of all things to *devise* a statue in verse. Judge whether I have succeeded in the statues of Elijah and Olympias:

> One was the Tishbite whom the raven fed,
> As when he stood on Carmel steeps
> With one arm stretched out bare, and mocked and said
> "Come cry aloud — he sleeps."

Tall, eager, lean and strong, his cloak wind-borne
  Behind, his forehead heavenly bright
From the clear marble pouring glorious scorn,
  Lit as with inner light.

One was Olympias: the floating snake
  Rolled round her ankles, round her waist
Knotted, and folded once about her neck,
  Her perfect lips to taste.

Round by the shoulder moved: she seeming blythe
  Declined her head: on every side
The dragon's curves melted and mingled with
  The woman's youthful pride
Of rounded limbs.

Or Venus in a snowy shell alone,
  Deep-shadowed in the glassy brine,
Moonlike glowed double on the blue, and shone
  A naked shape divine.

11, 99. *St. Cecily:* the patron saint of music, and supposed in some legends to have invented the organ.

11, 102. *Houris:* young women in the Mohammedan conception of Paradise.

11, 103. *Islamite:* Mohammedan.

12, 105. *mythic Uther's deeply wounded son:* King Arthur was the son of Uther, a shadowy legendary figure (*mythic*); he died of wounds received in battle.

12, 107. *Avalon:* an earthly paradise to which Arthur was borne by the *queens* referred to in the following line.

12, 108. The earlier, and weaker, reading was: Tended by crownèd queens.

12, 111. *the Ausonian king:* Numa, one of the earliest kings of Rome, was counselled, according to myth, by the nymph Egeria. *Ausonian* means belonging to Italy.

12, 113. *engrailed:* indented.

12, 115. *Indian Cama:* Camadev, god of love in Hindu myth.

12, 117–120. Europa, a beautiful princess of Phoenicia, carried off by Jupiter who assumed the guise of a bull.

12, 121–124. Ganymede, a beautiful Phrygian youth, carried off by Jupiter, who assumed the guise of an eagle, and made cupbearer to the gods.

12, 128. A long passage following the stanza ending here was removed in 1842; a part of it was inserted at an earlier point; but in all editions following 1851 two important philosophico-scientific stanzas were omitted altogether:

"From change to change four times within the womb
  The brain is moulded," she began,
"So thro' all phases of all thought I come
  Into the perfect man.

All nature widens upward: evermore
  The simpler essence lower lies,
More complex is more perfect, owning more
  Discourse, more widely wise."

Compare *In Memoriam*, Epilogue, and *Maud*, I, iv, 31 f.

12, 135–136. These lines developed from the earlier reading "Grim Dante pressed his lips."

12, 137. *The Ionian father of the rest:* Homer.

12, 137 f. At this point in the edition of 1833 appeared a long section on innocently sensuous joys, exotic fruits and liquors and colours, ending with the lines:

Thus her intense untold delight,
In deep or vivid colour, smell and sound,
Was flattered day and night.

In the course of the passage Tennyson couples with the beautiful flames of "precious oils" the "white streams of dazzling gas"!

148. *fail:* fade.

163. *Verulam:* Francis Bacon who was created Baron Verulam.

171. *Memnon:* a statue of Memnon in Egypt was believed to respond with music to the first beam of the dawn.

13, 186. *anadem:* garland.

13, 219. *Herod:* See *Acts*, XII, 21–23.

13, 223. *The abysmal deeps of Personality:* this phrase doubtless had emotional overtones for Tennyson, since in Hallam's *Remains* occur the words "the abysmal secrets of personality."

13, 227. *Mene:* one of the words written on the wall of King Belshazzar by an invisible hand and interpreted by the prophet Daniel. It means: "God hath numbered thy kingdom and finished it" (See *Daniel*, Ch. V).

13, 239. *phantasms:* unreal images, perceived by her alone.

14, 275. *dully:* dull.

14. THE LOTOS-EATERS

This poem first appeared in the *Poems* of 1833. Tennyson found the suggestion in the ninth book of the *Odyssey*, 82 f. The relevant part of the Homeric passage runs as follows (in Butcher and Lang's translation): "On the tenth day we set foot on the land of the lotos-eaters who eat a flowery food. So we stepped ashore and drew water. . . . When we had tasted meat and drink, I sent forth certain of my company to go and make search what manner of men they were who here live upon the earth by bread. . . . Then straightway they went and mixed with the men of the lotos-eaters and so it was that the lotos-eaters devised not death for our fellows but gave them of the lotos to taste. Now whosoever of them did eat the honey-sweet fruit of the lotos had no more wish to bring tidings nor to come back, but there he chose to abide with the lotos-eating men ever feeding on the lotos and forgetful of his homeward way. Therefore I led them back to the ships weeping and sore against their will . . . lest haply any should eat of the lotos and be forgetful of returning." In the last section of the "Choric Song" Tennyson follows Lucretius; see below.

Before republication in 1842 the poem underwent extensive revision, the final section of the "Choric Song" having been completely rewritten.

14, Introduction, 16. An excess of intensity probably led to the alteration of this line from a very beautiful earlier form:

Three thunder-cloven thrones of oldest snow

14, Introduction, 23, *galingale:* a grass.

15, Choric Song 61. *crisping:* curling.

16, 88. *amaranth:* an unfading flower. *moly:* an herb of divine powers.

16, 97. *acanthus:* a plant with pointed leaves.

16, 105 f. From this point to the end, the poem was completely rewritten for 1842. Few instances of Tennyson's reshaping of a passage are comparable with this. The whole of the text of 1833 is given for analysis:

We have had enough of motion,
Weariness and wild alarm,
Tossing on the tossing ocean,
Where the tuskèd sea-horse walloweth
In a stripe of grass-green calm,
At noontide beneath the lee;
And the monstrous narwhale swalloweth
His foam-fountains in the sea.
Long enough the wine-dark wave our weary bark did carry.
This is lovelier and sweeter,
Men of Ithaca, this is meeter,
In the hollow rosy vale to tarry,
Like a dreamy Lotos-eater, a delirious Lotos-eater!
We will eat the Lotos, sweet
As the yellow honeycomb,
In the valley some, and some
On the ancient heights divine;
And no more roam,
On the loud hoar foam,
To the melancholy home

At the limit of the brine,
The little isle of Ithaca, beneath the day's decline.
We'll lift no more the shattered oar,
No more unfurl the straining sail;
With the blissful Lotos-eaters pale
We will abide in the golden vale
Of the Lotos-land till the Lotos fail;
We will not wander more.
Hark! how sweet the horned ewes bleat
On the solitary steeps,
And the merry lizard leaps,
And the foam-white waters pour;
And the dark pine weeps,
And the lithe vine creeps,
And the heavy melon sleeps
On the level of the shore:
Oh! islanders of Ithaca, we will not wander more,
Surely, surely, slumber is more sweet than toil, the shore
Than labour in the ocean, and rowing with the oar,
Oh, islanders of Ithaca we will return no more.

The inferiority in music and diction is patent; almost every line in this earlier text has its false note, despite the different kind of beauty realized.

The picture of the gods which occupies so much of the last section in the later version appears to have satisfied Tennyson. Aubrey de Vere (*Memoir*, I, 504) reports him as "pointing out to me the improvement effected later by the introduction of the last paragraph setting forth the Lucretian philosophy respecting the Gods, their aloofness from all human interests and elevated action, an Epicurean and therefore hard-hearted repose, sweetened not troubled by the endless wail from the earth." De Vere goes on to say, aptly, that "the sudden change of metre in the last paragraph has a highly artistic effect, that of throwing the bulk of the poem as it were into a remote distance."

16, 107. *the wallowing monster:* the whale.

17, 124. *Elysian:* belonging to Paradise.

17. A DREAM OF FAIR WOMEN

This poem first appeared in the *Poems* of 1833. Collins rightly says (*Early Poems*, 115) that "there is no resemblance between [Tennyson's poem and Chaucer's *Legend of Good Women*] beyond the fact that both are visions and both have as their heroines illustrious women who have been unfortunate. Cleopatra is the only one common to the two poems."

The poem was extensively revised not only for republication in 1842 but at intervals up to 1853.

The emotional tone and philosophic outlook of the piece were admirably set forth in four stanzas which prefaced it in 1833 but were later removed:

As when a man, that sails in a balloon,
  Down looking sees the solid shining ground
Stream from beneath him in the broad blue noon,
  Tilth, hamlet, mead and mound:

And takes his flags and waves them to the mob,
  That shout below, all faces turned to where
Glows ruby-like the far up crimson globe,
  Filled with a finer air:

So lifted high, the Poet at his will
  Lets the great world flit from him, seeing all,
Higher through secret splendours mounting still,
  Self-poised, nor fears to fall,

Hearing apart the echoes of his fame.
  While I spoke thus, the seedsman, memory,
Sowed my deepfurrowed thought with many a name,
  Whose glory will not die.

The substance of these lines should be compared with that of *The Poet.* Tennyson did not admire them (*Memoir*, I, 121): it is not clear whether his dissatisfaction was with their relevance or with their intrinsic quality.

17, 2. *The Legend of Good Women:* see the general note on this poem.

17, 5. *Dan:* Master.

17, 27. *tortoise:* a literal translation of the Latin term *testudo* which has the meaning of soldiers hidden and sheltered under their shields and resembling, when seen from above, the shape of a tortoise.

17, 36. *seraglios:* harems.

17, 47. *leaguer'd:* besieged.

18, 85. *a lady:* Helen, of Troy.

18, 91. *immortal:* divine. Helen was the daughter of Jupiter by Leda a mortal.

18, 95–96. Helen was given to Paris, son of Priam, king of Troy, by Venus (Aphrodite) as the reward for his preferring her to Juno and Pallas. Helen's husband, Menelaus, summoned his fellow rulers in Greece (who had before Helen's marriage contracted to assure her eventual husband continuous possession of her) to help him recover her. In execution of their promise there followed the ten years war between the Greeks and the Trojans. There are varied accounts of her later life — all unhappy.

18, 100. *one:* Iphigenia, daughter of Agamemnon, who sacrificed her (according to some accounts) to propitiate Diana.

18, 105. *that sad place:* Aulis, in Boeotia. Tennyson names it in the next line. Prior to 1884 he did not name it, saying merely:

> Which yet to name my spirit loathes and fears.

It is unnecessary to emphasise the loss in intensity.

19, 127. *a queen:* Cleopatra.

19, 139. *that dull cold-blooded Caesar:* the reference is to Octavius, not to Julius, Caesar.

19, 145. *Libyan:* appertaining to Libya in north Africa, the region of Alexandria where Antony and Cleopatra revelled.

19, 146. *Canopus:* a star, invisible in western countries but clearly seen in Egypt.

19, 150. *Hercules:* Antony claimed descent from Hercules.

19, 151. *Bacchus:* the god of wine and accordingly of revels, and hence a prototype of Mark Antony.

19, 155. *worm:* serpent. See l. 160.

19, 178. *some one:* Jephtha's daughter. See *Judges*, ch. XI.

20, 197. *the warrior Gileadite:* Jephtha. Gilead lay across the Jordan from Samaria.

20, 199. *Mizpeh:* a city in Gilead, the home of Jephtha.

20, 237. *It is written:* in *Judges*, ch. XI, 33.

20, 238–239. *Ammon* lay to the south of Gilead; the word here stands for the inhabitants of the country. *Aroer* and *Minneth* were cities in *Ammon; Arnon* was the river dividing the Israelites from the Ammonites.

20, 243. *thridding:* threading.

21, 251. *Rosamond:* the mistress of Henry II, of England, supposed to have been poisoned by his wife, Eleanor.

21, 255. *Eleanor:* see note on l. 251.

21, 259. *Fulvia:* the wife of Mark Antony, who stood to Cleopatra in the same relation as Eleanor to Rosamond.

21, 266–267. The reference is to Margaret Roper, daughter of Sir Thomas More, who was beheaded by Henry VIII. She is believed to have purchased and embalmed her father's head.

21, 269. *her:* Eleanor of Aquitaine, wife of Edward I, of England, sucked poison from a wound her husband had suffered.

21. YOU ASK ME WHY, THO' ILL AT EASE

First published in 1842, but presumed to have been written much earlier. Aubrey de Vere suggests it was prompted by the tumult over the Reform Bill (1832).

22. OF OLD SAT FREEDOM ON THE HEIGHTS

First appeared in 1842, but like the preceding believed to have been written much earlier. Lines 13–20 occur in a letter written in 1834.

15. *triple forks:* trident, the Roman symbol of authority, *trisulca tela.*

22. LOVE THOU THY LAND

First published in 1842; but included entire in a letter of 1834.

23. MORTE D'ARTHUR

This poem was first published in 1842, but by 1835 it was sufficiently complete for Tennyson to read it to his friends FitzGerald and Spedding. The source is Malory's *Morte D'Arthur*, Bk. XXI, chs. 3–5. Tennyson dictated and approved the following comment: "How much of history we have in the story of Arthur is doubtful. Let not my readers press too hardly on details whether for history or for allegory. Some think that King Arthur may be taken to typify conscience. He is anyhow meant to be a man who spent himself in the cause of honour, duty, and self-sacrifice, who felt and aspired with his nobler knights, though with a stronger and clearer conscience than any of them, 'reverencing his conscience as his king.' 'There was no such perfect man since Adam' as an old writer says, 'Major praeteritis majorque futuris Regibus.'" *Memoir*, I, 194. "Morte D'Arthur" was subsequently incorporated in one of the *Idylls of the King*, "The Passing of Arthur."

23, 4. *Lyonnesse:* a legendary land, south of Cornwall, from which Arthur was believed to have come and to which he was destined to return.

23, 9. *chancel:* sanctuary.

23, 21. *Camelot:* the capital of Arthur.

23, 23. *Merlin:* a magician at Arthur's court.

23, 31. *samite:* a silken fabric.

23, 37. *into the middle mere:* into the middle of the lake.

25, 139. The reference is to the northern lights.

26, 210. *complaining:* wailing.

26, 232–233. The reference is to the star which led the three wise men to Bethlehem. (See *Matthew*, Ch. II, 7 f.)

27, 259. *Avilion:* Avalon, the paradise of Arthurian legend, an earthly paradise.

27. ULYSSES

This poem was first published in 1842, but composed much earlier. Tennyson's son reports his father as saying: "Ulysses was written soon after Arthur Hallam's death, and gave my feeling about the need of going forward, and braving the struggle of life perhaps more simply than anything in *In Memoriam*" (*Memoir*, I, 196). Sir James Knowles reports another remark of the poet's: "There is more about myself in 'Ulysses' [than in *In Memoriam*] which was written under the sense of loss and all that had gone by, but that still life must be fought out to the end. It was more written with the feeling of his loss upon me than many poems in *In Memoriam*." (*Nineteenth Century*, XXXIII, 1893.) Many commentators have emphasised how little the poem owes to Homer in its conception of the character of Ulysses. In essentials Tennyson follows Dante's representation of Ulysses in the twenty-sixth canto of the *Inferno*, from l. 90 to the end. Tennyson made no single alteration in the text after its first publication.

27, 10. *Hyades:* a group of stars which rises with the sun at time of the spring rains.

27, 34. *the isle:* Ulysses was King of Ithaca, an island off the west coast of Greece.

28, 60–62. Beyond the straits of Gibraltar, the Homeric age conceived that the waters led to a chasm through which Hades might be reached.

28, 63. *The Happy Isles:* the place where the heroes lived after death; it was supposed also to lie in the ocean beyond the straits of Gibraltar.

28, 64. *Achilles:* the mightiest in battle of the Greeks who took part in the Trojan War, was slain in the last year of the siege.

28. TITHONUS

This poem first appeared in the *Cornhill Magazine*, February, 1860. Tennyson has stated that the poem was "written upwards of a quarter of a century" earlier; but has offered no explanation why so finely moving and polished a poem was excluded from the volumes of 1842. Bush states (*Mythology and the Romantic Tradition*, 211) that the main source was the Homeric hymn to Aphrodite. In Greek mythology Tithonus was loved by the dawn, Eos, whose request that he be endowed with immortality was granted, but since it had not been stipulated that he be released from man's normal aging, Tithonus withered and weakened year after year beyond the human span, and prayed hopelessly for death.

28, 6. *thine arms:* the arms of Eos. See the general note on the poem.

28, 25. *the silver star:* the morning star.

28, 29. *kindly:* according to their nature.

28, 39–42. The reference is to the chariot and the steeds which were supposed in Greek myth to bear Eos (Aurora) on her morning journey to the top of Mount Olympus, the home of the gods.

28, 55. *mystic:* mysterious and supernatural.

29, 62–63. The walls of Troy (Ilion) were said to have risen to the sound of music, and in some versions of the myth the music was that of the lyre of Apollo, god of music.

29. LOCKSLEY HALL

This poem first appeared in the *Poems* of 1842. About it Tennyson has made a number of significant remarks. He explains the choice of the metre as the outcome of a chance observation by Henry Hallam that "English people liked verse in Trochaics" (*Memoir*, I, 195); he confesses an obligation to Sir William Jones's prose renderings of a series of old Arabian poems, the *Moallakát*, in one of which a lover utters a lament before the place from which his beloved with her tribe has lately removed; and he states that "the poem was a simple invention as to place, incidents and people" (*Memoir*, II, 379). He summed up the meaning of the poem with the remark that it "represents young life, its good side, its deficiencies and its yearnings" (*Memoir*, I, 195).

29, 3. *and all around it:* in 1842 he had written "and round the gables."

29, 4. *gleams:* the word does not refer to the curlews flying through the darkened sky. Tennyson stated that his meaning was "to express the flying gleams of light across a dreary moorland, when looking at it under peculiarly dreary circumstances" (*Memoir*, III, 82). Oddly in Tennyson's native Lincolnshire, from which he takes the landscape of the poem, *gleams* is applied to the *cry* of the curlew; but Tennyson did not know this local usage.

30, 31–32. This image was in the poet's opinion the finest he had conceived.

31, 75. *the poet:* Dante. See *Inferno*, canto V, 121–123.

33, 155. *Mahratta-battle:* the Mahrattas are an Indian people with which the British had many encounters in the early 19th century.

33, 160. "In the first, unpublished, edition of 'Locksley Hall,' after '*knots of Paradise*' came the following couplet, which was omitted lest the description should be too long:

> All about a summer ocean, leagues on leagues of golden calm,
> And within melodious waters rolling round the knolls of palm." (*Memoir*, I, 195.)

33, 162. *Swings:* up to 1850 the reading was "droops." Some commentators suggest the change was intended to stress the intense quiet of the scene by introducing one slight but definite movement; it is more likely that the change was to secure a balance both of meaning and of sound with "slide."

34, 180. *Joshua's moon.* See *Joshua*, X, 12.

34, 182. *the ringing grooves of change:* Tennyson has confessed the misconception which led to the metaphor, saying: "When I went by the first train from Liverpool to Manchester (1830) I thought that the wheels ran in a groove. It was a black night and there was such a vast crowd round the train at the station that we could not see the wheels. Then I made this line." (*Memoir*, I, 195.) Many of Tennyson's most striking images were worked out, as this one was, apart from their ultimate context.

34, 184. *Cathay:* China.

34. ST. AGNES' EVE

This poem was first published in 1837 in *The Keepsake*. This and a poem which was to become one of the sections of *Maud* were the only pieces Tennyson consented to print between 1833 and 1842.

This poem was entitled "St. Agnes" up to 1857. It is plausibly assumed that the change in title was intended to emphasize its likenesses and unlikenesses to Keats's *The Eve of St. Agnes*. St. Agnes was martyred at thirteen; although a medieval setting is suggested by many of the opening phrases she lived in the time of Diocletian. (283–304)

34, 16. *argent round:* silvery circle — the moon.

34, 17. *the Lamb:* Christ.

34, 31. *the Heavenly Bridegroom:* Christ.

34. SIR GALAHAD

First published in the *Poems* of 1842. McCallum points out (*Tennyson's Idylls and Arthurian Story,* 304) that just as the "Morte D'Arthur" is a sketch of the idyll *The Passing of Arthur*, "Sir Galahad," brief as it is, may be regarded as a sketch of *The Holy Grail*. No change has been made in the text since its first publication.

35, 25. *the stormy crescent:* the new moon when clouded before a storm.

35, 31. *stalls:* seats in the chancel or sanctuary.

35, 37. *meres:* lakes.

35, 42. *the holy Grail:* the cup (or plate) in which Joseph of Arimathea was said to have caught the drops of blood which fell from Christ on the cross. In Arthurian legend he is represented as having brought the grail to Britain.

35, 53. *leads:* of the roofs.

35. THE VISION OF SIN

This poem first appeared in the *Poems* of 1842.

35, 3. *a horse with wings:* Pegasus, a winged horse, was in Greek myth the steed of those inspired.

35, 10. *a crescent of eclipse:* reduced to the shape of a crescent in a partial eclipse.

36, 72. *the Dragon on the heath:* the inn where he serves.

36, 76. *spices:* spiced drinks.

36, 96. *rouse:* carouse.

36, 97–98. Until 1850 these lines stood:

> Every minute dies a man,
> Every minute one is born.

Collins reports a letter addressed to the poet by the celebrated mathematician Babbage (in obvious jest) in which it was protested: "that this calculation would tend to keep the sum total of the world's population in a state of perpetual equipoise, whereas it is a well-known fact that the said sum is constantly on the increase." Babbage suggested that "in the next edition of your excellent poem the erroneous calculation to which I refer should be corrected as follows:

> Every moment dies a man
> And one and a sixteenth is born."

Babbage conceded that even in his version the ratio would not be strictly correct: "the exact figures are 1.167, but something must, of course, be conceded to the laws of metre."

37, 142. *that cap upon her brows:* the figure of Liberty was often represented in Tennyson's time as a woman of the French Revolution, wearing a red cap.

37, 151. *stave:* song.

37, 172. *chap-fallen:* disconsolate, literally one whose jaw (*chap*) has fallen.

37, 189. *buss:* an archaic term meaning to kiss.

38, 208. *mystic:* mysterious.

38. BREAK, BREAK, BREAK

First appeared in the *Poems* of 1842. Tennyson has stated that it was composed not by the sea but "in a Lincolnshire lane at five o'clock in the morning between blossoming hedges."

38. SONGS FROM THE PRINCESS

The plan of *The Princess* Tennyson discussed with Miss Sellwood as early as 1839; the subject of higher education for women pre-occupied him to the point that he is reported to have declared that the two critical social problems of his time were "the housing and education of the poor man before making him our master and the higher education of women." His basic conception was that "woman was not undevelopt man but diverse"; and he was harassed by the fear that the provision of higher education for women — which he desired and believed inevitable — would not take account of this conception (*Memoir*, I, 249). The poem first appeared in 1847; but many of the Songs which

> The women sang
> Between the rougher voices of the men,
> Like linnets in the pauses of the wind

were not inserted until the third edition appeared in 1850. In his review of that edition Charles Kingsley aptly described the function of the songs: "At the end of the first canto fresh from the description of the female college, with its professoresses and hostleresses, and other Utopian monsters, we turn the page, and —

> As through the land at eve we went . . .
> O there above the little grave
> We kissed again with tears.

Between the next two cantos intervenes the well-known cradle-song, perhaps the best of all ["Sweet and low"]; and at the next interval is the equally well-known bugle-song, the idea of which is that of twin-labour and twin-fame in a pair of lovers ["The splendour falls on castle walls"]. In the next the memory of wife and child inspirits the soldier on the field ["Thy voice is heard"]; in the next the sight of the fallen hero's child opens the sluices of his widow's tears ["Home they brought her warrior dead"]; and in the last . . . the poet has succeeded in superadding a new form of emotion to a canto in which he seemed to have exhausted every resource of pathos which his subject allowed ["Ask me no more"]. In addition to these songs which intervene between the cantos there are a few others which are more directly interwoven into the structure of the poem's development.

38. I. *As thro' the land at eve we went.*

First appeared in the third edition (1850).

38. II. *Sweet and low.*

First appeared in 1850.

39. III. *The splendour falls on castle walls.*

First appeared in 1850.

39. IV. *Tears, idle tears.*

First appeared in 1847, in the original edition of the poem. Tennyson has stated: "The passion of the past, the abiding in the transient, was expressed in 'Tears, Idle Tears,' which was written in the yellowing autumn-tide at Tintern Abbey full for me of its bygone memories. Few know that it is a blank verse lyric" (*Memoir*, I, 253). The memories were of Hallam: see *In Memoriam*, XIX, and the notes thereon.

39. V. *O Swallow, Swallow.*

First appeared in the original edition of 1847.

40. VI. *Thy voice is heard thro' rolling drums.*

First appeared in 1850.

40. VII. *Home they brought her warrior dead.*

First appeared in 1850.

40. VIII. *Ask me no more.*

First appeared in 1850.

40. IX. *Now sleeps the crimson petal, now the white.*

First appeared in 1847.

40, 7. *Danaë:* a Greek princess imprisoned in a tower but visited by Jupiter in the guise of a golden shower.

40. X. *Come down, O maid, from yonder mountain height.*

First appeared in 1847. This poem is described in the text of the Princess as: "a small sweet Idyl." The *Memoir* reports that "for *simple* rhythm and vowel music [Tennyson] considered his 'Come down, O maid, from yonder mountain height,' written in Switzerland (chiefly at Lauterbrunnen and Grindelwald) and descriptive of the waste Alpine heights and gorges, and of the sweet, rich valleys below, as amongst his 'most successful work.'" (*Memoir*, I, 252.)

41, 13. *the Silver Horns:* the peaks of the mountains.

41, 15. *firths of ice:* glaciers.

41, 17. *dusky doors:* debris.

41, 25. *azure pillars:* of smoke.

41. IN MEMORIAM

In February, 1828, Alfred Tennyson matriculated at Trinity College, Cambridge; and shortly afterwards he made the acquaintance of Arthur Henry Hallam, a member of the same college, and the son of Henry Hallam, the historian of the Middle Ages. They were both elected to the group of brilliant undergraduates, known as the Apostles; in the summer of 1830 they travelled together to the Pyrenees, meeting there leaders of the Spanish insurgents; in other vacations they took more peaceful journeys together; and on one of his visits to the Tennyson household at Somersby Hallam became engaged to Alfred's sister, Emily.

In 1833 Hallam and his father travelled on the continent; and on September 15 Hallam died at Vienna. Tennyson soon began to compose elegies on his death. "The sections," he says, "were written at many different places, and as the phases of our intercourse came to my memory and suggested them. I did not write them with any view of weaving them into a whole, or for publication, until I found that I had written so many." (*Memoir*, I, 304.) A few of the sections can be precisely dated; but most of them cannot be dated at all or at best the evidence for dating them is conjectural. Tennyson has said that the earliest written sections were IX, XXX, XXIX, LXXXV; two sections were added after the poem's first publication in 1850, section XXXIX in 1872, section LIX in 1851.

The stanza of *In Memoriam* Tennyson believed he had invented; only after the work was published did he learn that Ben Jonson, Sir Philip Sidney and Lord Herbert of Cherbury had employed it. Tennyson himself employs the stanza elsewhere. He has supplied the key to the structure of the poem, in the remark "After the death of A. H. H. the divisions of the poem are made by First Xmas Eve (Section XXVIII), Second Xmas (LXXVIII), Third Xmas Eve (CIV and CV etc.)."

41. PROLOGUE

41, 1. *Love:* Tennyson explained that he intended the same meaning as St. John's (*John, First Epistle*, ch. iv). Note specially the eighth verse: "He that loveth not knoweth not God: for God is love"; and the ninth: "In this was manifested the love of God toward us because that God sent his only begotten Son in to the world, that we might live through Him" (See *Memoir*, I, 312).

41, 5. *orbs of light and shade:* the meaning is partly material, partly spiritual — pointing forward to lines 6–7.

41, 19. *broken lights:* refracted light as distinguished from pure light.

41. I

41, 1. *him:* Goethe.

42. II

42, 7. *the clock:* the clock of the church, concealed beneath the ivy.

42. III

42, 5. "This line states starkly the whole philosophic problem implicit in the poem . . . Tennyson goes to the heart of the difficulty. It is the problem of mechanism which appalls him" (A. N. Whitehead, *Science and the Modern World*, 96).

42, 9–12. It has been conjectured that the quotation marks have been wrongly placed. A better reading would appear to be that which would end Nature's speech with the close of the second stanza.

43. VII

43, 1. *Dark house:* the house of Hallam's father, at 67 Wimpole St., "the long unlovely street."

43, 9. *far away:* in the busy streets of London.

43. IX

43, 1. *Italian shore:* the ship bearing the body of Hallam put to sea from Trieste.

43, 10. *Phosphor:* the morning star.

44. X

44, 15–16. The elaborate image means no more than the church, specifically the chancel, where the congregation communicates. The stanza presents the alternative modes of burial, in the ground, or in a vault beneath the church.

44, 20. *tangle:* sea weed.

44. XI

44, 12. *bounding:* commentators differ as to the sense of the word in this line. It may mean limiting or else leaping: the latter appears to contrast effectively with the preceding lines.

44. XII

44, 6. *mortal ark:* his body. The choice of the word doubtless depended in part upon the previous use of dove, and the persistence through the passage of a sea setting.

44. XIII

44, 10. *an awful thought:* from having been a human-hearted man, his comrade has become an abstract idea, inspiring awe.

45. XV

45, 11. *a plane of molten glass:* the notion that a plane of glass intervened between earth and heaven was frequently held in the middle ages.

See also the phrase "a molten looking glass," applied to the sky in *Job*, XXXVII, 18.

46. XVIII

46, 2. *in English earth is laid:* actually Hallam was buried in Clevedon Church, not in the churchyard. The Hallams had a vault under the manor-aisle.

46. XIX

This poem is credibly reported to have been written in Tintern Abbey (Bradley: *Commentary on In Memoriam*, 100). Bradley's note on the use of the Severn and the Wye is admirably precise: "The tidal water, in flowing up the Bristol Channel, which, as it begins to narrow, is called the Severn, passes Clevedon and, further up, enters the Wye. . . . As the tide passes up the Wye, its silent flood deepens and hushes the river; but as it ebbs again, the river, growing shallower, becomes vocal and 'babbles.'"

46. XXI

46, 4. *pipes:* the musical instrument of a shepherd. This is one of the very few instances in the poem of Tennyson's employing the conventions of the pastoral elegy.

46, 15–16. Assumed, plausibly, to refer to Chartist tumults. See note on 20.

47, 20. *latest moon:* The discovery of Neptune had been established in 1846. "Moon" is probably used in the general sense of planetary body.

47. XXII

47, 3. *four sweet years:* Tennyson entered into residence in Cambridge in February, 1828, and met Hallam not long after.

47, 10. *autumnal slope:* Hallam died in September.

47. XXIII

47, 21–24. The stanza celebrates their shared delight in Greek philosophy and poetry (*Argive* and *Arcady*, denoting specific parts of Greece, suggest the variety of the Greek achievement).

47. XXIV

47, 3. *fount of Day:* the sun.

47, 4. *wandering isles of night:* sun-spots.

48. XXVI

48, 14. *Indian seas:* the suggestion of brilliant light contrasts effectively with the dimness of the landscape in the preceding sections.

48, 16. *proper:* own, *i.e.*, scorn of himself.

48. XXVII

48, 6. *field of time:* life on earth.

48. XXVIII

48, 1. References to the coming of Christmas give one of the clearest indications of progression and arrangement in the poem. See LXXVIII, CIV–CV.

48, 5–12. Bradley has clearly explained the involved meaning. Each church has four bells; they join to ring out the sounds represented by the phrases which compose lines 11–12.

48. XXX

In reading this section it is important to recall that Hallam had been engaged to Tennyson's sister and a frequent visitor in the Tennyson household.

49, 32. *Hope:* Christ as means to human immortality.

49. XXXI

The story of Lazarus, which occupies this and the succeeding section is told by St. John in the eleventh and twelfth chapters of his gospel.

49, 15. *he:* Lazarus.

49, 16. *that Evangelist:* St. John. None of the other writers of gospels tells the story.

49. XXXII

See note under XXXI.

49, 8. It was to Mary Magdalene that Jesus said "I am the resurrection and the life."

49, 12. *spikenard:* a sweet ointment (See *John*, Ch. XII, 1–3).

49. XXXIII

This poem presenting in contrast the faith of a brother and of a sister is clearly related to the preceding sections. The frequent references to his sister throughout the poem, and especially perhaps section XCVI, have led many to accept this contrast as autobiographical. This at least may be assumed: Lazarus had warrants for his faith which his sister could not have, yet it was his sister's faith which was "quicker unto good"; Lazarus could not possibly have communicated the grounds of his faith to her; he might perhaps have shown her that her grounds were inadequate if not mistaken. Men of metaphysical attainment should know that they cannot communicate the grounds of their belief and should refrain from shaking the ground others have.

49, 6. *her early Heaven:* Heaven as she conceived it from her early instruction. Here the reference cannot be to Mary Magdalene.

49, 16. *want of such a type:* failure to believe in the divinity of Christ incarnate. Tennyson's confessed belief in such a doctrine is presented as a reason against accepting this poem as autobiographical; but there is no assurance that his belief in it was continuous.

50. XXXV

50, 2. *narrow house:* the grave.

50, 11. *Aeonian:* which have endured for aeons.

50, 14. *forgetful shore:* the shore of forgetting, that is of the river Lethe, separating this world from the next.

50. XXXVI

50, 9. *the Word:* Christ. Tennyson has stated that he had here in mind St. John's use of the term (*John*, Ch. 1) which he took as meaning "the revelation of the eternal thought of the universe" (*Memoir*, I, 312).

50. XXXVII

50, 1. *Urania:* commonly the goddess of the heavens, and muse of astronomy. Milton had previously used the name to represent the goddess of divine poetry, and it is in this sense that Tennyson uses it here.

50, 6. *Parnassus:* the hill of the muses.

50, 7. *laurel:* laurel grows on the slopes of Parnassus and is habitually associated with greatness in poetry.

50, 9. *Melpomene:* the muse of tragedy, here representing the allied form of elegy.

50, 23. *master:* Hallam. If Christ were intended the first letter would have been capitalized.

50. XXXVIII

50, 2. *altered:* the comparison is with the time when Hallam was living.

51, 12. *ungrateful:* unpleasing.

51. XXXIX

This section was added in the edition of 1872, and composed in April, 1868. It should be closely compared with section II.

51, 3. *fruitful cloud and yellow smoke:* pollen.

51, 6. *golden hour:* the time of spring and love.

51, 11. *kindled at the tips:* with flowers.

51. XL

51, 19. The original reading was:

In such great offices as suit.

Tennyson disliked the coming together of sibilants and so changed the line.

51, 5. *strange:* alien.

51, 11. *grades of life and light:* Note the plural. Tennyson often conceived of life beyond the grave as a succession of distinct stages.

51, 15–16. The general reference is to the horrors of the underworld, Hell and Hades. *Forgotten* suggests exclusion from God, *howlings* the tortures inflicted.

51, 23. *secular:* enduring through ages.

52. XLIII

52, 1–8. The conception is of a period following death in which the soul is no more conscious than in a trance, and at the end of which it has acquired no new experience.

52, 3. *intervital:* between life on earth and the future life.

52, 10. *still garden of the souls:* the condition described above in the note on lines 1–8. Note the persistence through the section of the comparison with a flower.

52, 11–12. The meaning is: comprehends in a multitude of souls the entire range of human experience.

52. XLIV

This is the most difficult section in the poem. Bradley's commentary should be consulted, pp. 125–136. The interpretation of many phrases depends on whether one does or does not accept the sections as referring to an existence *before* earthly life; the notes below all suppose acceptance of the interpretation which insists on a pre-natal existence, but space does not permit this acceptance's being defended.

52, 3–4. A reference to existence before human life.

52, 4. *Shut the doorways of his head:* enclosed his spirit in the body.

52, 8. The meaning is: a suggestion, quick as lightning, mysterious and obscure, of a life before the earthly life.

52, 9–12. As those on earth occasionally have a reminiscence of life before they came on earth those in the future state may occasionally have a reminiscence of life on earth.

52. XLV

52, 9. Prior to earthly life, a being had no clear awareness (perhaps had no awareness) of separate identity; earthly life progressively quickens such awareness.

52. XLVI

52, 1. *this lower track:* the track or course of earthly life which takes us farther and farther away from a purely spiritual state of being.

52, 9–16. Commentators differ as to the sense of these lines, notably as to whether they refer to the poet or to his friend. It seems clear, however, that Tennyson would have thought it presumptuous to assert that the five years in which he knew Hallam were the *richest field* of the latter's earthly life. If this is so, the two stanzas must refer to the poet, although the logical connection with the preceding section would be clearer if the stanzas referred to Hallam.

52, 15–16. No clear meaning appears.

52. XLVII

52, 1–4. The idea, stated only to be rejected, is that just as in earthly life, the development of the personality follows upon enclosure of the spirit within the body, in the disembodied life beyond the grave the personality will pass away and the pure spirit will be resumed into the general soul (from which it separated to enter earthly life).

53, 14–16. Here Tennyson appears to conceive of an ultimate stage in the future life in which all spirits do "remerge in the general soul."

53. XLVIII

53, 5. *part:* sort out.

54. L

54, 14. *term:* limit.

53. LII

53, 11–12. The reference is to Christ.

54. LIII

54, 5. *fancy:* in the first edition the reading was *doctrine.* The change was clearly intended to emphasise Tennyson's disesteem for the position he is stating.

54, 7. *scarce had:* in the first edition the reading was *had not.* The alteration is similar in motive to that noticed in the comment on line 5.

54, 12. The reference is to those who are still in "the heats of youth."

54, 14. *divine:* the word praises, it is not descriptive.

54. LIV

54, 1. *Oh yet:* the phrase establishes a close connection with the preceding section.

54. LV

54, 4. *the likest God within the soul:* elements which are the most spiritual, as distinguished from the most natural (or sensational) within us.

54, 15. *the great world's altar-stairs:* the stairs that lead towards the divine.

54, 20. *the larger hope:* Tennyson is reported to have interpreted this as the hope "that the whole human race would through, perhaps, ages of suffering, be at length purified and saved" (*Memoir* I, 321).

54. LVI

54, 2. *scarped:* precipitous.

54, 2–3. The steep cliff and the stone exposed in the quarry are full of fossils — "a thousand types."

55, 20. *seal'd:* fossilized.

55, 21. Man is a monstrous being, the elements within him composing a completely incongruous whole, if his spirit is not immortal and the only survival allowed him that of a fossil.

55. LVIII

55, 11. *here:* by the grave.

55. LIX

This section appeared first in the fourth edition, 1851.

55. LX

55, 1. *nobler:* the comparison is not with the poet, but with mankind in general, the comparative being equivalent to the superlative, noblest.

55. LXI

55, 2. *ransom'd:* freed from the disabilities of the earthly life.

change: exchange.

55, 6. *character'd:* marked.

56, 9. *doubtful:* difficult to discern clearly.

56, 12. *Shakespeare:* the reference is apt, especially, because of Shakespeare's celebration of his love for a friend in the *Sonnets.*

56. LXII

56, 1–2. If reminiscence of the earthly life enfeebles for the life in the world beyond the grave. . . .

56, 5. *declined:* moved downward.

56. LXIII

56, 10–12. Tennyson compares Hallam with a planet which has a larger orbit than the earth's, himself with the earth.

56. LXVI

This section is not addressed to Hallam, but to another friend, still alive.

57. LXVII

57, 3. See notes on sections XVIII and XIX.

57, 11. *eaves:* eye-lids.

57, 15. *dark church:* in the first edition he had written "chancel," being misled by the use of that word by Hallam's father in his memoir of Arthur.

57. LXIX

57, 8. *a civic crown:* the general meaning is clear — a symbol of honor.

57. LXX

57, 2. In one of Hallam's poems occurs the line:

And *paint upon the gloom* thy mimic form.

57, 13. *beyond the will:* when sleep takes possession of him completely and the will is no longer active.

57. LXXI

57, 3. An evocation of the past, lasting the entire night.
57, 4. In 1830 Hallam and Tennyson visited the Pyrenees.
58, 13–16. A picture of scenes in the journey.

58. LXXII

58, 1. The dawn of the anniversary of Hallam's death.

58. LXXIII

58, 8. Nothing that exists can transgress against the constitution of the universe.
58, 15. *self-infolds:* encloses within itself.

58. LXXIV

58, 7. *the wise below:* probably below means "on earth." Tennyson would not, if he measured his words, place the wise in the underworld.

58. LXXV

58, 9. *these fading days:* the years of life which remain to the poet.

59. LXXVI

59, 6. *secular:* age-long.
59, 9. *the matin-songs:* the poetry of the early ages.

59. LXXVII

59, 4. The meaning is: seemingly shortened by the position from which they are regarded.

59. LXXVIII

59, 5. *Yule-clog: clog* is a dialectal variant for *log* used in the northern counties, including Tennyson's native Lincolnshire.

59, 11. A reference to the then frequent amusement of presenting tableaux resembling famous pictures (*tableaux-vivants*).

59. LXXIX

This section is addressed to one of the poet's brothers. Collins, without citing any authority, names his brother Charles, also a poet.

59, 4. *fee:* possession.

59. LXXX

60, 13. *credit:* probably meaning simply: the virtue I ascribe to him.
60, 15. *unused:* unexhausted.

60. LXXXI

As it stands this section appears imperfectly intelligible. The punctuation of line 4 must be changed, the period becoming either a mark of interrogation or a comma. Bradley has fully discussed (*Commentary*, pp. 172–174) the values of the two changes proposed. Either gives a good meaning.

60. LXXXIII

60, 5. *clouded noons:* noons which because of the spring's continued absence remain clouded.

61. LXXXV

This section was addressed to Edmund Lushington, a friend since undergraduate times, and subsequently the husband of the poet's sister, Cecilia. See the epilogue to *In Memoriam* which celebrates the marriage.

61, 28. *the cycled times:* the ages to come.
61, 35. *other:* other than human.
61, 33–36. This stanza is an interruption of the thought and the structure.

61, 53. *imaginative woe:* a misery in addition to the immediate one, produced by his imagination's being preoccupied with his grief.

61, 60. This line is variously interpreted. The clearest and simplest interpretation is that which considers the line as stating that man's dignity is bound up with his wish for immortality.

62, 67. *all-assuming:* all consuming.

62, 85. *clouds of nature:* earthly qualities.

62, 86. *the free:* those liberated from earthly life.

62, 95. *symbols:* ideas or images, or merely words, which suggest what they are powerless to express fully.

62. LXXXVI

This section was written at Barmouth, in Merionethshire, North Wales, on the Mawddach estuary.

62, 7. *horned:* curving.

62, 13–16. There is much controversy about the exact sense of the picture given here. Its general outline is clear. The poet is standing on the west coast of England; his fancy is caught by the succession of sunsets which will give a crimson colour to sea after sea (or some say, and very plausibly, *cloud* after *cloud*, taking sea as an image of the clouds) till the evening star, rising in the east, is reached. The star is a symbol of Jesus, and is properly associated with a, so to speak, absolute east for this reason.

62. LXXXVII

This section describes a visit to Cambridge.

62, 1. *the reverend walls:* of Trinity College, Cambridge, to which Tennyson and Hallam had belonged.

63, 15. The limes were in the garden of the college.

63, 21 f. Tennyson recalls the meetings of that group of students to which both he and Hallam belonged — the Apostles.

63, 40. *The bar of Michel Angelo:* a projecting ridge over the eyes. Tennyson reports Hallam as saying: "Alfred, look over my eyes; surely I have the bar of Michelangelo" (*Memoir*, I, 38). As frequently as possible Tennyson used phrases which he remembered from Hallam's conversation or writings; in this section he gives emphasis to the phrase by its position at the close both of the section and of a long sentence.

63. LXXXVIII

63, 1. *wild bird:* the nightingale.

63, 2. *quicks:* an expression used in rural regions of England for hedgerows.

63, 6. *darkening:* originally Tennyson had written *dusking*. The change was probably made because *dusk* is not an extreme but *dark* is.

63. LXXXIX

63, 1. *counterchange:* chequer.

63, 7. *liberal air: liberal* is here the opposite of confining, oppressive.

63, 24. *the Tuscan poets:* Tuscan is an Italian dialect and was the idiom of Florentine writers among others. Hallam undertook to edit Dante's *Vita Nuova* and read largely in "the older Italian literature" (*Memoir*, I, 44–45).

63, 36. *dream:* myth.

64, 47–48. *the crimson-circled star* is Venus, enfolded in the colours of the sunset, the sun is represented as father of Venus, and its setting as a sinking into the grave.

64. XCI

64, 2. *rarely:* with rare beauty.

64, 4. Tennyson commented humorously but firmly on this line in a letter to the Duke of Argyll: "As to 'sea-blue birds' etc., defendant states that he was walking one day in March by a deep-banked brook and under the leafless bushes he saw the kingfisher flitting or fleeting underneath him, and there came into his head a fragment of an old Greek lyric poet . . . 'the sea-purple or sea-shining bird of Spring,' spoken of as the halcyon. Defendant cannot say whether the Greek halcyon be the same as the British kingfisher, but as he never saw the kingfisher on this particular brook before March, he concludes that in that country at least, they go down to the sea during the hard weather and come up again with the spring . . ." (*Memoir*, II, 4).

64, 15. *thine after form:* the form assumed in the life following the earthly life.

64. XCII

64, 3. *canker:* disease.

64. XCIII

65, 9. *sightless:* invisible.

65, 15. *frame:* body.

65. XCV

For the full interpretation of this difficult section the *Memoir*, I, 320–321 should be consulted. No specific reference is made to this section; but the ideas are the essential framework of its key passages.

65, 8. *the fluttering urn:* the tea-*urn*, beneath which a flame *flutters*.

65, 10–12. According to Gatty's interpretation, sanctioned by Tennyson (who appears however to have sanctioned patent errors in this work) the reference is to night-moths.

65, 22. *year:* this term appears to stand for the whole period of their friendship, in retrospect so short.

65, 36–37. *The living soul, . . . and mine in this:* the original and long maintained readings were "His living soul," "and mine in his." Tennyson remarked rather enigmatically: "Perchance of the Deity, . . . My conscience was troubled by 'his.'" It is obvious at least that he was seeking to reduce the impression of a vision, making his experience less distinct.

65, 41. *Aeonian:* enduring through aeons.

65, 46. *matter-moulded:* formed out of sense-experiences.

66. XCVI

It is uncertain to whom this section was addressed. It seems clear, however, that the personage whose spiritual evolution is described is Hallam.

66, 18–20. The interpretation is to be sought in ll. 21–22, and in what these lines suggest.

66, 21–22. See *Exodus*, Ch. XIX, especially verses 9 (And The Lord said unto Moses, 'Lo, I come unto thee in a thick cloud, that the people may hear when I speak with thee and believe thee forever'), 18 (And mount Sinai was altogether on a smoke, because the Lord descended upon it in fire; and the smoke thereof ascended as the smoke of a furnace and the whole mount quaked greatly).

23. See Ch. XXXII, especially 3, 4 (And all the people brake off the golden earrings which were in their ears, and brought them unto Aaron. And he received them at their hand, and fashioned it with a graving tool, after he had made it a golden calf: and they said, 'These be thy gods, O Israel, which brought thee up out of the land of Egypt.') and 31 (And Moses returned unto the Lord, and said, 'Oh, this people have sinned a great sin, and have made them gods of gold').

66, 24. See Ch. XIX, 19 (And when the voice of the trumpet sounded long, and waxed louder and louder, Moses spake, and God answered him by a voice).

66. XCVII

Bradley has acutely pointed out that the tone of the first and purely prefatory stanza is not in accord with that of the remainder of the section.

66, 15. *earnest:* assurance, pledge.

66, 21. *thrids:* an archaic variant of thread.

66. XCVIII

This section was addressed to the poet's brother Charles and his bride, in 1836.

66, 3. In the summer of 1832.

66, 6. *that City:* Vienna.

67, 17. *gnarr:* snarl, from the same root as gnarl.

67. XCIX

The occasion of this section was the second anniversary of Hallam's death.

67. C

This is the first of a group dealing with the departure of the Tennysons from their home at Somersby, to which Hallam had frequently come.

67, 1. *I climb the hill:* the first edition read "I wake, I rise," a much weaker opening in that it does not indicate the place of vision, important for a clear understanding of the following lines.

67. CI

67, 11–12. *The lesser wain* is the constellation *ursa minor*, which moves about the "polar star."

68, 18. *blow:* blossom.

68. CII

68, 7. *Two spirits:* Hallam and the poet's father who had died in 1831. See *Memoir*, I, 72.

68, 23–24. The separate griefs are fused into one; there is a contrast between the states suggested by "mix" and by "pure."

68. CIII

Bradley has suggested that, although the dream here recorded may have been transmuted by the "waking imagination" of the poet, what is here set before us may not have the coherence and clarity of an allegory.

68, 6. *maidens:* representing, Tennyson suggested to Gatty, "the Muses, Arts etc."

68, 8. *river:* the river of life. It is easy to interpret the other references to water, in the light of this explanation.

68, 16. *the sea:* life beyond the grave.

68, 20. *flood:* river.

68, 31. *Anakim:* giants who were the sons of Anak (*Numbers*, Ch. XIII, 33), compared with whom men were as "grasshoppers."

68, 35. *that great race:* man in a later stage of his development.

68, 36. *star:* planet.

68, 45–52. Tennyson is here indicating the survival in life beyond the grave of high activities and qualities of the earthly life.

69. CV

69, 1–2. In the first edition these lines read:

> This holly by the cottage eave,
> To night, ungather'd, shall it stand.

The lines may have been altered to introduce the reference to the laurel, or else because in their earlier form the structure was awkward.

69, 9–12. At the previous celebrations of Christmas, in memory of those spent with Hallam, games had been played. The abandonment of these is linked with the departure from Somersby.

69, 14. *proved:* tested.

69, 27. *run out your measured arcs:* carry out the revolutions assigned to you.

69, 28. The last cycle or period of the world, which will bring back the golden age.

69. CVI

69, 32. The poet's son comments: "My father expressed his conviction that 'Christianity with its divine Morality but without the central figure of Christ, *the* Son of Man, would become cold, and that it is fatal for religion to lose its warmth'; that 'the Son of Man' was the most tremendous title possible; that the forms of Christian religion would alter; but that the Spirit of Christ would still grow from more to more, 'in the roll of the ages.'

> Till each man find his own in all men's good,
> And all men work in noble brotherhood.

'This is one of my meanings,' he said, 'of

> Ring in the Christ that is to be:

when Christianity without bigotry will triumph, when the controversies of creeds shall have vanished, and

> Shall bear false witness, each of each, no more,
> But find their limits by that larger light,
> And overstep them, moving easily
> Thro' after-ages in the Love of Truth,
> The truth of Love' " ("Akbar's Dream") (*Memoir*, I, 325–326).

70. CVII

70, 10. *yon hard crescent:* the moon.

70, 11. *grides:* clashes.

70, 13. *drifts:* the sense is doubtful, the simplest and least questionable meaning would perhaps be clouds.

70. CIX

70, 2. *household fountains:* personal sources.
70, 4. *the Muses' walk:* the place where the Muses gather.
70, 16. *the Celt:* the Irish.

70. CX

70, 2. *rathe:* younger.
70, 7. *the serpent:* a lying, deceiving person.
70, 13. *nearest:* in the first edition he had written "dearest." The older form presented Tennyson as *beloved by* Hallam, the revised form presents the relation between them as one of reciprocal affection.

71. CXI

71, 9. *act:* assume a part.
71, 18. *villain:* base, corresponding exactly with the "churl" of the first line in the section.
71, 21. *without abuse:* without doing it any wrong.

71. CXII

The key to this section lies in the *three* types presented: (i) the man of glorious insufficiencies, that is of noble imperfection, (ii) the man of limited perfectness, (iii) the man of noble perfectness. Hallam exemplifies the third type. The argument of the first stanza is as follows: Tennyson is criticized, by those who know his dissatisfaction with noble imperfection, for setting so little value on limited perfectness. The remainder of the section deals with this criticism, and indicates that to one who has known Hallam, neither noble imperfection nor limited perfectness can be impressive.
71, 2. *temperate eyes:* unstirred.
71, 4. *set light by:* think little of.
71, 8. *lesser lords of doom:* controlling their destiny, which is a limited one.

71. CXIII

71, 14. *has birth:* comes to birth.

71. CXIV

71, 12–13. Pallas was said to have been born of the brain of Zeus. Tennyson here conceives a disordered form of knowledge, born not of Zeus, but of devils.

72. CXV

72, 2. *maze of quick:* a hedge. See note on LXXXVIII, 2.
72, 8. *sightless:* invisible.
72, 14. *greening gleam:* the sea, the sense being almost as if he had written gleaming green.

72. CXVI

72, 6. *reorient:* reborn.
72, 11–12. *And that dear voice I once have known,*
Still speak . . .:

the original reading was

The dear, dear voice that I have known
Will speak . . .

The alteration has led to an awkward expression, . . . "once have known," but it has also avoided the repetition of "dear" which Tennyson may well have found excessive, and of "will" (see line 9).
72, 14. *commune:* communion.

72. CXVII

72, 11. *toothed wheels:* the reference is to the wheels of a clock.

72. CXVIII

72, 1. *contemplate:* the accent is on the second syllable, as was customary at the time Tennyson wrote
72, 4. *dying:* mortal.
Nature: the reference is to the physical body of man.
72, 6. *day:* life.
72, 11. *cyclic storms:* periodic upheavals.
72, 14. *a higher race:* not a superhuman race, but humanity elevated to a new level.

72, 15. *in higher place:* in a life beyond the grave.

72, 16. *type:* exemplify.

72, 17–20. Two alternatives are set forth, one follows the previous argument, representing man as developing to a higher level, the other presents him as drawing moral strength from his weaknesses and imperfections.

73. CXIX

Compare with section VII which records an earlier visit to Wimpole Street, in which Hallam lived.

73. CXX

73, 3. *magnetic mockeries:* merely electric machines.

73, 4. *like Paul with beasts:* In *I Corinthians*, Ch. XV, 32, Paul records having fought with beasts at Ephesus.

73, 12. *born:* This word was italicized in a late edition, and the stress emphasises the contrast between the man described in lines 9–11 and the poet.

73. CXXI

73, 1. *Hesper:* the evening star.

73, 5. *wain:* wagon.

73, 9. *Phosphor:* the morning star.

73, 19. Note that the morning star represents his present, the evening star his past youth.

73. CXXII

On this section Bradley (*Commentary*, 219–226) is suggestive and illuminating. There is no doubt that the state of mind described is that which the poet had sought to make clear in section XCV; but the mere recalling of section XCV will not suffice to explain everything.

For the relation of this section to earlier sections of the poem see *A Commentary*, 219–226, and especially section XCV.

73, 2. *doom:* loss and grief.

73. CXXIII

It is important to remember that although this section owes much to Tennyson's reading in modern geology, it also owes scarcely less to much earlier reflections on flux in the universe.

74. CXXIV

74, 3. The force behind or within the universe, however (and always inadequately) we may formulate it.

74, 5. The emphasis, Bradley wisely suggests, is strong on the "I." Others may find the force in natural forms, he did not.

74, 6. The reference is to the argument from design, which argues a God from the intricacy and aptness of natural organs.

74, 14. *colder:* than the heart, not than another part of the reason.

74, 21. *am:* in the first edition he had written "seem," which reduced the self to a mere appearance, against the general tone of the concluding sections of the poem.

74, 24. The word "thro' " is important, as suggesting that God is not within but beyond nature.

74. CXXV

74, 1. *said or sung:* the first term applies to conversation and soliloquy, only the second to poetry.

74, 8. *he:* love.

74. CXXVII

74, 1. *faith* and *form:* the reference is not purely religious, faith stands for reality, form for its passing vesture.

74, 3. *the storm:* upheaval, religious, or, as here, chiefly political and social.

74, 7–8. The Revolution of 1830, not that of 1848.

74, 16. *the great Æon:* the modern age. In the early editions Tennyson had "vast" instead of *great*.

74. CXXVIII

74, 3. *the lesser faith:* less tried, than by the experience of death.

75, 13–20. It is implied in each of the examples that nothing worth achieving is achieved, although in some cases Tennyson's expression does not make the failure plain.

75. CXXX

75, 7. *diffusive power:* rather than a separate entity.

75. CXXXI

75, 2. *seems:* the contrast is between that which merely *seems* and that which really *is.*

75, 3. *spiritual rock:* In *I Corinthians*, Ch. X, 4. Christ is termed a spiritual rock.

75. EPILOGUE

This is a marriage song for Edmund Lushington and the poet's sister, Cecelia. They were married in 1842.

Tennyson accounted for its place in the poem, saying that *In Memoriam* "begins with a funeral and ends with a marriage—begins with death and ends in promise of a new life—a sort of Divine Comedy, cheerful at the close."

76, 80. The reference is to champagne.

76, 90. *white-favour'd:* bearing white decorations.

77, 115. *friths:* firths, narrow inlets of the sea.

77. ODE ON THE DEATH OF THE DUKE OF WELLINGTON

The Duke of Wellington died on September 14, 1852; his funeral was not held until November 18, and on that day, in a pamphlet of sixteen pages, this poem appeared. It was, however, greatly modified before its republication (as a pamphlet) in the following year and again before it took its place in 1855 in a collection of Tennyson's poems. Henry Van Dyke in his *Poems of Tennyson* (439–440) has recorded the manner in which Tennyson read the poem aloud, giving to each strophe a marked and distinctive musical effect.

In reading the poem it is well to bear in mind that although Wellington's posthumous fame is based almost entirely upon his military career, which reached at once its climax and its conclusion with the battle of Waterloo, thirty-seven years before his death, nevertheless in 1852 it seemed entirely appropriate to lay almost equal emphasis upon his political career which began after Waterloo, led to the Prime Ministership in 1828, and ended in his retirement as late as 1846.

77, 5. In the first edition the reading was one much less apt to the general musical effect of the strophe:

When laurel-garlanded leaders fall.

77, 6. Generals in the national army carried the pall.

78, 9. Wellington was buried in the crypt of St. Paul's Cathedral, which was (and is) in the central part of the busiest district of London.

78, 21–22. These lines were added in 1853: they embody Tennyson's only personal impression of Wellington.

78, 42. *World-victor:* Napoleon.

78, 49–50. St. Paul's, itself a very high building is built upon a high place and crowned with a golden cross.

78, 56. *blazon'd deeds:* Wellington's military victories were inscribed upon the funeral chariot.

78, 64. He had won victories not only in Europe but in India.

78, 80 f. Lord Nelson, also buried in St. Paul's, addresses the question.

79, 97. Disraeli asserted that Wellington had never lost a gun, when he spoke in the House of Commons a few days before the funeral.

79, 99. *Assaye:* here, in northern India, Wellington defeated an Indian army eight times greater than his own.

79, 103–104. To protect Lisbon and maintain himself in the peninsula, Wellington built the triple lines of Torres Vedras.

79, 118. In the first two versions a line now excised followed 118:

He withdrew to brief repose.

Its absence may be regretted, since the line emphasises the termination of a chapter.

79, 121. *barking:* Tennyson maintained that no other word so well suggested the sound of an eagle in anger.

79, 123. *sabbath:* the battle of Waterloo was fought on a Sunday.

79, 137. At Copenhagen and on the Nile Nelson won two of his most overwhelming victories.

79, 152. *Powers:* rulers.
79, 172–173. Wellington advocated reinforcement of the coastal defenses, especially on the south.
80, 188. An early chronicler termed Alfred the Great *Ælfredus veridicus* (Alfred the truthful).
80, 194. In the funeral procession were delegations representing the armed powers of Europe.
80, 196. *stars:* indicating the various noble orders to which he had been named.
80, 235–236. The pain is not Wellington's, but rather that of his mourners.
80, 267. *the Dead March:* from Handel's *Saul.*

81. MAUD

Between 1833 and 1842 only two of Tennyson's poems were published; one was *St. Agnes Eve,* the other a lyric, entitled *Stanzas by Alfred Tennyson, Esq.* This latter poem appeared in 1837 in a collection, *The Tribute,* edited by Lord Northampton. These stanzas now form section IV in Part II of *Maud.*

The development of the short lyric into the monodrama *Maud* has been described by Aubrey de Vere: "Its origin and composition were, as he [Tennyson] described them, singular. He had accidentally lighted upon a poem of his own . . . which had long before been published in a selected volume got up by Lord Northampton for the aid of a sick clergyman. It had struck him in consequence of a suggestion made by Sir John Simeon [a neighbour of Tennyson on the Isle of Wight] that, to render the poem fully intelligible, a preceding one was necessary. He wrote it; the second poem too required a predecessor; and thus the whole work was written, as it were, *backwards.*" (*Memoir,* I, 379.)

Maud was written in the later months of 1854 and the winter of 1855. When published, in the latter year, it incurred much abuse; Tennyson believed that the account of its meaning given in *Maud Vindicated* by Dr. Mann cleared the poem of the misapprehensions it had aroused; when he was about to read it aloud—as he often did—he followed Mann's line of explanation in a preliminary statement; and towards the end of his life he asked that a central passage in Mann's work should be reprinted along with the poem. The passage follows:

"At the opening of the drama, the chief person or hero of the action is introduced with scenery and incidents artistically disposed around his figure, so as to make the reader at once acquainted with certain facts in his history, which it is essential should be known. Although still a young man, he has lost his father some years before by a sudden and violent death, following immediately upon unforeseen ruin brought about by an unfortunate speculation in which the deceased had engaged. Whether the death was the result of accident, or self-inflicted in a moment of despair, no one knows, but the son's mind has been painfully possessed by a suspicion of villainy and foul play somewhere, because an old friend of his family became suddenly and unaccountably rich by the same transaction that had brought ruin to the dead. Shortly after the decease of his father, the bereaved young man, by the death of his mother, is left quite alone in the world. He continues thenceforth to reside in the retired village in which his early days have been spent, but the sad experiences of his youth have confirmed the bent of a mind constitutionally prone to depression and melancholy. Brooding in loneliness upon miserable memories and bitter fancies, his temperament as a matter of course becomes more and more morbid and irritable. He can see nothing in human affairs that does not awaken in him disgust and contempt. Evil glares out from all social arrangements, and unqualified meanness and selfishness appear in every human form, so he keeps to himself and chews the cud of cynicism and discontent apart from his kind. Such in rough outline is the figure the poet has sketched as the foundation and centre of his plan. . . . Since the days of his early youth up to the period when the immediate action of the poem is supposed to commence, the dreamy recluse has seen nothing of the family of the man to whom circumstances have inclined him to attribute his misfortunes. This individual, although since his accession to prosperity the possessor of the neighbouring hall and of the manorial lands of the village, has been residing abroad. Just at this time however there are workmen up at the dark old place, and a rumour spreads that the absentees are about to return. This rumour, as a matter of course, stirs up afresh rankling memories in the breast of the recluse, and awakens there old griefs. But with the group of associated recollections that come crowding forth, there is one of the child Maud, who was in happier days his merry playfellow. She will now however be a child no longer. She will return as the lady mistress of the mansion (being the only daughter of the Squire, who is a widower). What will she be like? He, who wonders, has heard somewhere that she is singularly beautiful. But what is this to him? Even while he thinks of her he feels a chill presentiment, suggested no doubt by her close relationship to one who he considered had already worked him so much harm, that she will bring with her a curse for him."

Tennyson himself described *Maud* as "a little *Hamlet*" (*Memoir,* I, 396).

81. PART I

I

82, 36. *forges:* adulterates.

82, 41. *centre-bits:* a centre-bit is a burglar's tool.

82, 44. The pharmacist is represented as preparing a poisonous drug which he renders more poisonous, and hence perilous, by adulterating it.

82, 46. *Timour:* an alternative form of Tamerlane, a symbol of cruel oppression. Tamerlane is reported to have ordered his horsemen to ride down a thousand children.

82, 58. *made false haste to the grave:* committed suicide.

83, 76. *myself in myself:* this is what Tennyson had originally written, but in the early editions of the poem the reading was "myself in my books," a less effective characterization of this personage.

83. III

83, 4. *a gloom profound:* the despair of the speaker.

83, 14. *Orion:* a constellation of seventeen stars in the configuration of which some detect a resemblance to a man extending a sword.

84. IV

84, 9. This is the first of a number of references to the Crimean War of 1854–5. The Czar, Nicholas I, was charged with having lied in his claim that his intervention in Turkish affairs was exclusively prompted by concern for Christians in Turkey.

84, 23. *shrike:* butcher-bird.

84, 31. *eft:* newt.

85, 43. *an Isis:* an Egyptian female god.

85, 46. Poland had been partitioned in 1846; the Hungarians had suffered a defeat in 1849.

85. VI

86, 14. See Section IV, lines 15–18. *Courtesy* is used in the old sense of bow.

86, 44. *Assyrian Bull:* the bull with a human face was one of the deities worshipped in Assyria.

87. VII

87, 11. *vizier:* minister of state.

87. VIII

87, 10. *snowy-banded:* a clergyman's bands are the strips of white which hang from the neck in front.

87. X

This section, violent in tone, was in the original manuscript substantially longer. In the *Memoir*, I, 403, a part of the unprinted material is given; the remainder may be found in the *North American Review*, Oct., 1884. A few lines will suggest the hysterical tone:

Captain! he to hold a command!
He can hold a cue, he can pocket a ball;
And sure not bantam cockerel lives
With a weaker crow upon English land.

88, 41. The attire suggests a Quaker; and Tennyson was charged with having made here a personal onslaught on John Bright, a Quaker, a manufacturer and an orator, who sought to prevent war with Russia. Tennyson denied that any individual person had been in his mind.

88, 53–59. This stanza was added in the second edition (1856).

88, 67–68. This stanza also was added in 1856.

88. XII

88, 3. Tennyson's comment was that " 'Maud, Maud, Maud' is like the rook's caw" (*Memoir*, I, 403).

88, 11. His comment on this line was " 'Maud is here, here, here,' is like the call of the little birds."

89, 24. Tennyson explains this line as follows: "A woman's dress brushing across the daisies tilts their heads and lets us see the rosy under-petals" (Rawnsley: *Memories of the Tennysons*, 109).

89, 30. *little King Charley:* the King Charles is a breed of spaniel.

89. XIII

89, 11. *essences:* perfumes.

89, 21. *Gorgonised:* the Gorgons in Greek myth were three women with snaky locks whose glance turned a beholder to stone. To *Gorgonise* is to glance like a Gorgon.

89. XIV

89, 21. *seventh Heaven:* the highest of heavens, and, as such, the seat of supreme joy.

90. XV

90, 3–4. The someone else of line 3 is Maud, that of line 4 may be Maud or her other suitor. The relating of both to Maud herself gives a more dramatic meaning.

90. XVI

90, 8. *Oread:* mountain nymph.

90. XVII

90, 12. *glowing ships:* until 1872 the reading was "blowing ships." Note "blowing seas" in the line following. In avoiding a repetition which he must have thought ineffective, Tennyson has introduced an epithet which is less than apt.

91. XVIII

91, 15 f. Tennyson comments: "The sigh in the cedar branches seems to chime in with his own yearning" (*Memoir*, I, 404). *Lebanon:* a Syrian mountain.

91, 36. *sad astrology:* indifferent astronomy. Tennyson comments "*Sad astrology* is modern astronomy, for of old astrology was thought to sympathize with and rule man's fate."

92. XIX

This section was added in 1856.

94. XXII

94, 8. *the planet of Love:* Venus.

95. PART II

I

95, 26. *the Christless code:* the code of honour governing duels, incompatible with Christianity and unacknowledged by it.

95, 32. *the ghastly Wraith:* his hallucination that Maud was present, the first of his many hallucinations.

II

On the shell which is the theme of the first four stanzas of the section, Tennyson comments: "The shell undestroyed amid the storm perhaps symbolizes to him his own first and highest nature preserved amid the storms of passion" (*Memoir*, I, 404).

95, 32. *ancient fable:* Brittany was the scene of some of the most striking of medieval legends.

96, 48. *Lamech:* Lamech, in *Genesis*, Ch. IV, 23, says: "Hear my voice, ye wives of Lamech, hearken unto my speech; for I have slain a man to my wounding, and a young man to my hurt."

97. III

This section was added in 1856.

97. IV

This section was the nucleus of the poem. The original of 1837 was notably longer; some of the lines omitted here were included in other parts of *Maud*. Following the stanza which now ends the section came that which has been moved forward to constitute stanza 8; following it came six stanzas:

Would the happy Spirit descend,
In the chamber or the street
As she looks among the blest;
Should I fear to greet my friend,
Or to ask her, "Take me, sweet,
To the region of thy rest."

But she tarries in her place
And I paint the beauteous face
Of the maiden, that I lost,
In my inner eyes again,
Lest my heart be overborne
By the thing I hold in scorn,
By a dull mechanic ghost
And a juggle of the brain.

I can shadow forth my bride
As I knew her fair and kind,
As I woo'd her for my wife;
She is lovely by my side
In the silence of my life —
'Tis a phantom of the mind.

'Tis a phantom fair and good;
I can call it my side,
So to guard my life from ill,
Tho' its ghastly sister glide
And be moved around me still
With the moving of the blood,
That is moved not of the will.

Let it pass, the dreary brow,
Let the dismal face go by.
Will it lead me to the grave?
Then I lose it: it will fly:
Can it overlast the nerves?
Can it overlive the eye?

But the other, like a star,
Thro' the channel windeth far
Till it fade and fail and die,
To its Archetype that waits,
Clad in light by golden gates —
Clad in light the Spirit waits
To embrace me in the sky.

A multitude of other changes were made, notably in the stanzas which in the present version are numbered 6, 7, 10.

98. V

This section represents the madness of the hero. It is not always possible to explain precisely the function of images or their relation one to another.

98, 4. *wheels go over my head:* this is the first of a number of images which represent his delusion that he is living in the grave.

98, 22 f. It was a superstition that a person who had not received the rites of burial would not rest easily in his grave.

98, 42. It is uncertain what prophecy is intended but Collins plausibly suggests that recorded in *Luke*, Ch. XII, 2–3: "For there is nothing covered, that shall not be revealed; neither hid that shall not be known. Therefore whatsoever ye have spoken in darkness shall be heard in the light; and that which ye have spoken in the ear in closets shall be proclaimed upon the housetops."

99, 53 f. See I, XIII, 28.

99, 59. *in the Hanover ship:* with the House of Hanover which came to the British throne with the accession of George I (1714). The term *Hanoverian rat* was applied to the courtiers of the new regime, and to a new species of rat which then appeared in England.

99, 62–64. See I, I, 44–45.

99, 72 f. See I, XIV, 1–8.

99, 79–80. *The keeper* is Maud's brother, the *dead man* is the hero, the *spectral bride* is Maud.

99, 81. *Sultan:* See I, XX, 4.

99, 85. *a friend of mine:* the speaker's father.

99, 88. "The second corpse is Maud's brother," according to Tennyson's own explanation (*Memoir,* I, 404).

99, 92. *the Quaker:* See I, X, 41 f.

99. PART III

99, 6–9. Compare these lines with I, III, 14, for a striking instance of the use of nature to mirror mood.

99, 6. *the Charioteer:* the constellation Auriga.

100, 7. *the Gemini:* the stars Castor and Pollux.

100, 13–14. It is reported in the *Memoir* that in the spring of 1854 Tennyson observed the planet Mars "glowing" on the "breast" of the constellation of the Lion.

100, 45. *a giant liar:* The Czar, as in I, IV, 9.

100, 50. *For the peace, that I deem'd no peace:* the original reading was more bellicose still,

"For the long, long canker of peace."

101. NORTHERN FARMER, OLD STYLE

This poem, written in 1861, was first published in the collection *Enoch Arden and Other Poems,* in 1864. Tennyson has commented: "Roden Noel calls these two poems [the two Northern Farmer pieces] 'photographs,' but they are imaginative. The first [*Northern Farmer, Old Style*] is founded on the dying words of a farm-bailiff, as reported to me by a great uncle of mine, when verging upon eighty,—'God A'mighty little knows what He's about, a-taking me. An' Squire will be so mad an' all.' I conjectured the man from that one saying" (*Memoir,* II, 9).

103. NORTHERN FARMER, NEW STYLE

This poem first appeared in the collection of 1869, *The Holy Grail and Other Poems.* Tennyson comments upon it: "The 'Farmer, new style' . . . is likewise founded on a single sentence, 'When I canters my 'erse along the ramper (highway) I 'ears proputty, proputty, proputty.' I had been told that a rich farmer in our neighborhood was in the habit of saying this. I never saw the man and know no more of him. It was also reported of the wife of this worthy that, when she entered the *salle à manger* of a sea bathing-place, she slapt her pockets and said, 'When I married I brought him £5000 on each shoulder' " (*Memoir,* II, 9).

105. IN THE VALLEY OF CAUTERETZ

This poem first appeared in the collection *Enoch Arden and Other Poems,* in 1864. In the summer of 1861 Tennyson returned to the Pyrenees whither he had travelled with Hallam in 1830. This poem was written in August, 1861, after the poet had heard "the voice of the torrent seemingly sound deeper as the night grew" (*Memoir,* I, 474).

105, 4. *two and thirty:* Tennyson was exasperated by the inaccuracy: the interval had been thirty-one years.

105. THE HIGHER PANTHEISM

This poem first appeared in the collection of 1869, *The Holy Grail and Other Poems.* In the January of that year Tennyson spoke to his son of the idea here set forth: "Yes, it is true that there are moments when the flesh is nothing to me, when I feel and know the flesh to be the vision, God and the Spiritual the only real and true. Depend upon it, the Spiritual *is* the real; it belongs to one more than the hand and the foot. You may tell me that my hand and my foot are only imaginary symbols of my existence, I could believe you; but you never, never can convince me that the *I* is not an eternal Reality, and that the Spiritual is not the true and real part of me" (*Memoir,* II, 90).

The parody of this poem by Swinburne, "The Higher-Pantheism in a Nutshell" should be read as a comment on the present work.

105, 8. *to feel 'I am I':* to be aware of one's own personality.

105, 12. *closer is He:* closer to the individual's spirit (than that individual's body is).

105, 13. *God is law:* the conception of God as an impersonal force is unsatisfactory to Tennyson (see l. 15); it is unsatisfactory even if that force is conceived as imposing order on the universe.

105, 15. *no God, at all, says the fool:* the phrasing comes from *Psalms,* XIV, 1: "The fool hath said in his heart, 'There is no God.' "

105, 16. The image is intended to indicate that man cannot get outside his own consciousness and so is unable to conceive a god except in terms of his own nature.

106. FLOWER IN THE CRANNIED WALL

This poem first appeared in the collection of 1869, *The Holy Grail and Other Poems.*

106. IN THE GARDEN AT SWAINSTON

This poem first appeared in the collected edition of 1874. It commemorates Sir John Simeon, whose estate at Swainston was near Tennyson's on the Isle of Wight. Simeon who had prompted the elaboration of *Maud,* was one of the poet's closest friends. He died in 1870; and the poem was written almost immediately after the funeral (See *Memoir,* II, 97–98).

106, 5. *three dead men:* the others were Hallam and Henry Lushington, an early friend who had died in the 'fifties.

106. THE IDYLLS OF THE KING

The design of the *Idylls* shaped slowly. Tennyson had been interested in the Arthurian subject since his early youth. "The vision of Arthur as I have drawn him," he wrote, "had come upon me when, little more than a boy, I first lighted on Malory." His son Hallam observes that "it dwelt with him to the end; and we may perhaps say that now the completed poem, regarded as a whole, gives his innermost being more fully, though not more truly, than *In Memoriam* (*Memoir,* II, 128). In his early collections a number of brief poems on the Arthurian theme or subjects subsidiary to it appeared: for example in 1832, "The Lady of Shalott," in 1842 "Sir Galahad" and "Morte d'Arthur." At an early date in his development he wrote out plans for epics and for musical dramas on the Arthurian theme. The project of the idylls began to take definite form in the 'fifties; and in 1859 four appeared—*Enid* (subsequently *Geraint and Enid*), *Vivien* (subsequently *Merlin and Vivien*), *Elaine* (subsequently *Lancelot and Elaine*), and *Guinevere.* Tennyson offered a number of reasons, of varied weight, for deferring the completion of the series, which was to have twelve idylls; and it was not till 1869 that he added to his first four *The Coming of Arthur*, *The Holy Grail*, *Pelleas and Ettarre*, and *The Passing of Arthur.* Two years later appeared *The Last Tournament*, and the year following it *Gareth and Lynette.* In 1886 *Balin and Balan* was published, and with *The Marriage of Geraint*, it completes the cycle of twelve idylls.

Throughout the work runs an allegory, in some of the idylls very conspicuous (for example in *The Holy Grail*), in others scarcely to be discovered even by strenuous search. Tennyson, admitting and indeed professing that his intention was allegorical, was impatient of attempts to draw it out in black and white.

106. LANCELOT AND ELAINE

This was one of the first four *Idylls*, appearing (entitled *Elaine*) in 1859 along with *Enid* (subsequently entitled *Geraint and Enid*) *Vivien* (subsequently entitled *Merlin and Vivien*) and *Guinevere.* In the final arrangement of the *Idylls* it comes seventh, following *Merlin and Vivien* and preceding *The Holy Grail.* It should be compared with *The Lady of Shalott*, which is an earlier and more shadowy account of the main episode of the Idyll.

106, 2. *Astolat:* a variant of Shalott.

106, 10. *of her wit:* of her own invention (as distinguished from what she copied).

106, 22. *Caerlyle:* Carlisle, a city in Cumberland, in the northwest of England.

106, 23. *Caerleon:* Caerleon-upon-Usk, in South Wales.

106, 35. *Lyonnesse:* a mythical land, supposedly stretching to the southwest of Cornwall.

106, 39 f. No source for this episode is known.

106, 53. *scaur:* a precipitous cliff.

106, 75–76. *the place which now is this world's hugest:* London.

107, 134. *The low sun makes the colour:* the clouds take on bright colours only when the sun is setting or rising.

107, 181. *livest between the lips:* art known.

state: stature.

107, 195–196. The distinction between a blank and a blazoned shield is drawn by Tennyson in *Gareth and Lynette*, 405–409:

> When some good knight had done one noble deed,
> His arms were carven only; but if twain
> His arms were blazon'd also; but if none,
> The shield was blank and bare without a sign
> Saving the name beneath.

109, 212–214. The role of the water in Elaine's dream perhaps points forward to her journey after her death.

110, 263. *in a smaller time:* in a lesser age. This is probably a glancing reference to the poet's own period.

110, 279. *Badon hill:* At Mount Badon, in 520 A.D. the Britons defeated the Saxons and arrested their advance into the western parts of the country.

110, 287. *the violent Glem:* the reference is to a river but it is uncertain which of the Glem (Lincolnshire), Glen (Northumberland) or the Glevi (Devonshire) is intended.

110, 289. *Duglas:* there is a river Douglas in Lancashire.

Bassa: probably refers to Bashall Brook in same vicinity.

110, 291. *Celidon:* this is thought to lie in Cornwall.

110, 293. *our Lady's Head:* the head of Mary, the mother of Jesus, not Guinevere's.

110, 295. *lightened:* flashed.

110, 297. The white horse was the emblem of the Saxons; this line is purely figurative.

110, 299. *Agned-Cathregonion:* the identifications are conflicting and all conjectural.

110, 300. *Trath Treroit:* again the identifications are conflicting and conjectural.

111, 338. *rathe:* early.

111, 357. The meaning is that in asking she overcame an excitement which made speech difficult.

112, 422. *Pendragon:* The dragon was the emblem of the Britons; the title Pendragon was given to Uther, Arthur's father, and passed to Arthur.

114, 555–556. In the first edition instead of *Gareth* Tennyson had *Lamorak;* the change was doubtless made because Tennyson added another idyll, *Gareth and Lynette.* Gareth is an admirable character despite the evil in his race, Modred his brother turning traitor to Arthur, Gawain, another brother revealing, as in this idyll, his fundamental unlikeness to the Arthurian knightly ideal, and Lot, their father, being also a traitor to Arthur although married to his sister.

116, 653. *hern:* heron.

116, 707. *our courtesy:* courtesy was one of the rules of Arthur's knights.

118, 795. *the strange-statued gate:* a gate in Camelot on which were pictured Arthur's victories. See *Gareth and Lynette*, 209 f.

118, 796. *mystically:* symbolically.

118, 827. *No rest for me:* I need no rest.

119, 890. *passage:* a strain, in music.

119, 898. *burthen:* refrain.

120, 953. Lancelot's hereditary estates lay beyond the channel in Britanny.

121, 1036. *flood:* river.

122, 1092. *the ghostly man: ghostly* is used in the sense of spiritual and taken with *man* means a priest.

122, 1093. *shrive:* confess, or more precisely give absolution, a part of the confessor's function.

124, 1247–1251. Tennyson represents Arthur's birth as mysterious, in *Gareth and Lynette* letting it be suggested

> . . . that this King is not the King
> But only changeling out of Fairyland.

and, more emphatically, he foretells that Arthur will not die but pass to a hidden place in which he will prepare to come again.

125, 1316. *worship:* honour.

125, 1346. *affiance:* trust.

126, 1393 f. This account of Lancelot's childhood does not come from Malory, who has, indeed, little to say of Lancelot's life before his appearance at Arthur's court. In Malory the Lady of the Lake appears once as his helper when he is a full-fledged knight.

127. THE HOLY GRAIL

This poem appeared first in 1869; in the final arrangement of the *Idylls of the King*, it stands eighth following immediately upon *Lancelot and Elaine*, and preceding *Pelleas and Ettarre.* Tennyson's own comment on it establishes its importance in the moral and dramatic scheme of the *Idylls:* "*The Holy Grail* is one of the most imaginative of my poems. I have expressed there my strong feeling as to the Reality of the Unseen. The end, when the King speaks of his work and of his visions, is intended to be the summing up of all in the highest note by the highest of human men. These three lines in Arthur's speech are the (spiritually) central lines of the *Idylls:*

In moments when he feels he cannot die,
And knows himself no vision to himself,
Nor the High God a vision.

The general English view of God is as of an immeasurable clergyman; and some mistake the devil for God" (*Memoir*, II, 90).

127, 1. *noiseful:* famous, *i.e.*, noised abroad.

127, 2. *Sir Percivale:* in a prior form of the Grail legend Percivale had the role later assigned to Sir Galahad.

127, 15. *puff'd into smoke:* scattered the yellow pollen.

127, 26. *light:* carries a double meaning, first that of counterfeit coinage, lighter in weight than the genuine, second that of evil living.

127, 48. *Aromat:* a variant of Arimathea, the Greek form of the Hebrew Ramathaaim or Armathaim, a town close to Jerusalem.

127, 50. *Moriah:* the hill on which the temple at Jerusalem was built.

127, 51. *Joseph:* in each of the gospels he is represented as having taken the body of Jesus and given it burial. Mark's account of his intervention is as follows: "Joseph of Arimathea, an honorable counsellor, which also waited for the kingdom of God, came, and went in boldly unto Pilate, and craved the body of Jesus. And Pilate marvelled if he were already dead: and calling unto him the centurion, he asked him whether he had been anywhile dead. And when he knew it of the centurion, he gave the body to Joseph. And he brought fine linen, and took him down, and wrapped him in the linen, and laid him in a sepulchre which was hewn out of a rock, and rolled a stone unto the door of the sepulchre (*Mark*, Ch. XV, 43–7). In medieval legend he was supposed to have brought to England relics of Jesus, among them the Grail. Tennyson, in another idyll *Balin and Balan*, says:

Thorns of the crown and shivers of the cross,
. . . brought
By holy Joseph hither, that same spear
Wherewith the Roman pierced the side of Christ.

127, 52–53. The abbey at Glastonbury was reputed to have been founded about 60 A.D. by Joseph on his arrival in Britain; the thorn which flowers there at Christmas was believed to have sprouted from his staff.

127, 61. *Arviragus:* king of Britons in the first century A.D.

128, 80. *an adulterous race:* not merely Lancelot and Guinevere, but the society of Arthur's court in general at the time of its decline.

128, 97. "why it should not" is to be understood after *not.*

128, 118. *beatings:* pulsations.

129, 144. *a son of Lancelot:* "Galahad" had been used by earlier writers as the name of Lancelot in his youth. Subsequently he was described as Lancelot's son. Tennyson seeks to dissociate him from Lancelot, feeling that the gap between their natures is too large to make a relationship artistically plausible.

129, 148. *wanderingly lewd:* promiscuous.

129, 162. *the spiritual city:* Heaven, although in earlier versions of the legend, it was Sarras, the city in which Joseph of Arimathea had converted a pagan king.

129, 168. *past away:* vanished. Merlin was imprisoned by an enchantress.

129, 172. *the Siege perilous:* literally the dangerous seat. Joseph had made a table and chairs for the Grail, and one who had sat in a seat which was to be reserved (for Jesus or Judas, it is not clear which) had vanished. Merlin sought to reduplicate Joseph's table and chairs, and the seat reserved was for him who was to succeed in the quest of the Grail.

129, 174. *but he should lose himself:* there is a double meaning, losing oneself as perishing, and losing oneself as losing one's concern for oneself. Merlin perished by his lust for Vivien, Galahad lost all concern for himself.

129, 200. *cousin:* relative.

129, 209. *on:* for.

130, 240–241. The Northern Star is a symbol of fidelity, the east is the source of Christianity.

130, 263. *the golden dragon . . . over all:* the dragon was the emblem of the Britons.

131, 298. *the leader's bell:* the comparison is with sheep following the bell of their leader.

131, 300. *Taliessin:* a poet of the fifth century, Taliessin was preeminent among Welsh poets.

131, 312. *the strong White Horse:* the white horse was the emblem of the Saxons.

131, 350. *wyvern:* the wyvern was a dragon.

132, 358. *the Gate of the three Queens:* the Queens, who befriended Arthur are those who appear in *Morte D'Arthur*. The gate itself is described in *Gareth and Lynette*, 209 f.; it celebrated Arthur's great victories and honoured the queens.

133, 462. *sacring:* the consecration of the bread and wine by which, in Roman Catholic belief, they become the body and blood of Christ.

133, 490. *wintry water-courses:* courses in which a stream runs only in the wet seasons.

134, 509. *shoutings of all the sons of God:* an echo of *Job*, Ch. XXXVIII, 7: "When the morning stars sang together, and all the sons of God shouted for joy."

134, 513. *samite:* a rich silken fabric.

134, 539. *the gate of Arthur's wars:* see note on l. 358. It is the same gate.

134, 545. *breviary:* the book containing his prayers.

134, 547. *thorpe:* village.

135, 569. *eft:* newt.

135, 642–643. The references to the sluggard and the lion are echoes of *Proverbs*, Ch. XXVI, 13: "The slothful man saith there is a lion in the way."

136, 646–647. Lancelot's madness had been a cause of scandal because it resulted from a breach in his relations with Guinevere.

136, 659 f. The reference is to the Druidic religion.

136, 667. *he:* the sun.

136, 679. *scud:* the quickly-moving cloud.

136, 681. The reference is to the constellation of the Great Bear (*Ursa major*), sometimes called the Table Round.

137, 715. *basilisks:* crowned snakes.

cockatrices: winged snakes.

137, 716. *talbots:* huge dogs.

137, 759–760. A loose recollection of *John*, Ch. II, 2–11. The best wine was not kept at that feast; it was supposed to have been kept because of the consummate quality of the wine Jesus made from water.

138, 808. *shingle:* gravel on the beach.

138, 810. *Carbonek:* in it, built by the grandson of Joseph of Arimathea, the Grail was reputed to rest.

139, 862. *blue-eyed cat:* Darwin has observed that "cats which are entirely white and have blue eyes are generally deaf" (*Origin of Species*, Ch. 1).

139, 899–915. The explanation of Arthur's failure to pursue the quest is Tennyson's, and is essential to his conception of Arthur's character as to his moral principles in general.

139. THE LAST TOURNAMENT

This poem first appeared in the *Contemporary Review* for December, 1871; and was reprinted in the following year in the same volume with another idyll, *Gareth and Lynette*.

139, 1. *Dagonet:* this character was of Tennyson's creation. Hallam Tennyson remarks that the poet often "referred with pleasure" to Dagonet.

140, 37. *those diamonds:* in the idyll *Lancelot and Elaine*, Tennyson tells of the jousting for the last of nine great diamonds, of Lancelot's presenting them to Guinevere, and of her tossing them into the river which flows through Camelot.

140, 44–45. Elaine floated down the river in her bier, just after Guinevere, who had been jealous of her, flung the diamonds.

140, 47. *a brother-slayer:* Arthur had removed a crown containing the diamonds from a skull in Lyonnesse. The skull was that of one of a pair of brothers who had perished in single combat.

140, 53. *faded fields:* Autumn is the season for the *last* tournament.

140, 62. *for whom Christ died:* "equally as for a king" is implied.

140, 70. *the Red Knight:* Sir Pelleas, to whose perversion the preceding idyll, *Pelleas and Ettarre*, is largely devoted. Pelleas, at the outset of his knightly life an ideal character, is tricked by Gawain and comes to believe that the Round Table is a vast hypocrisy: he becomes the irreducible enemy of Arthur's knights and of Arthur's overlordship.

141, 90. *curiously:* carefully.

141, 92. *the heathen:* the Saxons.

141, 116. The person of whom it was written is "the wicked man," as judged by Eliphaz (*Job*, Ch. XV, 21). The reference to Isaiah given in some editions is merely misleading.

141, 132–133. In the first of the idylls, *The Coming of Arthur*, Merlin is reported to have sung the riddling words

> Sun, rain, and sun! and where is he who knows?
> From the great deep to the great deep he goes,

the reference being to Arthur.

141, 135–136. Those in earnest had in mind the actual story of the child, those who mocked turned the words to mean that virtue was dead in the land.

142, 150. *vail'd:* lowered.

142, 166. *Modred:* subsequently a traitor to Arthur, and already suspect because of his race. See note on *Lancelot and Elaine*, 555–6.

142, 174. *a spear, a harp, a bugle:* a spear because of his knighthood, a harp because of his special addiction to music, a bugle because of his special addiction to hunting.

142, 175–177. Tristram, in love with Iseult (or Isolt) of Ireland whom he conveyed to Cornwall for her marriage with King Mark, subsequently married Iseult (or Isolt) the White, or the White-Handed, a princess in Brittany.

142, 192. *Art thou the purest:* the question underlines the significance of the Queen's remark in offering the jewels for a prize:

> Perchance—who knows?—the purest of thy knights
> May win them for the purest of my maids. 49–50.

Tristram, far from being the purest of the knights is a symbol of lawless passion, and having won the jewels announces that he will offer them to his queen of beauty, whom the auditors will know to be Iseult of Ireland.

143, 211. *All courtesy is dead:* courtesy was one of the rules of the company of the Round Table.

143, 226. *he that tells the tale:* Malory, in his *Mort D'Arthur*.

143, 263. *Queen Isolt:* Iseult of Ireland.

143, 264–266. There is a play upon the meaning of broken music: technically it is (in one of its meanings) concerted music, *i.e.*, music in which there is more than one executant; the phrase *broken music* also means destroyed harmony.

144, 309. *a naked aught:* a pure nothing.

144, 321–322. Orpheus, a mythical Greek poet, was credited with power to make animals do his bidding when he sang and played. The term *harper* is used to emphasize the relation of the remark to Tristram himself.

144, 328. Orpheus was also credited with having had the privilege of redeeming his wife Eurydice from the underworld by his playing. He failed to redeem her because he infringed another condition by looking back to make sure that she was permitted to follow him above ground.

144, 333. *the harp of Arthur:* the constellation.

144, 341–342. The distinction between a king by courtesy and a king by right turns upon ancestry. In *The Coming of Arthur* Tennyson refers to the doubt whether Arthur was indeed Uther, his predecessor's son:

> . . . Arthur newly crown'd,
> Tho' not without an uproar made by those
> Who cried, 'He is not Uther's son.' . . .

145, 343. *the black king's highway:* the path to hell.

145, 371. *slot:* trail.

fewmets: excrement.

145, 391. *Tintagil:* a castle on the Cornish coast.

146, 421. *sallowy isle:* sallows are willows, and the phrase indicates an island full of willows.

146, 432. *field noir:* noir is the heraldic term for black.

146, 455. *the name:* Pelleas.

147, 479. *Alioth and Alcor:* stars in the constellation *ursa major*.

147, 481. *the water Moab saw:* an allusion to *II Kings*, Ch. III, 21–2: "And they rose up early in the morning and the sun shone upon the water, and the Moabites saw the water on the other side as red as blood."

147, 495. *she:* a note in Hallam Tennyson's edition of the *Works* purporting to give Tennyson's own view states that *she* refers to his wife, Iseult of Brittany. One hesitates to disagree with such an interpretation; but it seems both more dramatic and more straightforward to take *she* as referring to Iseult of Ireland, to whom he goes. Consideration of the tone of the conversation he holds with Iseult of Ireland will strengthen this interpretation.

147, 501. *roky:* misty.

147, 509. *the spiring stone:* a spiral staircase.

147, 543. The story of Mark's jealousy of Tristram and of their love for the lady of Sir Segwarides is told by Malory (VIII, 13). In the course of the affair Mark with two knights set upon Tristram whom they wounded but not before Tristram stunned Mark.

148, 549. *my Queen Paramount:* Guinivere. The phrase does not indicate any peculiar attachment to Guinivere on Tristram's part.

148, 570. *to sin in leading-strings:* to follow where guidance has been given in sin by a superior.

148, 611. *levin:* lightning.

149, 620. *leman:* paramour.

149, 627. *malkin:* wench or woman menial.

mast: beechnuts.

149, 629. This line was added, for emphasis, in 1872.

150, 692. When the ptarmigan takes on a white colour before winter comes, he makes himself conspicuous against a summer or autumn background, and so falls a victim to his enemies.

150, 695. *yaffingale:* woodpecker.

150, 725 f. The two stars symbolize the two Iseults.

151, 748. *Mark's way:* the phrase indicates that Mark has overheard the conversation throughout almost its whole extent: Iseult had used it in line 530.

151. LUCRETIUS

This poem first appeared in *Macmillan's Magazine* in May, 1868. Much of the material was skilfully drawn (along with many of the expressions) from the great philosophic poem of Lucretius (96–55 B.C.), *De Rerum Natura* (On the Nature of Things).

151, 11. *hexameter:* the measure in which the poem was written.

151, 13. *the Teacher:* Epicurus, a Greek philosopher, the first great exponent of atomistic materialism which Lucretius set forth in his poem.

151, 47. *Sylla:* a variant of Sulla, the military dictator of Rome in the age of Lucretius.

151, 50. *Cadmean teeth:* Cadmus, founder of the Greek city of Thebes, sowed the teeth of a dragon he had slain: armed men came forth from the earth.

151, 52. *hetairai:* courtesans.

151, 54. *mulberry-faced dictator:* Sulla.

152, 61. *the breasts of Helen:* Helen of Troy the most beautiful woman of her age, and for classical antiquity the symbol of perfect female beauty.

152, 65. *Ilion:* Troy.

152, 70. *prooemion:* preamble. In the opening passage of his poem Lucretius invoked Venus.

152, 82. *Mavors:* an archaic form of Mars, god of war.

152, 85–92. A retelling of the substance of the poem "Œnone."

152, 86. *Ida:* a mountain close to Troy.

152, 88. *Trojan:* Paris, son of Priam, king of Troy.

152, 89–90. Venus mourned her lover Adonis who was killed by a boar.

152, 91. *beardless apple-arbiter:* the reference is to Paris, who awarded the prize of a golden *apple* to Venus (Aphrodite) rather than to her rivals Pallas and Juno. *Beardless* means youthful.

152, 93. *the great Sicilian:* Empedocles, the philosopher-poet of Sicily who took his life by jumping into the crater of Mt. Etna in Sicily.

152, 94. *Calliope:* the muse of epic poetry.

152, 95. *Kypris:* the Cyprian. Venus was so called because she was believed to have first risen from the sea near the island of Cyprus.

152, 116. *my master:* Epicurus.

152, 119. *Memmius:* the friend to whom the *De Rerum Natura* was dedicated.

152, 125–126. The names *Apollo, Delius, Hyperion* are all applied in classical myth to the sun-god.

153, 148–149. Plato, in his dialogue, *Phaedo*, in which he treats of the immortality of the soul, argues in such terms that suicide is immoral.

153, 159. *miring:* dirtying.

153, 182. *Picus and Faunus:* early Italian rural deities.

153, 188. *oread:* mountain nymph.

153, 192. *satyr:* a creature half man half beast, supposed in classic myth to roam in wild places.

153, 194. *twy-natured:* two natured.

153, 201. *Mercury's ankle-wing:* Mercury, messenger of the gods, had wings attached to his ankles for speed.

154, 203. *goat-foot:* satyr. The satyrs had the form of goats from the waist down.

154, 224. *Heliconian:* appertaining to Mount Helicon or to its springs. Helicon was the home of the muses.

154, 235. *her:* Lucretia, wife of *Lucius Tarquinius Collatinus*, who was raped by Sextus, son of the Roman king *Tarquin*, and subsequently took her own life, after exposing the act of Sextus and thus provoking a rebellion in the state.

154, 241. *the Commonwealth:* the Roman republic.

154, 252. *momentary:* enduring but a moment in relation to the existence of nature.

154, 254. *fanes:* temples.

154, 260. *Ixionian wheel:* Ixion, for having seduced Juno, was by Jupiter's command bound to a wheel in hell which was to revolve forever.

154, 261. *the Fury's ringlet-snake:* the Furies were commonly represented as having snakes for their hair.

155. THE REVENGE

This poem first appeared in the *Nineteenth Century* for March, 1878, and was included in the collection of Tennyson's poems which came out in 1880. In 1873 Tennyson read "the account of Sir Richard Grenville in Froude" (*Memoir*, II, 142) that is in Froude's essay, *England's Forgotten Worthies;* Hallam Tennyson says that the first line of the poem was on his father's desk for years, and that "he finished the ballad at last all at once in a day or two." It is not clear whether it was in 1873 or later that the poem was written; but the only year in which there is evidence of his having occupied himself with materials for the poem is 1873.

155, 1. In 1591 an English squadron went to the Azores with the mission of cutting off and, if possible, capturing the Spanish fleet homeward bound with treasure from the West Indies. A fleet put out from Spain to destroy the English vessels, all of which, except the *Revenge*, a ship of five hundred tons, eluded the enemy. Grenville, in command of the *Revenge*, had been delayed bringing his sick on board.

155, 4. Lord Thomas Howard was in command of the squadron.

155, 33. The *Revenge*, for reasons that are not clear, elected to pass through the Spanish fleet.

156, 61. Four vessels were destroyed by the *Revenge*, two of them sinking immediately.

157, 108. The Spaniards because of his violence and because of the storm which followed the encounter and his death are said to have accounted him a devil, that is, one diabolically possessed.

157, 117. Only thirty-two of the Spanish ships survived to return to port.

157, 118–119. The *Revenge* sank by the island of St. Michael, one of the Azores group.

157. FRATER AVE ATQUE VALE

Written in the summer of 1880 in the course of a visit to Italy, this poem first appeared in the *Nineteenth Century* for March, 1883, and was included in the collection of 1885, *Tiresias and Other Poems.* Of the circumstances in which the poem was composed Hallam Tennyson tells us: "From Verona we returned home by the Lago di Garda and Milan. Over Sirmio, the peninsula of Catullus, we roamed all day. My father liked this, I think, the best of anything we had seen on our tour: its olives, its old ruins, and its green-sward stretching down to the blue lake with the mountains beyond. Here he made his *Frater Ave atque Vale*" (*Memoir*, II, 247). Catullus, a poet of the first century B.C., endeared himself with Tennyson "for his perfection in form and for his tenderness, he is the tenderest of Roman poets" (*Memoir*, I, 266). At the time of Tennyson's visit to Catullus' peninsula, he was specially attracted by Catullus' lament on the death of his brother: Tennyson's own "favourite brother Charles" had died in 1879; and in the present piece Tennyson is at once celebrating and evoking the spirit of Catullus and brooding over the death of his brother. On Catullus' lament he wrote to Gladstone in 1880: "nor can any modern elegy so long as men retain the least hope in the after-life of those whom they loved, equal in pathos the desolation of that everlasting farewell, 'Atque in perpetuum, frater, ave atque vale' " (*Memoir*, II, 239). A literal translation of the title is: Brother hail and farewell.

157, 1. *Desenzano:* a little town close to the peninsula of Sirmio (Italian, *Sirmione*) which projects into the Lago di Garda.

157, 2. *O venusta Sirmio: venusta* means lovely, the entire phrase occurs in one of Catullus' poems.

157, 3. The peninsula of Sirmione is planted over with olives.

157, 4. *the Roman ruin:* the ruin of Catullus' villa.

157, 8. *Lydian laughter* is a translation of one of Catullus' phrases. The Etruscans, who had dwelt near the lake, were believed to have taken their origin in Lydia in Asia Minor. Doubtless there lingers intentionally a suggestion of the usual connotation of "Lydian"—joyous and voluptuous.

157, 9. *all but island:* a translation of a phrase of Catullus' for the same peninsula.

157. TO VIRGIL

This poem first appeared in the *Nineteenth Century* for September, 1882, and was included in the collection of 1885, *Tiresias and Other Poems*.

157, 1–2. This stanza celebrates Virgil as author of the *Aeneid*.

157, 2. *Ilion:* Troy.

157, 3. *he that sang the Works and Days:* the Greek poet Hesiod.

157, 5–6. This stanza celebrates his achievement in the *Georgics*, *wheat* and *tilth* suggesting the first *Georgic*, *woodland* and *vineyard* the second, *horse* and *herd* the fourth and *hive* the third. The *Georgics* make up a comprehensive poetical treatment of farming in a liberal sense.

157, 7–10. These stanzas celebrate his achievement in his *Eclogues*. *Tityrus* suggesting the first, the *poet-satyr* the sixth and *Pollio* the fourth.

158, 18. A reminiscence of one of Virgil's allusions to Britain, *penitus toto divisos orbe Britannos*, *Eclogue*, I, 67. The poem abounds in reminiscences of Virgil's phrasing.

158, 19. *Mantovano:* an inhabitant of Mantua or its region. Virgil was born in the countryside near Mantua.

158, 20. *the stateliest measure:* the Latin hexameter.

158. LOCKSLEY HALL SIXTY YEARS AFTER

This poem first appeared in the collection of 1887 (actually published in 1886) *Locksley Hall Sixty Years After and Other Poems*. Tennyson drew up the following explanatory note: "A dramatic poem and Dramatis Personae are imaginary. Since it is so much the fashion in these days to regard each poem and story as a story of the poet's life or part of it, may I not be allowed to remind my readers of the possibility, that some event which comes to the poet's knowledge, some hint flashed from another mind, some thought or feeling arising in his own, or some mood coming—he knows not whence nor how—may strike a chord from which a poem evolves its life, and that this to other eyes may bear small relation to the thought, or fact, or feeling, to which the poem owes its birth, whether the tenor be dramatic, or given as a parable?" (*Memoir*, II, 329–30.) With special intensity Tennyson protested against any reading of an autobiographical meaning into either of the *Locksley Halls*. His opinion of the true significance of the two poems is revealed in Hallam Tennyson's report: "*Locksley Hall Sixty Years After* was dedicated to my mother, partly because it seemed to my father that the two *Locksley Halls* were likely to be in the future two of the most historically interesting of his poems, as descriptive of the tone of the age at two distant periods of his life." He goes on to say that the four lines about to be quoted were composed immediately after the death of Lionel Tennyson, one of the poet's sons. The lines are

> Truth for Truth is Truth, he worshipt, being true as he was brave;
> Good, for Good is Good, he follow'd, yet he look'd beyond the grave!
> Truth for Truth, and Good for Good! The Good, the True, the Pure, the Just!
> Take the charm "For ever" from them and they crumble into dust.

Tennyson considered that these described the chief characteristics of his dead son.

158, 3. The *curlews* called also in the first "Locksley Hall," l. 3.

158, 13. *Amy* was the heroine of the first poem.

158, 18. *amourist:* an uncomplimentary equivalent of lover.

159, 26. By the evidence of breeding in animals.

159, 29. *Cross'd:* a Crusader was buried with his feet crossed as a symbol of his devotion to Christianity.

159, 31. Amy was the speaker's cousin.

159, 40. There is an implied comparison of the planet and himself.

159, 43. *the tyrant of my youth:* probably the father of Amy who was his uncle and, his father being dead, his guardian.

160, 59–60. These lines recorded Tennyson's own estimate of his son Lionel who had died in 1886.

160, 75. *of my morning:* of the period of my youth. These marvels are celebrated in the first "Locksley Hall," especially ll. 11 f. and 119 f.

160, 82. *Timur:* Tamerlane.

160, 83. *Edward:* Edward I, King of England, conqueror of Wales and victor over the Scots.

160, 85. *the Greatest of the great:* Jesus.

160, 90. *Demos:* the Greek term for the people. It is used depreciatively here as an equivalent for populace.

161, 100. *St. Francis of Assisi:* St. Francis is pre-eminent as a lover of animals. He is reported to have preached to birds.

161, 101–102. In his *Laudes Creaturarum*, St. Francis calls the sun and fire his brothers and the moon, stars, and water his sisters, and praises the flowers. He does not actually call the flowers and beasts brothers and sisters.

161, 103. *Chaos, Cosmos:* the exact meaning of *cosmos* is order: the two terms are set in opposition and might more naturally be followed by a question mark.

161, 105. *fatal daughter of the Past:* determined ineluctably by the past.

161, 115. Fear of a conflict with Russia for the possession of India was strong throughout the 'eighties.

161, 117. *Imperial sceptre:* Victoria had been made Empress of India in 1877; prior to that time the English sovereign had no imperial title. The *three hundred millions* are the peoples of India.

162, 132. In 1884, to Tennyson's alarm, the franchise had been extended to an enormous number of men previously below the property qualification.

162, 136. By the *feet* the poet intends the lower, and less educated order of people whom he here opposes to the upper and better educated whom he intends by the term *brain.*

162, 145. *Zolaism:* Tennyson is thinking both of the works of Emile Zola who for twenty years had been writing naturalistic fiction and whose *Germinal* had in 1885 shocked many conservative readers, and also of the general trend toward frank and full realism in fiction and other forms of literature.

162, 157. *Jacobinism:* The Jacobins were one of the parties in the French Revolution, whose name came into general use as a term for revolutionary violence.

Jacquerie: in its exact meaning the revolt of the peasants of France in 1357, but used here, as frequently, in the general sense of a popular and violent insurrection.

162, 159 f. The image of the future presented in these lines should be compared with that presented in the first "Locksley Hall," 129 f.

163, 185. *Hesper:* the evening star.

164, 201. A reference to David's exclamation: "What is man, that thou art mindful of him?" (*Psalm VIII*, 4.)

164, 224. *warren:* strictly an area in which rabbits are kept, by extension any overcrowded area.

165, 248. *passant:* in heraldry, the posture of walking while looking to the right, three paws being upon the ground and the fourth, the right forepaw, raised.

166. FAR—FAR—AWAY

This poem first appeared in 1889, in the collection *Demeter and Other Poems.* Tennyson repeated it aloud in the summer of 1888.

166, 5. "Distant bells always charmed him with their 'lin-lan-lone' and when he heard them over the sea or a lake, he was never tired of listening to them" (*Memoir*, II, 366).

166, 8. Tennyson recorded that these words "far—far—away" had charmed him from his earliest days.

166. CROSSING THE BAR

This poem first appeared in 1889, in the collection *Demeter and Other Poems.* It was written in October of that year. When Tennyson showed it to his son Hallam, Hallam remarked, "That is the crown of your life's work." The poet rejoined: "It came in a moment," and went on to explain that "the Pilot" was "that Divine and Unseen Who is always guiding us." Shortly before his death Tennyson asked that this lyric should be printed at the end of all editions of his poems (*Memoir*, II, 366–367).

BIBLIOGRAPHY

167. ROBERT BROWNING

I. EDITIONS

Complete Works, 12 vols., ed. by C. Porter and H. A. Clarke, Crowell, 1898.
Works, 10 vols., ed. by Sir F. G. Kenyon, Smith Elder, 1912.
Complete Poetical Works, Macmillan, 1907.
New Poems of Robert Browning and Elizabeth Barrett Browning, ed. by Sir F. G. Kenyon, Macmillan, 1914.
Men and Women, ed. by G. E. Hadow, Oxford, 1911.
Selections from the Poems and Plays, ed. by Myra Reynolds, Scott, 1919.
The Reader's Browning, ed. by Walter Graham, American Book Co., 1936.
The Shorter Poems, ed. by W. C. DeVane, Crofts, 1934.
Hommes et Femmes [Men and Women], trans. and ed. by L. Cazamian, Aubier (Paris), 1938.
The Ring and the Book, ed. by A. K. Cook, Oxford, 1940.

II. BIOGRAPHY AND LETTERS

The Letters of Robert Browning and Elizabeth Barrett Browning, 2 vols., Smith Elder, 1899.
Robert Browning and Alfred Domett, ed. by Sir F. G. Kenyon, Smith Elder, 1906.
Letters of Robert Browning to Miss Isa Blagden, ed. by A. J. Armstrong, Baylor University Press, 1923.
Letters of Robert Browning, collected by T. J. Wise, ed. by T. L. Hood, Yale, 1933.
Chesterton, G. K.: *Robert Browning*, Macmillan, 1903.
Dowden, Edward: *The Life of Robert Browning*, Dent, 1904.
Griffin, W. H., and Minchin, H. C.: *The Life of Robert Browning*, Methuen, 1910. (2nd ed. revised, 1938.)
Herford, C. H.: *Robert Browning*, Dodd, 1905.
Lounsbury, T. R.: *The Early Literary Career of Robert Browning*, Scribner, 1911.
Orr, Mrs. Sutherland (revised by Sir F. G. Kenyon): *Life and Letters of Robert Browning*, Houghton, 1908.
Whiting, L.: *The Brownings, Their Life and Art*, Little Brown, 1917.

III. CRITICISM

I. Monographs

Alexander, W. J.: *An Introduction to the Poetry of Robert Browning*, Ginn, 1889.
Berdoe, E.: *The Browning Cyclopedia*, Macmillan, 1902.
Brockington, A. A.: *Browning and the Twentieth Century*, Oxford, 1932.
Broughton, L. N., and Stelter, B. F.: *A Concordance to the Poems of Robert Browning*, Stechert, 1924.
Brooke, S. A.: *The Poetry of Robert Browning*, Crowell, 1902.
Clarke, H. A.: *Browning's Italy*, Baker, 1907.
Cook, A. K.: *A Commentary upon Browning's 'The Ring and the Book,'* Oxford, 1920.
Cooke, G. W.: *A Guide-Book to the Poetic and Dramatic Works of Robert Browning*, Houghton, 1891.
Corson, H.: *An Introduction to the Study of Robert Browning's Poetry*, Heath, 1889.
DeVane, W. C.: *A Browning Handbook*, Crofts, 1935.
DeVane, W. C.: *Browning's 'Parleyings,' the Autobiography of a Mind*, Yale, 1927.
Duckworth, F. G. R.: *Browning, Background and Conflict*, Benn, 1931.
Hatcher, H. H.: *The Versification of Robert Browning*, Ohio State University Press, 1928.
Hodell, C. W.: *'The Ring and the Book': Its Moral Spirit and Motive*, Deitzer (Shelbyville, Ind.), 1894.
Jones, Sir H.: *Browning as a Philosophical and Religious Teacher*, Maclehose, 1892.
Mayne, E. C.: *Browning's Heroines*, Chatto, 1913.
Naish, E. M.: *Browning and Dogma*, Bell, 1906.
Nettleship, J. T.: *Robert Browning, Essays and Thoughts*, Matthews, 1890.

ORR, MRS. S.: *A Handbook to the Works of Robert Browning*, Smith Elder, 1886.
PHELPS, W. L.: *Robert Browning; How to Know Him*, Bobbs Merrill, 1915.
RUSSELL, F. T.: *One Word More on Browning*, Stanford, 1927.
TREVES, SIR F.: *The Country of 'The Ring and the Book,'* Cassell, 1913.
WENGER, C. N.: *The Aesthetics of Robert Browning*, Wahr, 1924.
WISE, T. J.: *A Complete Bibliography of the Writings in Prose and Verse of Robert Browning*, privately printed (London), 1897.

II. ESSAYS IN BOOKS

BAGEHOT, W.: "Wordsworth, Tennyson and Browning" in *Literary Studies* (3 vols.), Longmans, 1895.
CHAPMAN, J. J.: "Robert Browning" in *Emerson and Other Essays*, Scribner, 1898.
CHAUVET, P.: "Robert Browning" in *Sept essais de littérature anglaise*, Figuière, 1930.
ELLIOTT, G. R.: "The Whitmanism of Browning" in *The Cycle of Modern Poetry*, Princeton, 1929.
HEARN, L.: "Browning's 'Rabbi Ben Ezra' " in *Interpretations of Literature*, Dodd, 1915.
HEARN, L.: "Studies in Browning" in *Pre-Raphaelite and Other Poets*, Dodd, 1922.
HUTTON, R. H.: "Mr. Browning" in *Literary Essays*, Macmillan, 1888.
INGE, W. R.: "The Mysticism of Robert Browning" in *Studies of English Mystics*, Murray, 1906.
JAMES, H.: "The Novel in 'The Ring and the Book' " in *Notes on Novelists*, Scribner, 1914.
KER, W. P.: "Browning" in *Collected Essays*, 2 vols., Macmillan, 1925.
MACDONALD, J. F.: "Inhibitions in Browning's Poetry" in *Studies in English* (collected by M. W. Wallace), University of Toronto Press, 1932.
MORE, P. E.: "Why is Browning Popular?" in *Shelburne Essays, Third Series*, Putnam, 1905.
SAINTSBURY, G.: "Browning" in *Corrected Impressions*, Macmillan, 1895.
SANTAYANA, G.: "The Poetry of Barbarism" in *Interpretations of Poetry and Religion*, Scribner, 1900.
SCOTT, D.: "The Homeliness of Browning" in *Men of Letters*, Hodder, 1923.

III. ARTICLES IN PERIODICALS

BONNELL, J. K.: "Touch Images in the Poetry of Robert Browning" in *Publications of the Modern Language Association of America*, September, 1922.
CRAWFORD, A. W.: "Browning's Cleon" in *Journal of English and Germanic Philology*, October, 1927.
CRAWFORD, A. W.: "Browning's 'Saul' " in *Queen's Quarterly*, April–June, 1927.
CRESSMAN, E. D.: "Classical Poems of Robert Browning" in *Classical Journal*, December, 1927.
DEVANE, W. C.: "The Landscape of Browning's 'Childe Roland' " in *Publications of the Modern Language Association of America*, June, 1925.
FIRKINS, O. W.: "Paradoxical Ethics of Browning" in *Poet Lore*, September, 1912.
GOLDER, H.: "Browning's 'Childe Roland' " in *Publications of the Modern Language Association of America*, December, 1924.
HOOD, T. L.: "Browning's Ancient Classical Sources" in *Harvard Studies in Classical Philology*, 1922.
HOOD, T. L.: "The Meaning of the 'Childe Roland' " in *New England Magazine*, May, 1912.
KIRKCONNELL, W.: "The 'Epilogue' to 'Dramatis Personae' " in *Modern Language Notes*, April, 1926.
PALMER, G. H.: "The Monologue of Browning" in *Harvard Theological Review*, April, 1918.
RAYMOND, W. O.: "Browning and the Higher Criticism" in *Publications of the Modern Language Association of America*, June, 1929.
RAYMOND, W. O.: "Browning Fifty Years After" in *University of Toronto Quarterly*, January, 1940.
RUSSELL, F. T.: "A Poet's Portrayal of Emotion" in *The Psychological Review*, May, 1921.
RUSSELL, F. T.: "Browning the Artist in Theory and Practice" in *University of California Chronicle*, January, 1925.
RUSSELL, F. T.: "The Pessimism of Robert Browning" in *The Sewanee Review*, January, 1924.

NOTES AND COMMENTS

168. JOHANNES AGRICOLA IN MEDITATION

This poem first appeared in the *Monthly Repository* for January, 1836; reprinted in the collection of 1842, *Dramatic Lyrics*, it was grouped, as in the periodical, with "Porphyria." In the volume they bore jointly the caption, *Madhouse Cells*. Subsequently this poem was placed among *Men and Women*. Agricola, one of the great religious reformers of the sixteenth century was a disciple of Luther but deviated from him to found the sect of Antinomians. At its first appearance Browning printed with the text of the poem the following description of Antinomianism and comment on Agricola's relation to the sect, taken from Daniel Defoe's *Dictionary of All Religions:* "Antinomians, so denominated for rejecting the law as a thing of no use under the gospel dispensation: they say that good works do not further, nor evil works hinder salvation; that the child of God cannot sin, that God never chastiseth him, that murder, drunkenness, etc. are sins in the wicked, but not in him, that the child of grace, being once assured of salvation, afterwards never doubteth . . . that God doth not love any man for his holiness, that sanctification is no evidence of justification, etc. Potanus, in his *Catalogue of Heresies*, says John Agricola was the author of this sect, A.D. 1535." It is almost superfluous to point out that the description is a travesty.

168, 8. *my own abode:* as one of the elect.

168, 23. Agricola, convinced of his election, pronounces himself incapable of sin.

168, 29. *irreversibly:* originally Browning had written *irrevocably*. The shift is rather of sound than of sense.

168, 32. *no poison-gourd:* as one of those fore-ordained to be among the reprobate as he is fore-ordained to be among the elect.

168, 33 f. Compare the doctrine in these lines with that ascribed to the Antinomians by Defoe in the passage quoted above.

168, 42. *unexhausted:* inexhaustible.

168, 55–60. Agricola here attacks the doctrine of salvation by good works.

168. PORPHYRIA'S LOVER

This poem first appeared in the *Monthly Repository* for January, 1836, with the title "Porphyria"; it was reprinted in the collection of 1842, *Dramatic Lyrics*, grouped with "Johannes Agricola" under the caption *Madhouse Cells*. Subsequently it was placed among the *Dramatic Romances*. The personages are entirely imaginary.

169. CAVALIER TUNES

The three songs which are gathered together under this caption appeared in the collection of 1842, *Dramatic Lyrics*. In 1837 Browning had published his play *Strafford*, for which he had read widely in the period of the Commonwealth (1640–1660).

169. *Marching Along*

169, 1. *Sir Byng:* an imaginary personage.

169, 2. *the crop-headed Parliament:* The Parliament of 1640 was dominated by Puritans who clipped their hair short as a symbol of their convictions.

169, 3. *pressing:* enlisting. The word denotes forced service, but there is probably no emphasis on force here.

169, 7. *Pym:* John Pym was one of the pre-eminent Puritan opponents of the King.

carles: churls.

169, 8. *parles:* conspirings.

169, 14. *Hampden:* John Hampden, like Pym, was an outstanding Puritan opponent of the King, attacking the King's exaction of ship-money.

169, 15. *Hazelrig, Fiennes, and young Harry:* three Puritan leaders, Sir Arthur Hazelrig being one of the five members of Parliament whom the King sought to impeach, Nathaniel Fiennes, a friend of Cromwell, young Harry, Sir Henry Vane the younger, a son of the King's Secretary of State (who also bore the name Henry) but an adherent of the Puritan party.

170, 15. *Rupert:* Prince Rupert of Bavaria, nephew of King Charles, and a general in his army.

170, 22. *Nottingham:* here, in 1642, the Cavaliers made an attack on the army of the Puritans.

170. *Give a Rouse*

170, 1. *do him right:* do one's duty towards him.

170, 3. *rouse:* cheer.

170, 16. *Noll:* Oliver Cromwell.

170. *Boot and Saddle*

171, 10. *Brancepeth:* an actual castle near Durham.

171. MY LAST DUCHESS

This poem first appeared in the collection of 1842, *Dramatic Lyrics;* on its first appearance it was grouped with "Count Gismond" under the caption *Italy and France;* subsequently it was placed among the *Dramatic Romances*. Ferrara was, in the fifteenth and sixteenth centuries, one of the most cultivated and luxurious cities of Italy: Browning assumes a background for his duke of luxury, aesthetic appreciation and moral deterioration.

171, 3. *Frà Pandolf:* an imaginary artist. Some commentators attach importance to his being a friar (*fra* denotes his being such) as suggesting that the duke's jealousy would not permit a lay painter to approach his wife.

171, 6. *by design:* one interpretation suggests that the duke is here underlining the fact that the painter was a friar; but it is perhaps more likely that the phrase *by design* indicates the duke's awareness that rumour has linked the names of the duchess and the painter and his insistence that the duchess's punishment was not the consequence of adultery with the friar.

171, 22. The suspension points in this and in subsequent lines may denote the duke's awareness that he cannot fully explain why he was so dissatisfied with his wife's conduct; some commentators interpret them rather as proof of his haughtiness which prevented him from sympathetically investigating his wife's mode of feeling. The point at issue is whether pride or diffidence is indicated: there is no doubt that the duke was in the realm of feeling an inarticulate person.

171, 26. *dropping:* originally *drooping*, which does not accord with the notion of pleasure.

172, 45–46. Browning's own comment on these pregnant lines was: "the commands were that she should be put to death, or he might have had her shut up in a convent."

172, 54–56. W. L. Phelps suggests that the taming of the sea-horse is a symbol of the duke's desire for domination.

172, 56. *Claus of Innsbruck:* an imaginary artist.

172. SOLILOQUY OF THE SPANISH CLOISTER

This poem first appeared in the collection of 1842, *Dramatic Lyrics* and was on that appearance grouped with "An Incident of the French Camp," under the caption *Camp and Cloister;* it was then entitled "Cloister (Spanish)."

172, 4. *God's blood:* an oath based on the Roman Catholic belief of the transubstantiation of wine into the blood of Christ in the communion-service.

172, 10. *Salve tibi:* hail to you.

172, 31. *Barbary:* the northwest coast of Africa.

172, 37. *illustrate:* honour by the symbol.

172, 39. *Arian:* Arius was a theologian of the fourth century, who denied the equality of Christ with the Father and attacked the doctrine of the Trinity.

173, 49. *a great text in Galatians:* In St. Paul's epistle to the *Galatians*, Ch. V, 19–21, seventeen sinful practices are listed; Browning's use of twenty-nine, W. C. DeVane plausibly suggests, is probably in the sense of a great number.

173, 56. *Manichee:* a believer in the Manichean heresy which interprets the world as the theatre of conflict between eternally opposed principles of good and evil, neither powerful enough to destroy the other, rather than as the domain of an all-powerful and all-good Spirit such as the orthodox Christian conceives God to be.

173, 57–58. The reference is not to one of the frankly realistic works of French fiction, but to works purely pornographic, and exceedingly cheap in format.

173, 62. *woeful:* awful, in the colloquial sense.

print: illustration. The precision with which the speaker places the print in its sequence shows how he has pored over the book.

173, 70. *Hy, Zy, Hine:* the meaning of the three words is disputed.

173, 71. *Vespers:* Evening prayers, in a monastic order, the sixth of the seven canonical hours of prayer.

173, 71–72. *Plena gratia, Ave, Virgo:* the words serve to indicate the beginning of one of the prayers used at the vespers service (as at others) and commonly known, from a literal translation of the first two words, *Ave Maria*, as the Hail Mary. Browning's phrase, literally translated, means Hail, Virgin, full of grace.

173. IN A GONDOLA

This poem first appeared in the collection of 1842, *Dramatic Lyrics;* it was subsequently placed among the *Dramatic Romances*. In a letter probably written towards the end of 1841 Browning explains how the poem came into being. John Forster who was a friend of his and of the painter Maclise, told him of the subject of a painting Maclise had just completed and was about to exhibit, and asked him to write a few lines of verse to appear in the catalogue of the exhibition. The first section of the poem was so written; after Browning had seen the painting he then expanded the subject.

173, 22. *the Three:* they are subsequently called Paul, Gian, and Himself (that is her husband): see ll. 106–107.

173, 32. *loose:* free.

173, 33. *cruce:* crucible.

173, 34. *mage:* magician.

174, 106–107. See note to l. 22.

174, 108. *stylet:* stiletto.

174, 111. *sains:* protects.

174, 113. *Lido's wet accursed graves:* at the Lido, on an island, out from Venice towards the open sea, was a Jewish cemetery. The graves are called *wet* because at high tide they would be covered with water, *accursed* because those of heretics.

174, 127. *Giudecca:* a canal.

174, 129. *exactly waiting:* exactly corresponding.

175, 141. *lory:* parrot.

175, 151–154. Browning has in mind such a passage as the Roman epigrammatist Martial's, who says in one of his poems: "If Glaucilla twines a cold serpent round her neck."

175, 180. The reference is to a limpet on the beach coming forth from his shell at the sound of water.

175, 186. *Schidone:* or Schedone, an Italian painter of the late sixteenth and early seventeenth centuries.

175, 188. *Haste-thee-Luke:* Luca Giordano, a painter of a slightly later time. The nickname, a literal translation of the Italian *Luca-fa-presto*, arose from the reiterated demand by his father that he hurry.

175, 190. *Castelfranco:* an Italian painter of the sixteenth century generally known as Giorgione, but whose real name was Giorgio Barbarelli.

175, 192. *Ser:* gentleman.

175, 193. *Tizian:* a painting by Titian, whose Italian name was Tiziano Vecellio.

175, 206. *Zorzi:* his servant.

175, 207. *Zanze:* her servant.

175, 222. *Siora:* Signora, lady.

176. CRISTINA

This poem first appeared in the collection of 1842, *Dramatic Lyrics*, and was on that appearance grouped with "Rudel to the Lady of Tripoli" under the caption *Queen Worship*. Although Browning does not adhere to historical fact his Cristina derives from the Spanish Queen of that name, spouse of Ferdinand VII, and Queen Regent from 1833 to 1840, when she was obliged to abdicate by reason of the discovery that she was clandestinely married to an officer in the national army.

177. THE LABORATORY

This poem first appeared in *Hood's Magazine* for June, 1844; and was reprinted in the collection of 1845, *Dramatic Romances*. In its second appearance it was grouped with "The Confessional," under the caption *France and Spain*. It was subsequently placed among the *Dramatic Lyrics*. The characters are imaginary; and although the subtitle, *Ancien Régime*, establishes that the poem has to do with pre-revolutionary France, it is impossible to say whether the period is the sixteenth, the seventeenth, or the eighteenth century.

178. THE BISHOP ORDERS HIS TOMB AT ST. PRAXED'S CHURCH

This poem, under the title "The Tomb at St. Praxed's," first appeared in March, 1845, in *Hood's Magazine;* it was reprinted in the same year in the collection *Dramatic Romances*, and subsequently placed among *Men and Women*. In October, 1844, Browning saw the interior of the little church of S. Prassede at Rome; and it is probable that the poem was not composed before that time. Ruskin (in *Modern Painters*, Vol. IV) commends the poem in these words: "I know of no other piece of modern English, prose or poetry, in which there is so much told, as in these lines, of the Renaissance spirit,—its worldliness, inconsistency, pride, hypocrisy, ignorance of itself, love of art, of luxury, and of good Latin. It is nearly all that I have said of the central Renaissance in thirty pages of the *Stones of Venice*, put into as many lines, Browning's being also the antecedent work." The Bishop is an imaginary personage.

178, 1. The Bishop has in his memory the second verse of the first chapter of *Ecclesiastes:* "Vanity of vanities, saith the Preacher, vanity of vanities; all is vanity."

178, 3. *nephews-sons mine:* for propriety's sake the bishop habitually referred to his sons as nephews; on his death-bed he wavers between propriety and truthfulness.

178, 7. The implication is probably not that she had been his mistress before he took holy orders, but rather while he was a priest.

178, 21. *the epistle-side:* the right side of the altar, as one faces from the nave. The celebrant of a mass reads the gospel on the left side, the epistle on the right side of the altar.

179, 26. *tabernacle:* canopy.

179, 30. *pulse:* thrill.

179, 31. *onion-stone:* a cheap marble so called because it peels in layers as an onion does.

179, 41. *frail:* basket.

179, 46. *Frascati:* a beautiful suburb of Rome.

179, 49. *the Jesu Church:* the church of Il Jesu, in Rome.

179, 51. The Bishop is recalling a verse from *Job* (Ch. VII, 6): "My days are swifter than a weaver's shuttle, and are spent without hope."

179, 53–54. Basalt is black in color but less beautiful and costly than the kind of marble he now asks for.

179, 57. *Pans:* there is but one Pan, but the bishop wishes several figures of him on his tomb.

179, 58. *tripod:* an object with three feet: here a stool or table, associated with the oracle of Apollo at Delphi.

thyrsus: a staff, associated with Bacchus. It is intended that both the *thyrsus* and the *tripod* should suggest pagan religion.

179, 60. *Saint Praxed* (Prassede) was the virgin daughter of a Roman senator.

179, 62. *Moses with the tables:* Moses brought down from Mount Sinai the tables (or tablets) on which the ten commandments were written. See *Exodus*, Ch. XXIV.

179, 65. *revel down:* squander by the expense of their revels.

179, 66. *mouldy travertine:* a cheap stone which quickly flakes off.

179, 67. *Gandolf from his tomb-top:* an effigy of Gandolf was sculptured on the cover of his tomb.

179, 73–75. Browning here makes the confusion of values in the bishop's mind very clear: St. Praxed was a virgin who repudiated pagan civilisation.

180, 77. *Tully:* Cicero, whose full name was Marcus Tullius Cicero.

180, 79. *Ulpian:* Domitius Ulpianus, a late Latin writer, and one whose style and usage was doubtful.

180, 82. *God made and eaten:* in the course of the mass the priest is believed to convert the bread into the body of Christ, which is later consumed by himself and by the communicants.

180, 87. *a crook:* a crozier, as a symbol of the episcopal rank.

180, 89. *mortcloth:* a pall.

180, 95. The confusion of St. Praxed and Christ emphasizes how the bishop's mind is wandering. Of this way of indicating the bishop's state Browning has said: "he would not reveal himself as he does but for that."

180, 99. *elucescebat:* an inchoative form of the past where Cicero would have written *elucebat*, the meaning being "he shone," or "was famous."

180, 106–108. These lines were added in 1849.

180, 108. *vizor:* mask.

term: bust on pedestal.

180, 116. *gritstone:* sandstone, another cheap perishable material.

181. "HOW THEY BROUGHT THE GOOD NEWS FROM GHENT TO AIX"

This poem first appeared in the collection of 1845, *Dramatic Romances;* but it was subsequently placed among the *Dramatic Lyrics.* It is uncertain whether it was written on Browning's first trip to Italy, in 1838, or on his second, in 1844. He has himself made two important statements about the poem, both in letters: "There is no sort of historical foundation about 'Good News [from] Ghent.' I wrote it under the bulwark of a vessel, off the African Coast, after I had been at sea long enough to appreciate even the fancy of a gallop on a certain good horse 'York,' then in my stable at home. It was written in pencil on the flyleaf of Bartoli's *Simboli*, I remember." The second statement is as follows: "There is *no* historical incident whatever commemorated by the Poem you mention, which I wrote at sea, off the African coast, with a merely general impression of the characteristic warfare and besieging which abound in the Annals of Flanders. This accounts for some difficulties in the time and space occupied by the ride in one night." Browning was in Flanders in 1834, and again in 1838.

Ghent: a city in Belgium, about 100 miles (by direct route) from *Aix*, a city in Germany. By the route followed in the poem the distance is slightly greater, about 120 miles.

181, 5. *postern:* a back or side door or gate.

181, 10. *pique:* pommel.

181, 14. *Lokern:* a village on the route. All the proper names which follow are of places on the route, or of companions of the narrator, and their horses.

182. PICTOR IGNOTUS

This poem first appeared in the collection of 1845, *Dramatic Romances*, but was subsequently placed among *Men and Women.* The title means "An Unknown Painter." W. C. DeVane has pointed out that in this brief piece Browning for the first time addresses himself to the interpretation of the development of painting in Italy, a theme which, among others, "Andrea del Sarto," "Fra Lippo Lippi," and "Old Pictures in Florence" were to illustrate.

183, 22. *braved:* attacked.

183, 28. *Kaiser:* the emperor (of the Holy Roman Empire).

183, 56. *likes me:* pleases me.

183, 67. *travertine:* a limestone, cheap and very generally used.

184. THE ITALIAN IN ENGLAND

This poem first appeared in the collection of 1845, *Dramatic Romances*, under the title "Italy in England." No specific insurrection is described; but it is likely that Browning had in mind not only the rising in Northern Italy in 1823 but also the rebellion on the Neapolitan coast in 1844.

184, 8. *Charles:* Carlo Alberto, king of Sardinia at the time the poem was written. He had been a member of the revolutionary society, the Carbonari, and later repressed risings, but in his final stage—after Browning wrote—led an Italian movement against Austrian domination.

184, 19. *Metternich:* the principal Austrian statesman of the period, and the symbol of Austrian domination and oppression in Italy.

184, 20. *Charles's miserable end:* not his death, or abdication, both of which occurred after the poem was written, but his recreancy to the liberal cause.

184, 75. *duomo:* cathedral.

184, 76. *tenebrae:* the service in which, during Holy Week, the church commemorates the passion and crucifixion of Christ. The word itself means darkness; and in the course of the service candle after candle is extinguished.

185, 121–122. In the original manuscript Browning wrote, more moderately,

> I would grasp Metternich until
> I felt his throat and had my will.

But Miss Barrett found the moderation weak and suggested—in outline at least—the change to the present version.

185. THE ENGLISHMAN IN ITALY

This poem first appeared in the collection of 1845, *Dramatic Romances*, under the title, "England in Italy," and has borne its present title since 1849. It was still incomplete in the late summer of 1845, when it was submitted to Miss Barrett for emendation; the final section, ll. 287–92, was added after she first read the poem, and perhaps at her prompting.

Piano di Sorrento: the plain of Sorrento which is close to Naples.

185, 5. *scirocco:* a hot dry wind from the south.

185, 11. The original reading was much plainer and less suggestive:

All the memories plucked at Sorrento.

186, 47. *frails:* baskets made of rushes.

186, 53. *Amalfi:* a town on the coast near Naples.

186, 69. *Salerno:* another coastal town in the same region.

186, 87. *love-apple:* tomato.

186, 92. *regales:* feasts, or, more specifically, dainties.

186, 97. *lasagne:* macaroni in long strips.

187, 122. *medlar:* a tree bearing a fruit similar to a small, hard apple.

187, 138. *sorbs:* service-trees.

187, 171. *Calvano:* a mountain on the coast near Naples.

187, 196. This line is taken very plausibly to have a double meaning: beside the patent reference to the beauty of the immediate landscape, a passive beauty, Browning may be referring to the quality of Italian life in his period.

187, 199. *isles of the siren:* islands off the Neapolitan coast.

188, 250–251. *The Feast of the Rosary's Virgin:* October 7, the date of the victory (in 1571) of Christian over Turk at Lepanto.

188, 265. *Bellini:* an Italian composer who died not long before the poem was written.

Auber: a French composer still alive at the time Browning wrote.

188, 272. *stomp:* stamp, walk heavily.

188, 289. *Corn-laws:* laws which imposed a tax upon the import of grain and related products. They were repealed, after furious controversy, in 1846, in the wake of famine in Ireland.

189. THE LOST LEADER

This poem first appeared in the collection of 1845, *Dramatic Romances*, and was subsequently placed among the *Dramatic Lyrics*. Thirty years after the poem was written Browning stated, contritely, that he had had Wordsworth in mind when he wrote; from the form of his statement it is clear that he had not withheld from earlier inquirers that Wordsworth was his subject (see T. L. Hood: *Letters of Robert Browning*, 166–167). In 1843 Wordsworth became Poet Laureate; in 1842 he had accepted a Civil List pension. It was evident to all that he had reached the completely opposite position to his early revolutionary enthusiasm. W. C. DeVane (*A Browning Handbook*, 145) has pointed out the significance of the grouping of this poem with "The Italian in England" and "The Englishman in Italy."

189, 1. *a handful of silver:* the pension, referred to above, was no handful to Wordsworth, but £300.

189, 2. *a riband to stick in his coat:* This may perhaps refer to the laureateship, as an honorific post: but the laureateship is not accompanied by a riband.

189, 3. *us:* here and in following lines denotes not an organized revolutionary or radical group but the mass of individuals who believe in reform and progress.

189, 30. The original reading, less alliterative, but not perhaps less vigorous or apt was:

Aim at our heart ere we pierce through his own.

189. HOME-THOUGHTS FROM ABROAD

In the collection of 1845, *Dramatic Romances*, the poem "Home-Thoughts from Abroad" consisted of three sections. The first was what, with negligible verbal changes now constitutes the poem "Home-Thoughts from Abroad"; the second was the stanza now entitled "Here's to Nelson's Memory"; the third was what we know as "Home-Thoughts from the Sea." The second section disappeared in 1849 but was restored as an independent piece in 1863; the third was printed as a separate piece as early as 1849.

190. "HERE'S TO NELSON'S MEMORY"

See the note under "Home-Thoughts from Abroad." W. C. DeVane plausibly conjectures that it was written in 1844 when Browning was on his way to Italy by sea.

190, 9 f. No printed source of the anecdote is known.

190. HOME-THOUGHTS FROM THE SEA

See the note under "Home-Thoughts from Abroad." W. C. DeVane plausibly conjectures that these lines were written in 1844; they were doubtless at least conceived at that time.

190, 1. *Cape Saint Vincent:* a cape at the southwest of Portugal: here the Spanish fleet surrendered to Nelson in 1797.

190, 3. *Trafalgar:* here in 1805 Nelson met death defeating the joint fleet of France and Spain.

190, 7. *Jove's planet:* Jupiter.

190. MEETING AT NIGHT

This poem first appeared in the collection of 1845, *Dramatic Romances.* In that collection, under the caption *Night and Morning*, Browning grouped this poem and that now known as "Parting at Morning"; in 1849 the parts were separated and stood as they now do, one following the other.

190. PARTING AT MORNING

See the note under "Meeting at Night." In the year of his death Browning offered an elucidation of the two poems: "it [the two poems regarded as a unit] is *his* confession of how fleeting is the belief (implied in the first part) that such raptures are self-sufficient and enduring—as for the time they appear."

190, 3. *him:* the sun.

190, 4. *me:* the man, who speaks.

190. SAUL

The first nine sections of this poem first appeared in the collection of 1845, *Dramatic Romances.* In the collection of 1855, *Men and Women*, it was completed, the ninth section undergoing marked modification. Subsequently it was placed among the *Dramatic Lyrics.* The date when the poem was conceived was 1845, the year of its first publication: in January of that year Browning read the poetry of Christopher Smart; he has recorded in his *Parleying with Christopher Smart* some of his impressions. In a preface to his "Ode to Musick on Saint Cecilia's Day" Smart says:

It would not be right to conclude, without taking notice of a fine subject for an Ode on S. Cecilia's Day, which was suggested to the author by his friend the learned and ingenious Mr. Comber, late of Jesus College in this University [Cambridge]; that is David's playing to King Saul when he was troubled with the evil spirit. He was much pleased with the hint at first, but at length was deterred from improving it by the greatness of the subject, and he thinks not without reason. The choosing of too high subjects has been the ruin of many a tolerable Genius.

Alternative suggestions of sources for the poem have been examined and rejected by W. C. DeVane (*A Browning Handbook*, 226) who has also set forth in full Browning's obligation to Smart. The Biblical source of the poem's material is *I Samuel*, Ch. XVI, 14–23. Mr. DeVane conjectures that the poem was continued and completed in 1852–3.

The Speaker is David.

190, 1. *Abner:* the son of Ner, was Saul's uncle, and the commander of his army.

190, 3. *the King:* Saul.

191, 31. *waiting his change:* preparing to slough off his skin.

191, 45. *jerboa:* an animal of the rodent family, remarked for its leaps and jumps. It is because of his speed in bounding through the air that he is called in the next line "half-bird."

192, 57. *the great march:* a battle song.

192, 60. *Levites:* literally the sons of Levi. The priests of the temple were chosen from this tribe.

192, 65. *male-sapphires:* dazzling gems, sometimes called star-stones.

194, 162. The meaning is that when a boy he was not reflective, and the joys he experienced were less delightful than they would have been to a reflective consciousness such as he will be.

194, 175. *soul-wine:* insight into spiritual truth, as cheering to the soul as wine to the body.

194, 176. *actual:* existent.

194, 188. *paper-reeds:* sedge, from which papyrus was made.

195, 203. *Hebron:* a mountain in Judaea, on which stood a city of the same name.

195, 204. *Kidron:* a small river near Jerusalem.

195, 213. *error:* Saul had been commanded by God to destroy the Amalekites; but he preserved the best of their livestock and their king, Agag. His disobedience led God to decide that he should not remain king over Israel. (See *I Samuel*, Ch. XV.)

196, 291. *Sabaoth:* a Biblical term denoting armies. The term is here used metaphorically.

197, 331. *the new law:* that God is love.

198. LOVE AMONG THE RUINS

This poem first appeared as the first in the collection of 1855, *Men and Women;* it was subsequently placed among the *Dramatic Lyrics.* On its first appearance it consisted of fourteen six-lined stanzas; subsequently Browning regrouped the lines in seven twelve-lined stanzas, each breaking noticeably in the middle, thus emphasizing more effectively perhaps than in his original arrangement, the contrast between past and present which is essential to the poem. The poem was written in January, 1852, in one day. It is doubtful whether Browning intended to paint an Italian background, as was once confidently assumed. For a full consideration of the background see DeVane: *A Browning Handbook*, 191–192, and the bibliographical references there supplied.

198, 39. *caper:* a brambly bush.

199, 47. *minions:* creatures, more strictly darlings, or favorites.

199, 65. *causeys:* causeways, *i.e.*, raised paths.

199. EVELYN HOPE

This poem first appeared in the collection of 1855, *Men and Women;* it was subsequently placed among the *Dramatic Lyrics.* There is no evidence of an experience which might authorize the opinion that the poem was autobiographical: when it appeared however—it is not known when it was written—Browning was forty-three, almost three times the age of Evelyn Hope (see lines 9 and 21).

201. UP AT A VILLA—DOWN IN THE CITY

This poem first appeared in the collection of 1855, *Men and Women,* and was subsequently placed among the *Dramatic Lyrics.* It is conjectured that the poem was written in 1850 when Browning was living in the hills a little above Siena, or in 1853 when he was living in the country near Bagni di Lucca.

201, 4. *by Bacchus: Per Baccho*, a common and very mild Italian oath.

202, 29. *conch:* shell.

202, 42. *Pulcinello-trumpet:* Pulcinello was the buffoon in puppet-shows: the trumpet announced the coming of the show and suggested Pulcinello, the most amusing of the puppets.

202, 44. *liberal thieves:* men who were of the revolutionary party and accordingly antipathetic to the person of quality who speaks.

202, 47. *sonnet with flowery marge:* the poem's text was adorned with a marginal decoration of flowers.

202, 52. *seven swords:* denoting Our Lady of Sorrows. The Virgin is venerated as having endured seven great sorrows.

203. A WOMAN'S LAST WORD

This poem first appeared in the collection of 1855, *Men and Women;* it was subsequently placed among the *Dramatic Lyrics.*

203. FRA LIPPO LIPPI

This poem first appeared in the collection of 1855, *Men and Women.* W. C. DeVane plausibly conjectures that Browning was at work on it in 1853 (*A Browning Handbook*, 194). If the date of composition cannot be fixed with certainty, the sources to which Browning went for information and impressions are known. Besides his study of a number of Lippo's pictures (The Coronation of the Virgin, described in the closing section of the poem, 344 f., is at Florence) he consulted Vasari's vivid but not always veracious biographies of the painters (which he had read as early as 1846–7) and Baldinucci's *Delle Notizie del Disegno da Cimabue . . .*, which led him into one major distortion of fact.

Vasari's account of Lippo presents him as born in 1412 (instead of 1406); as orphaned at two; received into the care of his father's sister, Mona Lapaccia; in 1420, registered at the Carmine, a

Carmelite monastery in Florence; as filling his school-books with drawings and especially caricatures; as leaving the monastery, after taking holy orders, and enjoying a worldly life; as winning the patronage of Cosimo de' Medici; as on one occasion, when locked into the Medici palace to complete some paintings, escaping by knotting together his bedclothes and letting himself down to the street. Up to this point Lippo's history as given by Vasari is almost fully transferred to Browning's poem. After the time at which Browning represents him, he fell in love with a nun, abducted her, and at a much later time had his relation with her recognized by the church. He died in 1469. From Vasari Browning also formed his impression of Lippo's character.

Baldinucci misled Browning into placing Masaccio ("hulking Tom," in line 277) as Lippo's pupil rather than his master. As late as 1866 Browning was convinced that his presentation of this relationship was correct.

203, 3. *Zooks:* a mild oath.

203, 6. *sportive ladies:* prostitutes.

203, 7. *the Carmine:* the monastery of the Carmelites, the order to which Lippo belonged.

203, 12. *Aha, you know your betters:* at this point the officer of the guard approaches and the members who have apprehended Lippo salute their superior.

203, 17. *Cosimo of the Medici:* the head of the Medici family at the time, and the greatest power in the city of Florence.

203, 18. *Boh! you were best!:* as they withdraw their hands from his neck at the mention of his great patron, he compliments them on their discretion. *Were* is equivalent to "had."

204, 23. *pilchards:* a small fish common in the Mediterranean area.

204, 34. Vasari mentions that John the Baptist was a favorite subject for painting with Lippo.

204, 41. *they take you:* they please you.

204, 52. *whifts:* snatches.

204, 67. *Saint Laurence:* the church of San Lorenzo in one of the main streets.

204, 73. *Jerome:* Vasari mentions a picture of Jerome done by Lippo for the Duke Cosimo de' Medici.

205, 81–90. See the general note on the poem above for Vasari's account of Lippo's early life.

205, 117. *processional:* walking in procession.

fine: wearing special apparel, as taking part in a religious ceremony.

205, 121. *the Eight:* the magistracy of the city of Florence.

205, 130. *antiphonary:* the book containing the antiphons or responses sung by a church choir.

206, 139. *Camaldolese:* a religious order much less important than the Carmelites, but with a monastery in Florence, or than the *Preaching Friars*, or Dominicans.

206, 148. *cribs:* petty thievings.

206, 170. *the Prior:* the monk who presides over a monastery.

206, 172. *funked:* turned to smoke.

206, 183 f. Lippo is satirizing the scholastic explanations of the nature of the soul, which to him seem specious and fantastic.

207, 190. *Giotto:* the greatest of the early medieval artists (painter, sculptor, and architect). Here and in subsequent references to earlier painters such as Angelico and Lorenzo Monaco, Browning underlines the difference between Lippo's ideal and that of his predecessors. Giotto has many pictures which present a saint praising God.

207, 196. *Herodias:* the wife of Herod's brother. It was Salome her daughter who danced, but it was Herodias who devised the plot which led to John the Baptist's decapitation. See *Matthew*, Ch. XIV, 1–12. It may be that what Browning wishes to do is to suggest the prior's embarrassment and confusion.

207, 228. *rings:* rings secured to the wall at various levels, those on the lower levels intended for fastening horses, those above for holding flags.

207, 235. *Angelico:* also a monastic painter.

207, 236. *Lorenzo Monaco:* a painter who was a member of the rival Camaldolese order. He died when Lippo was beginning to paint. *Monaco* means the monk.

207, 239. *mistr . . .:* the incomplete word is *mistress.*

208, 262–263. The meaning of these lines is as follows: You pretend you don't like what your instinct leads you to value, you pretend you do like what, when you have it, seems wholly unsatisfying. The contrast is between the values of this world, and specifically of the flesh, and those which are spiritual and otherworldly.

208, 276–277. Lippo refers to Masaccio. See the introductory note.

209, 307. *cullion:* rascal.

209, 323. *Saint Laurence:* This saint was martyred by being burned on a gridiron.

209, 324. *Prato:* in a church in this town near Florence is some of Lippo's work.

209, 327. *phiz:* a vulgar equivalent of face.

209, 338. *Chianti wine:* wine from a region near Florence.

209, 344 f. The picture he refers to is the Coronation of the Virgin. See the introductory note.

209, 346. *a cast o' my office:* a work of my doing.

210, 353. *Saint John:* John the Baptist, a favorite subject of Lippo and the patron saint of Florence. The second circumstance may account for the addiction of Lippo to pictures of the saint.

210, 354. *Saint Ambrose:* the patron saint of the convent. Ambrogio (l. 345) is the Italian form of Ambrose.

210, 377. *Iste perfecit opus:* literally "this man made the work." In the Coronation of the Virgin these words appear in the lower right-hand corner, close to the head of the painter (see l. 362).

210, 381. *hot cockles:* a form of blind man's buff but another meaning, less innocent, is conceivable.

210. A TOCCATA OF GALUPPI'S

This poem first appeared in the collection of 1855, *Men and Women;* it was subsequently placed among the *Dramatic Lyrics.* Baldassaro Galuppi was a Venetian composer of the eighteenth century; his works ranged from ecclesiastical music to light operas: a *toccata,* or touch-piece, is a work light in character intended to exercise the technical power of the musician. W. C. DeVane (*A Browning Handbook,* 196–197) quotes an unidentified American as reporting Browning playing "a faint throbbing toccata of Galuppi" in 1847, and considers it certain that this poem was composed not later than 1853.

211, 6. *St. Mark's:* the cathedral of Venice.

Doges: the chief magistrate of Venice was called the *doge.*

wed the sea with rings: the ceremony of wedding the Adriatic sea, to symbolize that the sea was united and subject to Venice as wife to husband, went back to the middle ages, and was annually repeated, a ring being dropped into the sea.

211, 8. *Shylock's bridge:* the Rialto, a large bridge over the Grand Canal.

kept: held.

Through this line there is the evocation of the Venice of Shakespeare's play, *The Merchant of Venice.*

211, 18. *Toccatas:* see the general note on the poem.

clavichord: the first string instrument with a key-board, the earlier form of the piano.

211, 19–24. These lines, abounding as they do in technical musical terminology, are less difficult than they at first appear. The emotional significance of the terms (all that matters) is clarified by the context.

211, 26. *grave and gay:* see the general note to the poem.

211, 32. *a secret wrung from nature's close reserve:* the speaker is a scientist, see ll. 37–38.

211, 35 f. The passage within the quotation marks records the impression of the music on the speaker.

212. AN EPISTLE

This poem first appeared in the collection of 1855, *Men and Women.* Its source is in *John,* Ch. XI, 1–44; but the characters of Abib and Karshish are purely imaginary. The date is 66 A.D.

212, 1–2. Browning immediately sets before his reader the range of interest of his main character: although a scientist he is also a believer.

212, 12. *its source:* the world-soul, of which individual souls were temporarily separated parts.

212, 17. *snakestone:* substance thought effective in cases of snake-bite.

212, 21. *were brought to:* that is his account, in preceding letters, came to that point.

212, 28. *Vespasian:* The Holy Land was invaded in 66 A.D. by an army under the command of Vespasian, in 70 A.D. by another under the command of his son Titus, who destroyed Jerusalem.

212, 29. The Syrian lynx, as this line *suggests,* is marked by black ears.

212, 42. *viscid choler:* sticky humour.

212, 43. *tertian:* fever which recurs every third day.

212, 44. *falling-sickness:* epilepsy.

213, 46. *weaves no web:* belonging accordingly to the group of wandering spiders.

213, 55. *gum-tragacanth:* a medicinal gum from a shrub.

213, 57. *the porphyry:* the vessel made of rock porphyry on which the scientist would pound his pestle.

213, 60. *Zoar:* a city near the Dead Sea.

213, 82. *exhibition:* application.

213, 89. *conceit:* notion (some contempt is implied).

213, 93. *fancy-scrawls:* what fantasy has loosely written.

213, 100. *Nazarene physician:* Jesus, described as a physician because he had effected a physical cure.

213, 103. *fume:* diseased vapor.

213, 105. *the life of life:* the soul.

213, 109. *fifty:* Commentators have grappled with the problem of Lazarus' supposed age. An acceptable interpretation is that Browning makes Karshish describe Lazarus as fifty (when according to the Bible story he would be about sixty-five at the time Karshish met him) in order to demonstrate how fully Lazarus' physical life had been renewed by Jesus' miracle.

214, 146–147. A natural subject of discussion with the rumours mentioned in ll. 27–28.

214, 152. *Far as I see:* the phrase is thrown in to show that Karshish is not satisfied with his explanation.

214, 161. *pretermission:* interruption.

214, 177. *Greek fire:* a compound of sulphur, nitre and naphtha, used first at the siege of Constantinople, in 673 A.D. *Liquid* fire was known much earlier than the time of Vespasian.

215, 205. *'Sayeth:* the symbol preceding sayeth indicates an elision of the pronominal subject. The practice is peculiar to Browning.

215, 252. *the earthquake:* an earthquake occurred while Jesus hung on the cross. See *Matthew,* Ch. XXVII, 51.

216, 281. *blue-flowering borage:* this plant was believed to have stimulating powers.

Aleppo: a Syrian town.

216, 282. *It is strange!:* the purport of the phrase is intentionally ambiguous.

216. MY STAR

This poem first appeared in the collection of 1855, *Men and Women,* and was subsequently placed among the *Dramatic Lyrics.* In a selection from his poems brought out by Browning himself in 1872 this brief piece was placed first. The star may be the poet's wife, still alive when the poem was written, or it may be his imagination: there is no means of deciding.

216, 11. *Saturn:* a planet.

world: a planet, a much larger astronomical body than a star.

216. "CHILDE ROLAND TO THE DARK TOWER CAME"

This poem first appeared in the collection of 1855, *Men and Women,* and was subsequently placed among the *Dramatic Romances.* It was written in January, 1852, in a single day. W. C. DeVane aptly remarks that the circumstances of its composition—the poet had contracted with himself to write a poem a day—led to its being less intellectual, and closer to dream and fantasy than most of Browning's works. The poem invites speculation; and the question whether or not it contains symbols, or even an allegory, cannot be definitively answered. When shortly before his death Browning was asked whether he accepted one of the many allegorical interpretations, his answer was, in part: "Oh, no, not at all. Understand, I don't repudiate it either. I only mean I was conscious of no allegorical intention in writing it." An acceptable suggestion may be that while no clear allegory runs through the poem, informing all the details with meaning, the landscape, the characters and the moral dilemma all have definite meanings. On another occasion, also towards the close of his life, when he was asked whether the essential meaning of the poem could be expressed in the phrase: "He that endureth to the end shall be saved," Browning replied: "Yes, just about that."

In writing the poem Browning had in mind not only the Shakespearean reference given in the subtitle, but also a recollection of a tower in the Carrara Mountains, and of a figure of a horse in a tapestry. W. C. DeVane has established also that the landscape has close resemblances to that in Gerard de Lairesse's *The Art of Painting in All Its Branches,* ch. XVII, a work familiar to Browning since his childhood. (See DeVane: "The Landscape of Browning's Childe Roland," P.M.L.A., Vol. XL, pp. 426–432.)

Childe: the young son of a knight, who has not yet been admitted to knighthood.

217, 48. *estray:* strayer, in this instance one who, abandoning the path, becomes a victim.

218, 80. *colloped:* in folds.

218, 94. *fix me to the place:* strengthen my courage.

218, 114. *bespate:* spattered.

218, 133. *cirque:* arena, with an implication of circularity.

218, 143. *Tophet:* Hell.

218, 154. *palsied:* paralysed, in this case struck by lightning.

218, 160. *Apollyon:* a name for the devil, used in the following passage in *Revelation*, Ch. IX, 11: "And they had a king over them, which is the angel of the bottomless pit, whose name in the Hebrew tongue is Abaddon, but in the Greek tongue hath his name Apollyon."

218, 161. *dragon-penned:* dragon-pinioned.

218, 178. *scalped:* bare at the peak.

218, 189. *a cleft:* an opening in the hills.

219, 203. *slug-horn:* trumpet.

220. HOW IT STRIKES A CONTEMPORARY

This poem first appeared in the collection of 1855, *Men and Women.* It is unlikely that Browning ever visited the city of Valladolid, in Spain; and the reasons for his placing his ideas in such a setting are unknown. The speaker, as the last two lines make clear, is a worldling. W. C. DeVane conjectures (*A Browning Handbook*, 209–210) that the poem was written in 1851 or 1852.

220, 14. *breathed themselves:* took an airing.

220, 19. *Moorish work:* a survival of the period in which the Moors were masters of Spain. The time to which the poem refers cannot be precisely fixed. The Moors had been driven from Spain in the latter part of the fifteenth century; Titian (see l. 76) died in 1575; and it was in the late sixteenth and early seventeenth centuries that Spanish literature came to its greatest heights. It may be suggested with some plausibility that the poem refers to the late sixteenth or early seventeenth century. Valladolid was the Spanish capital for a short period in the seventeenth century.

220, 20. *ferrel:* the metal point.

220, 28. *fly-leaf ballads:* broadsides.

220, 44. *our Lord the King:* the King symbolizes God. In the first edition of the poem all the pronouns referring to him were capitalized.

221, 74. *Jewry:* ghetto.

221, 90. *Corregidor:* chief magistrate.

221, 96. *memorised:* celebrated.

221, 111–113. The passage *Bless us . . . you and I* is an aside; the passage *A second . . .* follows directly upon *for one thing.*

221, 115. *Prado:* promenade.

221. BISHOP BLOUGRAM'S APOLOGY

This poem first appeared in the collection of 1855, *Men and Women.* The character of Blougram was founded on that of Nicholas Wiseman, as Browning understood it: Wilfrid Ward, Wiseman's biographer, considers it entirely off the mark. Wiseman himself reviewed the poem (in *The Rambler*, January, 1856), approved it with reservations and obviously failed to detect any likeness, or intended likeness, to himself. Wiseman was in 1840 created Vicar Apostolic of the Central District of England and consecrated bishop of Melipotamus *in partibus infidelium* (see l. 973); in 1850 Archbishop of Westminster and Primate of the Roman Catholic Church in England.

221, 3. *our Abbey:* Westminster Abbey, which was lost to the Roman Catholic Church at the Reformation.

221, 4. *Basilica:* a building (originally denoting a palace, recently the term always implies a church) in the form of an oblong with double colonnade and apse. Blougram criticises such a form as exhausting to a preacher.

221, 6. *Pugin:* an English ecclesiastical architect converted to Roman Catholicism and author of a number of the nineteenth-century Gothic churches in Great Britain. Wiseman and he were close friends but had serious disagreements.

222, 13. *Gigadibs:* an imaginary personage. W. C. DeVane suggests that he was partially drawn from Browning's friend "Father" Prout, an ex-Jesuit priest.

222, 41. *their:* the Roman Catholics', or perhaps believers' in general.

222, 45. *Chè, chè:* an Italian phrase, impossible to translate literally, but roughly equivalent to "come, come!"

222, 54. *Count D'Orsay:* an arbiter of elegances in the London society of the period. The fact that he and Pugin died in 1852 leads to the conjecture that the poem was begun before that year.

223, 62. *They can't:* since the sixteenth century, all popes have been Italian.

223, 70. *tire-room:* dressing-room.

223, 77. *imperial:* absolute.

223, 107. *Balzac:* the novelist had died in 1850.

224, 112. *the Jerome:* Correggio's painting of St. Jerome, which is in the museum of Parma.

224, 113. *Correggio's fleeting glow:* one of the distinctive excellences of Correggio is his warm suggestive painting of flesh. Browning underlines the bishop's extreme worldliness by the reference to Correggio as a favorite painter (and his hypocrisy, perhaps, by the choice among Correggio's paintings of the St. Jerome). Wiseman, a man of taste and culture, delighted in art.

224, 116. *Modenese:* inhabitant of the city of Modena, or of the duchy. Correggio studied at Modena but was not born in the city.

225, 183. *a fancy from a flower-bell:* a notion conceived as one looks at a blossoming flower.

225, 190. *the grand Perhaps:* a literal translation of *le grand peut-être*, a phrase used, to denote the problem of the possibility of life beyond the grave, by Rabelais.

225, 204. *fresh:* recent.

225, 205–208. The doctrine here set forth is one employed by a number of religious and conservative minds of the period in an attempt to defend beliefs inconsistent with nineteenth-century scientific discoveries. A dramatic example is given in Edmund Gosse's *Father and Son*, Ch. V, which has reference to the decade following that in which Browning brought out this poem.

228, 316. *Peter's creed:* the doctrine of the Apostles, Peter being singled out from them, as the first pope.

Hildebrand's: Blougram here recognizes a distinction between the creed of the Apostles and that of the full-formed medieval church, in which Pope Gregory the Great (known also as Hildebrand) was one of the chief forces.

229, 377. *the last winking Virgin:* the statue of the Virgin Mary last claimed to have shown itself miraculously animated for the nonce.

229, 381. *Verdi:* an Italian composer, author of *Ernani* (1844), *Rigoletto* (1851), *Il Trovatore* (1853).

229, 386. *Rossini:* another, and more conservative, composer of the period.

229, 389. In the original text Browning wrote, more technically and less vividly, *thing within a thing*, instead of *wheel within a wheel.*

229, 397. *demirep:* demireputable, woman of doubtful morals.

229, 411. *Schelling:* a German idealistic philosopher, who based his system on Kant's, and accepted an organ of knowledge superior to the practical or critical reason. By such an acceptance one could affirm that what the practical reason found false the superior organ might find true.

230, 424. *coat bedropped with wax:* the implication probably is that the wax fell from candles as he prayed before a shrine.

230, 425. *Peter's chains:* the chains of St. Peter, who was imprisoned by Herod and, two chains having been placed upon him, binding him to two soldiers, escaped by the agency of an angel who struck off the chains (see *Acts*, Ch. XII, 3–11).

230, 426. *the needlework of Noodledom:* embroidery—doubtless of sacred subjects—done by foolish pious women.

231, 472. *an Austrian marriage:* Napoleon's second marriage was to Marie-Louise, an Austrian archduchess, and a member of the imperial family of Hapsburg.

231, 475. *Austerlitz:* a town northeast of Vienna where in 1805 Napoleon inflicted a catastrophic defeat upon the forces of Russia, Austria and Prussia.

231, 516. *Giulio Romano:* an Italian painter of the Renaissance.

Dowland: a musician and composer, contemporary with Shakespeare. Both are mentioned in Shakespeare's plays.

231, 519. *Pandulph, of fair Milan Cardinal:* words spoken by the Pope's Legate in *King John*, Act III, scene 1.

232, 533. *St. Gothard:* a mountain in the Swiss Alps.

232, 553. *Queen Bess:* Queen Elizabeth of England.

232, 572. *Re-opens a shut book:* During the period preceding Luther the Bible was read chiefly in Latin; and since few could read that language it was, to the vast majority, a shut book. Luther advocated translation of the Bible into the vernacular languages and provision of copies of the translation in places where all might read.

232, 573. The meaning is that Luther's energy of conviction was dependent on the energy of conviction of his contemporaries.

233, 577. *Strauss:* the author of *Leben Jesu* (The Life of Jesus) which appeared in 1835, and in an English translation, by George Eliot, in 1846. In saying he represents *the next advance*, Browning is taking Strauss as an example of the higher criticism of Biblical texts. Wiseman's early reputation was made in Biblical studies.

233, 582. *Read the text aright:* understand the text of the Bible in exactly the sense in which it was intended. It was the professed aim of the higher criticism to enable readers of the Bible to do this.

233, 608. *soul:* originally soil, which sustains the metaphor.

234, 640. *born in Rome:* Wiseman was born in Seville, in Spain. As Louis Cazamian suggests (*Hommes et Femmes*, 340) Browning probably did not wish the analogy between Blougram and Wiseman to be too exact.

234, 664. *ichors:* ichor was the fluid which, analogous to human blood flowed through the veins of the gods in Greek mythology.

234, 667. *Michael:* St. Michael the Archangel subdued Satan who had assumed the form of a snake.

234, 676. *These noodles:* stupid pious people.

235, 685. *the ark a-top of Ararat:* at Mount Ararat, in Asia Minor, the ark of Noah is stated to have come to rest. "And the ark rested in the seventh month, on the seventeenth day of the month, upon the mountains of Ararat" (*Genesis*, Ch. VIII, 4).

235, 703. *brother Newman:* John Henry Newman, who became a member of the Roman Catholic Church in 1845, maintained that the ordinary processes of nature could be varied by divine will. The reference may be to his *Essay on the Development of Christian Doctrine;* but the position is one he took on many occasions.

235, 704. *the Immaculate Conception:* the doctrine that Mary, the mother of Jesus, was conceived without sin, was proclaimed a dogma by Pope Pius IX, in 1854.

235, 715. *King Bomba:* Bomba was a nickname given to Ferdinand II, King of Sicily at the time Browning wrote.

lazzaroni: loafers, beggars.

235, 716. *Antonelli:* a prominent cardinal of the period.

235, 728. *Naples' liquefaction:* The blood of St. Januarius, the patron saint of Naples, is believed to liquefy every year on his feast-day, and from time to time on other days, for special purpose.

236, 732. *decrassify:* cleanse.

236, 744. *Fichte's clever cut at God himself:* Fichte was a German idealistic philosopher, who presented God as necessarily no more than an idea in the mind of man.

237, 791. *scouts:* ridicules.

238, 876. *you are God's sheep, not mine:* Gigadibs is not a member of the Roman Catholic Church, accordingly he is not one of Bishop Blougram's flock.

239, 913–915. Wiseman had founded the *Dublin Review*, a Catholic periodical of general information and opinion, and written many articles for it and other journals. His subjects were as varied as Blougram's; but there is no exact correspondence between their works.

240, 942. *drugget:* coarse woollen material, used for carpet more often than for dress.

240, 945. *Blackwood's Magazine:* a British periodical which at the time the poem was written had declined into unimportance.

240, 960. *our own reviews:* Roman Catholic periodicals.

240, 963. *The Outward-bound:* the phrase refers back to the image of the cabin and cabin-furniture.

240, 972–974. In 1850 Wiseman had become Archbishop of Westminster, the first Roman Catholic prelate with an episcopal see in England since the sixteenth century; the revival of Roman Catholic sees in England is what Browning glances at in the phrase "changed to by our novel hierarchy"; previously Wiseman, a vicar apostolic in England had been titular bishop of Melipotamus, *in partibus infidelium* (literally, in the territories of unbelievers).

240, 979. This line was added after the poem's first appearance.

241, 999. *oppugn:* attack.

241, 1014. *his last chapter of St. John:* in the last chapter of St. John's Gospel occurs the verse: "Then Peter, turning about, seeth the disciple whom Jesus loved following: which also leaned on his breast at supper [the reference is to St. John] and said, Lord, which is he that betrayeth thee?"

241. MEMORABILIA

This poem first appeared in the collection of 1855, *Men and Women;* subsequently it was placed among the *Dramatic Lyrics*. The incident on which the poem was based was recorded by W. G. Kingsland (*Poet Lore*, II, 131 f.): Browning "was in the shop of a then well-known London book seller, when a stranger to himself entered, and commenced a conversation with the bookseller on Shelley—stating, *inter alia*, that he had both seen and spoken to him. While thus conversing, the stranger suddenly turned round, and burst into a laugh on observing how Browning was staring at him with blanched face: 'and,' said the poet, 'I have not yet forgotten how strangely the sight of one who had spoken with Shelley affected me.'" Browning had in his youth admired Shelley above all other poets; and in 1852 had written a preface to a collection of spurious letters by Shelley.

Memorabilia: things worth remembering.

241. ANDREA DEL SARTO

This poem first appeared in the collection of 1855, *Men and Women.* Browning's munificent benefactor John Kenyon expressed the desire for a photographic reproduction of Andrea del Sarto's portrait of himself with his wife which hung in the Pitti Palace at Florence. Unable to find a photograph Browning composed and sent the poem. For a knowledge of the artist's work and character, apart from a study of his paintings, Browning consulted Vasari's *Lives* and Baldinucci's *Notizie,* the same texts which served him so well in preparing "Fra Lippo Lippi."

Andrea del Sarto (whose true name was Andrea d'Agnolo di Franciscon di Luca) was the son of a tailor (Sarto means tailor) and born in 1486. He rather early came to be known as "the faultless painter" (*il pittore senza errori*); and in 1513, already a notable artist, he married a widow, Lucrezia, who had served him as a model. Going to the court of the French King, Francis I, a great patron of art, in 1518 he added greatly to his fame; but his wife inveigled him into deserting the court to return to Florence, and into spending the money with which Francis furnished him to buy paintings for the new palaces for a house of his own in Florence. Browning presents him towards the end of his life, conceiving his last important picture, the portrait of himself with his wife. In 1523 he died of the plague, left to his misery by wife and servants. Such is Vasari's account; his conception of the character of Andrea and Lucrezia has the highest guarantees of authenticity: he had been apprenticed to Andrea. Doubt has, however, been cast on the statement that Andrea misappropriated the funds of Francis I. It is also doubted that the picture of Andrea and his wife was, at any rate in the form in which it now exists, entirely his own work.

241, 5. *friend's friend:* the friend was Lucrezia's "cousin," frequently mentioned below: who *his* friend was is not stated.

242, 15. *Fiesole:* a suburb of Florence, in the hills.

242, 24. *the five pictures we require:* presumably those to be done for the "friend's friend."

242, 26. The reference may be to her hair or to the graceful curves of her body.

242, 57. *cartoon:* a preliminary drawing for a painting.

242, 65. *Legate:* envoy of the Pope.

242, 66. *in France:* see the general note on the poem.

242, 76. *Someone:* Michael Angelo. See l. 199.

242, 83. *drop groundward:* are imperfect.

243, 93. *Morello:* a mountain near the city on the north.

243, 105. *The Urbinate:* Raphael, born at Urbino, near Ferrara.

243, 106. *copied:* hence of slight value, and not worth selling.

George Vasari: once Andrea's apprentice, later his biographer. Browning sometimes, as here, anglicises an Italian name, *George* standing for Giorgio.

243, 108. Raphael had commissions from many Italian nobles and from the Vatican.

243, 130. *Agnolo:* Michael Angelo.

243, 146 f. See the general note on the poem.

244, 178. *the Roman:* Raphael, whose last years were spent painting for the pope.

244, 189 f. In slightly differing form Vasari reports the remark: "There is a little fellow in Florence who will bring sweat to your brow if ever he is engaged in great works." The remark was not made to Raphael.

244, 210. *cue-owls:* little owls whose note resembles the sound "cue" or "ki-ou."

244, 214 f. See the general note on the poem.

244, 220. *Cousin:* really her lover, as Andrea well knows.

244, 230 f. The picture which he here begins to meditate is that in the Pitti Palace, of which the poet had sought a photographic reproduction. See general note.

245, 241. *scudi:* a *scudo* was roughly a dollar.

245, 262. *meted:* measured.

245, 263. *Leonard:* Leonardo da Vinci.

245. "DE GUSTIBUS —"

This poem first appeared in the collection of 1855, *Men and Women:* it was subsequently placed among the *Dramatic Lyrics.* The second part of the poem presents a setting near Naples. The title is an abridgement of the Latin proverb, *De gustibus non est disputandum* (There is no arguing about tastes).

245, 35. *king:* Ferdinand II, tyrant of the Two Sicilies who resided at Naples.

245, 36. *liver-wing:* right arm.

245, 37. *Bourbon:* he was a member of that family.

245, 40 f. The reference is to the remark said to have been made by Mary Tudor, in whose reign Calais was lost to the English, that after her death Calais would be found written on her heart.

246. CLEON

This poem first appeared in the collection of 1855, *Men and Women.* The personages are imaginary. The motto which follows the title is taken from Paul's speech from the Areopagus. In *Acts*, Ch. XVII, it is reported that Paul, having spoken in the synagogue, and in the market-place, was invited by Stoic and Epicurean philosophers to explain his teachings to them in an address at the Areopagus. Paul accepted the invitation, referred to the Athenian statue to the unknown God, stated that he served that God, and explained his religion as the service of a God who knew no limit of race or blood, who needed no temple, nor tangible sacrifice, briefly and obscurely referring also to Jesus, as raised by God from the dead. At the reference to the resurrection there was a divided response, some mocking, others, like the king in this poem wishing to hear more of the matter. The 28th verse is as follows: "For in him we live and move and have our being; as certain also of your own poets have said. For we are also his offspring." The quotation is from Aratus, a minor Greek poet.

246, 1. *the sprinkled isles:* a scattered group of islands called the Sporades, off the Greek coast, and near Crete.

246, 4. *tyranny:* in Greece a tyrant was an absolute ruler, but the term carried no suggestion of oppressive rule. *Tyranny* is a purely descriptive word here, analogous to duchy, republic, etc.

246, 10. The meaning is that the brilliant purple of the sunset is a royal colour; and further that Cleon thinks of Protus as brilliant, but belonging (like himself) to a life that comes to a close, gorgeous but final.

246, 15. *lyric:* this may mean knowing how to play the lyre or (more likely) having a beauty worth being celebrated on the lyre.

246, 35. *the East:* the source of light. It is not to be overlooked, when the poem is seen as a whole, that Palestine is east of where Protus reigns.

246, 43. *requirement:* request.

246, 47. *epos:* epic.

246, 51. *phare:* lighthouse. The word *phare* comes from an island near Alexandria where a great lighthouse had been erected.

246, 53. *the Poecile:* the Portico at Athens.

o'erstoried: its walls covered with a series of paintings, forming a narrative.

246, 60. *moods:* modes.

247, 83. *rhomb:* a figure similar to a square except that the angles are not right angles.

247, 84. *lozenge:* a diamond-shaped rhomb.

trapezoid: a four-sided figure, in which no two sides, or only two sides, are parallel.

247, 116 f. The taking on of human attributes by a God makes of him an eternal criterion of human character.

247, 140. *Terpander:* a Lesbian musician of an early period in Greek history (7th century B.C.) who added three strings to the lyre.

247, 141. *Phidias:* a sculptor of the fifth century B.C.

his friend: Many commentators suggest Pericles, the ruler of Athens in Phidias' time and a close friend of the sculptor; it seems more likely that another sculptor or painter is intended.

248, 185. *Imperfection means perfection hid:* An imperfect form implies incompleteness and so points to a perfect form which does not as yet exist but which the completing of the imperfect form will bring into existence.

249, 239–240. *capability for joy:* capacity to provide joy.

249, 249. *skills not:* is of no avail.

249, 252. *Naiad:* water-nymph.

249, 273 f. The position which Cleon here rejects was one advanced by many sceptics in Victorian England (notably by George Eliot and later by Samuel Butler) and often termed vicarious immortality. It asserted that although there was no personal survival after death, a soul might prolong its vitality as an influence on other souls. Browning has this contemporary position in mind here.

249, 288. *Phoebus:* Phoebus Apollo: the sun-god, also god of light and beauty. See l. 51.

249, 304. *Sappho:* an early Lesbian lyric poet (circa 600 B.C.).

250, 340. *Paulus:* Paul. See the general note on the poem.

250. A GRAMMARIAN'S FUNERAL

This poem first appeared in the collection of 1855, *Men and Women;* and was subsequently placed among the *Dramatic Romances.*

250, 3. *crofts:* small enclosed fields.

thorpes: villages.

250, 9. *that's the appropriate country:* the heights suit the character of the grammarian.

250, 13–16. The rich lands of the plain are given over to farming and are the dwelling-places of uncultivated men; on the hills are the towns, which rise even as high as the tops of mountains.

251, 34. *Apollo:* the sun god and also the god of light and art.

251, 47. *the scroll:* a scroll of manuscript.

251, 50. *gowned him:* turned to scholarship.

251, 59–60. In many manuscripts text and comment were interwoven.

252, 86. *Calculus:* the stone (*e.g.,* gall-stones).

252, 88. *Tussis:* a disease of the throat.

252, 127. *the rattle:* the death-rattle.

252, 129–131. The three words *Hoti, Oun* and *De* are insignificant Greek particles. The first means "that," the second "therefore" and the third "towards." When *De* is enclitic it is pronounced as part of the preceding word, so completely is it subordinated.

253. TWO IN THE CAMPAGNA

This poem first appeared in the collection of 1855, *Men and Women;* and was subsequently placed among the *Dramatic Lyrics.* W. C. DeVane plausibly conjectures that it was conceived in 1854 when the Brownings ventured out into the Roman campagna, a waste just beyond the city. Although it has always been tacitly assumed that the speaker is a man, there is no clear reason for the assumption; and it may be suggested that the utterance is more feminine than masculine: stanzas nine and ten are specially feminine.

253, 7–10. *has tantalised me many times . . . for rhymes to catch at and let go:* the meaning is that the line of thought which the speaker has sought to develop he has had to abandon because he could not find firm resting places at which to stop and then later start from. The resting-places are exemplified in the symbols of the following two stanzas.

253, 25. The campagna abounds in ruins of ancient Rome.

254. ABT VOGLER

This poem first appeared in the collection of 1864, *Dramatis Personae.* The choice of Vogler (the title *Abt* is equivalent not to abbot, but merely to abbé or father) as the medium of Browning in his most profound poem about music and one of his most impressive metaphysical formulations is not difficult to explain. It was essential to Browning's idea that the musician who was to unfold his ideas should be an improviser; and Vogler, a German who lived from 1749 to 1814, was noted for his powers in improvising, impressing Weber and Meyerbeer who were among his pupils, and vying with Beethoven. It furthered the effect of improvisation that the musician should play on an instrument extremely personal to himself, that is, of his own invention; the orchestrion, which Vogler invented, was a small organ, portable, and about three feet square. Browning was probably made familiar with Vogler's name and achievement by his musical instructor Relfe, who had studied under Vogler. It should be said that the metaphysical and spiritual eminence ascribed to Vogler is not substantiated by the records of his life and thought.

254, 3 f. In the Talmud, it is asserted that Solomon possessed a seal, with the divine name, which endowed him with power to have supernatural creatures do his bidding.

254, 7. *the ineffable Name:* the name of God.

254, 11. *dispart:* separate.

254, 17. *minion:* servant or creature.

254, 19. *rampired walls:* walls with ramparts.

255, 21–23. On great feasts the dome of St. Peter's at Rome is illuminated.

255, 25. *man's birth:* what man gave birth to.

255, 34. *Protoplast:* strictly, the first created, or formed man; but Browning is probably thinking more generally of the first life-substance.

255, 38. *an old world worth their new:* the old world is life on earth, the new, life beyond the grave. Vogler has made them one: there is no more near nor far.

255, 49. *the will that can:* the creative will.

255, 52. The meaning is that out of three sounds, a harmony is created as wonder-provoking as a new star.

256, 66. *houses not made with hands:* the phrase is taken from *II Corinthians*, Ch. V, 1: "For we know that if our earthly house of this tabernacle were dissolved, we have a building of God, an house not made with hands, eternal in the heavens." The analogy between Vogler's structure not made with hands, and that here described is clear.

256, 70. *silence implying sound:* silence whose function is that of a background for a succession of sounds, separating them and contributing to the effect they produce. Without sound, silence would have no function.

256, 72. *broken arcs:* fragmentary circles.

round: circle.

256, 74. *semblance:* in the first text, likeness.

256, 91. *common chord:* the fundamental tone.

256, 92 f. For a full explanation, with diagram, of the musical terms, see the edition of *Dramatis Personae* by Porter and Clarke, 309–10. The essence of the matter is not abstruse: the organist, returning from his great improvised heights, sinks to a minor tone, modulates away from the key in which he had been (thus reaching *alien ground*) and after a pause on the alien chord, he turns to *the C Major*, which DeVane describes (*Shorter Poems of Browning*) as the natural scale, and as such suggesting the common level of terrestrial life, to which Vogler now is returning. (The explanation of C Major in Porter and Clarke is somewhat different, but may be questioned as speculative.)

256. RABBI BEN EZRA

This poem first appeared in the collection of 1864, *Dramatis Personae.* The use of the image of potter and wheel (ll. 150 ff.) has encouraged the conjecture that in "Rabbi Ben Ezra" Browning is replying to FitzGerald's *Rubáiyát of Omar Khayyam;* and one critic, F. L. Sargent, has reprinted the two poems in one volume, and as if they constituted a dramatic debate (see his *Omar and the Rabbi*).

Abraham Ibn (or Ben) Ezra was a Spanish rabbi of the eleventh century; in middle life persecution drove him from Spain, and he came to know life in the near east and in many of the capitals of Europe; among his many contributions to knowledge were his commentaries upon the Old Testament. Browning may well, as W. C. DeVane conjectures, have been reminded as he read FitzGerald of Isaiah's verse: "But now, O Lord, thou art our father; we are the clay, and thou our potter; and we are all the work of thy hand." This verse may have led him on to think of Ibn Ezra's commentary on Isaiah, and thus shaped the poem. Although the poem accords with what is known of the rabbi, it is impregnated with Browning's personality, as with his opinions, and the effect it produces is not that produced by Lippo or by Karshish, great psychological portraits, but that of an expression of metaphysical and moral insight.

256, 3. The second half of Ibn Ezra's life, more arduous than the first, was also more productive and maturing.

256, 12. *figured:* imagined.

256, 14. *annulling:* rendering ineffective or null.

257, 17. *kinds:* species.

257, 42. *the scale:* the scale of being.

257, 45. The meaning is that the soul of such a person is active merely in the interest of his bodily nature.

257, 57. The meaning is that, having long recognized the universe as showing a great power at work, he now recognizes at work a love no less than the power.

257, 74. *youth's heritage:* what youth deserves to inherit.

257, 75. *term:* limit.

257, 81. *adventure brave and new:* life beyond the grave.

258, 100–101. Note that the example of error is an acquiescence, that of right, a rage. The values are characteristic not only of the Rabbi but of the poet.

258, 102. *proved:* tried.

258, 110. *uncouth:* unknowing, groping.

258, 113. *tempt:* try. The meaning is the same as that of *prove* in l. 102.

258, 112–114. The meaning is that meditation on the experience accumulated in youth will be more productive than accumulation of further experience.

258, 141. *passed:* neglected.

258, 147. The image is that of fish and a net.

258, 150. The image of the Potter and his wheel comes in *Isaiah*, Ch. LXIV, 8 (quoted above in the general note on the poem), in *Jeremiah*, Ch. XVIII, 2–6, and in FitzGerald's *Omar*, ll. 325 ff.

259, 164. *plastic:* moulding.

259, 174. *sterner stress:* heavier pressure.

259. CALIBAN UPON SETEBOS

This poem first appeared in the collection of 1864, *Dramatis Personae*. Caliban is a character, half-human, half-bestial, in Shakespeare's play *The Tempest;* Setebos is the god of Caliban's mother Sycorax. Browning was insistent upon the similarities between his Caliban and Shakespeare's, pointing to his interest in music, as shown in his composition and singing of a song, his having visions of Heaven, and intention of learning wisdom and "such grace," as being shared by the two (see *Letters of Browning*, ed. T. L. Hood, 228). The poem is a satire on natural theologians, who construct a conception of God from the nature of man and the universe; and it is also, at least implicitly, an attack on the doctrine of evolution as stated by Darwin in 1859. The motto comes from *Psalm* L, 21.

259, 5. *eft-things:* little creatures such as lizards.

259, 7. *pompion-plant:* a vine of the pumpkin species.

259, 16. *his dam:* his mother, emphasising his animality.

260, 20. *Prosper and Miranda: Prospero* is the magician who is master of the island on which Caliban lives, in Shakespeare's play; *Miranda* is his daughter.

260, 24. *Setebos:* see the introductory note. Observe also the peculiar effect of the repetition of name.

260, 27. *But not the stars:* the discrimination is entirely arbitrary, and suggests the inanity of Caliban's mind.

260, 30. *snaky:* the level of Caliban's apprehension of a natural phenomenon, suggesting how inadequate will be his reasoning about God.

260, 50. *pie:* magpie.

260, 57–58. Browning is revealing the superficiality of Caliban's reasoning: what Caliban denies on *a priori* grounds is what occurred when the Son was begotten by the Father and again when the Holy Spirit proceeded from the Two.

260, 71. *bladdery:* in bubbles.

260, 79. *hoopoe:* a bird with a large crest.

260, 83. *grigs:* grasshoppers.

261, 103. The position stated here is that of Calvinist thought which presents the will of God as arbitrary, and his disposition of men as determined before they are born.

261, 137. *This Quiet:* a conception original with Browning—there is no suggestion of it in *The Tempest.* Its introduction strengthens the attack implied on Caliban's conception of a God: it is shown as so inadequate that Caliban himself must invent another Being more nearly admirable and dependable.

262, 148. *hips:* haws.

262, 156. *oncelot:* a mountain panther.

262, 157. *ounce:* see note on preceding line.

262, 161. *Ariel:* a spirit in the service of Prospero.

262, 177. *orc:* a monstrous marine being.

262, 178. The emphasis is partly on *Now:* the rule of Setebos may end.

262, 196. *sloth:* a South American animal, slow in movement, like an ant-eater.

263, 214–215. A glance at palaeontology: the study of fossilized creatures. Evolutionists depended heavily on palaeontological evidence.

263, 229. *urchin:* hedgehog.

263, 266 f. Browning is satirizing the reduction of religion to sufferings self-inflicted to propitiate the Deity.

263, 276–278. Note the internal rhymes in Caliban's song.

264. CONFESSIONS

This poem first appeared in the collection of 1864, *Dramatis Personae.* Mrs. Browning's use of the phrase "say it's mad, and bad, and sad" in 1860 has led to the conjecture that this poem was written some time before it was printed.

264. YOUTH AND ART

This poem first appeared in the collection of 1864, *Dramatis Personae.* W. C. DeVane conjectures that it was written not later than 1861. The setting is in the cosmopolitan artistic group in Rome; but the speaker and the man she addresses are both English.

264, 8. *Gibson:* a sculptor, known to Browning, who was in Italy regarded as the greatest English sculptor of his time.
265, 12. *Grisi:* an Italian operatic singer, regarded as the greatest soprano of her time.
265, 31. *E in alt:* High E.
265, 57. *the Prince:* the Prince Consort, who died in 1861.
265, 58. *the Board:* probably the Board of Trade.
bals-paré: fancy-dress balls.
265, 60. *R. A.:* member of the Royal Academy (of Great Britain).

265. PROSPICE

This poem first appeared in the *Atlantic Monthly* for June, 1864; and was reprinted in the same year in the collection *Dramatis Personae.* It is conjectured, on purely internal evidence, to have been written soon after the death of Mrs. Browning in June, 1861. The title signifies: "Look forward."

25. *out of pain:* previously the reading had been "then a joy." The alteration, providing a rhyme and an alliterating phrase, is also an improvement dramatically, prolonging the struggle between pain and happiness, and removing a superfluous stage in the development of the happiness.

266. EPILOGUE

This group first appeared in the collection which it closed, *Dramatis Personae*, published in 1864.

First Speaker. Through David Browning expresses the position of modern ritualistic religion, both within and without the Roman Catholic Church. The service in the Temple is that of its dedication by Solomon: David, Solomon's father, had wished to build the Temple, but God had decreed that it be built by his son. (See *I Kings*, Chs. VIII, IX, and *II Chronicles*, V, VI, VII.)

266, 1–2. *the Feast of Feasts, the Dedication Day:* see the general note on the poem.
266, 3. *Levites:* the sons of Levi, dedicated to the service of God.
267. *Second Speaker.* Through Renan, whose *Vie de Jésus* (Life of Jesus) he had read with dislike in 1863 Browning expresses the position of modernist rationalism. Renan was the most persuasive of the higher critics of the Bible in the century.
267, 22. *Gone now:* this refers back to the conception of the preceding section.
267, 26. *a Face:* Christ.
267, 29. *gyre on gyre:* spirally.
267, 41–42. A purely rational conception of a God, without a personality.
267, 59 f. The meaning is that, in the modern view the universe would have developed exactly as it has even if there were no humanity in it. The poet is seeking to show the bleakness of a view which sees no special function for man.

Third Speaker: Browning himself, in one of his very rare personal pronouncements on philosophic and religious problems.

269. THE RING AND THE BOOK

This poem first appeared in four parts, the first and second in 1868, the third and fourth in 1869. Browning's principal source was a book, part in type, part in manuscript, which he bought in Florence in 1860. It contained twenty-one documents relating to the trial of Guido Franceschini, who, in 1698, had murdered his wife Pompilia. In 1862 Browning procured a pamphlet which gave a contemporary account of the murder and the execution which followed Guido's conviction. Both these sources were translated by Professor C. W. Hodell in his *The Old Yellow Book*, reprinted in Everyman's Library.

The story of the poem is as follows: In 1693 a poor and aging nobleman of Arezzo (in northern Italy), Count Guido Franceschini, married Francesca Pompilia, the supposed daughter of an obscure Roman commoner, Pietro Comparini and his wife Violante. The Comparini accompanied Pompilia to Arezzo; there, partly because of Guido's rage at finding that they were by no means so rich as he had thought, partly because he too was poorer than they had thought, friction almost immediately developed and the Comparini returned to Rome. They sued for the return of Pompilia's dowry and alleged that she was not in fact their daughter, but the child of a prostitute. Guido, always an unfeeling husband, now treated Pompilia with sharp cruelty and, according to her account, sought to foster an intrigue between her and a priest in Arezzo, Giuseppe Caponsacchi. In 1697, about to bear a child, Pompilia fled from Arezzo towards Rome, in the company of Caponsacchi. The fugitives were overtaken by Guido at Castelnouvo, within the papal dominion; they were arrested on the charge of adultery; and brought before a papal court which condemned Caponsacchi to three years banishment to Civita Vecchia because of his role in Pompilia's flight, his seduction of her and adultery with her, and Pompilia to detention in a nunnery until her case was further examined.

Under bond she was soon released to the Comparini at whose house she was to bear her child. Two weeks after the birth of the child, Guido, accompanied by four cutthroats, entered the house and killing the Comparini, wounded Pompilia so gravely that she died four days afterwards. Guido and his associates were almost immediately arrested and were soon brought to trial. The murder was admitted; but Guido's attorneys argued that his wife's conduct and that of the Comparini justified his deeds. The court's sentence was that Guido should be beheaded and his associates hanged. Guido thereupon appealed to the Pope, resting his right to such an appeal on his being in minor orders. The Pope declined to set aside the sentence of the court and Guido was executed.

Browning tells the story in a succession of dramatic monologues. His first book is introductory; the second, third and fourth give the opinions of representatives of elements in Roman society; the fifth is the plea to the court made by Guido; the sixth the opposing account given to the court by Caponsacchi; the seventh is a monologue by Pompilia on her deathbed; the eighth and ninth are speeches by the counsel; the tenth is the survey of the case by the Pope, leading to his judgment; the eleventh is another monologue by Guido as he awaits that judgment; the twelfth is Browning's conclusion.

269. *Pompilia*

This is a death-bed speech. Much of the material comes from the pamphlet *For Count Guido Franceschini and His Associates, Prisoners: Summary*, in *The Old Yellow Book* (*Everyman* edition, 87 f.), which contains a number of letters from the model for the character of Pompilia, and from the pamphlet *For the Fisc: Summary* (*id.* 47 f.). Critics have not accepted Browning's opinion that the Francesca whom he found in the documents was exactly the same as the Pompilia he drew ("I assure you I found her in the book just as she speaks and acts in my poem"); into his conception of Pompilia there has entered his love for his wife (who died just as the story was seizing his imagination) his pride in having freed her from a form of tyranny and imprisonment, and his grief for her death. In some measure he identified Caponsacchi's role in the story with his own in the flight from Wimpole Street; and the parallel between the story and the life of the poet may be pressed very far without much danger of erroneous analogies.

269, 4. *Lorenzo in Lucina:* this Roman church figures often in the poem. Here Pompilia was baptized and here with her foster-mother she crept out for the marriage ceremony. It is described at length at the beginning of the second book of the poem.

269, 6. *Francesca:* by this name she is known in the documents.

269, 17. *the Villa:* the house in the suburbs, where the Comparini, Pompilia's foster-parents, lived and where she took refuge after she fled from her husband.

269, 22 f. Browning, in 1864, asked his friend, the painter Frederick Leighton, to send him a detailed account of the interior of the church, which at an earlier time he had himself seen. There are lions in its portico.

269, 30. *Gaetano, for a reason:* see ll. 100 f. The saint, founder of a religious order, was canonized in 1671.

30–31. *the friar Don Celestine:* "the barefooted Augustinian" priest, Celestino Angelo of St. Anna, attended Pompilia after she had received her death-wound, and attested his unqualified admiration for her and his absolute conviction of her innocence of nature. See his testimony in *The Old Yellow Book* (*Everyman* edition), 57 f.

270, 42. The child was born on December 18, 1697; the assault which resulted in the immediate deaths of the foster-parents and in the death-wound to Pompilia took place on the following January 2; Pompilia died on January 6.

270, 97–98. Pietro and Violante Comparini were Pompilia's foster-parents.

140 f. In 1694 the Comparini, who had previously passed as the father and mother of Pompilia, disclosed to her, to her husband and to the courts the true fact of her birth and parentage. Their purpose was to escape paying over to Pompilia's husband the dowry which they had agreed to give; and they were led to dislike paying over such a sum because of the treatment they and Pompilia had received in the Franceschini home in Arezzo.

272, 145. *a woman known too well:* a woman whose immoral life was all to certain, *i.e.*, a prostitute.

272, 150. *my husband:* Count Guido Franceschini, whom she had married in 1693, when she was a child of 13.

272, 177. *letters:* these are given in *The Old Yellow Book* (*Everyman* edition), pp. 99–106. Browning follows Pompilia and Caponsacchi in branding them as forgeries: recent students (notably J. E. Shaw, "The 'Donna Angelicata' in *The Ring and the Book*," P.M.L.A., XLI, 55 f.) take them as genuine.

273, 230. *Our cause is gained:* the cause was probably that brought by the Comparini to recover Pompilia's dowry. There would have been no reason for Pompilia or the Comparini to rejoice very heartily in the decision in the cause of Guido against Pompilia and Caponsacchi, in the preceding September, when Caponsacchi had been banished for three years to Civita Vecchia (for seduction of Pompilia and being a party to her plan to desert her husband) and Pompilia sent to a nunnery from which she was, because of imminent childbirth, released under bond to the Comparini. It was distinctly possible that after she bore the child and returned to the nunnery a greater penalty might have been imposed.

273, 238. *sincere:* genuine.

274, 263. *San Giovanni:* the church of Saint John Lateran, one of the principal and most splendid churches in Rome.

274, 272–274. The original motive in passing off Pompilia as her own child was to secure an inheritance which would not belong to the Comparini if they were childless.

275, 323. *Paul:* Father Paolo Franceschini was an important ecclesiastical official in Rome, secretary to the order of St. John of Malta. He was the eldest of the family.

276, 361. *my friend:* Caponsacchi.

276, 371. *Don Celestine:* see note on ll. 30–1.

276, 390. *the slim young man:* Perseus, who rescued Andromeda from a dragon; or St. George (see l. 1323).

277, 405. *grime or glare:* the dulled surface of an old coin or the shining surface of a new.

277, 423. *Malpichi:* Malpighi, a papal physician of the century, who died in 1694.

277, 427. *the Lion's-mouth:* the street of the lion's mouth (Via della Bocca di Leone).

277, 428. *the Corso:* one of the main avenues of the city.

278, 507. *syllabub:* a dish in which milk, or cream, is one of the main ingredients.

279, 515. Violante is thinking of having passed off Pompilia as her child as well as of having agreed to her marrying Guido without Pietro's knowledge.

279, 557. *keep the house:* keep to the house as distinguished from seeking the society of other women.

280, 607–608. *the Square of the Spaniards:* the Piazza di Spagna, a square in Rome in which then and now foreign people are much seen. See l. 609.

the Spanish House: the palace of the Spanish ambassador from which the square takes its name.

282, 669. *wormy:* crooked and base.

282, 691. It was part of Pompilia's defence that she could not read—or write—and hence could not plausibly have carried on the charged correspondence with Caponsacchi.

283, 724. *the Archbishop:* actually the *bishop* of Arezzo.

283, 734. *twelve:* actually thirteen.

283, 762. The Bishop is quoting *Genesis,* Ch. I, 28, in which God bids "be fruitful, and multiply, and replenish the earth."

283, 769. *Molinists:* followers of Molinos, a Spanish priest from whose works sixty-eight propositions were condemned in 1687 and who, recanting his errors, had died in a prison in 1696, two years before the death of Pompilia. Molinos was a mystic and went beyond orthodox standards in urging emancipation of soul from body. There are frequent allusions to Molinos and his doctrines in the course of *The Ring and the Book.*

283, 771. *in your covenant:* in the terms of the marriage ceremony.

284, 798. *God's Bread:* an oath by the sacrament of communion in which, according to Roman Catholic doctrine, the bread is turned into the body of Christ.

284, 821. The bishop quotes *Matthew,* Ch. XIII, 34.

285, 833. *restif:* restive.

286, 885. *them:* the Comparini.

287, 951. *Carnival:* merrymaking preceding the Lenten season.

287, 967. *festa:* feast day.

287, 974 f. Pompilia's account of their meeting should be compared with Caponsacchi's, in Bk. VI, 393 f.

288, 987. *Conti:* he was the brother of Guido's sister's husband, and was to die in the month in which Pompilia also died—it was suspected he died by foul play.

288, 1015. *cornet:* a conical twist of paper.

288, 1029. This threat was reported by Pompilia in her testimony.

289, 1051 f. Compare the account of Margherita's role in Caponsacchi's monologue, Bk. VI, 505 f.

291, 1145. *imposthume:* abscess.

291, 1153. *Mirtillo:* a name of a pastoral lover, used in the original letters.

293, 1265. *the Governor:* Marzi-Medici, Governor of Arezzo.

293, 1267–1268. *gave a jewel or two:* the charge that Pompilia improperly restored such property to the Comparini was made by Guido before the Governor. The complete support which Marzi-Medici gave to the Franceschini family is shown in his letter to the eldest brother Father Paul, in *The Old Yellow Book* (*Everyman* edition, 89–90).

293, 1283. *The Roman:* Pompilia speaks of "an Augustinian father whom they call Romano" and of going to confess to him and ask his help in communicating with the Comparini. It was natural that she appeal to a presumed fellow-townsman. See *The Old Yellow Book* (*Everyman* edition, 92).

294, 1306. *Guillichini:* despite the refusal here mentioned Guido Franceschini proceeded against Guillichini (of whom scarcely anything is known) in the courts of Arezzo, and he was sentenced to the galleys; subsequently the sentence was softened.

294, 1323. *Saint George:* Note the tapestry described in l. 390 f.

294, 1326–1327. *that piece i' the Pieve:* the church of which Caponsacchi and Conti were canons. The *piece* was Vasari's statue of St. George.

296, 1410. The description of this meeting should be compared with Caponsacchi's in Bk. VI, 691 f.

297, 1450. *the House o' the Babe:* in Bethlehem.

298, 1485. "*He hath a devil*": The Pharisees made the charge when Jesus cast out devils, *Matthew*, Ch. IX, 34.

298, 1495. The original reading was:

I did think, do think, in the thought shall die.

It is obvious that the later form is more consonant with Pompilia's character in general, and with her mood at this time.

298, 1506. *votarist:* devotee.

298, 1517. *blow:* bloom.

298, 1528. With Pompilia's excited and not always easily grasped account of the journey from Arezzo to Castelnuovo, compare Caponsacchi's, in Bk. VI, 1151 f. The way lay about Perugia, near Assisi, past Foligno, to Castelnuovo in the Papal states.

299, 1555–1556. The story of the mother and her baby is also told, and at greater length by Caponsacchi. See Bk. VI, 1320 f.

301, 1649. The judgment on Pompilia's case had not been definitive: she was to remain with the Roman nuns while further inquiries were made and the order for her detention had been stretched to allow her to remain with the Comparini while she was expecting her baby.

303, 1793. *Civita:* Civita Vecchia, a city on the coast north of Rome, to which Caponsacchi had been banished for three years by the court.

304, 1845. The splendor of character which shines more and more powerfully as the monologue approaches its end is in large part the result of Browning's imposition upon the Pompilia he read about of the character of Mrs. Browning as her husband judged it. It is also, however, the result of Browning's belief in the evidence given by Father Celestine, who was with Pompilia at the end and wrote the following letter:

"I, the undersigned, barefooted Augustinian priest, pledge my faith that inasmuch as I was present, helping Signora Francesca Comparini from the first instant of her pitiable case, even to the very end of her life, I say and attest on my priestly oath, in the presence of the God who must judge me, that to my own confusion I have discovered and marvelled at an innocent and saintly conscience in that ever-blessed child. During the four days she survived, when exhorted by me to pardon her husband, she replied with tears in her eyes and with a placid and compassionate voice: 'May Jesus pardon him, as I have already done with all my heart.' But what is more to be wondered at is that, although she suffered great pain, I never heard her speak an offensive or impatient word, nor show the slightest outward vexation either toward God or those near by. But ever submissive to the Divine Will, she said: 'May God have pity on me,' in such a way, indeed, as would have been incompatible with a soul that was not at one with God. To such an union one does not attain in a moment, but rather by the habit of years.

"I say further that I have always seen her self-restrained, and especially during medical treatment. On these occasions, if her habit of life had not been good, she would not have minded certain details around her with a modesty well-noted and marvelled at by me; nor otherwise could a young girl have been in the presence of so many men with such modesty and calm as that in which the blessed child remained while dying. And you may well believe what the Holy Spirit speaks by the mouth of the Evangelist, in the words of St. Matthew, chapter 7: 'An evil tree cannot bring forth good fruit.' Note that he says 'cannot' and not 'does not'; that is making it impossible to infer the ability to do perfect deeds when oneself is imperfect and tainted with vice. You should therefore say that this girl was all goodness and modesty, since with all ease and all gladness she performed virtuous and modest deeds even at the very end of her life. Moreover she has died with strong love for God, with great composure, with all the sacred sacraments of the Church, and with the admiration of all bystanders, who blessed her as a saint. I do not say more lest I be taxed with partiality. I know very well that God alone is the searcher of hearts, but I also know that from the abundance of the heart the mouth speaks; and that my great St. Augustine says: 'As the life, so its end.'

"Therefore, having noted in that ever blessed child saintly words, virtuous deeds, most modest acts, and the death of a soul in great fear of God, for the relief of my conscience I am compelled to say, and cannot do otherwise, that necessarily she has ever been a good, modest, and honourable girl, etc.

This tenth of January, 1698,

I, Fra Celestino Angelo of St. Anna, barefooted Augustinian,
affirm as I have said above, with my own hand."

304. *The Pope*

Innocent XII, to whom Browning assigns this monologue, was elevated to the Papacy in 1691 and died in 1700. His secular name was Antonio Pignatelli (see l. 382). Prior to his elevation he had acquitted himself of many missions for the more famous Innocent XI; and had held episcopal and cardinalitial rank. He had, among other honors, been archbishop of Naples (see the last section of the monologue). His distinguishing character was simple virtue, which led him to purify administration and to attempt many undertakings in the interest of the unfortunate and poor. His reputation was for kindness and prudence.

Some commentators suggest that Browning has fused aspects of the character and career of Innocent XI (who reigned as Pope from 1676 to 1689) with those of Innocent XII. The earlier Innocent had condemned, with some reluctance, the heretical doctrines of Molinos (to which a number of references are made in the monologue) and had asserted the papal powers in violent opposition to Louis XIV. He, also, sought to purify administration and to quicken spiritual life.

In any event much of the monologue must be regarded as imaginative. There is little evidence in *The Old Yellow Book* of the motives of the pope in refusing to quash the sentence against Guido. The philosophic and religious views which the Pope advances are incompatible in part with Catholic doctrine and with the historical possibilities of the time, circumstances which have involved this monologue in critical controversy (see A. K. Cook: *A Commentary upon Browning's "The Ring and the Book,"* 198 f.).

304, 1. *Ahasuerus:* "Ahasuerus which reigned, from India even unto Ethiopia, over an hundred and seven and twenty provinces" (*Esther*, Ch. I, 1). When he was unable to sleep he bade his attendant read chronicles to him.

304, 2. He had been Pope seven years.

305, 11. St. Peter was the first Pope, the predecessor of Innocent was Alexander VIII, who died in 1691.

305, 23. *funeral cyst:* coffin.

305, 25. *Formosus:* Pope from 891 to 896. He had previously been bishop of Porto (see l. 46). His ecclesiastical life, prior to his election to the papacy appears to have been highly irregular.

305, 32. *Stephen . . . seventh of the name:* Pope from 896 to 897. He had been bishop of Arago (l. 61). Platina's account of his judgment of Formosus corresponds with Browning's: "Martin the historian says he hated [Formosus] to that degree that, in a council which he held, he ordered the body of Formosus to be dragged out of the grave, to be stripped of his pontifical habit and put into that of a layman, and then to be buried among secular persons, having first cut off those two fingers of his right hand which are principally used by priests in consecration, and thrown into the Tiber, because, contrary to his oath, as he said, he had returned to Rome and exercised his sacerdotal function, from which Pope John had legally degraded him. This proved a great controversy and of very ill example; for the succeeding popes made it almost a constant custom either to break or abrogate the acts of their predecessors, which was certainly far different from the practice of any of the good popes whose lives we have written." It is the last sentence which explains Browning's use of the story.

306, 89. The five letters of the Greek word for fish are the initial letters of the five Greek words for Jesus, Christ, God's, son, saviour. For this reason the symbol of a fish was much used in early Christian times, as a cryptic mode of communicating that Christians were present or near. The symbol has continued to be used.

306, 91. *Fisherman:* another reason for the use of the fish-symbol lies in Peter's having been a fisherman, whom Christ said he would convert into a fisher of men.

307, 104. *Romanus:* in his brief tenure of the papacy he sought to undo what Stephen had done.

307, 107. *Theodore:* Theodore II completed, as best he could in his even briefer reign, the restoration of the conditions existing before Stephen.

307, 121. *Luitprand:* a papal historian.

307, 128. *John:* John IX, 898–900, having a longer reign than any of the successors of Formosus up to his time, tried to remove the stigma left by Stephen, in a ceremonial and judicial manner of the greatest scope. He called a synod at Ravenna (where he had moved because of restlessness in Rome) and this synod condemned Stephen and his acts.

307, 133. *Eude:* crowned King of France in 888, died in 898.

307, 136. *Auxilius:* a French theologian of the tenth century who wrote on the subject of Pope Stephen's decision.

307, 141. *Sergius:* Sergius III of whose exploits Platina says: He "totally abolished all that Formosus had done before; so that priests, who had been by him admitted to holy orders, were forced to take new ordination. Nor was he content with thus dishonouring the dead pope; but he dragged his carcase again out of the grave, beheaded it as if it had been alive, and then threw it into the Tiber, as unworthy the honour of human burial. It is said that some fishermen, finding his body as they were fishing, brought it to St. Peter's church; and while the funeral rites were performing, the images of the saints which stood in the church bowed in veneration of his body [note that Browning has transferred this incident: ll. 122 f.] which gave them occasion to believe that Formosus was not justly persecuted with so great ignominy. But whether the fishermen did thus, or not, is a great question; especially it is not likely to have been done in Sergius' lifetime, who was a fierce persecutor of the favourers of Formosus, because he had hindered him before of obtaining the pontificate."

308, 168–169. *Once more appeal is made from man's assize to mine:* Guido had claimed the benefit of clergy, *i.e.*, the right, as in some sense a member of the clergy, to have his cause referred to an ecclesiastical tribunal, before sentence was executed. See ll. 438 f. of this monologue.

308, 203. *wonder they wait long:* because of the rank of the person accused and his connections with the papal court.

309, 211. *this sombre wintry day:* February 21.

309, 217. *certain five:* Guido had four hirelings from Arezzo with him.

309, 223. *torture's feat:* putting the accused to the torture was a normal part of the legal procedure.

309, 228. *rede:* design.

310, 292. *the sagacious Swede:* apparently a reference is intended to Swedenborg who was at the time when the Pope spoke less than ten years of age. A. K. Cook (207) questions this identification but proposes no other.

310, 296–297. The reference is to the *sortes Virgilianae* (Vergilian lots) which consisted of opening a copy of Virgil and placing the tip of a finger on a line, without looking, and finding guidance in it.

311, 327. *posset:* a drink, remedial in purpose, and mingling milk with wine or ale.

312, 375. *He:* Christ.

312, 385–386. *diocese domestic, legate-rule:* an Italian bishopric, and a nunciature abroad.

312, 416. *cirque:* arena.

313, 441. *priest's-exemption:* clerical privilege.

313, 465. *paravent:* screen.

ombrifuge: shade, or shelter.

314, 509. *the soldier crab:* a crab which occupies the shells of others.

316, 594. "Who" is to be understood before *else.*

317, 653. *Aretine:* inhabitant of Arezzo. The reference is to Pietro Aretino, a celebrated man of letters of the Renaissance and a master of obscenity.

317, 663. *for a fate to be:* starting from the ancient belief that human destinies were determined by the stars, Browning adds the dynamic notion of the stars actually in conflict to determine a specific human issue.

318, 696. *at the Pieve:* the church of the Pieve in Arezzo, of which Caponsacchi was a canon.

318, 699. Pompilia drew a sword when Guido threatened Caponsacchi and herself when he overtook them at the inn at Castelnuovo. See Pompilia's account, Bk. VII, 1619 f.

319, 747–750. The imagery is taken from *Genesis*, Ch. VIII: The Ark is Noah's, which rested on the top of Mount Ararat, whence he sent forth a dove which on its second flight returned with an olive branch to indicate the subsidence of the flood and the fertility of the earth.

319, 780. *when Saturn ruled:* in Greek mythology the golden age before Zeus brought law and order into the world. The Pope is satirizing the glorification of rural simplicity and the attribution of virtue to the natural man.

319, 781. *bards:* poets who glorify and attribute virtue in the manner criticized in the remarks explained in the preceding note.

320, 814. *hebetude:* stupidity.

320, 823. *the pick o' the post-house:* the best horses for travelling between places

320, 831. *the Tuscan Frontier:* Arezzo was in the domain of the grand-duke of Tuscany.

320, 835. *the Rota:* the supreme court.

321, 894. Paolo Franceschini left Rome in 1697 prior to the murder, losing his post because of the revelations concerning his role in the marriage.

322, 907–908. Girolamo Franceschini, whom Pompilia charged with making improper advances to her, had also fled.

322, 958. *poke:* pocket.

323, 972. No evidence of the kinship is known.

323, 986. *Archbishop:* really the *bishop* of Arezzo. His character appears in a letter to Guido Franceschini printed in *The Old Yellow Book* (*Everyman* edition, 99).

323, 990. *crook:* crozier. The Pope is using the word in two senses—the shepherd's staff and the bishop's, he being also a shepherd.

324, 1010. *the new splendid vesture:* that which she will wear in heaven.

324, 1021. *memorized:* recorded for the memory of posterity.

325, 1064. *only thine:* up to the time when she recognized that she was with child.

325, 1084. *him:* Caponsacchi.

325, 1096. *the other rose, the gold:* on the Fourth Sunday in Lent the Pope blesses a golden rose and subsequently it is sent either to a king (see l. 1098) or another individual of note, or to a group which has distinguished itself.

325, 1100. *ours the fault: ours* means the church's.

325, 1102 f. *leviathan:* the allusion is to the first verses in the forty-first chapter of *Job:* "Canst thou draw out leviathan with an hook? or his tongue with a cord which thou lettest down? Canst thou put an hook into his nose? or bore his jaw through with a thorn. . . . Wilt thou play with him as with a bird? or wilt thou bind him for thy maidens?"

326, 1128–1129. *this freak of thine:* the reference is not to any part of Caponsacchi's conduct in the case before the Pope but to his worldliness, although a priest. See Caponsacchi's account and explanation, Bk. VI, 220 f.

326, 1136. *our adversary:* the devil. Originally the word was capitalized.

326, 1167. *in mask and motley:* Caponsacchi took part (with full episcopal encouragement) in dances and masked balls, etc. He was *pledged* to such by a conversation with the bishop prior to his ordination.

327, 1201. Caponsacchi was urged by his bishop to pay court to important ladies of the town. See Bk. VI, 469 f.

328, 1242. *dispart:* separate.

328, 1244. *orb:* eye.

328, 1270. *misprision:* mistake.

329, 1307 f. The philosophic and religious ideas which the Pope expresses in the passage which begins here are such as no Pope has ever professed; there is no ground for attributing such ideas to Innocent XII; and further it is doubtful if any mind of the late seventeenth century could (or would) have held such ideas.

329, 1317. God's being is outside space (and time).

330, 1334. *new philosophy:* new science. The science of physics was termed natural philosophy up to a time much more recent than 1700.

330, 1338. *Thy transcendent act:* the taking on of human life by the second Person of the Trinity. Browning regards it as transcending all else in God because it is the supreme proof that God is loving, and God's love is the central doctrine of his theology. *Transcendent* means supreme, rising above all previous reality.

330, 1347. *a tale of Thee:* the New Testament, or perhaps the Bible as a whole.

330, 1350. *discept* (*from*): reject.

330, 1365. *isoscele:* an isosceles triangle, *i.e.*, one in which two sides are equal in length, here a triangle in which the base is shorter than the other two sides. Power and intelligence are the other two sides of Browning's triangle, love or virtue the short base.

331, 1383. *"I have said ye are Gods":* a reminiscence of *Psalm* LXXXII, 6, which runs: "I have said ye are Gods; and all of you are children of the most High."

331, 1387. Browning is suggesting that the life of Christ, as reported in the New Testament, may either be a historical fact or a spiritual symbol, and that, whichever it be, it is the key to life.

331, 1402. *choppy:* chapped.

331, 1406. *by God's gloved hand or the bare:* symbolically or actually.

332, 1470. There is no record of such a punishment having been inflicted on the bishop of Arezzo.

332, 1480 f. The reference is to an Augustinian monk whom Pompilia consulted in Arezzo and who promised to carry out her request to write to the Comparini. The Comparini received no message. See Pompilia's account, Bk. VII, 1282 f.

333, 1498. This community, of which the patron saint was Mary Magdalene, had been founded for the assistance and reformation of immoral women; and, having a right to the possessions of such women if they died in Rome, put in a claim to Pompilia's property.

333, 1503. Browning, for a dramatic purpose, alters the facts. Pompilia had not been in the custody of the Convertites but in that of the nuns of the convent of Scalette.

333, 1517. *the Fisc:* strictly the treasury or exchequer, and by extension the representative of these departments. Bk. IX records the argument of Bottinius, styled *Fisci et Rev. Cam. Apostol. Advocatus, i.e.*, advocate of the treasury and reverend apostolic chamber.

334, 1565–1569. The imagery is taken from St. Paul's *Epistle to the Ephesians*, Ch. VI, 13–7.

334, 1590. *To-kien:* Fo-Rien.

334, 1592. *Maigrot:* Vicar-Apostolic in China, who, in 1693, condemned the Jesuit tolerance of Chinese elements in a conception of Christian truth.

335, 1602. *Tournon:* legate in India, sent to China by Innocent's successor. He was elevated to the cardinalate in 1707.

335, 1618. *adept of the Rosy Cross:* Rosicrucian. The Rosicrucians claimed to have discovered a method of transmuting base metal into gold. See l. 1616.

335, 1619. *the Great Work:* transmutation.

335, 1638. The reference is to Jesus. Matthew remarks "there was darkness over all the land" during the three hours Jesus lay dying on the cross (*Matthew*, Ch. XXVII, 45).

336, 1669. Euripides is imagined as speaking; but Browning draws upon other ancient writers for the ideas embodied in the speech.

336, 1697. *Know thyself:* the counsel of Socrates.

Take the golden mean: the counsel of Horace, who added the "golden" to what Aristotle long before him advised.

337, 1706. When Euripides, an innovator in doctrine and in technique, followed upon Aeschylus and Sophocles.

337, 1717. *Paul spoke, Felix heard:* Paul explained his doctrine to Felix, the governor in Jerusalem (*Acts*, Ch. XXIV).

337, 1721–1722. Euripides was openly critical of the morality of some of the Greek divinities.

337, 1729. *Galileo's tube:* the telescope.

338, 1791. It was long a pious legend that St. Paul had held a correspondence with the Roman philosopher Seneca, establishing in it the truth of Christianity.

339, 1832. *Nero's cross:* for crucifixion.

339, 1851–1852. *that age my death will usher into life:* the eighteenth century. The prophecy of the Pope is in its main aspects correct: the challenge which the eighteenth century offered to Christianity led to a reinvigorated Christian faith in the early nineteenth century.

340, 1868. See note on Pompilia's monologue, l. 769.

340, 1903. *antimasque:* an interlude between acts of a mask.

kibe: heel, strictly a chilblain on the heel.

340, 1909. *the first experimentalist:* Caponsacchi.

341, 1924. *morrice:* a complex dance.

342, 1976. *the educated man's:* Bk. IV, *Tertium Quid*, formulates such a judgment.

342, 1985–1986. *nemini honorem trado:* I give my glory into no one's keeping. The phrase occurs twice in *Isaiah* (Ch. XLII, 8, and Ch. XLVIII, 11).

342, 2003. *Farinacci:* a Renaissance authority on canon law, and procurator-general to Pope Paul V.

343, 2055. *Barabbas' self:* Pilate offered to the Jews the freedom of Jesus or of Barabbas. They cried out for Barabbas (*Matthew*, Ch. XXVII, 17).

343, 2059. *the three little taps:* at the death of a pope the cardinal camerlengo is supposed to tap on his forehead thrice with a silver mallet.

343, 2068. *petit-maître priestlings:* worldly, contemptible priests. *Petit-maître* means literally little master.

343, 2069. *Sanctus et benedictus:* Holy and blessed.

344, 2087. *Priam:* King of Troy at the time of the Greek attack. The analogy is strengthened by Priam's great age.

344, 2088. *Hecuba:* his wife.

344, 2088–2089. *non tali auxilio:* literally, not with such aid. The phrase in its context (Virgil: *Aeneid*, Bk. II, 521) runs *non tali auxilio nec defensoribus istis tempus eget:* The situation dces not require such aid or such defenders.

344, 2099. *Quis pro Domino:* Guido had used the phrase in his first monologue (Bk. V, 1549).

344, 2110. *the People's Square:* the Piazza del Popolo, one of the great squares of Rome, at some distance from the Vatican.

345, 2130–2131. Browning attenuates the verdict by allowing his Pope to doubt the doctrine of eternal punishment.

345. HOUSE

This poem first appeared in the collection of 1876, *Pacchiarotto and How He Worked in Distemper, with Other Poems.* It is in part at least a comment on Wordsworth's lines (in his sonnet, "Scorn not the sonnet"):

With this same key [the sonnet-form]
Shakespeare unlocked his heart.

W. C. DeVane plausibly conjectures (*A Browning Handbook*, 356) that the poem is also a comment on the self-revelation in Rossetti's sonnet-sequence, *The House of Life* (1870). The poem was composed in February, 1874.

345, 4. See the general note on the poem.

345, 23–28. The details are consonant, at least, with the circumstances of Rossetti's life.

346, 35. *spirit-sense:* imagination.

346. SHOP

This poem first appeared in the collection of 1876, *Pacchiarotto and How He Worked in Distemper, with Other Poems.* In that volume it immediately followed "House," as it does here; and it was written a few days later in the same month, February, 1874.

346, 6 f. The shop sold jewelry and "notions."

347, 23. *City chaps:* business men. The central financial district of London is known as the City.

347, 30. *takes the rail:* does well for himself, takes the advantage.

347, 36. *Mayfair:* the fashionable residential district in London.

347, 38. *Hampstead:* a middle-class residential district, then in the suburbs.

347, 40. *country-box:* a little place in the country. The term is not intended to suggest poverty.

347, 54. *underscore:* stress.

347, 57. *cramp:* cramped.

348, 70. *scud:* rush.

348, 94. *chaffer:* bargaining.

349, 109–110. Browning twists a verse of *Matthew* (Ch. VI, 2)1: "For where your treasure is, there will your heart be."

349. ECHETLOS

This poem first appeared in the collection of 1880, *Dramatic Idyls* [Second Series]. The battle of Marathon, a village a short distance northeast of Athens, was won by a few thousand Athenians (supported by allies from other parts of Greece) over a Persian force many times as large. Browning drew mainly on Pausanias' *Description of Greece*, which records the achievement in the battle of an unknown peasant, who was called thereafter *echetlos, i.e.*, the holder of the ploughshare.

349, 2. *Barbarians:* the Greeks so described all foreigners, the term meaning literally "bearded ones."

349, 3. *Marathon:* see the general note on the poem.

349, 11. *clown:* peasant.

349, 13. *the weak mid-line:* the Persians broke through the Greek centre which had been weakened to strengthen the wings.

tunnies: small Mediterranean fish.

349, 15. *Kallimachos Polemarch:* Kallimachos, the *polemarch* (or military leader) of Athens, died in battle.

349, 16. *phalanx:* a square formation used by the Greeks in hand-to-hand fighting.

349, 18. *Sakian:* a Scythian tribe which supported the Persians.

Mede: Asiatics allied with the Persians in their empire.

350, 25. *Oracle:* at Delphi, the oracle of Apollo, the most famous in Greece.

350, 27. *the holder of the ploughshare:* see general note on the poem.

350, 28. *Miltiades:* the commander of the Greeks in the battle. On his defeat at *Paros isle* (l. 29) he was tried for treachery.

350, 29. *Themistokles:* a statesman-soldier who was also charged with treachery at a later time and took refuge among the Persians who treated him with honour.

350, 30. *Satrap:* governor.

Sardis: in Lydia, then under the Persian dominion.

350. NEVER THE TIME AND THE PLACE

This poem first appeared in the collection of 1883, *Jocoseria*. It is a tribute to his wife, now more than twenty years dead.

350. PROLOGUE TO ASOLANDO

The collection *Asolando*, to which this poem served as prologue, appeared on December 12, 1889, the day of Browning's death. This piece, written at Asolo, in northeastern Italy was dated September 6. His first visit to Asolo had taken place a little more than fifty years earlier; and throughout the poem the tempers of youth and age are contrasted.

350, 5. *iris-bow:* rainbow.

350, 8. *uncinct:* ungirt.

350, 13. *chrysopras:* apple-green chalcedony.

350, 21. *Asolo:* see general note on the poem.

350, 27. *the Bush:* the image came to Browning from *Exodus*, Ch. III, 2: "And the angel of the Lord appeared unto him [Moses] in a flame of fire out of the midst of a bush; and he looked, and, behold, the bush burned with fire, and the bush was not consumed."

351. DUBIETY

This poem first appeared in the collection of 1889, *Asolando*. The reference in the closing stanzas is to his wife and his love for her.

351. EPILOGUE

This poem appeared in the collection *Asolando: Fancies and Facts*, which came from the press on December 12, 1889, the day the poet died. In the *Pall Mall Gazette* for February 1, in the following year, appeared the statement: "One evening just before his death-illness, the poet was reading this [the third stanza of the "Epilogue"] from a proof to his daughter-in-law and sister. He said: 'It almost sounds like bragging to say this, and as if I ought to cancel it; but it's the simple truth; and as it's true, it shall stand.' "

BIBLIOGRAPHY

ELIZABETH BARRETT BROWNING

I. EDITIONS

Complete Works, ed. by C. Porter and H. A. Clarke, 6 vols., Crowell, 1900.
Poetical Works, ed. by Sir F. Kenyon, Macmillan, 1897.
New Poems by Robert Browning and Elizabeth Barrett Browning, ed. by Sir F. Kenyon, Macmillan, 1915.
Hitherto Unpublished Poems and Stories, 2 vols. Printed for members of the Bibliophile Society (Boston), 1914.

II. BIOGRAPHY AND LETTERS

Letters, ed. by Sir F. Kenyon, Macmillan, 1899.
Letters of Robert Browning and Elizabeth Barrett Barrett, 2 vols., Smith Elder, 1899.
Elizabeth Barrett Browning: Letters to Her Sister, ed. by L. Huxley, Murray, 1929.
Letters from Elizabeth Barrett to B. R. Haydon (1842–1845), ed. by M. H. Shackford, Oxford, 1939.
Burdett, O.: *The Brownings*, Houghton, 1929.
Lubbock, P.: *Elizabeth Barrett Browning in Her Letters*, Smith Elder, 1906.
Whiting, L.: *The Brownings: Their Life and Art*, Little Brown, 1917.

III. CRITICISM

I. Monographs

Royds, Kathleen: *Elizabeth Barrett Browning and Her Poetry*, Harrap, 1918.
Whiting, L.: *A Study of Elizabeth Barrett Browning*, Little Brown, 1899.
Wise, T. J.: *A Bibliography of the Writings in Prose and Verse of Elizabeth Barrett Browning*, Clay (London), 1918.

II. Essays in Books

Bald, M. A.: "Mrs. Browning" in *Women Writers of the Nineteenth Century*, Cambridge, 1923.
Benson, A. C.: "Elizabeth Barrett Browning" in *Essays*, Macmillan, 1896.
Chauvet, P.: "Elizabeth Barrett Browning" in *Sept essais de littérature anglaise*, Figuière (Paris), 1930.
Gosse, Sir Edmund: " 'The Sonnets from the Portuguese' " in *Critical Kitkats*, Scribners, 1896.

NOTES AND COMMENTS

353. COWPER'S GRAVE

This poem first appeared in the collection of 1838, *The Seraphim and Other Poems.* William Cowper, whose grave is at Dereham in Norfolk, died in 1800. He believed that he was predestined to eternal damnation: he was subject to accesses of insanity some of which lasted for periods of months and even years, and in these his conviction of damnation played a heavy part. He was the author of many moving hymns and in his secular poetry touched on the beauties of nature great and small, often finding solace in the charm of little creatures and of flowers and trees. All these facts are woven into the tribute Elizabeth Barrett pays to him.

353, 5. *a maniac's tongue:* see the general note to the poem.

353, 6. Cowper's conviction of eternal damnation (for which see the general note) did not lessen the fervour of his Christian belief.

353, 20. Nature was Cowper's resource in the periods of his deepest spiritual affliction.

353, 25. *hares:* hares were among Cowper's special favourites. At Olney he kept a number of them, and in *The Task,* as well as in his "Epitaph on a Hare" he expressed his affection for them.

354, 40. *Eyes:* the eyes of Christ.

354, 50. *Adam's sins:* original sin which, in the Calvinist scheme accepted by Cowper, taints all human beings is their inheritance from Adam.

354, 51. *Immanuel:* Jesus.

354, 52. *My God, I am forsaken:* the cry of Jesus as he lay dying on the cross. As recorded by St. Matthew the words were: "My God, my God, why hast thou forsaken me?" (*Matthew,* Ch. XXVII, 46.)

354. THE CRY OF THE CHILDREN

This poem first appeared in *Blackwood's Magazine* for August, 1843; it was subsequently reprinted in the *Poems* of 1844. The impetus for the poem came from a report on the employment of children in the mines and factories prepared by R. H. Horne, a friend of Elizabeth Barrett and the author of the once celebrated poem *Orion.*

The motto, taken from Euripides' play *Medea,* l. 1036, may be translated: "Alas, alas, why do you gaze at me with your eyes, my children?"

Mrs. Browning recognized the justice of criticism directed at the rhythm of the poem, writing to a friend in the following terms: "you are right in your complaint against the rhythm. The first stanza came into my head in a hurricane, and I was obliged to make the other stanzas like it—*that* is the whole mystery of the iniquity."

355, 40. *rime:* frost.

355, 50. *kirk:* church.

355, 56. *cerement:* grave-cloth.

357, 117. On this line Elizabeth Barrett appended the following note: "A fact rendered pathetically historical by Mr. Horne's report of his Commission. The name of the poet of *Orion* and *Cosmo de' Medici* has, however, a change of associations, and comes in time to remind me that we have some noble poetic heat of literature still,—however, open to the reproach of being somewhat gelid in our humanity."

357, 143. The meaning is that slaves have available to them the Christian faith—as the children in their ignorance, just illustrated, have not—and in its possession is spiritual freedom.

357, 144. *palm:* prize, as of a victory.

358. GRIEF

This poem first appeared in a group of sonnets without a title, in *Graham's Magazine,* for December, 1842, and was reprinted as one of the *Poems* of 1844.

358. THE DEAD PAN

This poem first appeared in the collection of 1844, *Poems*. Elizabeth Barrett prefaced to it the following acknowledgment: "Excited by Schiller's *Götter Griechenlands* [The Gods of Greece] and partly founded on a well-known tradition mentioned in a treatise of Plutarch (*De Oraculorum Defectu* [On the failing of the oracles]), according to which, at the hour of the Saviour's agony, a cry of 'Great Pan is dead!' swept across the waves in the hearing of certain mariners,—and the oracles ceased. It is in all veneration to the memory of the deathless Schiller that I oppose a doctrine still more dishonouring to poetry than to Christianity. As Mr. Kenyon's graceful and harmonious paraphrase of the German poem [the work of Schiller mentioned above] was the first occasion of the turning of my thoughts in this direction, I take advantage of the pretence to indulge my feelings (which overflow on other grounds) by inscribing my lyric to that dear friend and relative, with the earnestness of appreciating esteem as well as of affectionate gratitude." Pan was in Greek myth a nature god, the special custodian of animals and their herdsmen and hunters, as well as of gardens; he was also conceived as a god of fertility, and as such worshipped in orgiastic ceremonies. In appearance he was half human, and from the waist down resembled a goat. His delight in music, notably in playing a pipe of reeds, was to be the theme of Elizabeth Barrett Browning's "A Musical Instrument."

358, 1. *Hellas:* Greece.

358, 3. *mystic:* supernatural.

358, 9. *Aethiopia:* the modern Abyssinia, or in a more extended sense, the land of men of black skins.

358, 10. *Pygmies:* a race of small men believed to live far up the Nile.

358, 11. *mandragora:* a narcotic plant.

358, 23. *the silver spheres:* spheres believed to encompass the earth and to move around it, producing music as they moved.

358, 37. *Naiades:* water nymphs.

358, 41. *ay:* ever.

358, 44. *Dryads:* wood nymphs.

359, 51. *Oreads:* mountain nymphs.

359, 57. *Plato's vision:* in the *Phaedrus* Plato presents the gods in twelve bands, each accompanying one of the twelve principal gods.

359, 58. *starry wanderings:* in the *Phaedrus* the gods pass through the heavens following Zeus (Jupiter, Jove) in his chariot.

359, 64. *Jove:* Zeus, the chief of gods.

359, 65. *thunder:* thunder and lightning were Zeus's weapons. He was often represented with a faggot of thunderbolts in his right hand.

359, 68. *thine eagle:* he was often represented accompanied by an eagle, the king of birds.

359, 71. *Juno:* Hera, the wife of Jupiter.

359, 78. *Apollo:* god of many attributes but here conceived as god of the arts and, notably, of music and song.

359, 83. *Niobe:* Apollo slew her children.

359, 86. *Pallas:* Minerva, goddess of wisdom.

359, 89. *the olive:* the olive tree was sacred to her and groves of olives often surrounded her shrines.

359, 90. *Mars:* god of war, and persistent enemy of Pallas.

359, 92. *Bacchus:* god of wine, often represented as riding upon a *panther*.

359, 93. *vines:* he was usually represented as crowned with a wreath of vines.

359, 94. *Maenads:* women worshippers attending Bacchus.

359, 97. *Evohe:* a cry expressive of delight.

359, 99. *Neptune:* god of the sea, who carried a three-pronged spear (*trident*).

359, 101. *Pluto:* god of the underworld, a dark sunless land.

359, 103. *Ceres:* Demeter, goddess of earth and harvest. She was hostile to Pluto, who abducted her daughter Proserpine and made her his queen.

359, 104. *all:* Ceres had been desolate since the abduction of her daughter. See note on preceding line.

359, 106. *Aphrodite:* Venus, goddess of love.

359, 107. *foam:* Aphrodite was born of (or at least appeared from) the sea-foam.

359, 108. *cestus:* a girdle. Aphrodite's girdle was able to excite humans to passion.

359, 110. *Ai:* alas.

Adonis: a mortal youth whom Aphrodite loved and who was slain by a boar.

359, 115. *frore:* frozen.

359, 120. *Hermes:* Mercury, messenger of the gods, and himself a god.

359, 123. *caduceus:* staff.

360, 127. *Cybele:* Rhea, wife of Saturn and mother of the gods; her crown was in the form of a *turret.*

360, 129. Cybele was often represented as in a chariot drawn by lions.

360, 136. *Vesta:* goddess of the hearth.

360, 149. *obolus:* a Greek coin of small value.

360, 160. *Ida:* on Mt. Ida Zeus was believed to have been born.

360, 165. *Dark:* at the crucifixion darkness fell on the earth.

360, 198. The meaning is that they rent their Divinity as if it were a garment.

360, 201. *Dodona's oak:* at Dodona in Epirus Zeus had a shrine before which stood an oak.

360, 204. *Pythia:* priestess of Apollo's oracle at Delphi in Greece.

360, 207. *crispy fillets:* curled hair.

361, 214. *libations:* ceremonial drinking.

361, 220. *Schiller:* a German poet of the romantic period and the author of a poem which led to the composition of Elizabeth Barrett's. See the general note on this poem.

361, 227–228. The meaning is that the gods of classical myth represent gropings of humanity towards perfect truth, which Christianity embodies fully.

361, 230. *aureole:* halo.

361, 236. *Phoebus' chariot-course:* Phoebus Apollo was the sun god and was believed to ride through the skies daily in his chariot.

361, 248. *Poet:* the term means creator or maker.

361, 260–263. The passage echoes Paul saying in the *Epistle to the Philippians*, Ch. IV, 8: "Whatsoever things are true, whatsoever things are honest, whatsoever things are just, whatsoever things are pure, whatsoever things are lovely, whatsoever things are of good report: if there be any virtue, and if there be any praise, think on these things."

361. SONNETS FROM THE PORTUGUESE

This sequence of forty-four sonnets first appeared in 1850. When Robert Browning, admiring her *Poems* of 1844, called upon her, fell in love with her and in 1846 married her, Elizabeth Barrett recorded her feelings in this sequence. It is unknown at what time she began to write them; but they were not shown to Browning, or to any one until after the marriage. The first title they bore was *Sonnets Translated from the Bosnian:* doubtless Elizabeth Barrett hesitated to disclose without some veil the emotions which surge through them. Browning who admired a poem of love which had appeared in an earlier collection of Elizabeth Barrett's, the poem "Catarina to Camoens," suggested the present title. Camoens was the greatest epic and lyric poet of Portugal.

I

361, 1. *Theocritus:* a Greek lyrical and idyllic poet of the third century B.C. The allusion is to his fifteenth idyll.

361, 10. *mystic:* mysterious, supernatural.

361, 13. *Death:* the expectation was not melodramatic but natural, since she had for a long time supposed herself an incurable invalid, soon to die.

362. III

362, 7. *gages:* pledges of love.

362, 12. *cypress:* a symbol of death and grief.

362, 13. *chrism:* holy oil, marking the sanctification of the person receiving it. In this reference the consecration is aesthetic not religious.

362. V

362, 2. Electra, daughter of Agamemnon and Clytemnestra and sister of Orestes, conspired with her brother to avenge the murder of her father by her mother. In the course of their plot she carried an urn which was supposed to contain the ashes of Orestes. The image is emotionally of doubtful appropriateness.

362, 11. *laurels:* the branches of the laurel were used by the Greeks to crown poets.

362. VIII

362, 2–3. *gold and purple:* princely colors, continuing the image of l. 1.

363. XX

363, 2. *a year ago:* Browning wrote his first note to Elizabeth Barrett in January, 1845, saw her for the first time in May of that year and before the month was over had expressed his love.

363. XXI

363, 13. *iterance:* repetition.

364. XXVI

364, 1–2. The reference is to the years of invalidism and seclusion, from which Browning redeemed her.

364. XXXII

364, 2–3. *the moon to slacken all those bonds:* the moon was long associated with inconstancy in love.

364. XXXV

364, 1. *leave all:* Elizabeth Barrett appreciated before her marriage that she would be forced to pay for her happiness by a breach with her father and, so far as he could dictate, with all her brothers and sisters.

364, 8. *dead eyes:* the reference is to her mother.

364. XXXVIII

364, 5. *a ring of amethyst:* Elizabeth Barrett wore no ring nor in any way could indicate to her family or friends that she was affianced to Browning.

365, 10. *chrism:* holy oil.

365. XLIII

365, 3. *feeling out of sight:* passing beyond the range of existence, that is, of physical reality.

365, 9. *passion:* suffering.

365. A MUSICAL INSTRUMENT

This poem first appeared in the Cornhill Magazine for July, 1860, and was reprinted in the collection of 1862, *Last Poems.* She had already dealt with the theme of Pan in "The Dead Pan," a poem printed in the collection of 1844. Pan, a nature-god, was specially worshipped by hunters and shepherds. From the waist down he had the form of a goat. His favourite musical instrument was a flute of seven reeds.

365, 2. *reeds:* see the general note on the poem.

365, 3. *ban:* harm.

365, 4. *hoofs of a goat:* see the general note on the poem.

366, 37. *half a beast:* see the general note on the poem.

366. BIANCA AMONG THE NIGHTINGALES

This poem first appeared in the collections of 1862, *Last Poems.*

Bianca is the Italian name equivalent to Blanche. Bianca has followed from Florence to England her lover Giulio who had followed his English seductress.

366, 5. *crystallized:* gave the appearance of crystal to.

366, 20. *vow:* speak a vow.

366, 25. *heroic mails:* the mail worn by heroes.

366, 57. *Tuscan:* Tuscany is a large part of northern Italy. Florence, the scene of Bianca's idyll with her lover Giulio, is in Tuscany. See ll. 64 f.

367, 66. *the last feast-day of Saint John:* St. John the Baptist is the patron saint of Florence; his day is the occasion of festival.

367, 67. *Carraia bridge:* a bridge across the river Arno, which runs through Florence.

367, 69. *that river of ours:* the Arno.

367, 88. *Grazie tanto:* Many thanks.

88–89. *bruised to sweetness:* the commonplace phrase is attractive, spoken in an English accent.

367, 106. *pyx:* the receptacle for the wafers used in Communion when consecrated, and, according to Roman Catholic belief, converted into the body of Christ.

367, 127. *springe:* trap.

mio ben: my dear.

BIBLIOGRAPHY

EDWARD FITZGERALD

I. EDITIONS

Variorum and Definitive Edition, Poetical and Prose Writings, ed. by Sir Edmund Gosse and G. Bentham, 7 vols., Doubleday, 1902–3.

Rubáiyát of Omar Khayyám (the first and final texts, with variants in intervening texts), Macmillan, 1895.

II. BIOGRAPHY AND LETTERS

Letters and Literary Remains, ed. by W. A. Wright, 7 vols., Macmillan, 1902–3.

Letters to Fanny Kemble, 1871–1883, ed. by W. A. Wright, Macmillan, 1895.

Some New Letters, ed. by F. R. Barton, Williams and Norgate, 1923.

Edward FitzGerald and Bernard Barton: Letters Written by FitzGerald, 1839–1856, Putnam, 1924.

Letters to Bernard Quaritch 1853–1883, ed. by C. Q. Wrentmore, Quaritch, 1926.

Benson, A. C.: *Edward FitzGerald*, Macmillan, 1905.

Glyde, J.: *The Life of Edward FitzGerald*, Pearson (London), 1900.

Wright, T.: *The Life of Edward FitzGerald*, 2 vols., Scribner, 1904.

III. CRITICISM

Bradford, G.: "Edward FitzGerald" in *Bare Souls*, Harper, 1924.

Gosse, Sir Edmund: "Edward FitzGerald" in *Critical Kit-Kats*, Scribner, 1914.

Hutton, R. H.: "A Great Poet of Denial and Revolt" in *Brief Literary Criticisms*, Macmillan, 1906.

Johnson, Lionel: "Lucretius and Omar" in *Post-Liminium*, Mathews, 1911.

Platt, A.: "Edward FitzGerald" in *Nine Essays*, Cambridge, 1927.

Tutin, J. R.: *A Concordance to FitzGerald's Translation of the Rubáiyát of Omar Khayyám*, Macmillan, 1900.

Welby, T. Earle: "FitzGerald" in *Back Numbers*, Constable, 1929.

NOTES AND COMMENTS

369. THE RUBÁIYÁT OF OMAR KHAYYÁM

This poem first appeared in 1859; but it had been completed at least a year earlier and sent to *Fraser's Magazine*, the editors of which held it for so long that FitzGerald reclaimed it. In the first edition there were seventy-five quatrains (Rubáiyát is the Persian for quatrains); in the second one hundred and ten; in the third and fourth one hundred and one. For each of the later editions FitzGerald revised the work thoroughly, not always to its advantage. Some of the quatrains were suppressed; some altered beyond recognition. The beauty of the first two stanzas in the first version indicates how much has been lost in revision:

Awake! for Morning in the Bowl of Night
Has flung the Stone that puts the Stars to Flight:
  And Lo! the Hunter of the East has caught
The Sultán's Turret in a Noose of Light.

Dreaming when Dawn's Left Hand was in the Sky
I heard a Voice within the Tavern cry,
  "Awake, my Little ones, and fill the Cup
Before Life's Liquor in its Cup be dry."

369, 1–4. This stanza is original with FitzGerald.

369, 5. *False morning:* FitzGerald comments "a transient light on the horizon about an hour before the true dawn — a common phenomenon in the East."

369, 13. *the New Year:* the Persian new year began in the spring. Hence the reference to the "reviving."

369, 15. *the White Hand of Moses:* Moses put his hand into his breast and when he removed it it "was leprous as snow" (*Exodus*, Ch. IV, 6).

369, 16. *Jesus . . . suspires:* in Jesus' breath the Persians believed there was healing power.

369, 17. *Iram:* a garden in Arabia once famous, but in Omar's time completely covered with sand.

369, 18. *Jamshyd's Sev'n-ring'd cup:* Jamshyd was a Persian king; the cup was symbolical, seven being a mystic number, and had magical powers.

369, 20. *blows:* blooms.

369, 21–22. David exemplifies sacred song, which is represented as having fallen silent; Pehleví was the old literary language of the Persians, described as divine because of the works written in it.

370, 29. *Naishápúr:* the Persian village where Omar was born.

370, 36. *Jamshyd:* see note on l. 18.

Kaikobád: the founder of a dynasty of Persian kings.

370, 38. *Kaikhosrú:* the founder of the Persian empire.

370, 39. *Zál:* the "snow-haired Zal" of Arnold's *Sohrab and Rustum*, a hero among the Persians, and the father of Rustum.

Rustum: Zal's son and the greatest Persian hero of his age.

370, 40. *Hátim:* FitzGerald comments: "A type of Oriental Generosity."

370, 44. *Mahmud:* The Sultan, or, perhaps there is a reference to the specific figure of Mahmud the Great, conqueror of India.

370, 46. *Thou:* he is speaking to a nightingale.

370, 50. *the Prophet:* Mohammed.

370, 57. *the Golden grain:* money.

371, 65. *Caravanserai:* a resting-place for caravans. Here it is an image for life.

371, 70. *Jamshyd:* see note on l. 18.

371, 71. *Bahrám:* a Persian king who lost his life in hunting a wild ass.

371, 75. *Hyacinth:* the flower takes its name from a youth beloved of Apollo who killed him throwing a quoit which a jealous god directed towards Hyacinth.

371, 84. *Sev'n thousand Years:* a millennium for each of the seven planets known to Omar.

371, 96. *sans:* without.

371, 99. *Muezzín:* a crier who from the minaret of a mosque summons Mohammedans to prayer.

372, 106. *Doctor:* scholar.

372, 119. *forbidden:* wine is forbidden by Mohammed and avoided by orthodox Mohammedans.

372, 122. *Saturn:* god of the seventh heaven.

372, 127. *Me and Thee:* FitzGerald comments: "some dividual Existence or Personality distinct from the Whole."

372, 131. *Signs:* of the zodiac.

372, 133. *Thee in Me:* see note on l. 127. Here the opposite condition, the whole in the part, is affirmed.

372, 136. *Me within Thee blind:* the "Me" is now the whole, the "Thee" the part.

373, 146. *a Potter thumping his wet Clay:* here and in his later references to the potter and the clay FitzGerald is mindful of Biblical references, notably those in *Isaiah*, Ch. LXIV, 8.

373, 153–154. *a Drop that from our Cups we throw for Earth to drink of:* FitzGerald comments: "The custom of throwing a little Wine on the ground before drinking still continues in Persia, and perhaps generally in the East."

373, 164. *Minister of Wine:* the girl who bears the wine.

373, 169. *the darker Drink:* darker than wine, this drink is that of death. FitzGerald tells us that he had in mind an Oriental legend, which presented the Angel of Death as fulfilling his mission "by holding to the nostril an Apple from the Tree of Life."

373, 173. *the Dust:* the body.

374, 179. *Ferrásh:* servant.

374, 183. *Sáki:* wine-bearer.

374, 193. *spangle:* the word is used to indicate not only the brightness of life but much more its smallness.

374, 198. *Alif:* the first letter of the alphabet in the Arabic, and other Semitic languages.

374, 203. *from Máh to Máhi:* FitzGerald explains: "from fish to moon."

375, 221–224. This stanza is "a jest at his studies," FitzGerald says, Omar being a mathematician and logician as well as an astronomer.

375, 225–226. An allusion to his role in reforming the calendar.

375, 234. *The Two-and-Seventy jarring Sects:* FitzGerald comments that "Seventy-two Religions" were "supposed to divide the World, including Islamism as some think: but others not."

375, 237. *Mahmúd:* the reference is to the Sultan Mahmúd, conqueror of India.

375, 238. *the misbelieving and black Horde:* the image comes from the conquest of India.

377, 282. *Wit:* intelligence.

377, 298. *the Foal:* the constellation *Equuleus* (little horse).

377, 299. *Parwin and Mushtari:* the Pleiades and Jupiter.

377, 307–308. The meaning is that a moment's insight into the nature of the universe, even if it is intoxication that gives it, is better than no insight at all even if one practices all the observances of orthodox religion.

377, 309. *senseless:* unconscious.

378, 317. *gin:* snare.

378, 326. *Ramazán:* in Mohammedanism the month of fasting.

378, 346. *Súfi:* the Sufis were mystics, and the objects of Omar's attack.

379, 358. *the little Moon:* the new moon appearing at the end of the month of fasting.

379, 360. *shoulder-knot:* for carrying jars of wine.

379, 368. *overtaken unaware:* seduced into drinking, in violation of Mohammed's injunction.

379, 369. *Idols:* wine and similar material things.

380. *Tamám:* it is ended.

BIBLIOGRAPHY

381. ARTHUR HUGH CLOUGH

I. EDITIONS

Poems and Prose Remains, with a selection from his letters and a memoir, ed. by his wife, 2 vols., Macmillan, 1869.
Poetical Works, with a memoir by F. T. Palgrave, Routledge, 1906.
Poems, ed. by H. Milford, Oxford, 1910.

II. BIOGRAPHY AND LETTERS

Levy, G.: *Arthur Hugh Clough, 1819–1861*, Sidgwick and Jackson, 1938.
Osborne, J. I.: *Arthur Hugh Clough*, Constable, 1920.

III. CRITICISM

I. Monographs

Guyot, E.: *Essai sur la formation philosophique du poète A. H. Clough*, Hachette, 1913.
Waddington, S.: *Arthur Hugh Clough*, Bell, 1883.

II. Essays in Books

Bagehot, W.: "Mr. Clough's Poems" in *Literary Studies*, 3 vols., Longmans, 1895.
Brooke, S. A.: "Arthur Hugh Clough" in *Four Victorian Poets*, Putnam, 1908.
Garrod, H. W.: "Clough" in *Poetry and the Criticism of Life*, Harvard, 1931.
Gosse, Sir E.: "Clough" in *Books on the Table*, Heinemann, 1921.
Hutton, R. H.: "Arthur Hugh Clough" in *Literary Essays*, Macmillan, 1888.
Hutton, R. H.: "Amiel and Clough" and "The Unpopularity of Clough" in *Brief Literary Criticisms*, Macmillan, 1906.
Patmore, C.: "Arthur Hugh Clough" in *Principle in Art*, Bell, 1889.
Robertson, J. M.: "Clough" in *New Essays towards a Critical Method*, Lane, 1897.
Sidgwick, H.: "The Poems and Prose Remains of Arthur Hugh Clough" in *Miscellaneous Essays and Addresses*, Macmillan, 1904.
Welby, T. E.: "Clough" in *Back Numbers*, Constable, 1929.
Williams, S. T.: "Clough's Prose" in *Studies in Victorian Literature*, Dutton, 1918.
Wolfe, H.: "Arthur Hugh Clough" in *The Eighteen Sixties*, ed. by J. Drinkwater, Cambridge, 1932

NOTES AND COMMENTS

382. IN A LECTURE-ROOM

This poem first appeared in the collection of 1849, *Ambarvalia;* it was written nine years earlier.

382, 3. *bestead:* helped.

382. Τὸ Καλόν

This poem first appeared in the collection of 1849, *Ambarvalia;* but it was composed eight years earlier. The Greek title—which means "The Beautiful"—was not introduced until 1862: in 1849 this lyric was the tenth and last section of a sequence entitled *Blank Misgivings of a Creature moving about in Worlds not realised.*

382, 1. *these:* the circumstances of earthly existence.

382, 3. *ease:* satisfaction.

382, 8. *debt:* obligation.

382, 17. *summum Pulchrum:* the Supreme Beauty (the meaning is the same as that of the title).

382. QUA CURSUM VENTUS

This poem first appeared in the collection of 1849, *Ambarvalia.* The meaning of the title is: "where the wind guides the course." It is taken from the *Aeneid*, Bk. III. It is unknown to which of his friends (if to any individual person) the lyric was addressed.

383. THE NEW SINAI

This poem, originally entitled *When Israel Came Out of Egypt*, first appeared in the collection of 1849, *Ambarvalia.* On Mt. Sinai Moses received from God the tablets bearing the ten commandments; on returning to his people at the foot of the mount he found them preparing to adore a golden calf (see *Exodus*, Chs. XIX–XX, XXXIV).

383, 36. *Olympus:* the mountain on which, according to Greek mythology, the gods lived.

383, 37. *Avernian woods:* woods on the shores of the lake of Averno, near Naples. The lake was believed by the Romans to be an entrance to the underworld, which was known sometimes as Avernus.

383, 43. *Sinai:* see the general note on the poem.

383, 43–46. Clough is amplifying a passage in *Exodus* where it is reported that "there were thunders, and lightnings and a thick cloud upon the mount, and the voice of the trumpet exceeding loud. . . ." (*Exodus*, Ch. XIX, 16.)

383, 56. *Mécanique Céleste:* the literal translation of the French phrase is: a celestial mechanism.

383, 58. *a watch-work:* representing the idea of a complicated mechanical contrivance.

383, 66. *similitude of sense:* an image perceptible to the senses.

383, 81–82. See the general note on the poem.

384, 94. *own:* profess devotion to.

384, 105. The reference is to Moses. He has vanished since his report is no longer credited.

384, 112. The reference is to Moses' brother Aaron who prepared the golden calf and led in its worship while Moses was on Sinai.

384. THE LATEST DECALOGUE

This poem first appeared in the posthumous *Poems* of 1862; but it was composed much earlier and doubtless withheld from earlier volumes because of its provocative and cynical quality.

384. AT VENICE

This poem first appeared in the *Poems* of 1862 but was composed as early as 1849, when Clough visited Venice.

The Lido: a beach on an island farther out in the Adriatic than the main part of the city.

The Piazza: the Piazza San Marco, the cathedral place.

385, 8 f. The description is of the Cathedral of St. Mark, which forms one side of the place.

385, 14. *oriental:* the cathedral is Byzantine in style.

385, 16. *Campanile:* a campanile or bell-tower stands beside the cathedral.

385, 32. *San Giorgio* and *Redentore* (or Redeemer) are the names of two notable churches in Venice.

385, 41. *Palladio:* an architect, the designer of the church of San Giorgio mentioned in the preceding note.

pediment: a triangular part over the portico of classical or Renaissance buildings.

385, 44. *dim religious light:* an echo of Milton in *Il Penseroso.*

385, 50. *absolutely made:* perfectly achieved.

385. PESCHIERA

This poem first appeared in the collection of 1862, *Poems.* Peschiera is a fortified town in northern Italy. Captured from the Austrians in 1848, it reverted to them in 1849.

385, 3–4. An adaptation of the famous lines in *In Memoriam,* XXVII, 15–6.

385, 5. *the tricolor:* the Italian flag.

385, 9. *Croat:* a native of Croatia, which was at the time a part of the Austro-Hungarian monarchy.

385, 11. *the eagle with his black wings:* the flag of Austria-Hungary.

385, 14. *Brescia:* a city in northern Italy, the centre of revolt against the Austrians in 1848–9.

386, 20. *Lombard:* a native of Lombardy, an area in northern Italy.

386, 31. *the cause:* of Italian liberation from Austria-Hungary (and ultimately of Italian unification which presupposed the liberation).

386. QUI LABORAT, ORAT

This poem first appeared in the collection of 1849, *Ambarvalia.* The title means: He who labors, prays.

386, 17. *unowned;* unacknowledged.

387. WITH WHOM IS NO VARIABLENESS, NEITHER SHADOW OF TURNING

This poem first appeared in the posthumous collection of 1862, *Poems.*

387. SAY NOT THE STRUGGLE NOUGHT AVAILETH

This poem first appeared in the posthumous collection of 1862, *Poems.*

387. WHERE LIES THE LAND TO WHICH THE SHIP WOULD GO?

This poem first appeared in the posthumous *Poems* of 1862; but it was composed in 1852 on Clough's voyage to America.

BIBLIOGRAPHY

388. MATTHEW ARNOLD

I. EDITIONS

Works, 15 vols. (see vols. 1–3) Macmillan, 1903–1904.
Poetical Works, Macmillan, 1893.
Poems, 1849–1867, ed. by Sir A. Quiller-Couch, Oxford, 1913.
Selections, ed. by R. E. C. Houghton, Methuen, 1929.
Essays and Poems, ed. by F. W. Roe, Harcourt, 1928.
Poetry and Prose, ed. by Sir E. K. Chambers, Oxford, 1940.
Merope, ed. by J. Churton Collins, Oxford, 1906.

II. BIOGRAPHY AND LETTERS

Letters, 1848–1888, 2 vols., ed. by G. W. E. Russell, Macmillan, 1895.
Unpublished Letters, ed. by A. Whitridge, Yale, 1923.
Letters to A. H. Clough, ed. by H. F. Lowry, Oxford, 1932.
FITCH, SIR J.: *Thomas and Matthew Arnold and Their Influence on English Education*, Scribner, 1897.
PAUL, H. W.: *Matthew Arnold*, Macmillan, 1902.
RUSSELL, G. W. E.: *Matthew Arnold*, Scribners, 1904.
SAINTSBURY, G.: *Matthew Arnold*, Blackwood, 1899.

III. CRITICISM

I. MONOGRAPHS

BROWN, E. K.: *Studies in the Text of Matthew Arnold's Prose Works*, Droz, 1935.
DAWSON, W. H.: *Matthew Arnold and His Relation to the Thought of Our Time*, Putnam, 1904.
HOUGHTON, R. E. C.: *The Influence of the Classics on the Poetry of Matthew Arnold*, Blackwell, 1923.
KELSO, A. P.: *Matthew Arnold on Continental Life and Literature*, Blackwell, 1914.
ORRICK, J. B.: *Matthew Arnold and Goethe*, Moring (London), 1928.
SCHRAG, A.: *Matthew Arnold, Poet and Critic*, Reinhardt (Basel), 1904.
SHERMAN, S. P.: *Matthew Arnold, How to Know Him*, Bobbs Merrill, 1917.
SMART, T. B.: *The Bibliography of Matthew Arnold*, Davy (London), 1892. Also in Works, 1903–1904, vol. 15.
STANLEY, C.: *Matthew Arnold*, University of Toronto Press, 1938.
TINKER, C. B., and LOWRY, H. F.: *The Poetry of Matthew Arnold*, Oxford, 1940.
TRILLING, L.: *Matthew Arnold*, Norton, 1939.

II. ESSAYS IN BOOKS

BROOKE, S. A.: "Matthew Arnold" in *Four Victorian Poets*, Putnam, 1908.
BROWN, E. K.: "The French Reputation of Matthew Arnold" in *Studies in English* (collected by M. W. Wallace), University of Toronto Press, 1932.
BROWNELL, W. C.: "Matthew Arnold" in *Victorian Prose Masters*, Scribners, 1928.
COLLINS, J. C.: "Matthew Arnold" in *Posthumous Essays*, Dent, 1912.
ELLIOTT, G. R.: "The Arnoldian Lyric Melancholy" in *The Cycle of Modern Poetry*, Princeton, 1929.
FORMAN, H. B.: "Matthew Arnold" in *Our Living Poets*, Tinsley, 1871.
FRYE, P. H.: "Matthew Arnold" in *Visions and Revisions*, Jones (Boston), 1929.
GARROD, H. W.: "The Poetry of Matthew Arnold" in *Poetry and the Criticism of Life*, Harvard, 1931.
GATES, L. E.: "Matthew Arnold" in *Three Studies in Literature*, Macmillan, 1899.
HARPER, G. M.: "Matthew Arnold and the Zeitgeist" in *Spirit of Delight*, Holt, 1928.
HEARN, L.: "Matthew Arnold as Poet" in *Appreciations of Poetry*, Dodd, 1916.

HUTTON, R. H.: "The Poetry of Matthew Arnold" in *Literary Essays*, Macmillan, 1888.
HUTTON, R. H.: "The Poetic Place of Matthew Arnold," "Matthew Arnold's Popularity" and "Our Great Elegiac Poet" in *Brief Literary Criticisms*, Macmillan, 1906.
JOHNSON, LIONEL: "Matthew Arnold" in *Post-Liminium*, Matthews, 1911.
KER, W. P.: "Matthew Arnold" in *The Art of Poetry*, Oxford, 1923.
KNICKERBOCKER, W. S.: "Matthew Arnold" in *Creative Oxford*, Syracuse University Press, 1925.
QUILLER-COUCH, SIR A.: "Matthew Arnold" in *Studies in Literature*, Cambridge, 1920.
RALEIGH, SIR W.: "Matthew Arnold" in *Some Authors*, Oxford, 1923.
SWINBURNE, A. C.: "Matthew Arnold's 'New Poems' " in *Essays and Studies*, Chatto, 1875.
WARREN, SIR HERBERT: "Matthew Arnold" in *Essays of Poets and Poetry, Ancient and Modern*, Murray, 1909.
WILLIAMS, S. T.: "The Poetical Reputation of Matthew Arnold," "Matthew Arnold and His Contemporaries," "Three Aspects of Matthew Arnold's Poetry," "Theory and Practice in the Poetry of Matthew Arnold," in *Studies in Victorian Literature*, Dutton, 1923.
WOODBERRY, G. E.: "Matthew Arnold" in *Makers of Literature*, Macmillan, 1900.

III. ARTICLES IN PERIODICALS

BONNEROT, L.: "La jeunesse de Matthew Arnold" in *Revue anglo-américaine*, August, 1930.
BROWN, E. K.: "Matthew Arnold and the Eighteenth Century" in the *University of Toronto Quarterly*, January, 1940.
BROWN, E. K.: "The Scholar-Gipsy: An interpretation" in *Revue anglo-américaine*, April, 1935.
FOERSTER, N.: "Matthew Arnold and American Letters To-Day" in *Sewanee Review*, July, 1922.
HARRIS, A.: "Matthew Arnold: The 'Unknown Years' " in the *Nineteenth Century*, 1933.
KNICKERBOCKER, W. S.: "Semaphore: Arnold and Clough" in *Sewanee Review*, April, 1933.
LEWISOHN, L.: "A Study of Matthew Arnold" in *Sewanee Review*, October, 1901, April and July, 1902.
ORRICK, J. B.: "Matthew Arnold and Goethe" in *Publications of the English Goethe Society*, 1928.
TINKER, C. B.: "Arnold's Poetic Plans" in *Yale Review*, June, 1933.
WOODS, M. L.: "Matthew Arnold" in *Essays and Studies of the English Association*, 1929.

NOTES AND COMMENTS

389. MYCERINUS

This poem first appeared in the collection of 1849, *The Strayed Reveller, and Other Poems.* At J. A. Froude's suggestion Arnold appended in 1853 and later editions the passage from Herodotus which was his source: "After Chephren, Mycerinus, son of Cheops, reigned over Egypt. He abhorred his father's courses, and judged his subjects more justly than any of their kings had done.—To him there came an oracle from the city of Buto, to the effect that he was to live but six years longer, and to die in the seventh year from that time" (Book II, 133).

389, 1–2. See general note on the poem.

389, 5. *lips that cannot lie:* those of the priests of the oracle.

390, 18. *six years:* see the general note on the poem.

390, 22. *archetype:* great original.

390, 40. The reference is to the Nile's overflowing of its banks.

392. THE STRAYED REVELLER

This poem first appeared in the collection of 1849, in which it was the titular piece. The metre was probably influenced by Goethe as well as by Greek measures.

392, 4–5. The language is deliberately philosophic, and immediately discloses that the theme is not the sensuous one which the mention of Circe and *a wild train* would suggest. Circe cast a spell on Ulysses' men, making them bestial.

392, 12. *ivy-cinctured:* girt with ivy, at the middle.

392, 38. *Iacchus:* Bacchus.

392, 57. *creaming:* thickening.

393, 67. *Pan:* a god of the country, representative of the animal in man. The flute was his musical instrument and he was often represented playing it.

393, 78–80. The Greek gods were often represented as loving boys as well as women.

393, 135. *Tiresias:* a blind and famous prophet of advanced age.

393, 138. *Asopus:* a river in Boeotia, the country of Tiresias.

393, 142. *Thebes:* the capital city of Boeotia.

393, 143. *Centaurs:* creatures, half man and half horse.

393, 145. *Pelion:* a mountain in Thessaly where the centaurs dwelt.

394, 162. *Scythian:* an inhabitant of the region to the northeast of Greece. The term was often used to apply to the barbarous people to the east and north in general.

394, 163–200. Much of the material for this passage comes from the work of Alexander Burnes referred to in the notes on "Sohrab and Rustum."

394, 183. *Chorasmian stream:* the river Oxus which flows through the region then known as Chorasmia to the south of the Sea of Aral.

394, 206. *The Happy Islands:* the islands of the blest, on which heroes live after death. They were often supposed to lie in the Atlantic beyond the Straits of Gibraltar.

394, 220–222. Tiresias, bidden decide a dispute between Zeus and Hera (Juno) his wife, decided in favor of Zeus. Hera struck him blind: Zeus to compensate him for this calamity, gave him the gift of prophecy and lengthened his life.

394, 228. *Lapithae:* a warlike people at enmity with the Centaurs.

Theseus: a hero who aided the Lapithae in the conflict.

394, 231. *Alcmena's dreadful son:* Hercules, who also engaged in conflict with the Centaurs.

395, 259. *Argo:* the ship of the Argonauts who sailed to Crete for the golden fleece.

395, 260. After their gaining of the fleece, the Argonauts made their way by water around Europe, going northeast from the Black Sea and entering the Mediterranean by the Straits of Gibraltar.

395, 261. *Silenus:* a satyr.

395, 275. *Maenad:* a worshipper of Bacchus, wild from the drink and the dancing which accompanied his worship.

395. TO A FRIEND

This poem first appeared in the collection of 1849, *The Strayed Reveller, and Other Poems.* It is conjectured the friend was A. H. Clough.

395, 2. *the old man:* Homer.

395, 3. *The Wide Prospect:* Arnold explains the phrase saying "the name Europe (Εὐρώπη, *the wide prospect*) probably describes the appearance of the European coast to the Greeks on the coast of Asia Minor opposite."

the Asian Fen: Arnold comments: "the name Asia, again, comes, it has been thought, from the muddy fens of the rivers of Asia Minor, such as the Cayster or Maeander, which struck the imagination of the Greeks living near them."

395, 4. *Tmolus' hill:* a range near Smyrna.

Smyrna: a coastal city of Asia Minor, one of the seven cities laying claim to being the birthplace of Homer.

395, 6. *That halting slave:* Epictetus, who was lame.

Nicopolis: the city to which Epictetus withdrew when the philosophers were banished from Rome.

395, 7. *Arrian:* a disciple of Epictetus, who compiled a collection of his master's discourses.

Vespasian's brutal son: the emperor Domitian.

395, 8. *what most shamed him:* Philosophy.

395, 9 f. The rest of the sonnet celebrates Sophocles.

395, 10. *extreme old age:* at ninety he wrote one of his greatest plays, *Oedipus at Colonus.*

395, 12. This is the first use of the phrase which was to recur so often in Arnold's prose.

395, 14. *Colonus:* here, near Athens, Sophocles was born.

396. SHAKESPEARE

This poem first appeared in the collection of 1849, *The Strayed Reveller, and Other Poems.* The estimate of Shakespeare is much higher than Arnold ever pronounced in prose. For his critical opinion when fully considered, see the *Preface* to the *Poems* of 1853. See Tinker and Lowry: *The Poetry of Matthew Arnold*, 25–26 for Arnold's comments on the poem.

396, 1. *abide:* are subject to.

question: inquiry.

free: superior to our powers of inquiry.

396, 8. *mortality:* humanity.

396. THE FORSAKEN MERMAN

This poem first appeared in the collection of 1849, *The Strayed Reveller, and Other Poems.* Probable sources for it have been indicated by Professor C. B. Tinker and Professor H. F. Lowry (*The Poetry of Matthew Arnold*, 129 f.): Hans Andersen's account of an old Danish folk song of Agnete and the Merman (in *The True Story of My Life*, translated into English in 1847), a review by George Borrow (1825) and Borrow's ballad of The Deceived Merman in *Romantic Ballads translated from the Danish* (1826). There is no certainty that Arnold found his material or his stimulus in any of these sources; he may have known another version of the merman's tragedy not known to his commentators.

396, 6. *wild white horses:* white capped waves.

397, 81. *sealed to:* fixed on.

398, 91. *the bell:* the bell is rung at the consecration of the bread and of the wine, the central ceremonies in the Mass.

the holy well: the fount in the church where holy water is kept.

399. MEMORIAL VERSES

This poem first appeared in *Fraser's Magazine* in June, 1850; and was reprinted, with many revisions in the collection of 1852, *Empedocles on Etna and Other Poems.* Wordsworth's death, on April 23, 1850, was the occasion of the poem. It should be remembered that Wordsworth lived near the country home of the Arnolds; had been a friend of the family and especially of Thomas Arnold, the poet's father; and had shown much kindness to Matthew Arnold.

399, 1–2. Goethe died in 1832 and was buried in the town of Weimar (in western Germany) where he had lived most of his life; Byron died at Missolonghi in Greece in 1824.

399, 5. The original, and more moving version of this line was:

We stand to-day at Wordsworth's tomb.

399, 17. *Physician of the iron age:* Arnold thought that of modern men Goethe best understood the nature of the circumstances among which he lived and the weaknesses of which these circumstances were symptomatic: hence he styles him *physician. Iron age* is Arnold's term for the post-revolutionary period, the adjective suggesting the violence and coarseness of the time, and also (as compared with golden or silver) its inferiority to the great ages in the world's history.

399, 23. *Europe's dying hour:* Arnold considered that the old order had passed away with the Revolution in France and the rise of Napoleon; and that no new order had arisen by 1850 to replace it.

399, 24. *fitful dream:* the fantasies of the revolutionary idealists.

feverish power: the greed of unlimited power in other members of the revolutionary party.

399, 29–33. Arnold is here translating almost word for word a passage from Virgil's Georgics II, 490 f. The Virgilian passage begins: *Felix qui potuit rerum cognoscere causas.* Arnold expected his translation to be recognized as such.

399, 38. *Orpheus:* In Greek mythology he was, in return for the beauty of his playing and singing his poems, accorded the privilege of redeeming his wife Eurydice from the underworld, on condition that he did not look back to discover whether she was following him on the way up to the surface of the earth.

399, 47. In the first version three lines now suppressed, followed l. 47:

He tore us from the prison-cell
Of festering thoughts and personal fears,
Where we had long been doom'd to dwell.

It may be that Arnold considered that it was illegitimate to commend Wordsworth as an escape from subjectivism.

399, 48–49. Arnold asserts that Wordsworth restored those who read him sympathetically to a natural relation to the external world, and that this natural relation is also a happy one.

399, 72. *Rotha:* Wordsworth was buried in Grasmere churchyard, close to the river Rotha.

400. CADMUS AND HARMONIA

This poem (without its present title) was originally a song of Callicles in the philosophic drama, *Empedocles on Etna* (1852). Arnold resolved against reprinting that drama; but rescued from it a number of songs. In the collections of 1853, 1854 and 1857 this poem appeared as an independent work. In 1867 when *Empedocles on Etna* was reprinted, this song was restored to its original place. However in Arnold's own selection from his poems in the Golden Treasury Series (1878) he reprinted "Cadmus and Harmonia" as an independent work.

Cadmus was ruler of Thebes, Harmonia his wife.

400, 1. *here:* in Sicily.

400, 5. *brakes:* thickets.

400, 14. *where the Sphinx lived:* near the city of Thebes.

400, 24. Zeus gave Harmonia to Cadmus.

400. APOLLO

This poem (without a title) was originally a song of Callicles in the philosophic drama *Empedocles on Etna* (1852). In 1855, the drama having been suppressed from all the collections between 1852 and 1867, Arnold rescued a group of songs under the general title *The Harp-Player on Etna:* this, which had been the concluding song of the play, was the last of the group. Arnold reprinted *Empedocles on Etna* in 1867 and restored this song to its original—and important—function in the play; but in his selection from his own poems (1878) he reprinted it as an independent work under its present title.

400, 1–4. Empedocles has leapt into the crater of Etna; Callicles who is on the mountain side, well below the rim of the crater, sings.

400, 5. *Apollo:* here primarily the god of inspiration and beauty.

400, 7. *Helicon:* the mount of the Muses.

400, 9. *inlets:* of the Gulf of Corinth.

400, 11. *Thisbe:* a village in the valley below Helicon.

400, 30. *the Nine:* the Muses.

400, 39. *Olympus:* the mountain of the gods.

400, 47. *rest:* repose, not remainder.

401, 50. *palm:* reward.

401. TO MARGUERITE — *Continued*

This poem first appeared in the collection of 1852, *Empedocles on Etna and Other Poems*, under the title, To "Marguerite, in returning a volume of the Letters of Ortis." [The *Ultime Lettere di Jacopo Ortis*, by Ugo Foscolo, appeared in 1802: it was the Italian equivalent of Goethe's *Werther*, dealing with unfortunate lovers, but also with the patriotic aspirations of the nation, and ending in the suicide of Ortis.] Critics were very slow in accepting the reality of the Marguerite to whom this and many other of Arnold's lyrics were addressed; but a phrase in one of the letters to Clough (*Letters of M. A. to A. H. Clough*, ed. Lowry, 91) has set the reality of the girl beyond doubt. It remains, however, quite uncertain, how much of Arnold's representation of her and of his feelings for her is factual and how much imaginative. She was living in Switzerland in the 1840's, but she may well have been French.

401, 1. *enisled:* islanded, isolated.

401, 6. *endless:* eternal.

401. TRISTRAM AND ISEULT

This poem first appeared in the collection of 1852, *Empedocles on Etna and Other Poems.* It was written mainly on the continent and before the end of 1849 (see Tinker and Lowry, *The Poetry of Matthew Arnold*, 106 f.). Reprinted in the *Poems* of 1853, it was prefaced by the following passages from Dunlop's *History of Fiction*, introduced at the suggestion of J. A. Froude, who thought the poem would be more effective if the situation was given a preliminary explanation:

In the court of his uncle King Marc, the King of Cornwall who at this time resided at the castle of Tyntagel, Tristram became expert in all knightly exercises.—The king of Ireland, at Tristram's solicitations, promised to bestow his daughter Iseult in marriage on King Marc. The mother of Iseult gave to her daughter's confidante a philtre, or love-potion, to be administered on the night of her nuptials. Of this beverage Tristram and Iseult, on their voyage to Cornwall, unfortunately partook. Its influence, during the remainder of their lives, regulated the affections and destiny of the lovers.

After the arrival of Tristram and Iseult in Cornwall, and the nuptials of the latter with King Marc, a great part of the romance is occupied with their contrivances to procure secret interviews.—Tristram, being forced to leave Cornwall, on account of the displeasure of his uncle, repaired to Brittany, where lived Iseult with the White Hands.—He married her—more out of gratitude than love.—Afterwards he proceeded to the dominions of Arthur, which became the theatre of unnumbered exploits.

Tristram, subsequent to these events, returned to Brittany, and to his long-neglected wife. There, being wounded and sick, he was soon reduced to the lowest ebb. In this situation, he dispatched a confidant to the queen of Cornwall, to try if he could induce her to follow him to Brittany.

Arnold stated the sources of the poem in letters to Clough and Hill: they were articles in the *Revue de Paris* (1841) by Hersart de Villemarqué. The first of a series dealt with *les poèmes gallois et les romans de la Table-Ronde* (the Welsh poems and the tales of the Round Table).

In this article the legend of Tristram and Iseult is described as follows: In Tristram's earliest days as a knight, in Cornwall, at the court of his uncle King Marc, an Irish knight named Morhoult presents himself and demands a tribute to which he is not entitled. Tristram engages him and kills him; but having suffered a thigh-wound from a poisoned arrow, and not finding in Cornwall any physician clever enough to cure his wound, he disguises himself as a harp-player and goes to Ireland. There he sees the beautiful Iseult and describes her in such terms that his uncle the king wishes to marry her. On the mission of asking her hand on his uncle's behalf, Tristram, disguised as a merchant, leaves for Ireland and is returning to Cornwall with Iseult, now betrothed to Marc, when, without knowing what he is doing, he drinks—and then Iseult drinks also—from a cup containing a magic potion destined for Marc and confided to Branien, Iseult's servant. Tristram and Iseult at once feel love flowing through their veins. A few days after the marriage of Marc with Iseult, the seneschal and after him the court dwarf perceive the guilty liaison between Tristram and Iseult, inform the king of it and provide him with an opportunity of surprising them. Tristram, however, outwits their stratagems. Finally the two lovers are seized and are being brought to punishment when Tristram finds a method of escape and returning delivers the queen.

Three years pass, at the end of which, the king and his wife having been reconciled by a good hermit, the lover is ordered never again to present himself at the court. He reappears however: disguised as a jester, he is able to dupe every one and to renew his relations with Iseult. Three barons are however suspicious and communicate their suspicions to the king. The queen to bring about their undoing places herself under the protection of King Arthur and the knights of the Round Table, and proposes to her husband that she establish her innocence by a solemn oath. On the day fixed for this, as the retinue of Marc and Arthur proceed to the place designated for the oath, Tristram, disguised as a beggar, offers, at a ford, to carry the queen across. She accepts his offer; and on a sign from her her lover lets her fall. She is now able without perjury to make an oath that she has never been familiar with anyone but her husband and the clumsy beggar who has just let her fall to the ground. The queen having thus freed herself from the charge against her, every one devotes himself to gaiety: jousts are held. Tristram takes part in them disguised anew, and defeats one after another all the knights of the Round Table; Arthur amazed by his brilliance in combat, offers a great prize to any one who will bring to him this knight; but Tristram prudently avoids another combat and goes away. Although Iseult's innocence is recognized, her lover is not called back to the court of Marc; he withdraws to Brittany and decides to marry the daughter of Houel, king of the country, who also has the name Iseult. However, his attempt to forget his first love is vain; it is vain for him to engage in the most dangerous exploits; in them he finds no distraction, but instead a mortal wound. The wife of King Marc and she alone can cure him: he sends for her. But the daughter of the king of Brittany who has discovered her husband's love for Iseult of Cornwall, makes him believe that the queen refuses to do as he has asked, and Tristram dies of grief.

From Malory's *Morte d'Arthur* Arnold claimed to have drawn the material for the story of Merlin's fate in Part III (see his letter to Clough, May, 1853, in Lowry: *Letters of M. A. to Arthur Hugh Clough*). It is more likely that he resorted to Villemarqué's article *Visite au tombeau de Merlin* (a visit to the tomb of Merlin) in the *Revue de Paris* (1837).

Arnold's treatment of the characters should be compared with that in Tennyson's *The Last Tournament.*

401. I. TRISTRAM

The spelling, which was that in Villemarqué, was abandoned in 1857 for Tristan but was subsequently restored.

401, 16–17. The traditionally distinctive marks of Tristram, apart from his passion and traits which are related to it, are hunting and playing on the harp.

402, 20. After his love-affair with Iseult of Ireland he became a knight of the order of the Round Table.

402, 51. *Her snow-white hands:* Iseult of Brittany was also known as Iseult of the White Hands.

402, 61. *Tyntagel:* here on the coast of Cornwall, King Mark had his castle.

402, 64. *that spiced magic draught:* this, intended to assure lifelong love when drunk by Iseult and her affianced husband, Mark, was in error drunk by Iseult and Tristram. See 138–139 and the general note on the poem.

404, 161. *pleasaunce:* pleasure-garden, a garden with arbor, fountain, etc.

406, 236. *the chivalry of Rome:* medieval traditions reported that the Round Table (with Tristram one of the knights) had ranged as far as Rome in their sequence of conquests. See 253–254.

406, 258. *leaguer:* siege.

407, 284. *her:* Iseult of Ireland's.

409. II. ISEULT OF IRELAND

411, 85. *thy name shall be of sorrow:* Tristram comes from *tristis*, meaning sad.

412, 131–146. These lines, introduced in 1869, had formed part of the lyric "Lines Written by a Deathbed."

412, 153 f. The import of the huntsman and of the entire scene on the tapestry is obscure. It is an acceptable suggestion that Tristram's delight in hunting is closely related to the poet's choice of a huntsman as the central figure in the tapestry; the figure may indeed be Tristram in his youth, before he was the victim of passion. The question asked by the huntsman in ll. 175–179 emphasizes an affinity between Tristram and himself. However there is contrast as well as likeness: the huntsman is still, and emphatically, outside the main cause of Tristram's tragedy—his passion.

412, 159. *iron-figured:* with designs in iron.

412, 175. *glamour:* magic.

413, 186. *brake:* thicket.

413. III. ISEULT OF BRITTANY

413, 22. *fell-fare:* fieldfare, a thrush.

413, 26. *stagshorn:* coral.

414, 41. *swart:* swarthy.

415, 92. *prie-dieu:* kneeling desk, for prayer.

415, 112–150. This section, which formed part of the poem in the first printed version, was dropped in the second and third editions and then restored in 1857. In tone and manner it is open to aesthetic objection, in that unlike the other passages which comment on the tale, it is at times archaic (note especially ll. 134, 143).

416, 134. *gulls:* deceives.

416, 139. *fume:* vapors, disease.

416, 143. *wight:* person.

416, 143–150. Julius Caesar is reported by the historian Suetonius to have wept when he learned of the extent of the conquests and victories of Alexander the Great, son of Philip of Macedon.

416, 149. *Soudan:* Sultan.

416, 158. *Merlin:* The sage and magician of Arthur.

416, 159. *fay:* fairy.

416, 165. *the one Iseult chose:* The most obvious explanation of her choice is that she saw in Merlin a type of Tristram and in Vivian a type of the other Iseult. Such an explanation may seem unsatisfactory since it was a potion that bewitched Tristram to his undoing and not an evil woman. But it may be that the mother wished her children to think of love (and later on, when they were older and could interpret the story, of their father) in these terms. Another explanation represents Tristram as the Vivian who cast the spell, and Iseult, the speaker as the one it bewitched. This does not seem to agree with her character, since it suggests at least a measure of bitterness, or at least of dissatisfaction. If her meaning was the second one, of course, she did not expect, or wish, that the children would at the time comprehend it.

416, 174. *scored:* scratched.

417, 216. *wimple:* a covering for the head.

417. A SUMMER NIGHT

This poem first appeared in the collection of 1852, *Empedocles on Etna and Other Poems.* A reference to this poem in *A Southern Night*, ll. 13–6, may indicate that the setting of ll. 11–25 is Cette; the first lines of the poem are probably about London.

418, 11 f. See the general note on the poem.

418, 14–21. Compare the landscape with that described in *A Southern Night.*

418, 30. *whirls the spirit from itself away:* emancipates one from self-consciousness.

418, 58. The meaning is that there are fixed principles which the individual will cannot evade.

419, 69. *impossible:* which he cannot attain, although it may exist.

419, 83–85. The meaning is that he will not attribute a human feeling to the skies, finding, as he does, that it is more inspiriting to think of them as superior to man's weaknesses, instead of sympathetic with his hopes.

419, 91. *fair:* Arnold originally wrote *high* which expresses his meaning more clearly but is objectionable as seeming to carry on the picture of earth and skies *high* above it.

419. THE BURIED LIFE

This poem first appeared in the collection of 1852, *Empedocles on Etna and Other Poems*, following, as it does here, "A Summer Night," with which it is intimately related.

419, 1. *our:* More than one woman appears in Arnold's love poems; but it is probable that this reflective lyric, touched with love, is addressed to Marguerite.

419, 8. *anodyne:* palliative drug.

420, 23. *The same heart beats:* the original reading, which was superficially ambiguous, was *there beats one heart.*

421, 70. *at our call:* when we desire it.

421. STANZAS IN MEMORY OF THE AUTHOR OF "OBERMANN"

This poem first appeared in the collection of 1852, *Empedocles on Etna and Other Poems.* A note appended to l. 50 stated that the poem was composed in November, 1849. Arnold's subject was as little known to mid-Victorian readers as he is to readers of to-day; Arnold, appreciating that he was writing about an author with no English public, furnished in 1868 the following account of him in a footnote to "Obermann Once More," subsequently transferred to the notes on this poem.

The author of *Obermann*, Etienne Pivert de Senancour, has little celebrity in France, his own country; and out of France he is almost unknown. But the profound inwardness, the austere sincerity, of his principal work, *Obermann*, the delicate feeling for nature which it exhibits, and the melancholy eloquence of many passages of it, have attracted and charmed some of the most remarkable spirits of this century, such as George Sand and Sainte Beuve, and will probably always find a certain number of spirits whom they touch and interest.

Senancour was born in 1770. He was educated for the priesthood, and passed some time in the seminary of St. Sulpice [at Paris]; broke away from the Seminary and from France itself, and passed some years in Switzerland, where he married; returned to France in middle life [*Obermann* had appeared in 1804]; and followed thenceforward the career of a man of letters, but with hardly any fame or success. He died an old man in 1846, desiring that on his grave might be placed these words only: *Eternité, deviens mon asile!* [Eternity, be my refuge!].

The influence of Rousseau, and certain affinities with more famous and fortunate authors of his own day,—Chateaubriand and Madame de Staël,— are everywhere visible in Senancour. But though, like these eminent personages, he may be called a sentimental writer, and though *Obermann*, a collection of letters from Switzerland treating almost entirely of nature and of the human soul, may be called a work of sentiment, Senancour has a gravity and severity which distinguish him from all other writers of the sentimental school. The world is with him in his solitude far less than it is with them; of all writers he is the most perfectly isolated and the least attitudinising. His chief work, too, has a value and power of its own, apart from these merits of its author. The stir of all the main forces, by which modern life is and has been impelled, lives in the letters of *Obermann;* the dissolving agencies of the eighteenth century, the fiery storm of the French Revolution, the first faint promise and dawn of that new world which our own time is but now more fully bringing to light,—all these are to be felt, almost to be touched there. To me, indeed, it will always seem that the impressiveness of this production can hardly be rated too high.

Besides *Obermann* there is one other of Senancour's works which, for those spirits who feel his attraction, is very interesting; its title is *Libres Meditations d'un Solitaire Inconnu.*

In an article which appeared in *The Academy* for October 9, 1869, and which is reprinted in the Oxford edition of Arnold's *Essays*, Arnold amplified what he here says and illustrates copiously from Senancour's writings. In the concluding poem of Arnold's last collection (1867) he returned to Obermann under the title "Obermann Once More."

In a note to l. 5 Arnold tells that "the poem was conceived, and partly composed, in the valley going down from the foot of the Gemmi Pass towards the Rhone.

421, 3. *rack:* driven clouds.

421, 5. *baths:* the Baths of Leuk.

422, 50. Wordsworth was in the last year of his life when Arnold wrote.

422, 53–54. Wordsworth, although deeply convinced of the corruptive power of society over man, presents man almost exclusively as strengthened and purified by an intimate relationship with nature.

422, 66. *stormiest time:* the period of the Revolution and the Napoleonic wars, which deeply affected life in the duchy of Weimar (where Goethe was living), two of the great battles of the wars being fought not far from the capital city.

422, 67–68. Goethe was forty years old when the Revolution broke out.

422, 89. *the Son of Thetis:* Achilles.

422, 91. Achilles said to a prisoner who begged for his life that his friend Patroclus, "a better man than thou art" was dead (*Iliad*, Bk. XXI).

422, 94. *the poet's:* Arnold is speaking of himself although he uses the general term.

423, 114. *Jaman:* an Alpine peak.

423, 128. *Away:* Arnold means not simply that he is departing from the place and from Switzerland, but that he is about to abandon Obermann's mode of being for living actively in the world.

423, 143. The regenerate, that is those who have attained to a spiritual mode of being while yet in this life.

423, 150. *anchorite:* hermit.

423, 160. *Farewell:* it should be remembered that Senancour was only three years dead at the time Arnold conceived the poem.

423, 162. The reference is to Lake Geneva.

423, 164. *Vevey:* a town on Lake Geneva.

Meillerie: another town on the same lake.

423, 177. *granite terraces:* The Seine's banks as it flows through Paris, are lined with heavy stone walls.

423, 179. *the Capital of Pleasure:* Paris.

423. CONSOLATION

This poem first appeared in the collection of 1852, *Empedocles on Etna and Other Poems.* Arnold appended a note to l. 21, stating that it was "written during the siege of Rome by the French"; however some details of the pictures were added later (see Tinker and Lowry: *The Poetry of Matthew Arnold,* 62–63).

On its second and third appearances a motto was printed below the title:

The wide earth is still
Wider than one man's passion: there's no mood,
No meditation, no delight, no sorrow,
Cas'd in one man's dimensions, can distil
Such pregnant and infectious quality,
Six yards round shall not ring it.

423, 2–3. The impression he is seeking to give is that of a vague and undefined city landscape.
424, 14. *holy Lassa:* Lassa (or Lhassa) in Tibet is the seat of a celebrated temple.
424, 18–19. The gallery is that of the Vatican.
424, 21–22. See the general note on this poem.
424, 23. *Helicon:* the mount of the Muses, in Greece.

424. LINES WRITTEN IN KENSINGTON GARDENS

This poem first appeared in the collection of 1852, *Empedocles on Etna and Other Poems.* In *The Poetry of Matthew Arnold,* 196–197, Professors Tinker and Lowry have printed a first pencil draft (undated) which should be compared with the present version. Subsequent to its first publication this poem underwent notable revision, especially for its republication in 1867.

The Gardens are a park in London.

424, 17–20. Fishing was Arnold's favorite recreation.
425, 24. The reference is not to the poet's having been born in the country, but to his abiding devotion to it. Pan was in Greek myth a nature-god.

425. THE FUTURE

This poem first appeared in the collection of 1852, *Empedocles on Etna and Other Poems.* The form—unrhymed lines of uneven length—probably is modelled on some of the lyrics of Goethe.

On its second and third appearances this poem bore the prefatory motto, later suppressed:

For Nature has long kept this inn, the Earth,
And many a guest hath she therein received—

425, 36. *Rebekah:* She was found by the well of her town by the servant whom Abraham sent, under the guidance of an angel, to find a wife for his eldest son, Isaac (*Genesis,* Ch. XXIV).
425, 45. *Moses:* the Biblical account has been enriched by the poetical imagination; but the reference is to the incident recounted in *Exodus,* Ch. III, when God appeared to Moses, who was in the desert, in the guise of a burning bush.
425, 57. *shot:* variegated.
426, 87. *the infinite sea:* In interpreting this phrase and the poem as whole, it should be remembered that Arnold is presenting symbolically both the movement of the individual life from its first moment of separation from a greater whole to the last moment of its absorption into another (or the same) greater whole, and also the movement of human life as a historical development from the earliest times to the end of humanity's course. The infinite Sea, accordingly, signifies the world-soul, or sum of spiritual values, and also the final phase of human development.

426. MORALITY

This poem first appeared in the collection of 1852, *Empedocles on Etna and Other Poems.*
426, 23. *that strife divine:* the moral struggle is pronounced supernatural or at least supranatural by nature.
426, 31–32. *Time* and *Space* are presented as peculiar to physical being and absent from a purely spiritual being.
427, 35–36. Nature is presented as having emanated from Spirit.

427. SOHRAB AND RUSTUM

This poem first appeared in the *Poems* of 1853, having been composed early in that year. Arnold appended as a note a long paragraph from Sir John Malcolm's *History of Persia*, which was at first supposed to be the source of the poem. Two other sources were more important. The Persian poet Firdausi, in his long epic on Persian history, the *Sháh-Náma*, had sung the glories of Rustum, and narrated at length the encounter between Rustum and Sohrab; the *Sháh-Náma* had been translated into French by Mohl and the translation had led Sainte-Beuve to write an article on Firdausi. This article Arnold read and he states that it was the main source of his material. Much of the rich Oriental colouring comes from a narrative of travel in the East, Alexander Burnes's *Travels into Bokhara*.

Arnold often referred to "Sohrab and Rustum" in the letters he wrote during the time he was at work on it. In a letter of May, 1853 (*Letters*, ed. Russell, Vol. I, 301) he says to his mother: "All my spare time has been spent on a poem which I have just finished, and which I think by far the best thing I have yet done, and that it will be generally liked . . . I have had the greatest pleasure in composing it—a rare thing with me. . . . The story is a very noble and excellent one." To Clough, in a letter of the same month he speaks in much the same terms (*Letters of M. A. to A. H. Clough*, ed. Lowry, 136). Later, in August of the same year, he tells Clough that he has written out the poem and is less pleased with it. Finally in a letter of November 1853, after the poem has been published, he writes to Clough to say why he prefers "Sohrab and Rustum" to "The Scholar Gipsy," which Clough admired more than "Sohrab and Rustum." Arnold says that the great virtue of "Sohrab and Rustum" (a virtue which it shares with Homer and Shakespeare, although it has infinitely less than they have) is its power to *animate* (*Letters of M. A. to A. H. Clough* 146).

It was for the collection of 1853, in which "Sohrab and Rustum" was the most important piece, that Arnold wrote the famous preface which, starting with a justification of his refusal to reprint *Empedocles on Etna*, broadened out to state most of Arnold's controling ideas about poetry. (It did not come within the scope of his subject to deal with the nature and merit of lyrical poetry except incidentally.) In this preface he does not refer to "Sohrab and Rustum" by name; but there is no doubt that he is quietly asking his reader to compare it with the piece he had rejected.

The reason for suppressing *Empedocles on Etna* is given in these sentences: "Any accurate representation may therefore be expected to be interesting; but if the representation be a poetical one, more than this is demanded. It is demanded not only that it shall interest, but also that it shall inspirit and rejoice the reader; that it shall convey a charm and infuse delight . . . it is not enough that the poet should add to the knowledge of men, it is required of him also that he should add to their happiness. . . . In presence of the most tragic circumstances, represented in a work of art, the feeling of enjoyment, as is well known, may still subsist; the representation of the most utter calamity, of the liveliest anguish is not sufficient to destroy it; the more tragic the situation, the deeper becomes the enjoyment; and the situation is more tragic in proportion as it becomes more terrible. . . . What then are the situations, from the representations of which, though accurate, no poetical enjoyment can be derived? They are those in which the suffering finds no vent in action; in which a continuous state of mental distress is prolonged, unrelieved by incident, hope, or resistance; in which there is everything to be endured, nothing to be done. In such situations there is inevitably something morbid, in the description of them something monotonous. When they occur in actual life, they are painful, not tragic; the representation of them in poetry is painful also. To this class of situations poetically faulty, as it appears to me, that of Empedocles, as I have endeavoured to represent him, belongs; and I have therefore excluded the poem from the present collection.

The above passage—and indeed the entire preface—must be studied carefully in order to appreciate the central importance of "Sohrab and Rustum" in Arnold's poetry.

In brief one may say that the standards of poetry which Arnold affirms in the preface are these: I. The subject is all important, and no charm or power of treatment can compensate for a weak or inferior subject. II. The subject must appeal to the fundamental emotions of humanity, or to one of these emotions. III. The subject must not only be truly representative of human nature, it must issue in an action which moves and inspirits the reader. IV. The style and treatment must be rigorously subordinated to the subject. In "Sohrab and Rustum" the first three requisites are met; critics are in disagreement as to the fourth, many finding the abundance of long and complex similes distract the attention from the evolution of the action.

Stung by his friend J. D. Coleridge's charge (in a review in *The Christian Remembrancer*, April, 1854) that he had plagiarized, he appended to the edition of 1854 a long justificatory note, which was later suppressed but may be read in the Oxford edition of his poems (pp. 446–450).

427, 2. *Oxus stream:* The long river Oxus flows from the southeast, beginning not far from the border of what is now India, to empty in the Aral Sea.

427, 5. *Sohrab:* in Firdausi, and in Sainte Beuve, at the time of the episode Sohrab is not more than fourteen years of age; he has behind him, none the less, four years during which no one has dared to encounter him in single combat; his ambition is boundless and he has already schemed to make himself master of Tartary; despite his youth he is stately and leonine in appearance and demeanor.

427, 11. *Peran-Wisa:* the general in command of the Tartar forces.

427, 34. *Afrasiab:* King of the Tartars. Firdausi, followed by Sainte Beuve, represents Afrasiab as a designing monarch, who has sought to bring about a mortal conflict between Sohrab and Rustum. Afrasiab considered that if Sohrab could slay Rustum the whole Persian domain would be added to Afrasiab's territories and he could then despatch Sohrab "some night by binding him in endless sleep." If Rustum were to slay Sohrab, it would prey on Rustum's heart forever after and he would cease to be a threat; and, Sohrab once slain, Afrasiab would be more secure of his throne. Arnold completely excludes the plot which bulks so large in Firdausi, preferring to have the conflict between father and son appear the doing of fate.

428, 71–73. These lines were added after the first publication.

429, 101. *Kara-Kul:* lynx (literally 'black-ear').

429, 115. *frore:* frozen.

430, 160–168. All the details in this simile are taken from Burnes's account of his travels. See the general note on the poem.

430, 196. *Rustum:* Firdausi's account of Rustum emphasizes his hugeness, his indifference to the pleasures of love and revel, his fierce rages, boastfulness, and brutal simplicity.

431, 230. *girl:* in Firdausi the deceit practised upon Rustum was as to the age of the child not as to its sex.

432, 301. In Firdausi the encounter between Sohrab and Rustum extends over three separate days. At the first meeting in Firdausi's account Sohrab begins by insulting his opponent with gibes at his age. Rustum however takes no immediate offence and pleads with Sohrab not to fight with him, and so condemn himself to death.

434, 398. In Firdausi the duel begins with javelins, is continued with scimitars and then with maces and with bows and arrows. They had up to this time been on horse; thereupon they descend and wrestle. The first day ends. Rustum at night begins to doubt whether he will vanquish. On the second day, their horses left behind, they wrestle: Sohrab having felled Rustum, sits upon him and makes ready to cut off his head, when Rustum appeals to a mythical rule that a man must be felled twice before he is killed. Sohrab defers to this law. Overnight Rustum prays for a return of the strength of his prime. At the beginning of the third day, his strength restored, Rustum wounds Sohrab in the breast: this is the death wound. It is profitable to compare Firdausi's handling with Arnold's in some detail.

441, 772. In Firdausi it is Gudurz not Sohrab who begs Rustum not to take his own life. In Firdausi also Rustum seeks an elixir from the shah which will restore Sohrab's strength; but the shah, fearing the combined might of Sohrab and Rustum, refuses.

443. PHILOMELA

This poem first appeared as one of the *Poems* of 1853. Professor Tinker and Professor Lowry, in their *Poetry of Matthew Arnold*, 164–165, reproduce an incomplete first draft of importance. The legend on which the poem is based has many variations; but there is a constant nucleus which may be summarised as follows: Tereus, King of Thrace, married an Athenian, Procne (or Progne); falling in love with her sister Philomela, he outraged her and then cut out her tongue so that his conduct should not be known to any one else. Philomela found means to inform Procne of the deed; and Procne killed her infant son and persuaded Tereus, unaware of what he did, to eat the body. In some versions it is Procne who is dumb, in others Philomela, who was in any case transformed into a nightingale. Arnold represents Procne as dumb.

444, 18. See the general note on the poem.

444, 21. *thy dumb sister:* Procne, as noted above.

444, 27. *Daulis:* in Thrace.

the Cephissian vale: this, the valley of the river Cephissus, is really at some distance from Daulis, being in Phocis and Boeotia.

444, 28. *Eugenia:* it is unknown whom Arnold is here addressing. The name is doubtless invented.

444. REQUIESCAT

This poem first appeared in the *Poems* of 1853. It is unknown whether this poem has a personal meaning. The title means: May she rest; and the phrase, in peace (*in pace*), is understood.

444, 2. *yew:* indicating grief. The yew is associated with grave-yards.

444, 13. *cabin'd:* confined (by its earthly limitations).

444. THE SCHOLAR GIPSY

This poem first appeared in the *Poems* of 1853. It was probably composed in that year. Arnold appended to it the passage from Joseph Glanvil's *Vanity of Dogmatizing* which is given below, and which supplied him with the point of departure.

"There was very lately a lad in the University of Oxford, who was by his poverty forced to leave his studies there; and at last to join himself to a company of vagabond gipsies. Among these extravagant people, by the insinuating subtilty of his carriage, he quickly got so much of their love and esteem as that they discovered to him their mystery. After he had been a pretty while well exercised in the trade, there chanced to ride by a couple of scholars, who had formerly been of his acquaintance. They quickly spied out their old friend among the gipsies; and he gave them an account of the necessity which drove him to that kind of life, and told them that the people he went with were not such impostors as they were taken for, but that they had a traditional kind of learning among them, and could do wonders by the power of imagination, their fancy binding that of others: that himself had learned much of their art, and when he had compassed the whole secret, he intended, he said, to leave their company, and give the world an account of what he had learned."—Glanvil's *Vanity of Dogmatizing*, 1661.

The setting is described in detail by Sir Francis Wylie in his paper "The Scholar-Gipsy Country" reproduced in the appendix to Tinker and Lowry: *The Poetry of Matthew Arnold.*

The poem owes much of its formal beauty to Arnold's familiarity with the idylls of Theocritus, one of which he was subsequently to translate (in the course of his essay on "Pagan and Medieval Religious Sentiment," *Essays in Criticism, First Series*) and to his delight in pastoral poetry in general from the Greeks, down through Spenser and Milton to Wordsworth. For an appreciation of the formal qualities of such poetry as "The Scholar Gipsy" see Arnold's own comments on "Thyrsis" in the general note on that poem.

444, 2. *wattled cotes:* folds made of interlaced twigs and branches.

444, 13. *cruse:* jar.

444, 18. *folded:* penned up.

445, 31. *Glanvil's book:* see the passage appended in the general note to the poem.

445, 34. Note that these high qualities are not attributed to the scholar by Glanvil.
parts: abilities.

445, 50. *heaven-sent:* originally Arnold had said merely *happy*, which does not emphasize the loftiness of the scholar's conception.

445, 55. *antique:* previously *unique.*

445, 57. *the Hurst:* Cumner Hurst, a height in the parish of Cumner referred to below in l. 69.

445, 59. *ingle-bench:* bench near the chimney.
boors: peasants.

446, 74. *stripling:* the Thames is still near its source and has not attained its later breadth.

446, 75. After *trailing*, from a boat (*punt*), is implied.

446, 78. *fostering:* caressing.

446, 83. At Fyfield, around an elm of unusual size villagers and country folk danced on the first of May as about a maypole.

446, 95. *lasher:* a pool in a stream below a weir or dam.

446, 98. *outlandish:* foreign (in this instance foreign as to time, not region).

446, 114. The reference is to the clothes of the gipsies.

446, 120. *the spark from heaven.* See l. 50.

447, 129. *Christ-Church hall:* the dining hall of one of the large Oxford colleges.

447, 141 f. From this point on the gipsy is purely symbolic.

447, 149. *the just-pausing Genius:* the world-soul or sum of the spiritual force in the universe, to which in some fashion Arnold suggests that the individual returns at the time of his corporeal death.

447, 155. *peers:* contemporaries.

447, 167. *term or scope:* end or range.

447, 172. *casual:* adopted not from deep conviction but by the accident of inheritance or proximity.

448, 182. *one:* it is impossible to identify beyond question the person referred to; commentators have generally suggested Carlyle or Tennyson; and in 1883 Arnold is said to have explained that he was referring to Goethe. The suggestion of Tennyson is untenable for Arnold had no high opinion of Tennyson's intellectual or spiritual abilities. Without excluding the possibility that he is referring to Carlyle, one may venture the suggestion that the only nineteenth century writer of whom he elsewhere speaks in such terms (and this he does often) is Goethe.

448, 190. *anodynes:* palliatives, as distinguished from curative drugs.

448, 207. *bowering:* sheltering.

448, 208–210. Dido, whom Aeneas had abandoned despite her passionate love for him, was seen by him when he passed through Hades (*Aeneid*, VI) but turned away from him in anger and contempt.

448, 211. *the unconquerable hope:* the hope that the spark from heaven would fall.

448, 220. *dingles:* dells.

449, 231–250. The relevance of the simile which composes the last two stanzas has been much criticized. An acceptable suggestion is that the Tyrian trader represents the gipsy scholar (in his gravity, dislike of frivolity and contentiousness, and old-fashioned ways), the Greeks represent the world, especially Oxford, which was the gipsy-scholar's world before he became a gipsy (in its gaiety, affluence and energy) and the Iberians represent the gipsies (shy and dusky folk living a retired life).

449, 232. *Tyrian:* Tyre, one of the principal cities of Phoenicia, on the coast of Asia Minor. Prior to the Greeks the Tyrians were the chief traders in the Mediterranean world.

449, 234. *creepers:* foliage, overhanging the sea.

449, 238. *Chian:* Chios was one of the "Aegean isles" (see l. 236) and was inhabited by Greeks.

449, 244. *Midland waters:* the Mediterranean.

449, 247. *western straits:* the straits of Gibraltar beyond which the Mediterranean navigators in ancient times seldom passed.

449, 249. *Iberians:* the inhabitants of Spain and Portugal.

449. STANZAS FROM THE GRANDE CHARTREUSE

This poem first appeared in *Fraser's Magazine*, in April, 1855; and was reprinted in the collection of 1867, *New Poems.* Arnold was a frequent visitor to the Alps; at the monastery of the Grande Chartreuse, a Carthusian foundation of the eleventh century, he had stayed briefly in 1851. The monastery is in the French Alps, a short distance from the city of Grenoble.

449, 2. *blows:* blossoms.

449, 4. *Saint Laurent;* a village a few miles from the monastery.

449, 10. *Dead Guier's Stream:* the Guiers Mort river.

449, 14. *scars:* crags.

449, 18. *Courrerie:* another mountain village.

449, 27. *this outbuilding:* where guests were normally housed.

450, 40. *bare:* uncowled.

450, 42. *the Host:* the consecrated Bread, believed by Roman Catholics to be the Body of Christ. Arnold errs: it was the *Pax* (a crucifix) not the Host which was passed.

450, 51. The meaning is to recount the glorious episodes in the history of the Roman Catholic Church.

450, 54. *their drops of blood:* their spiritual agonies.

their death in life: probably the meaning is that these souls have purged themselves of all earthly concern. Possibly there is the deeper sense that the souls have reached a state in the mystic way in which aridity overtakes them: this state precedes, in mystics' accounts of their development, the final happiness.

450, 67. *Rigorous teachers:* there is no single person or definite group intended. Arnold is simply saying that his education was essentially a cultivation not of faith but of reason.

450, 68. *purged:* purified, of what a rationally minded person would regard as superstitious.

450, 69. *Truth:* as conceived by reason, not faith.

450, 77. *anchorites:* hermits.

ruth: fellow-feeling, perhaps, but the precise sense is not entirely clear.

450, 83. *Runic stone:* a tablet bearing lettering of an early Germanic kind.

450, 84. The early Germanic represents the Roman Catholic faith as held by the Carthusians, the Greek represents the type of belief which Arnold was subsequently to describe as "culture." The nineteenth century is the enemy of both Roman Catholicism and culture.

450, 85. *Two worlds:* one is pre-revolutionary Europe, the other the new order which will replace the pre-revolutionary, but which has not yet begun to shape itself clearly.

450, 99. *sciolists:* persons with but a smattering of knowledge.

450, 113. *engrave:* line.

450, 115. *Achilles:* the pre-eminent fighter among the Greeks of the Iliad; angered by a slight put upon him by Agamemnon, commander-in-chief of the Greek expedition to Troy, he remained within his tent and for a time refused to take part in battle.

450, 116. *the kings of modern thought are dumb:* the master thinkers of the nineteenth century have no solution to propose other than (as indicated in the following lines) to await the slow shaping of a new order.

450, 121. *our fathers:* the men of the revolutionary and romantic era.
their tears: melancholy was an outstanding feature of romantic literature and music.

451, 123–124. The revolutionaries and romantics abounded in power and energy.

451, 133 f. In this stanza Arnold is thinking especially of Byron's poem, in four long cantos, *Childe Harold's Pilgrimage*, in which the poet recounts European travels (in the first two cantos under a thin disguise, in the last two avowedly his own) which are infused with self-pity and despair.

451, 135. *Aetolian:* Aetolia is the ancient name for the region of Greece in which Missolonghi (where Byron died) is situated.

451, 139 f. In this stanza Arnold is thinking specially of the lyrics which Shelley wrote in his last years when he was an exile on the shore of the Bay of Spezzia in Italy. He was drowned in that bay.

451, 145 f. For Obermann, see the note on Arnold's poem "Stanzas in Memory of the Author of 'Obermann.'"

451, 149. *Fontainebleau:* in this town near Paris Obermann died.

451, 169 f. With this stanza and with the last section as a whole Professor Tinker and Professor Lowry compare a passage from Chateaubriand's *Le génie du Christianisme,* of which the following sentence forms part: "*Tout le monde a vu en Europe de vieilles abbayes cacheés dans les bois ou elles ne se décèlent aux voyageurs que par leurs clochers perdus dans la cîme des chênes.*" Arnold was reading Chateaubriand just before he visited the abbey.

451, 203–204. It should be noted that Arnold has here forgotten the specific character of the Carthusian order (although he had referred directly to their not permitting the playing of an organ, ll. 37–38) and is now thinking of Roman Catholic ceremonies as a whole.

452. A SOUTHERN NIGHT

This poem first appeared in *Victoria Regia*, in 1861, and was reprinted in the collection of 1867, *New Poems.* Arnold appended the note: "The Author's brother, William Delafield Arnold, Director of Public Instruction in the Punjab, and author of *Oakfield, or Fellowship in the East* [a striking treatment, in the form of a novel, of Indian problems], died at Gibraltar, on his way home from India, April the 9th, 1859." Arnold commemorated his brother and his wife (who had died before William set out on his return voyage, a man broken in health) also in the poem "Stanzas from Carnac." "Poor Fanny!" he exclaims in a letter written on receiving the news of his brother's death, "she at Dhurmsala and he by the Rock of Gibraltar" (*Letters*, ed. Russell, I, 80). He was in Paris at the time of his brother's death and travelling almost immediately to Brittany he there conceived the "Stanzas from Carnac" and probably wrote them out. Cette is a city on the French Riviera, which Arnold probably visited in 1859.

452, 1–12. These stanzas give a carefully accurate description of the site and view at Cette.

452, 13–16. A reminiscence of "A Summer Night," a poem from the collection of 1852.

452, 25–28. See the general note on this poem.

452, 43. *burnous:* an Arab garment for the upper part of the body, a fold of which can be raised to cover the head.

452, 51–52. See the general note on this poem.

452, 53–54. The Far East is, poetically, seen as the source of light.

453, 94. *Saint Louis:* Louis IX, King of France, died, in the course of a crusade in which he was the leading spirit, in 1270.

453, 97. *Troubadour:* a poet of medieval Provence, which bordered on the Mediterranean. The theme of Provençal poetry was love.

453. THYRSIS

This poem first appeared in *Macmillan's Magazine* for April 1866, five years after the death of the friend whom it commemorates, and was reprinted in the *New Poems* of 1867. The choice of an Oxford setting is easily explained. Shortly after the death of Clough Arnold wrote to the widow, saying that he was going to Oxford alone, and would, among the Cumner hills, be able to think of Clough uninterruptedly and in the way he would wish (See *Letters of M. A. to A. H. Clough, ed.* Lowry, 160) since among those hills they had so often rambled together. Further, Clough had greatly liked the "Scholar Gipsy"; and it is evident from "Thyrsis" that some of the symbols of the "Scholar Gipsy" had an esoteric meaning for the two friends. In Thyrsis, Arnold not only is setting his friend against the background, in which they had so often found themselves together; he is using the landscape of the "Scholar Gipsy" and its symbolic values. In form the poem is also intimately related to the

"Scholar Gipsy," using the same stanza, striking the same fusion of elegance and simplicity, and pointing back to Greek pastoral poetry. The debt to this latter body of poetry is made clear by Arnold in a letter to his mother in which he says: "The diction of the poem was modelled on that of Theocritus, whom I have been much reading during the two years the poem has been forming itself . . . I meant the diction to be so artless as to be almost heedless" (*Letters*, ed. Russell, II, 325). Arnold was apologetic for there not being "enough said about Clough in it" (*Letters*, II, 326). The setting of the poem is clearly described by Sir Francis Wylie in his paper "The Scholar Gipsy Country," reprinted in Tinker and Lowry: *The Poetry of Matthew Arnold.*

453. *Motto.* These lines are from a tragedy left incomplete partly because of the publication of Tennyson's dramatic monologue Lucretius. They were placed at the head of this poem when it was reprinted in 1867, and later removed; they are restored here not only because of their intrinsic beauty but because of the aid they give in the interpretation of this poem on its deeper levels of meaning.

453, 2: *the two Hinkseys:* two villages, North and South Hinksey.

453, 4. *Sibylla's name:* Sibella Kerr, who kept an inn in South Hinksey, had died in 1860.

453, 10. *Thyrsis:* throughout the poem Thyrsis represents Clough, Corydon (see l. 80) Arnold himself. These Greek names are commonly applied to shepherds in earlier pastoral poetry, in Virgil and in Milton for instance; there is no special fitness in calling Clough Thyris rather than any other pastoral name.

11. *Childsworth:* the modern Chiswell.

454, 15. *weirs:* dams.

youthful: still near its source.

454, 19. *dreaming spires:* Gothic towers and spires are the most prominent features of the Oxford landscape seen from a distance. The word dreaming is powerfully evocative, but is not susceptible of precise explanation.

454, 31. At the time of writing Arnold had not completed his second term as Professor of Poetry at Oxford; but the professor of poetry does not reside in Oxford, gives but three lectures a year; and moreover during Arnold's tenure of the chair he was still carrying his full burden of inspecting schools.

454, 35. *our shepherd pipes we first assayed:* the pastoral mode of saying that they began to try their powers in poetry. The statement is not strictly true: they had both composed poetry at Rugby before coming up to Oxford.

454, 36–37. Arnold wrote little poetry after 1857.

454, 40. Clough resigned his fellowship at Oriel College in protest against the requirement that fellows subscribe to the Thirty-Nine Articles of the Church of England.

454, 43. *keep:* stay.

454, 45. *silly:* in its older sense of innocent.

454, 46–50. Arnold interprets Clough's abandonment of Oxford and academic peace as the result of his acute consciousness of social injustice and oppression. The interpretation is only partially correct: Clough's temperament would not have permitted him lasting happiness at Oxford, in any event.

454, 48. *his piping took a troubled sound:* his poetry began to utter Clough's metaphysical and social doubts and fears.

454, 49. Clough in his poetry wrote much of the political upheavals and disturbances that came to a climax in the revolutions of 1848.

454, 51–70. These stanzas are reminiscences of Woodford, according to Arnold himself.

455, 79. Apart from the *Bothie of Tober-na-Vuolich*, Clough's verse failed to interest the general reading public.

455, 81–100. These stanzas are derived from the lament for the Sicilian Greek poet Bion by his friend the poet Moschus. They were contemporaries of Theocritus. G. C. Macaulay offers the following translation of the relevant part of the lament: "And I for this sorrow lament, shedding tears for thy fate: and if I might, even as Orpheus went down to Tartarus, as once Odysseus, as Alcides in former time, I too would have gone to the house of Pluto, that I might see thee, and if thou shouldest sing any song to Pluto, that I might hear what thou singest. Yet to Proserpine do thou play something, and sing some sweet pastoral strain: she too is Sicilian, and she played once in the valleys of Enna, and she knows the Dorian lay: not unrewarded shall be thy singing; and as to Orpheus once she gave back Eurydice for his sweet harping, so she shall send thee, Bion, back to the hills. And if I too had skill in piping, I myself would make music before Pluto."

455, 82. *shepherds:* the word continues the pastoral metaphor and is equivalent to poets.

455, 85. *unpermitted:* not permissible to living persons.

455, 86. *Pluto:* the ruler of the underworld.

455, 88. *Proserpine:* his queen.

455, 90. *Orpheus:* He was, in return for his music and song, allowed to bring back from the underworld his wife Eurydice provided he did not look back to see whether she was following him in the way up to the world of men.

455, 92. *Dorian:* the poetry of Theocritus and his contemporaries in Sicily was in the Doric, a Greek dialect.

455, 106. *the Fyfield tree:* the elm, referred to in "The Scholar Gipsy," l. 83. Many Oxford walkers claim that the tree was actually an oak.

456, 126. *shy:* the river at this point is not visible to one in the neighboring fields until one is almost on the bank. *Shy* is equivalent to unobtrusive.

456, 131 f. At the time when Arnold published this poem he was almost as old as his father at the time of his death. His grandfather had also died—and from the same cardiac trouble—in his early middle age. Arnold feared an early death for himself.

456, 135. *sprent:* sprinkled.

456, 153. *a troop of Oxford hunters:* a reference to "The Scholar Gipsy," l. 72.

456, 155. *Berkshire:* the county west of the Thames, Oxfordshire lying to the east.

457, 165. The statement has a symbolic meaning as well as a literal one: the writer's melancholy although lightened by the perception that the tree is still where it was, is still strong enough to prevent his attaining to confidence in a successful quest.

457, 167. *Arno-vale:* Clough died at Florence, which is in a valley through which the Arno flows, dividing the town.

457, 174. *lone sky-pointing tree:* there is a reference to the scholar gipsy implied: in that poem the gipsy is waiting for the spark from heaven to fall.

457, 175. *boon:* pleasant.

457, 177. *the great Mother:* Nature.

457, 180. *the Apennine:* a range of mountains east of Florence, (Italy).

457, 181. On this stanza Arnold appended a note: "Daphnis, the ideal Sicilian shepherd of Greek pastoral poetry, was said to have followed into Phrygia his mistress Piplea, who had been carried off by robbers, and to have found her in the power of the king of Phrygia, Lityerses. Lityerses used to make strangers try a contest with him in reaping corn, and to put them to death if he overcame them. Hercules arrived in time to save Daphnis, took upon him the reaping contest with Lityerses, overcame him, and slew him. The Lityerses-song, connected with this tradition, was, like the Linus-song, one of the early plaintive strains of Greek popular poetry, and used to be sung by corn-reapers. Other traditions represented Daphnis as beloved by a nymph, who exacted from him an oath to love no one else. He fell in love with a princess, and was struck blind by the jealous nymph. Mercury, who was his father, raised him to Heaven, and made a fountain spring up in the place from which he ascended. At this fountain the Sicilians offered yearly sacrifices."

457, 201 f. In this stanza Arnold is adumbrating in poetical terms the ideal he was subsequently to describe in critical prose as that of "culture."

458, 213. *Men gave thee nothing:* Clough found no post in keeping with his great abilities, and no adequate recognition of his poetic power.

458, 234. *the great town:* London.

458. DOVER BEACH

This poem, although written long before (See Tinker and Lowry, *The Poetry of Matthew Arnold*, 175 f.), first appeared in the collection of 1867, *New Poems*. The port of Dover on the English channel is so close to France that at night the lights projected from the French coast are visible. The shore is high and lined with white cliffs.

458, 3–5. See the general note on the poem.

458, 15–18. The reference is probably to one of the choruses in the *Antigone* which compares the threat of ruin to a house with the sound of an angry sea: "As the swelling wave, when driven by Thracian sea-blasts it rushes over the gloom which lies beneath the sea, rolls up the dark shingle from the depth, and the beach on which it breaks resounds with a stormy moan."

459. THE LAST WORD

This poem first appeared in the collection of 1867, *New Poems*.

459, 1. *thy narrow bed:* the grave.

459. RUGBY CHAPEL

This poem first appeared in the collection of 1867, *New Poems.* Despite the mention of November, 1857, in the subtitle, the poem cannot have been composed until the following year at the earliest. In 1858, reviewing *Tom Brown's School-days* for the *Edinburgh Review,* Fitzjames Stephen so dealt with Thomas Arnold that Matthew thought his father had been caricatured. In a letter to his mother written in August, 1867, Matthew Arnold says that it was Stephen's criticism which led to the composition of the poem, the aim of which was to give the character of Thomas Arnold as those truly intimate with him saw it. (See *Letters of M. A. to A. H. Clough,* 164.)

Thomas Arnold, born in 1795, educated in part at Winchester, went up to Oxford in 1811 and in 1815 was elected to a fellowship at Oriel College, Oxford. He married in 1820; Matthew, his eldest child was born in 1822; and in 1828, after some years of conducting a private school, he was appointed to the headmastership of Rugby College, which in a fourteen year tenure of the post he made the most effective educational institution in the country. In 1842, shortly after his election to the Regius Professorship of Modern History at Oxford, he died, with startling unexpectedness.

459, 2. *The Field:* the close of Rugby school.

459, 12–13. Thomas Arnold was buried under the communion table of the chapel.

459, 27–29. Thomas Arnold retired on June 11, 1842, in health; and was dead by eight o'clock the next morning.

461, 206. *stablish:* establish.

461. WESTMINSTER ABBEY

This poem appeared in the *Nineteenth Century* for January, 1882. *New Poems,* in 1867, was the last volume of Arnold's verse to appear: this poem and the half-dozen other poetical works of his last twenty years were obliged to await a collected edition (1885).

Arthur Penrhyn Stanley was a lifelong friend of Matthew Arnold. Born in 1815, he was educated at Rugby under Thomas Arnold, whose biography he wrote, and at Oxford. He was a liberal churchman (Canon of Canterbury, Professor of Ecclesiastical History at Oxford, and from 1863 to 1881, when he died, Dean of Westminster); the author of a study of the Old Testament which in 1863 Arnold singled out for the most enthusiastic praise (in his article for *Macmillan's Magazine,* February, 1863, entitled Dr. Stanley's Lectures on the Jewish Church); through his wife, Lady Augusta Bruce, sister of the Earl of Elgin, he had come into intimate association with the Queen and demonstrated his influence on the court.

461, 7. *child of light:* Arnold divided men into the groups of "children of light," barbarians, philistines, and populace. The children of light were those who possessed culture; no term of praise could be higher.

461, 11 f. To l. 4 Arnold appended the following passage from Dugdale's *Monasticon Anglicanum,* which is perhaps better given in connection with this stanza and the succeeding:

Aildred of Rievaulx, and several other writers, assert that Sebert, king of the East Saxons and nephew of Ethelbert, founded the Abbey of Westminster very early in the seventh century.

Sulcardus, who lived in the time of William the Conqueror, gives a minute account of the miracle supposed to have been worked at the consecration of the Abbey.

The church had been prepared against the next day for dedication. On the night preceding, St. Peter appeared on the opposite side of the water to a fisherman, desiring to be conveyed to the farther shore. Having left the boat, St. Peter ordered the fisherman to wait, promising him a reward on his return. An innumerable host from heaven accompanied the apostle, singing choral hymns, while everything was illuminated with a supernatural light. The dedication having been completed, St. Peter returned to the fisherman, quieted his alarm at what had passed, and announced himself as the apostle. He directed the fisherman to go as soon as it was day to the authorities, to state what he had seen and heard, and to inform them that, in corroboration of his testimony, they would find the marks of consecration on the walls of the church. In obedience to the apostle's direction, the fisherman waited on Mellitus, Bishop of London, who, going to the church, found not only marks of the chrism, but of the tapers with which the church had been illuminated. Mellitus therefore desisted from proceeding to a new consecration, and contented himself with the celebration of the mass.

Arnold refers to this tale as "a lovely legend," extremely well known up to the time of the Reformation, little known since, but familiar to Stanley (*Letters,* II, 195).

461, 15. *Thorney Isle:* the original church is believed to have been built upon this, an island in the Thames, no longer in existence.

461, 17. *Lambeth:* a district of London, on the south side of the Thames, where the bishop's palace is.

462, 49. *St. Peter's Church:* Peter was the patron saint of the Abbey.

462, 62. *dight:* arrayed.

462, 64. The reference is to theological speculations and formulations in general and perhaps specially to the medieval schoolmen.

462, 65. *childish wonderment:* superstition.

463, 66. *fond:* foolish.

463, 85. Arnold appended the note: "Demophoon, son of Celeus, King of Eleusis. See in the *Homeric Hymns*, the *Hymn to Demeter*, 184–298."

463, 86. *the Mighty Mother:* the mother of the gods, Rhea.

464, 124. *a cherish'd wife:* Lady Augusta Stanley had died in 1876.

464, 125. Stanley was frequently accused by conservative churchmen of holding heretical opinions.

464, 126. His death was ascribed, partially at least, to the noxious fumes coming from the imperfect drainage of the dean's house.

464, 134 f. Arnold appended the note: "Agamedes and Trophonius, the builders of the temple of Apollo at Delphi. See Plutarch, *Consolatio ad Apollonium*, c. 14."

464, 141 f. On certain of the odd words and odd usages of words Arnold wrote to his sister Fanny:

It is curious what happened about *cecity* [l. 155]. The word came into my mind as so suitable in that place that I determined to use it, as its formation from *cecitas* in Latin and *cecité* in French is as regular and simple as that of *levity*, from *levitas* in Latin and *levité* in French. Then I thought I would look in Richardson [a dictionary] for the word, though really not expecting to find it there, and I found that the word had been used by the great Hooker. Those Elizabethans had indeed a sense for diction. *Pullulate* [l. 160] is used by the Cambridge Platonists a good deal; *let* [l. 170] as a noun substantive is thorough good English, being used several times by Shakespeare (*Letters*, II, 197–198).

464, 160. *rites externe:* the reference is to the revival of ritualistic religion which was one of the consequences within the Church of England of the Oxford movement.

464, 168. *that well-recorded friend:* a tribute to Stanley's record of the life of Thomas Arnold (1844).

BIBLIOGRAPHY

466. DANTE GABRIEL ROSSETTI

I. EDITIONS

Collected Works, 2 vols., ed. by W. M. Rossetti, Ellis, 1890.
Works, 7 vols. ed. by W. M. Rossetti, Ellis, 1901.
Poems and Translations, 1850–70, Oxford, 1914.
The House of Life, ed. by P. F. Baum, Harvard, 1928.

II. BIOGRAPHY AND LETTERS

Family Letters, ed. by W. M. Rossetti, 2 vols., Ellis, 1895.
Rossetti Papers, ed. by W. M. Rossetti, Ellis, 1903.
Letters to William Allingham, ed. by G. B. Hill, Stokes, 1898.
Letters to His Publisher, ed. by O. Doughty, Scholartis (London), 1928.
Letters to Fanny Cornforth, ed. P. F. Baum, Johns Hopkins, 1940.
Beerbohm, Max: *Rossetti and His Circle*, Heinemann, 1922.
Benson, A. C.: *Rossetti*, Macmillan, 1904.
Caine, Sir Hall: *Recollections of Rossetti*, Cassell, 1882, 1928.
Dunn, H. T.: *Recollections of Dante Gabriel Rossetti and His Circle* (ed. G. Pedrick), Mathews, 1904.
Hunt, W. H.: *Pre-Raphaelitism and the Pre-Raphaelite Brotherhood*, Dutton, 2 vols.
Knight, J.: *Life of Dante Gabriel Rossetti*, Scott (London), 1887.
Marillier, H. C.: *Dante Gabriel Rossetti: an Illustrated Memorial of His Art and Life*, Bell, 1899.
Rossetti, W. M.: *Dante Gabriel Rossetti as Designer and Writer*, 1889.
Sharp, W.: *Dante Gabriel Rossetti: a Record and a Study*, Macmillan, 1882.
Waller, R. D.: *The Rossetti Family, 1824–1854*, Manchester University Press, 1932.
Waugh, E.: *Rossetti, His Life and Works*, Duckworth, 1928.

III. CRITICISM

I. Monographs

Buchanan, R. W.: *The Fleshly School of Poetry and Other Phenomena of the Day*, Strahan (London), 1872.
Hueffer, F. M. (later Ford, F. M.): *Rossetti, a Critical Essay on His Art*, Duckworth, 1902.
Rossetti, W. M.: *Bibliography of the Works of Dante Gabriel Rossetti*, Ellis, 1905.
Trombly, A. E.: *Rossetti the Poet*, University of Texas Bulletin, No. 2060.
Willoughby, L. A.: *Dante Gabriel Rossetti and German Literature*, Frowde (London), 1912.

II. Essays in Books

Brooke, S. A.: "Dante Gabriel Rossetti" in *Four Victorian Poets*, Putnam, 1908.
Forman, H. B.: "Dante Gabriel Rossetti" in *Our Living Poets*, Tinsley (London), 1871.
Hearn, L.: "Studies in Rossetti" in *Pre-Raphaelite and Other Poets*, Dodd, 1922.
Myers, F. W. H.: "Rossetti and the Religion of Beauty" in *Essays Modern*, Macmillan, 1885.
Pater, W.: "Dante Gabriel Rossetti" in *Appreciations*, Macmillan, 1889.
Patmore, C.: "Rossetti as a Poet" in *Principle in Art*, Bell, 1889.
Swinburne, A. C.: "The Poems of Dante Gabriel Rossetti" in *Essays and Studies*, Chatto, 1875.
Symons, A.: "Rossetti" in *Studies in Strange Souls*, Sawyer (London), 1929.
Williams, S. T.: "Two Poems by Rossetti" in *Studies in Victorian Literature*, Dutton, 1923.

III. Articles in Periodicals.

Burgum, E. B.: "Rossetti and the Ivory Tower" in the *Sewanee Review*, October, 1929.
Hamilton, G. L.: "Dante Gabriel Rossetti: a Review of His Poetry" in the *Criterion*, June, 1928.
Jones, H. F.: "Dante Gabriel Rossetti: Medievalist and Poet" in the *Quarterly Journal of the University of North Dakota*, May, 1926.

KNICKERBOCKER, K. L.: "Rossetti's 'The Blessed Damozel' " in *Studies in Philology*, July, 1932.

MORSE, B. J.: "Dante Gabriel Rossetti and Dante Alighieri" in *Englische Studien*, September, 1933.

ROSSETTI, W. M.: "Dante Gabriel Rossetti as Translator" in the *Sewanee Review*, October, 1909.

TISDEL, F. M.: "Rossetti's 'House of Life' " in *Modern Philology*, September, 1917.

WALLERSTEIN, R.: "Personal Experience in Rossetti's 'House of Life' " in *Publications of the Modern Language Association of America*, June, 1927.

WAUGH, E.: "D. G. Rossetti: a Centenary Criticism" in the *Fortnightly Review*, May, 1928.

WOLFF, L.: "Rossetti et le moyen-âge" in *Revue anglo-americaine*, June, 1928.

WORSFOLD, W. B.: "The Poetry of D. G. Rossetti" in the *Nineteenth Century*, August, 1893.

NOTES AND COMMENTS

467. THE BLESSED DAMOZEL

This poem first appeared in *The Germ* in 1850; with many and important revisions it was reprinted in the *Oxford and Cambridge Magazine* in 1856; revised substantially anew, it was one of the *Poems* of 1870. The poem should be compared with Rossetti's picture bearing the same name. Rossetti remarked, Sir Hall Caine reports, that he was led to compose the poem by Poe's "The Raven." "I saw that Poe had done the utmost it was possible to do with the grief of the lover on earth, and so I determined to reverse the conditions, and give utterance to the yearning of the loved one in heaven."

467. *Damozel* is a variant of the Old French word from which comes the English *damsel*, to which Rossetti's word is equivalent.

467, 5. *three:* a number with mystical value.

467, 6. *seven:* another number with mystical value.

467, 9–10. The meaning is that as a Virgin, and thus in the service of the Virgin Mary, she fittingly wore a flower which was a symbol of virginity.

467, 12. *like ripe corn:* like the *hair* of ripe corn.

467, 27–28. No detailed philosophic meaning is intended; Rossetti, accepting the current doctrine that space is only a form of human perception, indicates where the human world begins.

467, 34. *ridge:* mark out in alternate conspicuous strips.

467, 35. *as low as:* as far down as.

467, 36. *midge:* gnat.

468, 42. *flames:* indicating their purity.

468, 50. *Time:* like Space, it is presented as a part of the purely human world. Again no detailed philosophic meaning exists.

468, 54. Here and in l. 60 there is reminiscence of *Job*, Ch. XXXVIII, 7, where there is a reference to the singing of the stars (". . . the morning stars sang together . . .").

468, 86. *that living mystic tree:* "the tree of life which bare twelve manner of fruits, and yielded her fruit every month" (*Revelation*, Ch. XXII, 2).

468, 87. *the Dove:* the Holy Ghost.

468, 100. *unity:* union.

468, 107–108. Rossetti has chosen five names of saints which, taken together, produce a carefully considered musical effect. There is no clear justification for the choice of these five saints as the special attendants on the Virgin Mary.

468, 123. *unnumbered:* numberless.

468, 126. *citherns and citoles:* stringed instruments suggestive of the middle ages.

469. MY SISTER'S SLEEP

This poem first appeared in *The Germ* in 1850; it was subsequently reprinted in the *Poems* of 1870. On its appearance in the collection Rossetti appended the following note: "This little poem, written in 1847, was printed in a periodical at the outset of 1850. The metre, which is used by several old English writers, became celebrated a month or two later on the publication of *In Memoriam*." For the history of the metre see the note introducing *In Memoriam*. The poem has no basis in the circumstances of Rossetti's life.

469, 25. *dwindling years:* aged persons.

469. THE PORTRAIT

This poem first appeared as one of the *Poems* of 1870. W. M. Rossetti has commented on it as follows: "In printed notices of my brother's poems I have often seen the supposition advanced that this poem was written after the death of his wife, in relation to some portrait he had painted of her during her lifetime. The supposition is very natural, yet not correct. The poem was in fact an extremely early one, and purely imaginary,—perhaps in the first draft of it, as early as 1847; it was afterwards considerably revised."

471. JENNY

This poem first appeared in the *Poems* of 1870. It had been composed (in part at least) as early as 1848, and was read in manuscript by Ruskin in 1859. The degree to which it derived from personal experience is unknown. It should be compared with the painting *Found.*

471. *Motto:* See *The Merry Wives of Windsor*, Act IV, sc. i, 61.

471, 13. *Love's exuberant hotbed:* the meaning is that her life of passion has speeded her development which is already past its point of greatest beauty.

471, 17. *the whirlpool:* of vice.

471, 21. *lodestar:* magnet.

471, 31. *eyes of dancing seemed so fain:* eyes so tired that they seem continually to have figures moving about in front of them.

471, 49. *sweets:* beauties, specifically breasts.

471, 62. *revolved:* considered.

471, 75. The meaning is that by her *strength* (which is virtue) she refuses to lead such a life as Jenny's: a regimen of hard work and poor food keeps her *weak.*

472, 99. The gloved hand is here a mark of relative wealth and ease.

472, 102. *the ancient text:* "Consider the lilies of the field, how they grow; they toil not, neither do they spin: and yet I say unto you, that even Solomon in all his glory was not arrayed like one of these" (*Matthew*, Ch. VI, 28–9).

472, 117. *purfled:* adorned at the edges.

472, 142. *the Haymarket:* a street in the district in London where many of the theatres are. The term is sometimes applied to neighborhood as well as street.

472, 144. *your:* the reference is no longer to the individual girl but to her profession in its ups and downs.

472, 162. *dusty sense: Dusty* is intended to suggest immediately the condition of the book itself, and then of its purport (sense), which to one like Jenny would seem obscure and unreal.

472, 166. *Lethe:* the river of oblivion.

Of the middle street: running down the middle of the road. In older cities, the gutter was sometimes at the middle, instead of at the side of the road. Note that it is implied that Jenny's mind is a gutter.

472, 181. The Bible has a number of references to God as the potter and man as clay, notably that in *Isaiah*, Ch. LXIV, 8: "But now, O Lord, thou art our father; we are clay and thou our potter; and we are all the work of thy hand."

472, 185. *Nell:* there is no person especially intended.

473, 206. *a goblin:* a fiend.

473, 209. *till the world shall burn:* till the world comes to an end.

473, 230. *gilded aureole:* the halo about the head of a saint.

473, 258. *psyche-wings:* the superficial sense in which *psyche* is used here is that of a moth; but one is also intended to take the meaning soul.

473, 265. *puddled:* muddy.

473, 270. *sanguine:* red.

473, 282. *a toad within a stone:* a petrified fossil.

474, 322. *pierglass:* a mirror set in the wall between windows.

scrawled with diamond rings: her lovers had used their jewels to incise their names or sentiments, or patterns of an amorous kind.

474, 361. *Paphian Venus:* Venus was believed to have appeared from the foam at Paphos on the island of Crete, where she was worshipped with erotic rites. By *Paphian* Rossetti means sensual, distinguishing thus a lower type of love from others.

474, 365. *Priapus:* in Greek mythology a personification of lust.

474, 376. *Danae:* in Greek mythology the daughter of the King of Argos seduced by Jupiter who had assumed the form of a golden shower.

474, 377. *rang true:* a play on words, the meaning being that his love was genuine (in that it was disinterested) and that the money he left was genuine also.

475. THE CARD-DEALER

This poem first appeared as one of the *Poems* of 1870; it was written as early as 1849.

475, 24. *eyes:* jewels.

475, 28. *bann'd:* cursed.

475. SISTER HELEN

This poem first appeared in the English edition of the *Dusseldorf Artists' Annual* for 1853; it was later much revised, and for inclusion in the *Ballads and Poems* of 1881 greatly extended.

The theme of the poem is a widespread medieval belief that if one fabricated an image of a person one wished to harm, and observed certain rites, what was done to the image would befall the person also. The names of the personages are not derived from any earlier treatment of the theme.

475, 1. *your waxen man:* see the general note on the poem.

476, 15. *vesper-bell:* the bell calling to evening prayer.

476, 64. *Boyne Bar:* a bar at the mouth of the Irish river Boyne.

477, 114. *ban:* curse.

477, 148. *a broken coin:* as pledges Helen and Keith of Ewern had the two parts of a coin.

479. TROY TOWN

This poem first appeared in the *Poems* of 1870. The Roman historian Pliny has related a legendary tale of the dedication by Helen of Troy to Venus of a goblet shaped like one of her breasts.

479, 1. *Sparta's Queen:* Helen was the wife of Menelaus, one of the kings of Sparta.

479, 7. When the Greeks finally won possession of Troy, it was given to the flames.

479, 45–50. Venus (Aphrodite) was the successful goddess of the three who competed for the award of a golden apple by Paris. The others were Minerva (Pallas) and Juno (Hera).

480, 66. *drift:* meaning.

480, 92. *Paris:* a son of Priam, King of Troy, to whom the most beautiful woman in the world was promised by Venus, for awarding to her the apple.

480. AVE

This poem first appeared as one of the *Poems* of 1870.

480, 1. *the Fair Delight:* Jesus.

480, 2. *handmaid:* an echo of Mary's reply to the angel "Behold the handmaid of the Lord" (*Luke*, Ch. I, 38).

480, 3. Mary is said to sit on an equality with the Trinity because of her immeasurable superiority to all purely human creatures.

480, 6. *rood:* cross.

480, 11. *headstone:* keystone, principal strength.

480, 28–33. The story is told in *Luke*, Ch. I, 28–55.

480, 39. *Passover:* a Jewish feast commemorating the exemption of the Jews, when they were in Egypt, from the plague.

481, 47. An echo of Jesus' remark to Mary, when he was asked why he had delayed in Jerusalem disputing with the doctors in the temple, "Wist ye not that I must be about my Father's business?" (*Luke*, Ch. II, 49).

481, 63. *It was Finishèd:* The last words of Jesus on the cross, according to St. John, were "It is finished" (*John*, Ch. XIX, 30).

481, 65. *the house of John:* Jesus commended Mary to his disciple John as he was dying on the cross (*John*, Ch. XIX, 26–7); "and from that hour that disciple took her into his own home."

481, 89. Gabriel was the angel sent to announce to Mary that she was to bear Jesus (*Luke*, Ch. I, 26 f.).

481. THE HOUSE OF LIFE

The bibliographical history of this work is complex. In 1869 Rossetti published in the *Fortnightly Review* a sequence of sixteen sonnets which were to form part of the work (in the present numbering, which is that of 1881, they are sonnets XLIX–LII, XXXIX, XCI, XCV, XCVII, XXV–XXVI, XLVII, LXXXVI, LXV, LXVIII, XCIX, C). In the same year he had printed, but did not publish, a collection of poems, in which the above sixteen sonnets appeared along with, in the present numbering, sonnets II–IV, VI, VIII, XV, XXXVIII–XXXIX, XLV–XLVIII, LXIII, LXXXV, XC, XCII. In the *Poems* of 1870 fifty sonnets and eleven songs were grouped under the title, *Sonnets and Songs towards a Work to Be Called 'The House of Life.'* In a prefatory note he stated: "The first twenty-eight sonnets and the seven first songs treat of love. These and the others would belong to separate sections of the projected work." In the present text, each of the sonnets which appeared in the collection of 1870 bears in addition to its numbering in the scheme of 1881 the number it bore in 1870, this latter number being placed within square brackets. In 1881 the work consisted of one hundred and one sonnets, all the songs having been removed.

The House of Life is not in any usual sense of the term a sonnet sequence. There is no narrative, nor is there any steady or noticeable psychological development. It is best considered as a group, rather than a sequence, of sonnets on closely related themes. It must be admitted, however, that some few of the sonnets do not fit even the above description—these are simply occasional.

The title comes from astrology. The firmament was said to be divided into twelve *houses*, one of which was the house of life. Life, Rossetti coupled here, as he has said, with *love* and *death;* and his theme is nothing more specific than a series of reflections on life, love and death. When he was about to publish the collection of 1881 he weighed the desirability of warning in a prefatory note against the interpretation of the sonnets as records of his own experience, deciding finally against it.

Criticism has placed too much weight upon the correspondence of the sonnets with Rossetti's own life. Too much is known, or misknown, about that life for a confident ascription of these sonnets to particular moments in it or for a connection of even the most apparently intimate revelations with Rossetti's relationships. It is for example impossible to regard the sequence as primarily a celebration and commemoration of Elizabeth Siddal whom he married; there is no assurance how much of it sings the beauties and amorousness of models, especially of Fanny Schott; and it is at least probable that the central woman is a person whose very name we do not know. (For a full consideration of this problem, and all others relating to the series, see the introduction to P. F. Baum's *The House of Life*, Harvard, 1928).

481. THE SONNET (PREFATORY SONNET)

481, 4. *lustral:* purifying.

481, 11–14. Life, and the relations to it of Love and Death, Rossetti has described as his theme in the series.

481, 14. Charon was the ferryman over the river Styx across which, according to Greek myth, the dead were borne to the underworld. He required a fee.

482. II

482, 12–14. Through the strength of love, a spiritual level of being is reached; and through this strength, also, death can be surmounted.

482. III

This sonnet underwent notable revisions between its first publication in 1870 and its reappearance in 1881. The revisions specially affected the octave, which in 1870 read as follows:

O thou who at Love's hour ecstatically
Unto my lips dost evermore present
The body and blood of Love in sacrament;
Whom I have neared and felt thy breath to be
The inmost incense of his sanctuary;
Who without speech hast owned him, and, intent
Upon his will, thy life with mine hast blent,
And murmured o'er the cup, Remember me!—

The religious imagery is much more copious and emphatic in the earlier version.

482, 11–12. The meaning is: on the long descent to the shore of the river which separates life from death, and across that river to the underworld. Note that in the sestet the imagery is taken from pagan myth, whereas in the octave it was Christian.

483. V

483, 4. *that sea which Israel crossed dryshod:* the Red Sea, from which the waters were walled up to right and left so that Moses and the Israelites might cross on their departure from Egypt for the Promised Land (*Exodus*, Ch. XVI).

483, 12. *hill-fire:* light shining over, or upon, a hill.

483. VI

483, 1–2. The general meaning is: what injury or humiliation of this body . . ., the first line suggesting the degeneration of the body in a last illness, the second a sudden mutilation or disease.

483, 6. *consonant:* harmonious.

483, 7–8. Orpheus was permitted to bring back his wife Eurydice from the underworld in consideration of the beauty of his music and verse. However, he was not to look back to discover whether she was following; and doing so, lost the boon.
laurelled: as a sign of his achievement in poetry.

484. VI A

This sonnet, sharply attacked by Robert Buchanan, in his study *The Fleshly School of Poetry*, was in consequence of the outcry against it, removed from the collection of 1870 after its sixth printing, and did not reappear in the collection of 1881. Long after the poet's death, his brother and editor W. M. Rossetti restored it to the sequence.
484, 4. *singly:* separately.
484, 12. *watered light:* light seen dimly, as through water.

484. VII

484, 2. *harvest-field:* the original and more poetical word was *fallowfield*, rejected, doubtless, because it does not so fully or clearly carry out the meaning.
484, 6–8. The meaning is that for years love had longed for the first fulfillment of its desire; fate in bringing about that fulfillment has removed the possibility of longing for it, or attaining it.
484, 14. *sovereign:* complete.

484. VIII

484, 1. *zone:* girdle.

485. IX

485, 6. *hautboy:* oboe.
485, 14. *voluntary:* solo, really here the theme of its solo.

485. X

485, 1. *control:* some commentators find it a meaningless word but a clear, satisfactory and important meaning can be found by reading it as equivalent to dominion.
485, 5. *goal:* limit, not object.

485. XI

485, 4. *the smooth black stream:* of her hair.

487. XV

487, 5. *their father's children:* their half-brothers and sisters, offspring of his second marriage.
487, 12. The reference is to a pre-natal existence.

487. XVI

487, 2. *lonely:* because of the absence from it of the woman he celebrates.
487, 6. *an outworn populace:* a rabble which has lost what use and value it may ever have had.
487, 7. *echoing:* because empty.

487. XVII

487, 1–2. *last incarnate flower:* last born glory.
487, 2. *culminating:* reaching its highest and final beauty—at sunset.
487, 4. *full-quired:* by a complete chorus.
488, 11. *swan-stemmed galiot:* a small galley with a swan carved at the bow.

488. XVIII

488, 3. *Michael:* Michaelangelo.
furrowing: searching.
488, 10. *wires:* strings, as of a harp.

488. XIX

488, 4. *scatter and amass:* the clouds now separate and now collect.

488. XX

489, 12. *Queen Dian:* Dian is a variant of Diana, and refers to the moon.

489. XXI

489, 6. The "sweetness" has been gathered by the lover's kisses and by them imparted.

489, 13. *cloud-girt wayfaring:* the journey through life, represented as dark. Clouds are chosen to represent the darkness, since in the last four lines of the sonnet there is a sustained image of the sky, in which angels meet as they move.

489. XXII

489, 12. The meaning is that just as the old moon may be visible, faintly, between the tips of the new, so the presence of Love is faintly discerned through the song.

489. XXIII

490, 5–6. *And from one hand the petal and the core savoured of sleep:* when offered by one of the ladies (l. 3) both the slightest and the greatest tokens of love seemed merely sensuous spells, and had no deeper worth.

XXIV

490, 8. *night-rack:* a bank of clouds at night.

490, 14. *told:* recited.

490. XXV

490, 8. *contending joys:* the original reading was stronger: contending kisses.

491. XXVII

491, 6. *the sun-gate of the soul:* some commentators, for example Mr. Baum, see in this phrase a reference to the soul of the woman the poet celebrates. It is perhaps more likely that it refers to soul or spirit in general, as in the preceding line there is a reference to music in general and in the following a reference to the *heart of all life.* Through her eyes, he comes to a perception of the deepest ranges of spiritual life.

491, 11. *ambiguous:* deceitful, through dreams.

491. XXVIII

491, 7. *soul-winnowing:* soul-purifying.

491, 8. The image is that of a rainbow: but as Mr. Baum points out there is a suggestion, too, of the Biblical ark, in the sense of a repository of a precious treasure.

492. XXXI

492, 4. *hyacinth:* purplish.

493. XXXIII

The background of the poem is the rivalry of the goddesses Juno, representing power, Pallas, representing wisdom, and Venus, representing love and beauty, and their submission of their claims to Paris, to whom Venus, who was victorious, promised the most beautiful woman in the world, Helen.

493, 11. The meaning is that whether beauty, power or wisdom be placed first, his beloved, supreme in all, will be victor.

493, 13. *Victrix:* conquering.

493, 13–14. Venus and his beloved correspond (except that his beloved, as has already been said, has also the virtues of the other goddesses) and his beloved, the most beautiful of earthly women, corresponds to Helen as well.

493, 14. *guerdoning:* reward.

493. XXXIV

493, 14. *hour-girt:* earthly, time being a form of human perception and having no existence in spiritual being.

493. XXXV

494, 8. *chrysoprase:* a bright green precious stone.

basalt: a dark green (or brown) rock. Mr. Baum appropriately comments that it is an unusual choice for setting such a gem.

494. XXXVI

The poet addresses himself.

494, 2. *this lady:* his new love.

494, 8. *eventual:* to come.

494, 13. *the changeless night:* death.

494, 14. When the grave of his wife was opened seven years after her death, her golden hair was unaltered.

494. XXXVII

494, 7. *philtred euphrasy: euphrasy* is the eyebright used medicinally for the eyes; a *philtre* is not merely a potion, but a potion to induce love.

494, 10. *these twain:* the old love and the new.

494, 12. *Master:* Love.

494, 12–14. The meaning is that when the lover dies it will appear that he has perfected himself in love, as the moon progresses from its first phase to its culminating fullness.

495. XXXVIII

495, 8. *night-drift:* night-mists.

495, 9. *malisons:* curses.

495, 13. *thy life is still the sun's:* his life is still to proceed on earth.

495, 14. *the shadow of death:* consciousness or brooding about death.

495. XL

495, 3–4. The reference is to souls awaiting re-birth and in the meantime able only to recall indistinctly circumstances of their previous lives (l. 2).

495, 11–14. The love was in life, and is still, illicit: hence the kiss is soul-wrung and accompanied by a moan.

496. XLI

496, 1–5. The images in these lines are the "wild images of Death" mentioned in l. 7.

496, 6. *within some glass dimmed by our breath: glass* has the sense of mirror; the phrase as a whole is an imaginative expression of the idea that our selves obscure the picture that we see, introducing into it elements of our own peculiar natures.

496, 12. *angel-greeted door:* a door at which an angel stands. See the note to the following line.

496, 13. *threshing-floor:* W. M. Rossetti has pointed to an incident in *I Chronicles*, Ch. XXI, 18 f., in which David, accompanied by an angel, asks for the threshing-floor of Ornan the Jebusite, as the site for an altar. Doubtless this incident suggested also the preceding line of the sonnet.

497. XLIV

497, 4. *bond:* assurance.

497, 8. *gyres:* circlings.

497, 10. *lampless:* unseeing and unseen.

497. XLV

497, 4. *against:* towards.

497, 6. *annihilate:* by satisfying.

497, 13–14. The poet contrasts the love of the grove—private and (perhaps) illicit—with that ratified by society through the church.

497. XLVI

The poet addresses himself.

498. XLVII

498, 14. Commentators vary in interpretation of this line, W. M. Rossetti (among others) taking what is the most obvious meaning—the pain of a prayer which is not heard—and Mr. Baum suggesting the meaning—a prayer which, being improper, ought not to be prayed.

498. XLVIII

498, 2. *gonfalon:* banner.

498, 3. *web:* weave.

498. XLIX

The poem records a dream.

498, 5. The line is to be interpreted in the light of the succeeding sonnets within the group.

499. LI

499, 7. *their unforgotten food:* kisses, from the beloved.

499, 10. *tear-spurge, blood-wort:* the *spurge* and the *wort* are common plants; their conjunction with *tears* and *blood* is the work of the poet's imagination.

499. LII

499, 2. *wellaway:* moaning.

500, 14. *aureole:* halo.

500. LIII

Sir Hall Caine records Rossetti as saying he could not tell him "at what terrible moment it (LIII) was wrung" from him.

500. LIV

500, 1. In this line, and throughout the sonnet, there is a contrast (as well as a relation) between *Love* and physical passion (*Desire of Love*).

500. LV

500, 5. *consummate:* used probably in the sense of consummated or realized, not in the more usual one of supreme.

501. LVI

501, 4. *environing:* penetrating.

501, 6. *Philomel:* the nightingale.

501. LVII

501, 2. *lodestar:* magnet.

501. LVIII

501, 2. *the Seer:* Swedenborg, a mystical writer of the eighteenth century.

502. LX

502, 13–14. The poet echoes *I Kings*, Ch. XVIII, in which Elijah says to King Ahab "there is a sound of abundance of rain" (41), and shortly afterwards sending a servant to the top of Mount Carmel, learns from that servant that "there ariseth a little cloud out of the sea, like a man's hand" (44).

503. LXI

503, 9. *The Song-god—He the Sun-god:* Apollo was in Greek mythology both god of inspiration and of the sun.

503, 14. *inspir'd recoil:* the *recoil* (or rebound) is that of the shaft of Apollo; W. M. Rossetti suggests that the adjective *inspir'd* applies not so much to the shaft as to the emotion it images. So far as it does apply to the shaft it means no more than caused.

504. LXIV

504, 7. *valorous lusts:* strong pleasures.

504, 8. *daughters of the daybreak:* the birds. W. M. Rossetti's suggestion of "the powers and ministering spirits of the new day" is almost certainly to be rejected as too inclusive and also too vague.

504, 14. Mr. Baum helpfully points out that this line is governed by the "wind" of l. 11.

504. LXV

504, 13. *incommunicable:* uncommunicating.

504. LXVI

504, 3. The meaning is from a time in which there was trusting intimate love between the two to one in which (perhaps because the beloved had died) there was no more than recollection of past happiness.

504, 4. *ban:* curse (most commentators do not accept this, the usual, sense; but it fits perfectly the meaning of the line as a whole, which is an account of Rossetti's psychological development in the last years of his life).

504, 7. *primal:* original. The death of the body restores the soul to the condition in which it was before birth.

505. LXVII

505, 7. *unsought:* conspicuous.

505. LXVIII

505, 12–14. Rossetti stated to William Allingham that the practice he mentions was a frequent one in some regions of England.

505. LXIX

505, 12. The meaning is: I lose hours, reliving hours of past experience.

506. LXX

Rossetti has recorded writing this sonnet at the top of a hill in Warwickshire, which he had reached just after the sun set.

506, 7–8. The point of view is that of a traveller along a road in a wooded country: the sun is partially hidden by the growth, which it partially brightens also.

506–7. LXXI–III

This group of three is early work; Rossetti more than once expressed doubts about including it in the sequence, with which, indeed, it is not consonant either in method or in tone.

506. LXXI

506, 12–13. These lines read in 1870:

Through many days they toil; then comes a day
They die not,—never having lived,—but cease;

507. LXXIV

This sonnet emphasizes more heavily than anything else Rossetti wrote the religious quality which in other Pre-Raphaelites (notably in Holman Hunt) was central.

507, 4–5. The meaning is that in its early phases Christian art was not realistic but purely symbolic.

507, 7. *symbols also in some deeper way:* all natural things, being God's handiwork, illustrate his nature, and that of the spirit in general.

507, 10–11. The meaning is that in recent times (past noon l. 9) art has lost sight of its spiritual and representative aims and has become subjective and merely adroit.

508. LXXVI

508, 2. *these:* the early medieval painters such as Giotto and Angelico.

508, 3. *the husk of darkness:* the dark ages preceding the Middle Ages, properly so called.

508. LXXVII

In 1870 the sonnet was entitled *Sibylla Palmifera* (The Sibyl, bearing a palm): Between 1866 and 1870 Rossetti was engaged on a picture which was to be so named. It should be compared with the sonnet.

508, 10–11. *known to thee by flying hair and fluttering hem:* incompletely, despite one's earnest quest.

509. LXXVIII

In 1870 this sonnet was entitled *Lilith.* Shortly before he began to work on his picture *Sibylla Palmifera,* he had begun one to be named *Lady Lilith.* The picture and the sonnet should be compared. Lilith is a legendary figure, not alluded to in the Bible.

509, 7. *the bright web:* of her hair. The hair is again to be interpreted as a symbol.

509, 9. *rose and poppy:* the rose represents passion, the poppy the spell she casts.

509. LXXIX

Sir Hall Caine records that Rossetti's comment on this sonnet was "That sublimated mood of the soul in which a separate essence of itself seems to oversoar and survey it."

509. *Monochord:* an instrument with one string used to produce the pitch desired.

509, 3. *instinct:* inherent.

509, 7. *separate:* individual.

509, 11. *lifted shifted steeps:* the high places rising *and* changing.

510. LXXXI

510, 1–4. W. M. Rossetti "surmises" that his brother had in mind the conclusion of Poe's *Narrative of Arthur Gordon Pym;* but the difficult image is not much clarified by knowledge of its source.

510. LXXXIII

510, 11. The images are from *Genesis*, Ch. III, 1–5.

511. LXXXIV

This sonnet was written at Penkill Castle, the home of Miss Alice Boyd.

511. LXXXV

511, 7. *pit's pollution:* the image was stronger in the version of 1870, reading *scorching bridegroom.*

511, 9. *tribute:* in 1870 *garbage.*

511, 13. *destined:* in 1870 *worthier.*

511. LXXXVI

511, 8. In 1870, more powerfully, this line read:

The throats of men in Hell, who thirst alway.

In order to introduce the epithet *undying*, important for the sense, the concrete phrase "of men" was unfortunately sacrificed.

512. LXXXVII

Homer records the stratagem by which the Greeks, enclosed within a wooden horse, were able to enter the city of Troy, with Ulysses as their leader as also the passing of Ulysses' ship by the island of the sirens, the members of the crew with their ears stuffed so that they should not hear the songs the sirens sang, Ulysses, at his command, with his ears unstuffed but with his body bound to the mast so that he should be powerless to yield to the temptations they proposed.

512, 13–14. Rossetti echoes St. Paul's: "O death, where is thy sting? O grave where is thy victory?" (I *Corinthians*, Ch. XV, 55.)

512. LXXXVIII

Rossetti appended the note: "After the deaths of Leander and of Hero, the signal-lamp was dedicated to Anteros, with the edict that no man should light it unless his love had proved fortunate. He found his matter in Burton's *Anatomy of Melancholy.*

512, 1. *Eros:* god of love.

512, 2. *Sestian:* of Sestos, the town on the Hellespont (the modern Dardanelles) in which Hero lived.

512, 6. *life twice-ebb'd:* the reference is to the deaths of Hero and Leander.

512, 7. *Avernian:* belonging to the underworld.

512. LXXXIX

512, 8. *unabashed:* inscrutable.

513. XC

Retro Me, Sathana: Get thee behind me, Satan.

513. XCI

513, 3. *stark marriage-sheet:* the shroud of the beloved.

513, 4. The reference is to the death-knell.

513, 9–14. W. M. Rossetti has aptly suggested that his brother spoke of his rival ambitions towards poetry and painting.

513, 12–14. The original version read:

So from that soul, in mindful brotherhood,
(When silence may not be) sometimes they throng
Through high-streets and at many dusty inns.

Rossetti rightly found this reading "foggy."

514. XCIII

514, 2. *eld:* age.

514. XCIV

514, 6. *Colonna:* Vittoria Colonna, the love of his old age.

514, 9. A pun is here attempted. Bonarruoti was the sculptor's last name; it may be resolved into *bona* (good) and *ruota* (wheel). The real derivation of the word is quite different.

514. XCV

514, 1. *your:* the ordinary man's.

515, 4. *there:* sculpted (or painted) on the vase.

515, 9–11. These lines resist detailed interpretation. It is, for example, difficult to see why wine should represent blood, while blood, although included, represents something else.

515, 9–16. The person described in the sestet is contrasted with the youth on the vase in the octave.

515. XCVI

515, 8. *lovelihead:* loveliness.

515, 12–14. Rossetti's wife was buried in mid-winter.

515. XCVII

515, 3. *the dead-sea shell:* a shell from the sea of death, with the undercurrent of pictorial suggestion of a Dead Sea scene.

515, 4. *thy Life's foam-fretted feet:* the picture of a Dead Sea scene continues. The living man stands so close to its edge that the foam rises about his feet.

517. CI

517, 5–6. There may be a reference intended to Purgatory in l. 5, to Paradise in l. 6. If so they are rather symbols of varying destiny than theological ideas.

517, 10. *scriptured:* bearing letters, as the hyacinth was supposed to do, and which form the *spell* referred to in l. 12.

517, 12. *alien:* previously he had *written.* The increased power and stress is clear.

517, 13–14. Whether the name is that of Love or that of the beloved woman is impossible to decide.

517. THE KING'S TRAGEDY

This poem first appeared in the collection of 1881, *Ballads and Sonnets.* Rossetti appended to it the following explanatory note: "Tradition says that Catherine Douglas, in honour of her heroic act, when she barred the door with her arm against the murderers of James the First of Scots, received popularly the name of 'Barlass.' This name remains to her descendants, the Barlas family, in Scotland, who bear for their crest a broken arm. She married Alexander Lovell of Bolunnie. A few stanzas from King James's lovely poem, known as 'The King's Quair,' are quoted in the course of this ballad. The writer must express regret for the necessity which has compelled him to shorten the ten-syllabled lines to eight syllables, in order that they might harmonize with the ballade metre." King James the First of Scotland (1394–1437) was when a young boy captured by the English and held a prisoner for nineteen years; during his captivity he met the niece of King Henry IV, Joan Beaufort, whom he married; the poem *The King's Quair* (The King's Book) is attributed to him on good but not certain grounds.

517, 1–14. See the general note on the poem.

517, 8. *the palm-play:* the *jeu de paume,* a game played on courts and otherwise resembling tennis, but in which the hand is used to strike the ball.

517, 16. *King Robert:* Robert the Third, King of Scotland from 1390 to 1424.

517, 19. *pent:* see the general note.

517, 26. *the Bass Rock Fort:* a fort on an island off the east coast of Scotland.

517, 28–29. The reference is to King Henry IV.

517, 32. *approve:* prove.

517, 37. *a lady:* see the general note.

517, 41. *a sweeter Song: The King's Quair.*

518, 48. *Scone:* Here, in Perthshire, the kings of Scotland were crowned.

518, 68. *wrong:* The English raided the border of Scotland and tried to seize the young daughter of the King.

518, 72. *leaguer:* siege.
Roxbro': a castle on the border held by the English.
518, 120. *avow thy gage:* maintain your challenge.
519, 128. The reference is to the Highlands.
519, 138. *proper:* own.
519, 141. *The Black Friars Charterhouse of Perth:* the monastery of the black robed Dominicans at the city of Perth.
519, 146. *the Scotish Sea:* the Firth of Tay.
519, 157. *sea-wold:* the wild land along the shore.
519, 176. The meaning is — in Perthshire, these bodies of water being on two sides of it.
519, 179. *Inchkeith Isle:* an island in the Firth of Forth, near Edinburgh.
519, 181. *cerecloth:* cloth for burial.
520, 251. *lift:* sky.
520, 260. *Athole:* Atholl.
521, 291. *stark:* firmly.
521, 317. *kalends:* in the Roman calendar, the first day of a month.
521, 343. *aventure:* fortune.
521, 348. *rancor:* bitter fate.
522, 375. *astound:* astonished.
522, 388. *pearl-tir'd:* with a coronet of pearls.
522, 414. *Voidee-cup:* liquor drunk at bedtime.
522, 424. *brast:* broken.
523, 440. *ingle-nook:* chimney corner.
523, 445. *dight:* got ready.
523, 462. *dule:* grief.
dree: endure.
523, 469. *Aberdour:* a town near Edinburgh, on the Firth of Forth.
523, 515. *hardihood:* bravery.
524, 566. *stanchion-hold:* socket.
524, 610. *reck:* heed.
526, 710. *shrive:* confess, and especially (a part of the confession) absolve.
527, 757. *orb:* globe, a symbol of the royal power.
527, 818. *bale and ban:* evil and malediction.

BIBLIOGRAPHY

528. CHRISTINA ROSSETTI

I. EDITIONS

Poetical Works, ed. by W. M. Rossetti, Macmillan, 1924.
Poems, ed. by A. Meynell, Blackie, 1923.
Selected Poems, ed. by C. B. Burke, Macmillan, 1913.

II. BIOGRAPHY AND LETTERS

Family Letters, ed. by W. M. Rossetti, Scribner, 1908.
BELL, M.: *Christina Rossetti, a Biographical and Critical Study*, Roberts (Boston), 1908.
SANDARS, M. F.: *The Life of Christina Rossetti*, Hutchinson, 1930.
STUART, D. M.: *Christina Rossetti*, Macmillan, 1931.
THOMAS, E. W.: *Christina Georgina Rossetti*, Columbia, 1931.
WALLER, R. D.: *The Rossetti Family, 1824–1854*, Manchester University Press, 1932.

III. CRITICISM

BALD, M. A.: "Christina Rossetti" in *Women Writers of the Nineteenth Century*, Cambridge, 1923.
BENSON, A. C.: "Christina Rossetti" in *Essays*, Macmillan, 1896.
DE LA MARE, W.: "Christina Rossetti" in *The Royal Society of Literature, Essays by Divers Hands*, New Series, Vol. 6, Oxford, 1926.
EVANS, B. I.: "The Sources of Christina Rossetti's 'Goblin Market' " in *Modern Language Review*, April, 1933.
FORMAN, H. B.: "Christina Rossetti" in *Our Living Poets*, Tinsley (London), 1871.
GOSSE, SIR EDMUND: "Christina Rossetti" in *Critical Kit-Kats*, Dodd, 1896, reprinted in *Selected Essays*, Heinemann, 1928.
LUCAS, F. L.: "Christina Rossetti" in *Eight Victorian Poets*, Cambridge, 1931.
MORE, P. E.: "Christina Rossetti" in *Shelburne Essays*, Third Series, Putnam, 1905.
SHOVE, F.: *Christina Rossetti, a Study*, Cambridge, 1931.

NOTES AND COMMENTS

528. DREAM LAND

This poem first appeared in the first number of *The Germ*, in 1850; subsequently it was reprinted in the collection of 1862, *Goblin Market and Other Poems.*

529. SONG (OH ROSES FOR THE FLUSH OF YOUTH)

This poem first appeared in the second number of *The Germ*, in 1850. It was subsequently reprinted in the collection of 1862, *Goblin Market and Other Poems.*

529. UP-HILL

This poem first appeared in *Macmillan's Magazine* for February, 1861; it was subsequently reprinted in the collection of 1862, *Goblin Market and Other Poems.* It was the first piece by Christina Rossetti to appear in *Macmillan's*, or indeed in any magazine with a considerable circulation.

529. A BIRTHDAY

This poem first appeared in *Macmillan's Magazine* for April, 1861; subsequently it was reprinted in the collection of 1862, *Goblin Market and Other Poems.* William Michael Rossetti confessed his inability to account in biographical terms for the rapture and jubilation in this poem.

529, 6. *halcyon:* calm as on a bright day.

529, 10. *vair:* a gray fur.

529, 14. *fleur-de-lys:* lilies.

529. SONG (WHEN I AM DEAD, MY DEAREST)

This poem first appeared in the collection of 1862, *Goblin Market and Other Poems.* In December, 1848, when it was written, she was in the middle of the period of her engagement to James Collinson.

530. REMEMBER

This poem first appeared in the collection of 1862, *Goblin Market and Other Poems.* It is an expression of Christina Rossetti's love for James Collinson.

530. THE THREE ENEMIES

This poem first appeared in the collection of 1862, *Goblin Market and Other Poems.*

530, 6. There is a reminiscence of *Isaiah*, Ch. LXIII, 2–3, where the Lord speaks of having "trodden the winepress alone."

530, 34. *Get thee behind me:* the command of Jesus when tempted by Satan (see *Luke*, Ch. IV, 8).

530. ECHO

This poem first appeared in the collection of 1862, *Goblin Market and Other Poems.* Miss D. M. Stuart has aptly remarked (*Christina Rossetti*, 49) that this is among her lyrics one of the hardest to relate to a biographical experience.

531. GOBLIN MARKET

This poem first appeared in the collection of 1862, *Goblin Market and Other Poems.* William Michael Rossetti reports that the first title of the poem was "A Peep at the Goblins—To M. F. R."; M. F. R. was Maria Francesca Rossetti, Christina's sister. Although Christina Rossetti disclaimed profundity of meaning in the tale, the following suggestion, made by W. M. Rossetti, is suggestive: "The foundation of the narrative is this: That the goblins tempt women to eat their luscious but uncanny fruits; that a first taste produces a rabid craving for a second taste; but that the second taste is never accorded, and, in default of it, the woman pines away and dies. Then comes the central point: Laura having tasted the fruits once, and being at death's door through inability to get a second taste, her sister Lizzie determines to save her at all hazards; so she goes to the goblins, refuses to eat their fruits, and beguiles them into forcing the fruits upon her with so much insistency that her face is all smeared and steeped with the juices; she gets Laura to kiss and suck these juices off her face, and Laura, having thus obtained the otherwise impossible second taste, rapidly recovers."

531, 22. *bullaces:* small plums.
531, 24. *bilberries:* berries resembling the American blueberry.
531, 27. *barberries:* long red berries.
531, 75. *wombat:* an Australian marsupial resembling a badger.
531, 76. *ratel:* another animal resembling a badger, its habitat is in South Africa.
531, 83. *beck:* brook.
532, 158. *no grass will grow:* a sign of her damnation.
532, 161. *blow:* blossom.
533, 258. *succous:* juicy.
534, 284. *waxing:* growing.
534, 318. *rime:* frost.
534, 336. *mopping and mowing:* making grimaces.
534, 351. *panniers:* baskets.
535, 418. *virgin town:* a town never captured.
535, 451. *dingle:* dell.

536. A BETTER RESURRECTION

This poem first appeared in the collection of 1862, *Goblin Market and Other Poems.*
7. *everlasting hills:* a symbol of the divine power in the universe and hence a consolation.

537. PASSING AWAY, SAITH THE WORLD

This poem first appeared in the collection of 1862, *Goblin Market and Other Poems.* It was the last in a group of three poems entitled *Old and New Year Ditties;* and was itself originally entitled "The Knell of the Year." Written (or at least dated) December 31, 1860, it was the only poem composed by Christina Rossetti between July, 1860, and March, 1861. William Michael Rossetti regarded it as a "summit" of his sister's achievement; and states, discerningly, that the whole weight of the poem is borne by the meaning and sound, there being a minimum of adornment.

537, 5. Christina Rossetti was thirty years old when she wrote this poem: she had neither published a collection of verse nor won any recognition, beyond the Pre-Raphaelite group, for what lay in manuscript or had appeared in obscure places.

537, 22. *turtle:* turtle-dove.

537. WIFE TO HUSBAND

This poem first appeared in the collection of 1862, *Goblin Market and Other Poems.* William Michael Rossetti suggests, hesitatingly, that it may relate to Elizabeth Siddal, wife of Dante Gabriel Rossetti, who was grievously ill in 1861 and died in 1862.

538. AMOR MUNDI

This poem first appeared in *The Shilling Magazine* in 1865; it was subsequently reprinted, in the collected poems (1875).

The poem was thought by Christina and D. G. Rossetti to have a reminiscence of *The Demon Lover.* The meaning of the title is: Love of the World.

538, 18. Previously this line read, less powerfully and less simply: This way whereof thou weetest I fear is hell's own track.

538. PARADISE: IN A DREAM

This poem, of which the first title was "Easter Even," first appeared in the *Lyra Messianica* in 1865; it was subsequently reprinted in the collected poems (1875).

Christina Rossetti noted on a copy of her poems that this lyric did not record "a real dream."

538, 17. *the fourfold River:* a reminiscence of *Revelation*, Ch. XXII, 1: "a pure river of water of life, clear as crystal, proceeding out of the throne of God and of the Lamb."

538, 26. *its twelvefold fruits:* fruits for each month of the year (see *Revelation*, Ch. XXII, 2).

539. SOMEWHERE OR OTHER

This poem first appeared in the collection of 1866, *The Prince's Progress and Other Poems.* Between 1860 and 1866 Christina Rossetti and Charles Bagot Cayley were intimately drawn to each other in a relationship which was finally ended by Christina because of Cayley's religious opinions. She had much earlier rejected James Collinson also on religious grounds.

539. WEARY IN WELL-DOING

This poem first appeared in the collection of 1866, *The Prince's Progress and Other Poems.*

539, 12. *moil:* muddle.

539. THE LOWEST PLACE

This poem first appeared in the collection of 1866, *The Prince's Progress and Other Poems*, in which, significantly it occupied the last page. When this collection was reprinted along with *Goblin Market*, again this poem stood at the close. W. M. Rossetti remarks that it was because of its position in her works that he selected from it the second stanza to be engraved on Christina's tombstone.

539. A DIRGE

This poem first appeared in the first collected edition, in 1875.

539. BIRD RAPTURES

This poem first appeared in the collected edition of Christina Rossetti's poems in 1875.

540. MONNA INNOMINATA

This sequence of sonnets first appeared in the collection of 1881, *A Pageant and Other Poems.* It is somewhat clarified by the following note with which Christina Rossetti prefaced it:

Beatrice, immortalized by 'altissimo poeta . . . cotanto amante'—[the loftiest poet . . . and lover of equal height]; Laura, celebrated by a great though an inferior bard,—have alike paid the exceptional penalty of exceptional honour, and have come down to us resplendent with charms, but (at least, to my apprehension) scant of attractiveness.

These heroines of world-wide fame were preceded by a bevy of unnamed ladies, 'donne innominate,' sung by a school of less conspicuous poets; and in that land and that period which gave simultaneous birth to Catholics, to Albigenses, and to Troubadours, one can imagine many a lady as sharing her lover's poetic aptitude, while the barrier between them might be one held sacred by both, yet not such as to render mutual love incompatible with mutual honour.

Had such a lady spoken for herself, the portrait left us might have appeared more tender, if less dignified, than any drawn even by a devoted friend. Or had the Great Poetess of our own day and nation [Mrs. Browning] only been unhappy instead of happy, her circumstances would have invited her to bequeath to us, in lieu of the 'Portuguese Sonnets,' an inimitable 'donna innominata' drawn not from fancy but from feeling, and worthy to occupy a niche beside Beatrice and Laura.

Despite the claim in this comment that she is evoking a past age and an imaginary being, her brother William Michael is right in suggesting that it is her own love for Charles Cayley which is the real subject of the sequence.

541, (5) 59. *leal:* loyal.

541, (6) 74. *Lot's wife:* Lot was bidden by the Lord to escape from Sodom with his family, none of them pausing to look back. Lot obeyed; but "his wife looked back from behind him and she became a pillar of salt" (*Genesis*, Ch. XIX, 26).

541, 78. *sorriest:* poorest, most miserable.

541, (7) 96–98. The Book is the *Song of Songs;* in the eighth chapter, the sixth verse runs as follows: "Set me as a seal upon thine heart, as a seal upon thine arm; for love is strong as death; jealousy is cruel as the grave: the coals thereof are coals of fire, which hath a most vehement flame."

541, (8) 99. *Esther:* Esther, a Jewess, became the queen of Ahasuerus, King of Persia; when he allowed persecution of the Jews, she determined to go to him, saying to her counsellor *If I perish, I perish* (*Esther*, IV, 16); she put on "her royal apparel (*id.*, V, 1), charmed Ahasuerus, outwitted Haman, the enemy of the Jews, and secured from her husband freedom and power for her people.

543, (14) 190. *blow:* bloom.

BIBLIOGRAPHY

544. GEORGE MEREDITH

I. EDITIONS

Works, 29 vols., Scribner, 1909–12.
Works, 36 vols., Constable, 1914.
Poetical Works, ed. by G. M. Trevelyan, Constable, 1912.

II. BIOGRAPHY AND LETTERS

Letters, ed. by his son [W. M. Meredith], 2 vols., Scribner, 1912.
Letters to Alice Meynell, Nonesuch, 1923.
Butcher, Lady: *Memories of George Meredith*, Constable, 1919.
Ellis, S. M.: *George Meredith: His Life and Friends in Relation to His Work*, Richards, 1920.
Gretton, Mary: *The Writings and Life of George Meredith*, Oxford, 1926.
Photiadès, C.: *George Meredith* (translated by A. Price), Scribner, 1913.
Priestley, J. B.: *George Meredith*, Macmillan, 1926.
Sencourt, R. E.: *The Life of George Meredith*, Scribner, 1929.

III. CRITICISM

I. Monographs

Beach, J. W.: *The Comic Spirit in George Meredith*, Longmans, 1911.
Esdaile, A. J. K.: *Bibliography of the Writings in Prose and Verse of George Meredith*, Spencer (London), 1907.
Forman, M. B.: *A Bibliography of the Writings in Prose and Verse of George Meredith*, Dunedin Press (Edinburgh), 1922.
Forman, M. B.: (ed.) *George Meredith: Some Early Appreciations*, Chapman, 1909.
Galland, R.: *George Meredith: les cinquante premières années*, Presses universitaires (Paris), 1923.
Galland, R.: *George Meredith and British Criticism*, Presses universitaires (Paris), 1923.
Hammerton, J. A.: *George Meredith, His Life and Art in Anecdote and Criticism*, Grant (Edinburgh), 1911.
Le Gallienne, R.: *George Meredith, Some Characteristics*, Lane, 1900.
Trevelyan, G. M.: *The Poetry and Philosophy of George Meredith*, Constable, 1906.

II. Essays in Books

Clutton-Brock, A.: "George Meredith" in *More Essays on Books*, Dutton, 1921.
Dowden, E.: "Mr. Meredith in His Poems" in *New Studies in Literature*, Paul (London), 1895.
Elton, O.: "Mr. George Meredith" in *Modern Studies*, Arnold, 1907.
Figgis, D.: "George Meredith, the Philosopher in the Artist" in *Studies and Appreciations*, Dent, 1912.
Hearn, L.: "The Poetry of George Meredith" in *Pre-Raphaelite and Other Poets*, Dodd, 1922.
Quiller-Couch, Sir Arthur: "Meredith" in *Studies in Literature, First Series*, Cambridge, 1918.
Sherman, S. P.: "The Humanism of Meredith" in *On Contemporary Literature*, Holt, 1917.
Strong, A. T.: "An Essay on Nature in Wordsworth and Meredith" in *Three Studies in Shelley*, Oxford, 1921.
Symons, A.: "George Meredith as a Poet" in *Figures of Several Centuries*, Constable, 1916.
Welby, T. E.: "George Meredith" in *Back Numbers*, Constable, 1929.

III. Articles in Periodicals

Bailey, E. J.: "Meredith's 'Modern Love'" in the *Forum*, September, 1908.
Bailey, J.: "The Poetry of Meredith" in the *Fortnightly Review*, July, 1909.
Edgar, P.: "The Poetry of George Meredith" in the *Living Age*, December 21, 1907.
Foote, G. W.: "George Meredith, Free Thinker," in the *English Review*, March, 1913.
Hardy, T.: "George Meredith: A Reminiscence" in the *Nineteenth Century*, February, 1928.
Lowes, J. L.: "An Unacknowledged Imagist" in *The Nation*, February 24, 1916.
Lubbock, P.: "Meredith's Art" in the *Quarterly Review*, January, 1910.
Monroe, H.: "Meredith as a Poet" in *Poetry*, July, 1928.
Revell, W. F.: "George Meredith's Nature Poetry" in *Westminster Review*, November, 1894.
Russell, F. T.: "The Laurel for George Meredith" in the *South Atlantic Quarterly*, October, 1928.
Sinclair, May: "George Meredith" in the *Outlook*, June 19, 1909.
Trevelyan, G. M.: "George Meredith, 1828–1928," in *Nation Athenaeum*, February 11, 1928.

NOTES AND COMMENTS

545. LOVE IN THE VALLEY

This poem first appeared in *Poems*, the collection of 1851; it was subsequently revised and reappeared in its present form in *Macmillan's Magazine* for October, 1878.

545, 18. *her laces:* the laces of her bodice.

546, 36. *evejar:* the goatsucker, a bird resembling the whippoorwill.

546, 42. *raying:* shining.

547, 77. The meaning is that the dawn's light swallows up that of the morning star.

547, 107. *starry jasmine:* the jasmine has a circle shaped flower yellow in color.

548, 113. *birdfoot trefoil: trefoil* applies to a flower (or leaf) with three lobes; *birdfoot* is a small flower bearing a resemblance in shape to the foot of a bird.

548, 114. *cinquefoil:* having five lobes.

548, 117. *yaffle:* woodpecker.

548, 128. The meaning is that the brilliance of her beauty would blind the observer as the brightness of the sun.

548, 130. *link:* a loop in a river and the ground about it. The ground is intended here.

549, 165. *print-branches:* the shadows of branches.

549, 184. *our souls were in our names:* our souls expressed themselves fully by utterance of each other's names alone.

549, 203. *flushing like the dogwood:* the *dogwood* is the wild cornel; *flushing* refers to the coming of the autumn-colors to the leaves (see l. 205.)

549, 204. *whitebeam:* the leaves of this tree are very light on the underside.

550. JUGGLING JERRY

This poem first appeared in *Once a Week*, for September 3, 1859; it was reprinted in the collection of 1862, *Modern Love and Poems of the English Roadside*.

550, 3. *above the daisies:* alive.

550, 24. *shies:* flings.

550, 26. *wide:* far.

550, 27. *bale:* more usually *bail*, a cross-piece placed in grooves over the stumps or wicket before which the batsman stands in cricket. Two bails are now used; but formerly there was but one. The batsman is out when the ball (or bat) removes the bails.

550, 45. *professor:* here equivalent to magician.

550, 49. *topsy-turvy:* upside down position, that is, peculiar point of view.

550, 67. *bolus:* pill.

551, 78. *would hail you Cook:* would be happy to have you for cook.

551, 81. *chirper:* cup that cheers.

551. MODERN LOVE

This sequence of fifty sixteen-lined "sonnets" first appeared in the collection of 1862, *Modern Love and Poems of the English Roadside*. The sequence reflects a tragedy still recent and poignant in the poet's life. In 1849 he had married Mary Nicolls, daughter of Thomas Love Peacock and widow of a naval officer. Meredith's wife was a woman of sharp and fine intelligence, unusual knowledge, a great enthusiasm, and remarkable beauty. The poet's son has recorded the disaster that overtook the marriage: "Two highly strung temperaments—man and wife—each imaginative, emotional, quick to anger, cuttingly satirical in dispute, could not find domestic content within the narrow bounds of poverty and lodgings" (*Letters of George Meredith*, I, 7). They separated in 1858; and in 1861 Mrs. Meredith died. It is impossible to say whether or no Meredith in writing of his love for another woman, is recording his passion for Janet Ross: it was returned by friendship, not by love, and Miss Ross married in 1860. The intensity of his disappointment can be divined in his letters. The year after *Modern Love* appeared Meredith met Marie Vulliamy; and in 1864 they were married.

I

552, 15. *the sword between:* as a symbol of their separation (although this was not the significance on medieval tombs).

II

552, 3. *their sin:* passion without love.
552, 9. *brown:* dark, dull.
552, 14. *fainted on his vengefulness:* weakened in his vengefulness.

III

552, 1. *the man:* the wife's lover.
552, 12. *meet him there:* kiss where her lover has kissed.
552, 15. The meaning is that the woman with whom he shared a love, no longer exists: she has given place to another personality, dominated by a love for another man.

IV

552, 5–6. The meaning of these obscure lines is probably that although he would have welcomed illusion if it had brought happiness, the only illusion to come was that which presented each passing occupation as suggesting the futility and tastelessness of the one preceding it.
553, 14. *full worth:* a word such as "gets" is implied before this phrase.

V

553, 10. The meaning is that for a passing moment he imagines that their old relationship still exists.
553, 14. *to be looked at:* as distinguished from 'to look.'

VI

553, 5. *her:* nature.
553, 13. *the world's coward stroke:* condemnation for illicit passion.

VII

554, 4. *oiled:* with oiled hair.
554, 13. *filthiness:* carnality.

VIII

554, 1–2. The meaning is: she clearly struggled against her love for the other, and the fact of her struggling indicates an element of virtue in her which redeems her from real wickedness and renders her an object of pity.
554, 8 f. The poet is using the legend of Pan inventing the pipe with seven reeds.

IX

554, 14. *circle-glory:* the sun.

X

555, 2. *arraigned:* indicted, *i.e.* brought before a tribunal and the charge against one preferred.
555, 3. *sentence:* verdict.
555, 4. *nerveless:* flaccid (as opposed to the energy of a full life in which love is but a part).
555, 9. *are curled:* curl.

XI

555, 16. *a dead infant:* symbolizing their love.

XII

555, 5–6. *which begat distinction in old times:* which gave a special quality to their shared past.
555, 10–11. The meaning is: since his wife has sought a world of make-believe, in which only love exists.

XIII

556, 9. *urn:* funeral urn, symbolizing death.

XIV

556, 6–8. The first reference to the mistress, subsequently called "my lady."
556, 10. *the woman:* his wife.

XV

556, 5. The meaning is: The gloomy dramatic figure of an injured lover.
556, 7. *lid:* eyelid.
556, 11. *the burden:* an old letter.

XVII

557, 5. *ply the ball:* keep the conversation moving.
557, 12. *ephemeriae:* insects living but a day.

XVIII

557, 4. *signal:* notable.
557, 6. *one nut-brown stream:* a stream of nut brown ale.
557, 11. *a charmed Amphion-oak:* Amphion, one of Jupiter's sons, played so beautifully that the stones arose at the sound of his lyre and formed the walls of Thebes; he had similar power over trees.

XIX

558, 10. *goat-legged buyers;* Pan was represented in Greek art and poetry as having the legs of a goat, an animal taken as a symbol of lust.

XX

558, 9. *deuce:* devil.

XXI

558, 2. *My friend:* Probably there is a reference to Meredith's friend Maxse, engaged to be married in 1861. Meredith wrote to him two elaborate and intense letters on love in that year (see *Letters of George Meredith*, I, 38 f., 53 f.).
558, 14. *happy things:* the birth of children.

XXII

559, 16. *star:* place in the scale of being.

XXIII

559, 5. *the midnight's hollow door:* the dark and empty night.
559, 6. *the pit:* hell.

XXIV

559, 2. *sense:* conscience.
559, 6. *that cruel lovely pallor:* a mark of her suffering.
559, 7. *the low vibrating sounds:* the tones of her voice.

XXV

560, 1. *that French novel:* the account is too general for identification. The theme is that of a wife, who after a passing affair returns to her former love for her husband.
560, 9. *rosbif:* the French corruption of the words *roast beef.*
560, 10. *abused:* by infidelity.
560, 11. *Auguste:* the husband.

XXVI

560, 13. *side-lie:* bias.

XXVII

560, 3. *specific:* remedy against a particular ailment.
560, 14. *Lady:* not his wife but another woman to whom in other sonnets there are many references.

XXVIII

561, 8. *proper:* own.

561. *lessened in my proper sight:* belittled in my own opinion of myself (by having fallen into the Lady's clutches).

561, 13. *groan:* long.

561, 14. *sunflower:* taken as a symbol of conspicuous beauty of coarse quality.

XXIX

561, 2. *this head:* of the Lady, not his wife.

561, 3. *springing from the mould:* of an earthy sort.

561, 4. The meaning is: My present love does not exalt as my past love did.

561, 8. *at her worth:* for what she is.

561, 16. *eat our pot of honey:* enjoy our sensual pleasures.

on the grave: as mortal animals and no more.

XXX

561, 2. *at a leap:* at the first stage farther in our development, but that stage an immense advance.

561, 4. The meaning is: all that derives its force from the fact of our mortality.

561, 6. *the shadow loses form:* the awareness of mortality and the dread of it are blurred by love.

XXXII

562, 14. *her sex's antidote:* the poison effective to counteract the dangerous disease another woman has caused.

562, 16. *Shrieking Bacchantes:* the Bacchantes were the worshippers of Bacchus, god of wine; in their rites of worship intoxication and wild dancing were prominent, and as a consequence of their excitement they shrieked.

XXXIII

562. The picture described is Raphael's "St. Michael."

562, 2. *the sumptuously-feathered angel:* the archangel Michael.

562, 5. *Pharsalians:* the followers of Julius Caesar at the battle of Pharsalia in Thessaly, where Pompey's forces were annihilated or captured and Caesar's incurred only a trifling loss.

XXXIV

563, 1. *Madam:* his wife.

563, 2. *The Deluge or else Fire:* a deluge of tearful complaints or else a fiery attack. The image recurs in more concrete terms in *Niagara and Vesuvius* (ll. 7, 8).

XXXVII

564, 4. *the chariot:* the sun. In Greek myth Phoebus Apollo, the sun god, was believed to ride in a fiery chariot through the skies, beginning at the east in the morning and reaching the west in the evening.

564, 11. *rosed:* rose-coloured.

564, 12. *bars:* used in a double sense, that of bars of music, and that of the lines (as of trees) across the surface of the moon.

XXXVIII

564, 5. *Gogmagogs:* Gog and Magog were mythical tribes (*Revelation, Ch. XX*, 8).

564, 10. *arrowy:* speeds like an arrow.

564, 15. *she:* his wife, not the Lady whom he here addresses.

XL

565, 10. *this woman:* his wife.

XLI

565, 11. *A lifeless vow:* fidelity without love.

XLII

565, 5. *taken*: deceived.

565, 8. *Pallas:* Pallas Athene (Minerva) goddess of wisdom.

565, 13. *Hebe:* a daughter of Jupiter and Juno, worshipped as goddess of youth.

shamed: the poet may have had in mind the disgrace of Hebe at a banquet of the gods, when Jupiter, accusing her of immodesty, deprived her of her function as cup-bearer.

565, 14–16. He prevents her from taking her life.

XLIII

566, 10–11. *the unblest kisses which upbraid the full waked sense:* the kisses given were a consequence of unblest feelings quite unlike those of genuine love and now inspire disgust because he is now released from the spell under which he gave them.

566, 14. *wot:* knows.

XLIV

566, 2. *temple:* the temple of Love.

566, 12. *cheat:* counterfeit.

XLV

566, 5. *Hesper:* the evening star.

XLVI

566, 11. *rude:* violent.

566, 16. *widening:* with astonishment.

XLVII

566, 2. *osier:* willow.

XLVIII

566, 15. *my sentience of her:* what I feel to be the truth about her (see next line).

XLIX

568, 16. *Lethe:* Lethe was in classical myth the river of oblivion, passing through which, on the way to the world beyond the grave, men lost all memory of life on earth.

The meaning of the line as a whole is that as she was about to die she forgot all that had marred their life and remembered only the fact of their love; he was aware of how she felt although she could not express the whole of it. G. M. Trevelyan records Meredith's statement that the wife of the poem committed suicide (*Poems*, p. 584).

L

568, 10. *dole:* grief.

568. THE WOODS OF WESTERMAIN

This poem first appeared in the collection of 1883, *Poems and Lyrics of the Joy of Earth.* The woods of Westermain are in the county of Surrey (to the south of London) where the poet lived. The woods, as G. M. Trevelyan states, symbolize nature as a whole.

568, 9. *they quit their form:* they cease to be harmless, if one does not approach them boldly and happily.

568, 11. *have you by the hair:* fill you with fear.

568, 18. *yaffles:* woodpeckers.

568, 21. *the moth-winged jar:* the eve-jar (or night-jar), a bird.

568, 25. *roods:* spaces (strictly quarter-acres).

569, 46. *whins:* gorse.

569, 47. *minikins:* little creatures.

569, 68. *race:* current.

569, 77. *when mind was mud:* when *mind* (the distinctive feature of humanity) was in its primal form —the earth from which all has evolved.

569, 79. *timelessly:* through endless periods of time.

569, 80. *a slimy spine:* a ridge covered with slime (amidst the waters).

569, 81. *winging tons:* the planets and stars, weighty, and moving through the sky.

569, 84. *the Nurse of Seed:* the Mother of all (nature).

569, 92. *the white Foam-born:* Venus (Aphrodite) who appeared at Paphos, on the island of Cyprus, rising from the foam of the sea.

569, 94. *Phoebus:* Phoebus Apollo, god of music, whose special instrument was the lyre. His being god of the sun is also remembered in this allusion.

Phoebe: Diana, goddess of the moon.

569, 95. *reedy Pan: Pan* was god of nature. His instrument was a pipe of reeds.

569, 94–95. In these lines, Meredith selects gods representative of the sun, the moon and the earth. His purpose is to suggest that all the gods continue to have their place in his conception of the earth and of life.

569, 100. *the huntress moon:* Diana was also the goddess of hunting.

569, 103. *awn:* the soft spikes of grain.

569, 121. *centaur:* in Greek myth a creature half man, half horse.

570, 132. *the blossom-shoot:* the source.

570, 148. *casket-breasts:* hearts full of treasure.

570, 149–151. If man is tyrannical, craves a relationship with woman which ministers to his conceit, instead of acting according to the highest commands of intelligence, woman will be transformed into a deceiver.

570, 153. The meaning is that some of the tales end in violence, some even in death.

570, 158–159. The tiger represents man, the snake woman.

570, 180. *monkish glee:* unnatural envious delight.

570, 191. *quern:* hand mill.

570, 216–217. The meaning is that even if one approaches nature with the ideal attitude, there is danger: danger can be completely removed only when the ideal attitude is widely diffused.

570, 220. *Dragon-fowl:* According to Professor Trevelyan the dragon-fowl represents egoism.

570, 224. *stress:* dominion.

571, 267. *the Fount and Lure o' the chase:* Love.

571, 279. Professor Trevelyan describes as an old rural tradition the belief that in a section of the stem of the bracken, one can see as in miniature the form of an oak-tree.

571, 283. *her:* Nature.

571, 301. *Rosiest rosy:* the most beautiful of young girls.

crone: an old woman.

571, 333. *lighting:* tracking.

571, 335. The meaning is probably: through all the variety of its unsubstantial shapes, *shot* having the sense of varied.

571, 340. *misprised:* despised.

572, 354. *gnomes:* earth spirits, the custodians of the secrets and treasures of nature.

572, 363. *glassing:* mirroring.

572, 369. *ask:* the question unasked is what awaits man after death.

572, 374. *the chisel, axe and sword:* the *chisel* represents the arts, the *axe* the toils and the *sword* the struggles of life. The three together represent the achievement of man in society.

572, 379. *concordant:* agreeing.

572, 380. *ramped:* rampant.

572, 385. The meaning is: the river separating this life from what lies beyond the grave will have no terror but will appear harmlessly familiar.

572, 395. *the mind preserves:* even if the husk is discarded whatever element of significance it may have had, the mind — so that nothing whatever should be lost — will retain.

572, 401. *bent:* instinct.

572, 427. *marsh-damps:* the phosphorescent light in areas where there is decay.

572, 446. *the monster:* the dragon of egoism, repeatedly referred to above.

572, 451. *truncheon-saws: saws* has the meaning of proverbs (seen here as embodying narrow traditional views); the truncheon is at once a symbol and an instrument of social power, here considered as oppressive.

573, 457. *One whose eyes are out:* a symbol of death.

573, 459. *henbane and hellebore:* poisonous drugs derived from plants.

573, 466. *drums the sconce:* drums with her fingers on the skull.

573. EARTH AND MAN

This poem first appeared in the collection of 1883, *Poems and Lyrics of the Joy of Earth.* It represents, as Professor Trevelyan has said (*Poetical Works of George Meredith*, 591) the most complete expression of Meredith's idea of the earth as man's mother.

573, 6–7. *his heart involves his fate:* his fate is determined by his individual emotional nature, which earth does not seek to control.

573, 17–20. The general meaning is that unlike the other animals he has become conscious.
573, 19. *gnome:* an earth-spirit.
573, 30. *the Invisible:* the conception of a supernatural god, invented by man.
573, 36. *the eyeless Ghost:* a spirit without brain, and, accordingly, without perception in the human fashion.
574, 59. The reference is to the Darwinian doctrine of the survival of the fittest.
574, 60. *wanton:* a light woman. The choice is described as a wanton's because it appears totally unheeding of moral values.
574, 65. *read:* interpret.
574, 75. *shingle:* a pebbled shore.
574, 78. *the Invisible:* see note on l. 30.
574, 82. *some proofs of slaughtered nature:* some miracles, *i.e.*, some evidences of a power superior to nature and able to alter its normal processes.
574, 97–98. The reference is to cathedrals.
575, 144. *hoofed and horned:* hoofs and horns are symbols of the diabolical.
575, 158. *gapped readings:* fragmentary accounts.
575, 165. *her just Lord:* this, the true divine, is, as Professor Trevelyan points out, attainable only through nature: it is spiritual, but not supernatural.
576, 175. *twi-minded:* with two minds, or views.

576. LUCIFER IN STARLIGHT

This poem first appeared in the collection of 1883, *Poems and Lyrics of the Joy of Earth.*
576, 3. *the rolling ball:* the earth.
576, 10. *from Awe:* against God.
576, 14. The reference to the stars is continued.

576. THE SPIRIT OF SHAKESPEARE

This pair of sonnets first appeared in the collection of 1883, *Poems and Lyrics of the Joy of Earth.*

I

576, 3. *deflowered:* stripped.
576, 7. *the God:* Neptune (Poseidon) who was god of the sea.
576, 8. *intershifting:* blending.

II

576, 3. *a breast:* the breast of life.
576, 4. *glass:* mirror.

BIBLIOGRAPHY

577. WILLIAM MORRIS

I. EDITIONS

Collected Works, with introductions by May Morris, 24 vols., Longmans, 1910–1915.
Poetical Works, 11 vols., Longmans, 1896–1898.
Prose and Poetry, 1856–1870, Oxford, 1913.
Selected Writings, ed. by G. D. H. Cole, Nonesuch, 1934.

II. BIOGRAPHY AND LETTERS

Cary, E. L.: *William Morris, Poet, Craftsman, Socialist*, Putnam, 1902.
Clutton-Brock, A.: *William Morris, His Work and Influence*, Williams and Norgate, 1914.
Glaiser, J. B.: *William Morris and the Early Days of the Socialist Movement*, Longmans, 1921.
Mackail, J. W.: *The Life of William Morris*, Longmans, 2 vols., 1899.
Mackail, J. W.: *William Morris and His Circle*, Longmans, 1907.
Morris, May: *William Morris, Artist, Writer, Socialist*, 2 vols., Blackwell, 1936.
Noyes, A.: *William Morris*, Macmillan, 1908.
Sparling, H. H.: *The Kelmscott Press and William Morris, Master Craftsman*, Macmillan, 1924.
Vallance, A.: *William Morris, His Art, His Writings and His Public Life*, Bell, 1897.

III. CRITICISM

I. Monographs

Crow, G. H.: *William Morris, Designer*, Studio (London), 1935.
Drinkwater, J.: *William Morris, a Critical Study*, Secker, 1912.
Forman H. B.: *The Books of William Morris Described*, Hollings (London), 1897.
Hoare, D.: *The Works of Morris and Yeats in Relation to Early Saga Literature*, Cambridge, 1937.
Jackson, H.: *William Morris* (2nd ed.) Cape, 1926.
Phelan, A. A.: *The Social Philosophy of William Morris*, Duke University Press, 1927.
Scott, T.: *A Bibliography of the Works of William Morris*, Bell, 1897.
Shaw, G. B.: *William Morris As I Knew Him*, Dodd, 1936.
Vidalenc, G.: *William Morris*, Alcan, 1920.

II. Essays in Books

Brooke, S. A.: "William Morris" in *Four Victorian Poets*, Putnam, 1908.
Clutton-Brock, A.: "The Prose Romances of William Morris" in *Essays on Books*, Methuen, 1920.
Forman, H. B.: "William Morris" in *Our Living Poets*, Tinsley (London), 1871.
Guyot, E.: "Le socialisme de William Morris" in *Le socialisme et l'évolution de l'Angleterre contemporaine, 1880–1911*, Alcan, 1913.
Hearn, L., "William Morris" in *Pre-Raphaelite and Other Poets*, Dodd, 1922.
Lucas, F. L.: "William Morris" in *Eight Victorian Poets*, Cambridge, 1930.
Mackail, J. W.: "William Morris" in *Studies of English Poets*, Longmans, 1926.
More, P. E.: "William Morris" in *Shelburne Essays*, Seventh Series, Putnam, 1910.
Pater, W.: "Aesthetic Poetry" in *Appreciations* (1st edition only), Macmillan, 1889.
Saintsbury, G.: "Mr. William Morris" in *Corrected Impressions*, Macmillan, 1895.
Scott, Dixon: "The First Morris" in *Men of Letters*, Hodder, 1923.
Swinburne, A. C.: "Morris's 'Life and Death of Jason'" in *Essays and Studies*, Chatto, 1875.
Symons, A.: "William Morris" in *Studies in Two Literatures*, Secker, 1924.
Yeats, W. B.: "The Happiest of the Poets" in *Ideas of Good and Evil*, Bullen (London), 1903.

III. Articles from Periodicals

Hewlett, H. G.: "The Poems of Mr. Morris" in the *Contemporary Review*, December, 1874.
Lang, A.: "The Poetry of William Morris" in the *Contemporary Review*, August, 1882.
Lubbock, P.: "The Poetry of William Morris" in the *Quarterly Review*, October, 1911.

NOTES AND COMMENTS

578. RIDING TOGETHER

This poem first appeared in the *Oxford and Cambridge Magazine* for May, 1856; it was reprinted in the collection of 1858, *The Defence of Guenevere and Other Poems.* No source is known.

578, 4. *Our Lady's Feast:* the feast of the Annunciation, March 25.

578, 16. *bream:* a fresh water fish.

578, 18. *rood:* cross.

579. THE CHAPEL IN LYONESS

This poem first appeared in the *Oxford and Cambridge Magazine* for September, 1856; and was reprinted in the collection of 1858, *The Defence of Guenevere and Other Poems.*

Lyoness: a mythical country supposed to lie to the southwest of Cornwall; it frequently appears in Arthurian legend and Arthur himself was reported to have come from it.

Sir Ozana was a knight of Arthur and one of those who accompanied Guenevere when she was captured by Meliagrance (see Morris's poem *The Defence of Guenevere*); *Sir Bors*, like *Sir Galahad*, was one of the knights who set out in quest of the Holy Grail.

579, 11. *parclose:* a screen separating a chapel from the central part of the church.

579, 29. *Ozana of the hardy heart:* a literal translation of *Ozana le cure (cœur) hardy. Hardy* is the equivalent simply of brave.

579, 40. *Launcelot:* it is not clear why Lancelot should be mentioned; he was reputed to be the father of Galahad; he was the lover of Guenevere; it is likely that the introduction of his name is to be explained as follows: Sir Ozana may have received his death wound in the encounter with Meliagrance, which led to the capture of Guenevere; when Lancelot learns of that capture he will lead the rescue.

580. SUMMER DAWN

This poem first appeared, under the title "Pray but One Prayer for Me," in the *Oxford and Cambridge Magazine* for October, 1856; under its present title it was reprinted in the collection of 1858, *The Defence of Guenevere and Other Poems.*

580. THE DEFENCE OF GUENEVERE

This poem first appeared in the collection of 1858, *The Defence of Guenevere and Other Poems.* The source of the Poem is Malory's *Morte D'Arthur*, but Morris has departed from his source, and amplified it, whenever it suited his artistic purpose to do so. For instance, in Malory's account, Gawaine was a defender, not an accuser, of the Queen; in the battle which followed upon the discovery of Lancelot in Guenevere's chamber Lancelot did however slay two of Gawaine's brothers.

581, 11. *skill:* use.

581, 13. *wot:* knows.

581, 26. *my lord:* Gawaine, the chief accuser.

581, 47. The reference is to her relations with Lancelot through the years.

582, 86–87. *for a little word, scarce ever meant at all:* the acceptance of Arthur in the marriage service.

583, 126. *yellow-spotted singers:* the thrushes, mentioned in l. 106.

584, 138. *strained:* stretched.

584, 153. *your mother:* King Arthur's sister, slain by one of her sons when he convicted her of infidelity to his father.

584, 156. *drouth:* lack.

584, 157. *Agravaine:* a brother of Gawaine.

584, 165. *dress:* address.

584, 168. *Mellyagraunce:* Meliagrance was the leader of a band which captured Guenevere (see l. 161 f.); he charged her with adultery (see l. 173 f.); and died in combat with Lancelot who took up her cause (see l. 185 f.).

584, 169. *la Fausse Garde:* literally, the false prison; the meaning is that Meliagrance's conduct in attacking an unarmed group of knights, and carrying off the queen was unknightly, and that accordingly her capture was in violation of the code of war.

585, 201. *weet:* knew.

585, 205. *pen:* pennon.

585, 216. *the fire:* Guenevere had been sentenced to be burned for adultery.

586, 220. *shent:* destroyed.

586, 221. *against the Lord:* against the right.

586, 222. *blent:* involved (blended).

586, 239. *woof:* weave.

587, 295. *at good need:* in the nick of time (to save her from burning).

587. CONCERNING GEFFRAY TESTE NOIRE

This poem first appeared in the collection of 1858, *The Defence of Guenevere and Other Poems.* Geffray's exploits are recounted by the chronicler Jean Froissart, a canon of Chimay: he was a Gascon marauder of the late fourteenth century.

587, 1. *Chimay:* a Belgian town, just across the border from France.

587, 2. *Ortaise:* the palace of the feudal lord of Bearn, in southern France.

587, 3. *John of Castel Neuf:* John of Newcastle.

588, 7. *pilled:* pillaged.

588, 7. *lief:* in allegiance to.

588, 8. *King Charles:* Charles the Fifth of France.

588, 8. *St. Dennis:* the patron saint of France.

588, 9. *my lord:* a title of honour, not indicating allegiance on the part of the speaker.

588, 10. *the Duke of Berry:* the governor for the King of France in the south.

588, 13. *bastides:* towers run close to fortifications to assist in an assault.

588, 15. *the rock of Ventadour:* a castle on a height in Auvergne, in central France.

588, 25. *Alleyne Roux:* Alleyne the Red, a nephew of Geffray.

588, 26. *camaille:* armor for upper part of the body.

588, 29. *blackhead:* a literal translation of Teste Noire.

588, 33. *villaynes:* peasants.

588, 46. *sumpter:* pack.

588, 47. *Carcassonne:* a heavily fortified town in southern France.

589, 52. *the horse in Job:* The horse which "paweth in the valley, and rejoiceth in his strength; he goeth on to meet the armed men. He mocketh at fear, and is not affrighted; neither turneth he back from the sword" (*Job*, Ch. XXXIX, 21–22).

589, 80. *ceinture:* girdle.

589, 83. *coif:* cap.

590, 94. *this:* a bone, or the skeleton as a whole.

590, 99. *Jacquerie:* an uprising of the peasants (originally — and it is in this sense used here — the uprising of the French peasants in 1358).

590, 101. *Beauvais:* a city in northeastern France.

590, 103. *gentles:* nobles.

590, 107. *so great and fair:* the cathedral of Beauvais was conceived on a larger scale than any other of the French cathedrals; but it remained very incomplete.

591, 152. *overwinded harp:* a harp of which the strings have been stretched too tight.

592, 184. *natheless:* nonetheless.
the rood: the cross.

592, 190. *John Froissart:* the chronicler. See the general note on the poem.

592, 193. *the Eure:* a river in northern France.

592, 199. *Jaques Picard:* an imaginary artist.

592. OLD LOVE

This poem first appeared in the collection of 1858, *The Defence of Guenevere and Other Poems.*

592, 5. *basnet point:* helmet point.

592, 8. *natheless:* nonetheless.

592, 21–22. Venice held up to the middle of the fifteenth century the command of the eastern Mediterranean; but lost it to the Turks.

592, 23. *miscreants:* infidels.

592, 25. *Constantine:* Constantinople, which fell to the Turks in 1453.

593. THE GILLIFLOWER OF GOLD

This poem first appeared in the collection of 1858, *The Defence of Guenevere and Other Poems.*

593, 4. *la belle jaune giroflée:* the beautiful yellow gilliflower. This is the speaker's heraldic device and his war-cry.

593, 25. *Honneur aux fils des preux:* honor to the sons of the brave.

593, 30. *tabard:* cloak.

593, 31. *blame:* harm.

594. SHAMEFUL DEATH

This poem first appeared in the collection of 1858, *The Defence of Guenevere and Other Poems.* No source is known.

594, 2. *mass-priest:* chaplain.

594, 21. *hornbeams:* these trees, with smooth light-colored bark, were specially attractive to Morris and abounded in the parts of the Thames valley he knew best.

594. THE EVE OF CRECY

This poem first appeared in the collection of 1858, *The Defence of Guenevere and Other Poems.* At Crecy, in northern France, the English defeated the French in 1346.

594, 4. The line may be translated: Oh, how beautiful is Margaret. But it should be remembered that *marguerite* is also the French for a daisy.

595, 14. *arrière-ban:* proclamation to arms, or a body in arms in obedience to such a proclamation.

595, 15. *basnets:* helmets.

595, 39. *Philip:* Philip VI was King of France at the time of Crecy.

595, 41. *perdie:* a French oath of the mildest sort. Literally translated it means: By God (Par Dieu); but no such intensity of meaning attached to it.

595, 45. *rood:* cross.

595, 46. *banneret:* the word carries here its full meaning, which is twofold. First, that of a man knighted for valor in battle; second, that of a knight privileged to fight under a banner with his own heraldic device.

595, 51. *St. Ives:* a French saint, whose name was often used by the French as a warcry.

596. THE BLUE CLOSET

This poem first appeared in the collection of 1858, *The Defence of Guenevere and Other Poems;* it was composed as a verbal commentary on one of Rossetti's pictures.

596, 5. *laudate pueri:* praise, children. These are the opening words of a medieval hymn.

596, 13. *chevron:* a V-shaped bar.

597, 66. *Arthur:* King Arthur.

598. THE HAYSTACK IN THE FLOODS

This poem first appeared in the collection of 1858, *The Defence of Guenevere and Other Poems.* No source is known. The period is the middle of the fourteenth century.

598, 9. *kirtle:* skirt.

kilted: tucked up.

598, 35. *running:* rampant.

598, 39. *Robert:* her lover's full name was Robert de Marny, see l. 61.

598, 42. *coif:* a cap (often a helmet), coming down farther at the back of the head than in front. *the wrong way:* she turned the cap about so that the longer part (ordinarily behind) should be in front, over her eyes.

598, 45. *Poictiers:* at Poitiers, in 1356, the English, with the troops from those parts of France which they held, defeated the forces of France, although greatly outnumbered.

598, 47. *the Gascon frontier:* Gascony, in the southwest of France, was subject to England for most of the fourteenth century.

598, 51. *those six men:* the judges.

598, 52. *the gratings of the Chatelet:* the Châtelet was a prison in Paris, on the bank of the river Seine; *the gratings*, literally, frames of bars, suggest the cells of the prison.

598, 53 f. If she swam she would be pronounced guilty; innocent only if she sank.

598, 57. *him:* Godmar, their immediate enemy.

598, 61. *St. George:* the patron saint of England.

599, 109. *gag me Robert:* gag Robert for me.

599, 153. *fitte:* part (of a tale).

599. SIR GILES' WAR-SONG

This poem first appeared in the collection of 1858, *The Defence of Guenevere and Other Poems.* The source of the poem, if there was any, is unknown.

599, 1. *ride with me:* meet me in battle on horse.

599, 2. This line may be translated as: Sir Giles, good at assaults.

599, 7. *the leopards and lilies:* probably the device on his shield or perhaps on that of the leader of the army to which he belongs.

599, 8. *St. George Guienne: St. George* appears in this warcry as the patron saint of England, *Guienne* was a part of France held by the English during most of the fourteenth century.

599, 16. *basnet:* helmet.

600. PRAISE OF MY LADY

This poem first appeared in the collection of 1858, *The Defence of Guenevere and Other Poems.* The description exactly suits the beauty of Jane Burden, whom Morris met in 1856 and whom he was to marry the year after the collection was published.

600, 4. *Beata mea Domina:* my blessed lady.

600, 11. *crisped:* curled.

600, 14. *dead:* with the quality of sculpture.

601. SONGS FROM *THE LIFE AND DEATH OF JASON*

The Life and Death of Jason appeared in 1867. A poetic romance in eighteen books, it tells the tale of the quest of the golden fleece and also relates Jason's subsequent adventures. From time to time the narrative is interrupted by songs sung by a number of personages in the poem.

The first song given here ("I know a little garden close") occurs in Book IV (ll. 577–608). The Argonauts, bound for Colchis, put ashore in Mysia, in Asia Minor; and Hylas, a beautiful youth of their number, wandered inland. The water-nymphs fell in love with him; and one of them, adopting human form, placed herself in his way, affecting to be in profound distress. Hylas immediately fell in love with her; and at a pause in their wanderings she sang to him this song.

The second song ("O death, that maketh life so sweet") occurs in Book XII (ll. 335–402). The Argonauts, homeward bound, have left the Black Sea by a river to the north, have skirted the northern coasts of Europe, passing to the south of the British Isles, and are, when this song is sung by Orpheus, approaching the straits of Gibraltar. This they do not know: and having seen no land for many days, they are melancholy.

601, 9. *a poisonous unknown land:* no particular land is intended.

601, 20. *chequered:* by the sunlight shining through the trees.

601, 38. *outland:* foreign.

601, 43. The reference is to the golden fleece.

602, 60. *Argo:* the name of their ship.

602. THE EARTHLY PARADISE

This poem appeared in three sections (subsequently the first section was subdivided into two) between 1868 and 1870. It was conceived not earlier than 1865 (see Mackail, *Life of William Morris*, I, 178 f.). Following the brief apology, given among the selections in this volume, comes a long prologue which is almost a tale; twenty-four tales follow, joined by end-links (celebrating the twelve months of the year); the poem closes with an epilogue and an envoi. Half of the tales are drawn from Greek sources, half from medieval; three types of versification were used, the octosyllabic couplet, the heroic couplet and the seven-lined stanza of Morris's supreme master, Chaucer. Unity and a measure of aesthetic plausibility were given by the establishment, in the prologue, of a setting which could account for a succession of tales on varying themes and reflecting various civilizations. On a forgotten island survivors of Greek civilization are discovered by a group of mariners of the fourteenth century: Greek and medieval tales are thus not unnaturally exchanged.

602. AN APOLOGY

602, 1. *Heaven or Hell:* the themes of the greatest of narrative poets, Homer, Virgil, Dante, Milton.

602, 18. *names remembered:* most of the tales relate to legends well known to cultivated readers in his age, such legends as those of Atalanta, Paris, Hercules, etc.

602, 25. *the ivory gate:* according to Virgil, dreams which were merely false passed from the abode of Morpheus through a gate of ivory.

602, 29. *a wizard to a northern king:* the reference has not been clarified.

602, 31 f. The structure of the poem is supported by brief lyrics on the months of the year.

602. INTRODUCTION

These are the opening lines of the prologue, which is entitled "The Wanderers"; but they really serve to introduce the poem as a whole.

602, 1. *six counties:* the counties over parts of which, if not all, London and its suburbs extended in Morris's time.

603, 13. *Guienne:* in the Middle Ages, a southwestern province of France, possessed by the English for most of the fourteenth century, the period in which the poem is set.

603, 14–15. Chaucer was for some years a customs official.

603. ATALANTA'S RACE

This poem is the first tale in *The Earthly Paradise;* the section of that work to which it belongs appeared in 1868. In preparing to write the classical tales in that collection Morris read the relevant parts of Lemprière's *Classical Dictionary;* for this tale he also used Ovid's account in the *Metamorphoses,* Bk. X, 560 f. Inevitably he would have present to his mind Swinburne's *Atalanta in Calydon.* He prefixed to the poem the following "argument":

Atalanta, daughter of King Schoeneus, not willing to lose her virgin's estate, made it a law to all suitors that they should run a race with her in the public place, and if they failed to overcome her, should die unrevenged; and thus many brave men perished. At last came Milanion, the son of Amphidamas, who, outrunning her with the help of Venus, gained the virgin and wedded her.

603, 1. *Arcadian:* Arcadia lay to the north of Sparta in the same peninsula.

603, 14. *cornel:* cherrywood (or wood similar to it).

603, 28. *King Schoeneus' town:* for King Schoeneus see the general note to the poem. His *town* was Sciros.

604, 63. *the Fleet-foot One:* Mercury (Hermes) the messenger of the gods, whose feet had wings.

604, 73. *crisp-haired:* curly-haired.

604, 79. *Diana:* the virgin huntress.

606, 167. *centaur:* the centaurs were half-man, half-horse and lived in the forests.

606, 177. *saffron:* the bridal colour.

607, 184. *the Sea-born One:* Venus, goddess of love, appeared from the foam of the sea at Paphos on the island of Cyprus.

607, 206. *the Dryads:* wood nymphs.

607, 208. *Adonis' bane:* Adonis, a mortal beloved of Venus, was gored by the tusks of a boar, dying of the wounds.

607, 211. *Argive:* belonging to Argolis, a state to the east of Arcadia.

608, 275. *the three-formed goddess:* Diana (Artemis), so-called because she was confused with Proserpine and the moon.

608, 277. *saffron:* see note on l. 177.

609, 282. *the sea-born framer of delights:* Venus.

609, 291. *hardihead:* bravery.

609, 292. *marketstead:* market-place.

609, 301. *Artemis:* another name for Diana.

610, 336. *equal:* just.

610, 343. *heading:* beheading.

610, 352. *Argos:* a city in Argolis, to the east of Arcadia.
610, 354. *leech:* physician.
610, 358. *Argolis:* see note on l. 352.
610, 360. *the lion-bearing lands:* in northern Africa.
610, 363. *press:* wine-press.
611, 378. *the living treasures:* the beautiful women.
611, 403. *toils:* bonds.
613, 492. *unnamed:* unnamable, because unknown to man.
613, 516. *Damascus:* at this city in Syria was one of the most elaborate and frequented of the shrines of Venus.
614, 526. *scrip:* wallet.
614, 535. *Saturn's clime:* the golden age, before Saturn's sovereignty was replaced by the severer rule of Jupiter (Zeus).
614, 539. *the Helper of unhappy men:* Venus.
615, 585. *in other guise:* in less revealing garb.
616, 632. *Argive:* see note on l. 211.
617, 663. *the mighty Lord:* Jupiter (Zeus).
617, 671. *saffron:* see note on l. 177.
617, 674. *Love's servant:* Milanion.
617, 679. *zone:* girdle.
The *zone*, the *arrows* and the *bow* were the signs of Atalanta's service of Diana.

619. L'ENVOI

619, 4. *done on thee pilgrim's weed:* clothed you [in print] for your adventure.
619, 14. *soothly:* truly.
619, 33. *gain the Land of Matters Unforgot:* attain immortality.
619, 41. *bay:* laurel.
620, 71. *reading:* interpreting.
620, 93. The reference is to social and economic conditions in Victorian England, which Morris thought to be far more evil than those of the Middle Ages.
620, 97. *lovers dead:* notably Troilus and Cresseida, celebrated by Chaucer in the poem of that name.
620, 102. *the House of Fame:* there is a double meaning—in one sense Morris is saying that his poems may never attain immortality, in the other that they may not equal Chaucer's poem entitled *The House of Fame*.

620. SIGURD THE VOLSUNG

This poem, Morris's most important expression of his interest and admiration of the primitive north, appeared in 1876. He had given to it his leisure for a little less than two years. Of the place which it held in Morris's estimation Mackail remarks: "In his own judgment it stood apart from the rest of his poetry, less because it showed any higher perfection in craftsmanship than because the subject was the story which he counted the first in the world, and because he was convinced that he had treated the story with a fidelity and largeness of manner for which he could answer to his own conscience" (Mackail, *Life of William Morris*, I, 330). Morris himself said, prior to the composition of the poem: "This is the Great Story of the North, which should be to all our race what the Tale of Troy was to the Greeks: to all our race first, and afterwards, when the change of the world has made our race nothing more than a name of what has been, a story too, then should it be to those that come after us no less than the Tale of Troy has been to us." This judgment was expressed in the preface to the translation of the *Völsunga Saga*, carried through by Morris in collaboration with Eirikr Magnusson, and published in 1870. In that work Morris and his associate wove together parts of the Elder and the Younger *Eddas*. These works and the *Nibelungenlied*, a medieval German retelling of the saga material, provided him his main sources for *Sigurd the Volsung;* in his handling of landscape he was aided by his visits to Iceland, where both people and countryside made a deep impression upon his imagination.

The gist of the poem is as follows:

Sigurd is in four books, named *Sigmund*, *Regin*, *Brynhild*, and *Gudrun*. The first book is the tale of Sigurd's father, Sigmund. Volsung, King of the Midworld's Mark, has a daughter, Signy, who marries Siggeir, King of the Goths. Siggeir's army defeats Volsung's, slaying Volsung and all his sons save one, Sigmund. Sigmund, an exile among the Goths, rears Signy's son, Sinfiotli, in an unknown retreat, and with him destroys King Siggeir, his palace and his power. Sigmund reigns over the

Volsungs, marries Hiordis, daughter of the King of the Isles, and dies in battle leaving a son to be born after his death. Hiordis is given refuge by King Elf, the son of the Helper of Men.

In Book Two, Sigurd is born in the land of the Helper of Men; guided and counselled by Regin, the smith and adviser to the Helper. In concert with Regin he seeks to win the War-coat of Gold and the Helm of Aweing; slays the serpent Fafnir, brother to Regin, on the Glittering Heath; he eats of the heart of Fafnir, and detecting Regin's guile, slays him; he seizes the treasure of the Elf Andvari, the Helm of Aweing and the War-coat of Gold; and rouses from a spell Brynhild, whom he possesses but must quit.

Book Three introduces Giuki, king of the Niblungs, Grimhild his queen, his daughter Gudrun, and his three sons, Gunnar, Hogni and Guttorm. Gudrun goes to Brynhild, seeking an interpretation of her dream, which is of Sigurd. Sigurd, who has confessed his love to Brynhild, goes to the House of the Niblungs, where he allies himself with the sons of Giuki. He is given a magic potion which extinguishes all recollection of Brynhild and marries Gudrun. Adopting the form of Gunnar at the latter's request, and still under the spell of the potion, he wins Brynhild's consent to marry; but before the marriage of Brynhild and Gunnar, Sigurd's memory and love revive. His assumption of Gunnar's form becomes known to Brynhild, who demands Sigurd's death. Guttorm, at his brothers' bidding, slays Sigurd in a surprise attack at night, being killed in the grapple. Brynhild stabs herself and is placed on Sigurd's pyre.

Book Four presents Atli, king of the Outlands, who marries Gudrun. Gudrun persuades him to summon her brothers Gunnar and Hogni to his palace by golden promises. Hogni, suspicious, hides the treasure of the Elf Andvari; and then proceeding with Gunnar to Atli's hall, sustains the half-expected attack. After a long combat, the brothers are captured, Hogni's heart is torn out while he lives, and Gunnar—in the passage reproduced here—dies in the pit of the adders. Gudrun, the death of Sigurd thus avenged, avenges the deaths of her brothers by setting afire the house of Atli, in which her husband and all his men perish. She throws herself from a cliff into the sea.

620, 1. *Gunnar:* see introductory note to the poem.

620, 2. *Atli:* see introductory note.

620, 6. *the ransom of Odin:* a treasure in the possession of the Niblungs.

621, 13. *the Gold:* the treasure mentioned in l. 6.

621, 18. *Giuki:* king of the Niblungs before Gunnar, who was his son.

621, 19. *Gudrun:* sister of Gunnar, alienated from her brothers.

621, 20. *seeming:* expression.

621, 21. *groves of war:* fighting men. Elaborate expressions such as this abound in the Medieval Norse epics.

621, 25. *Sons of the Morning:* men from the east.

wain: wagon.

621, 30. *God-kin:* lesser Deity.

621, 32. *thorns of battle:* spears.

621, 41. *war-thorns:* see note on l. 32.

621, 48. *The folk that know not ruth:* these are the serpents already mentioned in line 26.

621, 53. *close:* the pit.

622, 71. *God-home:* Valhalla.

622, 72. *in the end:* at the final battle. In Norse myth the life of the gods and heroes in Valhalla is not conceived as eternal: ultimately a great battle will take place between the inhabitants of Valhalla and "the sons of destruction" piloted by the god Loki.

622, 76. *The World of Aforetime: the Gap of the Gaping*, mentioned in l. 81, the world before creation of the earth and its system. It was conceived as dark and empty.

622, 81. *the Gap of the Gaping:* see note on l. 76.

622, 86. *Mid-Earth:* the earth, conceived as in the middle of the world.

623, 117–118. The serpent mentioned here is the child of the god Loki, source of evil and of the undoing of man, hence described as the Midworld's (earth's) ancient curse.

623, 128. *fain:* eager, happy.

623, 134. *the Accuser:* Loki.

do on the death-shoon: put on the death-shoes, *i.e.*, make ready to die and go on the journey to Valhalla.

623, 138. *Odin:* the father of all the gods, the equivalent of the Greek Zeus and the Roman Jupiter.

623, 149. *war-fain:* battle-array.

624. THE DAY IS COMING

This poem appeared in the little pamphlet *Chants for Socialists* in 1884.

BIBLIOGRAPHY

626. A. C. SWINBURNE

I. EDITIONS

Complete Works, 20 vols., ed. by Sir Edmund Gosse and T. J. Wise, Heinemann, 1925–1927.
Collected Poetical Works, 2 vols., Heinemann, 1924.
Atalanta in Calydon, ed. by G. Lafourcade, Oxford, 1930.
Atalanta in Calydon and *Erechtheus*, ed. by M. C. Wier, Wahr (Ann Arbor), 1922.
Hyperion and Other Poems, ed. by G. Lafourcade (with an essay on Swinburne and Keats), Faber, 1927.
Posthumous Poems, ed. by Sir Edmund Gosse and T. J. Wise, Heinemann, 1917.
Selected Poems, ed. by L. Binyon, Oxford, 1939.
Selections, ed. by W. O. Raymond, Harcourt, 1925.
Selections, ed. by H. M. Burton, Cambridge, 1927.
The Best of Swinburne, ed. by C. K. Hyder and L. Chase, Ronald, 1937.

II. BIOGRAPHY AND LETTERS

Letters, with some personal recollections, ed. by T. Hake and A. Compton Rickett, Murray, 1918.
Letters, ed. by Sir Edmund Gosse and T. J. Wise, Heinemann, 1919.
GOSSE, SIR EDMUND: *The Life of Algernon Charles Swinburne*, Macmillan, 1917.
HYDER, C. K.: *Swinburne's Literary Career and Fame*, Duke University Press, 1933.
KERNAHAN, C.: *Swinburne as I Knew Him*, Lane, 1919.
LAFOURCADE, G.: *La jeunesse de Swinburne, 1837–1867*, 2 vols., (vol. 1), Publications de l'Université de Strasbourg, Oxford, 1928.
LAFOURCADE, G.: *Swinburne: a Literary Biography*, Bell, 1932.
LEITH, MRS. DISNEY: *The Boyhood of Algernon Charles Swinburne*, Chatto, 1917.
NICOLSON, H.: *Swinburne*, Macmillan, 1926.
WRATISLAW, T.: *Algernon Charles Swinburne*, Greening (London), 1900.

III. CRITICISM

I. MONOGRAPHS

BUCHANAN, R.: *The Fleshly School of Poetry and Other Phenomena of the Day*, Strahan (London), 1872.
CHEW, S. C.: *Swinburne*, Little Brown, 1929.
DRINKWATER, J.: *Swinburne, an Estimate*, Dent, 1924.
HENDERSON, W. B. D.: *Swinburne and Landor*, Macmillan, 1918.
LAFOURCADE, G.: *La jeunesse de Swinburne, 1837–1867*, 2 vols., (vol. 2), Publications de l'Université de Strasbourg, Oxford, 1928.
POUND, O.: *On the Application of the Principles of Greek Lyric Tragedy in the Classical Dramas of Swinburne*, University of Nebraska Studies, XIII, 4. 1913.
REUL, PAUL DE: *L'Oeuvre de Swinburne*, Sand (Brussels), 1922.
RUTLAND, W. R.: *Swinburne, a Nineteenth Century Hellene*, Blackwell, 1931.
THOMAS, E.: *Algernon Charles Swinburne, a Critical Study*, Secker, 1912.
WELBY, T. E.: *A Study of Swinburne* (2nd ed.), Doran, 1926.
WIER, M. C.: *The Influence of Aeschylus and Euripides on the Structure and Content of Swinburne's 'Atalanta in Calydon' and 'Erechtheus,'* Wahr (Ann Arbor), 1920.
WOODBERRY, G.: *Swinburne*, McClure, 1905.

II. ESSAYS IN BOOKS

BEERBOHM, MAX: "No. 2, The Pines: Reminiscences of Swinburne" in *And Even Now*, Dutton, 1921
CLUTTON-BROCK, A.: "Algernon Charles Swinburne" in *Essays on Books*, Methuen, 1921.
ELIOT, T. S.: "Swinburne as Poet" in *The Sacred Wood*, Methuen, 1920.

Elton, O.: "Mr. Swinburne's Poems" in *Modern Studies*, Arnold, 1907.

Forman, H. B.: "Algernon Charles Swinburne" in *Our Living Poets*, Tinsley (London), 1871.

Gosse, Sir Edmund: "Swinburne" in *Portraits and Sketches*, Scribner, 1912.

Gosse, Sir Edmund: "The First Draft of Swinburne's 'Anactoria'" in *Aspects and Impressions*, Cassell, 1922.

Hearn, L.: "Studies in Swinburne" in *Pre-Raphaelite and Other Poets*, Dodd, 1922.

Kellett, E. E.: "Swinburne" in *Reconsiderations*, Cambridge, 1928.

Lucas, F. L.: "Swinburne" in *Eight Victorian Poets*, Cambridge, 1931.

Lyall, A. C.: "Characteristics of Mr. Swinburne's Poetry" in *Studies in Literature and History*, Murray, 1915.

Mackail, J. W.: "Swinburne" in *Studies of English Poets*, Longmans, 1926.

Meynell, A.: "Swinburne's Lyrical Poetry" in *Hearts of Controversy*, Burns Oates, 1918.

More, P. E.: "Swinburne" in *Shelburne Essays*, Third Series, Putnam, 1905.

Saintsbury, G.: "Mr. Swinburne" in *Corrected Impressions*, Dodd, 1895.

Symons, A.: "Algernon Charles Swinburne" in *Figures of Several Centuries*, Constable, 1916.

Symons, A.: "Swinburne" in *Studies in Strange Souls*, Sawyer, 1929.

Woodberry, G. E.: "Swinburne" in *Literary Essays*, Harcourt, 1920.

III. Articles in Periodicals

Bailey, J.: "Swinburne" in *Quarterly Review*, July, 1917.

Brown, E. K. : "Swinburne: A Centenary Estimate" in *University of Toronto Quarterly*, January, 1937.

Hyder, C. K.: "Swinburne and the Popular Ballad" in *Publications of the Modern Language Association of America*, March, 1934.

Lafourcade, G.: "Le centenaire de Swinburne" in *Etudes Anglaises*, January, 1938.

Lafourcade, G.: "Swinburne et Baudelaire" in *Revue anglo-américaine*, February, 1924.

Lafourcade, G.: "Swinburne and Walt Whitman" in *Modern Language Review*, January, 1927.

Michaelides, C. C.: "Mr. Swinburne and the Sea" in *Independent Review*, January, 1906.

Morley, J.: "Mr. Swinburne's New Poems" in *Living Age*, June, 1926 (reprint of the attack in *The Spectator*, August 4, 1866).

Ratchford, F. E.: "The First Draft of Swinburne's 'Hertha'" in *Modern Language Notes*, January, 1924.

Russell, C. E.: "Swinburne and Music" in *North American Review*, November, 1907.

Warren, J. L. (Lord de Tabley): "'Atalanta in Calydon'" in *Fortnightly Review*, May 15, 1865.

NOTES AND COMMENTS

627. ATALANTA IN CALYDON

This poem first appeared in 1865, as an independent work. What impelled Swinburne to attempt a tragedy on the theme of Atalanta and Meleager is unknown. He was familiar with fragments of a lost tragedy of Euripides (a poet of whom he thought little), the *Meleager;* he knew the story of the boar-hunt as it was told in the *Iliad;* but his principal debts were to Ovid's *Metamorphoses* (VIII, 260 f.) and Apollodorus' *Bibliotheca* (I, viii). If it is unknown why he attempted this subject, it is quite clear what his motives were in writing a tragedy in the Greek form. He believed that no modern writer had succeeded in doing so. Shelley, whom he idolized, had in his *Prometheus Unbound* failed to attain the Hellenic manner, and had obtruded modern ideas. Arnold's *Merope*, published in 1858, when Arnold was professor of poetry at Oxford and Swinburne an undergraduate member of Balliol College, lacked, in Swinburne's view, vitality, impeccable as its structure might be. The conception of the character of Atalanta is in keeping with Swinburne's great delight in women who were masterful and masculine; and it is likely that the opportunity to express that delight was one of the main motives to the choice of the Atalanta-Meleager story.

In his handling of the theme Swinburne is often original. He deprives Meleager of the wife he had in Greek versions of the story, founding his conception of the character rather on the Greek character Hippolytus, who is untouched by love until Phaedra awakens him. He introduces Althaea's dream of giving birth to a firebrand. (On this and many other points see Bush: *Mythology and the Romantic Tradition*, 331 f.) His choral odes are more irregular than those in Greek tragedy, a difference which he later deemed a grave weakness. In general his conception and treatment are in dramatic power greatly inferior to Greek tragedy. The inferiority resides partly in the lack of human vitality in his characters (Althaea is a partial exception to this observation) and partly in the lack of condensation and intensity in the dialogue and the choral passages. Swinburne had few of the dramatist's gifts. He himself came to prefer to *Atalanta in Calydon* his later tragic poem *Erechtheus* (1876). But, if *Erechtheus* is more Greek than Atalanta, it is less dramatic and less poetic as well. It is the poetic power shown in Atalanta that substantiates the eulogies of M. Lafourcade. (See his edition of the work and his *La jeunesse de Swinburne*, II, 382 f.)

627, 1. *Maiden:* Diana (Artemis), who, as the moon, controls the *months*.

627, 4. *treble:* Diana was known as the three-formed because she was believed to be the same as the moon and Proserpine.

627, 5–6. *a foot swift on the hills:* Diana found in hunting her chief pleasure. It is as goddess of hunting that she presides over the poem.

628, 10. *thine eye's beam:* the moon's light.

628, 17. *O fair-faced sun:* Apollo, the sun-god.

628, 35. *horn of Acheloüs:* Acheloüs was a river-god in Epirus (in northwestern Greece); one of his horns having been torn off by Hercules, he took refuge in this river. The river has islands at its mouth, and in its division by them may be said to separate into a number of horns.

628, 36. *Euenus:* another river in Epirus.

628, 38. Apollo and Diana (*Artemis*) were twin children of Jupiter by Proserpine.

628, 43. *sanguine:* bloody.

628, 45. *Arcadian:* the daughter of Schoeneus, king of Scyros in Arcady (in western Greece).

628, 47. *Ladon:* a river in Arcady.

Maenalus: a mountain in Arcady.

628, 51. *Aetolian:* Aetolia was a section in western Greece, in the southern part of which Calydon lay.

628, 52. *Lelantian:* part of a district at the mouth of the Euenus.

628, 53. *the son of Zeus:* Hercules.

628, 55. *the wild god:* Achelous. See note on l. 35.

629, 66. *the mother of months:* see the note on l. 1.

629, 70. *Itylus:* son of Tereus and Procne. Tereus having raped Philomela, the sister of Procne his wife, Procne killed her child Itylus and served him as a feast to his father. Procne and Philomela then changed themselves into birds; according to some versions of the myth, Procne became a swallow and Philomela a nightingale, according to others the swallow was Philomela and the nightingale was Procne. See Swinburne's own development of the story in his poem "Itylus."

629, 71. *Thracian:* Tereus ruled in Thrace in northeastern Greece.

629, 72. Tereus tore out the tongue of Philomela that she might not relate his rape of her. See note on l. 70.

629, 102. *the oat:* a shepherd's pipe of straw.

629, 103. *a satyr:* a creature of the wilds, half-man and half-goat.

629, 105. *Pan:* god of shepherds and hunters, his fleetness, mentioned in the following line, is related to his having the form of a goat from the waist down.

Bacchus: god of wine. He was worshipped in wild passionate dances, in which the god himself was believed to take part. The rites were nocturnal.

630, 108. *Maenads* and *Bassarids* were types of worshippers of Bacchus, commonly women.

630, 113. *Bacchanal:* a woman worshipper of Bacchus.

630, 144. *Queen:* Althaea was the wife of Oeneus, king of Calydon.

630, 149. *four-foot plague:* the reference is to the boar.

631, 170. *the king:* Oeneus.

632, 186. *Euenus:* see note to l. 36.

632, 187. *Arcadia:* to the southward.

632, 189. *this maiden:* Atalanta.

632, 201. *light of wit:* of scant intelligence.

632, 203. *my brothers:* Toxeus and Plexippus.

632, 204. *my son:* Meleager.

633, 223. *holpen:* helped.

634, 271. *beaks:* prows.

634, 297. *gat:* got.

634, 299. *Eurythemis:* the wife of Thestius, king of Pleuron.

636, 376. *the tusked plague:* the boar.

636, 391. *Peleus the Larissæan:* Peleus was a Thessalian king exiled because of his complicity in the death of his brother. Larissa was a city in Thessaly.

636, 392. *the white sea-bred wife:* Peleus married one of the nereides or sea-nymphs.

636, 393. *their son:* the reference is probably to Achilles, but he was believed to be the offspring of Peleus by another marriage.

636, 397. *thy sister's sons:* Leda, sister of Althaea, had by Zeus (Jupiter) the twin sons Castor and Pollux.

636, 410. *Eurotas:* a river flowing through Laconia (Lacedaemon) and passing close to the city of Sparta.

637, 413. *Helen:* Helen of Troy.

637, 414. *Clytæmnestra:* later the wife and murderess of Agamemnon.

637, 429. *Telamon:* king of the island of Salamis, which lies just off the coast of Attica in the *Saronic sinus.*

637, 431. *Salamis:* See note to l. 429.

637, 433. *vine-chapleted:* crowned with vines.

637, 436. *Ancæus:* a king in Ionia, and one of Jason's chief companions in the quest of the golden fleece.

637, 439. *Cepheus:* also one of the Argonauts.

638, 461. *discreates:* annihilates.

639, 471. *his twin-born fate:* born when he is born.

639, 474. *equal-minded:* just.

639, 481. *mutual mouth:* agreement.

639, 492. In the tribute to an ideal old age Swinburne was consciously remembering Walter Savage Landor, whom he met in 1863, who died in 1865 and to whose memory the poem is dedicated. (See Lafourcade: *Atalanta in Calydon*, xi, n. 1.)

639, 504. *alien lips:* Landor's last years were spent in Italy.

640, 525. *terrene:* earthly.

640, 541–542. *burn from heaven among the stars:* be deified.

640, 549–552. The reference is to the wars attempted against King Oeneus by the neighbouring peoples. These wars in which Oeneus, with the aid of Meleager, was victorious, were inspired by Diana, angry because her worship was neglected, and shortly preceded her sending of the wild boar into Oeneus' dominions.

640, 557. *Ares:* Pallas (Minerva).

641, 584 f. The reference is to the voyage of the Argonauts in quest of the golden fleece.

641, 593. *Nereid:* sea-nymph.

641, 599. *irremeable:* impassable to ships propelled by oars.

Symplegades: two islands in the Black Sea, just inside the entrance from the Bosphorus. Ships passed between them; and the Greeks believed that the islands were movable and at the will of the gods closed together to crush ships bearing enemies of an angered god.

641, 601. *Colchis:* at the east side of the Black Sea.

641, 613. *Euxine:* the ancient name of the Black Sea.

641, 619. *a god:* equal to a god. The reference is to Atalanta.

643, 705. *molten:* melted.

644, 730. *Of sea-foam:* Aphrodite (Venus) was believed according to one myth to have been born of the foam of the sea.

644, 737. *weft:* web.

644, 753. *mere:* lake.

645, 793. *firth:* estuary.

645, 797. *girth:* girdle.

646, 854. *Tyro:* a nymph who lòved the river-god Enipeus, and was violated by Neptune who assumed the form of Enipeus to deceive her.

646, 855. The reference is to the severity with which Tyro was treated by her mother-in-law.

646, 858. *the seed of a king:* Tyro was the daughter of Salmoneus, king of Elis, to the west of Arcadia.

646, 864. *Enipeus:* the river-god with whom Tyro was in love. See note on l. 854.

646, 870. *the sun's white sister:* the moon, patron of chastity.

646, 874. *huntress:* Diana was usually represented as a huntress.

647, 884. *the starless fold o' the stars:* the sky, when the stars are invisible.

647, 899. *Elis:* see note on l. 858.

Acheloïan horn: see note on l. 35.

647, 902. *Iasius:* father of Atalanta, according to one myth.

647, 908. *whom all men praise:* Aphrodite.

647, 910. *habit:* constitution, way.

648, 932. *give her blood before the gods:* become a sacrifice.

648, 952. *King:* she addresses Oeneus.

648, 959–961. The reference is to Diana's slaying of the seven daughters of Niobe, daughter of Tantalus.

648, 962. *engraffed of Tantalus:* of the race of Tantalus, who was a son of Jupiter.

648, 973. *dances and the back-blowing torch:* the worship of the various gods and goddesses associated with passion and procreation was held at night, with the light of torches, and took the form of orgiastic dances.

649, 980. *footless:* slippery.

649, 983. *intermitting reed:* the *reed* was the instrument of Pan and shepherds; but here it is thought of as making a sound when blown by the wind. It is described as *intermitting*, because it is silent when the wind does not blow.

650, 1031. *Tegea:* Atalanta was born in Tegea, a town in Arcadia.

651, 1065. *guerdons:* rewards.

651, 1067. *bridal measure:* the music played at a wedding.

651, 1077. *the weeping Seven:* the muses.

652, 1112. *secular:* profane, as distinguished from religious or sacred.

652, 1139. *the lord:* the conception of a force superior to the gods and unknowable, was familiar to Greek thinking about the nature of the universe.

652, 1140. The conception of God, or the supreme force in the universe, as completely evil had been discovered by Swinburne in the works of the Marquis de Sade, introduced to his knowledge about 1861. (See Lafourcade; *La jeunesse de Swinburne,* I, 179.)

652, 1154. *hazardous:* exposed to hazard.

653, 1187. *casual breath:* life at the risk of accident which may end it.

654, 1230. *brakes:* thickets.

654, 1233. *Acarnania:* a land beyond the Acheloüs river and to the northwest of Calydon.

654, 1235. *Laertes island-born:* Laertes was king of Ithaca, an island off the west coast of Greece. He was the father (or foster-father) of Ulysses, and was a companion of Meleager in the voyage of the Argonauts.

654, 1236. *Gerenian Nestor:* Nestor was king of Pylos in Elis. At the village of Geranus, near-by, Nestor was said to have been born.

Panopeus: a hero of whom little is known. His son built the wooden horse in which the Greeks entered Troy.

654, 1237. *Cepheus and Ancæus:* see notes on ll. 426 and 429.

654, 1242. *braced:* belted.

655, 1246. *Iphicles:* the twin brother of Hercules.

655, 1247–1248. *Pirithous,* king of the Lapithae who dwelt in Thessaly, held a festival at the time of his marriage, and in the course of it the centaur *Eurytion,* having made improper advances to the bride, was killed. The *Eurytion* here mentioned is likely, however, to have been one of the Argonauts, who was the son of Hermes (Mercury) and hence styled *divine.*

655, 1249. *Æacides:* The word denotes merely *a* son of Æacus; but among his sons only Peleus married a goddess.

655, 1250. *Telamon:* also an Argonaut, and the father of Ajax.

Argive-born: born in Argo, the capital city of Argolis in the Peloponnesian peninsula of Greece.

655, 1252. *Amphiaraus:* an Argonaut, famous for his power of reading the future and after his death, honoured with a shrine to which persons resorted for divinations.

655, 1255. *Jason:* king of Iolchos near Thebes and the leader of the Argonauts in the quest of the golden fleece.

Dryas twin-begot with war: Dryas was a son of Mars. Since Mars was god of war, Dryas is described as war's twin.

655, 1257. *Idas:* another Argonaut.

655, 1258. *Lynceus:* another Argonaut; the epithet *keenest* is applied to his *eye* because he was credited with the power to see to the distance of nine miles and through solid earth. He and Idas were brothers.

Admetus twice espoused: another Argonaut. His marriages are mentioned because his second wife was famous for having laid down her life that he might live.

655, 1259. *Hippasus and Hyleus:* the reference is probably to two centaurs who bore these names.

656, 1300. *his comrade:* Eurytion, see l. 1304.

656, 1305. *Cadmean:* Theban. Amphiaraus was not a Theban but died at Thebes.

656, 1306. *sacred:* because of Amphiaraus' gift of divination which implies sanctity.

656, 1350. *melilote:* a species of lotus.

657, 1355. *faun:* a satyr, that is, a creature with half human form but with the legs and ears of a goat.

dryad: wood nymph.

658, 1400. *Thou:* Artemis.

658, 1402. *reluctant:* to separate and reveal the body.

658, 1404. *unbeholden:* unbeheld.

659, 1465. *Orion overthrown:* Diana slew Orion with arrows because he had made advances to her, or to one of her maiden attendants.

659, 1467. *zone:* girdle.

660, 1492. *double word:* word with ambiguous meaning.

661, 1537. *the Arcadian:* the reference is to the people of Arcadia as a whole.

662, 1552. *blanched:* whitened.

662, 1584. *relume:* relight.

662, 1590. *in lieu of these:* to replace these.

663, 1615. *false:* deceitful because imagined.

663, 1630. *privy:* stealthy.

664, 1668. *unholpen:* unhelped.

664, 1680. *a sect of thee:* a part of you (with the added suggestion that the part is cut off from you).

664, 1690. *ravin:* preying.

665, 1701. *the wheel of all necessities:* fate.

665, 1722. *wit:* intelligence.

666, 1755. *alien from the sun:* because committed to the underworld, Hades.

667, 1787. *weave:* move about.

668, 1825. *smitten:* struck.

668, 1838. The idea here expressed is again drawn from the Marquis de Sade. See note on l. 1131.

669, 1863–1864. The meaning is that fate is knit with her by as intimate relations as are conceivable. The references to *son* and *brother* have a double value.

669, 1868. *eaten fruits:* slain children.

669, 1879. *frankincense:* an aromatic incense.

670, 1914. *insatiate and intolerant:* unsatisfied and yet unable to endure what is sought as satisfaction.

674, 2039. *unchapleted hair:* a bride wore a chaplet, or wreath, in her hair.

674, 2040. *unfilleted cheek:* a maiden wore a fillet, or band, about her brow.

675, 2081. *among shadows a shadow:* the folk of the underworld were often represented as shadows.

impassable streams: the river (or rivers) over which the dead passed to the underworld could not be passed in the other direction.

675, 2103. *thawn:* thinned.

676, 2121. *the Acroceraunian snow:* the mountain peaks of the Acroceraunian range are in Epirus, at the northwest of Greece.

the ford of the fleece of gold: the Dardanelles, a narrow strait from the Mediterranean to the sea of Marmora, to be passed on the way to Colchis at the eastern shore of the Black Sea, where the fleece was seized by Jason and the Argonauts.

676, 2125. *the Chersonese:* a peninsula to the north of the Dardanelles. See note on l. 2121.

676, 2126. *the Bosphorus:* a strait between the Sea of Marmora and the Black Sea (or as it was sometimes called in ancient times, the *Pontic Sea*).

676, 2141. *narrowing Symplegades:* see note on l. 599.

the straits of Propontis: Propontis is the Sea of Marmora (see note on l. 2121) so called because it leads to the Pontic (or Black) Sea. The straits of Propontis are the same as what is now called the Bosphorus, a narrow passage joining the Sea of Marmora and the Black Sea.

676, 2151. *Helle:* the Hellespont.

678, 2202. *kingdom:* kingship.

678, 2230. *disbranched:* removed from its branch, *i.e.*, from the means of life.

678, 2231. *minished:* diminished.

679, 2277. *sons of my mother's sister:* Castor and Pollux, sons of Leda.

679, 2278. *that were in Colchis with me:* on the expedition of the Argonauts.

680. DEDICATION TO POEMS AND BALLADS [First Series]

This poem first appeared in the collection for which it served as dedication, in 1866.

680, 1. *shingle:* the pebbles on the shore, or in its representative force, as here, the shore itself.

680, 4. *first fruits:* they were his first *lyrics*, but not his first *poetry*.

680, 7. *bay-leaf:* laurel.

680, 13. The three colours suggest the many moods which recur in the collection.

680, 17. *seven years:* many of the poems are known to have been written at least as early as 1861. (See Lafourcade: *Swinburne: a Literary Biography*, 304.)

680, 23–24. The reference is to such poems in the collection as *Sapphics* and *Faustine*.

680, 27–28. All these names occur as those of important personages in the collection.

680, 35. *glasses:* mirrors.

681, 45. *class-time:* he left Oxford six years before he wrote this dedication, seven before the collection appeared.

681, 52. *reed:* pipe, such as Pan was believed to have used for his music.

681, 53. *your:* the collection was dedicated to [Sir] Edward Burne-Jones, a friend of long standing and one of the most eminent of the painters who, not founders of the Pre-Raphaelite Brotherhood, accepted its ideals. From this point on there are many references to Burne-Jones's paintings, with whose calm, often spiritual, beauty Swinburne contrasts the tone of his *Poems and Ballads*.

681. THE TRIUMPH OF TIME

This poem first appeared in the collection of 1866, *Poems and Ballads* [First Series]. It was inspired by the one normal love that Swinburne is known to have had. M. Lafourcade has given an account of the development of this love so far as it can now be reconstructed. In 1862 the poet met Jane Faulkner, the niece and adopted daughter of a doctor who was a friend of Ruskin and an admirer of the Pre-Raphaelites. Swinburne proposed to her but was rejected in favour of another suitor. In 1863 he composed *The Triumph of Time*, in which he laments not only the loss of a woman whom he loved but the loss of what possibility of a normal passional life he could perceive. (See Lafourcade: *Swinburne: A Literary Biography*, 100–2.)

681, 6–8. The poet is alluding, as he does repeatedly throughout the poem, to his sexual abnormality.

682, 17. *this fruit of my heart:* normal love.

683, 83. *the great third wave:* death, the image being taken from the legendary notion that after two smaller waves comes a larger one.

683, 91. *had:* would have.

683, 102. *his:* the rival suitor's.

683, 110–112. He makes a deliberately obscure allusion to his abnormality.

683, 115. *the cloven clay:* the earth dug for a grave.

684, 156. *the fates are three:* Man's fate was determined by the three goddesses, Clotho, Lachesis, and Atropos, known as the Fates in Greek myth.

684, 168. *I shall not be there:* He will be damned, losing the possibility of salvation because lapsing into his vicious abnormality, from which a normal love would have released him.

684, 191. *quick:* life, *i.e.*, core.

685, 228–229. *a sin . . . sure to dissolve and destroy me all through:* a sin completely corrupting.

685, 237. *What should such fellows as I do:* an echo of Hamlet's self-disgust.

685, 253. *seven:* as with the Virgin Mary whose seven chief sorrows were represented by seven swords.

685, 254. *doubtful:* uncertain.

685, 256. *reverberate:* instead of responding.

685, 268. *keen like pain:* and therefore to Swinburne desirable.

686, 321. *a singer:* Rudel, a Provençal poet of the twelfth century.

686, 322. *midland sea:* the Mediterranean.

686, 323. The reference is to Tripoli.

686, 324. *one woman:* the Countess of Tripoli.

686, 325–328. Rudel sailed to Tripoli to gaze on her beauty; falling sick on the way, he merely saw her as she came aboard, when he lay dying.

686, 353 f. In this stanza he appears to evoke the circumstances of his meetings with Jane Faulkner.

687. ITYLUS

This poem first appeared in the collection of 1866, *Poems and Ballads* [First Series]. Itylus (or Itys) was the son of Tereus, king of Thrace, and Procne his wife. After Tereus had raped Philomela, the sister of Procne, and removed her tongue to ensure her silence, Procne killed Itylus and served him at a feast to his father. Philomela assumed the form of a nightingale, and Procne that of a swallow, to escape. Philomela speaks.

687, 10. *the grief of the old time:* see the general note on the poem.

688, 47. *the slaying of Itylus:* see the general note.

688, 48. *Daulis:* a city in Phocis where Tereus unknowing ate the flesh of his son. See the general note.

688. HYMN TO PROSERPINE

This poem first appeared in the collection of 1866, *Poems and Ballads* [First Series]. Swinburne described it as "the deathsong of spiritual decadence." The words *Vicisti, Galilæe*, are reported to have been uttered by the Emperor Julian as he was dying. Julian was brought up a Christian; but on becoming emperor of Rome in 361 he abjured the Christian faith and so acquired the description *Julian the Apostate;* he received a mortal wound in battle in 363. Although he was bitterly attacked by Christian writers, from the purely pagan point of view he was a noble and admirable personality and attracted the admiration of Swinburne both by his hostility to Christianity and his exemplification of pagan excellence. The following poem is the speech not of Julian specifically but of a Roman pagan of Julian's approximate time.

Proserpine: an earth-goddess, wife of the king of the underworld.

Vicisti, Galilæe. Thou hast conquered, Galilean.

688, 6. *a goodlier gift is thine:* the gift of death.

688, 7. *Apollo:* conceived here as god of music.

688, 9. *bays:* laurels.

688, 13. *dethroned:* by the Christian religion.

688, 15. *new Gods:* the Christian saints.

689, 24. *brake:* thicket.

689, 36. *Lethean:* the river Lethe was crossed on the way from this world to the underworld of death: it brought oblivion of all memories.

689, 38. *May:* youth.

689, 43. The meaning is that life runs low in the Christians, who have suffered torture.

689, 44. *ghastly glories:* the relics are holy but horrible.

689, 71. *thine:* at this point he begins to address Jesus.

690, 73. *Cytherean:* Venus (Aphrodite) who according to one legend rose from the sea foam at the island of Cythera.

690, 78. *our mother:* Venus.

a blossom of flowering seas: see note on l. 73.

690, 80. *mother of Rome:* Venus was believed to have been the mother of Aeneas, who came to Italy from Troy and built the town of Lavinium close to the site of Rome.

690, 87. *viewless:* invisible.

690, 89. *wist:* thought.

690, 91. *her:* Proserpine.

690, 93. *daughter of earth:* Proserpine was the daughter of Demeter (Ceres), goddess of fertility of the earth.

690, 97. *poppies:* giving oblivion, they are specially sacred to Proserpine, goddess of the underworld.

690, 108. Swinburne appends as a note a phrase in the original Greek from Epictetus, a stoic philosopher living in Rome: it may be translated, "Thou art a little soul bearing up a corpse!"

690. FAUSTINE

This poem first appeared in the collection of 1866, *Poems and Ballads* [First Series]. In the pamphlet *Notes on Poems and Reviews* he explains that he was impelled to write it by "the sudden sight of a living face which recalled the well-known likeness of another dead for centuries: in this instance, the noble and faultless type of the elder Faustina [wife of the emperor Antonius as the younger Faustina, her daughter, was the wife of the emperor Marcus Aurelius] as seen in coin and bust." A more general idea lay behind the poem, that of "the transmigration of a single soul, doomed as though by accident from the first to all evil and no good, through many ages and forms, but clad always in the same type of fleshly beauty."

Ave Faustina Imperatrix, morituri te salutant: Hail, Faustina, Empress, those who are about to die salute you. It was customary for gladiators before their combats to salute the emperor (rather than the empress) in this fashion.

690, 6. *clean:* fully.

691, 15. *carved:* so perfectly formed that they resemble sculpture rather than physical life.

691, 60. *twice crown:* Swinburne suggests that the same nature, but in different bodies, characterized the two empresses Faustina. See general note on the poem.

691, 61. *sarcophagus:* tomb.

691, 69. One of the modes of gladiatorial combat was to match a man with a pike against a man whose weapon was a net in which he sought to involve his opponent.

691, 79. *circus:* arena.

691, 90. *teen:* grief.

692, 99. *Bacchanal:* devotee of Bacchus. Bacchus, god of wine, was worshipped in rites of frantic excitement, stimulated by wine and leading to acts of lust and cruelty.

692, 107. *coined in Roman gold:* placed her image on the imperial coinage.

692, 109–110. The reference is to transmigration into sub-human forms.

692, 117. *Sapphic:* by Sappho, the greatest woman poet of passion in the ancient world.

692, 118. *Mitylene:* in this city, on the island of Lesbos, near Asia Minor, Sappho was born.

692, 121. *the shameless nameless love:* a love not to be named because of its iniquity. The reference is to Lesbianism.

692, 122. *gin:* snare.

692, 130. *epicene:* with characteristics of both sexes.

692, 131–132. *without fruit of love:* abnormal.

692, 146. *the Lampsacene:* Priapus, god of generation and voluptuousness, was believed to have been born at Lampsacus in Asia Minor, where he was specially worshipped.

692, 147. Priapus was also god of gardens and in them his statue was usually erected.

metes: measures.

692. DOLORES

This poem first appeared in the collection of 1866, *Poems and Ballads* [First Series]. The poem is not an organic work: Swinburne wrote of it, when he was in the later stages of its composition that he had "added yet four more jets of boiling and gushing infamy to the perennial and poisonous fountain of *Dolores*"; and in a postscript to the same letter announced ten more jets, or stanzas. In his pamphlet *Notes on Poems and Reviews*, 1866, in which he seeks to defend the morality of *Poems and Ballads* [First Series], he asserts that "this poem, like *Faustine*, is so distinctly symbolic and fanciful that it cannot justly be amenable to judgment as a study in the school of realism." The plea cannot be accepted. The truth is rather that Swinburne is being as bold in the description of his abnormal nature as he dared to be, or as he thought consistent with art.

Notre Dame des Sept Douleurs: Our Lady of the Seven Sorrows, one of the attributions of the Virgin Mary.

692, 7. *mystic:* mysterious.

693, 13. *famishing:* longing for a repetition of the delights.

693, 14. *complete:* consummate.

control: lead (loosely used, probably for the rhyme).

693, 19. *tower not of ivory:* tower of ivory is one of the phrases applied to the Virgin Mary, in the Litany of the Blessed Virgin.

693, 21. *mystical rose:* another phrase from the same Litany.

693, 23. *fire:* passion.

693, 25 f. This is one of the passages where Swinburne is deliberately obscure. His fundamental idea is that Dolores takes delight (in the twin forms of *lust* and *laughter*) in the physical pain she inflicts upon him. The *snakes,* which are superficially related to her lips, are really whips, which *bite* into his flesh.

693, 37. *love thou despisest:* normal love and passion.

693, 51. *Libitina:* a goddess of passion, worshipped in Italy.

Priapus: a god of generation and sexual pleasure originally worshipped in Asia Minor, subsequently throughout the Graeco-Roman world.

693, 52. *Tuscan:* Libitina.

Greek: Priapus.

693, 57. *fruits fail: fruits* are a symbol here of the results of normal love.

693, 69–70. The two types of worship of Dolores: the inflictors and recipients of pain.

694, 103. *sanguine:* bloody, or blood-thirsty.

694, 131. *mortal:* ending in his death.

694, 135. *luxurious:* in the French sense of sensual to the extreme.

694, 146. *cross:* abnormal.

694, 166–167. The *kisses* on the *limbs* are blows.

694, 173. *the lords:* the gods.

694, 175–176. *the cypress:* normally associated with death, but by Swinburne with love.

the myrtle: normally associated with love, by Swinburne with death.

694, 177. *measure:* dance.

695, 186. *unknown of the sun:* and therefore associated with evil.

695, 197. *heavy caresses:* blows.

695, 209. *make redder:* by blows.

695, 221–222. *the pulse of thy passion smote kings:* making them cruel.

695, 223. *Thalassian:* literally, belonging to the sea. See note on line below. *Thalassa* is Greek for ocean.

695, 224. *Venus* (Aphrodite) arose from the foam of the sea. Swinburne makes the same claim for the goddess of pain. He associated the sea with the idea of pain, thinking of the effect of a strong sea buffeting the body of a swimmer.

695, 228. *the children of change:* the Christians.

695, 229–230. The meaning is: when the blood of Christians reddened the sand of the amphitheatre, sand never moistened by the sea but always by blood.

695, 240. *swords:* the swords of the gladiators.

695, 242. *bitter:* because of his exertions.

695, 244. *too delicious for death:* and therefore submitted to torture.

695, 245. *lit with live torches:* Nero is said to have illuminated his gardens with the bodies of living persons, among them Christians.

695, 251. The reference is to Nero, who was emperor of Rome from 54 to 68 A.D.

695, 254. *the flight of the fires:* Nero set Rome alight in a number of places and ordered musicians to play while the fires burned.

696, 267. *wealth:* beauty.

696, 278. *creeds:* Swinburne is thinking of the ascetic ideal of Christianity.

696, 281. *Vestal:* the Vestals, who were Virgins (and therefore associated by Swinburne with restraint and refusal, see l. 278) maintained the shrine of Vesta who was goddess of the hearth, keeping flames lit in it.

696, 289 f. This stanza is again deliberately obscure and for the usual reason.

696, 299. *Alciphron:* a Greek rhetorician who composed letters purporting to be by courtesans.

Arisbe: Priam's wife, divorced so that he might marry Hecuba.

696, 303. *the garden god:* Priapus, whose statues were usually erected in gardens. See note to l. 51.

696, 306. *one god:* Priapus.

696, 311. *thy father:* Priapus.

696, 318. *Bacchus:* god of wine.

696, 326. *Ipsithilla:* a lover mentioned in Catullus (*Carmina*, XXXII).

696, 330. *the Phrygian:* Cybele, a goddess of growth and generation, was originally worshipped in Phrygia, in Asia Minor. Her priests were eunuchs but the worship of the goddess was licentious.

696, 333. *Ida:* a mountain near Troy. Cybele was worshipped there.

696, 340. *Catullus:* a poet of the first century B.C., frankly passionate and also a master of verse-technique.

696, 341. *thy father's own city:* Lampsacus, in Asia Minor, notorious for voluptuousness.

696, 345. *Dindymus:* a mountain in Phrygia, seat of worship of Cybele, after whose mother the mountain was named.

696, 346. *lions:* Cybele was often represented in a chariot drawn by lions.

696, 347. *a mother:* The Virgin Mary.

697, 371–372. The image is taken from *Exodus*, Ch. VII, 8–10, where Aaron is bidden by the Lord to cast his rod before Pharaoh and it would become a serpent.

697, 375. *thy prophet:* probably the Marquis de Sade, the principal exponent of pleasure in pain.

697, 396. *do thee wrong:* by their inadequacy.

697, 405. *Lampsacus:* The city of Priapus. See note to l. 341.

697, 406. *Aphaca:* a town in Palestine, where Venus was worshipped.

697, 409. *Cotytto:* a goddess worshipped notably in Thrace. The exact function of the goddess is disputed; but licence and debauchery of all sorts abounded in her service.

697, 410. *Astarte or Ashtaroth:* alternative names of a Syrian goddess, the equivalent in Asiatic religion of the classical Venus or Aphrodite.

697, 425. *overmeasure:* excess.

698. THE GARDEN OF PROSERPINE

This poem first appeared in the collection of 1866, *Poems and Ballads* [First Series]. Proserpine, daughter of Demeter, the goddess of the earth and of Jupiter, was abducted by Pluto, king of the underworld, and shared his sovereignty. She was permitted to pass six months of the year with her mother, above ground; these months she passed notably in Sicily where she had lived before her abduction. The setting of the poem is in the fields of Sicily.

698, 14. *blown:* having blossomed.

698, 22. *wot:* know.

698, 31–32. Without her assent no person could die.

698, 49. *beyond porch and portal:* within the entrances to the underworld.

698, 50. *calm leaves:* the leaves of the poppy.

698, 59. *the earth her mother:* see the general note on the poem.

698, 72. This line describes only the *leaves*, of the preceding line.

698, 76. The image is that of the falcon, which darts down at its master's command.

lure: a bunch of feathers in which food is concealed during a falcon's training, and at the exhibition of which when he is in flight he returns to earth.

699, 94. *diurnal:* belonging to the day, as opposed to the night.

699. SAPPHICS

This poem first appeared in the collection of 1866, *Poems and Ballads* [First Series]. The name is derived from the verse-form, which is an adaptation for the English language of a form used by Sappho, an early Greek poetess.

699, 9. *Aphrodite:* the goddess of love (Venus).

699, 14. *reverted:* turning backwards.

699, 15. *Lesbos:* an island near the coast of Asia Minor.

699, 16. *Mitylene:* a town on this island, of which Sappho was a native.

699, 29. *the tenth:* Sappho was called the tenth muse because she was so great a poet and also a woman, as were all the muses.

699, 32–33. *laurel by laurel faded all their crowns:* the laurel was sacred to the muses, and used in crowning men of whose artistic achievements they approved.

699, 49. *the Lesbians:* the women of Lesbos.

smitten: struck.

700, 76. *Lethe:* the river which is crossed on the way to the underworld Hades, and in which all memories are lost.

700. PRELUDE TO SONGS BEFORE SUNRISE

Songs before Sunrise, Swinburne's second collection of lyrics, appeared in 1871. Its themes—philosophical and political—were in sharp opposition of tone to the celebration of passion in the first collection, *Poems and Ballads*. This *Prelude* seeks to explain and emphasize the psychological development.

700, 1 f. In this stanza the poet is evoking the quality of his first lyrical collection.

700, 19–20. The reference is to the celebration of forms of abnormal passion in *Poems and Ballads*.

700, 28–29. *his spirit's meat was freedom:* the political thesis of the collection was the need of freedom which is taken to be the prerequisite of all moral good.

700, 30. *his cloak woven of thought:* the consolations of the collection are found in ideas, not in sensations, as in *Poems and Ballads*.

700, 40. *strengthless dreams:* religions, especially Christianity, which is bitterly attacked in *Songs before Sunrise*.

701, 53. *miscreate:* fancifully attributed.

701, 64. *cerecloths:* garments for burial.

701, 75. *to time:* to life on this earth.

701, 78. *equal:* just.

701, 91. *we too have played:* in *Poems and Ballads*.

701, 95. *Maenads:* Bacchantes, women who worshipped Bacchus in an excitement amounting to temporary insanity.

701, 101. *star-proof:* so dense as to exclude the light of the stars.

701, 102. *Thyiades:* Thyas was the first worshipper of Bacchus. *Thyiades*, meaning literally the daughters of Thyas, came to denote his worshippers.

701, 104. *Bassarid:* Bassara was a town in Libya where Bacchus was worshipped with fervour. *Bassarid*, meaning literally an inhabitant of Bassara, was a term applied by the Persians to worshippers of Bacchus. The word was used in Thrace.

blood-feasts: sacrifice of living animals, or scourging of worshippers.

701, 114. *tabrets:* small drums.

701, 115. *high chill air:* hills were the favoured places for the rites.

701, 117. *Cotys:* Cotytto, a goddess worshipped at Mt. Edon in Thrace, with rites similar to those in the worship of Bacchus. She was associated with generation and growth.

701, 118. *Edonian:* appertaining to Mt. Edon. See note on line above.

701, 119. *maddened:* grew mad.

701, 135. *rime:* frost.

702, 141. *is man's God still:* is always the highest thing that man can discern.

702, 157. *equal:* smooth.

702, 163. *the lamplit race:* the race, in ancient Greece, in which a runner passed his lighted torch to another who took his place.

702, 172. *chime:* harmony, order.

702. SUPER FLUMINA BABYLONIS

This poem first appeared in the collection of 1871, *Songs before Sunrise*. The title is taken from the opening words of the one hundred and thirty-seventh psalm, as they appear in the Vulgate. The first verse of the psalm, "By the rivers of Babylon, there we sat down, yea, we wept, when we remembered Zion," describes the plight of the Jews and their feelings in the period of their captivity in Babylon; Swinburne uses the Biblical material as a symbol of the state of Italy.

702, 2. *thee:* Zion, symbolizing the idea of Italy, realized in the past.

703, 37. *their forefathers:* in the time of the Roman empire.

703, 45. *Eridanus:* the delta of the river Po, in northern Italy.

703, 57. *passion:* suffering.

704, 65. *Gethsemane:* a garden outside Jerusalem, where Jesus went through his spiritual agony and where he was seized for trial.

704, 67. *Aceldama:* another garden, where Judas took his own life after the betrayal.

sanguine: bloody.

704, 69. *the stone of the sepulchre:* rolled away so that Jesus might rise from the dead.

704, 73. *similitude:* likeness.

704, 99–100. A reminiscence of Jesus's saying: "Whosoever will save his life shall lose it; and whosoever will lose his life for my sake shall find it" (*Matthew*, Ch. XVI, 25).

705, 125. *Golgotha:* Calvary.

705, 127. The meaning is that captivity shall no longer exist.

705. HERTHA

This poem first appeared in the collection of 1871, *Songs before Sunrise.* Hertha was, in Germanic myth, goddess of earth, and of growth. Swinburne has deepened the ancient conception, his goddess being the primal being out of which all else has come. He considered (in 1875) that in this poem he had achieved his most satisfactory fusion of thought and music.

705, 4. *equal:* all of one nature.

705, 10. *thy soul:* the soul of man.

705, 15. *Before God was, I am:* an adaptation of the phrase of Jesus in John, Ch. VIII, 58: "Before Abraham was, I am."

706, 29. *uncreate:* uncreated, *i.e.*, eternal.

706, 30. *unbegotten:* the meaning is the same as that of *uncreate* in the preceding line.

706, 31 f. In this stanza Swinburne attacks through Hertha the conception of God and man as distinct, the one higher than the other.

706, 41 f. Swinburne adapts the questioning of Job by God in *Job*, Chapters XXXVIII–XXXIX.

706, 50. *my breast:* the earth.

706, 64. *tripod:* the *tripod* was the three cornered table or stool at the oracle of Delphi. It represents in this context the idea of priesthood.

707, 66. *Mother, not maker:* Man evolves, he is not created out of nothing; he (and all else in the universe) is of the same stuff as the greatest thing in the universe: Hertha, its primal source.

707, 70. *fashion:* making.

707, 71. *a rod:* an instrument of oppression.

707, 72. *of night:* a sign of ignorance and error.

707, 87. *overcast:* darkened.

707, 88. *the lights:* creeds discovered to be inadequate or mistaken.

707, 93. *the shadow:* as distinguished from substance.

707, 95. *the shadowless soul:* the soul which is in bondage to no figments.

707, 96 f. In this stanza Swinburne presents another symbol of Germanic myth: Yggdrasil, a tree which supports the universe.

707, 105. *the bark:* of the tree Yggdrasil.

708, 138. *guerdon:* reward, or outcome.

708, 140. *deathworms:* serpents.

709, 168. *dayspring:* dawn.

709, 190. *Republic:* it is to be remembered that the main theme of *Songs before Sunrise* was political and that the volume as a whole sought to contribute to revolutionary liberalism. Hertha supplies the metaphysics for the politics of the book. Hence the allusion to a *republic*—an ideal condition of social and political life—is relevant.

710. TO WALT WHITMAN IN AMERICA

This poem first appeared in the collection of 1871, *Songs before Sunrise.* Subsequently, an instance of his growing conservatism, literary and philosophical, Swinburne repudiated Whitman.

710, 6. *the twilight of terror:* when Swinburne wrote France was under the empire of Louis Napoleon, Germany under the military regime symbolized in the figure of Bismarck, Italy still far from unity. The reference is to the plight of Europe not to that of England in particular.

710, 19. *consonant:* appropriate to the substance they express, defined above.

710, 33. *our dead things:* the religious and political doctrines and practices which he thought outworn.

710, 38. *rollers:* large waves.

710, 43. *sea-steeds:* a variant of the more usual term "sea-horses."

710, 67. The meaning is that the specifically human qualities can be more fruitful than any reverence for a more than human being such as the Christian God.

710, 72. *bands:* swaddling-bands.

710, 73. *stake-net:* a fishing net supported by stakes driven into the bed of the water.

711, 95. *mail nor of lawn: mail* symbolizes the authority of an upper class, the knights alone having, for much of the medieval period, worn mail; *lawn* symbolizes the authority of the church, the symbol arising from the wearing of lawn-sleeves by bishops of the Church of England.

711, 106. In this stanza Swinburne deals with the argument, frequently and powerfully put in the Victorian period, that a non-personal God is no God.

711, 115. The God of whom Swinburne speaks is crucified over and over again, since he is in all human beings and suffers accordingly whenever a human being suffers.

711, 125. *stripe:* blow.
711, 130. *metres:* orbits measured.
711, 150. *king-stricken:* afflicted (and oppressed) by kings.
711, 153. *only:* alone.
711, 154. *only:* alone.

711. SIENA

This poem first appeared in *Lippincott's Magazine* for June, 1868; and was reprinted in the collection of 1871, *Songs before Sunrise.* Siena, a city between Florence and Rome, was in the time of St. Catherine (1347–80) the centre of a powerful state.

712, 31. *strange-shapen mountain-bound:* Siena spreads over a number of hills.

712, 38. *Saint Catherine:* Swinburne appended the following note: "Her pilgrimage to Avignon to recall the Pope into Italy as its redeemer from the distractions of the time is of course the central act of St. Catherine's life, the great abiding sign of the greatness of spirit and genius of heroism which distinguished this daughter of the people, and should yet keep her name fresh above the holy horde of saints in other records than the calendar; but there is no less significance in the story which tells how she succeeded in humanizing a criminal under sentence of death, and given over by the priests as a soul doomed and desperate; how the man thus raised and melted out of his fierce and brutal despair besought her to sustain him to the last by her presence; how having accompanied him with comfort and support to the very scaffold, and seen his head fall, she took it up, and turning to the spectators who stood doubtful whether the poor wretch could be 'saved' kissed it in sign of her faith that his sins were forgiven him. The high and fixed passion of her heroic temperament gives her a right to remembrance and honour of which the miracle-mongers have done their best to deprive her. Cleared of all the refuse rubbish of thaumaturgy, her life would deserve a chronicler who should do justice at once to the ardour of her religious imagination and to a thing far rarer and more precious—the strength and breadth of patriotic thought and devotion which sent this girl across the Alps to seek the living symbol of Italian hope and unity, and bring it back by force of simple appeal in the name of God and of the country. By the light of those solid and actual qualities which ensure to her no ignoble place on the noble roll of Italian women who have deserved well of Italy, the record of her visions and ecstasies may be read without contemptuous intolerance of hysterical disease. The rapturous visionary and passionate ascetic was in plain matters of earth as pure and practical a heroine as Joan of Arc."

712, 50. The Pope was then in residence at Avignon in Southern France.

712, 71. *Thou, God's heir:* The Pope is addressed.

712, 74–75. There is an echo of *Psalm* II.

712, 81. *require:* request.

712, 84 ff. The image of the shepherd is from the New Testament. See for example *John,* X.

712, 109. *You see her:* in the church of San Domenico, at Siena, there is a fresco of St. Catherine in a swoon.

713, 121. *the supreme Seven:* the highest seven spheres in heaven, where the saints are placed by Dante.

713, 129. *Razzi:* more famous by the nickname Il Sodoma, Giovanni Razzi painted frescoes at Siena depicting St. Catherine.

713, 131 ff. Razzi also painted Christ at the Column.

713, 166. *golden goddesses:* Swinburne appends the note: "In the Sienese Academy the two things notable to me were the detached wall-painting by Sodoma of the tortures of Christ bound to the pillar [see preceding note] and the divine though mutilated group of the Graces in the centre of the mail hall. The glory and beauty of ancient sculpture refresh and satisfy beyond expression a sense wholly wearied and well-nigh nauseated with contemplation of endless sanctities and agonies attempted by medieval art, while yet as handless as accident or barbarism has left the sculptured goddesses."

713, 167. *Idalian:* Idalium in Cyprus was a city associated with the rites of Venus. Here she was thought to have appeared from the sea.

713, 168. *Aphrodite:* Venus, goddess of love.

713, 170. *Paphian:* Paphos was another city in Cyprus, where Venus was thought to have appeared from the sea and where she was worshipped.

713, 172. *white three sisters:* the Graces, attendant on Venus.

713, 184. *Cytherean:* Cythera was an island off the Peloponnesian coast, where Venus was believed to have appeared from the sea.

713, 186. *Amathus:* a town in Cyprus, where Venus was worshipped.

713, 205–206. *Ricorditi di me, che son La Pia:* Remember me, who am Pia. The words occur in the *Purgatorio*, canto V. Swinburne appends the note: "Pia Guastelloni, a lady of Siena, married about 1295 to a Tolomei, afterwards to Nello or Paganello Pannoeschieschi, was suspected by her second husband of adultery with one Agosticio di Ghisi, and was imprisoned in Maremma till her death."

714, 227. The reference is to the Papacy.

714, 238. *Maremma:* see note to ll. 205–206.

714, 244. The reference is to Giacomo Leopardi, the chief poet of the Italian romantic period. Swinburne quotes in a note these lines from one of Leopardi's addresses to Italy:

O patria mia, vedo le mura e gli archi
E le colonne e i simulacri e l'erme
Torri degli avi nostri,
Ma la gloria non vedo,
Non vedo il lauro e il ferro ond' eran carchi
I nostri padri antichi.

(O my country, I see the walls, and the arches, and the columns, and the statues, and the empty towers of our ancestors, but I do not see the glory, I do not see the laurel, and the sword borne by our ancient sires).

Leopardi was born and passed most of his life at Recanati, a small town some distance to the east of Siena, with which he is not specifically associated.

714, 257. *quick:* alive.

714, 291. *equal:* just.

715, 313. *Trebia:* here, in northwestern Italy, Hannibal defeated the Romans in 218 B.C.

715, 314. *Mentana:* here, near Rome, Garibaldi was defeated by the French and others in 1867.

715, 323. *the Republic:* Swinburne's hope was for the unification of Italy in a republican regime.

715. COR CORDIUM

This poem first appeared in the collection of 1871, *Songs before Sunrise.* The title, literally translated in the first four words of the poem, was taken from the inscription on Shelley's tomb at Rome, suggested by Leigh Hunt. Swinburne considered Shelley not only one of the four greatest singers in English poetry but one of its main thinkers—the predecessor in revolutionary idealism of Swinburne himself.

715, 14. *the sepulchral sea:* Shelley was drowned in the Bay of Spezzia, in the Mediterranean.

715. MESSIDOR

This poem first appeared in the collection of 1871, *Songs before Sunrise.* The title is taken from the names assigned to the months in the French Revolution, *Messidor*, the harvest-month, beginning about the summer solstice.

In this poem, as in the collection taken as a whole, Swinburne writes as a citizen of Europe rather than of England: the revolution he expects and acclaims will involve England but is considered rather from the point of view of the entire continent.

715, 14. *the crescent:* the moon.

716, 66. *they:* the kings.

716, 67. *dread:* fearful.

716. A FORSAKEN GARDEN

This poem first appeared in the collection of 1878, *Poems and Ballads, Second Series.*

716, 7. *its roses:* sea-roses.

717, 74. *terrace and meadow:* this phrase is the object of *drink*.

718. FOR THE FEAST OF GIORDANO BRUNO: PHILOSOPHER AND MARTYR

This poem first appeared in the collection of 1878, *Poems and Ballads, Second Series.* Bruno, the author of a number of distinguished philosophical works, spent the last years of his life in detention by the Inquisition. Condemned by an ecclesiastical court he was given over to the civil power (for punishment) and was burned at the stake in 1600.

718, 6. *intolerable to sight:* too bright for men's eyes.

718, 11. Bruno was in England in the middle of the fifteen-eighties.

718, 12. *Sidney:* Sir Philip Sidney.
718, 23. *the ravening flame:* see the general note on the poem.
718, 25. *Lucretius:* in his philosophic poem *De Rerum Natura*, Lucretius expressed a bold antitheism. *such only:* only such.

718. THE HIGHER PANTHEISM IN A NUTSHELL

This poem first appeared in the *Heptalogia, or The Seven Against Sense, A Cap with Seven Bells*, a set of seven parodies (on Tennyson, Browning, Patmore, Rossetti, Owen Meredith (the son of Bulwer Lytton), Walt Whitman, and Swinburne himself). The work appeared in 1880 but was not then acknowledged by Swinburne. The present poem parodies Tennyson's "The Higher Pantheism," with which it should be carefully compared.
719, 19. *pterodactyls:* winged reptiles, of prehistoric periods.

719. NEPHELIDIA

This poem first appeared in 1880 in the volume entitled *The Heptalogia.* For a brief note on that work see the comment on "The Higher Pantheism in a Nutshell." "Nephelidia" is a self-parody. The title may be interpreted as meaning "cloudlets."
719, 7. *rathe:* early or rapid.
720, 14. *suspiring:* sighing.
720, 15. *Olympian:* in the manner of a god. Mt. Olympus was, in Greek myth, the home of the gods.
720, 17. *mirk:* murk.
720, 21. *beholden:* beheld.

720. AFTER LOOKING INTO CARLYLE'S REMINISCENCES

These sonnets first appeared in the collection of 1883, *A Century of Roundels.* Carlyle died in 1881; his *Reminiscences*, edited by J. A. Froude, his literary executor, appeared in 1883. Swinburne was hostile to Carlyle's political and social thought; and he disliked Froude because of his treatment of Mary Stuart in his *History of England* and for other reasons. For Swinburne's attitude towards Carlyle and Froude see S. C. Chew: *Swinburne*, 161–162. The sonnet *A Last Look* should also be read.
720, 2. *one:* Coleridge.
720, 3. *straining toward the sun:* seeking to penetrate to the essence of things.
720, 5. The reference is to Kubla Khan, which, after being interrupted in setting down the poem as it had come to him in a dream, Coleridge was unable to complete.
720, 8. *one:* Wordsworth.
720, 11. *one:* Lamb.
721, 27. *the gentlest:* a pun is intended.

721. NEAP-TIDE

This poem first appeared in the collection of 1889, *Poems and Ballads* [Third Series].
The title refers to the time of the month when the high water level is at its lowest.

722. ENGLAND: AN ODE

This poem first appeared in the collection of 1894, *Astrophel and Other Poems.*
722, 6. *quest:* expansion and exploration, or, more specifically perhaps, mission.
722, 10. *races of elder name:* the peoples of the east.
722, 17. *the murderous pyres:* the practice of widows' casting themselves on their husbands' funeral pyres was forbidden in India by the English.
722, 25–26. The reference is again to Asia.
722, 30. The *lightning* stands for oppressive and capricious rule; the *sun* for orderly and benevolent rule.
722, 34–35. *Shakespeare* expressed feeling for England notably by a speech of John of Gaunt in *Richard II*, Act II, sc. i; *Milton's* prose abounds in expressions of his belief in the superiority of England to other nations; *Wordsworth* expressed a similar belief in sonnets inspired by the war with France.
723, 40–42. The reference is to Shakespeare.

BIBLIOGRAPHY

THOMAS HARDY

I EDITIONS

Collected Poems, Macmillan, 1932.
The Dynasts, Macmillan, 1931.
The Famous Tragedy of the Queen of Cornwall, Macmillan, 1923.
Selected Poems, ed. by G. M. Young, Macmillan, 1940.

II. BIOGRAPHY AND LETTERS

BRENNECKE, E.: *The Life of Thomas Hardy*, Greenberg (New York), 1925.
HARDY, F. E.: *The Early Life of Thomas Hardy, 1840–1891*, Macmillan, 1928.
HARDY, F. E.: *The Later Years of Thomas Hardy, 1892–1928*, Macmillan, 1930.
WEBER, CARL J.: *Hardy of Wessex*, Columbia University Press, 1940.

III. CRITICISM

I. MONOGRAPHS

ABERCROMBIE, L.: *Thomas Hardy, a Critical Study*, Secker, 1912.
BRENNECKE, E.: *Thomas Hardy's Universe, a Study of a Poet's Mind*, Fisher Unwin, 1924.
CHEW, S. C.: *Thomas Hardy, Poet and Novelist* (2nd ed.), Knopf, 1928.
COLLINS, V. H.: *Talks with Thomas Hardy at Max Gate, 1920–1922*, Duckworth, 1928.
GARWOOD, H.: *Thomas Hardy, an Illustration of the Philosophy of Schopenhauer*, Winston, 1911.
HEDGCOCK, F. A.: *Thomas Hardy: Penseur et Artiste*, Hachette, 1910.
JOHNSON, LIONEL: *The Art of Thomas Hardy*, with a chapter on his poetry by J. E. Barton, Dodd, 1923.
MACDOWALL, A. S.: *Thomas Hardy, a Critical Study*, Faber, 1931.
RUTLAND, W. R.: *Thomas Hardy.* Blackwell, 1938.
SAXELBY, F. O.: *A Thomas Hardy Dictionary*, Routledge, 1911.
WEBB, A. P.: *A Bibliography of the Works of Thomas Hardy, 1865–1915*, Hollings (London), 1916.

II. ESSAYS IN BOOKS

ELLIOTT, G. R.: "Spectral Etching by Thomas Hardy" in *The Cycle of Modern Poetry*, Princeton, 1929.
ELLIS, S. M.: "Thomas Hardy: His Lyrics" in *Mainly Victorian*, Hutchinson (London), 1925.
FREEMAN, J.: "Thomas Hardy" in *The Moderns*, Crowell, 1917.
GOSSE, SIR EDMUND: "The Lyrical Poetry of Thomas Hardy" in *Some Diversions of a Man of Letters*, Scribner, 1919.
HARPER, G. M.: "Hardy, Housman, Hudson" in *Spirit of Delight*, Holt, 1928.
JOHNSON, LIONEL: "Mr. Hardy's Later Prose and Verse" in *Post Liminium*, Mathews, 1911.
LOWES, J. L.: "Two Readings of Earth" in *On Reading Books*, Houghton Mifflin, 1930.
MURRY, J. M.: "The Poetry of Thomas Hardy" in *Aspects of Literature*, Collins, 1920.
QUILLER-COUCH, SIR ARTHUR: "The Poetry of Thomas Hardy" in *Studies in Literature*, vol. 1, Cambridge.
SHAFER, R.: "Thomas Hardy" in *Christianity and Naturalism*, Yale, 1926.
STURGEON, M. C.: "Thomas Hardy" in *Studies of Contemporary Poets*, Harrap, 1920.

III. ARTICLES IN PERIODICALS

FLETCHER, J. G.: "The Spirit of Thomas Hardy" in *Yale Review*, January, 1924.
FLETCHER, J. G.: "Thomas Hardy: an American View" in *Poetry*, April, 1920.
HSIN-HAI, C.: "A Chinese Estimate of Hardy's Poetry" in the *Hibbert Journal*, October, 1928.
KING, R. W.: "The Lyrical Poems of Thomas Hardy" in *London Mercury*, December, 1926.
MAYNARD, T.: "The Poetry of Thomas Hardy" in *Catholic World*, April, 1926.
SMITH, R. M.: "Philosophy in Thomas Hardy's Poetry" in *North American Review*, December, 1924.
Southern Review, VI (Thomas Hardy centennial issue), 1940.
TRUEBLOOD, C. K.: "A Tragedian of Sentience" in the *Dial*, February, 1929.

NOTES AND COMMENTS

725. HAP

This poem first appeared in the collection of 1898, *Wessex Poems and Other Verses.* It was written more than thirty years earlier.

725, 8. *meted:* measured out.

725, 10. *unbloom:* a formation typical of Hardy's diction, carrying the meaning of the fading away of the blossoms of a plant without any fruit having ripened.

725, 13. *Doomsters:* masters of fate.

725. NATURE'S QUESTIONING

This poem first appeared in the collection of 1898, *Wessex Poems and Other Verses.*

726, 9. *lippings:* murmurings.

726, 21. *betides:* is in process.

726. THE IMPERCIPIENT

This poem first appeared in the collection of 1898, *Wessex Poems and Other Verses.*

726, 28. *liefer:* rather.

726. DRUMMER HODGE

This poem, one of a group entitled *War Poems,* first appeared in the collection of 1902, *Poems of the Past and Present.* No particular person is known to have been intended: it is probable that Hardy was mourning in the drummer-boy the loss of many thousands of soldiers in the South African War.

726, 3. *kopje:* the Dutch term for a small hill.

726, 4. *veldt:* the Dutch term for a prairie.

726, 5. *foreign constellations:* those which are visible in the southern hemisphere.

west: set.

726, 9. *Karoo:* a plateau in South Africa.

727. LAUSANNE

This poem first appeared in the collection of 1902, *Poems of the Past and the Present.* Edward Gibbon completed his historical work, *The Decline and Fall of the Roman Empire,* at midnight in his garden at Lausanne. In his autobiography he describes his feelings at the close of an undertaking which had occupied him for 14 years.

727, 11. *askance:* oblique.

727, 12. The meaning of the question is: Do orthodox theological writers affirm that what is really ridiculous and irrational is venerable in your time as in mine?

727, 15–16. Milton speaks to this effect towards the end of *Areopagitica.*

727. "I SAID TO LOVE"

This poem first appeared in the collection of 1902, *Poems of the Past and the Present.*

727, 5. *the Boy:* in Greek mythology Cupid (Love) was represented as the small male child of Venus.

727, 17–18. The *darts, swan* and *dove* frequently accompany classical descriptions or representations of Cupid; he is also represented and described as a *cherub,* that is, a child with wings.

727. BY THE EARTH'S CORPSE

This poem first appeared in the collection of 1902, *Poems of the Past and the Present.*

727, 1. *Lord:* The term Lord in this line and throughout the poem should not be interpreted as meaning the Christian (or Jewish) God.

728, 10. *readest:* understandest.

ween: think.

728, 23. *foredone:* done, with a stress upon the finality of what has occurred.

728, 25. *Noë:* Noah. Hardy uses an archaic form.

728. MUTE OPINION

This poem first appeared in the collection of 1902, *Poems of the Past and the Present.*

728, 12. *clamoured:* noisily proclaimed.

728, 14. *outwrought:* wrought out.

728. A BROKEN APPOINTMENT

This poem first appeared in the collection of 1902, *Poems of the Past and the Present.*

728, 7. *the hope-hour stroked its sum:* the hour of the appointment rang out the full number of its strokes.

729. THE DARKLING THRUSH

This poem first appeared in the collection of 1902, *Poems of the Past and the Present.*

729, 5. *bine:* a climbing plant, probably the hop.

scored: threw lines across.

729, 7. *haunted:* dwelt.

729, 10. *the Century:* the nineteenth.

729. IN TENEBRIS

This group of poems appeared first in the collection of 1902, *Poems of the Past and the Present.* The title means: *in darkness.*

729. I.

The motto is from the *Vulgate.* In the King James version it is translated as follows: "My heart is smitten, and withered like grass" (*Psalms*, CII, 4).

729. 21. *cope:* canopy.

729, 24. *unhope:* a typical Hardy formation, meaning the absence of hope.

729. II.

The motto is from the *Vulgate.* In the King James version it is translated as follows: "I looked on my right hand, and beheld, but there was no man that would know me . . . no man cared for my soul" (*Psalms*, CXLII, 4).

730. III.

The motto is from the *Vulgate.* In the King James version it is translated as follows: "Woe is me, that I sojourn in Mesech, that I dwell in the tents of Kedar. My soul hath long dwelt with him that hateth peace" (*Psalms*, CXX, 5–6). The phrase "in Mesech" has no equivalent in the *Vulgate* version.

730, 50. *Egdon:* a heath in Wessex.

730, 53. *quoin:* corner.

730, 54. *overgat:* overcame.

730, 57. *unweeting:* unwitting.

731. WHEN I SET OUT FOR LYONNESSE

This poem first appeared in the collection of 1914, *Satires of Circumstance, Lyrics and Reveries.* It was written in 1870, recording a visit Hardy made in the March of that year to St. Juliot's rectory in Cornwall, meeting in the course of it Emma Gifford, whom, in 1874, he married. Lyonnesse, a term much used in the Arthurian legends, indicates an area off what is now the coast of Cornwall, supposed to have been in early times a wild and mysterious country.

731, 3. *rime:* frost.

731, 10. *wizard:* the term is apt since Lyonnesse is associated with pagan and with mysterious life.

BIBLIOGRAPHY

GERARD MANLEY HOPKINS

I. EDITIONS

Poems, ed. by Robert Bridges, 2nd edition, with an appendix of additional poems, and a critical introduction by C. Williams, Oxford, 1930.

II. BIOGRAPHY AND LETTERS

LAHEY, G. F.: *Gerard Manley Hopkins*, Oxford, 1930.
Letters, ed. by C. C. Abbott, 2 vols., Oxford, 1934.
Further Letters, ed. by C. C. Abbott, Oxford, 1937.
Note-Books, ed. by H. House, Oxford, 1936.

III. CRITICISM

BINYON, L.: "Gerard Hopkins and His Influence" in *University of Toronto Quarterly*, April, 1939.
MURRY, J. M.: "G. M. Hopkins" in *Aspects of Literature*, Collins, 1920.
PHARE, E. E.: *The Poetry of Gerard Manley Hopkins*, Cambridge, 1933.
READ, HERBERT: "Gerard Manley Hopkins" in *Collected Essays in Literary Criticism*, Faber, 1938.
RICHARDS, I. A.: "Gerard Hopkins" in *The Dial*, September, 1926.
ZABEL, M. D.: "Gerard Manley Hopkins" in *Poetry*, December, 1930.

NOTES AND COMMENTS

732. THE WINDHOVER

This poem was composed in 1877, slightly altered in 1879, and appeared, for the first time, in 1918. The term "windhover" is applied to the kestrel because it hovers in the air, head to wind.

732, 1. *morning's minion:* the morning's darling.
dauphin: heir.
732, 3. *wimpling:* rippling.
733, 8. *achieve:* achievement.
733, 11. *sillion:* furrow.

733. PIED BEAUTY

This poem was composed in 1877, and first appeared in 1918. The form is the curtal sonnet, *i.e.*, according to Hopkins's own explanation, with a first unit of six lines, instead of eight, and a second of four instead of six, and with a half-line tail-piece.

733, 6. *trim:* synonymous with the two preceding nouns.
733, 7. *counter:* contrary.

734. FELIX RANDAL

This poem, composed in 1880, first appeared in the collection of 1918.

734, 6. *anointed:* the reference is to extreme unction, the last sacrament, in which the priest applies holy oils to the dying.

734, 7. *our sweet reprieve and ransom:* pardon for sin, assured by the sacrifice of Jesus.

734. THE LEADEN ECHO AND THE GOLDEN ECHO

This poem was composed in 1882 and first appeared in the collection of 1918. Hopkins considered that he "never did anything more musical."

734, 12. *ruck:* crease.
735, 26. *wimpled:* rippled.
735, 29. *an all youth:* complete youth.
735, 34. *beauty-in-the-ghost:* spiritual beauty.
735, 42. *care-coiled:* wrapt in care.
fashed: troubled.
cogged: probably in the sense of "deceived."

735. CARRION COMFORT

This poem, in Bridges' opinion, was composed in 1885, and first appeared in the collection of 1918. In that year Hopkins spoke of a sonnet "written in blood": Bridges assumes it was this.

735, 6. *wring-world:* so powerful as to be able to wring the whole universe.
735, 13. *each one: i.e.*, both.

BIBLIOGRAPHY

A. E. HOUSMAN

I. EDITIONS

Collected Poems, Holt, 1940.
The Name and Nature of Poetry, Cambridge, 1933.

II. BIOGRAPHY AND LETTERS

GOW, A. S. F.: *A. E. Housman, a Sketch Together with a List of His Writings and Indexes to His Classical Papers*, Cambridge, 1936.
HOUSMAN, L.: *A. E. H.: Some Poems, Some Letters and a Personal Memoir*, Cape, 1937.

III. CRITICISM

GARROD, H. W.: "Mr. A. E. Housman" in *The Profession of Poetry*, Oxford, 1929.
GOSSE, SIR EDMUND: "The Shropshire Lad" in *More Books on the Table*, Heinemann, 1923.
HARPER, G. M.: "Hardy, Hudson, Housman" in *Spirit of Delight*, Holt, 1928.
LUCAS, F. L.: "Few but Roses" in *Authors Dead and Living*, Macmillan, 1926.
PRIESTLEY, J. B.: "A. E. Housman" in *Figures in Modern Literature*, Dodd, 1924.
TINKER, C. B.: "Housman's Poetry" in *Yale Review*, 1936.
WILLIAMS, C.: "A. E. Housman" in *Poetry at Present*, Oxford, 1930.
WILSON, EDMUND: "A. E. Housman" in *The Triple Thinkers*, Harcourt, 1938.

NOTES AND COMMENTS

737. A SHROPSHIRE LAD

737, I. [From Clee to Heaven the beacon burns]

This poem first appeared in *A Shropshire Lad*, Housman's first collection, published in 1896. Unless there is a statement to the contrary, all the selections from Housman may be understood to have had their first publication in that volume. Numerals preceding poems mark their position in *A Shropshire Lad*.

1887: the year of Queen Victoria's Golden Jubilee, an occasion of national celebrations.

737, 1. *Clee:* a small town in southern Shropshire.

beacon: see the note on 1887, above.

737, 19. *the Nile:* during the eighteen nineties there was much fighting along the Nile in the Soudan.

737, 20. *the Severn:* this river flows through Shropshire.

737, 28. *the Fifty-third:* the Shropshire Regiment of Infantry.

737, II. [Loveliest of trees, the cherry now]

737, 3. *woodland ride:* a path for riding, through a wood.

737, IV. Reveille.

737, 1–4. The comparison between darkness and a sea is not unusual, but is made difficult by the use of *beach*, which ordinarily suggests a light colour, and by the disposition to take *rims*, as referring purely to hills, rather than to the darkness which is central to the image in this, as in the earlier lines.

737, 8. *straws:* strews.

738, XIV. [There pass the careless people]

738, 6. *sound:* fathom.

738, 13. *sain:* protect, especially by making the sign of the cross.

738, XIX. To an Athlete Dying Young.

738, 14. *cut:* broken.

738, 17. *rout:* number, assembly.

739, XXI. Bredon Hill.

Bredon is a high hill in the county of Worcestershire, which adjoins Shropshire on the southeast.

739, 3. *both the shires:* Worcestershire and Shropshire.

739, 8. *the coloured counties:* Housman records that the adjective "coloured" came to him in a dream, after he had completed the poem. It suggests the large range of view from the hill, from which the fields look like spaces in a checkerboard.

739, 24. *unbeknown:* unknown to the speaker.

739, XXVII. [Is my team ploughing?]

This lyric was of all Housman's work the most moving to Thomas Hardy.

740, XXVIII. *The Welsh Marches.* The Welsh marches are the borderlands between England and Wales, long the scene of forays and battles between English and Welsh.

740, 1. *Shrewsbury:* the principal city in Shropshire was once the seat of the palatine earldom of that name. In the time of Henry IV, it was the site of a battle against the insurgent Welsh.

740, 13. *Buildwas:* an early town a few miles nearer the mouth of the river.

740, 16. *got:* begot.

740, XXXI. [On Wenlock Edge the wood's in trouble]

740, 1. *Wenlock Edge:* hills in southeastern Shropshire.

740, 2. *the Wrekin:* an extinct volcano in the same area.

740, 3. *plies:* bends.

740, 5. *hanger:* a wood on the slope of a hill.

740, 6. *Uricon:* one of the main Roman cities in Britain, the capital of one of the provinces into which Roman Britain was divided. It was in what is now southeastern Shropshire.

740, XXXII. [From far, from eve and morning]

740, 2. *twelve-winded sky:* see l. 11, in which the *quarters* mentioned are *all* the points from which the wind can be described as coming.

740, XL. [Into my heart an air that kills]

740, 2. *yon far country:* Shropshire. The speaker is in London.

741, 5. *the land of lost content:* the meaning changes, the emphasis falling now not on Shropshire as contrasted with London, but on earlier years as contrasted with the present.

741, XLII. The Merry Guide

741, 2. *wold:* stretch of open ground, uncultivated.

741, 6. *youth:* the youth is Mercury (Hermes); he was commonly represented as wearing a cap with wings (see l. 7) and having winged sandals (see l. 59) and as bearing a staff of gold (l. 8) which was circled with serpents (l. 60).

741, 24. *folded:* having a sheepfold.

741, 36. *weald:* here equivalent to *wold* (l. 2).

741, 37. *granges:* barns, or buildings of a farm or estate as a whole.

741, L. [In valleys of springs of rivers]

The four villages mentioned in the introductory stanza are in southwestern Shropshire, in the vicinity of the river Clun, mentioned in l. 2.

741, 2. *Ony and Teme and Clun:* rivers in Shropshire.

741, 7. *Knighton:* a town on the river Teme.

742, 16. *handselled:* had a foretaste of.

742, LXI. Hughley Steeple

Hughley is a village in Shropshire, farther north than most of the places Housman refers to.

742, 12. *quick:* living.

742, LXII. [Terence, this is stupid stuff]

742, 1. *Terence:* Housman's original title for the collection was *The Poems of Terence Hearsay.*

742, 18. *Burton* (*upon Trent*): a city in Derbyshire, one of the chief centres of English brewing.

742, 19. *many a peer:* brewers ennobled.

743, 22. Housman echoes Milton's statement, of the aim of *Paradise Lost* (Bk. I, 26).

743, 29. *Ludlow:* a large town in southern Shropshire.

743, 51. *scored:* cut.

743, 59. *a king:* the tale of King Mithridates, of Pontus, a monarch of the second century B.C. comes from Pliny's *Natural History.*

743, LXIII. [I hoed and trenched and weeded]

This was the final poem in *A Shropshire Lad;* the flowers are his poems.

743, 4. *wear:* fashion.

743, 8. *out of mind:* forgotten.

743. LAST POEMS

743, IX. [The chestnut casts his flambeaux and the flowers]

Although this poem did not appear until 1922 it was composed in 1896, the year in which Housman published his earlier collection, *A Shropshire Lad.*

INDEX OF AUTHORS, TITLES, AND FIRST LINES OF POEMS

Authors' names are set in italic type, titles are set in capitals, and first lines of poems are set in body type. Entry is by first line only when the title repeats the first line.

This index has been prepared by Mr. G. H. Healey of Cornell University.

A Golden gilliflower to-day, 593
A happy lover who has come, 43
A message from her set his brain aflame, 553
A million emeralds break from the ruby-budded lime, 84
A sonnet is a moment's monument, 481
A spirit seems to pass, 727
A voice by the cedar tree, 85
A wanderer is a man from his birth, 425
ABT VOGLER, 254
AFTER LOOKING INTO CARLYLE'S REMINISCENCES, 720
Again at Christmas did we weave, 59
Ah, did you once see Shelley plain, 241
All along the valley, stream that flashest white, 105
All day long and every day, 579
All other joys of life he strove to warm, 552
All the night sleep came not upon my eyelids, 699
Along the field as we came by, 739
Along the garden terrace, under which, 564
Am I failing? For no longer can I cast, 561
AMOR MUNDI, 538
And all is well, tho' faith and form, 74
And if you meet the Canon of Chimay, 587
And now Love sang: but his was such a song, 499
And the first grey of morning fill'd the east, 427
And thou, O life, the lady of all bliss, 516
And was the day of my delight, 47
And yet, because thou overcomest so, 363
ANDREA DEL SARTO, 241
APOLLO, 400
ARDOUR AND MEMORY, 504
Are thine eyes weary? is thy heart too sick, 618
Arnold, Matthew, 388
Around the vase of Life at your slow pace, 514
As growth of form or momentary glance, 502
As ships, becalmed at eve, that lay, 382
As the child knows not if his mother's face, 509
As thro' the land at eve we went, 38
As thy friend's face, with shadow of soul o'erspread, 515
As two whose love, first foolish, widening scope, 504
As when desire, long darkling, dawns, and first, 482
As when two men have loved a woman well, 513
At dinner, she is hostess, I am host, 557
At Flores in the Azores Sir Richard Grenville lay, 155
At last we parley: we so strangely dumb, 567
At length their long kiss severed, with sweet smart, 484
At the midnight in the silence of the sleeptime, 351
AT VENICE, 384
ATALANTA IN CALYDON, 627
ATALANTA'S RACE, 603
AUTUMN IDLENESS, 505
Away, haunt thou not me, 382
AVE, 480

BARREN SPRING, 510
Be near me when my light is low, 53
Beautiful Evelyn Hope is dead! 199
Beauty like hers is genius. Not the call, 488
BEAUTY'S PAGEANT, 487
Because our talk was of the cloud-control, 497
Before our lives divide forever, 681
Beholding youth and hope in mockery caught, 513
Beloved, my Beloved, when I think, 363
Beloved, thou hast brought me many flowers, 365
BETTER RESURRECTION, A, 536
Between the green bud and the red, 700
BIANCA AMONG THE NIGHTINGALES, 366
BIRD RAPTURES, 539
Birds in the high Hall-garden, 88
BIRTH-BOND, THE, 487
BIRTHDAY, A, 529
BISHOP BLOUGRAM'S APOLOGY, 221
BISHOP ORDERS HIS TOMB AT ST. PRAXED'S CHURCH, THE, 178
Bless love and hope. Full many a withered year, 496
BLUE CLOSET, THE, 596
BODY'S BEAUTY, 509
BOOT AND SADDLE, 170
Boot, saddle, to horse and away! 170
Break, break, break, 38
BREDON HILL, 741
BRIDAL BIRTH, 482
BROKEN APPOINTMENT, A, 728
BROKEN MUSIC, 498
Browning, Elizabeth Barrett, 352
Browning, Robert, 167
BURIED LIFE, THE, 419
Bury the Great Duke, 77
But do not let us quarrel any more, 241
But if I praised the busy town, 64
But, knowing now that they would have her speak, 580
But where began the change; and what's my crime? 555
By night we linger'd on the lawn, 65
BY THE EARTH'S CORPSE, 727
By the waters of Babylon we sat down and wept, 702
By thine own tears thy song must tears beget, 503
By what word's power, the key of paths untrod, 483

CADMUS AND HARMONIA, 400
CALIBAN UPON SETEBOS, 259
Calm is the morn without a sound, 44
CARD-DEALER, THE, 475
CARRION COMFORT, 735
CAVALIER TUNES, 169
CHAPEL IN LYONESS, THE, 579
CHOICE, THE, 506
"CHILDE ROLAND TO THE DARK TOWER CAME," 216
CLARIBEL, 2
Cleon the poet (from the sprinkled isles, 246
CLOUD AND WIND, 497
Clough, Arthur Hugh, 381
Clunton and Clunbury, 741
Cold and clear-cut face, why come you so cruelly meek, 83
Cold eyelids that hide like a jewel, 692
Coldly, sadly descends, 459
Come back to me, who wait and watch for you:—540
Come, dear children, let us away; 396
Come hither, lads, and hearken, for a tale there is to tell, 624
Come into the garden, Maud, 94
Come not, when I am dead, 77
Come to me in the silence of the night, 530

Comrades, leave me here a little, while as yet 'tis early morn: 29
CONCERNING GEFFRAY TESTE NOIRE, 587
CONFESSIONS, 264
CONSOLATION, 423
Contemplate all this work of Time, 72
COR CORDIUM, 715
Could I have said while he was here, 60
Could Juno's self more sovereign presence wear, 493
Could we forget the widow'd hour, 51
Could you not drink her gaze like wine? 475
'Courage!' he said, and pointed toward the land, 14
Courage, poor heart of stone, 97
COWPER'S GRAVE, 353
Creep into thy narrow bed, 459
CRISTINA, 176
CROSSING THE BAR, 166
CRY OF THE CHILDREN, THE, 354

Dagonet, the fool, whom Gawain in his mood, 139
DARK DAY, A, 505
DARK GLASS, THE, 493
Dark house, by which once more I stand, 43
DARKLING THRUSH, THE, 729
DAY IS COMING, THE, 624
DAY OF LOVE, A, 487
Dead, long dead, 98
DEAD PAN, THE, 358
Dear friend, far off, my lost desire, 75
DEATH-IN-LOVE, 498
DEATH'S SONGSTERS, 512
DEDICATION TO POEMS AND BALLADS (Swinburne), 680
Deep on the convent-roof the snows, 34
DEFENCE OF GUENEVERE, THE, 580
"DE GUSTIBUS—" 245
Dip down upon the northern shore, 60
DIRGE, A, 539
Distraction is the panacea, Sir! 560
Does the road wind up-hill all the way? 529
Doesn't thou 'ear my 'erse's legs, as they canter awaäy? 103
Do we indeed desire the dead, 53
DOLORES, 692
Doors, where my heart was used to beat, 73
Dost thou look back on what hath been, 56
DOVER BEACH, 458
Do ye hear the children weeping, O my brothers, 354
DREAM LAND, 528
DREAM OF FAIR WOMEN, A, 17
DRUMMER HODGE, 726
DUBIETY, 351

Each hour until we meet is as a bird, 490
EAGLE, THE, 77
EARTH AND MAN, 573
EARTHLY PARADISE, THE, 602
Eat thou and drink; to-morrow thou shalt die. 506
ECHETLOS, 349
ECHO, 530
Elaine the fair, Elaine the loveable, 106
ENGLAND: AN ODE, 722
ENGLISHMAN IN ITALY, THE, 185
Enter these enchanted woods, 568
EPILOGUE, 266
EPILOGUE TO "ASOLANDO," 351
EPISTLE, AN, 212
EQUAL TROTH, 492
EVE OF CRECY, THE, 594
EVELYN HOPE, 199
Even as a child, of sorrow that we give, 490
Even as the moon grows queenlier in mid-space, 488

Fair ship, that from the Italian shore, 43
FAR—FAR—AWAY, 166
Far, far from here, 400
Far in a western brookland, 742
Far off is the sea, and the land is afar: 721
FAREWELL TO THE GLEN, 511
Faster, faster, 392
FAUSTINE, 690
Fear death?—to feel the fog in my throat, 265
FEBRUARY, 617
Felix Randal, the farrier, O he is dead then? my duty all ended, 734
First time he kissed me, he but only kissed, 364
FitzGerald, Edward, 368
Flower in the crannied wall, 106
For many, many days together, 578
FOR THE FEAST OF GIORDANO BRUNO, 718
Forget six countries overhung with smoke, 602
FORSAKEN GARDEN, A, 716
FORSAKEN MERMAN, THE, 396
Fortù, Fortù, my beloved one, 185
FRA LIPPO LIPPI, 203
'FRATER AVE ATQUE VALE,' 157
From art, from nature, from the schools, 53
From child to youth; from youth to arduous man; 504
From Clee to Heaven the beacon burns, 737
FROM DAWN TO NOON, 509
From far, from eve and morning, 740
From noiseful arms, and acts of prowess done, 127
From the depths of the dreamy decline of the dawn through a notable nimbus of nebulous moonshine, 719
Full faith I have she holds that rarest gift, 562
FUTURE, THE, 425

GARDEN OF PROSERPINE, THE, 698
GENIUS IN BEAUTY, 488
Get thee behind me. Even as, heavy-curled, 513
GILLIFLOWER OF GOLD, THE, 593
Girt in dark growths, yet glimmering with one star, 495
GIVE A ROUSE, 170
Give honour unto Luke Evangelist; 507
Give me the lowest place; not that I dare, 539
Give to imagination some pure light, 564
Glory be to God for dappled things—, 733
Go, for they call you, shepherd, from the hills; 444
Go from me. Yet I feel that I shall stand, 362
Go not, happy day, 90
GOBLIN MARKET, 531
GOD'S GRANDEUR, 733
Gods of Hellas, gods of Hellas, 358
Gold on her head, and gold on her feet, 594
Gr-r-r- there go, my heart's abhorrence! 172
GRACIOUS MOONLIGHT, 488
GRAMMARIAN'S FUNERAL, A, 250
Great Michelangelo, with age grown bleak, 514
GRIEF, 358
Grow old along with me! 256

Had I but plenty of money, money enough and to spare, 201
Had she come all the way for this, 598
HAP, 725
Hardy, Thomas, 724
Hark, ah, the nightingale—, 443
Have you not noted, in some family, 487
HAYSTACK IN THE FLOODS, THE, 598
HE AND I, 516
He clasps the crag with crooked hands; 77
He felt the wild beast in him betweenwhiles, 554
He found her by the ocean's moaning verge, 568
He past; a soul of nobler tone: 55
He tasted love with half his mind, 64
Heart-affluence in discursive talk, 70
HEART OF THE NIGHT, THE, 504
HEART'S COMPASS, 491
HEART'S HAVEN, 489
HEART'S HOPE, 483
Heavenborn Helen, Sparta's queen, 479
Her brother is coming back to-night, 92
Her eyes are homes of silent prayer, 49
HER GIFTS, 492
Here are we for the last time face to face, 619
Here is a story shall stir you! Stand up, Greeks dead and gone, 349
Here Jack and Tom are paired with Moll and Meg. 557
Here's to Nelson's memory! 190
Here, where the world is quiet; 698
HERO'S LAMP, 512
HERTHA, 705
High grace, the dower of queens; and therewithal, 492
High the vanes of Shrewsbury gleam, 738
High wisdom holds my wisdom less, 71
HIGHER PANTHEISM, THE, 105
HIGHER PANTHEISM IN A NUTSHELL, THE, 718
HILL SUMMIT, THE, 506
Ho! is there any will ride with me, 599
HOARDED JOY, 510
HOLY GRAIL, THE, 127
HOME-THOUGHTS, FROM ABROAD, 189
HOME-THOUGHTS, FROM THE SEA, 190
HOPE OVERTAKEN, 496
Hopkins, Gerard Manly, 732
HOUSE, 345
HOUSE OF LIFE, THE, 481
Housman, A. E., 736
How changed is here each spot man makes or fills! 453
How do I love thee? Let me count the ways. 365
How fares it with the happy dead? 52

HOW IT STRIKES A CONTEMPORARY, 220
How low when angels fall their black descent, 551
How many a father I have seen, 54
How many a thing which we cast to the ground, 565
How pure at heart and sound in head, 65
"HOW THEY BROUGHT THE GOOD NEWS FROM GHENT TO AIX," 181
How to keep—is there any any, is there none such, nowhere known some, bow or brooch or braid or brace, lace, latch or key to keep, 734
HUGHLEY STEEPLE, 742
HUSBANDMAN, THE, 508
HYMN TO PROSERPINE, 688

I am just seventeen years and five months old, 269
'I am not as these are,' the poet saith, 507
I am not of those miserable males, 558
I am poor brother Lippo, by your leave! 203
I am that which began; 705
I am to follow her. There is much grace, 565
I bade my Lady think what she might mean, 565
I built my soul a lordly pleasure-house, 10
I cannot love thee as I ought, 53
I cannot see the features right, 57
I Catherine am a Douglas born, 517
I caught this morning morning's minion, kingdom of daylight's dauphin, dapple-dawn-drawn Falcon, in his riding, 732
I climb the hill: from end to end, 67
I could have painted pictures like that youth's, 182
I deemed thy garments, O my Hope, were grey, 496
I dream of you, to wake: would that I might, 540
I dream'd there would be Spring no more, 57
I envy not in any moods, 48
I had a vision when the night was late: 35
I hate the dreadful hollow behind the little wood, 81
I have led her home, my love, my only friend. 91
I have lived long enough, having seen one thing, that love hath an end; 688
I have no wit, no words, no tears; 536
I have seen higher, holier things than these, 382
I hear the noise about thy keel; 44
I held it truth, with him who sings, 41
I hoed and trenched and weeded, 743
'I, if I perish, perish'—Esther spake: 541
I know a little garden close, 601
I know that this was Life,—the track, 47
I leant upon a coppice gate, 729
I leave thy praises unexpress'd, 58
I lift my heavy heart up solemnly, 362
I lived with visions for my company, 364
"I love you, sweet: how can you ever learn, 486
I loved you first: but afterwards your love, 540
I marked all kindred Powers the heart finds fair:—482
I must be flattered. The imperious, 561
I only knew one poet in my life: 220
I past beside the reverend walls, 62
'I play for Seasons; not Eternities!' 556
I read, before my eyelids dropt their shade, 17
I said: "Nay, pluck not,—let the first fruit be: 510
I said to Love, 727
I sat with Love upon a woodside well, 498
I send my heart up to thee, all my heart, 173
I send you here a sort of allegory, 10
I shall not see thee. Dare I say, 64
I sing to him that rests below, 46
I sometimes hold it half a sin, 42
I sprang to the stirrup, and Joris, and he; 181
I stood where Love in brimming armfuls bore, 489
I tell you, hopeless grief is passionless; 358
I thank all who have loved me in their hearts, 365
I think she sleeps: it must be sleep. when low, 556
I thought once how Theocritus had sung, 361
I traversed a dominion, 728
I trust I have not wasted breath, 73
I wage not any feud with Death, 60
I wake and feel the fell of dark, not day, 737
I will be happy if but for once: 351
I will not shut me from my kind, 70
I wish I could remember that first day, 540
I wonder do you feel to-day, 253
I would have gone; God bade me stay: 539
I vex my heart with fancies dim: 51
IDYLLS OF THE KING, 106
If any vague desire should rise, 59
If any vision should reveal, 64
If but some vengeful god would call to me, 725
If I could trust mine own self with your fate, 543
If I leave all for thee, wilt thou exchange, 364
If, in thy second state sublime, 55
If one should bring me this report, 45
If Sleep and Death be truly one, 52
If there be any one can take my place, 542
If these brief lays, of Sorrow born, 53
If thou must love me, let it be for nought, 362
If to grow old in Heaven is to grow young, 501
IMPERCIPIENT, THE, 726
In a coign of the cliff between lowland and highland, 716
IN A GONDOLA, 173
IN A LECTURE-ROOM, 382
In front the awful Alpine track, 421
IN MEMORIAM A. H. H., 41
In our old shipwrecked days there was an hour, 557
'In Paris, at the Louvre, there have I seen, 562
In summertime on Bredon, 739
IN TENEBRIS, 729
In the deserted moon-blanch'd street, 417
IN THE GARDEN AT SWAINSTON, 106
IN THE PIAZZA AT NIGHT, 384
IN THE VALLEY OF CAUTEREZ, 105
In this lone, open glade I lie, 424
In those sad words I took farewell: 55
INCLUSIVENESS, 503
Inside this northern summer's fold, 711
Into my heart an air that kills, 740
Is it, then, regret for buried time, 72
Is it this sky's vast vault or ocean's sound, 509
'Is my team ploughing, 739
Is she not come? The messenger was sure. 401
It chanced his lips did meet her forehead cool. 553
It ended, and the morrow brought the task. 552
It fortifies my soul to know, 387
It is a place where poets crowned may feel the heart's decaying; 353
It is no vulgar nature I have wived. 563
It is the day when I was born, 70
It is the season of the sweet wild rose, 566
It little profits that an idle king, 27
It once might have been, once only: 264
ITALIAN IN ENGLAND, THE, 184
ITYLUS, 687

JENNY, 471
JOHANNES AGRICOLA IN MEDITATION, 168
JUGGLING JERRY, 550
JUNE, 618
Just for a handful of silver he left us, 189

Karshish, the picker-up of learning's crumbs, 212
Kentish Sir Byng stood for his King, 169
King Charles, and who'll do him right now? 170
KING'S TRAGEDY, THE, 517
KNOWN IN VAIN, 504

LABORATORY, THE, 177
Lady Alice, Lady Louise, 596
Lady, I thank thee for thy loveliness, 491
LADY OF SHALOTT, THE, 4
LAMP'S SHRINE, THE, 493
LANCELOT AND ELAINE, 106
LANDMARK, THE, 505
LAST FIRE, 492
LAST POEMS, 743
LAST TOURNAMENT, THE, 139
LAST WORD, THE, 459
Late, my grandson! half the morning have I paced these sandy tracts, 158
LATEST DECALOGUE, THE, 384
LAUSANNE, 727
Lazy laughing languid Jenny, 471
LEADEN ECHO AND THE GOLDEN ECHO, THE, 734
Lean back, and get some minutes' peace; 690
L'ENVOI, 619
Let us begin and carry up this corpse, 250
Let's contend no more, Love, 203
LIFE-IN-LOVE, 494
LIFE THE BELOVED, 515
Light flows our war of mocking words, and yet, 419
Like labour-laden moonclouds faint to flee, 496
Like to Ahasuerus, that shrewd prince, 304
LINES WRITTEN IN KENSINGTON GARDENS, 424
Lo, as a dove when up she springs, 44
Lo, here is God, and there is God! 383
LOCKSLEY HALL, 29
LOCKSLEY HALL SIXTY YEARS AFTER, 158
Long have I sigh'd for a calm: God grant I may find it at last! 83
Look in my face; my name is Might-have-been; 515
LOST DAYS, 511
LOST LEADER, THE, 189

LOST ON BOTH SIDES, 513
LOTOS-EATERS, THE, 14
LOVE AMONG THE RUINS, 198
LOVE AND HOPE, 496
LOVE ENTHRONED, 482
Love ere he bleeds, an eagle in high skies, 560
LOVE IN THE VALLEY, 545
LOVE-LETTER, THE, 485
'Love me, for I love you'—and answer me, 541
LOVE-MOON, THE, 494
Love, should I fear death most for you or me? 497
LOVE-SWEETNESS, 489
Love thou thy land, with love far-brought, 22
Love, through your spirit and mine what summer eve, 492
Love to his singer held a glistening leaf, 502
Loveliest of trees, the cherry now, 737
LOVER'S WALK, THE, 486
LOVE'S BAUBLES, 489
LOVE'S FATALITY, 500
LOVE'S LAST GIFT, 502
LOVE'S LOVERS, 484
LOVESIGHT, 483
LOWEST PLACE, THE, 539
LUCIFER IN STARLIGHT, 576
Lucilia, wedded to Lucretius, found, 151
LUCRETIUS, 151

Madam would speak with me. So, now it comes: 563
Maiden, and mistress of the months and stars, 627
Many in aftertimes will say of you, 542
MARCHING ALONG, 169
MARIANA, 2
Mark where the pressing wind shoots javelin-like, 566
MAUD; A MONODRAMA, 81
Maud has a garden of roses, 89
MEETING AT NIGHT, 190
MEMORABILIA, 241
MEMORIAL THRESHOLDS, 510
MEMORIAL VERSES, 399
Meredith, George, 544
MERRY GUIDE, THE, 743
MESSIDOR, 715
MICHELANGELO'S KISS, 514
MID-RAPTURE, 490
Mist clogs the sunshine, 423
MODERN LOVE, 551
MONNA INNOMINATA, 540
MONOCHORD, THE, 509
MOONSTAR, THE, 491
MORALITY, 426
'More than my brothers are to me,'—59
Morning and evening, 531
Morning arises stormy and pale, 85
Morris, William, 577
MORROW'S MESSAGE, THE, 494
MORTE D'ARTHUR, 23
Mother of the Fair Delight, 480
MUSICAL INSTRUMENT, A, 365
MUTE OPINION, 728
My first thought was, he lied in every word, 216
My good blade carves the casques of men, 34
My heart is like a singing bird, 529
My hope and heart is with thee—thou wilt be, 4
My lady seems of ivory, 600
My Lady unto Madam makes her bow. 563
MY LAST DUCHESS, 171
My letters! all dead paper, . . . mute and white!—364
My life has crept so long on a broken wing, 99
My love has talk'd with rocks and trees; 66
My own dim life should teach me this, 49
MY SISTER'S SLEEP, 469
MYCERINUS, 389

NATURE'S QUESTIONING, 725
NEAP-TIDE, 721
NEPHELIDIA, 719
Never the time and the place, 350
NEW SINAI, THE, 383
NEWBORN DEATH, 516
Nightingales warbled without, 106
No more wine? Then we'll push back chairs and talk. 221
No state is enviable. To the luck alone, 558
Nobly, nobly Cape Saint Vincent to the North-west died away; 190
Noon—and the north-west sweeps the empty road, 617
NORTHERN FARMER (NEW STYLE), 103
NORTHERN FARMER (OLD STYLE), 101
NOT AS THESE, 507
'Not by justice that my father spurn'd, 389
Not by one measure mayst thou mete our love; 492
Not I myself know all my love for thee: 493
Not, I'll not, carrion comfort, Despair, not feast on thee; 735
Not in thy body is thy life at all, 494
Not solely that the Future she destroys, 555
NOVEMBER, 618
Now fades the last long streak of snow, 72
Now, sometimes in my sorrow shut, 47
Now that I, tying the glass mask tightly, 177
NUPTIAL SLEEP, 484

O beautiful beneath the magic moon, 384
O days and hours, your work in this, 72
O death, that maketh life so sweet, 601
O heart of hearts, the chalice of love's fire, 715
O June, O June, that we desired so, 618
O living will that shalt endure, 75
O Lord of all compassionate control. 485
"O Lord, why grievest Thou?—727
O my heart's heart, and you who are to me, 541
O only source of all our light and life, 386
O Sorrow, cruel fellowship, 42
O that 'twere possible, 97
O therefore from thy sightless range, 65
O thou that after toil and storm, 49
O thou who at Love's hour ecstatically, 482
O true and tried, so well and long, 75
"O ye, all ye that walk in Willowwood, 499
ODE ON THE DEATH OF THE DUKE OF WELLINGTON, 77
ŒNONE, 6
Of Adam's first wife, Lilith, it is told, 509
Of Heaven or Hell I have no power to sing, 602
Of old sat freedom on the heights, 22
Oh, Galuppi, Baldassaro, this is very sad to find! 210
Oh roses for the flush of youth, 529
Oh, to be in England, 189
Oh, wast thou with me, dearest, then, 73
'Oh, where are you going with your lovelocks flowing, 538
Oh yet we trust that somehow good, 54
OLD AND NEW ART, 507
OLD LOVE, 592
Old warder of these buried bones, 51
Old yew, which graspest at the stones, 42
On a starred night Prince Lucifer uprose, 576
On either side the river lie, 4
On her great venture, Man, 573
On her still lake the city sits, 384
On that last night before we went, 68
On the first of the Feasts of Feasts, 266
ON THE LIDO, 384
On this sweet bank your head thrice sweet and dear, 486
On Wenlock Edge the wood's in trouble, 740
Once in a dream I saw the flowers, 538
Once in the wind of morning, 741
Once more the changed year's turning wheel returns: 510
One flame-winged brought a white-winged harp-player, 485
ONE HOPE, THE, 517
One, who is not, we see: but one, whom we see not, is: 718
One writes, that 'Other friends remain,' 42
Others abide our question. Thou art free. 396
Out in the yellow meadows, where the bee, 555

PALACE OF ART, THE, 10
PARADISE: IN A DREAM, 538
Pardon the faults in me, 537
PARTED LOVE, 497
PARTING AT MORNING, 190
Passing away, saith the World, passing away: 537
PASSION AND WORSHIP, 485
Peace: come away: the song of woe, 55
PESCHIERA, 385
PHILOMELA, 443
PICTOR IGNOTUS, 182
PIED BEAUTY, 733
Pitch here the tent, while the old horse grazes: 550
POET, THE, 3
POMPILIA, 269
POPE, THE, 304
PORPHYRIA'S LOVER, 168
PORTRAIT, THE, 469
PORTRAIT, THE (THE HOUSE OF LIFE), 485
PRAISE OF MY LADY, 600
Pray but one prayer for me 'twixt thy closed lips, 580
PRELUDE TO SONGS BEFORE SUNRISE, 700

PRIDE OF YOUTH, 490
PROLOGUE TO "ASOLANDO," 350
PROSPICE, 265
Put in the sickles and reap; 715

QUA CURSUM VENTUS, 382
QUI LABORAT, ORAT, 386

RABBI BEN EZRA, 256
REMEMBER, 530
Remember me when I am gone away, 530
REQUIESCAT, 444
"RETRO ME, SATHANA!" 513
REVEILLE, 739
REVENGE, THE, 155
RIDING TOGETHER, 578
RING AND THE BOOK, THE, 269
Ring out, wild bells, to the wild sky, 69
Risest thou thus, dim dawn, again, 58
Risest thou thus, dim dawn, again, 67
Roman Virgil, thou that singest, 157
Rossetti, Christina, 528
Rossetti, Dante Gabriel, 466
Round the cape of a sudden came the sea, 190
Row us out from Desenzano, to your Sirmione row! 157
RUBAIYAT OF OMAR KHAYYAM OF NAISHAPUR, 369
RUGBY CHAPEL, 459

Sad Hesper o'er the Buried sun, 73
Said Abner, "At last thou art come! Ere I tell, ere thou speak, 190
ST. AGNES' EVE, 34
ST. LUKE THE PAINTER, 507
SAPPHICS, 699
SAUL, 190
Say not, the struggle nought availeth, 387
Say over again, and yet once over again, 363
SCHOLAR GIPSY, THE, 444
Scorn'd, to be scorn'd by one that I scorn, 89
Sea and strand, and a lordlier land than sea-tides rolling and rising sun, 722
SECRET PARTING, 497
See what a lovely shell, 96
Send but a song oversea for us, 710
SEVERED SELVES, 495
SHAKESPEARE, 396
Shall I sonnet-sing you about myself? 345
SHAMEFUL DEATH, 594
She came to the village church, 87
She fell asleep on Christmas Eve: 469
She issues radiant from her dressing-room, 553
She loves him; for her infinite soul is Love, 501
She should never have looked at me, 176
She yields: my Lady in her noblest mood, 564
SHOP, 346
SHROPSHIRE LAD, A, 737
Sick, am I sick of a jealous dread? 87
SIENA, 711
SIGURD THE VOLSUNG, 620
SILENT NOON, 488
SIR GALAHAD, 34
SIR GILES' WAR-SONG, 599
SISTER HELEN, 475
Sleep, kinsman thou to death and trance, 57
SLEEPLESS DREAMS, 495
So all day long the noise of battle roll'd, 23
'So careful of the type?' but no. 54
So dark a mind within me dwells, 90
So, friend, your shop was all your house! 346
So many worlds, so much to do, 58
So sang he: and as meeting rose and rose, 499
SOHRAB AND RUSTUM, 427
SOLILOQUY OF THE SPANISH CLOISTER, 172
Some ladies love the jewels in Love's zone, 484
Some prisoned moon in steep cloud-fastnesses,—503
Sometimes I fain would find in thee some fault, 493
Sometimes she is a child within mine arms, 489
Sometimes thou seem'st not as thyself alone, 491
Somewhere or other there must surely be, 539
SONG (OH ROSES FOR THE FLUSH OF YOUTH), 529
SONG (WHEN I AM DEAD MY DEAREST), 529
SONGS FROM *The Life and Death of Jason,* 601
SONGS FROM *The Princess,* 38
SONG-THROE, THE, 503
SONNETS FROM THE PORTUGUESE, 361
SOUL-LIGHT, 491
SOUL'S BEAUTY, 508
SOUL'S SPHERE, THE, 503
SOUTHERN NIGHT, A, 452
SPIRIT OF SHAKESPEARE, THE, 576
STANZAS FROM THE GRANDE CHARTREUSE, 449
STANZAS IN MEMORY OF THE AUTHOR OF "OBERMANN," 421
Still onward winds the dreary way; 48
STILLBORN LOVE, 500
Strange, that I felt so gay, 93
STRAYED REVELLER, THE, 392
Strew on her roses, roses, 444
Strong Son of God, immortal Love, 41
SUMMER DAWN, 580
SUN'S SHAME, THE, 513
Swallow, my sister, O sister swallow, 687
Sweet after showers, ambrosial air, 62
Sweet dimness of her loosened hair's downfall, 489
Sweet Love,—but oh! most dread Desire of Love, 500
Sweet soul, do with me as thou wilt; 56
Sweet stream-fed glen, why say "farewell" to thee, 511
'Sweet, thou art pale.' 530
Sweet twining hedgeflowers wind-stirred in no wise, 486
Swinburne, A. C., 626
Summer ends now; now, barbarous in beauty, the stooks arise, 733
SUMMER NIGHT, A, 417
Sunset and evening star, 166
SUPER FLUMENA BABYLONIS, 702
SUPERSCRIPTION, A, 515
SUPREME SURRENDER, 484

Take wings of fancy, and ascend, 59
Tears of the widower, when he sees, 44
Tennyson, Alfred, 1
'Terence, this is stupid stuff: 742
That each, who seems a separate whole, 52
That lamp thou fill'st in Eros' name to-night, 512
That second time they hunted me, 184
That which we dare invoke to bless; 74
That with this bright believing band, 726
That's my last duchess painted on the wall, 171
The baby new to earth and sky, 52
The blessed damozel leaned out, 467
The changing guests, each in a different mood, 503
The chestnut casts his flambeaux, and the flowers, 743
The churl in spirit, up or down, 71
The clink of arms is good to hear, 599
The cuckoo-throb, the heartbeat of the Spring; 504
The cypress stood up like a church, 366
The Danube to the Severn gave, 46
The face of all the world is changed, I think, 362
'The fault was mine, the fault was mine'—95
The first time that the sun rose on thine oath, 364
The gloom that breathes upon me with these airs, 505
The grey sea and the long black land, 190
The hour which might have been yet might not be, 500
The lesser griefs that may be said, 46
The love that rose on stronger wings, 74
The misery is greater, as I live! 559
The mother will not turn, who thinks she hears, 498
The path by which we twain did go, 47
The poet in a golden clime was born, 3
"The Poet's age is sad: for why? 350
The rain set early in to-night, 168
The sandy spits, the shorelock'd lakes, 452
The sea gives her shells to the shingle, 680
The sea is calm to-night. 458
The sun, the moon, the stars, the seas, the hills and the plains,—105
The sunrise wakes the lark to sing, 539
The time draws near the birth of Christ: 48
The time draws near the birth of Christ; 69
The time you won your town the race, 738
The vane on Hughley steeple, 742
The wish, that of the living whole, 54
The woods decay, the woods decay and fall, 28
The world is charged with the grandeur of God. 733
Their sense is with their senses all mixed in, 567
Then was Gunnar silent a little, and the shout in the hall had died, 620
There came an image in Life's retinue, 498
There have been times when I well might have passed and the ending have come—730
There lies a vale in Ida, lovelier, 6
There pass the careless people, 738
There rolls the deep where grew the tree. 73
There were four of us about that bed: 594
There's Heaven above, and night by night, 168
They say, that Pity in Love's service dwells, 566
They throw in Drummer Hodge, to rest, 726
Think thou and act; to-morrow thou shalt die, 507
Thinking of you, and all that was, and all, 542

This feast-day of the sun, his altar there, 506
This golden head has wit in it. I live, 562
This is her picture as she was: 469
This lump of earth has left his estate, 90
This sunlight shames November where he grieves, 505
This truth came borne with bier and pall, 61
This was the woman; what now of the man? 552
Tho' if an eye that's downward cast, 56
Tho' truths in manhood darkly join, 50
Those envied places which do know her well, 487
Thou art indeed just, Lord, if I contend, 737
Thou comest, much wept for: such a breeze, 45
"Thou Ghost," I said, "and is thy name To-day?—494
Thou lovely and beloved, thou my love; 490
Thou shalt have one God only; who, 284
Though God, as one that is a householder, 508
THREE ENEMIES, THE, 530
Three men lived yet when this dead man was young, 720
Through Alpine meadows soft-suffused, 449
THROUGH DEATH TO LOVE, 496
Through the black, rushing smoke-bursts, 400
Through thick Arcadian woods a hunter went, 603
Thus piteously Love closed what he begat: 568
Thy converse drew us with delight, 70
Thy greatness knew thee, Mother Earth; unsoured, 576
Thy spirit ere our fatal loss, 52
Thy voice is on the rolling air; 75
THYRSIS, 453
Time flies, hope flags, life plies a wearied wing; 542
'Tis Christmas weather, and a country house, 559
'Tis held that sorrow makes us wise; 71
'Tis well; 'tis something; we may stand, 46
TITHONUS, 28
TO—, 10
TO A FRIEND, 395
To all the spirits of love that wander by, 484
TO AN ATHLETE DYING YOUNG, 740
To be a sweetness more desired than Spring; 501
TO J. M. K., 4
Tò Καλόν, 382
TO MARGUERITE, 401
To Sleep I give my powers away; 42
TO VIRGIL, 157
TO WALT WHITMAN IN AMERICA, 710
TOCCATA OF GALUPPI'S, A, 210
To-day Death seems to me an infant child, 516
To-night the winds begin to rise, 45
To-night ungather'd let us leave, 69
TRANSFIGURED LIFE, 502
TREES OF THE GARDEN, THE, 512
TRISTRAM AND ISEULT, 401
TRIUMPH OF TIME, THE, 681
TROY TOWN, 479
TRUE WOMAN, 501
Trust me, I have not earned your dear rebuke,—541
TWO IN THE CAMPAGNA, 253
Two separate divided silences, 495

ULYSSES, 27
Under the arch of Life, where love and death, 508
Under yonder beech-tree single on the green-sward, 545
Unlike are we, unlike, O princely heart! 362
Unwatch'd, the garden bough shall sway, 67
UP AT A VILLA—DOWN IN THE CITY, 201
UP-HILL, 529
Urania speaks with darken'd brow: 50

VAIN VIRTUES, 511
Vanity, saith the preacher, vanity! 178
VASE OF LIFE, THE, 514
VENUS VICTRIX, 493
VISION OF SIN, THE, 35

Wake! For the Sun who scattered into flight, 369
Wake: the silver dusk returning, 737
Warmed by her hand and shadowed by her hair, 485
Was *that* the landmark? What,—the foolish well, 505
Watch thou and fear; tomorrow thou shalt die. 506
We cannot kindle when we will, 426
We leave the well-beloved place, 68
We ranging down this lower track, 52
We saw the swallows gathering in the sky, 567
We three are on the cedar-shadowed lawn, 558
WEARY IN WELL-DOING, 539
WELSH MARCHES, THE, 740
WESTMINSTER ABBEY, 461
What are we first? First, animals; and next, 561
What can I give thee back, O liberal, 362
What dawn-pulse at the heart of heaven, or last, 487
What! for a term so scant, 461
What hope is there for modern rhyme, 59
What is he buzzing in my ears? 264
What is the sorriest thing that enters Hell? 511
What may the woman labour to confess? 559
What of her glass without her? The blank gray, 500
What other woman could be loved like you, 491
What place so strange,—though unrevealed snow, 510
What shall be said of this embattled day, 497
What sight so lured him thro' the fields he knew, 166
What smouldering senses in death's sick delay, 483
What soul would bargain for a cure that brings, 556
What voice did on my spirit fall, 385
What was he doing, the great god Pan, 365
What words are these have fall'n from me? 45
Whatever I have said or sung, 74
Wheer 'asta beän saw long and meä liggin' 'ere aloän? 101
When do I see thee most, beloved one? 483
When first that horse, within whose populous womb, 512
When I am dead, my dearest, 529
When I contemplate all alone, 60
When I look forth at dawning, pool, 725
When I set out for Lyonesse, 731
When I watch the living meet, 738
When in the dawn I sink my head, 57
When Lazarus left his charnel-cave, 49
When on my bed the moonlight falls, 57
When our two souls stand up erect and strong, 363
When rosy plumelets tuft the larch, 64
"When that dead face, bowered in the furthest years, 494
When the clouds' swoln bosoms echo back the shouts of the many and strong, 729
When the hounds of spring are on winter's traces, 629
When the lad for longing sighs, 739
When vain desire at last and vain regret, 517
Whence came his feet into my field, and why? 516
Where Claribel low lieth, 2
Where lies the land to which the ship would go? 387
Where sunless rivers weep, 528
Where the quiet-coloured end of evening smiles, 198
Who loves not Knowledge? Who shall rail, 71
Who prop, thou ask'st, in these bad days, my mind?—395
Why did you melt your waxen man, 475
Why were you born when the snow was falling, 539
WIFE TO HUSBAND, 537
Wild bird, whose warble, liquid sweet, 63
['Will sprawl, now that the heat of day is best, 259
WILLOWWOOD, 498
WINDHOVER, THE, 732
WINGED HOURS, 490
Wintertime nighs; 729
Witch-elms that counterchange the floor, 63
With bleakest moss the flower-plots, 2
With rue my heart is laden, 742
With such compelling cause to grieve, 48
With trembling fingers did we weave, 48
With weary steps I loiter on, 50
"WITH WHOM IS NO VARIABLENESS, NEITHER SHADOW OF TURNING," 387
WITHOUT HER, 500
WOMAN'S LAST WORD, A, 203
WOODS OF WESTERMAIN, THE, 568
Would that the structure brave, the manifold music I build, 254

Ye who have passed Death's haggard hills; and ye, 512
Yes! in the sea of life enisled, 401
Yet if some voice that man could trust, 50
Yet it was plain she struggled, and that salt, 554
Yet pity for a horse o'er-driven, 56
You ask me, why, tho' ill at ease, 21
You did not come, 728
You leave us: you will see the Rhine, 66
You like not that French novel? Tell me why. 560
"You must be very old, Sir Giles," 592
You say, but with no touch of scorn, 66
You thought my heart too far diseased; 56
Your ghost will walk, you lover of trees, 245
Your hands lie open in the long fresh grass,—488
YOUTH AND ART, 264
Youth gone, and beauty gone if ever there, 543
YOUTH'S ANTIPHONY, 486
YOUTH'S SPRING-TRIBUTE, 486

PRIDE OF YOUTH, 490
PROLOGUE TO "ASOLANDO," 350
PROSPICE, 265
Put in the sickles and reap; 715

QUA CURSUM VENTUS, 382
QUI LABORAT, ORAT, 386

RABBI BEN EZRA, 256
REMEMBER, 530
Remember me when I am gone away, 530
REQUIESCAT, 444
"RETRO ME, SATHANA!" 513
REVEILLE, 739
REVENGE, THE, 155
RIDING TOGETHER, 578
RING AND THE BOOK, THE, 269
Ring out, wild bells, to the wild sky, 69
Risest thou thus, dim dawn, again, 58
Risest thou thus, dim dawn, again, 67
Roman Virgil, thou that singest, 157
Rossetti, Christina, 528
Rossetti, Dante Gabriel, 466
Round the cape of a sudden came the sea, 190
Row us out from Desenzano, to your Sirmione row! 157
RUBAIYÁT OF OMAR KHAYYÁM OF NAISHÁPÚR, 369
RUGBY CHAPEL, 459

Sad Hesper o'er the Buried sun, 73
Said Abner, "At last thou art come! Ere I tell, ere thou speak, 190
ST. AGNES' EVE, 34
ST. LUKE THE PAINTER, 507
SAPPHICS, 699
SAUL, 190
Say not, the struggle nought availeth, 387
Say over again, and yet once over again, 363
SCHOLAR GIPSY, THE, 444
Scorn'd, to be scorn'd by one that I scorn, 89
Sea and strand, and a lordlier land than sea-tides rolling and rising sun, 722
SECRET PARTING, 497
See what a lovely shell, 96
Send but a song oversea for us, 710
SEVERED SELVES, 495
SHAKESPEARE, 396
Shall I sonnet-sing you about myself? 345
SHAMEFUL DEATH, 594
She came to the village church, 87
She fell asleep on Christmas Eve: 469
She issues radiant from her dressing-room, 553
She loves him; for her infinite soul is Love, 501
She should never have looked at me, 176
She yields: my Lady in her noblest mood, 564
SHOP, 346
SHROPSHIRE LAD, A, 737
Sick, am I sick of a jealous dread? 87
SIENA, 711
SIGURD THE VOLSUNG, 620
SILENT NOON, 488
SIR GALAHAD, 34
SIR GILES' WAR-SONG, 599
SISTER HELEN, 475
Sleep, kinsman thou to death and trance, 57
SLEEPLESS DREAMS, 495
So all day long the noise of battle roll'd, 23
'So careful of the type?' but no. 54
So dark a mind within me dwells, 90
So, friend, your shop was all your house! 346
So many worlds, so much to do, 58
So sang he: and as meeting rose and rose, 499
SOHRAB AND RUSTUM, 427
SOLILOQUY OF THE SPANISH CLOISTER, 172
Some ladies love the jewels in Love's zone, 484
Some prisoned moon in steep cloud-fastnesses,—503
Sometimes I fain would find in thee some fault, 493
Sometimes she is a child within mine arms, 489
Sometimes thou seem'st not as thyself alone, 491
Somewhere or other there must surely be, 539
SONG (OH ROSES FOR THE FLUSH OF YOUTH), 529
SONG (WHEN I AM DEAD MY DEAREST), 529
SONGS FROM *The Life and Death of Jason,* 601
SONGS FROM *The Princess,* 38
SONG-THROE, THE, 503
SONNETS FROM THE PORTUGUESE, 361
SOUL-LIGHT, 491
SOUL'S BEAUTY, 508
SOUL'S SPHERE, THE, 503
SOUTHERN NIGHT, A, 452
SPIRIT OF SHAKESPEARE, THE, 576

STANZAS FROM THE GRANDE CHARTREUSE, 449
STANZAS IN MEMORY OF THE AUTHOR OF "OBERMANN," 421
Still onward winds the dreary way; 48
STILLBORN LOVE, 500
Strange, that I felt so gay, 93
STRAYED REVELLER, THE, 392
Strew on her roses, roses, 444
Strong Son of God, immortal Love, 41
SUMMER DAWN, 580
SUN'S SHAME, THE, 513
Swallow, my sister, O sister swallow, 687
Sweet after showers, ambrosial air, 62
Sweet dimness of her loosened hair's downfall, 489
Sweet Love,—but oh! most dread Desire of Love, 500
Sweet soul, do with me as thou wilt; 56
Sweet stream-fed glen, why say "farewell" to thee, 511
'Sweet, thou art pale.' 530
Sweet twining hedgeflowers wind-stirred in no wise, 486
Swinburne, A. C., 626
Summer ends now; now, barbarous in beauty, the stooks arise, 733
SUMMER NIGHT, A, 417
Sunset and evening star, 166
SUPER FLUMENA BABYLONIS, 702
SUPERSCRIPTION, A, 515
SUPREME SURRENDER, 484

Take wings of fancy, and ascend, 59
Tears of the widower, when he sees, 44
Tennyson, Alfred, 1
'Terence, this is stupid stuff: 742
That each, who seems a separate whole, 52
That lamp thou fill'st in Eros' name to-night, 512
That second time they hunted me, 184
That which we dare invoke to bless; 74
That with this bright believing band, 726
That's my last duchess painted on the wall, 171
The baby new to earth and sky, 52
The blessed damozel leaned out, 467
The changing guests, each in a different mood, 503
The chestnut casts his flambeaux, and the flowers, 743
The churl in spirit, up or down, 71
The clink of arms is good to hear, 599
The cuckoo-throb, the heartbeat of the Spring; 504
The cypress stood up like a church, 366
The Danube to the Severn gave, 46
The face of all the world is changed, I think, 362
'The fault was mine, the fault was mine'—95
The first time that the sun rose on thine oath, 364
The gloom that breathes upon me with these airs, 505
The grey sea and the long black land, 190
The hour which might have been yet might not be, 500
The lesser griefs that may be said, 46
The love that rose on stronger wings, 74
The misery is greater, as I live! 559
The mother will not turn, who thinks she hears, 498
The path by which we twain did go, 47
The poet in a golden clime was born, 3
"The Poet's age is sad: for why? 350
The rain set early in to-night, 168
The sandy spits, the shorelock'd lakes, 452
The sea gives her shells to the shingle, 680
The sea is calm to-night. 458
The sun, the moon, the stars, the seas, the hills and the plains,—105
The sunrise wakes the lark to sing, 539
The time draws near the birth of Christ: 48
The time draws near the birth of Christ; 69
The time you won your town the race, 738
The vane on Hughley steeple, 742
The wish, that of the living whole, 54
The woods decay, the woods decay and fall, 28
The world is charged with the grandeur of God. 733
Their sense is with their senses all mixed in, 567
Then was Gunnar silent a little, and the shout in the hall had died, 620
There came an image in Life's retinue, 498
There have been times when I well might have passed and the ending have come—730
There lies a vale in Ida, lovelier, 6
There pass the careless people, 738
There rolls the deep where grew the tree. 73
There were four of us about that bed: 594
There's Heaven above, and night by night, 168
They say, that Pity in Love's service dwells, 566
They throw in Drummer Hodge, to rest, 726
Think thou and act; to-morrow thou shalt die, 507
Thinking of you, and all that was, and all, 542